The
Poetical Works
of
Wordsworth

THE CAMBRIDGE EDITIONS

The
Poetical Works
of
Wordsworth

Cambridge Edition

Revised and with a New Introduction
by Paul D. Sheats

Houghton Mifflin Company Boston

Coyright © 1982 by Houghton Mifflin Company

ALL RIGHTS RESERVED.

For information about permission to reproduce selections
from this book, write to Permissions, Houghton Mifflin
Company, 2 Park Street, Boston, Massachusetts 02108.

Library of Congress Cataloging in Publication Data

Wordsworth, William, 1770-1850.
The poetical works of Wordsworth.

Rev. ed. of: The complete poetical works
of William Wordsworth. Cambridge ed. 1904.
Includes bibliographies and indexes.
I. Sheats, Paul D. II. Title.
PR5850.F80   821'.7   81—20175

ISBN 0–395–18496–7   AACR2

Printed in the United States of America

V 11 10 9 8 7 6 5 4 3 2

EDITOR'S NOTE

IN THE FOLLOWING PAGES the reader will find all the poems Wordsworth chose to publish in the edition of 1849–50, the last he saw through the press. To these are added: several poems published after his death, including *The Prelude* and *The Recluse*; the major critical essays; and the informal notes he dictated to his friend Isabella Fenwick in 1842–43. Placed in this edition at the head of each poem, the Fenwick notes introduce the poet as well as the poems. In them we find his personal reminiscences, unguarded comment on his contemporaries, his views on poetry, art, politics, and many other subjects. Taken together, the notes paint an intimate and varied portrait of Wordsworth near the close of a long and brilliant career.

Much has been discovered or rediscovered about the poet since 1904, when A. J. George published the first edition of this volume. In revising his edition I have attempted, accordingly, to correct errors of substance, typography, and punctuation. Dates have been revised, and the reader interested in the development of Wordsworth's art will find a chronological list of his poems, in order of composition, in the Appendix. The revised notes add a number of Wordsworth's own comments and in general seek to elucidate rather than interpret the poems. A select bibliography of modern studies of Wordsworth will be found in the Appendix, together with a bibliography of works published in the poet's lifetime and a map of the English Lake District, the locale of many of his poems.

In revising text and notes I have been guided by Ernest de Selincourt and Helen Darbishire, whose editions of *The Prelude* and *The Poetical Works* have not been superseded. Variant manuscript readings, of which Wordsworth left many, may be found in these editions and, in greater and more accurate detail, in the published volumes of the Cornell Wordsworth. All these works are listed in the Select Bibliography. My emendations of the 1850 text of *The Prelude*, listed in the notes to that poem, follow those first adopted by Professor Jack Stillinger in his *Selected Poems and Prefaces* (Houghton Mifflin, 1965); my debts to his excellent notes are recorded where incurred. The revised dating follows de Selincourt and (for the period before 1816) the *Chronology* of Professor Mark L. Reed (Harvard University Press, 1967–   ).

I would like to thank the Trustees of the Wordsworth Library for permitting me to consult the books and manuscripts in their keeping. I am particularly indebted, for help as gracious as it was informed, to the former Acting Librarian, Professor Beth Darlington. The Research Committee of the Academic Senate of the University of California, Los Angeles, provided a grant that aided preparation of the text. My editors at Houghton Mifflin, Arabel Porter, David Harris, and Lois Randall, gave encouragement and much patience. I am grateful, finally, to Gayle Shadduck for her willing and careful help in preparing the text.

Santa Monica, California, 1981   PAUL D. SHEATS

CONTENTS

CONTENTS

CONTENTS

CONTENTS

CONTENTS

CONTENTS

INTRODUCTION

WILLIAM WORDSWORTH frequently sought, on behalf of his poems, to divert interest from his life — a life he once described to a curious reader as "unusually barren of events." That phrase was perhaps overly modest; Wordsworth was the only major English poet of his generation to set foot in France during the stirring years of the French Revolution, and his visits there lacked neither adventure nor, at times, danger. In general, however, the outward facts that constitute his biography — his attachments, movements, decisions — are of personal and domestic, rather than literary or historical, interest. They are less important for themselves than for the kind and quality of feeling they imply — the poet's deep and abiding love for a particular place, his "native regions," for a very few human beings, most of them members of his family, and for his art. With a simplicity that in retrospect seems elemental, these attachments shaped his life.

He was born on April 7, 1770, in Cockermouth, a bustling market town that stands halfway between the mountains of the English Lake District and the Irish Sea. His father, John Wordsworth, was a successful and influential man, who managed the political and legal affairs of the most powerful (and unpopular) nobleman in the county, Sir James Lowther, afterward Earl of Lonsdale. William was the second of five children; his beloved sister Dorothy, who shares his fame, was born a year later, in 1771. The Wordsworth house still stands on the town's main street, its ample stone walls looking over a back garden and across a flagged walk to the noisy River Derwent, which the poet would salute in many of his poems. In 1778, when William was eight, his young mother died, probably of pneumonia. Dorothy went to live with a cousin in Yorkshire, and he and an older brother were sent to the grammar school in the village of Hawkshead, a two-day ride from Cockermouth in the heart of the Lake District. The sudden death of John Wordsworth five years later left the children in the care of two uncles. If not quite "destitute" (as Wordsworth would write), they were needlessly impoverished by the parsimony of their father's employer, the Earl, who for twenty years refused to pay them the nearly five thousand pounds he owed their father. This lesson in the abuse of aristocratic privilege was not lost on the young poet, who would not receive his inheritance until after 1802, when Lonsdale's more generous heir, William Lowther, agreed to repay the debt with interest.

Founded in 1585 under Elizabeth, the Hawkshead Grammar School enjoyed an excellent reputation in the later eighteenth century, especially for its teaching of mathematics. Many of its graduates, having studied Euclid's *Elements* as well as Latin and Greek, went on to distinguish themselves at the University of Cambridge and in later life; William's youngest brother, Christopher, would become the Master of Trinity College, Cambridge. The school can be found on the outskirts of the village, at the foot of the slope that leads up to the parish church; a much-carved desk in its single classroom bears Wordsworth's name, and from its

front door one can see across a meadow to the hamlet of Colthouse, where the
Wordsworth boys lodged with Ann Tyson, the kindly "grey-haired Dame"
William remembered with great affection. The school's rigorous curriculum left
time for play — for skating on the frozen lake of Esthwaite, not far from
the school, hunting expeditions on the moonlit fells, and climbs to the Yewdale
crags, where ravens nested. Years later Wordsworth celebrated these days, find-
ing in them the foundations of his mind and genius:

> Oh! when I have hung
> Above the raven's nest, by knots of grass
> And half-inch fissures in the slippery rock
> But ill sustained, and almost (so it seemed)
> Suspended by the blast that blew amain,
> Shouldering the naked crag, oh, at that time
> While on the perilous ridge I hung alone,
> With what strange utterance did the loud dry wind
> Blow through my ear! the sky seemed not a sky
> Of earth — and with what motion moved the clouds!

There was time, as well, for extracurricular reading, a good deal of which prob-
ably took place in the library of the headmaster who recognized and encouraged
Wordsworth's genius, William Taylor. Taylor assigned the boy's first poem,
and his library would have offered a wide selection of such popular lyric poets
of the age as Thomas Gray, James Beattie, Charlotte Smith, and Helen Maria
Williams. By the time he left for the University of Cambridge at the age of
seventeen, the schoolboy had filled several notebooks with verses that pay these
and other poets the compliment of assiduous imitation, verses that delight in the
then-fashionable poetic effects of Gothic terror and sentimental melancholy.

Wordsworth published his first poem in 1787, his last year at Hawkshead, in
the *European Magazine*. Entitled "Sonnet, On Seeing Miss Helen Maria Williams
Weep At a Tale of Distress," it is signed, with some bravado, in Greek:
"Axiologus," or "word's worth." Only the first two words of the sonnet refer to
the young poet's admired Miss Williams; the remainder dwells luxuriously on
his own fervid emotions:

> She Wept. — Life's purple tide began to flow
> In languid streams through every thrilling vein;
> Dim were my swimming eyes — my pulse beat slow,
> And my full heart was swell'd to dear delicious pain.
> Life left my loaded heart, and closing eye;
> A sigh recall'd the wanderer to my breast;
> Dear was the pause of life, and dear the sigh
> That call'd the wanderer home, and home to rest.
> That tear proclaims — in thee each virtue dwells,
> And bright will shine in misery's midnight hour;
> As the soft star of dewy evening tells
> What radiant fires were drown'd by day's malignant pow'r,
> That only wait the darkness of the night
> To cheer the wand'ring wretch with hospitable light.

The poem seeks both to describe emotion and to evoke it, and it does so in a lovingly artificial language that, for example, translates "blood" into "life's purple tide." Such elegant circumlocutions were imitated from the poets Wordsworth admired, and they offer a specimen of the "poetic diction" he would reject a few years later, with consequences that would change the course of English poetry.

In October 1787, the "stripling of the hills" entered St. John's College, Cambridge. His four years there would give him little cause for pride. If not an outright academic failure, Wordsworth by no means achieved the brilliant success he had predicted for himself. He did complete the required course of study, a curriculum shaped by the philosophy of John Locke and the cosmology of Isaac Newton. But he declined to read for a fellowship, and he refused to submit a poem in praise of a deceased headmaster, disappointing his uncles and perhaps himself. In later years he recalled the university as a kind of museum, in which the curiosities and oddities of human life were encased for casual inspection, a place that touched only the "suburbs of the mind." He was not, he summed up, "for that hour or that place," and his happiest memories of Cambridge were of leaving it: his first summer vacation back in the Lake District, when he composed a poem, "An Evening Walk," in honor of his sister and of the landscape, or his ambitious walking tour with a Cambridge friend from the English Channel to the Alps and back during the summer of 1790.

Wordsworth graduated in January 1791, but in the ten months that followed did nothing to recoup his losses. He appears to have drifted through London, Wales, and Cambridge. He toyed with the idea of entering the ministry, but at some future time. Then, in November, he asked his guardians to finance a journey to France, where he might perfect his French in preparation for a career as traveling-companion to some wealthy gentleman. Whatever his uncles may have thought of this scheme, they provided forty pounds, and, armed with letters of introduction from Charlotte Smith, Wordsworth embarked for France. After several days in Paris he moved south to the valley of the Loire, settling first at Orleans, then at Blois. There, during the most eventful year of his life, he witnessed the struggles that shook France during the third and fourth years of the Revolution: her successful repulse of Prussia, the fall of Louis XVI, and the declaration, in September 1792, of a republic. From the first, Wordsworth's own sympathies lay with the Revolution, or so he later claimed; as a youth in the Lake District he had known a "perfect Republic of Shepherds and Agriculturists," and he found nothing extraordinary in the French call for liberty, equality, and fraternity. Such rural predispositions may have been confirmed, however, by the political education he received in France from a new friend and partisan of the Revolution, Michel Beaupuy. A nobleman and captain in the Revolutionary Army, Beaupuy tutored the young Englishman in the revolutionary faith that the natural goodness of the human reason and heart, once freed of feudal inequities, would flower into a truly humane society. Nor was Beaupuy only a theoretician: "It is against *that*/That we are fighting," he said, pointing to a "hunger-bitten girl" on the banks of the Loire.

Wordsworth proved a willing listener, and by July, when Beaupuy left for the front, he had become an ardent patriot: "my heart was all/Given to the people, and my love was theirs." Like many of the moderate liberals with whom he associated, he saw the Revolution as a heroic cause that drew inspiration and example from republican Rome. As an Englishman and Protestant, he drew other parallels: he recalled the struggle of seventeenth-century patriots like John Milton to build a holy republic in England, and recognized in the French cause evidence of God's care for man, a millennial fulfillment of the covenant. In *Descriptive Sketches*, composed in the summer of 1792, he envisaged a mighty tide of freedom descending from the Alps, legendary home of liberty, to sweep the petty monarchs of Europe from their thrones. Years later, in his poetic biography, he recalled the joy known to those who believe they have the power to fashion a new world:

> O pleasant exercise of hope and joy!
> For mighty were the auxiliars which then stood
> Upon our side, we who were strong in love!
> Bliss was it in that dawn to be alive,
> But to be young was very Heaven! O times,
> In which the meagre, stale, forbidding ways
> Of custom, law, and statute, took at once
> The attraction of a country in romance!
>
> . . . .
>
> Not favoured spots alone, but the whole Earth,
> The beauty wore of promise — that which sets
> (As at some moments might not be unfelt
> Among the bowers of Paradise itself)
> The budding rose above the rose full blown.

Wordsworth's political commitment to the French people was surely deepened by his personal commitment to a particular Frenchwoman. Shortly after he arrived in Orleans, he met and fell in love with Marie-Anne Vallon, or "Annette," the twenty-five-year-old daughter of a surgeon of Blois. We may perhaps see Annette in the heroine of Wordsworth's later tale of two lovers in Revolutionary France, "Vaudracour and Julia," but few contemporary records of their attachment survive. In two letters to William and Dorothy that were impounded in a French post office in 1793, Annette shows herself to have been a frank and passionate woman, who loved her Englishman deeply. We know that on December 15, 1792, six weeks after William left for Paris and England, Annette bore him a daughter, Caroline. We know that he did not marry for ten years, that she never married, that they continued to correspond for years, and that Wordsworth made provision for Caroline when she married. Letters suggest that he and Annette intended to marry, and that they hoped to set up housekeeping in England with Dorothy. Wordsworth's uncles apparently opposed this idea forcefully, and it was perhaps to establish his maturity as well as his solvency that he hurriedly revised and published "An Evening Walk" and *Descriptive Sketches* in January 1793. By this time, however, the future of the two lovers no longer was theirs to plan. The French king was executed in January, and within weeks England and France were at war, a war that would drag on for twenty-two years.

The psychological effects of the war were shattering. Like many other young liberals, Wordsworth was abruptly alienated from his country:

> As a light
> And pliant harebell, swinging in the breeze
> On some grey rock — its birth-place — so had I
> Wantoned, fast rooted on the ancient tower
> Of my beloved country, wishing not
> A happier fortune than to wither there:
> Now was I from that pleasant station torn
> And tossed about in whirlwind.

He rejoiced, he confesses in *The Prelude*, when English soldiers were defeated by the French, and he silently "fed on the day of vengeance yet to come" — a day that would see the inevitable triumph of France. He may have undertaken a hazardous journey to France in the fall of 1793, to see Annette and Caroline. He wrote but did not publish a bitter attack on the war and the English monarchy, a "Letter to the Bishop of Llandaff." It may have been at this time that he first turned to the austere individualism of the English philosopher William Godwin, whose *Enquiry Concerning Political Justice*, published in 1793, demonstrated that the amelioration of society would be brought about not by political revolution but by the dispassionate exercise of the individual reason. And in a new narrative poem, "Salisbury Plain," he drew a starkly realistic picture of the sufferings inflicted on the poor by aristocracy and war.

In the spring of 1794 Wordsworth returned to the Lake District, where he was briefly reunited with his sister. That happiness did not, however, long postpone stresses that may have led toward, if not directly to, psychological breakdown: the separation from Annette and Caroline, and, of far broader implication, the spectacle of the moral disintegration of the Revolution itself into a reign of terror. What little he wrote at this time — a revision of "Salisbury Plain" in 1795 and the first draft of a tragedy, *The Borderers*, in 1796 — displays an introspective profundity, and in particular a preoccupation with the anatomy of guilt, that is new to his poetry. In the fall of 1795 a small annuity, the gift of a dying friend who believed in his talents, enabled him to move with Dorothy to a cottage in Dorset. Now free, for the first time in his life, of immediate financial worries, he could devote himself to poetry. Soon after, perhaps at a political meeting in the seaport of Bristol, he met another recent graduate of Cambridge, two years younger than he, Samuel Taylor Coleridge. A brilliant conversationalist and already an established poet, Coleridge proved a perceptive and enthusiastic supporter of Wordsworth's work, and their acquaintance soon ripened into friendship.

Wordsworth kept no journal, and his letters are seldom introspective. Our only index to his thinking at this time is therefore his poetry, which nevertheless makes abundantly clear that the development of his art and thought during these difficult years possesses a dimension that is historical as well as personal. He now questioned the fundamental moral assumptions of his age, the assumption, for example, that the human reason is necessarily true, or that human nature is intrinsically good. At the same time he discarded the traditional forms in which poets had framed serious verse, and turned instead to a language and style based less on convention than on immediate experience. He resembles the intellectual adventurer of his play, *The Borderers*: "sounding on, through words and things, a dim and perilous way," he gave the facts of human experience a new and powerful artistic form. To use his own deceptively simple formulation, which might describe many intellectual revolutions, he learned to "look steadily" at his object. He learned, in short, to *see* in a new way, and in doing so evolved the central assumptions and techniques of serious modern poetry. In his private struggles at this time we see an age struggling for and ultimately finding a new voice.

This troubled apprenticeship began to bear fruit in 1797. He completed a revised version of *The Borderers*, a work notable for psychological and ethical insight; and in *The Ruined Cottage*, a blank verse narrative that eventually became Book I of *The Excursion*, he achieved an elegiac profundity unmatched in his age. In June he and Dorothy moved north to the county of Somerset to be near Coleridge, and during the following twelve months the two poets entered into a creative collaboration that has few parallels in the history of literature. As Coleridge composed and revised "The Ancient Mariner," "Kubla Khan," the first part of "Christabel," and "Frost at Midnight," Wordsworth enlarged *The Ruined Cottage*, adding several philosophical sections that appeal to nature, not political action, to alleviate human suffering and despair. It was probably Coleridge who inspired him, in early March 1798, to undertake an extremely ambitious project, a grand philosophical poem that would, as Coleridge recalled it, take as its subject the "redemptive process" that embraces "the whole state of man and society." The title of this lofty work was to be "The Recluse: or Views of Nature, Man, and Society."

By the end of March, however, Wordsworth had apparently put aside the challenge of *The Recluse* in favor of the short, unpretentious pieces he would publish, together with several poems by Coleridge, that summer in *Lyrical Ballads*. This modest volume seems in retrospect to announce a new age in English poetry. Several of Wordsworth's contributions, such as "To My Sister" and "Expostulation and Reply," present a joyous faith in the moral power of nature. Others, like "The Idiot Boy" and "Simon Lee," are subtle exercises in the moral redemption of the reader, which direct attention to common subjects of the day — the poor, the outcast, the pathetic — and seek to transform conventional attitudes and feelings into authentic love and charity. The book sold slowly but steadily, and when a second edition was called for, in 1800, Wordsworth added a second volume of poems and a preface in which he attempted to explain his purposes. This famous statement sought to justify, in particular, the use of humble subjects and language, and made the bold (if not original) claim that prose and poetry are essentially the same. The controversy inspired by this preface far exceeded that aroused by the poems themselves, and certainly contributed, as Coleridge would point out, to the continued sales of the book, which appeared in new editions in 1802 and 1805.

The winter of 1798–99 found William and Dorothy in Germany, where during the coldest weather of the century he composed what may be his finest short lyrics, the "Lucy" and "Matthew" elegies. At the same time, in a series of blank verse studies of his childhood, he began his most substantial work, a poetic auto-biography addressed to Coleridge. He finished a first draft of this poem in 1805, but it was only after his death in 1850 that his wife published a much-revised version under the title of *The Prelude: or, Growth of a Poet's Mind*. Although it relates the story of Wordsworth's life from childhood through the stresses of the French Revolution to the consummation of 1798, *The Prelude* is far more than autobiography or, for that matter, than history. Drawing on a rich variety of literary precedents, among them the heroic epic and the long philosophical poem, it becomes a representative modern account of man's quest for spiritual wholeness.

Brother and sister returned to England in 1799, and in December, a few months before the poet's thirtieth birthday, they rented a small house — Dove Cottage — not far from Hawkshead, in a spot Wordsworth had coveted since his schooldays, the Vale of Grasmere. Henceforth the memorable events in his life are largely domestic. In 1802 he took advantage of a temporary armistice to travel to Calais, where he met Annette and Caroline. After a month's visit, the former lovers parted in apparent friendship, and in October of that year Wordsworth brought a bride back to Grasmere, a former schoolmate and friend, Mary Hutchinson. The Lowther debt was settled in 1802, and in good time, for the first of the Wordsworths' five children was born a year later. In 1813, with the help of his patron and friend, Sir George Beaumont, he was appointed Distributor of Stamps for Westmorland, a post that filled out his slender income. As an acceptance of patronage, however, it could seem a betrayal of the radicalism of his early years: "just for a handful of silver he left us," a younger, liberal Browning would write, decades later. In the same year, 1813, the Wordsworths moved to Rydal Mount, an ample home a few miles away from Grasmere, in order to escape the sight, in the village churchyard across the street from their house, of the graves of two of their children who had died suddenly in 1812. Except for occasional trips to London and the Continent, Wordsworth stayed at Rydal Mount for the rest of his life.

Although he remained a prolific poet during his later years, Wordsworth wrote most of the poems that support his reputation between 1797 and 1807, the so-called "golden decade." Many of these appeared in his collection of 1807, *Poems in Two Volumes*, including the "Ode: Intimations of Immortality" and a number of sonnets, among them some of the greatest political lyrics since Milton. *The Excursion* appeared in 1814; a long, moralistic poem in nine books, it was the only part of *The Recluse* — the grand project of 1798 — published in Words-worth's lifetime. *The White Doe of Rylstone* appeared in 1815, and two sonnet sequences, *The River Duddon* and *Ecclesiastical Sonnets*, in 1820 and 1822. Editions of the collected poems, each larger than its predecessors, appeared in 1815, 1820, 1827, 1832, 1836–37, 1845, and 1849. *The Prelude* was published posthumously in 1850, as was, in 1888, "Home at Grasmere," a fragment of the first book of *The Recluse*, composed in celebration of the Wordsworths' retirement to Grasmere in 1799.

As was clear to Wordsworth's contemporaries, his later work altered markedly in tone and apparent purpose. His youthful trust in natural influence gave way to an affirmation of the immortal and supernatural powers of the human mind, and ultimately to a more orthodox faith in the sacraments of the Anglican church, with their promise of "another and a better world." Although the death by shipwreck of his brother John, in 1805, undoubtedly hastened it, this transformation was gradual and can be detected in various forms in early as well as late works. As Wordsworth's philosophical and religious orientation changed, so did his style; the naked and plain style of 1798 grew comparatively artful and ornate in later years, returning in some respects to the eighteenth-century standards he had rejected. Although twentieth-century readers have so far decisively preferred the earlier poems, recent studies suggest a growing appreciation of the later work.

Fame came slowly to Wordsworth. An object of controversy and at times even ridicule during the first two decades of the nineteenth century, his poetry gradually succeeded (to borrow his phrase) in creating the taste by which it was to be relished. He was generally recognized as England's greatest living poet during the twenties and thirties. Oxford awarded him an honorary degree in 1839, citing, among other accomplishments, his labors on behalf of the poor. In 1843, on the death of his lifelong friend, Robert Southey, he was appointed Poet Laureate. With the advent of a new generation of poets, led by Tennyson and Browning, he assumed the role that would linger in the Victorian memory — that of a patriarch, a white-haired custodian of wisdom and probity, to whom the young and ambitious paid the compliment of pilgrimage.

To others, however, the "sage of Rydal" was less awesome. Visiting friends could count on a brisk walk over the fells, punctuated by enthusiastic lectures on the beauties of the landscape. Wordsworth's neighbors — farmers and laborers — found him distant but kind: "If any one was sick in the place," one said, "he wad be off to see til 'em." Often he could be seen and heard composing, muttering to himself as he strode back and forth on his garden walk. "He would set his head a bit forrard," recalled a neighbor, "and put his hands behint his back. And then he would start bumming, and it was bum, bum, bum, stop; then bum, bum, bum, reet down till t'other end, and then he'd set down and get a bit 'o paper out and write a bit; and then he'd git up, and bum, bum, bum, and go again."

If time spared Wordsworth to enjoy his fame, it left few to share it with him. Coleridge died in 1834, after many years of comparative estrangement, and Dorothy succumbed shortly after to a mental illness that impoverished their companionship, if not their affection. Others, friends and poets, died in the thirties and forties; as Wordsworth wrote in his great elegy for the poet James Hogg,

> How fast has brother followed brother,
> From sunshine to the sunless land!

Wordsworth's final grief was perhaps the keenest: the loss, in 1847, of his beloved daughter Dora. He himself died quietly, with Mary at his side, on April 23, 1850, not long after his eightieth birthday.

*

Although "Wordsworthianism" never became a European fashion, as did "Byronism," Wordsworth has never lacked admirers. He is at once an extremely various poet, whose work reflects human nature in many of its facets, and a poet who expects and seeks to win his reader's trust, and more. Like the hero of his "Poet's Epitaph,"

> you must love him, ere to you
> He will seem worthy of your love.

Frequently, therefore, the praise of one reader contradicts that of another, as both claim him for their own. The great Victorian poet and critic, Matthew Arnold — to take a common example — found Wordsworth an optimistic poet of nature and joy, whose "healing power" in a time of "distractions, doubts, fears," taught man how to feel again. The poet's "philosophy," however, he found to be an "illusion," notwithstanding those loyal readers who found in it a "system of belief." In a famous essay written two decades later at the turn of the century, the Oxford professor A. C. Bradley pointed to another Wordsworth, a poet of the yew as well as the daffodil, who with visionary power revealed a darker and more mysterious world than Arnold had dreamed of. Like others, this debate continues today, clothed in the altered language of a new generation of readers, and with a vigor that witnesses the abiding power of Wordsworth's art.

At the heart of that power lies a belief Wordsworth stated succinctly in his Preface of 1800. "Poetry," he wrote, "is the most philosophic of all writing; . . . its object is truth, not individual and local, but general and operative." To neither Wordsworth nor Coleridge did the term "philosophic" imply, as it does to many today, a subject matter that is abstruse and insubstantial and a style that is dry and abstract. For Wordsworth, as for the empirical philosopher John Locke, a "philosophic" language was a true language, in which words stood accurately and clearly for their objects, whether those objects happened to be things in the outer world or thoughts in the mind. Poetry, accordingly, could and should be "true" to its object — an ancient hope, which led in Wordsworth's practice to changes that were revolutionary, and deliberately so. In a spirit not unlike that of the natural scientist, he held the poetry of his contemporaries up to the test of "nature," and found it false in its report of both the outer world and the human heart. Why, he asked in the Prospectus to *The Excursion*, has art strayed from its proper subject, the real, substantial world?

> Paradise, and groves
> Elysian, Fortunate Fields — like those of old
> Sought in the Atlantic Main — why should they be
> A history only of departed things,
> Or a mere fiction of what never was?
> For the discerning intellect of Man,

> When wedded to this goodly universe
> In love and holy passion, shall find these
> A simple produce of the common day.

It was a bold and daring hope, then as now — that the poet need not look for a subject beyond the world of common, ordinary experience, if — and this is a crucial proviso — that world is perceived by a mind "wedded" to it in "love and holy passion."

Wordsworth's poetry characteristically seeks to accomplish this wedding of mind and nature, to enlarge our perceptions in ways that enrich our intellectual and moral being. Such large effects frequently turn on the choice of individual words, which not only predicate human attitudes but ways of knowing and feeling. A choice epithet for *grass* in the poetry of Wordsworth's day, for example, was "verdant herb." In a poem of 1797, the "Lines Left upon a Seat in a Yew-tree," Wordsworth mocked this phrase, addressing it to a fastidious connoisseur of natural scenery who cannot attend to, let alone feel, the ordinary things before his eyes:

> Nay, Traveller! rest. This lonely Yew-tree stands
> Far from all human dwelling: what if here
> No sparkling rivulet spread the verdant herb?

The Latinate circumlocution enshrines pride, a pride that seeks, by elevating language, to compensate for the assumed inferiority of its object, the grass. Authentic vision, on the other hand, will not trick out its objects in an attempt to suit polite tastes. It will express itself in a language that is true to the object, a language that is "philosophic":

> There is a blessing in the air,
> Which seems a sense of joy to yield
> To the bare trees, and mountains bare,
> And grass in the green field.

Here the "grass" seems quite at home in a landscape touched by sublimity; it seems transfigured. And yet it retains its common name, the bestowal of which, like an act of charity, allows the object to remain itself.

Like most of us, Wordsworth often applied the adjective "silent" to things capable of sound. At times, however, he used it redundantly, of a silence normally taken for granted:

> I felt a sense of pain when I beheld
> The silent trees, and saw the intruding sky.

> Far and wide the clouds were touched,
> And in their silent faces could he read
> Unutterable love.

> His triangles — they were the stars of heaven,
> The silent stars!

Trees, clouds, stars — to call attention to the silence of these usually silent things is to ask us to listen to what we habitually perceive with the eye. It suggests, furthermore, the act of listening with passionate intensity — as one might listen to a star — and thwarts what Wordsworth called the "tyranny" of the bodily eye over the other senses. The apparently redundant adjective endows the object with enhanced life, with a being, or presence, that is newly acknowledged in our altered perception of it.

Wordsworth enlists the humblest words in the language in this assault upon shrunken modes of perception. In "The Old Cumberland Beggar," for example, the verb "let" becomes a ringing exhortation:

> Then let him pass, a blessing on his head! . . .
> Let him be free of mountain solitudes; . . .
> And let him, *where* and *when* he will, sit down
> Beneath the trees, or on a grassy bank . . .

Addressed to "Statesmen" who propose to confine the old man in a workhouse, the repeated verbs solicit a voluntary surrender of political power; in effect, they extend the French Revolution to the minds of the reigning politicians, and ask relaxation of their governing will. In "Tintern Abbey," by contrast, the verb "let" implies the liberation of nature, as the speaker implores his sister to

> . . . let the moon
> Shine on thee in thy solitary walk;
> And let the misty mountain-winds be free
> To blow against thee.

Like the old beggar, the wind and moon are here perceived as being subject to the human will — a perception that at first seems contrary to experience, so that we are apt to take the passage as a circumlocution for "take moonlight walks, and walk among the mountains." The primary sense lingers, however, suggesting that in some sense the outer world is truly subject to the human will, which must indeed assent if man is to receive the blessing nature can give. Free these benign powers, the verb implies, so that they may save you — an irony that recalls other, Biblical, instances of man's determined refusal to receive the salvation offered him. Such effects, we may observe, are implicit; Wordsworth does not formulate these moral relations as abstractions, and claim them as "truths." Instead, he offers a version of the experience itself, incorporated — given body — within the permanent form of a poem. In such poems as these poetry becomes an act of presentation, which imitates the presentational activity of nature itself.

Given Wordsworth's concern for the conditions that shape perception, it is not difficult to see why, despite his many poems on patriotic, political, or religious subjects, he came to be remembered as a "nature" poet. It should be clear, too, that "nature" enters his poems less as an object of aesthetic contemplation than as an active agent, which can bring about a portentous change in the way we see and feel, an opening of the heart that can best be called "charity." We diminish the meaning of Wordsworth's idea of nature if, like many Victorians, we identify it with the small, fragile creatures he frequently addressed in the poems of the early 1800s — the cuckoo, the daisy, the butterfly. "Nature" had a far grander meaning for the poet; it comprehended not only the visible creation but the invisible law and spirit animating that creation. Its power is moral as well as physical, and hence immediately relevant to human concerns. The French Revolution was for Wordsworth a work of nature as well as man; a political prisoner of Napoleon, jailed for demanding the freedom of slaves, was nature's coworker. "Take comfort," he assured this man,

> Thou hast left behind
> Powers that will work for thee; air, earth, and skies;
> There's not a breathing of the common wind
> That will forget thee; thou hast great allies;
> Thy friends are exultations, agonies,
> And love, and man's unconquerable mind.

This grand "nature" inspires the great confession of faith at the center of "Tintern Abbey":

> And I have felt
> A presence that disturbs me with the joy
> Of elevated thoughts; a sense sublime
> Of something far more deeply interfused,
> Whose dwelling is the light of setting suns,
> And the round ocean and the living air,
> And the blue sky, and in the mind of man:
> A motion and a spirit, that impels
> All thinking things, all objects of all thought,
> And rolls through all things.

Not only in such lofty contexts, but in the most modest poems, Wordsworth conceives of nature as universal. He once corrected a reader who wrote of his poem "To a Daisy," pointing out that the correct title is "To *the* Daisy." "A mighty difference," he observed, implying that *a* daisy is individual and local, but that *the* daisy is everywhere, and will not pass away.

Like generations of poets before him, Wordsworth turned to this conception of nature in the hope that a poetry aligned with it would endure. As we have seen, he looked to it for another power as well, the power to redeem the minds and hearts of his readers. Around him in 1800 he saw the human mind subdued to "an almost savage torpor" by the monotony of work and life in cities, and by the thirst for mindless sensation born of that monotony. Nor was this degradation purely subjective; it was (and is) reflected in the outer world, in the things men make and influence, from the railroads and factories of Wordsworth's day to the polluted air and oceans of ours. All are the outward sign, Wordsworth might have said, of a human pride blind to the worth of anything beyond itself. To such evils he opposed poetry, an instrument that by itself hardly inspired confidence. "When I think upon this thirst after outrageous stimulation," he wrote in the Preface of 1800, "I am almost ashamed to have spoken of the feeble endeavour made in these volumes to counteract it; and, reflecting upon the magnitude of the general evil, I should be oppressed with no dishonourable melancholy, had I not a deep impression of certain inherent and indestructible qualities in the human mind, and likewise certain powers in the great and permanent objects that act upon it, which are equally inherent and indestructible."

The reciprocal "powers" and "qualities" of mind and nature form Wordsworth's central subject, the "haunt and main region" of his song. The "high argument" of *The Recluse* was to be "how exquisitely" the individual mind and the external world are "fitted," each to the other,

> And the creation (by no lower name
> Can it be called) which they with blended might
> Accomplish.

Wordsworth hails these processes with gratitude, calls his reader's attention to them, and describes them with a reverence that respects their mystery. The mind is built up, he wrote in *The Prelude*, "like harmony in music," a harmony that dances in the music of his lyrics:

> The stars of midnight shall be dear
> To her; and she shall lean her ear
> In many a secret place
> Where rivulets dance their wayward round,
> And beauty born of murmuring sound
> Shall pass into her face.

The process — or miracle — that transforms sound into the beauty of a human face is analyzed more closely in the great descriptive passages of *The Prelude*, where, for example, Wordsworth distinguishes between the various emotions exploited by nature to awaken and shape the mind. Several of the episodes in Books I and II portray the growth of love for "forms sublime or fair"; others, such as the boat-stealing episode of Book I, illustrate the benign effects of fear. At times nature takes advantage, as it were, of the unsuspecting openness of a young mind. In "There Was a Boy" the young hero listens intently for the owls to answer his "mimic hootings":

> Then, sometimes, in that silence, while he hung
> Listening, a gentle shock of mild surprise
> Has carried far into his heart the voice
> Of mountain-torrents; or the visible scene
> Would enter unawares into his mind,
> With all its solemn imagery, its rocks,
> Its woods, and that uncertain heaven, received
> Into the bosom of the steady lake.

Instead of the sounds desired by his conscious mind, the boy receives other, far more precious gifts "unawares": sights and sounds that, as memories, will remain formative and sustaining through life.

In "There Was a Boy," Wordsworth's attention is on the act of perception itself, considered as a process by which nature's gifts are internalized and made part of the mind. In other great poems attention turns to the psychology of intense feeling, or, as Wordsworth described his subject in the *Lyrical Ballads*, the "manner in which we associate ideas in a state of excitement." In "The Complaint of a Forsaken Indian Woman," for example, he adopts the language of a mind facing death; his speaker has been left by her people to starve by the trail. As in his descriptions of landscape, Wordsworth employs a "philosophic" language, but here his vocabulary and the structure of his poem are determined by what he observed to be the laws governing the mind. The woman begins in a state of despair, begging for death:

> Before I see another day,
> Oh let my body die away!

As she continues, however, the flux of her thoughts brings other, self-preserving emotions: resentment ("Alas! ye might have dragged me on"), selfless love ("Then do not weep and grieve for me"), and even hope ("I'll follow you across the snow"). At one point we see her mind creating a messenger wind to link her with her child and her people:

> O wind, that o'er my head art flying
> The way my friends their course did bend,
> I should not feel the pain of dying,
> Could I with thee a message send.

As a whole the poem enacts and implicitly celebrates the "inherent and indestructible" power of the human heart, and in particular its power to love, even in the face of death.

The "philosophy" that shapes such poems is not, then, the impediment Arnold supposed it to be. Like any authentic philosophy, it permeates the poetry, molding style as well as content. It is often most effective in those poems selected by Arnold as being, in their limpid power, least "philosophical." And it lends point to two practical requests Wordsworth put to his readers: First, he asked that we read his poems with careful attention, that we read what is really there. He was not a little discouraged, for example, when a reader of "I wandered lonely as a cloud" wrote admiringly of daffodils "reflected in the water." "What shall we think," he asked, "of criticism or judgement founded upon and exemplified by a Poem which must have been so inattentively perused?" The image praised by the reader is not in the poem: ". . . let me ask your friend how it is possible for flowers to be *reflected* in water where there are *waves*. They may indeed in still water — but the very object of my poem is the trouble or agitation both of the flowers and the Water." Second, he asked of us that, having seen accurately, we liberate our powers of response from any preconceived notion of propriety, or what he called our "pre-established codes of decision." Do not, he might have said, dismiss a poem about an idiot simply because you are accustomed to more polite subjects in poetry. Do not let an abstract idea of "poetry" prevent the heart from enjoying what it is qualified by nature to enjoy.

As we have seen, Wordsworth's poetry altered as he aged, and the principles and hopes of the Preface of 1800 are most fully realized in the early work, that composed between 1797 and 1800. Even then, however, it is clear that "nature" was for Wordsworth less an end in itself than an instrument by means of which he sought to reach other ends, humanistic and Christian. He came to manhood at the close of a century that had seen Christian revelation surrender much of its authority to the demonstrable truths of experience and natural science, and, as M. H. Abrams has pointed out, he stood with his age in his effort to base traditional Christian values on new and secular grounds. A number of modern readers have felt, further, that Wordsworth's advocacy of nature is psychologically ambivalent, and indeed that he hated or feared nature. Such views can be supported (and opposed) with textual justification, and they remind us that, after the failure of the French Revolution, the poet had reason to distrust the benignity of natural law. It was not without thought or risk that he wrote, in "Tintern Abbey," that nature "never did betray/The heart that loved her." Later poems are more clearly haunted by a fear that seldom finds easy consolation in the natural world: the fear of death. The poetry of the "golden decade" derives much of its power, indeed, from the tension between the daffodil and the yew, between Wordsworth's desire, even determination, to write an affirmative, humanistic poetry, and his honesty, which founded the excellence of poetry upon its truth, however painful that truth might be. Between 1798 and 1806 these opposites confronted each other in a series of great lyric poems: "Tintern Abbey," "Resolution and Independence," the Immortality Ode, and the "Elegiac Stanzas Suggested by a Picture of Peele Castle." In each, the speaker experiences a life crisis, usually sudden, usually precipitated by the recognition of a great and irredeemable loss. And in each, without taking refuge in nostalgia or self-pity (as did many eighteenth-century lyricists) and without escaping into lighthearted irrelevancies (as, frequently, did Byron), the speaker squarely confronts this loss and survives it, struggling toward a recovery of rational hope — a hope based upon reason and experience. It is perhaps obvious that such an outcome is uncommon in modern poetry, which only with difficulty enacts the survival — not to mention the growth — of the soul.

*

Despite the changes of a long and evolving career, then, Wordsworth's art was dedicated to one end — the welfare of man. "The poet," he wrote in 1802, "is the rock of defence for human nature, an upholder and preserver, carrying everywhere with him relationship and love. In spite of difference of soil and climate, of language and manners, of laws and customs: in spite of things gone silently out of mind, and things violently destroyed; the Poet binds together by passion and knowledge the vast empire of human society, as it is spread over the whole earth and over all time." His poems, he trusted, were active agents, empowered to "cooperate" with the "benign tendencies in human nature and society." They will, he wrote, "be efficacious in making men wiser, better, and happier."

The future tense is deliberate: the artist's skill and the mysterious power of words join in conferring on these poems the privilege of enduring life. Men must vanish, Wordsworth wrote in the last of the Duddon sonnets, but it is

> Enough, if something from our hands have power
> To live, and act, and serve the future hour.

Such was the poet's hope, a hope which the reader of the following poems may judge and, perhaps, fulfill.

If thou indeed derive thy light from Heaven,
Then, to the measure of that heaven-born light,
Shine, Poet! in thy place, and be content : —
The stars pre-eminent in magnitude,
And they that from the zenith dart their beams,
(Visible though they be to half the earth,
Though half a sphere be conscious of their brightness)
Are yet of no diviner origin,
No purer essence, than the one that burns,
Like an untended watch-fire on the ridge
Of some dark mountain ; or than those which seem
Humbly to hang, like twinkling winter lamps,
Among the branches of the leafless trees.
All are the undying offspring of one Sire :
Then, to the measure of the light vouchsafed,
Shine, Poet! in thy place, and be content.

LINES

WRITTEN AS A SCHOOL EXERCISE AT
HAWKSHEAD, ANNO ÆTATIS 14

1785. 1851

"AND has the Sun his flaming chariot
    driven
Two hundred times around the ring of
    heaven,
Since Science first, with all her sacred
    train,
Beneath yon roof began her heavenly
    reign?
While thus I mused, methought, before
    mine eyes,
The Power of EDUCATION seemed to rise;
Not she whose rigid precepts trained the boy
Dead to the sense of every finer joy;
Nor that vile wretch who bade the tender
    age
Spurn Reason's law and humour Passion's
    rage;   10
But she who trains the generous British
    youth
In the bright paths of fair majestic Truth:
Emerging slow from Academus' grove
In heavenly majesty she seemed to move.
Stern was her forehead, but a smile serene
'Softened the terrors of her awful mien.'
Close at her side were all the powers, de-
    signed
To curb, exalt, reform the tender mind:
With panting breast, now pale as winter
    snows,
Now flushed as Hebe, Emulation rose;   20
Shame followed after with reverted eye,
And hue far deeper than the Tyrian dye;
Last Industry appeared with steady pace,
A smile sat beaming on her pensive face.
I gazed upon the visionary train,
Threw back my eyes, returned, and gazed
    again.
When lo! the heavenly goddess thus began,
Through all my frame the pleasing accents
    ran.

"'When Superstition left the golden light
And fled indignant to the shades of night;   30
When pure Religion reared the peaceful
    breast
And lulled the warring passions into rest,
Drove far away the savage thoughts that
    roll
In the dark mansions of the bigot's soul,
Enlivening Hope displayed her cheerful ray,
And beamed on Britain's sons a brighter day;
So when on Ocean's face the storm subsides,
Hushed are the winds and silent are the
    tides;
The God of day, in all the pomp of light,
Moves through the vault of heaven, and dis-
    sipates the night;   40
Wide o'er the main a trembling lustre
    plays,
The glittering waves reflect the dazzling
    blaze;
Science with joy saw Superstition fly
Before the lustre of Religion's eye;
With rapture she beheld Britannia smile,
Clapped her strong wings, and sought the
    cheerful isle.
The shades of night no more the soul in-
    volve,
She sheds her beam, and, lo! the shades
    dissolve;
No jarring monks, to gloomy cell confined,
With mazy rules perplex the weary mind;
No shadowy forms entice the soul aside,   51
Secure she walks, Philosophy her guide.
Britain, who long her warriors had adored,
And deemed all merit centred in the sword;
Britain, who thought to stain the field was
    fame,
Now honoured Edward's less than Bacon's
    name.
Her sons no more in listed fields advance
To ride the ring, or toss the beamy lance;
No longer steel their indurated hearts
To the mild influence of the finer arts;   60
Quick to the secret grotto they retire
To court majestic truth, or wake the golden
    lyre;

By generous Emulation taught to rise,
The seats of learning brave the distant
    skies.
Then noble Sandys, inspired with great de-
    sign;
Reared Hawkshead's happy roof, and called
    it mine,
There have I loved to show the tender age
The golden precepts of the classic page;
To lead the mind to those Elysian plains
Where, throned in gold, immortal Science
    reigns;   70
Fair to the view is sacred Truth displayed,
In all the majesty of light arrayed,
To teach, on rapid wings, the curious soul
To roam from heaven to heaven, from pole
    to pole,
From thence to search the mystic cause of
    things
And follow Nature to her secret springs;
Nor less to guide the fluctuating youth
Firm in the sacred paths of moral truth,
To regulate the mind's disordered frame,
And quench the passions kindling into
    flame;   80
The glimmering fires of Virtue to enlarge,
And purge from Vice's dross my tender
    charge.
Oft have I said, the paths of Fame pursue,
And all that Virtue dictates, dare to do;
Go to the world, peruse the book of man,
And learn from thence thy own defects to
    scan;
Severely honest, break no plighted trust,
But coldly rest not here — be more than
    just;
Join to the rigours of the sires of Rome
The gentler manners of the private dome;
When Virtue weeps in agony of woe,   91
Teach from the heart the tender tear to
    flow;
If Pleasure's soothing song thy soul en-
    tice,
Or all the gaudy pomp of splendid Vice,
Arise superior to the Siren's power,
The wretch, the short-lived vision of an
    hour;
Soon fades her cheek, her blushing beauties
    fly,
As fades the chequered bow that paints the
    sky.
  So shall thy sire, whilst hope his breast
    inspires,
And wakes anew Life's glimmering trem-
    bling fires,   100

Hear Britain's sons rehearse thy praise with
    joy,
Look up to heaven, and bless his darling boy.
If e'er these precepts quelled the passions'
    strife,
If e'er they smoothed the rugged walks of
    life,
If e'er they pointed forth the blissful way
That guides the spirit to eternal day,
Do thou, if gratitude inspire thy breast,
Spurn the soft fetters of lethargic rest.
Awake, awake! and snatch the slumbering
    lyre,
Let this bright morn and Sandys the song
    inspire.'   110

" I looked obedience: the celestial Fair
Smiled like the morn, and vanished into
    air."

EXTRACT

FROM THE CONCLUSION OF A POEM,
COMPOSED IN ANTICIPATION OF LEAV-
ING SCHOOL

1787(?). 1815

Written at Hawkshead. The beautiful im-
age with which this poem concludes, suggested
itself to me while I was resting in a boat along
with my companions under the shade of a mag-
nificent row of sycamores, which then extended
their branches from the shore of the promon-
tory upon which stands the ancient, and at that
time the more picturesque, Hall of Coniston,
the seat of the Le Flemings from very early
times. The poem of which it was the conclu-
sion was of many hundred lines, and contained
thoughts and images most of which have been
dispersed through my other writings.

DEAR native regions, I foretell,
From what I feel at this farewell,
That, wheresoe'er my steps may tend,
And whensoe'er my course shall end,
If in that hour a single tie
Survive of local sympathy,
My soul will cast the backward view,
The longing look alone on you.

Thus, while the Sun sinks down to rest
Far in the regions of the west,
Though to the vale no parting beam
Be given, not one memorial gleam,
A lingering light he fondly throws
On the dear hills where first he rose.

WRITTEN IN VERY EARLY YOUTH

1788(?). 1802

CALM is all nature as a resting wheel.
The kine are couched upon the dewy grass;
The horse alone, seen dimly as I pass,
Is cropping audibly his later meal:
Dark is the ground; a slumber seems to
    steal
O'er vale, and mountain, and the starless
    sky.
Now, in this blank of things, a harmony,
Home-felt, and home-created, comes to heal
That grief for which the senses still supply
Fresh food; for only then, when memory
Is hushed, am I at rest. My Friends! re-
    strain
Those busy cares that would allay my pain;
Oh! leave me to myself, nor let me feel
The officious touch that makes me droop
    again.

AN EVENING WALK

ADDRESSED TO A YOUNG LADY

1788–93. 1793

The young Lady to whom this was ad-
dressed was my Sister. It was composed at
school, and during my two first College vaca-
tions. There is not an image in it which I
have not observed ; and now, in my seventy-
third year, I recollect the time and place where
most of them were noticed. I will confine my-
self to one instance : —

" Waving his hat, the shepherd, from the vale,
  Directs his winding dog the cliffs to scale, —
  The dog, loud barking, 'mid the glittering rocks,
  Hunts, where his master points, the intercepted
    flocks "

I was an eye-witness of this for the first time
while crossing the Pass of Dunmail Raise.
Upon second thought, I will mention another
image : —

" And, fronting the bright west, yon oak entwines
  Its darkening boughs and leaves, in stronger lines."

This is feebly and imperfectly expressed. but I
recollect distinctly the very spot where this first
struck me. It was in the way between Hawks-
head and Ambleside, and gave me extreme
pleasure. The moment was important in my
poetical history; for I date from it my con-
sciousness of the infinite variety of natural
appearances which had been unnoticed by the
poets of any age or country, so far as I was
acquainted with them ; and I made a resolu-
tion to supply, in some degree, the deficiency.
I could not have been at that time above
fourteen years of age. The description of the
swans, that follows, was taken from the daily
opportunities I had of observing their habits,
not as confined to the gentleman's park, but in a
state of nature. There were two pairs of them
that divided the lake of Esthwaite and its in-
and-out-flowing streams between them, never
trespassing a single yard upon each other's
separate domain. They were of the old mag-
nificent species, bearing in beauty and majesty
about the same relation to the Thames swan
which that does to the goose. It was from the
remembrance of those noble creatures I took,
thirty years after, the picture of the swan
which I have discarded from the poem of Dion.
While I was a school-boy, the late Mr. Curwen
introduced a little fleet of those birds, but of
the inferior species, to the lake of Windermere.
Their principal home was about his own island ;
but they sailed about into remote parts of the
lake, and, either from real or imagined injury
done to the adjoining fields, they were got rid
of at the request of the farmers and proprie-
tors, but to the great regret of all who had
become attached to them, from noticing their
beauty and quiet habits. I will conclude my
notice of this poem by observing that the plan
of it has not been confined to a particular walk
or an individual place, — a proof (of which I
was unconscious at the time) of my unwilling-
ness to submit the poetic spirit to the chains
of fact and real circumstance. The country is
idealised rather than described in any one of its
local aspects.

General Sketch of the Lakes — Author's re-
gret of his youth which was passed amongst
them — Short description of Noon — Cascade
— Noontide Retreat — Precipice and sloping
Lights — Face of Nature as the Sun declines
— Mountain-farm, and the Cock — Slate-
quarry — Sunset — Superstition of the Coun-
try connected with that moment — Swans —
Female Beggar — Twilight-sounds — West-
ern Lights — Spirits — Night — Moonlight
— Hope — Night-sounds — Conclusion.

FAR from my dearest Friend, 't is mine to
    rove
Through bare grey dell, high wood, and
    pastoral cove;
Where Derwent rests, and listens to the
    roar
That stuns the tremulous cliffs of high Lo-
    dore;

Where peace to Grasmere's lonely island
   leads,
To willowy hedge-rows, and to emerald
   meads;
Leads to her bridge, rude church, and cot-
   taged grounds,
Her rocky sheepwalks, and her woodland
   bounds;
Where, undisturbed by winds, Winander
   sleeps
'Mid clustering isles, and holly-sprinkled
   steeps;   10
Where twilight glens endear my Esthwaite's
   shore,
And memory of departed pleasures, more.
   Fair scenes, erewhile, I taught, a happy
     child,
The echoes of your rocks my carols wild:
The spirit sought not then, in cherished sad-
   ness,
A cloudy substitute for failing gladness.
In youth's keen eye the livelong day was
   bright,
The sun at morning, and the stars at night,
Alike, when first the bittern's hollow bill
Was heard, or woodcocks roamed the moon-
   light hill.   20
   In thoughtless gaiety I coursed the plain,
And hope itself was all I knew of pain;
For then, the inexperienced heart would beat
At times, while young Content forsook her
   seat,
And wild Impatience, pointing upward,
   showed,
Through passes yet unreached, a brighter
   road.
Alas! the idle tale of man is found
Depicted in the dial's moral round;
Hope with reflection blends her social rays
To gild the total tablet of his days;   30
Yet still, the sport of some malignant power,
He knows but from its shade the present
   hour.
   But why, ungrateful, dwell on idle pain?
To show what pleasures yet to me remain,
Say, will my Friend, with unreluctant ear,
The history of a poet's evening hear?
   When, in the south, the wan noon, brood-
     ing still,
Breathed a pale steam around the glaring
   hill,
And shades of deep-embattled clouds were
   seen,
Spotting the northern cliffs with lights be-
   tween;   40

When crowding cattle, checked by rails that
   make
A fence far stretched into the shallow lake,
Lashed the cool water with their restless
   tails,
Or from high points of rock looked out for
   fanning gales:
When school-boys stretched their length
   upon the green;
And round the broad-spread oak, a glim-
   mering scene,
In the rough fern-clad park, the herded deer
Shook the still-twinkling tail and glancing
   ear;   48
When horses in the sunburnt intake stood,
And vainly eyed below the tempting flood,
Or tracked the passenger, in mute distress,
With forward neck the closing gate to
   press —
Then, while I wandered where the huddling
   rill
Brightens with water-breaks the hollow
   ghyll
As by enchantment, an obscure retreat
Opened at once, and stayed my devious
   feet.
While thick above the rill the branches
   close,
In rocky basin its wild waves repose,
Inverted shrubs, and moss of gloomy green,
Cling from the rocks, with pale wood-weeds
   between;   60
And its own twilight softens the whole
   scene,
Save where aloft the subtle sunbeams shine
On withered briars that o'er the crags re-
   cline;
Save where, with sparkling foam, a small
   cascade
Illumines, from within, the leafy shade;
Beyond, along the vista of the brook,
Where antique roots its bustling course
   o'erlook,
The eye reposes on a secret bridge
Half grey, half shagged with ivy to its
   ridge;
There, bending o'er the stream, the listless
   swain   70
Lingers behind his disappearing wain.
— Did Sabine grace adorn my living line,
Blandusia's praise, wild stream, should yield
   to thine!
Never shall ruthless minister of death
'Mid thy soft glooms the glittering steel
   unsheath;

No goblets shall, for thee, be crowned with
flowers,
No kid with piteous outcry thrill thy
bowers;
The mystic shapes that by thy margin
rove
A more benignant sacrifice approve —
A mind, that, in a calm angelic mood   80
Of happy wisdom, meditating good,
Beholds, of all from her high powers re-
quired,
Much done, and much designed, and more
desired, —
Harmonious thoughts, a soul by truth re-
fined,
Entire affection for all human kind.
   Dear Brook, farewell! To-morrow's noon
again
Shall hide me, wooing long thy wildwood
strain;
But now the sun has gained his western
road,
And eve's mild hour invites my steps abroad.
   While, near the midway cliff, the silvered
kite   90
In many a whistling circle wheels her flight;
Slant watery lights, from parting clouds,
apace
Travel along the precipice's base;
Cheering its naked waste of scattered stone,
By lichens grey, and scanty moss, o'er-
grown;
Where scarce the foxglove peeps, or thistle's
beard;
And restless stone-chat, all day long, is
heard.
   How pleasant, as the sun declines, to view
The spacious landscape change in form and
hue!
Here, vanish, as in mist, before a flood   100
Of bright obscurity, hill, lawn, and wood;
There, objects, by the searching beams be-
trayed,
Come forth, and here retire in purple shade;
Even the white stems of birch, the cottage
white,
Soften their glare before the mellow light;
The skiffs, at anchor where with umbrage
wide
Yon chestnuts half the latticed boat-house
hide,
Shed from their sides, that face the sun's
slant beam,
Strong flakes of radiance on the tremulous
stream:

Raised by yon travelling flock, a dusty cloud
Mounts from the road, and spreads its mov-
ing shroud;   111
The shepherd, all involved in wreaths of
fire,
Now shows a shadowy speck, and now is
lost entire.
   Into a gradual calm the breezes sink,
A blue rim borders all the lake's still brink;
There doth the twinkling aspen's foliage
sleep,
And insects clothe, like dust, the glassy
deep:
And now, on every side, the surface breaks
Into blue spots, and slowly lengthening
streaks;
Here, plots of sparkling water tremble
bright   120
With thousand thousand twinkling points
of light;
There, waves that, hardly weltering, die
away,
Tip their smooth ridges with a softer ray;
And now the whole wide lake in deep re-
pose
Is hushed, and like a burnished mirror
glows,
Save where, along the shady western marge,
Coasts, with industrious oar, the charcoal
barge.
   Their panniered train a group of potters
goad,
Winding from side to side up the steep road;
The peasant, from yon cliff of fearful
edge   130
Shot, down the headlong path darts with his
sledge;
Bright beams the lonely mountain-horse il-
lume
Feeding 'mid purple heath, 'green rings,'
and broom;
While the sharp slope the slackened team
confounds,
Downward the ponderous timber-wain re-
sounds;
In foamy breaks the rill, with merry song,
Dashed o'er the rough rock, lightly leaps
along;
From lonesome chapel at the mountain's
feet,
Three humble bells their rustic chime
repeat;
Sounds from the water-side the hammered
boat;   140
And *blasted* quarry thunders, heard remote!

Even here, amid the sweep of endless
　　woods,
Blue pomp of lakes, high cliffs, and falling
　　floods,
Not undelightful are the simplest charms,
Found by the grassy door of mountain-
　　farms.
Sweetly ferocious, round his native walks,
Pride of his sister - wives, the monarch
　　stalks;
Spur-clad his nervous feet, and firm his
　　tread;
A crest of purple tops the warrior's head.
Bright sparks his black and rolling eye-ball
　　hurls　　　　　　　　　　　　　　150
Afar, his tail he closes and unfurls;
On tiptoe reared, he strains his clarion
　　throat,
Threatened by faintly - answering farms
　　remote:
Again with his shrill voice the mountain
　　rings,
While, flapped with conscious pride, re-
　　sound his wings.
　　Where, mixed with graceful birch, the
　　　　sombrous pine
And yew-tree o'er the silver rocks recline;
I love to mark the quarry's moving trains,
Dwarf panniered steeds, and men, and nu-
　　merous wains;
How busy all the enormous hive within,　160
While Echo dallies with its various din!
Some (hear you not their chisels' clinking
　　sound ?)
Toil, small as pigmies in the gulf profound;
Some, dim between the lofty cliffs descried,
O'erwalk the slender plank from side to
　　side;
These, by the pale-blue rocks that ceaseless
　　ring,
In airy baskets hanging, work and sing.
　　Just where a cloud above the mountain
　　　　rears
An edge all flame, the broadening sun ap-
　　pears;
A long blue bar its ægis orb divides,　　170
And breaks the spreading of its golden
　　tides;
And now that orb has touched the purple
　　steep
Whose softened image penetrates the deep.
'Cross the calm lake's blue shades the cliffs
　　aspire,
With towers and woods, a 'prospect all on
　　fire;'

While coves and secret hollows, through a
　　ray
Of fainter gold, a purple gleam betray.
Each slip of lawn the broken rocks between
Shines in the light with more than earthly
　　green:
Deep yellow beams the scattered stems
　　illume,　　　　　　　　　　　　　180
Far in the level forest's central gloom:
Waving his hat, the shepherd, from the vale,
Directs his winding dog the cliffs to scale, —
The dog, loud barking, 'mid the glittering
　　rocks,
Hunts, where his master points, the inter-
　　cepted flocks.
Where oaks o'erhang the road the radiance
　　shoots
On tawny earth, wild weeds, and twisted
　　roots;
The druid-stones a brightened ring unfold;
And all the babbling brooks are liquid gold;
Sunk to a curve, the day-star lessens still,
Gives one bright glance, and drops behind
　　the hill.　　　　　　　　　　　191
　　In these secluded vales, if village fame,
Confirmed by hoary hairs, belief may claim;
When up the hills, as now, retired the
　　light,
Strange apparitions mocked the shepherd's
　　sight.
　　The form appears of one that spurs his
　　　　steed
Midway along the hill with desperate speed;
Unhurt pursues his lengthened flight, while
　　all
Attend, at every stretch, his headlong fall.
Anon, appears a brave, a gorgeous show　200
Of horsemen-shadows moving to and fro;
At intervals imperial banners stream,
And now the van reflects the solar beam;
The rear through iron brown betrays a
　　sullen gleam.
While silent stands the admiring crowd
　　below,
Silent the visionary warriors go,
Winding in ordered pomp their upward
　　way
Till the last banner of their long array
Has disappeared, and every trace is fled
Of splendour — save the beacon's spiry
　　head　　　　　　　　　　　　210
Tipt with eve's latest gleam of burning red.
　　Now, while the solemn evening shadows
　　　　sail,
On slowly-waving pinions, down the vale;

And, fronting the bright west, yon oak
entwines
Its darkening boughs and leaves, in stronger
lines;
'T is pleasant near the tranquil lake to stray
Where, winding on along some secret bay,
The swan uplifts his chest, and backward
flings
His neck, a varying arch, between his
towering wings:
The eye that marks the gliding creature
sees   220
How graceful pride can be, and how ma-
jestic, ease.
While tender cares and mild domestic loves
With furtive watch pursue her as she moves,
The female with a meeker charm succeeds,
And her brown little-ones around her leads,
Nibbling the water lilies as they pass,
Or playing wanton with the floating grass.
She, in a mother's care, her beauty's pride
Forgetting, calls the wearied to her side;
Alternately they mount her back, and rest
Close by her mantling wings' embraces
prest.   231
  Long may they float upon this flood
serene;
Theirs be these holms untrodden, still, and
green,
Where leafy shades fence off the blustering
gale,
And breathes in peace the lily of the vale!
Yon isle, which feels not even the milk-
maid's feet,
Yet hears her song, "by distance made
more sweet,"
Yon isle conceals their home, their hut-like
bower;
Green water-rushes overspread the floor;
Long grass and willows form the woven wall,
And swings above the roof the poplar tall.
Thence issuing often with unwieldy stalk,
They crush with broad black feet their
flowery walk;   243
Or, from the neighbouring water, hear at
morn
The hound, the horse's tread, and mellow
horn;
Involve their serpent-necks in changeful
rings,
Rolled wantonly between their slippery
wings,
Or, starting up with noise and rude delight,
Force half upon the wave their cumbrous
flight.

Fair Swan! by all a mother's joys ca-
ressed,   250
Haply some wretch has eyed, and called
thee blessed;
When with her infants, from some shady
seat
By the lake's edge, she rose — to face the
noontide heat;
Or taught their limbs along the dusty road
A few short steps to totter with their load.
I see her now, denied to lay her head,
On cold blue nights, in hut or straw-built
shed,
Turn to a silent smile their sleepy cry,
By pointing to the gliding moon on high.
— When low-hung clouds each star of
summer hide,   260
And fireless are the valleys far and wide,
Where the brook brawls along the public
road
Dark with bat - haunted ashes stretching
broad,
Oft has she taught them on her lap to lay
The shining glow-worm; or, in heedless
play,
Toss it from hand to hand, disquieted;
While others, not unseen, are free to shed
Green unmolested light upon their mossy
bed.
  Oh! when the sleety showers her path
assail,
And like a torrent roars the headstrong
gale,   270
No more her breath can thaw their fingers
cold,
Their frozen arms her neck no more can
fold;
Weak roof a cowering form two babes to
shield,
And faint the fire a dying heart can yield!
Press the sad kiss, fond mother! vainly fears
Thy flooded cheek to wet them with its
tears;
No tears can chill them, and no bosom
warms,
Thy breast their death-bed, coffined in thine
arms!
  Sweet are the sounds that mingle from
afar,
Heard by calm lakes, as peeps the folding
star,   280
Where the duck dabbles 'mid the rustling
sedge,
And feeding pike starts from the water's
edge,

Or the swan stirs the reeds, his neck and
    bill
Wetting, that drip upon the water still;
And heron, as resounds the trodden shore,
Shoots upward, darting his long neck be-
    fore.
  Now, with religious awe, the farewell
    light
Blends with the solemn colouring of night;
'Mid groves of clouds that crest the moun-
    tain's brow,
And round the west's proud lodge their
    shadows throw,   290
Like Una shining on her gloomy way,
The half-seen form of Twilight roams
    astray;
Shedding, through paly loop-holes mild and
    small,
Gleams that upon the lake's still bosom
    fall;
Soft o'er the surface creep those lustres pale
Tracking the motions of the fitful gale.
With restless interchange at once the bright
Wins on the shade, the shade upon the
    light.
No favoured eye was e'er allowed to gaze
On lovelier spectacle in faery days;   300
When gentle Spirits urged a sportive chase,
Brushing with lucid wands the water's face:
While music, stealing round the glimmer-
    ing deeps,
Charmed the tall circle of the enchanted
    steeps.
— The lights are vanished from the watery
    plains:
No wreck of all the pageantry remains.
Unheeded night has overcome the vales:
On the dark earth the wearied vision fails;
The latest lingerer of the forest train,
The lone black fir, forsakes the faded
    plain;   310
Last evening sight, the cottage smoke, no
    more,
Lost in the thickened darkness, glimmers
    hoar;
And, towering from the sullen dark-brown
    mere,
Like a black wall, the mountain-steeps ap-
    pear.
— Now o'er the soothed accordant heart we
    feel
A sympathetic twilight slowly steal,
And ever, as we fondly muse, we find
The soft gloom deepening on the tranquil
    mind.

Stay ! pensive, sadly-pleasing visions, stay!
Ah no ! as fades the vale, they fade away:
Yet still the tender, vacant gloom remains;
Still the cold cheek its shuddering tear re-
    tains.   322
  The bird, who ceased, with fading light,
    to thread
Silent the hedge or steamy rivulet's bed,
From his grey re-appearing tower shall
    soon
Salute with gladsome note the rising moon,
While with a hoary light she frosts the
    ground,
And pours a deeper blue to Æther's bound;
Pleased, as she moves, her pomp of clouds
    to fold
In robes of azure, fleecy-white, and gold. 330
  Above yon eastern hill, where darkness
    broods
O'er all its vanished dells, and lawns, and
    woods;
Where but a mass of shade the sight can
    trace,
Even now she shews, half-veiled, her lovely
    face:
Across the gloomy valley flings her light,
Far to the western slopes with hamlets
    white;
And gives, where woods the chequered up-
    land strew,
To the green corn of summer, autumn's hue.
  Thus Hope, first pouring from her blessed
    horn
Her dawn, far lovelier than the moon's own
    morn,   340
Till higher mounted, strives in vain to cheer
The weary hills, impervious, blackening
    near;
Yet does she still, undaunted, throw the
    while
On darling spots remote her tempting smile.
  Even now she decks for me a distant
    scene,
(For dark and broad the gulf of time be-
    tween)
Gilding that cottage with her fondest ray,
(Sole bourn, sole wish, sole object of my
    way;
How fair its lawns and sheltering woods
    appear !
How sweet its streamlet murmurs in mine
    ear !)   350
Where we, my Friend, to happy days shall
    rise,
Till our small share of hardly-paining sighs

(For sighs will ever trouble human breath)
Creep hushed into the tranquil breast of
    death.
  But now the clear bright Moon her zenith
    gains,
And, rimy without speck, extend the plains:
The deepest cleft the mountain's front dis-
    plays
Scarce hides a shadow from her searching
    rays;
From the dark-blue faint silvery threads
    divide
The hills, while gleams below the azure
    tide ;   360
Time softly treads; throughout the land-
    scape breathes
A peace enlivened, not disturbed, by wreaths
Of charcoal-smoke, that o'er the fallen
    wood,
Steal down the hill, and spread along the
    flood.
  The song of mountain-streams, unheard
    by day,
Now hardly heard, beguiles my homeward
    way.
Air listens, like the sleeping water, still,
To catch the spiritual music of the hill,
Broke only by the slow clock tolling deep,
Or shout that wakes the ferry-man from
    sleep,   370
The echoed hoof nearing the distant shore,
The boat's first motion — made with dashing
    oar;
Sound of closed gate, across the water borne,
Hurrying the timid hare through rustling
    corn;
The sportive outcry of the mocking owl;
And at long intervals the mill-dog's howl;
The distant forge's swinging thump pro-
    found;
Or yell, in the deep woods, of lonely hound.

LINES

WRITTEN WHILE SAILING IN A BOAT AT EVENING

1788(?). 1798

  This title is scarcely correct. It was during
a solitary walk on the banks of the Cam that I
was first struck with this appearance, and ap-
plied it to my own feelings in the manner here
expressed, changing the scene to the Thames,
near Windsor. This, and the three stanzas of
the following poem, "Remembrance of Collins,"
formed one piece ; but, upon the recommenda-
tion of Coleridge, the three last stanzas were
separated from the other.

How richly glows the water's breast
Before us, tinged with evening hues,
While, facing thus the crimson west,
The boat her silent course pursues !
And see how dark the backward stream !
A little moment past so smiling !
And still, perhaps, with faithless gleam,
Some other loiterers beguiling.

Such views the youthful Bard allure;
But, heedless of the following gloom,
He deems their colours shall endure
Till peace go with him to the tomb.
— And let him nurse his fond deceit,
And what if he must die in sorrow !
Who would not cherish dreams so sweet,
Though grief and pain may come to-mor-
    row ?

REMEMBRANCE OF COLLINS

COMPOSED UPON THE THAMES NEAR RICHMOND

1788(?). 1798

GLIDE gently, thus for ever glide,
O Thames ! that other bards may see
As lovely visions by thy side
As now, fair river ! come to me.
O glide, fair stream ! for ever so,
Thy quiet soul on all bestowing,
Till all our minds for ever flow
As thy deep waters now are flowing.

Vain thought ! — Yet be as now thou art,
That in thy waters may be seen
The image of a poet's heart,
How bright, how solemn, how serene !
Such as did once the Poet bless,
Who murmuring here a later ditty,
Could find no refuge from distress
But in the milder grief of pity.

Now let us, as we float along,
For *him* suspend the dashing oar;
And pray that never child of song
May know that Poet's sorrows more.
How calm ! how still ! the only sound,
The dripping of the oar suspended !
— The evening darkness gathers round
By virtue's holiest Powers attended.

DESCRIPTIVE SKETCHES

TAKEN DURING A PEDESTRIAN TOUR AMONG THE ALPS

1792-93. 1793

Much the greatest part of this poem was composed during my walks upon the banks of the Loire in the years 1791, 1792. I will only notice that the description of the valley filled with mist, beginning — "In solemn shapes," was taken from that beautiful region of which the principal features are Lungarn and Sarnen. Nothing that I ever saw in nature left a more delightful impression on my mind than that which I have attempted, alas! how feebly, to convey to others in these lines. Those two lakes have always interested me especially, from bearing, in their size and other features, a resemblance to those of the North of England. It is much to be deplored that a district so beautiful should be so unhealthy as it is.

TO

THE REV. ROBERT JONES,

FELLOW OF ST. JOHN'S COLLEGE, CAMBRIDGE

DEAR SIR,

However desirous I might have been of giving you proofs of the high place you hold in my esteem, I should have been cautious of wounding your delicacy by thus publicly addressing you, had not the circumstance of my having accompanied you amongst the Alps, seemed to give this dedication a propriety sufficient to do away any scruples which your modesty might otherwise have suggested.

In inscribing this little work to you, I consult my heart. You know well how great is the difference between two companions lolling in a post-chaise, and two travellers plodding slowly along the road, side by side, each with his little knapsack of necessaries upon his shoulders. How much more of heart between the two latter!

I am happy in being conscious that I shall have one reader who will approach the conclusion of these few pages with regret. You they must certainly interest, in reminding you of moments to which you can hardly look back without a pleasure not the less dear from a shade of melancholy. You will meet with few images without recollecting the spot where we observed them together; consequently, whatever is feeble in my design, or spiritless in my colouring, will be amply supplied by your own memory.

With still greater propriety I might have inscribed to you a description of some of the features of your native mountains, through which we have wandered together, in the same manner, with so much pleasure. But the sea-sunsets, which give such splendour to the vale of Clwyd, Snowdon, the chair of Idris, the quiet village of Bethgelert, Menai and her Druids, the Alpine steeps of the Conway, and the still more interesting windings of the wizard stream of the Dee, remain yet untouched. Apprehensive that my pencil may never be exercised on these subjects, I cannot let slip this opportunity of thus publicly assuring you with how much affection and esteem

I am, dear Sir,
Most sincerely yours,
W. WORDSWORTH.

LONDON, 1793.

Happiness (if she had been to be found on earth) among the charms of Nature — Pleasures of the pedestrian Traveller — Author crosses France to the Alps — Present state of the Grande Chartreuse — Lake of Come — Time, Sunset — Same Scene, Twilight — Same Scene, Morning; its voluptuous Character; Old man and forest-cottage music — River Tusa — Via Mala and Grison Gipsy — Sckellenen-thal — Lake of Uri — Stormy sunset — Chapel of William Tell — Force of local emotion — Chamois-chaser — View of the higher Alps — Manner of life of a Swiss mountaineer, interspersed with views of the higher Alps — Golden age of the Alps — Life and views continued — Ranz des Vaches, famous Swiss Air — Abbey of Einsiedlen and its pilgrims — Valley of Chamouny — Mont Blanc — Slavery of Savoy — Influence of liberty on cottage-happiness — France — Wish for the Extirpation of Slavery — Conclusion.

WERE there, below, a spot of holy ground
Where from distress a refuge might be
      found,
And solitude prepare the soul for heaven;
Sure, nature's God that spot to man had
      given
Where falls the purple morning far and
      wide
In flakes of light upon the mountain side;
Where with loud voice the power of water
      shakes
The leafy wood, or sleeps in quiet lakes.
   Yet not unrecompensed the man shall
      roam,
Who at the call of summer quits his home,
And plods through some wide realm o'er
      vale and height,   11
Though seeking only holiday delight;

At least, not owning to himself an aim
To which the sage would give a prouder
name.
No gains too cheaply earned his fancy cloy,
Though every passing zephyr whispers joy;
Brisk toil, alternating with ready ease,
Feeds the clear current of his sympathies.
For him sod-seats the cottage-door adorn;
And peeps the far-off spire, his evening
bourn !   20
Dear is the forest frowning o'er his head,
And dear the velvet green-sward to his
tread:
Moves there a cloud o'er mid-day's flaming
eye ?
Upward he looks — "and calls it luxury:"
Kind Nature's charities his steps attend;
In every babbling brook he finds a friend;
While chastening thoughts of sweetest use,
bestowed
By wisdom, moralise his pensive road.
Host of his welcome inn, the noon-tide
bower,
To his spare meal he calls the passing poor;
He views the sun uplift his golden fire, 31
Or sink, with heart alive like Memnon's
lyre;
Blesses the moon that comes with kindly
ray,
To light him shaken by his rugged way.
Back from his sight no bashful children steal;
He sits a brother at the cottage-meal;
His humble looks no shy restraint impart;
Around him plays at will the virgin heart.
While unsuspended wheels the village
dance,   39
The maidens eye him with enquiring glance,
Much wondering by what fit of crazing care,
Or desperate love, bewildered, he came
there.
A hope, that prudence could not then ap-
prove,
That clung to Nature with a truant's love,
O'er Gallia's wastes of corn my footsteps led;
Her files of road-elms, high above my head
In long-drawn vista, rustling in the breeze;
Or where her pathways straggle as they
please
By lonely farms and secret villages.
But lo ! the Alps ascending white in air, 50
Toy with the sun and glitter from afar.
And now, emerging from the forest's
gloom,
I greet thee, Chartreuse, while I mourn thy
doom.

Whither is fled that Power whose frown
severe
Awed sober Reason till she crouched in
fear ?
That Silence, once in deathlike fetters
bound,
Chains that were loosened only by the sound
Of holy rites chanted in measured round ?
— The voice of blasphemy the fane alarms,
The cloister startles at the gleam of arms.
The thundering tube the aged angler hears,
Bent o'er the groaning flood that sweeps
away his tears.   62
Cloud-piercing pine-trees nod their troubled
heads,
Spires, rocks, and lawns a browner night
o'erspreads;
Strong terror checks the female peasant's
sighs,
And start the astonished shades at female
eyes.
From Bruno's forest screams the affrighted
jay,
And slow the insulted eagle wheels away.
A viewless flight of laughing Demons mock
The Cross, by angels planted on the aërial
rock.   70
The "parting Genius" sighs with hollow
breath
Along the mystic streams of Life and Death.
Swelling the outcry dull, that long resounds
Portentous through her old woods' trackless
bounds,
Vallombre, 'mid her falling fanes, deplores,
For ever broke, the sabbath of her bowers.
More pleased, my foot the hidden margin
roves
Of Como, bosomed deep in chestnut groves.
No meadows thrown between, the giddy
steeps
Tower, bare or sylvan, from the narrow
deeps.   80
— To towns, whose shades of no rude noise
complain,
From ringing team apart and grating
wain —
To flat-roofed towns, that touch the water's
bound,
Or lurk in woody sunless glens profound,
Or, from the bending rocks, obtrusive cling,
And o'er the whitened wave their shadows
fling —
The pathway leads, as round the steeps it
twines;
And Silence loves its purple roof of vines.

The loitering traveller hence, at evening, sees
From rock-hewn steps the sail between the trees;   90
Or marks, 'mid opening cliffs, fair dark-eyed maids
Tend the small harvest of their garden glades;
Or stops the solemn mountain-shades to view
Stretch o'er the pictured mirror broad and blue,
And track the yellow lights from steep to steep,
As up the opposing hills they slowly creep.
Aloft, here, half a village shines, arrayed
In golden light; half hides itself in shade;
While, from amid the darkened roofs, the spire,
Restlessly flashing, seems to mount like fire: 100
There, all unshaded, blazing forests throw
Rich golden verdure on the lake below.
Slow glides the sail along the illumined shore,
And steals into the shade the lazy oar;
Soft bosoms breathe around contagious sighs,
And amorous music on the water dies.
    How blest, delicious scene! the eye that greets
Thy open beauties, or thy lone retreats;
Beholds the unwearied sweep of wood that scales   109
Thy cliffs; the endless waters of thy vales;
Thy lowly cots that sprinkle all the shore,
Each with its household boat beside the door;
Thy torrents shooting from the clear-blue sky;
Thy towns, that cleave, like swallows' nests, on high;
That glimmer hoar in eve's last light, descried
Dim from the twilight water's shaggy side,
Whence lutes and voices down the enchanted woods
Steal, and compose the oar-forgotten floods;
Thy lake, that, streaked or dappled, blue or grey,
'Mid smoking woods gleams hid from morning's ray   120
Slow-travelling down the western hills, to enfold
Its green-tinged margin in a blaze of gold;

Thy glittering steeples, whence the matin bell
Calls forth the woodman from his desert cell,
And quickens the blithe sound of oars that pass
Along the steaming lake, to early mass.
But now farewell to each and all — adieu
To every charm, and last and chief to you,
Ye lovely maidens that in noontide shade   129
Rest near your little plots of wheaten glade;
To all that binds the soul in powerless trance,
Lip-dewing song, and ringlet-tossing dance;
Where sparkling eyes and breaking smiles illume
The sylvan cabin's lute-enlivened gloom.
— Alas! the very murmur of the streams
Breathes o'er the failing soul voluptuous dreams,
While Slavery, forcing the sunk mind to dwell
On joys that might disgrace the captive's cell,
Her shameless timbrel shakes on Como's marge   139
And lures from bay to bay the vocal barge.
    Yet are thy softer arts with power indued
To soothe and cheer the poor man's solitude.
By silent cottage doors, the peasant's home
Left vacant for the day, I loved to roam.
But once I pierced the mazes of a wood
In which a cabin undeserted stood;
There an old man an olden measure scanned
On a rude viol touched with withered hand.
As lambs or fawns in April clustering lie
Under a hoary oak's thin canopy,   150
Stretched at his feet, with stedfast upward eye,
His children's children listened to the sound;
— A Hermit with his family around!
    But let us hence; for fair Locarno smiles
Embowered in walnut slopes and citron isles:
Or seek at eve the banks of Tusa's stream,
Where, 'mid dim towers and woods, her waters gleam.
From the bright wave, in solemn gloom, retire
The dull-red steeps, and, darkening still, aspire
To where afar rich orange lustres glow   160
Round undistinguished clouds, and rocks, and snow:
Or, led where Via Mala's chasms confine
The indignant waters of the infant Rhine,

Hang o'er the abyss, whose else impervious
    gloom
His burning eyes with fearful light illume.
  The mind condemned, without reprieve,
    to go
O'er life's long deserts with its charge of
    woe,
With sad congratulation joins the train
Where beasts and men together o'er the
    plain
Move on — a mighty caravan of pain: 170
Hope, strength, and courage, social suffer-
    ing brings,
Freshening the wilderness with shades and
    springs.
— There be whose lot far otherwise is cast:
Sole human tenant of the piny waste,
By choice or doom a gipsy wanders here,
A nursling babe her only comforter;
Lo, where she sits beneath yon shaggy rock,
A cowering shape half hid in curling smoke !
  When lightning among clouds and moun-
    tain-snows   179
Predominates, and darkness comes and goes,
And the fierce torrent, at the flashes broad
Starts, like a horse, beside the glaring
    road —
She seeks a covert from the battering shower
In the roofed bridge; the bridge, in that
    dread hour,
Itself all trembling at the torrent's power.
  Nor is she more at ease on some *still* night,
When not a star supplies the comfort of its
    light;
Only the waning moon hangs dull and red
Above a melancholy mountain's head,
Then sets. In total gloom the Vagrant
    sighs,   190
Stoops her sick head, and shuts her weary
    eyes;
Or on her fingers counts the distant clock,
Or, to the drowsy crow of midnight cock,
Listens, or quakes while from the forest's
    gulf
Howls near and nearer yet the famished
    wolf.
  From the green vale of Urseren smooth
    and wide
Descend we now, the maddened Reuss our
    guide;
By rocks that, shutting out the blessed day,
Cling tremblingly to rocks as loose as they;
By cells upon whose image, while he prays,
The kneeling peasant scarcely dares to
    gaze;   201

By many a votive death-cross planted near,
And watered duly with the pious tear,
That faded silent from the upward eye
Unmoved with each rude form of peril nigh;
Fixed on the anchor left by Him who saves
Alike in whelming snows,and roaring waves.
  But soon a peopled region on the sight
Opens — a little world of calm delight;
Where mists, suspended on the expiring
    gale,   210
Spread rooflike o'er the deep secluded vale,
And beams of evening slipping in between,
Gently illuminate a sober scene: —
Here, on the brown wood-cottages they
    sleep,
There, over rock or sloping pasture creep.
On as we journey, in clear view displayed,
The still vale lengthens underneath its shade
Of low-hung vapour: on the freshened mead
The green light sparkles; — the dim bowers
    recede.
While pastoral pipes and streams the land-
    scape lull,   220
And bells of passing mules that tinkle dull,
In solemn shapes before the admiring eye
Dilated hang the misty pines on high,
Huge convent domes with pinnacles and
    towers,
And antique castles seen through gleamy
    showers.
  From such romantic dreams, my soul,
    awake !
To sterner pleasure, where, by Uri's lake,
In Nature's pristine majesty outspread,
Winds neither road nor path for foot to
    tread:
The rocks rise naked as a wall, or stretch
Far o'er the water, hung with groves of
    beech;   231
Aërial pines from loftier steeps ascend,
Nor stop but where creation seems to end.
Yet here and there, if mid the savage scene
Appears a scanty plot of smiling green,
Up from the lake a zigzag path will creep
To reach a small wood-hut hung boldly on
    the steep.
— Before those thresholds (never can they
    know
The face of traveller passing to and fro,)
No peasant leans upon his pole, to tell   240
For whom at morning tolled the funeral bell;
Their watch-dog ne'er his angry bark fore-
    goes,
Touched by the beggar's moan of human
    woes;

The shady porch ne'er offered a cool seat
To pilgrims overcome by summer's heat.
Yet thither the world's business finds its
    way
At times, and tales unsought beguile the
    day,
And *there* are those fond thoughts which
    Solitude,
However stern, is powerless to exclude.
There doth the maiden watch her lover's
    sail   250
Approaching, and upbraid the tardy gale;
At midnight listens till his parting oar,
And its last echo, can be heard no more.
   And what if ospreys, cormorants, herons,
    cry
Amid tempestuous vapours driving by,
Or hovering over wastes too bleak to rear
That common growth of earth, the foodful
    ear;
Where the green apple shrivels on the spray,
And pines the unripened pear in summer's
    kindliest ray;   259
Contentment shares the desolate domain
With Independence, child of high Disdain.
Exulting 'mid the winter of the skies,
Shy as the jealous chamois, Freedom flies,
And grasps by fits her sword, and often
    eyes;
And sometimes, as from rock to rock she
    bounds
The Patriot nymph starts at imagined
    sounds,
And, wildly pausing, oft she hangs aghast,
Whether some old Swiss air hath checked
    her haste
Or thrill of Spartan fife is caught between
    the blast.
   Swoln with incessant rains from hour to
    hour,   270
All day the floods a deepening murmur
    pour:
The sky is veiled, and every cheerful sight:
Dark is the region as with coming night;
But what a sudden burst of overpowering
    light!
Triumphant on the bosom of the storm,
Glances the wheeling eagle's glorious form!
Eastward, in long perspective glittering,
    shine
The wood-crowned cliffs that o'er the lake
    recline;
Those lofty cliffs a hundred streams unfold,
At once to pillars turned that flame with
    gold: 280

Behind his sail the peasant shrinks, to shun
The *west*, that burns like one dilated sun,
A crucible of mighty compass, felt
By mountains, glowing till they seem to
    melt.
   But, lo! the boatman, overawed, before
The pictured fane of Tell suspends his oar;
Confused the Marathonian tale appears,
While his eyes sparkle with heroic tears.
And who, that walks where men of ancient
    days
Have wrought with godlike arm the deeds
    of praise,   290
Feels not the spirit of the place control,
Or rouse and agitate his labouring soul?
Say, who, by thinking on Canadian hills,
Or wild Aosta lulled by Alpine rills,
On Zutphen's plain; or on that highland dell,
Through which rough Garry cleaves his
    way, can tell
What high resolves exalt the tenderest
    thought
Of him whom passion rivets to the spot,
Where breathed the gale that caught
    Wolfe's happiest sigh,
And the last sunbeam fell on Bayard's eye;
Where bleeding Sidney from the cup re-
    tired,   301
And glad Dundee in "faint huzzas" ex-
    pired?
   But now with other mind I stand alone
Upon the summit of this naked cone,
And watch the fearless chamois-hunter
    chase
His prey, through tracts abrupt of desolate
    space,
Through vacant worlds where Nature never
    gave
A brook to murmur or a bough to wave,
Which unsubstantial Phantoms sacred keep;
Thro' worlds where Life, and Voice, and
    Motion sleep;   310
Where silent Hours their deathlike sway
    extend,
Save when the avalanche breaks loose, to
    rend
Its way with uproar, till the ruin, drowned
In some dense wood or gulf of snow pro-
    found,
Mocks the dull ear of Time with deaf abor-
    tive sound.
— 'T is his, while wandering on from height
    to height,
To see a planet's pomp and steady light
In the least star of scarce-appearing night;

While the pale moon moves near him, on
    the bound   319
Of ether, shining with diminished round,
And far and wide the icy summits blaze,
Rejoicing in the glory of her rays:
To him the day-star glitters small and
    bright,
Shorn of its beams, insufferably white,
And he can look beyond the sun, and view
Those fast-receding depths of sable blue
Flying till vision can no more pursue!
— At once bewildering mists around him
    close,
And cold and hunger are his least of woes;
The Demon of the snow, with angry roar
Descending, shuts for aye his prison door.
Soon with despair's whole weight his spirits
    sink;   332
Bread has he none, the snow must be his
    drink;
And, ere his eyes can close upon the day,
The eagle of the Alps o'ershades her prey.
    Now couch thyself where, heard with fear
    afar,
Thunders through echoing pines the head-
    long Aar;
Or rather stay to taste the mild delights
Of pensive Underwalden's pastoral heights.
— Is there who 'mid these awful wilds has
    seen   340
The native Genii walk the mountain green?
Or heard, while other worlds their charms
    reveal,
Soft music o'er the aërial summit steal?
While o'er the desert, answering every
    close,
Rich steam of sweetest perfume comes and
    goes.
— And sure there is a secret Power that
    reigns
Here, where no trace of man the spot pro-
    fanes,
Nought but the *chalets*, flat and bare, on high
Suspended 'mid the quiet of the sky;
Or distant herds that pasturing upward
    creep,   350
And, not untended, climb the dangerous
    steep.
How still! no irreligious sound or sight
Rouses the soul from her severe delight.
An idle voice the sabbath region fills
Of Deep that calls to Deep across the hills,
And with that voice accords the soothing
    sound
Of drowsy bells, for ever tinkling round;

Faint wail of eagle melting into blue
Beneath the cliffs, and pine-woods' steady
    sugh;
The solitary heifer's deepened low;   360
Or rumbling, heard remote, of falling snow.
All motions, sounds, and voices, far and
    nigh,
Blend in a music of tranquillity;
Save when, a stranger seen below, the boy
Shouts from the echoing hills with savage
    joy.
    When, from the sunny breast of open
    seas,
And bays with myrtle fringed, the southern
    breeze
Comes on to gladden April with the sight
Of green isles widening on each snow-clad
    height;
When shouts and lowing herds the valley
    fill,   370
And louder torrents stun the noon-tide hill,
The pastoral Swiss begin the cliffs to scale,
Leaving to silence the deserted vale;
And like the Patriarchs in their simple age
Move, as the verdure leads, from stage to
    stage:
High and more high in summer's heat they
    go,
And hear the rattling thunder far below;
Or steal beneath the mountains, half-de-
    terred,
Where huge rocks tremble to the bellowing
    herd.
    One I behold who, 'cross the foaming
    flood,   380
Leaps with a bound of graceful hardihood;
Another, high on that green ledge; — he
    gained
The tempting spot with every sinew
    strained;
And downward thence a knot of grass he
    throws,
Food for his beasts in time of winter snows.
— Far different life from what Tradition
    hoar
Transmits of happier lot in times of yore!
Then Summer lingered long; and honey
    flowed
From out the rocks, the wild bees' safe
    abode:
Continual waters welling cheered the waste,
And plants were wholesome, now of deadly
    taste: 391
Nor Winter yet his frozen stores had piled,
Usurping where the fairest herbage smiled;

Nor Hunger driven the herds from pastures
     bare,
To climb the treacherous cliffs for scanty
     fare.
Then the milk-thistle flourished through the
     land,
And forced the full-swoln udder to demand,
Thrice every day, the pail and welcome
     hand.
Thus does the father to his children tell   399
Of banished bliss, by fancy loved too well.
Alas ! that human guilt provoked the rod
Of angry Nature to avenge her God.
Still, Nature, ever just, to him imparts
Joys only given to uncorrupted hearts.
'T is morn: with gold the verdant moun-
     tain glows;
More high, the snowy peaks with hues of
     rose.
Far-stretched beneath the many-tinted hills,
A mighty waste of mist the valley fills,
A solemn sea ! whose billows wide around
Stand motionless, to awful silence bound: 410
Pines, on the coast, through mist their tops
     uprear,
That like to leaning masts of stranded ships
     appear.
A single chasm, a gulf of gloomy blue,
Gapes in the centre of the sea — and,
     through
That dark mysterious gulf ascending, sound
Innumerable streams with roar profound.
Mount through the nearer vapours notes of
     birds,
And merry flageolet; the low of herds,
The bark of dogs, the heifer's tinkling
     bell,
Talk, laughter, and perchance a church-
     tower knell: 420
Think not the peasant from aloft has gazed
And heard with heart unmoved, with soul
     unraised:
Nor is his spirit less enrapt, nor less
Alive to independent happiness,
Then, when he lies, out-stretched, at even-
     tide,
Upon the fragrant mountain's purple side:
For as the pleasures of his simple day
Beyond his native valley seldom stray,
Nought round its darling precincts can he
     find   429
But brings some past enjoyment to his mind;
While Hope, reclining upon Pleasure's urn,
Binds her wild wreaths, and whispers his re-
     turn.

Once, Man entirely free, alone and wild,
Was blest as free — for he was Nature's
     child.
He, all superior but his God disdained,
Walked none restraining, and by none re-
     strained
Confessed no law but what his reason taught,
Did all he wished, and wished but what he
     ought.
As man in his primeval dower arrayed
The image of his glorious Sire displayed, 440
Even so, by faithful Nature guarded, here
The traces of primeval Man appear;
The simple dignity no forms debase;
The eye sublime, and surly lion-grace:
The slave of none, of beasts alone the lord,
His book he prizes, nor neglects his sword;
Well taught by that to feel his rights, pre-
     pared
With this " the blessings he enjoys to
     guard."
And, as his native hills encircle ground
For many a marvellous victory renowned,
The work of Freedom daring to oppose,   451
With few in arms, innumerable foes,
When to those famous fields his steps are led,
An unknown power connects him with the
     dead:
For images of other worlds are there;
Awful the light, and holy is the air.
Fitfully, and in flashes, through his soul,
Like sun-lit tempests, troubled transports
     roll;
His bosom heaves, his Spirit towers amain,
Beyond the senses and their little reign.   460
And oft, when that dread vision hath past
     by,
He holds with God himself communion high,
There where the peal of swelling torrents
     fills
The sky-roofed temple of the eternal hills;
Or when, upon the mountain's silent brow
Reclined, he sees, above him and below,
Bright stars of ice and azure fields of snow;
While needle peaks of granite shooting bare
Tremble in ever-varying tints of air.
And when a gathering weight of shadows
     brown   470
Falls on the valleys as the sun goes down;
And Pikes, of darkness named and fear and
     storms,
Uplift in quiet their illumined forms,
In sea-like reach of prospect round him
     spread,
Tinged like an angel's smile all rosy red —

Awe in his breast with holiest love unites,
And the near heavens impart their own de-
    lights.
  When downward to his winter hut he
    goes,
Dear and more dear the lessening circle
    grows;
That hut which on the hills so oft employs
His thoughts, the central point of all his
    joys.   481
And as a swallow, at the hour of rest,
Peeps often ere she darts into her nest,
So to the homestead, where the grandsire
    tends
A little prattling child, he oft descends,
To glance a look upon the well-matched
    pair;
Till storm and driving ice blockade him
    there.
There, safely guarded by the woods behind,
He hears the chiding of the baffled wind,
Hears Winter calling all his terrors round,
And, blest within himself, he shrinks not
    from the sound.   491
  Through Nature's vale his homely plea-
    sures glide,
Unstained by envy, discontent, and pride;
The bound of all his vanity, to deck,
With one bright bell, a favourite heifer's
    neck;
Well pleased upon some simple annual feast,
Remembered half the year and hoped the
    rest,
If dairy-produce, from his inner hoard,
Of thrice ten summers dignify the board.
— Alas! in every clime a flying ray   500
Is all we have to cheer our wintry way;
And here the unwilling mind may more than
    trace
The general sorrows of the human race;
The churlish gales of penury, that blow
Cold as the north-wind o'er a waste of snow,
To them the gentle groups of bliss deny
That on the noon-day bank of leisure lie.
Yet more; — compelled by Powers which
    only deign
That solitary man disturb their reign,
Powers that support an unremitting strife
With all the tender charities of life,   511
Full oft the father, when his sons have
    grown
To manhood, seems their title to disown;
And from his nest amid the storms of heaven
Drives, eagle-like, those sons as he was
    driven;

With stern composure watches to the
    plain —
And never, eagle-like, beholds again!
  When long-familiar joys are all resigned,
Why does their sad remembrance haunt the
    mind?
Lo! where through flat Batavia's willowy
    groves,   520
Or by the lazy Seine, the exile roves;
O'er the curled waters Alpine measures
    swell,
And search the affections to their inmost
    cell;
Sweet poison spreads along the listener's
    veins,
Turning past pleasures into mortal pains;
Poison, which not a frame of steel can brave,
Bows his young head with sorrow to the
    grave.
  Gay lark of hope, thy silent song resume!
Ye flattering eastern lights, once more the
    hills illume!
Fresh gales and dews of life's delicious
    morn,   530
And thou, lost fragrance of the heart, re-
    turn!
Alas! the little joy to man allowed
Fades like the lustre of an evening cloud;
Or like the beauty in a flower installed,
Whose season was, and cannot be recalled.
Yet, when opprest by sickness, grief, or care,
And taught that pain is pleasure's natural
    heir,
We still confide in more than we can know;
Death would be else the favourite friend of
    woe.
  'Mid savage rocks, and seas of snow that
    shine,   540
Between interminable tracts of pine,
Within a temple stands an awful shrine,
By an uncertain light revealed, that falls
On the mute Image and the troubled walls.
Oh! give not me that eye of hard disdain
That views, undimmed, Einsiedlen's wretch-
    ed fane.
While ghastly faces through the gloom ap-
    pear,
Abortive joy, and hope that works in fear;
While prayer contends with silenced agony,
Surely in other thoughts contempt may die.
If the sad grave of human ignorance bear
One flower of hope — oh, pass and leave it
    there!   552
  The tall sun, pausing on an Alpine spire,
Flings o'er the wilderness a stream of fire:

Now meet we other pilgrims ere the day
Close on the remnant of their weary way;
While they are drawing toward the sacred
floor
Where, so they fondly think, the worm shall
gnaw no more.
How gaily murmur and how sweetly taste
The fountains reared for them amid the
waste !   560
Their thirst they slake: — they wash their
toil-worn feet
And some with tears of joy each other greet.
Yes, I must see you when ye first behold
Those holy turrets tipped with evening gold;
In that glad moment will for you a sigh
Be heaved, of charitable sympathy;
In that glad moment when your hands are
prest
In mute devotion on the thankful breast !
    Last, let us turn to Chamouny that shields
With rocks and gloomy woods her fertile
fields: 570
Five streams of ice amid her cots descend,
And with wild flowers and blooming or-
chards blend; —
A scene more fair than what the Grecian
feigns
Of purple lights and ever-vernal plains;
Here all the seasons revel hand in hand:
'Mid lawns and shades by breezy rivulets
fanned,
They sport beneath that mountain's match-
less height
That holds no commerce with the summer
night.
From age to age, throughout his lonely
bounds
The crash of ruin fitfully resounds;   580
Appalling havoc! but serene his brow,
Where daylight lingers on perpetual snow;
Glitter the stars above, and all is black below.
    What marvel then if many a Wanderer
sigh,
While roars the sullen Arve in anger by,
That not for thy reward, unrivalled Vale!
Waves the ripe harvest in the autumnal
gale;
That thou, the slave of slaves, art doomed
to pine
And droop, while no Italian arts are thine,
To soothe or cheer, to soften or refine.   590
    Hail Freedom ! whether it was mine to
stray,
With shrill winds whistling round my lonely
way,

On the bleak sides of Cumbria's heath-clad
moors,
Or where dank sea-weed lashes Scotland's
shores;
To scent the sweets of Piedmont's breath-
ing rose,
And orange gale that o'er Lugano blows;
Still have I found, where Tyranny prevails,
That virtue languishes and pleasure fails,
While the remotest hamlets blessings share
In thy loved presence known, and only
there;   600
Heart-blessings — outward treasures, too,
which the eye
Of the sun peeping through the clouds can
spy,
And every passing breeze will testify.
There, to the porch, belike with jasmine
bound
Or woodbine wreaths, a smoother path is
wound;
The housewife there a brighter garden sees,
Where hum on busier wing her happy bees;
On infant cheeks there fresher roses blow;
And grey-haired men look up with livelier
brow, —
To greet the traveller needing food and
rest;   610
Housed for the night, or but a half-hour's
guest.
    And oh, fair France! though now the
traveller sees
Thy three-striped banner fluctuate on the
breeze;
Though martial songs have banished songs
of love,
And nightingales desert the village grove,
Scared by the fife and rumbling drum's
alarms,
And the short thunder, and the flash of arms;
That cease not till night falls, when far and
nigh,
Sole sound, the Sourd prolongs his mourn-
ful cry !
— Yet, hast thou found that Freedom spreads
her power   620
Beyond the cottage-hearth, the cottage-door:
All nature smiles, and owns beneath her eyes
Her fields peculiar, and peculiar skies.
Yes, as I roamed where Loiret's waters
glide
Through rustling aspens heard from side to
side,
When from October clouds a milder light
Fell where the blue flood rippled into white;

Methought from every cot the watchful bird
Crowed with ear-piercing power till then
    unheard;
Each clacking mill, that broke the murmur-
    ing streams,   630
Rocked the charmed thought in more de-
    lightful dreams;
Chasing those pleasant dreams, the falling
    leaf
Awoke a fainter sense of moral grief;
The measured echo of the distant flail
Wound in more welcome cadence down the
    vale;
With more majestic course the water rolled,
And ripening foliage shone with richer gold.
— But foes are gathering — Liberty must
    raise
Red on the hills her beacon's far-seen blaze;
Must bid the tocsin ring from tower to
    tower! —   640
Nearer and nearer comes the trying hour!
Rejoice, brave Land, though pride's per-
    verted ire
Rouse hell's own aid, and wrap thy fields in
    fire:
Lo, from the flames a great and glorious
    birth;
As if a new-made heaven were hailing a
    new earth!
— All cannot be: the promise is too fair
For creatures doomed to breathe terrestrial
    air:
Yet not for this will sober reason frown
Upon that promise, nor the hope disown; 649
She knows that only from high aims ensue
Rich guerdons, and to them alone are due.
    Great God! by whom the strifes of men
    are weighed
In an impartial balance, give thine aid
To the just cause; and, oh! do thou pre-
    side
Over the mighty stream now spreading
    wide:
So shall its waters, from the heavens sup-
    plied
In copious showers, from earth by whole-
    some springs,
Brood o'er the long-parched lands with Nile-
    like wings!
And grant that every sceptred child of clay
Who cries presumptuous, "Here the flood
    shall stay,"   660
May in its progress see thy guiding hand,
And cease the acknowledged purpose to
    withstand;

Or, swept in anger from the insulted shore,
Sink with his servile bands, to rise no more!
    To-night, my Friend, within this humble
    cot
Be scorn and fear and hope alike forgot
In timely sleep; and when, at break of
    day,
On the tall peaks the glistening sunbeams
    play,
With a light heart our course we may re-
    new,
The first whose footsteps print the mountain
    dew.   670

GUILT AND SORROW

OR INCIDENTS UPON SALISBURY PLAIN

1793–94. 1842

Unwilling to be unnecessarily particular, I have assigned this poem to the dates 1793 and '94; but in fact much of the " Female Vagrant's " story was composed at least two years before. All that relates to her sufferings as a sailor's wife in America, and her condition of mind during her voyage home, were faithfully taken from the report made to me of her own case by a friend who had been subjected to the same trials and affected in the same way. Mr. Coleridge, when I first became acquainted with him, was so much impressed with this poem, that it would have encouraged me to publish the whole as it then stood; but the mariner's fate appeared to me so tragical as to require a treatment more subdued and yet more strictly applicable in expression than I had at first given to it. This fault was corrected nearly fifty years afterwards, when I determined to publish the whole. It may be worth while to remark, that, though the incidents of this attempt do only in a small degree produce each other, and it deviates accordingly from the general rule by which narrative pieces ought to be governed, it is not therefore wanting in continuous hold upon the mind, or in unity, which is effected by the identity of moral interest that places the two personages upon the same footing in the reader's sympathies. My rambles over many parts of Salisbury Plain put me, as mentioned in the preface, upon writing this poem, and left on my mind imaginative impressions the force of which I have felt to this day. From that district I proceeded to Bath, Bristol, and so on to the banks of the Wye, where I took again to travelling on foot. In remembrance of that part of my journey, which was in '93, I began the verses — " Five years have passed."

ADVERTISEMENT

PREFIXED TO THE FIRST EDITION OF THIS POEM, PUBLISHED IN 1842

Not less than one third of the following poem, though it has from time to time been altered in the expression, was published so far back as the year 1798, under the title of " The Female Vagrant." The extract is of such length that an apology seems to be required for reprinting it here : but it was necessary to restore it to its original position, or the rest would have been unintelligible. The whole was written before the close of the year 1794, and I will detail, rather as matter of literary biography than for any other reason, the circumstances under which it was produced.

During the latter part of the summer of 1793, having passed a month in the Isle of Wight, in view of the fleet which was then preparing for sea off Portsmouth at the commencement of the war, I left the place with melancholy forebodings. The American war was still fresh in memory. The struggle which was beginning, and which many thought would be brought to a speedy close by the irresistible arms of Great Britain being added to those of the allies, I was assured in my own mind would be of long continuance, and productive of distress and misery beyond all possible calculation. This conviction was pressed upon me by having been a witness, during a long residence in revolutionary France, of the spirit which prevailed in that country. After leaving the Isle of Wight, I spent two days in wandering on foot over Salisbury Plain, which, though cultivation was then widely spread through parts of it, had upon the whole a still more impressive appearance than it now retains.

The monuments and traces of antiquity, scattered in abundance over that region, led me unavoidably to compare what we know or guess of those remote times with certain aspects of modern society, and with calamities, principally those consequent upon war, to which, more than other classes of men, the poor are subject. In those reflections, joined with particular facts that had come to my knowledge, the following stanzas originated.

In conclusion, to obviate some distraction in the minds of those who are well acquainted with Salisbury Plain, it may be proper to say, that of the features described as belonging to it, one or two are taken from other desolate parts of England.

I

A TRAVELLER on the skirt of Sarum's
    Plain
Pursued his vagrant way, with feet half
    bare;

Stooping his gait, but not as if to gain
Help from the staff he bore; for mien and
    air
Were hardy, though his cheek seemed worn
    with care
Both of the time to come, and time long
    fled:
Down fell in straggling locks his thin grey
    hair;
A coat he wore of military red
But faded, and stuck o'er with many a patch
    and shred.

II

While thus he journeyed, step by step led
    on,   10
He saw and passed a stately inn, full
    sure
That welcome in such house for him was
    none.
No board inscribed the needy to allure
Hung there, no bush proclaimed to old and
    poor
And desolate, " Here you will find a
    friend ! "
The pendent grapes glittered above the
    door ; —
On he must pace, perchance 'till night descend,
Where'er the dreary roads their bare white
    lines extend.

III

The gathering clouds grew red with stormy
    fire,
In streaks diverging wide and mounting
    high;   20
That inn he long had passed; the distant
    spire,
Which oft as he looked back had fixed his
    eye,
Was lost, though still he looked, in the blank
    sky.
Perplexed and comfortless he gazed around,
And scarce could any trace of man descry,
Save cornfields stretched and stretching
    without bound;
But where the sower dwelt was nowhere to
    be found.

IV

No tree was there, no meadow's pleasant
    green,
No brook to wet his lip or soothe his ear ;

Long files of corn-stacks here and there
    were seen, 30
But not one dwelling-place his heart to
    cheer.
Some labourer, thought he, may perchance
    be near;
And so he sent a feeble shout — in vain;
No voice made answer, he could only hear
Winds rustling over plots of unripe grain,
Or whistling thro' thin grass along the un-
    furrowed plain.

V

Long had he fancied each successive slope
Concealed some cottage, whither he might
    turn
And rest; but now along heaven's darken-
    ing cope
The crows rushed by in eddies, homeward
    borne. 40
Thus warned he sought some shepherd's
    spreading thorn
Or hovel from the storm to shield his head,
But sought in vain; for now, all wild, for-
    lorn,
And vacant, a huge waste around him
    spread;
The wet cold ground, he feared, must be
    his only bed.

VI

And be it so — for to the chill night shower
And the sharp wind his head he oft hath
    bared;
A Sailor he, who many a wretched hour
Hath told; for, landing after labour hard,
Full long endured in hope of just reward,
He to an armèd fleet was forced away 51
By seamen, who perhaps themselves had
    shared
Like fate; was hurried off, a helpless prey,
'Gainst all that in *his* heart, or theirs per-
    haps, said nay.

VII

For years the work of carnage did not
    cease,
And death's dire aspect daily he surveyed,
Death's minister; then came his glad re-
    lease,
And hope returned, and pleasure fondly
    made
Her dwelling in his dreams. By Fancy's
    aid
The happy husband flies, his arms to throw

Round his wife's neck; the prize of victory
    laid 61
In her full lap, he sees such sweet tears
    flow
As if thenceforth nor pain nor trouble she
    could know.

VIII

Vain hope! for fraud took all that he had
    earned.
The lion roars and gluts his tawny brood
Even in the desert's heart; but he, re-
    turned,
Bears not to those he loves their needful
    food.
His home approaching, but in such a mood
That from his sight his children might have
    run,
He met a traveller, robbed him, shed his
    blood; 70
And when the miserable work was done
He fled, a vagrant since, the murderer's
    fate to shun.

IX

From that day forth no place to him could
    be
So lonely, but that thence might come a
    pang
Brought from without to inward misery.
Now, as he plodded on, with sullen clang
A sound of chains along the desert rang;
He looked, and saw upon a gibbet high
A human body that in irons swang,
Uplifted by the tempest whirling by; 80
And, hovering, round it often did a raven
    fly.

X

It was a spectacle which none might view,
In spot so savage, but with shuddering
    pain;
Nor only did for him at once renew
All he had feared from man, but roused a
    train
Of the mind's phantoms, horrible as vain.
The stones, as if to cover him from day,
Rolled at his back along the living plain;
He fell, and without sense or motion lay;
But, when the trance was gone, feebly pur-
    sued his way. 90

XI

As one whose brain habitual phrensy fires
Owes to the fit in which his soul hath tossed

Profounder quiet, when the fit retires,
Even so the dire phantasma which had
    crossed
His sense, in sudden vacancy quite lost,
Left his mind still as a deep evening stream.
Nor, if accosted now, in thought engrossed,
Moody, or inly troubled, would he seem
To traveller who might talk of any casual
    theme.

XII

Hurtle the clouds in deeper darkness piled,
Gone is the raven timely rest to seek;   101
He seemed the only creature in the wild
On whom the elements their rage might
    wreak;
Save that the bustard, of those regions
    bleak
Shy tenant, seeing by the uncertain light
A man there wandering, gave a mournful
    shriek,
And half upon the ground, with strange
    affright,
Forced hard against the wind a thick un-
    wieldy flight.

XIII

All, all was cheerless to the horizon's
    bound;
The weary eye — which, wheresoe'er it
    strays,   110
Marks nothing but the red sun's setting
    round,
Or on the earth strange lines, in former
    days
Left by gigantic arms — at length surveys
What seems an antique castle spreading
    wide;
Hoary and naked are its walls, and raise
Their brow sublime: in shelter there to
    bide
He turned, while rain poured down smok-
    ing on every side.

XIV

Pile of Stone-henge! so proud to hint yet
    keep
Thy secrets, thou that lov'st to stand and
    hear
The Plain resounding to the whirlwind's
    sweep,   120
Inmate of lonesome Nature's endless year;
Even if thou saw'st the giant wicker rear
For sacrifice its throngs of living men,
Before thy face did ever wretch appear,

Who in his heart had groaned with deadlier
    pain
Than he who, tempest-driven, thy shelter
    now would gain.

XV

Within that fabric of mysterious form,
Winds met in conflict, each by turns su-
    preme;
And, from the perilous ground dislodged,
    through storm
And rain he wildered on, no moon to stream
From gulf of parting clouds one friendly
    beam,   131
Nor any friendly sound his footsteps led;
Once did the lightning's faint disastrous
    gleam
Disclose a naked guide-post's double head,
Sight which tho' lost at once a gleam of
    pleasure shed.

XVI

No swinging sign-board creaked from cot-
    tage elm
To stay his steps with faintness over-
    come;
'T was dark and void as ocean's watery
    realm
Roaring with storms beneath night's star-
    less gloom;
No gipsy cowered o'er fire of furze or
    broom;   140
No labourer watched his red kiln glaring
    bright,
Nor taper glimmered dim from sick man's
    room;
Along the waste no line of mournful light
From lamp of lonely toll-gate streamed
    athwart the night.

XVII

At length, though hid in clouds, the moon
    arose;
The downs were visible — and now revealed
A structure stands, which two bare slopes
    enclose.
It was a spot, where, ancient vows ful-
    filled,
Kind pious hands did to the Virgin build
A lonely Spital, the belated swain
From the night terrors of that waste to
    shield: 150
But there no human being could remain,
And now the walls are named the ' Dead
    House ' of the plain.

XVIII

Though he had little cause to love the abode
Of man, or covet sight of mortal face,
Yet when faint beams of light that ruin
    showed,
How glad he was at length to find some
    trace
Of human shelter in that dreary place.
Till to his flock the early shepherd goes,
Here shall much-needed sleep his frame
    embrace.   160
In a dry nook where fern the floor bestrows
He lays his stiffened limbs, — his eyes be-
    gin to close;

XIX

When hearing a deep sigh, that seemed to
    come
From one who mourned in sleep, he raised
    his head,
And saw a woman in the naked room
Outstretched, and turning on a restless
    bed:
The moon a wan dead light around her
    shed.
He waked her — spake in tone that would
    not fail,
He hoped, to calm her mind; but ill he sped,
For of that ruin she had heard a tale   170
Which now with freezing thoughts did all
    her powers assail;

XX

Had heard of one who, forced from storms
    to shroud,
Felt the loose walls of this decayed Retreat
Rock to incessant neighings shrill and
    loud,
While his horse pawed the floor with fu-
    rious heat;
Till on a stone, that sparkled to his feet,
Struck, and still struck again, the troubled
    horse:
The man half raised the stone with pain
    and sweat,
Half raised, for well his arm might lose its
    force
Disclosing the grim head of a late murdered
    corse.   180

XXI

Such tale of this lone mansion she had
    learned,
And, when that shape, with eyes in sleep
    half drowned,

By the moon's sullen lamp she first dis-
    cerned,
Cold stony horror all her senses bound.
Her he addressed in words of cheering
    sound;
Recovering heart, like answer did she
    make;
And well it was that, of the corse there
    found,
In converse that ensued she nothing spake;
She knew not what dire pangs in him such
    tale could wake.

XXII

But soon his voice and words of kind in-
    tent   190
Banished that dismal thought; and now the
    wind
In fainter howlings told its *rage* was spent:
Meanwhile discourse ensued of various
    kind,
Which by degrees a confidence of mind
And mutual interest failed not to create.
And, to a natural sympathy resigned,
In that forsaken building where they sate
The Woman thus retraced her own unto-
    ward fate.

XXIII

" By Derwent's side my father dwelt — a
    man
Of virtuous life, by pious parents bred;
And I believe that, soon as I began   201
To lisp, he made me kneel beside my bed,
And in his hearing there my prayers I said:
And afterwards, by my good father taught,
I read, and loved the books in which I
    read;
For books in every neighbouring house I
    sought,
And nothing to my mind a sweeter pleasure
    brought.

XXIV

" A little croft we owned — a plot of corn,
A garden stored with peas, and mint, and
    thyme,
And flowers for posies, oft on Sunday morn
Plucked while the church bells rang their
    earliest chime.   211
Can I forget our freaks at shearing time !
My hen's rich nest through long grass
    scarce espied;
The cowslip-gathering in June's dewy
    prime;

The swans that with white chests upreared
    in pride
Rushing and racing came to meet me at the
    water-side.

XXV

" The staff I well remember which upbore
The bending body of my active sire;
His seat beneath the honied sycamore
Where the bees hummed, and chair by
    winter fire;   220
When market-morning came, the neat
    attire
With which, though bent on haste, myself
    I decked;
Our watchful house-dog, that would tease
    and tire
The stranger till its barking-fit I checked;
The red-breast, known for years, which at
    my casement pecked.

XXVI

" The suns of twenty summers danced
    along, —
Too little marked how fast they rolled
    away:
But, through severe mischance and cruel
    wrong,
My father's substance fell into decay:
We toiled and struggled, hoping for a
    day   230
When Fortune might put on a kinder
    look;
But vain were wishes, efforts vain as they;
He from his old hereditary nook
Must part; the summons came; — our final
    leave we took.

XXVII

" It was indeed a miserable hour
When, from the last hill-top, my sire sur-
    veyed,
Peering above the trees, the steeple tower
That on his marriage day sweet music
    made !
Till then, he hoped his bones might there
    be laid
Close by my mother in their native bow-
    ers: 240
Bidding me trust in God, he stood and
    prayed ; —
I could not pray: — through tears that fell
    in showers
Glimmered our dear-loved home, alas ! no
    longer ours !

XXVIII

" There was a Youth whom I had loved so
    long,
That when I loved him not I cannot say:
'Mid the green mountains many a thought-
    less song
We two had sung, like gladsome birds in
    May;
When we began to tire of childish play,
We seemed still more and more to prize
    each other;
We talked of marriage and our marriage
    day;   250
And I in truth did love him like a bro-
    ther,
For never could I hope to meet with such
    another.

XXIX

" Two years were passed since to a distant
    town
He had repaired to ply a gainful trade:
What tears of bitter grief, till then un-
    known !
What tender vows, our last sad kiss de-
    layed !
To him we turned: — we had no other
    aid:
Like one revived, upon his neck I wept;
And her whom he had loved in joy, he
    said,
He well could love in grief; his faith he
    kept;   260
And in a quiet home once more my father
    slept.

XXX

" We lived in peace and comfort; and were
    blest
With daily bread, by constant toil sup-
    plied.
Three lovely babes had lain upon my
    breast;
And often, viewing their sweet smiles, I
    sighed,
And knew not why. My happy father
    died,
When threatened war reduced the children's
    meal:
Thrice happy ! that for him the grave
    could hide
The empty loom, cold hearth, and silent
    wheel,
And tears that flowed for ills which
    patience might not heal.   276

XXXI

" 'T was a hard change; an evil time was
   come;
We had no hope, and no relief could gain:
But soon, with proud parade, the noisy
   drum
Beat round to clear the streets of want and
   pain.
My husband's arms now only served to
   strain
Me and his children hungering in his view;
In such dismay my prayers and tears were
   vain:
To join those miserable men he flew,
And now to the sea-coast, with numbers
   more, we drew.

XXXII

" There were we long neglected, and we
   bore   280
Much sorrow ere the fleet its anchor
   weighed;
Green fields before us, and our native shore,
We breathed a pestilential air, that made
Ravage for which no knell was heard. We
   prayed
For our departure; wished and wished —
   nor knew,
'Mid that long sickness and those hopes
   delayed,
That happier days we never more must
   view.
The parting signal streamed — at last the
   land withdrew.

XXXIII

" But the calm summer season now was
   past.
On as we drove, the equinoctial deep   290
Ran mountains high before the howling
   blast,
And many perished in the whirlwind's
   sweep.
We gazed with terror on their gloomy sleep,
Untaught that soon such anguish must en-
   sue,
Our hopes such harvest of affliction reap,
That we the mercy of the waves should rue:
We reached the western world, a poor de-
   voted crew.

XXXIV

" The pains and plagues that on our heads
   came down,
Disease and famine, agony and fear,   299

In wood or wilderness, in camp or town,
It would unman the firmest heart to hear.
All perished — all in one remorseless year,
Husband and children ! one by one, by
   sword
And ravenous plague, all perished: every
   tear
Dried up, despairing, desolate, on board
A British ship I waked, as from a trance
   restored."

XXXV

Here paused she, of all present thought for-
   lorn,
Nor voice nor sound, that moment's pain
   expressed,
Yet Nature, with excess of grief o'erborne,
From her full eyes their watery load re-
   leased.   310
He too was mute; and, ere her weeping
   ceased,
He rose, and to the ruin's portal went,
And saw the dawn opening the silvery
   east
With rays of promise, north and southward
   sent;
And soon with crimson fire kindled the fir-
   mament.

XXXVI

" O come," he cried, " come, after weary
   night
Of such rough storm, this happy change to
   view."
So forth she came, and eastward looked;
   the sight
Over her brow like dawn of gladness threw;
Upon her cheek, to which its youthful hue
Seemed to return, dried the last lingering
   tear,   321
And from her grateful heart a fresh one
   drew:
The whilst her comrade to her pensive cheer
Tempered fit words of hope; and the lark
   warbled near.

XXXVII

They looked and saw a lengthening road,
   and wain
That rang down a bare slope not far re-
   mote:
The barrows glistered bright with drops of
   rain,
Whistled the waggoner with merry note,
The cock far off sounded his clarion throat;

But town, or farm, or hamlet, none they
    viewed, 330
Only were told there stood a lonely cot
A long mile thence. While thither they pur-
    sued
Their way, the Woman thus her mournful
    tale renewed.

XXXVIII

" Peaceful as this immeasurable plain
Is now, by beams of dawning light im-
    prest,
In the calm sunshine slept the glittering
    main;
The very ocean hath its hour of rest.
I too forgot the heavings of my breast.
How quiet 'round me ship and ocean were!
As quiet all within me. I was blest, 340
And looked, and fed upon the silent air
Until it seemed to bring a joy to my de-
    spair.

XXXIX

" Ah ! how unlike those late terrific sleeps,
And groans that rage of racking famine
    spoke;
The unburied dead that lay in festering
    heaps,
The breathing pestilence that rose like
    smoke,
The shriek that from the distant battle
    broke,
The mine's dire earthquake, and the pallid
    host
Driven by the bomb's incessant thunder-
    stroke
To loathsome vaults, where heart-sick an-
    guish tossed, 350
Hope died, and fear itself in agony was lost !

XL

" Some mighty gulf of separation past,
I seemed transported to another world;
A thought resigned with pain, when from
    the mast
The impatient mariner the sail unfurled,
And, whistling, called the wind that hardly
    curled
The silent sea. From the sweet thoughts
    of home
And from all hope I was for ever hurled.
For me — farthest from earthly port to
    roam
Was best, could I but shun the spot where
    man might come. 360

XLI

" And oft I thought (my fancy was so
    strong)
That I, at last, a resting-place had found;
' Here will I dwell,' said I, 'my whole life
    long,
Roaming the illimitable waters round;
Here will I live, of all but heaven dis-
    owned,
And end my days upon the peaceful flood.' —
To break my dream the vessel reached its
    bound;
And homeless near a thousand homes I
    stood,
And near a thousand tables pined and want-
    ed food.

XLII

" No help I sought; in sorrow turned adrift,
Was hopeless, as if cast on some bare rock;
Nor morsel to my mouth that day did
    lift, 372
Nor raised my hand at any door to knock.
I lay where, with his drowsy mates, the
    cock
From the cross - timber of an out-house
    hung:
Dismally tolled, that night, the city clock !
At morn my sick heart hunger scarcely
    stung,
Nor to the beggar's language could I fit
    my tongue.

XLIII

"So passed a second day; and, when the
    third
Was come, I tried in vain the crowd's re-
    sort. 380
— In deep despair, by frightful wishes
    stirred,
Near the sea-side I reached a ruined fort;
There, pains which nature could no more
    support,
With blindness linked, did on my vitals
    fall;
And, after many interruptions short
Of hideous sense, I sank, nor step could
    crawl:
Unsought for was the help that did my life
    recall.

XLIV

" Borne to a hospital, I lay with brain
Drowsy and weak, and shattered memory;

I heard my neighbours in their beds com-
plain 390
Of many things which never troubled me —
Of feet still bustling round with busy
glee,
Of looks where common kindness had no
part,
Of service done with cold formality,
Fretting the fever round the languid heart,
And groans which, as they said, might
make a dead man start.

XLV

" These things just served to stir the slum-
bering sense,
Nor pain nor pity in my bosom raised.
With strength did memory return; and,
thence
Dismissed, again on open day I gazed, 400
At houses, men, and common light, amazed.
The lanes I sought, and, as the sun re-
tired,
Came where beneath the trees a faggot
blazed,
The travellers saw me weep, my fate in-
quired,
And gave me food — and rest, more wel-
come, more desired.

XLVI

" Rough potters seemed they, trading so-
berly
With panniered asses driven from door to
door ;
But life of happier sort set forth to me,
And other joys my fancy to allure — 409
The bag-pipe dinning on the midnight moor
In barn uplighted ; and companions boon,
Well met from far with revelry secure
Among the forest glades, while jocund June
Rolled fast along the sky his warm and
genial moon.

XLVII

" But ill they suited me — those journeys
dark
O'er moor and mountain, midnight theft to
hatch !
To charm the surly house-dog's faithful
bark,
Or hang on tip-toe at the lifted latch.
The gloomy lantern, and the dim blue
match,
The black disguise, the warning whistle
shrill, 420

And ear still busy on its nightly watch,
Were not for me, brought up in nothing ill:
Besides, on griefs so fresh my thoughts
were brooding still.

XLVIII

" What could I do, unaided and unblest ?
My father ! gone was every friend of thine :
And kindred of dead husband are at best
Small help ; and, after marriage such as
mine,
With little kindness would to me incline.
Nor was I then for toil or service fit ;
My deep-drawn sighs no effort could con-
fine ; 430
In open air forgetful would I sit
Whole hours, with idle arms in moping sor-
row knit.

XLIX

" The roads I paced, I loitered through the
fields ;
Contentedly, yet sometimes self-accused,
Trusted my life to what chance bounty
yields,
Now coldly given, now utterly refused.
The ground I for my bed have often used :
But what afflicts my peace with keenest
ruth,
Is that I have my inner self abused,
Foregone the home delight of constant
truth, 440
And clear and open soul, so prized in fear-
less youth.

L

" Through tears the rising sun I oft have
viewed,
Through tears have seen him towards that
world descend
Where my poor heart lost all its fortitude :
Three years a wanderer now my course I
bend —
Oh ! tell me whither — for no earthly friend
Have I." — She ceased, and weeping turned
away ;
As if because her tale was at an end,
She wept ; because she had no more to say
Of that perpetual weight which on her
spirit lay. 450

LI

True sympathy the Sailor's looks expressed,
His looks — for pondering he was mute the
while.

Of social Order's care for wretchedness,
Of Time's sure help to calm and recon-
cile,
Joy's second spring and Hope's long-trea-
sured smile,
'T was not for *him* to speak — a man so
tried.
Yet, to relieve her heart, in friendly style
Proverbial words of comfort he applied,
And not in vain, while they went pacing
side by side.

LII

Erelong, from heaps of turf, before their
sight,   460
Together smoking in the sun's slant beam,
Rise various wreaths that into one unite
Which high and higher mounts with silver
gleam :
Fair spectacle, — but instantly a scream
Thence bursting shrill did all remark pre-
vent ;
They paused, and heard a hoarser voice
blaspheme,
And female cries. Their course they
thither bent,
And met a man who foamed with anger
vehement.

LIII

A woman stood with quivering lips and pale,
And, pointing to a little child that lay   470
Stretched on the ground, began a piteous
tale ;
How in a simple freak of thoughtless play
He had provoked his father, who straight-
way,
As if each blow were deadlier than the
last,
Struck the poor innocent. Pallid with dis-
may
The Soldier's Widow heard and stood
aghast ;
And stern looks on the man her grey-
haired Comrade cast.

LIV

His voice with indignation rising high
Such further deed in manhood's name for-
bade ;
The peasant, wild in passion, made reply
With bitter insult and revilings sad ;   481
Asked him in scorn what business there he
had ;
What kind of plunder he was hunting now ;

The gallows would one day of him be
glad ; —
Though inward anguish damped the Sail-
or's brow,
Yet calm he seemed as thoughts so poign-
ant would allow.

LV

Softly he stroked the child, who lay out-
stretched
With face to earth ; and, as the boy turned
round
His battered head, a groan the Sailor fetched
As if he saw — there and upon that ground —
Strange repetition of the deadly wound
He had himself inflicted. Through his
brain   492
At once the griding iron passage found ;
Deluge of tender thoughts then rushed
amain,
Nor could his sunken eyes the starting tear
restrain.

LVI

Within himself he said — What hearts have
we !
The blessing this a father gives his child !
Yet happy thou, poor boy ! compared with
me,
Suffering not doing ill — fate far more
mild.
The stranger's looks and tears of wrath be-
guiled   500
The father, and relenting thoughts awoke ;
He kissed his son — so all was recon-
ciled.
Then, with a voice which inward trouble
broke
Ere to his lips it came, the Sailor them be-
spoke.

LVII

"Bad is the world, and hard is the world's
law
Even for the man who wears the warmest
fleece ;
Much need have ye that time more closely
draw
The bond of nature, all unkindness cease,
And that among so few there still be peace :
Else can ye hope but with such numerous
foes   510
Your pains shall ever with your years in-
crease ? " —

While from his heart the appropriate lesson
flows,
A correspondent calm stole gently o'er his
woes.

LVIII

Forthwith the pair passed on ; and down
they look
Into a narrow valley's pleasant scene
Where wreaths of vapour tracked a wind-
ing brook,
That babbled on through groves and mead-
ows green ;
A low-roofed house peeped out the trees
between ;
The dripping groves resound with cheerful
lays,
And melancholy lowings intervene   520
Of scattered herds, that in the meadow
graze,
Some amid lingering shade, some touched
by the sun's rays.

LIX

They saw and heard, and, winding with the
road,
Down a thick wood, they dropt into the
vale;
Comfort, by prouder mansions unbestowed,
Their wearied frames, she hoped, would
soon regale.
Erelong they reached that cottage in the
dale:
It was a rustic inn; — the board was spread,
The milk-maid followed with her brimming
pail,
And lustily the master carved the bread,
Kindly the housewife pressed, and they in
comfort fed.   531

LX

Their breakfast done, the pair, though loth,
must part;
Wanderers whose course no longer now
agrees.
She rose and bade farewell ! and, while her
heart
Struggled with tears nor could its sorrow
ease,
She left him there ; for, clustering round
his knees,
With his oak-staff the cottage children
played;
And soon she reached a spot o'erhung with
trees

And banks of ragged earth; beneath the
shade
Across the pebbly road a little runnel
strayed.   540

LXI

A cart and horse beside the rivulet stood;
Chequering the canvas roof the sunbeams
shone.
She saw the carman bend to scoop the flood
As the wain fronted her, — wherein lay
one,
A pale-faced Woman, in disease far gone.
The carman wet her lips as well behoved;
Bed under her lean body there was none ;
Though even to die near one she most had
loved,
She could not of herself those wasted limbs
have moved.

LXII

The Soldier's Widow learned with honest
pain   550
And homefelt force of sympathy sincere,
Why thus that worn-out wretch must there
sustain
The jolting road and morning air severe.
The wain pursued its way; and following
near
In pure compassion she her steps retraced
Far as the cottage. "A sad sight is here,"
She cried aloud; and forth ran out in haste
The friends whom she had left but a few
minutes past.

LXIII

While to the door with eager speed they ran,
From her bare straw the Woman half up-
raised   560
Her bony visage — gaunt and deadly wan;
No pity asking, on the group she gazed
With a dim eye, distracted and amazed;
Then sank upon her straw with feeble moan.
Fervently cried the housewife — "God be
praised,
I have a house that I can call my own;
Nor shall she perish there, untended and
alone ! "

LXIV

So in they bear her to the chimney seat,
And busily, though yet with fear, untie
Her garments, and, to warm her icy feet
And chafe her temples, careful hands apply.
Nature reviving, with a deep-drawn sigh

She strove, and not in vain, her head to
　　rear;　　　　　　　　　　　　　　　573
Then said — " I thank you all; if I must
　　die,
The God in heaven my prayers for you will
　　hear;
Till now I did not think my end had been
　　so near.

LXV

" Barred every comfort labour could pro-
　　cure,
Suffering what no endurance could assuage,
I was compelled to seek my father's door,
Though loth to be a burthen on his age. 580
But sickness stopped me in an early stage
Of my sad journey; and within the wain
They placed me — there to end life's pil-
　　grimage,
Unless beneath your roof I may remain;
For I shall never see my father's door again.

LXVI

" My life, Heaven knows, hath long been
　　burthensome;
But, if I have not meekly suffered, meek
May my end be ! Soon will this voice be
　　dumb:
Should child of mine e'er wander hither,
　　speak
Of me, say that the worm is on my cheek. —
Torn from our hut, that stood beside the
　　sea　　　　　　　　　　　　　　　591
Near Portland lighthouse in a lonesome
　　creek,
My husband served in sad captivity
On shipboard, bound till peace or death
　　should set him free.

LXVII

" A sailor's wife I knew a widow's cares,
Yet two sweet little ones partook my
　　bed;
Hope cheered my dreams, and to my daily
　　prayers
Our heavenly Father granted each day's
　　bread;
Till one was found by stroke of violence
　　dead,
Whose body near our cottage chanced to
　　lie;　　　　　　　　　　　　　　　600
A dire suspicion drove us from our shed;
In vain to find a friendly face we try,
Nor could we live together those poor boys
　　and I;

LXVIII

" For evil tongues made oath how on that
　　day
My husband lurked about the neighbour-
　　hood;
Now he had fled, and whither none could
　　say,
And he had done the deed in the dark
　　wood —
Near his own home ! — but he was mild and
　　good;
Never on earth was gentler creature seen;
He 'd not have robbed the raven of its food.
My husband's lovingkindness stood between
Me and all worldly harms and wrongs how-
　　ever keen."　　　　　　　　　　　　612

LXIX

Alas ! the thing she told with labouring
　　breath
The Sailor knew too well. That wickedness
His hand had wrought; and when, in the
　　hour of death,
He saw his Wife's lips move his name to
　　bless
With her last words, unable to suppress
His anguish, with his heart he ceased to
　　strive;
And, weeping loud in this extreme distress,
He cried — " Do pity me ! That thou
　　shouldst live　　　　　　　　　　　620
I neither ask nor wish — forgive me, but
　　forgive ! "

LXX

To tell the change that Voice within her
　　wrought
Nature by sign or sound made no essay;
A sudden joy surprised expiring thought,
And every mortal pang dissolved away.
Borne gently to a bed, in death she lay,
Yet still while over her the husband bent,
A look was in her face which seemed to say,
" Be blest; by sight of thee from heaven
　　was sent
Peace to my parting soul, the fulness of
　　content."　　　　　　　　　　　　630

LXXI

She slept in peace, — his pulses throbbed
　　and stopped,
Breathless he gazed upon her face, — then
　　took
Her hand in his, and raised it, but both
　　dropped,

When on his own he cast a rueful look.
His ears were never silent; sleep forsook
His burning eyelids stretched and stiff as
    lead;
All night from time to time under him shook
The floor as he lay shuddering on his bed;
And oft he groaned aloud, " O God, that I
    were dead ! "

LXXII

The Soldier's Widow lingered in the cot,
And, when he rose, he thanked her pious
    care   641
Through which his Wife, to that kind shel-
    ter brought,
Died in his arms; and with those thanks a
    prayer
He breathed for her, and for that merciful
    pair.
The corse interred, not one hour he re-
    mained
Beneath their roof, but to the open air
A burthen, now with fortitude sustained,
He bore within a breast where dreadful
    quiet reigned.

LXXIII

Confirmed of purpose, fearlessly prepared
For act and suffering, to the city straight
He journeyed, and forthwith his crime
    declared: 651
" And from your doom," he added, " now I
    wait,
Nor let it linger long, the murderer's fate."
Not ineffectual was that piteous claim;
" O welcome sentence which will end though
    late,"
He said, " the pangs that to my conscience
    came
Out of that deed. My trust, Saviour ! is in
    thy name ! "

LXXIV

His fate was pitied. Him in iron case
(Reader, forgive the intolerable thought)
They hung not: — no one on *his* form or face
Could gaze, as on a show by idlers sought;
No kindred sufferer, to his death - place
    brought   662
By lawless curiosity or chance,
When into storm the evening sky is
    wrought,
Upon his swinging corse an eye can glance,
And drop, as he once dropped, in miserable
    trance.

LINES

LEFT UPON A SEAT IN A YEW-TREE,
WHICH STANDS NEAR THE LAKE OF
ESTHWAITE, ON A DESOLATE PART OF
THE SHORE, COMMANDING A BEAUTI-
FUL PROSPECT

1797. 1798

Composed in part at school at Hawkshead.
The tree has disappeared, and the slip of
Common on which it stood, that ran parallel to
the lake and lay open to it, has long been en-
closed; so that the road has lost much of its
attraction. This spot was my favourite walk
in the evenings during the latter part of my
school-time. The individual whose habits and
character are here given, was a gentleman of
the neighbourhood, a man of talent and learn-
ing, who had been educated at one of our Uni-
versities, and returned to pass his time in
seclusion on his own estate. He died a bachelor
in middle age. Induced by the beauty of the
prospect, he built a small summer-house on the
rocks above the peninsula on which the ferry-
house stands. This property afterwards passed
into the hands of the late Mr. Curwen. The
site was long ago pointed out by Mr. West in
his Guide, as the pride of the lakes, and now
goes by the name of "The Station." So much
used I to be delighted with the view from it,
while a little boy, that some years before the
first pleasure-house was built, I led thither
from Hawkshead a youngster about my own
age, an Irish boy, who was a servant to an
itinerant conjuror. My motive was to witness
the pleasure I expected the boy would receive
from the prospect of the islands below and the
intermingling water. I was not disappointed;
and I hope the fact, insignificant as it may ap-
pear to some, may be thought worthy of note
by others who may cast their eye over these
notes.

NAY, Traveller ! rest. This lonely Yew-
    tree stands
Far from all human dwelling: what if
    here
No sparkling rivulet spread the verdant
    herb ?
What if the bee love not these barren
    boughs ?
Yet, if the wind breathe soft, the curling
    waves,
That break against the shore, shall lull thy
    mind
By one soft impulse saved from vacancy.

Who he was
That piled these stones and with the mossy
      sod
First covered, and here taught this aged
      Tree   10
With its dark arms to form a circling
      bower,
I well remember. — He was one who owned
No common soul. In youth by science
      nursed,
And led by nature into a wild scene
Of lofty hopes, he to the world went forth
A favoured Being, knowing no desire
Which genius did not hallow; 'gainst the
      taint
Of dissolute tongues, and jealousy, and
      hate,
And scorn, — against all enemies prepared,
All but neglect. The world, for so it
      thought,   20
Owed him no service; wherefore he at
      once
With indignation turned himself away,
And with the food of pride sustained his
      soul
In solitude. — Stranger! these gloomy
      boughs
Had charms for him; and here he loved to
      sit,
His only visitants a straggling sheep,
The stone-chat, or the glancing sand-piper:
And on these barren rocks, with fern and
      heath,
And juniper and thistle, sprinkled o'er,
Fixing his downcast eye, he many an
      hour   30
A morbid pleasure nourished, tracing here
An emblem of his own unfruitful life:
And, lifting up his head, he then would
      gaze
On the more distant scene, — how lovely
      'tis

Thou seest, — and he would gaze till it
      became
Far lovelier, and his heart could not sustain
The beauty, still more beauteous! Nor,
      that time,
When nature had subdued him to herself,
Would he forget those Beings to whose
      minds,
Warm from the labours of benevolence, 40
The world, and human life, appeared a
      scene
Of kindred loveliness: then he would sigh,
Inly disturbed, to think that others felt
What he must never feel: and so, lost
      Man!
On visionary views would fancy feed,
Till his eye streamed with tears. In this
      deep vale
He died, — this seat his only monument.
   If Thou be one whose heart the holy
      forms
Of young imagination have kept pure,
Stranger! henceforth be warned; and
      know that pride,   50
Howe'er disguised in its own majesty,
Is littleness; that he, who feels contempt
For any living thing, hath faculties
Which he has never used; that thought
      with him
Is in its infancy. The man whose eye
Is ever on himself doth look on one,
The least of Nature's works, one who
      might move
The wise man to that scorn which wisdom
      holds
Unlawful, ever. O be wiser, Thou!
Instructed that true knowledge leads to
      love;   60
True dignity abides with him alone
Who, in the silent hour of inward thought,
Can still suspect, and still revere himself,
In lowliness of heart.

THE BORDERERS

A TRAGEDY

1796–97. 1842

Of this dramatic work I have little to say in addition to the short note which will be found at the end of the volume. It was composed at Racedown in Dorsetshire during the latter part of the year 1795, and in the course of the following year. Had it been the work of a later period of life, it would have been different in some respects from what it is now. The plot would have been something more complex, and a greater variety of characters introduced to relieve the mind from the pressure of incidents so mournful. The manners also would have been more attended to. My care was almost exclusively given to the passions and the characters, and the position in which the persons in the Drama stood relatively to each other, that the reader (for I had then no thought of the Stage) might be moved, and to a degree instructed, by lights penetrating somewhat into the depths of our nature. In this endeavour, I cannot think, upon a very late review, that I have failed. As to the scene and period of action, little more was required for my purpose than the absence of established law and government; so that the agents might be at liberty to act on their own impulses. Nevertheless I do remember that, having a wish to colour the manners in some degree from local history more than my knowledge enabled me to do, I read Redpath's History of the Borders, but found there nothing to my purpose. I once made an observation to Sir Walter Scott, in which he concurred, that it was difficult to conceive how so dull a book could be written on such a subject. Much about the same time, but a little after, Coleridge was employed in writing his tragedy of "Remorse," and it happened that soon after, through one of the Mr. Pooles, Mr. Knight the actor heard that we had been engaged in writing Plays, and upon his suggestion mine was curtailed, and I believe Coleridge's also was offered to Mr. Harris, manager of Covent Garden. For myself, I had no hope nor even a wish (though a successful play would, in the then state of my finances, have been a most welcome piece of good fortune) that he should accept my performance ; so that I incurred no disappointment when the piece was *judiciously* returned as not calculated for the Stage. In this judgment I entirely concurred, and had it been otherwise, it was so natural for me to shrink from public notice, that any hope I might have had of success would not have reconciled me altogether to such an exhibition. Mr. C.'s Play was, as is well known, brought forward several years after through the kindness of Mr. Sheridan. In conclusion I may observe that while I was composing this Play I wrote a short essay illustrative of that constitution and those tendencies of human nature which make the apparently *motiveless* actions of bad men intelligible to careful observers. This was partly done with reference to the character of Oswald, and his persevering endeavour to lead the man he disliked into so heinous a crime ; but still more to preserve in my distinct remembrance what I had observed of transition in character, and the reflections I had been led to make during the time I was a witness of the changes through which the French Revolution passed.

DRAMATIS PERSONÆ

MARMADUKE
OSWALD
WALLACE   } *Of the Band of Borderers.*
LACY
LENNOX
HERBERT.
WILFRED, *Servant to Marmaduke.*
Host.
Forester.
ELDRED, *a Peasant.*
Peasant, Pilgrims, etc.
IDONEA.
Female Beggar.
ELEANOR, *Wife to Eldred.*

SCENE — *Borders of England and Scotland.*
TIME — *The Reign of Henry III.*

Readers already acquainted with my Poems will recognise, in the following composition, some eight or ten lines which I have not scrupled to retain in the places where they originally stood. It is proper, however, to add, that they would not have been used elsewhere, if I had foreseen the time when I might be induced to publish this Tragedy.

February 28, 1842.

ACT I

SCENE — *Road in a Wood*

WALLACE *and* LACY

Lacy. The troop will be impatient; let us hie
Back to our post, and strip the Scottish Foray

Of their rich Spoil, ere they recross the
    Border.
— Pity that our young Chief will have no
    part
In this good service.
  Wal.   Rather let us grieve
That, in the undertaking which has caused
His absence, he hath sought, whate'er his
    aim,
Companionship with One of crooked ways,
From whose perverted soul can come no
    good
To our confiding, open-hearted, Leader. 10
  Lacy. True; and, remembering how the
    Band have proved
That Oswald finds small favour in our
    sight,
Well may we wonder he has gained such
    power
Over our much-loved Captain.
  Wal.   I have heard
Of some dark deed to which in early life
His passion drove him — then a Voyager
Upon the midland Sea. You knew his
    bearing
In Palestine ?
  Lacy.   Where he despised alike
Mahommedan and Christian. But enough;
Let us begone — the Band may else be
    foiled.   *[Exeunt.*

    Enter MARMADUKE *and* WILFRED.

  Wil. Be cautious, my dear Master !
  Mar.   I perceive 21
That fear is like a cloak which old men
    huddle
About their love, as if to keep it warm.
  Wil. Nay, but I grieve that we should
    part. This Stranger,
For such he is ——
  Mar.   Your busy fancies, Wilfred,
Might tempt me to a smile; but what of
    him ?
  Wil. You know that you have saved his
    life.
  Mar. I know it.
  Wil. And that he hates you ! — Pardon
    me, perhaps
That word was hasty.
  Mar.   Fy ! no more of it.
  Wil. Dear Master ! gratitude 's a heavy
    burden 30
To a proud Soul. — Nobody loves this
    Oswald —
Yourself, you do not love him.

  Mar.   I do more,
I honour him. Strong feelings to his heart
Are natural; and from no one can be learnt
More of man's thoughts and ways than his
    experience
Has given him power to teach: and then
    for courage
And enterprise — what perils hath he
    shunned ?
What obstacles hath he failed to overcome ?
Answer these questions, from our common
    knowledge,
And be at rest.
  Wil.   Oh, Sir !
  Mar.   Peace, my good Wilfred;
Repair to Liddesdale, and tell the Band 41
I shall be with them in two days, at far-
    thest.
  Wil. May He whose eye is over all pro-
    tect you !   *[Exit.*

Enter OSWALD (*a bunch of plants in his
    hand*).

  Osw. This wood is rich in plants and
    curious simples.
  Mar. (*looking at them*). The wild rose,
    and the poppy, and the nightshade:
Which is your favourite, Oswald ?
  Osw.   That which, while it is
Strong to destroy, is also strong to heal —
              [Looking forward.
Not yet in sight ! — We 'll saunter here
    awhile;
They cannot mount the hill, by us unseen.
  Mar. (*a letter in his hand*). It is no com-
    mon thing when one like you 50
Performs these delicate services, and there-
    fore
I feel myself much bounden to you, Oswald;
'T is a strange letter this ! — You saw her
    write it ?
  Osw. And saw the tears with which she
    blotted it.
  Mar. And nothing less would satisfy
    him ?
  Osw.   No less;
For that another in his Child's affection
Should hold a place, as if 't were robbery,
He seemed to quarrel with the very
    thought.
Besides, I know not what strange prejudice
Is rooted in his mind; this Band of ours, 60
Which you 've collected for the noblest
    ends,
Along the confines of the Esk and Tweed

To guard the Innocent — he calls us " Out-
   laws ";
And, for yourself, in plain terms he asserts
This garb was taken up that indolence
Might want no cover, and rapacity
Be better fed.
   Mar.   Ne'er may I own the heart
That cannot feel for one, helpless as he is.
   Osw. Thou know'st me for a Man not
     easily moved,
Yet was I grievously provoked to think 70
Of what I witnessed.
   Mar.   This day will suffice
To end her wrongs.
   Osw.   But if the blind Man's tale
Should *yet* be true ?
   Mar.   Would it were possible!
Did not the soldier tell thee that himself,
And others who survived the wreck, beheld
The Baron Herbert perish in the waves
Upon the coast of Cyprus ?
   Osw.   Yes, even so,
And I had heard the like before: in sooth
The tale of this his quondam Barony
Is cunningly devised; and, on the back 80
Of his forlorn appearance, could not fail
To make the proud and vain his tributaries,
And stir the pulse of lazy charity.
The seignories of Herbert are in Devon;
We, neighbours of the Esk and Tweed: 't is
   much
The Arch-Impostor ——
   Mar.   Treat him gently, Oswald;
Though I have never seen his face, me-
   thinks,
There cannot come a day when I shall
   cease
To love him. I remember, when a Boy
Of scarcely seven years' growth, beneath
   the Elm 90
That casts its shade over our village school,
'T was my delight to sit and hear Idonea
Repeat her Father's terrible adventures,
Till all the band of playmates wept to-
   gether;
And that was the beginning of my love.
And, through all converse of our later
   years,
An image of this old Man still was present,
When I had been most happy. Pardon me
If this be idly spoken.
   Osw.   See, they come, 99
Two Travellers !
   Mar. (points). The woman is Idonea.
   Osw. And leading Herbert.

   Mar.   We must let them pass —
This thicket will conceal us.
                   [*They step aside.*

Enter IDONEA, *leading* HERBERT *blind.*

   Idon. Dear Father, you sigh deeply;
     ever since
We left the willow shade by the brook-side,
Your natural breathing has been troubled.
   Her.   Nay,
You are too fearful; yet must I confess,
Our march of yesterday had better suited
A firmer step than mine.
   Idon.   That dismal Moor —
In spite of all the larks that cheered our
   path,
I never can forgive it: but how steadily
You paced along, when the bewildering
   moonlight 111
Mocked me with many a strange fantastic
   shape ! —
I thought the Convent never would appear;
It seemed to move away from us: and yet,
That you are thus the fault is mine; for
   the air
Was soft and warm, no dew lay on the
   grass,
And midway on the waste ere night had
   fallen
I spied a Covert walled and roofed with
   sods —
A miniature ; belike some Shepherd-
   boy,
Who might have found a nothing-doing
   hour 120
Heavier than work, raised it: within that hut
We might have made a kindly bed of heath
And thankfully there rested side by side
Wrapped in our cloaks, and, with recruited
   strength,
Have hailed the morning sun. But cheerily,
   Father, —
That staff of yours, I could have almost
   heart
To fling 't away from you: you make no use
Of me, or of my strength; — come, let me
   feel
That you do press upon me. There — in-
   deed
You are quite exhausted. Let us rest
   awhile 130
On this green bank.   [*He sits down.*
   Her. (after some time). Idonea, you are
   silent,
And I divine the cause.

Idon.   Do not reproach me :
I pondered patiently your wish and will
When I gave way to your request; and
    now,
When I behold the ruins of that face,
Those eyeballs dark — dark beyond hope of
    light,
And think that they were blasted for my
    sake,
The name of Marmaduke is blown away:
Father, I would not change that sacred
    feeling   139
For all this world can give.
  Her.   Nay, be composed:
Few minutes gone a faintness overspread
My frame, and I bethought me of two
    things
I ne'er had heart to separate — my grave,
And thee, my Child !
  Idon.   Believe me, honoured Sire !
'T is weariness that breeds these gloomy
    fancies,
And you mistake the cause: you hear the
    woods
Resound with music, could you see the sun,
And look upon the pleasant face of Na-
    ture ——
    Her. I comprehend thee — I should be
      as cheerful
As if we two were twins ; two. songsters
    bred   150
In the same nest, my spring-time one with
    thine.
My fancies, fancies if they be, are such
As come, dear Child ! from a far deeper
    source
Than bodily weariness. While here we sit
I feel my strength returning. — The be-
    quest
Of thy kind Patroness, which to receive
We have thus far adventured, will suffice
To save thee from the extreme of penury;
But when thy Father must lie down and
    die
How wilt thou stand alone ?
    Idon.   Is he not strong ?
Is he not valiant ?
    Her.   Am I then so soon 161
Forgotten ? have my warnings passed so
    quickly
Out of thy mind ? My dear, my only,
    Child;
Thou wouldst be leaning on a broken reed —
This Marmaduke ——
    Idon.   O could you hear his voice:

Alas ! you do not know him. He is one
(I wot not what ill tongue has wronged him
    with you)
All gentleness and love. His face bespeaks
A deep and simple meekness : and that
    Soul,
Which with the motion of a virtuous act
Flashes a look of terror upon guilt,   171
Is, after conflict, quiet as the ocean,
By a miraculous finger, stilled at once.
    Her. Unhappy Woman !
    Idon.   Nay, it was my duty
Thus much to speak; but think not I for-
    get —
Dear Father ! how *could* I forget and live —
You and the story of that doleful night
When, Antioch blazing to her topmost
    towers,
You rushed into the murderous flames, re-
    turned
Blind as the grave, but, as you oft have
    told me,   180
Clasping your infant Daughter to your
    heart.
    Her. Thy Mother too !— scarce had I
      gained the door,
I caught her voice; she threw herself upon
    me,
I felt thy infant brother in her arms;
She saw my blasted face — a tide of sol-
    diers
That instant rushed between us, and I heard
Her last death-shriek, distinct among a
    thousand.
    Idon. Nay, Father, stop not; let me hear
      it all.
    Her. Dear Daughter ! precious relic of
      that time —
For my old age, it doth remain with thee
To make it what thou wilt. Thou hast
      been told,   191
That when, on our return from Palestine,
I found how my domains had been usurped,
I took thee in my arms, and we began
Our wanderings together. Providence
At length conducted us to Rossland, —
    there,
Our melancholy story moved a Stranger
To take thee to her home — and for myself,
Soon after, the good Abbot of St. Cuth-
    bert's
Supplied my helplessness with food and rai-
    ment,   200
And, as thou know'st, gave me that hum-
    ble Cot

Where now we dwell. — For many years I
   bore
Thy absence, till old age and fresh infirmi-
   ties
Exacted thy return, and our reunion.
I did not think that, during that long ab-
   sence,
My Child, forgetful of the name of Herbert,
Had given her love to a wild Freebooter,
Who here, upon the borders of the Tweed,
Doth prey alike on two distracted Coun-
   tries,   209
Traitor to both.
   Idon.   Oh, could you hear his voice !
I will not call on Heaven to vouch for me,
But let this kiss speak what is in my heart.

Enter a PEASANT.

   Pea. Good morrow, Strangers ! If you
      want a Guide,
Let me have leave to serve you !
   Idon.   My Companion
Hath need of rest ; the sight of Hut or
   Hostel
Would be most welcome.
   Pea.   Yon white hawthorn gained,
You will look down into a dell, and there
Will see an ash from which a sign-board
   hangs ;
The house is hidden by the shade. Old
   Man,
You seem worn out with travel — shall I
   support you ?   220
   Her. I thank you ; but, a resting-place
      so near,
'T were wrong to trouble you.
   Pea.   God speed you both.
                            [*Exit* Peasant.
   Her. Idonea, we must part. Be not
      alarmed —
'T is but for a few days — a thought has
   struck me.
   Idon. That I should leave you at this
      house, and thence
Proceed alone. It shall be so ; for strength
Would fail you ere our journey's end be
   reached.
            [*Exit* Herbert *supported by* Idonea.

Re-enter MARMADUKE *and* OSWALD.

   Mar. This instant will we stop him ——
   Osw.   Be not hasty,
For, sometimes, in despite of my convic-
   tion,
He tempted me to think the Story true ;   230

'T is plain he loves the Maid, and what he
   said
That savoured of aversion to thy name
Appeared the genuine colour of his soul —
Anxiety lest mischief should befal her
After his death.
   Mar.   I have been much deceived.
   Osw. But sure he loves the Maiden, and
      never love
Could find delight to nurse itself so strange-
   ly,
Thus to torment her with *inventions !* —
   death —
There must be truth in this.
   Mar.   Truth in his story !
He must have felt it then, known what it
   was,   240
And in such wise to rack her gentle heart
Had been a tenfold cruelty.
   Osw.   Strange pleasures
Do we poor mortals cater for ourselves !
To see him thus provoke her tenderness
With tales of weakness and infirmity !
I 'd wager on his life for twenty years.
   Mar. We will not waste an hour in such
      a cause.
   Osw. Why, this is noble ! shake her off
      at once.
   Mar. Her virtues are his instruments. —
      A Man
Who has so practised on the world's cold
   sense,   250
May well deceive his Child — what ! leave
   her thus,
A prey to a deceiver ? — no — no — no —
'T is but a word and then ——
   Osw.   Something is here
More than we see, or whence this strong
   aversion ?
Marmaduke ! I suspect unworthy tales
Have reached his ear — you have had ene-
   mies.
   Mar. Enemies ! — of his own coinage.
   Osw.   That may be,
But wherefore slight protection such as you
Have power to yield ? perhaps he looks
   elsewhere, —
I am perplexed.
   Mar.   What hast thou heard or seen ?
   Osw. No — no — the thing stands clear
      of mystery ;   261
(As you have said) he coins himself the
   slander
With which he taints her ear ; — for a plain
   reason ;

He dreads the presence of a virtuous man
Like you; he knows your eye would search
   his heart,
Your justice stamp upon his evil deeds
The punishment they merit. All is plain:
It cannot be ——
   Mar.   What cannot be ?
   Osw.   Yet that a Father
Should in his love admit no rivalship,
And torture thus the heart of his own
   Child ——   270
   Mar. Nay, you abuse my friendship !
   Osw.   Heaven forbid ! —
There was a circumstance, trifling indeed —
It struck me at the time — yet I believe
I never should have thought of it again
But for the scene which we by chance have
   witnessed.
   Mar. What is your meaning ?
   Osw.   Two days gone I saw,
Though at a distance and he was disguised,
Hovering round Herbert's door, a man
   whose figure
Resembled much that cold voluptuary,
The villain, Clifford. He hates you, and he
   knows   280
Where he can stab you deepest.
   Mar.   Clifford never
Would stoop to skulk about a Cottage door —
It could not be.
   Osw.   And yet I now remember,
That, when your praise was warm upon my
   tongue,
And the blind Man was told how you had
   rescued
A maiden from the ruffian violence
Of this same Clifford, he became impatient
And would not hear me.
   Mar.   No — it cannot be —
I dare not trust myself with such a
   thought —
Yet whence this strange aversion ? You
   are a man   290
Not used to rash conjectures ——
   Osw.   If you deem it
A thing worth further notice, we must act
With caution, sift the matter artfully.
       [*Exeunt* Marmaduke *and* Oswald.

SCENE — *The Door of the Hostel*

HERBERT, IDONEA, *and* HOST.

   Her. (*seated*). As I am dear to you, re-
   member, Child !
This last request.

   Idon.   You know me, Sire; farewell !
   Her. And are you going then ? Come,
   come, Idonea,
We must not part, — I have measured many
   a league
When these old limbs had need of rest, —
   and now
I will not play the sluggard.
   Idon.   Nay, sit down.
                [*Turning to* Host.
Good Host, such tendance as you would
   expect   300
From your own Children, if yourself were
   sick,
Let this old Man find at your hands; poor
   Leader,   [*Looking at the dog.*
We soon shall meet again. If thou neglect
This charge of thine, then ill befall thee ! —
   Look,
The little fool is loth to stay behind.
Sir Host ! by all the love you bear to cour-
   tesy,
Take care of him, and feed the truant well.
   Host. Fear not, I will obey you; — but
   One so young,
And One so fair, it goes against my heart
That you should travel unattended, Lady ! —
I have a palfrey and a groom: the lad 311
Shall squire you, (would it not be better,
   Sir ?)
And for less fee than I would let him run
For any lady I have seen this twelvemonth
   Idon. You know, Sir, I have been too
   long your guard
Not to have learnt to laugh at little fears.
Why, if a wolf should leap from out a
   thicket,
A look of mine would send him scouring
   back,
Unless I differ from the thing I am   317
When you are by my side.
   Her.   Idonea, wolves
Are not the enemies that move my fears.
   Idon. No more, I pray, of this. Three
   days at farthest
Will bring me back — protect him, Saints
   — farewell !   [*Exit* Idonea.
   Host. 'T is never drought with us — St.
   Cuthbert and his Pilgrims,
Thanks to them, are to us a stream of com-
   fort:
Pity the Maiden did not wait a while;
She could not, Sir, have failed of company.
   Her. Now she is gone, I fain would call
   her back.

Host (calling). Holla !
Her.   No, no, the business must be
      done. —
What means this riotous noise?
Host.   The villagers
Are flocking in — a wedding festival — 331
That's all — God save you, Sir.

Enter OSWALD.

Osw.   Ha! as I live,
The Baron Herbert.
Host.   Mercy, the Baron Herbert !
Osw. So far into your journey ! on my life,
You are a lusty Traveller. But how fare
      you?
Her. Well as the wreck I am permits.
      And you, Sir?
Osw. I do not see Idonea.
Her.   Dutiful Girl,
She is gone before, to spare my weariness.
But what has brought you hither?
Osw.   A slight affair,
That will be soon despatched.
Her.   Did Marmaduke
Receive that letter?
Osw.   Be at peace. — The tie 341
Is broken, you will hear no more of *him.*
     Her. This is true comfort, thanks a thou-
      sand times ! —
That noise ! — would I had gone with her
      as far
As the Lord Clifford's Castle: I have heard
That, in his milder moods, he has expressed
Compassion for me. His influence is great
With Henry, our good King; — the Baron
      might
Have heard my suit, and urged my plea at
      Court.
No matter — he 's a dangerous Man. — That
      noise ! —   350
'T is too disorderly for sleep or rest.
Idonea would have fears for me, — the Con-
      vent
Will give me quiet lodging. You have a
      boy, good Host,
And he must lead me back.
Osw.   You are most lucky;
I have been waiting in the wood hard by
For a companion — here he comes; our
      journey

Enter MARMADUKE.

Lies on your way; accept us as your
      Guides.
Her. Alas ! I creep so slowly.

Osw.   Never fear;
We 'll not complain of that.
Her.   My limbs are stiff
And need repose. Could you but wait an
      hour ?   360
Osw. Most willingly ! — Come, let me
      lead you in,
And, while you take your rest, think not of
      us:
We 'll stroll into the wood; lean on my arm.
     [*Conducts* Herbert *into the house. Exit*
     Marmaduke.

Enter Villagers.

Osw. (*to himself coming out of the Hostel*).
      I have prepared a most apt Instru-
      ment —
The Vagrant must, no doubt, be loitering
      somewhere
About this ground; she hath a tongue well
      skilled,
By mingling natural matter of her own
With all the daring fictions I have taught
      her,
To win belief, such as my plot requires.
            [*Exit* Oswald.

Enter more Villagers, *a* Musician *among
      them.*

Host (*to them*). Into the court, my Friend,
      and perch yourself   370
Aloft upon the elm-tree. Pretty Maids,
Garlands and flowers, and cakes and merry
      thoughts,
Are here, to send the sun into the west
More speedily than you belike would wish.

SCENE *changes to the Wood adjoining the
      Hostel*

MARMADUKE *and* OSWALD *entering.*

Mar. I would fain hope that we deceive
      ourselves:
When first I saw him sitting there, alone,
It struck upon my heart I know not how.
Osw. To-day will clear up all. — You
      marked a Cottage,   378
That ragged Dwelling, close beneath a rock
By the brook-side: it is the abode of One,
A Maiden innocent till ensnared by Clifford,
Who soon grew weary of her; but, alas !
What she had seen and suffered turned her
      brain.
Cast off by her Betrayer, she dwells alone,

Nor moves her hands to any needful work:
She eats her food which every day the
    peasants
Bring to her hut; and so the Wretch has
    lived
Ten years; and no one ever heard her voice;
But every night at the first stroke of twelve
She quits her house, and, in the neighbour-
    ing Churchyard   390
Upon the self-same spot, in rain or storm,
She paces out the hour 'twixt twelve and
    one —
She paces round and round an Infant's
    grave,
And in the churchyard sod her feet have
    worn
A hollow ring; they say it is knee-deep ——
Ah! what is here?
        [*A female* Beggar *rises up, rubbing her
        eyes as if in sleep* — *a Child in her
        arms.*
Beg.   Oh! Gentlemen, I thank you;
I 've had the saddest dream that ever
    troubled
The heart of living creature. — My poor
    Babe
Was crying, as I thought, crying for bread
When I had none to give him; whereupon,
I put a slip of foxglove in his hand,   401
Which pleased him so, that he was hushed
    at once:
When, into one of those same spotted bells
A bee came darting, which the Child with
    joy
Imprisoned there, and held it to his ear,
And suddenly grew black, as he would die.
Mar. We have no time for this, my bab-
    bling Gossip;
Here 's what will comfort you.
                        [*Gives her money.*
Beg.   The Saints reward you
For this good deed! — Well, Sirs, this
    passed away;
And afterwards I fancied, a strange dog,
Trotting alone along the beaten road,   411
Came to my child as by my side he slept
And, fondling, licked his face, then on a
    sudden
Snapped fierce to make a morsel of his head:
But here he is (*kissing the Child*) it must
    have been a dream.
Osw. When next inclined to sleep, take
    my advice,
And put your head, good Woman, under
    cover.

Beg. Oh, sir, you would not talk thus, if
    you knew
What life is this of ours, how sleep will
    master
The weary-worn. — You gentlefolk have
    got   420
Warm chambers to your wish. I 'd rather
    be
A stone than what I am. — But two nights
    gone,
The darkness overtook me — wind and rain
Beat hard upon my head — and yet I saw
A glow-worm, through the covert of the
    furze,
Shine calmly as if nothing ailed the sky:
At which I half accused the God in
    Heaven. —
You must forgive me.
Osw.   Ay, and if you think
The Fairies are to blame, and you should
    chide
Your favourite saint — no matter — this
    good day   430
Has made amends.
Beg.   Thanks to you both; but, O sir!
How would you like to travel on whole
    hours
As I have done, my eyes upon the ground,
Expecting still, I knew not how, to find
A piece of money glittering through the
    dust?
Mar. This woman is a prater. Pray,
    good Lady!
Do you tell fortunes?
Beg.   Oh, Sir, you are like the rest.
This Little-one — it cuts me to the heart —
Well! they might turn a beggar from their
    doors,
But there are Mothers who can see the
    Babe   440
Here at my breast, and ask me where I
    bought it:
This they can do, and look upon my face —
But you, Sir, should be kinder.
Mar.   Come hither, Fathers,
And learn what nature is from this poor
    Wretch!
Beg. Ay, Sir, there 's nobody that feels
    for us.
Why now — but yesterday I overtook
A blind old Greybeard and accosted him,
I' th' name of all the Saints, and by the
    Mass
He should have used me better! — Charity!
If you can melt a rock, he is your man;

But I 'll be even with him — here again 451
Have I been waiting for him.
Osw.   Well, but softly,
Who is it that hath wronged you ?
Beg.   Mark you me;
I 'll point him out; — a Maiden is his guide,
Lovely as Spring's first rose; a little dog,
Tied by a woollen cord, moves on before
With look as sad as he were dumb; the cur,
I owe him no ill will, but in good sooth
He does his Master credit.
Mar.   As I live, 459
'T is Herbert and no other !
Beg.   'T is a feast to see him,
Lank as a ghost and tall, his shoulders bent,
And long beard white with age — yet ever-
        more,
As if he were the only Saint on earth,
He turns his face to heaven.
Osw.   But why so violent
Against this venerable Man ?
Beg.   I 'll tell you:
He has the very hardest heart on earth;
I had as lief turn to the Friars' school
And knock for entrance, in mid holiday.
Mar. But to your story.
Beg.   I was saying, Sir —
Well ! — he has often spurned me like a
        toad,   470
But yesterday was worse than all; — at last
I overtook him, Sirs, my Babe and I,
And begged a little aid for charity:
But he was snappish as a cottage cur.
Well then, says I — I 'll out with it; at
        which
I cast a look upon the Girl, and felt
As if my heart would burst; and so I left
        him.
Osw. I think, good Woman, you are the
        very person
Whom, but some few days past, I saw in
        Eskdale,   479
At Herbert's door.
Beg.   Ay; and if truth were known
I have good business there.
Osw.   I met you at the threshold,
And he seemed angry.
Beg.   Angry ! well he might;
And long as I can stir I 'll dog him. — Yes-
        terday,
To serve me so, and knowing that he owes
The best of all he has to me and mine.
But 't is all over now. — That good old
        Lady
Has left a power of riches; and, I say it,

If there 's a lawyer in the land, the knave
Shall give me half.
Osw. What 's this ? — I fear, good Wo-
        man,   489
You have been insolent.
Beg.   And there 's the Baron,
I spied him skulking in his peasant's dress.
Osw. How say you ? in disguise ? —
Mar.   But what 's your business
With Herbert or his Daughter ?
Beg.   Daughter ! truly —
But how 's the day ? — I fear, my little
        Boy,
We 've overslept ourselves. — Sirs, have
        you seen him ?   [*Offers to go.*
Mar. I must have more of this; — you
        shall not stir
An inch, till I am answered. Know you
        aught
That doth concern this Herbert ?
Beg.   You are provoked,
And will misuse me, Sir !   499
Mar.   No trifling, Woman !
Osw. You are as safe as in a sanctuary;
Speak.
Mar. Speak !
Beg.   He is a most hard-hearted Man.
Mar. Your life is at my mercy.
Beg.   Do not harm me,
And I will tell you all ! — You know not,
        Sir,
What strong temptations press upon the
        Poor.
Osw. Speak out.
Beg.   Oh Sir, I 've been a wicked Wo-
        man.
Osw. Nay, but speak out !
Beg.   He flattered me, and said
What harvest it would bring us both; and
        so,
I parted, with the Child.
Mar.   Parted with whom ?
Beg. Idonea, as he calls her; but the Girl
Is mine.
Mar. Yours, Woman ! are you Herbert's
        wife ?   510
Beg. Wife, Sir ! his wife — not I; my
        husband, Sir,
Was of Kirkoswald — many a snowy winter
We 've weathered out together. My poor
        Gilfred !
He has been two years in his grave.
Mar.   Enough.
Osw. We 've solved the riddle — Mis-
        creant !

Mar.   Do you,
Good Dame, repair to Liddesdale and wait
For my return; be sure you shall have
          justice.
     Osw. A lucky woman ! go, you have
          done good service.   [*Aside.*
     Mar. (to himself). Eternal praises on
          the power that saved her !—
     Osw. (gives her money). Here's for your
          little boy — and when you christen
          him   520
I'll be his Godfather.
     Beg.   Oh Sir, you are merry with me.
In grange or farm this Hundred scarcely
          owns
A dog that does not know me. — These
          good Folks,
For love of God, I must not pass their
          doors;
But I'll be back with my best speed: for
          you —
God bless and thank you both, my gentle
          Masters.   [*Exit* Beggar.
     Mar. (to himself). The cruel Viper !—
          Poor devoted Maid,
Now I *do* love thee.
     Osw.   I am thunderstruck.
     Mar. Where is she — holla !
     [*Calling to the* Beggar, *who returns ; he
          looks at her stedfastly.*
                    You are Idonea's mother ? —
Nay, be not terrified — it does me good 530
To look upon you.
     Osw. (interrupting). In a peasant's dress
You saw, who was it ?
     Beg.   Nay, I dare not speak;
He is a man, if it should come to his ears
I never shall be heard of more.
     Osw.   Lord Clifford ?
     Beg. What can I do ? believe me, gentle
          Sirs,
I love her, though I dare not call her
          daughter.
     Osw. Lord Clifford — did you see him
          talk with Herbert ?
     Beg. Yes, to my sorrow — under the
          great oak
At Herbert's door — and when he stood
          beside
The blind Man — at the silent Girl he
          looked   540
With such a look — it makes me tremble,
          Sir,
To think of it.
     Osw.   Enough ! you may depart.

Mar. (to himself). Father !— to God
          himself we cannot give
A holier name; and, under such a mask,
To lead a Spirit, spotless as the blessed,
To that abhorrèd den of brutish vice !—
Oswald, the firm foundation of my life
Is going from under me; these strange
          discoveries —
Looked at from every point of fear or hope,
Duty, or love — involve, I feel, my ruin.

ACT II

SCENE — *A Chamber in the Hostel*

OSWALD *alone, rising from a Table on which
          he had been writing.*

     Osw. They chose *him* for their Chief !—
          what covert part
He, in the preference, modest Youth, might
          take,
I neither know nor care. The insult bred
More of contempt than hatred; both are
          flown;
That either e'er existed is my shame:
'T was a dull spark — a most unnatural fire
That died the moment the air breathed
          upon it.
— These fools of feeling are mere birds of
          winter
That haunt some barren island of the north,
Where, if a famishing man stretch forth his
          hand,   10
They think it is to feed them. I have left
          him
To solitary meditation; — now
For a few swelling phrases, and a flash
Of truth, enough to dazzle and to blind,
And he is mine for ever — here he comes

Enter MARMADUKE.

     Mar. These ten years she has moved her
          lips all day
And never speaks !
     Osw.   Who is it ?
     Mar.   I have seen her.
     Osw. Oh ! the poor tenant of that ragged
          homestead,
Her whom the Monster, Clifford, drove to
          madness.
     Mar. I met a peasant near the spot; he
          told me,   20
These ten years she had sate all day alone
Within those empty walls.

Osw.   I too have seen her;
Chancing to pass this way some six months
    gone,
At midnight, I betook me to the Church-
    yard:
The moon shone clear, the air was still, so
    still
The trees were silent as the graves beneath
    them.
Long did I watch, and saw her pacing
    round
Upon the self-same spot, still round and
    round,
Her lips for ever moving.
Mar.   At her door
Rooted I stood; for, looking at the woman,
I thought I saw the skeleton of Idonea.   31
   Osw. But the pretended Father ——
   Mar.   Earthly law
Measures not crimes like his.
   Osw.   *We* rank not, happily,
With those who take the spirit of their rule
From that soft class of devotees who feel
Reverence for life so deeply, that they
    spare
The verminous brood, and cherish what
    they spare
While feeding on their bodies. Would that
    Idonea
Were present, to the end that we might hear
What she can urge in his defence; she loves
    him.   40
   Mar. Yes, loves him; 't is a truth that
    multiplies
His guilt a thousand-fold.
   Osw.   'T is most perplexing:
What must be done ?
   Mar.   We will conduct her hither;
These walls shall witness it — from first to
    last
He shall reveal himself.
   Osw.   Happy are we,
Who live in these disputed tracts, that own
No law but what each man makes for him-
    self ;
Here justice has indeed a field of triumph.
   Mar. Let us be gone and bring her
    hither ; — here
The truth shall be laid open, his guilt
    proved   50
Before her face. The rest be left to me.
   Osw. You will be firm: but though we
    well may trust
The issue to the justice of the cause,
Caution must not be flung aside ; remember,

Yours is no common life. Self-stationed
    here
Upon these savage confines, we have seen
    you
Stand like an isthmus 'twixt two stormy
    seas
That oft have checked their fury at your
    bidding.
Mid the deep holds of Solway's mossy
    waste,
Your single virtue has transformed a
    Band   60
Of fierce barbarians into Ministers
Of peace and order. Aged men with tears
Have blessed their steps, the fatherless re-
    tire
For shelter to their banners. But it is,
As you must needs have deeply felt, it is
In darkness and in tempest that we seek
The majesty of Him who rules the world.
Benevolence, that has not heart to use
The wholesome ministry of pain and evil,
Becomes at last weak and contemptible.   70
Your generous qualities have won due
    praise,
But vigorous Spirits look for something
    more
Than Youth's spontaneous products ; and
    to-day
You will not disappoint them ; and here-
    after ——
   Mar. You are wasting words ; hear me
    then, once for all :
You are a Man — and therefore, if com-
    passion,
Which to our kind is natural as life,
Be known unto you, you will love this
    Woman,
Even as I do ; but I should loathe the light,
If I could think one weak or partial feel-
    ing ——   80
   Osw. You will forgive me ——
   Mar.   If I ever knew
My heart, could penetrate its inmost core,
'T is at this moment. — Oswald, I have
    loved
To be the friend and father of the oppressed,
A comforter of sorrow ; — there is some-
    thing
Which looks like a transition in my soul,
And yet it is not. — Let us lead him hither.
   Osw. Stoop for a moment ; 't is an act of
    justice ;
And where 's the triumph if the delegate
Must fall in the execution of his office ?   90

The deed is done — if you will have it so —
Here where we stand — that tribe of vul-
  gar wretches
(You saw them gathering for the festival)
Rush in — the villains seize us ——
Mar.   Seize !
Osw.   Yes, they —
Men who are little given to sift and weigh —
Would wreak on us the passion of the mo-
  ment.
  Mar. The cloud will soon disperse —
  farewell — but stay,
Thou wilt relate the story.
  Osw.   Am I neither
To bear a part in this Man's punishment,
Nor be its witness ?
  Mar.   I had many hopes 100
That were most dear to me, and some will
  bear
To be transferred to thee.
  Osw.   When I 'm dishonoured !
  Mar. I would preserve thee. How may
  this be done ?
  Osw. By showing that you look beyond
  the instant.
A few leagues hence we shall have open
  ground,
And nowhere upon earth is place so fit
To look upon the deed. Before we enter
The barren Moor, hangs from a beetling
  rock
The shattered Castle in which Clifford oft
Has held infernal orgies — with the gloom,
And very superstition of the place, 111
Seasoning his wickedness. The Debauchee
Would there perhaps have gathered the
  first fruits
Of this mock Father's guilt.

  Enter HOST *conducting* HERBERT.

  Host.   The Baron Herbert
Attends your pleasure.
  Osw. (*to* Host).   We are ready —
                        (*To* Herbert) Sir !
I hope you are refreshed. — I have just
  written
A notice for your Daughter, that she may
  know
What is become of you. — You 'll sit down
  and sign it ;
'T will glad her heart to see her father's
  signature.
              [*Gives the letter he had written.*
  Her. Thanks for your care.
              [*Sits down and writes. Exit* Host.

  Osw. (*aside to* Marmaduke). Perhaps it
  would be useful   120
That you too should subscribe your name.
  [Marmaduke *overlooks* Herbert — *then
  writes — examines the letter eagerly.*
  Mar. I cannot leave this paper.
                  [*He puts it up, agitated.*
  Osw. (*aside*).   Dastard ! Come.
  [Marmaduke *goes towards* Herbert *and
  supports him* — Marmaduke *trem-
  blingly beckons* Oswald *to take his
  place.*
  Mar. (*as he quits* Herbert). There is a
  palsy in his limbs — he shakes.
  [*Exeunt* Oswald *and* Herbert — Mar-
  maduke *following.*

  SCENE *changes to a Wood*

  A group of Pilgrims, IDONEA *with them.*

  First Pil. A grove of darker and more
  lofty shade
I never saw.
  Second Pil. The music of the birds
Drops deadened from a roof so thick with
  leaves.
  Old Pil. This news ! It made my heart
  leap up with joy.
  Idon. I scarcely can believe it.
  Old Pil.   Myself, I heard
The Sheriff read, in open Court, a letter 129
Which purported it was the royal pleasure
The Baron Herbert, who, as was supposed,
Had taken refuge in this neighbourhood,
Should be forthwith restored. The hear-
  ing, Lady,
Filled my dim eyes with tears. — When I
  returned
From Palestine, and brought with me a
  heart,
Though rich in heavenly, poor in earthly,
  comfort,
I met your Father, then a wandering Out-
  cast :
He had a Guide, a Shepherd's boy ; but
  grieved
He was that One so young should pass his
  youth
In such sad service; and he parted with him.
We joined our tales of wretchedness to-
  gether,   141
And begged our daily bread from door to
  door.
I talk familiarly to you, sweet Lady !
For once you loved me.

Idon. You shall back with me
And see your Friend again. The good old
Man
Will be rejoiced to greet you.
Old Pil. It seems but yesterday
That a fierce storm o'ertook us, worn with
travel,
In a deep wood remote from any town.
A cave that opened to the road presented
A friendly shelter, and we entered in. 150
Idon. And I was with you?
Old Pil. If indeed 't was you —
But you were then a tottering Little-one —
We sate us down. The sky grew dark and
darker :
I struck my flint, and built up a small fire
With rotten boughs and leaves, such as the
winds
Of many autumns in the cave had piled.
Meanwhile the storm fell heavy on the
woods ;
Our little fire sent forth a cheering warmth
And we were comforted, and talked of
comfort ;
But 't was an angry night, and o'er our
heads 160
The thunder rolled in peals that would
have made
A sleeping man uneasy in his bed.
O Lady, you have need to love your Father.
His voice — methinks I hear it now, his
voice
When, after a broad flash that filled the cave,
He said to me, that he had seen his Child,
A face (no cherub's face more beautiful)
Revealed by lustre brought with it from
Heaven ;
And it was you, dear Lady !
Idon. God be praised,
That I have been his comforter till now ! 170
And will be so through every change of
fortune
And every sacrifice his peace requires. —
Let us be gone with speed, that he may hear
These joyful tidings from no lips but mine.
[*Exeunt* Idonea *and* Pilgrims.

SCENE — *The Area of a half-ruined Castle
— on one side the entrance to a dungeon*

OSWALD *and* MARMADUKE *pacing back-
wards and forwards.*

Mar. 'T is a wild night.
Osw. I 'd give my cloak and bonnet
For sight of a warm fire.

Mar. The wind blows keen;
My hands are numb.
Osw. Ha! ha! 't is nipping cold.
[*Blowing his fingers.*
I long for news of our brave Comrades;
Lacy
Would drive those Scottish Rovers to their
dens
If once they blew a horn this side the
Tweed. 180
Mar. I think I see a second range of
Towers;
This castle has another Area — come,
Let us examine it.
Osw. 'T is a bitter night;
I hope Idonea is well housed. That horse-
man,
Who at full speed swept by us where the
wood
Roared in the tempest, was within an ace
Of sending to his grave our precious Charge:
That would have been a vile mischance.
Mar. It would.
Osw. Justice had been most cruelly de-
frauded.
Mar. Most cruelly.
Osw. As up the steep we clomb,
I saw a distant fire in the north-east; 191
I took it for the blaze of Cheviot Beacon:
With proper speed our quarters may be
gained
To-morrow evening.
[*Looks restlessly towards the mouth of the
dungeon.*
Mar. When, upon the plank,
I had led him 'cross the torrent, his voice
blessed me:
You could not hear, for the foam beat the
rocks
With deafening noise, — the benediction fell
Back on himself; but changed into a
curse.
Osw. As well indeed it might.
Mar. And this you deem
The fittest place?
Osw. (*aside*). He is growing pitiful. 200
Mar. (*listening*). What an odd moaning
that is ! —
Osw. Mighty odd
The wind should pipe a little, while we
stand
Cooling our heels in this way ! — I 'll begin
And count the stars.
Mar. (*still listening*). That dog of his,
you are sure,

Could not come after us — he *must* have
    perished;
The torrent would have dashed an oak to
    splinters.
You said you did not like his looks — that he
Would trouble us; if he were here again,
I swear the sight of him would quail me
    more
Than twenty armies.
    Osw.   How?
    Mar.   The old blind Man,
When you had told him the mischance, was
    troubled   211
Even to the shedding of some natural tears
Into the torrent over which he hung,
Listening in vain.
    Osw.   He has a tender heart!
    [*Oswald offers to go down into the dun-*
      geon.
    Mar. How now, what mean you?
    Osw.   Truly, I was going
To waken our stray Baron. Were there not
A farm or dwelling-house within five leagues,
We should deserve to wear a cap and bells,
Three good round years, for playing the
    fool here
In such a night as this.
    Mar.   Stop, stop.
    Osw.   Perhaps,
You 'd better like we should descend to-
    gether,   221
And lie down by his side — what say you
    to it?
Three of us — we should keep each other
    warm:
I 'll answer for it that our four-legged friend
Shall not disturb us; further I 'll not engage;
Come, come, for manhood's sake!
    Mar.   These drowsy shiverings,
This mortal stupor which is creeping over
    me,
What do they mean? were this my single
    body
Opposed to armies, not a nerve would trem-
    ble:
Why do I tremble now? — Is not the depth
Of this Man's crimes beyond the reach of
    thought?   231
And yet, in plumbing the abyss for judg-
    ment,
Something I strike upon which turns my
    mind
Back on herself, I think, again — my breast
Concentres all the terrors of the Universe:
I look at him and tremble like a child.

    Osw. Is it possible?
    Mar.   One thing you noticed not:
Just as we left the glen a clap of thunder
Burst on the mountains with hell-rousing
    force.
This is a time, said he, when guilt may
    shudder;   240
But there 's a Providence for them who walk
In helplessness, when innocence is with
    them.
At this audacious blasphemy, I thought
The spirit of vengeance seemed to ride the
    air.
    Osw. Why are you not the man you were
    that moment?
    [*He draws* Marmaduke *to the dungeon.*
    Mar. You say he was asleep, — look at
    this arm,
And tell me if 't is fit for such a work.
Oswald, Oswald!   [*Leans upon* Oswald.
    Osw.   This is some sudden seizure !
    Mar. A most strange faintness, — will
    you hunt me out   249
A draught of water?
    Osw.   Nay, to see you thus
Moves me beyond my bearing. — I will try
To gain the torrent's brink.   [*Exit* Oswald.
    Mar. (after a pause).   It seems an age
Since that Man left me. — No, I am not lost.
    Her. (at the mouth of the dungeon). Give
    me your hand; where are you,
    Friends? and tell me
How goes the night.
    Mar.   'T is hard to measure time,
In such a weary night, and such a place.
    Her. I do not hear the voice of my friend
    Oswald.
    Mar. A minute past, he went to fetch a
    draught
Of water from the torrent. 'T is, you 'll say,
A cheerless beverage.
    Her.   How good it was in you
To stay behind! — Hearing at first no an-
    swer,   261
I was alarmed.
    Mar.   No wonder; this is a place
That well may put some fears into *your*
    heart.
    Her. Why so? a roofless rock had been
    a comfort,
Storm-beaten and bewildered as we were;
And in a night like this, to lend your cloaks
To make a bed for me ! — My Girl will
    weep
When she is told of it.

Mar.   This Daughter of yours
Is very dear to you.
 Her.   Oh! but you are young;
Over your head twice twenty years must
  roll,   270
With all their natural weight of sorrow and
  pain,
Ere can be known to you how much a Fa-
  ther
May love his Child.
 Mar.   Thank you, old Man, for this!
         [Aside.
 Her. Fallen am I, and worn out, a useless
  Man;
Kindly have you protected me to-night,
And no return have I to make but prayers;
May you in age be blest with such a daugh-
  ter ! —
When from the Holy Land I had returned
Sightless, and from my heritage was driven,
A wretched Outcast — but this strain of
  thought   280
Would lead me to talk fondly.
 Mar.   Do not fear;
Your words are precious to my ears; go on.
 Her. You will forgive me, but my heart
  runs over.
When my old Leader slipped into the flood
And perished, what a piercing outcry you
Sent after him. I have loved you ever since.
You start — where are we?
 Mar.   Oh, there is no danger;
The cold blast struck me.
 Her.   'T was a foolish question.
 Mar. But when you were an Outcast ? —
  Heaven is just;
Your piety would not miss its due reward;
The little Orphan then would be your suc-
  cour,   291
And do good service, though she knew it
  not.
 Her. I turned me from the dwellings of
  my Fathers,
Where none but those who trampled on my
  rights
Seemed to remember me. To the wide
  world
I bore her, in my arms; her looks won
  pity;
She was my Raven in the wilderness,
And brought me food. Have I not cause to
  love her ?   298
 Mar. Yes.
 Her. More than ever Parent loved a
  Child ?

Mar. Yes, yes.
 Her. I will not murmur, merciful God !
I will not murmur; blasted as I have
  been,
Thou hast left me ears to hear my Daugh-
  ter's voice,
And arms to fold her to my heart. Sub
  missively
Thee I adore, and find my rest in faith.

    Enter OSWALD.

 Osw. Herbert ! — confusion ! *(Aside.)*
  Here it is, my Friend,
      [Presents the Horn.
A charming beverage for you to carouse,
This bitter night.
 Her.   Ha ! Oswald ! ten bright crosses
I would have given, not many minutes gone,
To have heard your voice.
 Osw.   Your couch, I fear, good Baron,
Has been but comfortless; and yet that
  place,   310
When the tempestuous wind first drove us
  hither,
Felt warm as a wren's nest. You 'd better
  turn
And under covert rest till break of day,
Or till the storm abate.
(To Marmaduke *aside.)* He has restored
  you.
No doubt you have been nobly entertained ?
But soft ! — how came he forth ? The
  Night-mare Conscience
Has driven him out of harbour ?
 Mar.   I believe
You have guessed right.
 Her.   The trees renew their murmur:
Come, let us house together.
  [Oswald conducts him to the dungeon.
 Osw. (returns).   Had I not
Esteemed you worthy to conduct the affair
To its most fit conclusion, do you think 321
I would so long have struggled with my
  Nature,
And smothered all that 's man in me ? —
  away ! —
    [Looking towards the dungeon.
This man 's the property of him who best
Can feel his crimes. I have resigned a
  privilege;
It now becomes my duty to resume it.
 Mar. Touch not a finger ——
 Osw.   What then must be done ?
 Mar. Which way soe'er I turn, I am per-
  plexed.

Osw. Now, on my life, I grieve for you.
The misery
Of doubt is insupportable.   Pity, the facts
Did not admit of stronger evidence;   331
Twelve honest men, plain men, would set
us right;
Their verdict would abolish these weak
scruples.
Mar. Weak! I am weak — there does
my torment lie,
Feeding itself.
Osw.   Verily, when he said
How his old heart would leap to hear her
steps,
You thought his voice the echo of Idonea's.
Mar. And never heard a sound so terrible.
Osw. Perchance you think so now?
Mar.   I cannot do it:
Twice did I spring to grasp his withered
throat,   340
When such a sudden weakness fell upon
me,
I could have dropped asleep upon his breast.
Osw. Justice — is there not thunder in
the word?
Shall it be law to stab the petty robber
Who aims but at our purse; and shall this
Parricide —
Worse is he far, far worse (if foul dishonour
Be worse than death) to that confiding
Creature
Whom he to more than filial love and duty
Hath falsely trained — shall he fulfil his
purpose?   349
But you are fallen.
Mar.   Fallen should I be indeed —
Murder — perhaps asleep, blind, old, alone,
Betrayed, in darkness! Here to strike the
blow —
Away! away!──
                [Flings away his sword.
Osw.   Nay, I have done with you:
We'll lead him to the Convent. He shall
live,
And she shall love him. With unquestioned
title
He shall be seated in his Barony,
And we too chant the praise of his good
deeds.
I now perceive we do mistake our masters,
And most despise the men who best can
teach us:
Henceforth it shall be said that bad men
only   360

Are brave: Clifford is brave; and that old
Man
Is brave.
    *[Taking Marmaduke's sword and giving
    it to him.*
    To Clifford's arms he would have led
His Victim — haply to this desolate house.
Mar. (*advancing to the dungeon*). It
must be ended! —
Osw.   Softly; do not rouse him;
He will deny it to the last. He lies
Within the Vault, a spear's length to the
left.
    [Marmaduke descends to the dungeon.
(*Alone.*) The Villains rose in mutiny to destroy me;
I could have quelled the Cowards, but this
Stripling
Must needs step in, and save my life. The
look
With which he gave the boon — I see it
now!   370
The same that tempted me to loathe the
gift. —
For this old venerable Greybeard — faith
'T is his own fault if he hath got a face
Which doth play tricks with them that look
on it:
'T was this that put it in my thoughts — that
countenance —
His staff — his figure — Murder! — what,
of whom?
We kill a worn-out horse, and who but
women
Sigh at the deed?   Hew down a withered
tree,
And none look grave but dotards. He may
live
To thank me for this service. Rainbow
arches,   380
Highways of dreaming passion, have too
long,
Young as he is, diverted wish and hope
From the unpretending ground we mortals
tread; —
Then shatter the delusion, break it up
And set him free. What follows? I have
learned
That things will work to ends the slaves o'
the world
Do never dream of. I *have* been what he —
This Boy — when he comes forth with
bloody hands—
Might envy, and am now, — but he shall
know   389

What I am now —
> [*Goes and listens at the dungeon.*
> Praying or parleying ? — tut !

Is he not eyeless ? He has been half-dead
These fifteen years ——

Enter female Beggar *with two or three of her
Companions.*

(*Turning abruptly.*) Ha *!* speak — what
    Thing art thou ?
(*Recognizes her.*) Heavens ! my good
    Friend !   [*To her.*
  Beg.   Forgive me, gracious Sir ! —
  Osw. (*to her companions*). Begone, ye
    Slaves, or I will raise a whirlwind
And send ye dancing to the clouds, like
    leaves.   [*They retire affrighted.*
  Beg. Indeed we meant no harm; we
    lodge sometimes
In this deserted Castle — *I repent me.*
> [Oswald *goes to the dungeon — listens —
> returns to the* Beggar.

  Osw. Woman, thou hast a helpless Infant
    — keep
Thy secret for its sake, or verily
That wretched life of thine shall be the
    forfeit.   400
  Beg. I *do* repent me, Sir; I fear the curse
Of that blind Man. 'T was not your money,
    sir ——
  Osw. Begone !
  Beg. (*going*). There is some wicked deed
    in hand: [*Aside.*
Would I could find the old Man and his
    Daughter.   [*Exit* Beggar.

MARMADUKE (*re-enters from the dungeon*).

  Osw. It is all over then; — your foolish
    fears
Are hushed to sleep, by your own act and
    deed,
Made quiet as he is.
  Mar.   Why came you down ?
And when I felt your hand upon my arm
And spake to you, why did you give no
    answer ?
Feared you to waken him ? he must have
    been   410
In a deep sleep. I whispered to him thrice.
There are the strangest echoes in that
    place !
  Osw. Tut ! let them gabble till the day
    of doom.
  Mar. Scarcely, by groping, had I reached
    the Spot,

When round my wrist I felt a cord drawn
    tight,
As if the blind Man's dog were pulling at
    it.
  Osw. But after that ?
  Mar.   The features of Idonea
Lurked in his face ——
  Osw.   Psha ! Never to these eyes
Will retribution show itself again   419
With aspect so inviting. Why forbid me
To share your triumph ?
  Mar.   Yes, her very look,
Smiling in sleep ——
  Osw.   A pretty feat of Fancy !
  Mar. Though but a glimpse, it sent me
    to my prayers.
  Osw. Is he alive ?
  Mar.   What mean you ? who alive ?
  Osw. Herbert ! since you will have it,
    Baron Herbert;
He who will gain his Seignory when Idonea
Hath become Clifford's harlot — is *he* liv-
    ing ?
  Mar. The old Man in that dungeon *is*
    alive.
  Osw. Henceforth, then, will I never in
    camp or field
Obey you more. Your weakness, to the
    Band   430
Shall be proclaimed: brave Men, they all
    shall hear it.
You a protector of humanity !
Avenger you of outraged innocence !
  Mar. 'T was dark — dark as the grave;
    yet did I see,
Saw him — his face turned toward me; and
    I tell thee
Idonea's filial countenance was there
To baffle me — it put me to my prayers.
Upwards I cast my eyes, and, through a
    crevice,
Beheld a star twinkling above my head,
And, by the living God, I could not do
    it.   [*Sinks exhausted.*
  Osw. (*to himself*). Now may I perish if
    this turn do more   441
Than make me change my course.
(*To* Marmaduke.)   Dear Marmaduke,
My words were rashly spoken; I recall
    them:
I feel my error; shedding human blood
Is a most serious thing.
  Mar.   Not I alone,
Thou too art deep in guilt.
  Osw.   We have indeed

Been most presumptuous. There *is* guilt in
this,
Else could so strong a mind have ever
known
These trepidations ? Plain it is that Heaven
Has marked out this foul Wretch as one
whose crimes   450
Must never come before a mortal judgment-
seat,
Or be chastised by mortal instruments.
 Mar. A thought that's worth a thousand
 worlds ! [*Goes towards the dungeon.*
Osw.   I grieve
That, in my zeal, I have caused you so much
pain.
 Mar. Think not of that ! 't is over — we
are safe.
 Osw. (*as if to himself, yet speaking aloud*).
The truth is hideous, but how stifle
it ? [*Turning to* Marmaduke.
Give me your sword — nay, here are stones
and fragments,
The least of which would beat out a man's
brains;
Or you might drive your head against that
wall.   459
No ! this is not the place to hear the tale:
It should be told you pinioned in your bed,
Or on some vast and solitary plain,
Blown to you from a trumpet.
 Mar.   Why talk thus ?
Whate'er the monster brooding in your
breast
I care not: fear I have none, and cannot
fear ——
  [*The sound of a horn is heard.*
That horn again — 'T is some one of our
Troop;
What do they here ? Listen !
 Osw. What ! dogged like thieves !

 Enter WALLACE *and* LACY, etc.

 Lacy. You are found at last, thanks to
the vagrant Troop
For not misleading us.
 Osw. (*looking at* Wallace). That subtle
Greybeard —
I'd rather see my father's ghost.   470
 Lacy (*to* Marmaduke). My Captain,
We come by order of the Band. Belike
You have not heard that Henry has at
last
Dissolved the Barons' League, and sent
abroad
His Sheriffs with fit force to reinstate

The genuine owners of such Lands and
Baronies
As, in these long commotions, have been
seized.
His Power is this way tending. It befits us
To stand upon our guard, and with our
swords
Defend the innocent.
 Mar.   Lacy ! we look
But at the surfaces of things; we hear 480
Of towns in flames, fields ravaged, young
and old
Driven out in troops to want and nakedness;
Then grasp our swords and rush upon a cure
That flatters us, because it asks not thought:
The deeper malady is better hid;
The world is poisoned at the heart.
 Lacy.   What mean you ?
 Wal. (*whose eye has been fixed suspiciously
upon* Oswald). Ay, what is it you
mean ?
 Mar. Hark'e, my Friends; —
  [*Appearing gay.*
Were there a Man who, being weak and
helpless
And most forlorn, should bribe a Mother,
pressed
By penury, to yield him up her Daughter,
A little Infant, and instruct the Babe, 491
Prattling upon his knee, to call him
Father ——
 Lacy. Why, if his heart be tender, that
offence
I could forgive him.
 Mar. (*going on*). And should he make
the Child
An instrument of falsehood, should he teach
her
To stretch her arms, and dim the gladsome
light
Of infant playfulness with piteous looks
Of misery that was not ——
 Lacy.   Troth, 't is hard —
But in a world like ours ——
 Mar. (*changing his tone*). This selfsame
Man —
Even while he printed kisses on the cheek
Of this poor Babe, and taught its innocent
tongue   501
To lisp the name of Father — could he look
To the unnatural harvest of that time
When he should give her up, a Woman
grown,
To him who bid the highest in the market
Of foul pollution ——

Lacy.   The whole visible world
Contains not such a Monster !
Mar.   For this purpose
Should he resolve to taint her Soul by
    means
Which bathe the limbs in sweat to think of
    them;
Should he, by tales which would draw tears
    from iron,   510
Work on her nature, and so turn compas-
    sion
And gratitude to ministers of vice,
And make the spotless spirit of filial love
Prime mover in a plot to damn his Victim
Both soul and body ——
Wal.   'T is too horrible;
Oswald, what say you to it ?
Lacy.   Hew him down,
And fling him to the ravens.
Mar.   But his aspect
It is so meek, his countenance so venerable.
Wal. (*with an appearance of mistrust*).
    But how, what say you, Oswald ?
Lacy (*at the same moment*). Stab him,
    were it
Before the Altar.
Mar.   What, if he were sick,
Tottering upon the very verge of life,   521
And old, and blind ——
Lacy.   Blind, say you ?
Osw. (*coming forward*).   Are we Men,
Or own we baby Spirits ? Genuine cour-
    age
Is not an accidental quality,
A thing dependent for its casual birth
On opposition and impediment.
Wisdom, if Justice speak the word, beats
    down
The giant's strength; and, at the voice of
    Justice,
Spares not the worm. The giant and the
    worm —
She weighs them in one scale. The wiles
    of woman,   530
And craft of age, seducing reason, first
Made weakness a protection, and obscured
The moral shapes of things. His tender
    cries
And helpless innocence — do they protect
The infant lamb ? and shall the infirmities,
Which have enabled this enormous Culprit
To perpetrate his crimes, serve as a Sanc-
    tuary
To cover him from punishment ? Shame !
    — Justice,

Admitting no resistance, bends alike
The feeble and the strong.   She needs not
    here   540
Her bonds and chains, which make the
    mighty feeble.
— We recognize in this old Man a victim
Prepared already for the sacrifice.
Lacy. By heaven, his words are reason !
Osw.   Yes, my Friends,
His countenance is meek and venerable;
And, by the Mass, to see him at his
    prayers ! —
I am of flesh and blood, and may I perish
When my heart does not ache to think of
    it ! —
Poor Victim ! not a virtue under heaven
But what was made an engine to ensnare
    thee;   550
But yet I trust, Idonea, thou art safe.
Lacy. Idonea !
Wal.   How ! what ? your Idonea ?
                    (*To* Marmaduke.)
Mar.   Mine !
But now no longer mine. You know Lord
    Clifford;
He is the Man to whom the Maiden —
    pure
As beautiful, and gentle and benign,
And in her ample heart loving even me —
Was to be yielded up.
Lacy.   Now, by the head
Of my own child, this Man must die; my
    hand,
A worthier wanting, shall itself entwine
In his grey hairs ! —
Mar. (*to* Lacy). I love the Father in
    thee.   560
You know me, Friends; I have a heart to
    feel,
And I have felt, more than perhaps becomes
    me
Or duty sanctions.
Lacy.   We will have ample justice.
Who are we, Friends ? Do we not live on
    ground
Where Souls are self-defended, free to
    grow
Like mountain oaks rocked by the stormy
    wind.
Mark the Almighty Wisdom, which decreed
This monstrous crime to be laid open —
    here,
Where Reason has an eye that she can use,
And Men alone are Umpires.   To the
    Camp   570

He shall be led, and there, the Country
   round
All gathered to the spot, in open day
Shall Nature be avenged.
Osw.   'T is nobly thought;
His death will be a monument for ages.
  Mar. (*to* Lacy). I thank you for that
    hint. He shall be brought
Before the Camp, and would that best and
   wisest
Of every country might be present. There,
His crime shall be proclaimed; and for the
   rest
It shall be done as Wisdom shall decide:
Meanwhile, do you two hasten back and
   see   580
That all is well prepared.
  Wal.   We will obey you.
(*Aside.*) But softly ! we must look a little
   nearer.
  Mar. Tell where you found us. At some
    future time
I will explain the cause.   [*Exeunt.*

ACT III

SCENE—*The Door of the Hostel*

A group of Pilgrims *as before ;* IDONEA *and
the* HOST *among them.*

  Host. Lady, you 'll find your Father at the
   Convent
As I have told you: He left us yesterday
With two Companions; one of them, as
   seemed,
His most familiar Friend. (*Going.*) There
   was a letter
Of which I heard them speak, but that I
   fancy
Has been forgotten.
  Idon. (*to* Host). Farewell !
  Host.   Gentle pilgrims,
St. Cuthbert speed you on your holy errand.
      [*Exeunt* Idonea *and* Pilgrims.

SCENE — *A desolate Moor*

OSWALD (*alone*).

  Osw. Carry him to the Camp ! Yes, to
   the Camp.
Oh, Wisdom ! a most wise resolve ! and
   then,
That half a word should blow it to the
   winds !   10

This last device must end my work. — Me-
   thinks
It were a pleasant pastime to construct
A scale and table of belief — as thus —
Two columns, one for passion, one for
   proof;
Each rises as the other falls: and first,
Passion a unit and *against* us — proof —
Nay, we must travel in another path,
Or we 're stuck fast for ever; — passion,
   then,
Shall be a unit *for* us; proof — no, passion !
We 'll not insult thy majesty by time,   20
Person, and place — the where, the when,
   the how,
And all particulars that dull brains require
To constitute the spiritless shape of Fact,
They bow to, calling the idol, Demonstra-
   tion.
A whipping to the Moralists who preach
That misery is a sacred thing: for me,
I know no cheaper engine to degrade a
   man,
Nor any half so sure. This Stripling's
   mind
Is shaken till the dregs float on the surface;
And, in the storm and anguish of the heart,
He talks of a transition in his Soul,   31
And dreams that he is happy. We dissect
The senseless body, and why not the
   mind ? —
These are strange sights — the mind of man,
   upturned,
Is in all natures a strange spectacle;
In some a hideous one — hem ! shall I
   stop ?
No. — Thoughts and feelings will sink deep,
   but then
They have no substance. Pass but a few
   minutes,
And something shall be done which Memory
May touch, whene'er her Vassals are at
   work.   40

   Enter MARMADUKE, *from behind.*

  Osw. (*turning to meet him*). But listen,
    for my peace ——
  Mar.   Why, I *believe* you.
  Osw. But hear the proofs ——
  Mar.   Ay, prove that when two peas
Lie snugly in a pod, the pod must then
Be larger than the peas — prove this —
   't were matter
Worthy the hearing. Fool was I to dream
It ever could be otherwise !

Osw.   Last night
When I returned with water from the brook,
I overheard the Villains — every word
Like red-hot iron burnt into my heart.
Said one, " It is agreed on. The blind
    Man   50
Shall feign a sudden illness, and the Girl,
Who on her journey must proceed alone,
Under pretence of violence, be seized.
She is," continued the detested Slave,
" She is right willing — strange if she were
    not ! —
They say, Lord Clifford is a savage man;
But, faith, to see him in his silken tunic,
Fitting his low voice to the minstrel's harp,
There's witchery in 't. I never knew a
    maid
That could withstand it. True," continued
    he,   60
" When we arranged the affair, she wept a
    little
(Not the less welcome to my Lord for that)
And said, ' My Father he will have it so.' "
Mar. I am your hearer.
Osw.   This I caught, and more
That may not be retold to any ear.
The obstinate bolt of a small iron door
Detained them near the gateway of the
    Castle.
By a dim lantern's light I saw that wreaths
Of flowers were in their hands, as if de-
    signed
For festive decoration; and they said,   70
With brutal laughter and most foul allu-
    sion,
That they should share the banquet with
    their Lord
And his new Favourite.
Mar.   Misery ! —
Osw.   I knew
How you would be disturbed by this dire
    news,
And therefore chose this solitary Moor,
Here to impart the tale, of which, last
    night,
I strove to ease my mind, when our two
    Comrades,
Commissioned by the Band, burst in upon
    us.
Mar. Last night, when moved to lift the
    avenging steel,
I did believe all things were shadows —
    yea,   80
Living or dead all things were bodiless,
Or but the mutual mockeries of body,

Till that same star summoned me back
    again.
Now I could laugh till my ribs ached.   Oh
    Fool !
To let a creed, built in the heart of things,
Dissolve before a twinkling atom ! — Os-
    wald,
I could fetch lessons out of wiser schools
Than you have entered, were it worth the
    pains.
Young as I am, I might go forth a teacher,
And you should see how deeply I could
    reason   90
Of love in all its shapes, beginnings, ends;
Of moral qualities in their diverse aspects;
Of actions, and their laws and tendencies.
   Osw. You take it as it merits ——
   Mar.   One a King,
General or Cham, Sultan or Emperor,
Strews twenty acres of good meadow-
    ground
With carcases, in lineament and shape
And substance nothing differing from his
    own,
But that they cannot stand up of them-
    selves;
Another sits i' th' sun, and by the hour 100
Floats kingcups in the brook — a Hero one
We call, and scorn the other as Time's
    spendthrift;
But have they not a world of common
    ground
To occupy — both fools, or wise alike,
Each in his way ?
   Osw.   Troth, I begin to think so.
   Mar. Now for the corner-stone of my
    philosophy:
I would not give a denier for the man
Who, on such provocation as this earth
Yields, could not chuck his babe beneath
    the chin,
And send it with a fillip to its grave.   110
   Osw. Nay, you leave me behind.
   Mar.   That such a One,
So pious in demeanour ! in his look
So saintly and so pure ! —— Hark'e, my
    Friend,
I'll plant myself before Lord Clifford's
    Castle,
A surly mastiff kennels at the gate,
And he shall howl and I will laugh, a med-
    ley
Most tunable.
   Osw.   In faith, a pleasant scheme;
But take your sword along with you, for that

Might in such neighbourhood find seemly
  use. —
But first, how wash our hands of this old
  Man ?   120
  Mar. Oh yes, that mole, that viper in
    the path;
Plague on my memory, him I had forgotten.
  Osw. You know we left him sitting —
    see him yonder.
  Mar. Ha ! ha ! —
  Osw. As 't will be but a moment's work,
I will stroll on; you follow when 't is done.
                                  [*Exeunt.*

SCENE *changes to another part of the
  Moor at a short distance*

HERBERT *is discovered seated on a stone.*

  Her. A sound of laughter, too ! — 't is
    well — I feared,
The Stranger had some pitiable sorrow
Pressing upon his solitary heart.
Hush ! — 't is the feeble and earth-loving
  wind
That creeps along the bells of the crisp
  heather.   130
Alas ! 't is cold — I shiver in the sunshine —
What can this mean ? There is a psalm
  that speaks
Of God's parental mercies — with Idonea
I used to sing it. — Listen ! — what foot is
  there ?

          Enter MARMADUKE.

  Mar. (*aside — looking at* Herbert). And
    I have loved this Man ! and *she* hath
    loved him !
And I loved her, and she loves the Lord
  Clifford !
And there it ends; — if this be not enough
To make mankind merry for evermore,
Then plain it is as day, that eyes were made
For a wise purpose — verily to weep with !
                              [*Looking round.*
A pretty prospect this, a masterpiece   141
Of Nature, finished with most curious skill !
(*To* Herbert.) Good Baron, have you ever
    practised tillage ?
Pray tell me what this land is worth by the
  acre ?
  Her. How glad I am to hear your voice !
    I know not
Wherein I have offended you; — last night
I found in you the kindest of Protectors;
This morning, when I spoke of weariness,

You from my shoulder took my scrip and
  threw it
About your own; but for these two hours
  past   150
Once only have you spoken, when the lark
Whirred from among the fern beneath our
  feet,
And I, no coward in my better days,
Was almost terrified.
  Mar.   That 's excellent ! —
So, you bethought you of the many ways
In which a man may come to his end,
  whose crimes
Have roused all Nature up against him —
  pshaw ! —
  Her. For mercy's sake, is nobody in
    sight ?
No traveller, peasant, herdsman ?
  Mar.   Not a soul:
Here is a tree, raggèd, and bent, and
  bare,   160
That turns its goat's-beard flakes of pea-
  green moss
From the stern breathing of the rough sea-
  wind;
This have we, but no other company:
Commend me to the place. If a man
  should die
And leave his body here, it were all one
As he were twenty fathoms underground.
  Her. Where is our common Friend ?
  Mar.   A ghost, methinks —
The Spirit of a murdered man, for in-
  stance —
Might have fine room to ramble about here,
A grand domain to squeak and gibber
  in.   170
  Her. Lost Man ! if thou have any close-
    pent guilt
Pressing upon thy heart, and this the hour
Of visitation——
  Mar.   A bold word from *you !*
  Her. Restore him, Heaven !
  Mar.   The desperate Wretch ! — A
    Flower,
Fairest of all flowers, was she once, but
  now
They have snapped her from the stem —
  Poh ! let her lie
Besoiled with mire, and let the houseless
  snail
Feed on her leaves. You knew her well —
  ay, there,   178
Old Man ! you were a very Lynx, you knew
The worm was in her——

Her.   Mercy ! Sir, what mean you ?
Mar. You have a Daughter !
Her.   Oh that she were here ! —
She hath an eye that sinks into all hearts,
And if I have in aught offended you,
Soon would her gentle voice make peace
     between us.
Mar. (*aside*).   I do believe he weeps —
     I could weep too —
There is a vein of her voice that runs
     through his:
Even such a Man my fancy bodied forth
From the first moment that I loved the
     Maid;
And for his sake I loved her more: these
     tears —
I did not think that aught was left in me 190
Of what I have been — yes, I thank thee,
     Heaven !
One happy thought has passed across my
     mind.
— It may not be — I am cut off from man;
No more shall I be man — no more shall I
Have human feelings ! — (*To* Herbert) —
     Now, for a little more
About your Daughter !
Her.   Troops of armed men,
Met in the roads, would bless us; little chil-
     dren,
Rushing along in the full tide of play,
Stood silent as we passed them ! I have
     heard
The boisterous carman, in the miry road,
Check his loud whip and hail us with mild
     voice, 201
And speak with milder voice to his poor
     beasts.
Mar. And whither were you going ?
Her.   Learn, young Man,
To fear the virtuous, and reverence misery,
Whether too much for patience, or, like
     mine,
Softened till it becomes a gift of mercy.
Mar. Now, this is as it should be !
Her.   I am weak ! —
My Daughter does not know how weak I
     am;
And, as thou see'st, under the arch of
     heaven
Here do I stand, alone, to helplessness, 210
By the good God, our common Father,
     doomed ! —
But I had once a spirit and an arm ——
Mar. Now, for a word about your
     Barony:

I fancy when you left the Holy Land,
And came to — what's your title — eh ?
     your claims
Were undisputed !
Her.   Like a mendicant,
Whom no one comes to meet, I stood
     alone; —
I murmured — but, remembering Him who
     feeds
The pelican and ostrich of the desert,
From my own threshold I looked up to
     Heaven 220
And did not want glimmerings of quiet
     hope.
So, from the court I passed, and down the
     brook,
Led by its murmur, to the ancient oak
I came; and when I felt its cooling shade,
I sate me down, and cannot but believe —
While in my lap I held my little Babe
And clasped her to my heart, my heart that
     ached
More with delight than grief — I heard a
     voice
Such as by Cherith on Elijah called;
It said, "I will be with thee." A little
     boy, 230
A shepherd-lad, ere yet my trance was
     gone,
Hailed us as if he had been sent from
     heaven,
And said, with tears, that he would be our
     guide:
I had a better guide — that innocent
     Babe —
Her, who hath saved me, to this hour, from
     harm,
From cold, from hunger, penury, and
     death;
To whom I owe the best of all the good
I have, or wish for, upon earth — and more
And higher far than lies within earth's
     bounds:
Therefore I bless her: when I think of
     Man, 240
I bless her with sad spirit, — when of God,
I bless her in the fulness of my joy !
Mar. The name of daughter in his
     mouth, he prays !
With nerves so steady, that the very flies
Sit unmolested on his staff. — Innocent ! —
If he were innocent — then he would
     tremble
And be disturbed, as I am. (*Turning aside.*)
     I have read

In Story, what men now alive have wit-
  nessed,
How, when the People's mind was racked
  with doubt,
Appeal was made to the great Judge: the
  Accused   250
With naked feet walked over burning
  ploughshares.
Here is a Man by Nature's hand prepared
For a like trial, but more merciful.
Why else have I been led to this bleak
  Waste ?
Bare is it, without house or track, and
  destitute
Of obvious shelter, as a shipless sea.
Here will I leave him — here — All-seeing
  God !
Such as *he* is, and sore perplexed as I am,
I will commit him to this final *Ordeal !* —
He heard a voice — a shepherd-lad came to
  him   260
And was his guide; if once, why not again,
And in this desert ? If never — then the
  whole
Of what he says, and looks, and does, and
  is,
Makes up one damning falsehood. Leave
  him here
To cold and hunger ! — Pain is of the heart,
And what are a few throes of bodily suffer-
  ing
If they can waken one pang of remorse ?
                    [*Goes up to* Herbert.
Old Man ! my wrath is as a flame burnt
  out,
It cannot be rekindled. Thou art here
Led by my hand to save thee from perdi-
  tion;   270
Thou wilt have time to breathe and
  think ——
Her.   Oh, Mercy !
Mar. I know the need that all men have
  of mercy,
And therefore leave thee to a righteous
  judgment.
Her. My Child, my blessèd Child !
Mar.   No more of that;
Thou wilt have many guides if thou art
  innocent;
Yea, from the utmost corners of the earth,
That Woman will come o'er this Waste to
  save thee.
          [*He pauses and looks at* Herbert's *staff.*
Ha ! what is here ? and carved by her own
  hand !   [*Reads upon the staff.*

" I am eyes to the blind, saith the Lord.
He that puts his trust in me shall not
  fail ! "   280
Yes, be it so; — repent and be forgiven —
God and that staff are now thy only guides.
          [*He leaves* Herbert *on the Moor.*

SCENE — *An eminence, a Beacon on the*
          summit

LACY, WALLACE, LENNOX, etc. etc.

Several of the Band (confusedly). But
  patience !
One of the Band. Curses on that Traitor,
  Oswald ! —
Our Captain made a prey to foul device ! —
  Len. (to Wal.). His tool, the wandering
  Beggar, made last night
A plain confession, such as leaves no doubt,
Knowing what otherwise we know too well,
That she revealed the truth. Stand by me
  now;
For rather would I have a nest of vipers
Between my breast-plate and my skin, than
  make   290
Oswald my special enemy, if you
Deny me your support.
Lacy.   We have been fooled —
But for the motive ?
Wal.   Natures such as his
Spin motives out of their own bowels, Lacy !
I learned this when I was a Confessor.
I know him well; there needs no other
  motive
Than that most strange incontinence in
  crime
Which haunts this Oswald. Power is life
  to him
And breath and being; where he cannot
  govern,
He will destroy.
Lacy.   To have been trapped like
  moles ! —   300
Yes, you are right, we need not hunt for
  motives:
There is no crime from which this man
  would shrink;
He recks not human law; and I have
  noticed
That often when the name of God is
  uttered,
A sudden blankness overspreads his face.
Len. Yet, reasoner as he is, his pride has
  built
Some uncouth superstition of its own.

Wal. I have seen traces of it.

Len.   Once he headed
A band of Pirates in the Norway seas;
And when the King of Denmark summoned
    him   310
To the oath of fealty, I well remember,
'T was a strange answer that he made; he
    said,
"I hold of Spirits, and the Sun in heaven."

Lacy. He is no madman.

Wal.   A most subtle doctor
Were that man, who could draw the line
    that parts
Pride and her daughter, Cruelty, from
    Madness,
That should be scourged, not pitied. Rest-
    less Minds,
Such Minds as find amid their fellow-men
No heart that loves them, none that they
    can love,
Will turn perforce and seek for sympathy
In dim relation to imagined Beings.   321

One of the Band. What if he mean to
    offer up our Captain
An expiation and a sacrifice
To those infernal fiends !

Wal.   Now, if the event
Should be as Lennox has foretold, then
    swear,
My Friends, his heart shall have as many
    wounds
As there are daggers here.

Lacy.   What need of swearing !

One of the Band. Let us away!

Another.   Away !

A third.   Hark! how the horns
Of those Scotch Rovers echo through the
    vale.

Lacy. Stay you behind; and when the sun
    is down,   330
Light up this beacon.

One of the Band.   You shall be obeyed.
                     [They go out together.

SCENE — *The Wood on the edge of the
            Moor*

MARMADUKE (*alone*).

Mar. Deep, deep and vast, vast beyond
    human thought,
Yet calm. — I could believe, that there was
    here
The only quiet heart on earth. In terror,
Remembered terror, there is peace and
    rest.

Enter OSWALD.

Osw. Ha! my dear Captain.

Mar.   A later meeting, Oswald,
Would have been better timed.

Osw.   Alone, I see;
You have done your duty. I had hopes,
    which now
I feel that you will justify.

Mar.   I had fears,
From which I have freed myself — but 't is
    my wish   340
To be alone, and therefore we must part.

Osw. Nay, then — I am mistaken.
    There 's a weakness
About you still; you talk of solitude —
I am your friend.

Mar.   What need of this assurance
At any time ? and why given now ?

Osw.   Because
You are now in truth my Master; you have
    taught me
What there is not another living man
Had strength to teach; — and therefore
    gratitude
Is bold, and would relieve itself by praise.

Mar. Wherefore press this on me ?

Osw.   Because I feel
That you have shown, and by a signal in-
    stance,   351
How they who would be just must seek the
    rule
By diving for it into their own bosoms.
To-day you have thrown off a tyranny
That lives but in the torpid acquiescence
Of our emasculated souls, the tyranny
Of the world's masters, with the musty rules
By which they uphold their craft from age
    to age:
You have obeyed the only law that sense
Submits to recognise; the immediate law, 360
From the clear light of circumstances, flashed
Upon an independent Intellect.
Henceforth new prospects open on your path;
Your faculties should grow with the demand;
I still will be your friend, will cleave to you
Through good and evil, obloquy and scorn,
Oft as they dare to follow on your steps.

Mar. I would be left alone.

Osw. (*exultingly*). I know your motives !
I am not of the world's presumptuous judges,
Who damn where they can neither see nor
    feel,   370
With a hard-hearted ignorance; your strug-
    gles
I witnessed, and now hail your victory.

Mar. Spare me awhile that greeting.
Osw.   It may be,
That some there are, squeamish half-think-
ing cowards,
Who will turn pale upon you, call you mur-
derer,
And you will walk in solitude among them.
A mighty evil for a strong-built mind ! —
Join twenty tapers of unequal height
And light them joined, and you will see the
less
How 't will burn down the taller; and they
all   380
Shall prey upon the tallest.   Solitude ! —
The Eagle lives in Solitude.
Mar.   Even so,
The Sparrow so on the housetop, and I,
The weakest of God's creatures, stand re-
solved
To abide the issue of my act, alone.
Osw. Now would you ? and for ever ? —
My young Friend,
As time advances either we become
The prey or masters of our own past deeds.
Fellowship we *must* have, willing or no;
And if good Angels fail, slack in their duty,
Substitutes, turn our faces where we may,
Are still forthcoming; some which, though
they bear   392
Ill names, can render no ill services,
In recompense for what themselves re-
quired.
So meet extremes in this mysterious world,
And opposites thus melt into each other.
Mar. Time, since Man first drew breath,
has never moved
With such a weight upon his wings as now;
But they will soon be lightened.
Osw.   Ay, look up —
Cast round you your mind's eye, and you
will learn   400
Fortitude is the child of Enterprise:
Great actions move our admiration, chiefly
Because they carry in themselves an earnest
That we can suffer greatly.
Mar.   Very true.
Osw. Action is transitory — a step, a blow,
The motion of a muscle — this way or that —
'T is done, and in the after-vacancy
We wonder at ourselves like men betrayed:
Suffering is permanent, obscure and dark,
And shares the nature of infinity.   410
Mar. Truth — and I feel it.
Osw.   What ! if you had bid
Eternal farewell to unmingled joy

And the light dancing of the thoughtless
heart;
It is the toy of fools, and little fit
For such a world as this.   The wise abjure
All thoughts whose idle composition lives
In the entire forgetfulness of pain.
— I see I have disturbed you.
Mar.   By no means.
Osw. Compassion ! — pity ! — pride can
do without them;
And what if you should never know them
more ! —   420
He is a puny soul who, feeling pain,
Finds ease because another feels it too.
If e'er I open out this heart of mine
It shall be for a nobler end — to teach
And not to purchase puling sympathy.
— Nay, you are pale.
Mar.   It may be so.
Osw.   Remorse —
It cannot live with thought; think on, think
on,
And it will die.   What ! in this universe,
Where the least things control the greatest,
where
The faintest breath that breathes can move
a world;   430
What ! feel remorse, where, if a cat had
sneezed,
A leaf had fallen, the thing had never been
Whose very shadow gnaws us to the vitals.
Mar. Now, whither are you wandering ?
That a man
So used to suit his language to the time,
Should thus so widely differ from himself —
It is most strange.
Osw. Murder ! — what 's in the word ! —
I have no cases by me ready made
To fit all deeds.   Carry him to the Camp! —
A shallow project; — you of late have seen
More deeply, taught us that the institutes
Of Nature, by a cunning usurpation   442
Banished from human intercourse, exist
Only in our relations to the brutes
That make the fields their dwelling.   If a
snake
Crawl from beneath our feet we do not
ask
A license to destroy him: our good governors
Hedge in the life of every pest and plague
That bears the shape of man; and for what
purpose,
But to protect themselves from extirpa-
tion ? —   450
This flimsy barrier you have overleaped.

Mar. My Office is fulfilled — the Man is now

Delivered to the Judge of all things.

Osw. Dead!

Mar. I have borne my burthen to its destined end.

Osw. This instant we 'll return to our companions —

Oh how I long to see their faces again!

Enter IDONEA, *with* Pilgrims *who continue their journey.*

Idon. (*after some time*). What, Marmaduke! now thou art mine for ever.

And Oswald, too! (*To* Marmaduke.) On will we to my Father

With the glad tidings which this day hath brought; 459

We 'll go together, and, such proof received

Of his own rights restored, his gratitude

To God above will make him feel for ours.

Osw. I interrupt you?

Idon. Think not so.

Mar. Idonea,

That I should ever live to see this moment!

Idon. Forgive me. — Oswald knows it all — he knows,

Each word of that unhappy letter fell

As a blood drop from my heart.

Osw. 'T was even so.

Mar. I have much to say, but for whose ear? — not thine.

Idon. Ill can I bear that look — Plead for me, Oswald!

You are my Father's Friend.

(*To* Marmaduke.) Alas, you know not,

And never *can* you know, how much he loved me. 471

Twice had he been to me a father, twice

Had given me breath, and was I not to be

His daughter, once his daughter? could I withstand

His pleading face, and feel his clasping arms,

And hear his prayer that I would not forsake him

In his old age —— [*Hides her face.*

Mar. Patience — Heaven grant me patience! —

She weeps, she weeps — *my* brain shall burn for hours

Ere *I* can shed a tear.

Idon. I was a woman;

And, balancing the hopes that are the dearest 480

To womankind with duty to my Father,

I yielded up those precious hopes, which nought

On earth could else have wrested from me; — if erring,

Oh let me be forgiven!

Mar. I *do* forgive thee.

Idon. But take me to your arms — this breast, alas!

It throbs, and you have a heart that does not feel it.

Mar. (*exultingly*). She is innocent.

[*He embraces her.*

Osw. (*aside*). Were I a Moralist,

I should make wondrous revolution here;

It were a quaint experiment to show 489

The beauty of truth — [*Addressing them.*

I see I interrupt you;

I shall have business with you, Marmaduke;

Follow me to the Hostel. [*Exit* Oswald.

Idon. Marmaduke,

This is a happy day. My Father soon

Shall sun himself before his native doors;

The lame, the hungry, will be welcome there.

No more shall he complain of wasted strength,

Of thoughts that fail, and a decaying heart;

His good works will be balm and life to him.

Mar. This is most strange! — I know not what it was,

But there was something which most plainly said, 500

That thou wert innocent.

Idon. How innocent! —

Oh heavens! you 've been deceived.

Mar. Thou art a Woman,

To bring perdition on the universe.

Idon. Already I 've been punished to the height

Of my offence. [*Smiling affectionately.*

I see you love me still,

The labours of my hand are still your joy;

Bethink you of the hour when on your shoulder

I hung this belt.

[*Pointing to the belt on which was suspended* Herbert's *scrip.*

Mar. Mercy of Heaven! [*Sinks.*

Idon. What ails you! [*Distractedly.*

Mar. The scrip that held his food, and I forgot

To give it back again!

Idon. What mean your words?

Mar. I know not what I said — all may
  be well.   511
Idon. That smile hath life in it !
Mar.   This road is perilous;
I will attend you to a Hut that stands
Near the wood's edge — rest there to-night,
  I pray you:
For me, I have business, as you heard, with
  Oswald,
But will return to you by break of day.
          [*Exeunt.*

ACT IV

SCENE — *A desolate prospect — a ridge of
rocks — a Chapel on the summit of one
— Moon behind the rocks — night
stormy — irregular sound of a Bell*

HERBERT *enters exhausted.*

Her. That Chapel-bell in mercy seemed
  to guide me,
But now it mocks my steps; its fitful stroke
Can scarcely be the work of human hands.
Hear me, ye Men, upon the cliffs, if such
There be who pray nightly before the Altar.
Oh that I had but strength to reach the
  place !
My Child — my child — dark — dark — I
  faint — this wind —
These stifling blasts — God help me !

Enter ELDRED.

Eld.   Better this bare rock,
Though it were tottering over a man's head,
Than a tight case of dungeon walls for
  shelter   10
From such rough dealing.
          [*A moaning voice is heard.*
          Ha ! what sound is that ?
Trees creaking in the wind (but none are
  here)
Send forth such noises — and that weary
  bell !
Surely some evil Spirit abroad to-night
Is ringing it — 't would stop a Saint in
  prayer,
And that — what is it ? never was sound so
  like
A human groan. Ha ! what is here ?
  Poor Man —
Murdered ! alas ! speak — speak, I am your
  friend:
No answer — hush — lost wretch, he lifts
  his hand

And lays it to his heart — (*Kneels to him*).
  I pray you speak !   20
What has befallen you ?
Her. (*feebly*). A stranger has done this,
And in the arms of a stranger I must die.
Eld. Nay, think not so : come, let me
  raise you up: [*Raises him.*
This is a dismal place — well — that is
  well —
I was too fearful — take me for your guide
And your support — my hut is not far off.
          [*Draws him gently off the stage.*

SCENE — *A room in the Hostel*

MARMADUKE *and* OSWALD.

Mar. But for Idonea ! — I have cause to
  think
That she is innocent.
Osw.   Leave that thought awhile,
As one of those beliefs, which in their hearts
Lovers lock up as pearls, though oft no
  better   30
Than feathers clinging to their points of
  passion.
This day's event has laid on me the duty
Of opening out my story; you must hear it,
And without further preface. — In my
  youth,
Except for that abatement which is paid
By envy as a tribute to desert,
I was the pleasure of all hearts, the darling
Of every tongue — as you are now. You 've
  heard
That I embarked for Syria. On our voyage
Was hatched among the crew a foul Con-
  spiracy   40
Against my honour, in the which our Cap-
  tain
Was, I believed, prime Agent. The wind
  fell;
We lay becalmed week after week, until
The water of the vessel was exhausted;
I felt a double fever in my veins,
Yet rage suppressed itself; — to a deep still-
  ness
Did my pride tame my pride; — for many
  days,
On a dead sea under a burning sky,
I brooded o'er my injuries, deserted
By man and nature; — if a breeze had
  blown,   50
It might have found its way into my heart,
And I had been — no matter — do you mark
  me ?

Mar. Quick — to the point — if any un-
told crime
Doth haunt your memory.
   Osw.   Patience, hear me further ! —
One day in silence did we drift at noon
By a bare rock, narrow, and white, and
bare;
No food was there, no drink, no grass, no
shade,
No tree, nor jutting eminence, nor form
Inanimate large as the body of man,
Nor any living thing whose lot of life   60
Might stretch beyond the measure of one
moon.
To dig for water on the spot, the Captain
Landed with a small troop, myself being
one:
There I reproached him with his treachery.
Imperious at all times, his temper rose;
He struck me; and that instant had I killed
him,
And put an end to his insolence, but my
Comrades
Rushed in between us: then did I insist
(All hated him, and I was stung to mad-
ness)
That we should leave him there, alive ! —
we did so.   70
   Mar. And he was famished ?
   Osw.   Naked was the spot;
Methinks I see it now — how in the sun
Its stony surface glittered like a shield;
And in that miserable place we left him,
Alone but for a swarm of minute creatures
Not one of which could help him while
alive,
Or mourn him dead.
   Mar.   A man by men cast off,
Left without burial ! nay, not dead nor
dying,
But standing, walking, stretching forth his
arms,
In all things like ourselves, but in the
agony   80
With which he called for mercy; and —
even so —
He was forsaken ?
   Osw.   There is a power in sounds:
The cries he uttered might have stopped
the boat
That bore us through the water ——
   Mar.   You returned
Upon that dismal hearing — did you not ?
   Osw. Some scoffed at him with hellish
mockery,

And laughed so loud it seemed that the
smooth sea
Did from some distant region echo us.
   Mar. We all are of one blood, our veins
are filled   89
At the same poisonous fountain !
   Osw.   'T was an island
Only by sufferance of the winds and waves,
Which with their foam could cover it at
will.
I know not how he perished; but the calm,
The same dead calm, continued many days.
   Mar. But his own crime had brought on
him this doom,
His wickedness prepared it; these expe-
dients
Are terrible, yet ours is not the fault.
   Osw. The man was famished, and was
innocent !
   Mar. Impossible !
   Osw.   The man had never wronged me.
   Mar. Banish the thought, crush it, and
be at peace.   100
His guilt was marked — these things could
never be
Were there not eyes that see, and for good
ends,
Where ours are baffled.
   Osw.   I had been deceived.
   Mar. And from that hour the miserable
man
No more was heard of ?
   Osw.   I had been betrayed.
   Mar. And he found no deliverance !
   Osw.   The Crew
Gave me a hearty welcome; they had laid
The plot to rid themselves, at any cost,
Of a tyrannic Master whom they loathed.
So we pursued our voyage: when we landed,
The tale was spread abroad; my power at
once   111
Shrunk from me; plans and schemes, and
lofty hopes —
All vanished. I gave way — do you attend ?
   Mar. The Crew deceived you ?
   Osw.   Nay, command yourself.
   Mar. It is a dismal night — how the wind
howls !
   Osw. I hid my head within a Convent,
there
Lay passive as a dormouse in mid-winter.
That was no life for me — I was o'erthrown,
But not destroyed.
   Mar.   The proofs — you ought to have
seen

The guilt — have touched it — felt it at
   your heart —   120
As I have done.
  Osw.   A fresh tide of Crusaders
Drove by the place of my retreat: three
   nights
Did constant meditation dry my blood;
Three sleepless nights I passed in sounding
   on,
Through words and things, a dim and
   perilous way;
And, wheresoe'er I turned me, I beheld
A slavery compared to which the dungeon
And clanking chains are perfect liberty.
You understand me — I was comforted;
I saw that every possible shape of action
Might lead to good — I saw it and burst
   forth   131
Thirsting for some of those exploits that fill
The earth for sure redemption of lost peace.
     [*Marking* Marmaduke's *countenance.*
Nay, you have had the worst. Ferocity
Subsided in a moment, like a wind
That drops down dead out of a sky it
   vexed.
And yet I had within me evermore
A salient spring of energy; I mounted
From action up to action with a mind
That never rested — without meat or drink
Have I lived many days — my sleep was
   bound   141
To purposes of reason — not a dream
But had a continuity and substance
That waking life had never power to give.
  Mar. O wretched Human-kind ! — Until
   the mystery
Of all this world is solved, well may we
   envy
The worm, that, underneath a stone whose
   weight
Would crush the lion's paw with mortal
   anguish,
Doth lodge, and feed, and coil, and sleep,
   in safety.
Fell not the wrath of Heaven upon those
   traitors ?   150
  Osw. Give not to them a thought. From
   Palestine
We marched to Syria: oft I left the Camp,
When all that multitude of hearts was
   still,
And followed on, through woods of gloomy
   cedar,
Into deep chasms troubled by roaring
   streams;

Or from the top of Lebanon surveyed
The moonlight desert, and the moonlight
   sea:
In these my lonely wanderings I perceived
What mighty objects do impress their
   forms
To elevate our intellectual being;   160
And felt, if aught on earth deserves a
   curse,
'T is that worst principle of ill which dooms
A thing so great to perish self-consumed.
— So much for my remorse !
  Mar.   Unhappy Man !
  Osw. When from these forms I turned
   to contemplate
The World's opinions and her usages,
I seemed a Being who had passed alone
Into a region of futurity,
Whose natural element was freedom ——
  Mar.   Stop —
I may not, cannot, follow thee.
  Osw.   You must.
I had been nourished by the sickly food   171
Of popular applause. I now perceived
That we are praised, only as men in us
Do recognise some image of themselves,
An abject counterpart of what they are,
Or the empty thing that they would wish
   to be.
I felt that merit has no surer test
Than obloquy; that, if we wish to serve
The world in substance, not deceive by
   show,
We must become obnoxious to its hate,   180
Or fear disguised in simulated scorn.
  Mar. I pity, can forgive, you; but those
   wretches —
That monstrous perfidy !
  Osw.   Keep down your wrath.
False Shame discarded, spurious Fame de-
   spised,
Twin sisters both of Ignorance, I found
Life stretched before me smooth as some
   broad way
Cleared for a monarch's progress.   Priests
   might spin
Their veil, but not for me — 't was in fit
   place
Among its kindred cobwebs.   I had been,
And in that dream had left my native land,
One of Love's simple bondsmen — the soft
   chain   191
Was off for ever; and the men, from whom
This liberation came, you would destroy:
Join me in thanks for their blind services.

Mar. 'T is a strange aching that, when we
  would curse
And cannot. — You have betrayed me — I
  have done —
I am content — I know that he is guilt-
  less —
That both are guiltless, without spot or
  stain,
Mutually consecrated.   Poor old Man !
And I had heart for this, because thou
  lovedst   200
Her who from very infancy had been
Light to thy path, warmth to thy blood ! —
  Together   [*Turning to* Oswald.
We propped his steps, he leaned upon us
  both.
 Osw. Ay, we are coupled by a chain of
  adamant;
Let us be fellow-labourers, then, to enlarge
Man's intellectual empire.   We subsist
In slavery; all is slavery; we receive
Laws, but we ask not whence those laws
  have come;
We need an inward sting to goad us on.
 Mar. Have you betrayed me ?   Speak
  to that.
 Osw.   The mask,   210
Which for a season I have stooped to wear,
Must be cast off. — Know then that I was
  urged,
(For other impulse let it pass) was driven,
To seek for sympathy, because I saw
In you a mirror of my youthful self ;
I would have made us equal once again,
But that was a vain hope.   You have struck
  home,
With a few drops of blood cut short the
  business;
Therein for ever you must yield to me.
But what is done will save you from the
  blank   220
Of living without knowledge that you live:
Now you are suffering — for the future
  day,
'T is his who will command it. — Think of
  my story —
Herbert is *innocent.*
 Mar. (*in a faint voice, and doubtingly*).
     You do but echo
My own wild words ?
 Osw. Young Man, the seed must lie
Hid in the earth, or there can be no har-
  vest;
'T is Nature's law.   What I have done in
  darkness

I will avow before the face of day.
Herbert *is* innocent.
 Mar.   What fiend could prompt
This action ?   Innocent ! — oh, breaking
  heart ! —   230
Alive or dead, I 'll find him. [*Exit.*
 Osw. Alive — perdition ! [*Exit.*

SCENE — *The inside of a poor Cottage*

 ELEANOR *and* IDONEA *seated.*

Idon. The storm beats hard — Mercy
  for poor or rich,
Whose heads are shelterless in such a night !
A Voice without. Holla ! to bed, good
  Folks, within !
Elea.   O save us !
Idon. What can this mean ?
Elea. Alas, for my poor husband ! —
We 'll have a counting of our flocks to-
  morrow;
The wolf keeps festival these stormy nights:
Be calm, sweet Lady, they are wassailers
  [*The voices die away in the distance.*
Returning from their Feast — my heart
  beats so —
A noise at midnight does *so* frighten
  me.   240
Idon. Hush !   [*Listening.*
Elea. They are gone.   On such a
  night my husband,
Dragged from his bed, was cast into a dun-
  geon,
Where, hid from me, he counted many
  years,
A criminal in no one's eyes but theirs —
Not even in theirs — whose brutal violence
So dealt with him.
 Idon. I have a noble Friend
First among youths of knightly breeding,
  One
Who lives but to protect the weak or injured.
There again !   [*Listening.*
 Elea. 'T is my husband's foot.   Good
  Eldred
Has a kind heart; but his imprisonment 250
Has made him fearful, and he 'll never be
The man he was.
 Idon. I will retire; — good night !
       [*She goes within.*

 Enter ELDRED (*hides a bundle*).

 Eld. Not yet in bed, Eleanor ! — there
are stains in that frock which must be
washed out.

Elea. What has befallen you?

Eld. I am belated, and you must know the cause — (*speaking low*) that is the blood of an unhappy Man.

Elea. Oh! we are undone for ever. 260

Eld. Heaven forbid that I should lift my hand against any man. Eleanor, I have shed tears to-night, and it comforts me to think of it.

Elea. Where, where is he?

Eld. I have done him no harm, but —— it will be forgiven me; it would not have been so once.

Elea. You have not *buried* anything? You are no richer than when you left me? 271

Eld. Be at peace; I am innocent.

Elea. Then God be thanked —

[*A short pause; she falls upon his neck.*

Eld. To-night I met with an old Man lying stretched upon the ground — a sad spectacle: I raised him up with the hope that we might shelter and restore him.

Elea. (*as if ready to run*). Where is he? You were not able to bring him *all* the way with you; let us return, I can help you.   [*Eldred shakes his head.* 281

Eld. He did not seem to wish for life: as I was struggling on, by the light of the moon I saw the stains of blood upon my clothes — he waved his. hand, as if it were all useless; and I let him sink again to the ground.

Elea. Oh that I had been by your side!

Eld. I tell you his hands and his body were cold — how could I disturb his last moments? he strove to turn from me as if he wished to settle into sleep.   292

Elea. But, for the stains of blood —

Eld. He must have fallen, I fancy, for his head was cut; but I think his malady was cold and hunger.

Elea. Oh, Eldred, I shall never be able to look up at this roof in storm or fair but I shall tremble.   299

Eld. Is it not enough that my ill stars have kept me abroad to-night till this hour? I come home, and this is my comfort!

Elea. But did he say nothing which might have set you at ease?

Eld. I thought he grasped my hand while he was muttering something about his Child — his Daughter — (*starting as if he heard a noise*). What is that?

Elea. Eldred, you are a father.

Eld. God knows what was in my heart, and will not curse my son for my sake. 311

Elea. But you prayed by him? you waited the hour of his release?

Eld. The night was wasting fast; I have no friend; I am spited by the world — his wound terrified me — if I had brought him along with me, and he had died in my arms! —— I am sure I heard something breathing — and this chair!   319

Elea. Oh, Eldred, you will die alone. You will have nobody to close your eyes — no hand to grasp your dying hand — I shall be in my grave. A curse will attend us all.

Eld. Have you forgot your own troubles when I was in the dungeon?

Elea. And you left him alive?

Eld. Alive! — the damps of death were upon him — he could not have survived an hour.

Elea. In the cold, cold night.   330

Eld. (*in a savage tone*). Ay, and his head was bare; I suppose you would have had me lend my bonnet to cover it. — You will never rest till I am brought to a felon's end.

Elea. Is there nothing to be done? cannot we go to the Convent?

Eld. Ay, and say at once that I murdered him!   339

Elea. Eldred, I know that ours is the only house upon the Waste; let us take heart; this Man may be rich; and could he be saved by our means, his gratitude may reward us.

Eld. 'T is all in vain.

Elea. But let us make the attempt. This old Man may have a wife, and he may have children — let us return to the spot; we may restore him, and his eyes may yet open upon those that love him.   350

Eld. He will never open them more; even when he spoke to me, he kept them firmly sealed as if he had been blind.

Idon. (*rushing out*). It is, it is, my Father—

Eld. We are betrayed (*looking at Idonea*).

Elea. His Daughter! — God have mercy! (*turning to* Idonea).

Idon. (*sinking down*). Oh! lift me up and carry me to the place.   360
You are safe; the whole world shall not harm you.

Elea. This Lady is his Daughter.

Eld. (moved). I'll lead you to the spot.
Idon. (springing up).   Alive! — you
  heard him breathe? quick, quick —
                              [*Exeunt.*

ACT V

SCENE — *A wood on the edge of the Waste*

Enter OSWALD *and a* Forester.

For. He leaned upon the bridge that
  spans the glen,
And down into the bottom cast his eye,
That fastened there, as it would check the
  current.
Osw. He listened too; did you not say
  he listened?
For. As if there came such moaning
  from the flood
As is heard often after stormy nights.
Osw. But did he utter nothing?
For.   See him there!

MARMADUKE *appearing.*

Mar. Buzz, buzz, ye black and winged
  freebooters;
That is no substance which ye settle on!
For. His senses play him false; and see,
  his arms   10
Outspread, as if to save himself from fall-
  ing! —
Some terrible phantom I believe is now
Passing before him, such as God will not
Permit to visit any but a man
Who has been guilty of some horrid crime.
                        [Marmaduke *disappears.*
Osw. The game is up! —
For.   If it be needful, Sir,
I will assist you to lay hands upon
  him.
Osw. No, no, my Friend, you may pursue
  your business —
'T is a poor wretch of an unsettled mind,
Who has a trick of straying from his keep-
  ers;   20
We must be gentle. Leave him to my
  care.   [*Exit* Forester.
If his own eyes play false with him, these
  freaks
Of fancy shall be quickly tamed by mine;
The goal is reached. My Master shall be-
  come
A shadow of myself — made by myself.

SCENE — *The edge of the Moor*

MARMADUKE *and* ELDRED *enter from
  opposite sides.*

*Mar. (raising his eyes and perceiving
  Eldred).* In any corner of this
  savage Waste,
Have you, good Peasant, seen a blind old
  Man?
Eld. I heard ——
Mar.   You heard him, where? when
  heard him?
Eld.   As you know,
The first hours of last night were rough
  with storm: 29
I had been out in search of a stray heifer;
Returning late, I heard a moaning sound;
Then, thinking that my fancy had deceived
  me,
I hurried on, when straight a second moan,
A human voice distinct, struck on my ear,
So guided, distant a few steps, I found
An aged Man, and such as you describe.
Mar. You heard! — he called you to
  him? Of all men
The best and kindest! — but where is he?
  guide me,
That I may see him.
Eld.   On a ridge of rocks
A lonesome Chapel stands, deserted now:
The bell is left, which no one dares remove;
And, when the stormy wind blows o'er the
  peak,   42
It rings, as if a human hand were there
To pull the cord. I guess he must have
  heard it;
And it had led him towards the precipice,
To climb up to the spot whence the sound
  came;
But he had failed through weakness. From
  his hand
His staff had dropped, and close upon the
  brink
Of a small pool of water he was laid,
As if he had stooped to drink, and so re-
  mained   50
Without the strength to rise.
Mar.   Well, well, he lives,
And all is safe: what said he?
Eld.   But few words:
He only spake to me of a dear Daughter,
Who, so he feared, would never see him
  more;
And of a Stranger to him, One by whom
He had been sore misused; but he forgave

The wrong and the wrong-doer. You are
        troubled —
Perhaps you are his son ?
Mar.   The All-seeing knows,
I did not think he had a living Child. —
But whither did you carry him ?
Eld.   He was torn,
His head was bruised, and there was blood
        about him ——   61
Mar. That was no work of mine.
Eld.   Nor was it mine.
Mar. But had he strength to walk ?   I
        could have borne him
A thousand miles.
Eld.   I am in poverty,
And know how busy are the tongues of men;
My heart was willing, Sir, but I am one
Whose good deeds will not stand by their
        own light;
And, though it smote me more than words
        can tell,
I left him.
Mar. I believe that there are phantoms,
That in the shape of man do cross our path
On evil instigation, to make sport   71
Of our distress — and thou art one of them !
But things substantial have so pressed on
        me ——
Eld. My wife and children came into my
        mind.
Mar. Oh Monster ! Monster ! there are
        three of us,
And we shall howl together.
        [*After a pause and in a feeble voice.*
                        I am deserted
At my worst need, my crimes have in a net
(*Pointing to* Eldred) Entangled this poor
        man. — Where was it ? where ?
                        [*Dragging him along.*
Eld. 'T is needless; spare your violence.
        His Daughter ——
Mar. Ay, in the word a thousand scor-
        pions lodge   80
This old man *had* a Daughter.
Eld.   To the spot
I hurried back with her. — O save me, Sir,
From such a journey! —— there was a black
        tree,
A single tree; she thought it was her
        Father. —
Oh Sir, I would not see that hour again
For twenty lives. The daylight dawned,
        and now —
Nay; hear my tale, 't is fit that you should
        hear it —

As we approached, a solitary crow
Rose from the spot; — the Daughter
        clapped her hands,
And then I heard a shriek so terrible   90
        [*Marmaduke shrinks back.*
The startled bird quivered upon the wing.
Mar. Dead, dead ! —
Eld. (*after a pause*). A dismal matter,
        Sir, for me,
And seems the like for you; if 't is your
        wish,
I 'll lead you to his Daughter; but 't were
        best
That she should be prepared; I 'll go before.
Mar. There will be need of preparation.
                        [*Eldred goes off.*
Elea. (*enters*).   Master !
Your limbs sink under you, shall I support
        you ?
Mar. (*taking her arm*). Woman, I 've
        lent my body to the service
Which now thou tak'st upon thee. God for-
        bid
That thou shouldst ever meet a like occa-
        sion   100
With such a purpose in thine heart as mine
        was.
Elea. Oh, why have I to do with things
        like these ?   [*Exeunt.*

SCENE *changes to the door of* ELDRED'S
        cottage

IDONEA *seated — enter* ELDRED.

Eld. Your Father, Lady, from a wilful
        hand
Has met unkindness; so indeed he told me,
And you remember such was my report:
From what has just befallen me I have
        cause
To fear the very worst.
Idon.   My Father is dead;
Why dost thou come to me with words like
        these ?
Eld. A wicked Man should answer for
        his crimes.   109
Idon. Thou seest me what I am.
Eld.   It was most heinous,
And doth call out for vengeance.
Idon.   Do not add,
I prithee, to the harm thou 'st done already.
Eld. Hereafter you will thank me for
        this service.
Hard by, a Man I met, who, from plain
        proofs

Of interfering Heaven, I have no doubt,
Laid hands upon your Father. Fit it were
You should prepare to meet him.
    Idon.   I have nothing
To do with others; help me to my Father —
    [*She turns and sees* Marmaduke *leaning
    on* Eleanor — *throws herself upon his
    neck, and after some time,*
In joy I met thee, but a few hours past;
And thus we meet again; one human stay
Is left me still in thee. Nay, shake not so.
    Mar. In such a wildern. — to see no
        thing,   122
No, not the pitying moon !
    Idon.   And perish so.
    Mar. Without a dog to moan for him.
    Idon.   Think not of it,
But enter there and see him how he sleeps,
Tranquil as he had died in his own bed.
    Mar. Tranquil — why not ?
    Idon.   Oh, peace !
    Mar.   He is at peace;
His body is at rest: there was a plot,
A hideous plot, against the soul of man:
It took effect — and yet I baffled it,   130
In *some* degree.
    Idon.   Between us stood, I thought,
A cup of consolation, filled from Heaven
For both our needs; must I, and in thy pre-
    sence,
Alone partake of it? — Belovèd Marmaduke!
    Mar. Give me a reason why the wisest
    thing
That the earth owns shall never choose to
    die,
But some one must be near to count his
    groans.
The wounded deer retires to solitude,
And dies in solitude: all things but man,
All die in solitude.
    [*Moving towards the cottage door.*
    Mysterious God,   140
If she had never lived I had not done it ! —
    Idon. Alas, the thought of such a cruel
    death
Has overwhelmed him. — I must follow.
    Eld.   Lady !
You will do well; (*she goes*) unjust suspicion
    may
Cleave to this Stranger: if, upon his enter-
    ing,
The dead Man heave a groan, or from his
    side
Uplift his hand — that would be evidence.
    Elea. Shame ! Eldred, shame !

    Mar. (*both returning*).   The dead have
    but one face (*to himself*).
And such a Man — so meek and unoffend-
    ing —   149
Helpless and harmless as a babe: a Man,
By obvious signal to the world's protection,
Solemnly dedicated — to decoy him ! —
    Idon. Oh, had you seen him living ! —
    Mar.   I (so filled
With horror is this world) am unto thee
The thing most precious, that it now con-
    tains:
Therefore through me alone must be re-
    vealed
By whom thy Parent was destroyed, Idonea!
I have the proofs ! —
    Idon.   O miserable Father !
Thou didst command me to bless all man-
    kind;
Nor to this moment, have I ever wished 160
Evil to any living thing; but hear me,
Hear me, ye Heavens ! — (*kneeling*) — may
    vengeance haunt the fiend
For this most cruel murder: let him live
And move in terror of the elements;
The thunder send him on his knees to prayer
In the open streets, and let him think he
    sees,
If e'er he entereth the house of God,
The roof, self-moved, unsettling o'er his
    head;
And let him, when he would lie down at
    night,
Point to his wife the blood-drops on his
    pillow !   170
    Mar. My voice was silent, but my heart
    hath joined thee.
    Idon. (*leaning on* Marmaduke). Left to
    the mercy of that savage Man !
How could he call upon his Child ! — O
    Friend !   [*Turns to* Marmaduke.
My faithful true and only Comforter.
    Mar. Ay, come to me and weep. (*He
    kisses her.*) (*To* Eldred.) Yes, Var-
    let, look,
The devils at such sights do clap their hands.
        [*Eldred retires alarmed.*
    Idon. Thy vest is torn, thy cheek is dead-
    ly pale;
Hast thou pursued the monster ?
    Mar.   I have found him. —
Oh ! would that thou hadst perished in the
    flames !
    Idon. Here art thou, then can I be deso-
    late ? —   180

Mar. There was a time, when this protecting hand
Availed against the mighty; never more
Shall blessings wait upon a deed of mine.
Idon. Wild words for me to hear, for me,
    an orphan
Committed to thy guardianship by Heaven;
And, if thou hast forgiven me, let me hope,
In this deep sorrow, trust, that I am thine
For closer care; — here, is no malady.
                  [*Taking his arm.*
Mar. There, *is* a malady —
(*Striking his heart and forehead*). And here,
    and here,
A mortal malady. — I am accurst: 190
All nature curses me, and in my heart
Thy curse is fixed; the truth must be laid
    bare.
It must be told, and borne. I am the man,
(Abused, betrayed, but how it matters not)
Presumptuous above all that ever breathed,
Who, casting as I thought a guilty Person
Upon Heaven's righteous judgment, did become
An instrument of Fiends. Through me,
    through me
Thy Father perished.
Idon.   Perished — by what mischance?
Mar. Belovèd ! — if I dared, so would I
    call thee —   200
Conflict must cease, and, in thy frozen heart,
The extremes of suffering meet in absolute
    peace.   [*He gives her a letter.*
Idon. (*reads*). " Be not surprised if you
hear that some signal judgment has befallen
the man who calls himself your father; he
is now with me, as his signature will shew:
abstain from conjecture till you see me.
                " HERBERT.
               " MARMADUKE."
The writing Oswald's; the signature my
    Father's:
(*Looks steadily at the paper*). And here is
yours, — or do my eyes deceive me ?
You have then seen my Father ?
Mar.   He has leaned
Upon this arm.
Idon. You led him towards the Convent ?
Mar. That Convent was Stone-Arthur
    Castle. Thither   212
We were his guides. I on that night resolved
That he should wait thy coming till the day
Of resurrection.
Idon.   Miserable Woman,

Too quickly moved, too easily giving way,
I put denial on thy suit, and hence,
With the disastrous issue of last night,
Thy perturbation, and these frantic words.
Be calm, I pray thee !
Mar.   Oswald ——
Idon.   Name him not.

        Enter female Beggar.

Beg. And he is dead ! — that Moor —
    how shall I cross it ?   221
By night, by day, never shall I be able
To travel half a mile alone. — Good Lady !
Forgive me ! — Saints forgive me. Had I
    thought
It would have come to this ! —
Idon. What brings you hither ? speak !
Beg. (*pointing to* Marmaduke). This innocent Gentleman. Sweet heavens !
    I told him
Such tales of your dead Father ! — God is
    my judge,
I thought there was no harm: but that bad
    Man,
He bribed me with his gold, and looked so
    fierce.
Mercy ! I said I know not what — oh pity
    me —   230
I said, sweet Lady, you were not his Daughter —
Pity me, I am haunted; — thrice this day
My conscience made me wish to be struck
    blind;
And then I would have prayed, and had no
    voice.
Idon. (*to* Marmaduke). Was it my Father ? — no, no, no, for he
Was meek and patient, feeble, old and blind,
Helpless, and loved me dearer than his life.
— But hear me. For *one* question, I have
    a heart
That will sustain me. Did you murder him ?
Mar. No, not by stroke of arm. But
    learn the process: 240
Proof after proof was pressed upon me;
    guilt
Made evident, as seemed, by blacker guilt,
Whose impious folds enwrapped even thee;
    and truth
And innocence, embodied in his looks,
His words and tones and gestures, did but
    serve
With me to aggravate his crimes, and
    heaped
Ruin upon the cause for which they pleaded.

Then pity crossed the path of my resolve:
Confounded, I looked up to Heaven, and
    cast,
Idonea! thy blind Father, on the Ordeal 250
Of the bleak Waste — left him — and so he
    died ! —
     [*Idonea sinks senseless ; Beggar, Elea-
      nor, etc., crowd round, and bear her off.*
Why may we speak these things, and do no
    more;
Why should a thrust of the arm have such
    a power,
And words that tell these things be heard
    in vain ?
She is not dead. Why ! — if I loved this
    Woman,
I would take care she never woke again;
But she WILL wake, and she will weep for
    me,
And say, no blame was mine — and so, poor
    fool,
Will waste her curses on another name.
       [*He walks about distractedly.*

Enter OSWALD.

Osw. (to himself). Strong to o'erturn,
    strong also to build up.   260
               [*To* Marmaduke.
The starts and sallies of our last encounter
Were natural enough; but that, I trust,
Is all gone by. You have cast off the
    chains
That fettered your nobility of mind —
Delivered heart and head !
             Let us to Palestine;
This is a paltry field for enterprise.
  Mar. Ay, what shall we encounter next ?
    This issue —
'T was nothing more than darkness deepen-
    ing darkness,
And weakness crowned with the impotence
    of death ! —
Your pupil is, you see, an apt proficient.
    (*Ironically.*)   270
Start not ! — Here is another face hard by;
Come, let us take a peep at both together,
And, with a voice at which the dead will
    quake,
Resound the praise of your morality —
Of this too much.
     [*Drawing* Oswald *towards the Cottage
     — stops short at the door.*
        Men are there, millions, Oswald,
Who with bare hands would have plucked
    out thy heart

And flung it to the dogs: but I am raised
Above, or sunk below, all further sense
Of provocation. Leave me, with the weight
Of that old Man's forgiveness on thy
    heart,   280
Pressing as heavily as it doth on mine.
Coward I have been; know, there lies not
    now
Within the compass of a mortal thought,
A deed that I would shrink from; — but to
    endure,
That is my destiny. May it be thine:
Thy office, thy ambition, be henceforth
To feed remorse, to welcome every sting
Of penitential anguish, yea with tears.
When seas and continents shall lie between
    us —
The wider space the better — we may
    find   290
In such a course fit links of sympathy,
An incommunicable rivalship
Maintained, for peaceful ends beyond our
    view.
     [*Confused voices — several of the band
      enter — rush upon* Oswald, *and seize
      him.*
One of them. I would have dogged him
    to the jaws of hell —
Osw. Ha ! is it so ! — That vagrant Hag !
    — this comes
Of having left a thing like her alive !
                   [*Aside.*
Several voices. Despatch him !
Osw.   If I pass beneath a rock
And shout, and, with the echo of my voice,
Bring down a heap of rubbish, and it crush
    me,   299
I die without dishonour. Famished, starved,
A Fool and Coward blended to my wish !
     [*Smiles scornfully and exultingly at*
      Marmaduke.
Wal. 'T is done ! (*Stabs him*).
Another of the Band. The ruthless
    Traitor !
Mar.   A rash deed ! —
With that reproof I do resign a station
Of which I have been proud.
  Wil. (*approaching* Marmaduke). O my
    poor Master !
  Mar. Discerning Monitor, my faithful
    Wilfred,
Why art thou here ? [*Turning to* Wallace.
           Wallace, upon these Borders,
Many there be whose eyes will not want
    cause

To weep that I am gone. Brothers in
    arms !
Raise on that dreary Waste a monument
That may record my story: nor let words —
Few must they be, and delicate in their
    touch   311
As light itself — be there withheld from
    Her
Who, through most wicked arts, was made
    an orphan
By One who would have died a thousand
    times,
To shield her from a moment's harm. To
    you,
Wallace and Wilfred, I commend the Lady,
By lowly nature reared, as if to make
    her
In all things worthier of that noble birth,
Whose long-suspended rights are now on
    the eve   319
Of restoration: with your tenderest care
Watch over her, I pray — sustain her ——
    Several of the Band (*eagerly*). Captain !

Mar. No more of that; in silence hear
    my doom:
A hermitage has furnished fit relief
To some offenders: other penitents,
Less patient in their wretchedness, have
    fallen,
Like the old Roman, on their own sword's
    point.
They had their choice: a wanderer *must I* go,
The Spectre of that innocent Man, my
    guide.
No human ear shall ever hear me speak;
No human dwelling ever give me food, 330
Or sleep, or rest: but, over waste and
    wild,
In search of nothing, that this earth can
    give,
But expiation, will I wander on —
A Man by pain and thought compelled to
    live,
Yet loathing life — till anger is appeased
In Heaven, and Mercy gives me leave to
    die.

THE REVERIE OF POOR SUSAN
1797(?). 1800

This arose out of my observation of the af-
fecting music of these birds hanging in this
way in the London streets during the freshness
and stillness of the Spring morning.

AT the corner of Wood Street, when day-
    light appears,
Hangs a Thrush that sings loud, it has
    sung for three years:
Poor Susan has passed by the spot, and has
    heard
In the silence of morning the song of the
    Bird.

'T is a note of enchantment; what ails her ?
    She sees
A mountain ascending, a vision of trees;
Bright volumes of vapour through Lothbury
    glide,
And a river flows on through the vale of
    Cheapside.

Green pastures she views in the midst of
    the dale,
Down which she so often has tripped with
    her pail;

And a single small cottage, a nest like a
    dove's,
The one only dwelling on earth that she
    loves.

She looks, and her heart is in heaven: but
    they fade,
The mist and the river, the hill and the
    shade:
The stream will not flow, and the hill will
    not rise,
And the colours have all passed away from
    her eyes !

THE BIRTH OF LOVE
1792(?). 1795

Translated from some French stanzas by
Francis Wrangham, and printed in " Poems by
Francis Wrangham, M. A."

WHEN Love was born of heavenly line,
    What dire intrigues disturbed Cythera's
    joy !
Till Venus cried, " A mother's heart is
    mine;
    None but myself shall nurse my boy."

But, infant as he was, the child
  In that divine embrace enchanted lay;
And, by the beauty of the vase beguiled,
  Forgot the beverage — and pined away.

" And must my offspring languish in my
    sight ? "
(Alive to all a mother's pain,   10
The Queen of Beauty thus her court
    addressed)
" No: Let the most discreet of all my train
Receive him to her breast:
Think all, he is the God of young delight."

Then TENDERNESS with CANDOUR joined,
  And GAIETY the charming office sought;
Nor even DELICACY stayed behind:
  But none of those fair Graces brought
Wherewith to nurse the child — and still
    he pined.
Some fond hearts to COMPLIANCE seemed
    inclined;   20
  But she had surely spoiled the boy:
  And sad experience forbade a thought
On the wild Goddess of VOLUPTUOUS JOY.

Long undecided lay th' important choice,
Till of the beauteous court, at length, a voice
Pronounced the name of HOPE : — The
    conscious child
Stretched forth his little arms, and smiled.

'T is said ENJOYMENT (who averred
  The charge belonged to her alone)
Jealous that HOPE had been preferred   30
  Laid snares to make the babe her own.

Of INNOCENCE the garb she took,
The blushing mien and downcast look;
  And came her services to proffer:
And HOPE (what has not Hope believed !)
By that seducing air deceived,
  Accepted of the offer.

It happened that, to sleep inclined,
  Deluded HOPE for one short hour
To that false INNOCENCE'S power   40
Her little charge consigned.

The Goddess then her lap with sweetmeats
    filled
  And gave, in handfuls gave, the treacher-
    ous store:
A wild delirium first the infant thrilled;
  But soon upon her breast he sunk — to
    wake no more.

A NIGHT-PIECE

1798. 1815

Composed on the road between Nether Stowey and Alfoxden, extempore. I distinctly recollect the very moment when I was struck, as described, — " He looks up — the clouds are split," etc.

——— THE sky is overcast
With a continuous cloud of texture close,
Heavy and wan, all whitened by the Moon,
Which through that veil is indistinctly seen,
A dull, contracted circle, yielding light
So feebly spread, that not a shadow falls,
Chequering the ground — from rock, plant,
    tree, or tower.
At length a pleasant instantaneous gleam
Startles the pensive traveller while he
    treads
His lonesome path, with unobserving eye
Bent earthwards; he looks up — the clouds
    are split
Asunder, — and above his head he sees
The clear Moon, and the glory of the hea-
    vens.
There, in a black-blue vault she sails along,
Followed by multitudes of stars, that, small
And sharp, and bright, along the dark abyss
Drive as she drives: how fast they wheel
    away,
Yet vanish not ! — the wind is in the tree,
But they are silent; — still they roll along
Immeasurably distant; and the vault,
Built round by those white clouds, enor-
    mous clouds,
Still deepens its unfathomable depth.
At length the Vision closes; and the mind,
Not undisturbed by the delight it feels,
Which slowly settles into peaceful calm,
Is left to muse upon the solemn scene.

WE ARE SEVEN

1798. 1798

Written at Alfoxden in the spring of 1798, under circumstances somewhat remarkable. The little girl who is the heroine I met within the area of Goodrich Castle in the year 1793. Having left the Isle of Wight and crossed Salisbury Plain, as mentioned in the preface to " Guilt and Sorrow," I proceeded by Bristol up the Wye, and so on to North Wales, to the Vale of Clwydd, where I spent my summer under the roof of the father of my friend, Robert Jones. In reference to this Poem I will here mention one of the most remarkable facts in my own poetic history and that of Mr. Coleridge. In the spring of the year 1798, he, my Sister, and myself, started from Alfoxden, pretty late in the afternoon, with a view to visit Linton and the valley of Stones near it; and as our united funds were very small, we agreed to defray the expense of the tour by writing a poem, to be sent to the New Monthly Magazine set up by Phillips the bookseller, and edited by Dr. Aikin. Accordingly we set off and proceeded along the Quantock Hills towards Watchet, and in the course of this walk was planned the poem of the "Ancient Mariner," founded on a dream, as Mr. Coleridge said, of his friend, Mr. Cruikshank. Much the greatest part of the story was Mr. Coleridge's invention; but certain parts I myself suggested : — for example, some crime was to be committed which should bring upon the old Navigator, as Coleridge afterwards delighted to call him, the spectral persecution, as a consequence of that crime, and his own wanderings. I had been reading in Shelvock's Voyages a day or two before that while doubling Cape Horn they frequently saw Albatrosses in that latitude, the largest sort of sea-fowl, some extending their wings twelve or thirteen feet. "Suppose," said I, "you represent him as having killed one of these birds on entering the South Sea, and that the tutelary Spirits of those regions take upon them to avenge the crime." The incident was thought fit for the purpose and adopted accordingly. I also suggested the navigation of the ship by the dead men, but do not recollect that I had anything more to do with the scheme of the poem. The Gloss with which it was subsequently accompanied was not thought of by either of us at the time; at least, not a hint of it was given to me, and I have no doubt it was a gratuitous after-thought. We began the composition together on that, to me, memorable evening. I furnished two or three lines at the beginning of the poem, in particular : —

> "And listened like a three years' child ;
> The Mariner had his will."

These trifling contributions, all but one (which Mr. C. has with unnecessary scrupulosity recorded) slipt out of his mind as they well might. As we endeavoured to proceed conjointly (I speak of the same evening) our respective manners proved so widely different that it would have been quite presumptuous in me to do anything but separate from an undertaking upon which I could only have been a clog. We returned after a few days from a delightful tour, of which I have many pleas-

ant, and some of them droll-enough, recollections. We returned by Dulverton to Alfoxden. The "Ancient Mariner" grew and grew till it became too important for our first object, which was limited to our expectation of five pounds, and we began to talk of a Volume, which was to consist, as Mr. Coleridge has told the world, of poems chiefly on natural subjects taken from common life, but looked at, as much as might be, through an imaginative medium. Accordingly I wrote "The Idiot Boy," "Her eyes are wild," etc., "We are seven," "The Thorn," and some others. To return to "We are seven," the piece that called forth this note, I composed it while walking in the grove at Alfoxden. My friends will not deem it too trifling to relate that while walking to and fro I composed the last stanza first, having begun with the last line. When it was all but finished, I came in and recited it to Mr. Coleridge and my Sister, and said, "A prefatory stanza must be added, and I should sit down to our little tea-meal with greater pleasure if my task were finished." I mentioned in substance what I wished to be expressed, and Coleridge immediately threw off the stanza thus : —

> "A little child, dear brother Jem," —

I objected to the rhyme, "dear brother Jem," as being ludicrous, but we all enjoyed the joke of hitching-in our friend, James Tobin's name, who was familiarly called Jem. He was the brother of the dramatist, and this reminds me of an anecdote which it may be worth while here to notice. The said Jem got a sight of the Lyrical Ballads as it was going through the press at Bristol, during which time I was residing in that city. One evening he came to me with a grave face, and said, "Wordsworth, I have seen the volume that Coleridge and you are about to publish. There is one poem in it which I earnestly entreat you will cancel, for, if published, it will make you everlastingly ridiculous." I answered that I felt much obliged by the interest he took in my good name as a writer, and begged to know what was the unfortunate piece he alluded to. He said, "It is called 'We are seven.'" Nay! said I, that shall take its chance, however, and he left me in despair. I have only to add that in the spring of 1841 I revisited Goodrich Castle, not having seen that part of the Wye since I met the little Girl there in 1793. It would have given me greater pleasure to have found in the neighbouring hamlet traces of one who had interested me so much ; but that was impossible, as unfortunately I did not even know her name. The ruin, from its position and features, is a most impressive object. I could not but deeply regret that its solemnity was im-

paired by a fantastic new Castle set up on a
projection of the same ridge, as if to show how
far modern art can go in surpassing all that
could be done by antiquity and nature with
their united graces, remembrances, and associa-
tions. I could have almost wished for power,
so much the contrast vexed me, to blow away
Sir —— Meyrick's impertinent structure and
all the fopperies it contains.

—— A SIMPLE Child,
That lightly draws its breath,
And feels its life in every limb,
What should it know of death ?

I met a little cottage Girl:
She was eight years old, she said;
Her hair was thick with many a curl
That clustered round her head.

She had a rustic, woodland air,
And she was wildly clad: 10
Her eyes were fair, and very fair;
— Her beauty made me glad.

" Sisters and brothers, little Maid,
How many may you be ? "
" How many ? Seven in all," she said
And wondering looked at me.

" And where are they ? I pray you tell."
She answered, " Seven are we;
And two of us at Conway dwell,
And two are gone to sea.   20

" Two of us in the church-yard lie,
My sister and my brother;
And, in the church-yard cottage, I
Dwell near them with my mother."

" You say that two at Conway dwell,
And two are gone to sea,
Yet ye are seven ! — I pray you tell,
Sweet Maid, how this may be."

Then did the little Maid reply,
" Seven boys and girls are we;   30
Two of us in the church-yard lie,
Beneath the church-yard tree."

" You run about, my little Maid,
Your limbs they are alive;
If two are in the church-yard laid,
Then ye are only five."

" Their graves are green, they may be seen,"
The little Maid replied,

" Twelve steps or more from my mother's
    door,
And they are side by side.   40

" My stockings there I often knit,
My kerchief there I hem;
And there upon the ground I sit,
And sing a song to them.

" And often after sunset, Sir,
When it is light and fair,
I take my little porringer,
And eat my supper there.

" The first that died was sister Jane;
In bed she moaning lay,   50
Till God released her of her pain;
And then she went away.

" So in the church-yard she was laid;
And, when the grass was dry,
Together round her grave we played,
My brother John and I.

" And when the ground was white with
    snow,
And I could run and slide,
My brother John was forced to go,
And he lies by her side."   60

" How many are you, then," said I,
" If they two are in heaven ? "
Quick was the little Maid's reply,
" O Master ! we are seven."

" But they are dead; those two are dead !
Their spirits are in heaven ! "
'T was throwing words away; for still
The little Maid would have her will,
And said, " Nay, we are seven ! "

ANECDOTE FOR FATHERS

1798. 1798

" Retine vim istam, falsa enim dicam, si coges." —
EUSEBIUS.

This was suggested in front of Alfoxden.
The Boy was a son of my friend, Basil Mon-
tagu, who had been two or three years under
our care. The name of Kilve is from a village
on the Bristol Channel, about a mile from Al-
foxden; and the name of Liswyn Farm was
taken from a beautiful spot on the Wye.
When Mr. Coleridge, my Sister, and I, had

been visiting the famous John Thelwall, who had taken refuge from politics, after a trial for high treason, with a view to bring up his family by the profits of agriculture, which proved as unfortunate a speculation as that he had fled from, Coleridge and he had both been public lecturers; Coleridge mingling, with his politics, Theology, from which the other elocutionist abstained, unless it were for the sake of a sneer. This quondam community of public employment induced Thelwall to visit Coleridge at Nether Stowey, where he fell in my way. He really was a man of extraordinary talent, an affectionate husband, and a good father. Though brought up in the City on a tailor's board, he was truly sensible of the beauty of natural objects. I remember once, when Coleridge, he, and I were seated together upon the turf on the brink of a stream in the most beautiful part of the most beautiful glen of Alfoxden, Coleridge exclaimed, ''This is a place to reconcile one to all the jarrings and conflicts of the wide world.'' — ''Nay,'' said Thelwall, ''to make one forget them altogether.'' The visit of this man to Coleridge was, as I believe Coleridge has related, the occasion of a spy being sent by Government to watch our proceedings, which were, I can say with truth, such as the world at large would have thought ludicrously harmless.

I HAVE a boy of five years old;
His face is fair and fresh to see;
His limbs are cast in beauty's mould,
And dearly he loves me.

One morn we strolled on our dry walk,
Our quiet home all full in view,
And held such intermitted talk
As we are wont to do.

My thoughts on former pleasures ran;
I thought of Kilve's delightful shore,   10
Our pleasant home when spring began,
A long, long year before.

A day it was when I could bear
Some fond regrets to entertain;
With so much happiness to spare,
I could not feel a pain.

The green earth echoed to the feet
Of lambs that bounded through the glade,
From shade to sunshine, and as fleet
From sunshine back to shade.   20

Birds warbled round me — and each trace
Of inward sadness had its charm;

Kilve, thought I, was a favoured place,
And so is Liswyn farm.

My boy beside me tripped, so slim
And graceful in his rustic dress !
And, as we talked, I questioned him,
In very idleness.

"Now tell me, had you rather be,"
I said, and took him by the arm,   30
"On Kilve's smooth shore, by the green sea,
Or here at Liswyn farm ?"

In careless mood he looked at me,
While still I held him by the arm,
And said, "At Kilve I'd rather be
Than here at Liswyn farm."

"Now, little Edward, say why so:
My little Edward, tell me why." —
"I cannot tell, I do not know." —
"Why, this is strange," said I;   40

"For, here are woods, hills smooth and
    warm:
There surely must some reason be
Why you would change sweet Liswyn farm
For Kilve by the green sea."

At this, my boy hung down his head,
He blushed with shame, nor made reply;
And three times to the child I said,
"Why, Edward, tell me why ?"

His head he raised — there was in sight,
It caught his eye, he saw it plain —   50
Upon the house-top, glittering bright,
A broad and gilded vane.

Then did the boy his tongue unlock,
And eased his mind with this reply:
"At Kilve there was no weather-cock;
And that 's the reason why."

O dearest, dearest boy ! my·heart
For better lore would seldom yearn,
Could I but teach the hundredth part
Of what from thee I learn.   60

THE THORN

1798. 1798

Written at Alfoxden. Arose out of my observing, on the ridge of Quantock Hill, on a stormy day, a thorn which I had often past, in calm and bright weather, without noticing it. I said to myself, " Cannot I by some invention do as much to make this Thorn permanently an impressive object as the storm has made it to my eyes at this moment ? " I began the poem accordingly, and composed it with great rapidity. Sir George Beaumont painted a picture from which Wilkie thought his best. He gave it me ; though when he saw it several times at Rydal Mount afterwards, he said, " I could make a better, and would like to paint the same subject over again." The sky in this picture is nobly done, but it reminds one too much of Wilson. The only fault, however, of any consequence is the female figure, which is too old and decrepit for one likely to frequent an eminence on such a call.

I

" THERE is a Thorn — it looks so old,
In truth, you 'd find it hard to say
How it could ever have been young,
It looks so old and grey.
Not higher than a two years' child
It stands erect, this aged Thorn;
No leaves it has, no prickly points;
It is a mass of knotted joints,
A wretched thing forlorn.
It stands erect, and like a stone   10
With lichens is it overgrown.

II

" Like rock or stone, it is o'ergrown,
With lichens to the very top,
And hung with heavy tufts of moss,
A melancholy crop:
Up from the earth these mosses creep,
And this poor Thorn they clasp it round
So close, you 'd say that they are bent
With plain and manifest intent
To drag it to the ground;   20
And all have joined in one endeavour
To bury this poor Thorn for ever.

III

" High on a mountain's highest ridge,
Where oft the stormy winter gale
Cuts like a scythe, while through the clouds
It sweeps from vale to vale;
Not five yards from the mountain path,
This Thorn you on your left espy;
And to the left, three yards beyond,
You see a little muddy pond   30
Of water — never dry
Though but of compass small, and bare
To thirsty suns and parching air.

IV

" And, close beside this aged Thorn,
There is a fresh and lovely sight,
A beauteous heap, a hill of moss,
Just half a foot in height.
All lovely colours there you see,
All colours that were ever seen;
And mossy network too is there,   40
As if by hand of lady fair
The work had woven been;
And cups, the darlings of the eye,
So deep is their vermilion dye.

V

" Ah me ! what lovely tints are there
Of olive green and scarlet bright,
In spikes, in branches, and in stars,
Green, red, and pearly white !
This heap of earth o'ergrown with moss,
Which close beside the Thorn you see,   50
So fresh in all its beauteous dyes,
Is like an infant's grave in size,
As like as like can be:
But never, never any where,
An infant's grave was half so fair.

VI

" Now would you see this aged Thorn,
This pond, and beauteous hill of moss,
You must take care and choose your time
The mountain when to cross.
For oft there sits between the heap   60
So like an infant's grave in size,
And that same pond of which I spoke,
A Woman in a scarlet cloak,
And to herself she cries,
' Oh misery ! oh misery !
Oh woe is me ! oh misery !'

VII

" At all times of the day and night
This wretched Woman thither goes;
And she is known to every star,
And every wind that blows;   70
And there, beside the Thorn, she sits
When the blue daylight 's in the skies
And when the whirlwind 's on the hill,
Or frosty air is keen and still,
And to herself she cries,
' Oh misery ! oh misery !
Oh woe is me ! oh misery !'"

VIII

" Now wherefore, thus, by day and night,
In rain, in tempest, and in snow,

Thus to the dreary mountain-top   80
Does this poor Woman go ?
And why sits she beside the Thorn
When the blue daylight 's in the sky,
Or when the whirlwind 's on the hill,
Or frosty air is keen and still,
And wherefore does she cry ? —
O wherefore ? wherefore ? tell me why
Does she repeat that doleful cry ? "

IX

" I cannot tell; I wish I could;
For the true reason no one knows: 90
But would you gladly view the spot,
The spot to which she goes;
The hillock like an infant's grave,
The pond — and Thorn, so old and grey;
Pass by her door — 't is seldom shut —
And, if you see her in her hut —
Then to the spot away !
I never heard of such as dare
Approach the spot when she is there."

X

" " But wherefore to the mountain-top   100
Can this unhappy Woman go,
Whatever star is in the skies,
Whatever wind may blow ? "
" Full twenty years are past and gone
Since she (her name is Martha Ray)
Gave with a maiden's true good-will
Her company to Stephen Hill;
And she was blithe and gay,
While friends and kindred all approved
Of him whom tenderly she loved.   110

XI

" And they had fixed the wedding day,
The morning that must wed them both;
But Stephen to another Maid
Had sworn another oath;
And, with this other Maid, to church
Unthinking Stephen went —
Poor Martha ! on that woeful day
A pang of pitiless dismay
Into her soul was sent;
A fire was kindled in her breast,   120
Which might not burn itself to rest.

XII

" They say, full six months after this,
While yet the summer leaves were green,
She to the mountain-top would go,
And there was often seen.
What could she seek ? — or wish to hide ?

Her state to any eye was plain ;
She was with child, and she was mad ;
Yet often was she sober sad
From her exceeding pain.   130
O guilty Father — would that death
Had saved him from that breach of faith !

XIII

" Sad case for such a brain to hold
Communion with a stirring child !
Sad case, as you may think, for one
Who had a brain so wild !
Last Christmas-eve we talked of this,
And grey-haired Wilfred of the glen
Held that the unborn infant wrought
About its mother's heart, and brought   140
Her senses back again:
And, when at last her time drew near,
Her looks were calm, her senses clear.

XIV

" More know I not, I wish I did,
And it should all be told to you;
For what became of this poor child
No mortal ever knew;
Nay — if a child to her was born
No earthly tongue could ever tell;
And if 't was born alive or dead,   150
Far less could this with proof be said;
But some remember well,
That Martha Ray about this time
Would up the mountain often climb.

XV

" And all that winter, when at night
The wind blew from the mountain-peak,
'T was worth your while, though in the dark,
The churchyard path to seek!
For many a time and oft were heard
Cries coming from the mountain head: 16(
Some plainly living voices were;
And others, I 've heard many swear,
Were voices of the dead:
I cannot think, whate'er they say,
They had to do with Martha Ray.

XVI

" But that she goes to this old Thorn,
The Thorn which I described to you,
And there sits in a scarlet cloak
I will be sworn is true.
For one day with my telescope,   170
To view the ocean wide and bright,
When to this country first I came,
Ere I had heard of Martha's name,

I climbed the mountain's height: —
A storm came on, and I could see
No object higher than my knee.

XVII

" 'T was mist and rain, and storm and
    rain:
No screen, no fence could I discover;
And then the wind! in sooth, it was
A wind full ten times over.   180
I looked around, I thought I saw
A jutting crag, — and off I ran,
Head-foremost, through the driving rain,
The shelter of the crag to gain;
And, as I am a man,
Instead of jutting crag, I found
A Woman seated on the ground.

XVIII

" I did not speak — I saw her face;
Her face! — it was enough for me;
I turned about and heard her cry,   190
' Oh misery! oh misery!'
And there she sits, until the moon
Through half the clear blue sky will go;
And, when the little breezes make
The waters of the pond to shake,
As all the country know,
She shudders, and you hear her cry,
' Oh misery! oh misery!' "

XIX

" But what's the Thorn? and what the
    pond?
And what the hill of moss to her?   200
And what the creeping breeze that comes
The little pond to stir?"
" I cannot tell; but some will say
She hanged her baby on the tree;
Some say she drowned it in the pond,
Which is a little step beyond:
But all and each agree,
The little Babe was buried there,
Beneath that hill of moss so fair.

XX

" I 've heard, the moss is spotted red   210
With drops of that poor infant's blood;
But kill a new-born infant thus,
I do not think she could!
Some say, if to the pond you go,
And fix on it a steady view,
The shadow of a babe you trace,
A baby and a baby's face,
And that it looks at you;

Whene'er you look on it, 't is plain
The baby looks at you again.   220

XXI

" And some had sworn an oath that she
Should be to public justice brought;
And for the little infant's bones
With spades they would have sought.
But instantly the hill of moss
Before their eyes began to stir!
And, for full fifty yards around,
The grass — it shook upon the ground!
Yet all do still aver
The little Babe lies buried there,   230
Beneath that hill of moss so fair.

XXII

" I cannot tell how this may be,
But plain it is the Thorn is bound
With heavy tufts of moss that strive
To drag it to the ground;
And this I know, full many a time,
When she was on the mountain high,
By day, and in the silent night,
When all the stars shone clear and bright,
That I have heard her cry,   240
' Oh misery! oh misery!
Oh woe is me! oh misery!' "

GOODY BLAKE AND HARRY GILL

A TRUE STORY

1798. 1798

Written at Alfoxden. The incident from
Dr. Darwin's Zoönomia.

Oh! what's the matter? what 's the matter?
What is 't that ails young Harry Gill?
That evermore his teeth they chatter,
Chatter, chatter, chatter still!
Of waistcoats Harry has no lack,
Good duffle grey, and flannel fine;
He has a blanket on his back,
And coats enough to smother nine.

In March, December, and in July,
'T is all the same with Harry Gill;   10
The neighbours tell, and tell you truly,
His teeth they chatter, chatter still.
At night, at morning, and at noon,
'T is all the same with Harry Gill;
Beneath the sun, beneath the moon,
His teeth they chatter, chatter still!

Young Harry was a lusty drover,
And who so stout of limb as he?
His cheeks were red as ruddy clover;
His voice was like the voice of three.　20
Old Goody Blake was old and poor;
Ill fed she was, and thinly clad;
And any man who passed her door
Might see how poor a hut she had.

All day she spun in her poor dwelling:
And then her three hours' work at night,
Alas! 't was hardly worth the telling,
It would not pay for candle-light.
Remote from sheltered village-green,
On a hill's northern side she dwelt,　30
Where from sea-blasts the hawthorns
　　lean,
And hoary dews are slow to melt.

By the same fire to boil their pottage,
Two poor old Dames, as I have known,
Will often live in one small cottage;
But she, poor Woman! housed alone.
'T was well enough when summer came,
The long, warm, lightsome summer-day,
Then at her door the *canty* Dame
Would sit, as any linnet, gay.　40

But when the ice our streams did fet-
　　ter,
Oh then how her old bones would shake!
You would have said, if you had met her,
'T was a hard time for Goody Blake.
Her evenings then were dull and dead:
Sad case it was, as you may think,
For very cold to go to bed,
And then for cold not sleep a wink.

O joy for her! whene'er in winter
The winds at night had made a rout;　50
And scattered many a lusty splinter
And many a rotten bough about.
Yet never had she, well or sick,
As every man who knew her says,
A pile beforehand, turf or stick,
Enough to warm her for three days.

Now, when the frost was past enduring,
And made her poor old bones to ache,
Could any thing be more alluring
Than an old hedge to Goody Blake?　60
And, now and then, it must be said,
When her old bones were cold and chill,
She left her fire, or left her bed,
To seek the hedge of Harry Gill.

Now Harry he had long suspected
This trespass of old Goody Blake;
And vowed that she should be detected —
That he on her would vengeance take.
And oft from his warm fire he'd go,
And to the fields his road would take;　70
And there, at night, in frost and snow,
He watched to seize old Goody Blake.

And once, behind a rick of barley,
Thus looking out did Harry stand:
The moon was full and shining clearly,
And crisp with frost the stubble land.
— He hears a noise — he's all awake —
Again? — on tip-toe down the hill
He softly creeps — 't is Goody Blake;
She's at the hedge of Harry Gill!　80

Right glad was he when he beheld her:
Stick after stick did Goody pull:
He stood behind a bush of elder,
Till she had filled her apron full.
When with her load she turned about,
The by-way back again to take;
He started forward, with a shout,
And sprang upon poor Goody Blake.

And fiercely by the arm he took her,
And by the arm he held her fast,　90
And fiercely by the arm he shook her,
And cried, "I've caught you then at
　　last!" —
Then Goody, who had nothing said,
Her bundle from her lap let fall;
And, kneeling on the sticks, she prayed
To God that is the judge of all.

She prayed, her withered hand uprearing,
While Harry held her by the arm —
"God! who art never out of hearing,
O may he never more be warm!"　100
The cold, cold moon above her head,
Thus on her knees did Goody pray;
Young Harry heard what she had said:
And icy cold he turned away.

He went complaining all the morrow
That he was cold and very chill:
His face was gloom, his heart was sor-
　　row,
Alas! that day for Harry Gill!
That day he wore a riding-coat,
But not a whit the warmer he:　110
Another was on Thursday brought,
And ere the Sabbath he had three.

'T was all in vain, a useless matter,
And blankets were about him pinned;
Yet still his jaws and teeth they clatter;
Like a loose casement in the wind.
And Harry's flesh it fell away;
And all who see him say, 't is plain,
That, live as long as live he may,
He never will be warm again.   120

No word to any man he utters,
A-bed or up, to young or old;
But ever to himself he mutters,
" Poor Harry Gill is very cold."
A-bed or up, by night or day;
His teeth they chatter, chatter still.
Now think, ye farmers all, I pray,
Of Goody Blake and Harry Gill !

HER EYES ARE WILD

1798. 1798

Written at Alfoxden. The subject was re-
ported to me by a lady of Bristol, who had
seen the poor creature.

I

HER eyes are wild, her head is bare,
The sun has burnt her coal-black hair;
Her eyebrows have a rusty stain,
And she came far from over the main.
She has a baby on her arm,
Or else she were alone:
And underneath the hay-stack warm,
And on the greenwood stone,
She talked and sung the woods among,
And it was in the English tongue.   10

II

" Sweet babe ! they say that I am mad,
But nay, my heart is far too glad;
And I am happy when I sing
Full many a sad and doleful thing:
Then, lovely baby, do not fear !
I pray thee have no fear of me;
But safe as in a cradle, here,
My lovely baby ! thou shalt be:
To thee I know too much I owe;
I cannot work thee any woe.   20

III

" A fire was once within my brain;
And in my head a dull, dull pain;
And fiendish faces, one, two, three,
Hung at my breast, and pulled at me;

But then there came a sight of joy;
It came at once to do me good;
I waked, and saw my little boy,
My little boy of flesh and blood;
Oh joy for me that sight to see !
For he was here, and only he.   30

IV

" Suck, little babe, oh suck again !
It cools my blood; it cools my brain;
Thy lips I feel them, baby ! they
Draw from my heart the pain away.
Oh ! press me with thy little hand;
It loosens something at my chest;
About that tight and deadly band
I feel thy little fingers prest.
The breeze I see is in the tree:
It comes to cool my babe and me.   40

V

" Oh ! love me, love me, little boy !
Thou art thy mother's only joy;
And do not dread the waves below,
When o'er the sea-rock's edge we go;
The high crag cannot work me harm,
Nor leaping torrents when they howl;
The babe I carry on my arm,
He saves for me my precious soul;
Then happy lie; for blest am I;
Without me my sweet babe would die.   50

VI

" Then do not fear, my boy ! for thee
Bold as a lion will I be;
And I will always be thy guide,
Through hollow snows and rivers wide.
I 'll build an Indian bower; I know
The leaves that make the softest bed:
And, if from me thou wilt not go,
But still be true till I am dead,
My pretty thing ! then thou shalt sing
As merry as the birds in spring.   60

VII

" Thy father cares not for my breast,
'T is thine, sweet baby, there to rest;
'T is all thine own ! — and, if its hue
Be changed, that was so fair to view,
'T is fair enough for thee, my dove !
My beauty, little child, is flown,
But thou wilt live with me in love,
And what if my poor cheek be brown ?
'T is well for me, thou canst not see
How pale and wan it else would be.   70

VIII

"Dread not their taunts, my little Life;
I am thy father's wedded wife;
And underneath the spreading tree
We two will live in honesty.
If his sweet boy he could forsake,
With me he never would have stayed:
From him no harm my babe can take;
But he, poor man! is wretched made;
And every day we two will pray
For him that's gone and far away.   80

IX

"I'll teach my boy the sweetest things:
I'll teach him how the owlet sings.
My little babe! thy lips are still,
And thou hast almost sucked thy fill.
—Where art thou gone, my own dear
     child?
What wicked looks are those I see?
Alas! alas! that look so wild,
It never, never came from me:
If thou art mad, my pretty lad,
Then I must be for ever sad.   90

X

"Oh! smile on me, my little lamb!
For I thy own dear mother am:
My love for thee has well been tried:
I've sought thy father far and wide.
I know the poisons of the shade;
I know the earth-nuts fit for food:
Then, pretty dear, be not afraid:
We'll find thy father in the wood.
Now laugh and be gay, to the woods away!
And there, my babe, we'll live for aye."   100

SIMON LEE

THE OLD HUNTSMAN;
WITH AN INCIDENT IN WHICH HE WAS CONCERNED

1798. 1798

This old man had been huntsman to the squires of Alfoxden, which, at the time we occupied it, belonged to a minor. The old man's cottage stood upon the common, a little way from the entrance to Alfoxden Park. But it had disappeared. Many other changes had taken place in the adjoining village, which I could not but notice with a regret more natural than well-considered. Improvements but rarely appear such to those who, after long intervals of time, revisit places they have had much pleasure in. It is unnecessary to add, the fact was as mentioned in the poem; and I have, after an interval of forty-five years, the image of the old man as fresh before my eyes as if I had seen him yesterday. The expression when the hounds were out, "I dearly love their voices," was word for word from his own lips.

In the sweet shire of Cardigan,
Not far from pleasant Ivor-hall,
An old Man dwells, a little man, —
'T is said he once was tall.
Full five-and-thirty years he lived
A running huntsman merry;
And still the centre of his cheek
Is red as a ripe cherry.

No man like him the horn could sound,
And hill and valley rang with glee   10
When Echo bandied, round and round,
The halloo of Simon Lee.
In those proud days, he little cared
For husbandry or tillage;
To blither tasks did Simon rouse
The sleepers of the village.

He all the country could outrun,
Could leave both man and horse behind;
And often, ere the chase was done,
He reeled, and was stone-blind.   20
And still there's something in the world
At which his heart rejoices;
For when the chiming hounds are out,
He dearly loves their voices!

But, oh the heavy change! — bereft
Of health, strength, friends, and kindred,
     see!
Old Simon to the world is left
In liveried poverty.
His Master's dead, — and no one now
Dwells in the Hall of Ivor;   30
Men, dogs, and horses, all are dead;
He is the sole survivor.

And he is lean and he is sick;
His body, dwindled and awry,
Rests upon ankles swoln and thick;
His legs are thin and dry.
One prop he has, and only one,
His wife, an aged woman,
Lives with him, near the waterfall,
Upon the village Common.   40

Beside their moss-grown hut of clay,
Not twenty paces from the door,

A scrap of land they have, but they
Are poorest of the poor.
This scrap of land he from the heath
Enclosed when he was stronger;
But what to them avails the land
Which he can till no longer ?

Oft, working by her Husband's side,
Ruth does what Simon cannot do;   50
For she, with scanty cause for pride,
Is stouter of the two.
And, though you with your utmost skill
From labour could not wean them,
'T is little, very little — all
That they can do between them.

Few months of life has he in store
As he to you will tell,
For still, the more he works, the more
Do his weak ankles swell.   60
My gentle Reader, I perceive
How patiently you 've waited,
And now I fear that you expect
Some tale will be related.

O Reader ! had you in your mind
Such stores as silent thought can bring,
O gentle Reader ! you would find
A tale in every thing.
What more I have to say is short,
And you must kindly take it: 70
It is no tale; but, should you think,
Perhaps a tale you 'll make it.

One summer-day I chanced to see
This old Man doing all he could
To unearth the root of an old tree,
A stump of rotten wood.
The mattock tottered in his hand;
So vain was his endeavour,
That at the root of the old tree
He might have worked for ever.   80

" You 're overtasked, good Simon Lee,
Give me your tool," to him I said;
And at the word right gladly he
Received my proffered aid.
I struck, and with a single blow
The tangled root I severed,
At which the poor old Man so long
And vainly had endeavoured.

The tears into his eyes were brought,
And thanks and praises seemed to run   90

So fast out of his heart, I thought
They never would have done.
— I 've heard of hearts unkind, kind deeds
With coldness still returning;
Alas ! the gratitude of men
Hath oftener left me mourning.

LINES WRITTEN IN EARLY SPRING

1798. 1798

Actually composed while I was sitting by the
side of the brook that runs down from the
Comb, in which stands the village of Alford,
through the grounds of Alfoxden. It was a
chosen resort of mine. The brook fell down a
sloping rock so as to make a waterfall consid-
erable for that country, and across the pool be-
low had fallen a tree, an ash if I rightly remem-
ber, from which rose perpendicularly, boughs in
search of the light intercepted by the deep
shade above. The boughs bore leaves of green
that for want of sunshine had faded into almost
lily-white; and from the underside of this
natural sylvan bridge depended long and beau-
tiful tresses of ivy which waved gently in the
breeze that might poetically speaking be called
the breath of the waterfall. This motion varied
of course in proportion to the power of water in
the brook. When, with dear friends, I revisited
this spot, after an interval of more than forty
years, this interesting feature of the scene was
gone. To the owner of the place I could not
but regret that the beauty of this retired part
of the grounds had not tempted him to make it
more accessible by a path, not broad or obtru-
sive, but sufficient for persons who love such
scenes to creep along without difficulty.

I HEARD a thousand blended notes,
While in a grove I sate reclined,
In that sweet mood when pleasant thoughts
Bring sad thoughts to the mind.

To her fair works did Nature link
The human soul that through me ran;
And much it grieved my heart to think
What man has made of man.

Through primrose tufts, in that green
    bower,
The periwinkle trailed its wreaths;
And 't is my faith that every flower
Enjoys the air it breathes.

The birds around me hopped and played,
Their thoughts I cannot measure: —

But the least motion which they made
It seemed a thrill of pleasure.

The budding twigs spread out their fan,
To catch the breezy air;
And I must think, do all I can,
That there was pleasure there.

If this belief from heaven be sent,
If such be Nature's holy plan,
Have I not reason to lament
What man has made of man?

TO MY SISTER

1798. 1798

Composed in front of Alfoxden House. My little boy-messenger on this occasion was the son of Basil Montagu. The larch mentioned in the first stanza was standing when I revisited the place in May, 1841, more than forty years after. I was disappointed that it had not improved in appearance as to size, nor had it acquired anything of the majesty of age, which, even though less perhaps than any other tree, the larch sometimes does. A few score yards from this tree, grew, when we inhabited Alfoxden, one of the most remarkable beech-trees ever seen. The ground sloped both towards and from it. It was of immense size, and threw out arms that struck into the soil, like those of the banyan-tree, and rose again from it. Two of the branches thus inserted themselves twice, which gave to each the appearance of a serpent moving along by gathering itself up in folds. One of the large boughs of this tree had been torn off by the wind before we left Alfoxden, but five remained. In 1841 we could barely find the spot where the tree had stood. So remarkable a production of nature could not have been wilfully destroyed.

IT is the first mild day of March:
Each minute sweeter than before
The redbreast sings from the tall larch
That stands beside our door.

There is a blessing in the air,
Which seems a sense of joy to yield
To the bare trees, and mountains bare,
And grass in the green field.

My sister! ('t is a wish of mine)
Now that our morning meal is done,   10
Make haste, your morning task resign;
Come forth and feel the sun.

Edward will come with you; — and, pray,
Put on with speed your woodland dress:
And bring no book: for this one day
We 'll give to idleness.

No joyless forms shall regulate
Our living calendar:
We from to-day, my Friend, will date
The opening of the year.   20

Love, now a universal birth,
From heart to heart is stealing,
From earth to man, from man to earth:
— It is the hour of feeling.

One moment now may give us more
Than years of toiling reason:
Our minds shall drink at every pore
The spirit of the season.

Some silent laws our hearts will make,
Which they shall long obey: 30
We for the year to come may take
Our temper from to-day.

And from the blessed power that rolls
About, below, above,
We 'll frame the measure of our souls:
They shall be tuned to love.

Then come, my Sister! come, I pray,
With speed put on your woodland dress;
And bring no book: for this one day
We 'll give to idleness.   40

"A WHIRL-BLAST FROM BE-HIND THE HILL"

1798. 1800

Observed in the holly-grove at Alfoxden, where these verses were written in the spring of 1799. I had the pleasure of again seeing, with dear friends, this grove in unimpaired beauty forty-one years after.

A WHIRL-BLAST from behind the hill
Rushed o'er the wood with startling sound;
Then — all at once the air was still,
And showers of hailstones pattered round.
Where leafless oaks towered high above,
I sat within an undergrove
Of tallest hollies, tall and green;
A fairer bower was never seen.
From year to year the spacious floor
With withered leaves is covered o'er,

And all the year the bower is green.
But see ! where'er the hailstones drop
The withered leaves all skip and hop;
There's not a breeze — no breath of air —
Yet here, and there, and everywhere
Along the floor, beneath the shade
By those embowering hollies made,
The leaves in myriads jump and spring,
As if with pipes and music rare
Some Robin Good-fellow were there,
And all those leaves, in festive glee,
Were dancing to the minstrelsy.

EXPOSTULATION AND REPLY

1798. 1798

This poem is a favourite among the Quakers,
as I have learnt on many occasions. It was
composed in front of the house at Alfoxden, in
the spring of 1798.

" WHY, William, on that old grey stone,
Thus for the length of half a day,
Why, William, sit you thus alone,
And dream your time away ?

" Where are your books ? — that light be-
          queathed
To Beings else forlorn and blind !
Up ! up ! and drink the spirit•breathed
From dead men to their kind.

" You look round on your Mother Earth,
As if she for no purpose bore you;   10
As if you were her first-born birth,
And none had lived before you ! "

One morning thus, by Esthwaite lake,
When life was sweet, I knew not why,
To me my good friend Matthew spake,
And thus I made reply:

" The eye — it cannot choose but see;
We cannot bid the ear be still;
Our bodies feel, where'er they be,
Against or with our will.   20

" Nor less I deem that there are Powers
Which of themselves our minds impress;
That we can feed this mind of ours
In a wise passiveness.

" Think you, 'mid all this mighty sum
Of things for ever speaking,

That nothing of itself will come,
But we must still be seeking ?

" — Then ask not wherefore, here, alone,
Conversing as I may,   30
I sit upon this old grey stone,
And dream my time away."

THE TABLES TURNED

AN EVENING SCENE ON THE SAME SUBJECT

1798. 1798

UP ! up ! my Friend, and quit your books;
Or surely you 'll grow double:
Up ! up ! my Friend, and clear your looks;
Why all this toil and trouble ?

The sun, above the mountain's head,
A freshening lustre mellow
Through all the long green fields has
          spread,
His first sweet evening yellow.

Books ! 't is a dull and endless strife:
Come, hear the woodland linnet,   10
How sweet his music ! on my life,
There's more of wisdom in it.

And hark ! how blithe the throstle sings !
He, too, is no mean preacher:
Come forth into the light of things,
Let Nature be your teacher.

She has a world of ready wealth,
Our minds and hearts to bless —
Spontaneous wisdom breathed by health,
Truth breathed by cheerfulness.   20

One impulse from a vernal wood
May teach you more of man,
Of moral evil and of good,
Than all the sages can.

Sweet is the lore which Nature brings;
Our meddling intellect
Mis-shapes the beauteous forms of things: —
We murder to dissect.

Enough of Science and of Art;
Close up those barren leaves;   30
Come forth, and bring with you a heart
That watches and receives.

THE COMPLAINT

OF A FORSAKEN INDIAN WOMAN

1798. 1798

Written at Alfoxden, where I read Hearne's Journey with deep interest. It was composed for the volume of Lyrical Ballads.

When a Northern Indian, from sickness, is unable to continue his journey with his companions, he is left behind, covered over with deer-skins, and is supplied with water, food, and fuel, if the situation of the place will afford it. He is informed of the track which his companions intend to pursue, and if he be unable to follow, or overtake them, he perishes alone in the desert; unless he should have the good fortune to fall in with some other tribes of Indians. The females are equally, or still more, exposed to the same fate. See that very interesting work HEARNE's *Journey from Hudson's Bay to the Northern Ocean.* In the high northern latitudes, as the same writer informs us, when the northern lights vary their position in the air, they make a rustling and a crackling noise, as alluded to in the following poem.

I

BEFORE I see another day,
Oh let my body die away!
In sleep I heard the northern gleams;
The stars, they were among my dreams;
In rustling conflict through the skies,
I heard, I saw the flashes drive,
And yet they are upon my eyes,
And yet I am alive;
Before I see another day,
Oh let my body die away!   10

II

My fire is dead: it knew no pain;
Yet is it dead, and I remain:
All stiff with ice the ashes lie;
And they are dead, and I will die.
When I was well, I wished to live,
For clothes, for warmth, for food, and fire;
But they to me no joy can give,
No pleasure now, and no desire.
Then here contented will I lie!
Alone, I cannot fear to die.   20

III

Alas! ye might have dragged me on
Another day, a single one!
Too soon I yielded to despair;
Why did ye listen to my prayer?

When ye were gone my limbs were stronger;
And oh, how grievously I rue,
That, afterwards, a little longer,
My friends, I did not follow you!
For strong and without pain I lay,
Dear friends, when ye were gone away.   30

IV

My Child! they gave thee to another,
A woman who was not thy mother.
When from my arms my Babe they took,
On me how strangely did he look!
Through his whole body something ran,
A most strange working did I see;
— As if he strove to be a man,
That he might pull the sledge for me:
And then he stretched his arms, how wild!
Oh mercy! like a helpless child.   40

V

My little joy! my little pride!
In two days more I must have died.
Then do not weep and grieve for me;
I feel I must have died with thee.
O wind, that o'er my head art flying
The way my friends their course did bend,
I should not feel the pain of dying,
Could I with thee a message send;
Too soon, my friends, ye went away;
For I had many things to say.   50

VI

I'll follow you across the snow;
Ye travel heavily and slow;
In spite of all my weary pain
I'll look upon your tents again.
— My fire is dead, and snowy white
The water which beside it stood:
The wolf has come to me to-night,
And he has stolen away my food.
For ever left alone am I;
Then wherefore should I fear to die?   60

VII

Young as I am, my course is run,
I shall not see another sun;
I cannot lift my limbs to know
If they have any life or no.
My poor forsaken Child, if I
For once could have thee close to me,
With happy heart I then would die,
And my last thought would happy be;
But thou, dear Babe, art far away,
Nor shall I see another day.   70

THE LAST OF THE FLOCK

1798. 1798

Produced at the same time and for the same purpose. The incident occurred in the village of Holford, close by Alfoxden.

I

In distant countries have I been,
And yet I have not often seen
A healthy man, a man full grown,
Weep in the public roads, alone.
But such a one, on English ground,
And in the broad highway, I met;
Along the broad highway he came,
His cheeks with tears were wet:
Sturdy he seemed, though he was sad;
And in his arms a Lamb he had.   10

II

He saw me, and he turned aside,
As if he wished himself to hide:
And with his coat did then essay
To wipe those briny tears away.
I followed him, and said, " My friend,
What ails you ? wherefore weep you so ? "
— " Shame on me, Sir ! this lusty Lamb,
He makes my tears to flow.
To-day I fetched him from the rock;
He is the last of all my flock.   20

III

" When I was young, a single man,
And after youthful follies ran,
Though little given to care and thought,
Yet, so it was, an ewe I bought;
And other sheep from her I raised,
As healthy sheep as you might see;
And then I married, and was rich
As I could wish to be;
Of sheep I numbered a full score,
And every year increased my store.   30

IV

" Year after year my stock it grew;
And from this one, this single ewe,
Full fifty comely sheep I raised,
As fine a flock as ever grazed !
Upon the Quantock hills they fed;
They throve, and we at home did thrive:
— This lusty Lamb of all my store
Is all that is alive;
And now I care not if we die,
And perish all of poverty.   40

V

" Six Children, Sir ! had I to feed;
Hard labour in a time of need !
My pride was tamed, and in our grief
I of the Parish asked relief.
They said, I was a wealthy man;
My sheep upon the uplands fed,
And it was fit that thence I took
Whereof to buy us bread.
' Do this: how can we give to you,'
They cried, ' what to the poor is due ? '   50

VI

" I sold a sheep, as they had said,
And bought my little children bread,
And they were healthy with their food,
For me — it never did me good.
A woeful time it was for me,
To see the end of all my gains,
The pretty flock which I had reared
With all my care and pains,
To see it melt like snow away —
For me it was a woeful day.   60

VII

" Another still ! and still another !
A little lamb, and then its mother !
It was a vein that never stopped —
Like blood - drops from my heart they
    dropped.
Till thirty were not left alive
They dwindled, dwindled, one by one,
And I may say, that many a time
I wished they all were gone —
Reckless of what might come at last
Were but the bitter struggle past.   70

VIII

" To wicked deeds I was inclined,
And wicked fancies crossed my mind;
And every man I chanced to see,
I thought he knew some ill of me:
No peace, no comfort could I find,
No ease, within doors or without;
And, crazily and wearily
I went my work about;
And oft was moved to flee from home,   75
And hide my head where wild beasts roam.

IX

" Sir ! 't was a precious flock to me
As dear as my own children be;
For daily with my growing store
I loved my children more and more.
Alas ! it was an evil time;

God cursed me in my sore distress;
I prayed, yet every day I thought
I loved my children less;
And every week, and every day,
My flock it seemed to melt away. 90

X

"They dwindled, Sir, sad sight to see !
From ten to five, from five to three,
A lamb, a wether, and a ewe; —
And then at last from three to two;
And, of my fifty, yesterday
I had but only one:
And here it lies upon my arm,
Alas ! and I have none; —
To-day I fetched it from the rock;
It is the last of all my flock." 100

THE IDIOT BOY

1798. 1798

The last stanza — " The Cocks did crow to-whoo, to-whoo, And the sun did shine so cold " — was the foundation of the whole. The words were reported to me by my dear friend, Thomas Poole; but I have since heard the same repeated of other Idiots. Let me add that this long poem was composed in the groves of Alfoxden, almost extempore; not a word, I believe, being corrected, though one stanza was omitted. I mention this in gratitude to those happy moments, for, in truth, I never wrote anything with so much glee.

'T is eight o'clock, — a clear March night,
The moon is up, — the sky is blue,
The owlet, in the moonlight air,
Shouts from nobody knows where;
He lengthens out his lonely shout,
Halloo ! halloo ! a long halloo !

— Why bustle thus about your door,
What means this bustle, Betty Foy ?
Why are you in this mighty fret ?
And why on horseback have you set 10
Him whom you love, your Idiot Boy ?

Scarcely a soul is out of bed;
Good Betty, put him down again;
His lips with joy they burr at you;
But, Betty ! what has he to do
With stirrup, saddle, or with rein ?

But Betty 's bent on her intent;
For her good neighbour, Susan Gale,

Old Susan, she who dwells alone,
Is sick, and makes a piteous moan 20
As if her very life would fail.

There 's not a house within a mile,
No hand to help them in distress;
Old Susan lies a-bed in pain,
And sorely puzzled are the twain,
For what she ails they cannot guess.

And Betty's husband 's at the wood,
Where by the week he doth abide,
A woodman in the distant vale;
There 's none to help poor Susan Gale; 30
What must be done ? what will betide ?

And Betty from the lane has fetched
Her Pony, that is mild and good;
Whether he be in joy or pain,
Feeding at will along the lane,
Or bringing faggots from the wood.

And he is all in travelling trim, —
And, by the moonlight, Betty Foy
Has on the well-girt saddle set
(The like was never heard of yet) 40
Him whom she loves, her Idiot Boy.

And he must post without delay
Across the bridge and through the dale,
And by the church, and o'er the down,
To bring a Doctor from the town,
Or she will die, old Susan Gale.

There is no need of boot or spur,
There is no need of whip or wand;
For Johnny has his holly-bough,
And with a *hurly-burly* now 50
He shakes the green bough in his hand.

And Betty o'er and o'er has told
The Boy, who is her best delight,
Both what to follow, what to shun,
What do, and what to leave undone,
How turn to left, and how to right.

And Betty's most especial charge,
Was, " Johnny ! Johnny ! mind that you
Come home again, nor stop at all, —
Come home again, whate'er befall, 60
My Johnny, do, I pray you do."

To this did Johnny answer make,
Both with his head and with his hand,

And proudly shook the bridle too;
And then ! his words were not a few,
Which Betty well could understand.

And now that Johnny is just going,
Though Betty 's in a mighty flurry,
She gently pats the Pony's side,
On which her Idiot Boy must ride,   70
And seems no longer in a hurry.

But when the Pony moved his legs,
Oh ! then for the poor Idiot Boy !
For joy he cannot hold the bridle,
For joy his head and heels are idle,
He 's idle all for very joy.

And while the Pony moves his legs,
In Johnny's left hand you may see
The green bough motionless and dead:
The Moon that shines above his head   80
Is not more still and mute than he.

His heart it was so full of glee,
That till full fifty yards were gone,
He quite forgot his holly whip,
And all his skill in horsemanship:
Oh ! happy, happy, happy John.

And while the Mother, at the door,
Stands fixed, her face with joy o'erflows,
Proud of herself, and proud of him,
She sees him in his travelling trim,   90
How quietly her Johnny goes.

The silence of her Idiot Boy,
What hopes it sends to Betty's heart !
He 's at the guide-post — he turns right;
She watches till he 's out of sight,
And Betty will not then depart.

Burr, burr — now Johnny's lips they burr,
As loud as any mill, or near it;
Meek as a lamb the Pony moves,
And Johnny makes the noise he loves,   100
And Betty listens, glad to hear it.

Away she hies to Susan Gale:
Her Messenger 's in merry tune;
The owlets hoot, the owlets curr,
And Johnny's lips they burr, burr, burr,
As on he goes beneath the moon.

His steed and he right well agree;
For of this Pony there 's a rumour,

That, should he lose his eyes and ears,
And should he live a thousand years,   110
He never will be out of humour.

But then he is a horse that thinks !
And when he thinks, his pace is slack;
Now, though he knows poor Johnny well,
Yet, for his life, he cannot tell
What he has got upon his back.

So through the moonlight lanes they go,
And far into the moonlight dale,
And by the church, and o'er the down,
To bring a Doctor from the town,   120
To comfort poor old Susan Gale.

And Betty, now at Susan's side,
Is in the middle of her story,
What speedy help her Boy will bring,
With many a most diverting thing,
Of Johnny's wit, and Johnny's glory.

And Betty, still at Susan's side,
By this time is not quite so flurried:
Demure with porringer and plate
She sits, as if in Susan's fate   130
Her life and soul were buried.

But Betty, poor good woman ! she,
You plainly in her face may read it,
Could lend out of that moment's store
Five years of happiness or more
To any that might need it.

But yet I guess that now and then
With Betty all was not so well;
And to the road she turns her ears,
And thence full many a sound she hears,   140
Which she to Susan will not tell.

Poor Susan moans, poor Susan groans;
" As sure as there 's a moon in heaven,"
Cries Betty, " he 'll be back again;
They 'll both be here — 't is almost ten —
Both will be here before eleven."

Poor Susan moans, poor Susan groans;
The clock gives warning for eleven;
'T is on the stroke — " He must be near,"
Quoth Betty, " and will soon be here,   150
As sure as there 's a moon in heaven."

The clock is on the stroke of twelve,
And Johnny is not yet in sight:

—The Moon 's in heaven, as Betty sees,
But Betty is not quite at ease;
And Susan has a dreadful night.

And Betty, half an hour ago,
On Johnny vile reflections cast:
" A little idle sauntering Thing ! "
With other names, an endless string;   160
But now that time is gone and past.

And Betty 's drooping at the heart,
That happy time all past and gone,
" How can it be he is so late ?
The Doctor, he has made him wait;
Susan ! they 'll both be here anon."

And Susan 's growing worse and worse,
And Betty 's in a sad *quandary;*
And then there 's nobody to say
If she must go, or she must stay !   170
— She 's in a sad *quandary.*

The clock is on the stroke of one;
But neither Doctor nor his Guide
Appears along the moonlight road;
There 's neither horse nor man abroad,
And Betty 's still at Susan's side.

And Susan now begins to fear
Of sad mischances not a few:
That Johnny may perhaps be drowned,
Or lost, perhaps, and never found;   180
Which they must both for ever rue.

She prefaced half a hint of this
With, " God forbid it should be true ! "
At the first word that Susan said
Cried Betty, rising from the bed,
" Susan, I 'd gladly stay with you.

" I must be gone, I must away:
Consider, Johnny 's but half-wise;
Susan, we must take care of him,
If he is hurt in life or limb " —   190
" Oh God forbid ! " poor Susan cries.

" What can I do ? " says Betty, going,
" What can I do to ease your pain ?
Good Susan tell me, and I 'll stay;
I fear you 're in a dreadful way,
But I shall soon be back again."

" Nay, Betty, go ! good Betty, go !
There 's nothing that can ease my pain."

Then off she hies; but with a prayer
That God poor Susan's life would spare,   200
Till she comes back again.

So, through the moonlight lane she goes,
And far into the moonlight dale;
And how she ran, and how she walked,
And all that to herself she talked,
Would surely be a tedious tale.

In high and low, above, below,
In great and small, in round and square,
In tree and tower was Johnny seen,
In bush and brake, in black and green;   210
'T was Johnny, Johnny, every where.

And while she crossed the bridge, there came
A thought with which her heart is sore —
Johnny perhaps his horse forsook,
To hunt the moon within the brook,
And never will be heard of more.

Now is she high upon the down,
Alone amid a prospect wide;
There 's neither Johnny nor his Horse
Among the fern or in the gorse;   220
There 's neither Doctor nor his Guide.

" O saints ! what is become of him ?
Perhaps he 's climbed into an oak,
Where he will stay till he is dead;
Or, sadly he has been misled,
And joined the wandering gipsy-folk.

" Or him that wicked Pony 's carried
To the dark cave, the goblin's hall;
Or in the castle he 's pursuing
Among the ghosts his own undoing;   230
Or playing with the waterfall."

At poor old Susan then she railed,
While to the town she posts away;
" If Susan had not been so ill,
Alas ! I should have had him still,
My Johnny, till my dying day."

Poor Betty, in this sad distemper,
The Doctor's self could hardly spare:
Unworthy things she talked, and wild;
Even he, of cattle the most mild,   240
The Pony had his share.

But now she 's fairly in the town,
And to the Doctor's door she hies;

'T is silence all on every side;
The town so long, the town so wide,
Is silent as the skies.

And now she 's at the Doctor's door,
She lifts the knocker, rap, rap, rap;
The Doctor at the casement shows
His glimmering eyes that peep and doze !
And one hand rubs his old night-cap.   251

" O   Doctor !   Doctor !   where 's   my
        Johnny ? "
" I 'm here, what is 't you want with me ? "
" O Sir ! you know I 'm Betty Foy,
And I have lost my poor dear Boy,
You know him — him you often see;

" He 's not so wise as some folks be: "
" The devil take his wisdom ! " said
The Doctor, looking somewhat grim,
" What, Woman ! should I know of him ? "
And, grumbling, he went back to bed !   261

" O woe is me ! O woe is me !
Here will I die; here will I die;
I thought to find my lost one here,
But he is neither far nor near,
Oh ! what a wretched Mother I ! "

She stops, she stands, she looks about;
Which way to turn she cannot tell.
Poor Betty ! it would ease her pain
If she had heart to knock again;   270
— The clock strikes three — a dismal knell !

Then up along the town she hies,
No wonder if her senses fail;
This piteous news so much it shocked her,
She quite forgot to send the Doctor,
To comfort poor old Susan Gale.

And now she 's high upon the down,
And she can see a mile of road:
" O cruel ! I 'm almost threescore;
Such night as this was ne'er before,   280
There 's not a single soul abroad."

She listens, but she cannot hear
The foot of horse, the voice of man;
The streams with softest sound are flowing,
The grass you almost hear it growing,
You hear it now, if e'er you can.

The owlets through the long blue night
Are shouting to each other still:

Fond lovers ! yet not quite hob nob,
They lengthen out the tremulous sob,   290
That echoes far from hill to hill.

Poor Betty now has lost all hope,
Her thoughts are bent on deadly sin,
A green-grown pond she just has past,
And from the brink she hurries fast,
Lest she should drown herself therein.

And now she sits her down and weeps;
Such tears she never shed before;
" Oh dear, dear Pony ! my sweet joy !
Oh carry back my Idiot Boy !   300
And we will ne'er o'erload thee more."

A thought is come into her head:
The Pony he is mild and good,
And we have always used him well;
Perhaps he 's gone along the dell,
And carried Johnny to the wood.

Then up she springs as if on wings;
She thinks no more of deadly sin;
If Betty fifty ponds should see,
The last of all her thoughts would be   310
To drown herself therein.

O Reader ! now that I might tell
What Johnny and his Horse are doing,
What they 've been doing all this time,
Oh could I put it into rhyme,
A most delightful tale pursuing !

Perhaps, and no unlikely thought !
He with his Pony now doth roam
The cliffs and peaks so high that are,
To lay his hands upon a star,   320
And in his pocket bring it home.

Perhaps he 's turned himself about,
His face unto his horse's tail,
And, still and mute, in wonder lost,
All silent as a horseman-ghost,
He travels slowly down the vale.

And now, perhaps, is hunting sheep,
A fierce and dreadful hunter he;
Yon valley, now so trim and green,
In five months' time, should he be seen,   330
A desert wilderness will be !

Perhaps, with head and heels on fire,
And like the very soul of evil,

He's galloping away, away,
And so will gallop on for aye,
The bane of all that dread the devil !

I to the Muses have been bound
These fourteen years, by strong indentures.
O gentle Muses ! let me tell
But half of what to him befell;   340
He surely met with strange adventures.

O gentle Muses ! is this kind ?
Why will ye thus my suit repel ?
Why of your further aid bereave me ?
And can ye thus unfriended leave me,
Ye Muses ! whom I love so well ?

Who's yon, that, near the waterfall,
Which thunders down with headlong force,
Beneath the moon, yet shining fair,
As careless as if nothing were,   350
Sits upright on a feeding horse ?

Unto his horse — there feeding free,
He seems, I think, the rein to give;
Of moon or stars he takes no heed;
Of such we in romances read:
— 'T is Johnny ! Johnny ! as I live.

And that's the very Pony, too !
Where is she, where is Betty Foy ?
She hardly can sustain her fears;
The roaring waterfall she hears,   360
And cannot find her Idiot Boy.

Your Pony's worth his weight in gold:
Then calm your terrors, Betty Foy !
She's coming from among the trees,
And now all full in view she sees
Him whom she loves, her Idiot Boy.

And Betty sees the Pony too:
Why stand you thus, good Betty Foy ?
It is no goblin, 't is no ghost,
'T is he whom you so long have lost   370
He whom you love, your Idiot Boy.

She looks again — her arms are up —
She screams — she cannot move for joy;
She darts, as with a torrent's force,
She almost has o'erturned the Horse,
And fast she holds her Idiot Boy.

And Johnny burrs, and laughs aloud;
Whether in cunning or in joy

I cannot tell; but while he laughs,
Betty a drunken pleasure quaffs   380
To hear again her Idiot Boy.

And now she's at the Pony's tail,
And now is at the Pony's head, —
On that side now, and now on this;
And, almost stifled with her bliss,
A few sad tears does Betty shed.

She kisses o'er and o'er again
Him whom she loves, her Idiot Boy;
She's happy here, is happy there,
She is uneasy every where;   390
Her limbs are all alive with joy.

She pats the Pony, where or when
She knows not, happy Betty Foy !
The little Pony glad may be,
But he is milder far than she,
You hardly can perceive his joy.

"Oh ! Johnny, never mind the Doctor;
You've done your best, and that is all:"
She took the reins, when this was said,
And gently turned the Pony's head   400
From the loud waterfall.

By this the stars were almost gone,
The moon was setting on the hill,
So pale you scarcely looked at her:
The little birds began to stir,
Though yet their tongues were still.

The Pony, Betty, and her Boy,
Wind slowly through the woody dale;
And who is she, betimes abroad,
That hobbles up the steep rough road ? 410
Who is it, but old Susan Gale ?

Long time lay Susan lost in thought;
And many dreadful fears beset her,
Both for her Messenger and Nurse;
And, as her mind grew worse and worse,
Her body — it grew better.

She turned, she tossed herself in bed,
On all sides doubts and terrors met her;
Point after point did she discuss;
And, while her mind was fighting thus, 420
Her body still grew better.

"Alas ! what is become of them ?
These fears can never be endured;

I 'll to the wood." — The word scarce said,
Did Susan rise up from her bed,
As if by magic cured.

Away she goes up hill and down,
And to the wood at length is come;
She spies her Friends, she shouts a greet-
ing;
Oh me ! it is a merry meeting   430
As ever was in Christendom.

The owls have hardly sung their last,
While our four travellers homeward wend;
The owls have hooted all night long,
And with the owls began my song,
And with the owls must end.

For while they all were travelling home,
Cried Betty, " Tell us, Johnny, do,
Where all this long night you have been,
What you have heard, what you have
seen: 440
And, Johnny, mind you tell us true."

Now Johnny all night long had heard
The owls in tuneful concert strive;
No doubt too he the moon had seen;
For in the moonlight he had been
From eight o'clock till five.

And thus, to Betty's question, he
Made answer, like a traveller bold,
(His very words I give to you,)
" The cocks did crow to-whoo, to-whoo, 450
And the sun did shine so cold ! "
— Thus answered Johnny in his glory,
And that was all his travel's story.

LINES

COMPOSED A FEW MILES ABOVE TINTERN
ABBEY, ON REVISITING THE BANKS OF
THE WYE DURING A TOUR.   JULY 13,
1798

1798. 1798

No poem of mine was composed under cir-
cumstances more pleasant for me to remember
than this. I began it upon leaving Tintern,
after crossing the Wye, and concluded it just
as I was entering Bristol in the evening, after
a ramble of four or five days, with my Sister.
Not a line of it was altered, and not any part
of it written down till I reached Bristol. It
was published almost immediately after in the
little volume of which so much has been said
in these Notes. — (The Lyrical Ballads, as first
published at Bristol by Cottle.)

FIVE years have past; five summers, with
the length
Of five long winters ! and again I hear
These waters, rolling from their mountain-
springs
With a soft inland murmur. — Once again
Do I behold these steep and lofty cliffs,
That on a wild secluded scene impress
Thoughts of more deep seclusion; and con-
nect
The landscape with the quiet of the sky.
The day is come when I again repose
Here, under this dark sycamore, and view 10
These plots of cottage-ground, these
orchard-tufts,
Which at this season, with their unripe
fruits,
Are clad in one green hue, and lose them-
selves
'Mid groves and copses. Once again I see
These hedge-rows, hardly hedge-rows, little •
lines
Of sportive wood run wild: these pastoral
farms,
Green to the very door; and wreaths of
smoke
Sent up, in silence, from among the trees !
With some uncertain notice, as might seem
Of vagrant dwellers in the houseless
woods,   20
Or of some Hermit's cave, where by his fire
The Hermit sits alone.
                    These beauteous forms,
Through a long absence, have not been to
me
As is a landscape to a blind man's eye:
But oft, in lonely rooms, and 'mid the din
Of towns and cities, I have owed to them
In hours of weariness, sensations sweet,
Felt in the blood, and felt along the heart;
And passing even into my purer mind,
With tranquil restoration: — feelings too 30
Of unremembered pleasure: such, perhaps,
As have no slight or trivial influence
On that best portion of a good man's life,
His little, nameless, unremembered, acts
Of kindness and of love. Nor less, I trust,
To them I may have owed another gift,
Of aspect more sublime; that blessed
mood,
In which the burthen of the mystery,

In which the heavy and the weary weight
Of all this unintelligible world,   40
Is lightened: — that serene and blessed
      mood,
In which the affections gently lead us on, —
Until, the breath of this corporeal frame
And even the motion of our human blood
Almost suspended, we are laid asleep
In body, and become a living soul:
While with an eye made quiet by the power
Of harmony, and the deep power of joy,
We see into the life of things.
                              If this
Be but a vain belief, yet, oh ! how oft — 50
In darkness and amid the many shapes
Of joyless daylight; when the fretful stir
Unprofitable, and the fever of the world,
Have hung upon the beatings of my heart —
How oft, in spirit, have I turned to thee,
O sylvan Wye ! thou wanderer thro' the
      woods,
How often has my spirit turned to thee !
   And now, with gleams of half-extin-
      guished thought,
With many recognitions dim and faint,
And somewhat of a sad perplexity,   60
The picture of the mind revives again:
While here I stand, not only with the sense
Of present pleasure, but with pleasing
      thoughts
That in this moment there is life and food
For future years.   And so I dare to hope,
Though changed, no doubt, from what I
      was when first
I came among these hills; when like a roe
I bounded o'er the mountains, by the
      sides
Of the deep rivers, and the lonely streams,
Wherever nature led: more like a man   70
Flying from something that he dreads,
      than one
Who sought the thing he loved.   For na-
      ture then
(The coarser pleasures of my boyish days,
And their glad animal movements all gone
      by)
To me was all in all. — I cannot paint
What then I was.   The sounding cataract
Haunted me like a passion: the tall rock,
The mountain, and the deep and gloomy
      wood,
Their colours and their forms, were then
      to me
An appetite; a feeling and a love,   80
That had no need of a remoter charm,

By thought supplied, nor any interest
Unborrowed from the eye. — That time is
      past,
And all its aching joys are now no more,
And all its dizzy raptures.   Not for this
Faint I, nor mourn nor murmur; other
      gifts
Have followed; for such loss, I would be-
      lieve,
Abundant recompense.   For I have
      learned
To look on nature, not as in the hour
Of thoughtless youth; but hearing often-
      times   90
The still, sad music of humanity,
Nor harsh nor grating, though of ample
      power
To chasten and subdue.   And I have felt
A presence that disturbs me with the joy
Of elevated thoughts; a sense sublime
Of something far more deeply interfused,
Whose dwelling is the light of setting suns,
And the round ocean and the living air,
And the blue sky, and in the mind of man;
A motion and a spirit, that impels   100
All thinking things, all objects of all
      thought,
And rolls through all things.   Therefore
      am I still
A lover of the meadows and the woods,
And mountains; and of all that we behold
From this green earth; of all the mighty
      world
Of eye, and ear, — both what they half
      create,
And what perceive; well pleased to recog-
      nise
In nature and the language of the sense,
The anchor of my purest thoughts, the
      nurse,
The guide, the guardian of my heart, and
      soul   110
Of all my moral being.
                              Nor perchance,
If I were not thus taught, should I the
      more
Suffer my genial spirits to decay:
For thou art with me here upon the banks
Of this fair river; thou my dearest Friend,
My dear, dear Friend; and in thy voice I
      catch
The language of my former heart, and
      read
My former pleasures in the shooting lights
Of thy wild eyes.   Oh ! yet a little while

May I behold in thee what I was once, 120
My dear, dear Sister! and this prayer I
    make,
Knowing that Nature never did betray
The heart that loved her; 't is her privi-
    lege,
Through all the years of this our life, to
    lead
From joy to joy: for she can so inform
The mind that is within us, so impress
With quietness and beauty, and so feed
With lofty thoughts, that neither evil
    tongues,
Rash judgments, nor the sneers of selfish
    men,
Nor greetings where no kindness is, nor all
The dreary intercourse of daily life, 131
Shall e'er prevail against us, or disturb
Our cheerful faith, that all which we be-
    hold
Is full of blessings. Therefore let the moon
Shine on thee in thy solitary walk;
And let the misty mountain-winds be free
To blow against thee: and, in after years,
When these wild ecstasies shall be matured
Into a sober pleasure; when thy mind
Shall be a mansion for all lovely forms, 140
Thy memory be as a dwelling-place
For all sweet sounds and harmonies; oh!
    then,
If solitude, or fear, or pain, or grief,
Should be thy portion, with what healing
    thoughts
Of tender joy wilt thou remember me,
And these my exhortations! Nor, per-
    chance —
If I should be where I no more can hear
Thy voice, nor catch from thy wild eyes
    these gleams
Of past existence — wilt thou then forget
That on the banks of this delightful stream
We stood together; and that I, so long 151
A worshipper of Nature, hither came
Unwearied in that service: rather say
With warmer love — oh! with far deeper
    zeal
Of holier love. Nor wilt thou then for-
    get,
That after many wanderings, many years
Of absence, these steep woods and lofty
    cliffs,
And this green pastoral landscape, were to
    me
More dear, both for themselves and for thy
    sake!

THE OLD CUMBERLAND BEGGAR

1798. 1800

Observed, and with great benefit to my
own heart, when I was a child: written at
Racedown and Alfoxden in my twenty-eighth
year. The political economists were about that
time beginning their war upon mendicity in all
its forms, and by implication, if not directly,
on alms-giving also. This heartless process has
been carried as far as it can go by the AMENDED
poor-law bill, though the inhumanity that pre-
vails in this measure is somewhat disguised by
the profession that one of its objects is to throw
the poor upon the voluntary donations of their
neighbours; that is, if rightly interpreted, to
force them into a condition between relief in
the Union poorhouse, and alms robbed of their
Christian grace and spirit, as being *forced* ra-
ther from the benevolent than given by them;
while the avaricious and selfish, and all in fact
but the humane and charitable, are at liberty
to keep all they possess from their distressed
brethren.

The class of Beggars, to which the Old Man
here described belongs, will probably soon be
extinct. It consisted of poor, and, mostly, old
and infirm persons, who confined themselves to
a stated round in their neighbourhood, and had
certain fixed days, on which, at different houses,
they regularly received alms, sometimes in
money, but mostly in provisions.

I SAW an aged Beggar in my walk;
And he was seated, by the highway side,
On a low structure of rude masonry
Built at the foot of a huge hill, that they
Who lead their horses down the steep rough
    road
May thence remount at ease. The aged
    Man
Had placed his staff across the broad smooth
    stone
That overlays the pile; and, from a bag
All white with flour, the dole of village
    dames,
He drew his scraps and fragments, one by
    one; 10
And scanned them with a fixed and serious
    look
Of idle computation. In the sun,
Upon the second step of that small pile,
Surrounded by those wild unpeopled hills,
He sat, and ate his food in solitude:
And ever, scattered from his palsied hand,
That, still attempting to prevent the waste,
Was baffled still, the crumbs in little showers

Fell on the ground; and the small mountain birds,
Not venturing yet to peck their destined meal, 20
Approached within the length of half his staff.
　　Him from my childhood have I known;
and then
He was so old, he seems not older now;
He travels on, a solitary Man,
So helpless in appearance, that for him
The sauntering Horseman throws not with a slack
And careless hand his alms upon the ground,
But stops, — that he may safely lodge the coin
Within the old Man's hat; nor quits him so,
But still, when he has given his horse the rein, 30
Watches the aged Beggar with a look
Sidelong, and half-reverted. She who tends
The toll-gate, when in summer at her door
She turns her wheel, if on the road she sees
The aged beggar coming, quits her work,
And lifts the latch for him that he may pass.
The post-boy, when his rattling wheels o'er-take
The aged Beggar in the woody lane,
Shouts to him from behind; and if, thus warned,
The old man does not change his course, the boy 40
Turns with less noisy wheels to the roadside,
And passes gently by, without a curse
Upon his lips, or anger at his heart.
　　He travels on, a solitary Man;
His age has no companion. On the ground
His eyes are turned, and, as he moves along
They move along the ground; and, ever-more,
Instead of common and habitual sight 48
Of fields with rural works, of hill and dale,
And the blue sky, one little span of earth
Is all his prospect. Thus, from day to day,
Bow-bent, his eyes for ever on the ground,
He plies his weary journey; seeing still,
And seldom knowing that he sees, some straw,
Some scattered leaf, or marks which, in one track,
The nails of cart or chariot-wheel have left
Impressed on the white road, — in the same line,
At distance still the same. Poor Traveller!
His staff trails with him; scarcely do his feet

Disturb the summer dust; he is so still 60
In look and motion, that the cottage curs,
Ere he has passed the door, will turn away,
Weary of barking at him. Boys and girls,
The vacant and the busy, maids and youths,
And urchins newly breeched — all pass him by:
Him even the slow-paced waggon leaves behind.
　　But deem not this Man useless. — States-men! ye
Who are so restless in your wisdom, ye
Who have a broom still ready in your hands
To rid the world of nuisances; ye proud, 70
Heart-swoln, while in your pride ye con-template
Your talents, power, or wisdom, deem him not
A burthen of the earth! 'T is Nature's law
That none, the meanest of created things,
Or forms created the most vile and brute,
The dullest or most noxious, should exist
Divorced from good — a spirit and pulse of good,
A life and soul, to every mode of being
Inseparably linked. Then be assured
That least of all can aught — that ever owned 80
The heaven-regarding eye and front sub-lime
Which man is born to — sink, howe'er de-pressed,
So low as to be scorned without a sin;
Without offence to God cast out of view;
Like the dry remnant of a garden-flower
Whose seeds are shed, or as an implement
Worn out and worthless. While from door to door,
This old Man creeps, the villagers in him
Behold a record which together binds
Past deeds and offices of charity, 90
Else unremembered, and so keeps alive
The kindly mood in hearts which lapse of years,
And that half-wisdom half-experience gives,
Make slow to feel, and by sure steps resign
To selfishness and cold oblivious cares.
Among the farms and solitary huts,
Hamlets and thinly-scattered villages,
Where'er the aged Beggar takes his rounds,
The mild necessity of use compels
To acts of love; and habit does the work
Of reason; yet prepares that after-joy 101
Which reason cherishes. And thus the soul,
By that sweet taste of pleasure unpursued,

Doth find herself insensibly disposed
To virtue and true goodness.
                    Some there are,
By their good works exalted, lofty minds
And meditative, authors of delight
And happiness, which to the end of time
Will live, and spread, and kindle: even such
    minds
In childhood, from this solitary Being, 110
Or from like wanderer, haply have received
(A thing more precious far than all that
    books
Or the solicitudes of love can do !)
That first mild touch of sympathy and
    thought,
In which they found their kindred with a
    world
Where want and sorrow were. The easy
    man
Who sits at his own door, — and, like the
    pear
That overhangs his head from the green
    wall,
Feeds in the sunshine; the robust and young,
The prosperous and unthinking, they who
    live   120
Sheltered, and flourish in a little grove
Of their own kindred; — all behold in him
A silent monitor, which on their minds
Must needs impress a transitory thought
Of self-congratulation, to the heart
Of each recalling his peculiar boons,
His charters and exemptions; and, per-
    chance,
Though he to no one give the fortitude
And circumspection needful to preserve
His present blessings, and to husband up
The respite of the season, he, at least, 131
And 't is no vulgar service, makes them felt.
        Yet further. —— Many, I believe, there
            are
Who live a life of virtuous decency,
Men who can hear the Decalogue and feel
No self-reproach; who of the moral law
Established in the land where they abide
Are strict observers; and not negligent
In acts of love to those with whom they
    dwell,
Their kindred, and the children of their
    blood.   140
Praise be to such, and to their slumbers
    peace !
— But of the poor man ask, the abject poor;
Go, and demand of him, if there be here
In this cold abstinence from evil deeds,

And these inevitable charities,
Wherewith to satisfy the human soul ?
No — man is dear to man; the poorest poo
Long for some moments in a weary life
When they can know and feel that the;
    have been,
Themselves, the fathers and the dealers-ou
Of some small blessings; have been kind t(
    such   15
As needed kindness, for this single cause,
That we have all of us one human heart.
— Such pleasure is to one kind Being known,
My neighbour, when with punctual care,
    each week
Duly as Friday comes, though pressed her-
    self
By her own wants, she from her store of
    meal
Takes one unsparing handful for the scrip
Of this old Mendicant, and, from her doo
Returning with exhilarated heart,   16.
Sits by her fire, and builds her hope in
    heaven.
    Then let him pass, a blessing on his head !
And while in that vast solitude to which
The tide of things has borne him, he ap-
    pears
To breathe and live but for himself alone,
Unblamed, uninjured, let him bear about
The good which the benignant law of
    Heaven
Has hung around him: and, while life is his,
Still let him prompt the unlettered villagers
To tender offices and pensive thoughts. 170
— Then let him pass, a blessing on his
    head !
And, long as he can wander, let him breathe
The freshness of the valleys; let his blood
Struggle with frosty air and winter snows;
And let the chartered wind that sweeps the
    heath
Beat his grey locks against his withered
    face.
Reverence the hope whose vital anxiousness
Gives the last human interest to his heart.
May never HOUSE, misnamed of INDUSTRY,
Make him a captive ! — for that pent-up
    din,   180
Those life-consuming sounds that clog the
    air,
Be his the natural silence of old age !
Let him be free of mountain solitudes;
And have around him, whether heard or not,
The pleasant melody of woodland birds.
Few are his pleasures: if his eyes have now

Been doomed so long to settle upon earth
That not without some effort they behold
The countenance of the horizontal sun,
Rising or setting, let the light at least   190
Find a free entrance to their languid orbs.
And let him, *where* and *when* he will, sit
    down
Beneath the trees, or on a grassy bank
Of highway side, and with the little birds
Share his chance-gathered meal; and,
    finally,
As in the eye of Nature he has lived,
So in the eye of Nature let him die !

ANIMAL TRANQUILLITY AND DECAY

1797. 1798

THE little hedgerow birds,
That peck along the road, regard him not.
He travels on, and in his face, his step,
His gait, is one expression: every limb,
His look and bending figure, all bespeak
A man who does not move with pain, but
    moves
With thought. — He is insensibly subdued
To settled quiet: he is one by whom
All effort seems forgotten; one to whom
Long patience hath such mild composure
    given,
That patience now doth seem a thing of
    which
He hath no need.   He is by nature led
To peace so perfect that the young behold
With envy, what the Old Man hardly feels.

PETER BELL

A TALE

What 's in a *Name ?*

. . . .

Brutus will start a Spirit as soon as Cæsar !

1798. 1819

Written at Alfoxden. Founded upon an an-
ecdote, which I read in a newspaper, of an ass
being found hanging his head over a canal in a
wretched posture. Upon examination a dead
body was found in the water and proved to be
the body of its master. The countenance, gait,
and figure of Peter, were taken from a wild
rover with whom I walked from Builth, on the
river Wye, downwards nearly as far as the town
of Hay. He told me strange stories. It has
always been a pleasure to me through life to
catch at every opportunity that has occurred
in my rambles of becoming acquainted with
this class of people. The number of Peter's
wives was taken from the trespasses in this way
of a lawless creature who lived in the county
of Durham, and used to be attended by many
women, sometimes not less than half a dozen,
as disorderly as himself, and a story went in
the country that he had been heard to say while
they were quarrelling, "Why can't you be
quiet? There's none so many of you." Benoni,
or the child of sorrow, I knew when I was a
school-boy. His mother had been deserted by
a gentleman in the neighbourhood, she herself
being a gentlewoman by birth. The circum-
stances of her story were told me by my dear
old Dame, Anne Tyson, who was her confidante.
The Lady died broken-hearted. — In the woods
of Alfoxden I used to take great delight in
noticing the habits, tricks, and physiognomy of
asses; and I have no doubt that I was thus put
upon writing the poem out of liking for the
creature that is so often dreadfully abused. —
The crescent-moon, which makes such a figure
in the prologue, assumed this character one
evening while I was watching its beauty in
front of Alfoxden House. I intended this poem
for the volume before spoken of [*Lyrical Bal-
lads*], but it was not published for more than
twenty years afterwards. — The worship of
the Methodists or Ranters is often heard dur-
ing the stillness of the summer evening in the
country with affecting accompaniments of rural
beauty. In both the psalmody and the voice
of the preacher there is, not unfrequently, much
solemnity likely to impress the feelings of the
rudest characters under favourable circum-
stances.

TO

ROBERT SOUTHEY, ESQ., P.L.,
ETC. ETC.

MY DEAR FRIEND,
    The Tale of Peter Bell, which I now intro-
duce to your notice, and to that of the Pub-
lic, has, in its Manuscript state, nearly survived
its *minority :* — for it first saw the light in the
summer of 1798. During this long interval,
pains have been taken at different times to
make the production less unworthy of a favour-
able reception; or, rather, to fit it for filling
permanently a station, however humble, in the
Literature of our Country. This has, indeed,
been the aim of all my endeavours in Poetry,
which, you know, have been sufficiently labo-
rious to prove that I deem the Art not lightly
to be approached; and that the attainment of
excellence in it may laudably be made the prin-
cipal object of intellectual pursuit by any man,

who, with reasonable consideration of circumstances, has faith in his own impulses.

The Poem of Peter Bell, as the Prologue will show, was composed under a belief that the Imagination not only does not require for its exercise the intervention of supernatural agency, but that, though such agency be excluded, the faculty may be called forth as imperiously and for kindred results of pleasure, by incidents, within the compass of poetic probability, in the humblest departments of daily life. Since that Prologue was written, *you* have exhibited most splendid effects of judicious daring, in the opposite and usual course. Let this acknowledgment make my peace with the lovers of the supernatural ; and I am persuaded it will be admitted, that to you, as a Master in that province of the Art, the following Tale, whether from contrast or congruity, is not an unappropriate offering. Accept it, then, as a public testimony of affectionate admiration from one with whose name yours has been often coupled (to use your own words) for evil and for good; and believe me to be, with earnest wishes that life and health may be granted you to complete the many important works in which you are engaged, and with high respect,

Most faithfully yours,

WILLIAM WORDSWORTH.

RYDAL MOUNT, *April* 7, 1819.

PROLOGUE

THERE 's something in a flying horse,
There 's something in a huge balloon;
But through the clouds I 'll never float
Until I have a little Boat,
Shaped like the crescent-moon.

And now I *have* a little Boat,
In shape a very crescent-moon:
Fast through the clouds my boat can sail;
But if perchance your faith should fail,
Look up — and you shall see me soon !   10

The woods, my Friends, are round you roaring,
Rocking and roaring like a sea;
The noise of danger 's in your ears,
And ye have all a thousand fears
Both for my little Boat and me !

Meanwhile untroubled I admire
The pointed horns of my canoe;
And, did not pity touch my breast,
To see how ye are all distrest,
Till my ribs ached, I 'd laugh at you !   20

Away we go, my Boat and I —
Frail man ne'er sate in such another;
Whether among the winds we strive,
Or deep into the clouds we dive,
Each is contented with the other.

Away we go — and what care we
For treasons, tumults, and for wars ?
We are as calm in our delight
As is the crescent-moon so bright
Among the scattered stars.   30

Up goes my Boat among the stars
Through many a breathless field of light,
Through many a long blue field of ether,
Leaving ten thousand stars beneath her:
Up goes my little Boat so bright !

The Crab, the Scorpion, and the Bull —
We pry among them all; have shot
High o'er the red-haired race of Mars,
Covered from top to toe with scars;
Such company I like it not !   40

The towns in Saturn are decayed,
And melancholy Spectres throng them; —
The Pleiads, that appear to kiss
Each other in the vast abyss,
With joy I sail among them.

Swift Mercury resounds with mirth,
Great Jove is full of stately bowers;
But these, and all that they contain,
What are they to that tiny grain,
That little Earth of ours ?   50

Then back to Earth, the dear green Earth: —
Whole ages if I here should roam,
The world for my remarks and me
Would not a whit the better be;
I 've left my heart at home.

See ! there she is, the matchless Earth !
There spreads the famed Pacific Ocean !
Old Andes thrusts yon craggy spear
Through the grey clouds; the Alps are here,
Like waters in commotion !   60

Yon tawny slip is Libya's sands;
That silver thread the river Dnieper !
And look, where clothed in brightest green
Is a sweet Isle, of isles the Queen;
Ye fairies, from all evil keep her !

And see the town where I was born!
Around those happy fields we span
In boyish gambols; — I was lost
Where I have been, but on this coast
I feel I am a man.   70

Never did fifty things at once
Appear so lovely, never, never; —
How tunefully the forests ring!
To hear the earth's soft murmuring
Thus could I hang for ever!

"Shame on you!" cried my little Boat,
"Was ever such a homesick Loon,
Within a living Boat to sit,
And make no better use of it;
A Boat twin-sister of the crescent-moon! 80

"Ne'er in the breast of full-grown Poet
Fluttered so faint a heart before; —
Was it the music of the spheres
That overpowered your mortal ears?
— Such din shall trouble them no more.

"These nether precincts do not lack
Charms of their own; — then come with
     me;
I want a comrade, and for you
There's nothing that I would not do;
Nought is there that you shall not see.   90

"Haste! and above Siberian snows
We'll sport amid the boreal morning;
Will mingle with her lustres gliding
Among the stars, the stars now hiding,
And now the stars adorning.

"I know the secrets of a land
Where human foot did never stray;
Fair is that land as evening skies,
And cool, though in the depth it lies
Of burning Africa.   100

"Or we'll into the realm of Faery,
Among the lovely shades of things;
The shadowy forms of mountains bare,
And streams, and bowers, and ladies fair,
The shades of palaces and kings!

"Or, if you thirst with hardy zeal
Less quiet regions to explore,
Prompt voyage shall to you reveal
How earth and heaven are taught to feel
The might of magic lore!"   110

"My little vagrant Form of light,
My gay and beautiful Canoe,
Well have you played your friendly part;
As kindly take what from my heart
Experience forces — then adieu!

"Temptation lurks among your words;
But, while these pleasures you're pur-
     suing
Without impediment or let,
No wonder if you quite forget
What on the earth is doing.   120

"There was a time when all mankind
Did listen with a faith sincere
To tuneful tongues in mystery versed;
Then Poets fearlessly rehearsed
The wonders of a wild career.

"Go — (but the world's a sleepy world,
And 't is, I fear, an age too late)
Take with you some ambitious Youth!
For, restless Wanderer! I, in truth,
Am all unfit to be your mate.   130

"Long have I loved what I behold,
The night that calms, the day that cheers;
The common growth of mother-earth
Suffices me — her tears, her mirth,
Her humblest mirth and tears.

"The dragon's wing, the magic ring,
I shall not covet for my dower,
If I along that lowly way
With sympathetic heart may stray,
And with a soul of power.   140

"These given, what more need I desire
To stir, to soothe, or elevate?
What nobler marvels than the mind
May in life's daily prospect find,
May find or there create?

"A potent wand doth Sorrow wield;
What spell so strong as guilty Fear!
Repentance is a tender Sprite;
If aught on earth have heavenly might,
'T is lodged within her silent tear.   150

"But grant my wishes, — let us now
Descend from this ethereal height;
Then take thy way, adventurous Skiff,
More daring far than Hippogriff,
And be thy own delight!

"To the stone-table in my garden,
Loved haunt of many a summer hour,
The Squire is come: his daughter Bess
Beside him in the cool recess
Sits blooming like a flower.   160

"With these are many more convened;
They know not I have been so far; —
I see them there, in number nine,
Beneath the spreading Weymouth-pine !
I see them — there they are !

"There sits the Vicar and his Dame;
And there my good friend, Stephen Otter;
And, ere the light of evening fail,
To them I must relate the Tale
Of Peter Bell the Potter."   170

Off flew the Boat — away she flees,
Spurning her freight with indignation !
And I, as well as I was able,
On two poor legs, toward my stone-table
Limped on with sore vexation.

"O, here he is !" cried little Bess —
She saw me at the garden-door;
"We 've waited anxiously and long,"
They cried, and all around me throng,
Full nine of them or more !   180

"Reproach me not — your fears be still —
Be thankful we again have met; —
Resume, my Friends ! within the shade
Your seats, and quickly shall be paid
The well-remembered debt."

I spake with faltering voice, like one
Not wholly rescued from the pale
Of a wild dream, or worse illusion;
But, straight, to cover my confusion,
Began the promised Tale.   190

PART FIRST

ALL by the moonlight river side
Groaned the poor Beast — alas ! in vain;
The staff was raised to loftier height,
And the blows fell with heavier weight
As Peter struck — and struck again.

"Hold !" cried the Squire, "against the
    rules
Of common sense you 're surely sinning;
This leap is for us all too bold;
Who Peter was, let that be told,
And start from the beginning."   10

—— "A Potter, Sir, he was by trade,"
Said I, becoming quite collected;
"And wheresoever he appeared,
Full twenty times was Peter feared
For once that Peter was respected.

"He, two-and-thirty years or more,
Had been a wild and woodland rover;
Had heard the Atlantic surges roar
On farthest Cornwall's rocky shore,
And trod the cliffs of Dover.   20

"And he had seen Caernarvon's towers,
And well he knew the spire of Sarum;
And he had been where Lincoln bell
Flings o'er the fen that ponderous knell —
A far-renowned alarum !

"At Doncaster, at York, and Leeds,
And merry Carlisle had he been;
And all along the Lowlands fair,
All through the bonnie shire of Ayr
And far as Aberdeen.   30

"And he had been at Inverness;
And Peter, by the mountain-rills,
Had danced his round with Highland
    lasses;
And he had lain beside his asses
On lofty Cheviot Hills:

"And he had trudged through Yorkshire
    dales,
Among the rocks and winding *scars ;*
Where deep and low the hamlets lie
Beneath their little patch of sky
And little lot of stars: 40

"And all along the indented coast,
Bespattered with the salt-sea foam;
Where'er a knot of houses lay
On headland, or in hollow bay; —
Sure never man like him did roam !

"As well might Peter, in the Fleet,
Have been fast bound, a begging debtor; —
He travelled here, he travelled there; —
But not the value of a hair
Was heart or head the better.   50

"He roved among the vales and streams,
In the green wood and hollow dell;
They were his dwellings night and day, —
But nature ne'er could find the way
Into the heart of Peter Bell.

" In vain, through every changeful year,
Did Nature lead him as before;
A primrose by a river's brim
A yellow primrose was to him,
And it was nothing more.   60

''Small change it made in Peter's heart
To see his gentle panniered train
With more than vernal pleasure feeding,
Where'er the tender grass was leading
Its earliest green along the lane.

" In vain, through water, earth, and air,
The soul of happy sound was spread,
When Peter on some April morn,
Beneath the broom or budding thorn,
Made the warm earth his lazy bed.   70

" At noon, when, by the forest's edge
He lay beneath the branches high,
The soft blue sky did never melt
Into his heart; he never felt
The witchery of the soft blue sky !

" On a fair prospect some have looked
And felt, as I have heard them say,
As if the moving time had been
A thing as steadfast as the scene
On which they gazed themselves away.   80

" Within the breast of Peter Bell
These silent raptures found no place;
He was a Carl as wild and rude
As ever hue-and-cry pursued,
As ever ran a felon's race.

" Of all that lead a lawless life,
Of all that love their lawless lives,
In city or in village small,
He was the wildest far of all; —
He had a dozen wedded wives.   90

" Nay, start not ! — wedded wives — and
    twelve !
But how one wife could e'er come near
    him,
In simple truth I cannot tell;
For, be it said of Peter Bell,
To see him was to fear him.

" Though Nature could not touch his heart
By lovely forms, and silent weather,
And tender sounds, yet you might see
At once, that Peter Bell and she
Had often been together.   100

" A savage wildness round him hung
As of a dweller out of doors;
In his whole figure and his mien
A savage character was seen
Of mountains and of dreary moors.

" To all the unshaped half-human thoughts
Which solitary Nature feeds
'Mid summer storms or winter's ice,
Had Peter joined whatever vice
The cruel city breeds.   110

" His face was keen as is the wind
That cuts along the hawthorn-fence; —
Of courage you saw little there,
But, in its stead, a medley air
Of cunning and of impudence.

" He had a dark and sidelong walk,
And long and slouching was his gait;
Beneath his looks so bare and bold,
You might perceive, his spirit cold
Was playing with some inward bait.   120

" His forehead wrinkled was and furred;
A work, one half of which was done
By thinking of his ' *whens* ' and ' *hows* ; '
And half, by knitting of his brows
Beneath the glaring sun.

" There was a hardness in his cheek,
There was a hardness in his eye,
As if the man had fixed his face,
In many a solitary place,
Against the wind and open sky ! "   130

ONE NIGHT, (and now my little Bess !
We 've reached at last the promised Tale:)
One beautiful November night,
When the full moon was shining bright
Upon the rapid river Swale,

Along the river's winding banks
Peter was travelling all alone; —
Whether to buy or sell, or led
By pleasure running in his head,
To me was never known.   140

He trudged along through copse and brake,
He trudged along o'er hill and dale;
Nor for the moon cared he a tittle,
And for the stars he cared as little,
And for the murmuring river Swale.

But, chancing to espy a path
That promised to cut short the way,
As many a wiser man hath done,
He left a trusty guide for one
That might his steps betray.   150

To a thick wood he soon is brought
Where cheerily his course he weaves,
And whistling loud may yet be heard,
Though often buried, like a bird
Darkling, among the boughs and leaves.

But quickly Peter's mood is changed,
And on he drives with cheeks that burn
In downright fury and in wrath; —
There's little sign the treacherous path
Will to the road return !   160

The path grows dim, and dimmer still;
Now up, now down, the Rover wends,
With all the sail that he can carry,
Till brought to a deserted quarry —
And there the pathway ends.

He paused — for shadows of strange shape,
Massy and black, before him lay;
But through the dark, and through the cold,
And through the yawning fissures old,
Did Peter boldly press his way   170

Right through the quarry; — and behold
A scene of soft and lovely hue !
Where blue and grey, and tender green,
Together make as sweet a scene
As ever human eye did view.

Beneath the clear blue sky he saw
A little field of meadow ground;
But field or meadow name it not;
Call it of earth a small green plot,
With rocks encompassed round.   180

The Swale flowed under the grey rocks,
But he flowed quiet and unseen; —
You need a strong and stormy gale
To bring the noises of the Swale
To that green spot, so calm and green !

And is there no one dwelling here,
No hermit with his beads and glass ?
And does no little cottage look
Upon this soft and fertile nook ?
Does no one live near this green grass ?   190

Across the deep and quiet spot
Is Peter driving through the grass —
And now has reached the skirting trees;
When, turning round his head, he sees
A solitary Ass.

" A Prize ! " cries Peter — but he first
Must spy about him far and near:
There's not a single house in sight,
No woodman's hut, no cottage light —
Peter, you need not fear !   200

There's nothing to be seen but woods,
And rocks that spread a hoary gleam,
And this one Beast, that from the bed
Of the green meadow hangs his head
Over the silent stream.

His head is with a halter bound;
The halter seizing, Peter leapt
Upon the Creature's back, and plied
With ready heels his shaggy side;
But still the Ass his station kept.   210

Then Peter gave a sudden jerk,
A jerk that from a dungeon-floor
Would have pulled up an iron ring;
But still the heavy-headed Thing
Stood just as he had stood before !

Quoth Peter, leaping from his seat,
" There is some plot against me laid; "
Once more the little meadow-ground
And all the hoary cliffs around
He cautiously surveyed.   220

All, all is silent — rocks and woods,
All still and silent — far and near !
Only the Ass, with motion dull,
Upon the pivot of his skull
Turns round his long left ear.

Thought Peter, What can mean all this ?
Some ugly witchcraft must be here !
— Once more the Ass, with motion dull,
Upon the pivot of his skull
Turned round his long left ear.   230

Suspicion ripened into dread;
Yet with deliberate action slow,
His staff high-raising, in the pride
Of skill, upon the sounding hide,
He dealt a sturdy blow.

The poor Ass staggered with the shock;
And then, as if to take his ease,
In quiet uncomplaining mood,
Upon the spot where he had stood,
Dropped gently down upon his knees: 240

As gently on his side he fell;
And by the river's brink did lie;
And, while he lay like one that mourned,
The patient Beast on Peter turned
His shining hazel eye.

'T was but one mild, reproachful look,
A look more tender than severe;
And straight in sorrow, not in dread,
He turned the eye-ball in his head   249
Towards the smooth river deep and clear.

Upon the Beast the sapling rings;
His lank sides heaved, his limbs they
       stirred;
He gave a groan, and then another,
Of that which went before the brother,
And then he gave a third.

All by the moonlight river side
He gave three miserable groans;
And not till now hath Peter seen
How gaunt the Creature is, — how lean
And sharp his staring bones !   260

With legs stretched out and stiff he lay: —
No word of kind commiseration
Fell at the sight from Peter's tongue;
With hard contempt his heart was wrung,
With hatred and vexation.

The meagre beast lay still as death;
And Peter's lips with fury quiver;
Quoth he, " You little mulish dog,
I 'll fling your carcase like a log
Head-foremost down the river !"   270

An impious oath confirmed the threat —
Whereat from the earth on which he lay
To all the echoes, south and north,
And east and west, the Ass sent forth
A long and clamorous bray !

This outcry, on the heart of Peter,
Seems like a note of joy to strike, —
Joy at the heart of Peter knocks;
But in the echo of the rocks
Was something Peter did not like.   280

Whether to cheer his coward breast,
Or that he could not break the chain,
In this serene and solemn hour,
Twined round him by demoniac power,
To the blind work he turned again.

Among the rocks and winding crags;
Among the mountains far away;
Once more the Ass did lengthen out
More ruefully a deep-drawn shout,   289
The hard dry see-saw of his horrible bray !

What is there now in Peter's heart ?
Or whence the might of this strange sound ?
The moon uneasy looked and dimmer,
The broad blue heavens appeared to glim-
       mer,
And the rocks staggered all around —

From Peter's hand the sapling dropped !
Threat has he none to execute;
" If any one should come and see
That I am here, they 'll think," quoth he,
" I 'm helping this poor dying brute."   300

He scans the Ass from limb to limb,
And ventures now to uplift his eyes;
More steady looks the moon, and clear,
More like themselves the rocks appear
And touch more quiet skies.

His scorn returns — his hate revives;
He stoops the Ass's neck to seize
With malice — that again takes flight;
For in the pool a startling sight
Meets him, among the inverted trees.   310

Is it the moon's distorted face ?
The ghost-like image of a cloud ?
Is it a gallows there portrayed ?
Is Peter of himself afraid ?
Is it a coffin, — or a shroud ?

A grisly idol hewn in stone ?
Or imp from witch's lap let fall ?
Perhaps a ring of shining fairies ?
Such as pursue their feared vagaries
In sylvan bower, or haunted hall ?   320

Is it a fiend that to a stake
Of fire his desperate self is tethering ?
Or stubborn spirit doomed to yell
In solitary ward or cell,
Ten thousand miles from all his brethren ?

Never did pulse so quickly throb,
And never heart so loudly panted;
He looks, he cannot choose but look;
Like some one reading in a book —
A book that is enchanted.   330

Ah, well-a-day for Peter Bell !
He will be turned to iron soon,
Meet Statue for the court of Fear !
His hat is up — and every hair
Bristles, and whitens in the moon !

He looks, he ponders, looks again;
He sees a motion — hears a groan;
His eyes will burst — his heart will break —
He gives a loud and frightful shriek,
And back he falls, as if his life were
        flown !   340

PART SECOND

WE left our Hero in a trance,
Beneath the alders, near the river;
The Ass is by the river-side,
And, where the feeble breezes glide,
Upon the stream the moonbeams quiver.

A happy respite ! but at length
He feels the glimmering of the moon;
Wakes with glazed eye, and feebly sigh-
        ing —
To sink, perhaps, where he is lying,
Into a second swoon !   10

He lifts his head, he sees his staff;
He touches — 't is to him a treasure !
Faint recollection seems to tell
That he is yet where mortals dwell —
A thought received with languid pleasure !

His head upon his elbow propped,
Becoming less and less perplexed,
Sky-ward he looks — to rock and wood —
And then — upon the glassy flood
His wandering eye is fixed.   20

Thought he, that is the face of one
In his last sleep securely bound !
So toward the stream his head he bent,
And downward thrust his staff, intent
The river's depth to sound.

Now — like a tempest-shattered bark,
That overwhelmed and prostrate lies,
And in a moment to the verge

Is lifted of a foaming surge —
Full suddenly the Ass doth rise !   30

His staring bones all shake with joy,
And close by Peter's side he stands:
While Peter o'er the river bends,
The little Ass his neck extends,
And fondly licks his hands.

Such life is in the Ass's eyes,
Such life is in his limbs and ears;
That Peter Bell, if he had been
The veriest coward ever seen,
Must now have thrown aside his fears.   40

The Ass looks on — and to his work
Is Peter quietly resigned;
He touches here — he touches there —
And now among the dead man's hair
His sapling Peter has entwined.

He pulls — and looks — and pulls again;
And he whom the poor Ass had lost,
The man who had been four days dead,
Head-foremost from the river's bed
Uprises like a ghost !   50

And Peter draws him to dry land;
And through the brain of Peter pass
Some poignant twitches, fast and faster;
"No doubt," quoth he, "he is the Master
Of this poor miserable Ass !"

The meagre Shadow that looks on —
What would he now ? what is he doing ?
His sudden fit of joy is flown, —
He on his knees hath laid him down,
As if he were his grief renewing;   60

But no — that Peter on his back
Must mount, he shows well as he can:
Thought Peter then, come weal or woe,
I 'll do what he would have me do,
In pity to this poor drowned man.

With that resolve he boldly mounts
Upon the pleased and thankful Ass;
And then, without a moment's stay,
That earnest Creature turned away
Leaving the body on the grass.   70

Intent upon his faithful watch,
The Beast four days and nights had past;
A sweeter meadow ne'er was seen,
And there the Ass four days had been,
Nor ever once did break his fast:

Yet firm his step, and stout his heart;
The mead is crossed — the quarry's mouth
Is reached; but there the trusty guide
Into a thicket turns aside,
And deftly ambles towards the south.   80

When hark a burst of doleful sound!
And Peter honestly might say,
The like came never to his ears,
Though he has been, full thirty years,
A rover — night and day!

'T is not a plover of the moors,
'T is not a bittern of the fen;
Nor can it be a barking fox,
Nor night-bird chambered in the rocks,
Nor wild-cat in a woody glen!   90

The Ass is startled — and stops short
Right in the middle of the thicket;
And Peter, wont to whistle loud
Whether alone or in a crowd,
Is silent as a silent cricket.

What ails you now, my little Bess?
Well may you tremble and look grave!
This cry — that rings along the wood,
This cry — that floats adown the flood,
Comes from the entrance of a cave: 100

I see a blooming Wood-boy there,
And if I had the power to say
How sorrowful the wanderer is,
Your heart would be as sad as his
Till you had kissed his tears away!

Grasping a hawthorn branch in hand,
All bright with berries ripe and red,
Into the cavern's mouth he peeps;
Thence back into the moonlight creeps;
Whom seeks he — whom? — the silent
        dead: 110

His father! — Him doth he require —
Him hath he sought with fruitless pains,
Among the rocks, behind the trees;
Now creeping on his hands and knees,
Now running o'er the open plains.

And hither is he come at last,
When he through such a day has gone,
By this dark cave to be distrest
Like a poor bird — her plundered nest
Hovering around with dolorous moan!   120

Of that intense and piercing cry
The listening Ass conjectures well;
Wild as it is, he there can read
Some intermingled notes that plead
With touches irresistible.

But Peter — when he saw the Ass
Not only stop but turn, and change
The cherished tenor of his pace
That lamentable cry to chase —
It wrought in him conviction strange;   130

A faith that, for the dead man's sake
And this poor slave who loved him well,
Vengeance upon his head will fall,
Some visitation worse than all
Which ever till this night befell.

Meanwhile the Ass to reach his home,
Is striving stoutly as he may;
But, while he climbs the woody hill,
The cry grows weak — and weaker still;
And now at last it dies away.   140

So with his freight the Creature turns
Into a gloomy grove of beech,
Along the shade with footsteps true
Descending slowly, till the two
The open moonlight reach.

And there, along the narrow dell,
A fair smooth pathway you discern,
A length of green and open road —
As if it from a fountain flowed —
Winding away between the fern.   150

The rocks that tower on either side
Build up a wild fantastic scene;
Temples like those among the Hindoos,
And mosques, and spires, and abbey windows,
And castles all with ivy green!

And, while the Ass pursues his way,
Along this solitary dell,
As pensively his steps advance,
The mosques and spires change countenance
And look at Peter Bell!   160

That unintelligible cry
Hath left him high in preparation, —
Convinced that he, or soon or late,
This very night will meet his fate —
And so he sits in expectation!

The strenuous Animal hath clomb
With the green path; and now he wends
Where, shining like the smoothest sea,
In undisturbed immensity
A level plain extends. 170

But whence this faintly-rustling sound
By which the journeying pair are chased?
— A withered leaf is close behind,
Light plaything for the sportive wind
Upon that solitary waste.

When Peter spied the moving thing,
It only doubled his distress;
"Where there is not a bush or tree,
The very leaves they follow me —
So huge hath been my wickedness!" 180

To a close lane they now are come,
Where, as before, the enduring Ass
Moves on without a moment's stop,
Nor once turns round his head to crop
A bramble-leaf or blade of grass.

Between the hedges as they go,
The white dust sleeps upon the lane;
And Peter, ever and anon
Back-looking, sees, upon a stone,
Or in the dust, a crimson stain. 190

A stain — as of a drop of blood
By moonlight made more faint and wan;
Ha! why these sinkings of despair?
He knows not how the blood comes there —
And Peter is a wicked man.

At length he spies a bleeding wound,
Where he had struck the Ass's head;
He sees the blood, knows what it is, —
A glimpse of sudden joy was his,
But then it quickly fled; 200

Of him whom sudden death had seized
He thought, — of thee, O faithful Ass!
And once again those ghastly pains,
Shoot to and fro through heart and reins,
And through his brain like lightning pass.

PART THIRD

I 'VE heard of one, a gentle Soul,
Though given to sadness and to gloom,
And for the fact will vouch, — one night
It chanced that by a taper's light
This man was reading in his room;

Bending, as you or I might bend
At night o'er any pious book,
When sudden blackness overspread
The snow-white page on which he read,
And made the good man round him look. 10

The chamber walls were dark all round, —
And to his book he turned again;
— The light had left the lonely taper,
And formed itself upon the paper
Into large letters — bright and plain!

The godly book was in his hand —
And, on the page, more black than coal,
Appeared, set forth in strange array,
A *word* — which to his dying day
Perplexed the good man's gentle soul. 20

The ghostly word, thus plainly seen,
Did never from his lips depart;
But he hath said, poor gentle wight!
It brought full many a sin to light
Out of the bottom of his heart.

Dread Spirits! to confound the meek
Why wander from your course so far,
Disordering colour, form, and stature!
— Let good men feel the soul of nature,
And see things as they are. 30

Yet, potent Spirits! well I know,
How ye, that play with soul and sense,
Are not unused to trouble friends
Of goodness, for most gracious ends —
And this I speak in reverence!

But might I give advice to you,
Whom in my fear I love so well;
From men of pensive virtue go,
Dread Beings! and your empire show
On hearts like that of Peter Bell. 40

Your presence often have I felt
In darkness and the stormy night;
And, with like force, if need there be,
Ye can put forth your agency
When earth is calm, and heaven is bright.

Then, coming from the wayward world,
That powerful world in which ye dwell,
Come, Spirits of the Mind! and try
To-night, beneath the moonlight sky,
What may be done with Peter Bell! 50

— O, would that some more skilful voice
My further labour might prevent!

Kind Listeners, that around me sit,
I feel that I am all unfit
For such high argument.

I 've played, I 've danced, with my narra-
    tion;
I loitered long ere I began:
Ye waited then on my good pleasure;
Pour out indulgence still, in measure
As liberal as ye can!   60

Our Travellers, ye remember well,
Are thridding a sequestered lane;
And Peter many tricks is trying,
And many anodynes applying,
To ease his conscience of its pain.

By this his heart is lighter far;
And, finding that he can account
So snugly for that crimson stain,
His evil spirit up again
Does like an empty bucket mount.   70

And Peter is a deep logician
Who hath no lack of wit mercurial;
" Blood drops — leaves rustle — yet," quoth
    he,
" This poor man never, but for me,
Could have had Christian burial.

" And, say the best you can, 't is plain,
That here has been some wicked dealing;
No doubt the devil in me wrought;
I 'm not the man who could have thought
An Ass like this was worth the steal-
    ing !"   80

So from his pocket Peter takes
His shining horn tobacco-box;
And, in a light and careless way,
As men who with their purpose play,
Upon the lid he knocks.

Let them whose voice can stop the clouds,
Whose cunning eye can see the wind,
Tell to a curious world the cause
Why, making here a sudden pause,
The Ass turned round his head, and
    grinned.   90

Appalling process ! I have marked
The like on heath, in lonely wood;
And, verily, have seldom met
A spectacle more hideous — yet
It suited Peter's present mood.

And, grinning in his turn, his teeth
He in jocose defiance showed —
When, to upset his spiteful mirth,
A murmur, pent within the earth,
In the dead earth beneath the road   100

Rolled audibly ! it swept along,
A muffled noise — a rumbling sound ! —
'T was by a troop of miners made,
Plying with gunpowder their trade,
Some twenty fathoms under ground.

Small cause of dire effect ! for, surely,
If ever mortal, King or Cotter,
Believed that earth was charged to quake
And yawn for his unworthy sake,
'T was Peter Bell the Potter.   110

But, as an oak in breathless air
Will stand though to the centre hewn;
Or as the weakest things, if frost
Have stiffened them, maintain their post;
So he, beneath the gazing moon ! —

The Beast bestriding thus, he reached
A spot where, in a sheltering cove,
A little chapel stands alone,
With greenest ivy overgrown,
And tufted with an ivy grove;   120

Dying insensibly away
From human thoughts and purposes,
It seemed — wall, window, roof and tower
To bow to some transforming power,
And blend with the surrounding trees.

As ruinous a place it was,
Thought Peter, in the shire of Fife
That served my turn, when following still
From land to land a reckless will
I married my sixth wife !   13c

The unheeding Ass moves slowly on,
And now is passing by an inn
Brim-full of a carousing crew,
That make, with curses not a few,
An uproar and a drunken din.

I cannot well express the thoughts
Which Peter in those noises found; —
A stifling power compressed his frame,
While-as a swimming darkness came
Over that dull and dreary sound.   140

For well did Peter know the sound;
The language of those drunken joys

To him, a jovial soul, I ween,
But a few hours ago, had been
A gladsome and a welcome noise.

Now, turned adrift into the past,
He finds no solace in his course;
Like planet-stricken men of yore,
He trembles, smitten to the core
By strong compunction and remorse. 150

But, more than all, his heart is stung
To think of one, almost a child;
A sweet and playful Highland girl,
As light and beauteous as a squirrel,
As beauteous and as wild !

Her dwelling was a lonely house,
A cottage in a heathy dell;
And she put on her gown of green,
And left her mother at sixteen,
And followed Peter Bell. 160

But many good and pious thoughts
Had she; and, in the kirk to pray,
Two long Scotch miles, through rain or
snow
To kirk she had been used to go,
Twice every Sabbath-day.

And, when she followed Peter Bell,
It was to lead an honest life;
For he, with tongue not used to falter,
Had pledged his troth before the altar
To love her as his wedded wife. 170

A mother's hope is hers; — but soon
She drooped and pined like one forlorn,
From Scripture she a name did borrow;
Benoni, or the child of sorrow,
She called her babe unborn.

For she had learned how Peter lived,
And took it in most grievous part;
She to the very bone was worn,
And, ere that little child was born,
Died of a broken heart. 180

And now the Spirits of the Mind
Are busy with poor Peter Bell;
Upon the rights of visual sense
Usurping, with a prevalence
More terrible than magic spell.

Close by a brake of flowering furze
(Above it shivering aspens play)

He sees an unsubstantial creature,
His very self in form and feature,
Not four yards from the broad high-
way: 190

And stretched beneath the furze he sees
The Highland girl — it is no other;
And hears her crying as she cried,
The very moment that she died,
" My mother ! oh my mother ! "

The sweat pours down from Peter's face,
So grievous is his heart's contrition;
With agony his eye-balls ache
While he beholds by the furze-brake
This miserable vision ! 200

Calm is the well-deserving brute,
His peace hath no offence betrayed;
But now, while down that slope he wends,
A voice to Peter's ear ascends,
Resounding from the woody glade:

The voice, though clamorous as a horn
Re-echoed by a naked rock,
Comes from that tabernacle — List !
Within, a fervent Methodist
Is preaching to no heedless flock ! 210

" Repent ! repent ! " he cries aloud,
" While yet ye may find mercy; — strive
To love the Lord with all your might;
Turn to him, seek him day and night,
And save your souls alive !

" Repent ! repent ! though ye have gone,
Through paths of wickedness and woe,
After the Babylonian harlot;
And, though your sins be red as scarlet,
They shall be white as snow ! " 220

Even as he passed the door, these words
Did plainly come to Peter's ears;
And they such joyful tidings were,
The joy was more than he could bear ! —
He melted into tears.

Sweet tears of hope and tenderness !
And fast they fell, a plenteous shower !
His nerves, his sinews seemed to melt;
Through all his iron frame was felt
A gentle, a relaxing power ! 230

Each fibre of his frame was weak;
Weak all the animal within;

But, in its helplessness, grew mild
And gentle as an infant child,
An infant that has known no sin.

'T is said, meek Beast! that, through
    Heaven's grace,
He not unmoved did notice now
The cross upon thy shoulder scored,
For lasting impress, by the Lord
To whom all human-kind shall bow;   240

Memorial of his touch — that day
When Jesus humbly deigned to ride,
Entering the proud Jerusalem,
By an immeasurable stream
Of shouting people deified!

Meanwhile the persevering Ass
Turned towards a gate that hung in view
Across a shady lane; his chest
Against the yielding gate he pressed
And quietly passed through.   250

And up the stony lane he goes;
No ghost more softly ever trod;
Among the stones and pebbles, he
Sets down his hoofs inaudibly,
As if with felt his hoofs were shod.

Along the lane the trusty Ass
Went twice two hundred yards or more,
And no one could have guessed his aim, —
Till to a lonely house he came,
And stopped beside the door.   260

Thought Peter, 't is the poor man's home!
He listens — not a sound is heard
Save from the trickling household rill;
But, stepping o'er the cottage-sill,
Forthwith a little Girl appeared.

She to the Meeting-house was bound
In hopes some tidings there to gather:
No glimpse it is, no doubtful gleam;
She saw — and uttered with a scream,
"My father! here's my father!"   270

The very word was plainly heard,
Heard plainly by the wretched Mother —
Her joy was like a deep affright:
And forth she rushed into the light,
And saw it was another!

And, instantly, upon the earth,
Beneath the full moon shining bright,

Close to the Ass's feet she fell;
At the same moment Peter Bell
Dismounts in most unhappy plight.   280

As he beheld the Woman lie
Breathless and motionless, the mind
Of Peter sadly was confused;
But, though to such demands unused,
And helpless almost as the blind,

He raised her up; and, while he held
Her body propped against his knee,
The Woman waked — and when she spied
The poor Ass standing by her side,
She moaned most bitterly.   290

"Oh! God be praised — my heart's at
    ease —
For he is dead — I know it well!"
— At this she wept a bitter flood;
And, in the best way that he could,
His tale did Peter tell.

He trembles — he is pale as death;
His voice is weak with perturbation;
He turns aside his head, he pauses;
Poor Peter, from a thousand causes,
Is crippled sore in his narration.   300

At length she learned how he espied
The Ass in that small meadow-ground;
And that her Husband now lay dead,
Beside that luckless river's bed
In which he had been drowned.

A piercing look the Widow cast
Upon the Beast that near her stands;
She sees 't is he, that 't is the same;
She calls the poor Ass by his name,
And wrings, and wrings her hands.   310

"O wretched loss — untimely stroke!
If he had died upon his bed!
He knew not one forewarning pain;
He never will come home again —
Is dead, for ever dead!"

Beside the woman Peter stands;
His heart is opening more and more;
A holy sense pervades his mind;
He feels what he for human kind
Had never felt before.   320

At length, by Peter's arm sustained,
The Woman rises from the ground —

"Oh, mercy ! something must be done,
My little Rachel, you must run, —
Some willing neighbour must be found.

"Make haste — my little Rachel — do,
The first you meet with — bid him come,
Ask him to lend his horse to-night,
And this good Man, whom Heaven re-
    quite,
Will help to bring the body home."   330

Away goes Rachel weeping loud; —
An Infant, waked by her distress,
Makes in the house a piteous cry;
And Peter hears the Mother sigh,
"Seven are they, and all fatherless !"

And now is Peter taught to feel
That man's heart is a holy thing;
And Nature, through a world of death,
Breathes into him a second breath,   339
More searching than the breath of spring.

Upon a stone the Woman sits
In agony of silent grief —
From his own thoughts did Peter start;
He longs to press her to his heart,
From love that cannot find relief.

But roused, as if through every limb
Had past a sudden shock of dread,
The Mother o'er the threshold flies,
And up the cottage stairs she hies,   349
And on the pillow lays her burning head.

And Peter turns his steps aside
Into a shade of darksome trees,
Where he sits down, he knows not how,
With his hands pressed against his brow,
His elbows on his tremulous knees.

There, self-involved, does Peter sit
Until no sign of life he makes,
As if his mind were sinking deep
Through years that have been long asleep
The trance is passed away — he wakes;   360

He lifts his head — and sees the Ass
Yet standing in the clear moonshine;
"When shall I be as good as thou ?
Oh ! would, poor beast, that I had now
A heart but half as good as thine !"

But *He* — who deviously hath sought
His Father through the lonesome woods,

Hath sought, proclaiming to the ear
Of night his grief and sorrowful fear —   369
He comes, escaped from fields and floods; —

With weary pace is drawing nigh;
He sees the Ass — and nothing living
Had ever such a fit of joy
As hath this little orphan Boy,
For he has no misgiving !

Forth to the gentle Ass he springs,
And up about his neck he climbs;
In loving words he talks to him,
He kisses, kisses face and limb, —
He kisses him a thousand times !   380

This Peter sees, while in the shade
He stood beside the cottage-door;
And Peter Bell, the ruffian wild,
Sobs loud, he sobs even like a child,
"O God ! I can endure no more !"

— Here ends my Tale: for in a trice
Arrived a neighbour with his horse;
Peter went forth with him straightway;
And, with due care, ere break of day,
Together they brought back the Corse.   390

And many years did this poor Ass,
Whom once it was my luck to see
Cropping the shrubs of Leming-Lane,
Help by his labour to maintain
The Widow and her family.

And Peter Bell, who, till that night,
Had been the wildest of his clan,
Forsook his crimes, renounced his folly,
And, after ten months' melancholy,
Became a good and honest man.   400

THE SIMPLON PASS

1804(?). 1845

—— Brook and road
Were fellow-travellers in this gloomy Pass,
And with them did we journey several hours
At a slow step. The immeasurable height
Of woods decaying, never to be decayed,
The stationary blasts of waterfalls,
And in the narrow rent, at every turn,
Winds thwarting winds bewildered and for-
    lorn,
The torrents shooting from the clear blue
    sky,

The rocks that muttered close upon our
    ears,
Black drizzling crags that spake by the way-
    side
As if a voice were in them, the sick sight
And giddy prospect of the raving stream,
The unfettered clouds and region of the
    heavens,
Tumult and peace, the darkness and the
    light —
Were all like workings of one mind, the
    features
Of the same face, blossoms upon one tree,
Characters of the great Apocalypse,
The types and symbols of Eternity,
Of first, and last, and midst, and without
    end.

INFLUENCE OF NATURAL OBJECTS

IN CALLING FORTH AND STRENGTHENING THE IMAGINATION IN BOYHOOD AND EARLY YOUTH

1798. 1809

Written in Germany. This Extract is re-
printed from The Friend.

WISDOM and Spirit of the universe !
Thou Soul, that art the Eternity of thought !
And giv'st to forms and images a breath
And everlasting motion ! not in vain,
By day or star-light, thus from my first
    dawn
Of childhood didst thou intertwine for me
The passions that build up our human soul;
Not with the mean and vulgar works of
    Man;
But with high objects, with enduring things,
With life and nature; purifying thus   10
The elements of feeling and of thought,
And sanctifying by such discipline
Both pain and fear, — until we recognise
A grandeur in the beatings of the heart.
    Nor was this fellowship vouchsafed to
    me
With stinted kindness. In November days,
When vapours rolling down the valleys
    made
A lonely scene more lonesome; among
    woods
At noon; and 'mid the calm of summer
    nights,   19
When, by the margin of the trembling lake,

Beneath the gloomy hills, homeward I went
In solitude, such intercourse was mine:
Mine was it in the fields both day and
    night,
And by the waters, all the summer long.
And in the frosty season, when the sun
Was set, and, visible for many a mile,
The cottage-windows through the twilight
    blazed,
I heeded not the summons: happy time
It was indeed for all of us; for me
It was a time of rapture ! Clear and loud
The village-clock tolled six — I wheeled
    about,   31
Proud and exulting like an untired horse
That cares not for his home. — All shod
    with steel
We hissed along the polished ice, in games
Confederate, imitative of the chase
And woodland pleasures, — the resounding
    horn,
The pack loud-chiming, and the hunted
    hare.
So through the darkness and the cold we
    flew,
And not a voice was idle: with the din
Smitten, the precipices rang aloud;   40
The leafless trees and every icy crag
Tinkled like iron; while far-distant hills
Into the tumult sent an alien sound
Of melancholy, not unnoticed while the
    stars,
Eastward, were sparkling clear, and in the
    west
The orange sky of evening died away.
    Not seldom from the uproar I retired
Into a silent bay, or sportively
Glanced sideway, leaving the tumultuous
    throng,
To cut across the reflex of a star;   50
Image, that, flying still before me, gleamed
Upon the glassy plain: and oftentimes,
When we had given our bodies to the wind,
And all the shadowy banks on either side
Came sweeping through the darkness, spin-
    ning still
The rapid line of motion, then at once
Have I, reclining back upon my heels,
Stopped short; yet still the solitary cliffs
Wheeled by me — even as if the earth had
    rolled
With visible motion her diurnal round ! 60
Behind me did they stretch in solemn train,
Feebler and feebler, and I stood and watched
Till all was tranquil as a summer sea.

THERE WAS A BOY

1798. 1800

Written in Germany. This is an extract from the poem on my own poetical education. This practice of making an instrument of their own fingers is known to most boys, though some are more skilful at it than others. William Raincock of Rayrigg, a fine spirited lad, took the lead of all my schoolfellows in this art.

THERE was a Boy; ye knew him well, ye cliffs
And islands of Winander ! — many a time,
At evening, when the earliest stars began
To move along the edges of the hills,
Rising or setting, would he stand alone,
Beneath the trees, or by the glimmering lake;
And there, with fingers interwoven, both hands
Pressed closely palm to palm and to his mouth
Uplifted, he, as through an instrument,
Blew mimic hootings to the silent owls,　10
That they might answer him. — And they would shout
Across the watery vale, and shout again,
Responsive to his call, — with quivering peals,
And long halloos, and screams, and echoes loud
Redoubled and redoubled; concourse wild
Of jocund din ! And, when there came a pause
Of silence such as baffled his best skill:
Then, sometimes, in that silence, while he hung
Listening, a gentle shock of mild surprise
Has carried far into his heart the voice　20
Of mountain-torrents; or the visible scene
Would enter unawares into his mind
With all its solemn imagery, its rocks,
Its woods, and that uncertain heaven received
Into the bosom of the steady lake.
　This boy was taken from his mates, and died
In childhood, ere he was full twelve years old.
Pre-eminent in beauty is the vale
Where he was born and bred: the church-yard hangs
Upon a slope above the village-school;　30

And, through that church-yard when my way has led
On summer-evenings, I believe, that there
A long half-hour together I have stood
Mute — looking at the grave in which he lies !

NUTTING

1798. 1800

Written in Germany; intended as part of a poem on my own life, but struck out as not being wanted there. Like most of my schoolfellows I was an impassioned nutter. For this pleasure, the vale of Esthwaite, abounding in coppice-wood, furnished a very wide range. These verses arose out of the remembrance of feelings I had often had when a boy, and particularly in the extensive woods that still stretch from the side of Esthwaite Lake towards Graythwaite, the seat of the ancient family of Sandys.

———— It seems a day
(I speak of one from many singled out)
One of those heavenly days that cannot die;
When, in the eagerness of boyish hope,
I left our cottage-threshold, sallying forth
With a huge wallet o'er my shoulders slung,
A nutting-crook in hand; and turned my steps
Tow'rd some far-distant wood, a Figure quaint,
Tricked out in proud disguise of cast-off weeds
Which for that service had been husbanded,
By exhortation of my frugal Dame —　11
Motley accoutrement, of power to smile
At thorns, and brakes, and brambles, — and, in truth,
More raggèd than need was ! O'er pathless rocks,
Through beds of matted fern, and tangled thickets,
Forcing my way, I came to one dear nook
Unvisited, where not a broken bough
Drooped with its withered leaves, ungracious sign
Of devastation; but the hazels rose　19
Tall and erect, with tempting clusters hung,
A virgin scene ! — A little while I stood,
Breathing with such suppression of the heart
As joy delights in; and, with wise restraint
Voluptuous, fearless of a rival, eyed
The banquet; — or beneath the trees I sate

Among the flowers, and with the flowers I
  played;
A temper known to those, who, after long
And weary expectation, have been blest
With sudden happiness beyond all hope.
Perhaps it was a bower beneath whose leaves
The violets of five seasons re-appear   31
And fade, unseen by any human eye;
Where fairy water-breaks do murmur on
For ever; and I saw the sparkling foam,
And — with my cheek on one of those green
  stones
That, fleeced with moss, under the shady
  trees,
Lay round me, scattered like a flock of
  sheep —
I heard the murmur and the murmuring
  sound,
In that sweet mood when pleasure loves to
  pay
Tribute to ease; and, of its joy secure,   40
The heart luxuriates with indifferent things,
Wasting its kindliness on stocks and stones,
And on the vacant air.   Then up I rose,
And dragged to earth both branch and
  bough, with crash
And merciless ravage: and the shady nook
Of hazels, and the green and mossy bower,
Deformed and sullied, patiently gave up
Their quiet being: and, unless I now
Confound my present feelings with the past,
Ere from the mutilated bower I turned   50
Exulting, rich beyond the wealth of kings,
I felt a sense of pain when I beheld
The silent trees, and saw the intruding sky —
Then, dearest Maiden, move along these
  shades
In gentleness of heart; with gentle hand
Touch — for there is a spirit in the woods.

"STRANGE FITS OF PASSION HAVE I KNOWN"

1798. 1800

Written in Germany.

STRANGE fits of passion have I known:
And I will dare to tell,
But in the Lover's ear alone,
What once to me befell.

When she I loved looked every day
Fresh as a rose in June,
I to her cottage bent my way,
Beneath an evening-moon.

Upon the moon I fixed my eye,
All over the wide lea;
With quickening pace my horse drew nigh
Those paths so dear to me.

And now we reached the orchard-plot;
And, as we climbed the hill,
The sinking moon to Lucy's cot
Came near, and nearer still.

In one of those sweet dreams I slept,
Kind Nature's gentlest boon!
And all the while my eyes I kept
On the descending moon.

My horse moved on; hoof after hoof
He raised, and never stopped:
When down behind the cottage roof,
At once, the bright moon dropped.

What fond and wayward thoughts will slide
Into a Lover's head!
"O mercy!" to myself I cried,
"If Lucy should be dead!"

"SHE DWELT AMONG THE UN-TRODDEN WAYS"

1798. 1800

Written in Germany.

SHE dwelt among the untrodden ways
  Beside the springs of Dove,
A Maid whom there were none to praise
  And very few to love:

A violet by a mossy stone
  Half hidden from the eye!
— Fair as a star, when only one
  Is shining in the sky.

She lived unknown, and few could know
  When Lucy ceased to be;
But she is in her grave, and, oh,
  The difference to me!

"I TRAVELLED AMONG UN-KNOWN MEN"

1801. 1807

Written in Germany.

I TRAVELLED among unknown men,
  In lands beyond the sea;
Nor, England! did I know till then
  What love I bore to thee.

'T is past, that melancholy dream !
  Nor will I quit thy shore
A second time; for still I seem
  To love thee more and more.

Among thy mountains did I feel
  The joy of my desire;
And she I cherished turned her wheel
  Beside an English fire.

Thy mornings showed, thy nights concealed
  The bowers where Lucy played;
And thine too is the last green field
  That Lucy's eyes surveyed.

"THREE YEARS SHE GREW IN SUN AND SHOWER"

1799. 1800

Composed in the Hartz Forest.

THREE years she grew in sun and shower,
Then Nature said, " A lovelier flower
On earth was never sown;
This Child I to myself will take;
She shall be mine, and I will make
A Lady of my own.

" Myself will to my darling be
Both law and impulse: and with me
The Girl, in rock and plain,
In earth and heaven, in glade and bower,   10
Shall feel an overseeing power
To kindle or restrain.

" She shall be sportive as the fawn
That wild with glee across the lawn,
Or up the mountain springs;
And hers shall be the breathing balm,
And hers the silence and the calm
Of mute insensate things.

" The floating clouds their state shall lend
To her; for her the willow bend;   20
Nor shall she fail to see
Even in the motions of the Storm
Grace that shall mould the Maiden's form
By silent sympathy.

" The stars of midnight shall be dear
To her; and she shall lean her ear
In many a secret place
Where rivulets dance their wayward round,
And beauty born of murmuring sound
Shall pass into her face.   30

" And vital feelings of delight
Shall rear her form to stately height,
Her virgin bosom swell;
Such thoughts to Lucy I will give
While she and I together live
Here in this happy dell."

Thus Nature spake — The work was done —
How soon my Lucy's race was run !
She died, and left to me
This heath, this calm, and quiet scene;   40
The memory of what has been,
And never more will be.

"A SLUMBER DID MY SPIRIT SEAL"

1798. 1800

Written in Germany.

A SLUMBER did my spirit seal;
  I had no human fears:
She seemed a thing that could not feel
  The touch of earthly years.

No motion has she now, no force;
  She neither hears nor sees;
Rolled round in earth's diurnal course,
  With rocks, and stones, and trees.

A POET'S EPITAPH

1798(?). 1800

ART thou a Statist in the van
Of public conflicts trained and bred ?
— First learn to love one living man;
Then may'st thou think upon the dead.

A Lawyer art thou ? — draw not nigh !
Go, carry to some fitter place
The keenness of that practised eye,
The hardness of that sallow face.

Art thou a Man of purple cheer ?
A rosy Man, right plump to see ?   10
Approach; yet, Doctor, not too near,
This grave no cushion is for thee.

Or art thou one of gallant pride,
A Soldier and no man of chaff ?
Welcome ! — but lay thy sword aside,
And lean upon a peasant's staff.

Physician art thou ? one, all eyes,
Philosopher ! a fingering slave,
One that would peep and botanise
Upon his mother's grave ?   20

Wrapt closely in thy sensual fleece,
O turn aside, — and take, I pray,
That he below may rest in peace,
Thy ever-dwindling soul, away !

A Moralist perchance appears;
Led, Heaven knows how ! to this poor sod:
And he has neither eyes nor ears;
Himself his world, and his own God;

One to whose smooth-rubbed soul can
            cling
Nor form, nor feeling, great or small;   30
A reasoning, self-sufficing thing,
An intellectual All-in-all !

Shut close the door; press down the latch;
Sleep in thy intellectual crust;
Nor lose ten tickings of thy watch
Near this unprofitable dust.

But who is He, with modest looks,
And clad in homely russet brown ?
He murmurs near the running brooks
A music sweeter than their own.   40

He is retired as noontide dew,
Or fountain in a noon-day grove;
And you must love him, ere to you
He will seem worthy of your love.

The outward shows of sky and earth,
Of hill and valley, he has viewed;
And impulses of deeper birth
Have come to him in solitude.

In common things that round us lie
Some random truths he can impart, —   50
The harvest of a quiet eye
That broods and sleeps on his own heart.

But he is weak; both Man and Boy,
Hath been an idler in the land;
Contented if he might enjoy
The things which others understand.

— Come hither in thy hour of strength:
Come, weak as is a breaking wave !
Here stretch thy body at full length;
Or build thy house upon this grave.   60

ADDRESS TO THE SCHOLARS OF THE VILLAGE SCHOOL OF ——

1798(?). 1842

Composed at Goslar, in Germany.

I COME, ye little noisy Crew,
Not long your pastime to prevent;
I heard the blessing which to you
Our common Friend and Father sent.
I kissed his cheek before he died;
And when his breath was fled,
I raised, while kneeling by his side,
His hand: — it dropped like lead.
Your hands, dear Little-ones, do all
That can be done, will never fall   10
Like his till they are dead.
By night or day blow foul or fair,
Ne'er will the best of all your train
Play with the locks of his white hair,
Or stand between his knees again.
   Here did he sit confined for hours;
But he could see the woods and plains,
Could hear the wind and mark the showers
Come streaming down the streaming panes.
Now stretched beneath his grass - green
            mound   20
He rests a prisoner of the ground.
He loved the breathing air,
He loved the sun, but if it rise
Or set, to him where now he lies,
Brings not a moment's care.
Alas ! what idle words; but take
The Dirge which for our Master's sake
And yours, love prompted me to make.
The rhymes so homely in attire
With learned ears may ill agree,   30
But chanted by your Orphan Quire
Will make a touching melody.

DIRGE

Mourn, Shepherd, near thy old grey stone;
Thou Angler, by the silent flood;
And mourn when thou art all alone,
Thou Woodman, in the distant wood !

Thou one blind Sailor, rich in joy
Though blind, thy tunes in sadness hum;
And mourn, thou poor half-witted Boy !
Born deaf, and living deaf and dumb.   40

Thou drooping sick Man, bless the Guide
Who checked or turned thy headstrong
            youth,

As he before had sanctified
Thy infancy with heavenly truth.

Ye Striplings, light of heart and gay,
Bold settlers on some foreign shore,
Give, when your thoughts are turned this way,
A sigh to him whom we deplore.

For us who here in funeral strain
With one accord our voices raise,   50
Let sorrow overcharged with pain
Be lost in thankfulness and praise.

And when our hearts shall feel a sting
From ill we meet or good we miss,
May touches of his memory bring
Fond healing, like a mother's kiss.

BY THE SIDE OF THE GRAVE SOME YEARS
AFTER

Long time his pulse hath ceased to beat,
But benefits, his gift, we trace —
Expressed in every eye we meet
Round this dear Vale, his native place.   60

To stately Hall and Cottage rude
Flowed from his life what still they hold,
Light pleasures, every day, renewed;
And blessings half a century old.

Oh true of heart, of spirit gay,
Thy faults, where not already gone
From memory, prolong their stay
For charity's sweet sake alone.

Such solace find we for our loss;
And what beyond this thought we crave   70
Comes in the promise from the Cross,
Shining upon thy happy grave.

MATTHEW
1798(?). 1800

In the School of —— is a tablet, on which
are inscribed, in gilt letters, the Names of the
several persons who have been Schoolmasters
there since the foundation of the School, with
the time at which they entered upon and quitted
their office. Opposite to one of those names the
Author wrote the following lines.

Such a Tablet as is here spoken of continued
to be preserved in Hawkshead School, though
the inscriptions were not brought down to our
time. This and other poems connected with
Matthew would not gain by a literal detail of

facts. Like the Wanderer in "The Excursion,"
this Schoolmaster was made up of several both
of his class and men of other occupations. I do
not ask pardon for what there is of untruth in
such verses, considered strictly as matters of
fact. It is enough if, being true and consistent
in spirit, they move and teach in a manner not
unworthy of a Poet's calling.

If Nature, for a favourite child,
In thee hath tempered so her clay,
That every hour thy heart runs wild,
Yet never once doth go astray,

Read o'er these lines; and then review
This tablet, that thus humbly rears
In such diversity of hue
Its history of two hundred years.

— When through this little wreck of fame,
Cipher and syllable ! thine eye   10
Has travelled down to Matthew's name,
Pause with no common sympathy.

And, if a sleeping tear should wake,
Then be it neither checked nor stayed:
For Matthew a request I make
Which for himself he had not made.

Poor Matthew, all his frolics o'er,
Is silent as a standing pool;
Far from the chimney's merry roar,
And murmur of the village school.   20

The sighs which Matthew heaved were sighs
Of one tired out with fun and madness;
The tears which came to Matthew's eyes
Were tears of light, the dew of gladness.

Yet, sometimes, when the secret cup
Of still and serious thought went round,
It seemed as if he drank it up —
He felt with spirit so profound.

— Thou soul of God's best earthly mould !
Thou happy Soul ! and can it be   30
That these two words of glittering gold
Are all that must remain of thee ?

THE TWO APRIL MORNINGS
1798(?). 1800

We walked along, while bright and red
Uprose the morning sun;
And Matthew stopped, he looked, and said,
" The will of God be done ! "

A village schoolmaster was he,
With hair of glittering grey;
As blithe a man as you could see
On a spring holiday.

And on that morning, through the grass,
And by the steaming rills,   10
We travelled merrily, to pass
A day among the hills.

" Our work," said I, " was well begun,
Then, from thy breast what thought,
Beneath so beautiful a sun,
So sad a sigh has brought ? "

A second time did Matthew stop;
And fixing still his eye
Upon the eastern mountain-top,
To me he made reply: 20

" Yon cloud with that long purple cleft
Brings fresh into my mind
A day like this which I have left
Full thirty years behind.

" And just above yon slope of corn
Such colours, and no other,
Were in the sky, that April morn,
Of this the very brother.

" With rod and line I sued the sport
Which that sweet season gave,   30
And, to the church - yard come, stopped
        short
Beside my daughter's grave.

" Nine summers had she scarcely seen,
The pride of all the vale;
And then she sang; — she would have been
A very nightingale.

" Six feet in earth my Emma lay;
And yet I loved her more,
For so it seemed, than till that day
I e'er had loved before.   40

" And, turning from her grave, I met,
Beside the church-yard yew,
A blooming Girl, whose hair was wet
With points of morning dew.

" A basket on her head she bare;
Her brow was smooth and white:
To see a child so very fair,
It was a pure delight !

" No fountain from its rocky cave
E'er tripped with foot so free;   50
She seemed as happy as a wave
That dances on the sea.

" There came from me a sigh of pain
Which I could ill confine;
I looked at her, and looked again:
And did not wish her mine ! "

Matthew is in his grave, yet now,
Methinks, I see him stand,
As at that moment, with a bough
Of wilding in his hand.   60

THE FOUNTAIN

A CONVERSATION

1798(?). 1800

WE talked with open heart, and tongue
Affectionate and true,
A pair of friends, though I was young,
And Matthew seventy-two.

We lay beneath a spreading oak,
Beside a mossy seat;
And from the turf a fountain broke,
And gurgled at our feet.

" Now, Matthew ! " said I, " let us match
This water's pleasant tune   10
With some old border-song, or catch
That suits a summer's noon;

" Or of the church-clock and the chimes
Sing here beneath the shade,
That half-mad thing of witty rhymes
Which you last April made ! "

In silence Matthew lay, and eyed
The spring beneath the tree;
And thus the dear old Man replied,
The grey-haired man of glee: 20

" No check, no stay, this Streamlet fears;
How merrily it goes !
'T will murmur on a thousand years,
And flow as now it flows.

" And here, on this delightful day,
I cannot choose but think
How oft, a vigorous man, I lay
Beside this fountain's brink.

" My eyes are dim with childish tears,
My heart is idly stirred,   30
For the same sound is in my ears
Which in those days I heard.

" Thus fares it still in our decay:
And yet the wiser mind
Mourns less for what age takes away
Than what it leaves behind.

" The blackbird amid leafy trees,
The lark above the hill,
Let loose their carols when they please,
Are quiet when they will.   40

" With Nature never do *they* wage
A foolish strife; they see
A happy youth, and their old age
Is beautiful and free:

" But we are pressed by heavy laws;
And often, glad no more,
We wear a face of joy, because
We have been glad of yore.

" If there be one who need bemoan
His kindred laid in earth,   50
The household hearts that were his own;
It is the man of mirth.

" My days, my Friend, are almost gone,
My life has been approved,
And many love me; but by none
Am I enough beloved."

" Now both himself and me he wrongs,
The man who thus complains;
I live and sing my idle songs
Upon these happy plains;   60

" And, Matthew, for thy children dead
I 'll be a son to thee ! "
At this he grasped my hand, and said,
" Alas ! that cannot be."

We rose up from the fountain-side;
And down the smooth descent
Of the green sheep-track did we glide;
And through the wood we went;

And, ere we came to Leonard's rock,
He sang those witty rhymes   70
About the crazy old church-clock,
And the bewildered chimes.

TO A SEXTON

1798(?). 1800
Written in Germany.

LET thy wheel-barrow alone —
Wherefore, Sexton, piling still
In thy bone-house bone on bone?
'T is already like a hill
In a field of battle made,
Where three thousand skulls are laid;
These died in peace each with the other, —
Father, sister, friend, and brother.

Mark the spot to which I point !
From this platform, eight feet square,   10
Take not even a finger-joint:
Andrew's whole fire-side is there.
Here, alone, before thine eyes,
Simon's sickly daughter lies,
From weakness now, and pain defended,
Whom he twenty winters tended.

Look but at the gardener's pride —
How he glories, when he sees
Roses, lilies, side by side,
Violets in families !   20
By the heart of Man, his tears,
By his hopes and by his fears,
Thou, too heedless, art the Warden
Of a far superior garden.

Thus then, each to other dear,
Let them all in quiet lie,
Andrew there, and Susan here,
Neighbours in mortality.
And, should I live through sun and rain
Seven widowed years without my Jane,   30
O Sexton, do not then remove her,
Let one grave hold the Loved and Lover !

THE DANISH BOY

A FRAGMENT
1798(?). 1800

Written in Germany. It was entirely a fancy;
but intended as a prelude to a ballad poem
never written.

I

BETWEEN two sister moorland rills
There is a spot that seems to lie
Sacred to flowerets of the hills,
And sacred to the sky.

And in this smooth and open dell
There is a tempest-stricken tree;
A corner-stone by lightning cut,
The last stone of a lonely hut;
And in this dell you see
A thing no storm can e'er destroy,   10
The shadow of a Danish Boy.

II

In clouds above, the lark is heard,
But drops not here to earth for rest;
Within this lonesome nook the bird
Did never build her nest.
No beast, no bird hath here his home;
Bees, wafted on the breezy air,
Pass high above those fragrant bells
To other flowers: — to other dells
Their burthens do they bear;   20
The Danish Boy walks here alone:
The lovely dell is all his own.

III

A Spirit of noon-day is he;
Yet seems a form of flesh and blood;
Nor piping shepherd shall he be,
Nor herd-boy of the wood.
A regal vest of fur he wears,
In colour like a raven's wing;
It fears not rain, nor wind, nor dew;
But in the storm 't is fresh and blue   30
As budding pines in spring;
His helmet has a vernal grace,
Fresh as the bloom upon his face.

IV

A harp is from his shoulder slung;
Resting the harp upon his knee,
To words of a forgotten tongue
He suits its melody.
Of flocks upon the neighbouring hill
He is the darling and the joy;
And often, when no cause appears,   40
The mountain-ponies prick their ears,
— They hear the Danish Boy,
While in the dell he sings alone
Beside the tree and corner-stone.

V

There sits he; in his face you spy
No trace of a ferocious air,
Nor ever was a cloudless sky
So steady or so fair.
The lovely Danish Boy is blest
And happy in his flowery cove: 50

From bloody deeds his thoughts are far ;
And yet he warbles songs of war,
That seem like songs of love,
For calm and gentle is his mien;
Like a dead Boy he is serene.

LUCY GRAY

OR, SOLITUDE

1798(?). 1800

Written at Goslar in Germany. It was founded on a circumstance told me by my Sister, of a little girl who, not far from Halifax in Yorkshire, was bewildered in a snow-storm. Her footsteps were traced by her parents to the middle of the lock of a canal, and no other vestige of her, backward or forward, could be traced. The body however was found in the canal. The way in which the incident was treated and the spiritualising of the character might furnish hints for contrasting the imaginative influences which I have endeavoured to throw over common life with Crabbe's matter of fact style of treating subjects of the same kind. This is not spoken to his disparagement, far from it, but to direct the attention of thoughtful readers, into whose hands these notes may fall, to a comparison that may both enlarge the circle of their sensibilities, and tend to produce in them a catholic judgment.

Oft I had heard of Lucy Gray:
And, when I crossed the wild,
I chanced to see at break of day
The solitary child.

No mate, no comrade Lucy knew;
She dwelt on a wide moor,
— The sweetest thing that ever grew
Beside a human door !

You yet may spy the fawn at play,
The hare upon the green;   10
But the sweet face of Lucy Gray
Will never more be seen.

" To-night will be a stormy night —
You to the town must go;
And take a lantern, Child, to light
Your mother through the snow."

" That, Father ! will I gladly do:
'T is scarcely afternoon —
The minster-clock has just struck two,
And yonder is the moon ! "   20

At this the Father raised his hook,
And snapped a faggot-band;
He plied his work; — and Lucy took
The lantern in her hand.

Not blither is the mountain roe:
With many a wanton stroke
Her feet disperse the powdery snow,
That rises up like smoke.

The storm came on before its time:
She wandered up and down;   30
And many a hill did Lucy climb:
But never reached the town.

The wretched parents all that night
Went shouting far and wide;
But there was neither sound nor sight
To serve them for a guide.

At day-break on a hill they stood
That overlooked the moor;
And thence they saw the bridge of wood,
A furlong from their door.   40

They wept — and, turning homeward, cried,
" In heaven we all shall meet;"
— When in the snow the mother spied
The print of Lucy's feet.

Then downwards from the steep hill's
        edge
They tracked the footmarks small;
And through the broken hawthorn hedge,
And by the long stone-wall;

And then an open field they crossed:
The marks were still the same;   50
They tracked them on, nor ever lost;
And to the bridge they came.

They followed from the snowy bank
Those footmarks, one by one,
Into the middle of the plank;
And further there were none !

— Yet some maintain that to this day
She is a living child;
That you may see sweet Lucy Gray
Upon the lonesome wild.   60

O'er rough and smooth she trips along,
And never looks behind;
And sings a solitary song
That whistles in the wind

RUTH
1798(?). 1800

Written in Germany. Suggested by an ac-
count I had of a wanderer in Somersetshire.

WHEN Ruth was left half desolate,
Her Father took another Mate;
And Ruth, not seven years old,
A slighted child, at her own will
Went wandering over dale and hill,
In thoughtless freedom, bold.

And she had made a pipe of straw,
And music from that pipe could draw
Like sounds of winds and floods;
Had built a bower upon the green,   10
As if she from her birth had been
An infant of the woods.

Beneath her father's roof, alone
She seemed to live; her thoughts her own;
Herself her own delight;
Pleased with herself, nor sad, nor gay;
And, passing thus the live-long day,
She grew to woman's height.

There came a Youth from Georgia's
        shore —
A military casque he wore,   20
With splendid feathers drest;
He brought them from the Cherokees;
The feathers nodded in the breeze,
And made a gallant crest.

From Indian blood you deem him sprung:
But no ! he spake the English tongue,
And bore a soldier's name;
And, when America was free
From battle and from jeopardy,
He 'cross the ocean came.   30

With hues of genius on his cheek
In finest tones the Youth could speak:
— While he was yet a boy,
The moon, the glory of the sun,
And streams that murmur as they run,
Had been his dearest joy.

He was a lovely youth ! I guess
The panther in the wilderness
Was not so fair as he;
And, when he chose to sport and play,   40
No dolphin ever was so gay
Upon the tropic sea.

Among the Indians he had fought,
And with him many tales he brought
Of pleasure and of fear;
Such tales as told to any maid
By such a Youth, in the green shade,
Were perilous to hear.

He told of girls — a happy rout!
Who quit their fold with dance and shout,
Their pleasant Indian town,   51
To gather strawberries all day long;
Returning with a choral song
When daylight is gone down.

He spake of plants that hourly change
Their blossoms, through a boundless range
Of intermingling hues;
With budding, fading, faded flowers
They stand the wonder of the bowers
From morn to evening dews.   60

He told of the magnolia, spread
High as a cloud, high over head!
The cypress and her spire;
— Of flowers that with one scarlet gleam
Cover a hundred leagues, and seem
To set the hills on fire.

The Youth of green savannahs spake,
And many an endless, endless lake,
With all its fairy crowds
Of islands, that together lie   70
As quietly as spots of sky
Among the evening clouds.

"How pleasant," then he said, "it were
A fisher or a hunter there,
In sunshine or in shade
To wander with an easy mind;
And build a household fire, and find
A home in every glade!

"What days and what bright years! Ah me!
Our life were life indeed, with thee   80
So passed in quiet bliss,
And all the while," said he, "to know
That we were in a world of woe,
On such an earth as this!"

And then he sometimes interwove
Fond thoughts about a father's love;
"For there," said he, "are spun
Around the heart such tender ties,
That our own children to our eyes
Are dearer than the sun.   90

"Sweet Ruth! and could you go with me
My helpmate in the woods to be,
Our shed at night to rear;
Or run, my own adopted bride,
A sylvan huntress at my side,
And drive the flying deer!

"Belovèd Ruth!"—No more he said,
The wakeful Ruth at midnight shed
A solitary tear:
She thought again — and did agree   100
With him to sail across the sea,
And drive the flying deer.

"And now, as fitting is and right,
We in the church our faith will plight,
A husband and a wife."
Even so they did; and I may say
That to sweet Ruth that happy day
Was more than human life.

Through dream and vision did she sink,
Delighted all the while to think   110
That on those lonesome floods,
And green savannahs, she should share
His board with lawful joy, and bear
His name in the wild woods.

But, as you have before been told,
This Stripling, sportive, gay, and bold,
And, with his dancing crest,
So beautiful, through savage lands
Had roamed about, with vagrant bands
Of Indians in the West.   120

The wind, the tempest roaring high,
The tumult of a tropic sky,
Might well be dangerous food
For him, a Youth to whom was given
So much of earth — so much of heaven,
And such impetuous blood.

Whatever in those climes he found
Irregular in sight or sound
Did to his mind impart
A kindred impulse, seemed allied   130
To his own powers, and justified
The workings of his heart.

Nor less, to feed voluptuous thought,
The beauteous forms of nature wrought,
Fair trees and gorgeous flowers;
The breezes their own languor lent;
The stars had feelings, which they sent
Into those favoured bowers.

Yet, in his worst pursuits, I ween
That sometimes there did intervene   140
Pure hopes of high intent:
For passions linked to forms so fair
And stately, needs must have their share
Of noble sentiment.

But ill he lived, much evil saw,
With men to whom no better law
Nor better life was known;
Deliberately, and undeceived,
Those wild men's vices he received,
And gave them back his own.   150

His genius and his moral frame
Were thus impaired, and he became
The slave of low desires:
A Man who without self-control
Would seek what the degraded soul
Unworthily admires.

And yet he with no feigned delight
Had wooed the Maiden, day and night
Had loved her, night and morn:
What could he less than love a Maid   160
Whose heart with so much nature played?
So kind and so forlorn!

Sometimes, most earnestly, he said,
"O Ruth! I have been worse than dead;
False thoughts, thoughts bold and vain,
Encompassed me on every side
When I, in confidence and pride,
Had crossed the Atlantic main.

"Before me shone a glorious world —
Fresh as a banner bright, unfurled   170
To music suddenly:
I looked upon those hills and plains,
And seemed as if let loose from chains,
To live at liberty.

"No more of this; for now, by thee
Dear Ruth! more happily set free
With nobler zeal I burn;
My soul from darkness is released,
Like the whole sky when to the east
The morning doth return."   180

Full soon that better mind was gone;
No hope, no wish remained, not one, —
They stirred him now no more;
New objects did new pleasure give,
And once again he wished to live
As lawless as before.

Meanwhile, as thus with him it fared,
They for the voyage were prepared,
And went to the sea-shore,
But, when they thither came the Youth   190
Deserted his poor Bride, and Ruth
Could never find him more.

God help thee, Ruth! — Such pains she had,
That she in half a year was mad,
And in a prison housed;
And there, with many a doleful song
Made of wild words, her cup of wrong
She fearfully caroused.

Yet sometimes milder hours she knew,
Nor wanted sun, nor rain, nor dew,   200
Nor pastimes of the May;
— They all were with her in her cell;
And a clear brook with cheerful knell
Did o'er the pebbles play.

When Ruth three seasons thus had lain,
There came a respite to her pain;
She from her prison fled;
But of the Vagrant none took thought;
And where it liked her best she sought
Her shelter and her bread.   210

Among the fields she breathed again:
The master-current of her brain
Ran permanent and free;
And, coming to the Banks of Tone,
There did she rest; and dwell alone
Under the greenwood tree.

The engines of her pain, the tools
That shaped her sorrow, rocks and pools,
And airs that gently stir
The vernal leaves — she loved them still;
Nor ever taxed them with the ill   221
Which had been done to her.

A Barn her *winter* bed supplies;
But, till the warmth of summer skies
And summer days is gone,
(And all do in this tale agree)
She sleeps beneath the greenwood tree,
And other home hath none.

An innocent life, yet far astray!
And Ruth will, long before her day,   230
Be broken down and old:
Sore aches she needs must have! but less
Of mind, than body's wretchedness,
From damp, and rain, and cold.

If she is prest by want of food,
She from her dwelling in the wood
Repairs to a road-side;
And there she begs at one steep place
Where up and down with easy pace
The horsemen-travellers ride.   240

That oaten pipe of hers is mute,
Or thrown away; but with a flute
Her loneliness she cheers:
This flute, made of a hemlock stalk,
At evening in his homeward walk
The Quantock woodman hears.

I, too, have passed her on the hills
Setting her little water-mills
By spouts and fountains wild —
Such small machinery as she turned   250
Ere she had wept, ere she had mourned,
A young and happy Child !

Farewell ! and when thy days are told,
Ill-fated Ruth, in hallowed mould
Thy corpse shall buried be,
For thee a funeral bell shall ring,
And all the congregation sing
A Christian psalm for thee.

WRITTEN IN GERMANY

ON ONE OF THE COLDEST DAYS OF THE CENTURY

1798(?). 1800

A bitter winter it was when these verses were composed by the side of my Sister, in our lodgings at a draper's house in the romantic imperial town of Goslar, on the edge of the Hartz Forest. In this town the German emperors of the Franconian line were accustomed to keep their court, and it retains vestiges of ancient splendour. So severe was the cold of this winter, that when we passed out of the parlour warmed by the stove, our cheeks were struck by the air as by cold iron. I slept in a room over a passage which was not ceiled. The people of the house used to say, rather unfeelingly, that they expected I should be frozen to death some night; but, with the protection of a pelisse lined with fur, and a dog's-skin bonnet, such as was worn by the peasants, I walked daily on the ramparts, or in a sort of public ground or garden, in which was a pond. Here, I had no companion but a kingfisher, a beautiful creature, that used to glance by me. I consequently became much attached to it.

During these walks I composed "The Poet's Epitaph."

The Reader must be apprised, that the Stoves in North-Germany generally have the impression of a galloping horse upon them, this being part of the Brunswick Arms.

A PLAGUE on your languages, German and
          Norse !
Let me have the song of the kettle;
And the tongs and the poker, instead of
          that horse
That gallops away with such fury and
          force
On this dreary dull plate of black metal.

See that Fly, — a disconsolate creature !
          perhaps
A child of the field or the grove;
And, sorrow for him ! the dull treacherous
          heat
Has seduced the poor fool from his winter
          retreat,
And he creeps to the edge of my stove.   10

Alas ! how he fumbles about the domains
Which this comfortless oven environ !
He cannot find out in what track he must
          crawl,
Now back to the tiles, then in search of the
          wall,
And now on the brink of the iron.

Stock-still there he stands like a traveller
          bemazed:
The best of his skill he has tried;
His feelers, methinks, I can see him put
          forth
To the east and the west, to the south and
          the north;
But he finds neither guide-post nor guide.   20

His spindles sink under him, foot, leg, and
          thigh !
His eyesight and hearing are lost;
Between life and death his blood freezes
          and thaws;
And his two pretty pinions of blue dusky
          gauze
Are glued to his sides by the frost.

No brother, no mate has he near him —
          while I
Can draw warmth from the cheek of my
          Love;

As blest and as glad, in this desolate gloom,
As if green summer grass were the floor of
    my room,
And woodbines were hanging above.   30

Yet, God is my witness, thou small helpless
    Thing !
Thy life I would gladly sustain
Till summer come up from the south, and
    with crowds
Of thy brethren a march thou should'st
    sound through the clouds,
And back to the forests again !

"BLEAK SEASON WAS IT, TURBULENT AND BLEAK"

1800–1806(?). 1851

BLEAK season was it, turbulent and bleak,
When hitherward we journeyed, side by
    side,
Through burst of sunshine and through
    flying showers,
Paced the long vales, — how long they
    were, and yet
How fast that length of way was left be-
    hind —
Wensley's rich vale, and Sedbergh's naked
    heights.
The frosty wind, as if to make amends
For its keen breath, was aiding to our
    steps
And drove us onward like two ships at
    sea ;
Or like two birds, companions in mid-air,
Parted and reunited by the blast.
Stern was the face of Nature ; we rejoiced
In that stern countenance, for our Souls
    thence drew
A feeling of their strength.
                              The naked trees,
The icy brooks, as on we passed, appeared
To question us. ''Whence come ye? to
    what end?''

"ON NATURE'S INVITATION DO I COME"

1800–1806(?). 1851

ON Nature's invitation do I come,
By Reason sanctioned. Can the choice mis-
    lead,

That made the calmest, fairest spot of
    earth,
With all its unappropriated good,
My own ; and not mine only, for with me
Entrenched — say rather, peacefully em-
    bowered —
Under yon orchard, in yon humble cot,
A younger orphan of a home extinct,
The only daughter of my parents, dwells :
Aye, think on that, my heart, and cease to
    stir ;   10
Pause upon that, and let the breathing
    frame
No longer breathe, but all be satisfied.
Oh, if such silence be not thanks to God
For what hath been bestowed, then where,
    where then
Shall gratitude find rest ?   Mine eyes did
    ne'er
Fix on a lovely object, nor my mind
Take pleasure in the midst of happy
    thoughts
But either she, whom now I have, who now
Divides with me this loved abode, was
    there,
Or not far off. Where'er my footsteps
    turned,   20
Her voice was like a hidden bird that sang ;
The thought of her was like a flash of light,
Or an *unseen* companionship ; a breath
Or fragrance independent of the wind.
In all my goings, in the new and old
Of all my meditations, and in this
Favourite of all, in this the most of all. . . .
Embrace me then, ye hills, and close me in ;
Now in the clear and open day I feel   29
Your guardianship ; I take it to my heart ;
'T is like the solemn shelter of the night.
But I would call thee beautiful, for mild
And soft, and gay, and beautiful thou art,
Dear Valley, having in thy face a smile
Though peaceful, full of gladness. Thou
    art pleased,
Pleased with thy crags, and woody steeps,
    thy lake,
Its one green island, and its winding shores,
The multitude of little rocky hills,
Thy church, and cottages of mountain stone
Clustered like stars some few, but single
    most,   40
And lurking dimly in their shy retreats,
Or glancing at each other cheerful looks
Like separated stars with clouds between.

THE PRELUDE, OR, GROWTH OF A POET'S MIND;

AN AUTOBIOGRAPHICAL POEM;

1798–1805. 1850

ADVERTISEMENT

The following Poem was commenced in the beginning of the year 1799, and completed in the summer of 1805.

The design and occasion of the work are described by the Author in his Preface to the " Excursion," first published in 1814, where he thus speaks : —

"Several years ago, when the Author retired to his native mountains with the hope of being enabled to construct a literary work that might live, it was a reasonable thing that he should take a review of his own mind, and examine how far Nature and Education had qualified him for such an employment.

"As subsidiary to this preparation, he undertook to record, in verse, the origin and progress of his own powers, as far as he was acquainted with them.

"That work, addressed to a dear friend, most distinguished for his knowledge and genius, and to whom the Author's intellect is deeply indebted, has been long finished ; and the result of the investigation which gave rise to it, was a determination to compose a philosophical Poem, containing views of Man, Nature, and Society, and to be entitled the 'Recluse ; ' as having for its principal subject the sensations and opinions of a poet living in retirement.

"The preparatory poem is biographical, and conducts the history of the Author's mind to the point when he was emboldened to hope that his faculties were sufficiently matured for entering upon the arduous labour which he had proposed to himself ; and the two works have the same kind of relation to each other, if he may so express himself, as the Ante-chapel has to the body of a Gothic church. Continuing this allusion, he may be permitted to add, that his minor pieces, which have been long before the public, when they shall be properly arranged, will be found by the attentive reader to have such connection with the main work as may give them claim to be likened to the little cells, oratories, and sepulchral recesses, ordinarily included in those edifices."

Such was the Author's language in the year 1814.

It will thence be seen, that the present Poem was intended to be introductory to the " Recluse," and that the " Recluse," if completed, would have consisted of Three Parts. Of these, the Second Part alone : viz. the " Excursion," was finished, and given to the world by the Author.

The First Book of the First Part of the " Recluse " still remains in manuscript ; but the Third Part was only planned. The materials of which it would have been formed have, however, been incorporated, for the most part, in the Author's other Publications, written subsequently to the " Excursion."

The Friend, to whom the present Poem is addressed, was the late SAMUEL TAYLOR COLERIDGE, who was resident in Malta, for the restoration of his health, when the greater part of it was composed.

Mr. Coleridge read a considerable portion of the Poem while he was abroad ; and his feelings, on hearing it recited by the Author (after his return to his own country), are recorded in his Verses, addressed to Mr. Wordsworth, which will be found in the *Sibylline Leaves*, p. 197, ed. 1817, or *Poetical Works, by S. T. Coleridge*, vol. i. p. 206.

RYDAL MOUNT, *July 13th*, 1850.

BOOK FIRST

INTRODUCTION — CHILDHOOD AND SCHOOL-TIME

OH there is blessing in this gentle breeze,
A visitant that while it fans my cheek
Doth seem half-conscious of the joy it brings
From the green fields, and from yon azure
   sky.

Whate'er its mission, the soft breeze can
   come
To none more grateful than to me ; escaped
From the vast city, where I long had pined
A discontented sojourner : now free,
Free as a bird to settle where I will.
What dwelling shall receive me ? in what
   vale   10
Shall be my harbour ? underneath what grove

Shall I take up my home ? and what clear
          stream
Shall with its murmur lull me into rest ?
The earth is all before me. With a heart
Joyous, nor scared at its own liberty,
I look about; and should the chosen guide
Be nothing better than a wandering cloud,
I cannot miss my way. I breathe again !
Trances of thought and mountings of the
          mind
Come fast upon me: it is shaken off,   20
That burthen of my own unnatural self,
The heavy weight of many a weary day
Not mine, and such as were not made for me.
Long months of peace (if such bold word
          accord
With any promises of human life),
Long months of ease and undisturbed de-
          light
Are mine in prospect; whither shall I turn,
By road or pathway, or through trackless
          field,
Up hill or down, or shall some floating thing
Upon the river point me out my course ? 30

, Dear Liberty ! Yet what would it avail
But for a gift that consecrates the joy ?
For I, methought, while the sweet breath
          of heaven
Was blowing on my body, felt within
A correspondent breeze, that gently moved
With quickening virtue, but is now become
A tempest, a redundant energy,
Vexing its own creation. Thanks to both,
And their congenial powers, that, while they
          join
In breaking up a long-continued frost,   40
Bring with them vernal promises, the hope
Of active days urged on by flying hours, —
Days of sweet leisure, taxed with patient
          thought
Abstruse, nor wanting punctual service high,
Matins and vespers of harmonious verse !

     Thus far, O Friend ! did I, not used to
          make
A present joy the matter of a song,
Pour forth that day my soul in measured
          strains
That would not be forgotten, and are here
Recorded: to the open fields I told   50
A prophecy: poetic numbers came
Spontaneously to clothe in priestly robe
A renovated spirit singled out,
Such hope was mine, for holy services.

My own voice cheered me, and, far more,
          the mind's
Internal echo of the imperfect sound;
To both I listened, drawing from them both
A cheerful confidence in things to come.

     Content and not unwilling now to give
A respite to this passion, I paced on   60
With brisk and eager steps; and came, at
          length,
To a green shady place, where down I sate
Beneath a tree, slackening my thoughts by
          choice
And settling into gentler happiness.
'T was autumn, and a clear and placid day,
With warmth, as much as needed, from a
          sun
Two hours declined towards the west; a
          day
With silver clouds, and sunshine on the
          grass,
And in the sheltered and the sheltering grove
A perfect stillness. Many were the thoughts
Encouraged and dismissed, till choice was
          made   71
Of a known Vale, whither my feet should
          turn,
Nor rest till they had reached the very door
Of the one cottage which methought I saw.
No picture of mere memory ever looked
So fair; and while upon the fancied scene
I gazed with growing love, a higher power
Than Fancy gave assurance of some work
Of glory there forthwith to be begun,
Perhaps too there performed. Thus long I
          mused,   80
Nor e'er lost sight of what I mused upon,
Save when, amid the stately grove of oaks,
Now here, now there, an acorn, from its cup
Dislodged, through sere leaves rustled, or
          at once
To the bare earth dropped with a startling
          sound.
From that soft couch I rose not, till the sun
Had almost touched the horizon; casting
          then
A backward glance upon the curling cloud
Of city smoke, by distance ruralised;
Keen as a Truant or a Fugitive,   90
But as a Pilgrim resolute, I took,
Even with the chance equipment of that
          hour,
The road that pointed toward the chosen
          Vale.
It was a splendid evening, and my soul

Once more made trial of her strength, nor
    lacked
Æolian visitations; but the harp
Was soon defrauded, and the banded host
Of harmony dispersed in straggling sounds,
And lastly utter silence ! " Be it so;   99
Why think of anything but present good?"
So, like a home-bound labourer, I pursued
My way beneath the mellowing sun, that
    shed
Mild influence; nor left in me one wish
Again to bend the Sabbath of that time
To a servile yoke. What need of many
    words ?
A pleasant loitering journey, through three
    days
Continued, brought me to my hermitage.
I spare to tell of what ensued, the life
In common things — the endless store of
    things,
Rare, or at least so seeming, every day 110
Found all about me in one neighbourhood —
The self-congratulation, and, from morn
To night, unbroken cheerfulness serene.
But speedily an earnest longing rose
To brace myself to some determined aim,
Reading or thinking; either to lay up
New stores, or rescue from decay the old
By timely interference: and therewith
Came hopes still higher, that with outward
    life
I might endue some airy phantasies 120
That had been floating loose about for years,
And to such beings temperately deal forth
The many feelings that oppressed my heart.
That hope hath been discouraged; welcome
    light
Dawns from the east, but dawns to disap-
    pear
And mock me with a sky that ripens not
Into a steady morning: if my mind,
Remembering the bold promise of the past,
Would gladly grapple with some noble
    theme,
Vain is her wish; where'er she turns she
    finds 130
Impediments from day to day renewed.

And now it would content me to yield up
Those lofty hopes awhile, for present gifts
Of humbler industry. But, oh, dear Friend !
The Poet, gentle creature as he is,
Hath, like the Lover, his unruly times;
His fits when he is neither sick nor well,
Though no distress be near him but his own

Unmanageable thoughts: his mind, best
    pleased 139
While she as duteous as the mother dove
Sits brooding, lives not always to that end,
But like the innocent bird, hath goadings on
That drive her as in trouble through the
    groves;
With me is now such passion, to be blamed
No otherwise than as it lasts too long.

When, as becomes a man who would pre-
    pare
For such an arduous work, I through myself
Make rigorous inquisition, the report
Is often cheering; for I neither seem
To lack that first great gift, the vital soul,
Nor general Truths, which are themselves
    a sort 151
Of Elements and Agents, Under-powers,
Subordinate helpers of the living mind:
Nor am I naked of external things,
Forms, images, nor numerous other aids
Of less regard, though won perhaps with toil
And needful to build up a Poet's praise.
Time, place, and manners do I seek, and
    these
Are found in plenteous store, but nowhere
    such 159
As may be singled out with steady choice;
No little band of yet remembered names
Whom I, in perfect confidence, might hope
To summon back from lonesome banish-
    ment,
And make them dwellers in the hearts of
    men
Now living, or to live in future years.
Sometimes the ambitious Power of choice,
    mistaking
Proud spring-tide swellings for a regular
    sea,
Will settle on some British theme, some old
Romantic tale by Milton left unsung;
More often turning to some gentle place
Within the groves of Chivalry, I pipe 171
To shepherd swains, or seated harp in hand,
Amid reposing knights by a river side
Or fountain, listen to the grave reports
Of dire enchantments faced and overcome
By the strong mind, and tales of warlike
    feats,
Where spear encountered spear, and sword
    with sword
Fought, as if conscious of the blazonry
That the shield bore, so glorious was the
    strife;

Whence inspiration for a song that winds
Through ever changing scenes of votive
    quest   181
Wrongs to redress, harmonious tribute paid
To patient courage and unblemished truth,
To firm devotion, zeal unquenchable,
And Christian meekness hallowing faithful
    loves.
Sometimes, more sternly moved, I would
    relate
How vanquished Mithridates northward
    passed,
And, hidden in the cloud of years, became
Odin, the Father of a race by whom
Perished the Roman Empire : how the
    friends   190
And followers of Sertorius, out of Spain
Flying, found shelter in the Fortunate Isles,
And left their usages, their arts and laws,
To disappear by a slow gradual death,
To dwindle and to perish one by one,
Starved in those narrow bounds: but not the
    soul
Of Liberty, which fifteen hundred years
Survived, and, when the European came
With skill and power that might not be
    withstood,
Did, like a pestilence, maintain its hold   200
And wasted down by glorious death that
    race
Of natural heroes: or I would record
How, in tyrannic times, some high-souled
    man,
Unnamed among the chronicles of kings,
Suffered in silence for Truth's sake: or tell,
How that one Frenchman, through contin-
    ued force
Of meditation on the inhuman deeds
Of those who conquered first the Indian
    Isles,
Went single in his ministry across
The Ocean; not to comfort the oppressed,
But, like a thirsty wind, to roam about   211
Withering the Oppressor: how Gustavus
    sought
Help at his need in Dalecarlia's mines:
How Wallace fought for Scotland; left the
    name
Of Wallace to be found, like a wild flower,
All over his dear Country; left the deeds
Of Wallace, like a family of Ghosts,
To people the steep rocks and river banks,
Her natural sanctuaries, with a local soul
Of independence and stern liberty.   220
Sometimes it suits me better to invent

A tale from my own heart, more near
    akin
To my own passions and habitual thoughts;
Some variegated story, in the main
Lofty, but the unsubstantial structure melts
Before the very sun that brightens it,
Mist into air dissolving ! Then a wish,
My best and favourite aspiration, mounts
With yearning toward some philosophic
    song
Of Truth that cherishes our daily life; 230
With meditations passionate from deep
Recesses in man's heart, immortal verse
Thoughtfully fitted to the Orphean lyre;
But from this awful burthen I full soon
Take refuge and beguile myself with trust
That mellower years will bring a riper
    mind
And clearer insight. Thus my days are past
In contradiction; with no skill to part
Vague longing, haply bred by want of
    power,
From paramount impulse not to be with-
    stood,   240
A timorous capacity from prudence,
From circumspection, infinite delay.
Humility and modest awe themselves
Betray me, serving often for a cloak
To a more subtle selfishness; that now
Locks every function up in blank reserve,
Now dupes me, trusting to an anxious eye
That with intrusive restlessness beats off
Simplicity and self-presented truth.
Ah ! better far than this, to stray about
Voluptuously through fields and rural
    walks,   251
And ask no record of the hours, resigned
To vacant musing, unreproved neglect
Of all things, and deliberate holiday.
Far better never to have heard the name
Of zeal and just ambition, than to live
Baffled and plagued by a mind that every
    hour
Turns recreant to her task; takes heart
    again,
Then feels immediately some hollow
    thought
Hang like an interdict upon her hopes. 260
This is my lot; for either still I find
Some imperfection in the chosen theme,
Or see of absolute accomplishment
Much wanting, so much wanting, in myself,
That I recoil and droop, and seek repose
In listlessness from vain perplexity,
Unprofitably travelling toward the grave,

Like a false steward who hath much re-
ceived
And renders nothing back.
                    Was it for this
That one, the fairest of all rivers, loved   270
To blend his murmurs with my nurse's song,
And, from his alder shades and rocky falls,
And from his fords and shallows, sent a
voice
That flowed along my dreams ? For this,
didst thou,
O Derwent ! winding among grassy holms
Where I was looking on, a babe in arms,
Make ceaseless music that composed my
thoughts
To more than infant softness, giving me
Amid the fretful dwellings of mankind
A foretaste, a dim earnest, of the calm   280
That Nature breathes among the hills and
groves.

When he had left the mountains and re-
ceived
On his smooth breast the shadow of those
towers
That yet survive, a shattered monument
Of feudal sway, the bright blue river passed
Along the margin of our terrace walk;
A tempting playmate whom we dearly
loved.
Oh, many a time have I, a five years' child,
In a small mill-race severed from his
stream,
Made one long bathing of a summer's
day;   290
Basked in the sun, and plunged and basked
again
Alternate, all a summer's day, or scoured
The sandy fields, leaping through flowery
groves
Of yellow ragwort; or, when rock and hill,
The woods, and distant Skiddaw's lofty
height,
Were bronzed with deepest radiance, stood
alone
Beneath the sky, as if I had been born
On Indian plains, and from my mother's hut
Had run abroad in wantonness, to sport
A naked savage, in the thunder shower.   300

Fair seed-time had my soul, and I grew
up
Fostered alike by beauty and by fear:
Much favoured in my birth-place, and no
less

In that beloved Vale to which erelong
We were transplanted — there were we
let loose
For sports of wider range. Ere I had told
Ten birth-days, when among the mountain
slopes
Frost, and the breath of frosty wind, had
snapped
The last autumnal crocus, 't was my joy
With store of springes o'er my shoulder
hung   310
To range the open heights where wood-
cocks run
Along the smooth green turf. Through
half the night,
Scudding away from snare to snare, I plied
That anxious visitation; — moon and stars
Were shining o'er my head. I was alone,
And seemed to be a trouble to the peace
That dwelt among them. Sometimes it
befell
In these night wanderings, that a strong
desire
O'erpowered my better reason, and the bird
Which was the captive of another's toil   320
Became my prey; and when the deed was
done
I heard among the solitary hills
Low breathings coming after me, and
sounds
Of undistinguishable motion, steps
Almost as silent as the turf they trod.

Nor less when spring had warmed the
cultured Vale,
Roved we as plunderers where the mother-
bird
Had in high places built her lodge; though
mean
Our object and inglorious, yet the end
Was not ignoble. Oh ! when I have
hung   330
Above the raven's nest, by knots of grass
And half-inch fissures in the slippery rock
But ill sustained, and almost (so it seemed)
Suspended by the blast that blew amain,
Shouldering the naked crag, oh, at that
time
While on the perilous ridge I hung alone,
With what strange utterance did the loud
dry wind
Blow through my ear ! the sky seemed not
a sky
Of earth — and with what motion moved
the clouds !

Dust as we are, the immortal spirit
grows   340
Like harmony in music; there is a dark
Inscrutable workmanship that reconciles
Discordant elements, makes them cling to-
gether
In one society. How strange, that all
The terrors, pains, and early miseries,
Regrets, vexations, lassitudes interfused
Within my mind, should e'er have borne a
part,
And that a needful part, in making up
The calm existence that is mine when I
Am worthy of myself ! Praise to the end !
Thanks to the means which Nature deigned
to employ;   351
Whether her fearless visitings, or those
That came with soft alarm, like hurtless
light
Opening the peaceful clouds; or she would
use
Severer interventions, ministry
More palpable, as best might suit her aim.

One summer evening (led by her) I
found
A little boat tied to a willow tree
Within a rocky cave, its usual home.
Straight I unloosed her chain, and step-
ping in   360
Pushed from the shore. It was an act of
stealth
And troubled pleasure, nor without the
voice
Of mountain-echoes did my boat move on;
Leaving behind her still, on either side,
Small circles glittering idly in the moon,
Until they melted all into one track
Of sparkling light. But now, like one who
rows,
Proud of his skill, to reach a chosen point
With an unswerving line, I fixed my view
Upon the summit of a craggy ridge,   370
The horizon's utmost boundary; for above
Was nothing but the stars and the grey
sky.
She was an elfin pinnace; lustily
I dipped my oars into the silent lake,
And, as I rose upon the stroke, my boat
Went heaving through the water like a
swan;
When, from behind that craggy steep till
then
The horizon's bound, a huge peak, black
and huge,

As if with voluntary power instinct
Upreared its head. I struck and struck
again,   380
And growing still in stature the grim shape
Towered up between me and the stars, and
still,
For so it seemed, with purpose of its own
And measured motion like a living thing,
Strode after me. With trembling oars I
turned,
And through the silent water stole my way
Back to the covert of the willow tree;
There in her mooring-place I left my
bark, —
And through the meadows homeward went,
in grave
And serious mood; but after I had seen 390
That spectacle, for many days, my brain
Worked with a dim and undetermined
sense
Of unknown modes of being; o'er my
thoughts
There hung a darkness, call it solitude
Or blank desertion. No familiar shapes
Remained, no pleasant images of trees,
Of sea or sky, no colours of green fields;
But huge and mighty forms, that do not
live
Like living men, moved slowly through the
mind
By day, and were a trouble to my dreams.

Wisdom and Spirit of the universe !   401
Thou Soul that art the eternity of thought,
That givest to forms and images a breath
And everlasting motion, not in vain
By day or star-light thus from my first
dawn
Of childhood didst thou intertwine for me
The passions that build up our human soul;
Not with the mean and vulgar works of
man,
But with high objects, with enduring
things —
With life and nature, purifying thus   410
The elements of feeling and of thought,
And sanctifying, by such discipline,
Both pain and fear, until we recognise
A grandeur in the beatings of the heart.
Nor was this fellowship vouchsafed to me
With stinted kindness. In November days,
When vapours rolling down the valley
made
A lonely scene more lonesome, among
woods,

At noon and 'mid the calm of summer
    nights,
When, by the margin of the trembling
    lake,   420
Beneath the gloomy hills homeward I
    went
In solitude, such intercourse was mine;
Mine was it in the fields both day and
    night,
And by the waters, all the summer long.

    And in the frosty season, when the sun
Was set, and visible for many a mile
The cottage windows blazed through twi-
    light gloom,
I heeded not their summons: happy time
It was indeed for all of us — for me
It was a time of rapture! Clear and
    loud   430
The village clock tolled six, — I wheeled
    about,
Proud and exulting like an untired horse
That cares not for his home. All shod
    with steel,
We hissed along the polished ice in games
Confederate, imitative of the chase
And woodland pleasures, — the resounding
    horn,
The pack loud chiming, and the hunted
    hare.
So through the darkness and the cold we
    flew,
And not a voice was idle; with the din
Smitten, the precipices rang aloud;   440
The leafless trees and every icy crag
Tinkled like iron; while far distant hills
Into the tumult sent an alien sound
Of melancholy not unnoticed, while the stars
Eastward were sparkling clear, and in the
    west
The orange sky of evening died away.
Not seldom from the uproar I retired
Into a silent bay, or sportively
Glanced sideway, leaving the tumultuous
    throng,
To cut across the reflex of a star   450
That fled, and, flying still before me,
    gleamed
Upon the glassy plain; and oftentimes,
When we had given our bodies to the wind,
And all the shadowy banks on either side
Came sweeping through the darkness, spin-
    ning still
The rapid line of motion, then at once
Have I, reclining back upon my heels,

Stopped short; yet still the solitary cliffs
Wheeled by me — even as if the earth had
    rolled
With visible motion her diurnal round!   460
Behind me did they stretch in solemn train,
Feebler and feebler, and I stood and
    watched
Till all was tranquil as a dreamless sleep.

    Ye Presences of Nature in the sky
And on the earth! Ye Visions of the hills!
And Souls of lonely places! can I think
A vulgar hope was yours when ye employed
Such ministry, when ye through many a
    year
Haunting me thus among my boyish sports,
On caves and trees, upon the woods and
    hills,   470
Impressed upon all forms the characters
Of danger or desire; and thus did make
The surface of the universal earth
With triumph and delight, with hope and
    fear,
Work like a sea?
                Not uselessly employed,
Might I pursue this theme through every
    change
Of exercise and play, to which the year
Did summon us in his delightful round.

    We were a noisy crew; the sun in heaven
Beheld not vales more beautiful than ours;
Nor saw a band in happiness and joy   481
Richer, or worthier of the ground they trod.
I could record with no reluctant voice
The woods of autumn, and their hazel
    bowers
With milk-white clusters hung; the rod and
    line,
True symbol of hope's foolishness, whose
    strong
And unreproved enchantment led us on
By rocks and pools shut out from every
    star,
All the green summer, to forlorn cascades
Among the windings hid of mountain
    brooks.   490
— Unfading recollections! at this hour
The heart is almost mine with which I felt,
From some hill-top on sunny afternoons,
The paper kite high among fleecy clouds
Pull at her rein like an impetuous courser;
Or, from the meadows sent on gusty days,
Beheld her breast the wind, then suddenly
Dashed headlong, and rejected by the storm.

Ye lowly cottages wherein we dwelt,
A ministration of your own was yours; 500
Can I forget you, being as you were
So beautiful among the pleasant fields
In which ye stood ? or can I here forget
The plain and seemly countenance with
    which
Ye dealt out your plain comforts ? Yet
    had ye
Delights and exultations of your own.
Eager and never weary we pursued
Our home-amusements by the warm peat-
    fire
At evening, when with pencil, and smooth
    slate
In square divisions parcelled out and all
With crosses and with cyphers scribbled
    o'er, 511
We schemed and puzzled, head opposed to
    head
In strife too humble to be named in verse:
Or round the naked table, snow-white deal,
Cherry or maple, sate in close array,
And to the combat, Loo or Whist, led on
A thick-ribbed army; not, as in the world,
Neglected and ungratefully thrown by
Even for the very service they had wrought,
But husbanded through many a long cam-
    paign. 520
Uncouth assemblage was it, where no few
Had changed their functions: some, ple-
    beian cards
Which Fate, beyond the promise of their
    birth,
Had dignified, and called to represent
The persons of departed potentates.
Oh, with what echoes on the board they fell !
Ironic diamonds, — clubs, hearts, diamonds,
    spades,
A congregation piteously akin !
Cheap matter offered they to boyish wit,
Those sooty knaves, precipitated down 530
With scoffs and taunts, like Vulcan out of
    heaven:
The paramount ace, a moon in her eclipse,
Queens gleaming through their splendour's
    last decay,
And monarchs surly at the wrongs sus-
    tained
By royal visages. Meanwhile abroad
Incessant rain was falling, or the frost
Raged bitterly, with keen and silent tooth;
And, interrupting oft that eager game,
From under Esthwaite's splitting fields of
    ice

The pent-up air, struggling to free itself,
Gave out to meadow grounds and hills a
    loud 541
Protracted yelling, like the noise of wolves
Howling in troops along the Bothnic Main.

Nor, sedulous as I have been to trace
How Nature by extrinsic passion first
Peopled the mind with forms sublime or
    fair,
And made me love them, may I here omit
How other pleasures have been mine, and
    joys
Of subtler origin; how I have felt,
Not seldom even in that tempestuous time,
Those hallowed and pure motions of the
    sense 551
Which seem, in their simplicity, to own
An intellectual charm; that calm delight
Which, if I err not, surely must belong
To those first-born affinities that fit
Our new existence to existing things,
And, in our dawn of being, constitute
The bond of union between life and joy.

Yes, I remember when the changeful
    earth,
And twice five summers on my mind had
    stamped 560
The faces of the moving year, even then
I held unconscious intercourse with beauty
Old as creation, drinking in a pure
Organic pleasure from the silver wreaths
Of curling mist, or from the level plain
Of waters coloured by impending clouds.

The sands of Westmoreland, the creeks
    and bays
Of Cumbria's rocky limits, they can tell
How, when the Sea threw off his evening
    shade,
And to the shepherd's hut on distant
    hills 570
Sent welcome notice of the rising moon,
How I have stood, to fancies such as these
A stranger, linking with the spectacle
No conscious memory of a kindred sight,
And bringing with me no peculiar sense
Of quietness or peace; yet have I stood,
Even while mine eye hath moved o'er many
    a league
Of shining water, gathering as it seemed,
Through every hair-breadth in that field of
    light,
New pleasure like a bee among the flowers.

Thus oft amid those fits of vulgar joy 581
Which, through all seasons, on a child's
    pursuits
Are prompt attendants, 'mid that giddy
    bliss
Which, like a tempest, works along the
    blood
And is forgotten; even then I felt
Gleams like the flashing of a shield; — the
    earth
And common face of Nature spake to me
Rememberable things; sometimes, 't is true,
By chance collisions and quaint accidents
(Like those ill-sorted unions, work supposed
Of evil-minded fairies), yet not vain 591
Nor profitless, if haply they impressed
Collateral objects and appearances,
Albeit lifeless then, and doomed to sleep
Until maturer seasons called them forth
To impregnate and to elevate the mind.
— And if the vulgar joy by its own weight
Wearied itself out of the memory,
The scenes which were a witness of that joy
Remained in their substantial lineaments
Depicted on the brain, and to the eye 601
Were visible, a daily sight; and thus
By the impressive discipline of fear,
By pleasure and repeated happiness,
So frequently repeated, and by force
Of obscure feelings representative
Of things forgotten, these same scenes so
    bright,
So beautiful, so majestic in themselves,
Though yet the day was distant, did be-
    come
Habitually dear, and all their forms 610
And changeful colours by invisible links
Were fastened to the affections.
                              I began
My story early — not misled, I trust,
By an infirmity of love for days
Disowned by memory — ere the breath of
    spring
Planting my snowdrops among winter
    snows:
Nor will it seem to thee, O Friend! so
    prompt
In sympathy, that I have lengthened out
With fond and feeble tongue a tedious tale.
Meanwhile, my hope has been, that I might
    fetch 620
Invigorating thoughts from former years;
Might fix the wavering balance of my mind,
And haply meet reproaches too, whose
    power

May spur me on, in manhood now mature,
To honourable toil. Yet should these hopes
Prove vain, and thus should neither I be
    taught
To understand myself, nor thou to know
With better knowledge how the heart was
    framed
Of him thou lovest; need I dread from thee
Harsh judgments, if the song be loth to quit
Those recollected hours that have the charm
Of visionary things, those lovely forms 632
And sweet sensations that throw back our
    life,
And almost make remotest infancy
A visible scene, on which the sun is shining ?

One end at least hath been attained; my
    mind
Hath been revived, and if this genial mood
Desert me not, forthwith shall be brought
    down
Through later years the story of my life.
The road lies plain before me; — 't is a
    theme 640
Single and of determined bounds; and
    hence
I choose it rather at this time, than work
Of ampler or more varied argument,
Where I might be discomfited and lost:
And certain hopes are with me, that to thee
This labour will be welcome, honoured
    Friend !

BOOK SECOND

SCHOOL-TIME (*continued*)

THUS far, O Friend ! have we, though
    leaving much
Unvisited, endeavoured to retrace
The simple ways in which my childhood
    walked;
Those chiefly that first led me to the love
Of rivers, woods, and fields. The passion yet
Was in its birth, sustained as might befall
By nourishment that came unsought; for
    still
From week to week, from month to month,
    we lived
A round of tumult.   Duly were our games
Prolonged in summer till the daylight failed;
No chair remained before the doors; the
    bench 11
And threshold steps were empty; fast asleep
The labourer, and the old man who had sate

A later lingerer; yet the revelry
Continued and the loud uproar: at last,
When all the ground was dark, and twin-
  kling stars
Edged the black clouds, home and to bed
  we went,
Feverish with weary joints and beating
  minds.
Ah! is there one who ever has been young,
Nor needs a warning voice to tame the
  pride   20
Of intellect and virtue's self-esteem?
One is there, though the wisest and the best
Of all mankind, who covets not at times
Union that cannot be; — who would not give
If so he might, to duty and to truth
The eagerness of infantine desire?
A tranquillising spirit presses now
On my corporeal frame, so wide appears
The vacancy between me and those days
Which yet have such self-presence in my
  mind,   30
That, musing on them, often do I seem
Two consciousnesses, conscious of myself
And of some other Being. A rude mass
Of native rock, left midway in the square
Of our small market village, was the goal
Or centre of these sports; and when, re-
  turned
After long absence, thither I repaired,
Gone was the old grey stone, and in its place
A smart Assembly-room usurped the ground
That had been ours. There let the fiddle
  scream,   40
And be ye happy! Yet, my Friends! I
  know
That more than one of you will think with
  me
Of those soft starry nights, and that old
  Dame
From whom the stone was named, who
  there had sate,
And watched her table with its huckster's
  wares
Assiduous, through the length of sixty years.

  We ran a boisterous course; the year
    span round
With giddy motion. But the time ap-
  proached
That brought with it a regular desire
For calmer pleasures, when the winning
  forms   50
Of Nature were collaterally attached
To every scheme of holiday delight

And every boyish sport, less grateful else
And languidly pursued.
                     When summer came,
Our pastime was, on bright half-holidays,
To sweep along the plain of Windermere
With rival oars; and the selected bourne
Was now an Island musical with birds
That sang and ceased not; now a Sister Isle
Beneath the oaks' umbrageous covert, sown
With lilies of the valley like a field;   61
And now a third small Island, where sur-
  vived
In solitude the ruins of a shrine
Once to Our Lady dedicate, and served
Daily with chaunted rites.   In such a race
So ended, disappointment could be none,
Uneasiness, or pain, or jealousy:
We rested in the shade, all pleased alike,
Conquered and conqueror. Thus the pride
  of strength,
And the vain-glory of superior skill,   70
Were tempered; thus was gradually pro-
  duced
A quiet independence of the heart:
And to my Friend who knows me I may
  add,
Fearless of blame, that hence for future days
Ensued a diffidence and modesty,
And I was taught to feel, perhaps too much,
The self-sufficing power of Solitude.

  Our daily meals were frugal, Sabine fare!
More than we wished we knew the blessing
  then
Of vigorous hunger — hence corporeal
  strength   80
Unsapped by delicate viands; for, exclude
A little weekly stipend, and we lived
Through three divisions of the quartered
  year
In penniless poverty. But now to school
From the half-yearly holidays returned,
We came with weightier purses, that suf-
  ficed
To furnish treats more costly than the
  Dame
Of the old grey stone, from her scant board,
  supplied.
Hence rustic dinners on the cool green
  ground,
Or in the woods, or by a river side   90
Or shady fountains, while among the leaves
Soft airs were stirring, and the mid-day sun
Unfelt shone brightly round us in our joy.
Nor is my aim neglected if I tell

How sometimes, in the length of those half-
    years,
We from our funds drew largely; — proud
    to curb,
And eager to spur on, the galloping steed;
And with the courteous inn-keeper, whose
    stud
Supplied our want, we haply might employ
Sly subterfuge, if the adventure's bound 100
Were distant: some famed temple where
    of yore
The Druids worshipped, or the antique
    walls
Of that large abbey, where within the Vale
Of Nightshade, to St. Mary's honour built,
Stands yet a mouldering pile with fractured
    arch,
Belfry, and images, and living trees;
A holy scene ! — Along the smooth green
    turf
Our horses grazed. To more than inland
    peace
Left by the west wind sweeping overhead
From a tumultuous ocean, trees and tow-
    ers   110
In that sequestered valley may be seen,
Both silent and both motionless alike;
Such the deep shelter that is there, and
    such
The safeguard for repose and quietness.

Our steeds remounted and the summons
    given,
With whip and spur we through the chaun-
    try flew
In uncouth race, and left the cross-legged
    knight,
And the stone-abbot, and that single wren
Which one day sang so sweetly in the nave
Of the old church, that — though from re-
    cent showers   120
The earth was comfortless, and touched
    by faint
Internal breezes, sobbings of the place
And respirations, from the roofless walls
The shuddering ivy dripped large drops —
    yet still
So sweetly 'mid the gloom the invisible
    bird
Sang to herself, that there I could have
    made
My dwelling-place, and lived for ever there
To hear such music. Through the walls
    we flew
And down the valley, and, a circuit made

In wantonness of heart, through rough and
    smooth   130
We scampered homewards. Oh, ye rocks
    and streams,
And that still spirit shed from evening air !
Even in this joyous time I sometimes felt
Your presence, when with slackened step
    we breathed
Along the sides of the steep hills, or when
Lighted by gleams of moonlight from the
    sea
We beat with thundering hoofs the level
    sand.

Midway on long Winander's eastern
    shore,
Within the crescent of a pleasant bay,
A tavern stood; no homely - featured
    house,   140
Primeval like its neighbouring cottages,
But 't was a splendid place, the door beset
With chaises, grooms, and liveries, and
    within
Decanters, glasses, and the blood-red wine.
In ancient times, and ere the Hall was
    built
On the large island, had this dwelling been
More worthy of a poet's love, a hut,
Proud of its own bright fire and sycamore
    shade.
But — though the rhymes were gone that
    once inscribed
The threshold, and large golden charac-
    ters,   150
Spread o'er the spangled sign-board, had
    dislodged
The old Lion and usurped his place, in
    slight
And mockery of the rustic painter's hand —
Yet, to this hour, the spot to me is dear
With all its foolish pomp. The garden lay
Upon a slope surmounted by a plain
Of a small bowling-green; beneath us
    stood
A grove, with gleams of water through the
    trees
And over the tree-tops; nor did we want
Refreshment, strawberries and mellow
    cream.   160
There, while through half an afternoon we
    played
On the smooth platform, whether skill pre-
    vailed
Or happy blunder triumphed, bursts of
    glee

Made all the mountains ring. But, ere
    night-fall,
When in our pinnace we returned at lei-
    sure
Over the shadowy lake, and to the beach
Of some small island steered our course
    with one,
The Minstrel of the Troop, and left him
    there,
And rowed off gently, while he blew his
    flute
Alone upon the rock — oh, then, the calm
And dead still water lay upon my mind 171
Even with a weight of pleasure, and the
    sky,
Never before so beautiful, sank down
Into my heart, and held me like a dream!
Thus were my sympathies enlarged, and
    thus
Daily the common range of visible things
Grew dear to me: already I began
To love the sun; a boy I loved the sun,
Not as I since have loved him, as a pledge
And surety of our earthly life, a light 180
Which we behold and feel we are alive;
Nor for his bounty to so many worlds —
But for this cause, that I had seen him lay
His beauty on the morning hills, had seen
The western mountain touch his setting
    orb,
In many a thoughtless hour, when, from
    excess
Of happiness, my blood appeared to flow
For its own pleasure, and I breathed with
    joy.
And, from like feelings, humble though in-
    tense,
To patriotic and domestic love   190
Analogous, the moon to me was dear;
For I could dream away my purposes,
Standing to gaze upon her while she hung
Midway between the hills as if she knew
No other region, but belonged to thee,
Yea, appertained by a peculiar right
To thee and thy grey huts, thou one dear
    Vale!

    Those incidental charms which first at-
        tached
My heart to rural objects, day by day
Grew weaker, and I hasten on to tell 200
How Nature, intervenient till this time
And secondary, now at length was sought
For her own sake. But who shall parcel
    out

His intellect by geometric rules,
Split like a province into round and square?
Who knows the individual hour in which
His habits were first sown, even as a seed?
Who that shall point as with a wand and
    say
"This portion of the river of my mind
Came from yon fountain?" Thou, my
    Friend! art one   210
More deeply read in thy own thoughts; to
    thee
Science appears but what in truth she is,
Not as our glory and our absolute boast,
But as a succedaneum, and a prop
To our infirmity. No officious slave
Art thou of that false secondary power
By which we multiply distinctions, then
Deem that our puny boundaries are things
That we perceive, and not that we have
    made.
To thee, unblinded by these formal arts, 220
The unity of all hath been revealed,
And thou wilt doubt, with me less aptly
    skilled
Than many are to range the faculties
In scale and order, class the cabinet
Of their sensations, and in voluble phrase
Run through the history and birth of each
As of a single independent thing.
Hard task, vain hope, to analyse the mind,
If each most obvious and particular
    thought,
Not in a mystical and idle sense,   230
But in the words of Reason deeply weighed,
Hath no beginning.
                    Blest the infant Babe,
(For with my best conjecture I would trace
Our Being's earthly progress,) blest the
    Babe,
Nursed in his Mother's arms, who sinks to
    sleep
Rocked on his Mother's breast; who with
    his soul
Drinks in the feelings of his Mother's eye!
For him, in one dear Presence, there exists
A virtue which irradiates and exalts
Objects through widest intercourse of
    sense.   240
No outcast he, bewildered and depressed:
Along his infant veins are interfused
The gravitation and the filial bond
Of nature that connect him with the world.
Is there a flower, to which he points with
    hand
Too weak to gather it, already love

Drawn from love's purest earthly fount for
    him
Hath beautified that flower; already shades
Of pity cast from inward tenderness
Do fall around him upon aught that
    bears   250
Unsightly marks of violence or harm.
Emphatically such a Being lives,
Frail creature as he is, helpless as frail,
An inmate of this active universe.
For feeling has to him imparted power
That through the growing faculties of sense
Doth like an agent of the one great Mind
Create, creator and receiver both,
Working but in alliance with the works
Which it beholds. — Such, verily, is the first
Poetic spirit of our human life,   261
By uniform control of after years,
In most, abated or suppressed; in some,
Through every change of growth and of
    decay,
Pre-eminent till death.

             From early days,
Beginning not long after that first time
In which, a Babe, by intercourse of touch
I held mute dialogues with my Mother's
    heart,
I have endeavoured to display the means
Whereby this infant sensibility,   270
Great birthright of our being, was in me
Augmented and sustained.   Yet is a path
More difficult before me; and I fear
That in its broken windings we shall need
The chamois' sinews, and the eagle's wing:
For now a trouble came into my mind
From unknown causes.   I was left alone
Seeking the visible world, nor knowing why.
The props of my affections were removed,
And yet the building stood, as if sustained
By its own spirit!   All that I beheld   281
Was dear, and hence to finer influxes
The mind lay open to a more exact
And close communion.   Many are our joys
In youth, but oh! what happiness to live
When every hour brings palpable access
Of knowledge, when all knowledge is de-
    light,
And sorrow is not there! The seasons came,
And every season wheresoe'er I moved
Unfolded transitory qualities,   290
Which, but for this most watchful power of
    love,
Had been neglected; left a register
Of permanent relations, else unknown.
Hence life, and change, and beauty, solitude

More active even than "best society" —
Society made sweet as solitude
By silent inobtrusive sympathies,
And gentle agitations of the mind
From manifold distinctions, difference
Perceived in things, where, to the unwatch-
    ful eye,   300
No difference is, and hence, from the same
    source,
Sublimer joy; for I would walk alone,
Under the quiet stars, and at that time
Have felt whate'er there is of power in
    sound
To breathe an elevated mood, by form
Or image unprofaned; and I would stand,
If the night blackened with a coming storm,
Beneath some rock, listening to notes that
    are
The ghostly language of the ancient earth,
Or make their dim abode in distant winds.
Thence did I drink the visionary power;   311
And deem not profitless those fleeting moods
Of shadowy exultation: not for this,
That they are kindred to our purer mind
And intellectual life; but that the soul,
Remembering how she felt, but what she
    felt
Remembering not, retains an obscure sense
Of possible sublimity, whereto
With growing faculties she doth aspire,   319
With faculties still growing, feeling still
That whatsoever point they gain, they yet
Have something to pursue.

             And not alone,
'Mid gloom and tumult, but no less 'mid fair
And tranquil scenes, that universal power
And fitness in the latent qualities
And essences of things, by which the mind
Is moved with feelings of delight, to me
Came, strengthened with a superadded soul,
A virtue not its own.   My morning walks
Were early; — oft before the hours of
    school   330
I travelled round our little lake, five miles
Of pleasant wandering. Happy time! more
    dear
For this, that one was by my side, a Friend,
Then passionately loved; with heart how
    full
Would he peruse these lines! For many
    years
Have since flowed in between us, and, our
    minds
Both silent to each other, at this time
We live as if those hours had never been.

Nor seldom did I lift our cottage latch 339
Far earlier, ere one smoke-wreath had risen
From human dwelling, or the vernal thrush
Was audible; and sate among the woods
Alone upon some jutting eminence,
At the first gleam of dawn-light, when the
    Vale,
Yet slumbering, lay in utter solitude.
How shall I seek the origin ? where find
Faith in the marvellous things which then I
    felt ?
Oft in these moments such a holy calm
Would overspread my soul, that bodily eyes
Were utterly forgotten, and what I saw 350
Appeared like something in myself, a dream,
A prospect in the mind.
                    'T were long to tell
What spring and autumn, what the winter
    snows,
And what the summer shade, what day and
    night,
Evening and morning, sleep and waking,
    thought
From sources inexhaustible, poured forth
To feed the spirit of religious love
In which I walked with Nature.   But let
    this
Be not forgotten, that I still retained
My first creative sensibility;   360
That by the regular action of the world
My soul was unsubdued.   A plastic power
Abode with me; a forming hand, at times
Rebellious, acting in a devious mood;
A local spirit of his own, at war
With general tendency, but, for the most,
Subservient strictly to external things
With which it communed.   An auxiliar light
Came from my mind, which on the setting
    sun
Bestowed new splendour; the melodious
    birds,   370
The fluttering breezes, fountains that run on
Murmuring so sweetly in themselves,
    obeyed
A like dominion, and the midnight storm
Grew darker in the presence of my eye:
Hence my obeisance, my devotion hence,
And hence my transport.
                Nor should this, perchance,
Pass unrecorded, that I still had loved
The exercise and produce of a toil,
Than analytic industry to me
More pleasing, and whose character I deem
Is more poetic as resembling more   381
Creative agency.   The song would speak

Of that interminable building reared
By observation of affinities
In objects where no brotherhood exists
To passive minds.   My seventeenth year
    was come;
And, whether from this habit rooted now
So deeply in my mind, or from excess
In the great social principle of life
Coercing all things into sympathy,   390
To unorganic natures were transferred
My own enjoyments; or the power of truth
Coming in revelation, did converse
With things that really are; I, at this time,
Saw blessings spread around me like a sea.
Thus while the days flew by, and years
    passed on,
From Nature and her overflowing soul,
I had received so much, that all my
    thoughts
Were steeped in feeling; I was only then
Contented, when with bliss ineffable   400
I felt the sentiment of Being spread
O'er all that moves and all that seemeth
    still;
O'er all that, lost beyond the reach of
    thought
And human knowledge, to the human eye
Invisible, yet liveth to the heart;
O'er all that leaps and runs, and shouts and
    sings,
Or beats the gladsome air; o'er all that
    glides
Beneath the wave, yea, in the wave itself,
And mighty depth of waters.   Wonder not
If high the transport, great the joy I felt,
Communing in this sort through earth and
    heaven   411
With every form of creature, as it looked
Towards the Uncreated with a countenance
Of adoration, with an eye of love.
One song they sang, and it was audible,
Most audible, then, when the fleshly ear,
O'ercome by humblest prelude of that strain,
Forgot her functions, and slept undisturbed.

If this be error, and another faith
Find easier access to the pious mind,   420
Yet were I grossly destitute of all
Those human sentiments that make this
    earth
So dear, if I should fail with grateful voice
To speak of you, ye mountains, and ye lakes
And sounding cataracts, ye mists and winds
That dwell among the hills where I was
    born.

If in my youth I have been pure in heart,
If, mingling with the world, I am content
With my own modest pleasures, and have
    lived
With God and Nature communing, re-
    moved   430
From little enmities and low desires —
The gift is yours; if in these times of fear,
This melancholy waste of hopes o'erthrown,
If, 'mid indifference and apathy,
And wicked exultation when good men
On every side fall off, we know not how,
To selfishness, disguised in gentle names
Of peace and quiet and domestic love,
Yet mingled not unwillingly with sneers
On visionary minds; if, in this time   440
Of dereliction and dismay, I yet
Despair not of our nature, but retain
A more than Roman confidence, a faith
That fails not, in all sorrow my support,
The blessing of my life — the gift is yours,
Ye winds and sounding cataracts! 'tis yours,
Ye mountains! thine, O Nature! Thou hast
    fed
My lofty speculations; and in thee,
For this uneasy heart of ours, I find
A never-failing principle of joy   450
And purest passion.
                Thou, my Friend! wert reared
In the great city, 'mid far other scenes;
But we, by different roads, at length have
    gained
The selfsame bourne. And for this cause
    to thee
I speak, unapprehensive of contempt,
The insinuated scoff of coward tongues,
And all that silent language which so oft
In conversation between man and man
Blots from the human countenance all trace
Of beauty and of love. For thou hast
    sought   460
The truth in solitude, and, since the days
That gave thee liberty, full long desired,
To serve in Nature's temple, thou hast
    been
The most assiduous of her ministers;
In many things my brother, chiefly here
In this our deep devotion.
                        Fare thee well!
Health and the quiet of a healthful mind
Attend thee! seeking oft the haunts of
    men,
And yet more often living with thyself,
And for thyself, so haply shall thy days   470
Be many, and a blessing to mankind.

BOOK THIRD

RESIDENCE AT CAMBRIDGE

IT was a dreary morning when the wheels
Rolled over a wide plain o'erhung with
    clouds,
And nothing cheered our way till first we
    saw
The long-roofed chapel of King's College
    lift
Turrets and pinnacles in answering files,
Extended high above a dusky grove.

Advancing, we espied upon the road
A student clothed in gown and tasselled
    cap,
Striding along as if o'ertasked by Time,
Or covetous of exercise and air;   10
He passed — nor was I master of my eyes
Till he was left an arrow's flight behind.
As near and nearer to the spot we drew,
It seemed to suck us in with an eddy's
    force.
Onward we drove beneath the Castle; caught,
While crossing Magdalene Bridge, a glimpse
    of Cam;
And at the *Hoop* alighted, famous Inn.

My spirit was up, my thoughts were full
    of hope;
Some friends I had, acquaintances who there
Seemed friends, poor simple schoolboys, now
    hung round   20
With honour and importance: in a world
Of welcome faces up and down I roved;
Questions, directions, warnings and advice,
Flowed in upon me, from all sides; fresh
    day
Of pride and pleasure! to myself I seemed
A man of business and expense, and went
From shop to shop about my own affairs,
To Tutor or to Tailor, as befell,
From street to street with loose and careless
    mind.

I was the Dreamer, they the Dream; I
    roamed   30
Delighted through the motley spectacle;
Gowns grave, or gaudy, doctors, students,
    streets,
Courts, cloisters, flocks of churches, gate-
    ways, towers:
Migration strange for a stripling of the
    hills,
A northern villager.

As if the change
Had waited on some Fairy's wand, at once
Behold me rich in monies, and attired
In splendid garb, with hose of silk, and
        hair
Powdered like rimy trees, when frost is
        keen.
My lordly dressing-gown, I pass it by,   40
With other signs of manhood that supplied
The lack of beard. — The weeks went
        roundly on,
With invitations, suppers, wine and fruit,
Smooth housekeeping within, and all with-
        out
Liberal, and suiting gentleman's array.

The Evangelist St. John my patron was:
Three Gothic courts are his, and in the first
Was my abiding-place, a nook obscure;
Right underneath, the College kitchens
        made
A humming sound, less tuneable than
        bees,   50
But hardly less industrious; with shrill
        notes
Of sharp command and scolding inter-
        mixed.
Near me hung Trinity's loquacious clock,
Who never let the quarters, night or day,
Slip by him unproclaimed, and told the
        hours
Twice over with a male and female voice.
Her pealing organ was my neighbour too;
And from my pillow, looking forth by light
Of moon or favouring stars, I could behold
The antechapel where the statue stood   60
Of Newton with his prism and silent face,
The marble index of a mind for ever
Voyaging through strange seas of Thought,
        alone.

Of College labours, of the Lecturer's
        room
All studded round, as thick as chairs could
        stand,
With loyal students, faithful to their books,
Half-and-half idlers, hardy recusants,
And honest dunces — of important days,
Examinations, when the man was weighed
As in a balance ! of excessive hopes,   70
Tremblings withal and commendable fears,
Small jealousies, and triumphs good or
        bad,
Let others that know more speak as they
        know.

Such glory was but little sought by me,
And little won. Yet from the first crude
        days
Of settling time in this untried abode,
I was disturbed at times by prudent thoughts,
Wishing to hope without a hope, some fears
About my future worldly maintenance,
And, more than all, a strangeness in the
        mind,   80
A feeling that I was not for that hour,
Nor for that place. But wherefore be cast
        down ?
For (not to speak of Reason and her pure
Reflective acts to fix the moral law
Deep in the conscience, nor of Christian
        Hope,
Bowing her head before her sister Faith
As one far mightier), hither I had come,
Bear witness Truth, endowed with holy
        powers
And faculties, whether to work or feel.
Oft when the dazzling show no longer new
Had ceased to dazzle, ofttimes did I quit 91
My comrades, leave the crowd, buildings
        and groves,
And as I paced alone the level fields
Far from those lovely sights and sounds
        sublime
With which I had been conversant, the
        mind
Drooped not; but there into herself return-
        ing,
With prompt rebound seemed fresh as here-
        tofore.
At least I more distinctly recognised
Her native instincts: let me dare to speak
A higher language, say that now I felt 100
What independent solaces were mine,
To mitigate the injurious sway of place
Or circumstance, how far soever changed
In youth, or to be changed in manhood's
        prime;
Or for the few who shall be called to look
On the long shadows in our evening years,
Ordained precursors to the night of death.
As if awakened, summoned, roused, con-
        strained,
I looked for universal things; perused
The common countenance of earth and sky :
Earth, nowhere unembellished by some trace
Of that first Paradise whence man was
        driven;
And sky, whose beauty and bounty are
        expressed   113

By the proud name she bears — the name
    of Heaven.
I called on both to teach me what they
    might;
Or turning the mind in upon herself
Pored, watched, expected, listened, spread
    my thoughts
And spread them with a wider creeping;
    felt
Incumbencies more awful, visitings
Of the Upholder of the tranquil soul,   120
That tolerates the indignities of Time,
And, from the centre of Eternity
All finite motions overruling, lives
In glory immutable. But peace ! enough
Here to record that I was mounting now
To such community with highest truth —
A track pursuing, not untrod before,
From strict analogies by thought supplied
Or consciousnesses not to be subdued.
To every natural form, rock, fruit, or
    flower,   130
Even the loose stones that cover the high-
    way,
I gave a moral life: I saw them feel,
Or linked them to some feeling: the great
    mass
Lay bedded in a quickening soul, and all
That I beheld respired with inward mean-
    ing.
Add that whate'er of Terror or of Love
Or Beauty, Nature's daily face put on
From transitory passion, unto this
I was as sensitive as waters are
To the sky's influence in a kindred mood
Of passion; was obedient as a lute   141
That waits upon the touches of the wind.
Unknown, unthought of, yet I was most
    rich —
I had a world about me — 't was my own;
I made it, for it only lived to me,
And to the God who sees into the heart.
Such sympathies, though rarely, were be-
    trayed
By outward gestures and by visible looks:
Some called it madness — so indeed it was,
If child-like fruitfulness in passing joy,   150
If steady moods of thoughtfulness matured
To inspiration, sort with such a name;
If prophecy be madness; if things
    viewed
By poets in old time, and higher up
By the first men, earth's first inhabitants,
May in these tutored days no more be seen
With undisordered sight. But leaving
    this,

It was no madness, for the bodily eye
Amid my strongest workings evermore
Was searching out the lines of difference
As they lie hid in all external forms,   161
Near or remote, minute or vast, an eye
Which, from a tree, a stone, a withered
    leaf,
To the broad ocean and the azure heavens
Spangled with kindred multitudes of stars,
Could find no surface where its power
    might sleep;
Which spake perpetual logic to my soul,
And by an unrelenting agency
Did bind my feelings even as in a chain.

And here, O Friend ! have I retraced
    my life   170
Up to an eminence, and told a tale
Of matters which not falsely may be called
The glory of my youth. Of genius,
    power,
Creation and divinity itself
I have been speaking, for my theme has
    been
What passed within me. Not of outward
    things
Done visibly for other minds, words, signs,
Symbols or actions, but of my own heart
Have I been speaking, and my youthful
    mind.
O Heavens! how awful is the might of
    souls,   180
And what they do within themselves while
    yet
The yoke of earth is new to them, the
    world
Nothing but a wild field where they were
    sown.
This is, in truth, heroic argument,
This genuine prowess, which I wished to
    touch
With hand however weak, but in the main
It lies far hidden from the reach of words.
Points have we all of us within our souls
Where all stand single; this I feel, and
    make
Breathings for incommunicable powers;   190
But is not each a memory to himself?
And, therefore, now that we must quit this
    theme,
I am not heartless, for there 's not a
    man
That lives who hath not known his god-
    like hours,
And feels not what an empire we inherit
As natural beings in the strength of Nature.

No more: for now into a populous plain
We must descend.   A Traveller I am,
Whose tale is only of himself; even so,
So be it, if the pure of heart be prompt
To follow, and if thou, my honoured
        Friend!   201
Who in these thoughts art ever at my side,
Support, as heretofore, my fainting steps.

It hath been told, that when the first de-
        light
That flashed upon me from this novel show
Had failed, the mind returned into her-
        self;
Yet true it is, that I had made a change
In climate, and my nature's outward coat
Changed also slowly and insensibly.
Full oft the quiet and exalted thoughts   210
Of loneliness gave way to empty noise
And superficial pastimes; now and then
Forced labour, and more frequently forced
        hopes;
And, worst of all, a treasonable growth
Of indecisive judgments, that impaired
And shook the mind's simplicity. — And
        yet
This was a gladsome time.   Could I be-
        hold —
Who, less insensible than sodden clay
In a sea-river's bed at ebb of tide,
Could have beheld — with undelighted
        heart,   220
So many happy youths, so wide and fair
A congregation in its budding-time
Of health, and hope, and beauty, all at
        once
So many divers samples from the growth
Of life's sweet season — could have seen
        unmoved
That miscellaneous garland of wild flowers
Decking the matron temples of a place
So famous through the world ?   To me, at
        least,
It was a goodly prospect: for, in sooth,
Though I had learnt betimes to stand un-
        propped,   230
And independent musings pleased me so
That spells seemed on me when I was alone,
Yet could I only cleave to solitude
In lonely places; if a throng was near
That way I leaned by nature; for my heart
Was social, and loved idleness and joy.

Not seeking those who might participate
My deeper pleasures (nay, I had not once,

Though not unused to mutter lonesome
        songs,
Even with myself divided such delight,   240
Or looked that way for aught that might
        be clothed
In human language), easily I passed
From the remembrances of better things,
And slipped into the ordinary works
Of careless youth, unburthened, unalarmed.
Caverns there were within my mind which
        sun
Could never penetrate, yet did there not
Want store of leafy *arbours* where the light
Might enter in at will.   Companionships,
Friendships, acquaintances, were welcome
        all.   250
We sauntered, played, or rioted; we talked
Unprofitable talk at morning hours;
Drifted about along the streets and
        walks,
Read lazily in trivial books, went forth
To gallop through the country in blind zeal
Of senseless horsemanship, or on the breast
Of Cam sailed boisterously, and let the
        stars
Come forth, perhaps without one quiet
        thought.

Such was the tenor of the second act
In this new life.   Imagination slept,   260
And yet not utterly.   I could not print
Ground where the grass had yielded to the
        steps
Of generations of illustrious men,
Unmoved.   I could not always lightly pass
Through the same gateways, sleep where
        they had slept,
Wake where they waked, range that in-
        closure old,
That garden of great intellects, undisturbed.
Place also by the side of this dark sense
Of noble feeling, that those spiritual men,
Even the great Newton's own ethereal self,
Seemed humbled in these precincts thence
        to be   271
The more endeared.   Their several memo-
        ries here
(Even like their persons in their portraits
        clothed
With the accustomed garb of daily life)
Put on a lowly and a touching grace
Of more distinct humanity, that left
All genuine admiration unimpaired.

Beside the pleasant Mill of Trompington
I laughed with Chaucer in the hawthorn
        shade;

Heard him, while birds were warbling, tell
    his tales   280
Of amorous passion. And that gentle Bard,
Chosen by the Muses for their Page of
    State —
Sweet Spenser, moving through his clouded
    heaven
With the moon's beauty and the moon's soft
    pace,
I called him Brother, Englishman, and
    Friend!
Yea, our blind Poet, who, in his later day,
Stood almost single; uttering odious truth—
Darkness before, and danger's voice behind,
Soul awful — if the earth has ever lodged
An awful soul — I seemed to see him here
Familiarly, and in his scholar's dress 291
Bounding before me, yet a stripling youth —
A boy, no better, with his rosy cheeks
Angelical, keen eye, courageous look,
And conscious step of purity and pride.
Among the band of my compeers was one
Whom chance had stationed in the very
    room
Honoured by Milton's name. O temperate
    Bard!
Be it confest that, for the first time, seated
Within thy innocent lodge and oratory, 300
One of a festive circle, I poured out
Libations, to thy memory drank, till pride
And gratitude grew dizzy in a brain
Never excited by the fumes of wine
Before that hour, or since. Then, forth I
    ran
From the assembly; through a length of
    streets,
Ran, ostrich-like, to reach our chapel door
In not a desperate or opprobrious time,
Albeit long after the importunate bell
Had stopped, with wearisome Cassandra
    voice   310
No longer haunting the dark winter night.
Call back, O Friend! a moment to thy mind
The place itself and fashion of the rites.
With careless ostentation shouldering up
My surplice, through the inferior throng I
    clove
Of the plain Burghers, who in audience
    stood
On the last skirts of their permitted ground,
Under the pealing organ. Empty thoughts!
I am ashamed of them: and that great Bard,
And thou, O Friend! who in thy ample
    mind   320
Hast placed me high above my best deserts,

Ye will forgive the weakness of that hour,
In some of its unworthy vanities,
Brother to many more.
                  In this mixed sort
The months passed on, remissly, not given
    up
To wilful alienation from the right,
Or walks of open scandal, but in vague
And loose indifference, easy likings, aims
Of a low pitch — duty and zeal dismissed,
Yet Nature, or a happy course of things 330
Not doing in their stead the needful work.
The memory languidly revolved, the heart
Reposed in noontide rest, the inner pulse
Of contemplation almost failed to beat.
Such life might not inaptly be compared
To a floating island, an amphibious spot
Unsound, of spongy texture, yet withal
Not wanting a fair face of water weeds
And pleasant flowers. The thirst of living
    praise,
Fit reverence for the glorious Dead, the
    sight   340
Of those long vistas, sacred catacombs,
Where mighty *minds* lie visibly entombed,
Have often stirred the heart of youth, and
    bred
A fervent love of rigorous discipline. —
Alas! such high emotion touched not me.
Look was there none within these walls to
    shame
My easy spirits, and discountenance
Their light composure, far less to instil
A calm resolve of mind, firmly addressed
To puissant efforts. Nor was this the blame
Of others but my own; I should, in truth,
As far as doth concern my single self, 352
Misdeem most widely, lodging it elsewhere:
For I, bred up 'mid Nature's luxuries,
Was a spoiled child, and, rambling like the
    wind,
As I had done in daily intercourse
With those crystalline rivers, solemn
    heights,
And mountains, ranging like a fowl of the
    air,
I was ill-tutored for captivity;
To quit my pleasure, and, from month to
    month,   360
Take up a station calmly on the perch
Of sedentary peace. Those lovely forms
Had also left less space within my mind,
Which, wrought upon instinctively, had
    found
A freshness in those objects of her love,

A winning power, beyond all other power.
Not that I slighted books, — that were to
    lack
All sense, — but other passions in me ruled,
Passions more fervent, making me less
    prompt   369
To in-door study than was wise or well,
Or suited to those years. Yet I, though
    used
In magisterial liberty to rove,
Culling such flowers of learning as might
    tempt
A random choice, could shadow forth a
    place
(If now I yield not to a flattering dream)
Whose studious aspect should have bent me
    down
To instantaneous service; should at once
Have made me pay to science and to arts
And written lore, acknowledged my liege
    lord,   379
A homage frankly offered up, like that
Which I had paid to Nature. Toil and
    pains
In this recess, by thoughtful Fancy built,
Should spread from heart to heart; and
    stately groves,
Majestic edifices, should not want
A corresponding dignity within.
The congregating temper that pervades
Our unripe years, not wasted, should be
    taught
To minister to works of high attempt —
Works which the enthusiast would perform
    with love.   389
Youth should be awed, religiously possessed
With a conviction of the power that waits
On knowledge, when sincerely sought and
    prized
For its own sake, on glory and on praise
If but by labour won, and fit to endure
The passing day; should learn to put aside
Her trappings here, should strip them off
    abashed
Before antiquity and stedfast truth
And strong book-mindedness; and over all
A healthy sound simplicity should reign,
A seemly plainness, name it what you will,
Republican or pious.
                    If these thoughts
Are a gratuitous emblazonry   402
That mocks the recreant age *we* live in,
    then
Be Folly and False-seeming free to affect
Whatever formal gait of discipline

Shall raise them highest in their own es-
    teem —
Let them parade among the Schools at will,
But spare the House of God. Was ever
    known   408
The witless shepherd who persists to drive
A flock that thirsts not to a pool disliked ?
A weight must surely hang on days begun
And ended with such mockery. Be wise,
Ye Presidents and Deans, and, till the spirit
Of ancient times revive, and youth be
    trained
At home in pious service, to your bells
Give seasonable rest, for 't is a sound
Hollow as ever vexed the tranquil air ; 417
And your officious doings bring disgrace
On the plain steeples of our English Church,
Whose worship, 'mid remotest village trees,
Suffers for this. Even Science, too, at hand
In daily sight of this irreverence,
Is smitten thence with an unnatural taint,
Loses her just authority, falls beneath
Collateral suspicion, else unknown.   425
This truth escaped me not, and I confess,
That having 'mid my native hills given loose
To a schoolboy's vision, I had raised a pile
Upon the basis of the coming time,
That fell in ruins round me. Oh, what joy
To see a sanctuary for our country's youth
Informed with such a spirit as might be
Its own protection ; a primeval grove,
Where, though the shades with cheerfulness
    were filled,   434
Nor indigent of songs warbled from crowds
In under-coverts, yet the countenance
Of the whole place should bear a stamp of
    awe;
A habitation sober and demure
For ruminating creatures ; a domain
For quiet things to wander in ; a haunt 440
In which the heron should delight to feed
By the shy rivers, and the pelican
Upon the cypress spire in lonely thought
Might sit and sun himself. — Alas ! Alas !
In vain for such solemnity I looked ;
Mine eyes were crossed by butterflies, ears
    vexed
By chattering popinjays; the inner heart
Seemed trivial, and the impresses without
Of a too gaudy region.
                    Different sight
Those venerable Doctors saw of old,   450
When all who dwelt within these famous
    walls
Led in abstemiousness a studious life;

When, in forlorn and naked chambers
　　cooped　　　　　　　　　　　453
And crowded, o'er the ponderous books
　　they hung
Like caterpillars eating out their way
In silence, or with keen devouring noise
Not to be tracked or fathered. Princes then
At matins froze, and couched at curfew-
　　time,　　　　　　　　　　　　458
Trained up through piety and zeal to prize
Spare diet, patient labour, and plain weeds.
O seat of Arts ! renowned throughout the
　　world !
Far different service in those homely days
The Muses' modest nurslings underwent
From their first childhood: in that glorious
　　time
When Learning, like a stranger come from
　　far,
Sounding through Christian lands her
　　trumpet, roused
Peasant and king; when boys and youths,
　　the growth
Of raggèd villages and crazy huts,
Forsook their homes, and, errant in the quest
Of Patron, famous school or friendly nook,
Where, pensioned, they in shelter might sit
　　down,　　　　　　　　　　　　471
From town to town and through wide scat-
　　tered realms
Journeyed with ponderous folios in their
　　hands;
And often, starting from some covert place,
Saluted the chance comer on the road,
Crying, " An obolus, a penny give
To a poor scholar ! " — when illustrious
　　men,
Lovers of truth, by penury constrained,
Bucer, Erasmus, or Melancthon, read
Before the doors or windows of their cells
By moonshine through mere lack of taper
　　light.　　　　　　　　　　　　481

But peace to vain regrets ! We see but
　　darkly
Even when we look behind us, and best
　　things
Are not so pure by nature that they needs
Must keep to all, as fondly all believe,
Their highest promise. If the mariner,
When at reluctant distance he hath passed
Some tempting island, could but know the
　　ills
That must have fallen upon him had he
　　brought

His bark to land upon the wished-for shore,
Good cause would oft be his to thank the
　　surf　　　　　　　　　　　　491
Whose white belt scared him thence, or
　　wind that blew
Inexorably adverse: for myself
I grieve not; happy is the gownèd youth,
Who only misses what I missed, who falls
No lower than I fell.
　　　　　　　　　　I did not love,
Judging not ill perhaps, the timid course
Of our scholastic studies; could have wished
To see the river flow with ampler range
And freer pace; but more, far more, I
　　grieved　　　　　　　　　　　500
To see displayed among an eager few,
Who in the field of contest persevered,
Passions unworthy of youth's generous heart
And mounting spirit, pitiably repaid,
When so disturbed, whatever palms are
　　won.
From these I turned to travel with the shoal
Of more unthinking natures, easy minds
And pillowy; yet not wanting love that
　　makes
The day pass lightly on, when foresight
　　sleeps,
And wisdom and the pledges interchanged
With our own inner being are forgot. 511

Yet was this deep vacation not given up
To utter waste. Hitherto I had stood
In my own mind remote from social life,
(At least from what we commonly so name,)
Like a lone shepherd on a promontory,
Who lacking occupation looks far forth
Into the boundless sea, and rather makes
Than finds what he beholds. And sure it is,
That this first transit from the smooth de-
　　lights　　　　　　　　　　　520
And wild outlandish walks of simple youth
To something that resembles an approach
Towards human business, to a privileged
　　world
Within a world, a midway residence
With all its intervenient imagery,
Did better suit my visionary mind,
Far better, than to have been bolted forth,
Thrust out abruptly into Fortune's way
Among the conflicts of substantial life;
By a more just gradation did lead on 530
To higher things; more naturally matured,
For permanent possession, better fruits,
Whether of truth or virtue, to ensue.
In serious mood, but oftener, I confess,

With playful zest of fancy did we note
(How could we less?) the manners and the
    ways
Of those who lived distinguished by the
    badge
Of good or ill report; or those with whom
By frame of Academic discipline
We were perforce connected, men whose
    sway   540
And known authority of office served
To set our minds on edge, and did no more.
Nor wanted we rich pastime of this kind,
Found everywhere, but chiefly in the ring
Of the grave Elders, men unscoured, gro-
    tesque
In character, tricked out like aged trees
Which through the lapse of their infirmity
Give ready place to any random seed
That chooses to be reared upon their trunks.

Here on my view, confronting vividly
Those shepherd swains whom I had lately
    left   551
Appeared a different aspect of old age;
How different! yet both distinctly marked,
Objects embossed to catch the general eye,
Or portraitures for special use designed,
As some might seem, so aptly do they serve
To illustrate Nature's book of rudiments —
That book upheld as with maternal care
When she would enter on her tender scheme
Of teaching comprehension with delight,
And mingling playful with pathetic thoughts.

The surfaces of artificial life   562
And manners finely wrought, the delicate
    race
Of colours, lurking, gleaming up and down
Through that state arras woven with silk
    and gold;
This wily interchange of snaky hues,
Willingly or unwillingly revealed,
I neither knew nor cared for; and as such
Were wanting here, I took what might be
    found
Of less elaborate fabric. At this day   570
I smile, in many a mountain solitude
Conjuring up scenes as obsolete in freaks
Of character, in points of wit as broad,
As aught by wooden images performed
For entertainment of the gaping crowd
At wake or fair. And oftentimes do flit
Remembrances before me of old men —
Old humourists, who have been long in their
    graves,

And having almost in my mind put off
Their human names, have into phantoms
    passed   580
Of texture midway between life and books.

I play the loiterer: 't is enough to note
That here in dwarf proportions were ex-
    pressed
The limbs of the great world; its eager
    strifes
Collaterally pourtrayed, as in mock fight,
A tournament of blows, some hardly dealt
Though short of mortal combat; and what-
    e'er
Might in this pageant be supposed to hit
An artless rustic's notice, this way less,
More that way, was not wasted upon me —
And yet the spectacle may well demand
A more substantial name, no mimic show,
Itself a living part of a live whole,   593
A creek in the vast sea; for, all degrees
And shapes of spurious fame and short-lived
    praise
Here sate in state, and fed with daily alms
Retainers won away from solid good;
And here was Labour, his own bond-slave;
    Hope,
That never set the pains against the prize;
Idleness halting with his weary clog,   600
And poor misguided Shame, and witless
    Fear,
And simple Pleasure foraging for Death;
Honour misplaced, and Dignity astray;
Feuds, factions, flatteries, enmity, and guile,
Murmuring submission, and bald govern-
    ment,
(The idol weak as the idolater),
And Decency and Custom starving Truth,
And blind Authority beating with his staff
The child that might have led him; Empti-
    ness   609
Followed as of good omen, and meek Worth
Left to herself unheard of and unknown.

Of these and other kindred notices
I cannot say what portion is in truth
The naked recollection of that time,
And what may rather have been called to
    life
By after-meditation. But delight
That, in an easy temper lulled asleep,
Is still with Innocence its own reward,
This was not wanting. Carelessly I roamed
As through a wide museum from whose
    stores   620

A casual rarity is singled out
And has its brief perusal, then gives way
To others, all supplanted in their turn;
Till 'mid this crowded neighbourhood of
    things
That are by nature most unneighbourly,
The head turns round and cannot right
    itself;
And though an aching and a barren sense
Of gay confusion still be uppermost,
With few wise longings and but little love,
Yet to the memory something cleaves at
    last,   630
Whence profit may be drawn in times to
    come.

Thus in submissive idleness, my Friend!
The labouring time of autumn, winter,
    spring,
Eight months! rolled pleasingly away; the
    ninth
Came and returned me to my native hills.

BOOK FOURTH

SUMMER VACATION

BRIGHT was the summer's noon when quick-
    ening steps
Followed each other till a dreary moor
Was crossed, a bare ridge clomb, upon whose
    top
Standing alone, as from a rampart's edge,
I overlooked the bed of Windermere,
Like a vast river, stretching in the sun.
With exultation, at my feet I saw
Lake, islands, promontories, gleaming bays,
A universe of Nature's fairest forms
Proudly revealed with instantaneous burst,
Magnificent, and beautiful, and gay.   11
I bounded down the hill shouting amain
For the old Ferryman; to the shout the
    rocks
Replied, and when the Charon of the flood
Had staid his oars, and touched the jutting
    pier,
I did not step into the well-known boat
Without a cordial greeting. Thence with
    speed
Up the familiar hill I took my way
Towards that sweet Valley where I had been
    reared;
'T was but a short hour's walk, ere veering
    round   20
I saw the snow-white church upon her hill

Sit like a thronèd Lady, sending out
A gracious look all over her domain.
Yon azure smoke betrays the lurking town;
With eager footsteps I advance and reach
The cottage threshold where my journey
    closed.
Glad welcome had I, with some tears, per-
    haps,
From my old Dame, so kind and motherly,
While she perused me with a parent's pride.
The thoughts of gratitude shall fall like
    dew   30
Upon thy grave, good creature! While my
    heart
Can beat never will I forget thy name.
Heaven's blessing be upon thee where thou
    liest
After thy innocent and busy stir
In narrow cares, thy little daily growth
Of calm enjoyments, after eighty years,
And more than eighty, of untroubled life,
Childless, yet by the strangers to thy blood
Honoured with little less than filial love.   39
What joy was mine to see thee once again,
Thee and thy dwelling, and a crowd of
    things
About its narrow precincts all beloved,
And many of them seeming yet my own!
Why should I speak of what a thousand
    hearts
Have felt, and every man alive can guess?
The rooms, the court, the garden were not
    left
Long unsaluted, nor the sunny seat
Round the stone table under the dark pine,
Friendly to studious or to festive hours;
Nor that unruly child of mountain birth,   50
The froward brook, who, soon as he was
    boxed
Within our garden, found himself at once,
As if by trick insidious and unkind,
Stripped of his voice and left to dimple
    down
(Without an effort and without a will)
A channel paved by man's officious care.
I looked at him and smiled, and smiled
    again,
And in the press of twenty thousand
    thoughts,
"Ha," quoth I, "pretty prisoner, are you
    there!"
Well might sarcastic Fancy then have
    whispered,   60
" An emblem here behold of thy own life;
In its late course of even days with all

Their smooth enthralment; " but the heart
was full,
Too full for that reproach. My aged Dame
Walked proudly at my side: she guided me;
I willing, nay — nay, wishing to be led.
— The face of every neighbour whom I met
Was like a volume to me; some were hailed
Upon the road, some busy at their work,
Unceremonious greetings interchanged   70
With half the length of a long field between.
Among my schoolfellows I scattered round
Like recognitions, but with some constraint
Attended, doubtless, with a little pride,
But with more shame, for my habiliments,
The transformation wrought by gay attire.
Not less delighted did I take my place
At our domestic table: and, dear Friend !
In this endeavour simply to relate
A Poet's history, may I leave untold   80
The thankfulness with which I laid me down
In my accustomed bed, more welcome now
Perhaps than if it had been more desired
Or been more often thought of with regret;
That lowly bed whence I had heard the wind
Roar and the rain beat hard, where I so
oft
Had lain awake on summer nights to watch
The moon in splendour couched among the
leaves
Of a tall ash, that near our cottage stood;
Had watched her with fixed eyes while to
and fro   90
In the dark summit of the waving tree
She rocked with every impulse of the breeze.

Among the favourites whom it pleased me
well
To see again, was one by ancient right
Our inmate, a rough terrier of the hills;
By birth and call of nature pre-ordained
To hunt the badger and unearth the fox
Among the impervious crags, but having
been
From youth our own adopted, he had passed
Into a gentler service. And when first 100
The boyish spirit flagged, and day by day
Along my veins I kindled with the stir,
The fermentation, and the vernal heat
Of poesy, affecting private shades
Like a sick Lover, then this dog was used
To watch me, an attendant and a friend,
Obsequious to my steps early and late,
Though often of such dilatory walk
Tired, and uneasy at the halts I made. 109
A hundred times when, roving high and low,

I have been harassed with the toil of verse,
Much pains and little progress, and at once
Some lovely Image in the song rose up
Full-formed, like Venus rising from the
sea;
Then have I darted forwards to let loose
My hand upon his back with stormy joy,
Caressing him again and yet again.
And when at evening on the public way
I sauntered, like a river murmuring
And talking to itself when all things else 120
Are still, the creature trotted on before;
Such was his custom; but whene'er he met
A passenger approaching, he would turn
To give me timely notice, and straightway,
Grateful for that admonishment, I hushed
My voice, composed my gait, and, with the
air
And mien of one whose thoughts are free,
advanced
To give and take a greeting that might save
My name from piteous rumours, such as wait
On men suspected to be crazed in brain. 130

Those walks well worthy to be prized and
loved —
Regretted ! — that word, too, was on my
tongue,
But they were richly laden with all good,
And cannot be remembered but with thanks
And gratitude, and perfect joy of heart —
Those walks in all their freshness now came
back
Like a returning Spring. When first I
made
Once more the circuit of our little lake,
If ever happiness hath lodged with man,
That day consummate happiness was mine,
Wide-spreading, steady, calm, contempla-
tive.   141
The sun was set, or setting, when I left
Our cottage door, and evening soon brought
on
A sober hour, not winning or serene,
For cold and raw the air was, and untuned:
But as a face we love is sweetest then
When sorrow damps it, or, whatever look
It chance to wear, is sweetest if the heart
Have fulness in herself; even so with me
It fared that evening. Gently did my soul
Put off her veil, and, self-transmuted, stood
Naked, as in the presence of her God. 152
While on I walked, a comfort seemed to
touch
A heart that had not been disconsolate:

Strength came where weakness was not
    known to be,
At least not felt; and restoration came
Like an intruder knocking at the door
Of unacknowledged weariness. I took
The balance, and with firm hand weighed
    myself.
— Of that external scene which round me
    lay,   160
Little, in this abstraction, did I see;
Remembered less; but I had inward hopes
And swellings of the spirit, was rapt and
    soothed,
Conversed with promises, had glimmering
    views
How life pervades the undecaying mind;
How the immortal soul with God-like
    power
Informs, creates, and thaws the deepest
    sleep
That time can lay upon her; how on earth,
Man, if he do but live within the light   169
Of high endeavours, daily spreads abroad
His being armed with strength that cannot
    fail.
Nor was there want of milder thoughts, of
    love,
Of innocence, and holiday repose;
And more than pastoral quiet, 'mid the stir
Of boldest projects, and a peaceful end
At last, or glorious, by endurance won.
Thus musing, in a wood I sate me down
Alone, continuing there to muse: the slopes
And heights meanwhile were slowly over-
    spread   179
With darkness, and before a rippling breeze
The long lake lengthened out its hoary line,
And in the sheltered coppice where I sate,
Around me from among the hazel leaves,
Now here, now there, moved by the strag-
    gling wind,
Came ever and anon a breath-like sound,
Quick as the pantings of the faithful dog,
The off and on companion of my walk;
And such, at times, believing them to be,
I turned my head to look if he were there;
Then into solemn thought I passed once
    more.   190

A freshness also found I at this time
In human Life, the daily life of those
Whose occupations really I loved;
The peaceful scene oft filled me with sur-
    prise
Changed like a garden in the heat of spring

After an eight-days' absence. For (to omit
The things which were the same and yet
    appeared
Far otherwise) amid this rural solitude,
A narrow Vale where each was known to
    all,
'T was not indifferent to a youthful mind
To mark some sheltering bower or sunny
    nook   201
Where an old man had used to sit alone,
Now vacant; pale-faced babes whom I had
    left
In arms, now rosy prattlers at the feet
Of a pleased grandame tottering up and
    down;
And growing girls whose beauty, filched
    away
With all its pleasant promises, was gone
To deck some slighted playmate's homely
    cheek.

Yes, I had something of a subtler sense,
And often looking round was moved to
    smiles   210
Such as a delicate work of humour breeds;
I read, without design, the opinions,
    thoughts,
Of those plain-living people now observed
With clearer knowledge; with another eye
I saw the quiet woodman in the woods,
The shepherd roam the hills. With new
    delight,
This chiefly, did I note my grey-haired
    Dame;
Saw her go forth to church or other work
Of state, equipped in monumental trim,
Short velvet cloak, (her bonnet of the like),
A mantle such as Spanish Cavaliers   221
Wore in old time. Her smooth domestic
    life,
Affectionate without disquietude,
Her talk, her business, pleased me; and
    no less
Her clear though shallow stream of piety
That ran on Sabbath days a fresher course;
With thoughts unfelt till now I saw her
    read
Her Bible on hot Sunday afternoons,
And loved the book, when she had dropped
    asleep
And made of it a pillow for her head.   230

Nor less do I remember to have felt,
Distinctly manifested at this time,
A human-heartedness about my love

For objects hitherto the absolute wealth
Of my own private being and no more;
Which I had loved, even as a blessed spirit
Or Angel, if he were to dwell on earth,
Might love in individual happiness.
But now there opened on me other thoughts
Of change, congratulation or regret,   240
A pensive feeling ! It spread far and wide;
The trees, the mountains shared it, and the
    brooks,
The stars of Heaven, now seen in their old
    haunts —
White Sirius glittering o'er the southern
    crags,
Orion with his belt, and those fair Seven,
Acquaintances of every little child,
And Jupiter, my own belovèd star !
Whatever shadings of mortality,
Whatever imports from the world of death
Had come among these objects hereto-
    fore,   250
Were, in the main, of mood less tender:
    strong,
Deep, gloomy were they, and severe; the
    scatterings
Of awe or tremulous dread, that had given
    way
In later youth to yearnings of a love
Enthusiastic, to delight and hope.

As one who hangs down-bending from
    the side
Of a slow-moving boat, upon the breast
Of a still water, solacing himself
With such discoveries as his eye can make
Beneath him in the bottom of the deep,   260
Sees many beauteous sights — weeds, fishes,
    flowers,
Grots, pebbles, roots of trees, and fancies
    more,
Yet often is perplexed, and cannot part
The shadow from the substance, rocks and
    sky,
Mountains and clouds, reflected in the depth
Of the clear flood, from things which there
    abide
In their true dwelling; now is crossed by
    gleam
Of his own image, by a sunbeam now,
And wavering motions sent he knows not
    whence,
Impediments that make his task more
    sweet;   270
Such pleasant office have we long pursued
Incumbent o'er the surface of past time

With like success, nor often have appeared
Shapes fairer or less doubtfully discerned
Than these to which the Tale, indulgent
    Friend !
Would now direct thy notice. Yet in spite
Of pleasure won, and knowledge not with-
    held,
There was an inner falling off — I loved,
Loved deeply all that had been loved before,
More deeply even than ever: but a swarm
Of heady schemes jostling each other,
    gawds,   281
And feast and dance, and public revelry,
And sports and games (too grateful in
    themselves,
Yet in themselves less grateful, I believe,
Than as they were a badge glossy and fresh
Of manliness and freedom) all conspired
To lure my mind from firm habitual quest
Of feeding pleasures, to depress the zeal
And damp those yearnings which had once
    been mine —
A wild, unworldly-minded youth, given
    up   290
To his own eager thoughts. It would de-
    mand
Some skill, and longer time than may be
    spared
To paint these vanities, and how they
    wrought
In haunts where they, till now, had been
    unknown.
It seemed the very garments that I wore
Preyed on my strength, and stopped the
    quiet stream
Of self-forgetfulness.
             Yes, that heartless chase
Of trivial pleasures was a poor exchange
For books and nature at that early age.
'T is true, some casual knowledge might be
    gained   300
Of character or life; but at that time,
Of manners put to school I took small note,
And all my deeper passions lay elsewhere.
Far better had it been to exalt the mind
By solitary study, to uphold
Intense desire through meditative peace;
And yet, for chastisement of these regrets,
The memory of one particular hour
Doth here rise up against me. 'Mid a
    throng
Of maids and youths, old men, and matrons
    staid,   310
A medley of all tempers, I had passed
The night in dancing, gaiety, and mirth,

With din of instruments and shuffling feet,
And glancing forms, and tapers glittering,
And unaimed prattle flying up and down;
Spirits upon the stretch, and here and there
Slight shocks of young love-liking inter-
    spersed,
Whose transient pleasure mounted to the
    head,
And tingled through the veins. Ere we
    retired,
The cock had crowed, and now the eastern
    sky   320
Was kindling, not unseen, from humble
    copse
And open field, through which the pathway
    wound,
And homeward led my steps. Magnificent
The morning rose, in memorable pomp,
Glorious as e'er I had beheld — in front,
The sea lay laughing at a distance; near,
The solid mountains shone, bright as the
    clouds,
Grain-tinctured, drenched in empyrean
    light;
And in the meadows and the lower grounds
Was all the sweetness of a common
    dawn —   330
Dews, vapours, and the melody of birds,
And labourers going forth to till the fields.
Ah! need I say, dear Friend! that to the
    brim
My heart was full; I made no vows, but
    vows
Were then made for me; bond unknown to
    me
Was given, that I should be, else sinning
    greatly,
A dedicated Spirit. On I walked
In thankful blessedness, which yet survives.

Strange rendezvous! My mind was at
    that time
A parti-coloured show of grave and gay, 340
Solid and light, short-sighted and profound;
Of inconsiderate habits and sedate,
Consorting in one mansion unreproved.
The worth I knew of powers that I pos-
    sessed,
Though slighted and too oft misused. Be-
    sides,
That summer, swarming as it did with
    thoughts
Transient and idle, lacked not intervals
When Folly from the frown of fleeting
    Time

Shrunk, and the mind experienced in her-
    self
Conformity as just as that of old   350
To the end and written spirit of God's
    works,
Whether held forth in Nature or in Man,
Through pregnant vision, separate or con-
    joined.

When from our better selves we have
    too long
Been parted by the hurrying world, and
    droop,
Sick of its business, of its pleasures tired,
How gracious, how benign, is Solitude;
How potent a mere image of her sway;
Most potent when impressed upon the mind
With an appropriate human centre — her-
    mit,   360
Deep in the bosom of the wilderness;
Votary (in vast cathedral, where no foot
Is treading, where no other face is seen)
Kneeling at prayers; or watchman on the
    top
Of lighthouse, beaten by Atlantic waves;
Or as the soul of that great Power is met
Sometimes embodied on a public road,
When, for the night deserted, it assumes
A character of quiet more profound
Than pathless wastes.   Once, when those summer months
Were flown, and autumn brought its annual
    show   371
Of oars with oars contending, sails with
    sails,
Upon Winander's spacious breast, it
    chanced
That — after I had left a flower-decked
    room
(Whose in-door pastime, lighted up, sur-
    vived
To a late hour), and spirits overwrought
Were making night do penance for a day
Spent in a round of strenuous idleness —
My homeward course led up a long ascent,
Where the road's watery surface, to the
    top   380
Of that sharp rising, glittered to the moon
And bore the semblance of another stream
Stealing with silent lapse to join the brook
That murmured in the vale. All else was
    still;
No living thing appeared in earth or air,
And, save the flowing water's peaceful
    voice,

Sound there was none — but, lo! an un-
    couth shape,
Shown by a sudden turning of the road,
So near that, slipping back into the shade
Of a thick hawthorn, I could mark him
    well,   390
Myself unseen. He was of stature tall,
A span above man's common measure, tall,
Stiff, lank, and upright; a more meagre
    man
Was never seen before by night or day.
Long were his arms, pallid his hands; his
    mouth
Looked ghastly in the moonlight: from
    behind,
A mile-stone propped him; I could also ken
That he was clothed in military garb,
Though faded, yet entire. Companionless,
No dog attending, by no staff sustained, 400
He stood, and in his very dress appeared
A desolation, a simplicity,
To which the trappings of a gaudy world
Make a strange back-ground. From his
    lips, ere long,
Issued low muttered sounds, as if of pain
Or some uneasy thought; yet still his form
Kept the same awful steadiness — at his
    feet
His shadow lay, and moved not. From
    self-blame
Not wholly free, I watched him thus; at
    length
Subduing my heart's specious cowardice, 410
I left the shady nook where I had stood
And hailed him. Slowly from his resting-
    place
He rose, and with a lean and wasted arm
In measured gesture lifted to his head
Returned my salutation; then resumed
His station as before; and when I asked
His history, the veteran, in reply,
Was neither slow nor eager; but, unmoved,
And with a quiet uncomplaining voice,
A stately air of mild indifference, 420
He told in few plain words a soldier's
    tale —
That in the Tropic Islands he had served,
Whence he had landed scarcely three weeks
    past;
That on his landing he had been dismissed,
And now was travelling towards his native
    home.
This heard, I said, in pity, "Come with me."
He stooped, and straightway from the
    ground took up

An oaken staff by me yet unobserved —
A staff which must have dropped from his
    slack hand
And lay till now neglected in the grass. 430
Though weak his step and cautious, he ap-
    peared
To travel without pain, and I beheld,
With an astonishment but ill suppressed,
His ghostly figure moving at my side;
Nor could I, while we journeyed thus, for-
    bear
To turn from present hardships to the past,
And speak of war, battle, and pestilence,
Sprinkling this talk with questions, better
    spared,
On what he might himself have seen or
    felt.
He all the while was in demeanour calm, 440
Concise in answer; solemn and sublime
He might have seemed, but that in all he
    said
There was a strange half-absence, as of
    one
Knowing too well the importance of his
    theme,
But feeling it no longer. Our discourse
Soon ended, and together on we passed
In silence through a wood gloomy and still.
Up-turning, then, along an open field,
We reached a cottage. At the door I
    knocked,
And earnestly to charitable care 450
Commended him as a poor friendless man,
Belated and by sickness overcome.
Assured that now the traveller would repose
In comfort, I entreated that henceforth
He would not linger in the public ways,
But ask for timely furtherance and help
Such as his state required. At this reproof,
With the same ghastly mildness in his look,
He said, "My trust is in the God of Hea-
    ven, 459
And in the eye of him who passes me!"

    The cottage door was speedily unbarred,
And now the soldier touched his hat once
    more
With his lean hand, and in a faltering voice,
Whose tone bespake reviving interests
Till then unfelt, he thanked me; I returned
The farewell blessing of the patient man,
And so we parted. Back I cast a look,
And lingered near the door a little space,
Then sought with quiet heart my distant
    home.

BOOK FIFTH

BOOKS

When Contemplation, like the night-calm
    felt
Through earth and sky, spreads widely, and
    sends deep
Into the soul its tranquillising power,
Even then I sometimes grieve for thee, O
    Man,
Earth's paramount Creature ! not so much
    for woes
That thou endurest; heavy though that
    weight be,
Cloud-like it mounts, or touched with light
    divine
Doth melt away; but for those palms
    achieved
Through length of time, by patient exercise
Of study and hard thought; there, there,
    it is   10
That sadness finds its fuel.   Hitherto,
In progress through this Verse, my mind
    hath looked
Upon the speaking face of earth and heaven
As her prime teacher, intercourse with man
Established by the sovereign Intellect,
Who through that bodily image hath dif-
    fused,
As might appear to the eye of fleeting time,
A deathless spirit.   Thou also, man ! hast
    wrought,
For commerce of thy nature with herself,
Things that aspire to unconquerable life;
And yet we feel — we cannot choose but
    feel —   21
That they must perish.   Tremblings of the
    heart
It gives, to think that our immortal being
No more shall need such garments; and yet
    man,
As long as he shall be the child of earth,
Might almost " weep to have " what he may
    lose,
Nor be himself extinguished, but survive,
Abject, depressed, forlorn, disconsolate.
A thought is with me sometimes, and I
    say, —
Should the whole frame of earth by inward
    throes   30
Be wrenched, or fire come down from far
    to scorch
Her pleasant habitations, and dry up
Old Ocean, in his bed left singed and bare,
Yet would the living Presence still subsist

Victorious, and composure would ensue,
And kindlings like the morning — presage
    sure
Of day returning and of life revived.
But all the meditations of mankind,
Yea, all the adamantine holds of truth
By reason built, or passion, which itself   40
Is highest reason in a soul sublime;
The consecrated works of Bard and Sage,
Sensuous or intellectual, wrought by men,
Twin labourers and heirs of the same hopes;
Where would they be ?   Oh ! why hath not
    the Mind
Some element to stamp her image on
In nature somewhat nearer to her own ?
Why, gifted with such powers to send
    abroad
Her spirit, must it lodge in shrines so frail ?

One day, when from my lips a like com-
    plaint   50
Had fallen in presence of a studious friend,
He with a smile made answer, that in truth
'Twas going far to seek disquietude;
But on the front of his reproof confessed
That he himself had oftentimes given way
To kindred hauntings.   Whereupon I told,
That once in the stillness of a summer's
    noon,
While I was seated in a rocky cave
By the sea-side, perusing, so it chanced,
The famous history of the errant knight   60
Recorded by Cervantes, these same
    thoughts
Beset me, and to height unusual rose,
While listlessly I sate, and, having closed
The book, had turned my eyes toward the
    wide sea.
On poetry and geometric truth,
And their high privilege of lasting life,
From all internal injury exempt,
I mused; upon these chiefly: and at length,
My senses yielding to the sultry air,   69
Sleep seized me, and I passed into a dream.
I saw before me stretched a boundless plain
Of sandy wilderness, all black and void,
And as I looked around, distress and fear
Came creeping over me, when at my side,
Close at my side, an uncouth shape ap-
    peared
Upon a dromedary, mounted high.
He seemed an Arab of the Bedouin tribes:
A lance he bore, and underneath one arm
A stone, and in the opposite hand a shell
Of a surpassing brightness.   At the sight 80

Much I rejoiced, not doubting but a guide
Was present, one who with unerring skill
Would through the desert lead me; and
while yet   85
I looked and looked, self-questioned what
this freight
Which the new-comer carried through the
waste
Could mean, the Arab told me that the
stone
(To give it in the language of the dream)
Was "Euclid's Elements," and "This,"
said he,
"Is something of more worth;" and at the
word
Stretched forth the shell, so beautiful in
shape,   90
In colour so resplendent, with command
That I should hold it to my ear. I did so,
And heard that instant in an unknown tongue,
Which yet I understood, articulate sounds,
A loud prophetic blast of harmony;
An Ode, in passion uttered, which foretold
Destruction to the children of the earth
By deluge, now at hand. No sooner ceased
The song, than the Arab with calm look de-
clared
That all would come to pass of which the
voice   100
Had given forewarning, and that he himself
Was going then to bury those two books:
The one that held acquaintance with the
stars,
And wedded soul to soul in purest bond
Of reason, undisturbed by space or time;
The other that was a god, yea many gods,
Had voices more than all the winds, with
power
To exhilarate the spirit, and to soothe,
Through every clime, the heart of human
kind.
While this was uttering, strange as it may
seem,   110
I wondered not, although I plainly saw
The one to be a stone, the other a shell;
Nor doubted once but that they both were
books,
Having a perfect faith in all that passed.
Far stronger, now, grew the desire I felt
To cleave unto this man; but when I prayed
To share his enterprise, he hurried on
Reckless of me: I followed, not unseen,
For oftentimes he cast a backward look,
Grasping his twofold treasure. — Lance in
rest,   120

He rode, I keeping pace with him; and now
He, to my fancy, had become the knight
Whose tale Cervantes tells; yet not the
knight,
But was an Arab of the desert too;
Of these was neither, and was both at once.
His countenance, meanwhile, grew more
disturbed;
And, looking backwards when he looked,
mine eyes
Saw, over half the wilderness diffused,
A bed of glittering light: I asked the cause:
"It is," said he, "the waters of the deep   130
Gathering upon us;" quickening then the
pace
Of the unwieldy creature he bestrode,
He left me: I called after him aloud;
He heeded not; but, with his twofold charge
Still in his grasp, before me, full in view,
Went hurrying o'er the illimitable waste,
With the fleet waters of a drowning world
In chase of him; whereat I waked in terror,
And saw the sea before me, and the book,
In which I had been reading, at my side.

Full often, taking from the world of
sleep   140
This Arab phantom, which I thus beheld,
This semi-Quixote, I to him have given
A substance, fancied him a living man,
A gentle dweller in the desert, crazed
By love and feeling, and internal thought
Protracted among endless solitudes;
Have shaped him wandering upon this quest!
Nor have I pitied him; but rather felt
Reverence was due to a being thus em-
ployed;   150
And thought that, in the blind and awful
lair
Of such a madness, reason did lie couched.
Enow there are on earth to take in charge
Their wives, their children, and their virgin
loves,
Or whatsoever else the heart holds dear;
Enow to stir for these; yea, will I say,
Contemplating in soberness the approach
Of an event so dire, by signs in earth
Or heaven made manifest, that I could share
That maniac's fond anxiety, and go   160
Upon like errand. Oftentimes at least
Me hath such strong entrancement over-
come,
When I have held a volume in my hand,
Poor earthly casket of immortal verse,
Shakespeare, or Milton, labourers divine!

Great and benign, indeed, must be the
power
Of living nature, which could thus so long
Detain me from the best of other guides
And dearest helpers, left unthanked, un-
praised,
Even in the time of lisping infancy;   170
And later down, in prattling childhood even,
While I was travelling back among those
days,
How could I ever play an ingrate's part ?
Once more should I have made those bowers
resound,
By intermingling strains of thankfulness
With their own thoughtless melodies; at
least
It might have well beseemed me to repeat
Some simply fashioned tale, to tell again,
In slender accents of sweet verse, some tale
That did bewitch me then, and soothes me
now.   180
O Friend ! O Poet ! brother of my soul,
Think not that I could pass along untouched
By these remembrances. Yet wherefore
speak ?
Why call upon a few weak words to say
What is already written in the hearts
Of all that breathe ? — what in the path of
all
Drops daily from the tongue of every child,
Wherever man is found ? The trickling tear
Upon the cheek of listening Infancy
Proclaims it, and the insuperable look   190
That drinks as if it never could be full.

That portion of my story I shall leave
There registered: whatever else of power
Or pleasure sown, or fostered thus, may be
Peculiar to myself, let that remain
Where still it works, though hidden from
all search
Among the depths of time. Yet is it just
That here, in memory of all books which lay
Their sure foundations in the heart of man,
Whether by native prose, or numerous verse,
That in the name of all inspired souls —   201
From Homer the great Thunderer, from
the voice
That roars along the bed of Jewish song,
And that more varied and elaborate,
Those trumpet-tones of harmony that shake
Our shores in England, — from those loftiest
notes
Down to the low and wren-like warblings,
made

For cottagers and spinners at the wheel,
And sun-burnt travellers resting their tired
limbs,
Stretched under wayside hedge-rows, ballad
tunes,   210
Food for the hungry ears of little ones,
And of old men who have survived their
joys —
'T is just that in behalf of these, the works,
And of the men that framed them, whether
known
Or sleeping nameless in their scattered
graves,
That I should here assert their rights, attest
Their honours, and should, once for all, pro-
nounce
Their benediction; speak of them as Powers
For ever to be hallowed; only less,
For what we are and what we may become,
Than Nature's self, which is the breath of
God,   221
Or His pure Word by miracle revealed.

Rarely and with reluctance would I stoop
To transitory themes; yet I rejoice,
And, by these thoughts admonished, will
pour out
Thanks with uplifted heart, that I was
reared
Safe from an evil which these days have
laid
Upon the children of the land, a pest
That might have dried me up, body and soul.
This verse is dedicate to Nature's self,   230
And things that teach as Nature teaches.
then,
Oh ! where had been the Man, the Poet
where,
Where had we been, we two, beloved Friend!
If in the season of unperilous choice,
In lieu of wandering, as we did, through
vales
Rich with indigenous produce, open ground
Of Fancy, happy pastures ranged at will,
We had been followed, hourly watched, and
noosed,
Each in his several melancholy walk
Stringed like a poor man's heifer at its
feed,   240
Led through the lanes in forlorn servitude;
Or rather like a stalled ox debarred
From touch of growing grass, that may
not taste
A flower till it have yielded up its sweets
A prelibation to the mower's scythe.

Behold the parent hen amid her brood,
Though fledged and feathered, and well
  pleased to part
And straggle from her presence, still a
  brood,
And she herself from the maternal bond 249
Still undischarged; yet doth she little more
Than move with them in tenderness and
  love,
A centre to the circle which they make;
And now and then, alike from need of theirs
And call of her own natural appetites,
She scratches, ransacks up the earth for
  food,
Which they partake at pleasure. Early
  died
My honoured Mother, she who was the
  heart
And hinge of all our learnings and our
  loves:
She left us destitute, and, as we might,
Trooping together. Little suits it me   260
To break upon the sabbath of her rest
With any thought that looks at others'
  blame;
Nor would I praise her but in perfect love.
Hence am I checked: but let me boldly say,
In gratitude, and for the sake of truth,
Unheard by her, that she, not falsely taught,
Fetching her goodness rather from times
  past,
Than shaping novelties for times to come,
Had no presumption, no such jealousy,   269
Nor did by habit of her thoughts mistrust
Our nature, but had virtual faith that He
Who fills the mother's breast with innocent
  milk,
Doth also for our nobler part provide,
Under His great correction and control,
As innocent instincts, and as innocent food;
Or draws, for minds that are left free to
  trust
In the simplicities of opening life,
Sweet honey out of spurned or dreaded
  weeds.
This was her creed, and therefore she was
  pure
From anxious fear of error or mishap,   280
And evil, overweeningly so called;
Was not puffed up by false unnatural hopes,
Nor selfish with unnecessary cares,
Nor with impatience from the season asked
More than its timely produce; rather loved
The hours for what they are, than from
  regard

Glanced on their promises in restless pride.
Such was she — not from faculties more
  strong
Than others have, but from the times, per-
  haps,
And spot in which she lived, and through a
  grace   290
Of modest meekness, simple-mindedness,
A heart that found benignity and hope,
Being itself benign.
                         My drift I fear
Is scarcely obvious; but, that common sense
May try this modern system by its fruits,
Leave let me take to place before her sight
A specimen pourtrayed with faithful hand.
Full early trained to worship seemliness,
This model of a child is never known
To mix in quarrels; that were far beneath
Its dignity; with gifts he bubbles o'er   301
As generous as a fountain; selfishness
May not come near him, nor the little throng
Of flitting pleasures tempt him from his
  path;
The wandering beggars propagate his name,
Dumb creatures find him tender as a nun,
And natural or supernatural fear,
Unless it leap upon him in a dream,
Touches him not. To enhance the wonder,
  see
How arch his notices, how nice his sense
Of the ridiculous; not blind is he   311
To the broad follies of the licensed world,
Yet innocent himself withal, though shrewd,
And can read lectures upon innocence;
A miracle of scientific lore,
Ships he can guide across the pathless sea,
And tell you all their cunning; he can read
The inside of the earth, and spell the stars;
He knows the policies of foreign lands;
Can string you names of districts, cities,
  towns,   320
The whole world over, tight as beads of
  dew
Upon a gossamer thread; he sifts, he
  weighs;
All things are put to question; he must live
Knowing that he grows wiser every day
Or else not live at all, and seeing too
Each little drop of wisdom as it falls
Into the dimpling cistern of his heart:
For this unnatural growth the trainer blame,
Pity the tree. — Poor human vanity,   329
Wert thou extinguished, little would be left
Which he could truly love; but how escape?
For, ever as a thought of purer birth

Rises to lead him toward a better clime,
Some intermeddler still is on the watch
To drive him back, and pound him, like a stray,
Within the pinfold of his own conceit.
Meanwhile old grandame earth is grieved to find
The playthings, which her love designed for him,
Unthought of: in their woodland beds the flowers
Weep, and the river sides are all forlorn. 340
Oh ! give us once again the wishing-cap
Of Fortunatus, and the invisible coat
Of Jack the Giant-killer, Robin Hood,
And Sabra in the forest with St. George !
The child, whose love is here, at least, doth reap
One precious gain, that he forgets himself.

These mighty workmen of our later age,
Who, with a broad highway, have over-bridged
The froward chaos of futurity,
Tamed to their bidding; they who have the skill 350
To manage books, and things, and make them act
On infant minds as surely as the sun
Deals with a flower; the keepers of our time,
The guides and wardens of our faculties,
Sages who in their prescience would control
All accidents, and to the very road
Which they have fashioned would confine us down,
Like engines; when will their presumption learn,
That in the unreasoning progress of the world
A wiser spirit is at work for us, 360
A better eye than theirs, most prodigal
Of blessings, and most studious of our good,
Even in what seem our most unfruitful hours ?

There was a Boy: ye knew him well, ye cliffs
And islands of Winander ! — many a time
At evening, when the earliest stars began
To move along the edges of the hills,
Rising or setting, would he stand alone
Beneath the trees or by the glimmering lake,
And there, with fingers interwoven, both hands 370

Pressed closely palm to palm, and to his mouth
Uplifted, he, as through an instrument,
Blew mimic hootings to the silent owls,
That they might answer him; and they would shout
Across the watery vale, and shout again,
Responsive to his call, with quivering peals,
And long halloos and screams, and echoes loud,
Redoubled and redoubled, concourse wild
Of jocund din; and, when a lengthened pause
Of silence came and baffled his best skill,
Then sometimes, in that silence while he hung 381
Listening, a gentle shock of mild surprise
Has carried far into his heart the voice
Of mountain torrents; or the visible scene
Would enter unawares into his mind,
With all its solemn imagery, its rocks,
Its woods, and that uncertain heaven, received
Into the bosom of the steady lake.

This Boy was taken from his mates, and died
In childhood, ere he was full twelve years old. 390
Fair is the spot, most beautiful the vale
Where he was born; the grassy church-yard hangs
Upon a slope above the village school,
And through that churchyard when my way has led
On summer evenings, I believe that there
A long half hour together I have stood
Mute, looking at the grave in which he lies !
Even now appears before the mind's clear eye
That self-same village church; I see her sit
(The thronèd Lady whom erewhile we hailed)
On her green hill, forgetful of this Boy 401
Who slumbers at her feet, — forgetful, too,
Of all her silent neighbourhood of graves,
And listening only to the gladsome sounds
That, from the rural school ascending, play
Beneath her and about her. May she long
Behold a race of young ones like to those
With whom I herded ! — (easily, indeed,
We might have fed upon a fatter soil
Of arts and letters — but be that forgiven)—
A race of real children; not too wise, 411
Too learned, or too good; but wanton, fresh,
And bandied up and down by love and hate;

Not unresentful where self-justified;
Fierce, moody, patient, venturous, modest,
   shy;
Mad at their sports like withered leaves in
   winds;
Though doing wrong and suffering, and full
   oft
Bending beneath our life's mysterious weight
Of pain, and doubt, and fear, yet yielding not
In happiness to the happiest upon earth.   420
Simplicity in habit, truth in speech,
Be these the daily strengtheners of their
   minds;
May books and Nature be their early joy !
And knowledge, rightly honoured with that
   name —
Knowledge not purchased by the loss of
   power !

Well do I call to mind the very week
When I was first intrusted to the care
Of that sweet Valley; when its paths, its
   shores,
And brooks were like a dream of novelty
To my half-infant thoughts; that very week,
While I was roving up and down alone,   431
Seeking I knew not what, I chanced to cross
One of those open fields, which, shaped like
   ears,
Make green peninsulas on Esthwaite's Lake:
Twilight was coming on, yet through the
   gloom
Appeared distinctly on the opposite shore
A heap of garments, as if left by one
Who might have there been bathing. Long
   I watched,
But no one owned them; meanwhile the
   calm lake
Grew dark with all the shadows on its breast,
And, now and then, a fish up-leaping
   snapped   441
The breathless stillness. The succeeding
   day,
Those unclaimed garments telling a plain
   tale
Drew to the spot an anxious crowd; some
   looked
In passive expectation from the shore,
While from a boat others hung o'er the
   deep,
Sounding with grappling irons and long
   poles.
At last, the dead man, 'mid that beauteous
   scene
Of trees and hills and water, bolt upright

Rose, with his ghastly face, a spectre
   shape   450
Of terror; yet no soul-debasing fear,
Young as I was, a child not nine years old,
Possessed me, for my inner eye had seen
Such sights before, among the shining
   streams
Of faëry land, the forest of romance.
Their spirit hallowed the sad spectacle
With decoration of ideal grace;
A dignity, a smoothness, like the works
Of Grecian art, and purest poesy.

A precious treasure had I long pos-
   sessed,   460
A little yellow, canvas-covered book,
A slender abstract of the Arabian tales;
And, from companions in a new abode,
When first I learnt, that this dear prize of
   mine
Was but a block hewn from a mighty
   quarry —
That there were four large volumes, laden
   all
With kindred matter, 't was to me, in truth,
A promise scarcely earthly. Instantly,
With one not richer than myself, I made
A covenant that each should lay aside   470
The moneys he possessed, and hoard up
   more
Till our joint savings had amassed enough
To make this book our own. Through
   several months,
In spite of all temptation, we preserved
Religiously that vow; but firmness failed,
Nor were we ever masters of our wish.

And when thereafter to my father's house
The holidays returned me, there to find
That golden store of books which I had
   left,
What joy was mine ! How often in the
   course   480
Of those glad respites, though a soft west
   wind
Ruffled the waters to the angler's wish
For a whole day together, have I lain
Down by thy side, O Derwent ! murmur-
   ing stream,
On the hot stones, and in the glaring sun,
And there have read, devouring as I read,
Defrauding the day's glory, desperate !
Till with a sudden bound of smart reproach,
Such as an idler deals with in his shame,
I to the sport betook myself again.   490

A gracious spirit o'er this earth presides,
And o'er the heart of man; invisibly
It comes, to works of unreproved delight,
And tendency benign, directing those
Who care not, know not, think not what
    they do.
The tales that charm away the wakeful night
In Araby, romances; legends penned
For solace by dim light of monkish lamps;
Fictions, for ladies of their love, devised
By youthful squires; adventures endless,
    spun   500
By the dismantled warrior in old age,
Out of the bowels of those very schemes
In which his youth did first extravagate;
These spread like day, and something in
    the shape
Of these will live till man shall be no more.
Dumb yearnings, hidden appetites, are ours,
And *they must* have their food. Our child-
    hood sits,
Our simple childhood, sits upon a throne
That hath more power than all the ele-
    ments.
I guess not what this tells of Being past,   510
Nor what it augurs of the life to come;
But so it is; and, in that dubious hour —
That twilight — when we first begin to see
This dawning earth, to recognise, expect,
And, in the long probation that ensues,
The time of trial, ere we learn to live
In reconcilement with our stinted powers;
To endure this state of meagre vassalage,
Unwilling to forego, confess, submit,
Uneasy and unsettled, yoke-fellows   520
To custom, mettlesome, and not yet tamed
And humbled down — oh ! then we feel, we
    feel,
We know where we have friends. Ye
    dreamers, then,
Forgers of daring tales ! we bless you then,
Impostors, drivellers, dotards, as the ape
Philosophy will call you: *then* we feel
With what, and how great might ye are in
    league,
Who make our wish, our power, our thought
    a deed,
An empire, a possession, — ye whom time
And seasons serve; all Faculties to whom   530
Earth crouches, the elements are potter's
    clay,
Space like a heaven filled up with northern
    lights,
Here, nowhere, there, and everywhere at
    once.

Relinquishing this lofty eminence
For ground, though humbler, not the less **a**
    tract
Of the same isthmus, which our spirits
    cross
In progress from their native continent
To earth and human life, the Song might
    dwell
On that delightful time of growing youth,
When craving for the marvellous gives
    way   540
To strengthening love for things that we
    have seen ;
When sober truth and steady sympathies,
Offered to notice by less daring pens,
Take firmer hold of us, and words them-
    selves
Move us with conscious pleasure.
                                     I am sad
At thought of raptures now for ever flown ;
Almost to tears I sometimes could be sad
To think of, to read over, many a page,
Poems withal of name, which at that time
Did never fail to entrance me, and are
    now   550
Dead in my eyes, dead as a theatre
Fresh emptied of spectators. Twice five
    years
Or less I might have seen, when first my
    mind
With conscious pleasure opened to the
    charm
Of words in tuneful order, found them
    sweet
For their own *sakes*, a passion, and a power;
And phrases pleased me chosen for delight,
For pomp, or love. Oft, in the public roads
Yet unfrequented, while the morning light
Was yellowing the hill tops, I went
    abroad   560
With a dear friend, and for the better part
Of two delightful hours we strolled along
By the still borders of the misty lake,
Repeating favourite verses with one voice,
Or conning more, as happy as the birds
That round us chaunted. Well might we
    be glad,
Lifted above the ground by airy fancies,
More bright than madness or the dreams
    of wine;
And, though full oft the objects of our love
Were false, and in their splendour over-
    wrought,   570
Yet was there surely then no vulgar power
Working within us, — nothing less, in truth,

Than that most noble attribute of man,
Though yet untutored and inordinate,
That wish for something loftier, more adorned,
Than is the common aspect, daily garb,
Of human life. What wonder, then, if sounds
Of exultation echoed through the groves !
For, images, and sentiments, and words,
And everything encountered or pursued 580
In that delicious world of poesy,
Kept holiday, a never-ending show,
With music, incense, festival, and flowers !

Here must we pause: this only let me add,
From heart-experience, and in humblest sense
Of modesty, that he, who in his youth
A daily wanderer among woods and fields
With living Nature hath been intimate,
Not only in that raw unpractised time
Is stirred to ecstasy, as others are, 590
By glittering verse; but further, doth receive,
In measure only dealt out to himself,
Knowledge and increase of enduring joy
From the great Nature that exists in works
Of mighty Poets. Visionary power
Attends the motions of the viewless winds,
Embodied in the mystery of words:
There, darkness makes abode, and all the host
Of shadowy things work endless changes, — there,
As in a mansion like their proper home, 600
Even forms and substances are circumfused
By that transparent veil with light divine,
And, through the turnings intricate of verse,
Present themselves as objects recognised,
In flashes, and with glory not their own.

BOOK SIXTH

CAMBRIDGE AND THE ALPS

THE leaves were fading when to Esthwaite's banks
And the simplicities of cottage life
I bade farewell; and, one among the youth
Who, summoned by that season, reunite
As scattered birds troop to the fowler's lure,
Went back to Granta's cloisters, not so prompt

Or eager, though as gay and undepressed
In mind, as when I thence had taken flight
A few short months before. I turned my face
Without repining from the coves and heights 10
Clothed in the sunshine of the withering fern;
Quitted, not loth, the mild magnificence
Of calmer lakes and louder streams; and you,
Frank-hearted maids of rocky Cumberland,
You and your not unwelcome days of mirth,
Relinquished, and your nights of revelry,
And in my own unlovely cell sate down
In lightsome mood — such privilege has youth
That cannot take long leave of pleasant thoughts.

The bonds of indolent society 20
Relaxing in their hold, henceforth I lived
More to myself. Two winters may be passed
Without a separate notice: many books
Were skimmed, devoured, or studiously perused,
But with no settled plan. I was detached
Internally from academic cares;
Yet independent study seemed a course
Of hardy disobedience toward friends
And kindred, proud rebellion and unkind.
This spurious virtue, rather let it bear 30
A name it more deserves, this cowardice,
Gave treacherous sanction to that over-love
Of freedom which encouraged me to turn
From regulations even of my own
As from restraints and bonds. Yet who can tell —
Who knows what thus may have been gained, both then
And at a later season, or preserved;
What love of nature, what original strength
Of contemplation, what intuitive truths,
The deepest and the best, what keen research, 40
Unbiassed, unbewildered, and unawed ?

The Poet's soul was with me at that time;
Sweet meditations, the still overflow
Of present happiness, while future years
Lacked not anticipations, tender dreams,
No few of which have since been realised;
And some remain, hopes for my future life.
Four years and thirty, told this very week,

Have I been now a sojourner on earth,
By sorrow not unsmitten; yet for me   50
Life's morning radiance hath not left the
    hills,
Her dew is on the flowers. Those were
    the days
Which also first emboldened me to trust
With firmness, hitherto but lightly touched
By such a daring thought, that I might
    leave
Some monument behind me which pure
    hearts
Should reverence.   The instinctive humble-
    ness,
Maintained even by the very name and
    thought
Of printed books and authorship, began
To melt away; and further, the dread awe
Of mighty names was softened down and
    seemed   61
Approachable, admitting fellowship
Of modest sympathy. Such aspect now,
Though not familiarly, my mind put on,
Content to observe, to admire, and to enjoy.

All winter long, whenever free to choose,
Did I by night frequent the College groves
And tributary walks; the last, and oft
The only one, who had been lingering there
Through hours of silence, till the porter's
    bell,   70
A punctual follower on the stroke of nine,
Rang with its blunt unceremonious voice,
Inexorable summons! Lofty elms,
Inviting shades of opportune recess,
Bestowed composure on a neighbourhood
Unpeaceful in itself.   A single tree
With sinuous trunk, boughs exquisitely
    wreathed,
Grew there; an ash which Winter for him-
    self
Decked as in pride, and with outlandish
    grace:
Up from the ground, and almost to the top,
The trunk and every master branch were
    green   81
With clustering ivy, and the lightsome twigs
And outer spray profusely tipped with seeds
That hung in yellow tassels, while the air
Stirred them, not voiceless. Often have I
    stood
Foot-bound uplooking at this lovely tree
Beneath a frosty moon. The hemisphere
Of magic fiction, verse of mine perchance
May never tread; but scarcely Spenser's self

Could have more tranquil visions in his
    youth,   90
Or could more bright appearances create
Of human forms with superhuman powers,
Than I beheld, loitering on calm clear
    nights
Alone, beneath this fairy work of earth.

On the vague reading of a truant youth
'T were idle to descant. My inner judgment
Not seldom differed from my taste in books,
As if it appertained to another mind,
And yet the books which then I valued
    most
Are dearest to me now; for, having scanned,
Not heedlessly, the laws, and watched the
    forms   101
Of Nature, in that knowledge I possessed
A standard, often usefully applied,
Even when unconsciously, to things re-
    moved
From a familiar sympathy. — In fine,
I was a better judge of thoughts than words,
Misled in estimating words, not only
By common inexperience of youth,
But by the trade in classic niceties,
The dangerous craft of culling term and
    phrase   110
From languages that want the living voice
To carry meaning to the natural heart;
To tell us what is passion, what is truth,
What reason, what simplicity and sense.

Yet may we not entirely overlook
The pleasure gathered from the rudiments
Of geometric science. Though advanced
In these inquiries, with regret I speak,
No farther than the threshold, there I found
Both elevation and composed delight: 120
With Indian awe and wonder, ignorance
    pleased
With its own struggles, did I meditate
On the relation those abstractions bear
To Nature's laws, and by what process led,
Those immaterial agents bowed their heads
Duly to serve the mind of earth-born man;
From star to star, from kindred sphere to
    sphere,
From system on to system without end.

More frequently from the same source I
    drew
A pleasure quiet and profound, a sense   131
Of permanent and universal sway,
And paramount belief; there, recognised

A type, for finite natures, of the one
Supreme Existence, the surpassing life
Which — to the boundaries of space and
    time,
Of melancholy space and doleful time,
Superior, and incapable of change,
Nor touched by welterings of passion — is,
And hath the name of, God. Transcendent
    peace   139
And silence did await upon these thoughts
That were a frequent comfort to my youth.

'T is told by one whom stormy waters
    threw,
With fellow-sufferers by the shipwreck
    spared,
Upon a desert coast, that having brought
To land a single volume, saved by chance,
A treatise of Geometry, he wont,
Although of food and clothing destitute,
And beyond common wretchedness de-
    pressed,
To part from company and take this book
(Then first a self-taught pupil in its
    truths)   150
To spots remote, and draw his diagrams
With a long staff upon the sand, and thus
Did oft beguile his sorrow, and almost
Forget his feeling: so (if like effect
From the same cause produced, 'mid out-
    ward things
So different, may rightly be compared),
So was it then with me, and so will be
With Poets ever. Mighty is the charm
Of those abstractions to a mind beset
With images, and haunted by herself,   160
And specially delightful unto me
Was that clear synthesis built up aloft
So gracefully; even then when it appeared
Not more than a mere plaything, or a toy
To sense embodied: not the thing it is
In verity, an independent world,
Created out of pure intelligence.

Such dispositions then were mine un-
    earned
By aught, I fear, of genuine desert —
Mine, through heaven's grace and inborn
    aptitudes.   170
And not to leave the story of that time
Imperfect, with these habits must be joined,
Moods melancholy, fits of spleen, that loved
A pensive sky, sad days, and piping winds,
The twilight more than dawn, autumn than
    spring;

A treasured and luxurious gloom of choice
And inclination mainly, and the mere
Redundancy of youth's contentedness.
— To time thus spent, add multitudes of
    hours   179
Pilfered away, by what the Bard who sang
Of the Enchanter Indolence hath called
" Good-natured lounging," and behold a map
Of my collegiate life — far less intense
Than duty called for, or, without regard
To duty, *might* have sprung up of itself
By change of accidents, or even, to speak
Without unkindness, in another place.
Yet why take refuge in that plea ? — the
    fault,
This I repeat, was mine; mine be the blame.

In summer, making quest for works of
    art,   190
Or scenes renowned for beauty, I explored
That streamlet whose blue current works
    its way
Between romantic Dovedale's spiry rocks;
Pried into Yorkshire dales, or hidden tracts
Of my own native region, and was blest
Between these sundry wanderings with a joy
Above all joys, that seemed another morn
Risen on mid noon; blest with the presence,
    Friend!
Of that sole Sister, her who hath been long
Dear to thee also, thy true friend and mine,
Now, after separation desolate,   201
Restored to me — such absence that she
    seemed
A gift then first bestowed. The varied
    banks
Of Emont, hitherto unnamed in song,
And that monastic castle, 'mid tall trees,
Low-standing by the margin of the stream,
A mansion visited (as fame reports)
By Sidney, where, in sight of our Helvellyn,
Or stormy Cross-fell, snatches he might pen
Of his Arcadia, by fraternal love   210
Inspired; — that river and those mouldering
    towers
Have seen us side by side, when, having
    clomb
The darksome windings of a broken stair,
And crept along a ridge of fractured wall,
Not without trembling, we in safety looked
Forth, through some Gothic window's open
    space,
And gathered with one mind a rich reward
From the far-stretching landscape, by the
    light

Of morning beautified, or purple eve;
Or, not less pleased, lay on some turret's
    head, 220
Catching from tufts of grass and hare-bell
    flowers
Their faintest whisper to the passing breeze,
Given out while mid-day heat oppressed the
    plains.

Another maid there was, who also shed
A gladness o'er that season, then to me,
By her exulting outside look of youth
And placid under - countenance, first en-
    deared;
That other spirit, Coleridge ! who is now
So near to us, that meek confiding heart,
So reverenced by us both. O'er paths and
    fields 230
In all that neighbourhood, through narrow
    lanes
Of eglantine, and through the shady woods
And o'er the Border Beacon, and the waste
Of naked pools, and common crags that lay
Exposed on the bare fell, were scattered
    love,
The spirit of pleasure, and youth's golden
    gleam.
O Friend ! we had not seen thee at that
    time,
And yet a power is on me, and a strong
Confusion, and I seem to plant thee there.
Far art thou wandered now in search of
    health 240
And milder breezes, — melancholy lot !
But thou art with us, with us in the past,
The present, with us in the times to come.
There is no grief, no sorrow, no despair,
No languor, no dejection, no dismay,
No absence scarcely can there be, for those
Who love as we do. Speed thee well ! divide
With us thy pleasure; thy returning
    strength,
Receive it daily as a joy of ours;
Share with us thy fresh spirits, whether gift
Of gales Etesian or of tender thoughts. 251

I, too, have been a wanderer; but, alas !
How different the fate of different men.
Though mutually unknown, yea nursed and
    reared
As if in several elements, we were framed
To bend at last to the same discipline,
Predestined, if two beings ever were,
To seek the same delights, and have one
    health,

One happiness. Throughout this narrative,
Else sooner ended, I have borne in mind 260
For whom it registers the birth, and marks
    the growth,
Of gentleness, simplicity, and truth,
And joyous loves, that hallow innocent days
Of peace and self-command. Of rivers,
    fields,
And groves I speak to thee, my Friend ! to
    thee,
Who, yet a liveried schoolboy, in the depths
Of the huge city, on the leaded roof
Of that wide edifice, thy school and home,
Wert used to lie and gaze upon the clouds
Moving in heaven; or, of that pleasure tired,
To shut thine eyes, and by internal light 271
See trees, and meadows, and thy native
    stream,
Far distant, thus beheld from year to year
Of a long exile. Nor could I forget,
In this late portion of my argument,
That scarcely, as my term of pupilage
Ceased, had I left those academic bowers
When thou wert thither guided. From the
    heart
Of London, and from cloisters there, thou
    camest, 279
And didst sit down in temperance and peace,
A rigorous student. What a stormy course
Then followed. Oh ! it is a pang that calls
For utterance, to think what easy change
Of circumstances might to thee have spared
A world of pain, ripened a thousand hopes,
For ever withered. Through this retrospect
Of my collegiate life I still have had
Thy after-sojourn in the self-same place
Present before my eyes, have played with
    times
And accidents as children do with cards, 290
Or as a man, who, when his house is built,
A frame locked up in wood and stone, doth
    still,
As impotent fancy prompts, by his fireside,
Rebuild it to his liking. I have thought
Of thee, thy learning, gorgeous eloquence,
And all the strength and plumage of thy
    youth,
Thy subtle speculations, toils abstruse
Among the schoolmen, and Platonic forms
Of wild ideal pageantry, shaped out
From things well-matched or ill, and words
    for things, 300
The self-created sustenance of a mind
Debarred from Nature's living images,
Compelled to be a life unto herself,

And unrelentingly possessed by thirst
Of greatness, love, and beauty. Not alone,
Ah ! surely not in singleness of heart
Should I have seen the light of evening fade
From smooth Cam's silent waters: had we
    met,
Even at that early time, needs must I trust
In the belief, that my maturer age,   310
My calmer habits, and more steady voice,
Would with an influence benign have soothed,
Or chased away, the airy wretchedness
That battened on thy youth. But thou hast
    trod
A march of glory, which doth put to shame
These vain regrets; health suffers in thee,
    else
Such grief for thee would be the weakest
    thought
That ever harboured in the breast of man.

A passing word erewhile did lightly
    touch
On wanderings of my own, that now em-
    braced   320
With livelier hope a region wider far.

When the third summer freed us from
    restraint,
A youthful friend, he too a mountaineer,
Not slow to share my wishes, took his staff,
And sallying forth, we journeyed side by
    side,
Bound to the distant Alps. A hardy slight,
Did this unprecedented course imply,
Of college studies and their set rewards;
Nor had, in truth, the scheme been formed
    by me
Without uneasy forethought of the pain,   330
The censures, and ill-omening, of those
To whom my worldly interests were dear.
But Nature then was sovereign in my mind,
And mighty forms, seizing a youthful fancy,
Had given a charter to irregular hopes.
In any age of uneventful calm
Among the nations, surely would my heart
Have been possessed by similar desire;
But Europe at that time was thrilled with
    joy,
France standing on the top of golden
    hours,   340
And human nature seeming born again.

Lightly equipped, and but a few brief
    looks
Cast on the white cliffs of our native shore
From the receding vessel's deck, we
    chanced
To land at Calais on the very eve
Of that great federal day; and there we
    saw,
In a mean city, and among a few,
How bright a face is worn when joy of one
Is joy for tens of millions. Southward
    thence
We held our way, direct through hamlets,
    towns,   350
Gaudy with reliques of that festival,
Flowers left to wither on triumphal arcs,
And window-garlands. On the public
    roads,
And, once, three days successively, through
    paths
By which our toilsome journey was
    abridged,
Among sequestered villages we walked
And found benevolence and blessedness
Spread like a fragrance everywhere, when
    spring
Hath left no corner of the land untouched;
Where elms for many and many a league
    in files   360
With their thin umbrage, on the stately
    roads
Of that great kingdom, rustled o'er our
    heads,
For ever near us as we paced along:
How sweet at such a time, with such de-
    light
On every side, in prime of youthful
    strength,
To feed a Poet's tender melancholy
And fond conceit of sadness, with the sound
Of undulations varying as might please
The wind that swayed them; once, and
    more than once,
Unhoused beneath the evening star we
    saw   370
Dances of liberty, and, in late hours
Of darkness, dances in the open air
Deftly prolonged, though grey-haired
    lookers on
Might waste their breath in chiding.
                              Under hills —
The vine-clad hills and slopes of Burgundy,
Upon the bosom of the gentle Saone
We glided forward with the flowing stream.
Swift Rhone ! thou wert the *wings* on
    which we cut
A winding passage with majestic ease
Between thy lofty rocks. Enchanting show

Those woods and farms and orchards did
    present,   381
And single cottages and lurking towns,
Reach after reach, succession without end
Of deep and stately vales ! A lonely pair
Of strangers, till day closed, we sailed
    along
Clustered together with a merry crowd
Of those emancipated, a blithe host
Of travellers, chiefly delegates, returning
From the great spousals newly solemnised
At their chief city, in the sight of Heaven.
Like bees they swarmed, gaudy and gay as
    bees;   391
Some vapoured in the unruliness of joy,
And with their swords flourished as if to
    fight
The saucy air. In this proud company
We landed — took with them our evening
    meal,
Guests welcome almost as the angels were
To Abraham of old. The supper done,
With flowing cups elate and happy thoughts
We rose at signal given, and formed a ring
And, hand in hand, danced round and
    round the board;   400
All hearts were open, every tongue was
    loud
With amity and glee; we bore a name
Honoured in France, the name of English-
    men,
And hospitably did they give us hail,
As their forerunners in a glorious course;
And round and round the board we danced
    again.
With these blithe friends our voyage we
    renewed
At early dawn. The monastery bells
Made a sweet jingling in our youthful ears;
The rapid river flowing without noise,   410
And each uprising or receding spire
Spake with a sense of peace, at intervals
Touching the heart amid the boisterous
    crew
By whom we were encompassed. Taking
    leave
Of this glad throng, foot-travellers side by
    side,
Measuring our steps in quiet, we pursued
Our journey, and ere twice the sun had
    set
Beheld the Convent of Chartreuse, and
    there
Rested within an awful *solitude:*
Yes; for even then no other than a place   420

Of soul-affecting *solitude* appeared
That far-famed region, though our eyes
    had seen,
As toward the sacred mansion we advanced,
Arms flashing, and a military glare
Of riotous men commissioned to expel
The blameless inmates, and belike subvert
That frame of social being, which so long
Had bodied forth the ghostliness of things
In silence visible and perpetual calm.
— "Stay, stay your sacrilegious hands !" —
    The voice   430
Was Nature's, uttered from her Alpine
    throne;
I heard it then and seem to hear it now —
" Your impious work forbear, perish what
    may,
Let this one temple last, be this one spot
Of earth devoted to eternity ! "
She ceased to speak, but while St. Bruno's
    pines
Waved their dark tops, not silent as they
    waved,
And while below, along their several beds,
Murmured the·sister streams of Life and
    Death,
Thus by conflicting passions pressed, my
    heart   440
Responded; " Honour to the patriot's zeal !
Glory and hope to new-born Liberty !
Hail to the mighty projects of the time !
Discerning sword that Justice wields, do
    thou
Go forth and prosper; and, ye purging
    fires,
Up to the loftiest towers of Pride ascend,
Fanned by the breath of angry Providence.
But oh ! if Past and Future be the wings
On whose support harmoniously conjoined
Moves the great spirit of human knowledge,
    spare   450
These courts of mystery, where a step ad-
    vanced
Between the portals of the shadowy rocks
Leaves far behind life's treacherous vani-
    ties,
For penitential tears and trembling hopes
Exchanged — to equalise in God's pure
    sight
Monarch and peasant: be the house re-
    deemed
With its unworldly votaries, for the sake
Of conquest over sense, hourly achieved
Through faith and meditative reason, rest-
    ing

Upon the word of heaven - imparted
   truth,   460
Calmly triumphant; and for humbler claim
Of that imaginative impulse sent
From these majestic floods, yon shining
   cliffs,
The untransmuted shapes of many worlds,
Cerulean ether's pure inhabitants,
These forests unapproachable by death,
That shall endure as long as man endures,
To think, to hope, to worship, and to feel,
To struggle, to be lost within himself
In trepidation, from the blank abyss   470
To look with bodily eyes, and be consoled."
Not seldom since that moment have I
   wished
That thou, O Friend ! the trouble or the
   calm
Hadst shared, when, from profane regards
   apart,
In sympathetic reverence we trod
The floors of those dim cloisters, till that
   hour,
From their foundation, strangers to the
   presence
Of unrestricted and unthinking man.
Abroad, how cheeringly the sunshine lay
Upon the open lawns ! Vallombre's
   groves   480
Entering, we fed the soul with darkness;
   thence
Issued, and with uplifted eyes beheld,
In different quarters of the bending sky,
The cross of Jesus stand erect, as if
Hands of angelic powers had fixed it there,
Memorial reverenced by a thousand storms;
Yet then, from the undiscriminating sweep
And rage of one State-whirlwind, insecure.

'T is not my present purpose to retrace
That variegated journey step by step.   490
A march it was of military speed,
And Earth did change her images and forms
Before us, fast as clouds are changed in
   heaven.
Day after day, up early and down late,
From hill to vale we dropped, from vale to
   hill
Mounted — from province on to province
   swept,
Keen hunters in a chase of fourteen weeks,
Eager as birds of prey, or as a ship
Upon the stretch, when winds are blowing
   fair: 499
Sweet coverts did we cross of pastoral life,

Enticing valleys, greeted them and left
Too soon, while yet the very flash and
   gleam
Of salutation were not passed away.
Oh ! sorrow for the youth who could have
   seen,
Unchastened, unsubdued, unawed, unraised
To patriarchal dignity of mind,
And pure simplicity of wish and will,
Those sanctified abodes of peaceful man,
Pleased (though to hardship born, and com-
   passed round   509
With danger, varying as the seasons change),
Pleased with his daily task, or, if not pleased,
Contented, from the moment that the dawn
(Ah ! surely not without attendant gleams
Of soul-illumination) calls him forth
To industry, by glistenings flung on rocks,
Whose evening shadows lead him to repose.

   Well might a stranger look with bound-
   ing heart
Down on a green recess, the first I saw
Of those deep haunts, an aboriginal vale,
Quiet and lorded over and possessed   520
By naked huts, wood-built, and sown like
   tents
Or Indian cabins over the fresh lawns
And by the river side.
                      That very day,
From a bare ridge we also first beheld
Unveiled the summit of Mont Blanc, and
   grieved
To have a soulless image on the eye
That had usurped upon a living thought
That never more could be. The wondrous
   Vale
Of Chamouny stretched far below, and
   soon
With its dumb cataracts and streams of
   ice,   530
A motionless array of mighty waves,
Five rivers broad and vast, made rich
   amends,
And reconciled us to realities;
There small birds warble from the leafy
   trees,
The eagle soars high in the element,
There doth the reaper bind the yellow
   sheaf,
The maiden spread the haycock in the sun,
While Winter like a well-tamed lion walks,
Descending from the mountain to make
   sport
Among the cottages by beds of flowers.   540

Whate'er in this wide circuit we beheld,
Or heard, was fitted to our unripe state
Of intellect and heart.   With such a book
Before our eyes, we could not choose but
     read
Lessons of genuine brotherhood, the plain
And universal reason of mankind,
The truths of young and old. Nor, side by
     side
Pacing, two social pilgrims, or alone
Each with his humour, could we fail to
     abound
In dreams and fictions, pensively composed:
Dejection taken up for pleasure's sake, 551
And gilded sympathies, the willow wreath,
And sober posies of funereal flowers,
Gathered among those solitudes sublime
From formal gardens of the lady Sorrow,
Did sweeten many a meditative hour.

Yet still in me with those soft luxuries
Mixed something of stern mood, an under-
     thirst
Of vigour seldom utterly allayed:
And from that source how different a sad-
     ness   560
Would issue, let one incident make known.
When from the Vallais we had turned, and
     clomb
Along the Simplon's steep and rugged road,
Following a band of muleteers, we reached
A halting-place, where all together took
Their noon-tide meal. Hastily rose our
     guide,
Leaving us at the board; awhile we lin-
     gered,
Then paced the beaten downward way that
     led
Right to a rough stream's edge, and there
     broke off;
The only track now visible was one   570
That from the torrent's further brink held
     forth
Conspicuous invitation to ascend
A lofty mountain.   After brief delay
Crossing the unbridged stream, that road
     we took,
And clomb with eagerness, till anxious
     fears
Intruded, for we failed to overtake
Our comrades gone before. By fortunate
     chance,
While every moment added doubt to doubt,
A peasant met us, from whose mouth we
     learned

That to the spot which had perplexed us
     first   580
We must descend, and there should find the
     road,
Which in the stony channel of the stream
Lay a few steps, and then along its banks;
And, that our future course, all plain to
     sight,
Was downwards, with the current of that
     stream.
Loth to believe what we so grieved to hear,
For still we had hopes that pointed to the
     clouds,
We questioned him again, and yet again;
But every word that from the peasant's lips
Came in reply, translated by our feelings,
Ended in this, — *that we had crossed the
     Alps.*   591

Imagination — here the Power so called
Through sad incompetence of human speech,
That awful Power rose from the mind's
     abyss
Like an unfathered vapour that enwraps,
At once, some lonely traveller. I was lost;
Halted without an effort to break through;
But to my conscious soul I now can say —
" I recognise thy glory: " in such strength
Of usurpation, when the light of sense 600
Goes out, but with a flash that has revealed
The invisible world, doth greatness make
     abode,
There harbours; whether we be young or
     old,
Our destiny, our being's heart and home,
Is with infinitude, and only there;
With hope it is, hope that can never die,
Effort, and expectation, and desire,
And something evermore about to be.
Under such banners militant, the soul
Seeks for no trophies, struggles for no
     spoils   610
That may attest her prowess, blest in
     thoughts
That are their own perfection and reward,
Strong in herself and in beatitude
That hides her, like the mighty flood of
     Nile
Poured from his fount of Abyssinian clouds
To fertilise the whole Egyptian plain.

The melancholy slackening that ensued
Upon those tidings by the peasant given
Was soon dislodged. Downwards we hur-
     ried fast,

And, with the half-shaped road which we
    had missed,   620
Entered a narrow chasm. The brook and
    road
Were fellow-travellers in this gloomy strait,
And with them did we journey several hours
At a slow pace. The immeasurable height
Of woods decaying, never to be decayed,
The stationary blasts of waterfalls,
And in the narrow rent at every turn
Winds thwarting winds, bewildered and for-
    lorn,
The torrents shooting from the clear blue
    sky,
The rocks that muttered close upon our
    ears,   630
Black drizzling crags that spake by the
    way-side
As if a voice were in them, the sick sight
And giddy prospect of the raving stream,
The unfettered clouds and region of the
    Heavens,
Tumult and peace, the darkness and the
    light—
Were all like workings of one mind, the
    features
Of the same face, blossoms upon one tree;
Characters of the great Apocalypse,
The types and symbols of Eternity,
Of first, and last, and midst, and without
    end.   640

That night our lodging was a house that
    stood
Alone within the valley, at a point
Where, tumbling from aloft, a torrent
    swelled
The rapid stream whose margin we had
    trod;
A dreary mansion, large beyond all need,
With high and spacious rooms, deafened
    and stunned
By noise of waters, making innocent sleep
Lie melancholy among weary bones.

Uprisen betimes, our journey we re-
    newed,
Led by the stream, ere noon-day magni-
    fied   650
Into a lordly river, broad and deep,
Dimpling along in silent majesty,
With mountains for its neighbours, and in
    view
Of distant mountains and their snowy tops,
And thus proceeding to Locarno's Lake,

Fit resting-place for such a visitant.
Locarno! spreading out in width like
    Heaven,
How dost thou cleave to the poetic heart,
Bask in the sunshine of the memory;
And Como! thou, a treasure whom the
    earth   660
Keeps to herself, confined as in a depth
Of Abyssinian privacy. I spake
Of thee, thy chestnut woods, and garden
    plots
Of Indian corn tended by dark-eyed maids;
Thy lofty steeps, and pathways roofed with
    vines,
Winding from house to house, from town
    to town,
Sole link that binds them to each other;
    walks,
League after league, and cloistral avenues,
Where silence dwells if music be not there:
While yet a youth undisciplined in verse,
Through fond ambition of that hour I
    strove   671
To chant your praise; nor can approach
    you now
Ungreeted by a more melodious Song,
Where tones of Nature smoothed by learned
    Art
May flow in lasting current. Like a breeze
Or sunbeam over your domain I passed
In motion without pause; but ye have
    left
Your beauty with me, a serene accord
Of forms and colours, passive, yet endowed
In their submissiveness with power as sweet
And gracious, almost, might I dare to say,
As virtue is, or goodness; sweet as love, 682
Or the remembrance of a generous deed,
Or mildest visitations of pure thought,
When God, the giver of all joy, is thanked
Religiously, in silent blessedness;
Sweet as this last herself, for such it is.

With those delightful pathways we ad-
    vanced,
For two days' space, in presence of the
    Lake,
That, stretching far among the Alps, as-
    sumed   690
A character more stern. The second night,
From sleep awakened, and misled by sound
Of the church clock telling the hours with
    strokes
Whose import then we had not learned, we
    rose

By moonlight, doubting not that day was
    nigh,
And that meanwhile, by no uncertain path,
Along the winding margin of the lake,
Led, as before, we should behold the scene
Hushed in profound repose. We left the
    town
Of Gravedona with this hope; but soon   700
Were lost, bewildered among woods im-
    mense,
And on a rock sate down, to wait for day.
An open place it was, and overlooked,
From high, the sullen water far beneath,
On which a dull red image of the moon
Lay bedded, changing oftentimes its form
Like an uneasy snake. From hour to hour
We sate and sate, wondering, as if the
    night
Had been ensnared by witchcraft. On the
    rock
At last we stretched our weary limbs for
    sleep,   710
But *could not* sleep, tormented by the stings
Of insects, which, with noise like that of
    noon,
Filled all the woods: the cry of unknown
    birds;
The mountains more by blackness visible
And their own size, than any outward
    light;
The breathless wilderness of clouds; the
    clock
That told, with unintelligible voice,
The widely parted hours; the noise of
    streams,
And sometimes rustling motions nigh at
    hand,
That did not leave us free from personal
    fear;   720
And, lastly, the withdrawing moon, that
    set
Before us, while she still was high in
    heaven; —
These were our food; and such a summer's
    night
Followed that pair of golden days that
    shed
On Como's Lake, and all that round it lay,
Their fairest, softest, happiest influence.

    But here I must break off, and bid fare-
    well
To days, each offering some new sight, or
    fraught
With some untried adventure, in a course

Prolonged till sprinklings of autumnal
    snow   730
Checked our unwearied steps. Let this
    alone
Be mentioned as a parting word, that not
In hollow exultation, dealing out
Hyperboles of praise comparative;
Not rich one moment to be poor for ever;
Not prostrate, overborne, as if the mind
Herself were nothing, a mere pensioner
On outward forms — did we in presence
    stand
Of that magnificent region. On the front
Of this whole Song is written that my
    heart   740
Must, in such Temple, needs have offered
    up
A different worship. Finally, whate'er
I saw, or heard, or felt, was but a stream
That flowed into a kindred stream; a gale,
Confederate with the current of the soul,
To speed my voyage; every sound or sight,
In its degree of power, administered
To grandeur or to tenderness, — to the one
Directly, but to tender thoughts by means
Less often instantaneous in effect;   750
Led me to these by paths that, in the main,
Were more circuitous, but not less sure
Duly to reach the point marked out by
    Heaven.

    Oh, most belovèd Friend! a glorious
    time,
A happy time that was; triumphant looks
Were then the common language of all
    eyes;
As if awaked from sleep, the Nations hailed
Their great expectancy: the fife of war
Was then a spirit-stirring sound indeed,
A blackbird's whistle in a budding grove.
We left the Swiss exulting in the fate   761
Of their near neighbours; and, when
    shortening fast
Our pilgrimage, nor distant far from home,
We crossed the Brabant armies on the fret
For battle in the cause of Liberty.
A stripling, scarcely of the household then
Of social life, I looked upon these things
As from a distance; heard, and saw, and
    felt,
Was touched, but with no intimate concern;
I seemed to move along them, as a bird   770
Moves through the air, or as a fish pursues
Its sport, or feeds in its proper element;
I wanted not that joy, I did not need

Such help; the ever-living universe,
Turn where I might, was opening out its
    glories,
And the independent spirit of pure youth
Called forth, at every season, new delights,
Spread round my steps like sunshine o'er
    green fields.

BOOK SEVENTH

RESIDENCE IN LONDON

Six changeful years have vanished since I
    first
Poured out (saluted by that quickening
    breeze
Which met me issuing from the City's
    walls)
A glad preamble to this Verse: I sang
Aloud, with fervour irresistible
Of short-lived transport, like a torrent
    bursting,
From a black thunder-cloud, down Scafell's
    side
To rush and disappear. But soon broke
    forth
(So willed the Muse) a less impetuous
    stream,   9
That flowed awhile with unabating strength,
Then stopped for years; not audible again
Before last primrose-time. Belovèd Friend !
The assurance which then cheered some
    heavy thoughts
On thy departure to a foreign land
Has failed; too slowly moves the promised
    work.
Through the whole summer have I been at
    rest,
Partly from voluntary holiday,
And part through outward hindrance. But
    I heard,
After the hour of sunset yester-even,
Sitting within doors between light and
    dark,   20
A choir of redbreasts gathered somewhere
    near
My threshold, — minstrels from the distant
    woods
Sent in on Winter's service, to announce,
With preparation artful and benign,
That the rough lord had left the surly
    North
On his accustomed journey. The delight,
Due to this timely notice, unawares
Smote me, and, listening, I in whispers said,

" Ye heartsome Choristers, ye and I will be
Associates, and, unscared by blustering
    winds,   30
Will chant together." Thereafter, as the
    shades
Of twilight deepened, going forth, I spied
A glow-worm underneath a dusky plume
Or canopy of yet unwithered fern,
Clear-shining, like a hermit's taper seen
Through a thick forest. Silence touched
    me here
No less than sound had done before; the
    child
Of Summer, lingering, shining, by herself,
The voiceless worm on the unfrequented
    hills,
Seemed sent on the same errand with the
    choir   40
Of Winter that had warbled at my door,
And the whole year breathed tenderness
    and love.

    The last night's genial feeling overflowed
Upon this morning, and my favourite grove,
Tossing in sunshine its dark boughs aloft,
As if to make the strong wind visible,
Wakes in me agitations like its own,
A spirit friendly to the Poet's task,
Which we will now resume with lively hope,
Nor checked by aught of tamer argument
That lies before us, needful to be told.   51

    Returned from that excursion, soon I bade
Farewell for ever to the sheltered seats
Of gownèd students, quitted hall and
    bower,
And every comfort of that privileged
    ground,
Well pleased to pitch a vagrant tent among
The unfenced regions of society.

    Yet, undetermined to what course of life
I should adhere, and seeming to possess
A little space of intermediate time   60
At full command, to London first I turned,
In no disturbance of excessive hope,
By personal ambition unenslaved,
Frugal as there was need, and, though
    self-willed,
From dangerous passions free. Three
    years had flown
Since I had felt in heart and soul the shock
Of the huge town's first presence, and had
    paced
Her endless streets, a transient visitant:

Now, fixed amid that concourse of mankind
Where Pleasure whirls about incessantly, 70
And life and labour seem but one, I filled
An idler's place; an idler well content
To have a house (what matter for a home ?)
That owned him; living cheerfully abroad
With unchecked fancy ever on the stir,
And all my young affections out of doors.

There was a time when whatsoe'er is
    feigned
Of airy palaces, and gardens built
By Genii of romance; or hath in grave
Authentic history been set forth of Rome,
Alcairo, Babylon, or Persepolis;   81
Or given upon report by pilgrim friars,
Of golden cities ten months' journey deep
Among Tartarian wilds — fell short, far
    short,
Of what my fond simplicity believed
And thought of London — held me by a
    chain
Less strong of wonder and obscure delight.
Whether the bolt of childhood's Fancy shot
For me beyond its ordinary mark,
'T were vain to ask; but in our flock of
    boys   90
Was One, a cripple from his birth, whom
    chance
Summoned from school to London; fortu-
    nate
And envied traveller ! When the Boy
    returned,
After short absence, curiously I scanned
His mien and person, nor was free, in sooth,
From disappointment, not to find some
    change
In look and air, from that new region
    brought,
As if from Fairy-land. Much I questioned
    him;
And every word he uttered, on my ears
Fell flatter than a cagèd parrot's note,   100
That answers unexpectedly awry,
And mocks the prompter's listening. Mar-
    vellous things
Had vanity (quick Spirit that appears
Almost as deeply seated and as strong
In a Child's heart as fear itself) conceived
For my enjoyment. Would that I could
    now
Recall what then I pictured to myself,
Of mitred Prelates, Lords in ermine clad,
The King, and the King's Palace, and, not
    last,

Nor least, Heaven bless him ! the renowned
    Lord Mayor.   110
Dreams not unlike to those which once begat
A change of purpose in young Whittington,
When he, a friendless and a drooping boy,
Sate on a stone, and heard the bells speak
    out
Articulate music. Above all, one thought
Baffled my understanding: how men lived
Even next-door neighbours, as we say, yet
    still
Strangers, not knowing each the other's
    name.

Oh, wondrous power of words, by simple
    faith   119
Licensed to take the meaning that we love !
Vauxhall and Ranelagh ! I then had heard
Of your green groves, and wilderness of
    lamps
Dimming the stars, and fireworks magical,
And gorgeous ladies, under splendid domes,
Floating in dance, or warbling high in air
The songs of spirits ! Nor had Fancy
    fed
With less delight upon that other class
Of marvels, broad-day wonders permanent:
The River proudly bridged; the dizzy top
And Whispering Gallery of St. Paul's; the
    tombs   130
Of Westminster; the Giants of Guildhall;
Bedlam, and those carved maniacs at the
    gates,
Perpetually recumbent; Statues — man,
And the horse under him — in gilded pomp
Adorning flowery gardens, 'mid vast
    squares;
The Monument, and that Chamber of the
    Tower
Where England's sovereigns sit in long
    array,
Their steeds bestriding, — every mimic
    shape
Cased in the gleaming mail the monarch
    wore,
Whether for gorgeous tournament ad-
    dressed,   140
Or life or death upon the battle-field.
Those bold imaginations in due time
Had vanished, leaving others in their stead:
And now I looked upon the living scene;
Familiarly perused it; oftentimes,
In spite of strongest disappointment, pleased
Through courteous self-submission, as a tax
Paid to the object by prescriptive right.

Rise up, thou monstrous ant-hill on the
　　plain
Of a too busy world ! Before me flow,　150
Thou endless stream of men and moving
　　things !
Thy every-day appearance, as it strikes —
With wonder heightened, or sublimed by
　　awe —
On strangers, of all ages; the quick dance
Of colours, lights, and forms; the deafening
　　din;
The comers and the goers face to face,
Face after face; the string of dazzling wares,
Shop after shop, with symbols, blazoned
　　names,
And all the tradesman's honours overhead:
Here, fronts of houses, like a title-page,　160
With letters huge inscribed from top to
　　toe,
Stationed above the door, like guardian
　　saints;
There, allegoric shapes, female or male,
Or physiognomies of real men,
Land-warriors, kings, or admirals of the
　　sea,
Boyle, Shakspeare, Newton, or the attrac-
　　tive head
Of some quack-doctor, famous in his day.

Meanwhile the roar continues, till at
　　length,
Escaped as from an enemy, we turn
Abruptly into some sequestered nook,　170
Still as a sheltered place when winds blow
　　loud !
At leisure, thence, through tracts of thin
　　resort,
And sights and sounds that come at inter-
　　vals,
We take our way.　A raree-show is here,
With children gathered round; another
　　street
Presents a company of dancing dogs,
Or dromedary, with an antic pair
Of monkeys on his back; a minstrel band
Of Savoyards; or, single and alone,
An English ballad-singer.　Private courts,
Gloomy as coffins, and unsightly lanes　181
Thrilled by some female vendor's scream,
　　belike
The very shrillest of all London cries,
May then entangle our impatient steps;
Conducted through those labyrinths, un-
　　awares,
To privileged regions and inviolate,

Where from their airy lodges studious
　　lawyers
Look out on waters, walks, and gardens
　　green.

Thence back into the throng, until we
　　reach,
Following the tide that slackens by degrees,
Some half-frequented scenes, where wider
　　streets　　　191
Bring straggling breezes of suburban air.
Here files of ballads dangle from dead walls;
Advertisements, of giant-size, from high
Press forward, in all colours, on the sight;
These, bold in conscious merit, lower down;
That, fronted with a most imposing word,
Is, peradventure, one in masquerade.
As on the broadening causeway we advance,
Behold, turned upwards, a face hard and
　　strong　　　200
In lineaments, and red with over-toil.
'T is one encountered here and everywhere;
A travelling cripple, by the trunk cut short,
And stumping on his arms.　In sailor's garb
Another lies at length, beside a range
Of well-formed characters, with chalk in-
　　scribed
Upon the smooth flat stones: the Nurse is
　　here,
The Bachelor, that loves to sun himself,
The military Idler, and the Dame,
That field-ward takes her walk with decent
　　steps.　　　210

Now homeward through the thickening
　　hubbub, where
See, among less distinguishable shapes,
The begging scavenger, with hat in hand;
The Italian, as he thrids his way with care,
Steadying, far-seen, a frame of images
Upon his head; with basket at his breast
The Jew; the stately and slow-moving Turk,
With freight of slippers piled beneath his
　　arm !

Enough; — the mighty concourse I sur-
　　veyed
With no unthinking mind, well pleased to
　　note　　　220
Among the crowd all specimens of man,
Through all the colours which the sun be-
　　stows,
And every character of form and face:
The Swede, the Russian; from the genial
　　south,

The Frenchman and the Spaniard; from re-
mote
America, the Hunter-Indian; Moors,
Malays, Lascars, the Tartar, the Chinese,
And Negro Ladies in white muslin gowns.

At leisure, then, I viewed, from day to
day,
The spectacles within doors, — birds and
beasts   230
Of every nature, and strange plants con-
vened
From every clime; and, next, those sights
that ape
The absolute presence of reality,
Expressing, as in mirror, sea and land,
And what earth is, and what she has to
show.
I do not here allude to subtlest craft,
By means refined attaining purest ends,
But imitations, fondly made in plain
Confession of man's weakness and his loves.
Whether the Painter, whose ambitious skill
Submits to nothing less than taking in   241
A whole horizon's circuit, do with power,
Like that of angels or commissioned spirits,
Fix us upon some lofty pinnacle,
Or in a ship on waters, with a world
Of life, and life-like mockery beneath,
Above, behind, far stretching and before;
Or more mechanic artist represent
By scale exact, in model, wood or clay,   249
From blended colours also borrowing help,
Some miniature of famous spots or things, —
St. Peter's Church; or, more aspiring aim,
In microscopic vision, Rome herself;
Or, haply, some choice rural haunt, — the
Falls
Of Tivoli; and, high upon that steep,
The Sibyl's mouldering Temple ! every tree,
Villa, or cottage, lurking among rocks
Throughout the landscape; tuft, stone
scratch minute —
All that the traveller sees when he is there.

Add to these exhibitions, mute and still,
Others of wider scope, where living men,
Music, and shifting pantomimic scenes,   262
Diversified the allurement.   Need I fear
To mention by its name, as in degree,
Lowest of these and humblest in attempt,
Yet richly graced with honours of her own,
Half-rural Sadler's Wells ?   Though at that
time
Intolerant, as is the way of youth

Unless itself be pleased, here more than
once   269
Taking my seat, I saw (nor blush to add,
With ample recompense) giants and dwarfs,
Clowns, conjurors, posture-masters, harle-
quins,
Amid the uproar of the rabblement,
Perform their feats.   Nor was it mean de-
light
To watch crude Nature work in untaught
minds;
To note the laws and progress of belief;
Though obstinate on this way, yet on that
How willingly we travel, and how far !
To have, for instance, brought upon the
scene   279
The champion, Jack the Giant-killer: Lo !
He dons his coat of darkness; on the stage
Walks, and achieves his wonders, from the
eye
Of living Mortal covert, "as the moon
Hid in her vacant interlunar cave."
Delusion bold ! and how can it be wrought ?
The garb he wears is black as death, the
word
" *Invisible* " flames forth upon his chest.

Here, too, were " forms and pressures of
the time,"
Rough, bold, as Grecian comedy displayed
When Art was young; dramas of living
men,   290
And recent things yet warm with life; a
sea-fight,
Shipwreck, or some domestic incident
Divulged by Truth and magnified by Fame;
Such as the daring brotherhood of late
Set forth, too serious theme for that light
place —
I mean, O distant Friend ! a story drawn
From our own ground, — the Maid of But-
termere, —
And how, unfaithful to a virtuous wife
Deserted and deceived, the Spoiler came
And wooed the artless daughter of the hills,
And wedded her, in cruel mockery   301
Of love and marriage bonds.   These words
to thee
Must needs bring back the moment when
we first,
Ere the broad world rang with the maiden's
name,
Beheld her serving at the cottage inn;
Both stricken, as she entered or withdrew,
With admiration of her modest mien

And carriage, marked by unexampled grace.
We since that time not unfamiliarly
Have seen her, — her discretion have ob-
    served,   310
Her just opinions, delicate reserve,
Her patience, and humility of mind
Unspoiled by commendation and the excess
Of public notice — an offensive light
To a meek spirit suffering inwardly.

From this memorial tribute to my theme
I was returning, when, with sundry forms
Commingled — shapes which met me in the
    way
That we must tread — thy image rose again,
Maiden of Buttermere ! She lives in peace
Upon the spot where she was born and reared;
Without contamination doth she live   322
In quietness, without anxiety:
Beside the mountain chapel, sleeps in earth
Her new-born infant, fearless as a lamb
That, thither driven from some unsheltered
    place,
Rests underneath the little rock-like pile
When storms are raging. Happy are they
    both —
Mother and child ! — These feelings, in
    themselves   329
Trite, do yet scarcely seem so when I think
On those ingenuous moments of our youth
Ere we have learnt by use to slight the
    crimes
And sorrows of the world. Those simple
    days
Are now my theme; and, foremost of the
    scenes,
Which yet survive in memory, appears
One, at whose centre sate a lovely Boy,
A sportive infant, who, for six months'
    space,
Not more, had been of age to deal about
Articulate prattle — Child as beautiful
As ever clung around a mother's neck,   340
Or father fondly gazed upon with pride.
There, too, conspicuous for stature tall
And large dark eyes, beside her infant stood
The mother; but, upon her cheeks diffused,
False tints too well accorded with the glare
From play-house lustres thrown without re-
    serve
On every object near. The Boy had been
The pride and pleasure of all lookers-on
In whatsoever place, but seemed in this
A sort of alien scattered from the clouds.
Of lusty vigour, more than infantine   351

He was in limb, in cheek a summer rose
Just three parts blown — a cottage-child —
    if e'er,
By cottage-door on breezy mountain-side,
Or in some sheltering vale, was seen a
    babe
By Nature's gifts so favoured. Upon a
    board
Decked with refreshments had this child
    been placed,
His little stage in the vast theatre,
And there he sate, surrounded with a
    throng
Of chance spectators, chiefly dissolute men
And shameless women, treated and ca-
    ressed;   361
Ate, drank, and with the fruit and glasses
    played,
While oaths and laughter and indecent
    speech
Were rife about him as the songs of birds
Contending after showers. The mother
    now
Is fading out of memory, but I see
The lovely Boy as I beheld him then
Among the wretched and the falsely gay,
Like one of those who walked with hair
    unsinged   369
Amid the fiery furnace. Charms and spells
Muttered on black and spiteful instigation
Have stopped, as some believe, the kind-
    liest growths.
Ah, with how different spirit might a prayer
Have been preferred, that this fair creature,
    checked
By special privilege of Nature's love,
Should in his childhood be detained for
    ever !
But with its universal freight the tide
Hath rolled along, and this bright innocent,
Mary ! may now have lived till he could
    look   379
With envy on thy nameless babe that sleeps,
Beside the mountain chapel, undisturbed.

Four rapid years had scarcely then been
    told
Since, travelling southward from our pas-
    toral hills,
I heard, and for the first time in my life,
The voice of woman utter blasphemy —
Saw woman as she is, to open shame
Abandoned, and the pride of public vice;
I shuddered, for a barrier seemed at once
Thrown in that from humanity divorced

Humanity, splitting the race of man　　390
In twain, yet leaving the same outward
　　form.　　　　　　　.
Distress of mind ensued upon the sight,
And ardent meditation.　Later years
Brought to such spectacle a milder sadness,
Feelings of pure commiseration, grief
For the individual and the overthrow
Of her soul's beauty; farther I was then
But seldom led, or wished to go; in truth
The sorrow of the passion stopped me
　　there.

　　But let me now, less moved, in order
　　take　　　　　　　400
Our argument.　Enough is said to show
How casual incidents of real life,
Observed where pastime only had been
　　sought,
Outweighed, or put to flight, the set events
And measured passions of the stage, albeit
By Siddons trod in the fulness of her power.
Yet was the theatre my dear delight;
The very gilding, lamps and painted scrolls,
And all the mean upholstery of the place,
Wanted not animation, when the tide　　410
Of pleasure ebbed but to return as fast
With the ever-shifting figures of the scene,
Solemn or gay: whether some beauteous
　　dame
Advanced in radiance through a deep recess
Of thick entangled forest, like the moon
Opening the clouds; or sovereign king,
　　announced
With flourishing trumpet, came in full-
　　blown state
Of the world's greatness, winding round
　　with train
Of courtiers, banners, and a length of
　　guards;
Or captive led in abject weeds, and jin-
　　gling　　　　　　　420
His slender manacles; or romping girl
Bounced, leapt, and pawed the air; or
　　mumbling sire,
A scare-crow pattern of old age dressed up
In all the tatters of infirmity
All loosely put together, hobbled in,
Stumping upon a cane with which he smites,
From time to time, the solid boards, and
　　makes them
Prate somewhat loudly of the whereabout
Of one so overloaded with his years.
But what of this! the laugh, the grin, gri-
　　mace,　　　　　　　430

The antics striving to outstrip each other,
Were all received, the least of them not
　　lost,
With an unmeasured welcome.　Through
　　the night,
Between the show, and many-headed mass
Of the spectators, and each several nook
Filled with its fray or brawl, how eagerly
And with what flashes, as it were, the mind
Turned this way — that way! sportive and
　　alert
And watchful, as a kitten when at play,
While winds are eddying round her, among
　　straws　　　　　　　440
And rustling leaves.　Enchanting age and
　　sweet!
Romantic almost, looked at through a space,
How small, of intervening years!　For then,
Though surely no mean progress had been
　　made
In meditations holy and sublime,
Yet something of a girlish child-like gloss
Of novelty survived for scenes like these;
Enjoyment haply handed down from times
When at a country-playhouse, some rude
　　barn
Tricked out for that proud use, if I per-
　　chance　　　　　　　450
Caught, on a summer evening through a
　　chink
In the old wall, an unexpected glimpse
Of daylight, the bare thought of where I
　　was
Gladdened me more than if I had been led
Into a dazzling cavern of romance,
Crowded with Genii busy among works
Not to be looked at by the common sun.

　　The matter that detains us now may
　　seem,
To many, neither dignified enough
Nor arduous, yet will not be scorned by
　　them,　　　　　　　460
Who, looking inward, have observed the
　　ties
That bind the perishable hours of life
Each to the other, and the curious props
By which the world of memory and thought
Exists and is sustained.　More lofty themes,
Such as at least do wear a prouder face,
Solicit our regard; but when I think
Of these, I feel the imaginative power
Languish within me; even then it slept,
When, pressed by tragic sufferings, the
　　heart　　　　　　　470

Was more than full; amid my sobs and
   tears
It slept, even in the pregnant season of
   youth.
For though I was most passionately moved
And yielded to all changes of the scene
With an obsequious promptness, yet the
   storm
Passed not beyond the suburbs of the mind;
Save when realities of act and mien,
The incarnation of the spirits that move
In harmony amid the Poet's world,
Rose to ideal grandeur, or, called forth   480
By power of contrast, made me recognise,
As at a glance, the things which I had
   shaped,
And yet not shaped, had seen and scarcely
   seen,
When, having closed the mighty Shak-
   speare's page,
I mused, and thought, and felt, in soli-
   tude.

Pass we from entertainments, that are
   such
Professedly, to others titled higher,
Yet, in the estimate of youth at least,
More near akin to those than names im-
   ply, —
I mean the brawls of lawyers in their courts
Before the ermined judge, or that great
   stage   491
Where senators, tongue-favoured men, per-
   form,
Admired and envied. Oh! the beating
   heart,
When one among the prime of these rise
   up, —
One, of whose name from childhood we had
   heard
Familiarly, a household term, like those,
The Bedfords, Glosters, Salsburys, of old,
Whom the fifth Harry talks of. Silence!
   hush!
This is no trifler, no short-flighted wit,
No stammerer of a minute, painfully   500
Delivered. No! the Orator hath yoked
The Hours, like young Aurora, to his car:
Thrice welcome Presence! how can patience
   e'er
Grow weary of attending on a track
That kindles with such glory! All are
   charmed,
Astonished; like a hero in romance,
He winds away his never-ending horn;

Words follow words, sense seems to follow
   sense:
What memory and what logic! till the
   strain   509
Transcendent, superhuman as it seemed,
Grows tedious even in a young man's ear.

Genius of Burke! forgive the pen se-
   duced
By specious wonders, and too slow to tell
Of what the ingenuous, what bewildered
   men,
Beginning to mistrust their boastful guides,
And wise men, willing to grow wiser,
   caught,
Rapt auditors! from thy most eloquent
   tongue —
Now mute, for ever mute in the cold grave.
I see him, — old, but vigorous in age, —
Stand like an oak whose stag-horn branches
   start   520
Out of its leafy brow, the more to awe
The younger brethren of the grove. But
   some —
While he forewarns, denounces, launches
   forth,
Against all systems built on abstract rights,
Keen ridicule; the majesty proclaims
Of Institutes and Laws, hallowed by time;
Declares the vital power of social ties
Endeared by Custom; and with high dis-
   dain,
Exploding upstart Theory, insists
Upon the allegiance to which men are
   born —   530
Some — say at once a froward multitude —
Murmur (for truth is hated, where not
   loved)
As the winds fret within the Æolian cave,
Galled by their monarch's chain. The times
   were big
With ominous change, which, night by
   night, provoked
Keen struggles, and black clouds of passion
   raised;
But memorable moments intervened,
When Wisdom, like the Goddess from
   Jove's brain,
Broke forth in armour of resplendent words,
Startling the Synod. Could a youth, and
   one   540
In ancient story versed, whose breast had
   heaved
Under the weight of classic eloquence,
Sit, see, and hear, unthankful, uninspired?

Nor did the Pulpit's oratory fail
To achieve its higher triumph. Not unfelt
Were its admonishments, nor lightly heard
The awful truths delivered thence by
    tongues
Endowed with various power to search the
    soul;
Yet ostentation, domineering, oft
Poured forth harangues, how sadly out of
    place ! —   550
There have I seen a comely bachelor,
Fresh from a toilette of two hours, ascend
His rostrum, with seraphic glance look up,
And, in a tone elaborately low
Beginning, lead his voice through many a
    maze
A minuet course; and, winding up his
    mouth,
From time to time, into an orifice
Most delicate, a lurking eyelet, small,
And only not invisible, again
Open it out, diffusing thence a smile   560
Of rapt irradiation, exquisite.
Meanwhile the Evangelists, Isaiah, Job,
Moses, and he who penned, the other day,
The Death of Abel, Shakspeare, and the
    Bard
Whose genius spangled o'er a gloomy theme
With fancies thick as his inspiring stars,
And Ossian (doubt not — 't is the naked
    truth)
Summoned from streamy Morven — each
    and all
Would, in their turns, lend ornaments and
    flowers
To entwine the crook of eloquence that
    helped   570
This pretty Shepherd, pride of all the plains,
To rule and guide his captivated flock.

I glance but at a few conspicuous marks,
Leaving a thousand others, that, in hall,
Court, theatre, conventicle, or shop,
In public room or private, park or street,
Each fondly reared on his own pedestal,
Looked out for admiration. Folly, vice,
Extravagance in gesture, mien, and dress,
And all the strife of singularity,   580
Lies to the ear, and lies to every sense —
Of these, and of the living shapes they
    wear,
There is no end. Such candidates for re-
    gard,
Although well pleased to be where they
    were found,

I did not hunt after, nor greatly prize,
Nor made unto myself a secret boast
Of reading them with quick and curious
    eye;
But, as a common produce, things that are
To-day, to-morrow will be, took of them
Such willing note, as, on some errand bound
That asks not speed, a traveller might be-
    stow   591
On sea-shells that bestrew the sandy beach,
Or daisies swarming through the fields of
    June.

But foolishness and madness in parade,
Though most at home in this their dear
    domain,
Are scattered everywhere, no rarities,
Even to the rudest novice of the Schools.
Me, rather, it employed, to note, and keep
In memory, those individual sights
Of courage, or integrity, or truth,   600
Or tenderness, which there, set off by foil,
Appeared more touching. One will I se-
    lect —
A Father — for he bore that sacred
    name; —
Him saw I, sitting in an open square,
Upon a corner-stone of that low wall,
Wherein were fixed the iron pales that
    fenced
A spacious grass-plot; there, in silence,
    sate
This One Man, with a sickly babe out-
    stretched
Upon his knee, whom he had thither
    brought
For sunshine, and to breathe the fresher
    air.   610
Of those who passed, and me who looked at
    him,
He took no heed; but in his brawny arms
(The Artificer was to the elbow bare,
And from his work this moment had been
    stolen)
He held the child, and, bending over it,
As if he were afraid both of the sun
And of the air, which he had come to seek,
Eyed the poor babe with love unutterable.

As the black storm upon the mountain top
Sets off the sunbeam in the valley, so   620
That huge fermenting mass of human-kind
Serves as a solemn back-ground, or relief,
To single forms and objects, whence they
    draw,

For feeling and contemplative regard,
More than inherent liveliness and power.
How oft, amid those overflowing streets,
Have I gone forward with the crowd, and said
Unto myself, " The face of every one
That passes by me is a mystery ! "
Thus have I looked, nor ceased to look, op-
pressed   630
By thoughts of what and whither, when
and how,
Until the shapes before my eyes became
A second-sight procession, such as glides
Over still mountains, or appears in dreams;
And once, far-travelled in such mood, be-
yond
The reach of common indication, lost
Amid the moving pageant, I was smitten
Abruptly, with the view (a sight not rare)
Of a blind Beggar, who, with upright face,
Stood, propped against a wall, upon his
chest   640
Wearing a written paper, to explain
His story, whence he came, and who he
was.
Caught by the spectacle my mind turned
round
As with the might of waters; an apt type
This label seemed of the utmost we can
know,
Both of ourselves and of the universe;
And, on the shape of that unmoving man,
His steadfast face and sightless eyes, I
gazed,
As if admonished from another world.

Though reared upon the base of outward
things,   650
Structures like these the excited spirit
mainly
Builds for herself; scenes different there
are,
Full-formed, that take, with small internal
help,
Possession of the faculties, — the peace
That comes with night; the deep solemnity
Of nature's intermediate hours of rest,
When the great tide of human life stands
still:
The business of the day to come, unborn,
Of that gone by, locked up, as in the grave;
The blended calmness of the heavens and
earth,   660
Moonlight and stars, and empty streets, and
sounds

Unfrequent as in deserts; at late hours
Of winter evenings, when unwholesome
rains
Are falling hard, with people yet astir,
The feeble salutation from the voice
Of some unhappy woman, now and then
Heard as we pass, when no one looks about,
Nothing is listened to. But these, I fear,
Are falsely catalogued; things that are, are
not,
As the mind answers to them, or the
heart   670
Is prompt, or slow, to feel. What say you,
then,
To times, when half the city shall break
out
Full of one passion, vengeance, rage, or
fear ?
To executions, to a street on fire,
Mobs, riots, or rejoicings ? From these
sights
Take one, — that ancient festival, the Fair,
Holden where martyrs suffered in past
time,
And named of St. Bartholomew; there, see
A work completed to our hands, that lays,
If any spectacle on earth can do,   680
The whole creative powers of man
asleep ! —
For once, the Muse's help will we implore,
And she shall lodge us, wafted on her
wings,
Above the press and danger of the crowd,
Upon some showman's platform. What a
shock
For eyes and ears ! what anarchy and din,
Barbarian and infernal, — a phantasma,
Monstrous in colour, motion, shape, sight,
sound !
Below, the open space, through every nook
Of the wide area, twinkles, is alive   690
With heads; the midway region, and above,
Is thronged with staring pictures and huge
scrolls,
Dumb proclamations of the Prodigies;
With chattering monkeys dangling from
their poles,
And children whirling in their roundabouts;
With those that stretch the neck and strain
the eyes,
And crack the voice in rivalship, the crowd
Inviting; with buffoons against buffoons
Grimacing, writhing, screaming, — him who
grinds
The hurdy-gurdy, at the fiddle weaves,   700

Rattles the salt-box, thumps the kettle-
drum,
And him who at the trumpet puffs his
cheeks,
The silver-collared Negro with his timbrel,
Equestrians, tumblers, women, girls, and
boys,
Blue-breeched, pink-vested, with high-
towering plumes. —
All moveables of wonder, from all parts,
Are here — Albinos, painted Indians,
Dwarfs,
The Horse of knowledge, and the learned
Pig,
The Stone-eater, the man that swallows fire,
Giants, Ventriloquists, the Invisible Girl,
The Bust that speaks and moves its gog-
gling eyes,   711
The Wax-work, Clock-work, all the mar-
vellous craft
Of modern Merlins, Wild Beasts, Puppet-
shows,
All out-o'-the-way, far-fetched, perverted
things,
All freaks of nature, all Promethean
thoughts
Of man, his dulness, madness, and their
feats
All jumbled up together, to compose
A Parliament of Monsters. Tents and
Booths
Meanwhile, as if the whole were one vast
mill,
Are vomiting, receiving on all sides,   720
Men, Women, three-years' Children, Babes
in arms.

Oh, blank confusion! true epitome
Of what the mighty City is herself,
To thousands upon thousands of her sons,
Living amid the same perpetual whirl
Of trivial objects, melted and reduced
To one identity, by differences
That have no law, no meaning, and no
end —
Oppression, under which even highest
minds
Must labour, whence the strongest are not
free.   730
But though the picture weary out the
eye,
By nature an unmanageable sight,
It is not wholly so to him who looks
In steadiness, who hath among least things
An under-sense of greatest; sees the parts

As parts, but with a feeling of the whole.
This, of all acquisitions, first awaits
On sundry and most widely different modes
Of education, nor with least delight
On that through which I passed. Atten-
tion springs,   740
And comprehensiveness and memory flow,
From early converse with the works of God
Among all regions; chiefly where appear
Most obviously simplicity and power.
Think, how the everlasting streams and
woods,
Stretched and still stretching far and wide,
exalt
The roving Indian. On his desert sands
What grandeur not unfelt, what pregnant
show
Of beauty, meets the sun-burnt Arab's eye:
And, as the sea propels, from zone to
zone,   750
Its currents; magnifies its shoals of life
Beyond all compass; spreads, and sends
aloft
Armies of clouds, — even so, its powers and
aspects
Shape for mankind, by principles as fixed,
The views and aspirations of the soul
To majesty. Like virtue have the forms
Perennial of the ancient hills; nor less
The changeful language of their counte-
nances
Quickens the slumbering mind, and aids
the thoughts,
However multitudinous, to move   760
With order and relation. This, if still,
As hitherto, in freedom I may speak,
Not violating any just restraint,
As may be hoped, of real modesty, —
This did I feel, in London's vast domain.
The Spirit of Nature was upon me there;
The soul of Beauty and enduring Life
Vouchsafed her inspiration, and diffused,
Through meagre lines and colours, and the
press
Of self-destroying, transitory things,   770
Composure, and ennobling Harmony.

BOOK EIGHTH

RETROSPECT — LOVE OF NATURE LEAD-
ING TO LOVE OF MAN

WHAT sounds are those, Helvellyn, that
are heard
Up to thy summit, through the depth of air

Ascending, as if distance had the power
To make the sounds more audible ? What crowd
Covers, or sprinkles o'er, yon village green ?
Crowd seems it, solitary hill ! to thee,
Though but a little family of men,
Shepherds and tillers of the ground — be-
times
Assembled with their children and their wives,
And here and there a stranger interspersed.
They hold a rustic fair — a festival, 11
Such as, on this side now, and now on that,
Repeated through his tributary vales,
Helvellyn, in the silence of his rest,
Sees annually, if clouds towards either ocean
Blown from their favourite resting-place, or mists
Dissolved, have left him an unshrouded head.
Delightful day it is for all who dwell
In this secluded glen, and eagerly
They give it welcome. Long ere heat of noon, 20
From byre or field the kine were brought; the sheep
Are penned in cotes; the chaffering is begun.
The heifer lows, uneasy at the voice
Of a new master; bleat the flocks aloud.
Booths are there none; a stall or two is here;
A lame man or a blind, the one to beg,
The other to make music; hither, too,
From far, with basket, slung upon her arm,
Of hawker's wares —books, pictures, combs, and pins —
Some aged woman finds her way again, 30
Year after year, a punctual visitant !
There also stands a speech-maker by rote,
Pulling the strings of his boxed raree-show;
And in the lapse of many years may come
Prouder itinerant, mountebank, or he
Whose wonders in a covered wain lie hid.
But one there is, the loveliest of them all,
Some sweet lass of the valley, looking out
For gains, and who that sees her would not buy ?
Fruits of her father's orchard are her wares,
And with the ruddy produce she walks round 41
Among the crowd, half pleased with, half ashamed
Of, her new office, blushing restlessly.

The children now are rich, for the old to-day
Are generous as the young; and, if content
With looking on, some ancient wedded pair
Sit in the shade together; while they gaze,
" A cheerful smile unbends the wrinkled brow,
The days departed start again to life,
And all the scenes of childhood reappear,
Faint, but more tranquil, like the changing sun 51
To him who slept at noon and wakes at eve."
Thus gaiety and cheerfulness prevail,
Spreading from young to old, from old to young,
And no one seems to want his share. —
Immense
Is the recess, the circumambient world
Magnificent, by which they are embraced:
They move about upon the soft green turf:
How little they, they and their doings, seem,
And all that they can further or obstruct !
Through utter weakness pitiably dear, 61
As tender infants are: and yet how great !
For all things serve them: them the morn-
ing light
Loves, as it glistens on the silent rocks;
And them the silent rocks, which now from high
Look down upon them; the reposing clouds;
The wild brooks prattling from invisible haunts;
And old Helvellyn, conscious of the stir
Which animates this day their calm abode.

With deep devotion, Nature, did I feel, 70
In that enormous City's turbulent world
Of men and things, what benefit I owed
To thee, and those domains of rural peace,
Where to the sense of beauty first my heart
Was opened; tract more exquisitely fair
Than that famed paradise of ten thousand trees,
Or Gehol's matchless gardens, for delight
Of the Tartarian dynasty composed
(Beyond that mighty wall, not fabulous, 79
China's stupendous mound) by patient toil
Of myriads and boon nature's lavish help;
There, in a clime from widest empire chosen,
Fulfilling (could enchantment have done more ?)
A sumptuous dream of flowery lawns, with domes
Of pleasure sprinkled over, shady dells
For eastern monasteries, sunny mounts

With temples crested, bridges, gondolas,
Rocks, dens, and groves of foliage taught
    to melt
Into each other their obsequious hues,
Vanished and vanishing in subtle chase, 90
Too fine to be pursued; or standing forth
In no discordant opposition, strong
And gorgeous as the colours side by side
Bedded among rich plumes of tropic birds;
And mountains over all, embracing all;
And all the landscape, endlessly enriched
With waters running, falling, or asleep.

But lovelier far than this, the paradise
Where I was reared; in Nature's primitive
    gifts
Favoured no less, and more to every sense
Delicious, seeing that the sun and sky, 101
The elements, and seasons as they change,
Do find a worthy fellow-labourer there —
Man free, man working for himself, with
    choice
Of time, and place, and object; by his
    wants,
His comforts, native occupations, cares,
Cheerfully led to individual ends
Or social, and still followed by a train
Unwooed, unthought-of even — simplicity,
And beauty, and inevitable grace.   110

Yea, when a glimpse of those imperial
    bowers
Would to a child be transport over-great,
When but a half-hour's roam through such
    a place
Would leave behind a dance of images,
That shall break in upon his sleep for weeks;
Even then the common haunts of the green
    earth,
And ordinary interests of man,
Which they embosom, all without regard
As both may seem, are fastening on the
    heart
Insensibly, each with the other's help.   120
For me, when my affections first were led
From kindred, friends, and playmates, to
    partake
Love for the human creature's absolute self,
That noticeable kindliness of heart
Sprang out of fountains, there abounding
    most,
Where sovereign Nature dictated the tasks
And occupations which her beauty adorned,
And Shepherds were the men that pleased
    me first;

Not such as Saturn ruled 'mid Latian wilds,
With arts and laws so tempered, that their
    lives   130
Left, even to us toiling in this late day,
A bright tradition of the golden age;
Not such as, 'mid Arcadian fastnesses
Sequestered, handed down among them-
    selves
Felicity, in Grecian song renowned;
Nor such as — when an adverse fate had
    driven,
From house and home, the courtly band
    whose fortunes
Entered, with Shakspeare's genius, the wild
    woods
Of Arden — amid sunshine or in shade
Culled the best fruits of Time's uncounted
    hours,   140
Ere Phœbe sighed for the false Ganymede;
Or there where Perdita and Florizel
Together danced, Queen of the feast, and
    King;
Nor such as Spenser fabled. True it is,
That I had heard (what he perhaps had
    seen)
Of maids at sunrise bringing in from far
Their May-bush, and along the streets in
    flocks
Parading with a song of taunting rhymes,
Aimed at the laggards slumbering within
    doors;
Had also heard, from those who yet remem-
    bered,   150
Tales of the May-pole dance, and wreaths
    that decked
Porch, door-way, or kirk-pillar; and of
    youths,
Each with his maid, before the sun was up,
By annual custom, issuing forth in troops,
To drink the waters of some sainted well,
And hang it round with garlands. Love
    survives;
But, for such purpose, flowers no longer
    grow:
The times, too sage, perhaps too proud, have
    dropped
These lighter graces; and the rural ways
And manners which my childhood looked
    upon   160
Were the unluxuriant produce of a life
Intent on little but substantial needs,
Yet rich in beauty, beauty that was felt.
But images of danger and distress,
Man suffering among awful Powers and
    Forms;

Of this I heard, and saw enough to make
Imagination restless; nor was free
Myself from frequent perils; nor were tales
Wanting, — the tragedies of former times,
Hazards and strange escapes, of which the
    rocks   170
Immutable, and everflowing streams,
Where'er I roamed, were speaking monu-
    ments.

    Smooth life had flock and shepherd in
    old time,
Long springs and tepid winters, on the
    banks
Of delicate Galesus; and no less
Those scattered along Adria's myrtle
    shores:
Smooth life had herdsman, and his snow-
    white herd
To triumphs and to sacrificial rites
Devoted, on the inviolable stream
Of rich Clitumnus; and the goat-herd
    lived   180
As calmly, underneath the pleasant brows
Of cool Lucretilis, where the pipe was heard
Of Pan, Invisible God, thrilling the rocks
With tutelary music, from all harm
The fold protecting. I myself, mature
In manhood then, have seen a pastoral tract
Like one of these, where Fancy might run
    wild,
Though under skies less generous, less
    serene:
There, for her own delight had Nature
    framed
A pleasure-ground, diffused a fair ex-
    panse   190
Of level pasture, islanded with groves
And banked with woody risings; but the
    Plain
Endless, here opening widely out, and there
Shut up in lesser lakes or beds of lawn
And intricate recesses, creek or bay
Sheltered within a shelter, where at large
The shepherd strays, a rolling hut his
    home.
Thither he comes with spring-time, there
    abides
All summer, and at sunrise ye may hear
His flageolet to liquid notes of love   200
Attuned, or sprightly fife resounding far.
Nook is there none, nor tract of that vast
    space
Where passage opens, but the same shall
    have

In turn its visitant, telling there his hours
In unlaborious pleasure, with no task
More toilsome than to carve a beechen
    bowl
For spring or fountain, which the traveller
    finds,
When through the region he pursues at
    will
His devious course. A glimpse of such
    sweet life
I saw when, from the melancholy walls   210
Of Goslar, once imperial, I renewed
My daily walk along that wide champaign,
That, reaching to her gates, spreads east
    and west,
And northwards, from beneath the moun-
    tainous verge
Of the Hercynian forest. Yet, hail to you
Moors, mountains, headlands, and ye hol-
    low vales,
Ye long deep channels for the Atlantic's
    voice,
Powers of my native region! Ye that
    seize
The heart with firmer grasp! Your snows
    and streams   219
Ungovernable, and your terrifying winds,
That howl so dismally for him who treads
Companionless your awful solitudes!
There, 't is the shepherd's task the winter
    long
To wait upon the storms: of their approach
Sagacious, into sheltering coves he drives
His flock, and thither from the homestead
    bears
A toilsome burden up the craggy ways,
And deals it out, their regular nourishment
Strewn on the frozen snow. And when the
    spring
Looks out, and all the pastures dance with
    lambs,   230
And when the flock, with warmer weather,
    climbs
Higher and higher, him his office leads
To watch their goings, whatsoever track
The wanderers choose. For this he quits
    his home
At day-spring, and no sooner doth the sun
Begin to strike him with a fire-like heat,
Than he lies down upon some shining rock,
And breakfasts with his dog. When they
    have stolen,
As is their wont, a pittance from strict
    time,
For rest not needed or exchange of love, 240

Then from his couch he starts; and now
  his feet
Crush out a livelier fragrance from the
  flowers
Of lowly thyme, by Nature's skill en-
  wrought
In the wild turf: the lingering dews of
  morn
Smoke round him, as from hill to hill he
  hies,
His staff protending like a hunter's spear,
Or by its aid leaping from crag to crag,
And o'er the brawling beds of unbridged
  streams.
Philosophy, methinks, at Fancy's call,
Might deign to follow him through what
  he does   250
Or sees in his day's march; himself he
  feels,
In those vast regions where his service lies,
A freeman, wedded to his life of hope
And hazard, and hard labour interchanged
With that majestic indolence so dear
To native man. A rambling schoolboy,
  thus,
I felt his presence in his own domain,
As of a lord and master, or a power,
Or genius, under Nature, under God,
Presiding; and severest solitude   260
Had more commanding looks when he was
  there.
When up the lonely brooks on rainy days
Angling I went, or trod the trackless hills
By mists bewildered, suddenly mine eyes
Have glanced upon him distant a few steps,
In size a giant, stalking through thick fog,
His sheep like Greenland bears; or, as he
  stepped
Beyond the boundary line of some hill-
  shadow,
His form hath flashed upon me, glorified
By the deep radiance of the setting sun: 270
Or him have I descried in distant sky,
A solitary object and sublime,
Above all height ! like an aerial cross
Stationed alone upon a spiry rock
Of the Chartreuse, for worship. Thus was
  man
Ennobled outwardly before my sight,
And thus my heart was early introduced
To an unconscious love and reverence
Of human nature; hence the human form
To me became an index of delight,   280
Of grace and honour, power and worthi-
  ness.

Meanwhile this creature — spiritual almost
As those of books, but more exalted far;
Far more of an imaginative form
Than the gay Corin of the groves, who
  lives
For his own fancies, or to dance by the
  hour,
In coronal, with Phyllis in the midst —
Was, for the purposes of kind, a man
With the most common; husband, father;
  learned,
Could teach, admonish; suffered with the
  rest   290
From vice and folly, wretchedness and
  fear;
Of this I little saw, cared less for it,
But something must have felt.
              Call ye these appearances —
Which I beheld of shepherds in my youth,
This sanctity of Nature given to man —
A shadow, a delusion, ye who pore
On the dead letter, miss the spirit of
  things;
Whose truth is not a motion or a shape
Instinct with vital functions, but a block
Or waxen image which yourselves have
  made,   300
And ye adore ! But blessèd be the God
Of Nature and of Man that this was so;
That men before my inexperienced eyes
Did first present themselves thus purified,
Removed, and to a distance that was fit:
And so we all of us in some degree
Are led to knowledge, wheresoever led,
And howsoever; were it otherwise,
And we found evil fast as we find good
In our first years, or think that it is
  found,   310
How could the innocent heart bear up and
  live !
But doubly fortunate my lot; not here
Alone, that something of a better life
Perhaps was round me than it is the privi-
  lege
Of most to move in, but that first I looked
At Man through objects that were great or
  fair;
First communed with him by their help.
  And thus
Was founded a sure safeguard and defence
Against the weight of meanness, selfish
  cares,
Coarse manners, vulgar passions, that beat
  in   320
On all sides from the ordinary world

In which we traffic. Starting from this
point
I had my face turned toward the truth,
began
With an advantage furnished by that kind
Of prepossession, without which the soul
Receives no knowledge that can bring forth
good,
No genuine insight ever comes to her.
From the restraint of over-watchful eyes
Preserved, I moved about, year after year,
Happy, and now most thankful that my
walk   330
Was guarded from too early intercourse
With the deformities of crowded life,
And those ensuing laughters and contempts,
Self-pleasing, which, if we would wish to
think
With a due reverence on earth's rightful
lord,
Here placed to be the inheritor of heaven,
Will not permit us; but pursue the mind,
That to devotion willingly would rise,
Into the temple and the temple's heart.

Yet deem not, Friend ! that human kind
with me   340
Thus early took a place pre-eminent;
Nature herself was, at this unripe time,
But secondary to my own pursuits
And animal activities, and all
Their trivial pleasures; and when these had
drooped
And gradually expired, and Nature, prized
For her own sake, became my joy, even
then —
And upwards through late youth, until not
less
Than two-and-twenty summers had been
told —
Was Man in my affections and regards 350
Subordinate to her, her visible forms
And viewless agencies: a passion, she,
A rapture often, and immediate love
Ever at hand; he, only a delight
Occasional, an accidental grace,
His hour being not yet come. Far less had
then
The inferior creatures, beast or bird, at-
tuned
My spirit to that gentleness of love,
(Though they had long been carefully ob-
served),
Won from me those minute obeisances 360
Of tenderness, which I may number now

With my first blessings. Nevertheless, on
these
The light of beauty did not fall in vain,
Or grandeur circumfuse them to no end.

But when that first poetic faculty
Of plain Imagination and severe,
No longer a mute influence of the soul,
Ventured, at some rash Muse's earnest call,
To try her strength among harmonious
words;
And to book-notions and the rules of art 370
Did knowingly conform itself; there came
Among the simple shapes of human life
A wilfulness of fancy and conceit;
And Nature and her objects beautified
These fictions, as in some sort, in their turn,
They burnished her. From touch of this
new power
Nothing was safe: the elder-tree that grew
Beside the well-known charnel-house had
then
A dismal look: the yew-tree had its ghost,
That took his station there for ornament:
The dignities of plain occurrence then 381
Were tasteless, and truth's golden mean, a
point
Where no sufficient pleasure could be found.
Then, if a widow, staggering with the blow
Of her distress, was known to have turned
her steps
To the cold grave in which her husband
slept,
One night, or haply more than one, through
pain
Or half-insensate impotence of mind,
The fact was caught at greedily, and there
She must be visitant the whole year through,
Wetting the turf with never-ending tears.

Through quaint obliquities I might pur-
sue   392
These cravings; when the foxglove, one by
one,
Upwards through every stage of the tall
stem,
Had shed beside the public way its bells,
And stood of all dismantled, save the last
Left at the tapering ladder's top, that
seemed
To bend as doth a slender blade of grass
Tipped with a rain-drop, Fancy loved to
seat,
Beneath the plant despoiled, but crested still
With this last relic, soon itself to fall, 401

Some vagrant mother, whose arch little
ones,
All unconcerned by her dejected plight,
Laughed as with rival eagerness their hands
Gathered the purple cups that round them
lay,
Strewing the turf's green slope.
     A diamond light
(Whene'er the summer sun, declining,
smote
A smooth rock wet with constant springs)
was seen
Sparkling from out a copse-clad bank that
rose
Fronting our cottage. Oft beside the hearth
Seated, with open door, often and long 411
Upon this restless lustre have I gazed,
That made my fancy restless as itself.
'T was now for me a burnished silver shield
Suspended over a knight's tomb, who lay
Inglorious, buried in the dusky wood:
An entrance now into some magic cave
Or palace built by fairies of the rock;
Nor could I have been bribed to disen-
chant
The spectacle, by visiting the spot. 420
Thus wilful Fancy, in no hurtful mood,
Engrafted far-fetched shapes on feelings
bred
By pure Imagination: busy Power
She was, and with her ready pupil turned
Instinctively to human passions, then
Least understood. Yet, 'mid the fervent
swarm
Of these vagaries, with an eye so rich
As mine was through the bounty of a grand
And lovely region, I had forms distinct 429
To steady me: each airy thought revolved
Round a substantial centre, which at once
Incited it to motion, and controlled.
I did not pine like one in cities bred,
As was thy melancholy lot, dear Friend!
Great Spirit as thou art, in endless dreams
Of sickliness, disjoining, joining, things
Without the light of knowledge. Where
the harm,
If, when the woodman languished with dis-
ease
Induced by sleeping nightly on the ground
Within his sod-built cabin, Indian-wise, 440
I called the pangs of disappointed love,
And all the sad etcetera of the wrong,
To help him to his grave? Meanwhile the
man,
If not already from the woods retired

To die at home, was haply, as I knew,
Withering by slow degrees, 'mid gentle airs,
Birds, running streams, and hills so beauti-
ful
On golden evenings, while the charcoal pile
Breathed up its smoke, an image of his ghost
Or spirit that full soon must take her flight.
Nor shall we not be tending towards that
point 451
Of sound humanity to which our Tale
Leads, though by sinuous ways, if here I
show
How Fancy, in a season when she wove
Those slender cords, to guide the uncon-
scious Boy
For the Man's sake, could feed at Nature's
call
Some pensive musings which might well
beseem
Maturer years.
    A grove there is whose boughs
Stretch from the western marge of Thur-
stonmere,
With length of shade so thick, that whoso
glides 460
Along the line of low-roofed water, moves
As in a cloister. Once — while, in that
shade
Loitering, I watched the golden beams of
light
Flung from the setting sun, as they reposed
In silent beauty on the naked ridge
Of a high eastern hill — thus flowed my
thoughts
In a pure stream of words fresh from the
heart:
Dear native Regions, wheresoe'er shall
close
My mortal course, there will I think on
you; 469
Dying, will cast on you a backward look;
Even as this setting sun (albeit the Vale
Is no where touched by one memorial
gleam)
Doth with the fond remains of his last
power
Still linger, and a farewell lustre sheds,
On the dear mountain-tops where first he
rose.

Enough of humble arguments; recall,
My Song! those high emotions which thy
voice
Has heretofore made known; that bursting
forth

Of sympathy, inspiring and inspired,
When everywhere a vital pulse was felt, 480
And all the several frames of things, like
    stars,
Through every magnitude distinguishable,
Shone mutually indebted, or half lost
Each in the other's blaze, a galaxy
Of life and glory. In the midst stood
    Man,
Outwardly, inwardly contemplated,
As, of all visible natures, crown, though
    born
Of dust, and kindred to the worm; a Being,
Both in perception and discernment, first
In every capability of rapture,   490
Through the divine effect of power and
    love;
As, more than anything we know, instinct
With godhead, and, by reason and by will,
Acknowledging dependency sublime.

    Ere long, the lonely mountains left, I
        moved,
Begirt, from day to day, with temporal
    shapes
Of vice and folly thrust upon my view,
Objects of sport, and ridicule, and scorn,
Manners and characters discriminate,
And little bustling passions that eclipse, 500
As well they might, the impersonated
    thought,
The idea, or abstraction of the kind.

    An idler among academic bowers,
Such was my new condition, as at large
Has been set forth; yet here the vulgar
    light
Of present, actual, superficial life,
Gleaming through colouring of other times,
Old usages and local privilege,
Was welcomed, softened, if not solemnised.
This notwithstanding, being brought more
    near   510
To vice and guilt, forerunning wretchedness,
I trembled, — thought, at times, of human
    life
With an indefinite terror and dismay,
Such as the storms and angry elements
Had bred in me; but gloomier far, a dim
Analogy to uproar and misrule,
Disquiet, danger, and obscurity.

    It might be told (but whereof speak of
        things
Common to all?) that, seeing, I was led

Gravely to ponder — judging between good
And evil, not as for the mind's delight   521
But for her guidance — one who was to
    act,
As sometimes to the best of feeble means
I did, by human sympathy impelled:
And, through dislike and most offensive
    pain,
Was to the truth conducted; of this faith
Never forsaken, that, by acting well,
And understanding, I should learn to love
The end of life, and everything we know.

    Grave Teacher, stern Preceptress! for at
        times   530
Thou canst put on an aspect most severe;
London, to thee I willingly return.
Erewhile my verse played idly with the
    flowers
Enwrought upon thy mantle; satisfied
With that amusement, and a simple look
Of child-like inquisition now and then
Cast upwards on thy countenance, to de-
    tect
Some inner meanings which might harbour
    there.
But how could I in mood so light in-
    dulge,
Keeping such fresh remembrance of the
    day,   540
When, having thridded the long labyrinth
Of the suburban villages, I first
Entered thy vast dominion? On the roof
Of an itinerant vehicle I sate,
With vulgar men about me, trivial forms
Of houses, pavement, streets, of men and
    things, —
Mean shapes on every side: but, at the
    instant,
When to myself it fairly might be said,
The threshold now is overpast, (how strange
That aught external to the living mind   550
Should have such mighty sway! yet so it
    was),
A weight of ages did at once descend
Upon my heart; no thought embodied, no
Distinct remembrances, but weight and
    power, —
Power growing under weight: alas! I feel
That I am trifling: 't was a moment's
    pause, —
All that took place within me came and
    went
As in a moment; yet with Time it dwells,
And grateful memory, as a thing divine.

The curious traveller, who, from open day,
Hath passed with torches into some huge
   cave,   561
The Grotto of Antiparos, or the Den
In old time haunted by that Danish Witch,
Yordas; he looks around and sees the vault
Widening on all sides; sees, or thinks he
   sees,
Erelong, the massy roof above his head,
That instantly unsettles and recedes, —
Substance and shadow, light and darkness,
   all
Commingled, making up a canopy
Of shapes and forms and tendencies to shape
That shift and vanish, change and inter-
   change   571
Like spectres,— ferment silent and sublime !
That after a short space works less and less,
Till, every effort, every motion gone,
The scene before him stands in perfect view
Exposed, and lifeless as a written book ! —
But let him pause awhile, and look again,
And a new quickening shall succeed, at
   first
Beginning timidly, then creeping fast,
Till the whole cave, so late a senseless mass,
Busies the eye with images and forms   581
Boldly assembled, — here is shadowed forth
From the projections, wrinkles, cavities,
A variegated landscape, — there the shape
Of some gigantic warrior clad in mail,
The ghostly semblance of a hooded monk,
Veiled nun, or pilgrim resting on his staff :
Strange congregation ! yet not slow to meet
Eyes that perceive through minds that can
   inspire.

Even in such sort had I at first been
   moved,   590
Nor otherwise continued to be moved,
As I explored the vast metropolis,
Fount of my country's destiny and the
   world's;
That great emporium, chronicle at once
And burial-place of passions, and their home
Imperial, their chief living residence.

With strong sensations teeming as it did
Of past and present, such a place must
   needs
Have pleased me, seeking knowledge at
   that time
Far less than craving power; yet knowledge
   came,   600
Sought or unsought, and influxes of power

Came, of themselves, or at her call derived
In fits of kindliest apprehensiveness,
From all sides, when whate'er was in itself
Capacious found, or seemed to find, in me
A correspondent amplitude of mind;
Such is the strength and glory of our youth !
The human nature unto which I felt
That I belonged, and reverenced with love,
Was not a punctual presence, but a spirit
Diffused through time and space, with aid
   derived   611
Of evidence from monuments, erect,
Prostrate, or leaning towards their common
   rest
In earth, the widely scattered wreck sublime
Of vanished nations, or more clearly drawn
From books and what they picture and
   record.

'T is true, the history of our native land—
With those of Greece compared and popular
   Rome,
And in our high-wrought modern narratives
Stript of their harmonising soul, the life 620
Of manners and familiar incidents —
Had never much delighted me. And less
Than other intellects had mine been used
To lean upon extrinsic circumstance
Of record or tradition; but a sense
Of what in the Great City had been done
And suffered, and was doing, suffering, still,
Weighed with me, could support the test of
   thought;
And, in despite of all that had gone by,
Or was departing never to return,   630
There I conversed with majesty and power
Like independent natures. Hence the place
Was thronged with impregnations like the
   Wilds
In which my early feelings had been
   nursed —
Bare hills and valleys, full of caverns, rocks,
And audible seclusions, dashing lakes,
Echoes and waterfalls, and pointed crags
That into music touch the passing wind.
Here then my young imagination found
No uncongenial element; could here   640
Among new objects serve or give command,
Even as the heart's occasions might re-
   quire,
To forward reason's else too-scrupulous
   march.
The effect was, still more elevated views
Of human nature. Neither vice nor guilt,
Debasement undergone by body or mind,

Nor all the misery forced upon my sight,
Misery not lightly passed, but sometimes
   scanned
Most feelingly, could overthrow my trust
In what we *may* become; induce belief 650
That I was ignorant, had been falsely
   taught,
A solitary, who with vain conceits
Had been inspired, and walked about in
   dreams.
From those sad scenes when meditation
   turned,
Lo! everything that was indeed divine
Retained its purity inviolate,
Nay brighter shone, by this portentous
   gloom
Set off; such opposition as aroused
The mind of Adam, yet in Paradise
Though fallen from bliss, when in the East
   he saw 660
Darkness ere day's mid course, and morn-
   ing light
More orient in the western cloud, that drew
O'er the blue firmament a radiant white,
Descending slow with something heavenly
   fraught.

Add also, that among the multitudes
Of that huge city, oftentimes was seen
Affectingly set forth, more than elsewhere
Is possible, the unity of man,
One spirit over ignorance and vice
Predominant, in good and evil hearts; 670
One sense for moral judgments, as one eye
For the sun's light. The soul when smit-
   ten thus
By a sublime *idea*, whencesoe'er
Vouchsafed for union or communion, feeds
On the pure bliss, and takes her rest with
   God.

Thus from a very early age, O Friend!
My thoughts by slow gradations had been
   drawn
To human-kind, and to the good and ill
Of human life: Nature had led me on;
And oft amid the " busy hum " I seemed
To travel independent of her help, 681
As if I had forgotten her; but no,
The world of human-kind outweighed not
   hers
In my habitual thoughts; the scale of love,
Though filling daily, still was light, com-
   pared
With that in which *her* mighty objects lay.

BOOK NINTH

RESIDENCE IN FRANCE

EVEN as a river, — partly (it might seem)
Yielding to old remembrances, and swayed
In part by fear to shape a way direct,
That would engulph him soon in the raven-
   ous sea —
Turns, and will measure back his course,
   far back,
Seeking the very regions which he crossed
In his first outset; so have we, my Friend!
Turned and returned with intricate delay.
Or as a traveller, who has gained the brow
Of some aerial Down, while there he halts
For breathing-time, is tempted to review 11
The region left behind him; and, if aught
Deserving notice have escaped regard,
Or been regarded with too careless eye,
Strives, from that height, with one and yet
   one more
Last look, to make the best amends he
   may:
So have we lingered. Now we start afresh
With courage, and new hope risen on our
   toil.
Fair greetings to this shapeless eagerness,
Whene'er it comes! needful in work so
   long, 20
Thrice needful to the argument which now
Awaits us! Oh, how much unlike the past!

Free as a colt at pasture on the hill,
I ranged at large, through London's wide
   domain,
Month after month. Obscurely did I live,
Not seeking frequent intercourse with men,
By literature, or elegance, or rank,
Distinguished. Scarcely was a year thus
   spent
Ere I forsook the crowded solitude,
With less regret for its luxurious pomp, 30
And all the nicely-guarded shows of art,
Than for the humble book-stalls in the
   streets,
Exposed to eye and hand where'er I turned.

France lured me forth; the realm that I
   had crossed
So lately, journeying toward the snow-clad
   Alps.
But now, relinquishing the scrip and staff,
And all enjoyment which the summer sun
Sheds round the steps of those who meet
   the day

With motion constant as his own, I went
Prepared to sojourn in a pleasant town, 40
Washed by the current of the stately Loire.

Through Paris lay my readiest course,
    and there
Sojourning a few days, I visited
In haste, each spot of old or recent fame,
The latter chiefly; from the field of Mars
Down to the suburbs of St. Antony,
And from Mont Martyr southward to the
    Dome
Of Geneviève. In both her clamorous
    Halls,
The National Synod and the Jacobins,
I saw the Revolutionary Power 50
Toss like a ship at anchor, rocked by
    storms;
The Arcades I traversed, in the Palace
    huge
Of Orleans; coasted round and round the
    line
Of Tavern, Brothel, Gaming-house, and
    Shop,
Great rendezvous of worst and best, the
    walk
Of all who had a purpose, or had not;
I stared and listened, with a stranger's
    ears,
To Hawkers and Haranguers, hubbub wild!
And hissing Factionists with ardent eyes,
In knots, or pairs, or single. Not a look 60
Hope takes, or Doubt or Fear is forced to
    wear,
But seemed there present; and I scanned
    them all,
Watched every gesture uncontrollable,
Of anger, and vexation, and despite,
All side by side, and struggling face to
    face,
With gaiety and dissolute idleness.

Where silent zephyrs sported with the
    dust
Of the Bastille, I sate in the open sun,
And from the rubbish gathered up a stone,
And pocketed the relic, in the guise 70
Of an enthusiast: yet, in honest truth,
I looked for something that I could not find,
Affecting more emotion than I felt;
For 't is most certain, that these various
    sights,
However potent their first shock, with me
Appeared to recompense the traveller's
    pains

Less than the painted Magdalene of Le
    Brun,
A beauty exquisitely wrought, with hair
Dishevelled, gleaming eyes, and rueful
    cheek 79
Pale and bedropped with overflowing tears.

But hence to my more permanent abode
I hasten; there, by novelties in speech,
Domestic manners, customs, gestures, looks,
And all the attire of ordinary life,
Attention was engrossed; and, thus amused,
I stood 'mid those concussions, unconcerned,
Tranquil almost, and careless as a flower
Glassed in a green-house, or a parlour
    shrub
That spreads its leaves in unmolested peace,
While every bush and tree, the country
    through, 90
Is shaking to the roots: indifference this
Which may seem strange: but I was un-
    prepared
With needful knowledge, had abruptly
    passed
Into a theatre, whose stage was filled
And busy with an action far advanced.
Like others, I had skimmed, and some-
    times read
With care, the master pamphlets of the
    day;
Nor wanted such half-insight as grew wild
Upon that meagre soil, helped out by talk
And public news; but having never seen
A chronicle that might suffice to show 101
Whence the main organs of the public
    power
Had sprung, their transmigrations, when
    and how
Accomplished, giving thus unto events
A form and body; all things were to me
Loose and disjointed, and the affections
    left
Without a vital interest. At that time,
Moreover, the first storm was overblown,
And the strong hand of outward violence
Locked up in quiet. For myself, I fear 110
Now, in connection with so great a theme,
To speak (as I must be compelled to do)
Of one so unimportant; night by night
Did I frequent the formal haunts of men,
Whom, in the city, privilege of birth
Sequestered from the rest, societies
Polished in arts, and in punctilio versed;
Whence, and from deeper causes, all dis-
    course

Of good and evil of the time was shunned
With scrupulous care; but these restric-
    tions soon   120
Proved tedious, and I gradually withdrew
Into a noisier world, and thus ere long
Became a patriot; and my heart was all
Given to the people, and my love was
    theirs.

    A band of military Officers,
Then stationed in the city, were the chief
Of my associates: some of these wore
    swords
That had been seasoned in the wars, and
    all
Were men well-born; the chivalry of
    France.
In age and temper differing, they had yet
One spirit ruling in each heart; alike   131
(Save only one, hereafter to be named)
Were bent upon undoing what was done:
This was their rest and only hope; there-
    with
No fear had they of bad becoming worse,
For worst to them was come; nor would
    have stirred,
Or deemed it worth a moment's thought to
    stir,
In anything, save only as the act
Looked thitherward. One, reckoning by
    years,
Was in the prime of manhood, and ere-
    while   140
He had sate lord in many tender hearts;
Though heedless of such honours now, and
    changed:
His temper was quite mastered by the
    times,
And they had blighted him, had eaten away
The beauty of his person, doing wrong
Alike to body and to mind: his port,
Which once had been erect and open, now
Was stooping and contracted, and a face,
Endowed by Nature with her fairest gifts
Of symmetry and light and bloom, ex-
    pressed,   150
As much as any that was ever seen,
A ravage out of season, made by thoughts
Unhealthy and vexatious. With the hour,
That from the press of Paris duly brought
Its freight of public news, the fever came,
A punctual visitant, to shake this man,
Disarmed his voice and fanned his yellow
    cheek
Into a thousand colours; while he read,

Or mused, his sword was haunted by his
    touch
Continually, like an uneasy place   160
In his own body. 'T was in truth an hour
Of universal ferment; mildest men
Were agitated; and commotions, strife
Of passion and opinion, filled the walls
Of peaceful houses with unquiet sounds.
The soil of common life was, at that time,
Too hot to tread upon. Oft said I then,
And not then only, "What a mockery
    this
Of history, the past and that to come !
Now do I feel how all men are deceived, 170
Reading of nations and their works, in
    faith,
Faith given to vanity and emptiness;
Oh ! laughter for the page that would re-
    flect
To future times the face of what now
    is ! "
The land all swarmed with passion, like a
    plain
Devoured by locusts, — Carra, Gorsas, —
    add
A hundred other names, forgotten now,
Nor to be heard of more; yet they were
    powers,
Like earthquakes, shocks repeated day by
    day,
And felt through every nook of town and
    field.   180

    Such was the state of things. Mean-
    while the chief
Of my associates stood prepared for flight
To augment the band of emigrants in arms
Upon the borders of the Rhine, and leagued
With foreign foes mustered for instant
    war.
This was their undisguised intent, and they
Were waiting with the whole of their de-
    sires
The moment to depart.
                      An Englishman,
Born in a land whose very name appeared
To license some unruliness of mind;   190
A stranger, with youth's further privilege,
And the indulgence that a half-learnt
    speech
Wins from the courteous; I, who had been
    else
Shunned and not tolerated, freely lived
With these defenders of the Crown, and
    talked,

And heard their notions; nor did they dis-
    dain
The wish to bring me over to their cause.

  But though untaught by thinking or by
    books
To reason well of polity or law,
And nice distinctions, then on every
    tongue,   200
Of natural rights and civil; and to acts
Of nations and their passing interests
(If with unworldly ends and aims com-
    pared)
Almost indifferent, even the historian's
    tale
Prizing but little otherwise than I prized
Tales of the poets, as it made the heart
Beat high, and filled the fancy with fair
    forms,
Old heroes and their sufferings and their
    deeds;
Yet in the regal sceptre, and the pomp
Of orders and degrees, I nothing found 210
Then, or had ever, even in crudest youth,
That dazzled me, but rather what I
    mourned
And ill could brook, beholding that the
    best
Ruled not, and feeling that they ought to
    rule.

  For, born in a poor district, and which
    yet
Retaineth more of ancient homeliness,
Than any other nook of English ground,
It was my fortune scarcely to have seen,
Through the whole tenor of my school-day
    time,
The face of one, who, whether boy or
    man,   220
Was vested with attention or respect
Through claims of wealth or blood; nor
    was it least
Of many benefits, in later years
Derived from academic institutes
And rules, that they held something up to
    view
Of a Republic, where all stood thus far
Upon equal ground; that we were brothers
    all
In honour, as in one community,
Scholars and gentlemen; where, further-
    more,
Distinction open lay to all that came,   230
And wealth and titles were in less esteem

Than talents, worth, and prosperous indus-
    try.
Add unto this, subservience from the first
To presences of God's mysterious power
Made manifest in Nature's sovereignty,
And fellowship with venerable books,
To sanction the proud workings of the soul,
And mountain liberty. It could not be
But that one tutored thus should look with
    awe
Upon the faculties of man, receive   240
Gladly the highest promises, and hail,
As best, the government of equal rights
And individual worth. And hence, O
    Friend !
If at the first great outbreak I rejoiced
Less than might well befit my youth, the
    cause
In part lay here, that unto me the events
Seemed nothing out of nature's certain
    course,
A gift that was come rather late than soon.
No wonder, then, if advocates like these,
Inflamed by passion, blind with preju-
    dice,   250
And stung with injury, at this riper day,
Were impotent to make my hopes put on
The shape of theirs, my understanding
    bend
In honour to their honour: zeal, which yet
Had slumbered, now in opposition burst
Forth like a Polar summer: every word
They uttered was a dart, by counter-winds
Blown back upon themselves; their reason
    seemed
Confusion-stricken by a higher power
Than human understanding, their dis-
    course   260
Maimed, spiritless; and, in their weakness
    strong,
I triumphed.
              Meantime, day by day, the roads
Were crowded with the bravest youth of
    France,
And all the promptest of her spirits, linked
In gallant soldiership, and posting on
To meet the war upon her frontier bounds.
Yet at this very moment do tears start
Into mine eyes: I do not say I weep —
I wept not then, — but tears have dimmed
    my sight,
In memory of the farewells of that time,
Domestic severings, female fortitude   271
At dearest separation, patriot love
And self-devotion, and terrestrial hope,

Encouraged with a martyr's confidence;
Even files of strangers merely seen but
   once,
And for a moment, men from far with
   sound
Of music, martial tunes, and banners spread,
Entering the city, here and there a face,
Or person, singled out among the rest,   279
Yet still a stranger and beloved as such;
Even by these passing spectacles my heart
Was oftentimes uplifted, and they seemed
Arguments sent from Heaven to prove the
   cause
Good, pure, which no one could stand up
   against,
Who was not lost, abandoned, selfish, proud,
Mean, miserable, wilfully depraved,
Hater perverse of equity and truth.

   Among that band of Officers was one,
Already hinted at, of other mould —
A patriot, thence rejected by the rest,   290
And with an oriental loathing spurned,
As of a different caste. A meeker man
Than this lived never, nor a more benign,
Meek though enthusiastic. Injuries
Made *him* more gracious, and his nature
   then
Did breathe its sweetness out most sensibly,
As aromatic flowers on Alpine turf,
When foot hath crushed them. He through
   the events
Of that great change wandered in perfect
   faith,   299
As through a book, an old romance, or tale
Of Fairy, or some dream of actions wrought
Behind the summer clouds. By birth he
   ranked
With the most noble, but unto the poor
Among mankind he was in service bound,
As by some tie invisible, oaths professed
To a religious order. Man he loved
As man; and, to the mean and the obscure,
And all the homely in their homely works,
Transferred a courtesy which had no air
Of condescension; but did rather seem   310
A passion and a gallantry, like that
Which he, a soldier, in his idler day
Had paid to woman: somewhat vain he was,
Or seemed so, yet it was not vanity,
But fondness, and a kind of radiant joy
Diffused around him, while he was intent
On works of love or freedom, or revolved
Complacently the progress of a cause,
Whereof he was a part: yet this was meek

And placid, and took nothing from the man
That was delightful. Oft in solitude   321
With him did I discourse about the end
Of civil government, and its wisest forms;
Of ancient loyalty, and chartered rights,
Custom and habit, novelty and change;
Of self-respect, and virtue in the few
For patrimonial honour set apart,
And ignorance in the labouring multitude.
For he, to all intolerance indisposed,   329
Balanced these contemplations in his mind;
And I, who at that time was scarcely dipped
Into the turmoil, bore a sounder judgment
Than later days allowed; carried about me,
With less alloy to its integrity,
The experience of past ages, as, through
   help
Of books and common life, it makes sure
   way
To youthful minds, by objects over near
Not pressed upon, nor dazzled or misled
By struggling with the crowd for present
   ends.

   But though not deaf, nor obstinate to find
Error without excuse upon the side   341
Of them who strove against us, more de-
   light
We took, and let this freely be confessed,
In painting to ourselves the miseries
Of royal courts, and that voluptuous life
Unfeeling, where the man who is of soul
The meanest thrives the most; where
   dignity,
True personal dignity, abideth not;
A light, a cruel, and vain world cut off
From the natural inlets of just sentiment,
From lowly sympathy and chastening
   truth;   351
Where good and evil interchange their
   names,
And thirst for bloody spoils abroad is paired
With vice at home. We added dearest
   themes —
Man and his noble nature, as it is
The gift which God has placed within his
   power,
His blind desires and steady faculties
Capable of clear truth, the one to break
Bondage, the other to build liberty
On firm foundations, making social life,   360
Through knowledge spreading and imper-
   ishable,
As just in regulation, and as pure
As individual in the wise and good.

We summoned up the honourable deeds
Of ancient Story, thought of each bright
    spot,
That would be found in all recorded time,
Of truth preserved and error passed away;
Of single spirits that catch the flame from
    Heaven,
And how the multitudes of men will feed
And fan each other; thought of sects, how
    keen   370
They are to put the appropriate nature on,
Triumphant over every obstacle
Of custom, language, country, love, or hate,
And what they do and suffer for their creed;
How far they travel, and how long endure;
How quickly mighty Nations have been
    formed,
From least beginnings; how, together locked
By new opinions, scattered tribes have made
One body, spreading wide as clouds in
    heaven.
To aspirations then of our own minds   380
Did we appeal; and, finally, beheld
A living confirmation of the whole
Before us, in a people from the depth
Of shameful imbecility uprisen,
Fresh as the morning star. Elate we looked
Upon their virtues; saw, in rudest men,
Self-sacrifice the firmest; generous love,
And continence of mind, and sense of right,
Uppermost in the midst of fiercest strife.

Oh, sweet it is, in academic groves,   390
Or such retirement, Friend! as we have
    known
In the green dales beside our Rotha's
    stream,
Greta, or Derwent, or some nameless rill,
To ruminate, with interchange of talk,
On rational liberty, and hope in man,
Justice and peace. But far more sweet
    such toil —
Toil, say I, for it leads to thoughts ab-
    struse —
If nature then be standing on the brink
Of some great trial, and we hear the voice
Of one devoted, — one whom circumstance
Hath called upon to embody his deep
    sense   401
In action, give it outwardly a shape,
And that of benediction, to the world.
Then doubt is not, and truth is more than
    truth, —
A hope it is, and a desire; a creed
Of zeal, by an authority Divine

Sanctioned, of danger, difficulty, or death.
Such conversation, under Attic shades,
Did Dion hold with Plato; ripened thus
For a Deliverer's glorious task, — and such
He, on that ministry already bound,   411
Held with Eudemus and Timonides,
Surrounded by adventurers in arms,
When those two vessels with their daring
    freight,
For the Sicilian Tyrant's overthrow,
Sailed from Zacynthus, — philosophic war,
Led by Philosophers. With harder fate,
Though like ambition, such was he, O
    Friend !
Of whom I speak. So Beaupuis (let the
    name
Stand near the worthiest of Antiquity)   420
Fashioned his life; and many a long dis-
    course,
With like persuasion honoured, we main-
    tained:
He, on his part, accoutred for the worst,
He perished fighting, in supreme command,
Upon the borders of the unhappy Loire,
For liberty, against deluded men,
His fellow-countrymen; and yet most
    blessed
In this, that he the fate of later times
Lived not to see, nor what we now behold,
Who have as ardent hearts as he had
    then.   430

Along that very Loire, with festal mirth
Resounding at all hours, and innocent yet
Of civil slaughter, was our frequent walk;
Or in wide forests of continuous shade,
Lofty and over-arched, with open space
Beneath the trees, clear footing many a
    mile —
A solemn region. Oft amid those haunts,
From earnest dialogues I slipped in thought,
And let remembrance steal to other times,
When, o'er those interwoven roots, moss-
    clad,   440
And smooth as marble or a waveless sea,
Some Hermit, from his cell forth-strayed,
    might pace
In sylvan meditation undisturbed;
As on the pavement of a Gothic church
Walks a lone Monk, when service hath ex-
    pired,
In peace and silence. But if e'er was
    heard, —
Heard, though unseen, — a devious travel-
    ler,

Retiring or approaching from afar
With speed and echoes loud of trampling
      hoofs
From the hard floor reverberated, then   450
It was Angelica thundering through the
      woods
Upon her palfrey, or that gentle maid
Erminia, fugitive as fair as she.
Sometimes methought I saw a pair of
      knights
Joust underneath the trees, that as in storm
Rocked high above their heads; anon, the
      din
Of boisterous merriment, and music's roar,
In sudden proclamation, burst from haunt
Of Satyrs in some viewless glade, with
      dance
Rejoicing o'er a female in the midst,   460
A mortal beauty, their unhappy thrall.
The width of those huge forests, unto me
A novel scene, did often in this way
Master my fancy while I wandered on
With that revered companion.   And some-
      times —
When to a convent in a meadow green,
By a brook-side, we came, a roofless pile,
And not by reverential touch of Time
Dismantled, but by violence abrupt —
In spite of those heart-bracing collo-
      quies,   470
In spite of real fervour, and of that
Less genuine and wrought up within my-
      self —
I could not but bewail a wrong so harsh,
And for the Matin-bell to sound no more
Grieved, and the twilight taper, and the
      cross
High on the topmost pinnacle, a sign
(How welcome to the weary traveller's
      eyes !)
Of hospitality and peaceful rest.
And when the partner of those varied walks
Pointed upon occasion to the site   480
Of Romorentin, home of ancient kings,
To the imperial edifice of Blois,
Or to that rural castle, name now slipped
From my remembrance, where a lady
      lodged,
By the first Francis wooed, and bound to
      him
In chains of mutual passion, from the
      tower,
As a tradition of the country tells,
Practised to commune with her royal
      knight

By cressets and love-beacons, intercourse
'Twixt her high-seated residence and
      his   490
Far off at Chambord on the plain beneath;
Even here, though less than with the peace-
      ful house
Religious, 'mid those frequent monuments
Of Kings, their vices and their better deeds,
Imagination, potent to inflame
At times with virtuous wrath and noble
      scorn,
Did also often mitigate the force
Of civic prejudice, the bigotry,
So call it, of a youthful patriot's mind;
And on these spots with many gleams I
      looked   500
Of chivalrous delight.   Yet not the less,
Hatred of absolute rule, where will of one
Is law for all, and of that barren pride
In them who, by immunities unjust,
Between the sovereign and the people
      stand,
His helper and not theirs, laid stronger hold
Daily upon me, mixed with pity too
And love; for where hope is, there love
      will be
For the abject multitude.   And when we
      chanced
One day to meet a hunger-bitten girl,   510
Who crept along fitting her languid gait
Unto a heifer's motion, by a cord
Tied to her arm, and picking thus from the
      lane
Its sustenance, while the girl with pallid
      hands
Was busy knitting in a heartless mood
Of solitude, and at the sight my friend
In agitation said, " 'T is against *that*
That we are fighting," I with him believed
That a benignant spirit was abroad
Which might not be withstood, that
      poverty   520
Abject as this would in a little time
Be found no more, that we should see the
      earth
Unthwarted in her wish to recompense
The meek, the lowly, patient child of toil,
All institutes for ever blotted out
That legalised exclusion, empty pomp
Abolished, sensual state and cruel power
Whether by edict of the one or few;
And finally, as sum and crown of all,   529
Should see the people having a strong hand
In framing their own laws; whence better
      days

To all mankind. But, these things set
    apart,
Was not this single confidence enough
To animate the mind that ever turned
A thought to human welfare? That
    henceforth
Captivity by mandate without law
Should cease; and open accusation lead
To sentence in the hearing of the world,
And open punishment, if not the air
Be free to breathe in, and the heart of
    man   540
Dread nothing. From this height I shall
    not stoop
To humbler matter that detained us oft
In thought or conversation, public acts,
And public persons, and emotions wrought
Within the breast, as ever-varying winds
Of record or report swept over us;
But I might here, instead, repeat a tale,
Told by my Patriot friend, of sad events,
That prove to what low depth had struck
    the roots,
How widely spread the boughs, of that old
    tree   550
Which, as a deadly mischief, and a foul
And black dishonour, France was weary of.

Oh, happy time of youthful lovers, (thus
The story might begin,) oh, balmy time,
In which a love-knot, on a lady's brow,
Is fairer than the fairest star in Heaven!
So might — and with that prelude *did*
    begin
The record ; and, in faithful verse, was
    given
The doleful sequel.
                        But our little bark
On a strong river boldly hath been
    launched;   560
And from the driving current should we
    turn
To loiter wilfully within a creek,
Howe'er attractive, Fellow voyager!
Would'st thou not chide? Yet deem not
    my pains lost:
For Vaudracour and Julia (so were named
The ill-fated pair) in that plain tale will
    draw
Tears from the hearts of others, when their
    own
Shall beat no more. Thou, also, there
    may'st read,
At leisure, how the enamoured youth was
    driven,

By public power abased, to fatal crime,   570
Nature's rebellion against monstrous law;
How, between heart and heart, oppression
    thrust
Her mandates, severing whom true love
    had joined,
Harassing both; until he sank and pressed
The couch his fate had made for him;
    supine,
Save when the stings of viperous remorse,
Trying their strength, enforced him to
    start up,
Aghast and prayerless. Into a deep wood
He fled, to shun the haunts of human kind;
There dwelt, weakened in spirit more and
    more;   580
Nor could the voice of Freedom, which
    through France
Full speedily resounded, public hope,
Or personal memory of his own worst
    wrongs,
Rouse him; but, hidden in those gloomy
    shades,
His days he wasted, — an imbecile mind.

BOOK TENTH

RESIDENCE IN FRANCE (*continued*)

IT was a beautiful and silent day
That overspread the countenance of earth,
Then fading with unusual quietness, —
A day as beautiful as e'er was given
To soothe regret, though deepening what it
    soothed,
When by the gliding Loire I paused, and
    cast
Upon his rich domains, vineyard and tilth,
Green meadow-ground, and many-coloured
    woods,
Again, and yet again, a farewell look;
Then from the quiet of that scene passed
    on,   10
Bound to the fierce Metropolis. From his
    throne
The King had fallen, and that invading
    host —
Presumptuous cloud, on whose black front
    was written
The tender mercies of the dismal wind
That bore it — on the plains of Liberty
Had burst innocuous. Say in bolder words,
They — who had come elate as eastern
    hunters
Banded beneath the Great Mogul, when he

Erewhile went forth from Agra or Lahore,
Rajahs and Omrahs in his train, intent   20
To drive their prey enclosed within a ring
Wide as a province, but, the signal given,
Before the point of the life-threatening
    spear
Narrowing itself by moments — they, rash
    men,
Had seen the anticipated quarry turned
Into avengers, from whose wrath they fled
In terror. Disappointment and dismay
Remained for all whose fancies had run
    wild
With evil expectations; confidence   29
And perfect triumph for the better cause.

The State — as if to stamp the final seal
On her security, and to the world
Show what she was, a high and fearless
    soul,
Exulting in defiance, or heart-stung
By sharp resentment, or belike to taunt
With spiteful gratitude the baffled League,
That had stirred up her slackening faculties
To a new transition — when the King was
    crushed,
Spared not the empty throne, and in proud
    haste
Assumed the body and venerable name   40
Of a Republic. Lamentable crimes,
'T is true, had gone before this hour, dire
    work
Of massacre, in which the senseless sword
Was prayed to as a judge; but these were
    past,
Earth free from them for ever, as was
    thought, —
Ephemeral monsters, to be seen but once !
Things that could only show themselves
    and die.

Cheered with this hope, to Paris I re-
    turned,
And ranged, with ardour heretofore unfelt,
The spacious city, and in progress passed
The prison where the unhappy Monarch
    lay,   51
Associate with his children and his wife
In bondage; and the palace, lately stormed
With roar of cannon by a furious host.
I crossed the square (an empty area then !)
Of the Carrousel, where so late had lain
The dead, upon the dying heaped, and gazed
On this and other spots, as doth a man
Upon a volume whose contents he knows

Are memorable, but from him locked up,   60
Being written in a tongue he cannot read,
So that he questions the mute leaves with
    pain,
And half upbraids their silence. But that
    night
I felt most deeply in what world I was,
What ground I trod on, and what air I
    breathed.
High was my room and lonely, near the
    roof
Of a large mansion or hotel, a lodge
That would have pleased me in more quiet
    times;
Nor was it wholly without pleasure then.
With unextinguished taper I kept watch,   70
Reading at intervals; the fear gone by
Pressed on me almost like a fear to come.
I thought of those September massacres,
Divided from me by one little month,
Saw them and touched: the rest was con-
    jured up
From tragic fictions or true history,
Remembrances and dim admonishments.
The horse is taught his manage, and no
    star
Of wildest course but treads back his own
    steps;
For the spent hurricane the air provides   80
As fierce a successor; the tide retreats
But to return out of its hiding-place
In the great deep; all things have second
    birth;
The earthquake is not satisfied at once;
And in this way I wrought upon myself,
Until I seemed to hear a voice that cried,
To the whole city, " Sleep no more." The
    trance
Fled with the voice to which it had given
    birth;
But vainly comments of a calmer mind
Promised soft peace and sweet forgetful-
    ness.   90
The place, all hushed and silent as it was,
Appeared unfit for the repose of night,
Defenceless as a wood where tigers roam.

With early morning towards the Palace-
    walk
Of Orleans eagerly I turned: as yet
The streets were still; not so those long
    Arcades;
There, 'mid a peal of ill-matched sounds
    and cries,
That greeted me on entering, I could hear

Shrill voices from the hawkers in the throng,
Bawling, "Denunciation of the Crimes 100
Of Maximilian Robespierre;" the hand,
Prompt as the voice, held forth a printed speech,
The same that had been recently pronounced,
When Robespierre, not ignorant for what mark
Some words of indirect reproof had been
Intended, rose in hardihood, and dared
The man who had an ill surmise of him
To bring his charge in openness; whereat,
When a dead pause ensued, and no one stirred,
In silence of all present, from his seat 110
Louvet walked single through the avenue,
And took his station in the Tribune, saying,
"I, Robespierre, accuse thee!" Well is known
The inglorious issue of that charge, and how
He, who had launched the startling thunderbolt,
The one bold man, whose voice the attack had sounded,
Was left without a follower to discharge
His perilous duty, and retire lamenting
That Heaven's best aid is wasted upon men
Who to themselves are false.
                    But these are things
Of which I speak, only as they were storm
Or sunshine to my individual mind, 122
No further. Let me then relate that now —
In some sort seeing with my proper eyes
That Liberty, and Life, and Death, would soon
To the remotest corners of the land
Lie in the arbitrement of those who ruled
The capital City; what was struggled for,
And by what combatants victory must be won;
The indecision on their part whose aim 130
Seemed best, and the straightforward path of those
Who in attack or in defence were strong
Through their impiety — my inmost soul
Was agitated; yea, I could almost
Have prayed that throughout earth upon all men,
By patient exercise of reason made
Worthy of liberty, all spirits filled
With zeal expanding in Truth's holy light,
The gift of tongues might fall, and power arrive

From the four quarters of the winds to do
For France, what without help she could not do, 141
A work of honour; think not that to this
I added, work of safety: from all doubt
Or trepidation for the end of things
Far was I, far as angels are from guilt.

Yet did I grieve, nor only grieved, but thought
Of opposition and of remedies:
An insignificant stranger and obscure,
And one, moreover, little graced with power
Of eloquence even in my native speech, 150
And all unfit for tumult or intrigue,
Yet would I at this time with willing heart
Have undertaken for a cause so great
Service however dangerous. I revolved,
How much the destiny of Man had still
Hung upon single persons; that there was,
Transcendent to all local patrimony,
One nature, as there is one sun in heaven;
That objects, even as they are great, thereby
Do come within the reach of humblest eyes; 160
That Man is only weak through his mistrust
And want of hope where evidence divine
Proclaims to him that hope should be most sure;
Nor did the inexperience of my youth
Preclude conviction, that a spirit strong
In hope, and trained to noble aspirations,
A spirit thoroughly faithful to itself,
Is for Society's unreasoning herd
A domineering instinct, serves at once
For way and guide, a fluent receptacle 170
That gathers up each petty straggling rill
And vein of water, glad to be rolled on
In safe obedience; that a mind, whose rest
Is where it ought to be, in self-restraint,
In circumspection and simplicity,
Falls rarely in entire discomfiture
Below its aim, or meets with, from without,
A treachery that foils it or defeats;
And, lastly, if the means on human will,
Frail human will, dependent should betray
Him who too boldly trusted them, I felt 181
That 'mid the loud distractions of the world
A sovereign voice subsists within the soul,
Arbiter undisturbed of right and wrong,
Of life and death, in majesty severe
Enjoining, as may best promote the aims
Of truth and justice, either sacrifice,
From whatsoever region of our cares

Or our infirm affections Nature pleads,
Earnest and blind, against the stern decree.

On the other side, I called to mind those
    truths   191
That are the commonplaces of the schools —
(A theme for boys, too hackneyed for their
    sires,)
Yet, with a revelation's liveliness,
In all their comprehensive bearings known
And visible to philosophers of old,
Men who, to business of the world un-
    trained,
Lived in the shade; and to Harmodius
    known
And his compeer Aristogiton, known   199
To Brutus — that tyrannic power is weak,
Hath neither gratitude, nor faith, nor love,
Nor the support of good or evil men
To trust in; that the godhead which is ours
Can never utterly be charmed or stilled;
That nothing hath a natural right to last
But equity and reason; that all else
Meets foes irreconcilable, and at best
Lives only by variety of disease.

Well might my wishes be intense, my
    thoughts
Strong and perturbed, not doubting at that
    time   210
But that the virtue of one paramount mind
Would have abashed those impious crests
    — have quelled
Outrage and bloody power, and — in despite
Of what the People long had been and were
Through ignorance and false teaching, sad-
    der proof
Of immaturity, and — in the teeth
Of desperate opposition from without —
Have cleared a passage for just govern-
    ment,
And left a solid birthright to the State,
Redeemed, according to example given   220
By ancient lawgivers.
                 In this frame of mind,
Dragged by a chain of harsh necessity,
So seemed it, — now I thankfully acknow-
    ledge,
Forced by the gracious providence of
    Heaven, —
To England I returned, else (though as-
    sured
That I both was and must be of small
    weight,
No better than a landsman on the deck

Of a ship struggling with a hideous storm)
Doubtless, I should have then made com-
    mon cause
With some who perished; haply perished
    too,   230
A poor mistaken and bewildered offering, —
Should to the breast of Nature have gone
    back,
With all my resolutions, all my hopes,
A Poet only to myself, to men
Useless, and even, beloved Friend ! a soul
To thee unknown !
            Twice had the trees let fall
Their leaves, as often Winter had put on
His hoary crown, since I had seen the surge
Beat against Albion's shore, since ear of
    mine   239
Had caught the accents of my native speech
Upon our native country's sacred ground.
A patriot of the world, how could I glide
Into communion with her sylvan shades,
Erewhile my tuneful haunt ? It pleased
    me more
To abide in the great City, where I found
The general air still busy with the stir
Of that first memorable onset made
By a strong levy of humanity
Upon the traffickers in Negro blood;
Effort which, though defeated, had recalled
To notice old forgotten principles,   251
And through the nation spread a novel heat
Of virtuous feeling. For myself, I own
That this particular strife had wanted power
To rivet my affections; nor did now
Its unsuccessful issue much excite
My sorrow; for I brought with me the
    faith
That, if France prospered, good men would
    not long
Pay fruitless worship to humanity,
And this most rotten branch of human
    shame,   260
Object, so seemed it, of superfluous pains,
Would fall together with its parent tree.
What, then, were my emotions, when in
    arms
Britain put forth her free-born strength in
    league,
Oh, pity and shame ! with those confeder-
    ate Powers !
Not in my single self alone I found,
But in the minds of all ingenuous youth,
Change and subversion from that hour. No
    shock
Given to my moral nature had I known   269

Down to that very moment; neither lapse
Nor turn of sentiment that might be named
A revolution, save at this one time;
All else was progress on the self-same path
On which, with a diversity of pace,
I had been travelling: this a stride at once
Into another region. As a light
And pliant harebell, swinging in the breeze
On some grey rock — its birth-place — so
    had I
Wantoned, fast rooted on the ancient tower
Of my beloved country, wishing not   280
A happier fortune than to wither there:
Now was I from that pleasant station torn
And tossed about in whirlwind. I rejoiced,
Yea, afterwards — truth most painful to
    record ! —
Exulted, in the triumph of my soul,
When Englishmen by thousands were o'er-
    thrown,
Left without glory on the field, or driven,
Brave hearts ! to shameful flight. It was
    a grief, —
Grief call it not, 't was anything but that, —
A conflict of sensations without name,   290
Of which *he* only, who may love the sight
Of a village steeple, as I do, can judge,
When, in the congregation bending all
To their great Father, prayers were offered
    up,
Or praises for our country's victories;
And, 'mid the simple worshippers, perchance
I only, like an uninvited guest
Whom no one owned, sate silent, shall I
    add,
Fed on the day of vengeance yet to come.

    Oh ! much have they to account for, who
    could tear,   300
By violence, at one decisive rent,
From the best youth in England their dear
    pride,
Their joy, in England; this, too, at a time
In which worst losses easily might wear
The best of names, when patriotic love
Did of itself in modesty give way,
Like the Precursor when the Deity
Is come Whose harbinger he was; a time
In which apostasy from ancient faith
Seemed but conversion to a higher creed;
Withal a season dangerous and wild,   311
A time when sage Experience would have
    snatched
Flowers out of any hedge-row to compose
A chaplet in contempt of his grey locks.

When the proud fleet that bears the red-
    cross flag
In that unworthy service was prepared
To mingle, I beheld the vessels lie,
A brood of gallant creatures, on the deep;
I saw them in their rest, a sojourner
Through a whole month of calm and glassy
    days   320
In that delightful island which protects
Their place of convocation — there I heard,
Each evening, pacing by the still sea-shore,
A monitory sound that never failed, —
The sunset cannon. While the orb went
    down
In the tranquillity of nature, came
That voice, ill requiem ! seldom heard by
    me
Without a spirit overcast by dark
Imaginations, sense of woes to come,
Sorrow for human kind, and pain of heart.

    In France, the men, who, for their des-
    perate ends,   331
Had plucked up mercy by the roots, were
    glad
Of this new enemy. Tyrants, strong before
In wicked pleas, were strong as demons
    now;
And thus, on every side beset with foes,
The goaded land waxed mad; the crimes
    of few
Spread into madness of the many; blasts
From hell came sanctified like airs from
    heaven.
The sternness of the just, the faith of those
Who doubted not that Providence had
    times   340
Of vengeful retribution, theirs who throned
The human Understanding paramount
And made of that their God, the hopes of
    men
Who were content to barter short-lived
    pangs
For a paradise of ages, the blind rage
Of insolent tempers, the light vanity
Of intermeddlers, steady purposes
Of the suspicious, slips of the indiscreet,
And all the accidents of life — were pressed
Into one service, busy with one work.   350
The Senate stood aghast, her prudence
    quenched,
Her wisdom stifled, and her justice scared,
Her frenzy only active to extol
Past outrages, and shape the way for new,
Which no one dared to oppose or mitigate.

Domestic carnage now filled the whole
    year
With feast-days; old men from the chimney-
    nook,
The maiden from the bosom of her love,
The mother from the cradle of her babe,
The warrior from the field — all perished,
    all —   360
Friends, enemies, of all parties, ages, ranks,
Head after head, and never heads enough
For those that bade them fall. They found
    their joy,
They made it proudly, eager as a child,
(If like desires of innocent little ones
May with such heinous appetites be com-
    pared),
Pleased in some open field to exercise
A toy that mimics with revolving wings
The motion of a wind-mill; though the air
Do of itself blow fresh, and make the vanes
Spin in his eyesight, *that* contents him not,
But with the plaything at arm's length, he
    sets   372
His front against the blast, and runs amain,
That it may whirl the faster.
                    Amid the depth
Of those enormities, even thinking minds
Forgot, at seasons, whence they had their
    being,
Forgot that such a sound was ever heard
As Liberty upon earth: yet all beneath
Her innocent authority was wrought,
Nor could have been, without her blessed
    name.   380
The illustrious wife of Roland, in the hour
Of her composure, felt that agony,
And gave it vent in her last words. O
    Friend!
It was a lamentable time for man,
Whether a hope had e'er been his or not:
A woful time for them whose hopes survived
The shock; most woful for those few who
    still
Were flattered, and had trust in human
    kind:
They had the deepest feeling of the grief.
Meanwhile the Invaders fared as they de-
    served: 390
The Herculean Commonwealth had put
    forth her arms,
And throttled with an infant godhead's
    might
The snakes about her cradle; that was
    well,
And as it should be; yet no cure for them

Whose souls were sick with pain of what
    would be
Hereafter brought in charge against man-
    kind.
Most melancholy at that time, O Friend!
Were my day-thoughts, — my nights were
    miserable;
Through months, through years, long after
    the last beat
Of those atrocities, the hour of sleep   400
To me came rarely charged with natural
    gifts,
Such ghastly visions had I of despair
And tyranny, and implements of death;
And innocent victims sinking under fear,
And momentary hope, and worn-out prayer,
Each in his separate cell, or penned in crowds
For sacrifice, and struggling with forced
    mirth
And levity in dungeons, where the dust
Was laid with tears. Then suddenly the
    scene
Changed, and the unbroken dream entangled
    me   410
In long orations, which I strove to plead
Before unjust tribunals, — with a voice
Labouring, a brain confounded, and a sense,
Death-like, of treacherous desertion, felt
In the last place of refuge — my own soul.

    When I began in youth's delightful prime
To yield myself to Nature, when that strong
And holy passion overcame me first,
Nor day nor night, evening or morn, was
    free
From its oppression. But, O Power Su-
    preme!   420
Without Whose call this world would cease
    to breathe,
Who from the fountain of Thy grace dost
    fill
The veins that branch through every frame
    of life,
Making man what he is, creature divine,
In single or in social eminence,
Above the rest raised infinite ascents
When reason that enables him to be
Is not sequestered — what a change is here!
How different ritual for this after-worship,
What countenance to promote this second
    love!   430
The first was service paid to things which
    lie
Guarded within the bosom of Thy will.
Therefore to serve was high beatitude;

Tumult was therefore gladness, and the fear
Ennobling, venerable; sleep secure,
And waking thoughts more rich than hap-
  piest dreams.

But as the ancient Prophets, borne aloft
In vision, yet constrained by natural laws
With them to take a troubled human heart,
Wanted not consolations, nor a creed   440
Of reconcilement, then when they de-
  nounced,
On towns and cities, wallowing in the abyss
Of their offences, punishment to come;
Or saw, like other men, with bodily eyes,
Before them, in some desolated place,
The wrath consummate and the threat
  fulfilled;
So, with devout humility be it said,
So did a portion of that spirit fall
On me uplifted from the vantage-ground
Of pity and sorrow to a state of being   450
That through the time's exceeding fierceness
  saw
Glimpses of retribution, terrible,
And in the order of sublime behests:
But, even if that were not, amid the awe
Of unintelligible chastisement,
Not only acquiescences of faith
Survived, but daring sympathies with power,
Motions not treacherous or profane, else
  why
Within the folds of no ungentle breast
Their dread vibration to this hour prolonged ?
Wild blasts of music thus could find their
  way   461
Into the midst of turbulent events;
So that worst tempests might be listened to.
Then was the truth received into my heart,
That, under heaviest sorrow earth can bring,
If from the affliction somewhere do not
  grow
Honour which could not else have been, a
  faith,
An elevation, and a sanctity,
If new strength be not given nor old restored,
The blame is ours, not Nature's. When a
  taunt   470
Was taken up by scoffers in their pride,
Saying, " Behold the harvest that we reap
From popular government and equality,"
I clearly saw that neither these nor aught
Of wild belief engrafted on their names
By false philosophy had caused the woe,
But a terrific reservoir of guilt
And ignorance filled up from age to age,

That could no longer hold its loathsome
  charge,
But burst and spread in deluge through the
  land.   480

And as the desert hath green spots, the
  sea
Small islands scattered amid stormy waves,
So *that* disastrous period did not want
Bright sprinklings of all human excellence,
To which the silver wands of saints in
  Heaven
Might point with rapturous joy. Yet not
  the less,
For those examples, in no age surpassed,
Of fortitude and energy and love,
And human nature faithful to herself
Under worst trials, was I driven to think   490
Of the glad times when first I traversed
  France
A youthful pilgrim; above all reviewed
That eventide, when under windows bright
With happy faces and with garlands hung,
And through a rainbow-arch that spanned
  the street,
Triumphal pomp for liberty confirmed,
I paced, a dear companion at my side,
The town of Arras, whence with promise
  high
Issued, on delegation to sustain
Humanity and right, *that* Robespierre,   500
He who thereafter, and in how short time !
Wielded the sceptre of the Atheist crew.
When the calamity spread far and wide —
And this same city, that did then appear
To outrun the rest in exultation, groaned
Under the vengeance of her cruel son,
As Lear reproached the winds — I could
  almost
Have quarrelled with that blameless spec-
  tacle
For lingering yet an image in my mind
To mock me under such a strange reverse.

O Friend ! few happier moments have
  been mine   511
Than that which told the downfall of this
  Tribe
So dreaded, so abhorred. The day deserves
A separate record. Over the smooth sands
Of Leven's ample estuary lay
My journey, and beneath a genial sun,
With distant prospect among gleams of sky
And clouds and intermingling mountain
  tops,

In one inseparable glory clad,
Creatures of one ethereal substance met   520
In consistory, like a diadem
Or crown of burning seraphs as they sit
In the empyrean.   Underneath that pomp
Celestial, lay unseen the pastoral vales
Among whose happy fields I had grown up
From childhood.   On the fulgent spectacle,
That neither passed away nor changed, I
    gazed
Enrapt; but brightest things are wont to
    draw
Sad opposites out of the inner heart,
As even their pensive influence drew from
    mine.   530
How could it otherwise ? for not in vain
That very morning had I turned aside
To seek the ground where, 'mid a throng
    of graves,
An honoured teacher of my youth was laid,
And on the stone were graven by his desire
Lines from the churchyard elegy of Gray.
This faithful guide, speaking from his
    death-bed,
Added no farewell to his parting counsel,
But said to me, " My head will soon lie
    low; "
And when I saw the turf that covered
    him,   540
After the lapse of full eight years, those
    words,
With sound of voice and countenance of
    the Man,
Came back upon me, so that some few tears
Fell from me in my own despite. But now
I thought, still traversing that widespread
    plain,
With tender pleasure of the verses graven
Upon his tombstone, whispering to myself:
He loved the Poets, and, if now alive,
Would have loved me, as one not destitute
Of promise, nor belying the kind hope   550
That he had formed, when I, at his com-
    mand,
Began to spin, with toil, my earliest songs.

    As I advanced, all that I saw or felt
Was gentleness and peace.   Upon a small
And rocky island near, a fragment stood,
(Itself like a sea rock) the low remains
(With shells encrusted, dark with briny
    weeds)
Of a dilapidated structure, once
A Romish chapel, where the vested priest
Said matins at the hour that suited those

Who crossed the sands with ebb of morning
    tide.   561
Not far from that still ruin all the plain
Lay spotted with a variegated crowd
Of vehicles and travellers, horse and foot,
Wading beneath the conduct of their guide
In loose procession through the shallow
    stream
Of inland waters; the great sea meanwhile
Heaved at safe distance, far retired.   I
    paused,
Longing for skill to paint a scene so bright
And cheerful, but the foremost of the band
As he approached, no salutation given   571
In the familiar language of the day,
Cried, " Robespierre is dead ! " nor was a
    doubt,
After strict question, left within my mind
That he and his supporters all were fallen.

    Great was my transport, deep my grati-
    tude
To everlasting Justice, by this fiat
Made manifest. " Come now, ye golden
    times,"
Said I forth-pouring on those open sands
A hymn of triumph: " as the morning
    comes   580
From out the bosom of the night, come ye :
Thus far our trust is verified; behold !
They who with clumsy desperation brought
A river of Blood, and preached that nothing
    else
Could cleanse the Augean stable, by the
    might
Of their own helper have been swept away;
Their madness stands declared and visible;
Elsewhere will safety now be sought, and
    earth
March firmly towards righteousness and
    peace." —
Then schemes I framed more calmly, when
    and how   590
The madding factions might be tranquil-
    lised,
And how through hardships manifold and
    long
The glorious renovation would proceed.
Thus interrupted by uneasy bursts
Of exultation, I pursued my way
Along that very shore which I had skimmed
In former days, when — spurring from the
    Vale
Of Nightshade, and St. Mary's mouldering
    fane,

And the stone abbot, after circuit made
In wantonness of heart, a joyous band   600
Of schoolboys hastening to their distant
    home
Along the margin of the moonlight sea —
We beat with thundering hoofs the level
    sand.

BOOK ELEVENTH

FRANCE (*concluded*)

FROM that time forth, Authority in France
Put on a milder face; Terror had ceased,
Yet everything was wanting that might give
Courage to them who looked for good by
    light   .
Of rational Experience, for the shoots
And hopeful blossoms of a second spring:
Yet, in me, confidence was unimpaired;
The Senate's language, and the public acts
And measures of the Government, though
    both
Weak, and of heartless omen, had not
    power   10
To daunt me; in the People was my trust:
And, in the virtues which mine eyes had
    seen,
I knew that wound external could not take
Life from the young Republic; that new
    foes
Would only follow, in the path of shame,
Their brethren, and her triumphs be in the
    end
Great, universal, irresistible.
This intuition led me to confound
One victory with another, higher far, —
Triumphs of unambitious peace at home,   20
And noiseless fortitude. Beholding still
Resistance strong as heretofore, I thought
That what was in degree the same was
    likewise
The same in quality, — that, as the worse
Of the two spirits then at strife remained
Untired, the better, surely, would preserve
The heart that first had roused him. Youth
    maintains,
In all conditions of society,
Communion more direct and intimate
With Nature, — hence, ofttimes, with rea-
    son too —   30
Than age or manhood, even. To Nature
    then,
Power had reverted: habit, custom, law,
Had left an interregnum's open space

For *her* to move about in, uncontrolled.
Hence could I see how Babel-like their
    task,
Who, by the recent deluge stupified,
With their whole souls went culling from
    the day
Its petty promises, to build a tower
For their own safety; laughed with my
    compeers
At gravest heads, by enmity to France   40
Distempered, till they found, in every blast
Forced from the street-disturbing news-
    man's horn,
For her great cause record or prophecy
Of utter ruin. How might we believe
That wisdom could, in any shape, come
    near
Men clinging to delusions so insane?
And thus, experience proving that no few
Of our opinions had been just, we took
Like credit to ourselves where less was due,
And thought that other notions were as
    sound,   50
Yea, could not but be right, because we saw
That foolish men opposed them.
                    To a strain
More animated I might here give way,
And tell, since juvenile errors are my theme,
What in those days, through Britain, was
    performed
To turn *all* judgments out of their right
    course;
But this is passion over-near ourselves,
Reality too close and too intense,
And intermixed with something, in my mind,
Of scorn and condemnation personal,   60
That would profane the sanctity of verse.
Our Shepherds, this say merely, at that time
Acted, or seemed at least to act, like men
Thirsting to make the guardian crook of
    law
A tool of murder; they who ruled the
    State —
Though with such awful proof before their
    eyes
That he, who would sow death, reaps death,
    or worse,
And can reap nothing better — child-like
    longed
To imitate, not wise enough to avoid;
Or left (by mere timidity betrayed)   70
The plain straight road, for one no better
    chosen
Than if their wish had been to undermine
Justice, and make an end of Liberty.

But from these bitter truths I must return
To my own history. It hath been told
That I was led to take an eager part
In arguments of civil polity,
Abruptly, and indeed before my time:
I had approached, like other youths, the
    shield
Of human nature from the golden side,   80
And would have fought, even to the death,
    to attest
The quality of the metal which I saw.
What there is best in individual man,
Of wise in passion, and sublime in power,
Benevolent in small societies,
And great in large ones, I had oft revolved,
Felt deeply, but not thoroughly understood
By reason: nay, far from it; they were yet,
As cause was given me afterwards to learn,
Not proof against the injuries of the day;
Lodged only at the sanctuary's door,   91
Not safe within its bosom. Thus prepared,
And with such general insight into evil,
And of the bounds which sever it from good,
As books and common intercourse with life
Must needs have given — to the inexpe-
    rienced mind,
When the world travels in a beaten road,
Guide faithful as is needed — I began
To meditate with ardour on the rule
And management of nations; what it is   100
And ought to be; and strove to learn how
    far
Their power or weakness, wealth or poverty,
Their happiness or misery, depends
Upon their laws, and fashion of the State.

O pleasant exercise of hope and joy !
For mighty were the auxiliars which then
    stood
Upon our side, us who were strong in love !
Bliss was it in that dawn to be alive,
But to be young was very Heaven ! O
    times,   109
In which the meagre, stale, forbidding ways
Of custom, law, and statute, took at once
The attraction of a country in romance !
When Reason seemed the most to assert her
    rights,
When most intent on making of herself
A prime enchantress — to assist the work,
Which then was going forward in her name !
Not favoured spots alone, but the whole
    Earth,
The beauty wore of promise — that which
    sets

(As at some moments might not be unfelt
Among the bowers of Paradise itself)   120
The budding rose above the rose full blown.
What temper at the prospect did not wake
To happiness unthought of ? The inert
Were roused, and lively natures rapt away !
They who had fed their childhood upon
    dreams,
The play-fellows of fancy, who had made
All powers of swiftness, subtilty, and
    strength
Their ministers, — who in lordly wise had
    stirred
Among the grandest objects of the sense,
And dealt with whatsoever they found there
As if they had within some lurking right   131
To wield it; — they, too, who of gentle
    mood
Had watched all gentle motions, and to
    these
Had fitted their own thoughts, schemers
    more mild,
And in the region of their peaceful selves;—
Now was it that *both* found, the meek and
    lofty
Did both find, helpers to their hearts' desire,
And stuff at hand, plastic as they could
    wish, —
Were called upon to exercise their skill,
Not in Utopia, — subterranean fields, —   140
Or some secreted island, Heaven knows
    where !
But in the very world, which is the world
Of all of us, — the place where, in the end,
We find our happiness, or not at all !

Why should I not confess that Earth was
    then
To me, what an inheritance, new-fallen,
Seems, when the first time visited, to one
Who thither comes to find in it his home ?
He walks about and looks upon the spot
With cordial transport, moulds it and re-
    moulds,   150
And is half-pleased with things that are
    amiss,
'T will be such joy to see them disappear.

An active partisan, I thus convoked
From every object pleasant circumstance
To suit my ends; I moved among mankind
With genial feelings still predominant;
When erring, erring on the better part,
And in the kinder spirit; placable,
Indulgent, as not uninformed that men   159

See as they have been taught — Antiquity
Gives rights to error; and aware, no less
That throwing off oppression must be work
As well of License as of Liberty;
And above all — for this was more than
    all —
Not caring if the wind did now and then
Blow keen upon an eminence that gave
Prospect so large into futurity;
In brief, a child of Nature, as at first,
Diffusing only those affections wider
That from the cradle had grown up with
    me,   170
And losing, in no other way than light
Is lost in light, the weak in the more strong.

    In the main outline, such it might be
        said
Was my condition, till with open war
Britain opposed the liberties of France.
This threw me first out of the pale of love;
Soured and corrupted, upwards to the
        source,
My sentiments; was not, as hitherto,   178
A swallowing up of lesser things in great,
But change of them into their contraries;
And thus a way was opened for mistakes
And false conclusions, in degree as gross,
In kind more dangerous. What had been
        a pride,
Was now a shame; my likings and my loves
Ran in new channels, leaving old ones dry;
And hence a blow that, in maturer age,
Would but have touched the judgment,
        struck more deep
Into sensations near the heart: meantime,
As from the first, wild theories were afloat,
To whose pretensions, sedulously urged,   190
I had but lent a careless ear, assured
That time was ready to set all things right,
And that the multitude, so long oppressed,
Would be oppressed no more.
                        But when events
Brought less encouragement, and unto these
The immediate proof of principles no more
Could be entrusted, while the events them-
        selves,
Worn out in greatness, stripped of novelty,
Less occupied the mind, and sentiments
Could through my understanding's natural
        growth   200
No longer keep their ground, by faith main-
        tained
Of inward consciousness, and hope that laid
Her hand upon her object — evidence

Safer, of universal application, such
As could not be impeached, was sought else-
    where.

    But now, become oppressors in their turn,
Frenchmen had changed a war of self-
    defence
For one of conquest, losing sight of all
Which they had struggled for: now mounted
        up,
Openly in the eye of earth and heaven,   210
The scale of liberty. I read her doom.
With anger vexed, with disappointment
        sore,
But not dismayed, nor taking to the shame
Of a false prophet. While resentment rose,
Striving to hide, what nought could heal,
        the wounds
Of mortified presumption, I adhered
More firmly to old tenets, and, to prove
Their temper, strained them more; and
        thus, in heat
Of contest, did opinions every day
Grow into consequence, till round my
        mind   220
They clung, as if they were its life, nay
        more,
The very being of the immortal soul.

    This was the time, when, all things tend-
        ing fast
To depravation, speculative schemes —
That promised to abstract the hopes of
        Man
Out of his feelings, to be fixed thenceforth
For ever in a purer element —
Found ready welcome. Tempting region
        that
For Zeal to enter and refresh herself,
Where passions had the privilege to work,
And never hear the sound of their own
        names.   231
But, speaking more in charity, the dream
Flattered the young, pleased with ex-
        tremes, nor least
With that which makes our Reason's naked
        self
The object of its fervour. What delight!
How glorious! in self-knowledge and self-
        rule,
To look through all the frailties of the
        world,
And, with a resolute mastery shaking off
Infirmities of nature, time, and place,
Build social upon personal Liberty,   240

Which, to the blind restraints of general
    laws,
Superior, magisterially adopts
One guide, the light of circumstances,
    flashed
Upon an independent intellect.
Thus expectation rose again; thus hope,
From her first ground expelled, grew proud
    once more.
Oft, as my thoughts were turned to human
    kind,
I scorned indifference; but, inflamed with
    thirst
Of a secure intelligence, and sick   249
Of other longing, I pursued what seemed
A more exalted nature; wished that Man
Should start out of his earthly, worm-like
    state,
And spread abroad the wings of Liberty,
Lord of himself, in undisturbed delight —
A noble aspiration ! *yet* I feel
(Sustained by worthier as by wiser
    thoughts)
The aspiration, nor shall ever cease
To feel it; — but return we to our course.

Enough, 't is true — could such a plea
    excuse
Those aberrations — had the clamorous
    friends   260
Of ancient Institutions said and done
To bring disgrace upon their very names;
Disgrace, of which, custom and written law,
And sundry moral sentiments as props
Or emanations of those institutes,
Too justly bore a part. A veil had been
Uplifted; why deceive ourselves ? in
    sooth,
'T was even so; and sorrow for the man
Who either had not eyes wherewith to
    see,
Or, seeing, had forgotten ! A strong
    shock   270
Was given to old opinions; all men's minds
Had felt its power, and mine was both let
    loose,
Let loose and goaded. After what hath
    been
Already said of patriotic love,
Suffice it here to add, that, somewhat stern
In temperament, withal a happy man,
And therefore bold to look on painful
    things,
Free likewise of the world, and thence
    more bold,

I summoned my best skill, and toiled, in-
    tent
To anatomise the frame of social life;   280
Yea, the whole body of society
Searched to its heart. Share with me,
    Friend ! the wish
That some dramatic tale, endued with
    shapes
Livelier, and flinging out less guarded
    words
Than suit the work we fashion, might set
    forth
What then I learned, or think I learned, of
    truth,
And the errors into which I fell, betrayed
By present objects, and by reasonings false
From their beginnings, inasmuch as drawn
Out of a heart that had been turned aside
From Nature's way by outward accidents,
And which was thus confounded, more and
    more   292
Misguided, and misguiding. So I fared,
Dragging all precepts, judgments, maxims,
    creeds,
Like culprits to the bar; calling the mind,
Suspiciously, to establish in plain day
Her titles and her honours; now believing,
Now disbelieving; endlessly perplexed
With impulse, motive, right and wrong,
    the ground
Of obligation, what the rule and whence
The sanction; till, demanding formal *proof*,
And seeking it in every thing, I lost   302
All feeling of conviction, and, in fine,
Sick, wearied out with contrarieties,
Yielded up moral questions in despair.

This was the crisis of that strong disease,
This the soul's last and lowest ebb; I
    drooped,
Deeming our blessèd reason of least use
Where wanted most: "The lordly attri-
    butes
Of will and choice," I bitterly exclaimed,
"What are they but a mockery of a Being
Who hath in no concerns of his a test   312
Of good and evil; knows not what to fear
Or hope for, what to covet or to shun;
And who, if those could be discerned,
    would yet
Be little profited, would see, and ask
Where is the obligation to enforce ?
And, to acknowledged law rebellious, still,
As selfish passion urged, would act amiss;
The dupe of folly, or the slave of crime."

Depressed, bewildered thus, I did not
    walk   321
With scoffers, seeking light and gay re-
    venge
From indiscriminate laughter, nor sate
    down
In reconcilement with an utter waste
Of intellect; such sloth I could not brook,
(Too well I loved, in that my spring of
    life,
Pains-taking thoughts, and truth, their dear
    reward)
But turned to abstract science, and there
    sought
Work for the reasoning faculty enthroned
Where the disturbances of space and
    time —   330
Whether in matter's various properties
Inherent, or from human will and power
Derived — find no admission. Then it
    was —
Thanks to the bounteous Giver of all
    good ! —
That the belovèd Sister in whose sight
Those days were passed, now speaking in
    a voice
Of sudden admonition — like a brook
That did but *cross* a lonely road, and now
Is seen, heard, felt, and caught at every
    turn,
Companion never lost through many a
    league —   340
Maintained for me a saving intercourse
With my true self; for, though bedimmed
    and changed
Much, as it seemed, I was no further
    changed
Than as a clouded and a waning moon:
She whispered still that brightness would
    return;
She, in the midst of all, preserved me still
A Poet, made me seek beneath that name,
And that alone, my office upon earth;
And, lastly, as hereafter will be shown,
If willing audience fail not, Nature's self,
By all varieties of human love   351
Assisted, led me back through opening day
To those sweet counsels between head and
    heart
Whence grew that genuine knowledge,
    fraught with peace,
Which, through the later sinkings of this
    cause,
Hath still upheld me, and upholds me now
In the catastrophe (for so they dream,

And nothing less), when, finally to close
And seal up all the gains of France, a
    Pope
Is summoned in, to crown an Emperor —
This last opprobrium, when we see a peo-
    ple,   361
That once looked up in faith, as if to Heaven
For manna, take a lesson from the dog
Returning to his vomit; when the sun
That rose in splendour, was alive, and
    moved
In exultation with a living pomp
Of clouds — his glory's natural retinue —
Hath dropped all functions by the gods
    bestowed,
And, turned into a gewgaw, a machine,
Sets like an Opera phantom.
                      Thus, O Friend !
Through times of honour and through times
    of shame   371
Descending, have I faithfully retraced
The perturbations of a youthful mind
Under a long-lived storm of great events—
A story destined for thy ear, who now,
Among the fallen of nations, dost abide
Where Etna, over hill and valley, casts
His shadow stretching towards Syracuse,
The city of Timoleon ! Righteous Heaven !
How are the mighty prostrated ! They
    first,
They first of all that breathe should have
    awaked   381
When the great voice was heard from out
    the tombs
Of ancient heroes. If I suffered grief
For ill-requited France, by many deemed
A trifler only in her proudest day;
Have been distressed to think of what she
    once
Promised, now is; a far more sober cause
Thine eyes must see of sorrow in a land,
To the reanimating influence lost
Of memory, to virtue lost and hope,   390
Though with the wreck of loftier years
    bestrewn.

But indignation works where hope is not,
And thou, O Friend ! wilt be refreshed.
    There is
One great society alone on earth:
The noble Living and the noble Dead.

Thine be such converse strong and
    sanative,
A ladder for thy spirit to reascend

To health and joy and pure contentedness;
To me the grief confined, that thou art
 gone
From this last spot of earth, where Freedom
 now   400
Stands single in her only sanctuary;
A lonely wanderer, art gone, by pain
Compelled and sickness, at this latter day,
This sorrowful reverse for all mankind.
I feel for thee, must utter what I feel:
The sympathies erewhile in part discharged,
Gather afresh, and will have vent again:
My own delights do scarcely seem to me
My own delights; the lordly Alps them-
 selves,
Those rosy peaks, from which the Morning
 looks   410
Abroad on many nations, are no more
For me that image of pure gladsomeness
Which they were wont to be. Through
 kindred scenes,
For purpose, at a time, how different !
Thou tak'st thy way, carrying the heart and
 soul
That Nature gives to Poets, now by thought
Matured, and in the summer of their
 strength.
Oh ! wrap him in your shades, ye giant
 woods,
On Etna's side; and thou, O flowery field
Of Enna ! is there not some nook of thine,
From the first play-time of the infant world
Kept sacred to restorative delight, 422
When from afar invoked by anxious love ?

Child of the mountains, among shepherds
 reared,
Ere yet familiar with the classic page,
I learnt to dream of Sicily; and lo,
The gloom, that, but a moment past, was
 deepened
At thy command, at her command gives
 way;
A pleasant promise, wafted from her shores,
Comes o'er my heart: in fancy I behold 430
Her seas yet smiling, her once happy vales;
Nor can my tongue give utterance to a
 name
Of note belonging to that honoured isle,
Philosopher or Bard, Empedocles,
Or Archimedes, pure abstracted soul !
That doth not yield a solace to my grief:
And, O Theocritus, so far have some
Prevailed among the powers of heaven and
 earth,

By their endowments, good or great, that
 they
Have had, as thou reportest, miracles 440
Wrought for them in old time: yea, not
 unmoved,
When thinking on my own beloved friend,
I hear thee tell how bees with honey fed
Divine Comates, by his impious lord
Within a chest imprisoned; how they came
Laden from blooming grove or flowery field,
And fed him there, alive, month after
 month,
Because the goatherd, blessèd man ! had
 lips
Wet with the Muses' nectar.
       Thus I soothe
The pensive moments by this calm fire-side,
And find a thousand bounteous images 451
To cheer the thoughts of those I love, and
 mine.
Our prayers have been accepted; thou wilt
 stand
On Etna's summit, above earth and sea,
Triumphant, winning from the invaded
 heavens
Thoughts without bound, magnificent de-
 signs,
Worthy of poets who attuned their harps
In wood or echoing cave, for discipline
Of heroes; or, in reverence to the gods,
'Mid temples, served by sapient priests, and
 choirs   460
Of virgins crowned with roses. Not in vain
Those temples, where they in their ruins yet
Survive for inspiration, shall attract
Thy solitary steps: and on the brink
Thou wilt recline of pastoral Arethuse;
Or, if that fountain be in truth no more,
Then, near some other spring — which, by
 the name
Thou gratulatest, willingly deceived —
I see thee linger a glad votary,
And not a captive pining for his home. 470

BOOK TWELFTH

IMAGINATION AND TASTE, HOW IMPAIRED AND RESTORED

LONG time have human ignorance and guilt
Detained us, on what spectacles of woe
Compelled to look, and inwardly oppressed
With sorrow, disappointment, vexing
 thoughts,
Confusion of the judgment, zeal decayed,

And, lastly, utter loss of hope itself
And things to hope for ! Not with these
  began
Our song, and not with these our song
  must end.
Ye motions of delight, that haunt the sides
Of the green hills; ye breezes and soft
  airs,   10
Whose subtle intercourse with breathing
  flowers,
Feelingly watched, might teach Man's
  haughty race
How without injury to take, to give
Without offence; ye who, as if to show
The wondrous influence of power gently
  used,
Bend the complying heads of lordly pines,
And, with a touch, shift the stupendous
  clouds
Through the whole compass of the sky; ye
  brooks,
Muttering along the stones, a busy noise
By day, a quiet sound in silent night;   20
Ye waves, that out of the great deep steal
  forth
In a calm hour to kiss the pebbly shore,
Not mute, and then retire, fearing no
  storm;
And you, ye groves, whose ministry it is
To interpose the covert of your shades,
Even as a sleep, between the heart of
  man
And outward troubles, between man him-
  self,
Not seldom, and his own uneasy heart:
Oh ! that I had a music and a voice
Harmonious as your own, that I might tell
What ye have done for me. The morning
  shines,   31
Nor heedeth Man's perverseness; Spring
  returns, —
I saw the Spring return, and could rejoice,
In common with the children of her love,
Piping on boughs, or sporting on fresh
  fields,
Or boldly seeking pleasure nearer heaven
On wings that navigate cerulean skies.
So neither were complacency, nor peace,
Nor tender yearnings, wanting for my good
Through these distracted times; in Nature
  still   40
Glorying, I found a counterpoise in her,
Which, when the spirit of evil reached its
  height,
Maintained for me a secret happiness.

This narrative, my Friend ! hath chiefly
  told
Of intellectual power, fostering love,
Dispensing truth, and, over men and things,
Where reason yet might hesitate, diffusing
Prophetic sympathies of genial faith:
So was I favoured — such my happy lot —
Until that natural graciousness of mind   50
Gave way to overpressure from the times
And their disastrous issues. What availed,
When spells forbade the voyager to land,
That fragrant notice of a pleasant shore
Wafted, at intervals, from many a bower
Of blissful gratitude and fearless love ?
Dare I avow that wish was mine to see,
And hope that future times *would* surely
  see,
The man to come, parted, as by a gulph,
From him who had been; that I could no
  more   60
Trust the elevation which had made me one
With the great family that still survives
To illuminate the abyss of ages past,
Sage, warrior, patriot, hero; for it seemed
That their best virtues were not free from
  taint
Of something false and weak, that could
  not stand
The open eye of Reason. Then I said,
"Go to the Poets, they will speak to thee
More perfectly of purer creatures; — yet
If reason be nobility in man,   70
Can aught be more ignoble than the man
Whom they delight in, blinded as he is
By prejudice, the miserable slave
Of low ambition or distempered love ? "

In such strange passion, if I may once
  more
Review the past, I warred against myself —
A bigot to a new idolatry —
Like a cowled monk who hath forsworn
  the world,
Zealously laboured to cut off my heart
From all the sources of her former strength;
And as, by simple waving of a wand,   81
The wizard instantaneously dissolves
Palace or grove, even so could I unsoul
As readily by syllogistic words
Those mysteries of being which have made,
And shall continue evermore to make,
Of the whole human race one brotherhood.

What wonder, then, if, to a mind so far
Perverted, even the visible Universe

Fell under the dominion of a taste 90
Less spiritual, with microscopic view
Was scanned, as I had scanned the moral
   world ?

O Soul of Nature ! excellent and fair !
That didst rejoice with me, with whom I,
   too,
Rejoiced through early youth, before the
   winds
And roaring waters, and in lights and
   shades
That marched and countermarched about
   the hills
In glorious apparition, Powers on whom
I daily waited, now all eye and now 99
All ear; but never long without the heart
Employed, and man's unfolding intellect:
O Soul of Nature ! that, by laws divine
Sustained and governed, still dost overflow
With an impassioned life, what feeble ones
Walk on this earth ! how feeble have I
   been
When thou wert in thy strength ! Nor this
   through stroke
Of human suffering, such as justifies
Remissness and inaptitude of mind,
But through presumption; even in pleasure
   pleased
Unworthily, disliking here, and there 110
Liking; by rules of mimic art transferred
To things above all art; but more, — for
   this,
Although a strong infection of the age,
Was never much my habit — giving way
To a comparison of scene with scene,
Bent overmuch on superficial things,
Pampering myself with meagre novelties
Of colour and proportion; to the moods
Of time and season, to the moral power,
The affections and the spirit of the place,
Insensible. Nor only did the love 121
Of sitting thus in judgment interrupt
My deeper feelings, but another cause,
More subtle and less easily explained,
That almost seems inherent in the creature,
A twofold frame of body and of mind.
I speak in recollection of a time
When the bodily eye, in every stage of life
The most despotic of our senses, gained
Such strength in *me* as often held my mind
In absolute dominion. Gladly here, 131
Entering upon abstruser argument,
Could I endeavour to unfold the means
Which Nature studiously employs to thwart

This tyranny, summons all the senses each
To counteract the other, and themselves,
And makes them all, and the objects with
   which all
Are conversant, subservient in their turn
To the great ends of Liberty and Power.
But leave we this: enough that my de-
   lights 140
(Such as they were) were sought insatiably.
Vivid the transport, vivid though not pro-
   found;
I roamed from hill to hill, from rock to
   rock,
Still craving combinations of new forms,
New pleasure, wider empire for the sight,
Proud of her own endowments, and re-
   joiced
To lay the inner faculties asleep.
Amid the turns and counterturns, the strife
And various trials of our complex being,
As we grow up, such thraldom of that sense
Seems hard to shun. And yet I knew a
   maid, 151
A young enthusiast, who escaped these
   bonds;
Her eye was not the mistress of her heart;
Far less did rules prescribed by passive
   taste,
Or barren intermeddling subtleties,
Perplex her mind; but, wise as women are
When genial circumstance hath favoured
   them,
She welcomed what was given, and craved
   no more;
Whate'er the scene presented to her view
That was the best, to that she was attuned
By her benign simplicity of life, 161
And through a perfect happiness of soul,
Whose variegated feelings were in this
Sisters, that they were each some new de-
   light.
Birds in the bower, and lambs in the green
   field,
Could they have known her, would have
   loved; methought
Her very presence such a sweetness breathed,
That flowers, and trees, and even the silent
   hills,
And everything she looked on, should have
   had
An intimation how she bore herself 170
Towards them and to all creatures. God
   delights
In such a being; for, her common thoughts
Are piety, her life is gratitude.

Even like this maid, before I was called
       forth
From the retirement of my native hills,
I loved whate'er I saw: nor lightly loved,
But most intensely; never dreamt of aught
More grand, more fair, more exquisitely
       framed
Than those few nooks to which my happy
       feet
Were limited. I had not at that time   180
Lived long enough, nor in the least sur-
       vived
The first diviner influence of this world,
As it appears to unaccustomed eyes.
Worshipping then among the depth of
       things,
As piety ordained, could I submit
To measured admiration, or to aught
That should preclude humility and love ?
I felt, observed, and pondered; did not
       judge,
Yea, never thought of judging; with the gift
Of all this glory filled and satisfied.   190
And afterwards, when through the gorgeous
       Alps
Roaming, I carried with me the same heart:
In truth, the degradation — howsoe'er
Induced, effect, in whatsoe'er degree,
Of custom that prepares a partial scale
In which the little oft outweighs the great;
Or any other cause that hath been named;
Or lastly, aggravated by the times
And their impassioned sounds, which well
       might make
The milder minstrelsies of rural scenes 200
Inaudible — was transient; I had known
Too forcibly, too early in my life,
Visitings of imaginative power
For this to last: I shook the habit off
Entirely and for ever, and again
In Nature's presence stood, as now I stand,
A sensitive being, a *creative* soul.

       There are in our existence spots of time,
That with distinct pre-eminence retain 209
A renovating virtue, whence — depressed
By false opinion and contentious thought,
Or aught of heavier or more deadly weight,
In trivial occupations, and the round
Of ordinary intercourse — our minds
Are nourished and invisibly repaired;
A virtue, by which pleasure is enhanced,
That penetrates, enables us to mount,
When high, more high, and lifts us up
       when fallen.

This efficacious spirit chiefly lurks
Among those passages of life that give 220
Profoundest knowledge to what point, and
       how,
The mind is lord and master — outward
       sense
The obedient servant of her will. Such
       moments
Are scattered everywhere, taking their date
From our first childhood. I remember well,
That once, while yet my inexperienced
       hand
Could scarcely hold a bridle, with proud
       hopes
I mounted, and we journeyed towards the
       hills:
An ancient servant of my father's house
Was with me, my encourager and guide:
We had not travelled long, ere some mis-
       chance   231
Disjoined me from my comrade; and,
       through fear
Dismounting, down the rough and stony
       moor
I led my horse, and, stumbling on, at length
Came to a bottom, where in former times
A murderer had been hung in iron chains.
The gibbet-mast had mouldered down, the
       bones
And iron case were gone; but on the turf,
Hard by, soon after that fell deed was
       wrought,
Some unknown hand had carved the mur-
       derer's name.   240
The monumental letters were inscribed
In times long past; but still, from year to
       year
By superstition of the neighbourhood,
The grass is cleared away, and to this hour
The characters are fresh and visible:
A casual glance had shown them, and I fled,
Faltering and faint, and ignorant of the
       road:
Then, reascending the bare common, saw
A naked pool that lay beneath the hills,
The beacon on the summit, and, more near,
A girl, who bore a pitcher on her head, 251
And seemed with difficult steps to force
       her way
Against the blowing wind. It was, in truth,
An ordinary sight; but I should need
Colours and words that are unknown to man,
To paint the visionary dreariness
Which, while I looked all round for my
       lost guide,

Invested moorland waste and naked pool,
The beacon crowning the lone eminence,
The female and her garments vexed and
    tossed   260
By the strong wind.   When, in the blessèd
    hours
Of early love, the loved one at my side,
I roamed, in daily presence of this scene,
Upon the naked pool and dreary crags,
And on the melancholy beacon, fell
A spirit of pleasure and youth's golden
    gleam;
And think ye not with radiance more sub-
    lime
For these remembrances, and for the power
They had left behind ?   So feeling comes
    in aid
Of feeling, and diversity of strength   270
Attends us, if but once we have been
    strong.
Oh ! mystery of man, from what a depth
Proceed thy honours.   I am lost, but see
In simple childhood something of the base
On which thy greatness stands; but this I
    feel,
That from thyself it comes, that thou must
    give,
Else never canst receive.   The days gone by
Return upon me almost from the dawn
Of life: the hiding-places of man's power
Open; I would approach them, but they
    close.   280
I see by glimpses now; when age comes on,
May scarcely see at all; and I would give,
While yet we may, as far as words can
    give,
Substance and life to what I feel, enshrin-
    ing,
Such is my hope, the spirit of the Past
For future restoration. — Yet another
Of these memorials : —
                            One Christmas-time,
On the glad eve of its dear holidays,
Feverish, and tired, and restless, I went
    forth
Into the fields, impatient for the sight   290
Of those led palfreys that should bear us
    home;
My brothers and myself.   There rose a
    crag,
That, from the meeting-point of two high-
    ways
Ascending, overlooked them both, far
    stretched;
Thither, uncertain on which road to fix

My expectation, thither I repaired,
Scout-like, and gained the summit; 't was
    a day
Tempestuous, dark, and wild, and on the
    grass
I sate half-sheltered by a naked wall;
Upon my right hand couched a single
    sheep,   300
Upon my left a blasted hawthorn stood;
With those companions at my side, I
    watched,
Straining my eyes intensely, as the mist
Gave intermitting prospect of the copse
And plain beneath.   Ere we to school re-
    turned, —
That dreary time, — ere we had been ten
    days
Sojourners in my father's house, he died;
And I and my three brothers, orphans then,
Followed his body to the grave.   The
    event,
With all the sorrow that it brought, ap-
    peared   310
A chastisement; and when I called to mind
That day so lately past, when from the
    crag
I looked in such anxiety of hope;
With trite reflections of morality,
Yet in the deepest passion, I bowed low
To God, Who thus corrected my desires;
And, afterwards, the wind and sleety rain,
And all the business of the elements,
The single sheep, and the one blasted tree,
And the bleak music from that old stone
    wall,   320
The noise of wood and water, and the mist
That on the line of each of those two roads
Advanced in such indisputable shapes;
All these were kindred spectacles and
    sounds
To which I oft repaired, and thence would
    drink,
As at a fountain; and on winter nights,
Down to this very time, when storm and
    rain
Beat on my roof, or, haply, at noon-day,
While in a grove I walk, whose lofty trees,
Laden with summer's thickest foliage, rock
In a strong wind, some working of the
    spirit,   331
Some inward agitations thence are brought,
Whate'er their office, whether to beguile
Thoughts over busy in the course they
    took,
Or animate an hour of vacant ease.

BOOK THIRTEENTH

IMAGINATION AND TASTE, HOW IMPAIRED
AND RESTORED (*concluded*)

FROM Nature doth emotion come, and
    moods
Of calmness equally are Nature's gift:
This is her glory; these two attributes
Are sister horns that constitute her strength.
Hence Genius, born to thrive by inter-
    change
Of peace and excitation, finds in her
His best and purest friend; from her re-
    ceives
That energy by which he seeks the truth,
From her that happy stillness of the mind
Which fits him to receive it when unsought.

Such benefit the humblest intellects   11
Partake of, each in their degree; 't is mine
To speak, what I myself have known and
    felt;
Smooth task! for words find easy way, in-
    spired
By gratitude, and confidence in truth.
Long time in search of knowledge did I
    range
The field of human life, in heart and mind
Benighted; but, the dawn beginning now
To re-appear, 't was proved that not in vain
I had been taught to reverence a Power   20
That is the visible quality and shape
And image of right reason; that matures
Her processes by steadfast laws; gives birth
To no impatient or fallacious hopes,
No heat of passion or excessive zeal,
No vain conceits; provokes to no quick
    turns
Of self-applauding intellect; but trains
To meekness, and exalts by humble faith;
Holds up before the mind intoxicate
With present objects, and the busy dance   30
Of things that pass away, a temperate show
Of objects that endure; and by this course
Disposes her, when over-fondly set
On throwing off incumbrances, to seek
In man, and in the frame of social life,
Whate'er there is desirable and good
Of kindred permanence, unchanged in form
And function, or, through strict vicissitude
Of life and death, revolving. Above all
Were re-established now those watchful
    thoughts   40
Which, seeing little worthy or sublime
In what the Historian's pen so much delights

To blazon — power and energy detached
From moral purpose — early tutored me
To look with feelings of fraternal love
Upon the unassuming things that hold
A silent station in this beauteous world.

Thus moderated, thus composed, I found
Once more in Man an object of delight,
Of pure imagination, and of love;   50
And, as the horizon of my mind enlarged,
Again I took the intellectual eye
For my instructor, studious more to see
Great truths, than touch and handle little
    ones.
Knowledge was given accordingly; my trust
Became more firm in feelings that had stood
The test of such a trial; clearer far
My sense of excellence — of right and
    wrong:
The promise of the present time retired   59
Into its true proportion; sanguine schemes,
Ambitious projects, pleased me less; I sought
For present good in life's familiar face,
And built thereon my hopes of good to come.

With settling judgments now of what
    would last
And what would disappear; prepared to
    find
Presumption, folly, madness, in the men
Who thrust themselves upon the passive
    world
As Rulers of the world; to see in these,
Even when the public welfare is their aim,
Plans without thought, or built on theories
Vague and unsound; and having brought
    the books   71
Of modern statists to their proper test,
Life, human life, with all its sacred claims
Of sex and age, and heaven-descended
    rights,
Mortal, or those beyond the reach of death;
And having thus discerned how dire a thing
Is worshipped in that idol proudly named
"The Wealth of Nations," *where* alone that
    wealth
Is lodged, and how increased; and having
    gained
A more judicious knowledge of the worth
And dignity of individual man,   81
No composition of the brain, but man
Of whom we read, the man whom we be-
    hold
With our own eyes — I could not but en-
    quire —

Not with less interest than heretofore,
But greater, though in spirit more sub-
    dued —
Why is this glorious creature to be found
One only in ten thousand ? What one is,
Why may not millions be ? What bars are
    thrown
By Nature in the way of such a hope ?   90
Our animal appetites and daily wants,
Are these obstructions insurmountable ?
If not, then others vanish into air.
" Inspect the basis of the social pile:
Enquire," said I, " how much of mental
    power
And genuine virtue they possess who live
By bodily toil, labour exceeding far
Their due proportion, under all the weight
Of that injustice which upon ourselves   99
Ourselves entail." Such estimate to frame
I chiefly looked (what need to look beyond ?)
Among the natural abodes of men,
Fields with their rural works; recalled to
    mind
My earliest notices; with these compared
The observations made in later youth,
And to that day continued. — For, the time
Had never been when throes of mighty
    Nations
And the world's tumult unto me could yield,
How far soe'er transported and possessed,
Full measure of content; but still I craved
An intermingling of distinct regards   111
And truths of individual sympathy
Nearer ourselves. Such often might be
    gleaned
From the great City, else it must have
    proved
To me a heart-depressing wilderness;
But much was wanting: therefore did I turn
To you, ye pathways, and ye lonely roads;
Sought you enriched with everything I
    prized,
With human kindnesses and simple joys.

Oh ! next to one dear state of bliss,
    vouchsafed,   120
Alas ! to few in this untoward world,
The bliss of walking daily in life's prime
Through field or forest with the maid we
    love,
While yet our hearts are young, while yet
    we breathe
Nothing but happiness, in some lone nook,
Deep vale, or anywhere, the home of both,
From which it would be misery to stir:

Oh ! next to such enjoyment of our youth,
In my esteem, next to such dear delight,
Was that of wandering on from day to day
Where I could meditate in peace, and cull
Knowledge that step by step might lead
    me on   132
To wisdom; or, as lightsome as a bird
Wafted upon the wind from distant lands,
Sing notes of greeting to strange fields or
    groves,
Which lacked not voice to welcome me in
    turn;
And, when that pleasant toil had ceased to
    please,
Converse with men, where if we meet a face
We almost meet a friend, on naked heaths
With long long ways before, by cottage
    bench,   140
Or well-spring where the weary traveller
    rests.

Who doth not love to follow with his eye
The windings of a public way ? the sight,
Familiar object as it is, hath wrought
On my imagination since the morn
Of childhood, when a disappearing line,
One daily present to my eyes, that crossed
The naked summit of a far-off hill
Beyond the limits that my feet had trod,
Was like an invitation into space   150
Boundless, or guide into eternity.
Yes, something of the grandeur which in-
    vests
The mariner, who sails the roaring sea
Through storm and darkness, early in my
    mind
Surrounded, too, the wanderers of the earth;
Grandeur as much, and loveliness far more.
Awed have I been by strolling Bedlamites;
From many other uncouth vagrants (passed
In fear) have walked with quicker step; but
    why
Take note of this ? When I began to en-
    quire,   160
To watch and question those I met, and
    speak
Without reserve to them, the lonely roads
Were open schools in which I daily read
With most delight the passions of mankind,
Whether by words, looks, sighs, or tears,
    revealed;
There saw into the depth of human souls,
Souls that appear to have no depth at all
To careless eyes. And — now convinced at
    heart

How little those formalities, to which
With overweening trust alone we give 170
The name of Education, have to do
With real feeling and just sense; how vain
A correspondence with the talking world
Proves to the most; and called to make good
    search
If man's estate, by doom of Nature yoked
With toil, be therefore yoked with igno-
    rance;
If virtue be indeed so hard to rear,
And intellectual strength so rare a boon —
I prized such walks still more, for there I
    found
Hope to my hope, and to my pleasure peace
And steadiness, and healing and repose 181
To every angry passion. There I heard,
From mouths of men obscure and lowly,
    truths
Replete with honour; sounds in unison
With loftiest promises of good and fair.

There are who think that strong affection,
    love
Known by whatever name, is falsely deemed
A gift, to use a term which they would use,
Of vulgar nature; that its growth requires
Retirement, leisure, language purified 190
By manners studied and elaborate;
That whoso feels such passion in its strength
Must live within the very light and air
Of courteous usages refined by art.
True is it, where oppression worse than
    death
Salutes the being at his birth, where grace
Of culture hath been utterly unknown,
And poverty and labour in excess
From day to day pre-occupy the ground
Of the affections, and to Nature's self 200
Oppose a deeper nature; there, indeed,
Love cannot be; nor does it thrive with ease
Among the close and overcrowded haunts
Of cities, where the human heart is sick,
And the eye feeds it not, and cannot feed.
— Yes, in those wanderings deeply did I
    feel
How we mislead each other; above all,
How books mislead us, seeking their reward
From judgments of the wealthy Few, who
    see
By artificial lights; how they debase 210
The Many for the pleasure of those Few;
Effeminately level down the truth
To certain general notions, for the sake
Of being understood at once, or else

Through want of better knowledge in the
    heads
That framed them; flattering self-conceit
    with words,
That, while they most ambitiously set forth
Extrinsic differences, the outward marks
Whereby society has parted man
From man, neglect the universal heart. 220

Here, calling up to mind what then I
    saw,
A youthful traveller, and see daily now
In the familiar circuit of my home,
Here might I pause, and bend in reverence
To Nature, and the power of human minds,
To men as they are men within themselves.
How oft high service is performed within,
When all the external man is rude in
    show, —
Not like a temple rich with pomp and gold,
But a mere mountain chapel, that pro-
    tects 230
Its simple worshippers from sun and
    shower.
Of these, said I, shall be my song; of these,
If future years mature me for the task,
Will I record the praises, making verse
Deal boldly with substantial things; in
    truth
And sanctity of passion, speak of these,
That justice may be done, obeisance paid
Where it is due: thus haply shall I teach,
Inspire; through unadulterated ears
Pour rapture, tenderness, and hope, — my
    theme 240
No other than the very heart of man,
As found among the best of those who
    live —
Not unexalted by religious faith,
Nor uninformed by books, good books,
    though few —
In Nature's presence: thence may I select
Sorrow, that is not sorrow, but delight;
And miserable love, that is not pain
To hear of, for the glory that redounds
Therefrom to human kind, and what we
    are.
Be mine to follow with no timid step 250
Where knowledge leads me: it shall be my
    pride
That I have dared to tread this holy
    ground,
Speaking no dream, but things oracular;
Matter not lightly to be heard by those
Who to the letter of the outward promise

Do read the invisible soul; by men adroit
In speech, and for communion with the
world
Accomplished; minds whose faculties are
then
Most active when they are most eloquent,
And elevated most when most admired. 260
Men may be found of other mould than
these,
Who' are their own upholders, to them-
selves
Encouragement, and energy, and will,
Expressing liveliest thoughts in lively
words
As native passion dictates. Others, too,
There are among the walks of homely life
Still higher, men for contemplation framed,
Shy, and unpractised in the strife of
phrase;
Meek men, whose very souls perhaps would
sink
Beneath them, summoned to such inter-
course: 270
Theirs is the language of the heavens, the
power,
The thought, the image, and the silent
joy:
Words are but under-agents in their souls;
When they are grasping with their greatest
strength,
They do not breathe among them: this I
speak
In gratitude to God, Who feeds our hearts
For His own service; knoweth, loveth us,
When we are unregarded by the world.

Also, about this time did I receive
Convictions still more strong than hereto-
fore, 280
Not only that the inner frame is good,
And graciously composed, but that, no less,
Nature for all conditions wants not power
To consecrate, if we have eyes to see,
The outside of her creatures, and to breathe
Grandeur upon the very humblest face
Of human life. I felt that the array
Of act and circumstance, and visible form,
Is mainly to the pleasure of the mind
What passion makes them; that meanwhile
the forms 290
Of Nature have a passion in themselves,
That intermingles with those works of man
To which she summons him; although the
works
Be mean, have nothing lofty of their own;

And that the Genius of the Poet hence
May boldly take his way among mankind
Wherever Nature leads; that he hath
stood
By Nature's side among the men of old,
And so shall stand for ever. Dearest
Friend !
If thou partake the animating faith 300
That Poets, even as Prophets, each with
each
Connected in a mighty scheme of truth,
Have each his own peculiar faculty,
Heaven's gift, a sense that fits him to per-
ceive
Objects unseen before, thou wilt not blame
The humblest of this band who dares to
hope
That unto him hath also been vouchsafed
An insight that in some sort he possesses,
A privilege whereby a work of his,
Proceeding from a source of untaught
things, 310
Creative and enduring, may become
A power like one of Nature's. To a hope
Not less ambitious once among the wilds
Of Sarum's Plain, my youthful spirit was
raised;
There, as I ranged at will the pastoral
downs
Trackless and smooth, or paced the bare
white roads
Lengthening in solitude their dreary line,
Time with his retinue of ages fled
Backwards, nor checked his flight until I
saw
Our dim ancestral Past in vision clear; 320
Saw multitudes of men, and, here and
there,
A single Briton clothed in wolf-skin vest,
With shield and stone-axe, stride across the
wold;
The voice of spears was heard, the rattling
spear
Shaken by arms of mighty bone, in
strength,
Long mouldered, of barbaric majesty.
I called on Darkness — but before the word
Was uttered, midnight darkness seemed to
take
All objects from my sight; and lo ! again
The Desert visible by dismal flames; 330
It is the sacrificial altar, fed
With living men — how deep the groans ! the
voice
Of those that crowd the giant wicker thrills

The monumental hillocks, and the pomp
Is for both worlds, the living and the dead.
At other moments — (for through that
    wide waste
Three summer days I roamed) where'er
    the Plain
Was figured o'er with circles, lines, or
    mounds,
That yet survive, a work, as some divine,
Shaped by the Druids, so to represent   340
Their knowledge of the heavens, and image
    forth
The constellations — gently was I charmed
Into a waking dream, a reverie
That, with believing eyes, where'er I
    turned,
Beheld long-bearded teachers, with white
    wands
Uplifted, pointing to the starry sky,
Alternately, and plain below, while breath
Of music swayed their motions, and the
    waste
Rejoiced with them and me in those sweet
    sounds.

  This for the past, and things that may
    be viewed   350
Or fancied in the obscurity of years
From monumental hints: and thou, O
    Friend !
Pleased with some unpremeditated strains
That served those wanderings to beguile,
    hast said
That then and there my mind had exercised
Upon the vulgar forms of present things,
The actual world of our familiar days,
Yet higher power; had caught from them
    a tone,
An image, and a character, by books
Not hitherto reflected. Call we this   360
A partial judgment — and yet why ? for
    then
We were as strangers; and I may not
    speak
Thus wrongfully of verse, however rude,
Which on thy young imagination, trained
In the great City, broke like light from
    far.
Moreover, each man's Mind is to herself
Witness and judge; and I remember well
That in life's every-day appearances
I seemed about this time to gain clear sight
Of a new world — a world, too, that was fit
To be transmitted, and to other eyes   371
Made visible; as ruled by those fixed laws

Whence spiritual dignity originates,
Which do both give it being and maintain
A balance, an ennobling interchange
Of action from without and from within;
The excellence, pure function, and best
    power
Both of the object seen, and eye that sees.

BOOK FOURTEENTH

CONCLUSION

In one of those excursions (may they ne'er
Fade from remembrance !) through the
    Northern tracts
Of Cambria ranging with a youthful friend,
I left Bethgelert's huts at couching-time,
And westward took my way, to see the sun
Rise, from the top of Snowdon. To the
    door
Of a rude cottage at the mountain's base
We came, and roused the shepherd who
    attends
The adventurous stranger's steps, a trusty
    guide;
Then, cheered by short refreshment, sallied
    forth.   10

  It was a close, warm, breezeless summer
    night,
Wan, dull, and glaring, with a dripping fog
Low-hung and thick that covered all the
    sky;
But, undiscouraged, we began to climb
The mountain-side. The mist soon girt us
    round,
And, after ordinary travellers' talk
With our conductor, pensively we sank
Each into commerce with his private
    thoughts:
Thus did we breast the ascent, and by my-
    self
Was nothing either seen or heard that
    checked   20
Those musings or diverted, save that once
The shepherd's lurcher, who, among the
    crags,
Had to his joy unearthed a hedgehog, teased
His coiled-up prey with barkings turbulent.
This small adventure, for even such it
    seemed
In that wild place and at the dead of night,
Being over and forgotten, on we wound
In silence as before. With forehead bent
Earthward, as if in opposition set

Against an enemy, I panted up   30
With eager pace, and no less eager thoughts.
Thus might we wear a midnight hour away,
Ascending at loose distance each from each,
And I, as chanced, the foremost of the
    band;
When at my feet the ground appeared to
    brighten,
And with a step or two seemed brighter
    still;
Nor was time given to ask or learn the
    cause,
For instantly a light upon the turf
Fell like a flash, and lo ! as I looked up
The Moon hung naked in a firmament   40
Of azure without cloud, and at my feet
Rested a silent sea of hoary mist.
A hundred hills their dusky backs upheaved
All over this still ocean; and beyond,
Far, far beyond, the solid vapours stretched,
In headlands, tongues, and promontory
    shapes,
Into the main Atlantic, that appeared
To dwindle, and give up his majesty,
Usurped upon far as the sight could reach.
Not so the ethereal vault; encroachment
    none   50
Was there, nor loss; only the inferior stars
Had disappeared, or shed a fainter light
In the clear presence of the full-orbed Moon,
Who, from her sovereign elevation, gazed
Upon the billowy ocean, as it lay
All meek and silent, save that through a
    rift —
Not distant from the shore whereon we
    stood,
A fixed, abysmal, gloomy, breathing-
    place —
Mounted the roar of waters, torrents,
    streams
Innumerable, roaring with one voice !   60
Heard over earth and sea, and, in that hour,
For so it seemed, felt by the starry heavens.

When into air had partially dissolved
That vision, given to spirits of the night
And three chance human wanderers, in calm
    thought
Reflected, it appeared to me the type
Of a majestic intellect, its acts
And its possessions, what it has and craves,
What in itself it is, and would become.
There I beheld the emblem of a mind   70
That feeds upon infinity, that broods
Over the dark abyss, intent to hear

Its voices issuing forth to silent light
In one continuous stream; a mind sustained
By recognitions of transcendent power,
In sense conducting to ideal form,
In soul of more than mortal privilege.
One function, above all, of such a mind
Had Nature shadowed there, by putting
    forth,
'Mid circumstances awful and sublime,   80
That mutual domination which she loves
To exert upon the face of outward things,
So moulded, joined, abstracted, so endowed
With interchangeable supremacy,
That men, least sensitive, see, hear, per-
    ceive,
And cannot choose but feel. The power,
    which all
Acknowledge when thus moved, which Na-
    ture thus
To bodily sense exhibits, is the express
Resemblance of that glorious faculty
That higher minds bear with them as their
    own.   90
This is the very spirit in which they deal
With the whole compass of the universe:
They from their native selves can send
    abroad
Kindred mutations; for themselves create
A like existence; and, whene'er it dawns
Created for them, catch it, or are caught
By its inevitable mastery,
Like angels stopped upon the wing by sound
Of harmony from Heaven's remotest
    spheres.
Them the enduring and the transient both
Serve to exalt; they build up greatest
    things   101
From least suggestions; ever on the watch,
Willing to work and to be wrought upon,
They need not extraordinary calls
To rouse them; in a world of life they
    live,
By sensible impressions not enthralled,
But by their quickening impulse made more
    prompt
To hold fit converse with the spiritual world,
And with the generations of mankind
Spread over time, past, present, and to
    come,   110
Age after age, till Time shall be no more.
Such minds are truly from the Deity,
For they are Powers; and hence the high-
    est bliss
That flesh can know is theirs — the con-
    sciousness

Of Whom they are, habitually infused
Through every image and through every
  thought,
And all affections by communion raised
From earth to heaven, from human to di-
  vine;
Hence endless occupation for the Soul,
Whether discursive or intuitive;   120
Hence cheerfulness for acts of daily life,
Emotions which best foresight need not fear,
Most worthy then of trust when most in-
  tense.
Hence, amid ills that vex and wrongs that
  crush
Our hearts — if here the words of Holy Writ
May with fit reverence be applied — that
  peace
Which passeth understanding, that repose
In moral judgments which from this pure
  source
Must come, or will by man be sought in vain.

  Oh ! who is he that hath his whole life
  long   130
Preserved, enlarged, this freedom in him-
  self ?
For this alone is genuine liberty:
Where is the favoured being who hath held
That course unchecked, unerring, and un-
  tired,
In one perpetual progress smooth and
  bright ? —
A humbler destiny have we retraced,
And told of lapse and hesitating choice,
And backward wanderings along thorny
  ways:
Yet — compassed round by mountain soli-
  tudes,
Within whose solemn temple I received 140
My earliest visitations, careless then
Of what was given me; and which now I
  range,
A meditative, oft a suffering, man —
Do I declare — in accents which, from
  truth
Deriving cheerful confidence, shall blend
Their modulation with these vocal streams—
That, whatsoever falls my better mind,
Revolving with the accidents of life,
May have sustained, that, howsoe'er mis-
  led,
Never did I, in quest of right and wrong, 150
Tamper with conscience from a private
  aim;
Nor was in any public hope the dupe

Of selfish passions; nor did ever yield
Wilfully to mean cares or low pursuits,
But shrunk with apprehensive jealousy
From every combination which might aid
The tendency, too potent in itself,
Of use and custom to bow down the soul
Under a growing weight of vulgar sense,
And substitute a universe of death   160
For that which moves with light and life
  informed,
Actual, divine, and true. To fear and love,
To love as prime and chief, for there fear
  ends,
Be this ascribed; to early intercourse,
In presence of sublime or beautiful forms,
With the adverse principles of pain and
  joy —
Evil as one is rashly named by men
Who know not what they speak. By love
  subsists
All lasting grandeur, by pervading love;
That gone, we are as dust. — Behold the
  fields   170
In balmy spring-time full of rising flowers
And joyous creatures; see that pair, the
  lamb
And the lamb's mother, and their tender
  ways
Shall touch thee to the heart; thou callest
  this love,
And not inaptly so, for love it is,
Far as it carries thee. In some green
  bower
Rest, and be not alone, but have thou there
The One who is thy choice of all the world:
There linger, listening, gazing, with delight
Impassioned, but delight how pitiable !   180
Unless this love by a still higher love
Be hallowed, love that breathes not without
  awe;
Love that adores, but on the knees of
  prayer,
By heaven inspired; that frees from chains
  the soul,
Lifted, in union with the purest, best,
Of earth-born passions, on the wings of
  praise
Bearing a tribute to the Almighty's Throne.

  This spiritual Love acts not nor can exist
Without Imagination, which, in truth,
Is but another name for absolute power   190
And clearest insight, amplitude of mind,
And Reason in her most exalted mood.
This faculty hath been the feeding source

Of our long labour: we have traced the
    stream
From the blind cavern whence is faintly
    heard
Its natal murmur; followed it to light
And open day; accompanied its course
Among the ways of Nature, for a time
Lost sight of it bewildered and engulphed;
Then given it greeting as it rose once
    more   200
In strength, reflecting from its placid breast
The works of man and face of human life;
And lastly, from its progress have we
    drawn
Faith in life endless, the sustaining thought
Of human Being, Eternity, and God.

    Imagination having been our theme,
So also hath that intellectual Love,
For they are each in each, and cannot stand
Dividually. — Here must thou be, O Man!
Power to thyself; no Helper hast thou
    here;   210
Here keepest thou in singleness thy state:
No other can divide with thee this work:
No secondary hand can intervene
To fashion this ability; 't is thine,
The prime and vital principle is thine
In the recesses of thy nature, far
From any reach of outward fellowship,
Else is not thine at all.   But joy to him,
Oh, joy to him who here hath sown, hath
    laid
Here, the foundation of his future years! 220
For all that friendship, all that love can do,
All that a darling countenance can look
Or dear voice utter, to complete the man,
Perfect him, made imperfect in himself,
All shall be his: and he whose soul hath
    risen
Up to the height of feeling intellect
Shall want no humbler tenderness; his
    heart
Be tender as a nursing mother's heart;
Of female softness shall his life be full,
Of humble cares and delicate desires,   230
Mild interests and gentlest sympathies.

    Child of my parents! Sister of my soul!
Thanks in sincerest verse have been else-
    where
Poured out for all the early tenderness
Which I from thee imbibed: and 't is most
    true
That later seasons owed to thee no less;

For, spite of thy sweet influence and the
    touch
Of kindred hands that opened out the
    springs
Of genial thought in childhood, and in spite
Of all that unassisted I had marked   240
In life or nature of those charms minute
That win their way into the heart by
    stealth
(Still to the very going-out of youth)
I too exclusively esteemed *that* love,
And sought *that* beauty, which, as Milton
    sings,
Hath terror in it.   Thou didst soften down
This over-sternness; but for thee, dear
    Friend!
My soul, too reckless of mild grace, had
    stood
In her original self too confident,
Retained too long a countenance severe; 250
A rock with torrents roaring, with the
    clouds
Familiar, and a favourite of the stars:
But thou didst plant its crevices with flowers,
Hang it with shrubs that twinkle in the
    breeze,
And teach the little birds to build their
    nests
And warble in its chambers.   At a time
When Nature, destined to remain so long
Foremost in my affections, had fallen back
Into a second place, pleased to become
A handmaid to a nobler than herself,   260
When every day brought with it some new
    sense
Of exquisite regard for common things,
And all the earth was budding with these
    gifts
Of more refined humanity, thy breath,
Dear Sister! was a kind of gentler spring
That went before my steps.   Thereafter
    came
One whom with thee friendship had early
    paired;
She came, no more a phantom to adorn
A moment, but an inmate of the heart,
And yet a spirit, there for me enshrined 270
To penetrate the lofty and the low;
Even as one essence of pervading light
Shines, in the brightest of ten thousand stars
And the meek worm that feeds her lonely
    lamp
Couched in the dewy grass.
                    With such a theme,
Coleridge! with this my argument, of thee

Shall I be silent ? O capacious Soul !
Placed on this earth to love and understand,
And from thy presence shed the light of love,
Shall I be mute, ere thou be spoken of ? 280
Thy kindred influence to my heart of hearts
Did also find its way. Thus fear relaxed
Her overweening grasp; thus thoughts and things
In the self-haunting spirit learned to take
More rational proportions; mystery,
The incumbent mystery of sense and soul,
Of life and death, time and eternity,
Admitted more habitually a mild
Interposition — a serene delight
In closelier gathering cares, such as become
A human creature, howsoe'er endowed, 291
Poet, or destined for a humbler name;
And so the deep enthusiastic joy,
The rapture of the hallelujah sent
From all that breathes and is, was chastened, stemmed
And balanced by pathetic truth, by trust
In hopeful reason, leaning on the stay
Of Providence; and in reverence for duty,
Here, if need be, struggling with storms, and there
Strewing in peace life's humblest ground with herbs, 300
At every season green, sweet at all hours.

And now, O Friend ! this history is brought
To its appointed close: the discipline
And consummation of a Poet's mind,
In everything that stood most prominent,
Have faithfully been pictured; we have reached
The time (our guiding object from the first)
When we may, not presumptuously, I hope,
Suppose my powers so far confirmed, and such
My knowledge, as to make me capable 310
Of building up a Work that shall endure.
Yet much hath been omitted, as need was;
Of books how much ! and even of the other wealth
That is collected among woods and fields,
Far more: for Nature's secondary grace
Hath hitherto been barely touched upon,
The charm more superficial that attends
Her works, as they present to Fancy's choice
Apt illustrations of the moral world,
Caught at a glance, or traced with curious pains. 320

Finally, and above all, O Friend ! (I speak
With due regret) how much is overlooked
In human nature and her subtle ways,
As studied first in our own hearts, and then
In life among the passions of mankind,
Varying their composition and their hue,
Where'er we move, under the diverse shapes
That individual character presents
To an attentive eye. For progress meet,
Along this intricate and difficult path, 330
Whate'er was wanting, something had I gained,
As one of many schoolfellows compelled,
In hardy independence, to stand up
Amid conflicting interests, and the shock
Of various tempers; to endure and note
What was not understood, though known to be;
Among the mysteries of love and hate,
Honour and shame, looking to right and left,
Unchecked by innocence too delicate,
And moral notions too intolerant, 340
Sympathies too contracted. Hence, when called
To take a station among men, the step
Was easier, the transition more secure,
More profitable also; for, the mind
Learns from such timely exercise to keep
In wholesome separation the two natures,
The one that feels, the other that observes.

Yet one word more of personal concern; —
Since I withdrew unwillingly from France,
I led an undomestic wanderer's life 350
In London chiefly harboured, whence I roamed,
Tarrying at will in many a pleasant spot
Of rural England's cultivated vales
Or Cambrian solitudes. A youth — (he bore
The name of Calvert — it shall live, if words
Of mine can give it life,) in firm belief
That by endowments not from me withheld
Good might be furthered — in his last decay
By a bequest sufficient for my needs
Enabled me to pause for choice, and walk
At large and unrestrained; nor damped too soon 361
By mortal cares. Himself no Poet, yet
Far less a common follower of the world,
He deemed that my pursuits and labours lay

Apart from all that leads to wealth, or
    even
A necessary maintenance insures,
Without some hazard to the finer sense;
He cleared a passage for me, and the stream
Flowed in the bent of Nature.
                    Having now
Told what best merits mention, further
    pains   370
Our present purpose seems not to require,
And I have other tasks.   Recall to mind
The mood in which this labour was begun,
O Friend ! The termination of my course
Is nearer now, much nearer; yet even then,
In that distraction and intense desire,
I said unto the life which I had lived,
Where art thou ?   Hear I not a voice from
    thee
Which 't is reproach to hear ?   Anon I rose
As if on wings, and saw beneath me
    stretched   380
Vast prospect of the world which I had
    been
And was; and hence this Song, which, like
    a lark,
I have protracted, in the unwearied heavens
Singing, and often with more plaintive
    voice
To earth attempered and her deep-drawn
    sighs,
Yet centring all in love, and in the end
All gratulant, if rightly understood.

Whether to me shall be allotted life,
And, with life, power to accomplish aught
    of worth,
That will be deemed no insufficient plea 390
For having given the story of myself,
Is all uncertain: but, beloved Friend !
When, looking back, thou seest, in clearer
    view
Than any liveliest sight of yesterday,
That summer, under whose indulgent skies,
Upon smooth Quantock's airy ridge we
    roved
Unchecked, or loitered 'mid her sylvan
    combs,
Thou in bewitching words, with happy
    heart,
Didst chaunt the vision of that Ancient
    Man,
The bright-eyed Mariner, and rueful woes
Didst utter of the Lady Christabel;   401
And I, associate with such labour, steeped
In soft forgetfulness the livelong hours,

Murmuring of him who, joyous hap, was
    found,
After the perils of his moonlight ride,
Near the loud waterfall; or her who sate
In misery near the miserable Thorn —
When thou dost to that summer turn thy
    thoughts,
And hast before thee all which then we
    were,
To thee, in memory of that happiness,   410
It will be known, by thee at least, my
    Friend !
Felt, that the history of a Poet's mind
Is labour not unworthy of regard;
To thee the work shall justify itself.

The last and later portions of this gift
Have been prepared, not with the buoyant
    spirits
That were our daily portion when we first
Together wantoned in wild Poesy,
But, under pressure of a private grief,
Keen and enduring, which the mind and
    heart,   420
That in this meditative history
Have been laid open, needs must make me
    feel
More deeply, yet enable me to bear
More firmly; and a comfort now hath risen
From hope that thou art near, and wilt be
    soon
Restored to us in renovated health;
When, after the first mingling of our tears,
'Mong other consolations, we may draw
Some pleasure from this offering of my love.

Oh ! yet a few short years of useful life,
And all will be complete, thy race be run,
Thy monument of glory will be raised;   430
Then, though (too weak to tread the ways
    of truth)
This age fall back to old idolatry,
Though men return to servitude as fast
As the tide ebbs, to ignominy and shame,
By nations, sink together, we shall still
Find solace — knowing what we have learnt
    to know,
Rich in true happiness if allowed to be
Faithful alike in forwarding a day   440
Of firmer trust, joint labourers in the work
(Should Providence such grace to us vouch-
    safe)
Of their deliverance, surely yet to come.
Prophets of Nature, we to them will speak
A lasting inspiration, sanctified

By reason, blest by faith: what we have
    loved,
Others will love, and we will teach them
    how;
Instruct them how the mind of man becomes
A thousand times more beautiful than the
    earth

On which he dwells, above this frame of
    things   450
(Which, 'mid all revolution in the hopes
And fears of men, doth still remain un-
    changed)
In beauty exalted, as it is itself
Of quality and fabric more divine.

THE RECLUSE

1800–1806(?). 1888

PART FIRST

BOOK FIRST — HOME AT GRASMERE

ONCE to the verge of yon steep barrier
    came
A roving school-boy; what the adventurer's
    age
Hath now escaped his memory — but the
    hour,
One of a golden summer holiday,
He well remembers, though the year be
    gone.
Alone and devious from afar he came;
And, with a sudden influx overpowered
At sight of this seclusion, he forgot
His haste, for hasty had his footsteps been
As boyish his pursuits; and sighing said, 10
" What happy fortune were it here to live !
And, if a thought of dying, if a thought
Of mortal separation, could intrude
With paradise before him, here to die ! "
No Prophet was he, had not even a hope,
Scarcely a wish, but one bright pleasing
    thought,
A fancy in the heart of what might be
The lot of others, never could be his.
    The station whence he looked was soft
    and green,
Not giddy yet aerial, with a depth   20
Of vale below, a height of hills above.
For rest of body perfect was the spot,
All that luxurious nature could desire;
But stirring to the spirit; who could gaze
And not feel motions there ?   He thought
    of clouds
That sail on winds: of breezes that delight
To play on water, or in endless chase
Pursue each other through the yielding
    plain
Of grass or corn, over and through and
    through,

In billow after billow, evermore   30
Disporting — nor unmindful was the boy
Of sunbeams, shadows, butterflies and birds;
Of fluttering sylphs and softly-gliding Fays,
Genii, and winged angels that are Lords
Without restraint of all which they behold.
The illusion strengthening as he gazed, he
    felt
That such unfettered liberty was his,
Such power and joy; but only for this end,
To flit from field to rock, from rock to field,
From shore to island, and from isle to
    shore,   40
From open ground to covert, from a bed
Of meadow-flowers into a tuft of wood;
From high to low, from low to high, yet
    still
Within the bound of this huge concave;
    here
Must be his home, this valley be his world.
    Since that day forth the Place to him —
      to me
(For I who live to register the truth
Was that same young and happy Being)
    became
As beautiful to thought, as it had been
When present, to the bodily sense; a haunt
Of pure affections, shedding upon joy   51
A brighter joy; and through such damp
    and gloom
Of the gay mind, as ofttimes splenetic youth
Mistakes for sorrow, darting beams of light
That no self-cherished sadness could with-
    stand;
And now 't is mine, perchance for life, dear
    Vale,
Beloved Grasmere (let the wandering
    streams
Take up, the cloud-capt hills repeat, the
    Name)
One of thy lowly Dwellings is my Home.

And was the cost so great ? and could it
   seem   60
An act of courage, and the thing itself
A conquest ? who must bear the blame ?
   Sage man
Thy prudence, thy experience, thy desires,
Thy apprehensions — blush thou for them
   all.
Yes the realities of life so cold,
So cowardly, so ready to betray,
So stinted in the measure of their grace
As we pronounce them, doing them much
   wrong,
Have been to me more bountiful than hope,
Less timid than desire — but that is past. 70
On Nature's invitation do I come,
By Reason sanctioned.   Can the choice mis-
   lead,
That made the calmest, fairest spot of earth
With all its unappropriated good
My own; and not mine only, for with me
Entrenched, say rather peacefully embow-
   ered,
Under yon orchard, in yon humble cot,
A younger Orphan of a home extinct,
The only Daughter of my Parents dwells.
   Ay, think on that, my heart, and cease to
      stir,   80
Pause upon that and let the breathing frame
No longer breathe, but all be satisfied.
— Oh, if such silence be not thanks to God
For what hath been bestowed, then where,
   where then
Shall gratitude find rest ?   Mine eyes did
   ne'er
Fix on a lovely object, nor my mind
Take pleasure in the midst of happy
   thoughts,
But either She whom now I have, who now
Divides with me this loved abode, was
   there
Or not far off.   Where'er my footsteps
   turned,   90
Her voice was like a hidden Bird that sang.
The thought of her was like a flash of light,
Or an *unseen* companionship, a breath
Of fragrance independent of the Wind.
In all my goings, in the new and old
Of all my meditations, and in this
Favourite of all, in this the most of all.
— What being, therefore, since the birth of
   Man
Had ever more abundant cause to speak
Thanks, and if favours of the Heavenly
   Muse   100

Make him more thankful, then to call on
   Verse
To aid him and in song resound his joy ?
The boon is absolute; surpassing grace
To me hath been vouchsafed; among the
   bowers
Of blissful Eden this was neither given
Nor could be given, possession of the good
Which had been sighed for, ancient thought
   fulfilled,
And dear Imaginations realised,
Up to their highest measure, yea and more.
   Embrace me then, ye Hills, and close me
   in;   110
Now in the clear and open day I feel
Your guardianship; I take it to my heart;
'T is like the solemn shelter of the night.
But I would call thee beautiful, for mild,
And soft, and gay, and beautiful thou art,
Dear Valley, having in thy face a smile,
Though peaceful, full of gladness.   Thou
   art pleased,
Pleased with thy crags and woody steeps,
   thy Lake,
Its one green island and its winding shores;
The multitude of little rocky hills,   120
Thy Church and cottages of mountain stone
Clustered like stars some few, but single
   most,
And lurking dimly in their shy retreats,
Or glancing at each other cheerful looks
Like separated stars with clouds between.
What want we ? have we not perpetual
   streams,
Warm woods, and sunny hills, and fresh
   green fields,
And mountains not less green, and flocks
   and herds,
And thickets full of songsters, and the voice
Of lordly birds, an unexpected sound   130
Heard now and then from morn to latest eve,
Admonishing the man who walks below
Of solitude and silence in the sky ?
These have we, and a thousand nooks of
   earth
Have also these, but nowhere else is found,
Nowhere (or is it fancy ?) can be found
The one sensation that is here; 't is here,
Here as it found its way into my heart
In childhood, here as it abides by day,
By night, here only; or in chosen minds 140
That take it with them hence, where'er they
   go.
— 'T is, but I cannot name it, 't is the sense
Of majesty, and beauty, and repose,

A blended holiness of earth and sky,
Something that makes this individual spot,
This small abiding-place of many men,
A termination, and a last retreat,
A centre, come from wheresoe'er you will,
A whole without dependence or defect,
Made for itself, and happy in itself,   150
Perfect contentment, Unity entire.
　　Bleak season was it, turbulent and bleak,
When hitherward we journeyed side by side
Through burst of sunshine and through fly-
　　ing showers;
Paced the long vales — how long they were
　　— and yet
How fast that length of way was left be-
　　hind,
Wensley's rich Vale, and Sedbergh's naked
　　heights.
The frosty wind, as if to make amends
For its keen breath, was aiding to our steps,
And drove us onward like two ships at sea,
Or like two birds, companions in mid-air,
Parted and reunited by the blast.   162
　　Stern was the face of nature; we rejoiced
In that stern countenance, for our souls
　　thence drew
A feeling of their strength. The naked
　　trees,
The icy brooks, as on we passed, appeared
To question us. "Whence come ye, to
　　what end?"
They seemed to say. "What would ye,"
　　said the shower,
"Wild Wanderers, whither through my
　　dark domain?"
The sunbeam said, "Be happy." When
　　this vale   170
We entered, bright and solemn was the sky
That faced us with a passionate welcoming,
And led us to our threshold. Daylight
　　failed
Insensibly, and round us gently fell
Composing darkness, with a quiet load
Of full contentment, in a little shed
Disturbed, uneasy in itself as seemed,
And wondering at its new inhabitants.
It loves us now, this Vale so beautiful
Begins to love us! by a sullen storm,   180
Two months unwearied of severest storm,
It put the temper of our minds to proof,
And found us faithful through the gloom,
　　and heard
The poet mutter his prelusive songs
With cheerful heart, an unknown voice of
　　joy

Among the silence of the woods and hills;
Silent to any gladsomeness of sound
With all their shepherds.
　　　　　　　But the gates of Spring
Are opened; churlish winter hath given
　　leave
That she should entertain for this one day,
Perhaps for many genial days to come,   191
His guests, and make them jocund. — They
　　are pleased,
But most of all the birds that haunt the
　　flood,
With the mild summons; inmates though
　　they be
Of Winter's household, they keep festival
This day, who drooped, or seemed to droop,
　　so long;
They show their pleasure, and shall I do
　　less?
Happier of happy though I be, like them
I cannot take possession of the sky,
Mount with a thoughtless impulse, and
　　wheel there   200
One of a mighty multitude, whose way
Is a perpetual harmony and dance
Magnificent. Behold how with a grace
Of ceaseless motion, that might scarcely
　　seem
Inferior to angelical, they prolong
Their curious pastime, shaping in mid-air,
And sometimes with ambitious wing that
　　soars
High as the level of the mountain tops,
A circuit ampler than the lake beneath,   209
Their own domain; — but ever, while intent
On tracing and retracing that large round,
Their jubilant activity evolves
Hundreds of curves and circlets, to and fro,
Upwards and downwards; progress intricate
Yet unperplexed, as if one spirit swayed
Their indefatigable flight. 'T is done,
Ten times and more I fancied it had ceased,
But lo! the vanished company again
Ascending, they approach. I hear their
　　wings   219
Faint, faint at first; and then an eager sound
Passed in a moment — and as faint again!
They tempt the sun to sport among their
　　plumes;
Tempt the smooth water, or the gleaming
　　ice,
To show them a fair image, — 't is them-
　　selves,
Their own fair forms upon the glimmering
　　plain

Painted more soft and fair as they descend,
Almost to touch, — then up again aloft,
Up with a sally and a flash of speed,
As if they scorned both resting-place and
    rest !
— This day is a thanksgiving, 't is a day   230
Of glad emotion and deep quietness;
Not upon me alone hath been bestowed,
Me rich in many onward-looking thoughts,
The penetrating bliss; oh surely these
Have felt it, not the happy choirs of spring,
Her own peculiar family of love
That sport among green leaves, a blither
    train !
But two are missing, two, a lonely pair
Of milk-white Swans; wherefore are they
    not seen
Partaking this day's pleasure ? From afar
They came, to sojourn here in solitude,   241
Choosing this Valley, they who had the
    choice
Of the whole world. We saw them day by
    day,
Through those two months of unrelenting
    storm,
Conspicuous at the centre of the Lake
Their safe retreat, we knew them well, I
    guess
That the whole valley knew them; but to us
They were more dear than may be well be-
    lieved,
Not only for their beauty, and their still
And placid way of life, and constant love
Inseparable, not for these alone,   251
But that *their* state so much resembled ours,
They having also chosen this abode;
They strangers, and we strangers, they a
    pair,
And we a solitary pair like them.
They should not have departed; many days
Did I look forth in vain, nor on the wing
Could see them, nor in that small open
    space
Of blue unfrozen water, where they lodged
And lived so long in quiet, side by side.   260
Shall we behold them consecrated friends,
Faithful companions, yet another year
Surviving, they for us, and we for them,
And neither pair be broken ? nay perchance
It is too late already for such hope;
The Dalesmen may have aimed the deadly
    tube,
And parted them; or haply both are gone
One death, and that were mercy given to
    both.

Recall, my song, the ungenerous thought;
    forgive,
Thrice favoured Region, the conjecture harsh
Of such inhospitable penalty   271
Inflicted upon confidence so pure.
Ah ! if I wished to follow where the sight
Of all that is before my eyes, the voice
Which speaks from a presiding spirit here,
Would lead me, I should whisper to myself:
They who are dwellers in this holy place
Must needs themselves be hallowed, they
    require
No benediction from the stranger's lips,
For they are blessed already; none would
    give   280
The greeting " peace be with you " unto
    them,
For peace they have; it cannot but be theirs,
And mercy, and forbearance — nay — not
    these —
Their healing offices a pure good-will
Precludes, and charity beyond the bounds
Of charity — an overflowing love;
Not for the creature only, but for all
That is around them; love for everything
Which in this happy Region they behold!
    Thus do we soothe ourselves, and when
        the thought   290
Is passed, we blame it not for having come.
— What if I floated down a pleasant stream,
And now am landed, and the motion gone,
Shall I reprove myself ? Ah no, the stream
Is flowing, and will never cease to flow,
And I shall float upon that stream again.
By such forgetfulness the soul becomes,
Words cannot say how beautiful: then hail,
Hail to the visible Presence, hail to thee,
Delightful Valley, habitation fair !   300
And to whatever else of outward form
Can give us inward help, can purify,
And elevate, and harmonise, and soothe,
And steal away, and for a while deceive
And lap in pleasing rest, and bear us on
Without desire in full complacency,
Contemplating perfection absolute,
And entertained as in a placid sleep.
    But not betrayed by tenderness of mind
That feared, or wholly overlooked the truth,
Did we come hither, with romantic hope   311
To find in midst of so much loveliness
Love, perfect love: of so much majesty
A like majestic frame of mind in those
Who here abide, the persons like the place.
Not from such hope, or aught of such be-
    lief,

Hath issued any portion of the joy
Which I have felt this day. An awful voice
'T is true hath in my walks been often heard,
Sent from the mountains or the sheltered
    fields,   320
Shout after shout — reiterated whoop,
In manner of a bird that takes delight
In answering to itself: or like a hound
Single at chase among the lonely woods,
His yell repeating; yet it was in truth
A human voice — a spirit of coming night;
How solemn when the sky is dark, and earth
Not dark, nor yet enlightened, but by snow
Made visible, amid a noise of winds
And bleatings manifold of mountain sheep,
Which in that iteration recognise   331
Their summons, and are gathering round
    for food,
Devoured with keenness, ere to grove or
    bank
Or rocky bield with patience they retire.
    That very voice, which, in some timid
        mood
Of superstitious fancy, might have seemed
Awful as ever stray demoniac uttered,
His steps to govern in the wilderness;
Or as the Norman Curfew's regular beat
To hearths when first they darkened at the
    knell: 340
That shepherd's voice, it may have reached
    mine ear
Debased and under profanation, made
The ready organ of articulate sounds
From ribaldry, impiety, or wrath,
Issuing when shame hath ceased to check
    the brawls
Of some abused Festivity — so be it.
I came not dreaming of unruffled life,
Untainted manners; born among the hills,
Bred also there, I wanted not a scale
To regulate my hopes; pleased with the
    good   350
I shrink not from the evil with disgust,
Or with immoderate pain. I look for Man,
The common creature of the brotherhood,
Differing but little from the Man elsewhere,
For selfishness and envy and revenge,
Ill neighbourhood — pity that this should
    be —
Flattery and double-dealing, strife and
    wrong.
    Yet is it something gained, it is in truth
A mighty gain, that Labour here preserves
His rosy face, a servant only here   360
Of the fireside or of the open field,

A Freeman therefore sound and unimpaired:
That extreme penury is here unknown,
And cold and hunger's abject wretchedness
Mortal to body and the heaven-born mind:
That they who want are not too great a
    weight
For those who can relieve; here may the
    heart
Breathe in the air of fellow-suffering
Dreadless, as in a kind of fresher breeze
Of her own native element, the hand   370
Be ready and unwearied without plea,
From tasks too frequent or beyond its
    power,
For languor or indifference or despair.
And as these lofty barriers break the force
Of winds, — this deep Vale, as it doth in
    part
Conceal us from the storm, so here abides
A power and a protection for the mind,
Dispensed indeed to other solitudes
Favoured by noble privilege like this,
Where kindred independence of estate   380
Is prevalent, where he who tills the field,
He, happy man ! is master of the field,
And treads the mountains which his Fathers
    trod.
    Not less than halfway up yon mountain's
        side,
Behold a dusky spot, a grove of Firs
That seems still smaller than it is; this
    grove
Is haunted — by what ghost ? a gentle spirit
Of memory faithful to the call of love;
For, as reports the Dame, whose fire sends
    up
Yon curling smoke from the grey cot below,
The trees (her first-born child being then a
    babe)   391
Were planted by her husband and herself,
That ranging o'er the high and houseless
    ground
Their sheep might neither want, from per-
    ilous storm
Of winter nor from summer's sultry heat,
A friendly covert; " and they knew it well,"
Said she, " for thither as the trees grew up
We to the patient creatures carried food
In times of heavy snow." She then began
In fond obedience to her private thoughts
To speak of her dead husband; is there not
An art, a music, and a strain of words   402
That shall be life, the acknowledged voice
    of life,
Shall speak of what is done among the fields,

Done truly there, or felt, of solid good
And real evil, yet be sweet withal,
More grateful, more harmonious than the breath,
The idle breath of softest pipe attuned
To pastoral fancies ? Is there such a stream
Pure and unsullied flowing from the heart
With motions of true dignity and grace ?
Or must we seek that stream where Man is not ?   412
Methinks I could repeat in tuneful verse,
Delicious as the gentlest breeze that sounds
Through that aerial fir-grove — could preserve
Some portion of its human history
As gathered from the Matron's lips, and tell
Of tears that have been shed at sight of it,
And moving dialogues between this Pair
Who in their prime of wedlock, with joint hands   420
Did plant the grove, now flourishing, while they
No longer flourish, he entirely gone,
She withering in her loneliness. Be this
A task above my skill — the silent mind
Has her own treasures, and I think of these,
Love what I see, and honour humankind.
  No, we are not alone, we do not stand,
My sister here misplaced and desolate,
Loving what no one cares for but ourselves.
We shall not scatter through the plains and rocks   430
Of this fair Vale, and o'er its spacious heights,
Unprofitable kindliness, bestowed
On objects unaccustomed to the gifts
Of feeling, which were cheerless and forlorn
But few weeks past, and would be so again
Were we not here; we do not tend a lamp
Whose lustre we alone participate,
Which shines dependent upon us alone,
Mortal though bright, a dying, dying flame.
Look where we will, some human hand has been   440
Before us with its offering; not a tree
Sprinkles these little pastures, but the same
Hath furnished matter for a thought; perchance
For some one serves as a familiar friend.
Joy spreads, and sorrow spreads; and this whole Vale,
Home of untutored shepherds as it is,
Swarms with sensation, as with gleams of sunshine,

Shadows or breezes, scents or sounds. Nor deem
These feelings, though subservient more than ours
To every day's demand for daily bread,   450
And borrowing more their spirit and their shape
From self-respecting interests; deem them not
Unworthy therefore, and unhallowed — no,
They lift the animal being, do themselves
By nature's kind and ever-present aid
Refine the selfishness from which they spring,
Redeem by love the individual sense
Of anxiousness, with which they are combined.
And thus it is that fitly they become
Associates in the joy of purest minds: 460
They blend therewith congenially: meanwhile
Calmly they breathe their own undying life
Through this their mountain sanctuary; long
Oh long may it remain inviolate,
Diffusing health and sober cheerfulness,
And giving to the moments as they pass
Their little boons of animating thought
That sweeten labour, make it seen and felt
To be no arbitrary weight imposed,
But a glad function natural to man.   470
  Fair proof of this, newcomer though I be,
Already have I gained; the inward frame,
Though slowly opening, opens every day
With process not unlike to that which cheers
A pensive stranger journeying at his leisure
Through some Helvetian Dell; when low-hung mists
Break up and are beginning to recede;
How pleased he is where thin and thinner grows
The veil, or where it parts at once, to spy
The dark pines thrusting forth their spiky heads;   480
To watch the spreading lawns with cattle grazed;
Then to be greeted by the scattered huts
As they shine out; and *see* the streams whose murmur
Had soothed his ear while *they* were hidden; how pleased
To have about him which way e'er he goes
Something on every side concealed from view,
In every quarter something visible
Half seen or wholly, lost and found again,

Alternate progress and impediment,
And yet a growing prospect in the main.   490
  Such pleasure now is mine, albeit forced,
Herein less happy than the Traveller,
To cast from time to time a painful look
Upon unwelcome things which unawares
Reveal themselves, not therefore is my heart
Depressed, nor does it fear what is to come;
But confident, enriched at every glance,
The more I see the more delight my mind
Receives, or by reflection can create:
Truth justifies herself, and as she dwells
With Hope, who would not follow where
    she leads ?   501
  Nor let me pass unheeded other loves
Where no fear is, and humbler sympathies.
Already hath sprung up within my heart
A liking for the small grey horse that bears
The paralytic man, and for the brute
In Scripture sanctified — the patient brute
On which the cripple, in the quarry maimed,
Rides to and fro: I know them and their
    ways.
The famous sheep-dog, first in all the
    vale,   510
Though yet to me a stranger, will not be
A stranger long; nor will the blind man's
    guide,
Meek and neglected thing, of no renown !
Soon will peep forth the primrose, ere it
    fades
Friends shall I have at dawn, blackbird
    and thrush
To rouse me, and a hundred warblers
    more !
And if those Eagles to their ancient hold
Return, Helvellyn's Eagles ! with the Pair
From my own door I shall be free to claim
Acquaintance, as they sweep from cloud to
    cloud.   520
The owl that gives the name to Owlet-Crag
Have I heard whooping, and he soon will
    be
A chosen one of my regards. See there
The heifer in yon little croft belongs
To one who holds it dear; with duteous
    care
She reared it, and in speaking of her charge
I heard her scatter some endearing words
Domestic, and in spirit motherly,
She being herself a mother; happy Beast,
If the caresses of a human voice   530
Can make it so, and care of human hands.
  And ye as happy under Nature's care,
Strangers to me and all men, or at least

Strangers to all particular amity,
All intercourse of knowledge or of love
That parts the individual from his kind.
Whether in large communities ye keep
From year to year, not shunning man's
    abode,
A settled residence, or be from far
Wild creatures, and of many homes, that
    come   540
The gift of winds, and whom the winds
    again
Take from us at your pleasure; yet shall ye
Not want for this your own subordinate
    place
In my affections.   Witness the delight
With which erewhile I saw that multitude
Wheel through the sky, and see them now
    at rest,
Yet not at rest upon the glassy lake:
They *cannot* rest — they gambol like young
    whelps;
Active as lambs, and overcome with joy
They try all frolic motions; flutter, plunge,
And beat the passive water with their
    wings.   551
Too distant are they for plain view, but lo !
Those little fountains, sparkling in the sun,
Betray their occupation, rising up
First one and then another silver spout,
As one or other takes the fit of glee,
Fountains and spouts, yet somewhat in the
    guise
Of plaything fireworks, that on festal nights
Sparkle about the feet of wanton boys.
— How vast the compass of this theatre, 560
Yet nothing to be seen but lovely pomp
And silent majesty; the birch-tree woods
Are hung with thousand thousand diamond
    drops
Of melted hoar-frost, every tiny knot
In the bare twigs, each little budding-place
Cased with its several beads; what myriads
    there
Upon one tree, while all the distant grove,
That rises to the summit of the steep,
Shows like a mountain built of silver light:
See yonder the same pageant, and again 570
Behold the universal imagery
Inverted, all its sun-bright features touched
As with the varnish and the gloss of
    dreams.
Dreamlike the blending also of the whole
Harmonious landscape: all along the shore
The boundary lost — the line invisible
That parts the image from reality;

And the clear hills, as high as they ascend
Heavenward, so deep piercing the lake be-
low.
Admonished of the days of love to come 580
The raven croaks, and fills the upper air
With a strange sound of genial harmony;
And in and all about that playful band,
Incapable although they be of rest,
And in their fashion very rioters,
There is a stillness; and they seem to make
Calm revelry in that their calm abode.
Them leaving to their joyous hours I pass,
Pass with a thought the life of the whole
        year
That is to come: the throng of woodland
        flowers   590
And lilies that will dance upon the waves.

Say boldly then that solitude is not
Where these things are: he truly is alone,
He of the multitude whose eyes are doomed
To hold a vacant commerce day by day
With Objects wanting life — repelling love;
He by the vast metropolis immured,
Where pity shrinks from unremitting calls,
Where numbers overwhelm humanity,
And neighbourhood serves rather to divide
Than to unite — what sighs more deep than
        his,   601
Whose nobler will hath long been sacrificed;
Who must inhabit under a black sky
A city, where, if indifference to disgust
Yield not to scorn or sorrow, living men
Are ofttimes to their fellow-men no more
Than to the forest Hermit are the leaves
That hang aloft in myriads; nay, far less,
For they protect his walk from sun and
        shower,
Swell his devotion with their voice in
        storms,   610
And whisper while the stars twinkle among
        them
His lullaby. From crowded streets remote,
Far from the living and dead Wilderness
Of the thronged world, Society is here
A true community — a genuine frame
Of many into one incorporate.
That must be looked for here: paternal
        sway,
One household, under God, for high and
        low,
One family and one mansion; to themselves
Appropriate, and divided from the world,
As if it were a cave, a multitude   621
Human and brute, possessors undisturbed
Of this Recess — their legislative Hall,

Their Temple, and their glorious Dwelling-
        place.
Dismissing therefore all Arcadian dreams,
All golden fancies of the golden age,
The bright array of shadowy thoughts from
        times
That were before all time, or are to be
Ere time expire, the pageantry that stirs
And will be stirring, when our eyes are fixed
On lovely objects, and we wish to part   631
With all remembrance of a jarring world,
— Take we at once this one sufficient hope,
What need of more ? that we shall neither
        droop
Nor pine for want of pleasure in the life
Scattered about us, nor through dearth of
        aught
That keeps in health the insatiable mind.
— That we shall have for knowledge and
        for love
Abundance, and that feeling as we do
How goodly, how exceeding fair, how pure
From all reproach is yon ethereal vault,   641
And this deep Vale, its earthly counterpart,
By which and under which we are enclosed
To breathe in peace; we shall moreover find
(If sound, and what we ought to be our-
        selves,
If rightly we observe and justly weigh)
The inmates not unworthy of their home,
The Dwellers of their Dwelling.
                                And if this
Were otherwise, we have within ourselves
Enough to fill the present day with joy,   650
And overspread the future years with hope,
Our beautiful and quiet home, enriched
Already with a stranger whom we love
Deeply, a stranger of our Father's house,
A never-resting Pilgrim of the Sea,
Who finds at last an hour to his content
Beneath our roof. And others whom we
        love
Will seek us also, Sisters of our hearts,
And one, like them, a Brother of our hearts,
Philosopher and Poet, in whose sight   660
These mountains will rejoice with open joy.
— Such is our wealth ! O Vale of Peace
        we are
And must be, with God's will, a happy
        Band.
Yet 't is not to enjoy that we exist,
For that end only; something must be done:
I must not walk in unreproved delight
These narrow bounds, and think of nothing
        more,

No duty that looks further, and no care.
Each Being has his office, lowly some
And common, yet all worthy if fulfilled   670
With zeal, acknowledgment that with the
    gift
Keeps pace a harvest answering to the seed.
Of ill-advised Ambition and of Pride
I would stand clear, but yet to me I feel
That an internal brightness is vouchsafed
That must not die, that must not pass
    away.
Why does this inward lustre fondly seek
And gladly blend with outward fellowship?
Why do *they* shine around me whom I love?
Why do they teach me, whom I thus revere?
Strange question, yet it answers not itself.
That humble Roof embowered among the
    trees,   682
That calm fireside, it is not even in them,
Blest as they are, to furnish a reply
That satisfies and ends in perfect rest.
Possessions have I that are solely mine,
Something within which yet is shared by
    none,
Not even the nearest to me and most dear,
Something which power and effort may im-
    part;
I would impart it, I would spread it wide:
Immortal in the world which is to come —
Forgive me if I add another claim —   692
And would not wholly perish even in this,
Lie down and be forgotten in the dust,
I and the modest Partners of my days
Making a silent company in death;
Love, knowledge, all my manifold delights,
All buried with me without monument
Or profit unto any but ourselves!
It must not be, if I, divinely taught,   700
Be privileged to speak as I have felt
Of what in man is human or divine.
    While yet an innocent little one, with a
        heart
That doubtless wanted not its tender moods,
I breathed (for this I better recollect)
Among wild appetites and blind desires,
Motions of savage instinct my delight
And exaltation.   Nothing at that time
So welcome, no temptation half so dear
As that which urged me to a daring feat,
Deep pools, tall trees, black chasms, and
    dizzy crags,   711
And tottering towers: I loved to stand and
    read
Their looks forbidding, read and disobey,
Sometimes in act and evermore in thought.

With impulses, that scarcely were by these
Surpassed in strength, I heard of danger
    met
Or sought with courage; enterprise forlorn
By one, sole keeper of his own intent,
Or by a resolute few, who for the sake
Of glory fronted multitudes in arms.   720
Yea, to this hour I cannot read a Tale
Of two brave vessels matched in deadly
    fight,
And fighting to the death, but I am pleased
More than a wise man ought to be; I wish,
Fret, burn, and struggle, and in soul am
    there.
But me hath Nature tamed, and bade to
    seek
For other agitations, or be calm;
Hath dealt with me as with a turbulent
    stream,
Some nursling of the mountains which she
    leads
Through quiet meadows, after he has learnt
His strength, and had his triumph and his
    joy,   731
His desperate course of tumult and of glee.
That which in stealth by Nature was per-
    formed
Hath Reason sanctioned: her deliberate
    Voice
Hath said; be mild, and cleave to gentle
    things,
Thy glory and thy happiness be there.
Nor fear, though thou confide in me, a want
Of aspirations that *have* been — of foes
To wrestle with, and victory to complete,
Bounds to be leapt, darkness to be explored;
All that inflamed thy infant heart, the love,
The longing, the contempt, the undaunted
    quest,   742
All shall survive, though changed their of-
    fice, all
Shall live, it is not in their power to die.
    Then farewell to the Warrior's Schemes,
        farewell
The forwardness of soul which looks that
    way
Upon a less incitement than the Cause
Of Liberty endangered, and farewell
That other hope, long mine, the hope to fill
The heroic trumpet with the Muse's breath!
Yet in this peaceful Vale we will not spend
Unheard-of days, though loving peaceful
    thoughts,   752
A voice shall speak, and what will be the
    theme?

On Man, on Nature, and on Human Life
Musing in solitude, I oft perceive
Fair trains of imagery before me rise,
Accompanied by feelings of delight
Pure, or with no unpleasing sadness mixed;
And I am conscious of affecting thoughts
And dear remembrances, whose presence
    soothes   760
Or elevates the Mind, intent to weigh
The good and evil of our mortal state.
— To these emotions, whencesoe'er they
    come,
Whether from breath of outward circum-
    stance,
Or from the Soul — an impulse to herself —
I would give utterance in numerous verse.
Of Truth, of Grandeur, Beauty, Love, and
    Hope,
And melancholy Fear subdued by Faith;
Of blessèd consolations in distress;
Of moral strength, and intellectual Power;
Of joy in widest commonalty spread;   771
Of the individual Mind that keeps her own
Inviolate retirement, subject there
To Conscience only, and the law supreme
Of that Intelligence which governs all —
I sing: — " fit audience let me find though
    few ! "
    So prayed, more gaining than he asked,
    the Bard —
In holiest mood. Urania, I shall need
Thy guidance, or a greater Muse, if such
Descend to earth or dwell in highest heaven !
For I must tread on shadowy ground, must
    sink   781
Deep — and, aloft ascending, breathe in
    worlds
To which the heaven of heavens is but a veil,
All strength — all terror, single or in bands,
That ever was put forth in personal form —
Jehovah — with his thunder, and the choir
Of shouting Angels, and the empyreal
    thrones —
I pass them unalarmed. Not Chaos, not
The darkest pit of lowest Erebus,
Nor aught of blinder vacancy, scooped out
By help of dreams — can breed such fear
    and awe   791
As fall upon us often when we look
Into our Minds, into the Mind of Man —
My haunt, and the main region of my song
— Beauty — a living Presence of the earth,
Surpassing the most fair ideal Forms
Which craft of delicate Spirits hath com-
    posed

From earth's materials — waits upon my
    steps;
Pitches her tents before me as I move,
An hourly neighbour. Paradise, and groves
Elysian, Fortunate Fields — like those of
    old   801
Sought in the Atlantic Main — why should
    they be
A history only of departed things,
Or a mere fiction of what never was ?
For the discerning intellect of Man,
When wedded to this goodly universe
In love and holy passion, shall find these
A simple produce of the common day.
— I, long before the blissful hour arrives,
Would chant, in lonely peace, the spousal
    verse   810
Of this great consummation : — and, by
    words
Which speak of nothing more than what we
    are,
Would I arouse the sensual from their sleep
Of Death, and win the vacant and the vain
To noble raptures; while my voice proclaims
How exquisitely the individual Mind
(And the progressive powers perhaps no less
Of the whole species) to the external World
Is fitted: — and how exquisitely, too —   819
Theme this but little heard of among men—
The external World is fitted to the Mind;
And the creation (by no lower name
Can it be called) which they with blended
    might
Accomplish: — this is our high argument.
— Such grateful haunts foregoing, if I oft
Must turn elsewhere — to travel near the
    tribes
And fellowships of men, and see ill sights
Of madding passions mutually inflamed;
Must hear Humanity in fields and groves
Pipe solitary anguish; or must hang   830
Brooding above the fierce confederate storm
Of sorrow, barricadoed evermore
Within the walls of cities — may these
    sounds
Have their authentic comment; that even
    these
Hearing, I be not downcast or forlorn ! —
Descend, prophetic Spirit ! that inspir'st
The human Soul of universal earth,
Dreaming on things to come; and dost pos-
    sess
A metropolitan temple in the hearts
Of mighty Poets: upon me bestow   840
A gift of genuine insight; that my Song

With star-like virtue in its place may shine,
Shedding benignant influence, and secure,
Itself, from all malevolent effect
Of those mutations that extend their sway
Throughout the nether sphere ! — And if
  with this
I mix more lowly matter; with the thing
Contemplated, describe the mind and Man
Contemplating; and who, and what he
  was —
The transitory Being that beheld   850
This Vision; — when and where, and how
  he lived;

Be not this labour useless. If such theme
May sort with highest objects, then — dread
  Power !
Whose gracious favour is the primal source
Of all illumination — may my Life
Express the image of a better time,
More wise desires, and simpler manners; —
  nurse
My Heart in genuine freedom: — all pure
  thoughts
Be with me; — so shall thy unfailing love
Guide, and support, and cheer me to the
  end !   860

THE BROTHERS

1799. 1800

This poem was composed in a grove at the north-eastern end of Grasmere lake, which grove was in a great measure destroyed by turning the high-road along the side of the water. The few trees that are left were spared at my intercession. The poem arose out of the fact, mentioned to me at Ennerdale, that a shepherd had fallen asleep upon the top of the rock called The Pillar, and perished as here described, his staff being left midway on the rock.

"THESE Tourists, heaven preserve us !
      needs must live
A profitable life: some glance along,
Rapid and gay, as if the earth were air,
And they were butterflies to wheel about
Long as the summer lasted: some, as wise,
Perched on the forehead of a jutting crag,
Pencil in hand and book upon the knee,
Will look and scribble, scribble on and look,
Until a man might travel twelve stout miles,
Or reap an acre of his neighbour's corn.   10
But, for that moping Son of Idleness,
Why can he tarry *yonder* ? — In our church-
      yard
Is neither epitaph nor monument,
Tombstone nor name — only the turf we
      tread
And a few natural graves."
                  To Jane, his wife,
Thus spake the homely Priest of Ennerdale.
It was a July evening; and he sate
Upon the long stone-seat beneath the eaves
Of his old cottage, — as it chanced, that day,
Employed in winter's work. Upon the
      stone   20

His wife sate near him, teasing matted
      wool,
While, from the twin cards toothed with
      glittering wire,
He fed the spindle of his youngest child,
Who, in the open air, with due accord
Of busy hands and back-and-forward steps
Her large round wheel was turning. To-
      wards the field
In which the Parish Chapel stood alone,
Girt round with a bare ring of mossy wall,
While half an hour went by, the Priest had
      sent
Many a long look of wonder: and at last, 30
Risen from his seat, beside the snow-white
      ridge
Of carded wool which the old man had piled
He laid his implements with gentle care,
Each in the other locked; and, down the
      path
That from his cottage to the church-yard
      led,
He took his way, impatient to accost
The Stranger, whom he saw still lingering
      there.
  'T was one well known to him in former
      days,
A Shepherd-lad; who ere his sixteenth year
Had left that calling, tempted to entrust 40
His expectations to the fickle winds
And perilous waters; with the mariners
A fellow-mariner; — and so had fared
Through twenty seasons; but he had been
      reared
Among the mountains, and he in his heart
Was half a shepherd on the stormy seas.
Oft in the piping shrouds had Leonard
      heard
The tones of waterfalls, and inland sounds

Of caves and trees:— and, when the regular
      wind
Between the tropics filled the steady sail, 50
And blew with the same breath through
      days and weeks,
Lengthening invisibly its weary line
Along the cloudless Main, he, in those hours
Of tiresome indolence, would often hang
Over the vessel's side, and gaze and gaze;
And, while the broad blue wave and spar-
      kling foam
Flashed round him images and hues that
      wrought
In union with the employment of his heart,
He, thus by feverish passion overcome,
Even with the organs of his bodily eye, 60
Below him, in the bosom of the deep,
Saw mountains; saw the forms of sheep
      that grazed
On verdant hills — with dwellings among
      trees,
And shepherds clad in the same country
      grey
Which he himself had worn.
                    And now, at last,
From perils manifold, with some small
      wealth
Acquired by traffic 'mid the Indian Isles,
To his paternal home he is returned,
With a determined purpose to resume
The life he had lived there; both for the
      sake 70
Of many darling pleasures, and the love
Which to an only brother he has borne
In all his hardships, since that happy time
When, whether it blew foul or fair, they two
Were brother-shepherds on their native
      hills.
— They were the last of all their race: and
      now,
When Leonard had approached his home,
      his heart
Failed in him; and, not venturing to enquire
Tidings of one so long and dearly loved,
He to the solitary churchyard turned; 80
That, as he knew in what particular spot
His family were laid, he thence might learn
If still his Brother lived, or to the file
Another grave was added. — He had found
Another grave,— near which a full half-
      hour
He had remained; but, as he gazed, there
      grew
Such a confusion in his memory,
That he began to doubt; and even to hope

That he had seen this heap of turf before,—
That it was not another grave; but one 90
He had forgotten.   He had lost his path,
As up the vale, that afternoon, he walked
Through fields which once had been well
      known to him:
And oh what joy this recollection now
Sent to his heart! he lifted up his eyes,
And, looking round, imagined that he saw
Strange alteration wrought on every side
Among the woods and fields, and that the
      rocks,
And everlasting hills themselves were
      changed.
    By this the Priest, who down the field
      had come, 100
Unseen by Leonard, at the churchyard gate
Stopped short, — and thence, at leisure,
      limb by limb
Perused him with a gay complacency.
Ay, thought the Vicar, smiling to himself,
'T is one of those who needs must leave the
      path
Of the world's business to go wild alone:
His arms have a perpetual holiday;
The happy man will creep about the fields,
Following his fancies by the hour, to bring
Tears down his cheek, or solitary smiles 110
Into his face, until the setting sun
Write fool upon his forehead. — Planted
      thus
Beneath a shed that over-arched the gate
Of this rude churchyard, till the stars ap-
      peared
The good Man might have communed with
      himself,
But that the Stranger, who had left the
      grave,
Approached; he recognised the Priest at
      once,
And, after greetings interchanged, and
      given
By Leonard to the Vicar as to one
Unknown to him, this dialogue ensued. 120
    Leonard. You live, Sir, in these dales, a
      quiet life:
Your years make up one peaceful family;
And who would grieve and fret, if, wel-
      come come
And welcome gone, they are so like each
      other,
They cannot be remembered? Scarce a
      funeral
Comes to this churchyard once in eighteen
      months;

And yet, some changes must take place
　　among you:
And you, who dwell here, even among these
　　rocks,
Can trace the finger of mortality,
And see, that with our threescore years
　　and ten　　　　　　　　　　　130
We are not all that perish. —— I remember,
(For many years ago I passed this road)
There was a foot-way all along the fields
By the brook-side — 't is gone — and that
　　dark cleft !
To me it does not seem to wear the face
Which then it had !
　　Priest.　　　Nay, Sir, for aught I know,
That chasm is much the same —
　　Leonard.　　　But, surely, yonder —
　　Priest. Ay, there, indeed, your memory
　　is a friend
That does not play you false. — On that
　　tall pike
(It is the loneliest place of all these hills)
There were two springs which bubbled side
　　by side,　　　　　　　　　　141
As if they had been made that they might
　　be
Companions for each other: the huge crag
Was rent with lightning — one hath dis-
　　appeared;
The other, left behind, is flowing still.
For accidents and changes such as these,
We want not store of them; — a water-
　　spout
Will bring down half a mountain; what a
　　feast
For folks that wander up and down like
　　you　　　　　　　　　　　149
To see an acre's breadth of that wide cliff
One roaring cataract ! a sharp May-storm
Will come with loads of January snow,
And in one night send twenty score of
　　sheep
To feed the ravens; or a shepherd dies
By some untoward death among the rocks:
The ice breaks up and sweeps away a
　　bridge;
A wood is felled: — and then for our own
　　homes !
A child is born or christened, a field
　　ploughed,
A daughter sent to service, a web spun,
The old house-clock is decked with a new
　　face;　　　　　　　　　　160
And hence, so far from wanting facts or
　　dates

To chronicle the time, we all have here
A pair of diaries, — one serving, Sir,
For the whole dale, and one for each fire-
　　side —
Yours was a stranger's judgment: for
　　historians,
Commend me to these valleys !
　　Leonard.　　　　　Yet your Churchyard
Seems, if such freedom may be used with
　　you,
To say that you are heedless of the past:
An orphan could not find his mother's
　　grave:
Here 's neither head nor foot stone, plate of
　　brass,　　　　　　　　　　170
Cross-bones nor skull, — type of our earthly
　　state
Nor emblem of our hopes: the dead man's
　　home
Is but a fellow to that pasture-field.
　　Priest. Why, there, Sir, is a thought
　　that 's new to me !
The stone-cutters, 't is true, might beg their
　　bread
If every English churchyard were like ours;
Yet your conclusion wanders from the truth:
We have no need of names and epitaphs;
We talk about the dead by our firesides.
And then, for our immortal part ! *we* want
No symbols, Sir, to tell us that plain
　　tale:　　　　　　　　　　181
The thought of death sits easy on the man
Who has been born and dies among the
　　mountains.
　　Leonard. Your Dalesmen, then, do in
　　each other's thoughts
Possess a kind of second life: no doubt
You, Sir, could help me to the history
Of half these graves ?
　　Priest.　　　For eight-score winters past,
With what I 've witnessed, and with what
　　I 've heard,
Perhaps I might; and, on a winter-evening,
If you were seated at my chimney's
　　nook,　　　　　　　　　　190
By turning o'er these hillocks one by one,
We two could travel, Sir, through a strange
　　round;
Yet all in the broad highway of the world.
Now there 's a grave — your foot is half
　　upon it, —
It looks just like the rest; and yet that man
Died broken-hearted.
　　Leonard.　　　　　'T is a common case.
We 'll take another: who is he that lies

Beneath yon ridge, the last of those three
    graves ?
It touches on that piece of native rock   199
Left in the church-yard wall.
    Priest.   That 's Walter Ewbank.
He had as white a head and fresh a cheek
As ever were produced by youth and age
Engendering in the blood of hale fourscore.
Through five long generations had the
    heart
Of Walter's forefathers o'erflowed the
    bounds
Of their inheritance, that single cottage —
You see it yonder ! and those few green
    fields.
They toiled and wrought, and still, from
    sire to son,
Each struggled, and each yielded as before
A little — yet a little, — and old Walter,   210
They left to him the family heart, and land
With other burthens than the crop it bore.
Year after year the old man still kept up
A cheerful mind, — and buffeted with bond,
Interest, and mortgages; at last he sank,
And went into his grave before his time.
Poor Walter ! whether it was care that
    spurred him
God only knows, but to the very last
He had the lightest foot in Ennerdale:
His pace was never that of an old man: 220
I almost see him tripping down the path
With his two grandsons after him: — but
    you,
Unless our Landlord be your host to-night,
Have far to travel, — and on these rough
    paths
Even in the longest day of midsummer —
    Leonard. But those two Orphans !
    Priest. Orphans ! — Such they were —
Yet not while Walter lived: for, though
    their parents
Lay buried side by side as now they lie,
The old man was a father to the boys,
Two fathers in one father: and if tears,   230
Shed when he talked of them where they
    were not,
And hauntings from the infirmity of love,
Are aught of what makes up a mother's
    heart,
This old Man, in the day of his old age,
Was half a mother to them. — If you weep,
    Sir,
To hear a stranger talking about strangers,
Heaven bless you when you are among
    your kindred !

Ay — you may turn that way — it is a grave
Which will bear looking at.
    Leonard.   These boys — I hope
They loved this good old Man ? —
    Priest.   They did — and truly: 240
But that was what we almost overlooked,
They were such darlings of each other.
    Yes,
Though from the cradle they had lived with
    Walter,
The only kinsman near them, and though
    he
Inclined to both by reason of his age,
With a more fond, familiar, tenderness;
They, notwithstanding, had much love to
    spare,
And it all went into each other's hearts.
Leonard, the elder by just eighteen months,
Was two years taller: 't was a joy to see,
To hear, to meet them ! — From their house
    the school   251
Is distant three short miles, and in the time
Of storm and thaw, when every watercourse
And unbridged stream, such as you may
    have noticed
Crossing our roads at every hundred steps,
Was swoln into a noisy rivulet,
Would Leonard then, when elder boys re-
    mained
At home, go staggering through the slippery
    fords,
Bearing his brother on his back. I have
    seen him,
On windy days, in one of those stray
    brooks,   260
Ay, more than once I have seen him, mid-
    leg deep,
Their two books lying both on a dry stone,
Upon the hither side: and once I said,
As I remember, looking round these rocks
And hills on which we all of us were born,
That God who made the great book of the
    world
Would bless such piety —
    Leonard.   It may be then —
    Priest. Never did worthier lads break
    English bread:
The very brightest Sunday Autumn saw
With all its mealy clusters of ripe nuts, 270
Could never keep those boys away from
    church,
Or tempt them to an hour of sabbath
    breach.
Leonard and James ! I warrant, every cor-
    ner

Among these rocks, and every hollow place
That venturous foot could reach, to one or
  both
Was known as well as to the flowers that
  grow there.
Like roe-bucks they went bounding o'er the
  hills;
They played like two young ravens on the
  crags:
Then they could write, ay and speak too,
  as well
As many of their betters — and for Leonard!
The very night before he went away,   281
In my own house I put into his hand
A Bible, and I 'd wager house and field
That, if he be alive, he has it yet.
   Leonard. It seems, these Brothers have
  not lived to be
A comfort to each other —
   Priest.   That they might
Live to such end is what both old and young
In this our valley all of us have wished,
And what, for my part, I have often prayed:
But Leonard —
   Leonard. Then James still is left among
  you !   290
   Priest. 'T is of the elder brother I am
  speaking:
They had an uncle; — he was at that time
A thriving man, and trafficked on the seas:
And, but for that same uncle, to this hour
Leonard had never handled rope or shroud:
For the boy loved the life which we lead
  here;
And though of unripe years, a stripling only,
His soul was knit to this his native soil.
But, as I said, old Walter was too weak
To strive with such a torrent; when he
  died,   300
The estate and house were sold; and all
  their sheep,
A pretty flock, and which, for aught I know,
Had clothed the Ewbanks for a thousand
  years: —
Well — all was gone, and they were desti-
  tute,
And Leonard, chiefly for his Brother's sake,
Resolved to try his fortune on the seas.
Twelve years are past since we had tidings
  from him.
If there were one among us who had heard
That Leonard Ewbank was come home
  again,
From the Great Gavel, down by Leeza's
  banks,   310

And down the Enna, far as Egremont,
The day would be a joyous festival;
And those two bells of ours, which there
  you see —
Hanging in the open air — but, O good Sir !
This is sad talk — they 'll never sound for
  him —
Living or dead. — When last we heard of
  him,
He was in slavery among the Moors
Upon the Barbary coast. — 'T was not a
  little
That would bring down his spirit; and no
  doubt,
Before it ended in his death, the Youth   320
Was sadly crossed. — Poor Leonard ! when
  we parted,
He took me by the hand, and said to me,
If e'er he should grow rich, he would return,
To live in peace upon his father's land,
And lay his bones among us.
   Leonard.   If that day
Should come, 't would needs be a glad day
  for him;
He would himself, no doubt, be happy then
As any that should meet him —
   Priest.   Happy ! Sir —
   Leonard. You said his kindred all were
  in their graves,   329
And that he had one Brother —
   Priest.   That is but
A fellow-tale of sorrow.   From his youth
James, though not sickly, yet was delicate;
And Leonard being always by his side
Had done so many offices about him,
That, though he was not of a timid nature,
Yet still the spirit of a mountain-boy
In him was somewhat checked; and, when
  his Brother
Was gone to sea, and he was left alone,
The little colour that he had was soon
Stolen from his cheek; he drooped, and
  pined, and pined —   340
   Leonard. But these are all the graves of
  full-grown men !
   Priest. Ay, Sir, that passed away: we
  took him to us;
He was the child of all the dale — he lived
Three months with one, and six months with
  another,
And wanted neither food, nor clothes, nor
  love:
And many, many happy days were his.
But, whether blithe or sad, 't is my belief
His absent Brother still was at his heart.

And, when he dwelt beneath our roof, we
  found
(A practice till this time unknown to him)
That often, rising from his bed at night, 351
He in his sleep would walk about, and sleep-
  ing
He sought his brother Leonard. — You are
  moved!
Forgive me, Sir: before I spoke to you,
I judged you most unkindly.
  Leonard.   But this Youth,
How did he die at last?
  Priest.   One sweet May-morning,
(It will be twelve years since when Spring
  returns)
He had gone forth among the new-dropped
  lambs,
With two or three companions, whom their
  course
Of occupation led from height to height 360
Under a cloudless sun — till he, at length,
Through weariness, or, haply, to indulge
The humour of the moment, lagged behind.
You see yon precipice; — it wears the shape
Of a vast building made of many crags;
And in the midst is one particular rock
That rises like a column from the vale,
Whence by our shepherds it is called, THE
  PILLAR.
Upon its aëry summit crowned with heath,
The loiterer, not unnoticed by his comrades,
Lay stretched at ease; but, passing by the
  place 371
On their return, they found that he was gone.
No ill was feared; till one of them by chance
Entering, when evening was far spent, the
  house
Which at that time was James's home, there
  learned
That nobody had seen him all that day:
The morning came, and still he was unheard
  of:
The neighbours were alarmed, and to the
  brook
Some hastened; some ran to the lake: ere
  noon
They found him at the foot of that same
  rock 380
Dead, and with mangled limbs. The third
  day after
I buried him, poor Youth, and there he lies!
  Leonard. And that then *is* his grave! —
  Before his death
You say that he saw many happy years?
  Priest. Ay, that he did —

Leonard. And all went well with him? —
Priest. If he had one, the Youth had
  twenty homes.
Leonard. And you believe, then, that his
  mind was easy? —
Priest. Yes, long before he died, he found
  that time
Is a true friend to sorrow; and unless
His thoughts were turned on Leonard's
  luckless fortune, 390
He talked about him with a cheerful love.
  Leonard. He could not come to an un-
  hallowed end!
  Priest. Nay, God forbid! — You recollect
  I mentioned
A habit which disquietude and grief
Had brought upon him; and we all con-
  jectured
That, as the day was warm, he had lain
  down
On the soft heath, — and, waiting for his
  comrades,
He there had fallen asleep; that in his sleep
He to the margin of the precipice
Had walked, and from the summit had
  fallen headlong: 400
And so no doubt he perished. When the
  Youth
Fell, in his hand he must have grasped, we
  think,
His shepherd's staff; for on that Pillar of
  rock
It had been caught mid-way; and there for
  years
It hung; — and mouldered there.
                The Priest here ended —
The Stranger would have thanked him, but
  he felt
A gushing from his heart, that took away
The power of speech. Both left the spot in
  silence;
And Leonard, when they reached the
  churchyard gate,
As the Priest lifted up the latch, turned
  round, — 410
And, looking at the grave, he said, "My
  Brother!"
The Vicar did not hear the words: and now,
He pointed towards his dwelling-place, en-
  treating
That Leonard would partake his homely
  fare:
The other thanked him with an earnest
  voice;
But added, that, the evening being calm,

He would pursue his journey. So they
    parted.
   It was not long ere Leonard reached a
    grove
That overhung the road: he there stopped
    short,
And, sitting down beneath the trees, re-
    viewed   420
All that the Priest had said: his early years
Were with him: — his long absence, cher-
    ished hopes,
And thoughts which had been his an hour
    before,
All pressed on him with such a weight, that
    now,
This vale, where he had been so happy,
    seemed
A place in which he could not bear to live:
So he relinquished all his purposes.
He travelled back to Egremont: and thence,
That night, he wrote a letter to the Priest,
Reminding him of what had passed between
    them;   430
And adding, with a hope to be forgiven,
That it was from the weakness of his heart
He had not dared to tell him who he was.
This done, he went on shipboard, and is now
A Seaman, a grey-headed Mariner.

MICHAEL

A PASTORAL POEM

1800. 1800

Written at Town-end, Grasmere, about the
same time as " The Brothers." The Sheepfold,
on which so much of the poem turns, remains,
or rather the ruins of it. The character and
circumstances of Luke were taken from a
family to whom had belonged, many years be-
fore, the house we lived in at Town-end, along
with some fields and woodlands on the eastern
shore of Grasmere. The name of the Evening
Star was not in fact given to this house, but to
another on the same side of the valley, more to
the north.

If from the public way you turn your steps
Up the tumultuous brook of Greenhead
    Ghyll,
You will suppose that with an upright path
Your feet must struggle; in such bold as-
    cent
The pastoral mountains front you, face to
    face.

But, courage ! for around that boisterous
    brook
The mountains have all opened out them-
    selves,
And made a hidden valley of their own.
No habitation can be seen; but they
Who journey thither find themselves alone
With a few sheep, with rocks and stones,
    and kites   11
That overhead are sailing in the sky.
It is in truth an utter solitude;
Nor should I have made mention of this
    Dell
But for one object which you might pass
    by,
Might see and notice not. Beside the brook
Appears a straggling heap of unhewn
    stones !
And to that simple object appertains
A story — unenriched with strange events,
Yet not unfit, I deem, for the fireside,   20
Or for the summer shade. It was the first
Of those domestic tales that spake to me
Of shepherds, dwellers in the valleys, men
Whom I already loved; not verily
For their own sakes, but for the fields and
    hills
Where was their occupation and abode.
And hence this Tale, while I was yet a Boy
Careless of books, yet having felt the power
Of Nature, by the gentle agency
Of natural objects, led me on to feel   30
For passions that were not my own, and
    think
(At random and imperfectly indeed)
On man, the heart of man, and human life.
Therefore, although it be a history
Homely and rude, I will relate the same
For the delight of a few natural hearts;
And, with yet fonder feeling, for the sake
Of youthful Poets, who among these hills
Will be my second self when I am gone.
    Upon the forest-side in Grasmere Vale 40
There dwelt a Shepherd, Michael was his
    name;
An old man, stout of heart, and strong of
    limb.
His bodily frame had been from youth to
    age
Of an unusual strength: his mind was keen,
Intense, and frugal, apt for all affairs,
And in his shepherd's calling he was prompt
And watchful more than ordinary men.
Hence had he learned the meaning of all
    winds,

Of blasts of every tone; and, oftentimes,
When others heeded not, He heard the South   50
Make subterraneous music, like the noise
Of bagpipers on distant Highland hills.
The Shepherd, at such warning, of his flock
Bethought him, and he to himself would say,
"The winds are now devising work for me!"
And, truly, at all times, the storm, that drives
The traveller to a shelter, summoned him
Up to the mountains: he had been alone
Amid the heart of many thousand mists,
That came to him, and left him, on the heights.   60
So lived he till his eightieth year was past.
And grossly that man errs, who should suppose
That the green valleys, and the streams and rocks,
Were things indifferent to the Shepherd's thoughts.
Fields, where with cheerful spirits he had breathed
The common air; hills, which with vigorous step
He had so often climbed; which had impressed
So many incidents upon his mind   68
Of hardship, skill or courage, joy or fear;
Which, like a book, preserved the memory
Of the dumb animals, whom he had saved,
Had fed or sheltered, linking to such acts
The certainty of honourable gain;
Those fields, those hills — what could they less? had laid
Strong hold on his affections, were to him
A pleasurable feeling of blind love,
The pleasure which there is in life itself.
  His days had not been passed in singleness.
His Helpmate was a comely matron, old —
Though younger than himself full twenty years.   80
She was a woman of a stirring life,
Whose heart was in her house: two wheels she had
Of antique form; this large, for spinning wool;
That small, for flax; and if one wheel had rest
It was because the other was at work.
The Pair had but one inmate in their house,

An only Child, who had been born to them
When Michael, telling o'er his years, began
To deem that he was old, — in shepherd's phrase,
With one foot in the grave. This only Son,
With two brave sheep-dogs tried in many a storm,   91
The one of an inestimable worth,
Made all their household. I may truly say,
That they were as a proverb in the vale
For endless industry. When day was gone,
And from their occupations out of doors
The Son and Father were come home, even then,
Their labour did not cease; unless when all
Turned to the cleanly supper-board, and there,
Each with a mess of pottage and skimmed milk,   100
Sat round the basket piled with oaten cakes,
And their plain home-made cheese. Yet when the meal
Was ended, Luke (for so the Son was named)
And his old Father both betook themselves
To such convenient work as might employ
Their hands by the fireside; perhaps to card
Wool for the Housewife's spindle, or repair
Some injury done to sickle, flail, or scythe,
Or other implement of house or field.
  Down from the ceiling, by the chimney's edge,   110
That in our ancient uncouth country style
With huge and black projection overbrowed
Large space beneath, as duly as the light
Of day grew dim the Housewife hung a lamp;
An aged utensil, which had performed
Service beyond all others of its kind.
Early at evening did it burn — and late,
Surviving comrade of uncounted hours,
Which, going by from year to year, had found,
And left, the couple neither gay perhaps
Nor cheerful, yet with objects and with hopes,   121
Living a life of eager industry.
And now, when Luke had reached his eighteenth year,
There by the light of this old lamp they sate,
Father and Son, while far into the night
The Housewife plied her own peculiar work,
Making the cottage through the silent hours

Murmur as with the sound of summer flies.
This light was famous in its neighbourhood,
And was a public symbol of the life   130
That thrifty Pair had lived. For, as it
     chanced,
Their cottage on a plot of rising ground
Stood single, with large prospect, north
     and south,
High into Easedale, up to Dunmail-Raise,
And westward to the village near the lake;
And from this constant light, so regular
And so far seen, the House itself, by all
Who dwelt within the limits of the vale,
Both old and young, was named THE
     EVENING STAR.
    Thus living on through such a length of
     years,   140
The Shepherd, if he loved himself, must
     needs
Have loved his Helpmate; but to Michael's
     heart
This son of his old age was yet more dear —
Less from instinctive tenderness, the same
Fond spirit that blindly works in the blood
     of all —
Than that a child, more than all other gifts
That earth can offer to declining man,
Brings hope with it, and forward-looking
     thoughts,
And stirrings of inquietude, when they
By tendency of nature needs must fail.   150
Exceeding was the love he bare to him,
His heart and his heart's joy ! For often-
     times
Old Michael, while he was a babe in arms,
Had done him female service, not alone
For pastime and delight, as is the use
Of fathers, but with patient mind enforced
To acts of tenderness; and he had rocked
His cradle, as with a woman's gentle hand.
    And, in a later time, ere yet the Boy
Had put on boy's attire, did Michael love,
Albeit of a stern unbending mind,   161
To have the Young-one in his sight, when
     he
Wrought in the field, or on his shepherd's
     stool
Sate with a fettered sheep before him
     stretched
Under the large old oak, that near his door
Stood single, and, from matchless depth of
     shade,
Chosen for the Shearer's covert from the
     sun,
Thence in our rustic dialect was called

The CLIPPING TREE, a name which yet it
     bears.
There, while they two were sitting in the
     shade,   170
With others round them, earnest all and
     blithe,
Would Michael exercise his heart with looks
Of fond correction and reproof bestowed
Upon the Child, if he disturbed the sheep
By catching at their legs, or with his
     shouts
Scared them, while they lay still beneath
     the shears.
    And when by Heaven's good grace the
     boy grew up
A healthy Lad, and carried in his cheek
Two steady roses that were five years old;
Then Michael from a winter coppice cut 180
With his own hand a sapling, which he
     hooped
With iron, making it throughout in all
Due requisites a perfect shepherd's staff,
And gave it to the Boy; wherewith equipt
He as a watchman oftentimes was placed
At gate or gap, to stem or turn the flock;
And, to his office prematurely called,
There stood the urchin, as you will divine,
Something between a hindrance and a help;
And for this cause not always, I believe, 190
Receiving from his Father hire of praise;
Though nought was left undone which
     staff, or voice,
Or looks, or threatening gestures, could
     perform.
    But soon as Luke, full ten years old,
     could stand
Against the mountain blasts; and to the
     heights,
Not fearing toil, nor length of weary ways,
He with his Father daily went, and they
Were as companions, why should I relate
That objects which the Shepherd loved
     before
Were dearer now ? that from the Boy there
     came   200
Feelings and emanations — things which
     were
Light to the sun and music to the wind;
And that the old Man's heart seemed born
     again ?
    Thus in his Father's sight the Boy grew
     up:
And now, when he had reached his eight-
     eenth year,
He was his comfort and his daily hope.

While in this sort the simple household
   lived
From day to day, to Michael's ear there
   came
Distressful tidings. Long before the time
Of which I speak, the Shepherd had been
   bound   210
In surety for his brother's son, a man
Of an industrious life, and ample means;
But unforeseen misfortunes suddenly
Had prest upon him; and old Michael now
Was summoned to discharge the forfeiture,
A grievous penalty, but little less
Than half his substance. This unlooked-for
   claim,
At the first hearing, for a moment took
More hope out of his life than he supposed
That any old man ever could have lost. 220
As soon as he had armed himself with
   strength
To look his trouble in the face, it seemed
The Shepherd's sole resource to sell at once
A portion of his patrimonial fields.
Such was his first resolve; he thought again,
And his heart failed him. "Isabel," said he,
Two evenings after he had heard the news,
"I have been toiling more than seventy
   years,
And in the open sunshine of God's love 229
Have we all lived; yet if these fields of ours
Should pass into a stranger's hand, I think
That I could not lie quiet in my grave.
Our lot is a hard lot; the sun himself
Has scarcely been more diligent than I;
And I have lived to be a fool at last
To my own family. An evil man
That was, and made an evil choice, if he
Were false to us; and if he were not false,
There are ten thousand to whom loss like
   this   239
Had been no sorrow. I forgive him; — but
'T were better to be dumb than to talk thus.
   When I began, my purpose was to speak
Of remedies and of a cheerful hope.
Our Luke shall leave us, Isabel; the land
Shall not go from us, and it shall be free;
He shall possess it, free as is the wind
That passes over it. We have, thou know'st,
Another kinsman — he will be our friend
In this distress. He is a prosperous man,
Thriving in trade — and Luke to him shall
   go,   250
And with his kinsman's help and his own
   thrift
He quickly will repair this loss, and then

He may return to us. If here he stay,
What can be done? Where every one is
   poor,
What can be gained?"
               At this the old Man paused,
And Isabel sat silent, for her mind
Was busy, looking back into past times.
There's Richard Bateman, thought she to
   herself,
He was a parish-boy — at the church-door
They made a gathering for him, shillings,
   pence   260
And halfpennies, wherewith the neighbours
   bought
A basket, which they filled with pedlar's
   wares;
And, with this basket on his arm, the lad
Went up to London, found a master there,
Who, out of many, chose the trusty boy
To go and overlook his merchandise
Beyond the seas; where he grew wondrous
   rich,
And left estates and monies to the poor.
And, at his birth-place, built a chapel,
   floored
With marble which he sent from foreign
   lands.   270
These thoughts, and many others of like
   sort,
Passed quickly through the mind of Isabel,
And her face brightened. The old Man
   was glad,
And thus resumed: — "Well, Isabel! this
   scheme
These two days, has been meat and drink
   to me.
Far more than we have lost is left us yet.
— We have enough — I wish indeed that I
Were younger; — but this hope is a good
   hope.
— Make ready Luke's best garments, of
   the best
Buy for him more, and let us send him
   forth   280
To-morrow, or the next day, or to-night:
— If he *could* go, the Boy should go to-
   night."
   Here Michael ceased, and to the fields
   went forth
With a light heart. The Housewife for
   five days
Was restless morn and night, and all day
   long
Wrought on with her best fingers to pre-
   pare

Things needful for the journey of her son.
But Isabel was glad when Sunday came
To stop her in her work: for, when she
    lay
By Michael's side, she through the last two
    nights   290
Heard him, how he was troubled in his
    sleep:
And when they rose at morning she could
    see
That all his hopes were gone. That day
    at noon
She said to Luke, while they two by them-
    selves
Were sitting at the door, " Thou must not
    go:
We have no other Child but thee to lose —
None to remember — do not go away,
For if thou leave thy Father he will die."
The Youth made answer with a jocund
    voice;
And Isabel, when she had told her fears,
Recovered heart. That evening her best
    fare   301
Did she bring forth, and all together sat
Like happy people round a Christmas fire.
With daylight Isabel resumed her work;
And all the ensuing week the house ap-
    peared
As cheerful as a grove in Spring: at length
The expected letter from their kinsman
    came,
With kind assurances that he would do
His utmost for the welfare of the Boy;
To which, requests were added, that forth-
    with   310
He might be sent to him. Ten times or
    more
The letter was read over; Isabel
Went forth to show it to the neighbours
    round;
Nor was there at that time on English land
A prouder heart than Luke's. When Isabel
Had to her house returned, the old Man
    said,
" He shall depart to-morrow." To this
    word
The Housewife answered, talking much of
    things
Which, if at such short notice he should
    go,   319
Would surely be forgotten. But at length
She gave consent, and Michael was at ease.
    Near the tumultuous brook of Greenhead
        Ghyll,

In that deep valley, Michael had designed
To build a Sheep-fold; and, before he heard
The tidings of his melancholy loss,
For this same purpose he had gathered up
A heap of stones, which by the streamlet's
    edge
Lay thrown together, ready for the work.
With Luke that evening thitherward he
    walked:
And soon as they had reached the place he
    stopped,   330
And thus the old Man spake to him: —
    " My Son,
To-morrow thou wilt leave me: with full
    heart
I look upon thee, for thou art the same
That wert a promise to me ere thy birth,
And all thy life hast been my daily joy.
I will relate to thee some little part
Of our two histories; 't will do thee good
When thou art from me, even if I should
    touch
On things thou canst not know of. ——
    After thou
First cam'st into the world — as oft befalls
To new-born infants — thou didst sleep
    away   341
Two days, and blessings from thy Father's
    tongue
Then fell upon thee. Day by day passed
    on,
And still I loved thee with increasing love.
Never to living ear came sweeter sounds
Than when I heard thee by our own fireside
First uttering, without words, a natural
    tune;
While thou, a feeding babe, didst in thy joy
Sing at thy Mother's breast. Month fol-
    lowed month,
And in the open fields my life was passed
And on the mountains; else I think that
    thou   351
Hadst been brought up upon thy Father's
    knees.
But we were playmates, Luke: among
    these hills,
As well thou knowest, in us the old and
    young
Have played together, nor with me didst
    thou
Lack any pleasure which a boy can know."
Luke had a manly heart; but at these
    words
He sobbed aloud. The old Man grasped
    his hand,

And said, " Nay, do not take it so — I see
That these are things of which I need not
    speak.   360
— Even to the utmost I have been to thee
A kind and a good Father: and herein
I but repay a gift which I myself
Received at others' hands; for, though now
    old
Beyond the common life of man, I still
Remember them who loved me in my youth.
Both of them sleep together: here they
    lived,
As all their Forefathers had done; and
    when
At length their time was come, they were
    not loth
To give their bodies to the family mould.
I wished that thou should'st live the life
    they lived: 371
But, 't is a long time to look back, my Son,
And see so little gain from threescore years.
These fields were burthened when they
    came to me;
Till I was forty years of age, not more
Than half of my inheritance was mine.
I toiled and toiled; God blessed me in my
    work,
And till these three weeks past the land
    was free.
— It looks as if it never could endure
Another Master. Heaven forgive me,
    Luke,   380
If I judge ill for thee, but it seems good
That thou should'st go."
                    At this the old Man paused;
Then, pointing to the stones near which
    they stood,
Thus, after a short silence, he resumed:
" This was a work for us; and now, my Son,
It is a work for me. But, lay one stone —
Here, lay it for me, Luke, with thine own
    hands.
Nay, Boy, be of good hope; — we both
    may live
To see a better day. At eighty-four
I still am strong and hale; — do thou thy
    part;   390
I will do mine. — I will begin again
With many tasks that were resigned to
    thee:
Up to the heights, and in among the storms,
Will I without thee go again, and do
All works which I was wont to do alone,
Before I knew thy face. — Heaven bless
    thee, Boy !

Thy heart these two weeks has been beat-
    ing fast
With many hopes; it should be so — yes —
    yes —
I knew that thou could'st never have a wish
To leave me, Luke: thou hast been bound
    to me   400
Only by links of love: when thou art gone,
What will be left to us ! — But, I forget
My purposes. Lay now the corner-stone,
As I requested; and hereafter, Luke,
When thou art gone away, should evil men
Be thy companions, think of me, my Son,
And of this moment; hither turn thy
    thoughts,
And God will strengthen thee: amid all fear
And all temptation, Luke, I pray that thou
May'st bear in mind the life thy Fathers
    lived,   410
Who, being innocent, did for that cause
Bestir them in good deeds. Now, fare thee
    well —
When thou return'st, thou in this place wilt
    see
A work which is not here: a covenant
'T will be between us; but, whatever fate
Befall thee, I shall love thee to the last,
And bear thy memory with me to the
    grave."
    The Shepherd ended here; and Luke
        stooped down,
And, as his Father had requested, laid
The first stone of the Sheep-fold. At the
    sight   420
The old Man's grief broke from him; to
    his heart
He pressed his Son, he kissèd him and wept;
And to the house together they returned.
— Hushed was that House in peace, or
    seeming peace,
Ere the night fell: — with morrow's dawn
    the Boy
Began his journey, and when he had reached
The public way, he put on a bold face;
And all the neighbours, as he passed their
    doors,
Came forth with wishes and with farewell
    prayers,
That followed him till he was out of sight.
    A good report did from their Kinsman
        come,   431
Of Luke and his well-doing: and the Boy
Wrote loving letters, full of wondrous news,
Which, as the Housewife phrased it, were
    throughout

" The prettiest letters that were ever seen."
Both parents read them with rejoicing
  hearts.
So, many months passed on: and once again
The Shepherd went about his daily work
With confident and cheerful thoughts; and
  now   439
Sometimes when he could find a leisure hour
He to that valley took his way, and there
Wrought at the Sheep-fold. Meantime
  Luke began
To slacken in his duty; and, at length,
He in the dissolute city gave himself
To evil courses: ignominy and shame
Fell on him, so that he was driven at last
To seek a hiding-place beyond the seas.

  There is a comfort in the strength of love;
'T will make a thing endurable, which else
Would overset the brain, or break the heart:
I have conversed with more than one who
  well   451
Remember the old Man, and what he was
Years after he had heard this heavy news.
His bodily frame had been from youth to age
Of an unusual strength. Among the rocks
He went, and still looked up to sun and
  cloud,
And listened to the wind; and, as before,
Performed all kinds of labour for his sheep,
And for the land, his small inheritance. 459
And to that hollow dell from time to time
Did he repair, to build the Fold of which
His flock had need. 'T is not forgotten yet
The pity which was then in every heart
For the old Man — and 't is believed by all
That many and many a day he thither went,
And never lifted up a single stone.
  There, by the Sheep-fold, sometimes
    was he seen
Sitting alone, or with his faithful Dog,
Then old, beside him, lying at his feet.
The length of full seven years, from time to
  time,   470
He at the building of this Sheep-fold
  wrought,
And left the work unfinished when he died.
Three years, or little more, did Isabel
Survive her Husband: at her death the estate
Was sold, and went into a stranger's hand.
The Cottage which was named the EVEN-
  ING STAR
Is gone — the ploughshare has been through
  the ground
On which it stood; great changes have been
  wrought

In all the neighbourhood: — yet the oak is
  left
That grew beside their door; and the re-
  mains   480
Of the unfinished Sheep-fold may be seen
Beside the boisterous brook of Greenhead
  Ghyll.

THE IDLE SHEPHERD-BOYS

OR, DUNGEON-GHYLL FORCE

A PASTORAL

1800. 1800

Written at Town-end, Grasmere. I will only
add a little monitory anecdote concerning this
subject. When Coleridge and Southey were
walking together upon the Fells, Southey
observed that, if I wished to be considered a
faithful painter of rural manners, I ought not
to have said that my Shepherd-boys trimmed
their rustic hats as described in the poem. Just
as the words had passed his lips two boys ap-
peared with the very plant entwined round
their hats. I have often wondered that Southey,
who rambled so much about the mountains,
should have fallen into this mistake, and I re-
cord it as a warning for others who, with far
less opportunity than my dear friend had of
knowing what things are, and far less sagacity,
give way to presumptuous criticism, from
which he was free, though in this matter mis-
taken. In describing a tarn under Helvellyn,
I say —

> " There sometimes doth a leaping fish
>   Send through the tarn a lonely cheer."

This was branded by a critic of these days, in
a review ascribed to Mrs. Barbauld, as unnatu-
ral and absurd. I admire the genius of Mrs.
Barbauld, and am certain that, had her educa-
tion been favourable to imaginative influences,
no female of her day would have been more
likely to sympathise with that image, and to
acknowledge the truth of the sentiment.

THE valley rings with mirth and joy;
Among the hills the echoes play
A never never ending song,
To welcome in the May.
The magpie chatters with delight;
The mountain raven's youngling brood
Have left the mother and the nest;
And they go rambling east and west
In search of their own food;
Or through the glittering vapours dart   10
In very wantonness of heart.

Beneath a rock, upon the grass,
Two boys are sitting in the sun;
Their work, if any work they have,
Is out of mind — or done.
On pipes of sycamore they play
The fragments of a Christmas hymn;
Or with that plant which in our dale
We call stag-horn, or fox's tail,
Their rusty hats they trim: 20
And thus, as happy as the day,
Those Shepherds wear the time away.

Along the river's stony marge
The sand-lark chants a joyous song;
The thrush is busy in the wood,
And carols loud and strong.
A thousand lambs are on the rocks,
All newly born ! both earth and sky
Keep jubilee, and more than all,
Those boys with their green coronal;   30
They never hear the cry,
That plaintive cry ! which up the hill
Comes from the depth of Dungeon-Ghyll.

Said Walter, leaping from the ground,
" Down to the stump of yon old yew
We 'll for our whistles run a race."
—— Away the shepherds flew;
They leapt — they ran — and when they
            came
Right opposite to Dungeon-Ghyll,
Seeing that he should lose the prize,   40
" Stop ! " to his comrade Walter cries —
James stopped with no good will:
Said Walter then, exulting; " Here
You 'll find a task for half a year.

" Cross, if you dare, where I shall cross —
Come on, and tread where I shall tread."
The other took him at his word,
And followed as he led.
It was a spot which you may see
If ever you to Langdale go;   50
Into a chasm a mighty block
Hath fallen, and made a bridge of rock:
The gulf is deep below;
And, in a basin black and small,
Receives a lofty waterfall.

With staff in hand across the cleft
The challenger pursued his march;
And now, all eyes and feet, hath gained
The middle of the arch.
When list ! he hears a piteous moan —   60
Again ! — his heart within him dies —

His pulse is stopped, his breath is lost,
He totters, pallid as a ghost,
And, looking down, espies
A lamb, that in the pool is pent
Within that black and frightful rent.

The lamb had slipped into the stream,
And safe without a bruise or wound
The cataract had borne him down
Into the gulf profound.   70
His dam had seen him when he fell,
She saw him down the torrent borne;
And, while with all a mother's love
She from the lofty rocks above
Sent forth a cry forlorn,
The lamb, still swimming round and round,
Made answer to that plaintive sound.

When he had learnt what thing it was,
That sent this rueful cry; I ween
The Boy recovered heart, and told   80
The sight which he had seen.
Both gladly now deferred their task;
Nor was there wanting other aid —
A Poet, one who loves the brooks
Far better than the sages' books,
By chance had thither strayed;
And there the helpless lamb he found
By those huge rocks encompassed round.

He drew it from the troubled pool,
And brought it forth into the light: 90
The Shepherds met him with his charge,
An unexpected sight !
Into their arms the lamb they took,
Whose life and limbs the flood had spared;
Then up the steep ascent they hied,
And placed him at his mother's side;
And gently did the Bard
Those idle Shepherd-boys upbraid,
And bade them better mind their trade.

THE PET-LAMB

A PASTORAL

1800. 1800

Written at Town-end, Grasmere. Barbara
Lewthwaite, now living at Ambleside (1843),
though much changed as to beauty, was one of
two most lovely sisters. Almost the first words
my poor brother John said, when he visited us
for the first time at Grasmere, were, " Were
those two Angels that I have just seen ? " and
from his description I have no doubt they were
those two sisters. The mother died in childbed;

and one of our neighbours at Grasmere told me that the loveliest sight she had ever seen was that mother as she lay in her coffin with her babe in her arm. I mention this to notice what I cannot but think a salutary custom once universal in these vales. Every attendant on a funeral made it a duty to look at the corpse in the coffin before the lid was closed, which was never done (nor I believe is now) till a minute or two before the corpse was removed. Barbara Lewthwaite was not in fact the child whom I had seen and overheard as described in the poem. I chose the name for reasons implied in the above; and will here add a caution against the use of names of living persons. Within a few months after the publication of this poem, I was much surprised, and more hurt, to find it in a child's school-book which, having been compiled by Lindley Murray, had come into use at Grasmere School where Barbara was a pupil; and, alas! I had the mortification of hearing that she was very vain of being thus distinguished; and, in after-life, she used to say that she remembered the incident and what I said to her upon the occasion.

THE dew was falling fast, the stars began
    to blink;
I heard a voice; it said, " Drink, pretty
    creature, drink ! "
And, looking o'er the hedge, before me I
    espied
A snow-white mountain-lamb with a Maiden
    at its side.

Nor sheep nor kine were near; the lamb
    was all alone,
And by a slender cord was tethered to a
    stone;
With one knee on the grass did the little
    Maiden kneel,
While to that mountain-lamb she gave its
    evening meal.

The lamb, while from her hand he thus his
    supper took,
Seemed to feast with head and ears; and
    his tail with pleasure shook.   10
" Drink, pretty creature, drink," she said
    in such a tone
That I almost received her heart into my
    own.

'T was little Barbara Lewthwaite, a child of
    beauty rare !
I watched them with delight, they were a
    lovely pair.

Now with her empty can the Maiden turned
    away:
But ere ten yards were gone her footsteps
    did she stay.

Right towards the lamb she looked; and
    from a shady place
I unobserved could see the workings of her
    face:
If Nature to her tongue could measured
    numbers bring,
Thus, thought I, to her lamb that little
    Maid might sing: 20

" What ails thee, young One ? what ? Why
    pull so at thy cord ?
Is it not well with thee ? well both for bed
    and board ?
Thy plot of grass is soft, and green as grass
    can be;
Rest, little young One, rest; what is 't that
    aileth thee ?

" What is it thou wouldst seek ? What is
    wanting to thy heart ?
Thy limbs are they not strong ? And beautiful thou art:
This grass is tender grass; these flowers
    they have no peers;
And that green corn all day is rustling in
    thy ears !

" If the sun be shining hot, do but stretch
    thy woollen chain,
This beech is standing by, its covert thou
    canst gain;   30
For rain and mountain-storms ! the like
    thou need'st not fear,
The rain and storm are things that scarcely
    can come here.

" Rest, little young One, rest; thou hast forgot the day
When my father found thee first in places
    far away;
Many flocks were on the hills, but thou
    wert owned by none,
And thy mother from thy side for evermore
    was gone.

" He took thee in his arms, and in pity
    brought thee home:
A blessed day for thee ! then whither
    wouldst thou roam ?

A faithful nurse thou hast; the dam that
    did thee yean
Upon the mountain-tops no kinder could
    have been.   40

" Thou know'st that twice a day I have
    brought thee in this can
Fresh water from the brook, as clear as ever
    ran;
And twice in the day, when the ground is
    wet with dew,
I bring thee draughts of milk, warm milk
    it is and new.

" Thy limbs will shortly be twice as stout
    as they are now,
Then I 'll yoke thee to my cart like a pony
    in the plough;
My playmate thou shalt be; and when the
    wind is cold
Our hearth shall be thy bed, our house shall
    be thy fold.

" It will not, will not rest ! — Poor creature,
    can it be
That 't is thy mother's heart which is work-
    ing so in thee ?   50
Things that I know not of belike to thee are
    dear,
And dreams of things which thou canst
    neither see nor hear.

" Alas, the mountain-tops that look so green
    and fair !
I 've heard of fearful winds and darkness
    that come there;
The little brooks that seem all pastime and
    all play,
When they are angry, roar like lions for
    their prey.

" Here thou need'st not dread the raven in
    the sky;
Night and day thou art safe, — our cottage
    is hard by.
Why bleat so after me ?   Why pull so at
    thy chain ?
Sleep — and at break of day I will come to
    thee again ! "   60

— As homeward through the lane I went
    with lazy feet,
This song to myself did I oftentimes re-
    peat;

And it seemed, as I retraced the ballad line
    by line,
That but half of it was hers, and one half
    of it was *mine.*

Again, and once again, did I repeat the
    song;
" Nay," said I, " more than half to the
    damsel must belong,
For she looked with such a look and she
    spake with such a tone,
That I almost received her heart into my
    own."

POEMS ON THE NAMING OF PLACES

1800. 1800

ADVERTISEMENT

By persons resident in the country and at-
tached to rural objects, many places will be
found unnamed or of unknown names, where
little Incidents must have occurred, or feelings
been experienced, which will have given to
such places a private and peculiar interest.
From a wish to give some sort of record to such
Incidents, and renew the gratification of such
feelings, Names have been given to Places by
the Author and some of his Friends, and the
following Poems written in consequence.

I

Written at Grasmere. This poem was sug-
gested on the banks of the brook that runs
through Easedale, which is, in some parts of
its course, as wild and beautiful as brook can
be. I have composed thousands of verses by
the side of it.

IT was an April morning: fresh and clear
The Rivulet, delighting in its strength,
Ran with a young man's speed; and yet the
    voice
Of waters which the winter had supplied
Was softened down into a vernal tone.
The spirit of enjoyment and desire,
And hopes and wishes, from all living things
Went circling, like a multitude of sounds.
The budding groves seemed eager to urge
    on   9
The steps of June; as if their various hues
Were only hindrances that stood between
Them and their object: but, meanwhile,
    prevailed
Such an entire contentment in the air

That every naked ash, and tardy tree
Yet leafless, showed as if the countenance
With which it looked on this delightful day
Were native to the summer. — Up the brook
I roamed in the confusion of my heart,
Alive to all things and forgetting all.
At length I to a sudden turning came   20
In this continuous glen, where down a rock
The Stream, so ardent in its course before,
Sent forth such sallies of glad sound, that all
Which I till then had heard, appeared the voice
Of common pleasure: beast and bird, the lamb,
The shepherd's dog, the linnet and the thrush
Vied with this waterfall, and made a song,
Which, while I listened, seemed like the wild growth
Or like some natural produce of the air,
That could not cease to be.   Green leaves were here;   30
But 't was the foliage of the rocks — the birch,
The yew, the holly, and the bright green thorn,
With hanging islands of resplendent furze:
And, on a summit, distant a short space,
By any who should look beyond the dell,
A single mountain-cottage might be seen.
I gazed and gazed, and to myself I said,
" Our thoughts at least are ours; and this wild nook,
My EMMA, I will dedicate to thee."
—— Soon did the spot become my other home,   40
My dwelling, and my out-of-doors abode.
And, of the Shepherds who have seen me there,
To whom I sometimes in our idle talk
Have told this fancy, two or three, perhaps,
Years after we are gone and in our graves,
When they have cause to speak of this wild place,
May call it by the name of EMMA'S DELL.

II

TO JOANNA

Written at Grasmere. The effect of her
laugh is an extravagance ; though the effect
of the reverberation of voices in some parts
of the mountains is very striking. There is, in
the " Excursion," an allusion to the bleat of a
lamb thus re-echoed, and described without
any exaggeration, as I heard it, on the side of
Stickle Tarn, from the precipice that stretches
on to Langdale Pikes.

AMID the smoke of cities did you pass
The time of early youth; and there you learned,
From years of quiet industry, to love
The living Beings by your own fireside,
With such a strong devotion, that your heart
Is slow to meet the sympathies of them
Who look upon the hills with tenderness,
And make dear friendships with the streams and groves.
Yet we, who are transgressors in this kind,
Dwelling retired in our simplicity   10
Among the woods and fields, we love you well,
Joanna ! and I guess, since you have been
So distant from us now for two long years,
That you will gladly listen to discourse,
However trivial, if you thence be taught
That they, with whom you once were happy, talk
Familiarly of you and of old times.
    While I was seated, now some ten days past,
Beneath those lofty firs, that overtop
Their ancient neighbour, the old steeple-tower,   20
The Vicar from his gloomy house hard by
Came forth to greet me; and when he had asked,
" How fares Joanna, that wild - hearted Maid !
And when will she return to us ? " he paused;
And, after short exchange of village news,
He with grave looks demanded, for what cause,
Reviving obsolete idolatry,
I, like a Runic Priest, in characters
Of formidable size had chiselled out
Some uncouth name upon the native rock,
Above the Rotha, by the forest-side.   31
— Now, by those dear immunities of heart
Engendered between malice and true love,
I was not loth to be so catechised,
And this was my reply: — " As it befell,
One summer morning we had walked abroad
At break of day, Joanna and myself.
— 'T was that delightful season when the broom,

Full-flowered, and visible on every steep,
Along the copses runs in veins of gold. 40
Our pathway led us on to Rotha's banks;
And when we came in front of that tall rock
That eastward looks, I there stopped short
  — and stood
Tracing the lofty barrier with my eye
From base to summit; such delight I found
To note in shrub and tree, in stone and
  flower
That intermixture of delicious hues,
Along so vast a surface, all at once,
In one impression, by connecting force
Of their own beauty, imaged in the heart.
— When I had gazed perhaps two minutes'
  space,   51
Joanna, looking in my eyes, beheld
That ravishment of mine, and laughed
  aloud.
The Rock, like something starting from a
  sleep,
Took up the Lady's voice, and laughed
  again;
That ancient Woman seated on Helm-crag
Was ready with her cavern; Hammar-scar,
And the tall Steep of Silver-how, sent forth
A noise of laughter; southern Loughrigg
  heard,
And Fairfield answered with a mountain
  tone;   60
Helvellyn far into the clear blue sky
Carried the Lady's voice, — old Skiddaw
  blew
His speaking-trumpet; — back out of the
  clouds
Of Glaramara southward came the voice;
And Kirkstone tossed it from his misty
  head.
— Now whether (said I to our cordial
  Friend,
Who in the hey-day of astonishment
Smiled in my face) this were in simple
  truth
A work accomplished by the brotherhood
Of ancient mountains, or my ear was
  touched   70
With dreams and visionary impulses
To me alone imparted, sure I am
That there was a loud uproar in the hills.
And, while we both were listening, to my
  side
The fair Joanna drew, as if she wished
To shelter from some object of her fear.
— And hence, long afterwards, when eight-
  een moons

Were wasted, as I chanced to walk alone
Beneath this rock, at sunrise, on a calm
And silent morning, I sat down, and there,
In memory of affections old and true,   81
I chiselled out in those rude characters
Joanna's name deep in the living stone: —
And I, and all who dwell by my fireside,
Have called the lovely rock, JOANNA'S
  ROCK."

III

It is not accurate that the Eminence here al-
luded to could be seen from our orchard-seat.
It rises above the road by the side of Gras-
mere lake, towards Keswick, and its name is
Stone-Arthur.

THERE is an Eminence, — of these our
  hills
The last that parleys with the setting sun;
We can behold it from our orchard-seat;
And, when at evening we pursue our walk
Along the public way, this Peak, so high
Above us, and so distant in its height,
Is visible; and often seems to send
Its own deep quiet to restore our hearts.
The meteors make of it a favourite haunt:
The star of Jove, so beautiful and large
In the mid heavens, is never half so fair
As when he shines above it.   'T is in truth
The loneliest place we have among the
  clouds.
And She who dwells with me, whom I have
  loved
With such communion, that no place on
  earth
Can ever be a solitude to me,
Hath to this lonely Summit given my
  Name.

IV

The character of the eastern shore of Gras-
mere lake is quite changed, since these verses
were written, by the public road being carried
along its side. The friends spoken of were
Coleridge and my Sister, and the fact occurred
strictly as recorded.

A NARROW girdle of rough stones and
  crags,
A rude and natural causeway, interposed
Between the water and a winding slope
Of copse and thicket, leaves the eastern
  shore
Of Grasmere safe in its own privacy:

And there myself and two belovèd Friends,
One calm September morning, ere the mist
Had altogether yielded to the sun,
Sauntered on this retired and difficult way.
—— Ill suits the road with one in haste;
   but we   10
Played with our time; and, as we strolled
   along,
It was our occupation to observe
Such objects as the waves had tossed
   ashore —
Feather, or leaf, or weed, or withered
   bough,
Each on the other heaped, along the line
Of the dry wreck. And, in our vacant
   mood,
Not seldom did we stop to watch some
   tuft
Of dandelion seed or thistle's beard,
That skimmed the surface of the dead calm
   lake,
Suddenly halting now — a lifeless stand ! 20
And starting off again with freak as sudden;
In all its sportive wanderings, all the while,
Making report of an invisible breeze
That was its wings, its chariot, and its
   horse,
Its playmate, rather say, its moving soul.
—— And often, trifling with a privilege
Alike indulged to all, we paused, one now,
And now the other, to point out, perchance
To pluck, some flower or water-weed, too
   fair
Either to be divided from the place   30
On which it grew, or to be left alone
To its own beauty. Many such there are,
Fair ferns and flowers, and chiefly that tall
   fern,
So stately, of the queen Osmunda named;
Plant lovelier, in its own retired abode
On Grasmere's beach, than Naiad by the
   side
Of Grecian brook, or Lady of the Mere,
Sole-sitting by the shores of old romance.
— So fared we that bright morning: from
   the fields
Meanwhile, a noise was heard, the busy
   mirth   40
Of reapers, men and women, boys and girls.
Delighted much to listen to those sounds,
And feeding thus our fancies, we advanced
Along the indented shore; when suddenly,
Through a thin veil of glittering haze was
   seen
Before us, on a point of jutting land,
The tall and upright figure of a Man

Attired in peasant's garb, who stood alone,
Angling beside the margin of the lake.
" Improvident and reckless," we exclaimed,
" The Man must be, who thus can lose a
   day   51
Of the mid harvest, when the labourer's
   hire
Is ample, and some little might be stored
Wherewith to cheer him in the winter time."
Thus talking of that Peasant, we approached
Close to the spot where with his rod and
   line
He stood alone; whereat he turned his
   head
To greet us — and we saw a Man worn
   down
By sickness, gaunt and lean, with sunken
   cheeks   59
And wasted limbs, his legs so long and lean
That for my single self I looked at them,
Forgetful of the body they sustained. —
Too weak to labour in the harvest field,
The Man was using his best skill to gain
A pittance from the dead unfeeling lake
That knew not of his wants. I will not say
What thoughts immediately were ours, nor
   how
The happy idleness of that sweet morn,
With all its lovely images, was changed
To serious musing and to self-reproach.   70
Nor did we fail to see within ourselves
What need there is to be reserved in speech,
And temper all our thoughts with charity.
— Therefore, unwilling to forget that day,
My Friend, Myself, and She who then re-
   ceived
The same admonishment, have called the
   place
By a memorial name, uncouth indeed
As e'er by mariner was given to bay
Or foreland, on a new-discovered coast;
And POINT RASH-JUDGMENT is the name
   it bears.

V

TO M. H.

1799. 1800

The pool alluded to is in Rydal Upper Park.

OUR walk was far among the ancient trees:
There was no road, nor any woodman's
   path;
But a thick umbrage — checking the wild
   growth

Of weed and sapling, along soft green turf
Beneath the branches — of itself had made
A track, that brought us to a slip of lawn,
And a small bed of water in the woods.
All round this pool both flocks and herds
    might drink
On its firm margin, even as from a well,
Or some stone-basin which the herdsman's
    hand
Had shaped for their refreshment; nor did
    sun,
Or wind from any quarter, ever come,
But as a blessing to this calm recess,
This glade of water and this one green
    field.
The spot was made by Nature for herself;
The travellers know it not, and 't will re-
    main
Unknown to them; but it is beautiful;
And if a man should plant his cottage near,
Should sleep beneath the shelter of its trees,
And blend its waters with his daily meal,
He would so love it, that in his death-hour
Its image would survive among his thoughts:
And therefore, my sweet MARY, this still
    Nook,
With all its beeches, we have named from
    You !

THE WATERFALL AND THE EGLANTINE

1800. 1800

Suggested nearer to Grasmere, on the same
mountain track as that referred to in the fol-
lowing Note. The Eglantine remained many
years afterwards, but is now gone.

I

" BEGONE, thou fond presumptuous Elf,"
Exclaimed an angry Voice,
" Nor dare to thrust thy foolish self
Between me and my choice ! "
A small Cascade fresh swoln with snows
Thus threatened a poor Briar-rose,
That, all bespattered with his foam,
And dancing high and dancing low,
Was living, as a child might know,
In an unhappy home.   10

II

" Dost thou presume my course to block ?
Off, off ! or, puny Thing !

I 'll hurl thee headlong with the rock
To which thy fibres cling."
The Flood was tyrannous and strong;
The patient Briar suffered long,
Nor did he utter groan or sigh,
Hoping the danger would be past;
But, seeing no relief, at last,
He ventured to reply.   20

III

" Ah ! " said the Briar, " blame me not;
Why should we dwell in strife ?
We who in this sequestered spot
Once lived a happy life !
You stirred me on my rocky bed —
What pleasure through my veins you spread
The summer long, from day to day,
My leaves you freshened and bedewed;
Nor was it common gratitude
That did your cares repay.   30

IV

" When spring came on with bud and
    bell,
Among these rocks did I
Before you hang my wreaths to tell
That gentle days were nigh !
And in the sultry summer hours,
I sheltered you with leaves and flowers;
And in my leaves — now shed and gone,
The linnet lodged, and for us two
Chanted his pretty songs, when you
Had little voice or none.   40

V

" But now proud thoughts are in your
    breast —
What grief is mine you see,
Ah ! would you think, even yet how blest
Together we might be !
Though of both leaf and flower bereft,
Some ornaments to me are left —
Rich store of scarlet hips is mine,
With which I, in my humble way,
Would deck you many a winter day,
A happy Eglantine ! "   50

VI

What more he said I cannot tell,
The Torrent down the rocky dell
Came thundering loud and fast;
I listened, nor aught else could hear;
The Briar quaked — and much I fear
Those accents were his last.

THE OAK AND THE BROOM

A PASTORAL

1800. 1800

Suggested upon the mountain pathway that leads from Upper Rydal to Grasmere. The ponderous block of stone which is mentioned in the poem remains, I believe, to this day, a good way up Nab-Scar. Broom grows under it, and in many places on the side of the precipice.

I

His simple truths did Andrew glean
Beside the babbling rills;
A careful student he had been
Among the woods and hills.
One winter's night, when through the trees
The wind was roaring, on his knees
His youngest born did Andrew hold:
And while the rest, a ruddy quire,
Were seated round their blazing fire,
This Tale the Shepherd told.   10

II

" I saw a crag, a lofty stone
As ever tempest beat !
Out of its head an Oak had grown,
A Broom out of its feet.
The time was March, a cheerful noon —
The thaw-wind, with the breath of June,
Breathed gently from the warm south-west:
When, in a voice sedate with age,
This Oak, a giant and a sage,
His neighbour thus addressed : —   20

III

" ' Eight weary weeks, through rock and clay,
Along this mountain's edge,
The Frost hath wrought both night and day,
Wedge driving after wedge.
Look up ! and think, above your head
What trouble, surely, will be bred;
Last night I heard a crash — 't is true,
The splinters took another road —
I see them yonder — what a load
For such a Thing as you !   30

IV

" ' You are preparing as before,
To deck your slender shape;
And yet, just three years back — no more —
You had a strange escape:

Down from yon cliff a fragment broke;
It thundered down, with fire and smoke,
And hitherward pursued its way;
This ponderous block was caught by me,
And o'er your head, as you may see,
'T is hanging to this day !   40

V

" ' If breeze or bird to this rough steep
Your kind's first seed did bear;
The breeze had better been asleep,
The bird caught in a snare:
For you and your green twigs decoy
The little witless shepherd-boy
To come and slumber in your bower;
And, trust me, on some sultry noon,
Both you and he, Heaven knows how soon
Will perish in one hour.   50

VI

" ' From me this friendly warning take ' —
The Broom began to doze,
And thus, to keep herself awake,
Did gently interpose:
' My thanks for your discourse are due;
That more than what you say is true,
I know, and I have known it long;
Frail is the bond by which we hold
Our being, whether young or old,
Wise, foolish, weak, or strong.   60

VII

" ' Disasters, do the best we can,
Will reach both great and small;
And he is oft the wisest man,
Who is not wise at all.
For me, why should I wish to roam ?
This spot is my paternal home,
It is my pleasant heritage;
My father many a happy year,
Spread here his careless blossoms, here
Attained a good old age.   70

VIII

" ' Even such as his may be my lot.
What cause have I to haunt
My heart with terrors ? Am I not
In truth a favoured plant !
On me such bounty Summer pours,
That I am covered o'er with flowers;
And, when the Frost is in the sky,
My branches are so fresh and gay
That you might look at me and say,
This Plant can never die.   80

IX

"'The butterfly, all green and gold,
To me hath often flown,
Here in my blossoms to behold
Wings lovely as his own.
When grass is chill with rain or dew,
Beneath my shade, the mother-ewe
Lies with her infant lamb; I see
The love they to each other make,
And the sweet joy which they partake,
It is a joy to me.' 90

X

" Her voice was blithe, her heart was light:
The Broom might have pursued
Her speech, until the stars of night
Their journey had renewed;
But in the branches of the oak
Two ravens now began to croak
Their nuptial song, a gladsome air;
And to her own green bower the breeze
That instant brought two stripling bees
To rest, or murmur there. 100

XI

" One night, my Children ! from the north
There came a furious blast;
At break of day I ventured forth,
And near the cliff I passed.
The storm had fallen upon the Oak,
And struck him with a mighty stroke,
And whirled, and whirled him far away;
And, in one hospitable cleft,
The little careless Broom was left
To live for many a day." 110

HART-LEAP WELL

1800. 1800

Written at Town-end, Grasmere. The first eight stanzas were composed extempore one winter evening in the cottage ; when, after having tired myself with labouring at an awkward passage in "The Brothers," I started with a sudden impulse to this to get rid of the other, and finished it in a day or two. My Sister and I had past the place a few weeks before in our wild winter journey from Sockburn on the banks of the Tees to Grasmere. A peasant whom we met near the spot told us the story so far as concerned the name of the Well, and the Hart, and pointed out the Stones. Both the Stones and the Well are objects that may easily be missed ; the tradition by this time may be extinct in the neighbourhood : the man who related it to us was very old.

Hart-Leap Well is a small spring of water, about five miles from Richmond in Yorkshire, and near the side of the road that leads from Richmond to Askrigg. Its name is derived from a remarkable Chase, the memory of which is preserved by the monuments spoken of in the second Part of the following Poem, which monuments do now exist as I have there described them.

PART FIRST

THE Knight had ridden down from Wensley Moor
With the slow motion of a summer's cloud,
And now, as he approached a vassal's door,
" Bring forth another horse ! " he cried aloud.

" Another horse ! " — That shout the vassal heard
And saddled his best Steed, a comely grey;
Sir Walter mounted him; he was the third
Which he had mounted on that glorious day.

Joy sparkled in the prancing courser's eyes;
The horse and horseman are a happy pair; 10
But, though Sir Walter like a falcon flies,
There is a doleful silence in the air.

A rout this morning left Sir Walter's Hall,
That as they galloped made the echoes roar;
But horse and man are vanished, one and all;
Such race, I think, was never seen before.

Sir Walter, restless as a veering wind,
Calls to the few tired dogs that yet remain:
Blanch, Swift, and Music, noblest of their kind,
Follow, and up the weary mountain strain. 20

The knight hallooed, he cheered and chid them on
With suppliant gestures and upbraidings stern;
But breath and eyesight fail; and, one by one,
The dogs are stretched among the mountain fern.

Where is the throng, the tumult of the race ?
The bugles that so joyfully were blown ?
— This chase it looks not like an earthly chase;
Sir Walter and the Hart are left alone.

The poor Hart toils along the mountain-
side;
I will not stop to tell how far he fled,   30
Nor will I mention by what death he died;
But now the Knight beholds him lying dead.

Dismounting, then, he leaned against a
thorn;
He had no follower, dog, nor man, nor boy:
He neither cracked his whip, nor blew his
horn,
But gazed upon the spoil with silent joy.

Close to the thorn on which Sir Walter
leaned,
Stood his dumb partner in this glorious feat;
Weak as a lamb the hour that it is yeaned;
And white with foam as if with cleaving
sleet.   40

Upon his side the Hart was lying stretched:
His nostril touched a spring beneath a hill,
And with the last deep groan his breath had
fetched
The waters of the spring were trembling
still.

And now, too happy for repose or rest,
(Never had living man such joyful lot!)
Sir Walter walked all round, north, south,
and west,
And gazed and gazed upon that darling spot.

And climbing up the hill — (it was at least
Four roods of sheer ascent) Sir Walter
found   50
Three several hoof-marks which the hunted
Beast
Had left imprinted on the grassy ground.

Sir Walter wiped his face, and cried, " Till
now
Such sight was never seen by human eyes:
Three leaps have borne him from this lofty
brow,
Down to the very fountain where he lies.

" I 'll build a pleasure-house upon this spot,
And a small arbour, made for rural joy;
'T will be the traveller's shed, the pilgrim's
cot,   59
A place of love for damsels that are coy.

" A cunning artist will I have to frame
A basin for that fountain in the dell!

And they who do make mention of the
same,
From this day forth, shall call it HART-
LEAP WELL.

" And, gallant Stag! to make thy praises
known,
Another monument shall here be raised;
Three several pillars, each a rough-hewn
stone,
And planted where thy hoofs the turf have
grazed.

" And, in the summer-time when days are
long,
I will come hither with my Paramour;   70
And with the dancers and the minstrel's
song
We will make merry in that pleasant bower.

" Till the foundations of the mountains fail
My mansion with its arbour shall endure; —
The joy of them who till the fields of
Swale,
And them who dwell among the woods of
Ure!"

Then home he went, and left the Hart,
stone-dead,
With breathless nostrils stretched above the
spring.
— Soon did the Knight perform what he
had said;   79
And far and wide the fame thereof did ring.

Ere thrice the Moon into her port had
steered,
A cup of stone received the living well;
Three pillars of rude stone Sir Walter
reared,
And built a house of pleasure in the dell.

And near the fountain, flowers of stature
tall
With trailing plants and trees were inter-
twined, —
Which soon composed a little sylvan hall,
A leafy shelter from the sun and wind.

And thither, when the summer days were
long,
Sir Walter led his wondering Paramour;   90
And with the dancers and the minstrel's
song
Made merriment within that pleasant bower

The Knight, Sir Walter, died in course of
time,
And his bones lie in his paternal vale. —
But there is matter for a second rhyme,
And I to this would add another tale.

PART SECOND

THE moving accident is not my trade;
To freeze the blood I have no ready arts:
'T is my delight, alone in summer shade,
To pipe a simple song for thinking hearts.

As I from Hawes to Richmond did repair,
It chanced that I saw standing in a dell
Three aspens at three corners of a square;
And one, not four yards distant, near a well.

What this imported I could ill divine:
And, pulling now the rein my horse to stop,
I saw three pillars standing in a line, — 11
The last stone-pillar on a dark hill-top.

The trees were grey, with neither arms nor
head;
Half wasted the square mound of tawny
green;
So that you just might say, as then I said,
"Here in old time the hand of man hath
been."

I looked upon the hill both far and near,
More doleful place did never eye survey;
It seemed as if the spring-time came not
here,
And Nature here were willing to decay. 20

I stood in various thoughts and fancies lost,
When one, who was in shepherd's garb
attired,
Came up the hollow: — him did I accost,
And what this place might be I then
inquired.

The Shepherd stopped, and that same story
told
Which in my former rhyme I have re-
hearsed.
"A jolly place," said he, "in times of old !
But something ails it now: the spot is curst.

"You see these lifeless stumps of aspen
wood —
Some say that they are beeches, others
elms — 30

These were the bower; and here a mansion
stood,
The finest palace of a hundred realms !

"The arbour does its own condition tell;
You see the stones, the fountain, and the
stream;
But as to the great Lodge ! you might as
well
Hunt half a day for a forgotten dream.

"There 's neither dog nor heifer, horse nor
sheep,
Will wet his lips within that cup of stone;
And oftentimes, when all are fast asleep, 39
This water doth send forth a dolorous groan.

"Some say that here a murder has been
done,
And blood cries out for blood: but, for my
part,
I 've guessed, when I 've been sitting in the
sun,
That it was all for that unhappy Hart.

"What thoughts must through the crea-
ture's brain have past !
Even from the topmost stone, upon the
steep,
Are but three bounds — and look, Sir, at
this last —
O Master ! it has been a cruel leap.

"For thirteen hours he ran a desperate
race;
And in my simple mind we cannot tell 50
What cause the Hart might have to love
this place,
And come and make his deathbed near the
well.

"Here on the grass perhaps asleep he sank,
Lulled by the fountain in the summer-
tide;
This water was perhaps the first he drank
When he had wandered from his mother's
side.

"In April here beneath the flowering thorn
He heard the birds their morning carols
sing;
And he, perhaps, for aught we know, was
born
Not half a furlong from that self-same
spring. 60

"Now, here is neither grass nor pleasant
  shade;
The sun on drearier hollow never shone;
So will it be, as I have often said,
Till trees, and stones, and fountain, all are
  gone."

"Grey-headed Shepherd, thou hast spoken
  well;
Small difference lies between thy creed and
  mine:
This Beast not unobserved by Nature fell;
His death was mourned by sympathy divine.

"The Being, that is in the clouds and air,
That is in the green leaves among the
  groves,   70
Maintains a deep and reverential care
For the unoffending creatures whom he
  loves.

"The pleasure-house is dust: — behind,
  before;
This is no common waste, no common
  gloom;
But Nature, in due course of time, once
  more
Shall here put on her beauty and her bloom.

"She leaves these objects to a slow decay,
That what we are, and have been, may be
  known;
But at the coming of the milder day,
These monuments shall all be overgrown. 80

"One lesson, Shepherd, let us two divide,
Taught both by what she shows, and what
  conceals;
Never to blend our pleasure or our pride
With sorrow of the meanest thing that
  feels."

"'T IS SAID, THAT SOME HAVE DIED FOR LOVE"

1800. 1800

'T is said, that some have died for love:
And here and there a churchyard grave is
  found
In the cold north's unhallowed ground,
Because the wretched man himself had slain,
His love was such a grievous pain.
And there is one whom I five years have
  known;

He dwells alone
Upon Helvellyn's side:
He loved — the pretty Barbara died;
And thus he makes his moan: 10
Three years had Barbara in her grave been
  laid
When thus his moan he made:

"Oh, move, thou Cottage, from behind
  that oak !
Or let the aged tree uprooted lie,
That in some other way yon smoke
May mount into the sky !
The clouds pass on; they from the heavens
  depart.
I look — the sky is empty space;
I know not what I trace;
But when I cease to look, my hand is on
  my heart.   20

"Oh ! what a weight is in these shades !
  Ye leaves,
That murmur once so dear, when will it
  cease ?
Your sound my heart of rest bereaves,
It robs my heart of peace.
Thou Thrush, that singest loud — and loud
  and free,
Into yon row of willows flit,
Upon that alder sit;
Or sing another song, or choose another
  tree.

"Roll back, sweet Rill ! back to thy
  mountain-bounds,
And there for ever be thy waters chained !
For thou dost haunt the air with sounds 31
That cannot be sustained;
If still beneath that pine - tree's ragged
  bough
Headlong yon waterfall must come,
Oh let it then be dumb !
Be anything, sweet Rill, but that which
  thou art now.

"Thou Eglantine, so bright with sunny
  showers,
Proud as a rainbow spanning half the vale,
Thou one fair shrub, oh ! shed thy flowers,
And stir not in the gale.   40
For thus to see thee nodding in the air,
To see thy arch thus stretch and bend,
Thus rise and thus descend, —
Disturbs me till the sight is more than I can
  bear."

The Man who makes this feverish complaint
Is one of giant stature, who could dance
Equipped from head to foot in iron mail.
Ah gentle Love ! if ever thought was thine
To store up kindred hours for me, thy face
Turn from me, gentle Love ! nor let me
    walk   50
Within the sound of Emma's voice, nor
    know
Such happiness as I have known to-day.

THE CHILDLESS FATHER

1800. 1800

Written at Town-end, Grasmere. When I
was a child at Cockermouth, no funeral took
place without a basin filled with sprigs of box-
wood being placed upon a table covered with
a white cloth in front of the house. The hunt-
ings on foot, in which the old man is supposed
to join as here described, were of common, al-
most habitual, occurrence in our vales when I
was a boy ; and the people took much delight in
them. They are now less frequent.

" Up, Timothy, up with your staff and away !
Not a soul in the village this morning will
    stay;
The hare has just started from Hamilton's
    grounds,
And Skiddaw is glad with the. cry of the
    hounds."

— Of coats and of jackets grey, scarlet, and
    green,
On the slopes of the pastures all colours
    were seen;
With their comely blue aprons, and caps
    white as snow,
The girls on the hills made a holiday show.

Fresh sprigs of green box-wood, not six
    months before,
Filled the funeral basin at Timothy's door;
A coffin through Timothy's threshold had
    past;
One Child did it bear, and that Child was
    his last.

Now fast up the dell came the noise and the
    fray,
The horse and the horn, and the hark !
    hark away !
Old Timothy took up his staff, and he shut
With a leisurely motion the door of his hut.

Perhaps to himself at that moment he said;
" The key I must take, for my Ellen is dead."
But of this in my ears not a word did he
    speak;
And he went to the chase with a tear on his
    cheek.

SONG

FOR THE WANDERING JEW

1800. 1800

Though the torrents from their fountains
Roar down many a craggy steep,
Yet they find among the mountains
Resting-places calm and deep.

Clouds that love through air to hasten,
Ere the storm its fury stills,
Helmet-like themselves will fasten
On the heads of towering hills.

What, if through the frozen centre
Of the Alps the Chamois bound,
Yet he has a home to enter
In some nook of chosen ground:

And the Sea-horse, though the ocean
Yield him no domestic cave,
Slumbers without sense of motion,
Couched upon the rocking wave.

If on windy days the Raven
Gambol like a dancing skiff,
Not the less she loves her haven
In the bosom of the cliff.

The fleet Ostrich, till day closes,
Vagrant over desert sands,
Brooding on her eggs reposes
When chill night that care demands.

Day and night my toils redouble,
Never nearer to the goal;
Night and day, I feel the trouble
Of the Wanderer in my soul.

RURAL ARCHITECTURE

1800. 1800

Written at Town-end, Grasmere. These
structures, as every one knows, are common
amongst our hills, being built by shepherds, as
conspicuous marks, and occasionally by boys in
sport.

There 's George Fisher, Charles Fleming,
　and Reginald Shore,
Three rosy-cheeked school-boys, the highest
　not more
Than the height of a counsellor's bag;
To the top of GREAT How did it please
　them to climb:
And there they built up, without mortar or
　lime,
A Man on the peak of the crag.

They built him of stones gathered up as
　they lay:
They built him and christened him all in
　one day,
An urchin both vigorous and hale;
And so without scruple they called him
　Ralph Jones.
Now Ralph is renowned for the length of
　his bones;
The Magog of Legberthwaite dale.

Just half a week after, the wind sallied forth,
And, in anger or merriment, out of the north,
Coming on with a terrible pother,
From the peak of the crag blew the giant
　away.
And what did these school-boys? — The
　very next day
They went and they built up another.

— Some little I've seen of blind boisterous
　works
By Christian disturbers more savage than
　Turks,
Spirits busy to do and undo:
At remembrance whereof my blood some-
　times will flag;
Then, light-hearted Boys, to the top of the
　crag!
And I'll build up a giant with you.

ELLEN IRWIN

OR, THE BRAES OF KIRTLE

1798(?). 1800

It may be worth while to observe that as
there are Scotch Poems on this subject in
simple ballad strain, I thought it would be
both presumptuous and superfluous to attempt
treating it in the same way; and, accordingly,
I chose a construction of stanza quite new in
our language; in fact, the same as that of
Bürger's *Leonora*, except that the first and
third lines do not, in my stanzas, rhyme. At
the outset I threw out a classical image to pre-
pare the reader for the style in which I meant
to treat the story, and so to preclude all com-
parison.

FAIR Ellen Irwin, when she sate
Upon the braes of Kirtle,
Was lovely as a Grecian maid
Adorned with wreaths of myrtle;
Young Adam Bruce beside her lay,
And there did they beguile the day
With love and gentle speeches,
Beneath the budding beeches.

From many knights and many squires
The Bruce had been selected;　　　10
And Gordon, fairest of them all,
By Ellen was rejected.
Sad tidings to that noble Youth!
For it may be proclaimed with truth,
If Bruce hath loved sincerely,
That Gordon loves as dearly.

But what are Gordon's form and face,
His shattered hopes and crosses,
To them, 'mid Kirtle's pleasant braes,
Reclined on flowers and mosses?　　20
Alas that ever he was born!
The Gordon, couched behind a thorn,
Sees them and their caressing;
Beholds them blest and blessing.

Proud Gordon, maddened by the thoughts
That through his brain are travelling,
Rushed forth, and at the heart of Bruce
He launched a deadly javelin!
Fair Ellen saw it as it came,
And, starting up to meet the same,　　30
Did with her body cover
The Youth, her chosen lover.

And, falling into Bruce's arms,
Thus died the beauteous Ellen,
Thus, from the heart of her True-love,
The mortal spear repelling.
And Bruce, as soon as he had slain
The Gordon, sailed away to Spain;
And fought with rage incessant
Against the Moorish crescent.　　40

But many days, and many months,
And many years ensuing,
This wretched Knight did vainly seek
The death that he was wooing.

So, coming his last help to crave,
Heart-broken, upon Ellen's grave
His body he extended,
And there his sorrow ended.

Now ye, who willingly have heard
The tale I have been telling,   50
May in Kirkconnel churchyard view
The grave of lovely Ellen:
By Ellen's side the Bruce is laid;
And, for the stone upon his head,
May no rude hand deface it,
And its forlorn 𝔥𝔦𝔠 𝔧𝔞𝔠𝔢𝔱!

ANDREW JONES

1798(?). 1800

I HATE that Andrew Jones; he'll breed
His children up to waste and pillage.
I wish the press-gang or the drum
Would, with its rattling music, come,
And sweep him from the village!

I said not this, because he loves
Through the long day to swear and tipple;
But for the poor dear sake of one
To whom a foul deed he had done,
A friendless man, a travelling cripple!   10

For this poor crawling helpless wretch,
Some horseman who was passing by,
A penny on the ground had thrown;
But the poor cripple was alone
And could not stoop — no help was nigh.

Inch-thick the dust lay on the ground
For it had long been droughty weather;
So with his staff the cripple wrought
Among the dust till he had brought
The half-pennies together.   20

It chanced that Andrew passed that way
Just at the time; and there he found
The cripple in the mid-day heat
Standing alone, and at his feet
He saw the penny on the ground.

He stooped and took the penny up:
And when the cripple nearer drew,
Quoth Andrew, " Under half-a-crown,
What a man finds is all his own,
And so, my Friend, good-day to you."   30

And *hence* I say, that Andrew's boys
Will all be trained to waste and pillage;
And wished the press-gang, or the drum
Would, with its rattling music, come,
And sweep him from the village.

THE TWO THIEVES

OR, THE LAST STAGE OF AVARICE

1800. 1800

This is described from the life, as I was in
the habit of observing when a boy at Hawks-
head School. Daniel was more than eighty
years older than myself when he was daily,
thus occupied, under my notice. No book could
have so early taught me to think of the changes
to which human life is subject; and while
looking at him I could not but say to myself —
we may, any one of us, I or the happiest of my
playmates, live to become still more the object
of pity than this old man, this half-doating
pilferer!

O NOW that the genius of Bewick were mine,
And the skill which he learned on the banks
     of the Tyne.
Then the Muses might deal with me just as
     they chose,
For I'd take my last leave both of verse
     and of prose.

What feats would I work with my magical
     hand!
Book-learning and books should be banished
     the land:
And, for hunger and thirst and such trouble-
     some calls,
Every ale-house should then have a feast
     on its walls.

The traveller would hang his wet clothes
     on a chair;
Let them smoke, let them burn, not a straw
     would he care!   10
For the Prodigal Son, Joseph's Dream and
     his sheaves,
Oh, what would they be to my tale of two
     Thieves?

The One, yet unbreeched, is not three birth-
     days old,
His Grandsire that age more than thirty
     times told;

There are ninety good seasons of fair and
  foul weather
Between them, and both go a - pilfering
  together.

With chips is the carpenter strewing his
  floor ?
Is a cart-load of turf at an old woman's
  door ?
Old Daniel his hand to the treasure will
  slide !
And his Grandson 's as busy at work by his
  side.   20

Old Daniel begins; he stops short — and
  his eye,
Through the lost look of dotage, is cunning
  and sly:
'T is a look which at this time is hardly his
  own,
But tells a plain tale of the days that are
  flown.

He once had a heart which was moved by
  the wires
Of manifold pleasures and many desires:
And what if he cherished his purse? 'T was
  no more
Than treading a path trod by thousands
  before.

'T was a path trod by thousands; but Daniel
  is one
Who went something farther than others
  have gone,   30
And now with old Daniel you see how it
  fares;
You see to what end he has brought his
  grey hairs.

The pair sally forth hand in hand: ere the
  sun
Has peered o'er the beeches, their work is
  begun:
And yet, into whatever sin they may fall,
This child but half knows it, and that, not
  at all.

They hunt through the streets with delib-
  erate tread,
And each, in his turn, becomes leader or led;
And, wherever they carry their plots and
  their wiles,
Every face in the village is dimpled with
  smiles.   40

Neither checked by the rich nor the needy
  they roam;
For the grey-headed Sire has a daughter at
  home,
Who will gladly repair all the damage
  that 's done;
And three, were it asked, would be ren-
  dered for one.

Old Man ! whom so oft I with pity have eyed,
I love thee, and love the sweet Boy at thy
  side:
Long yet may'st thou live! for a teacher we
  see
That lifts up the veil of our nature in thee.

A CHARACTER

1797(?). 1800

  The principal features are taken from that
of my friend Robert Jones.

I MARVEL how Nature could ever find space
For so many strange contrasts in one human
  face:
There 's thought and no thought, and there 's
  paleness and bloom
And bustle and sluggishness, pleasure and
  gloom.

There 's weakness, and strength both re-
  dundant and vain;
Such strength as, if ever affliction and pain
Could pierce through a temper that 's soft to
  disease,
Would be rational peace — a philosopher's
  ease.

There 's indifference, alike when he fails or
  succeeds,
And attention full ten times as much as
  there needs;
Pride where there 's no envy, there 's so
  much of joy;
And mildness, and spirit both forward and
  coy.

There 's freedom, and sometimes a diffident
  stare
Of shame scarcely seeming to know that
  she 's there,
There 's virtue, the title it surely may claim,
Yet wants heaven knows what to be worthy
  the name.

This picture from nature may seem to depart,
Yet the Man would at once run away with your heart;
And I for five centuries right gladly would be
Such an odd, such a kind happy creature as he.

INSCRIPTIONS

FOR THE SPOT WHERE THE HERMITAGE STOOD ON ST. HERBERT'S ISLAND, DERWENTWATER

1800. 1800

IF thou in the dear love of some one Friend
Hast been so happy that thou know'st what thoughts
Will sometimes in the happiness of love
Make the heart sink, then wilt thou reverence
This quiet spot; and, Stranger! not unmoved
Wilt thou behold this shapeless heap of stones,
The desolate ruins of St. Herbert's Cell.
Here stood his threshold; here was spread the roof
That sheltered him, a self-secluded Man,
After long exercise in social cares
And offices humane, intent to adore
The Deity, with undistracted mind,
And meditate on everlasting things,
In utter solitude. — But he had left
A Fellow-labourer, whom the good Man loved
As his own soul. And, when with eye upraised
To heaven he knelt before the crucifix,
While o'er the lake the cataract of Lodore
Pealed to his orisons, and when he paced
Along the beach of this small isle and thought
Of his Companion, he would pray that both
(Now that their earthly duties were fulfilled)
Might die in the same moment. Nor in vain
So prayed he: — as our chronicles report,
Though here the Hermit numbered his last day
Far from St. Cuthbert his belovèd Friend,
Those holy Men both died in the same hour.

WRITTEN WITH A PENCIL UPON A STONE IN THE WALL OF THE HOUSE (AN OUTHOUSE), ON THE ISLAND AT GRASMERE

1800. 1800

RUDE is this Edifice, and Thou hast seen
Buildings, albeit rude, that have maintained
Proportions more harmonious, and approached
To closer fellowship with ideal grace.
But take it in good part: — alas! the poor
Vitruvius of our village had no help
From the great City; never, upon leaves
Of red Morocco folio, saw displayed,
In long succession, pre-existing ghosts   9
Of Beauties yet unborn — the rustic Lodge
Antique, and Cottage with verandah graced,
Nor lacking, for fit company, alcove,
Green-house, shell-grot, and moss-lined hermitage.
Thou see'st a homely Pile, yet to these walls
The heifer comes in the snow-storm, and here
The new-dropped lamb finds shelter from the wind.
And hither does one Poet sometimes row
His pinnace, a small vagrant barge, up-piled
With plenteous store of heath and withered fern,
(A lading which he with his sickle cuts,   20
Among the mountains) and beneath this roof
He makes his summer couch, and here at noon
Spreads out his limbs, while, yet unshorn, the Sheep,
Panting beneath the burthen of their wool,
Lie round him, even as if they were a part
Of his own Household: nor, while from his bed
He looks, through the open door-place, toward the lake
And to the stirring breezes, does he want
Creations lovely as the work of sleep —
Fair sights, and visions of romantic joy!   30

WRITTEN WITH A SLATE PENCIL UPON A STONE, THE LARGEST OF A HEAP LYING NEAR A DESERTED QUARRY, UPON ONE OF THE ISLANDS AT RYDAL

1800. 1800

STRANGER! this hillock of mis-shapen stones
Is not a Ruin spared or made by time,

Nor, as perchance thou rashly deem'st, the
    Cairn
Of some old British Chief: 't is nothing
    more
Than the rude embryo of a little Dome
Or Pleasure-house, once destined to be
    built
Among the birch-trees of this rocky isle.
But, as it chanced, Sir William having
    learned
That from the shore a full-grown man
    might wade,   9
And make himself a freeman of this spot
At any hour he chose, the prudent Knight
Desisted, and the quarry and the mound
Are monuments of his unfinished task.
The block on which these lines are traced,
    perhaps,
Was once selected as the corner-stone
Of that intended Pile, which would have
    been
Some quaint odd plaything of elaborate
    skill,
So that, I guess, the linnet and the thrush,
And other little builders who dwell here,
Had wondered at the work. But blame
    him not,   20
For old Sir William was a gentle Knight,
Bred in this vale, to which he appertained
With all his ancestry. Then peace to him,
And for the outrage which he had devised
Entire forgiveness ! — But if thou art one
On fire with thy impatience to become
An inmate of these mountains, — if, dis-
    turbed
By beautiful conceptions, thou hast hewn
Out of the quiet rock the elements
Of thy trim Mansion destined soon to blaze
In snow-white splendour, — think again;
    and, taught   31
By old Sir William and his quarry, leave
Thy fragments to the bramble and the
    rose;
There let the vernal slow-worm sun him-
    self,
And let the redbreast hop from stone to
    stone.

THE SPARROW'S NEST

1802. 1807

Written in the Orchard, Town-end, Gras-
mere. At the end of the garden of my father's
house at Cockermouth was a high terrace that
commanded a fine view of the river Derwent
and Cockermouth Castle. This was our favour-
ite play-ground. The terrace-wall, a low one,
was covered with closely-clipt privet and roses,
which gave an almost impervious shelter to
birds that built their nests there. The latter
of these stanzas alludes to one of those nests.

BEHOLD, within the leafy shade,
Those bright blue eggs together laid !
On me the chance-discovered sight
Gleamed like a vision of delight.
I started — seeming to espy
The home and sheltered bed,
The Sparrow's dwelling, which, hard by
My Father's house, in wet or dry
My sister Emmeline and I
    Together visited.

She looked at it and seemed to fear it;
Dreading, tho' wishing, to be near it:
Such heart was in her, being then
A little Prattler among men.
The Blessing of my later years
Was with me when a boy:
She gave me eyes, she gave me ears;
And humble cares, and delicate fears;
A heart, the fountain of sweet tears;
    And love, and thought, and joy.

"PELION AND OSSA FLOURISH SIDE BY SIDE"

1802(?). 1815

PELION and Ossa flourish side by side,
Together in immortal books enrolled:
His ancient dower Olympus hath not sold;
And that inspiring Hill, which "did di-
    vide
Into two ample horns his forehead wide,"
Shines with poetic radiance as of old;
While not an English Mountain we be-
    hold
By the celestial Muses glorified.
Yet round our sea-girt shore they rise in
    crowds:
What was the great Parnassus' self to
    Thee,
Mount Skiddaw? In his natural sover-
    eignty
Our British Hill is nobler far; he shrouds
His double front among Atlantic clouds,
And pours forth streams more sweet than
    Castaly.

THE PRIORESS'S TALE

FROM CHAUCER

1801. 1820

" Call up him who left half told
The story of Cambuscan bold."

In the following Poem no further deviation
from the original has been made than was
necessary for the fluent reading and instant un-
derstanding of the Author: so much, however,
is the language altered since Chaucer's time, es-
pecially in pronunciation, that much was to be
removed, and its place supplied with as little
incongruity as possible. The ancient accent
has been retained in a few conjunctions, as
alsò and *alwày*, from a conviction that such
sprinklings of antiquity would be admitted, by
persons of taste, to have a graceful accordance
with the subject. The fierce bigotry of the
Prioress forms a fine background for her ten-
der-hearted sympathies with the Mother and
Child; and the mode in which the story is told
amply atones for the extravagance of the
miracle.

I

" O LORD, our Lord! how wondrously,"
(quoth she)
" Thy name in this large world is spread
abroad !
For not alone by men of dignity
Thy worship is performed and precious
laud;
But by the mouths of children, gracious
God !
Thy goodness is set forth; they when they
lie
Upon the breast thy name do glorify.

II

" Wherefore in praise, the worthiest that I
may,
Jesu ! of thee, and the white Lily-flower
Which did thee bear, and is a Maid for
aye,   10
To tell a story I will use my power;
Not that I may increase her honour's
dower,
For she herself is honour, and the root
Of goodness, next her Son, our soul's best
boot.

III

" O Mother Maid ! O Maid and Mother
free !
O bush unburnt ! burning in Moses' sight !

That down didst ravish from the Deity,
Through humbleness, the spirit that did
alight
Upon thy heart, whence, through that
glory's might,
Conceivèd was the Father's sapience,   20
Help me to tell it in thy reverence !

IV

" Lady ! thy goodness, thy magnificence,
Thy virtue, and thy great humility,
Surpass all science and all utterance;
For sometimes, Lady ! ere men pray to thee
Thou goest before in thy benignity,
The light to us vouchsafing of thy prayer,
To be our guide unto thy Son so dear.

V

" My knowledge is so weak, O blissful
Queen !
To tell abroad thy mighty worthiness,   30
That I the weight of it may not sustain;
But as a child of twelvemonths old or less,
That laboureth his language to express,
Even so fare I; and therefore, I thee pray,
Guide thou my song which I of thee shall
say.

VI

" There was in Asia, in a mighty town,
'Mong Christian folk, a street where Jews
might be,
Assigned to them and given them for their
own
By a great Lord, for gain and usury,
Hateful to Christ and to his company;   40
And through this street who list might ride
and wend;
Free was it, and unbarred at either end.

VII

" A little school of Christian people stood
Down at the farther end, in which there
were
A nest of children come of Christian blood,
That learned in that school from year to
year
Such sort of doctrine as men usèd there,
That is to say, to sing and read alsò,
As little children in their childhood do.

VIII

" Among these children was a Widow's
son,   50
A little scholar, scarcely seven years old,

Who day by day unto this school hath gone,
And eke, when he the image did behold
Of Jesu's Mother, as he had been told,
This Child was wont to kneel adown and say
Ave Marie, as he goeth by the way.

IX

"This Widow thus her little Son hath taught
Our blissful Lady, Jesu's Mother dear,
To worship aye, and he forgat it not;
For simple infant hath a ready ear.   60
Sweet is the holiness of youth: and hence,
Calling to mind this matter when I may,
Saint Nicholas in my presence standeth aye,
For he so young to Christ did reverence.

X

"This little Child, while in the school he sate
His Primer conning with an earnest cheer,
The whilst the rest their anthem-book repeat
The *Alma Redemptoris* did he hear;
And as he durst he drew him near and near,
And hearkened to the words and to the note,   70
Till the first verse he learned it all by rote.

XI

"This Latin knew he nothing what it said,
For he too tender was of age to know;
But to his comrade he repaired, and prayed
That he the meaning of this song would show,
And unto him declare why men sing so;
This oftentimes, that he might be at ease,
This child did him beseech on his bare knees.

XII

"His Schoolfellow, who elder was than he,
Answered him thus: — 'This song, I have heard say,   80
Was fashioned for our blissful Lady free;
Her to salute, and also her to pray
To be our help upon our dying day:
If there is more in this, I know it not;
Song do I learn, — small grammar I have got.'

XIII

"'And is this song fashioned in reverence
Of Jesu's Mother?' said this Innocent;

'Now, certès, I will use my diligence
To con it all ere Christmas-tide be spent;
Although I for my Primer shall be shent,   90
And shall be beaten three times in an hour,
Our Lady I will praise with all my power.'

XIV

"His Schoolfellow, whom he had so besought,
As they went homeward taught him privily,
And then he sang it well and fearlessly,
From word to word according to the note:
Twice in a day it passèd through his throat;
Homeward and schoolward whensoe'er he went,
On Jesu's Mother fixed was his intent.

XV

"Through all the Jewry (this before said I)   100
This little Child, as he came to and fro,
Full merrily then would he sing and cry,
O *Alma Redemptoris!* high and low:
The sweetness of Christ's Mother piercèd so
His heart, that her to praise, to her to pray,
He cannot stop his singing by the way.

XVI

"The Serpent, Satan, our first foe, that hath
His wasp's nest in Jew's heart, upswelled
      — 'O woe,
O Hebrew people!' said he in his wrath,
'Is it an honest thing? Shall this be so?   110
That such a Boy where'er he lists shall go
In your despite, and sing his hymns and saws,
Which is against the reverence of our laws!'

XVII

"From that day forward have the Jews conspired
Out of the world this Innocent to chase;
And to this end a Homicide they hired,
That in an alley had a privy place,
And, as the Child 'gan to the school to pace,
This cruel Jew him seized, and held him fast
And cut his throat, and in a pit him cast.   120

XVIII

"I say that him into a pit they threw,
A loathsome pit, whence noisome scents exhale;
O cursèd folk! away, ye Herods new!
What may your ill intentions you avail?
Murder will out; certès it will not fail;

Know, that the honour of high God may
. spread,
The blood cries out on your accursèd deed.

XIX

" O Martyr 'stablished in virginity !
Now may'st thou sing for aye before the
    throne,   129
Following the Lamb celestial," quoth she,
" Of which the great Evangelist, Saint John,
In Patmos wrote, who saith of them that go
Before the Lamb singing continually,
That never fleshly woman they did know.

XX

" Now this poor widow waiteth all that
    night
After her little Child, and he came not;
For which, by earliest glimpse of morning
    light,
With face all pale with dread and busy
    thought,
She at the School and elsewhere him hath
    sought
Until thus far she learned, that he had
    been   140
In the Jews' street, and there he last was
    seen.

XXI

" With Mother's pity in her breast enclosed
She goeth, as she were half out of her
    mind,
To every place wherein she hath supposed
By likelihood her little Son to find;
And ever on Christ's Mother meek and kind
She cried, till to the Jewry she was brought,
And him among the accursèd Jews she
    sought.

XXII

" She asketh, and she piteously doth pray
To every Jew that dwelleth in that place 150
To tell her if her child had passed that
    way;
They all said — Nay; but Jesu of his grace
Gave to her thought, that in a little space
She for her Son in that same spot did cry
Where he was cast into a pit hard by.

XXIII

" O thou great God that dost perform thy
    laud
By mouths of Innocents, lo ! here thy
    might;

This gem of chastity, this emerald,
And eke of martyrdom this ruby bright,
There, where with mangled throat he lay
    upright,   160
The *Alma Redemptoris* 'gan to sing,
So loud, that with his voice the place did
    ring.

XXIV

" The Christian folk that through the Jewry
    went
Come to the spot in wonder at the thing;
And hastily they for the Provost sent;
Immediately he came, not tarrying,
And praiseth Christ that is our heavenly
    King,
And eke his Mother, honour of Mankind:
Which done he bade that they the Jews
    should bind.

XXV

" This Child with piteous lamentation then
Was taken up, singing his song alwày; 171
And with procession great and pomp of
    men
To the next Abbey him they bare away;
His Mother swooning by the body lay:
And scarcely could the people that were
    near
Remove this second Rachel from the bier.

XXVI

" Torment and shameful death to every
    one
This Provost doth for those bad Jews pre-
    pare
That of this murder wist, and that anon:
Such wickedness his judgments cannot
    spare;   180
Who will do evil, evil shall he bear;
Them therefore with wild horses did he
    draw,
And after that he hung them by the law.

XXVII

" Upon his bier this Innocent doth lie
Before the altar while the Mass doth last:
The Abbot with his convent's company
Then sped themselves to bury him full
    fast;
And, when they holy water on him cast,
Yet spake this Child when sprinkled was
    the water,
And sang, O *Alma Redemptoris Mater !* 190

XXVIII

"This Abbot, for he was a holy man,
As all Monks are, or surely ought to be,
In supplication to the Child began
Thus saying, 'O dear Child! I summon thee
In virtue of the holy Trinity
Tell me the cause why thou dost sing this hymn
Since that thy throat is cut, as it doth seem.'

XXIX

"'My throat is cut unto the bone, I trow,'
Said this young Child, 'and by the law of kind
I should have died, yea many hours ago; 200
But Jesus Christ, as in the books ye find,
Will that his glory last, and be in mind;
And, for the worship of his Mother dear,
Yet may I sing O *Alma!* loud and clear.

XXX

"'This well of mercy, Jesu's Mother sweet,
After my knowledge I have loved alwày;
And in the hour when I my death did meet
To me she came, and thus to me did say,
"Thou in thy dying sing this holy lay," 209
As ye have heard; and soon as I had sung
Methought she laid a grain upon my tongue.

XXXI

"'Wherefore I sing, nor can from song refrain,
In honour of that blissful Maiden free,
Till from my tongue off-taken is the grain;
And after that thus said she unto me;
"My little Child, then will I come for thee
Soon as the grain from off thy tongue they take:
Be not dismayed, I will not thee forsake!"'

XXXII

"This holy Monk, this Abbot — him mean I,
Touched then his tongue, and took away the grain; 220
And he gave up the ghost full peacefully;
And, when the Abbot had this wonder seen,
His salt tears trickled down like showers of rain;
And on his face he dropped upon the ground,
And still he lay as if he had been bound.

XXXIII

"Eke the whole Convent on the pavement lay,
Weeping and praising Jesu's Mother dear;
And after that they rose, and took their way,
And lifted up this Martyr from the bier,
And in a tomb of precious marble clear 230
Enclosed his uncorrupted body sweet. —
Where'er he be, God grant us him to meet!

XXXIV

"Young Hew of Lincoln! in like sort laid low
By cursèd Jews — thing well and widely known,
For it was done a little while ago —
Pray also thou for us, while here we tarry
Weak sinful folk, that God, with pitying eye,
In mercy would his mercy multiply
On us, for reverence of his Mother Mary!"

THE CUCKOO AND THE NIGHTINGALE

FROM CHAUCER

1801. 1841

I

THE God of Love — *ah, benedicite!*
How mighty and how great a Lord is he!
For he of low hearts can make high, of high
He can make low, and unto death bring nigh;
And hard hearts he can make them kind and free.

II

Within a little time, as hath been found,
He can make sick folk whole and fresh and sound:
Them who are whole in body and in mind,
He can make sick, — bind can he and unbind
All that he will have bound, or have unbound. 10

III

To tell his might my wit may not suffice;
Foolish men he can make them out of wise; —
For he may do all that he will devise;

Loose livers he can make abate their vice,
And proud hearts can make tremble in a
    trice.

IV

In brief, the whole of what he will, he may;
Against him dare not any wight say nay;
To humble or afflict whome'er he will,
To gladden or to grieve, he hath like skill;
But most his might he sheds on the eve of
    May.   20

V

For every true heart, gentle heart and free,
That with him is, or thinketh so to be,
Now against May shall have some stirring
    — whether
To joy, or be it to some mourning; never
At other time, methinks, in like degree.

VI

For now when they may hear the small
    birds' song,
And see the budding leaves the branches
    throng,
This unto their remembrance doth bring
All kinds of pleasure mixed with sorrowing;
And longing of sweet thoughts that ever
    long.   30

VII

And of that longing heaviness doth come,
Whence oft great sickness grows of heart
    and home:
Sick are they all for lack of their desire;
And thus in May their hearts are set on fire,
So that they burn forth in great martyrdom.

VIII

In sooth, I speak from feeling, what though
    now
Old am I, and to genial pleasure slow;
Yet have I felt of sickness through the May,
Both hot and cold, and heart-aches every
    day, —
How hard, alas ! to bear, I only know.   40

IX

Such shaking doth the fever in me keep
Through all this May that I have little
    sleep;
And also 't is not likely unto me,
That any living heart should sleepy be
In which Love's dart its fiery point doth
    steep.

X

But tossing lately on a sleepless bed,
I of a token thought which Lovers heed;
How among them it was a common tale,
That it was good to hear the Nightingale,
Ere the vile Cuckoo's note be utterèd.   50

XI

And then I thought anon as it was day,
I gladly would go somewhere to essay
If I perchance a Nightingale might hear,
For yet had I heard none, of all that year,
And it was then the third night of the
    May.

XII

And soon as I a glimpse of day espied,
No longer would I in my bed abide,
But straightway to a wood that was hard
    by,
Forth did I go, alone and fearlessly,
And held the pathway down by a brook-
    side;   60

XIII

Till to a lawn I came all white and green,
I in so fair a one had never been.
The ground was green, with daisy powdered
    over;
Tall were the flowers, the grove a lofty
    cover,
All green and white; and nothing else was
    seen.

XIV

There sate I down among the fair fresh
    flowers,
And saw the birds come tripping from their
    bowers,
Where they had rested them all night; and
    they,
Who were so joyful at the light of day,   69
Began to honour May with all their powers.

XV

Well did they know that service all by
    rote,
And there was many and many a lovely
    note,
Some, singing loud, as if they had com-
    plained;
Some with their notes another manner
    feigned;
And some did sing all out with the full
    throat.

XVI

They pruned themselves, and made them-
    selves right gay,
Dancing and leaping light upon the spray;
And ever two and two together were,
The same as they had chosen for the year,
Upon Saint Valentine's returning day.   80

XVII

Meanwhile the stream, whose bank I sate
    upon,
Was making such a noise as it ran on
Accordant to the sweet Birds' harmony;
Methought that it was the best melody
Which ever to man's ear a passage won.

XVIII

And for delight, but how I never wot,
I in a slumber and a swoon was caught,
Not all asleep and yet not waking wholly;
And as I lay, the Cuckoo, bird unholy,
Broke silence, or I heard him in my
    thought.   90

XIX

And that was right upon a tree fast by,
And who was then ill satisfied but I ?
Now, God, quoth I, that died upon the
    rood,
From thee and thy base throat, keep all
    that's good,
Full little joy have I now of thy cry.

XX

And, as I with the Cuckoo thus 'gan chide,
In the next bush that was me fast beside,
I heard the lusty Nightingale so sing,
That her clear voice made a loud rioting,
Echoing thorough all the green wood
    wide.   100

XXI

Ah ! good sweet Nightingale ! for my
    heart's cheer,
Hence hast thou stayed a little while too
    long;
For we have had the sorry Cuckoo here,
And she hath been before thee with her
    song;
Evil light on her ! she hath done me wrong.

XXII

But hear you now a wondrous thing, I
    pray;
As long as in that swooning-fit I lay,

Methought I wist right well what these
    birds meant,
And had good knowing both of their intent,
And of their speech, and all that they
    would say.   110

XXIII

The Nightingale thus in my hearing
    spake : —
Good Cuckoo, seek some other bush or
    brake,
And, prithee, let us that can sing dwell here;
For every wight eschews thy song to hear,
Such uncouth singing verily dost thou make.

XXIV

What ! quoth she then, what is 't that ails
    thee now ?
It seems to me I sing as well as thou;
For mine's a song that is both true and
    plain, —
Although I cannot quaver so in vain
As thou dost in thy throat, I wot not
    how.   120

XXV

All men may understanding have of me,
But, Nightingale, so may they not of thee;
For thou hast many a foolish and quaint
    cry : —
Thou say'st OSEE, OSEE, then how may I
Have knowledge, I thee pray, what this
    may be ?

XXVI

Ah, fool ! quoth she, wist thou not what it
    is ?
Oft as I say OSEE, OSEE, I wis,
Then mean I, that I should be wonderous
    fain
That shamefully they one and all were
    slain,
Whoever against Love mean aught amiss. 130

XXVII

And also would I that they all were dead,
Who do not think in love their life to lead;
For who is loth the God of Love to obey,
Is only fit to die, I dare well say,
And for that cause OSEE I cry; take heed !

XXVIII

Ay, quoth the Cuckoo, that is a quaint law,
That all must love or die; but I withdraw,
And take my leave of all such company,

For mine intent it neither is to die, 139
Nor ever while I live Love's yoke to draw.

XXIX

For lovers of all folk that be alive,
The most disquiet have and least do thrive;
Most feeling have of sorrow, woe and care,
And the least welfare cometh to their share;
What need is there against the truth to
strive ?

XXX

What ! quoth she, thou art all out of thy
mind,
That in thy churlishness a cause canst find
To speak of Love's true Servants in this
mood;
For in this world no service is so good
To every wight that gentle is of kind. 150

XXXI

For thereof comes all goodness and all
worth;
All gentiless and honour thence come forth;
Thence worship comes, content and true
heart's pleasure,
And full-assurèd trust, joy without measure,
And jollity, fresh cheerfulness, and mirth;

XXXII

And bounty, lowliness, and courtesy,
And seemliness, and faithful company,
And dread of shame that will not do amiss;
For he that faithfully Love's servant is,
Rather than be disgraced, would chuse to
die. 160

XXXIII

And that the very truth it is which I
Now say — in such belief I 'll live and
die;
And Cuckoo, do thou so, by my advice.
Then, quoth she, let me never hope for
bliss,
If with that counsel I do e'er comply.

XXXIV

Good Nightingale ! thou speakest wondrous
fair,
Yet for all that, the truth is found else-
where;
For Love in young folk is but rage, I wis:
And Love in old folk a great dotage is;
Who most it useth, him 't will most im-
pair. 170

XXXV

For thereof come all contraries to gladness !
Thence sickness comes, and overwhelming
sadness,
Mistrust and jealousy, despite, debate,
Dishonour, shame, envy importunate,
Pride, anger, mischief, poverty, and mad-
ness.

XXXVI

Loving is aye an office of despair,
And one thing is therein which is not fair;
For whoso gets of love a little bliss,
Unless it alway stay with him, I wis 179
He may full soon go with an old man's hair.

XXXVII

And, therefore, Nightingale ! do thou keep
nigh,
For trust me well, in spite of thy quaint
cry,
If long time from thy mate thou be, or far
Thou 'lt be as others that forsaken are;
Then shalt thou raise a clamour as do I.

XXXVIII

Fie, quoth she, on thy name, Bird ill be-
seen !
The God of Love afflict thee with all teen,
For thou art worse than mad a thousand
fold;
For many a one hath virtues manifold,
Who had been nought, if Love had never
been. 190

XXXIX

For evermore his servants Love amendeth,
And he from every blemish them defendeth;
And maketh them to burn, as in a fire,
In loyalty, and worshipful desire,
And, when it likes him, joy enough them
sendeth.

XL

Thou Nightingale ! the Cuckoo said, be still,
For Love no reason hath but his own will; —
For to th' untrue he oft gives ease and joy;
True lovers doth so bitterly annoy,
He lets them perish through that grievous
ill. 200

XLI

With such a master would I never be;
For he, in sooth, is blind, and may not
see,

And knows not when he hurts and when he
heals;
Within this court full seldom Truth avails,
So diverse in his wilfulness is he.

XLII

Then of the Nightingale did I take note,
How from her inmost heart a sigh she
brought,
And said, Alas! that ever I was born,
Not one word have I now, I am so forlorn, —
And with that word, she into tears burst out.

XLIII

Alas, alas! my very heart will break,   211
Quoth she, to hear this churlish bird thus
speak
Of Love, and of his holy services;
Now, God of Love; thou help me in some
wise,
That vengeance on this Cuckoo I may
wreak.

XLIV

And so methought I started up anon,
And to the brook I ran and got a stone,
Which at the Cuckoo hardily I cast,
And he for dread did fly away full fast;   219
And glad, in sooth, was I when he was gone.

XLV

And as he flew, the Cuckoo, ever and aye,
Kept crying "Farewell! — farewell, Pop-
injay!"
As if in scornful mockery of me;
And on I hunted him from tree to tree,
Till he was far, all out of sight, away.

XLVI

Then straightway came the Nightingale to
me,
And said, Forsooth, my friend, do I thank
thee,
That thou wert near to rescue me; and
now,
Unto the God of Love I make a vow,   229
That all this May I will thy songstress be.

XLVII

Well satisfied, I thanked her, and she said,
By this mishap no longer be dismayed,
Though thou the Cuckoo heard, ere thou
heard'st me;
Yet if I live it shall amended be,
When next May comes, if I am not afraid.

XLVIII

And one thing will I counsel thee alsò,
The Cuckoo trust not thou, nor his Love's
saw;
All that she said is an outrageous lie.
Nay, nothing shall me bring thereto, quoth
I,   239
For Love, and it hath done me mighty woe.

XLIX

Yea, hath it? use, quoth she, this medicine;
This May-time, every day before thou dine,
Go look on the fresh daisy; then say I,
Although for pain thou may'st be like to
die,
Thou wilt be eased, and less wilt droop and
pine.

L

And mind always that thou be good and
true,
And I will sing one song, of many new,
For love of thee, as loud as I may cry;
And then did she begin this song full high,
"Beshrew all them that are in love untrue."

LI

And soon as she had sung it to the end,   251
Now farewell, quoth she, for I hence must
wend;
And, God of Love, that can right well and
may,
Send unto thee as mickle joy this day,
As ever he to Lover yet did send.

LII

Thus takes the Nightingale her leave of
me;
I pray to God with her always to be,
And joy of love to send her evermore;
And shield us from the Cuckoo and her lore,
For there is not so false a bird as she.   260

LIII

Forth then she flew, the gentle Nightingale,
To all the Birds that lodged within that
dale,
And gathered each and all into one place;
And them besought to hear her doleful case
And thus it was that she began her tale.

LIV

The Cuckoo — 't is not well that I should
hide
How she and I did each the other chide,

And without ceasing, since it was daylight;
And now I pray you all to do me right 269
Of that false Bird whom Love can not abide.

LV

Then spake one Bird, and full assent all
        gave;
This matter asketh counsel good as grave,
For birds we are—all here together brought;
And, in good sooth, the Cuckoo here is not;
And therefore we a Parliament will have.

LVI

And thereat shall the Eagle be our Lord,
And other Peers whose names are on record;
A summons to the Cuckoo shall be sent,
And judgment there be given; or that intent
Failing, we finally shall make accord. 280

LVII

And all this shall be done, without a nay,
The morrow after Saint Valentine's day,
Under a maple that is well beseen,
Before the chamber-window of the Queen,
At Woodstock, on the meadow green and
        gay.

LVIII

She thankèd them; and then her leave she
        took,
And flew into a hawthorn by that brook;
And there she sate and sung — upon that
        tree —
" For term of life Love shall have hold of
        me " —
So loudly, that I with that song awoke. 290

Unlearned Book and rude, as well I know,
For beauty thou hast none, nor eloquence,
Who did on thee the hardiness bestow
To appear before my Lady ? but a sense
Thou surely hast of her benevolence,
Whereof her hourly bearing proof doth
        give;
For of all good she is the best alive.

Alas, poor Book ! for thy unworthiness,
To show to her some pleasant meanings
        writ
In winning words, since through her gen-
        tiless, 300
Thee she accepts as for her service fit !
Oh ! it repents me I have neither wit
Nor leisure unto thee more worth to give;
For of all good she is the best alive.

Beseech her meekly with all lowliness,
Though I be far from her I reverence,
To think upon my truth and stedfastness,
And to abridge my sorrow's violence,
Caused by the wish, as knows your sapience,
She of her liking proof to me would give;
For of all good she is the best alive. 311

L'ENVOY

Pleasure's Aurora, Day of gladsomeness !
Luna by night, with heavenly influence
Illumined ! root of beauty and goodnesse,
Write, and allay, by your beneficence,
My sighs breathed forth in silence, — com-
        fort give !
Since of all good, you are the best alive.

EXPLICIT

TROILUS AND CRESIDA

FROM CHAUCER

1801. 1841

NEXT morning Troilus began to clear
His eyes from sleep, at the first break of
        day,
And unto Pandarus, his own Brother dear,
For love of God, full piteously did say,
We must the Palace see of Cresida;
For since we yet may have no other feast,
Let us behold her Palace at the least !

And therewithal to cover his intent
A cause he found into the Town to go,
And they right forth to Cresid's Palace
        went; 10
But, Lord, this simple Troilus was woe,
Him thought his sorrowful heart would
        break in two;
For when he saw her doors fast bolted all,
Well nigh for sorrow down he 'gan to fall

Therewith when this true Lover 'gan be-
        hold,
How shut was every window of the place,
Like frost he thought his heart was icy
        cold;
For which, with changèd, pale, and deadly
        face,
Without word uttered, forth he 'gan to
        pace;
And on his purpose bent so fast to ride, 20
That no wight his continuance espied.

Then said he thus, — O Palace desolate !
O house of houses, once so richly dight !
O Palace empty and disconsolate !
Thou lamp of which extinguished is the
    light;
O Palace whilom day that now art night,
Thou ought'st to fall and I to die; since
    she
Is gone who held us both in sovereignty.

O, of all houses once the crownèd boast !
Palace illumined with the sun of bliss;   30
O ring of which the ruby now is lost,
O cause of woe, that cause has been of
    bliss:
Yet, since I may no better, would I kiss
Thy cold doors; but I dare not for this rout;
Farewell, thou shrine of which the Saint is
    out.

Therewith he cast on Pandarus an eye,
With changèd face, and piteous to behold;
And when he might his time aright espy,
Aye as he rode, to Pandarus he told
Both his new sorrow and his joys of old,   40
So piteously, and with so dead a hue,
That every wight might on his sorrow rue.

Forth from the spot he rideth up and down,
And everything to his rememberànce
Came as he rode by places of the town
Where he had felt such perfect pleasure
    once.
Lo, yonder saw I mine own Lady dance,
And in that Temple she with her bright
    eyes,
My Lady dear, first bound me captive-wise.

And yonder with joy-smitten heart have I
Heard my own Cresid's laugh; and once
    at play   51
I yonder saw her eke full blissfully;
And yonder once she unto me 'gan say —
Now, my sweet Troilus, love me well, I
    pray !
And there so graciously did me behold,
That hers unto the death my heart I hold.

And at the corner of that self-same house
Heard I my most belovèd Lady dear,
So womanly, with voice melodious
Singing so well, so goodly, and so clear,   60
That in my soul methinks I yet do hear
The blissful sound; and in that very place
My Lady first me took unto her grace.

O blissful God of Love ! then thus he cried,
When I the process have in memory,
How thou hast wearied me on every side,
Men thence a book might make, a history;
What need to seek a conquest over me,
Since I am wholly at thy will ? what joy
Hast thou thy own liege subjects to de-
    stroy ?   70

Dread Lord ! so fearful when provoked,
    thine ire
Well hast thou wreaked on me by pain and
    grief.
Now mercy, Lord ! thou know'st well I
    desire
Thy grace above all pleasures first and
    chief;
And live and die I will in thy belief;
For which I ask for guerdon but one boon,
That Cresida again thou send me soon.

Constrain her heart as quickly to return,
As thou dost mine with longing her to see,
Then know I well that she would not so-
    journ.   80
Now, blissful Lord, so cruel do not be
Unto the blood of Troy, I pray of thee,
As Juno was unto the Theban blood,
From whence to Thebes came griefs in mul-
    titude.

And after this he to the gate did go,
Whence Cresid rode, as if in haste she was;
And up and down there went, and to and fro,
And to himself full oft he said, alas !
From hence my hope, and solace forth did
    pass.
O would the blissful God now for his joy,
I might her see again coming to Troy !   91

And up to yonder hill was I her guide;
Alas, and there I took of her my leave;
Yonder I saw her to her Father ride,
For very grief of which my heart shall
    cleave; —
And hither home I came when it was eve;
And here I dwell an outcast from all joy,
And shall, unless I see her soon in Troy.

And of himself did he imagine oft,
That he was blighted, pale, and waxen less
Than he was wont; and that in whispers
    soft   101
Men said, what may it be, can no one guess
Why Troilus hath all this heaviness ?

All which he of himself conceited wholly
Out of his weakness and his melancholy.

Another time he took into his head,
That every wight, who in the way passed
 by,
Had of him ruth, and fancied that they
 said,
I am right sorry Troilus will die:
And thus a day or two drove wearily;   110
As ye have heard; such life 'gan he to lead
As one that standeth betwixt hope and
 dread.

For which it pleased him in his songs to
 show
The occasion of his woe, as best he might;
And made a fitting song, of words but few,
Somewhat his woeful heart to make more
 light;
And when he was removed from all men's
 sight,
With a soft voice, he of his Lady
 dear,
That absent was, 'gan sing as ye may hear.

O star, of which I lost have all the light,   120
With a sore heart well ought I to bewail,
That ever dark in torment, night by night,
Toward my death with wind I steer and
 sail;
For which upon the tenth night if thou fail
With thy bright beams to guide me but
 one hour,
My ship and me Charybdis will devour.

As soon as he this song had thus sung
 through,
He fell again into his sorrows old;
And every night, as was his wont to do,
Troilus stood the bright moon to behold;   130
And all his trouble to the moon he told,
And said; I wis, when thou art horn'd
 anew,
I shall be glad if all the world be true.

Thy horns were old as now upon that
 morrow,
When hence did journey my bright Lady
 dear,
That cause is of my torment and my sor-
 row;
For which, oh, gentle Luna, bright and
 clear;
For love of God, run fast about thy sphere;

For when thy horns begin once more to
 spring,
Then shall she come, that with her bliss
 may bring.   140

The day is more, and longer every night
Than they were wont to be — for he thought
 so;
And that the sun did take his course not
 right,
By longer way than he was wont to go;
And said, I am in constant dread I trow,
That Phäeton his son is yet alive,
His too fond father's car amiss to drive.

Upon the walls fast also would he walk,
To the end that he the Grecian host might
 see;   149
And ever thus he to himself would talk: —
Lo! yonder is my own bright Lady free;
Or yonder is it that the tents must be;
And thence does come this air which is so
 sweet,
That in my soul I feel the joy of it.

And certainly this wind, that more and
 more
By moments thus increaseth in my face,
Is of my Lady's sighs heavy and sore;
I prove it thus; for in no other space
Of all this town, save only in this place,   159
Feel I a wind, that soundeth so like pain;
It saith, Alas, why severed are we twain?

A weary while in pain he tosseth thus,
Till fully past and gone was the ninth
 night;
And ever at his side stood Pandarus,
Who busily made use of all his might
To comfort him, and make his heart more
 light;
Giving him always hope, that she the
 morrow
Of the tenth day will come, and end his
 sorrow.

THE SAILOR'S MOTHER
1802. 1807

Written at Town-end, Grasmere. I met this
woman near the Wishing-gate, on the high-
road that then led from Grasmere to Amble-
side. Her appearance was exactly as here
described, and such was her account, nearly to
the letter.

ONE morning (raw it was and wet —
A foggy day in winter time)
A Woman on the road I met,
Not old, though something past her
　　prime:
Majestic in her person, tall and straight;
And like a Roman matron's was her mien
　　and gait.

The ancient spirit is not dead;
Old times, thought I, are breathing there;
Proud was I that my country bred
Such strength, a dignity so fair:　　　10
She begged an alms, like one in poor
　　estate;
I looked at her again, nor did my pride
　　abate.

When from these lofty thoughts I woke,
"What is it," said I, "that you bear,
Beneath the covert of your Cloak,
Protected from this cold damp air ? "
She answered, soon as she the question
　　heard,
"A simple burthen, Sir, a little Singing-
　　bird."

And, thus continuing, she said,
"I had a Son, who many a day　　　20
Sailed on the seas, but he is dead;
In Denmark he was cast away:
And I have travelled weary miles to
　　see
If aught which he had owned might still
　　remain for me.

"The bird and cage they both were
　　his:
'T was my Son's bird; and neat and
　　trim
He kept it: many voyages
The singing-bird had gone with him;
When last he sailed, he left the bird
　　behind;
From bodings, as might be, that hung upon
　　his mind.　　　30

"He to a fellow-lodger's care
Had left it, to be watched and fed,
And pipe its song in safety; — there
I found it when my Son was dead;
And now, God help me for my little
　　wit !
I bear it with me, Sir; — he took so much
　　delight in it."

ALICE FELL

OR, POVERTY

1802. 1807

Written to gratify Mr. Graham of Glasgow,
brother of the Author of " The Sabbath." He
was a zealous coadjutor of Mr. Clarkson, and a
man of ardent humanity. The incident had
happened to himself, and he urged me to put
it into verse, for humanity's sake. The hum-
bleness, meanness if you like, of the subject,
together with the homely mode of treating it,
brought upon me a world of ridicule by the
small critics, so that in policy I excluded it
from many editions of my Poems, till it was
restored at the request of my son-in-law,
Edward Quillinan.

THE post-boy drove with fierce career,
For threatening clouds the moon had
　　drowned;
When, as we hurried on, my ear
Was smitten with a startling sound.

As if the wind blew many ways,
I heard the sound, — and more and more,
It seemed to follow with the chaise,
And still I heard it as before.

At length I to the boy called out;
He stopped his horses at the word,　　　10
But neither cry, nor voice, nor shout,
Nor aught else like it, could be heard.

The boy then smacked his whip, and fast
The horses scampered through the rain;
But, hearing soon upon the blast
The cry, I bade him halt again.

Forthwith alighting on the ground,
"Whence comes," said I, "this piteous
　　moan ? "
And there a little Girl I found,
Sitting behind the chaise, alone.　　　20

"My cloak ! " no other word she spake,
But loud and bitterly she wept,
As if her innocent heart would break;
And down from off her seat she leapt.

"What ails you, child ? " — she sobbed
　　" Look here ! "
I saw it in the wheel entangled,
A weather-beaten rag as e'er
From any garden scare-crow dangled.

There, twisted between nave and spoke,
It hung, nor could at once be freed;   30
But our joint pains unloosed the cloak,
A miserable rag indeed!

"And whither are you going, child,
To-night along these lonesome ways?"
"To Durham," answered she, half wild—
"Then come with me into the chaise."

Insensible to all relief
Sat the poor girl, and forth did send
Sob after sob, as if her grief
Could never, never have an end.   40

"My child, in Durham do you dwell?"
She checked herself in her distress,
And said, "My name is Alice Fell;
I'm fatherless and motherless.

"And I to Durham, Sir, belong."
Again, as if the thought would choke
Her very heart, her grief grew strong;
And all was for her tattered cloak!

The chaise drove on; our journey's end
Was nigh; and, sitting by my side,   50
As if she had lost her only friend
She wept, nor would be pacified.

Up to the tavern-door we post;
Of Alice and her grief I told;
And I gave money to the host,
To buy a new cloak for the old.

"And let it be of duffil grey,
As warm a cloak as man can sell!"
Proud creature was she the next day,
The little orphan, Alice Fell!   60

BEGGARS

1802. 1807

Written at Town-end, Grasmere. Met, and
described to me by my Sister, near the quarry
at the head of Rydal lake, a place still a chosen
resort of vagrants travelling with their fami-
lies.

SHE had a tall man's height or more;
Her face from summer's noontide heat
No bonnet shaded, but she wore
A mantle, to her very feet

Descending with a graceful flow,
And on her head a cap as white as new-fallen
snow.

Her skin was of Egyptian brown:
Haughty, as if her eye had seen
Its own light to a distance thrown,
She towered, fit person for a Queen   10
To lead those ancient Amazonian files;
Or ruling Bandit's wife among the Grecian
isles.

Advancing, forth she stretched her hand
And begged an alms with doleful plea
That ceased not; on our English land
Such woes, I knew, could never be;
And yet a boon I gave her, for the crea-
ture
Was beautiful to see — a weed of glorious
feature.

I left her, and pursued my way;
And soon before me did espy   20
A pair of little Boys at play,
Chasing a crimson butterfly;
The taller followed with his hat in hand,
Wreathed round with yellow flowers the
gayest of the land.

The other wore a rimless crown
With leaves of laurel stuck about;
And, while both followed up and down,
Each whooping with a merry shout,
In their fraternal features I could trace
Unquestionable lines of that wild Suppli-
ant's face.   30

Yet *they*, so blithe of heart, seemed fit
For finest tasks of earth or air:
Wings let them have, and they might flit
Precursors to Aurora's car,
Scattering fresh flowers; though happier
far, I ween,
To hunt their fluttering game o'er rock and
level green.

They dart across my path — but lo,
Each ready with a plaintive whine!
Said I, "not half an hour ago
Your Mother has had alms of mine."   40
"That cannot be," one answered — "she
is dead:" —
I looked reproof — they saw — but neither
hung his head.

" She has been dead, Sir, many a day." —
" Hush, boys ! you 're telling me a lie;
It was your Mother, as I say ! "
And, in the twinkling of an eye,
" Come ! Come ! " cried one, and without
　　more ado,
Off to some other play the joyous Vagrants
　　flew !

TO A BUTTERFLY

1802. 1807

Written in the orchard, Town-end, Grasmere.
My sister and I were parted immediately after
the death of our mother, who died in 1778,
both being very young.

STAY near me — do not take thy flight !
A little longer stay in sight !
Much converse do I find in thee,
Historian of my infancy !
Float near me; do not yet depart !
Dead times revive in thee:
Thou bring'st, gay creature as thou art !
A solemn image to my heart,
My father's family !

Oh ! pleasant, pleasant were the days,
The time, when, in our childish plays,
My sister Emmeline and I
Together chased the butterfly !
A very hunter did I rush
Upon the prey: — with leaps and springs
I followed on from brake to bush;
But she, God love her, feared to brush
The dust from off its wings.

THE EMIGRANT MOTHER

1802. 1807

Suggested by what I have noticed in more
than one French fugitive during the time of
the French Revolution. If I am not mistaken,
the lines were composed at Sockburn, when I
was on a visit to Mrs. Wordsworth and her
brother.

ONCE in a lonely hamlet I sojourned
In which a Lady driven from France did
　　dwell;
The big and lesser griefs with which she
　　mourned,
In friendship she to me would often tell.
This Lady, dwelling upon British ground,
Where she was childless, daily would repair

To a poor neighbouring cottage; as I found,
For sake of a young Child whose home was
　　there.

Once having seen her clasp with fond em-
　　brace
This Child, I chanted to myself a lay,　10
Endeavouring, in our English tongue, to
　　trace
Such things as she unto the Babe might
　　say:
And thus, from what I heard and knew, or
　　guessed,
My song the workings of her heart ex-
　　pressed.

I

" Dear Babe, thou daughter of another,
One moment let me be thy mother !
An infant's face and looks are thine,
And sure a mother's heart is mine:
Thy own dear mother 's far away,
At labour in the harvest field:　20
Thy little sister is at play; —
What warmth, what comfort would it yield
To my poor heart, if thou wouldst be
One little hour a child to me !

II

" Across the waters I am come,
And I have left a babe at home:
A long, long way of land and sea !
Come to me — I 'm no enemy:
I am the same who at thy side
Sate yesterday, and made a nest　30
For thee, sweet Baby ! — thou hast tried,
Thou know'st the pillow of my breast;
Good, good art thou: — alas ! to me
Far more than I can be to thee.

III

" Here, little Darling, dost thou lie;
An infant thou, a mother I !
Mine wilt thou be, thou hast no fears;
Mine art thou — spite of these my tears.
Alas ! before I left the spot,
My baby and its dwelling-place;　40
The nurse said to me, ' Tears should not
Be shed upon an infant's face,
It was unlucky ' — no, no, no;
No truth is in them who say so !

IV

" My own dear Little-one will sigh,
Sweet Babe ! and they will let him die.

'He pines,' they 'll say, 'it is his doom,
And you may see his hour is come.'
Oh ! had he but thy cheerful smiles,
Limbs stout as thine, and lips as gay,   50
Thy looks, thy cunning, and thy wiles,
And countenance like a summer's day,
They would have hopes of him; — and
     then
I should behold his face again !

V

" 'T is gone — like dreams that we forget;
There was a smile or two — yet — yet
I can remember them, I see
The smiles, worth all the world to me.
Dear Baby ! I must lay thee down;
Thou troublest me with strange alarms;   60
Smiles hast thou, bright ones of thy own;
I cannot keep thee in my arms;
For they confound me; — where — where is
That last, that sweetest smile of his ?

VI

"Oh ! how I love thee ! — we will stay
Together here this one half day.
My sister's child, who bears my name,
From France to sheltering England came;
She with her mother crossed the sea;
The babe and mother near me dwell: 70
Yet does my yearning heart to thee
Turn rather, though I love her well:
Rest, little Stranger, rest thee here !
Never was any child more dear !

VII

" — I cannot help it; ill intent
I 've none, my pretty Innocent !
I weep — I know they do thee wrong,
These tears — and my poor idle tongue.
Oh, what a kiss was that ! my cheek
How cold it is ! but thou art good;   80
Thine eyes are on me — they would speak,
I think, to help me if they could.
Blessings upon that soft, warm face,
My heart again is in its place !

VIII

" While thou art mine, my little Love,
This cannot be a sorrowful grove;
Contentment, hope, and mother's glee,
I seem to find them all in thee:
Here 's grass to play with, here are flowers;
I 'll call thee by my darling's name;   90
Thou hast, I think, a look of ours,
Thy features seem to me the same;

His little sister thou shalt be;
And, when once more my home I see,
I 'll tell him many tales of Thee."

"MY HEART LEAPS UP WHEN I BEHOLD"

1802. 1807

Written at Town-end, Grasmere.

My heart leaps up when I behold
     A rainbow in the sky:
So was it when my life began;
So is it now I am a man;
So be it when I shall grow old,
     Or let me die !
The Child is father of the Man;
And I could wish my days to be
Bound each to each by natural piety.

"AMONG ALL LOVELY THINGS MY LOVE HAD BEEN"

1802. 1807

Among all lovely things my Love had been;
Had noted well the stars, all flowers that
     grew
About her home; but she had never seen
A glow-worm, never one, and this I knew.

While riding near her home one stormy
     night
A single glow-worm did I chance to espy;
I gave a fervent welcome to the sight,
And from my horse I leapt; great joy had I.

Upon a leaf the glow-worm did I lay,
To bear it with me through the stormy
     night:
And, as before, it shone without dismay;
Albeit putting forth a fainter light.

When to the dwelling of my Love I came,
I went into the orchard quietly;
And left the glow-worm, blessing it by name,
Laid safely by itself, beneath a tree.

The whole next day, I hoped, and hoped
     with fear;
At night the glow-worm shone beneath the
     tree;
I led my Lucy to the spot, " Look here,"
Oh ! joy it was for her, and joy for me !

WRITTEN IN MARCH

WHILE RESTING ON THE BRIDGE AT THE FOOT OF BROTHER'S WATER

1802. 1807

Extempore. This little poem was a favourite with Joanna Baillie.

THE Cock is crowing,
The stream is flowing,
The small birds twitter,
The lake doth glitter,
The green field sleeps in the sun;
The oldest and youngest
Are at work with the strongest;
The cattle are grazing,
Their heads never raising;
There are forty feeding like one !

Like an army defeated
The snow hath retreated,
And now doth fare ill
On the top of the bare hill;
The ploughboy is whooping — anon — anon:
There 's joy in the mountains;
There 's life in the fountains;
Small clouds are sailing,
Blue sky prevailing;
The rain is over and gone !

THE REDBREAST CHASING THE BUTTERFLY

1802. 1807

Observed, as described, in the then beautiful orchard, Town-end, Grasmere.

ART thou the bird whom Man loves best,
The pious bird with the scarlet breast,
    Our little English Robin;
The bird that comes about our doors
When Autumn-winds are sobbing ?
Art thou the Peter of Norway Boors ?
    Their Thomas in Finland,
    And Russia far inland ?
The bird, that by some name or other
All men who know thee call their brother,
The darling of children and men ?   11
Could Father Adam open his eyes
And see this sight beneath the skies,
He 'd wish to close them again.

— If the butterfly knew but his friend,
Hither his flight he would bend;
And find his way to me,
Under the branches of the tree:
In and out, he darts about;
Can this be the bird, to man so good,   20
That, after their bewildering,
Covered with leaves the little children,
    So painfully in the wood ?
What ailed thee, Robin, that thou could'st pursue
    A beautiful creature,
That is gentle by nature ?
Beneath the summer sky
From flower to flower let him fly;
'T is all that he wishes to do.   29
The cheerer Thou of our in-door sadness,
He is the friend of our summer gladness:
What hinders, then, that ye should be
Playmates in the sunny weather,
And fly about in the air together !
His beautiful wings in crimson are drest,
A crimson as bright as thine own:
Would'st thou be happy in thy nest,
O pious Bird ! whom man loves best,
Love him, or leave him alone !

TO A BUTTERFLY

1802. 1807

Written in the orchard, Town-end, Grasmere.

I 'VE watched you now a full half-hour,
Self-poised upon that yellow flower;
And, little Butterfly ! indeed
I know not if you sleep or feed.
How motionless ! — not frozen seas
More motionless ! and then
What joy awaits you, when the breeze
Hath found you out among the trees,
And calls you forth again !

This plot of orchard-ground is ours;
My trees they are, my sister's flowers;
Here rest your wings when they are weary;
Here lodge as in a sanctuary !
Come often to us, fear no wrong;
Sit near us on the bough !
We 'll talk of sunshine and of song,
And summer days, when we were young;
Sweet childish days, that were as long
As twenty days are now.

FORESIGHT

1802. 1807

Also composed in the orchard, Town-end, Grasmere.

THAT is work of waste and ruin —
Do as Charles and I are doing!
Strawberry-blossoms, one and all,
We must spare them — here are many:
Look at it — the flower is small,
Small and low, though fair as any:
Do not touch it! summers two
I am older, Anne, than you.

Pull the primrose, sister Anne!
Pull as many as you can.   10
— Here are daisies, take your fill;
Pansies, and the cuckoo-flower:
Of the lofty daffodil
Make your bed, or make your bower;
Fill your lap, and fill your bosom;
Only spare the strawberry-blossom!

Primroses, the Spring may love them —
Summer knows but little of them:
Violets, a barren kind,
Withered on the ground must lie;   30
Daisies leave no fruit behind
When the pretty flowerets die;
Pluck them, and another year
As many will be blowing here.

God has given a kindlier power
To the favoured strawberry-flower.
Hither soon as spring is fled
You and Charles and I will walk;
Lurking berries, ripe and red,
Then will hang on every stalk,   30
Each within its leafy bower;
And for that promise spare the flower!

TO THE SMALL CELANDINE

1802. 1807

Written at Town-end, Grasmere. It is remarkable that this flower, coming out so early in the spring as it does, and so bright and beautiful, and in such profusion, should not have been noticed earlier in English verse. What adds much to the interest that attends it is its habit of shutting itself up and opening out according to the degree of light and temperature of the air.

PANSIES, lilies, kingcups, daisies,
Let them live upon their praises;
Long as there's a sun that sets,
Primroses will have their glory;
Long as there are violets,
They will have a place in story:
There's a flower that shall be mine,
'T is the little Celandine.

Eyes of some men travel far
For the finding of a star;   10
Up and down the heavens they go,
Men that keep a mighty rout!
I'm as great as they, I trow,
Since the day I found thee out,
Little Flower! — I'll make a stir,
Like a sage astronomer.

Modest, yet withal an Elf
Bold, and lavish of thyself;
Since we needs must first have met
I have seen thee, high and low,   20
Thirty years or more, and yet
'T was a face I did not know;
Thou hast now, go where I may,
Fifty greetings in a day.

Ere a leaf is on a bush,
In the time before the thrush
Has a thought about her nest,
Thou wilt come with half a call,
Spreading out thy glossy breast
Like a careless Prodigal;   30
Telling tales about the sun,
When we've little warmth, or none.

Poets, vain men in their mood!
Travel with the multitude:
Never heed them; I aver
That they all are wanton wooers;
But the thrifty cottager,
Who stirs little out of doors,
Joys to spy thee near her home;
Spring is coming, Thou art come!   40

Comfort have thou of thy merit,
Kindly, unassuming Spirit!
Careless of thy neighbourhood,
Thou dost show thy pleasant face
On the moor, and in the wood,
In the lane; — there's not a place,
Howsoever mean it be,
But 't is good enough for thee.

Ill befall the yellow flowers,
Children of the flaring hours!   50

Buttercups, that will be seen,
Whether we will see or no;
Others, too, of lofty mien;
They have done as worldlings do,
Taken praise that should be thine,
Little, humble Celandine !

Prophet of delight and mirth,
Ill-requited upon earth;
Herald of a mighty band,
Of a joyous train ensuing,   60
Serving at my heart's command,
Tasks that are no tasks renewing,
I will sing, as doth behove,
Hymns in praise of what I love !

TO THE SAME FLOWER

1802. 1807

PLEASURES newly found are sweet
When they lie about our feet:
February last, my heart
First at sight of thee was glad;
All unheard of as thou art,
Thou must needs, I think, have had,
Celandine ! and long ago,
Praise of which I nothing know.

I have not a doubt but he,
Whosoe'er the man might be,   10
Who the first with pointed rays
(Workman worthy to be sainted)
Set the sign-board in a blaze,
When the rising sun he painted
Took the fancy from a glance
At thy glittering countenance.

Soon as gentle breezes bring
News of winter's vanishing,
And the children build their bowers,
Sticking 'kerchief-plots of mould   20
All about with full-blown flowers,
Thick as sheep in shepherd's fold !
With the proudest thou art there,
Mantling in the tiny square.

Often have I sighed to measure
By myself a lonely pleasure,
Sighed to think, I read a book
Only read, perhaps, by me;
Yet I long could overlook
Thy bright coronet and Thee,   30
And thy arch and wily ways,
And thy store of other praise.

Blithe of heart, from week to week
Thou dost play at hide-and-seek;
While the patient primrose sits
Like a beggar in the cold,
Thou, a flower of wiser wits,
Slipp'st into thy sheltering hold;
Liveliest of the vernal train
When ye all are out again.   40

Drawn by what peculiar spell,
By what charm of sight or smell,
Does the dim-eyed curious Bee,
Labouring for her waxen cells,
Fondly settle upon Thee
Prized above all buds and bells
Opening daily at thy side,
By the season multiplied ?

Thou art not beyond the moon,
But a thing " beneath our shoon: "   50
Let the bold Discoverer thrid
In his bark the polar sea;
Rear who will a pyramid;
Praise it is enough for me,
If there be but three or four
Who will love my little Flower.

RESOLUTION AND INDE-PENDENCE

1802. 1807

Written at Town-end, Grasmere. This old Man I met a few hundred yards from my cottage ; and the account of him is taken from his own mouth. I was in the state of feeling described in the beginning of the poem, while crossing over Barton Fell from Mr. Clarkson's, at the foot of Ullswater, towards Askham. The image of the hare I then observed on the ridge of the Fell.

I

THERE was a roaring in the wind all night;
The rain came heavily and fell in floods;
But now the sun is rising calm and bright;
The birds are singing in the distant woods;
Over his own sweet voice the Stock-dove
     broods;
The Jay makes answer as the Magpie
     chatters;
And all the air is filled with pleasant noise
     of waters.

II

All things that love the sun are out of doors;
The sky rejoices in the morning's birth;

The grass is bright with rain-drops; — on
   the moors   10
The hare is running races in her mirth;
And with her feet she from the plashy
   earth
Raises a mist, that, glittering in the sun,
Runs with her all the way, wherever she
   doth run.

III

I was a Traveller then upon the moor,
I saw the hare that raced about with joy;
I heard the woods and distant waters roar;
Or heard them not, as happy as a boy:
The pleasant season did my heart employ:
My old remembrances went from me wholly;
And all the ways of men, so vain and mel-
   ancholy.   21

IV

But, as it sometimes chanceth, from the
   might
Of joy in minds that can no further go,
As high as we have mounted in delight
In our dejection do we sink as low;
To me that morning did it happen so;
And fears and fancies thick upon me came;
Dim sadness — and blind thoughts, I knew
   not, nor could name.

V

I heard the sky-lark warbling in the sky;
And I bethought me of the playful hare:
Even such a happy Child of earth am I; 31
Even as these blissful creatures do I fare;
Far from the world I walk, and from all
   care;
But there may come another day to me —
Solitude, pain of heart, distress, and poverty.

VI

My whole life I have lived in pleasant
   thought,
As if life's business were a summer mood;
As if all needful things would come un-
   sought
To genial faith, still rich in genial good;
But how can He expect that others should
Build for him, sow for him, and at his call
Love him, who for himself will take no heed
   at all?   42

VII

I thought of Chatterton, the marvellous Boy,
The sleepless Soul that perished in his
   pride;

Of Him who walked in glory and in joy
Following his plough, along the mountain-
   side:
By our own spirits are we deified:
We Poets in our youth begin in gladness;
But thereof come in the end despondency
   and madness.

VIII

Now, whether it were by peculiar grace, 50
A leading from above, a something given,
Yet it befell, that, in this lonely place,
When I with these untoward thoughts had
   striven,
Beside a pool bare to the eye of heaven
I saw a Man before me unawares:
The oldest man he seemed that ever wore
   grey hairs.

IX

As a huge stone is sometimes seen to lie
Couched on the bald top of an eminence;
Wonder to all who do the same espy,
By what means it could thither come, and
   whence;   60
So that it seems a thing endued with sense:
Like a sea-beast crawled forth, that on a
   shelf
Of rock or sand reposeth, there to sun itself;

X

Such seemed this Man, not all alive nor
   dead,
Nor all asleep — in his extreme old age:
His body was bent double, feet and head
Coming together in life's pilgrimage;
As if some dire constraint of pain, or rage
Of sickness felt by him in times long past,
A more than human weight upon his frame
   had cast.   70

XI

Himself he propped, limbs, body, and pale
   face,
Upon a long grey staff of shaven wood:
And, still as I drew near with gentle pace,
Upon the margin of that moorish flood
Motionless as a cloud the old Man stood,
That heareth not the loud winds when they
   call
And moveth all together, if it move at all.

XII

At length, himself unsettling, he the pond
Stirred with his staff, and fixedly did look

Upon the muddy water, which he conned,
As if he had been reading in a book: 81
And now a stranger's privilege I took;
And, drawing to his side, to him did say,
" This morning gives us promise of a glo-
rious day."

XIII

A gentle answer did the old Man make,
In courteous speech which forth he slowly
drew:
And him with further words I thus bespake,
" What occupation do you there pursue ?
This is a lonesome place for one like you."
Ere he replied, a flash of mild surprise 90
Broke from the sable orbs of his yet-vivid
eyes.

XIV

His words came feebly, from a feeble chest,
But each in solemn order followed each,
With something of a lofty utterance drest —
Choice word and measured phrase, above
the reach
Of ordinary men; a stately speech;
Such as grave Livers do in Scotland use,
Religious men, who give to God and man
their dues.

XV

He told, that to these waters he had come
To gather leeches, being old and poor: 100
Employment hazardous and wearisome !
And he had many hardships to endure:
From pond to pond he roamed, from moor
to moor;
Housing, with God's good help, by choice or
chance,
And in this way he gained an honest main-
tenance.

XVI

The old Man still stood talking by my side;
But now his voice to me was like a stream
Scarce heard; nor word from word could
I divide;
And the whole body of the Man did seem
Like one whom I had met with in a dream;
Or like a man from some far region sent,
To give me human strength, by apt admon-
ishment. 112

XVII

My former thoughts returned: the fear that
kills;
And hope that is unwilling to be fed;

Cold, pain, and labour, and all fleshly ills;
And mighty Poets in their misery dead.
— Perplexed, and longing to be comforted,
My question eagerly did I renew,
" How is it that you live, and what is it you
do ? "

XVIII

He with a smile did then his words repeat;
And said that, gathering leeches, far and
wide 121
He travelled ; stirring thus about his feet
The waters of the pools where they abide.
" Once I could meet with them on every
side;
But they have dwindled long by slow decay;
Yet still I persevere, and find them where I
may."

XIX

While he was talking thus, the lonely place,
The old Man's shape, and speech — all trou-
bled me:
In my mind's eye I seemed to see him pace
About the weary moors continually, 130
Wandering about alone and silently.
While I these thoughts within myself pur-
sued,
He, having made a pause, the same discourse
renewed.

XX

And soon with this he other matter blended,
Cheerfully uttered, with demeanour kind,
But stately in the main; and when he ended,
I could have laughed myself to scorn to
find
In that decrepit Man so firm a mind.
" God," said I, " be my help and stay se-
cure;
I 'll think of the Leech-gatherer on the
lonely moor ! " 140

"I GRIEVED FOR BUONAPARTÉ"

1802. 1802

I GRIEVED for Buonaparté, with a vain
And an unthinking grief ! The tenderest
mood
Of that Man's mind — what can it be ?
what food
Fed his first hopes ? what knowledge could
he gain ?

'T is not in battles that from youth we
 train
The Governor who must be wise and good,
And temper with the sternness of the brain
Thoughts motherly, and meek as woman-
 hood.
Wisdom doth live with children round her
 knees:
Books, leisure, perfect freedom, and the
 talk
Man holds with week-day man in the hourly
 walk
Of the mind's business: these are the
 degrees
By which true Sway doth mount; this is
 the stalk
True Power doth grow on; and her rights
 are these.

A FAREWELL

1802. 1815

Composed just before my sister and I went
to fetch Mrs. Wordsworth from Gallow-hill,
near Scarborough.

FAREWELL, thou little Nook of mountain-
 ground,
Thou rocky corner in the lowest stair
Of that magnificent temple which doth
 bound
One side of our whole vale with grandeur
 rare;
Sweet garden-orchard, eminently fair,
The loveliest spot that man hath ever
 found,
Farewell ! — we leave thee to Heaven's
 peaceful care,
Thee, and the Cottage which thou dost
 surround.

Our boat is safely anchored by the shore,
And there will safely ride when we are
 gone; 10
The flowering shrubs that deck our humble
 door
Will prosper, though untended and alone:
Fields, goods, and far-off chattels we have
 none:
These narrow bounds contain our private
 store
Of things earth makes, and sun doth shine
 upon;
Here are they in our sight — we have no
 more.

Sunshine and shower be with you, bud and
 bell !
For two months now in vain we shall be
 sought:
We leave you here in solitude to dwell
With these our latest gifts of tender
 thought; 20
Thou, like the morning, in thy saffron coat,
Bright gowan, and marsh-marigold, fare-
 well !
Whom from the borders of the Lake we
 brought,
And placed together near our rocky Well.

We go for One to whom ye will be dear;
And she will prize this Bower, this Indian
 shed,
Our own contrivance, Building without
 peer !
— A gentle Maid, whose heart is lowly bred,
Whose pleasures are in wild fields gatherèd,
With joyousness, and with a thoughtful
 cheer, 30
Will come to you; to you herself will wed;
And love the blessed life that we lead here.

Dear Spot ! which we have watched with
 tender heed,
Bringing thee chosen plants and blossoms
 blown
Among the distant mountains, flower and
 weed,
Which thou hast taken to thee as thy own,
Making all kindness registered and known;
Thou for our sakes, though Nature's child
 indeed,
Fair in thyself and beautiful alone,
Hast taken gifts which thou dost little
 need. 40

And O most constant, yet most fickle Place,
Thou hast thy wayward moods, as thou
 dost show
To them who look not daily on thy face;
Who, being loved, in love no bounds dost
 know,
And say'st, when we forsake thee, " Let
 them go ! "
Thou easy-hearted Thing, with thy wild race
Of weeds and flowers, till we return be slow,
And travel with the year at a soft pace.

Help us to tell Her tales of years gone by,
And this sweet spring, the best beloved and
 best; 50

Joy will be flown in its mortality;
Something must stay to tell us of the rest.
Here, thronged with primroses, the steep
 rock's breast
Glittered at evening like a starry sky;
And in this bush our sparrow built her nest,
Of which I sang one song that will not die.

O happy Garden! whose seclusion deep
Hath been so friendly to industrious hours;
And to soft slumbers, that did gently steep
Our spirits, carrying with them dreams of
 flowers,   60
And wild notes warbled among leafy bowers;
Two burning months let summer overleap,
And, coming back with Her who will be
 ours,
Into thy bosom we again shall creep.

"THE SUN HAS LONG BEEN SET"

1802. 1807

Reprinted at the request of my Sister, in whose presence the lines were thrown off.

This *Impromptu* appeared, many years ago, among the Author's poems, from which, in subsequent editions, it was excluded.

THE sun has long been set,
 The stars are out by twos and threes,
The little birds are piping yet
 Among the bushes and trees;
There's a cuckoo, and one or two thrushes,
And a far-off wind that rushes,
And a sound of water that gushes,
And the cuckoo's sovereign cry
Fills all the hollow of the sky.
 Who would go "parading"
In London, and "masquerading,"
On such a night of June
With that beautiful soft half-moon,
And all these innocent blisses?
On such a night as this is!

COMPOSED UPON WESTMINSTER BRIDGE, SEPT. 3, 1802

1802. 1807

Written on the roof of a coach, on my way to France.

EARTH has not anything to show more fair:
Dull would he be of soul who could pass by
A sight so touching in its majesty:

This City now doth, like a garment, wear
The beauty of the morning; silent, bare,
Ships, towers, domes, theatres, and temples
 lie
Open unto the fields, and to the sky;
All bright and glittering in the smokeless
 air.
Never did sun more beautifully steep
In his first splendour, valley, rock, or hill;
Ne'er saw I, never felt, a calm so deep!
The river glideth at his own sweet will:
Dear God! the very houses seem asleep;
And all that mighty heart is lying still!

COMPOSED BY THE SEA-SIDE, NEAR CALAIS, AUGUST 1802

1802. 1807

FAIR Star of evening, Splendour of the west,
Star of my Country! — on the horizon's
 brink
Thou hangest, stooping, as might seem, to
 sink
On England's bosom; yet well pleased to
 rest,
Meanwhile, and be to her a glorious crest
Conspicuous to the Nations. Thou, I think,
Should'st be my Country's emblem; and
 should'st wink,
Bright Star! with laughter on her banners, drest
In thy fresh beauty. There! that dusky
 spot
Beneath thee, that is England; there she lies.
Blessings be on you both! one hope, one lot,
One life, one glory! — I, with many a fear
For my dear Country, many heartfelt sighs,
Among men who do not love her, linger
 here.

CALAIS, AUGUST 1802

1802. 1803

Is it a reed that's shaken by the wind,
Or what is it that ye go forth to see?
Lords, lawyers, statesmen, squires of low
 degree,
Men known, and men unknown, sick, lame,
 and blind,
Post forward all, like creatures of one kind,
With first-fruit offerings crowd to bend the
 knee
In France, before the new-born Majesty.

'T is ever thus. Ye men of prostrate mind,
A seemly reverence may be paid to power;
But that 's a loyal virtue, never sown
In haste, nor springing with a transient
    shower:
When truth, when sense, when liberty were
    flown,
What hardship had it been to wait an
    hour ?
Shame on you, feeble Heads, to slavery
    prone !

COMPOSED NEAR CALAIS, ON THE ROAD LEADING TO AR-DRES, AUGUST 7, 1802

1802. 1807

JONES ! as from Calais southward you and I
Went pacing side by side, this public Way
Streamed with the pomp of a too-credulous
    day,
When faith was pledged to new-born Lib-
    erty:
A homeless sound of joy was in the sky:
From hour to hour the antiquated Earth
Beat like the heart of Man: songs, gar-
    lands, mirth,
Banners, and happy faces, far and nigh !
And now, sole register that these things
    were,
Two solitary greetings have I heard,
" *Good-morrow, Citizen !* " a hollow word,
As if a dead man spake it ! Yet despair
Touches me not, though pensive as a bird
Whose vernal coverts winter hath laid bare.

CALAIS, AUGUST 15, 1802

1802. 1803

FESTIVALS have I seen that were not
    names:
This is young Buonaparté's natal day,
And his is henceforth an established sway—
Consul for life. With worship France pro-
    claims
Her approbation, and with pomps and
    games.
Heaven grant that other Cities may be
    gay !
Calais is not: and I have bent my way
To the sea-coast, noting that each man
    frames

His business as he likes. Far other show
My youth here witnessed, in a prouder
    time;
The senselessness of joy was then sublime !
Happy is he, who, caring not for Pope,
Consul, or King, can sound himself to know
The destiny of Man, and live in hope.

"IT IS A BEAUTEOUS EVEN-ING, CALM AND FREE"

1802. 1807

This was composed on the beach near Calais,
in the autumn of 1802.

IT is a beauteous evening, calm and free,
The holy time is quiet as a Nun
Breathless with adoration; the broad sun
Is sinking down in its tranquillity;
The gentleness of heaven broods o'er the
    Sea:
Listen ! the mighty Being is awake,
And doth with his eternal motion make
A sound like thunder — everlastingly.
Dear Child ! dear Girl ! that walkest with
    me here,
If thou appear untouched by solemn
    thought,
Thy nature is not therefore less divine:
Thou liest in Abraham's bosom all the year;
And worship'st at the Temple's inner shrine,
God being with thee when we know it not.

ON THE EXTINCTION OF THE VENETIAN REPUBLIC

1802. 1807

ONCE did She hold the gorgeous east in
    fee;
And was the safeguard of the west: the
    worth
Of Venice did not fall below her birth,
Venice, the eldest Child of Liberty.
She was a maiden City, bright and free;
No guile seduced, no force could violate;
And, when she took unto herself a Mate,
She must espouse the everlasting Sea.
And what if she had seen those glories fade,
Those titles vanish, and that strength
    decay;
Yet shall some tribute of regret be paid
When her long life hath reached its final
    day:

Men are we, and must grieve when even
the Shade
Of that which once was great, is passed
away.

THE KING OF SWEDEN

1804(?). 1807

THE Voice of song from distant lands shall
call
To that great King; shall hail the crownèd
Youth
Who, taking counsel of unbending Truth,
By one example hath set forth to all
How they with dignity may stand; or fall,
If fall they must. Now, whither doth it
tend ?
And what to him and his shall be the end ?
That thought is one which neither can
appal
Nor cheer him; for the illustrious Swede
hath done
The thing which ought to be; is raised
above
All consequences: work he hath begun
Of fortitude, and piety, and love,
Which all his glorious ancestors approve:
The heroes bless him, him their rightful son.

TO TOUSSAINT L'OUVERTURE

1802. 1803

TOUSSAINT, the most unhappy man of
men !
Whether the whistling Rustic tend his
plough
Within thy hearing, or thy head be now
Pillowed in some deep dungeon's earless
den; —
O miserable Chieftain ! where and when
Wilt thou find patience ? Yet die not; do
thou
Wear rather in thy bonds a cheerful brow:
Though fallen thyself, never to rise again,
Live, and take comfort. Thou hast left
behind
Powers that will work for thee; air, earth,
and skies;
There 's not a breathing of the common
wind
That will forget thee; thou hast great allies;
Thy friends are exultations, agonies,
And love, and man's unconquerable mind.

COMPOSED IN THE VALLEY NEAR DOVER, ON THE DAY OF LANDING

1802. 1807

HERE, on our native soil, we breathe once
more.
The cock that crows, the smoke that curls,
that sound
Of bells; those boys who in yon meadow-
ground
In white-sleeved shirts are playing; and
the roar
Of the waves breaking on the chalky
shore; —
All, all are English. Oft have I looked
round
With joy in Kent's green vales; but never
found
Myself so satisfied in heart before.
Europe is yet in bonds; but let that pass,
Thought for another moment. Thou art
free,
My Country ! and 't is joy enough and
pride
For one hour's perfect bliss, to tread the
grass
Of England once again, and hear and see,
With such a dear Companion at my side.

SEPTEMBER 1, 1802

1802. 1803

Among the capricious acts of tyranny that
disgraced those times, was the chasing of all
Negroes from France by decree of the govern-
ment: we had a Fellow-passenger who was one
of the expelled.

WE had a female Passenger who came
From Calais with us, spotless in array, —
A white-robed Negro, like a lady gay,
Yet downcast as a woman fearing blame;
Meek, destitute, as seemed, of hope or aim
She sate, from notice turning not away,
But on all proffered intercourse did lay
A weight of languid speech, or to the same
No sign of answer made by word or face:
Yet still her eyes retained their tropic fire,
That, burning independent of the mind,
Joined with the lustre of her rich attire
To mock the Outcast. — O ye Heavens, be
kind !
And feel, thou Earth, for this afflicted Race !

NEAR DOVER, September 1802

1802. 1807

INLAND, within a hollow vale, I stood;
And saw, while sea was calm and air was
  clear,
The coast of France — the coast of France
  how near!
Drawn almost into frightful neighbourhood.
I shrunk; for verily the barrier flood
Was like a lake, or river bright and fair,
A span of waters; yet what power is there!
What mightiness for evil and for good!
Even so doth God protect us if we be
Virtuous and wise. Winds blow, and waters
  roll,
Strength to the brave, and Power, and
  Deity;
Yet in themselves are nothing! One decree
Spake laws to *them*, and said that by the
  soul
Only, the Nations shall be great and free.

IN LONDON, September 1802

1802. 1807

This was written immediately after my re-
turn from France to London, when I could not
but be struck, as here described, with the vanity
and parade of our own country, especially in
great towns and cities, as contrasted with the
quiet, and I may say the desolation, that the
revolution had produced in France. This must
be borne in mind, or else the reader may think
that in this and the succeeding Sonnets I have
exaggerated the mischief engendered and fos-
tered among us by undisturbed wealth. It
would not be easy to conceive with what a depth
of feeling I entered into the struggle carried
on by the Spaniards for their deliverance from
the usurped power of the French. Many times
have I gone from Allan Bank in Grasmere vale,
where we were then residing, to the top of the
Raise-gap as it is called, so late as two o'clock
in the morning, to meet the carrier bringing
the newspaper from Keswick. Imperfect traces
of the state of mind in which I then was may
be found in my Tract on the Convention of
Cintra, as well as in these Sonnets.

O FRIEND! I know not which way I must
  look
For comfort, being, as I am, opprest,
To think that now our life is only drest
For show; mean handy-work of craftsman,
  cook,

Or groom! — We must run glittering like
  a brook
In the open sunshine, or we are unblest:
The wealthiest man among us is the best:
No grandeur now in nature or in book
Delights us. Rapine, avarice, expense,
This is idolatry; and these we adore:
Plain living and high thinking are no more:
The homely beauty of the good old cause
Is gone; our peace, our fearful innocence,
And pure religion breathing household
  laws.

LONDON, 1802

1802. 1807

MILTON! thou should'st be living at this
  hour:
England hath need of thee: she is a fen
Of stagnant waters: altar, sword, and pen,
Fireside, the heroic wealth of hall and
  bower,
Have forfeited their ancient English dower
Of inward happiness. We are selfish men;
Oh! raise us up, return to us again;
And give us manners, virtue, freedom,
  power.
Thy soul was like a Star, and dwelt apart:
Thou hadst a voice whose sound was like
  the sea:
Pure as the naked heavens, majestic, free,
So didst thou travel on life's common way,
In cheerful godliness; and yet thy heart
The lowliest duties on herself did lay.

"GREAT MEN HAVE BEEN AMONG US"

1802. 1807

GREAT men have been among us; hands
  that penned
And tongues that uttered wisdom — better
  none:
The later Sidney, Marvel, Harrington,
Young Vane, and others who called Milton
  friend.
These moralists could act and comprehend:
They knew how genuine glory was put on;
Taught us how rightfully a nation shone
In splendour: what strength was, that
  would not bend
But in magnanimous meekness. France,
  't is strange,

Hath brought forth no such souls as we had
then.
Perpetual emptiness ! unceasing change !
No single volume paramount, no code,
No master spirit, no determined road;
But equally a want of books and men !

"IT IS NOT TO BE THOUGHT OF"

1802. 1803

IT is not to be thought of that the Flood
Of British freedom, which, to the open sea
Of the world's praise, from dark antiquity
Hath flowed, " with pomp of waters, un-
    withstood,"
Roused though it be full often to a mood
Which spurns the check of salutary bands,
That this most famous Stream in bogs and
    sands
Should perish; and to evil and to good
Be lost for ever. In our halls is hung
Armoury of the invincible Knights of old:
We must be free or die, who speak the
    tongue
That Shakspeare spake; the faith and
    morals hold
Which Milton held. — In everything we are
    sprung
Of Earth's first blood, have titles manifold.

"WHEN I HAVE BORNE IN MEMORY"

1802. 1803

WHEN I have borne in memory what has
    tamed
Great Nations, how ennobling thoughts
    depart
When men change swords for ledgers, and
    desert
The student's bower for gold, some fears
    unnamed
I had, my Country ! — am I to be blamed ?
Now, when I think of thee, and what thou art,
Verily, in the bottom of my heart,
Of those unfilial fears I am ashamed.
For dearly must we prize thee; we who find
In thee a bulwark for the cause of men:
And I by my affection was beguiled:
What wonder if a Poet now and then,
Among the many movements of his mind,
Felt for thee as a lover or a child !

COMPOSED AFTER A JOURNEY ACROSS THE HAMBLETON HILLS, YORKSHIRE

1802. 1807

Composed October 4th, 1802, after a jour-
ney over the Hambleton Hills, on a day mem-
orable to me — the day of my marriage.
The horizon commanded by those hills is most
magnificent. — The next day, while we were
travelling in a post-chaise up Wensleydale, we
were stopt by one of the horses proving rest-
ive, and were obliged to wait two hours in a
severe storm before the post-boy could fetch
from the inn another to supply its place. The
spot was in front of Bolton Hall, where Mary
Queen of Scots was kept prisoner soon after
her unfortunate landing at Workington. The
place then belonged to the Scroopes, and me-
morials of her are yet preserved there. To
beguile the time I composed a Sonnet. The
subject was our own confinement contrasted
with hers ; but it was not thought worthy of
being preserved.

DARK and more dark the shades of evening
    fell;
The wished-for point was reached — but at
    an hour
When little could be gained from that rich
    dower
Of prospect, whereof many thousands tell.
Yet did the glowing west with marvellous
    power
Salute us; there stood Indian citadel,
Temple of Greece, and minster with its
    tower
Substantially expressed — a place for bell
Or clock to toll from ! Many a tempting
    isle,
With groves that never were imagined, lay
'Mid seas how steadfast ! objects all for
    the eye
Of silent rapture; but we felt the while
We should forget them; they are of the sky,
And from our earthly memory fade away.

STANZAS

WRITTEN IN MY POCKET-COPY OF THOM-SON'S "CASTLE OF INDOLENCE"

1802. 1815

Composed in the orchard, Town-end, Gras-
mere, Coleridge living with us much at the
time : his son Hartley has said, that his father's

character and habits are here preserved in a livelier way than in anything that has been written about him.

WITHIN our happy Castle there dwelt One
Whom without blame I may not overlook;
For never sun on living creature shone
Who more devout enjoyment with us took:
Here on his hours he hung as on a book,
On his own time here would he float away,
As doth a fly upon a summer brook;
But go to-morrow, or belike to-day,
Seek for him, — he is fled; and whither none can say.

Thus often would he leave our peaceful home,   10
And find elsewhere his business or delight;
Out of our Valley's limits did he roam:
Full many a time, upon a stormy night,
His voice came to us from the neighbouring height:
Oft could we see him driving full in view
At mid-day when the sun was shining bright;
What ill was on him, what he had to do,
A mighty wonder bred among our quiet crew.

Ah! piteous sight it was to see this Man
When he came back to us, a withered flower, —   20
Or like a sinful creature, pale and wan.
Down would he sit; and without strength or power
Look at the common grass from hour to hour:
And oftentimes, how long I fear to say,
Where apple-trees in blossom made a bower,
Retired in that sunshiny shade he lay;
And, like a naked Indian, slept himself away.

Great wonder to our gentle tribe it was
Whenever from our Valley he withdrew;
For happier soul no living creature has   30
Than he had, being here the long day through.
Some thought he was a lover, and did woo:
Some thought far worse of him, and judged him wrong;
But verse was what he had been wedded to;

And his own mind did like a tempest strong
Come to him thus, and drove the weary Wight along.

With him there often walked in friendly guise,
Or lay upon the moss by brook or tree,
A noticeable Man with large gray eyes,   39
And a pale face that seemed undoubtedly
As if a blooming face it ought to be;
Heavy his low-hung lip did oft appear,
Deprest by weight of musing Phantasy;
Profound his forehead was, though not severe;
Yet some did think that he had little business here.

Sweet heaven forfend! his was a lawful right;
Noisy he was, and gamesome as a boy;
His limbs would toss about him with delight
Like branches when strong winds the trees annoy.
Nor lacked his calmer hours device or toy
To banish listlessness and irksome care;   51
He would have taught you how you might employ
Yourself; and many did to him repair, —
And certes not in vain; he had inventions rare.

Expedients, too, of simplest sort he tried:
Long blades of grass, plucked round him as he lay,
Made, to his ear attentively applied,
A pipe on which the wind would deftly play;
Glasses he had, that little things display,
The beetle panoplied in gems and gold,   60
A mailèd angel on a battle-day;
The mysteries that cups of flowers enfold,
And all the gorgeous sights which fairies do behold.

He would entice that other Man to hear
His music, and to view his imagery:
And, sooth, these two were each to the other dear:
No livelier love in such a place could be:
There did they dwell — from earthly labour free,
As happy spirits as were ever seen;
If but a bird, to keep them company,   70
Or butterfly sate down, they were, I ween,
As pleased as if the same had been a Maiden-queen.

TO H. C.

SIX YEARS OLD

1802. 1807

O THOU! whose fancies from afar are
    brought;
Who of thy words dost make a mock apparel,
And fittest to unutterable thought
The breeze-like motion and the self-born
    carol;
Thou faery voyager! that dost float
In such clear water, that thy boat
May rather seem
To brood on air than on an earthly stream;
Suspended in a stream as clear as sky,
Where earth and heaven do make one
    imagery;   10
O blessed vision! happy child!
Thou art so exquisitely wild,
I think of thee with many fears
For what may be thy lot in future years.
    I thought of times when Pain might be
      thy guest,
Lord of thy house and hospitality;
And Grief, uneasy lover! never rest
But when she sate within the touch of thee.
O too industrious folly!
O vain and causeless melancholy!   20
Nature will either end thee quite;.
Or, lengthening out thy season of delight,
Preserve for thee, by individual right,
A young lamb's heart among the full-grown
    flocks.
What hast thou to do with sorrow,
Or the injuries of to-morrow?
Thou art a dew-drop, which the morn
    brings forth,
Ill fitted to sustain unkindly shocks,
Or to be trailed along the soiling earth;
A gem that glitters while it lives,   30
And no forewarning gives;
But, at the touch of wrong, without a strife
Slips in a moment out of life.

TO THE DAISY

1802. 1807

This, "To the Same Flower," and "The
Green Linnet" were composed in the orchard,
Town-end, Grasmere, where the bird [the lin-
net] was often seen as here described.

"Her divine skill taught me this,
    That from every thing I saw
    I could some instruction draw,

And raise pleasure to the height
Through the meanest object's sight.
By the murmur of a spring,
Or the least bough's rustelling;
By a Daisy whose leaves spread
Shut when Titan goes to bed;
Or a shady bush or tree;
She could more infuse in me
Than all Nature's beauties can
In some other wiser man."
                G. WITHER.

IN youth from rock to rock I went,
From hill to hill in discontent
Of pleasure high and turbulent,
    Most pleased when most uneasy;
But now my own delights I make, —
My thirst at every rill can slake,
And gladly Nature's love partake,
    Of Thee, sweet Daisy!

Thee Winter in the garland wears
That thinly decks his few grey hairs;   10
Spring parts the clouds with softest airs,
    That she may sun thee;
Whole Summer-fields are thine by right;
And Autumn, melancholy Wight!
Doth in thy crimson head delight
    When rains are on thee.

In shoals and bands, a morrice train,
Thou greet'st the traveller in the lane;
Pleased at his greeting thee again;
    Yet nothing daunted,   20
Nor grieved if thou be set at nought:
And oft alone in nooks remote
We meet thee, like a pleasant thought,
    When such are wanted.

Be violets in their secret mews
The flowers the wanton Zephyrs choose;
Proud be the rose, with rains and dews
    Her head impearling,
Thou liv'st with less ambitious aim,
Yet hast not gone without thy fame;   30
Thou art indeed by many a claim
    The Poet's darling.

If to a rock from rains he fly,
Or, some bright day of April sky,
Imprisoned by hot sunshine lie
    Near the green holly,
And wearily at length should fare;
He needs but look about, and there
Thou art! — a friend at hand, to scare
    His melancholy.   40

A hundred times, by rock or bower,
Ere thus I have lain couched an hour,

Have I derived from thy sweet power
    Some apprehension;
Some steady love; some brief delight;
Some memory that had taken flight;
Some chime of fancy wrong or right;
    Or stray invention.

If stately passions in me burn,
And one chance look to Thee should turn,
I drink out of an humbler urn   51
    A lowlier pleasure;
The homely sympathy that heeds
The common life, our nature breeds;
A wisdom fitted to the needs
    Of hearts at leisure.

Fresh-smitten by the morning ray,
When thou art up, alert and gay,
Then, cheerful Flower ! my spirits play
    With kindred gladness: 60
And when, at dusk, by dews opprest
Thou sink'st, the image of thy rest
Hath often eased my pensive breast
    Of careful sadness.

And all day long I number yet,
All seasons through, another debt,
Which I, wherever thou art met,
    To thee am owing;
An instinct call it, a blind sense;
A happy, genial influence,   70
Coming one knows not how, or whence,
    Nor whither going.

Child of the Year ! that round dost run
Thy pleasant course, — when day 's begun
As ready to salute the sun
    As lark or leveret,
Thy long-lost praise thou shalt regain;
Nor be less dear to future men
Than in old time; — thou not in vain
    Art Nature's favourite.   80

TO THE SAME FLOWER

1802. 1807

WITH little here to do or see
Of things that in the great world be,
Daisy ! again I talk to thee,
    For thou art worthy,
Thou unassuming Common-place
Of Nature, with that homely face,
And yet with something of a grace,
    Which love makes for thee !

Oft on the dappled turf at ease
I sit, and play with similes,   10
Loose types of things through all degrees,
    Thoughts of thy raising:
And many a fond and idle name
I give to thee, for praise or blame,
As is the humour of the game,
    While I am gazing.

A nun demure of lowly port;
Or sprightly maiden, of Love's court,
In thy simplicity the sport
    Of all temptations;   20
A queen in crown of rubies drest;
A starveling in a scanty vest;
Are all, as seems to suit thee best,
    Thy appellations.

A little cyclops, with one eye
Staring to threaten and defy,
That thought comes next — and instantly
    The freak is over,
The shape will vanish — and behold
A silver shield with boss of gold,   30
That spreads itself, some faery bold
    In fight to cover !

I see thee glittering from afar —
And then thou art a pretty star;
Not quite so fair as many are
    In heaven above thee !
Yet like a star, with glittering crest,
Self-poised in air thou seem'st to rest; —
May peace come never to his nest,
    Who shall reprove thee !   40

Bright *Flower !* for by that name at last,
When all my reveries are past,
I call thee, and to that cleave fast,
    Sweet silent creature !
That breath'st with me in sun and air,
Do thou, as thou art wont, repair
My heart with gladness, and a share
    Of thy meek nature !

TO THE DAISY

1802. 1807

This and the other Poems addressed to the
same flower were composed at Town-end, Gras-
mere, during the earlier part of my residence
there. I have been censured for the last line
but one — " thy function apostolical " — as be-
ing little less than profane. How could it be

thought so ? The word is adopted with reference to its derivation, implying something sent on a mission ; and assuredly this little flower, especially when the subject of verse, may be regarded, in its humble degree, as administering both to moral and to spiritual purposes.

BRIGHT Flower! whose home is everywhere,
Bold in maternal Nature's care,
And all the long year through the heir
    Of joy and sorrow;
Methinks that there abides in thee
Some concord with humanity,
Given to no other flower I see
    The forest thorough!

Is it that Man is soon deprest ?
A thoughtless Thing ! who, once unblest,
Does little on his memory rest,
    Or on his reason,
And Thou would'st teach him how to find
A shelter under every wind,
A hope for times that are unkind
    And every season ?

Thou wander'st the wide world about,
Unchecked by pride or scrupulous doubt,
With friends to greet thee, or without,
    Yet pleased and willing;
Meek, yielding to the occasion's call,
And all things suffering from all,
Thy function apostolical
    In peace fulfilling.

THE GREEN LINNET

1802(?). 1807

BENEATH these fruit-tree boughs that shed
Their snow-white blossoms on my head,
With brightest sunshine round me spread
    Of spring's unclouded weather,
In this sequestered nook how sweet
To sit upon my orchard-seat !
And birds and flowers once more to greet,
    My last year's friends together.

One have I marked, the happiest guest
In all this covert of the blest: 10
Hail to Thee, far above the rest
    In joy of voice and pinion !
Thou, Linnet ! in thy green array,
Presiding Spirit here to-day,
Dost lead the revels of the May;
    And this is thy dominion.

While birds, and butterflies, and flowers,
Make all one band of paramours,
Thou, ranging up and down the bowers,
    Art sole in thy employment: 20
A life, a Presence like the Air,
Scattering thy gladness without care,
Too blest with any one to pair;
    Thyself thy own enjoyment.

Amid yon tuft of hazel trees,
That twinkle to the gusty breeze,
Behold him perched in ecstasies,
    Yet seeming still to hover;
There ! where the flutter of his wings
Upon his back and body flings   30
Shadows and sunny glimmerings,
    That cover him all over.

My dazzled sight he oft deceives,
A Brother of the dancing leaves;
Then flits, and from the cottage-eaves
    Pours forth his song in gushes;
As if by that exulting strain
He mocked and treated with disdain
The voiceless Form he chose to feign,
    While fluttering in the bushes.   40

YEW-TREES

1804(?). 1815

Written at Grasmere. These yew-trees are still standing, but the spread of that at Lorton is much diminished by mutilation. I will here mention that a little way up the hill, on the road leading from Rosthwaite to Stonethwaite (in Borrowdale), lay the trunk of a yew-tree, which appeared as you approached, so vast was its diameter, like the entrance of a cave, and not a small one. Calculating upon what I have observed of the slow growth of this tree in rocky situations, and of its durability, I have often thought that the one I am describing must have been as old as the Christian era. The tree lay in the line of a fence. Great masses of its ruins were strewn about, and some had been rolled down the hillside and lay near the road at the bottom. As you approached the tree, you were struck with the number of shrubs and young plants, ashes, etc., which had found a bed upon the decayed trunk and grew to no inconsiderable height, forming, as it were, a part of the hedgerow. In no part of England, or of Europe, have I ever seen a yew-tree at all approaching this in magnitude, as it must have stood. By the bye, Hutton, the old Guide, of Keswick, had been so im-

pressed with the remains of this tree, that he
used gravely to tell strangers that there could
be no doubt of its having been in existence be-
fore the flood.

THERE is a Yew-tree, pride of Lorton Vale,
Which to this day stands single, in the
    midst
Of its own darkness, as it stood of yore;
Not loth to furnish weapons for the bands
Of Umfraville or Percy ere they marched
To Scotland's heaths; or those that crossed
    the sea
And drew their sounding bows at Azincour,
Perhaps at earlier Crecy, or Poictiers.
Of vast circumference and gloom profound
This solitary Tree ! a living thing   10
Produced too slowly ever to decay;
Of form and aspect too magnificent
To be destroyed. But worthier still of
    note
Are those fraternal Four of Borrowdale,
Joined in one solemn and capacious grove;
Huge trunks ! and each particular trunk a
    growth
Of intertwisted fibres serpentine
Up-coiling, and inveterately convolved;
Nor uninformed with Phantasy, and looks
That threaten the profane; — a pillared
    shade,   20
Upon whose grassless floor of red-brown
    hue,
By sheddings from the pining umbrage
    tinged
Perennially — beneath whose sable roof
Of boughs, as if for festal purpose, decked
With unrejoicing berries — ghostly Shapes
May meet at noontide; Fear and trembling
    Hope,
Silence and Foresight; Death the Skeleton
And Time the Shadow; — there to cele-
    brate,
As in a natural temple scattered o'er
With altars undisturbed of mossy stone, 30
United worship; or in mute repose
To lie, and listen to the mountain flood
Murmuring from Glaramara's inmost caves.

"WHO FANCIED WHAT A PRETTY SIGHT"

1804(?). 1807

WHO fancied what a pretty sight
This Rock would be if edged around

With living snow-drops ? circlet bright !
How glorious to this orchard-ground !
Who loved the little Rock, and set
Upon its head this coronet ?

Was it the humour of a child ?
Or rather of some gentle maid,
Whose brows, the day that she was styled
The shepherd-queen, were thus arrayed ?
Of man mature, or matron sage ?
Or old man toying with his age ?

I asked — 't was whispered; The device
To each and all might well belong:
It is the Spirit of Paradise
That prompts such work, a Spirit strong,
That gives to all the self-same bent
Where life is wise and innocent.

"IT IS NO SPIRIT WHO FROM HEAVEN HATH FLOWN"

1802(?). 1807

Written at Town-end, Grasmere. I remem-
ber the instant my sister, S. H., called me to
the window of our Cottage, saying, "Look
how beautiful is yon star ! It has the sky
all to itself." I composed the verses imme-
diately.

IT is no Spirit who from heaven hath flown,
And is descending on his embassy;
Nor Traveller gone from earth the heavens
    to espy !
'T is Hesperus — there he stands with glit-
    tering crown,
First admonition that the sun is down !
For yet it is broad day-light: clouds pass
    by;
A few are near him still — and now the sky,
He hath it to himself — 't is all his own.
O most ambitious Star ! an inquest wrought
Within me when I recognised thy light;
A moment I was startled at the sight:
And, while I gazed, there came to me a
    thought
That I might step beyond my natural race
As thou seem'st now to do; might one day
    trace
Some ground not mine; and, strong her
    strength above,
My Soul, an Apparition in the place,
Tread there with steps that no one shall
    reprove !

MEMORIALS OF A TOUR IN SCOTLAND

1803

Mr. Coleridge, my Sister, and myself started together from Town-end to make a tour in Scotland. Poor Coleridge was at that time in bad spirits, and somewhat too much in love with his own dejection; and he departed from us, as is recorded in my Sister's Journal, soon after we left Loch Lomond. The verses that stand foremost among these Memorials were not actually written for the occasion, but transplanted from my " Epistle to Sir George Beaumont."

I

DEPARTURE FROM THE VALE OF GRASMERE

AUGUST 1803

1811. 1827

THE gentlest Shade that walked Elysian
　　plains
Might sometimes covet dissoluble chains;
Even for the tenants of the zone that lies
Beyond the stars, celestial Paradise,
Methinks 't would heighten joy, to overleap
At will the crystal battlements, and peep
Into some other region, though less fair,
To see how things are made and managed
　　there.
Change for the worse might please, incur-
　　sion bold
Into the tracts of darkness and of cold;　10
O'er Limbo lake with aëry flight to steer,
And on the verge of Chaos hang in fear.
Such animation often do I find,
Power in my breast, wings growing in my
　　mind,
Then, when some rock or hill is overpast,
Perchance without one look behind me cast,
Some barrier with which Nature, from the
　　birth
Of things, has fenced this fairest spot on
　　earth.
O pleasant transit, Grasmere ! to resign
Such happy fields, abodes so calm as
　　thine;　　20
Not like an outcast with himself at strife;
The slave of business, time, or care for
　　life,
But moved by choice; or, if constrained in
　　part,
Yet still with Nature's freedom at the
　　heart; —
To cull contentment upon wildest shores,
And luxuries extract from bleakest moors;
With prompt embrace all beauty to enfold,
And having rights in all that we behold.

— Then why these lingering steps ? — A
　　bright adieu,
For a brief absence, proves that love is
　　true;　　30
Ne'er can the way be irksome or for-
　　lorn
That winds into itself for sweet return.

II

AT THE GRAVE OF BURNS

1803

SEVEN YEARS AFTER HIS DEATH

1803. 1842

For illustration, see my Sister's Journal. It may be proper to add that the second of these pieces, though *felt* at the time, was not composed till many years after.

I SHIVER, Spirit fierce and bold,
At thought of what I now behold:
As vapours breathed from dungeons cold,
　　Strike pleasure dead,
So sadness comes from out the mould
　　Where Burns is laid.

And have I then thy bones so near,
And thou forbidden to appear ?
As if it were thyself that 's here
　　I shrink with pain;　　10
And both my wishes and my fear
　　Alike are vain.

Off weight — nor press on weight ! — away
Dark thoughts ! — they came, but not to
　　stay;
With chastened feelings would I pay
　　The tribute due
To him, and aught that hides his clay
　　From mortal view.

Fresh as the flower, whose modest worth
He sang, his genius " glinted " forth,　　20

Rose like a star that touching earth,
    For so it seems,
Doth glorify its humble birth
    With matchless beams.

The piercing eye, the thoughtful brow,
The struggling heart, where be they
        now ? —
Full soon the Aspirant of the plough,
    The prompt, the brave,
Slept, with the obscurest, in the low
    And silent grave.   30

I mourned with thousands, but as one
More deeply grieved, for He was gone
Whose light I hailed when first it shone,
    And showed my youth
How Verse may build a princely throne
    On humble truth.

Alas ! where'er the current tends,
Regret pursues and with it blends, —
Huge Criffel's hoary top ascends
    By Skiddaw seen, —   40
Neighbours we were, and loving friends
    We might have been;

True friends though diversely inclined;
But heart with heart and mind with mind,
Where the main fibres are entwined,
    Through Nature's skill,
May even by contraries be joined
    More closely still.

The tear will start, and let it flow;
Thou " poor Inhabitant below,"   50
At this dread moment — even so —
    Might we together
Have sate and talked where gowans blow,
    Or on wild heather.

What treasures would have then been
        placed
Within my reach; of knowledge graced
By fancy what a rich repast !
    But why go on ? —
Oh ! spare to sweep, thou mournful blast,
    His grave grass-grown.   60

There, too, a Son, his joy and pride,
(Not three weeks past the Stripling died,)
Lies gathered to his Father's side,
    Soul-moving sight !
Yet one to which is not denied
    Some sad delight:

For *he* is safe, a quiet bed
Hath early found among the dead,
Harboured where none can be misled,
    Wronged, or distrest;   70
And surely here it may be said
    That such are blest.

And oh for Thee, by pitying grace
Checked oft-times in a devious race,
May He who halloweth the place
    Where Man is laid
Receive thy Spirit in the embrace
    For which it prayed !

Sighing I turned away; but ere
Night fell I heard, or seemed to hear,   80
Music that sorrow comes not near,
    A ritual hymn,
Chaunted in love that casts out fear
    By Seraphim.

III

THOUGHTS

SUGGESTED THE DAY FOLLOWING, ON
THE BANKS OF NITH, NEAR THE POET'S
RESIDENCE

1839. 1842

Too frail to keep the lofty vow
That must have followed when his brow
Was wreathed — " The Vision " tells us
        how —
    With holly spray,
He faltered, drifted to and fro,
    And passed away.

Well might such thoughts, dear Sister,
        throng
Our minds when, lingering all too long,
Over the grave of Burns we hung
    In social grief —   10
Indulged as if it were a wrong
    To seek relief.

But, leaving each unquiet theme
Where gentlest judgments may misdeem,
And prompt to welcome every gleam
    Of good and fair,
Let us beside the limpid Stream
    Breathe hopeful air.

Enough of sorrow, wreck, and blight;
Think rather of those moments bright   20

When to the consciousness of right
    His course was true,
When Wisdom prospered in his sight
    And virtue grew.

Yes, freely let our hearts expand,
Freely as in youth's season bland,
When side by side, his Book in hand,
    We wont to stray,
Our pleasure varying at command
    Of each sweet Lay.   30

How oft inspired must he have trod
These pathways, yon far-stretching road!
There lurks his home; in that Abode,
    With mirth elate,
Or in his nobly-pensive mood,
    The Rustic sate.

Proud thoughts that Image overawes,
Before it humbly let us pause,
And ask of Nature, from what cause
    And by what rules   40
She trained her Burns to win applause
    That shames the Schools.

Through busiest street and loneliest glen
Are felt the flashes of his pen;
He rules 'mid winter snows, and when
    Bees fill their hives;
Deep in the general heart of men
    His power survives.

What need of fields in some far clime
Where Heroes, Sages, Bards sublime,   50
And all that fetched the flowing rhyme
    From genuine springs,
Shall dwell together till old Time
    Folds up his wings?

Sweet Mercy! to the gates of Heaven
This Minstrel lead, his sins forgiven;
The rueful conflict, the heart riven
    With vain endeavour,
And memory of Earth's bitter leaven,
    Effaced for ever.   60

But why to Him confine the prayer,
When kindred thoughts and yearnings
    bear
On the frail heart the purest share
    With all that live? —
The best of what we do and are,
    Just God, forgive!

IV

TO THE SONS OF BURNS

AFTER VISITING THE GRAVE OF THEIR FATHER

1805(?). 1807

"The Poet's grave is in a corner of the church-yard. We looked at it with mélancholy and painful reflections, repeating to each other his own verses —

"'Is there a man whose judgment clear,' etc."
Extract from the Journal of my Fellow-Traveller.

'MID crowded obelisks and urns
I sought the untimely grave of Burns;
Sons of the Bard, my heart still mourns
    With sorrow true;
And more would grieve, but that it turns
    Trembling to you!

Through twilight shades of good and ill
Ye now are panting up life's hill,
And more than common strength and skill
    Must ye display;   10
If ye would give the better will
    Its lawful sway.

Hath Nature strung your nerves to bear
Intemperance with less harm, beware!
But if the Poet's wit ye share,
    Like him can speed
The social hour — of tenfold care
    There will be need;

For honest men delight will take
To spare your failings for his sake,   20
Will flatter you, — and fool and rake
    Your steps pursue;
And of your Father's name will make
    A snare for you.

Far from their noisy haunts retire,
And add your voices to the quire
That sanctify the cottage fire
    With service meet;
There seek the genius of your Sire,
    His spirit greet;   30

Or where, 'mid "lonely heights and hows,"
He paid to Nature tuneful vows;
Or wiped his honourable brows
    Bedewed with toil,
While reapers strove, or busy ploughs
    Upturned the soil;

His judgment with benignant ray
Shall guide, his fancy cheer, your way;
But ne'er to a seductive lay
    Let faith be given;   40
Nor deem that " light which leads astray,
    Is light from Heaven."

Let no mean hope your souls enslave;
Be independent, generous, brave;
Your Father such example gave,
    And such revere;
But be admonished by his grave,
    And think, and fear !

V

TO A HIGHLAND GIRL

AT INVERSNEYDE, UPON LOCH LOMOND

1803. 1807

This delightful creature and her demeanour are particularly described in my Sister's Journal. The sort of prophecy with which the verses conclude has, through God's goodness, been realised; and now, approaching the close of my 73d year, I have a most vivid remembrance of her and the beautiful objects with which she was surrounded. She is alluded to in the Poem of "The Three Cottage Girls" among my Continental Memorials. In illustration of this class of poems I have scarcely anything to say beyond what is anticipated in my Sister's faithful and admirable Journal.

Sweet Highland Girl, a very shower
Of beauty is thy earthly dower !
Twice seven consenting years have shed
Their utmost bounty on thy head:
And these grey rocks; that household
    lawn;
Those trees, a veil just half withdrawn;
This fall of water that doth make
A murmur near the silent lake;
This little bay; a quiet road
That holds in shelter thy Abode —   10
In truth together do ye seem
Like something fashioned in a dream;
Such Forms as from their covert peep
When earthly cares are laid asleep !
But, O fair Creature ! in the light
Of common day, so heavenly bright,
I bless Thee, Vision as thou art,
I bless thee with a human heart;
God shield thee to thy latest years !
Thee, neither know I, nor thy peers;   20
And yet my eyes are filled with tears.

With earnest feeling I shall pray
For thee when I am far away:
For never saw I mien, or face,
In which more plainly I could trace
Benignity and home-bred sense
Ripening in perfect innocence.
Here scattered, like a random seed,
Remote from men, Thou dost not need
The embarrassed look of shy distress,   30
And maidenly shamefacedness:
Thou wear'st upon thy forehead clear
The freedom of a Mountaineer:
A face with gladness overspread !
Soft smiles, by human kindness bred !
And seemliness complete, that sways
Thy courtesies, about thee plays;
With no restraint, but such as springs
From quick and eager visitings
Of thoughts that lie beyond the reach   40
Of thy few words of English speech:
A bondage sweetly brooked, a strife
That gives thy gestures grace and life !
So have I, not unmoved in mind,
Seen birds of tempest-loving kind —
Thus beating up against the wind.
    What hand but would a garland cull
For thee who art so beautiful ?
O happy pleasure ! here to dwell
Beside thee in some heathy dell;   50
Adopt your homely ways, and dress,
A Shepherd, thou a Shepherdess !
But I could frame a wish for thee
More like a grave reality:
Thou art to me but as a wave
Of the wild sea; and I would have
Some claim upon thee, if I could,
Though but of common neighbourhood.
What joy to hear thee, and to see !
Thy elder Brother I would be,   60
Thy Father — anything to thee !
    Now thanks to Heaven ! that of its
        grace
Hath led me to this lonely place.
Joy have I had; and going hence
I bear away my recompence.
In spots like these it is we prize
Our Memory, feel that she hath eyes:
Then, why should I be loth to stir ?
I feel this place was made for her;
To give new pleasure like the past,   70
Continued long as life shall last.
Nor am I loth, though pleased at heart,
Sweet Highland Girl ! from thee to part:
For I, methinks, till I grow old,
As fair before me shall behold,

As I do now, the cabin small,
The lake, the bay, the waterfall;
And Thee, the Spirit of them all !

VI

GLEN-ALMAIN

OR, THE NARROW GLEN

1805. 1807

IN this still place, remote from men,
Sleeps Ossian, in the NARROW GLEN;
In this still place, where murmurs on
But one meek streamlet, only one:
He sang of battles, and the breath
Of stormy war, and violent death;
And should, methinks, when all was past,
Have rightfully been laid at last
Where rocks were rudely heaped, and rent
As by a spirit turbulent;   10
Where sights were rough, and sounds were
        wild,
And everything unreconciled;
In some complaining, dim retreat,
For fear and melancholy meet;
But this is calm; there cannot be
A more entire tranquillity.
    Does then the Bard sleep here indeed ?
Or is it but a groundless creed ?
What matters it ? — I blame them not
Whose Fancy in this lonely Spot   20
Was moved; and in such way expressed
Their notion of its perfect rest.
A convent, even a hermit's cell,
Would break the silence of this Dell:
It is not quiet, is not ease;
But something deeper far than these:
The separation that is here
Is of the grave; and of austere
Yet happy feelings of the dead:
And, therefore, was it rightly said   30
That Ossian, last of all his race !
Lies buried in this lonely place.

VII

STEPPING WESTWARD

1805. 1807

While my Fellow-traveller and I were walk-
ing by the side of Loch Ketterine, one fine
evening after sunset, in our road to a Hut
where, in the course of our Tour, we had been
hospitably entertained some weeks before, we
met, in one of the loneliest parts of that solitary
region, two well-dressed Women, one of whom
said to us, by way of greeting, " What, you are
stepping westward ? "

" *What, you are stepping westward ?* " —
    " *Yea.*"
— 'T would be a *wildish* destiny,
If we, who thus together roam
In a strange Land, and far from home,
Were in this place the guests of Chance:
Yet who would stop, or fear to advance,
Though home or shelter he had none,
With such a sky to lead him on ?

The dewy ground was dark and cold;
Behind, all gloomy to behold;
And stepping westward seemed to be
A kind of *heavenly* destiny:
I liked the greeting; 't was a sound
Of something without place or bound;
And seemed to give me spiritual right
To travel through that region bright.

The voice was soft, and she who spake
Was walking by her native lake:
The salutation had to me
The very sound of courtesy:
Its power was felt; and while my eye
Was fixed upon the glowing Sky,
The echo of the voice enwrought
A human sweetness with the thought
Of travelling through the world that lay
Before me in my endless way.

VIII

THE SOLITARY REAPER

1805. 1807

BEHOLD her, single in the field,
Yon solitary Highland Lass !
Reaping and singing by herself;
Stop here, or gently pass !
Alone she cuts and binds the grain,
And sings a melancholy strain;
O listen ! for the Vale profound
Is overflowing with the sound.

No Nightingale did ever chaunt
More welcome notes to weary bands   10
Of travellers in some shady haunt,
Among Arabian sands:

A voice so thrilling ne'er was heard
In spring-time from the Cuckoo-bird,
Breaking the silence of the seas
Among the farthest Hebrides.

Will no one tell me what she sings ? —
Perhaps the plaintive numbers flow
For old, unhappy, far-off things,
And battles long ago: 20
Or is it some more humble lay,
Familiar matter of to-day ?
Some natural sorrow, loss, or pain,
That has been, and may be again ?

Whate'er the theme, the Maiden sang
As if her song could have no ending;
I saw her singing at her work,
And o'er the sickle bending; —
I listened, motionless and still;
And, as I mounted up the hill   30
The music in my heart I bore,
Long after it was heard no more.

IX

ADDRESS TO KILCHURN CASTLE,
UPON LOCH AWE

1803. 1827

The first three lines were thrown off at the
moment I first caught sight of the Ruin from a
small eminence by the wayside ; the rest was
added many years after.

" From the top of the hill a most impressive
scene opened upon our view, — a ruined Castle
on an Island (for an Island the flood had made
it) at some distance from the shore, backed by
a Cove of the Mountain Cruachan, down which
came a foaming stream.   The Castle occupied
every foot of the Island that was visible to us,
appearing to rise out of the water, — mists
rested upon the mountain side, with spots of
sunshine ; there was a mild desolation in the
low grounds, a solemn grandeur in the moun-
tains, and the Castle was wild, yet stately —
not dismantled of turrets — nor the walls broken
down, though obviously a ruin." — *Extract
from the Journal of my Companion.*

CHILD of loud-throated War ! the moun-
     tain Stream
Roars in thy hearing; but thy hour of rest
Is come, and thou art silent in thy age;
Save when the wind sweeps by and sounds
     are caught
Ambiguous, neither wholly thine nor theirs.

Oh ! there is life that breathes not; Powers
     there are
That touch each other to the quick in
     modes
Which the gross world no sense hath to
     perceive,
No soul to dream of.   What art Thou,
     from care
Cast off — abandoned by thy rugged Sire, 10
Nor by soft Peace adopted; though, in
     place
And in dimension, such that thou might'st
     seem
But a mere footstool to yon sovereign Lord,
Huge Cruachan, (a thing that meaner hills
Might crush, nor know that it had suffered
     harm;)
Yet he, not loth, in favour of thy claims
To reverence, suspends his own; submit-
     ting
All that the God of Nature hath conferred,
All that he holds in common with the stars,
To the memorial majesty of Time   20
Impersonated in thy calm decay !
Take, then, thy seat, Vicegerent unre-
     proved !
Now, while a farewell gleam of evening
     light
Is fondly lingering on thy shattered front,
Do thou, in turn, be paramount; and rule
Over the pomp and beauty of a scene
Whose mountains, torrents, lake, and
     woods, unite
To pay thee homage; and with these are
     joined,
In willing admiration and respect,
Two Hearts, which in thy presence might
     be called   30
Youthful as Spring. — Shade of departed
     Power,
Skeleton of unfleshed humanity,
The chronicle were welcome that should
     call
Into the compass of distinct regard
The toils and struggles of thy infant years !
Yon foaming flood seems motionless as
     ice;
Its dizzy turbulence eludes the eye,
Frozen by distance; so, majestic Pile,
To the perception of this Age, appear
Thy fierce beginnings, softened and sub-
     dued   40
And quieted in character — the strife,
The pride, the fury uncontrollable,
Lost on the aërial heights of the Crusades !

X

ROB ROY'S GRAVE

1805. 1807

I have since been told that I was misinformed as to the burial-place of Rob Roy. If so, I may plead in excuse that I wrote on apparently good authority, namely, that of a well-educated Lady who lived at the head of the Lake, within a mile or less of the point indicated as containing the remains of One so famous in the neighbourhood.

The history of Rob Roy is sufficiently known; his grave is near the head of Loch Ketterine, in one of those small pinfold-like Burial-grounds, of neglected and desolate appearance, which the traveller meets with in the Highlands of Scotland.

A FAMOUS man is Robin Hood,
The English ballad-singer's joy !
And Scotland has a thief as good,
An outlaw of as daring mood ;
She has her brave ROB ROY !
Then clear the weeds from off his Grave,
And let us chant a passing stave,
In honour of that Hero brave !

Heaven gave Rob Roy a dauntless heart
And wondrous length and strength of
  arm :
Nor craved he more to quell his foes,   11
  Or keep his friends from harm.

Yet was Rob Roy as *wise* as brave ;
Forgive me if the phrase be strong ; —
A Poet worthy of Rob Roy
  Must scorn a timid song.

Say, then, that he was wise as brave ;
As wise in thought as bold in deed :
For in the principles of things
  He sought his moral creed.   20

Said generous Rob, " What need of books ?
Burn all the statutes and their shelves :
They stir us up against our kind ;
  And worse, against ourselves.

" We have a passion — make a law,
Too false to guide us or control !
And for the law itself we fight
  In bitterness of soul.

" And, puzzled, blinded thus, we lose
Distinctions that are plain and few :   30
These find I graven on my heart :
  That tells me what to do.

" The creatures see of flood and field,
And those that travel on the wind !
With them no strife can last ; they live
  In peace, and peace of mind.

" For why ? — because the good old rule
Sufficeth them, the simple plan,
That they should take, who have the power,
  And they should keep who can.   40

" A lesson that is quickly learned,
A signal this which all can see !
Thus nothing here provokes the strong
  To wanton cruelty.

" All freakishness of mind is checked ;
He tamed, who foolishly aspires ;
While to the measure of his might
  Each fashions his desires.

" All kinds, and creatures, stand and fall
By strength of prowess or of wit :   50
'T is God's appointment who must sway,
  And who is to submit.

" Since, then, the rule of right is plain,
And longest life is but a day ;
To have my ends, maintain my rights,
  I 'll take the shortest way."

And thus among these rocks he lived,
Through summer heat and winter snow :
The Eagle, he was lord above,
  And Rob was lord below.   60

So was it — *would*, at least, have been
But through untowardness of fate ;
For Polity was then too strong —
  He came an age too late ;

Or shall we say an age too soon ?
For, were the bold Man living *now*,
How might he flourish in his pride,
  With buds on every bough !

Then rents and factors, rights of chase,
Sheriffs, and lairds and their domains,   70
Would all have seemed but paltry things,
  Not worth a moment's pains.

Rob Roy had never lingered here,
To these few meagre Vales confined;
But thought how wide the world, the times
    How fairly to his mind !

And to his Sword he would have said,
" Do Thou my sovereign will enact
From land to land through half the earth !
    Judge thou of law and fact !   80

" 'T is fit that we should do our part,
Becoming, that mankind should learn
That we are not to be surpassed
    In fatherly concern.

" Of old things all are over old,
Of good things none are good enough: —
We 'll show that we can help to frame
    A world of other stuff.

" I, too, will have my kings that take
From me the sign of life and death: 90
Kingdoms shall shift about, like clouds,
    Obedient to my breath."

And, if the word had been fulfilled,
As *might* have been, then, thought of joy !
France would have had her present Boast,
    And we our own Rob Roy !

Oh ! say not so; compare them not;
I would not wrong thee, Champion brave !
Would wrong thee nowhere; least of all
    Here standing by thy grave.   100

For Thou, although with some wild thoughts,
Wild Chieftain of a savage Clan !
Hadst this to boast of; thou didst love
    The *liberty* of man.

And, had it been thy lot to live
With us who now behold the light,
Thou would'st have nobly stirred thyself,
    And battled for the Right.

For thou wert still the poor man's stay,
The poor man's heart, the poor man's
    hand;   110
And all the oppressed, who wanted strength,
    Had thine at their command.

Bear witness many a pensive sigh
Of thoughtful Herdsman when he strays
Alone upon Loch Veol 's heights,
    And by Loch Lomond 's braes.

And, far and near, through vale and hill,
Are faces that attest the same;
The proud heart flashing through the eyes,
    At sound of Rob Roy's name.   120

XI

SONNET

COMPOSED AT ——— CASTLE

1803. 1807

    The Castle here mentioned was Nidpath
near Peebles. The person alluded to was the
then Duke of Queensbury. The fact was told
me by Walter Scott.

DEGENERATE Douglas ! oh, the unworthy
    Lord !
Whom mere despite of heart could so far
    please,
And love of havoc, (for with such disease
Fame taxes him,) that he could send forth
    word
To level with the dust a noble horde,
A brotherhood of venerable Trees,
Leaving an ancient dome, and towers like
    these,
Beggared and outraged ! — Many hearts
    deplored
The fate of those old Trees; and oft with
    pain
The traveller, at this day, will stop and gaze
On wrongs, which Nature scarcely seems
    to heed:
For sheltered places, bosoms, nooks, and
    bays,
And the pure mountains, and the gentle
    Tweed,
And the green silent pastures, yet remain.

XII

YARROW UNVISITED

1803. 1807

    See the various Poems the scene of which is
laid upon the banks of the Yarrow ; in particu-
lar, the exquisite Ballad of Hamilton begin-
ning
    " Busk ye, busk ye, my bonny, bonny Bride,
    Busk ye, busk ye, my winsome Marrow ! — "

FROM Stirling castle we had seen
The mazy Forth unravelled;
Had trod the banks of Clyde, and Tay,
And with the Tweed had travelled;

And when we came to Clovenford,
Then said my " *winsome Marrow*,"
" Whate'er betide, we 'll turn aside,
And see the Braes of Yarrow."

" Let Yarrow folk, *frae* Selkirk town,
Who have been buying, selling,   10
Go back to Yarrow, 't is their own;
Each maiden to her dwelling !
On Yarrow's banks let herons feed,
Hares couch, and rabbits burrow !
But we will downward with the Tweed,
Nor turn aside to Yarrow.

" There 's Galla Water, Leader Haughs,
Both lying right before us;
And Dryborough, where with chiming
          Tweed
The lintwhites sing in chorus;   20
There 's pleasant Tiviot-dale, a land
Made blithe with plough and harrow:
Why throw away a needful day
To go in search of Yarrow ?

" What 's Yarrow but a river bare,
That glides the dark hills under ?
There are a thousand such elsewhere
As worthy of your wonder."
— Strange words they seemed of slight and
          scorn;
My True-love sighed for sorrow;   30
And looked me in the face, to think
I thus could speak of Yarrow !

" Oh ! green," said I, " are Yarrow's holms,
And sweet is Yarrow flowing !
Fair hangs the apple frae the rock,
But we will leave it growing.
O'er hilly path, and open Strath,
We 'll wander Scotland thorough;
But, though so near, we will not turn
Into the dale of Yarrow.   40

" Let beeves and home-bred kine partake
The sweets of Burn-mill meadow;
The swan on still St. Mary's Lake
Float double, swan and shadow !
We will not see them; will not go,
To-day, nor yet to-morrow;
Enough if in our hearts we know
There 's such a place as Yarrow.

" Be Yarrow stream unseen, unknown !
It must, or we shall rue it: 50
We have a vision of our own;
Ah ! why should we undo it ?

The treasured dreams of times long past,
We 'll keep them, winsome Marrow !
For when we 're there, although 't is fair,
'T will be another Yarrow !

" If Care with freezing years should come,
And wandering seem but folly, —
Should we be loth to stir from home,
And yet be melancholy;   60
Should life be dull, and spirits low,
'T will soothe us in our sorrow,
That earth has something yet to show,
The bonny holms of Yarrow ! "

XIII

THE MATRON OF JEDBOROUGH AND HER HUSBAND

1804. 1807

At Jedborough, my companion and I went
into private lodgings for a few days; and
the following Verses were called forth by
the character and domestic situation of our
Hostess.

AGE ! twine thy brows with fresh spring
          flowers,
And call a train of laughing Hours;
And bid them dance, and bid them sing;
And thou, too, mingle in the ring !
Take to thy heart a new delight;
If not, make merry in despite
That there is One who scorns thy power: —
But dance ! for under Jedborough Tower,
A Matron dwells who, though she bears
The weight of more than seventy years,   10
Lives in the light of youthful glee,
And she will dance and sing with thee.

Nay ! start not at that Figure — there !
Him who is rooted to his chair !
Look at him — look again ! for he
Hath long been of thy family.
With legs that move not, if they can,
And useless arms, a trunk of man,
He sits, and with a vacant eye;
A sight to make a stranger sigh !   20
Deaf, drooping, that is now his doom:
His world is in this single room:
Is this a place for mirthful cheer ?
Can merry-making enter here ?
The joyous Woman is the Mate
Of him in that forlorn estate !
He breathes a subterraneous damp;
But bright as Vesper shines her lamp:

He is as mute as Jedborough Tower:
She jocund as it was of yore, 30
With all its bravery on; in times
When all alive with merry chimes,
Upon a sun-bright morn of May,
It roused the Vale to holiday.

I praise thee, Matron! and thy due
Is praise, heroic praise, and true!
With admiration I behold
Thy gladness unsubdued and bold:
Thy looks, thy gestures, all present
The picture of a life well spent: 40
This do I see; and something more;
A strength unthought of heretofore!
Delighted am I for thy sake;
And yet a higher joy partake:
Our Human-nature throws away
Its second twilight, and looks gay;
A land of promise and of pride
Unfolding, wide as life is wide.

Ah! see her helpless Charge! enclosed
Within himself as seems, composed; 50
To fear of loss, and hope of gain,
The strife of happiness and pain,
Utterly dead! yet in the guise
Of little infants, when their eyes
Begin to follow to and fro
The persons that before them go,
He tracks her motions, quick or slow,
Her buoyant spirit can prevail
Where common cheerfulness would fail;
She strikes upon him with the heat 60
Of July suns; he feels it sweet;
An animal delight though dim!
'T is all that now remains for him!

The more I looked, I wondered more —
And, while I scanned them o'er and o'er,
Some inward trouble suddenly
Broke from the Matron's strong black eye—
A remnant of uneasy light,
A flash of something over-bright!
Nor long this mystery did detain 70
My thoughts; — she told in pensive strain
That she had borne a heavy yoke,
Been stricken by a twofold stroke;
Ill health of body; and had pined
Beneath worse ailments of the mind.

So be it! — but let praise ascend
To Him who is our lord and friend!
Who from disease and suffering
Hath called for thee a second spring;
Repaid thee for that sore distress 80
By no untimely joyousness;
Which makes of thine a blissful state;
And cheers thy melancholy Mate!

XIV

"FLY, SOME KIND HARBINGER, TO GRASMERE-DALE!"

1803. 1815

This was actually composed the last day of our tour between Dalston and Grasmere.

FLY, some kind Harbinger, to Grasmere-
dale!
Say that we come, and come by this day's
light;
Fly upon swiftest wing round field and
height,
But chiefly let one Cottage hear the tale;
There let a mystery of joy prevail,
The kitten frolic, like a gamesome sprite,
And Rover whine, as at a second sight
Of near-approaching good that shall not
fail:
And from that Infant's face let joy appear;
Yea, let our Mary's one companion child —
That hath her six weeks' solitude beguiled
With intimations manifold and dear,
While we have wandered over wood and
wild —
Smile on his Mother now with bolder cheer.

XV

THE BLIND HIGHLAND BOY

A TALE TOLD BY THE FIRE-SIDE, AFTER
RETURNING TO THE VALE OF GRASMERE

1804(?). 1807

The story was told me by George Mackereth, for many years parish-clerk of Grasmere. He had been an eye-witness of the occurrence. The vessel in reality was a washing-tub, which the little fellow had met with on the shore of the Loch.

Now we are tired of boisterous joy,
Have romped enough, my little Boy!
Jane hangs her head upon my breast,
And you shall bring your stool and rest;
This corner is your own.

There! take your seat, and let me see
That you can listen quietly:
And, as I promised, I will tell
That strange adventure which befell
A poor blind Highland Boy. 10

A *Highland* Boy ! — why call him so ?
Because, my Darlings, ye must know
That, under hills which rise like towers,
Far higher hills than these of ours !
    He from his birth had lived.

He ne'er had seen one earthly sight,
The sun, the day; the stars, the night;
Or tree, or butterfly, or flower,
Or fish in stream, or bird in bower,
    Or woman, man, or child.   20

And yet he neither drooped nor pined,
Nor had a melancholy mind;
For God took pity on the Boy,
And was his friend; and gave him joy
    Of which we nothing know.

His Mother, too, no doubt, above
Her other children him did love:
For, was she here, or was she there,
She thought of him with constant care,
    And more than mother's love.   30

And proud she was of heart, when, clad
In crimson stockings, tartan plaid,
And bonnet with a feather gay,
To Kirk he on the Sabbath day
    Went hand in hand with her.

A dog, too, had he; not for need,
But one to play with and to feed;
Which would have led him, if bereft
Of company or friends, and left
    Without a better guide.   40

And then the bagpipes he could blow —
And thus from house to house would go;
And all were pleased to hear and see,
For none made sweeter melody
    Than did the poor blind Boy.

Yet he had many a restless dream;
Both when he heard the eagles scream,
And when he heard the torrents roar,
And heard the water beat the shore
    Near which their cottage stood.   50

Beside a lake their cottage stood,
Not small like ours, a peaceful flood;
But one of mighty size, and strange;
That, rough or smooth, is full of change,
    And stirring in its bed.

For to this lake, by night and day,
The great Sea-water finds its way

Through long, long windings of the hills
And drinks up all the pretty rills
    And rivers large and strong: 60

Then hurries back the road it came —
Returns, on errand still the same;
This did it when the earth was new;
And this for evermore will do
    As long as earth shall last.

And, with the coming of the tide,
Come boats and ships that safely ride
Between the woods and lofty rocks;
And to the shepherds with their flocks
    Bring tales of distant lands.   70

And of those tales, whate'er they were,
The blind Boy always had his share;
Whether of mighty towns, or vales
With warmer suns and softer gales,
    Or wonders of the Deep.

Yet more it pleased him, more it stirred,
When from the water-side he heard
The shouting, and the jolly cheers;
The bustle of the mariners
    In stillness or in storm.   80

But what do his desires avail ?
For He must never handle sail;
Nor mount the mast, nor row, nor float
In sailor's ship, or fisher's boat,
    Upon the rocking waves.

His Mother often thought, and said,
What sin would be upon her head
If she should suffer this: " My Son,
Whate'er you do, leave this undone;
    The danger is so great."   90

Thus lived he by Loch Leven's side
Still sounding with the sounding tide,
And heard the billows leap and dance,
Without a shadow of mischance,
    Till he was ten years old.

When one day (and now mark me well,
Ye soon shall know how this befell)
He in a vessel of his own,
On the swift flood is hurrying down,
    Down to the mighty Sea.   100

In such a vessel never more
May human creature leave the shore !
If this or that way he should stir,

Woe to the poor blind Mariner !
  For death will be his doom.

But say what bears him ? — Ye have seen
The Indian's bow, his arrows keen,
Rare beasts, and birds with plumage bright;
Gifts which, for wonder or delight,
  Are brought in ships from far.   110

Such gifts had those seafaring men
Spread round that haven in the glen;
Each hut, perchance, might have its own,
And to the Boy they all were known —
  He knew and prized them all.

The rarest was a Turtle-shell
Which he, poor Child, had studied well;
A shell of ample size, and light
As the pearly car of Amphitrite,
  That sportive dolphins drew.   120

And, as a Coracle that braves
On Vaga's breast the fretful waves,
This shell upon the deep would swim,
And gaily lift its fearless brim
  Above the tossing surge.

And this the little blind Boy knew:
And he a story strange yet true
Had heard, how in a shell like this
An English Boy, O thought of bliss !
  Had stoutly launched from shore;   130

Launched from the margin of a bay
Among the Indian isles, where lay
His father's ship, and had sailed far —
To join that gallant ship of war,
  In his delightful shell.

Our Highland Boy oft visited
The house that held this prize; and, led
By choice or chance, did thither come
One day when no one was at home,
  And found the door unbarred.   140

While there he sate, alone and blind,
That story flashed upon his mind; —
A bold thought roused him, and he took
The shell from out its secret nook,
  And bore it on his head.

He launched his vessel, — and in pride
Of spirit, from Loch Leven's side,
Stepped into it — his thoughts all free
As the light breezes that with glee   149
  Sang through the adventurer's hair.

A while he stood upon his feet;
He felt the motion — took his seat;
Still better pleased as more and more
The tide retreated from the shore,
  And sucked, and sucked him in.

And there he is in face of Heaven.
How rapidly the Child is driven !
The fourth part of a mile, I ween,
He thus had gone, ere he was seen
  By any human eye.   160

But when he was first seen, oh me
What shrieking and what misery !
For many saw; among the rest
His Mother, she who loved him best,
  She saw her poor blind Boy.

But for the child, the sightless Boy,
It is the triumph of his joy !
The bravest traveller in balloon,
Mounting as if to reach the moon,
  Was never half so blessed.   170

And let him, let him go his way,
Alone, and innocent, and gay !
For, if good Angels love to wait
On the forlorn unfortunate,
  This Child will take no harm.

But now the passionate lament,
Which from the crowd on shore was sent,
The cries which broke from old and young
In Gaelic, or the English tongue,
  Are stifled — all is still.   180

And quickly with a silent crew
A boat is ready to pursue;
And from the shore their course they take,
And swiftly down the running lake
  They follow the blind Boy.

But soon they move with softer pace;
So have ye seen the fowler chase
On Grasmere's clear unruffled breast
A youngling of the wild-duck's nest
  With deftly-lifted oar;   190

Or as the wily sailors crept
To seize (while on the Deep it slept)
The hapless creature which did dwell
Erewhile within the dancing shell,
  They steal upon their prey.

With sound the least that can be made,
They follow, more and more afraid,

More cautious as they draw more near;
But in his darkness he can hear,
   And guesses their intent.   200

" *Lei-gha — Lei-gha* " — he then cried out,
" *Lei-gha — Lei-gha* " — with eager shout;
Thus did he cry, and thus did pray,
And what he meant was, " Keep away,
   And leave me to myself ! "

Alas ! and when he felt their hands ——
You 've often heard of magic wands,
That with a motion overthrow
A palace of the proudest show,
   Or melt it into air: 210

So all his dreams — that inward light
With which his soul had shone so bright —
All vanished; — 't was a heartfelt cross
To him, a heavy, bitter loss,
   As he had ever known.

But hark ! a gratulating voice,
With which the very hills rejoice:
'T is from the crowd, who tremblingly
Have watched the event, and now can see
   That he is safe at last.   220

And then, when he was brought to land,
Full sure they were a happy band,
Which, gathering round, did on the banks

Of that great Water give God thanks,
   And welcomed the poor Child.

And in the general joy of heart
The blind Boy's little dog took part;
He leapt about, and oft did kiss
His master's hands in sign of bliss,
   With sound like lamentation.   230

But most of all, his Mother dear,
She who had fainted with her fear,
Rejoiced when waking she espies
The Child; when she can trust her eyes,
   And touches the blind Boy.

She led him home, and wept amain,
When he was in the house again:
Tears flowed in torrents from her eyes;
She kissed him — how could she chastise ?
   She was too happy far.   240

Thus, after he had fondly braved
The perilous Deep, the Boy was saved;
And, though his fancies had been wild,
Yet he was pleased and reconciled
   To live in peace on shore.

And in the lonely Highland dell
Still do they keep the Turtle-shell
And long the story will repeat
Of the blind Boy's adventurous feat,
   And how he was preserved.   250

OCTOBER 1803

1803. 1807

ONE might believe that natural miseries
Had blasted France, and made of it a land
Unfit for men; and that in one great band
Her sons were bursting forth, to dwell at ease.
But 't is a chosen soil, where sun and breeze
Shed gentle favours: rural works are there,
And ordinary business without care;
Spot rich in all things that can soothe and please !
How piteous then that there should be such dearth
Of knowledge; that whole myriads should unite
To work against themselves such fell despite:

Should come in phrensy and in drunken mirth,
Impatient to put out the only light
Of Liberty that yet remains on earth !

" THERE IS A BONDAGE WORSE, FAR WORSE, TO BEAR "

1802. 1807

THERE is a bondage worse, far worse, to bear
Than his who breathes, by roof, and floor, and wall,
Pent in, a Tyrant's solitary Thrall:
'T is his who walks about in the open air,
One of a Nation who, henceforth, must wear
Their fetters in their souls. For who could be,
Who, even the best, in such condition, free

From self-reproach, reproach that he must
    share
With Human-nature ?   Never be it ours
To see the sun how brightly it will shine,
And know that noble feelings, manly
    powers,
Instead of gathering strength, must droop
    and pine;
And earth with all her pleasant fruits and
    flowers
Fade, and participate in man's decline.

OCTOBER 1803

1803. 1807

THESE times strike monied worldlings with
    dismay:
Even rich men, brave by nature, taint the
    air
With words of apprehension and despair:
While tens of thousands, thinking on the
    affray,
Men unto whom sufficient for the day
And minds not stinted or untilled are given,
Sound, healthy, children of the God of
    heaven,
Are cheerful as the rising sun in May.
What do we gather hence but firmer faith
That every gift of noble origin
Is breathed upon by Hope's perpetual
    breath;
That virtue and the faculties within
Are vital, — and that riches are akin
To fear, to change, to cowardice, and death ?

"ENGLAND ! THE TIME IS COME WHEN THOU SHOULD'ST WEAN "

1802. 1807

ENGLAND ! the time is come when thou
    should'st wean
Thy heart from its emasculating food;
The truth should now be better understood;
Old things have been unsettled; we have
    seen
Fair seed-time, better harvest might have
    been
But for thy trespasses; and, at this day,
If for Greece, Egypt, India, Africa,
Aught good were destined, thou would'st
    step between.
England ! all nations in this charge agree:
But worse, more ignorant in love and hate,

Far — far more abject, is thine Enemy:
Therefore the wise pray for thee, though
    the freight
Of thy offences be a heavy weight:
Oh grief that Earth's best hopes rest all
    with Thee !

OCTOBER 1803

1803. 1807

WHEN, looking on the present face of
    things,
I see one man, of men the meanest too !
Raised up to sway the world, to do, undo,
With mighty Nations for his underlings,
The great events with which old story rings
Seem vain and hollow; I find nothing great:
Nothing is left which I can venerate;
So that a doubt almost within me springs
Of Providence, such emptiness at length
Seems at the heart of all things. But, great
    God !
I measure back the steps which I have trod:
And tremble, seeing whence proceeds the
    strength
Of such poor Instruments, with thoughts
    sublime
I tremble at the sorrow of the time.

TO THE MEN OF KENT

OCTOBER 1803

1803. 1807

VANGUARD of Liberty, ye men of Kent,
Ye children of a Soil that doth advance
Her haughty brow against the coast of
    France,
Now is the time to prove your hardiment !
To France be words of invitation sent !
They from their fields can see the counte-
    nance
Of your fierce war, may ken the glittering
    lance
And hear you shouting forth your brave
    intent.
Left single, in bold parley, ye, of yore,
Did from the Norman win a gallant wreath;
Confirmed the charters that were yours
    before; —
No parleying now. In Britain is one breath;
We all are with you now from shore to
    shore: —
Ye men of Kent, 't is victory or death !

IN THE PASS OF KILLICRANKY

1803. 1807

An invasion being expected, October 1803.

SIX thousand veterans practised in war's
    game,
Tried men, at Killicranky were arrayed
Against an equal host that wore the plaid,
Shepherds and herdsmen. — Like a whirl-
    wind came
The Highlanders, the slaughter spread like
    flame;
And Garry, thundering down his mountain-
    road,
Was stopped, and could not breathe be-
    neath the load
Of the dead bodies. — 'T was a day of shame
For them whom precept and the pedantry
Of cold mechanic battle do enslave.
O for a single hour of that Dundee,
Who on that day the word of onset gave !
Like conquest would the Men of England
    see;
And her Foes find a like inglorious grave.

ANTICIPATION, OCTOBER 1803

1803. 1803

SHOUT, for a mighty Victory is won !
On British ground the Invaders are laid
    low;
The breath of Heaven has drifted them
    like snow,
And left them lying in the silent sun,
Never to rise again ! — the work is done.
Come forth, ye old men, now in peaceful
    show
And greet your sons ! drums beat and
    trumpets blow !
Make merry, wives ! ye little children,
    stun
Your grandame's ears with pleasure of your
    noise !
Clap, infants, clap your hands ! Divine
    must be
That triumph, when the very worst, the
    pain,
And even the prospect of our brethren
    slain,
Hath something in it which the heart
    enjoys: —
In glory will they sleep and endless sanc-
    tity.

LINES ON THE EXPECTED INVASION, 1803

1803. 1842

COME ye — who, if (which Heaven avert !)
    the Land
Were with herself at strife, would take
    your stand,
Like gallant Falkland, by the Monarch's
    side,
And, like Montrose, make Loyalty your
    pride —
Come ye — who, not less, zealous, might
    display
Banners at enmity with regal sway,
And, like the Pyms and Miltons of that day,
Think that a State would live in sounder
    health
If Kingship bowed its head to Common-
    wealth —
Ye too — whom no discreditable fear
Would keep, perhaps with many a fruitless
    tear,
Uncertain what to choose and how to
    steer —
And ye — who might mistake for sober
    sense
And wise reserve the plea of indolence —
Come ye — whate'er your creed — O waken
    all,
Whate'er your temper, at your Country's
    call;
Resolving (this a free-born Nation can)
To have one Soul, and perish to a man,
Or save this honoured Land from every
    Lord
But British reason and the British sword.

THE FARMER OF TILSBURY VALE

1797(?). 1800

The character of this man was described to
me, and the incident upon which the verses turn
was told me, by Mr. Pool of Nether Stowey,
with whom I became acquainted through our
common friend, S. T. Coleridge. During my
residence at Alfoxden I used to see much of
him and had frequent occasions to admire the
course of his daily life, especially his conduct
to his labourers and poor neighbours: their
virtues he carefully encouraged, and weighed
their faults in the scales of charity. If I seem
in these verses to have treated the weaknesses
of the farmer, and his transgression, too ten-

derly, it may in part be ascribed to my having received the story from one so averse to all harsh judgment. After his death, was found in his escritoir a lock of grey hair carefully preserved, with a notice that it had been cut from the head of his faithful shepherd, who had served him for a length of years. I need scarcely add that he felt for all men as his brothers. He was much beloved by distinguished persons — Mr. Coleridge, Mr. Southey, Sir H. Davy, and many others; and in his own neighbourhood was highly valued as a magistrate, a man of business, and in every other social relation. The latter part of the poem, perhaps, requires some apology as being too much of an echo to the "Reverie of Poor Susan."

'Tis not for the unfeeling, the falsely re-
    fined,
The squeamish in taste, and the narrow of
    mind,
And the small critic wielding his delicate
    pen,
That I sing of old Adam, the pride of old
    men.

He dwells in the centre of London's wide
    Town;
His staff is a sceptre — his grey hairs a
    crown;
And his bright eyes look brighter, set off
    by the streak
Of the unfaded rose that still blooms on his
    cheek.

'Mid the dews, in the sunshine of morn, —
    'mid the joy
Of the fields, he collected that bloom, when
    a boy,   10
That countenance there fashioned, which,
    spite of a stain
That his life hath received, to the last will
    remain.

A Farmer he was; and his house far and
    near
Was the boast of the country for excellent
    cheer:
How oft have I heard in sweet Tilsbury
    Vale
Of the silver-rimmed horn whence he dealt
    his mild ale!

Yet Adam was far as the farthest from ruin,
His fields seemed to know what their Mas-
    ter was doing:

And turnips, and corn-land, and meadow,
    and lea,   19
All caught the infection — as generous as he.

Yet Adam prized little the feast and the
    bowl, —
The fields better suited the ease of his soul:
He strayed through the fields like an indo-
    lent wight,
The quiet of nature was Adam's delight.

For Adam was simple in thought; and the
    poor,
Familiar with him, made an inn of his door:
He gave them the best that he had; or, to say
What less may mislead you, they took it
    away.

Thus thirty smooth years did he thrive on
    his farm:
The Genius of plenty preserved him from
    harm: 30
At length, what to most is a season of
    sorrow,
His means are run out, — he must beg, or
    must borrow.

To the neighbours he went, — all were free
    with their money;
For his hive had so long been replenished
    with honey,
That they dreamt not of dearth; — He con-
    tinued his rounds,
Knocked here — and knocked there, pounds
    still adding to pounds.

He paid what he could with his ill-gotten
    pelf,
And something, it might be, reserved for
    himself:
Then (what is too true) without hinting a
    word,
Turned his back on the country — and off
    like a bird.   40

You lift up your eyes! — but I guess that
    you frame
A judgment too harsh of the sin and the
    shame;
In him it was scarcely a business of art,
For this he did all in the *ease* of his heart.

To London — a sad emigration I ween —
With his grey hairs he went from the brook
    and the green;

And there, with small wealth but his legs
    and his hands,
As lonely he stood as a crow on the
    sands.

All trades, as need was, did old Adam as-
    sume, —
Served as stable-boy, errand-boy, porter,
    and groom;   50
But nature is gracious, necessity kind,
And, in spite of the shame that may lurk in
    his mind,

He seems ten birthdays younger, is green
    and is stout;
Twice as fast as before does his blood run
    about;
You would say that each hair of his beard
    was alive,
And his fingers as busy as bees in a hive.

For he 's not like an Old Man that leisurely
    goes
About work that he knows, in a track that
    he knows;
But often his mind is compelled to demur,
And you guess that the more then his body
    must stir.   60

In the throng of the town like a stranger is
    he,
Like one whose own country 's far over the
    sea;
And Nature, while through the great city
    he hies,
Full ten times a day takes his heart by
    surprise.

This gives him the fancy of one that is
    young,
More of soul in his face than of words on
    his tongue;
Like a maiden of twenty he trembles and
    sighs,
And tears of fifteen will come into his eyes.

What 's a tempest to him, or the dry parch-
    ing heats ?
Yet he watches the clouds that pass over
    the streets;   70
With a look of such earnestness often will
    stand,
You might think he 'd twelve reapers at
    work in the Strand.

Where proud Covent-garden, in desolate
    hours
Of snow and hoar-frost, spreads her fruits
    and her flowers,
Old Adam will smile at the pains that have
    made
Poor winter look fine in such strange
    masquerade.

'Mid coaches and chariots, a waggon of
    straw,
Like a magnet, the heart of old Adam can
    draw;
With a thousand soft pictures his memory
    will teem,
And his hearing is touched with the sounds
    of a dream.   80

Up the Haymarket hill he oft whistles his
    way,
Thrusts his hands in a waggon, and smells
    at the hay;
He thinks of the fields he so often hath
    mown,
And is happy as if the rich freight were his
    own.

But chiefly to Smithfield he loves to re-
    pair, —
If you pass by at morning, you 'll meet with
    him there.
The breath of the cows you may see him
    inhale,
And his heart all the while is in Tilsbury
    Vale.

Now farewell, old Adam ! when low thou
    art laid,
May one blade of grass spring up over thy
    head;   90
And I hope that thy grave, wheresoever it
    be,
Will hear the wind sigh through the leaves
    of a tree.

TO THE CUCKOO

1802. 1807

Composed in the orchard, Town-end, Gras-
mere.

O BLITHE New-comer ! I have heard,
    I hear thee and rejoice.
O Cuckoo ! shall I call thee Bird,
    Or but a wandering Voice ?

While I am lying on the grass
Thy twofold shout I hear,
From hill to hill it seems to pass,
At once far off, and near.

Though babbling only to the Vale,
Of sunshine and of flowers,   10
Thou bringest unto me a tale
Of visionary hours.

Thrice welcome, darling of the Spring !
Even yet thou art to me
No bird, but an invisible thing,
A voice, a mystery;

The same whom in my school-boy days
I listened to; that Cry
Which made me look a thousand ways
In bush, and tree, and sky.   20

To seek thee did I often rove
Through woods and on the green;
And thou wert still a hope, a love;
Still longed for, never seen.

And I can listen to thee yet;
Can lie upon the plain
And listen, till I do beget
That golden time again.

O blessèd Bird ! the earth we pace
Again appears to be   30
An unsubstantial, faery place;
That is fit home for Thee !

"SHE WAS A PHANTOM OF DELIGHT"

1803(?). 1807

Written at Town-end, Grasmere. The germ
of this poem was four lines composed as a part
of the verses on the Highland Girl. Though
beginning in this way, it was written from my
heart, as is sufficiently obvious.

SHE was a Phantom of delight
When first she gleamed upon my sight;
A lovely Apparition, sent
To be a moment's ornament;
Her eyes as stars of Twilight fair;
Like Twilight's, too, her dusky hair;
But all things else about her drawn
From May-time and the cheerful Dawn;
A dancing Shape, an Image gay,
To haunt, to startle, and way-lay.   10

I saw her upon nearer view,
A Spirit, yet a Woman too !
Her household motions light and free,
And steps of virgin-liberty;
A countenance in which did meet
Sweet records, promises as sweet;
A Creature not too bright or good
For human nature's daily food;
For transient sorrows, simple wiles,
Praise, blame, love, kisses, tears, and
    smiles.   20

And now I see with eye serene
The very pulse of the machine;
A Being breathing thoughtful breath,
A Traveller between life and death;
The reason firm, the temperate will,
Endurance, foresight, strength, and skill;
A perfect Woman, nobly planned,
To warn, to comfort, and command;
And yet a Spirit still, and bright
With something of angelic light.   30

"I WANDERED LONELY AS A CLOUD"

1804(?). 1807

Written at Town-end, Grasmere. The two
best lines in it are by Mary. The Daffodils
grew and still grow on the margin of Ullswater,
and probably may be seen to this day as beauti-
ful in the month of March, nodding their golden
heads beside the dancing and foaming waves.

I WANDERED lonely as a cloud
That floats on high o'er vales and hills,
When all at once I saw a crowd,
A host, of golden daffodils;
Beside the lake, beneath the trees,
Fluttering and dancing in the breeze.

Continuous as the stars that shine
And twinkle on the milky way,
They stretched in never-ending line
Along the margin of a bay:
Ten thousand saw I at a glance,
Tossing their heads in sprightly dance.

The waves beside them danced; but they
Out-did the sparkling waves in glee:
A poet could not but be gay,
In such a jocund company:
I gazed — and gazed — but little thought
What wealth the show to me had brought:

For oft, when on my couch I lie
In vacant or in pensive mood,
They flash upon that inward eye
Which is the bliss of solitude;
And then my heart with pleasure fills,
And dances with the daffodils.

THE AFFLICTION OF MARGARET

1800(?). 1807

Written at Town-end, Grasmere. This was
taken from the case of a poor widow who lived
in the town of Penrith. Her sorrow was well
known to Mrs. Wordsworth, to my Sister, and,
I believe, to the whole town. She kept a shop,
and when she saw a stranger passing by, she
was in the habit of going out into the street to
enquire of him after her son.

I

WHERE art thou, my beloved Son,
Where art thou, worse to me than dead?
Oh find me, prosperous or undone!
Or, if the grave be now thy bed,
Why am I ignorant of the same
That I may rest; and neither blame
Nor sorrow may attend thy name?

II

Seven years, alas! to have received
No tidings of an only child;
To have despaired, have hoped, believed, 10
And been for evermore beguiled;
Sometimes with thoughts of very bliss!
I catch at them, and then I miss;
Was ever darkness like to this?

III

He was among the prime in worth,
An object beauteous to behold;
Well born, well bred; I sent him forth
Ingenuous, innocent, and bold:
If things ensued that wanted grace,
As hath been said, they were not base; 20
And never blush was on my face.

IV

Ah! little doth the young one dream,
When full of play and childish cares,
What power is in his wildest scream,
Heard by his mother unawares!
He knows it not, he cannot guess:
Years to a mother bring distress;
But do not make her love the less.

V

Neglect me! no, I suffered long
From that ill thought; and, being blind, 30
Said, "Pride shall help me in my wrong;
Kind mother have I been, as kind
As ever breathed:" and that is true;
I've wet my path with tears like dew,
Weeping for him when no one knew.

VI

My Son, if thou be humbled, poor,
Hopeless of honour and of gain,
Oh! do not dread thy mother's door;
Think not of me with grief and pain:
I now can see with better eyes;   40
And worldly grandeur I despise,
And fortune with her gifts and lies.

VII

Alas! the fowls of heaven have wings,
And blasts of heaven will aid their flight;
They mount — how short a voyage brings
The wanderers back to their delight!
Chains tie us down by land and sea;
And wishes, vain as mine, may be
All that is left to comfort thee.

VIII

Perhaps some dungeon hears thee groan, 50
Maimed, mangled by inhuman men;
Or thou upon a desert thrown
Inheritest the lion's den;
Or hast been summoned to the deep,
Thou, thou and all thy mates, to keep
An incommunicable sleep.

IX

I look for ghosts; but none will force
Their way to me: 'tis falsely said
That there was ever intercourse
Between the living and the dead;   60
For, surely, then I should have sight
Of him I wait for day and night,
With love and longings infinite.

X

My apprehensions come in crowds;
I dread the rustling of the grass;
The very shadows of the clouds
Have power to shake me as they pass:
I question things and do not find
One that will answer to my mind;
And all the world appears unkind.   70

XI

Beyond participation lie
My troubles, and beyond relief:
If any chance to heave a sigh,
They pity me, and not my grief.
Then come to me, my Son, or send
Some tidings that my woes may end;
I have no other earthly friend !

THE FORSAKEN

1800(?). 1842

This was an overflow from the " Affliction of Margaret ——," and was excluded as superfluous there, but preserved in the faint hope that it may turn to account by restoring a shy lover to some forsaken damsel. My poetry has been complained of as deficient in interests of this sort, — a charge which the piece beginning, " Lyre ! though such power do in thy magic live," will scarcely tend to obviate. The natural imagery of these verses was supplied by frequent, I might say intense, observation of the Rydal torrent. What an animating contrast is the ever-changing aspect of that, and indeed of every one of our mountain brooks, to the monotonous tone and unmitigated fury of such streams among the Alps as are fed all the summer long by glaciers and melting snows. A traveller observing the exquisite purity of the great rivers, such as the Rhine at Geneva, and the Reuss at Lucerne, when they issue out of their respective lakes, might fancy for a moment that some power in nature produced this beautiful change, with a view to make amends for those Alpine sullyings which the waters exhibit near their fountain heads; but, alas ! how soon does that purity depart before the influx of tributary waters that have flowed through cultivated plains and the crowded abodes of men.

THE peace which others seek they find;
The heaviest storms not longest last;
Heaven grants even to the guiltiest mind
An amnesty for what is past;
When will my sentence be reversed ?
I only pray to know the worst;
And wish as if my heart would burst.

O weary struggle ! silent years
Tell seemingly no doubtful tale;
And yet they leave it short, and fears
And hopes are strong and will prevail.
My calmest faith escapes not pain;
And, feeling that the hope is vain,
I think that he will come again.

REPENTANCE

A PASTORAL BALLAD

1801–02(?). 1820

Written at Town-end, Grasmere. Suggested by the conversation of our next neighbour, Margaret Ashburner.

THE fields which with covetous spirit we sold,
Those beautiful fields, the delight of the day,
Would have brought us more good than a burthen of gold,
Could we but have been as contented as they.

When the troublesome Tempter beset us, said I,
" Let him come, with his purse proudly grasped in his hand;
But, Allan, be true to me, Allan, — we 'll die
Before he shall go with an inch of the land ! "

There dwelt we, as happy as birds in their bowers;
Unfettered as bees that in gardens abide; 10
We could do what we liked with the land, it was ours;
And for us the brook murmured that ran by its side.

But now we are strangers, go early or late;
And often, like one overburthened with sin,
With my hand on the latch of the half-opened gate,
I look at the fields, but I cannot go in !

When I walk by the hedge on a bright summer's day,
Or sit in the shade of my grandfather's tree,
A stern face it puts on, as if ready to say,
" What ails you, that you must come creeping to me ! " 20

With our pastures about us, we could not be sad;
Our comfort was near if we ever were crost;
But the comfort, the blessings, and wealth that we had,
We slighted them all, — and our birth-right was lost.

Oh, ill-judging sire of an innocent son
Who must now be a wanderer ! but peace
　　to that strain !
Think of evening's repose when our labour
　　was done,
The sabbath's return; and its leisure's soft
　　chain !

And in sickness, if night had been sparing
　　of sleep,
How cheerful, at sunrise, the hill where I
　　stood,　　　　　　　　　　　　　　30
Looking down on the kine, and our treasure
　　of sheep
That besprinkled the field; 't was like youth
　　in my blood !

Now I cleave to the house, and am dull as a
　　snail;
And, oftentimes, hear the church-bell with
　　a sigh,
That follows the thought —We 've no land
　　in the vale,
Save six feet of earth where our forefathers
　　lie !

THE SEVEN SISTERS

OR, THE SOLITUDE OF BINNORIE

1800. 1800

I

SEVEN Daughters had Lord Archibald,
All children of one mother:
You could not say in one short day
What love they bore each other.
A garland, of seven lilies, wrought !
Seven Sisters that together dwell;
But he, bold Knight as ever fought,
Their Father, took of them no thought,
He loved the wars so well.
Sing, mournfully, oh ! mournfully,　　　10
The solitude of Binnorie !

II

Fresh blows the wind, a western wind,
And from the shores of Erin,
Across the wave, a Rover brave
To Binnorie is steering:
Right onward to the Scottish strand
The gallant ship is borne;
The warriors leap upon the land,
And hark ! the Leader of the band
Hath blown his bugle horn.　　　　　20

Sing, mournfully, oh ! mournfully,
The solitude of Binnorie.

III

Beside a grotto of their own,
With boughs above them closing,
The Seven are laid, and in the shade
They lie like fawns reposing.
But now, upstarting with affright
At noise of man and steed,
Away they fly to left, to right —
Of your fair household, Father-knight,　　30
Methinks you take small heed !
Sing, mournfully, oh ! mournfully,
The solitude of Binnorie.

IV

Away the seven fair Campbells fly,
And, over hill and hollow,
With menace proud, and insult loud,
The youthful Rovers follow.
Cried they, " Your Father loves to roam:
Enough for him to find
The empty house when he comes home;　　40
For us your yellow ringlets comb,
For us be fair and kind ! "
Sing, mournfully, oh ! mournfully,
The solitude of Binnorie.

V

Some close behind, some side by side,
Like clouds in stormy weather;
They run, and cry, " Nay, let us die,
And let us die together."
A lake was near; the shore was steep;
There never foot had been;　　　　　50
They ran, and with a desperate leap
Together plunged into the deep,
Nor ever more were seen.
Sing, mournfully, oh ! mournfully,
The solitude of Binnorie.

VI

The stream that flows out of the lake,
As through the glen it rambles,
Repeats a moan o'er moss and stone,
For those seven lovely Campbells.
Seven little Islands, green and bare,　　60
Have risen from out the deep:
The fishers say, those sisters fair,
By faeries all are buried there,
And there together sleep.
Sing, mournfully, oh ! mournfully,
The solitude of Binnorie.

ADDRESS TO MY INFANT DAUGHTER, DORA

ON BEING REMINDED THAT SHE WAS A
MONTH OLD THAT DAY, SEPTEMBER 16

1804. 1815

—— HAST thou then survived —
Mild Offspring of infirm humanity,
Meek Infant ! among all forlornest things
The most forlorn — one life of that bright
    star,
The second glory of the Heavens ? — Thou
    hast,
Already hast survived that great decay,
That transformation through the wide earth
    felt,
And by all nations.   In that Being's sight
From whom the Race of human kind pro-
    ceed,
A thousand years are but as yesterday;   10
And one day's narrow circuit is to Him
Not less capacious than a thousand years.
But what is time ?   What outward glory ?
    neither
A measure is of Thee, whose claims extend
Through "heaven's eternal year." — Yet
    hail to Thee,
Frail, feeble Monthling ! — by that name,
    methinks,
Thy scanty breathing-time is portioned out
Not idly. — Hadst thou been of Indian birth,
Couched on a casual bed of moss and leaves,
And rudely canopied by leafy boughs,   20
Or to the churlish elements exposed
On the blank plains, — the coldness of the
    night,
Or the night's darkness, or its cheerful
    face
Of beauty, by the changing moon adorned,
Would, with imperious admonition, then
Have scored thine age, and punctually
    timed
Thine infant history, on the minds of those
Who might have wandered with thee. —
    Mother's love,
Nor less than mother's love in other breasts,
Will, among us warm-clad and warmly
    housed,   30
Do for thee what the finger of the heavens
Doth all too often harshly execute
For thy unblest coevals, amid wilds
Where fancy hath small liberty to grace
The affections, to exalt them or refine;
And the maternal sympathy itself,

Though strong, is, in the main, a joyless
    tie
Of naked instinct, wound about the heart.
Happier, far happier is thy lot and ours !
Even now — to solemnise thy helpless state,
And to enliven in the mind's regard   41
Thy passive beauty — parallels have risen,
Resemblances, or contrasts, that connect,
Within the region of a father's thoughts,
Thee and thy mate and sister of the sky.
And first; — thy sinless progress, through a
    world
By sorrow darkened and by care disturbed,
Apt likeness bears to hers, through gathered
    clouds,
Moving untouched in silver purity,
And cheering oft-times their reluctant
    gloom.   50
Fair are ye both, and both are free from
    stain:
But thou, how leisurely thou fill'st thy
    horn
With brightness ! leaving her to post along,
And range about, disquieted in change,
And still impatient of the shape she wears.
Once up, once down the hill, one journey,
    Babe,
That will suffice thee; and it seems that
    now
Thou hast fore-knowledge that such task is
    thine;
Thou travellest so contentedly, and sleep'st
In such a heedless peace.   Alas ! full soon
Hath this conception, grateful to behold,   61
Changed countenance, like an object sullied
    o'er
By breathing mist; and thine appears
    to be
A mournful labour, while to her is given
Hope, and a renovation without end.
— That smile forbids the thought; for on
    thy face
Smiles are beginning, like the beams of
    dawn,
To shoot and circulate; smiles have there
    been seen,
Tranquil assurances that Heaven supports
The feeble motions of thy life, and cheers
Thy 'loneliness: or shall those smiles be
    called   71
Feelers of love, put forth as if to explore
This untried world, and to prepare thy
    way
Through a strait passage intricate and
    dim ?

Such are they; and the same are tokens, signs,
Which, when the appointed season hath arrived,
Joy, as her holiest language, shall adopt;
And Reason's godlike Power be proud to own.

THE KITTEN AND FALLING LEAVES

1804(?). 1807

Seen at Town-end, Grasmere. The elder-bush has long since disappeared : it hung over the wall near the Cottage ; and the Kitten continued to leap up, catching the leaves as here described. The infant was Dora.

THAT way look, my Infant, lo !
What a pretty baby-show !
See the Kitten on the wall,
Sporting with the leaves that fall,
Withered leaves — one — two — and three —
From the lofty elder-tree !
Through the calm and frosty air
Of this morning bright and fair,
Eddying round and round they sink
Softly, slowly: one might think,   10
From the motions that are made,
Every little leaf conveyed
Sylph or Faery hither tending, —
To this lower world descending,
Each invisible and mute,
In his wavering parachute.
—— But the Kitten, how she starts,
Crouches, stretches, paws, and darts !
First at one, and then its fellow
Just as light and just as yellow;   20
There are many now — now one —
Now they stop and there are none.
What intenseness of desire
In her upward eye of fire !
With a tiger-leap half-way
Now she meets the coming prey,
Lets it go as fast, and then
Has it in her power again:
Now she works with three or four,
Like an Indian conjurer;   30
Quick as he in feats of art,
Far beyond in joy of heart.
Were her antics played in the eye
Of a thousand standers-by,
Clapping hands with shout and stare,
What would little Tabby care
For the plaudits of the crowd ?

Over happy to be proud,
Over wealthy in the treasure
Of her own exceeding pleasure !   40
'T is a pretty baby-treat;
Nor, I deem, for me unmeet;
Here, for neither Babe nor me,
Other play-mate can I see.
Of the countless living things,
That with stir of feet and wings
(In the sun or under shade,
Upon bough or grassy blade)
And with busy revellings,
Chirp and song, and murmurings,   50
Made this orchard's narrow space,
And this vale so blithe a place;
Multitudes are swept away
Never more to breathe the day:
Some are sleeping; some in bands
Travelled into distant lands;
Others slunk to moor and wood,
Far from human neighbourhood;
And, among the Kinds that keep
With us closer fellowship,   60
With us openly abide,
All have laid their mirth aside.
  Where is he that giddy Sprite,
Blue-cap, with his colours bright,
Who was blest as bird could be,
Feeding in the apple-tree;
Made such wanton spoil and rout,
Turning blossoms inside out;
Hung — head pointing towards the ground —
Fluttered, perched, into a round   70
Bound himself, and then unbound;
Lithest, gaudiest Harlequin !
Prettiest Tumbler ever seen !
Light of heart and light of limb;
What is now become of Him ?
Lambs, that through the mountains went
Frisking, bleating merriment.
When the year was in its prime,
They are sobered by this time.
If you look to vale or hill,   80
If you listen, all is still,
Save a little neighbouring rill,
That from out the rocky ground
Strikes a solitary sound.
Vainly glitter hill and plain,
And the air is calm in vain;
Vainly Morning spreads the lure
Of a sky serene and pure;
Creature none can she decoy
Into open sign of joy: 90
Is it that they have a fear
Of the dreary season near ?

Or that other pleasures be
Sweeter even than gaiety?
 Yet, whate'er enjoyments dwell
In the impenetrable cell
Of the silent heart which Nature
Furnishes to every creature;
Whatsoe'er we feel and know
Too sedate for outward show,   100
Such a light of gladness breaks,
Pretty Kitten! from thy freaks, —
Spreads with such a living grace
O'er my little Dora's face;
Yes, the sight so stirs and charms
Thee, Baby, laughing in my arms,
That almost I could repine
That your transports are not mine,
That I do not wholly fare
Even as ye do, thoughtless pair!   110
And I will have my careless season
Spite of melancholy reason,
Will walk through life in such a way
That, when time brings on decay,
Now and then I may possess
Hours of perfect gladsomeness.
— Pleased by any random toy;
By a kitten's busy joy,
Or an infant's laughing eye
Sharing in the ecstasy;   120
I would fare like that or this,
Find my wisdom in my bliss;
Keep the sprightly soul awake,
And have faculties to take,
Even from things by sorrow wrought,
Matter for a jocund thought,
Spite of care, and spite of grief,
To gambol with Life's falling Leaf.

TO THE SPADE OF A FRIEND

(AN AGRICULTURIST)

COMPOSED WHILE WE WERE LABOURING
TOGETHER IN HIS PLEASURE-GROUND

1806. 1807

 This person was Thomas Wilkinson, a quaker
by religious profession; by natural constitution
of mind, or shall I venture to say, by God's
grace, he was something better. He had in-
herited a small estate, and built a house upon
it near Yanwath, upon the banks of the Emont.
I have heard him say that his heart used to
beat, in his boyhood, when he heard the sound
of a drum and fife. Nevertheless, the spirit of
enterprise in him confined itself to tilling his
ground, and conquering such obstacles as stood
in the way of its fertility. Persons of his reli-
gious persuasion do now, in a far greater degree
than formerly, attach themselves to trade and
commerce. He kept the old track. As repre-
sented in this poem, he employed his leisure
hours in shaping pleasant walks by the side of
his beloved river, where he also built some-
thing between a hermitage and a summer-
house, attaching to it inscriptions after the
manner of Shenstone at his Leasowes. He used
to travel from time to time, partly from love of
nature, and partly with religious friends in the
service of humanity. His admiration of genius
in every department did him much honour.
Through his connection with the family in
which Edmund Burke was educated, he be-
came acquainted with that great man, who
used to receive him with great kindness and
consideration; and many times have I heard
Wilkinson speak of those interesting interviews.
He was honoured also by the friendship of
Elizabeth Smith, and of Thomas Clarkson and
his excellent wife, and was much esteemed by
Lord and Lady Lonsdale, and every member
of that family. Among his verses (he wrote
many) are some worthy of preservation — one
little poem in particular upon disturbing, by
prying curiosity, a bird while hatching her
young in his garden. The latter part of this
innocent and good man's life was melancholy.
He became blind, and also poor by becoming
surety for some of his relations. He was a
bachelor. He bore, as I have often witnessed,
his calamities with unfailing resignation. I will
only add that, while working in one of his
fields, he unearthed a stone of considerable
size, then another, then two more, and, observ-
ing that they had been placed in order as if
forming the segment of a circle, he proceeded
carefully to uncover the soil, and brought into
view a beautiful Druid's temple of perfect
though small dimensions. In order to make
his farm more compact, he exchanged this
field for another; and, I am sorry to add, the
new proprietor destroyed this interesting relic
of remote ages for some vulgar purpose.

SPADE! with which Wilkinson hath tilled
      his lands,
And shaped these pleasant walks by
      Emont's side,
Thou art a tool of honour in my hands;
I press thee through the yielding soil, with
      pride.

Rare master has it been thy lot to know;
Long hast Thou served a man to reason
      true;

Whose life combines the best of high and
    low,
The labouring many and the resting few;

Health, meekness, ardour, quietness se-
    cure,
And industry of body and of mind;   10
And elegant enjoyments, that are pure
As nature is; too pure to be refined.

Here often hast Thou heard the Poet sing
In concord with his river murmuring by;
Or in some silent field, while timid spring
Is yet uncheered by other minstrelsy.

Who shall inherit Thee when death has
    laid
Low in the darksome cell thine own dear
    lord ?
That man will have a trophy, humble
    Spade !   19
A trophy nobler than a conqueror's sword.

If he be one that feels, with skill to part
False praise from true, or, greater from
    the less,
Thee will he welcome to his hand and
    heart,
Thou monument of peaceful happiness !

He will not dread with Thee a toilsome
    day —
Thee his loved servant, his inspiring mate !
And, when thou art past service, worn
    away,
No dull oblivious nook shall hide thy fate.

His thrift thy uselessness will never scorn;
An *heir-loom* in his cottage wilt thou
    be: —   30
High will he hang thee up, well pleased to
    adorn
His rustic chimney with the last of Thee !

THE SMALL CELANDINE

1804. 1807

THERE is a Flower, the lesser Celandine,
That shrinks, like many more, from cold
    and rain;
And, the first moment that the sun may
    shine,
Bright as the sun himself, 't is out again !

When hailstones have been falling, swarm
    on swarm,
Or blasts the green field and the trees
    distrest,
Oft have I seen it muffled up from harm,
In close self-shelter, like a Thing at rest.

But lately, one rough day, this Flower I
    passed
And recognised it, though an altered form,
Now standing forth an offering to the blast,
And buffeted at will by rain and storm.

I stopped, and said with inly - muttered
    voice,
" It doth not love the shower, nor seek the
    cold:
This neither is its courage nor its choice,
But its necessity in being old.

" The sunshine may not cheer it, nor the
    dew;
It cannot help itself in its decay;
Stiff in its members, withered, changed of
    hue."
And, in my spleen, I smiled that it was
    grey.

To be a Prodigal's Favourite — then, worse
    truth,
A Miser's Pensioner — behold our lot !
O Man, that from thy fair and shining
    youth
Age might but take the things Youth
    needed not !

AT APPLETHWAITE, NEAR KESWICK

1803(?). 1842

This place was presented to me by Sir
George Beaumont with a view to the erection
of a house upon it, for the sake of being near
to Coleridge, then living, and likely to remain,
at Greta Hall near Keswick. The *severe* neces-
sities that prevented this arose from his do-
mestic situation. This little property, with a
considerable addition that still leaves it very
small, lies beautifully upon the banks of a rill
that gurgles down the side of Skiddaw, and the
orchard and other parts of the grounds com-
mand a magnificent prospect of Derwent
Water, and of the mountains of Borrowdale and
Newlands. Many years ago I gave the place
to my daughter.

BEAUMONT ! it was thy wish that I should rear
A seemly Cottage in this sunny Dell,
On favoured ground, thy gift, where I might dwell
In neighbourhood with One to me most dear,
That undivided we from year to year
Might work in our high Calling — a bright hope
To which our fancies, mingling, gave free scope
Till checked by some necessities severe.
And should these slacken, honoured BEAU-MONT ! still
Even then we may perhaps in vain implore
Leave of our fate thy wishes to fulfil.
Whether this boon be granted us or not,
Old Skiddaw will look down upon the Spot
With pride, the Muses love it evermore.

TO THE SUPREME BEING

FROM THE ITALIAN OF MICHAEL ANGELO

1805. 1806

THE prayers I make will then be sweet indeed
If Thou the spirit give by which I pray:
My unassisted heart is barren clay,
That of its native self can nothing feed:
Of good and pious works thou art the seed,
That quickens only where thou say'st it may:
Unless Thou show to us thine own true way
No man can find it: Father ! Thou must lead.
Do Thou, then, breathe those thoughts into my mind
By which such virtue may in me be bred
That in thy holy footsteps I may tread;
The fetters of my tongue do Thou unbind,
That I may have the power to sing of thee,
And sound thy praises everlastingly.

ODE TO DUTY

1804. 1807

This ode is on the model of Gray's Ode to Adversity, which is copied from Horace's Ode to Fortune. Many and many a time have I been twitted by my wife and sister for having forgotten this dedication of myself to the stern lawgiver. Transgressor indeed I have been,
from hour to hour, from day to day : I would fain hope, however, not more flagrantly or in a worse way than most of my tuneful brethren. But these last words are in a wrong strain. We should be rigorous to ourselves and forbearing, if not indulgent, to others, and, if we make comparisons at all, it ought to be with those who have morally excelled us.

"Jam non consilio bonus, sed more eò perductus, ut non tantum rectè facere possim, sed nisi rectè facere non possim."

STERN Daughter of the Voice of God !
O Duty ! if that name thou love
Who art a light to guide, a rod
To check the erring, and reprove;
Thou, who art victory and law
When empty terrors overawe;
From vain temptations dost set free;
And calm'st the weary strife of frail humanity !

There are who ask not if thine eye
Be on them; who, in love and truth,   10
Where no misgiving is, rely
Upon the genial sense of youth:
Glad Hearts ! without reproach or blot
Who do thy work, and know it not:
Oh ! if through confidence misplaced
They fail, thy saving arms, dread Power !
around them cast.

Serene will be our days and bright,
And happy will our nature be,
When love is an unerring light,
And joy its own security.   20
And they a blissful course may hold
Even now, who, not unwisely bold,
Live in the spirit of this creed;
Yet seek thy firm support, according to their need.

I, loving freedom, and untried;
No sport of every random gust,
Yet being to myself a guide,
Too blindly have reposed my trust:
And oft, when in my heart was heard
Thy timely mandate, I deferred   30
The task, in smoother walks to stray;
But thee I now would serve more strictly, if I may.

Through no disturbance of my soul,
Or strong compunction in me wrought,
I supplicate for thy control;
But in the quietness of thought:

Me this unchartered freedom tires;
I feel the weight of chance-desires:
My hopes no more must change their name,
I long for a repose that ever is the same. 40

Stern Lawgiver! yet thou dost wear
The Godhead's most benignant grace;
Nor know we anything so fair
As is the smile upon thy face:
Flowers laugh before thee on their beds
And fragrance in thy footing treads;
Thou dost preserve the stars from wrong;
And the most ancient heavens, through
  Thee, are fresh and strong.

To humbler functions, awful Power!
I call thee: I myself commend   50
Unto thy guidance from this hour;
Oh, let my weakness have an end!
Give unto me, made lowly wise,
The spirit of self-sacrifice;
The confidence of reason give;
And in the light of truth thy Bondman let
  me live!

TO A SKY-LARK

1802. 1807

UP with me! up with me into the clouds!
  For thy song, Lark, is strong;
Up with me, up with me into the clouds!
  Singing, singing,
With clouds and sky about thee ringing,
  Lift me, guide me till I find
That spot which seems so to thy mind!

I have walked through wildernesses dreary
And to-day my heart is weary;
Had I now the wings of a Faery,   10
Up to thee would I fly.
There is madness about thee, and joy divine
In that song of thine;
Lift me, guide me high and high
To thy banqueting-place in the sky.

    Joyous as morning
Thou art laughing and scorning;
Thou hast a nest for thy love and thy rest,
And, though little troubled with sloth,
Drunken Lark! thou would'st be loth   20
To be such a traveller as I.
Happy, happy Liver,
With a soul as strong as a mountain river
Pouring out praise to the Almighty Giver,
  Joy and jollity be with us both!

Alas! my journey, rugged and uneven,
Through prickly moors or dusty ways must
  wind;
But hearing thee, or others of thy kind,
As full of gladness and as free of heaven,
I, with my fate contented, will plod on, 30
And hope for higher raptures, when life's
  day is done.

FIDELITY

1805. 1807

The young man whose death gave occasion
to this poem was named Charles Gough, and
had come early in the spring to Patterdale for
the sake of angling. While attempting to
cross over Helvellyn to Grasmere he slipped
from a steep part of the rock where the ice
was not thawed, and perished. His body was
discovered as is told in this poem. Walter
Scott heard of the accident, and both he and
I, without either of us knowing that the other
had taken up the subject, each wrote a poem
in admiration of the dog's fidelity. His con-
tains a most beautiful stanza: —

"How long didst thou think that his silence
      was slumber?
When the wind waved his garment how oft
      didst thou start?"

I will add that the sentiment in the last four
lines of the last stanza in my verses was uttered
by a shepherd with such exactness, that a
traveller, who afterwards reported his account
in print, was induced to question the man
whether he had read them, which he had not.

A BARKING sound the Shepherd hears,
A cry as of a dog or fox;
He halts — and searches with his eyes
Among the scattered rocks:
And now at distance can discern
A stirring in a brake of fern;
And instantly a dog is seen,
Glancing through that covert green.

The Dog is not of mountain breed;
Its motions, too, are wild and shy;   10
With something, as the Shepherd thinks,
Unusual in its cry:
Nor is there any one in sight
All round, in hollow or on height;
Nor shout, nor whistle strikes his ear;
What is the creature doing here?

It was a cove, a huge recess,
That keeps, till June, December's snow;

A lofty precipice in front,
A silent tarn below !   20
Far in the bosom of Helvellyn,
Remote from public road or dwelling,
Pathway, or cultivated land;
From trace of human foot or hand.

There sometimes doth a leaping fish
Send through the tarn a lonely cheer;
The crags repeat the raven's croak,
In symphony austere;
Thither the rainbow comes — the cloud —
And mists that spread the flying shroud;   30
And sunbeams; and the sounding blast,
That, if it could, would hurry past;
But that enormous barrier holds it fast.

Not free from boding thoughts, a while
The Shepherd stood; then makes his way
O'er rocks and stones, following the Dog
As quickly as he may;
Nor far had gone before he found
A human skeleton on the ground;
The appalled Discoverer with a sigh   40
Looks round, to learn the history.

From those abrupt and perilous rocks
The Man had fallen, that place of fear !
At length upon the Shepherd's mind
It breaks, and all is clear:
He instantly recalled the name,
And who he was, and whence he came;
Remembered, too, the very day
On which the Traveller passed this way.

But hear a wonder, for whose sake   50
This lamentable tale I tell !
A lasting monument of words
This wonder merits well.
The Dog which still was hovering nigh,
Repeating the same timid cry,
This Dog had been through three months'
        space
A dweller in that savage place.

Yes, proof was plain that, since the day
When this ill-fated Traveller died,
The Dog had watched about the spot,   60
Or by his master's side:
How nourished here through such long
        time
He knows, who gave that love sublime;
And gave that strength of feeling, great
Above all human estimate !

INCIDENT

CHARACTERISTIC OF A FAVOURITE DOG

1805. 1807

This Dog I knew well. It belonged to Mrs.
Wordsworth's brother, Mr. Thomas Hutchin-
son, who then lived at Sockburn on the Tees, a
beautiful retired situation where I used to visit
him and his sisters before my marriage. My
sister and I spent many months there after our
return from Germany in 1799.

ON his morning rounds the Master
Goes to learn how all things fare;
Searches pasture after pasture,
Sheep and cattle eyes with care;
And, for silence or for talk,
He hath comrades in his walk;
Four dogs, each pair a different breed,
Distinguished two for scent, and two for
        speed.

See a hare before him started !
— Off they fly in earnest chase;   10
Every dog is eager-hearted,
All the four are in the race:
And the hare whom they pursue,
Knows from instinct what to do;
Her hope is near: no turn she makes;
But, like an arrow, to the river takes.

Deep the river was, and crusted
Thinly by a one night's frost;
But the nimble Hare hath trusted
To the ice, and safely crost;   20
She hath crost, and without heed
All are following at full speed,
When, lo ! the ice, so thinly spread,
Breaks — and the greyhound, DART, is over-
        head !

Better fate have PRINCE and SWALLOW —
See them cleaving to the sport !
MUSIC has no heart to follow,
Little MUSIC, she stops short.
She hath neither wish nor heart,
Hers is now another part: 30
A loving creature she, and brave !
And fondly strives her struggling friend to
        save.

From the brink her paws she stretches,
Very hands as you would say !
And afflicting moans she fetches,
As he breaks the ice away.

For herself she hath no fears, —
Him alone she sees and hears, —
Makes efforts with complainings; nor gives
o'er   39
Until her fellow sinks to re-appear no more.

TRIBUTE

TO THE MEMORY OF THE SAME DOG

1805. 1807

LIE here, without a record of thy worth,
Beneath a covering of the common earth!
It is not from unwillingness to praise,
Or want of love, that here no Stone we raise;
More thou deserv'st; but *this* man gives to
man,
Brother to brother, *this* is all we can.
Yet they to whom thy virtues made thee
dear
Shall find thee through all changes of the
year:
This Oak points out thy grave; the silent
tree
Will gladly stand a monument of thee.   10
  We grieved for thee, and wished thy end
were past;
And willingly have laid thee here at last:
For thou hadst lived till everything that
cheers
In thee had yielded to the weight of years;
Extreme old age had wasted thee away,
And left thee but a glimmering of the day:
Thy ears were deaf, and feeble were thy
knees, —
I saw thee stagger in the summer breeze,
Too weak to stand against its sportive
breath,
And ready for the gentlest stroke of death.
It came, and we were glad; yet tears were
shed;   21
Both man and woman wept when thou wert
dead;
Not only for a thousand thoughts that were,
Old household thoughts, in which thou hadst
thy share;
But for some precious boons vouchsafed to
thee,
Found scarcely anywhere in like degree!
For love, that comes wherever life and sense
Are given by God, in thee was most intense;
A chain of heart, a feeling of the mind,
A tender sympathy, which did thee bind   30
Not only to us Men, but to thy Kind:

Yea, for thy fellow-brutes in thee we saw
A soul of love, love's intellectual law: —
Hence, if we wept, it was not done in shame;
Our tears from passion and from reason
came,
And, therefore, shalt thou be an honoured
name!

"WHEN TO THE ATTRACTIONS OF THE BUSY WORLD"

1800. 1815

The grove still exists, but the plantation has
been walled in, and is not so accessible as when
my brother John wore the path in the manner
here described. The grove was a favourite
haunt with us all while we lived at Town-end.

WHEN, to the attractions of the busy world,
Preferring studious leisure, I had chosen
A habitation in this peaceful Vale,
Sharp season followed of continual storm
In deepest winter; and, from week to week,
Pathway, and lane, and public road, were
clogged
With frequent showers of snow. Upon a
hill
At a short distance from my cottage, stands
A stately Fir-grove, whither I was wont
To hasten, for I found, beneath the roof   10
Of that perennial shade, a cloistral place
Of refuge, with an unincumbered floor.
Here, in safe covert, on the shallow snow,
And, sometimes, on a speck of visible earth,
The redbreast near me hopped; nor was I
loth
To sympathise with vulgar coppice birds
That, for protection from the nipping blast,
Hither repaired. — A single beech-tree grew
Within this grove of firs! and, on the fork
Of that one beech, appeared a thrush's
nest;   20
A last year's nest, conspicuously built
At such small elevation from the ground
As gave sure sign that they, who in that
house
Of nature and of love had made their home
Amid the fir-trees, all the summer long
Dwelt in a tranquil spot. And oftentimes,
A few sheep, stragglers from some moun-
tain-flock,
Would watch my motions with suspicious
stare,
From the remotest outskirts of the grove, —

Some nook where they had made their final
 stand,   30
Huddling together from two fears — the
 fear
Of me and of the storm. Full many an
 hour
Here did I lose. But in this grove the
 trees
Had been so thickly planted, and had
 thriven
In such perplexed and intricate array ;
That vainly did I seek, beneath their stems
A length of open space, where to and fro
My feet might move without concern or
 care;
And, baffled thus, though earth from day
 to day
Was fettered, and the air by storm dis-
 turbed,   40
I ceased the shelter to frequent, — and
 prized,
Less than I wished to prize, that calm
 recess.
 The snows dissolved, and genial Spring
 returned
To clothe the fields with verdure. Other
 haunts
Meanwhile were mine ; till, one bright
 April day,
By chance retiring from the glare of noon
To this forsaken covert, there I found
A hoary pathway traced between the trees,
And winding on with such an easy line
Along a natural opening, that I stood   50
Much wondering how I could have sought
 in vain
For what was now so obvious. To abide,
For an allotted interval of ease,
Under my cottage-roof, had gladly come
From the wild sea a cherished Visitant ;
And with the sight of this same path —
 begun,
Begun and ended, in the shady grove,
Pleasant conviction flashed upon my mind
That, to this opportune recess allured,
He had surveyed it with a finer eye,   60
A heart more wakeful ; and had worn the
 track
By pacing here, unwearied and alone,
In that habitual restlessness of foot
That haunts the Sailor measuring o'er and
 o'er
His short domain upon the vessel's deck,
While she pursues her course through the
 dreary sea.

When thou hadst quitted Esthwaite's
 pleasant shore,
And taken thy first leave of those green
 hills
And rocks that were the play-ground of thy
 youth,
Year followed year, my Brother ! and we
 two,   70
Conversing not, knew little in what mould
Each other's mind was fashioned; and at
 length,
When once again we met in Grasmere Vale,
Between us there was little other bond
Than common feelings of fraternal love.
But thou, a Schoolboy, to the sea hadst
 carried
Undying recollections ! Nature there
Was with thee; she, who loved us both, she
 still
Was with thee; and even so didst thou
 become
A *silent* Poet; from the solitude   80
Of the vast sea didst bring a watchful
 heart
Still couchant, an inevitable ear,
And an eye practised like a blind man's
 touch.
— Back to the joyless Ocean thou art gone;
Nor from this vestige of thy musing hours
Could I withhold thy honoured name, —
 and now
I love the fir-grove with a perfect love.
Thither do I withdraw when cloudless suns
Shine hot, or wind blows troublesome and
 strong;
And there I sit at evening, when the steep
Of Silver-how, and Grasmere's peaceful
 lake,   91
And one green island, gleam between the
 stems
Of the dark firs, a visionary scene !
And, while I gaze upon the spectacle
Of clouded splendour, on this dream-like
 sight
Of solemn loveliness, I think on thee,
My Brother, and on all which thou hast
 lost.
Nor seldom, if I rightly guess, while Thou,
Muttering the verses which I muttered first
Among the mountains, through the mid-
 night watch   100
Art pacing thoughtfully the vessel's deck
In some far region, here, while o'er my
 head,
At every impulse of the moving breeze,

The fir-grove murmurs with a sea-like
 sound,
Alone I tread this path; — for aught I
 know,
Timing my steps to thine; and, with a
 store
Of undistinguishable sympathies,
Mingling most earnest wishes for the day
When we, and others whom we love, shall
 meet
A second time, in Grasmere's happy Vale. 110

ELEGIAC VERSES

IN MEMORY OF MY BROTHER, JOHN WORDSWORTH,

COMMANDER OF THE E. I. COMPANY'S SHIP THE
EARL OF ABERGAVENNY, IN WHICH HE PER-
ISHED BY CALAMITOUS SHIPWRECK, FEB. 6,
1805

1805. 1842

Composed near the Mountain track that leads
from Grasmere through Grisdale Hawes, where
it descends toward Patterdale.

" Here did we stop ; and here looked round,
 While each into himself descends."

The point is two or three yards below the
outlet of Grisdale tarn, on a foot-road by
which a horse may pass to Patterdale — a ridge
of Helvellyn on the left, and the summit of
Fairfield on the right.

I

THE Sheep-boy whistled loud, and lo !
That instant, startled by the shock,
The Buzzard mounted from the rock
Deliberate and slow:
Lord of the air, he took his flight;
Oh ! could he on that woeful night
Have lent his wing, my Brother dear,
For one poor moment's space to Thee,
And all who struggled with the Sea,
When safety was so near. 10

II

Thus in the weakness of my heart
I spoke (but let that pang be still)
When rising from the rock at will,
I saw the Bird depart.
And let me calmly bless the Power
That meets me in this unknown Flower.
Affecting type of him I mourn !
With calmness suffer and believe,
And grieve, and know that I must grieve,
Not cheerless, though forlorn. 20

III

Here did we stop; and here looked round
While each into himself descends,
For that last thought of parting Friends
That is not to be found.
Hidden was Grasmere Vale from sight,
Our home and his, his heart's delight,
His quiet heart's selected home.
But time before him melts away,
And he hath feeling of a day
Of blessedness to come. 30

IV

Full soon in sorrow did I weep,
Taught that the mutual hope was dust,
In sorrow, but for higher trust,
How miserably deep !
All vanished in a single word,
A breath, a sound, and scarcely heard:
Sea — Ship — drowned — Shipwreck — so
 it came,
The meek, the brave, the good, was gone;
He who had been our living John
Was nothing but a name. 40

V

That was indeed a parting ! oh,
Glad am I, glad that it is past;
For there were some on whom it cast
Unutterable woe.
But they as well as I have gains; —
From many a humble source, to pains
Like these, there comes a mild release;
Even here I feel it, even this Plant
Is in its beauty ministrant
To comfort and to peace. 50

VI

He would have loved thy modest grace,
Meek Flower ! To Him I would have said,
" It grows upon its native bed
Beside our Parting-place;
There, cleaving to the ground, it lies
With multitude of purple eyes,
Spangling a cushion green like moss;
But we will see it, joyful tide !
Some day, to see it in its pride,
The mountain will we cross." 60

VII

— Brother and Friend, if verse of mine
Have power to make thy virtues known,
Here let a monumental Stone
Stand — sacred as a Shrine;

And to the few who pass this way,
Traveller or Shepherd, let it say,
Long as these mighty rocks endure, -
Oh do not Thou too fondly brood,
Although deserving of all good,
On any earthly hope, however pure !   70

TO THE DAISY

1805. 1815

SWEET Flower ! belike one day to have
A place upon thy Poet's grave,
I welcome thee once more;
But He, who was on land, at sea,
My Brother, too, in loving thee,
Although he loved more silently,
Sleeps by his native shore.

Ah ! hopeful, hopeful was the day
When to that Ship he bent his way,
To govern and to guide: 10
His wish was gained: a little time
Would bring him back in manhood's prime
And free for life, these hills to climb;
With all his wants supplied.

And full of hope day followed day
While that stout Ship at anchor lay
Beside the shores of Wight;
The May had then made all things green;
And, floating there, in pomp serene,
That Ship was goodly to be seen,   20
His pride and his delight !

Yet then, when called ashore, he sought
The tender peace of rural thought:
In more than happy mood
To your abodes, bright daisy Flowers !
He then would steal at leisure hours,
And loved you glittering in your bowers
A starry multitude.

But hark the word ! — the ship is gone; —
Returns from her long course: — anon   30
Sets sail: — in season due,
Once more on English earth they stand:
But, when a third time from the land
They parted, sorrow was at hand
For Him and for his crew.

Ill-fated Vessel ! — ghastly shock !
— At length delivered from the rock,
The deep she hath regained;
And through the stormy night they steer;
Labouring for life, in hope and fear,   40

To reach a safer shore — how near,
Yet not to be attained !

" Silence ! " the brave Commander cried:
To that calm word a shriek replied,
It was the last death-shriek.
— A few (my soul oft sees that sight)
Survive upon the tall mast's height;
But one dear remnant of the night —
For Him in vain I seek.

Six weeks beneath the moving sea   50
He lay in slumber quietly;
Unforced by wind or wave
To quit the Ship for which he died,
(All claims of duty satisfied;)
And there they found him at her side;
And bore him to the grave.

Vain service ! yet not vainly done
For this, if other end were none,
That He, who had been cast
Upon a way of life unmeet   60
For such a gentle Soul and sweet,
Should find an undisturbed retreat
Near what he loved, at last —

That neighbourhood of grove and field
To Him a resting-place should yield,
A meek man and a brave !
The birds shall sing and ocean make
A mournful murmur for *his* sake;
And Thou, sweet Flower, shalt sleep and
    wake
Upon his senseless grave.   70

ELEGIAC STANZAS

SUGGESTED BY A PICTURE OF PEELE
CASTLE, IN A STORM, PAINTED BY SIR
GEORGE BEAUMONT

1806. 1807

Sir George Beaumont painted two pictures
of this subject, one of which he gave to Mrs.
Wordsworth saying she ought to have it; but
Lady Beaumont interfered, and after Sir
George's death she gave it to Sir Uvedale
Price, in whose house at Foxley I have seen
it —, rather grudgingly, shown.

I WAS thy neighbour once, thou rugged
    Pile !
Four summer weeks I dwelt in sight of
    thee:
I saw thee every day; and all the while
Thy Form was sleeping on a glassy sea.

So pure the sky, so quiet was the air !
So like, so very like, was day to day !
Whene'er I looked, thy Image still was
 there;
It trembled, but it never passed away.

How perfect was the calm ! it seemed no
 sleep;
No mood, which season takes away, or
 brings: 10
I could have fancied that the mighty Deep
Was even the gentlest of all gentle Things.

Ah ! THEN, if mine had been the Painter's
 hand,
To express what then I saw; and add the
 gleam,
The light that never was, on sea or land,
The consecration, and the Poet's dream;

I would have planted thee, thou hoary
 Pile
Amid a world how different from this !
Beside a sea that could not cease to smile;
On tranquil land, beneath a sky of bliss. 20

Thou shouldst have seemed a treasure-
 house divine
Of peaceful years; a chronicle of heaven; —
Of all the sunbeams that did ever shine
The very sweetest had to thee been given.

A Picture had it been of lasting ease,
Elysian quiet, without toil or strife;
No motion but the moving tide, a breeze,
Or merely silent Nature's breathing life.

Such, in the fond illusion of my heart,
Such Picture would I at that time have
 made: 30
And seen the soul of truth in every part,
A stedfast peace that might not be betrayed.

So once it would have been, — 't is so no
 more;
I have submitted to a new control:
A power is gone, which nothing can re-
 store;
A deep distress hath humanised my Soul.

Not for a moment could I now behold
A smiling sea, and be what I have been:
The feeling of my loss will ne'er be old;
This, which I know, I speak with mind
 serene.   40

Then, Beaumont, Friend ! who would have
 been the Friend,
If he had lived, of Him whom I deplore,
This work of thine I blame not, but com-
 mend;
This sea in anger, and that dismal shore.

O 't is a passionate Work ! — yet wise and
 well,
Well chosen is the spirit that is here;
That Hulk which labours in the deadly
 swell,
This rueful sky, this pageantry of fear !

And this huge Castle, standing here sub-
 lime,   49
I love to see the look with which it braves,
Cased in the unfeeling armour of old time,
The lightning, the fierce wind, and tram-
 pling waves.

Farewell, farewell the heart that lives
 alone,
Housed in a dream, at distance from the
 Kind !
Such happiness, wherever it be known,
Is to be pitied; for 't is surely blind.

But welcome fortitude, and patient cheer,
And frequent sights of what is to be borne !
Such sights, or worse, as are before me
 here. —   59
Not without hope we suffer and we mourn.

LOUISA

AFTER ACCOMPANYING HER ON A
MOUNTAIN EXCURSION

1802. 1807

Written at Town-end, Grasmere.

I MET Louisa in the shade,
And, having seen that lovely Maid,
Why should I fear to say
That, nymph-like, she is fleet and strong,
And down the rocks can leap along
Like rivulets in May ?

She loves her fire, her cottage-home;
Yet o'er the moorland will she roam
In weather rough and bleak;
And, when against the wind she strains,
Oh ! might I kiss the mountain rains
That sparkle on her cheek.

Take all that's mine "beneath the moon,"
If I with her but half a noon
May sit beneath the walls
Of some old cave, or mossy nook,
When up she winds along the brook
To hunt the waterfalls.

TO A YOUNG LADY

WHO HAD BEEN REPROACHED FOR TAK-
ING LONG WALKS IN THE COUNTRY

1802. 1802

Composed at the same time and on the same view as "I met Louisa in the shade": indeed they were designed to make one piece.

DEAR Child of Nature, let them rail !
— There is a nest in a green dale,
A harbour and a hold;
Where thou, a Wife and Friend, shalt see
Thy own heart-stirring days, and be
A light to young and old.

There, healthy as a shepherd boy,
And treading among flowers of joy
Which at no season fade,
Thou, while thy babes around thee cling,
Shalt show us how divine a thing
A Woman may be made.

Thy thoughts and feelings shall not die,
Nor leave thee, when grey hairs are nigh,
A melancholy slave;
But an old age serene and bright,
And lovely as a Lapland night,
Shall lead thee to thy grave.

VAUDRACOUR AND JULIA

1804. 1820

Written at Town-end, Grasmere. Faithfully narrated, though with the omission of many pathetic circumstances, from the mouth of a French lady, who had been an eye-and-ear-witness of all that was done and said. Many long years after, I was told that Dupligne was then a monk in the Convent of La Trappe.

The following tale was written as an Episode, in a work from which its length may perhaps exclude it. The facts are true ; no invention as to these has been exercised, as none was needed.

O HAPPY time of youthful lovers (thus
My story may begin) O balmy time,
In which a love-knot on a lady's brow
Is fairer than the fairest star in heaven !
To such inheritance of blessed fancy
(Fancy that sports more desperately with
    minds
Than ever fortune hath been known to do)
The high-born Vaudracour was brought,
    by years
Whose progress had a little overstepped
His stripling prime. A town of small re-
    pute,   10
Among the vine-clad mountains of Au-
    vergne,
Was the Youth's birth-place. There he
    wooed a Maid
Who heard the heart-felt music of his suit
With answering vows. Plebeian was the
    stock,
Plebeian, though ingenuous, the stock,
From which her graces and her honours
    sprung:
And hence the father of the enamoured
    Youth,
With haughty indignation, spurned the
    thought
Of such alliance. — From their cradles up,
With but a step between their several
    homes,   20
Twins had they been in pleasure; after
    strife
And petty quarrels, had grown fond again;
Each other's advocate, each other's stay;
And, in their happiest moments, not con-
    tent,
If more divided than a sportive pair
Of sea-fowl, conscious both that they are
    hovering
Within the eddy of a common blast,
Or hidden only by the concave depth
Of neighbouring billows from each other's
    sight.   29
Thus, not without concurrence of an age
Unknown to memory, was an earnest given
By ready nature for a life of love,
For endless constancy, and placid truth;
But whatsoe'er of such rare treasure lay
Reserved, had fate permitted, for support
Of their maturer years, his present mind
Was under fascination; — he beheld
A vision, and adored the thing he saw.
Arabian fiction never filled the world
With half the wonders that were wrought
    for him.   40

Earth breathed in one great presence of the
    spring;
Life turned the meanest of her implements,
Before his eyes, to price above all gold;
The house she dwelt in was a sainted
    shrine;
Her chamber-window did surpass in glory
The portals of the dawn; all paradise
Could, by the simple opening of a door,
Let itself in upon him: — pathways, walks,
Swarmed with enchantment, till his spirit
    sank,
Surcharged, within him, overblest to move
Beneath a sun that wakes a weary world   51
To its dull round of ordinary cares;
A man too happy for mortality !
    So passed the time, till whether through
    effect
Of some unguarded moment that dissolved
Virtuous restraint — ah, speak it, think it,
    not !
Deem rather that the fervent Youth, who
    saw
So many bars between his present state
And the dear haven where he wished to be
In honourable wedlock with his Love,   60
Was in his judgment tempted to decline
To perilous weakness, and entrust his cause
To nature for a happy end of all;
Deem that by such fond hope the Youth
    was swayed,
And bear with their transgression, when I
    add
That Julia, wanting yet the name of wife,
Carried about her for a secret grief
The promise of a mother.
              To conceal
The threatened shame, the parents of the
    Maid
Found means to hurry her away by night,
And unforewarned, that in some distant
    spot   71
She might remain shrouded in privacy,
Until the babe was born. When morning
    came
The Lover, thus bereft, stung with his loss,
And all uncertain whither he should turn,
Chafed like a wild beast in the toils; but
    soon
Discovering traces of the fugitives,
Their steps he followed to the Maid's re-
    treat.
Easily may the sequel be divined —
Walks to and fro — watchings at every
    hour;   80

And the fair Captive, who, whene'er she
    may,
Is busy at her casement as the swallow
Fluttering its pinions, almost within reach,
About the pendent nest, did thus espy
Her Lover ! — thence a stolen interview,
Accomplished under friendly shade of
    night.
    I pass the raptures of the pair; — such
    theme
Is, by innumerable poets, touched
In more delightful verse than skill of mine
Could fashion; chiefly by that darling bard
Who told of Juliet and her Romeo,   91
And of the lark's note heard before its
    time,
And of the streaks that laced the severing
    clouds
In the unrelenting east. — Through all her
    courts
The vacant city slept; the busy winds,
That keep no certain intervals of rest,
Moved not; meanwhile the galaxy dis-
    played
Her fires, that like mysterious pulses beat
Aloft; — momentous but uneasy bliss !
To their full hearts the universe seemed
    hung   100
On that brief meeting's slender filament !
    They parted; and the generous Vaudra-
    cour
Reached speedily the native threshold, bent
On making (so the Lovers had agreed)
A sacrifice of birthright to attain
A final portion from his father's hand;
Which granted, Bride and Bridegroom then
    would flee
To some remote and solitary place,
Shady as night, and beautiful as heaven,
Where they may live, with no one to be-
    hold   110
Their happiness, or to disturb their love.
But now of this no whisper; not the less,
If ever an obtrusive word were dropped
Touching the matter of his passion, still,
In his stern father's hearing, Vaudracour
Persisted openly that death alone
Should abrogate his human privilege
Divine, of swearing everlasting truth,
Upon the altar, to the Maid he loved.
    "You shall be baffled in your mad in-
    tent   120
If there be justice in the court of France,"
Muttered the Father. — From these words
    the Youth

Conceived a terror; and, by night or day,
Stirred nowhere without weapons, that full
    soon
Found dreadful provocation: for at night
When to his chamber he retired, attempt
Was made to seize him by three armèd
    men,
Acting, in furtherance of the father's will,
Under a private signet of the State.
One the rash Youth's ungovernable hand
Slew, and as quickly to a second gave 131
A perilous wound — he shuddered to be-
    hold
The breathless corse; then peacefully re-
    signed
His person to the law, was lodged in prison,
And wore the fetters of a criminal.
   Have you observed a tuft of wingèd seed
That, from the dandelion's naked stalk,
Mounted aloft, is suffered not to use
Its natural gifts for purposes of rest,
Driven by the autumnal whirlwind to and
    fro 140
Through the wide element ? or have you
    marked
The heavier substance of a leaf-clad bough,
Within the vortex of a foaming flood,
Tormented ? by such aid you may con-
    ceive
The perturbation that ensued; — ah, no !
Desperate the Maid — the Youth is stained
    with blood;
Unmatchable on earth is their disquiet !
Yet as the troubled seed and tortured
    bough
Is Man, subjected to despotic sway.
   For him, by private influence with the
    Court, 150
Was pardon gained, and liberty procured;
But not without exaction of a pledge,
Which liberty and love dispersed in air.
He flew to her from whom they would
    divide him —
He clove to her who could not give him
    peace —
Yea, his first word of greeting was, — "All
    right
Is gone from me; my lately-towering hopes,
To the least fibre of their lowest root,
Are withered; thou no longer canst be
    mine,
I thine — the conscience-stricken must not
    woo 160
The unruffled Innocent, — I see thy face,
Behold thee, and my misery is complete ! "

"One, are we not ? " exclaimed the
    Maiden — " One,
For innocence and youth, for weal and
    woe ? "
Then with the father's name she coupled
    words
Of vehement indignation; but the Youth
Checked her with filial meekness; for no
    thought
Uncharitable crossed his mind, no sense
Of hasty anger rising in the eclipse
Of true domestic loyalty, did e'er 170
Find place within his bosom. — Once again
The persevering wedge of tyranny
Achieved their separation: and once more
Were they united, — to be yet again
Disparted, pitiable lot ! But here
A portion of the tale may well be left
In silence, though my memory could add
Much how the Youth, in scanty space of
    time,
Was traversed from without; much, too,
    of thoughts
That occupied his days in solitude 180
Under privation and restraint; and what,
Through dark and shapeless fear of things
    to come,
And what, through strong compunction for
    the past,
He suffered — breaking down in heart and
    mind !
   Doomed to a third and last captivity,
His freedom he recovered on the eve
Of Julia's travail. When the babe was
    born,
Its presence tempted him to cherish schemes
Of future happiness. "You shall return,
Julia," said he, "and to your father's
    house 190
Go with the child. — You have been
    wretched; yet
The silver shower, whose reckless burthen
    weighs
Too heavily upon the lily's head,
Oft leaves a saving moisture at its root.
Malice, beholding you, will melt away.
Go ! — 't is a town where both of us were
    born;
None will reproach you, for our truth is
    known;
And if, amid those once-bright bowers, our
    fate
Remain unpitied, pity is not in man.
With ornaments — the prettiest, nature
    yields 200

Or art can fashion, shall you deck our boy,
And feed his countenance with your own
    sweet looks
Till no one can resist him. — Now, even
    now,
I see him sporting on the sunny lawn;
My father from the window sees him too;
Startled, as if some new-created thing
Enriched the earth, or Faery of the woods
Bounded before him; — but the unweeting
    Child
Shall by his beauty win his grandsire's
    heart   209
So that it shall be softened, and our loves
End happily, as they began!"
                 These gleams
Appeared but seldom; oftener was he seen
Propping a pale and melancholy face
Upon the Mother's bosom; resting thus
His head upon one breast, while from the
    other
The Babe was drawing in its quiet food.
— That pillow is no longer to be thine,
Fond Youth! that mournful solace now
    must pass
Into the list of things that cannot be!
Unwedded Julia, terror-smitten, hears   220
The sentence, by her mother's lip pro-
    nounced,
That dooms her to a convent. — Who shall
    tell,
Who dares report, the tidings to the lord
Of her affections? so they blindly asked
Who knew not to what quiet depths a weight
Of agony had pressed the Sufferer down:
The word, by others dreaded, he can hear
Composed and silent, without visible sign
Of even the least emotion. Noting this,
When the impatient object of his love   230
Upbraided him with slackness, he returned
No answer, only took the Mother's hand
And kissed it; seemingly devoid of pain,
Or care, that what so tenderly he pressed,
Was a dependant on the obdurate heart
Of one who came to disunite their lives
For ever — sad alternative! preferred,
By the unbending Parents of the Maid,
To secret 'spousals meanly disavowed.
— So be it!
         In the city he remained   240
A season after Julia had withdrawn
To those religious walls. He, too, de-
    parts —
Who with him? — even the senseless Lit-
    tle-one.

With that sole charge he passed the city-
    gates,
For the last time, attendant by the side
Of a close chair, a litter, or sedan,
In which the Babe was carried. To a hill,
That rose a brief league distant from the
    town,
The dwellers in that house where he had
    lodged
Accompanied his steps, by anxious love   250
Impelled; — they parted from him there,
    and stood
Watching below till he had disappeared
On the hill top. His eyes he scarcely took,
Throughout that journey, from the vehicle
(Slow-moving ark of all his hopes!) that
    veiled
The tender infant: and, at every inn,
And under every hospitable tree
At which the bearers halted or reposed,
Laid him with timid care upon his knees,
And looked, as mothers ne'er were known
    to look,   260
Upon the nursling which his arms em-
    braced.
    This was the manner in which Vaudra-
    cour
Departed with his infant; and thus reached
His father's house, where to the innocent
    child
Admittance was denied. The young man
    spake
No word of indignation or reproof,
But of his father begged, a last request,
That a retreat might be assigned to him
Where in forgotten quiet he might dwell,
With such allowance as his wants required;
For wishes he had none. To a lodge that
    stood   271
Deep in a forest, with leave given, at the
    age
Of four-and-twenty summers he withdrew;
And thither took with him his motherless
    Babe,
And one domestic for their common needs,
An aged woman. It consoled him here
To attend upon the orphan, and perform
Obsequious service to the precious child,
Which, after a short time, by some mis-
    take
Or indiscretion of the Father, died. —   280
The Tale I follow to its last recess
Of suffering or of peace, I know not which:
Theirs be the blame who caused the woe,
    not mine!

From this time forth he never shared a
    smile
With mortal creature. An Inhabitant
Of that same town, in which the pair had left
So lively a remembrance of their griefs,
By chance of business, coming within
    reach
Of his retirement, to the forest lodge
Repaired, but only found the matron there,
Who told him that his pains were thrown
    away,   291
For that her Master never uttered word
To living thing — not even to her. — Be-
    hold !
While they were speaking, Vaudracour
    approached;
But, seeing some one near, as on the latch
Of the garden-gate his hand was laid, he
    shrunk —
And, like a shadow, glided out of view.
Shocked at his savage aspect, from the
    place
The visitor retired.
                  Thus lived the Youth
Cut off from all intelligence with man, 300
And shunning even the light of common
    day;
Nor could the voice of Freedom, which
    through France
Full speedily resounded, public hope,
Or personal memory of his own deep
    wrongs,
Rouse him: but in those solitary shades
His days he wasted, an imbecile mind !

THE COTTAGER TO HER INFANT

BY MY SISTER

1805. 1815

Suggested to her while beside my sleeping
children.

THE days are cold, the nights are long,
The north-wind sings a doleful song;
Then hush again upon my breast;
All merry things are now at rest,
    Save thee, my pretty Love !

The kitten sleeps upon the hearth,
The crickets long have ceased their mirth ;
There 's nothing stirring in the house
Save one *wee*, hungry, nibbling mouse,
    Then why so busy thou ?

Nay ! start not at that sparkling light;
'T is but the moon that shines so bright
On the window pane bedropped with rain:
Then, little Darling ! sleep again,
    And wake when it is day.

THE WAGGONER

1806. 1819

Written at Town-end, Grasmere. The char-
acters and story from fact.

> In Cairo's crowded streets
> The impatient Merchant, wondering, waits in vain,
> And Mecca saddens at the long delay.
>   THOMSON.

TO
CHARLES LAMB, ESQ.

MY DEAR FRIEND,

    When I sent you, a few weeks ago, the tale
of Peter Bell, you asked "why 'The Wag-
goner' was not added ? "— To say the truth
— from the higher tone of imagination, and
the deeper touches of passion aimed at in the
former, I apprehended this little Piece could
not accompany it without disadvantage. In
the year 1806, if I am not mistaken, "The
Waggoner" was read to you in manuscript,
and, as you have remembered it for so long a
time, I am the more encouraged to hope, that,
since the localities on which the Poem partly
depends did not prevent its being interesting to
you, it may prove acceptable to others. Being
therefore in some measure the cause of its
present appearance, you must allow me the
gratification of inscribing it to you; in ac-
knowledgment of the pleasure I have derived
from your Writings, and of the high esteem
with which
                I am very truly yours,
                WILLIAM WORDSWORTH.

RYDAL MOUNT, *May* 20, 1819.

CANTO FIRST

'T IS spent — this burning day of June !
Soft darkness o'er its latest gleams is
    stealing;
The buzzing dor-hawk, round and round,
    is wheeling, —
That solitary bird
Is all that can be heard
In silence deeper far than that of deepest
    noon !
Confiding Glow-worms, 't is a night
Propitious to your earth-born light !

But, where the scattered stars are seen
In hazy straits the clouds between,   10
Each, in his station twinkling not,
Seems changed into a pallid spot.
The mountains against heaven's grave
                weight
Rise up, and grow to wondrous height.
The air, as in a lion's den,
Is close and hot; — and now and then
Comes a tired and sultry breeze
With a haunting and a panting,
Like the stifling of disease;
But the dews allay the heat,   20
And the silence makes it sweet.
Hush, there is some one on the stir !
'T is Benjamin the Waggoner;
Who long hath trod this toilsome way,
Companion of the night and day.
That far-off tinkling's drowsy cheer,
Mixed with a faint yet grating sound
In a moment lost and found,
The Wain announces — by whose side
Along the banks of Rydal Mere   30
He paces on, a trusty Guide, —
Listen ! you can scarcely hear !
Hither he his course is bending; —
Now he leaves the lower ground,
And up the craggy hill ascending
Many a stop and stay he makes,
Many a breathing-fit he takes; —
Steep the way and wearisome,
Yet all the while his whip is dumb !
    The Horses have worked with right
                good-will,   40
And so have gained the top of the hill;
He was patient, they were strong,
And now they smoothly glide along,
Recovering breath, and pleased to win
The praises of mild Benjamin.
Heaven shield him from mishap and snare !
But why so early with this prayer ? —
Is it for threatenings in the sky ?
Or for some other danger nigh ?
No; none is near him yet, though he   50
Be one of much infirmity;
For at the bottom of the brow,
Where once the DOVE and OLIVE-BOUGH
Offered a greeting of good ale
To all who entered Grasmere Vale;
And called on him who must depart
To leave it with a jovial heart;
There, where the DOVE and OLIVE-BOUGH
Once hung, a Poet harbours now,
A simple water-drinking Bard;   60
Why need our Hero then (though frail

His best resolves) be on his guard ?
He marches by, secure and bold;
Yet while he thinks on times of old,
It seems that all looks wondrous cold;
He shrugs his shoulders, shakes his head,
And, for the honest folk within,
It is a doubt with Benjamin
Whether they be alive or dead !
    Here is no danger, — none at all !   70
Beyond his wish he walks secure;
But pass a mile — and *then* for trial, —
Then for the pride of self-denial;
If he resist that tempting door,
Which with such friendly voice will call;
If he resist those casement panes,
And that bright gleam which thence will
                fall
Upon his Leaders' bells and manes,
Inviting him with cheerful lure:
For still, though all be dark elsewhere,   80
Some shining notice will be *there*,
Of open house and ready fare.
    The place to Benjamin right well
Is known, and by as strong a spell
As used to be that sign of love
And hope — the OLIVE-BOUGH and DOVE;
He knows it to his cost, good Man !
Who does not know the famous SWAN ?
Object uncouth ! and yet our boast,
For it was painted by the Host;   90
His own conceit the figure planned,
'T was coloured all by his own hand;
And that frail Child of thirsty clay,
Of whom I sing this rustic lay,
Could tell with self-dissatisfaction
Quaint stories of the bird's attraction !
    Well ! that is past — and in despite
Of open door and shining light.
And now the conqueror essays
The long ascent of Dunmail-raise;   100
And with his team is gentle here
As when he clomb from Rydal Mere;
His whip they do not dread — his voice
They only hear it to rejoice.
To stand or go is at *their* pleasure;
Their efforts and their time they measure
By generous pride within the breast;
And, while they strain, and while they rest,
He thus pursues his thoughts at leisure.
    Now am I fairly safe to-night —   110
And with proud cause my heart is light:
I trespassed lately worse than ever —
But Heaven has blest a good endeavour;
And, to my soul's content, I find
The evil One is left behind.

Yes, let my master fume and fret,
Here am I — with my horses yet!
My jolly team, he finds that ye
Will work for nobody but me!
Full proof of this the Country gained;   120
It knows how ye were vexed and strained,
And forced unworthy stripes to bear,
When trusted to another's care.
Here was it — on this rugged slope,
Which now ye climb with heart and hope,
I saw you, between rage and fear,
Plunge, and fling back a spiteful ear,
And ever more and more confused,
As ye were more and more abused:
As chance would have it, passing by   130
I saw you in that jeopardy:
A word from me was like a charm;
Ye pulled together with one mind;
And your huge burthen, safe from harm,
Moved like a vessel in the wind!
— Yes, without me, up hills so high
'T is vain to strive for mastery.
Then grieve not, jolly team! though tough
The road we travel, steep, and rough;
Though Rydal-heights and Dunmail-raise,
And all their fellow banks and braes,   141
Full often make you stretch and strain,
And halt for breath and halt again,
Yet to their sturdiness 't is owing
That side by side we still are going!
    While Benjamin in earnest mood
His meditations thus pursued,
A storm, which had been smothered long,
Was growing inwardly more strong;
And, in its struggles to get free,   150
Was busily employed as he.
The thunder had begun to growl —
He heard not, too intent of soul;
The air was now without a breath —
He marked not that 't was still as death.
But soon large rain-drops on his head
Fell with the weight of drops of lead; —
He starts — and takes, at the admonition,
A sage survey of his condition.
The road is black before his eyes,   160
Glimmering faintly where it lies;
Black is the sky — and every hill,
Up to the sky, is blacker still —
Sky, hill, and dale, one dismal room,
Hung round and overhung with gloom;
Save that above a single height
Is to be seen a lurid light,
Above Helm-crag — a streak half dead,
A burning of portentous red;
And near that lurid light, full well   170

The ASTROLOGER, sage Sidrophel,
Where at his desk and book he sits,
Puzzling aloft his curious wits;
He whose domain is held in common
With no one but the ANCIENT WOMAN,
Cowering beside her rifted cell,
As if intent on magic spell; —
Dread pair that, spite of wind and weather,
Still sit upon Helm-crag together!
    The ASTROLOGER was not unseen   180
By solitary Benjamin;
But total darkness came anon,
And he and everything was gone:
And suddenly a ruffling breeze,
(That would have rocked the sounding
    trees
Had aught of sylvan growth been there)
Swept through the Hollow long and bare:
The rain rushed down — the road was bat-
    tered,
As with the force of billows shattered;
The horses are dismayed, nor know   190
Whether they should stand or go;
And Benjamin is groping near them,
Sees nothing, and can scarcely hear them.
He is astounded, — wonder not, —
With such a charge in such a spot;
Astounded in the mountain gap
With thunder-peals, clap after clap,
Close-treading on the silent flashes —
And somewhere, as he thinks, by crashes
Among the rocks; with weight of rain,   200
And sullen motions long and slow,
That to a dreary distance go —
Till, breaking in upon the dying strain,
A rending o'er his head begins the fray
    again.
    Meanwhile, uncertain what to do,
And oftentimes compelled to halt,
The horses cautiously pursue
Their way, without mishap or fault;
And now have reached that pile of stones,
Heaped over brave King Dunmail's bones;
He who had once supreme command,   211
Last king of rocky Cumberland;
His bones, and those of all his Power
Slain here in a disastrous hour!
    When, passing through this narrow strait,
Stony, and dark, and desolate,
Benjamin can faintly hear
A voice that comes from some one near,
A female voice: — "Whoe'er you be,
Stop," it exclaimed, "and pity me!"   220
And, less in pity than in wonder,
Amid the darkness and the thunder,

The Waggoner, with prompt command,
Summons his horses to a stand.
   While, with increasing agitation,
The Woman urged her supplication,
In rueful words, with sobs between —
The voice of tears that fell unseen;
There came a flash — a startling glare,
And all Seat-Sandal was laid bare !   230
'T is not a time for nice suggestion,
And Benjamin, without a question,
Taking her for some way-worn rover,
Said, " Mount, and get you under cover ! "
   Another voice, in tone as hoarse
As a swoln brook with rugged course,
Cried out, " Good brother, why so fast ?
I 've had a glimpse of you — *avast !*
Or, since it suits you to be civil,
Take her at once — for good and evil ! " 240
" It is my Husband," softly said
The Woman, as if half afraid:
By this time she was snug within,
Through help of honest Benjamin;
She and her Babe, which to her breast
With thankfulness the Mother pressed;
And now the same strong voice more near
Said cordially, " My Friend, what cheer ?
Rough doings these ! as God 's my judge
The sky owes somebody a grudge !   250
We 've had in half an hour or less
A twelvemonth's terror and distress ! "
   Then Benjamin entreats the Man
Would mount, too, quickly as he can:
The Sailor — Sailor now no more,
But such he had been heretofore —
To courteous Benjamin replied,
" Go you your way, and mind not me;
For I must have, whate'er betide,
My Ass and fifty things beside, —   260
Go, and I 'll follow speedily ! "
   The Waggon moves — and with its load
Descends along the sloping road;
And the rough Sailor instantly
Turns to a little tent hard by:
For when, at closing-in of day,
The family had come that way,
Green pasture and the soft warm air
Tempted them to settle there. —
Green is the grass for beast to graze,   270
Around the stones of Dunmail-raise !
   The Sailor gathers up his bed,
Takes down the canvas overhead;
And, after farewell to the place,
A parting word — though not of grace,
Pursues, with Ass and all his store,
The way the Waggon went before.

CANTO SECOND

IF Wytheburn's modest House of prayer,
As lowly as the lowliest dwelling,
Had, with its belfry's humble stock,
A little pair that hang in air,
Been mistress also of a clock,
(And one, too, not in crazy plight)
Twelve strokes that clock would have been
   telling
Under the brow of old Helvellyn —
Its bead-roll of midnight,
Then, when the Hero of my tale   10
Was passing by, and, down the vale
(The vale now silent, hushed I ween
As if a storm had never been)
Proceeding with a mind at ease;
While the old Familiar of the seas,
Intent to use his utmost haste,
Gained ground upon the Waggon fast,
And gives another lusty cheer;
For, spite of rumbling of the wheels,
A welcome greeting he can hear; —   20
It is a fiddle in its glee
Dinning from the CHERRY TREE !
   Thence the sound — the light is there —
As Benjamin is now aware,
Who, to his inward thoughts confined,
Had almost reached the festive door,
When, startled by the Sailor's roar,
He hears a sound and sees the light,
And in a moment calls to mind
That 't is the village MERRY-NIGHT !   30
   Although before in no dejection,
At this insidious recollection
His heart with sudden joy is filled, —
His ears are by the music thrilled,
His eyes take pleasure in the road
Glittering before him bright and broad;
And Benjamin is wet and cold,
And there are reasons manifold
That make the good, tow'rds which he 's
   yearning,
Look fairly like a lawful earning.   40
   Nor has thought time to come and go,
To vibrate between yes and no;
For, cries the Sailor, " Glorious chance
That blew us hither ! — let him dance,
Who can or will ! — my honest soul,
Our treat shall be a friendly bowl ! "
He draws him to the door — " Come in,
Come, come," cries he to Benjamin !
And Benjamin — ah, woe is me !
Gave the word — the horses heard   50
And halted, though reluctantly.

"Blithe souls and lightsome hearts have
    we,
Feasting at the CHERRY TREE!"
This was the outside proclamation,
This was the inside salutation;
What bustling — jostling — high and low!
A universal overflow!
What tankards foaming from the tap!
What store of cakes in every lap!
What thumping — stumping — overhead!
The thunder had not been more busy: 61
With such a stir you would have said,
This little place may well be dizzy!
'T is who can dance with greatest vigour —
'T is what can be most prompt and eager;
As if it heard the fiddle's call,
The pewter clatters on the wall;
The very bacon shows its feeling,
Swinging from the smoky ceiling!
    A steaming bowl, a blazing fire,   70
What greater good can heart desire?
'T were worth a wise man's while to try
The utmost anger of the sky:
To *seek* for thoughts of a gloomy cast,
If such the bright amends at last.
Now should you say I judge amiss,
The CHERRY TREE shows proof of this;
For soon of all the happy there,
Our Travellers are the happiest pair;
All care with Benjamin is gone —   80
A Cæsar past the Rubicon!
He thinks not of his long, long strife; —
The Sailor, Man by nature gay,
Hath no resolves to throw away;
And he hath now forgot his Wife,
Hath quite forgotten her — or may be
Thinks her the luckiest soul on earth,
Within that warm and peaceful berth,
        Under cover,
        Terror over,   90
Sleeping by her sleeping Baby.
    With bowl that sped from hand to hand,
The gladdest of the gladsome band,
Amid their own delight and fun,
They hear — when every dance is done,
When every whirling bout is o'er —
The fiddle's *squeak* — that call to bliss,
Ever followed by a kiss;
They envy not the happy lot,
But enjoy their own the more!   100
    While thus our jocund Travellers fare,
Up springs the Sailor from his chair —
Limps (for I might have told before
That he was lame) across the floor —
Is gone — returns — and with a prize;

With what? — a Ship of lusty size;
A gallant stately Man-of-war,
Fixed on a smoothly-sliding car.
Surprise to all, but most surprise
To Benjamin, who rubs his eyes,   110
Not knowing that he had befriended
A Man so gloriously attended!
    "This," cries the Sailor, "a Third-rate
        is —
Stand back, and you shall see her gratis!
This was the Flag-ship at the Nile,
The Vanguard — you may smirk and smile,
But, pretty Maid, if you look near,
You 'll find you 've much in little here!
A nobler ship did never swim,
And you shall see her in full trim: 120
I 'll set, my friends, to do you honour,
Set every inch of sail upon her."
So said, so done; and masts, sails, yards,
He names them all; and interlards
His speech with uncouth terms of art,
Accomplished in the showman's part;
And then, as from a sudden check,
Cries out — "'T is there, the quarter-deck
On which brave Admiral Nelson stood —
A sight that would have roused your blood!
One eye he had, which, bright as ten,   131
Burned like a fire among his men;
Let this be land, and that be sea,
Here lay the French — and *thus* came we!"
    Hushed was by this the fiddle's sound,
The dancers all were gathered round,
And, such the stillness of the house,
You might have heard a nibbling mouse;
While, borrowing helps where'er he may,
The Sailor through the story runs   140
Of ships to ships and guns to guns;
And does his utmost to display
The dismal conflict, and the might
And terror of that marvellous night!
"A bowl, a bowl of double measure,"
Cries Benjamin, "a draught of length,
To Nelson, England's pride and treasure
Her bulwark and her tower of strength!"
When Benjamin had seized the bowl,
The mastiff, from beneath the waggon,   150
Where he lay, watchful as a dragon,
Rattled his chain; — 't was all in vain,
For Benjamin, triumphant soul!
He heard the monitory growl;
Heard — and in opposition quaffed
A deep, determined, desperate draught!
Nor did the battered Tar forget,
Or flinch from what he deemed his debt:
Then, like a hero crowned with laurel,

Back to her place the ship he led;   160
Wheeled her back in full apparel;
And so, flag flying at mast head,
Re-yoked her to the Ass: — anon
Cries Benjamin, "We must be gone."
Thus, after two hours' hearty stay,
Again behold them on their way !

CANTO THIRD

RIGHT gladly had the horses stirred,
When they the wished-for greeting heard,
The whip's loud notice from the door,
That they were free to move once more.
You think, those doings must have bred
In them disheartening doubts and dread;
No, not a horse of all the eight,
Although it be a moonless night,
Fears either for himself or freight;
For this they know (and let it hide,   10
In part, the offences of their guide)
That Benjamin, with clouded brains,
Is worth the best with all their pains;
And, if they had a prayer to make,
The prayer would be that they may take
With him whatever comes in course,
The better fortune or the worse;
That no one else may have business near
    them,
And, drunk or sober, he may steer them.
  So, forth in dauntless mood they fare, 20
And with them goes the guardian pair.
  Now, heroes, for the true commotion,
The triumph of your late devotion !
Can aught on earth impede delight,
Still mounting to a higher height;
And higher still — a greedy flight !
Can any low-born care pursue her ?
Can any mortal clog come to her ?
No notion have they — not a thought,
That is from joyless regions brought !   30
And, while they coast the silent lake,
Their inspiration I partake;
Share their empyreal spirits — yea,
With their enraptured vision, see —
O fancy — what a jubilee !
What shifting pictures — clad in gleams
Of colour bright as feverish dreams !
Earth, spangled sky, and lake serene,
Involved and restless all — a scene
Pregnant with mutual exaltation,   40
Rich change, and multiplied creation !
This sight to me the Muse imparts; —
And then, what kindness in their hearts !
What tears of rapture, what vow-making,

Profound entreaties, and hand-shaking !
What solemn, vacant, interlacing,
As if they'd fall asleep embracing !
Then, in the turbulence of glee,
And in the excess of amity,
Says Benjamin, "That Ass of thine,   50
He spoils thy sport, and hinders mine:
If he were tethered to the waggon,
He'd drag as well what he is dragging,
And we, as brother should with brother,
Might trudge it alongside each other !"
  Forthwith, obedient to command,
The horses made a quiet stand;
And to the waggon's skirts was tied
The Creature, by the Mastiff's side,
The Mastiff wondering, and perplext   60
With dread of what will happen next;
And thinking it but sorry cheer,
To have such company so near !
  This new arrangement made, the Wain
Through the still night proceeds again;
No Moon hath risen her light to lend;
But indistinctly may be kenned
The VANGUARD, following close behind,
Sails spread, as if to catch the wind !
  "Thy wife and child are snug and warm,
Thy ship will travel without harm;   71
I like," said Benjamin, "her shape and
    stature:
And this of mine — this bulky creature
Of which I have the steering — this,
Seen fairly, is not much amiss !
We want your streamers, friend, you know;
But, altogether as we go,
We make a kind of handsome show !
Among these hills, from first to last,
We 've weathered many a furious blast; 80
Hard passage forcing on, with head
Against the storm, and canvas spread.
I hate a boaster; but to thee
Will say 't, who know'st both land and
    sea,
The unluckiest hulk that stems the brine
Is hardly worse beset than mine,
When cross-winds on her quarter beat;
And, fairly lifted from my feet,
I stagger onward — heaven knows how;
But not so pleasantly as now: 90
Poor pilot I, by snows confounded,
And many a foundrous pit surrounded !
Yet here we are, by night and day
Grinding through rough and smooth our
    way;
Through foul and fair our task fulfilling;
And long shall be so yet — God willing !"

"Ay," said the Tar, "through fair and foul —
But save us from yon screeching owl!"
That instant was begun a fray
Which called their thoughts another way:
The mastiff, ill-conditioned carl!   101
What must he do but growl and snarl,
Still more and more dissatisfied
With the meek comrade at his side!
Till, not incensed though put to proof,
The Ass, uplifting a hind hoof,
Salutes the Mastiff on the head;
And so were better manners bred,
And all was calmed and quieted.
　　"Yon screech-owl," says the Sailor, turning   110
Back to his former cause of mourning,
"Yon owl! — pray God that all be well!
'T is worse than any funeral bell;
As sure as I 've the gift of sight,
We shall be meeting ghosts to-night!"
— Said Benjamin, "This whip shall lay
A thousand, if they cross our way.
I know that Wanton's noisy station,
I know him and his occupation;
The jolly bird hath learned his cheer   120
Upon the banks of Windermere;
Where a tribe of them make merry,
Mocking the Man that keeps the ferry;
Hallooing from an open throat,
Like travellers shouting for a boat.
— The tricks he learned at Windermere
This vagrant owl is playing here —
That is the worst of his employment:
He 's at the top of his enjoyment!"
　　This explanation stilled the alarm,   130
Cured the foreboder like a charm;
This, and the manner, and the voice,
Summoned the Sailor to rejoice;
His heart is up — he fears no evil
From life or death, from man or devil;
He wheels — and, making many stops,
Brandished his crutch against the mountain tops;
And, while he talked of blows and scars,
Benjamin, among the stars,
Beheld a dancing — and a glancing;   140
Such retreating and advancing
As, I ween, was never seen
In bloodiest battle since the days of Mars!

CANTO FOURTH

THUS they, with freaks of proud delight,
Beguile the remnant of the night;

And many a snatch of jovial song
Regales them as they wind along;
While to the music, from on high,
The echoes make a glad reply. —
But the sage Muse the revel heeds
No farther than her story needs;
Nor will she servilely attend
The loitering journey to its end.   10
— Blithe spirits of her own impel
The Muse, who scents the morning air,
To take of this transported pair
A brief and unreproved farewell;
To quit the slow-paced waggon's side,
And wander down yon hawthorn dell,
With murmuring Greta for her guide.
— There doth she ken the awful form
Of Raven-crag — black as a storm —
Glimmering through the twilight pale;   20
And Ghimmer-crag, his tall twin brother,
Each peering forth to meet the other: —
And, while she roves through St. John's Vale,
Along the smooth unpathwayed plain,
By sheep-track or through cottage lane,
Where no disturbance comes to intrude
Upon the pensive solitude,
Her unsuspecting eye, perchance,
With the rude shepherd's favoured glance,
Beholds the faeries in array,   30
Whose party-coloured garments gay
The silent company betray:
Red, green, and blue; a moment's sight!
For Skiddaw-top with rosy light
Is touched — and all the band take flight.
— Fly also, Muse! and from the dell
Mount to the ridge of Nathdale Fell;
Thence, look thou forth o'er wood and lawn
Hoar with the frost-like dews of dawn;
Across yon meadowy bottom look,   40
Where close fogs hide their parent brook;
And see, beyond that hamlet small,
The ruined towers of Threlkeld-hall,
Lurking in a double shade,
By trees and lingering twilight made!
There, at Blencathara's rugged feet,
Sir Lancelot gave a safe retreat
To noble Clifford; from annoy
Concealed the persecuted boy,
Well pleased in rustic garb to feed   50
His flock, and pipe on shepherd's reed
Among this multitude of hills,
Crags, woodlands, waterfalls, and rills;
Which soon the morning shall enfold,
From east to west, in ample vest
Of massy gloom and radiance bold.

The mists, that o'er the streamlet's bed
Hung low, begin to rise and spread;
Even while I speak, their skirts of grey
Are smitten by a silver ray;   60
And lo ! — up Castrigg's naked steep
(Where, smoothly urged, the vapours sweep
Along — and scatter and divide,
Like fleecy clouds self-multiplied)
The stately waggon is ascending,
With faithful Benjamin attending,
Apparent now beside his team —
Now lost amid a glittering steam :
And with him goes his Sailor-friend,
By this time near their journey's end;   70
And, after their high-minded riot,
Sickening into thoughtful quiet;
As if the morning's pleasant hour
Had for their joys a killing power.
And, sooth, for Benjamin a vein
Is opened of still deeper pain
As if his heart by notes were stung
From out the lowly hedge-rows flung;
As if the Warbler lost in light
Reproved his soarings of the night,   80
In strains of rapture pure and holy
Upbraided his distempered folly.

Drooping is he, his step is dull;
But the horses stretch and pull;
With increasing vigour climb,
Eager to repair lost time;
Whether, by their own desert,
Knowing what cause there is for shame,
They are labouring to avert
As much as may be of the blame,   90
Which, they foresee, must soon alight
Upon *his* head, whom, in despite
Of all his failings, they love best;
Whether for him they are distrest,
Or, by length of fasting roused,
Are impatient to be housed:
Up against the hill they strain
Tugging at the iron chain,
Tugging all with might and main,
Last and foremost, every horse   100
To the utmost of his force !
And the smoke and respiration,
Rising like an exhalation,
Blend with the mist — a moving shroud —
To form an undissolving cloud;
Which, with slant ray, the merry sun
Takes delight to play upon.
Never golden-haired Apollo,
Pleased some favourite chief to follow
Through accidents of peace or war,   110
In a perilous moment threw

Around the object of his care
Veil of such celestial hue;
Interposed so bright a screen —
Him and his enemies between !
Alas ! what boots it ? — who can hide,
When the malicious Fates are bent
On working out an ill intent ?
Can destiny be turned aside ?
No — sad progress of my story !   120
Benjamin, this outward glory
Cannot shield thee from thy Master,
Who from Keswick has pricked forth,
Sour and surly as the north;
And, in fear of some disaster,
Comes to give what help he may,
And to hear what thou canst say;
If, as needs he must forebode,
Thou hast been loitering on the road !
His fears, his doubts, may now take
        flight —   130
The wished-for object is in sight;
Yet, trust the Muse, it rather hath
Stirred him up to livelier wrath;
Which he stifles, moody man !
With all the patience that he can;
To the end that, at your meeting,
He may give thee decent greeting.

There he is — resolved to stop,
Till the waggon gains the top;
But stop he cannot — must advance: 140
Him Benjamin, with lucky glance,
Espies — and instantly is ready,
Self-collected, poised, and steady:
And, to be the better seen,
Issues from his radiant shroud,
From his close-attending cloud,
With careless air and open mien.
Erect his port, and firm his going;
So struts yon cock that now is crowing;
And the morning light in grace   150
Strikes upon his lifted face,
Hurrying the pallid hue away
That might his trespasses betray.
But what can all avail to clear him,
Or what need of explanation,
Parley or interrogation ?
For the Master sees, alas !
That unhappy Figure near him,
Limping o'er the dewy grass,
Where the road it fringes, sweet,   160
Soft and cool to way-worn feet;
And, O indignity ! an Ass,
By his noble Mastiff's side,
Tethered to the waggon's tail:
And the ship, in all her pride,

Following after in full sail !
Not to speak of babe and mother;
Who, contented with each other,
And snug as birds in leafy arbour,
Find, within, a blessed harbour !　　170
　　With eager eyes the Master pries;
Looks in and out, and through and through;
Says nothing — till at last he spies
A wound upon the Mastiff's head,
A wound, where plainly might be read
What feats an Ass's hoof can do !
But drop the rest: — this aggravation,
This complicated provocation,
A hoard of grievances unsealed;
All past forgiveness it repealed;　　180
And thus, and through distempered blood
On both sides, Benjamin the good,
The patient, and the tender-hearted,
Was from his team and waggon parted;
When duty of that day was o'er,
Laid down his whip — and served no more. —
Nor could the waggon long survive,
Which Benjamin had ceased to drive:
It lingered on; — guide after guide
Ambitiously the office tried;　　190
But each unmanageable hill
Called for *his* patience and *his* skill; —
And sure it is, that through this night,
And what the morning brought to light,
Two losses had we to sustain,
We lost both WAGGONER and WAIN !

———

Accept, O Friend, for praise or blame,
The gift of this adventurous song;
A record which I dared to frame,
Though timid scruples checked me long;
They checked me — and I left the theme
Untouched — in spite of many a gleam
Of fancy which thereon was shed,
Like pleasant sunbeams shifting still
Upon the side of a distant hill:
But Nature might not be gainsaid;　　10
For what I have and what I miss
I sing of these; — it makes my bliss !
Nor is it I who play the part,
But a shy spirit in my heart,
That comes and goes — will sometimes
　　leap
From hiding-places ten years deep;
Or haunts me with familiar face,
Returning, like a ghost unlaid,
Until the debt I owe be paid.
Forgive me, then; for I had been　　20

On friendly terms with this Machine:
In him, while he was wont to trace
Our roads, through many a long year's
　　space,
A living almanack had we;
We had a speaking diary,
That in this uneventful place
Gave to the days a mark and name
By which we knew them when they came.
— Yes, I, and all about me here,
Through all the changes of the year,　　30
Had seen him through the mountains go,
In pomp of mist or pomp of snow,
Majestically huge and slow:
Or, with a milder grace adorning
The landscape of a summer's morning;
While Grasmere smoothed her liquid plain
The moving image to detain;
And mighty Fairfield, with a chime
Of echoes, to his march kept time;
When little other business stirred,　　40
And little other sound was heard;
In that delicious hour of balm,
Stillness, solitude, and calm,
While yet the valley is arrayed,
On this side with a sober shade;
On that is prodigally bright —
Crag, lawn, and wood — with rosy light.
— But most of all, thou Lordly Wain !
I wish to have thee here again,
When windows flap and chimney roars,　　50
And all is dismal out of doors;
And, sitting by my fire, I see
Eight sorry carts, no less a train;
Unworthy successors of thee,
Come straggling through the wind and
　　rain !
And oft, as they pass slowly on,
Beneath my windows, one by one,
See, perched upon the naked height
The summit of a cumbrous freight,
A single traveller — and there　　60
Another; then perhaps a pair —
The lame, the sickly, and the old;
Men, women, heartless with the cold;
And babes in wet and starveling plight;
Which once, be weather as it might,
Had still a nest within a nest,
Thy shelter — and their mother's breast!
Then most of all, then far the most,
Do I regret what we have lost;
Am grieved for that unhappy sin　　70
Which robbed us of good Benjamin;
And of his stately Charge, which none
Could keep alive when He was gone !

FRENCH REVOLUTION

AS IT APPEARED TO ENTHUSIASTS AT
ITS COMMENCEMENT. REPRINTED FROM
THE FRIEND

1804. 1809

An extract from the long poem on my own
poetical education. It was first published by
Coleridge in his Friend, which is the reason
of its having had a place in every edition of
my poems since.

OH ! pleasant exercise of hope and joy !
For mighty were the auxiliars which then
   stood
Upon our side, we who were strong in love !
Bliss was it in that dawn to be alive,
But to be young was very heaven ! — Oh !
   times,
In which the meagre, stale, forbidding ways
Of custom, law, and statute, took at once
The attraction of a country in romance !
When Reason seemed the most to assert
   her rights,
When most intent on making of herself   10
A prime Enchantress — to assist the work,
Which then was going forward in her
   name !
Not favoured spots alone, but the whole
   earth,
The beauty wore of promise, that which
   sets
(As at some moment might not be unfelt
Among the bowers of paradise itself)
The budding rose above the rose full blown.
What temper at the prospect did not wake
To happiness unthought of ? The inert
Were roused, and lively natures rapt
   away !   20
They who had fed their childhood upon
   dreams,
The playfellows of fancy, who had made
All powers of swiftness, subtilty, and
   strength
Their ministers, — who in lordly wise had
   stirred
Among the grandest objects of the sense,
And dealt with whatsoever they found there
As if they had within some lurking right
To wield it; — they, too, who, of gentle
   mood,
Had watched all gentle motions, and to
   these
Had fitted their own thoughts, schemers
   more mild,   30

And in the region of their peaceful selves; —
Now was it that both found, the meek and
   lofty
Did both find, helpers to their heart's
   desire,
And stuff at hand, plastic as they could
   wish;
Were called upon to exercise their skill,
Not in Utopia, subterranean fields,
Or some secreted island, Heaven knows
   where !
But in the very world, which is the world
Of all of us, — the place where in the
   end
We find our happiness, or not at all !   40

CHARACTER OF THE HAPPY WARRIOR

1805–06. 1807

The course of the great war with the French
naturally fixed one's attention upon the mili-
tary character, and, to the honour of our coun-
try, there were many illustrious instances of the
qualities that constitute its highest excellence.
Lord Nelson carried most of the virtues that
the trials he was exposed to in his department
of the service necessarily call forth and sus-
tain, if they do not produce the contrary vices.
But his public life was stained with one great
crime, so that, though many passages of these
lines were suggested by what was generally
known as excellent in his conduct, I have not
been able to connect his name with the poem
as I could wish, or even to think of him with
satisfaction in reference to the idea of what a
warrior ought to be. For the sake of such of
my friends as may happen to read this note I
will add, that many elements of the character
here pourtrayed were found in my brother John,
who perished by shipwreck as mentioned else-
where. His messmates used to call him the
Philosopher, from which it must be inferred
that the qualities and dispositions I allude to
had not escaped their notice. He often ex-
pressed his regret, after the war had continued
some time, that he had not chosen the Naval,
instead of the East India Company's service. to
which his family connection had led him. He
greatly valued moral and religious instruction
for youth, as tending to make good sailors.
The best, he used to say, came from Scotland;
the next to them, from the North of England,
especially from Westmoreland and Cumber-
land, where, thanks to the piety and local at-
tachments of our ancestors, endowed, or, as
they are commonly called, free, schools abound.

WHO is the happy Warrior? Who is he
That every man in arms should wish to be?
— It is the generous Spirit, who, when
   brought
Among the tasks of real life, hath wrought
Upon the plan that pleased his boyish
   thought:
Whose high endeavours are an inward light
That makes the path before him always
   bright:
Who, with a natural instinct to discern
What knowledge can perform, is diligent
   to learn;
Abides by this resolve, and stops not
   there,   10
But makes his moral being his prime care;
Who, doomed to go in company with Pain,
And Fear, and Bloodshed, miserable train!
Turns his necessity to glorious gain;
In face of these doth exercise a power
Which is our human nature's highest dower;
Controls them and subdues, transmutes,
   bereaves
Of their bad influence, and their good re-
   ceives:
By objects, which might force the soul to
   abate
Her feeling, rendered more compassion-
   ate;   20
Is placable — because occasions rise
So often that demand such sacrifice;
More skilful in self-knowledge, even more
   pure,
As tempted more; more able to endure,
As more exposed to suffering and distress;
Thence, also, more alive to tenderness.
— 'T is he whose law is reason; who de-
   pends
Upon that law as on the best of friends;
Whence, in a state where men are tempted
   still
To evil for a guard against worse ill,   30
And what in quality or act is best
Doth seldom on a right foundation rest,
He labours good on good to fix, and owes
To virtue every triumph that he knows:
— Who, if he rise to station of command,
Rises by open means; and there will stand
On honourable terms, or else retire,
And in himself possess his own desire;
Who comprehends his trust, and to the
   same
Keeps faithful with a singleness of aim;   40
And therefore does not stoop, nor lie in wait
For wealth, or honours, or for worldly state;

Whom they must follow; on whose head
   must fall,
Like showers of manna, if they come at all:
Whose powers shed round him in the com-
   mon strife,
Or mild concerns of ordinary life,
A constant influence, a peculiar grace;
But who, if he be called upon to face
Some awful moment to which Heaven has
   joined
Great issues, good or bad for human kind,
Is happy as a Lover; and attired   51
With sudden brightness, like a Man in-
   spired;
And, through the heat of conflict, keeps the
   law
In calmness made, and sees what he foresaw;
Or if an unexpected call succeed,
Come when it will, is equal to the need:
— He who, though thus endued as with a
   sense
And faculty for storm and turbulence,
Is yet a Soul whose master-bias leans
To homefelt pleasures and to gentle scenes;
Sweet images! which, wheresoe'er he be, 61
Are at his heart; and such fidelity
It is his darling passion to approve;
More brave for this, that he hath much to
   love: —
'T is, finally, the Man, who, lifted high,
Conspicuous object in a Nation's eye,
Or left unthought-of in obscurity, —
Who, with a toward or untoward lot,
Prosperous or adverse, to his wish or not —
Plays, in the many games of life, that one
Where what he most doth value must be
   won: 71
Whom neither shape of danger can dismay,
Nor thought of tender happiness betray;
Who, not content that former worth stand
   fast,
Looks forward, persevering to the last,
From well to better, daily self-surpast:
Who, whether praise of him must walk the
   earth
For ever, and to noble deeds give birth,
Or he must fall, to sleep without his fame,
And leave a dead unprofitable name —   80
Finds comfort in himself and in his cause;
And, while the mortal mist is gathering,
   draws
His breath in confidence of Heaven's
   applause:
This is the happy Warrior; this is He
That every Man in arms should wish to be

THE HORN OF EGREMONT CASTLE

1806. 1807

A tradition transferred from the ancient mansion of Hutton John, the seat of the Huddlestones, to Egremont Castle.

ERE the Brothers through the gateway
Issued forth with old and young,
To the Horn Sir Eustace pointed
Which for ages there had hung.
Horn it was which none could sound,
No one upon living ground,
Save He who came as rightful Heir
To Egremont's Domains and Castle fair.

Heirs from times of earliest record
Had the House of Lucie born,   10
Who of right had held the Lordship
Claimed by proof upon the Horn:
Each at the appointed hour
Tried the Horn, — it owned his power;
He was acknowledged: and the blast,
Which good Sir Eustace sounded, was the last.

With his lance Sir Eustace pointed,
And to Hubert thus said he,
" What I speak this Horn shall witness
For thy better memory.   20
Hear, then, and neglect me not !
At this time, and on this spot,
The words are uttered from my heart,
As my last earnest prayer ere we depart.

" On good service we are going
Life to risk by sea and land,
In which course if Christ our Saviour
Do my sinful soul demand,
Hither come thou back straightway,
Hubert, if alive that day;   30
Return, and sound the Horn, that we
May have a living House still left in thee ! "

" Fear not," quickly answered Hubert;
" As I am thy Father's son,
What thou askest, noble Brother,
With God's favour shall be done."
So were both right well content:
Forth they from the Castle went,
And at the head of their Array
To Palestine the Brothers took their way.

Side by side they fought (the Lucies   41
Were a line for valour famed),

And where'er their strokes alighted,
There the Saracens were tamed.
Whence, then, could it come — the thought —
By what evil spirit brought ?
Oh ! can a brave Man wish to take
His Brother's life, for Lands' and Castle's sake ?

" Sir ! " the Ruffians said to Hubert,
" Deep he lies in Jordan flood."   50
Stricken by this ill assurance,
Pale and trembling Hubert stood.
" Take your earnings." — Oh ! that I
Could have *seen* my Brother die !
It was a pang that vexed him then;
And oft returned, again, and yet again.

Months passed on, and no Sir Eustace !
Nor of him were tidings heard;
Wherefore, bold as day, the Murderer
Back again to England steered.   60
To his Castle Hubert sped;
Nothing has he now to dread.
But silent and by stealth he came,
And at an hour which nobody could name.

None could tell if it were night-time,
Night or day, at even or morn;
No one's eye had seen him enter,
No one's ear had heard the Horn.
But bold Hubert lives in glee:
Months and years went smilingly;   70
With plenty was his table spread;
And bright the Lady is who shares his bed.

Likewise he had sons and daughters;
And, as good men do, he sate
At his board by these surrounded,
Flourishing in fair estate.
And while thus in open day
Once he sate, as old books say,
A blast was uttered from the Horn,
Where by the Castle-gate it hung forlorn.

'T is the breath of good Sir Eustace !   81
He is come to claim his right:
Ancient castle, woods, and mountains
Hear the challenge with delight.
Hubert ! though the blast be blown
He is helpless and alone:
Thou hast a dungeon, speak the word !
And there he may be lodged, and thou be Lord.

Speak ! — astounded Hubert cannot;
And, if power to speak he had, 90
All are daunted, all the household
Smitten to the heart, and sad.
'T is Sir Eustace; if it be
Living man, it must be he !
Thus Hubert thought in his dismay,
And by a postern-gate he slunk away.

Long, and long was he unheard of:
To his Brother then he came,
Made confession, asked forgiveness,
Asked it by a brother's name, 100
And by all the saints in heaven;
And of Eustace was forgiven:
Then in a convent went to hide
His melancholy head, and there he died.

But Sir Eustace, whom good angels
Had preserved from murderers' hands,
And from Pagan chains had rescued,
Lived with honour on his lands.
Sons he had, saw sons of theirs:
And through ages, heirs of heirs, 110
A long posterity renowned,
Sounded the Horn which they alone could
sound.

A COMPLAINT

1806(?). 1807

Written at Town-end, Grasmere. Suggested
by a change in the manner of a friend.

THERE is a change — and I am poor;
Your love hath been, not long ago,
A fountain at my fond heart's door,
Whose only business was to flow;
And flow it did: not taking heed
Of its own bounty, or my need.

What happy moments did I count !
Blest was I then all bliss above !
Now, for that consecrated fount
Of murmuring, sparkling, living love,
What have I ? shall I dare to tell ?
A comfortless and hidden well.

A well of love — it may be deep —
I trust it is, — and never dry:
What matter ? if the waters sleep
In silence and obscurity.
— Such change, and at the very door
Of my fond heart, hath made me poor.

STRAY PLEASURES

1806. 1807

" —— *Pleasure is spread through the earth
In stray gifts to be claimed by whoever shall find.*"

Suggested on the Thames by the sight of
one of those floating mills that used to be seen
there. This I noticed on the Surrey side be-
tween Somerset House and Blackfriars Bridge.
Charles Lamb was with me at the time ; and I
thought it remarkable that I should have to
point out to *him*, an idolatrous Londoner, a sight
so interesting as the happy group dancing on
the platform. Mills of this kind used to be,
and perhaps still are, not uncommon on the
Continent. I noticed several upon the river
Saone in the year 1790, particularly near the
town of Chalons, where my friend Jones and I
halted a day when we crossed France ; so far
on foot : there we embarked and floated down
to Lyons.

BY their floating mill,
That lies dead and still,
Behold yon Prisoners three,
The Miller with two Dames, on the breast
of the Thames !
The platform is small, but gives room for
them all;
And they 're dancing merrily.

From the shore come the notes
To their mill where it floats,
To their house and their mill tethered fast:
To the small wooden isle where, their work
to beguile, 10
They from morning to even take whatever
is given; —
And many a blithe day they have past.

In sight of the spires,
All alive with the fires
Of the sun going down to his rest,
In the broad open eye of the solitary sky,
They dance, — there are three, as jocund as
free,
While they dance on the calm river's breast.

Man and Maidens wheel,
They themselves make the reel, 20
And their music 's a prey which they seize;
It plays not for them, — what matter ? 't is
theirs;
And if they had care, it has scattered their
cares
While they dance, crying, " Long as ye
please ! "

They dance not for me,
Yet mine is their glee !
Thus pleasure is spread through the earth
In stray gifts to be claimed by whoever
    shall find;
Thus a rich loving-kindness, redundantly
    kind,
Moves all nature to gladness and mirth. 30

The showers of the spring
Rouse the birds, and they sing;
If the wind do but stir for his proper de-
    light,
Each leaf, that and this, his neighbour will
    kiss;
Each wave, one and t' other, speeds after
    his brother:
They are happy, for that is their right !

POWER OF MUSIC

1806. 1807

Taken from life.

An Orpheus ! an Orpheus ! yes, Faith may
    grow bold,
And take to herself all the wonders of
    old; —
Near the stately Pantheon you 'll meet with
    the same
In the street that from Oxford hath bor-
    rowed its name.

His station is there; and he works on the
    crowd,
He sways them with harmony merry and
    loud;
He fills with his power all their hearts to
    the brim —
Was aught ever heard like his fiddle and
    him ?

What an eager assembly ! what an empire
    is this !
The weary have life, and the hungry have
    bliss;   10
The mourner is cheered, and the anxious
    have rest;
And the guilt-burthened soul is no longer
    opprest.

As the Moon brightens round her the clouds
    of the night,
So He, where he stands, is a centre of
    light;

It gleams on the face, there, of dusky-
    browed Jack,
And the pale-visaged Baker's, with basket
    on back.

That errand-bound 'Prentice was passing in
    haste —
What matter ! he 's caught — and his time
    runs to waste;
The Newsman is stopped, though he stops
    on the fret;
And the half-breathless Lamplighter —
    he 's in the net !   20

The Porter sits down on the weight which
    he bore;
The Lass with her barrow wheels hither her
    store; —
If a thief could be here he might pilfer at
    ease;
She sees the Musician, 't is all that she sees !

He stands, backed by the wall; — he abates
    not his din;
His hat gives him vigour, with boons drop-
    ping in,
From the old and the young, from the
    poorest; and there !
The one-pennied Boy has his penny to spare.

O blest are the hearers, and proud be the
    hand
Of the pleasure it spreads through so thank-
    ful a band;   30
I am glad for him, blind as he is ! — all the
    while
If they speak 't is to praise, and they praise
    with a smile.

That tall Man, a giant in bulk and in
    height,
Not an inch of his body is free from delight;
Can he keep himself still, if he would ? oh,
    not he !
The music stirs in him like wind through a
    tree.

Mark that Cripple who leans on his crutch;
    like a tower
That long has leaned forward, leans hour
    after hour ! —
That Mother, whose spirit in fetters is
    bound,
While she dandles the Babe in her arms to
    the sound.   40

Now, coaches and chariots! roar on like a
 stream;
Here are twenty souls happy as souls in a
 dream:
They are deaf to your murmurs — they care
 not for you,
Nor what ye are flying, nor what ye pursue!

STAR–GAZERS

1806. 1807

Observed by me in Leicester-square, as here
described.

WHAT crowd is this? what have we here!
 we must not pass it by;
A Telescope upon its frame, and pointed to
 the sky:
Long is it as a barber's pole, or mast of
 little boat,
Some little pleasure-skiff, that doth on
 Thames's waters float.

The Showman chooses well his place, 't is
 Leicester's busy Square;
And is as happy in his night, for the
 heavens are blue and fair;
Calm, though impatient, is the crowd; each
 stands ready with the fee,
And envies him that's looking; — what an
 insight must it be!

Yet, Showman, where can lie the cause?
 Shall thy Implement have blame,
A boaster, that when he is tried, fails, and
 is put to shame?   10
Or is it good as others are, and be their
 eyes in fault?
Their eyes, or minds? or, finally, is yon
 resplendent vault?

Is nothing of that radiant pomp so good as
 we have here?
Or gives a thing but small delight that
 never can be dear?
The silver moon with all her vales, and
 hills of mightiest fame,
Doth she betray us when they're seen? or
 are they but a name?

Or is it rather that Conceit rapacious is and
 strong,
And bounty never yields so much but it
 seems to do her wrong?

Or is it, that when human Souls a journey
 long have had
And are returned into themselves, they
 cannot but be sad?   20

Or must we be constrained to think that
 these Spectators rude,
Poor in estate, of manners base, men of the
 multitude,
Have souls which never yet have risen, and
 therefore prostrate lie?
No, no, this cannot be; — men thirst for
 power and majesty!

Does, then, a deep and earnest thought the
 blissful mind employ
Of him who gazes, or has gazed? a grave
 and steady joy,
That doth reject all show of pride, admits
 no outward sign,
Because not of this noisy world, but silent
 and divine!

Whatever be the cause, 't is sure that they
 who pry and pore
Seem to meet with little gain, seem less
 happy than before: 30
One after One they take their turn, nor
 have I one espied
That doth not slackly go away, as if dis-
 satisfied.

"YES, IT WAS THE MOUNTAIN ECHO"

1806. 1807

Written at Town-end, Grasmere. The echo
came from Nab-scar, when I was walking on
the opposite side of Rydal Mere. I will here
mention, for my dear Sister's sake, that, while
she was sitting alone one day high up on this
part of Loughrigg Fell, she was so affected by
the voice of the Cuckoo heard from the crags
at some distance that she could not suppress a
wish to have a stone inscribed with her name
among the rocks from which the sound pro-
ceeded. On my return from my walk I recited
these verses to Mary, who was then confined
with her son Thomas, who died in his 7th year,
as is recorded on his head-stone in Grasmere
Church-yard.

YES, it was the mountain Echo,
Solitary, clear, profound,
Answering to the shouting Cuckoo,
Giving to her sound for sound!

Unsolicited reply
To a babbling wanderer sent;
Like her ordinary cry,
Like — but oh, how different !

Hears not also mortal Life ?
Hear not we, unthinking Creatures !
Slaves of folly, love, or strife —
Voices of two different natures ?

Have not *we* too ? — yes, we have
Answers, and we know not whence;
Echoes from beyond the grave,
Recognised intelligence !

Such rebounds our inward ear
Catches sometimes from afar —
Listen, ponder, hold them dear;
For of God, — of God they are.

"NUNS FRET NOT AT THEIR CONVENT'S NARROW ROOM"

1802(?). 1807

In the cottage, Town-end, Grasmere, one
afternoon in 1801, my sister read to me the
Sonnets of Milton. I had long been well ac-
quainted with them, but I was particularly
struck on that occasion with the dignified sim-
plicity and majestic harmony that runs through
most of them, — in character so totally dif-
ferent from the Italian, and still more so from
Shakspeare's fine Sonnets. I took fire, if I
may be allowed to say so, and produced three
Sonnets the same afternoon, the first I ever
wrote except an irregular one at school. Of
these three, the only one I distinctly remember
is — "I grieved for Buonaparté." One was
never written down : the third, which was, I
believe, preserved, I cannot particularise.

NUNS fret not at their convent's narrow
        room;
And hermits are contented with their cells;
And students with their pensive citadels;
Maids at the wheel, the weaver at his loom,
Sit blithe and happy; bees that soar for
        bloom,
High as the highest Peak of Furness-fells,
Will murmur by the hour in foxglove bells:
In truth the prison, unto which we doom
Ourselves, no prison is: and hence for me,
In sundry moods, 't was pastime to be bound
Within the Sonnet's scanty plot of ground;
Pleased if some Souls (for such there needs
        must be)

Who have felt the weight of too much lib-
        erty,
Should find brief solace there, as I have
        found.

PERSONAL TALK

1802(?). 1807

Written at Town-end, Grasmere. The last
line but two stood, at first, better and more
characteristically, thus :

   " By my half-kitchen and half-parlour fire."

My Sister and I were in the habit of having the
tea-kettle in our little sitting-room ; and we
toasted the bread ourselves, which reminds me
of a little circumstance not unworthy of being
set down among these minutiæ. Happening
both of us to be engaged a few minutes one
morning when we had a young prig of a Scotch
lawyer to breakfast with us, my dear Sister, with
her usual simplicity, put the toasting-fork with
a slice of bread into the hands of this Edin-
burgh genius. Our little book-case stood on
one side of the fire. To prevent loss of time,
he took down a book, and fell to reading, to
the neglect of the toast, which was burnt to a
cinder. Many a time have we laughed at this
circumstance, and other cottage simplicities of
that day. By the bye, I have a spite at one
of this series of Sonnets (I will leave the reader
to discover which) as having been the means
of nearly putting off for ever our acquaintance
with dear Miss Fenwick, who has always stig-
matised one line of it as vulgar, and worthy
only of having been composed by a country
squire.

I

I AM not One who much or oft delight
To season my fireside with personal talk. —
Of friends, who live within an easy walk,
Or neighbours, daily, weekly, in my sight:
And, for my chance-acquaintance, ladies
        bright,
Sons, mothers, maidens withering on the
        stalk,
These all wear out of me, like Forms, with
        chalk
Painted on rich men's floors, for one feast-
        night.
Better than such discourse doth silence
        long,
Long, barren silence, square with my de-
        sire;   10
To sit without emotion, hope, or aim,
In the loved presence of my cottage-fire,

And listen to the flapping of the flame,
Or kettle whispering its faint undersong.

II

" Yet life," you say, " is life; we have seen
  and see,
And with a living pleasure we describe;
And fits of sprightly malice do but bribe
The languid mind into activity.
Sound sense, and love itself, and mirth and
  glee
Are fostered by the comment and the gibe."
Even be it so; yet still among your tribe, 21
Our daily world's true Worldlings, rank not
  me !
Children are blest, and powerful; their
  world lies
More justly balanced; partly at their feet,
And part far from them: sweetest melodies
Are those that are by distance made more
  sweet;
Whose mind is but the mind of his own
  eyes,
He is a Slave; the meanest we can meet !

III

Wings have we, — and as far as we can go,
We may find pleasure: wilderness and
  wood, 30
Blank ocean and mere sky, support that
  mood
Which with the lofty sanctifies the low.
Dreams, books, are each a world; and
  books, we know,
Are a substantial world, both pure and
  good:
Round these, with tendrils strong as flesh
  and blood,
Our pastime and our happiness will grow.
There find I personal themes, a plenteous
  store,
Matter wherein right voluble I am,
To which I listen with a ready ear;
Two shall be named, pre-eminently dear, —
The gentle Lady married to the Moor; 41
And heavenly Una with her milk-white
  Lamb.

IV

Nor can I not believe but that hereby
Great gains are mine; for thus I live remote
From evil-speaking; rancour, never sought,
Comes to me not; malignant truth, or lie.
Hence have I genial seasons, hence have I

Smooth passions, smooth discourse, and joy-
  ous thought:
And thus from day to day my little boat
Rocks in its harbour, lodging peaceably. 50
Blessings be with them — and eternal
  praise,
Who gave us nobler loves, and nobler
  cares —
The Poets, who on earth have made us heirs
Of truth and pure delight by heavenly lays !
Oh ! might my name be numbered among
  theirs,
Then gladly would I end my mortal days.

ADMONITION

1804(?). 1807

Intended more particularly for the perusal of
those who may have happened to be enamoured
of some beautiful Place of Retreat, in the
Country of the Lakes.

WELL may'st thou halt — and gaze with
  brightening eye !
The lovely Cottage in the guardian nook
Hath stirred thee deeply; with its own dear
  brook,
Its own small pasture, almost its own sky !
But covet not the Abode; — forbear to sigh,
As many do, repining while they look;
Intruders — who would tear from Nature's
  book
This precious leaf, with harsh impiety.
Think what the home must be if it were
  thine,
Even thine, though few thy wants ! — Roof,
  window, door,
The very flowers are sacred to the Poor,
The roses to the porch which they entwine:
Yea, all, that now enchants thee, from the
  day
On which it should be touched, would melt
  away.

"BELOVED VALE!" I SAID, "WHEN I SHALL CON "

1802(?). 1807

" BELOVED Vale !" I said, "when I shall con
Those many records of my childish years,
Remembrance of myself and of my peers
Will press me down: to think of what is
  gone

Will be an awful thought, if life have one."
But, when into the Vale I came, no fears
Distressed me; from mine eyes escaped no
    tears;
Deep thought, or dread remembrance, had
    I none.
By doubts and thousand petty fancies crost
I stood, of simple shame the blushing
    Thrall;
So narrow seemed the brooks, the fields so
    small !
A Juggler's balls old Time about him
    tossed;
I looked, I stared, I smiled, I laughed;
    and all
The weight of sadness was in wonder lost.

"HOW SWEET IT IS, WHEN MOTHER FANCY ROCKS"

1802(?). 1807

How sweet it is, when mother Fancy rocks
The wayward brain, to saunter through a
    wood !
An old place, full of many a lovely brood,
Tall trees, green arbours, and ground-
    flowers in flocks;
And wild rose tip-toe upon hawthorn stocks,
Like a bold Girl, who plays her agile pranks
At Wakes and Fairs with wandering
    Mountebanks, —
When she stands cresting the Clown's head,
    and mocks
The crowd beneath her. Verily I think,
Such place to me is sometimes like a dream
Or map of the whole world: thoughts, link
    by link,
Enter through ears and eyesight, with such
    gleam
Of all things, that at last in fear I shrink,
And leap at once from the delicious stream.

"THOSE WORDS WERE UTTERED AS IN PENSIVE MOOD"

1802(?). 1807

"—— they are of the sky,
  And from our earthly memory fade away."

THOSE words were uttered as in pensive
    mood
We turned, departing from that solemn
    sight:

A contrast and reproach to gross delight,
And life's unspiritual pleasures daily
    wooed !
But now upon this thought I cannot brood;
It is unstable as a dream of night;
Nor will I praise a cloud, however bright,
Disparaging Man's gifts, and proper food.
Grove, isle, with every shape of sky-built
    dome,
Though clad in colours beautiful and pure,
Find in the heart of man no natural home:
The immortal Mind craves objects that
    endure:
These cleave to it; from these it cannot
    roam,
Nor they from it: their fellowship is secure.

COMPOSED BY THE SIDE OF GRASMERE LAKE

1807(?). 1819

CLOUDS, lingering yet, extend in solid bars
Through the grey west; and lo ! these
    waters, steeled
By breezeless air to smoothest polish, yield
A vivid repetition of the stars;
Jove, Venus, and the ruddy crest of Mars
Amid his fellows beauteously revealed
At happy distance from earth's groaning
    field,
Where ruthless mortals wage incessant
    wars.
Is it a mirror ? — or the nether Sphere
Opening to view the abyss in which she feeds
Her own calm fires ? — But list ! a voice is
    near;
Great Pan himself low-whispering through
    the reeds,
"Be thankful, thou; for, if unholy deeds
Ravage the world, tranquillity is here !"

"WITH HOW SAD STEPS, O MOON, THOU CLIMB'ST THE SKY"

1802(?). 1807

"WITH how sad steps, O Moon, thou
    climb'st the sky,
How silently, and with how wan a face !"
Where art thou ? Thou so often seen on
    high
Running among the clouds a Wood-nymph's
    race !

Unhappy Nuns, whose common breath's a
  sigh
Which they would stifle, move at such a
  pace !
The northern Wind, to call thee to the
  chase,
Must blow to-night his bugle horn. Had I
The power of Merlin, Goddess ! this should
  be:
And all the stars, fast as the clouds were
  riven,
Should sally forth, to keep thee company,
Hurrying and sparkling through the clear
  blue heaven.
But, Cynthia ! should to thee the palm be
  given,
Queen both for beauty and for majesty.

"THE WORLD IS TOO MUCH WITH US; LATE AND SOON"

1802(?). 1807

THE world is too much with us; late and
  soon,
Getting and spending, we lay waste our
  powers:
Little we see in Nature that is ours;
We have given our hearts away, a sordid
  boon !
The Sea that bares her bosom to the moon;
The winds that will be howling at all hours,
And are up-gathered now like sleeping
  flowers;
For this, for everything, we are out of
  tune;
It moves us not. — Great God ! I 'd rather be
A Pagan suckled in a creed outworn;
So might I, standing on this pleasant lea,
Have glimpses that would make me less
  forlorn;
Have sight of Proteus rising from the sea;
Or hear old Triton blow his wreathèd horn.

"WITH SHIPS THE SEA WAS SPRINKLED FAR AND NIGH"

1802(?). 1807

WITH Ships the sea was sprinkled far and
  nigh,
Like stars in heaven, and joyously it
  showed;

Some lying fast at anchor in the road,
Some veering up and down, one knew not
  why.
A goodly Vessel did I then espy
Come like a giant from a haven broad;
And lustily along the bay she strode,
Her tackling rich, and of apparel high.
This Ship was nought to me, nor I to her,
Yet I pursued her with a Lover's look;
This Ship to all the rest did I prefer:
When will she turn, and whither ? She
  will brook
No tarrying; where She comes the winds
  must stir:
On went She, and due north her journey
  took.

"WHERE LIES THE LAND TO WHICH YON SHIP MUST GO?"

1802(?). 1807

WHERE lies the Land to which yon Ship
  must go?
Fresh as a lark mounting at break of day,
Festively she puts forth in trim array;
Is she for tropic suns, or polar snow ?
What boots the inquiry ? — Neither friend
  nor foe
She cares for; let her travel where she may,
She finds familiar names, a beaten way
Ever before her, and a wind to blow.
Yet still I ask, what haven is her mark ?
And, almost as it was when ships were rare,
(From time to time, like Pilgrims, here and
  there
Crossing the waters) doubt, and something
  dark,
Of the old Sea some reverential fear,
Is with me at thy farewell, joyous Bark !

TO SLEEP

1802. 1807

O GENTLE SLEEP ! do they belong to thee,
These twinklings of oblivion ? Thou dost
  love
To sit in meekness, like the brooding Dove,
A captive never wishing to be free.
This tiresome night, O Sleep ! thou art to
  me
A Fly, that up and down himself doth shove
Upon a fretful rivulet, now above
Now on the water vexed with mockery.

I have no pain that calls for patience, no;
Hence am I cross and peevish as a child:
Am pleased by fits to have thee for my
foe,
Yet ever willing to be reconciled:
O gentle Creature ! do not use me so,
But once and deeply let me be beguiled.

TO SLEEP

1802. 1807

A FLOCK of sheep that leisurely pass by,
One after one; the sound of rain, and bees
Murmuring; the fall of rivers, winds and
seas,
Smooth fields, white sheets of water, and
pure sky;
I have thought of all by turns, and yet do
lie
Sleepless ! and soon the small birds' melo-
dies
Must hear, first uttered from my orchard
trees;
And the first cuckoo's melancholy cry.
Even thus last night, and two nights more,
I lay,
And could not win thee, Sleep ! by any
stealth:
So do not let me wear to-night away:
Without Thee what is all the morning's
wealth ?
Come, blessed barrier between day and day,
Dear mother of fresh thoughts and joyous
health !

TO SLEEP

1802. 1807

FOND words have oft been spoken to thee,
Sleep !
And thou hast had thy store of tenderest
names;
The very sweetest, Fancy culls or frames,
When thankfulness of heart is strong and
deep !
Dear Bosom-child we call thee, that dost
steep
In rich reward all suffering; Balm that
tames
All anguish; Saint that evil thoughts and
aims
Takest away, and into souls dost creep,

Like to a breeze from heaven. Shall I alone,
I surely not a man ungently made,
Call thee worst Tyrant by which Flesh is
crost ?
Perverse, self-willed to own and to disown,
Mere slave of them who never for thee
prayed,
Still last to come where thou art wanted
most !

TWO TRANSLATIONS FROM MICHAEL ANGELO, AND A TRANSLATION FROM THE LATIN OF THOMAS WARTON

1805(?). 1883

Night speaks

GRATEFUL is Sleep, my life in stone bound
fast
More grateful still: while wrong and shame
shall last,
On me can Time no happier state bestow
Than to be left unconscious of the woe.
Ah then, lest you awaken me, speak low.

GRATEFUL is Sleep, more grateful still to be
Of marble; for while shameless wrong and
woe
Prevail, 't is best to neither hear nor see;
Then wake me not, I pray you. Hush,
speak low.

COME, gentle Sleep, Death's image tho'
thou art,
Come share my couch, nor speedily depart;
How sweet thus living without life to lie,
Thus without death how sweet it is to die.

FROM THE ITALIAN OF MICHAEL ANGELO

1805. 1806

Translations from Michael Angelo, done at
the request of Mr. Duppa, whose acquaintance
I made through Mr. Southey. Mr. Duppa was
engaged in writing the life of Michael Angelo,
and applied to Mr. Southey and myself to fur-
nish some specimens of his poetic genius.

I

YES ! hope may with my strong desire
keep pace,
And I be undeluded, unbetrayed;

For if of our affections none finds grace
In sight of Heaven, then, wherefore hath
    God made
The world which we inhabit ? Better plea
Love cannot have, than that in loving thee
Glory to that eternal Peace is paid,
Who such divinity to thee imparts
As hallows and makes pure all gentle
    hearts.
His hope is treacherous only whose love
    dies
With beauty, which is varying every hour;
But, in chaste hearts uninfluenced by the
    power
Of outward change, there blooms a death-
    less flower,
That breathes on earth the air of paradise.

FROM THE SAME

1805. 1807

II

No mortal object did these eyes behold
When first they met the placid light of
    thine,
And my Soul felt her destiny divine,
And hope of endless peace in me grew bold:
Heaven-born, the Soul a heaven-ward
    course must hold;
Beyond the visible world she soars to seek
(For what delights the sense is false and
    weak)
Ideal Form, the universal mould.
The wise man, I affirm, can find no rest
In that which perishes: nor will he lend
His heart to aught which doth on time de-
    pend.
'T is sense, unbridled will, and not true
    love,
That kills the soul: love betters what is
    best,
Even here below, but more in heaven above.

TO THE MEMORY OF RAISLEY
CALVERT

1802(?). 1807

This young man, Raisley Calvert, to whom I
was so much indebted, died at Penrith, 1795.

CALVERT ! it must not be unheard by them
Who may respect my name, that I to thee

Owed many years of early liberty.
This care was thine when sickness did con-
    demn
Thy youth to hopeless wasting, root and
    stem —
That I, if frugal and severe, might stray
Where'er I liked; and finally array
My temples with the Muse's diadem.
Hence, if in freedom I have loved the
    truth;
If there be aught of pure, or good, or
    great,
In my past verse; or shall be, in the lays
Of higher mood, which now I meditate; —
It gladdens me, O worthy, short-lived,
    Youth !
To think how much of this will be thy
    praise.

"METHOUGHT I SAW THE FOOT-
STEPS OF A THRONE"

1802. 1807

The latter part of this Sonnet was a great
favourite with my sister S. H. When I saw
her lying in death, I could not resist the im-
pulse to compose the Sonnet that follows it.

[See the editor's note.]

METHOUGHT I saw the footsteps of a
    throne
Which mists and vapours from mine eyes
    did shroud —
Nor view of who might sit thereon al-
    lowed;
But all the steps and ground about were
    strown
With sights the ruefullest that flesh and
    bone
Ever put on; a miserable crowd,
Sick, hale, old, young, who cried before
    that cloud,
"Thou art our king, O Death ! to thee we
    groan."
Those steps I clomb; the mists before me
    gave
Smooth way; and I beheld the face of one
Sleeping alone within a mossy cave,
With her face up to heaven; that seemed
    to have
Pleasing remembrance of a thought fore-
    gone;
A lovely Beauty in a summer grave !

LINES

1806. 1807

Composed at Grasmere, during a walk one
Evening, after a stormy day, the Author hav-
ing just read in a Newspaper that the dissolu-
tion of Mr. Fox was hourly expected.

LOUD is the Vale ! the Voice is up
With which she speaks when storms are
      gone,
A mighty unison of streams !
Of all her Voices, One !

Loud is the Vale ; — this inland Depth
In peace is roaring like the Sea ;
Yon star upon the mountain-top
Is listening quietly.

Sad was I, even to pain deprest,
Importunate and heavy load !
The Comforter hath found me here,
Upon this lonely road ;

And many thousands now are sad —
Wait the fulfilment of their fear ;
For he must die who is their stay,
Their glory disappear.

A Power is passing from the earth
To breathless Nature's dark abyss ;
But when the great and good depart
What is it more than this —

That Man, who is from God sent forth,
Doth yet again to God return ? —
Such ebb and flow must ever be,
Then wherefore should we mourn ?

NOVEMBER 1806

1806. 1807

ANOTHER year ! — another deadly blow !
Another mighty Empire overthrown !
And We are left, or shall be left, alone ;
The last that dare to struggle with the
      Foe.
'T is well ! from this day forward we shall
      know
That in ourselves our safety must be sought ;
That by our own right hands it must be
      wrought ;
That we must stand unpropped, or be laid
      low.

O dastard whom such foretaste doth not
      cheer !
We shall exult, if they who rule the land
Be men who hold its many blessings dear,
Wise, upright, valiant ; not a servile band,
Who are to judge of danger which they
      fear,
And honour which they do not understand.

ADDRESS TO A CHILD

DURING A BOISTEROUS WINTER EVENING

BY MY SISTER

1805. 1815

Written at Town-end, Grasmere.

WHAT way does the wind come ? What
      way does he go ?
He rides over the water, and over the snow,
Through wood, and through vale ; and, o'er
      rocky height
Which the goat cannot climb, takes his
      sounding flight ;
He tosses about in every bare tree,
As, if you look up, you plainly may see ;
But how he will come, and whither he goes,
There's never a scholar in England knows.

He will suddenly stop in a cunning nook
And ring a sharp 'larum ; — but, if you
      should look,   10
There's nothing to see but a cushion of snow
Round as a pillow, and whiter than milk,
And softer than if it were covered with silk.
Sometimes he'll hide in the cave of a rock,
Then whistle as shrill as the buzzard cock ;
— Yet seek him, — and what shall you find
      in the place ?
Nothing but silence and empty space ;
Save, in a corner, a heap of dry leaves,
That he's left, for a bed, to beggars or
      thieves !
As soon as 't is daylight to-morrow, with me
You shall go to the orchard, and then you
      will see   21
That he has been there, and made a great
      rout,
And cracked the branches, and strewn them
      about ;
Heaven grant that he spare but that one
      upright twig
That looked up at the sky so proud and big
All last summer, as well you know,
Studded with apples, a beautiful show !

Hark ! over the roof he makes a pause,
And growls as if he would fix his claws
Right in the slates, and with a huge rattle
Drive them down, like men in a battle: ₃₁
— But let him range round; he does us no
    harm,
We build up the fire, we 're snug and warm;
Untouched by his breath see the candle
    shines bright,
And burns with a clear and steady light;
Books have we to read, — but that half-
    stifled knell,
Alas ! 't is the sound of the eight o'clock
    bell.
— Come, now we 'll to bed ! and when we
    are there
He may work his own will, and what shall
    we care ?
He may knock at the door, — we 'll not let
    him in; ₄₀
May drive at the windows, — we 'll laugh at
    his din;
Let him seek his own home wherever it
    be;
Here 's a *cozie* warm house for Edward and
    me.

ODE

INTIMATIONS OF IMMORTALITY FROM RECOLLECTIONS OF EARLY CHILDHOOD

1802–04. 1807

This was composed during my residence at Town-end, Grasmere. Two years at least passed between the writing of the four first stanzas and the remaining part. To the attentive and competent reader the whole sufficiently explains itself; but there may be no harm in adverting here to particular feelings or *experiences* of my own mind on which the structure of the poem partly rests. Nothing was more difficult for me in childhood than to admit the notion of death as a state applicable to my own being. I have said elsewhere —

> " A simple child,
> That lightly draws its breath,
> And feels its life in every limb,
> What should it know of death ! " —

But it was not so much from feelings of animal vivacity that *my* difficulty came as from a sense of the indomitableness of the Spirit within me. I used to brood over the stories of Enoch and Elijah, and almost to persuade myself that, whatever might become of others, I should be translated, in something of the same way, to heaven. With a feeling congenial to this, I was often unable to think of external things as having external existence, and I communed with all that I saw as something not apart from, but inherent in, my own immaterial nature. Many times while going to school have I grasped at a wall or tree to recall myself from this abyss of idealism to the reality. At that time I was afraid of such processes. In later periods of life I have deplored, as we have all reason to do, a subjugation of an opposite character, and have rejoiced over the remembrances, as is expressed in the lines —

> " Obstinate questionings
> Of sense and outward things,
> Fallings from us, vanishings ; " etc.

To that dream-like vividness and splendour which invest objects of sight in childhood, every one, I believe, if he would look back, could bear testimony, and I need not dwell upon it here : but having in the poem regarded it as presumptive evidence of a prior state of existence, I think it right to protest against a conclusion, which has given pain to some good and pious persons, that I meant to inculcate such a belief. It is far too shadowy a notion to be recommended to faith, as more than an element in our instincts of immortality. But let us bear in mind that, though the idea is not advanced in revelation, there is nothing there to contradict it, and the fall of Man presents an analogy in its favour. Accordingly, a pre-existent state has entered into the popular creeds of many nations; and, among all persons acquainted with classic literature, is known as an ingredient in Platonic philosophy. Archimedes said that he could move the world if he had a point whereon to rest his machine. Who has not felt the same aspirations as regards the world of his own mind ? Having to wield some of its elements when I was impelled to write this poem on the " Immortality of the Soul," I took hold of the notion of pre-existence as having sufficient foundation in humanity for authorising me to make for my purpose the best use of it I could as a poet.

> " The Child is Father of the Man ;
> And I could wish my days to be
> Bound each to each by natural piety. "

I

THERE was a time when meadow, grove,
    and stream,
The earth, and every common sight,
      To me did seem
      Apparelled in celestial light,
The glory and the freshness of a dream.
It is not now as it hath been of yore; —

Turn wheresoe'er I may,
By night or day,
The things which I have seen I now can
see no more.

II

The Rainbow comes and goes,   10
And lovely is the Rose,
The Moon doth with delight
Look round her when the heavens are bare,
Waters on a starry night
Are beautiful and fair;
The sunshine is a glorious birth;
But yet I know, where'er I go,
That there hath past away a glory from the
earth.

III

Now, while the birds thus sing a joyous
song,
And while the young lambs bound   20
As to the tabor's sound,
To me alone there came a thought of grief:
A timely utterance gave that thought relief,
And I again am strong:
The cataracts blow their trumpets from the
steep;
No more shall grief of mine the season
wrong;
I hear the Echoes through the mountains
throng,
The Winds come to me from the fields of
sleep,
And all the earth is gay;
Land and sea   30
Give themselves up to jollity,
And with the heart of May
Doth every Beast keep holiday; —
Thou Child of Joy,
Shout round me, let me hear thy shouts,
thou happy Shepherd-boy!

IV

Ye blessèd Creatures, I have heard the call
Ye to each other make; I see
The heavens laugh with you in your jubilee;
My heart is at your festival,   40
My head hath its coronal,
The fulness of your bliss, I feel — I feel it
all.
Oh evil day! if I were sullen
While Earth herself is adorning,
This sweet May-morning,
And the Children are culling
On every side,

In a thousand valleys far and wide,
Fresh flowers; while the sun shines
warm,
And the Babe leaps up on his Mother's
arm: —   49
I hear, I hear, with joy I hear!
— But there's a Tree, of many, one,
A single Field which I have looked upon,
Both of them speak of something that is
gone:
The Pansy at my feet
Doth the same tale repeat:
Whither is fled the visionary gleam?
Where is it now, the glory and the dream?

V

Our birth is but a sleep and a forgetting:
The Soul that rises with us, our life's Star,
Hath had elsewhere its setting,   60
And cometh from afar:
Not in entire forgetfulness,
And not in utter nakedness,
But trailing clouds of glory do we come
From God, who is our home:
Heaven lies about us in our infancy!
Shades of the prison-house begin to close
Upon the growing Boy,
But He
Beholds the light, and whence it flows,   70
He sees it in his joy;
The Youth, who daily farther from the east
Must travel, still is Nature's Priest,
And by the vision splendid
Is on his way attended;
At length the Man perceives it die away,
And fade into the light of common day.

VI

Earth fills her lap with pleasures of her own;
Yearnings she hath in her own natural kind,
And, even with something of a Mother's
mind,   80
And no unworthy aim,
The homely Nurse doth all she can
To make her Foster-child, her Inmate Man,
Forget the glories he hath known,
And that imperial palace whence he came.

VII

Behold the Child among his new-born
blisses,
A six years' Darling of a pigmy size!
See, where 'mid work of his own hand he
lies,
Fretted by sallies of his mother's kisses,

With light upon him from his father's
   eyes !   90
See, at his feet, some little plan or chart,
Some fragment from his dream of human
   life,
Shaped by himself with newly-learned art;
   A wedding or a festival,
   A mourning or a funeral;
      And this hath now his heart,
      And unto this he frames his song:
      Then will he fit his tongue
To dialogues of business, love, or strife;
   But it will not be long   100
   Ere this be thrown aside,
   And with new joy and pride
The little Actor cons another part;
Filling from time to time his " humorous
   stage "
With all the Persons, down to palsied Age,
That Life brings with her in her equipage;
   As if his whole vocation
   Were endless imitation.

VIII

Thou, whose exterior semblance doth belie
   Thy Soul's immensity;   110
Thou best Philosopher, who yet dost keep
Thy heritage, thou Eye among the blind,
That, deaf and silent, read'st the eternal
   deep,
Haunted for ever by the eternal mind, —
   Mighty Prophet ! Seer blest !
   On whom those truths do rest,
Which we are toiling all our lives to find,
In darkness lost, the darkness of the grave;
Thou, over whom thy Immortality
Broods like the Day, a Master o'er a Slave,
A Presence which is not to be put by;   121
Thou little Child, yet glorious in the might
Of heaven-born freedom on thy being's
   height,
Why with such earnest pains dost thou
   provoke
The years to bring the inevitable yoke,
Thus blindly with thy blessedness at strife ?
Full soon thy Soul shall have her earthly
   freight,
And custom lie upon thee with a weight,
Heavy as frost, and deep almost as life !

IX

O joy ! that in our embers   130
Is something that doth live,
That nature yet remembers
What was so fugitive !

The thought of our past years in me doth
   breed
Perpetual benediction: not indeed
For that which is most worthy to be blest;
Delight and liberty, the simple creed
Of Childhood, whether busy or at rest,
With new-fledged hope still fluttering in
   his breast: —
   Not for these I raise   140
   The song of thanks and praise;
But for those obstinate questionings
Of sense and outward things,
Fallings from us, vanishings;
Blank misgivings of a Creature
Moving about in worlds not realised,
High instincts before which our mortal
   Nature
Did tremble like a guilty Thing surprised:
   But for those first affections,
   Those shadowy recollections,   150
   Which, be they what they may,
Are yet the fountain light of all our day,
Are yet a master light of all our seeing;
   Uphold us, cherish, and have power to
   make
Our noisy years seem moments in the being
Of the eternal Silence: truths that wake,
   To perish never:
Which neither listlessness, nor mad en-
   deavour,
   Nor Man nor Boy,
Nor all that is at enmity with joy,   160
Can utterly abolish or destroy !
   Hence in a season of calm weather
   Though inland far we be,
Our Souls have sight of that immortal sea
   Which brought us hither,
   Can in a moment travel thither,
And see the Children sport upon the shore,
And hear the mighty waters rolling ever-
   more.

X

Then sing, ye Birds, sing, sing a joyous
   song !
   And let the young Lambs bound   170
   As to the tabor's sound !
We in thought will join your throng,
   Ye that pipe and ye that play,
   Ye that through your hearts to-day
   Feel the gladness of the May !
What though the radiance which was once
   so bright
Be now for ever taken from my sight,
   Though nothing can bring back the hour

Of splendour in the grass, of glory in the
   flower;
We will grieve not, rather find   180
Strength in what remains behind;
In the primal sympathy
Which having been must ever be;
In the soothing thoughts that spring
Out of human suffering;
In the faith that looks through death,
In years that bring the philosophic mind.

XI

And O, ye Fountains, Meadows, Hills, and
   Groves,
Forebode not any severing of our loves !
Yet in my heart of hearts I feel your might;
I only have relinquished one delight   191
To live beneath your more habitual sway.
I love the Brooks which down their chan-
   nels fret,
Even more than when I tripped lightly as
   they;
The innocent brightness of a new-born Day
   Is lovely yet;
The Clouds that gather round the setting
   sun
Do take a sober colouring from an eye
That hath kept watch o'er man's mortality;
Another race hath been, and other palms
   are won.   200
Thanks to the human heart by which we
   live,
Thanks to its tenderness, its joys, and fears,
To me the meanest flower that blows can
   give
Thoughts that do often lie too deep for
   tears.

A PROPHECY. FEBRUARY 1807

1807. 1807

HIGH deeds, O Germans, are to come
   from you !
Thus in your books the record shall be
   found,
" A watchword was pronounced, a potent
   sound —
ARMINIUS ! — all the people quaked like
   dew
Stirred by the breeze; they rose, a Nation,
   true,
True to herself — the mighty Germany,
She of the Danube and the Northern Sea,
She rose, and off at once the yoke she threw.

All power was given her in the dreadful
   trance;
Those new-born Kings she withered like a
   flame.''
— Woe to them all ! but heaviest woe and
   shame
To that Bavarian who could first advance
His banner in accursed league with France,
First open traitor to the German name !

THOUGHT OF A BRITON ON THE SUBJUGATION OF SWITZER-LAND

1806(?). 1807

This was composed while pacing to and fro
between the Hall of Coleorton, then rebuilding,
and the principal Farm-house of the Estate, in
which we lived for nine or ten months. I will
here mention that the Song on the Restoration
of Lord Clifford, as well as that on the feast of
Brougham Castle, were produced on the same
ground.

Two Voices are there; one is of the sea,
One of the mountains; each a mighty Voice:
In both from age to age thou didst rejoice,
They were thy chosen music, Liberty !
There came a Tyrant, and with holy glee
Thou fought'st against him; but hast vainly
   striven:
Thou from thy Alpine holds at length art
   driven,
Where not a torrent murmurs heard by thee.
Of one deep bliss thine ear hath been be-
   reft:
Then cleave, O cleave to that which still is
   left;
For, high-souled Maid, what sorrow would
   it be
That Mountain floods should thunder as be-
   fore,
And Ocean bellow from his rocky shore,
And neither awful Voice be heard by thee !

TO THOMAS CLARKSON

ON THE FINAL PASSING OF THE BILL
FOR THE ABOLITION OF THE SLAVE
TRADE

1807. 1807

CLARKSON ! it was an obstinate hill to
   climb:
How toilsome — nay, how dire — it was, by
   thee

Is known; by none, perhaps, so feelingly:
But thou, who, starting in thy fervent
    prime,
Didst first lead forth that enterprise sub-
    lime,
Hast heard the constant Voice its charge
    repeat,
Which, out of thy young heart's oracular
    seat,
First roused thee. — O true yoke-fellow of
    Time,
Duty's intrepid liegeman, see, the palm
Is won, and by all Nations shall be worn!
The blood-stained Writing is for ever torn;
And thou henceforth wilt have a good man's
    calm,
A great man's happiness; thy zeal shall find
Repose at length, firm friend of human
    kind!

THE MOTHER'S RETURN

BY MY SISTER

1807. 1815

Written at Town-end, Grasmere.

A MONTH, sweet Little-ones, is past
Since your dear Mother went away, —
And she to-morrow will return;
To-morrow is the happy day.

O blessèd tidings! thought of joy!
The eldest heard with steady glee;
Silent he stood; then laughed amain, —
And shouted, "Mother, come to me."

Louder and louder did he shout,
With witless hope to bring her near;　10
"Nay, patience! patience, little boy!
Your tender mother cannot hear."

I told of hills, and far-off towns,
And long, long vales to travel through; —
He listens, puzzled, sore perplexed,
But he submits; what can he do?

No strife disturbs his sister's breast;
She wars not with the mystery
Of time and distance, night and day;
The bonds of our humanity.　20

Her joy is like an instinct, joy
Of kitten, bird, or summer fly;

She dances, runs without an aim,
She chatters in her ecstasy.

Her brother now takes up the note,
And echoes back his sister's glee;
They hug the infant in my arms,
As if to force his sympathy.

Then, settling into fond discourse,
We rested in the garden bower;　30
While sweetly shone the evening sun
In his departing hour.

We told o'er all that we had done, —
Our rambles by the swift brook's side
Far as the willow-skirted pool,
Where two fair swans together glide.

We talked of change, of winter gone,
Of green leaves on the hawthorn spray,
Of birds that build their nests and sing,
And all "since Mother went away!"　40

To her these tales they will repeat,
To her our new-born tribes will show,
The goslings green, the ass's colt,
The lambs that in the meadow go.

— But, see, the evening star comes forth!
To bed the children must depart;
A moment's heaviness they feel,
A sadness at the heart:

'T is gone — and in a merry fit
They run upstairs in gamesome race;　50
I, too, infected by their mood,
I could have joined the wanton chase.

Five minutes past — and, O the change!
Asleep upon their beds they lie;
Their busy limbs in perfect rest,
And closed the sparkling eye.

GIPSIES

1807. 1807

Composed at Coleorton. I had observed
them, as here described, near Castle Donning-
ton, on my way to and from Derby.

YET are they here the same unbroken knot
Of human Beings, in the self-same spot!
    Men, women, children, yea the frame
    Of the whole spectacle the same!
Only their fire seems bolder, yielding light,
Now deep and red, the colouring of night;

That on their Gipsy-faces falls,
Their bed of straw and blanket-walls.
— Twelve hours, twelve bounteous hours
    are gone, while I
Have been a traveller under open sky,
    Much witnessing of change and cheer,
    Yet as I left I find them here !
The weary Sun betook himself to rest; —
Then issued Vesper from the fulgent west,
    Outshining like a visible God
    The glorious path in which he trod.
And now, ascending, after one dark hour
And one night's diminution of her power,
    Behold the mighty Moon ! this way
    She looks as if at them — but they
Regard not her: — oh better wrong and
    strife
(By nature transient) than this torpid life;
    Life which the very stars reprove
    As on their silent tasks they move !
Yet, witness all that stirs in heaven or earth !
In scorn I speak not; — they are what their
    birth
    And breeding suffer them to be;
    Wild outcasts of society !

"O NIGHTINGALE! THOU SURELY ART"

1807. 1807

Written at Town-end, Grasmere. (*Mrs. W.
says in a note* — " AT COLEORTON.")

O NIGHTINGALE ! thou surely art
A creature of a " fiery heart ": —
These notes of thine — they pierce and
    pierce;
Tumultuous harmony and fierce !
Thou sing'st as if the God of wine
Had helped thee to a Valentine;
A song in mockery and despite
Of shades, and dews, and silent night;
And steady bliss, and all the loves
Now sleeping in these peaceful groves.

I heard a Stock-dove sing or say
His homely tale, this very day;
His voice was buried among trees,
Yet to be come at by the breeze:
He did not cease; but cooed — and cooed;
And somewhat pensively he wooed:
He sang of love, with quiet blending,
Slow to begin, and never ending;
Of serious faith, and inward glee;
That was the song — the song for me !

TO LADY BEAUMONT

1807. 1807

The winter garden of Coleorton, fashioned
out of an old quarry under the superintendence
and direction of Mrs. Wordsworth and my sis-
ter Dorothy, during the winter and spring we
resided there.

LADY ! the songs of Spring were in the
    grove
While I was shaping beds for winter
    flowers;
While I was planting green unfading
    bowers,
And shrubs — to hang upon the warm al-
    cove,
And sheltering wall; and still, as Fancy
    wove
The dream, to time and nature's blended
    powers
I gave this paradise for winter hours,
A labyrinth, Lady ! which your feet shall
    rove.
Yes ! when the sun of life more feebly
    shines,
Becoming thoughts, I trust, of solemn
    gloom
Or of high gladness you shall hither bring;
And these perennial bowers and murmur-
    ing pines
Be gracious as the music and the bloom
And all the mighty ravishment of spring.

" THOUGH NARROW BE THAT OLD MAN'S CARES "

1806(?). 1807

" —— gives to airy nothing
A local habitation and a name."

Written at Coleorton. This old man's name
was Mitchell. He was, in all his ways and con-
versation, a great curiosity, both individually
and as a representative of past times. His chief
employment was keeping watch at night by
pacing round the house, at that time building,
to keep off depredators. He has often told me
gravely of having seen the Seven Whistlers and
the Hounds as here described. Among the
groves of Coleorton, where I became familiar
with the habits and notions of old Mitchell,
there was also a labourer of whom, I regret, I
had no personal knowledge ; for, more than
forty years after, when he was become an old
man, I learnt that while I was composing
verses, which I usually did aloud, he took

much pleasure, unknown to me, in following my steps that he might catch the words I uttered; and, what is not a little remarkable, several lines caught in this way kept their place in his memory. My volumes have lately been given to him by my informant, and surely he must have been gratified to meet in print his old acquaintances.

THOUGH narrow be that old Man's cares,
    and near,
The poor old Man is greater than he seems:
For he hath waking empire, wide as
    dreams;
An ample sovereignty of eye and ear.
Rich are his walks with supernatural cheer;
The region of his inner spirit teems
With vital sounds and monitory gleams
Of high astonishment and pleasing fear.
He the seven birds hath seen, that never
    part,
Seen the SEVEN WHISTLERS in their nightly
    rounds,
And counted them: and oftentimes will
    start —
For overhead are sweeping GABRIEL'S
    HOUNDS
Doomed, with their impious Lord, the
    flying Hart
To chase for ever, on aërial grounds !

SONG AT THE
FEAST OF BROUGHAM CASTLE

UPON THE RESTORATION OF LORD CLIF-
FORD, THE SHEPHERD, TO THE ESTATES
AND HONOURS OF HIS ANCESTORS

1806(?). 1807

This poem was composed at Coleorton while I was walking to and fro along the path that led from Sir George Beaumont's Farm-house, where we resided, to the Hall which was building at that time.

HIGH in the breathless Hall the Minstrel
    sate,
And Emont's murmur mingled with the
    Song. —
The words of ancient time I thus translate,
A festal strain that hath been silent
    long: —
" From town to town, from tower to tower,
The red rose is a gladsome flower.
Her thirty years of winter past,
The red rose is revived at last;

She lifts her head for endless spring,
For everlasting blossoming: 10
Both roses flourish, red and white:
In love and sisterly delight
The two that were at strife are blended,
And all old troubles now are ended. —
Joy ! joy to both ! but most to her
Who is the flower of Lancaster !
Behold her how She smiles to-day
On this great throng, this bright array !
Fair greeting doth she send to all
From every corner of the hall;   20
But chiefly from above the board
Where sits in state our rightful Lord,
A Clifford to his own restored !

    They came with banner, spear, and shield;
And it was proved in Bosworth-field.
Not long the Avenger was withstood —
Earth helped him with the cry of blood:
St. George was for us, and the might
Of blessed Angels crowned the right.
Loud voice the Land has uttered forth,   30
We loudest in the faithful north:
Our fields rejoice, our mountains ring,
Our streams proclaim a welcoming;
Our strong-abodes and castles see
The glory of their loyalty.

    How glad is Skipton at this hour —
Though lonely, a deserted Tower;
Knight, squire, and yeoman, page and
    groom:
We have them at the feast of Brough'm.
How glad Pendragon — though the sleep   40
Of years be on her ! — She shall reap
A taste of this great pleasure, viewing
As in a dream her own renewing.
Rejoiced is Brough, right glad I deem
Beside her little humble stream;
And she that keepeth watch and ward
Her statelier Eden's course to guard;
They both are happy at this hour,
Though each is but a lonely Tower: —
But here is perfect joy and pride   50
For one fair House by Emont's side,
This day, distinguished without peer
To see her Master and to cheer —
Him, and his Lady-mother dear !

    Oh ! it was a time forlorn
When the fatherless was born —
Give her wings that she may fly,
Or she sees her infant die !
Swords that are with slaughter wild
Hunt the Mother and the Child.   60
Who will take them from the light ?
— Yonder is a man in sight —

Yonder is a house — but where ?
No, they must not enter there.
To the caves, and to the brooks,
To the clouds of heaven she looks;
She is speechless, but her eyes
Pray in ghostly agonies.
Blissful Mary, Mother mild,
Maid and Mother undefiled,   70
Save a Mother and her Child !
　Now Who is he that bounds with joy
On Carrock's side, a Shepherd-boy ?
No thoughts hath he but thoughts that
　　　pass
Light as the wind along the grass.
Can this be He who hither came
In secret, like a smothered flame ?
O'er whom such thankful tears were shed
For shelter, and a poor man's bread ?
God loves the Child; and God hath willed 80
That those dear words should be fulfilled,
The Lady's words, when forced away,
The last she to her Babe did say:
' My own, my own, thy Fellow-guest
I may not be; but rest thee, rest,
For lowly shepherd's life is best !'
　Alas ! when evil men are strong
No life is good, no pleasure long.
The Boy must part from Mosedale's groves,
And leave Blencathara's rugged coves,   90
And quit the flowers that summer brings
To Glenderamakin's lofty springs;
Must vanish, and his careless cheer
Be turned to heaviness and fear.
— Give Sir Lancelot Threlkeld praise !
Hear it, good man, old in days !
Thou tree of covert and of rest
For this young Bird that is distrest;
Among thy branches safe he lay,
And he was free to sport and play,   100
When falcons were abroad for prey.
　A recreant harp, that sings of fear
And heaviness in Clifford's ear !
I said, when evil men are strong,
No life is good, no pleasure long,
A weak and cowardly untruth !
Our Clifford was a happy Youth,
And thankful through a weary time,
That brought him up to manhood's prime.
— Again he wanders forth at will,   110
And tends a flock from hill to hill:
His garb is humble; ne'er was seen
Such garb with such a noble mien;
Among the shepherd grooms no mate
Hath he, a Child of strength and state !
Yet lacks not friends for simple glee,

Nor yet for higher sympathy.
To his side the fallow-deer
Came, and rested without fear;
The eagle, lord of land and sea,   120
Stooped down to pay him fealty;
And both the undying fish that swim
Through Bowscale-tarn did wait on him;
The pair were servants of his eye
In their immortality;
And glancing, gleaming, dark or bright,
Moved to and fro, for his delight.
He knew the rocks which Angels haunt
Upon the mountains visitant;
He hath kenned them taking wing: 130
And into caves where Faeries sing
He hath entered; and been told
By Voices how men lived of old.
Among the heavens his eye can see
The face of thing that is to be;
And, if that men report him right,
His tongue could whisper words of might.
— Now another day is come,
Fitter hope, and nobler doom;
He hath thrown aside his crook,   140
And hath buried deep his book;
Armour rusting in his halls
On the blood of Clifford calls; —
' Quell the Scot,' exclaims the Lance —
Bear me to the heart of France,
Is the longing of the Shield —
Tell thy name, thou trembling Field;
Field of death, where'er thou be,
Groan thou with our victory !
Happy day, and mighty hour,   150
When our Shepherd, in his power,
Mailed and horsed, with lance and sword,
To his ancestors restored
Like a re-appearing Star,
Like a glory from afar,
First shall head the flock of war ! "

Alas ! the impassioned minstrel did not
　　know
How, by Heaven's grace, this Clifford's
　　heart was framed,
How he, long forced in humble walks to go,
Was softened into feeling, soothed, and
　　tamed.   160

Love had he found in huts where poor men
　　lie;
His daily teachers had been woods and
　　rills,
The silence that is in the starry sky,
The sleep that is among the lonely hills.

In him the savage virtue of the Race,
Revenge, and all ferocious thoughts were
    dead:
Nor did he change; but kept in lofty
    place
The wisdom which adversity had bred.

Glad were the vales, and every cottage hearth;
The Shepherd-lord was honoured more and
    more;   170
And, ages after he was laid in earth,
    " The good Lord Clifford " was the name
    he bore.

THE WHITE DOE OF RYLSTONE

OR, THE FATE OF THE NORTONS

1807. 1815

The earlier half of this Poem was composed at Stockton-upon-Tees, when Mrs. Wordsworth and I were on a visit to her eldest Brother, Mr. Hutchinson, at the close of the year 1807. The country is flat, and the weather was rough. I was accustomed every day to walk to and fro under the shelter of a row of stacks in a field at a small distance from the town, and there poured forth my verses aloud as freely as they would come. Mrs. Wordsworth reminds me that her brother stood upon the punctilio of not sitting down to dinner till I joined the party; and it frequently happened that I did not make my appearance till too late, so that she was made uncomfortable. I here beg her pardon for this and similar transgressions during the whole course of our wedded life. To my beloved Sister the same apology is due.

When, from the visit just mentioned, we returned to Town-end, Grasmere, I proceeded with the Poem; and it may be worth while to note, as a caution to others who may cast their eye on these memoranda, that the skin having been rubbed off my heel by my wearing too tight a shoe, though I desisted from walking I found that the irritation of the wounded part was kept up, by the act of composition, to a degree that made it necessary to give my constitution a holiday. A rapid cure was the consequence. Poetic excitement, when accompanied by protracted labour in composition, has throughout my life brought on more or less bodily derangement. Nevertheless, I am, at the close of my seventy-third year, in what may be called excellent health; so that intellectual labour is not necessarily unfavourable to longevity. But perhaps I ought here to add that mine has been generally carried on out of doors.

Let me here say a few words of this Poem in the way of criticism. The subject being taken from feudal times has led to its being compared to some of Walter Scott's poems that belong to the same age and state of society. The comparison is inconsiderate. Sir Walter pursued the customary and very natural course of conducting an action, presenting various turns of fortune, to some outstanding point on which the mind might rest as a termination or catastrophe. The course I attempted to pursue is entirely different. Everything that is attempted by the principal personages in " The White Doe " fails, so far as its object is external and substantial. So far as it is moral and spiritual it succeeds. The Heroine of the Poem knows that her duty is not to interfere with the current of events, either to forward or delay them, but

> " To abide
> The shock, and finally secure
> O'er pain and grief a triumph pure."

This she does in obedience to her brother's injunction, as most suitable to a mind and character that, under previous trials, had been proved to accord with his. She achieves this not without aid from the communication with the inferior Creature, which often leads her thoughts to revolve upon the past with a tender and humanising influence that exalts rather than depresses her. The anticipated beatification, if I may so say, of her mind, and the apotheosis of the companion of her solitude, are the points at which the Poem aims, and constitute its legitimate catastrophe, far too spiritual a one for instant or widely-spread sympathy, but not therefore the less fitted to make a deep and permanent impression upon that class of minds who think and feel more independently, than the many do, of the surfaces of things and interests transitory because belonging more to the outward and social forms of life than to its internal spirit. How insignificant a thing, for example, does personal prowess appear, compared with the fortitude of patience and heroic martyrdom ; in other words, with struggles for the sake of principle, in preference to victory gloried in for its own sake.

ADVERTISEMENT

During the Summer of 1807 I visited, for the first time, the beautiful country that surrounds Bolton Priory, in Yorkshire ; and the Poem of " The White Doe," founded upon a Tradition connected with that place, was composed at the close of the same year.

DEDICATION

In trellised shed with clustering roses gay,
And, MARY! oft beside our blazing fire,
When years of wedded life were as a day
Whose current answers to the heart's desire,
Did we together read in Spenser's Lay
How Una, sad of soul — in sad attire,
The gentle Una, of celestial birth,
To seek her Knight went wandering o'er the earth.

Ah, then, Belovèd! pleasing was the smart,
And the tear precious in compassion shed   10
For Her, who, pierced by sorrow's thrilling dart,
Did meekly bear the pang unmerited ;
Meek as that emblem of her lowly heart
The milk-white Lamb which in a line she led, —
And faithful, loyal in her innocence,
Like the brave Lion slain in her defence.

Notes could we hear as of a faery shell
Attuned to words with sacred wisdom fraught ;
Free Fancy prized each specious miracle,
And all its finer inspiration caught ;   20
Till in the bosom of our rustic Cell,
We by a lamentable change were taught
That " bliss with mortal Man may not abide : "
How nearly joy and sorrow are allied !

For us the stream of fiction ceased to flow,
For us the voice of melody was mute.
— But, as soft gales dissolve the dreary snow,
And give the timid herbage leave to shoot,
Heaven's breathing influence failed not to bestow
A timely promise of unlooked-for fruit,   30
Fair fruit of pleasure and serene content
From blossoms wild of fancies innocent.

It soothed us — it beguiled us — then, to hear
Once more of troubles wrought by magic spell ;
And griefs whose aery motion comes not near
The pangs that tempt the Spirit to rebel :
Then, with mild Una in her sober cheer,
High over hill and low adown the dell
Again we wandered, willing to partake
All that she suffered for her dear Lord's sake.   40

Then, too, this Song of mine once more could please,
Where anguish, strange as dreams of restless sleep,
Is tempered and allayed by sympathies
Aloft ascending, and descending deep,
Even to the inferior Kinds ; whom forest-trees
Protect from beating sunbeams, and the sweep
Of the sharp winds ; — fair Creatures ! — to whom Heaven
A calm and sinless life, with love, hath given.

This tragic Story cheered us ; for it speaks
Of female patience winning firm repose ;   50
And, of the recompense that conscience seeks,
A bright, encouraging, example shows ;
Needful when o'er wide realms the tempest breaks,
Needful amid life's ordinary woes ; —
Hence, not for them unfitted who would bless
A happy hour with holier happiness.

He serves the Muses erringly and ill,
Whose aim is pleasure light and fugitive :
Oh, that my mind were equal to fulfil
The comprehensive mandate which they give —   60
Vain aspiration of an earnest will !
Yet in this moral Strain a power may live,
Belovèd Wife ! such solace to impart
As it hath yielded to thy tender heart.

RYDAL MOUNT, WESTMORELAND,
        April 20, 1815.

" Action is transitory — a step, a blow,
The motion of a muscle — this way or that —
'T is done ; and in the after-vacancy
We wonder at ourselves like men betrayed :
Suffering is permanent, obscure and dark,
And has the nature of infinity.
Yet through that darkness (infinite though it seem
And irremoveable) gracious openings lie,
By which the soul — with patient steps of thought
Now toiling, wafted now on wings of prayer —
May pass in hope, and, though from mortal bonds
Yet undelivered, rise with sure ascent
Even to the fountain-head of peace divine."

" They that deny a God, destroy Man's nobility : for certainly Man is of kinn to the Beast by his Body ; and if he be not of kinn to God by his Spirit, he is a base, ignoble Creature. It destroys likewise Magnanimity, and the raising of humane Nature : for take an example of a Dogg, and mark what a generosity and courage he will put on, when he finds himself maintained by a Man, who to him is instead of a God, or Melior Natura. Which courage is manifestly such, as that Creature without that confidence of a better Nature than his own could never attain. So Man, when he resteth and assureth himself upon Divine protection and favour, gathereth a force and faith which human Nature in itself could not obtain."
        LORD BACON.

CANTO FIRST

FROM Bolton's old monastic tower
The bells ring loud with gladsome power ;
The sun shines bright ; the fields are gay
With people in their best array
Of stole and doublet, hood and scarf
Along the banks of crystal Wharf,
Through the Vale retired and lowly,
Trooping to that summons holy.
And, up among the moorlands, see
What sprinklings of blithe company !   10
Of lasses and of shepherd grooms,
That down the steep hills force their way,
Like cattle through the budded brooms ;
Path, or no path, what care they ?
And thus in joyous mood they hie
To Bolton's mouldering Priory.

What would they there? — Full fifty
    years
That sumptuous Pile, with all its peers,
Too harshly hath been doomed to taste
The bitterness of wrong and waste: 20
Its courts are ravaged; but the tower
Is standing with a voice of power,
That ancient voice which wont to call
To mass or some high festival;
And in the shattered fabric's heart
Remaineth one protected part;
A Chapel, like a wild-bird's nest,
Closely embowered and trimly drest;
And thither young and old repair,
This Sabbath-day, for praise and prayer. 30

Fast the churchyard fills; — anon
Look again, and they all are gone;
The cluster round the porch, and the folk
Who sate in the shade of the Prior's Oak!
And scarcely have they disappeared
Ere the prelusive hymn is heard: —
With one consent the people rejoice,
Filling the church with a lofty voice!
They sing a service which they feel:
For 't is the sunrise now of zeal; 40
Of a pure faith the vernal prime —
In great Eliza's golden time.

A moment ends the fervent din,
And all is hushed, without and within;
For though the priest, more tranquilly,
Recites the holy liturgy,
The only voice which you can hear
Is the river murmuring near.
— When soft! — the dusky trees between,
And down the path through the open green,
Where is no living thing to be seen; 51
And through yon gateway, where is found,
Beneath the arch with ivy bound,
Free entrance to the churchyard ground —
Comes gliding in with lovely gleam,
Comes gliding in serene and slow,
Soft and silent as a dream,
A solitary Doe!
White she is as lily of June,
And beauteous as the silver moon 60
When out of sight the clouds are driven
And she is left alone in heaven;
Or like a ship some gentle day
In sunshine sailing far away,
A glittering ship, that hath the plain
Of ocean for her own domain.

Lie silent in your graves, ye dead!
Lie quiet in your churchyard bed!
Ye living, tend your holy cares;
Ye multitude, pursue your prayers; 70

And blame not me if my heart and sight
Are occupied with one delight!
'T is a work for sabbath hours
If I with this bright Creature go:
Whether she be of forest bowers,
From the bowers of earth below;
Or a Spirit for one day given,
A pledge of grace from purest heaven.

What harmonious pensive changes
Wait upon her as she ranges 80
Round and through this Pile of state
Overthrown and desolate!
Now a step or two her way
Leads through space of open day,
Where the enamoured sunny light
Brightens her that was so bright;
Now doth a delicate shadow fall,
Falls upon her like a breath,
From some lofty arch or wall,
As she passes underneath: 90
Now some gloomy nook partakes
Of the glory that she makes, —
High-ribbed vault of stone, or cell,
With perfect cunning framed as well
Of stone, and ivy, and the spread
Of the elder's bushy head;
Some jealous and forbidding cell,
That doth the living stars repel,
And where no flower hath leave to dwell.

The presence of this wandering Doe 100
Fills many a damp obscure recess
With lustre of a saintly show;
And, reappearing, she no less
Sheds on the flowers that round her blow
A more than sunny liveliness.
But say, among these holy places,
Which thus assiduously she paces,
Comes she with a votary's task,
Rite to perform, or boon to ask?
Fair Pilgrim! harbours she a sense 110
Of sorrow, or of reverence?
Can she be grieved for quire or shrine,
Crushed as if by wrath divine?
For what survives of house where God
Was worshipped, or where Man abode;
For old magnificence undone;
Or for the gentler work begun
By Nature, softening and concealing,
And busy with a hand of healing?
Mourns she for lordly chamber's hearth 120
That to the sapling ash gives birth;
For dormitory's length laid bare
Where the wild rose blossoms fair;
Or altar, whence the cross was rent,
Now rich with mossy ornament?

— She sees a warrior carved in stone,
Among the thick weeds, stretched alone;
A warrior, with his shield of pride
Cleaving humbly to his side,
And hands in resignation prest,   130
Palm to palm, on his tranquil breast;
As little she regards the sight
As a common creature might:
If she be doomed to inward care,
Or service, it must lie elsewhere.
— But hers are eyes serenely bright,
And on she moves — with pace how light !
Nor spares to stoop her head, and taste
The dewy turf with flowers bestrown;
And thus she fares, until at last   140
Beside the ridge of a grassy grave
In quietness she lays her down;
Gentle as a weary wave
Sinks, when the summer breeze hath died
Against an anchored vessel's side;
Even so, without distress, doth she
Lie down in peace, and lovingly.
    The day is placid in its going,
To a lingering motion bound,
Like the crystal stream now flowing   150
With its softest summer sound:
So the balmy minutes pass,
While this radiant Creature lies
Couched upon the dewy grass,
Pensively with downcast eyes.
— But now again the people raise
With awful cheer a voice of praise;
It is the last, the parting song;
And from the temple forth they throng,
And quickly spread themselves abroad,   160
While each pursues his several road.
But some — a variegated band
Of middle-aged, and old, and young,
And little children by the hand
Upon their leading mothers hung —
With mute obeisance gladly paid
Turn towards the spot where, full in view,
The white Doe, to her service true,
Her sabbath couch has made.
    It was a solitary mound;   170
Which two spears' length of level ground
Did from all other graves divide:
As if in some respect of pride;
Or melancholy's sickly mood,
Still shy of human neighbourhood;
Or guilt, that humbly would express
A penitential loneliness.
    "Look, there she is, my Child ! draw
          near;
She fears not, wherefore should we fear ?

She means no harm;" — but still the
          Boy,   180
To whom the words were softly said,
Hung back, and smiled, and blushed for
          joy,
A shame-faced blush of glowing red !
Again the Mother whispered low,
" Now you have seen the famous Doe;
From Rylstone she hath found her way
Over the hills this sabbath day;
Her work, whate'er it be, is done,
And she will depart when we are gone;
Thus doth she keep, from year to year,   190
Her sabbath morning, foul or fair."
    Bright was the Creature, as in dreams
The Boy had seen her, yea, more bright;
But is she truly what she seems ?
He asks with insecure delight,
Asks of himself, and doubts, — and still
The doubt returns against his will:
Though he, and all the standers-by,
Could tell a tragic history
Of facts divulged, wherein appear   200
Substantial motive, reason clear,
Why thus the milk-white Doe is found
Couchant beside that lonely mound;
And why she duly loves to pace
The circuit of this hallowed place.
Nor to the Child's inquiring mind
Is such perplexity confined:
For, spite of sober Truth that sees
A world of fixed remembrances
Which to this mystery belong,   210
If, undeceived, my skill can trace
The characters of every face,
There lack not strange delusion here,
Conjecture vague, and idle fear,
And superstitious fancies strong,
Which do the gentle Creature wrong.
    That bearded, staff-supported Sire —
Who in his boyhood often fed
Full cheerily on convent-bread
And heard old tales by the convent-fire,   220
And to his grave will go with scars,
Relics of long and distant wars —
That Old Man, studious to expound
The spectacle, is mounting high
To days of dim antiquity;
When Lady Aäliza mourned
Her Son, and felt in her despair
The pang of unavailing prayer;
Her Son in Wharf's abysses drowned,
The noble Boy of Egremound.   230
From which affliction — when the grace
Of God had in her heart found place —

A pious structure, fair to see,
Rose up, this stately Priory !
The Lady's work; — but now laid low;
To the grief of her soul that doth come
    and go,
In the beautiful form of this innocent
    Doe:
Which, though seemingly doomed in its
    breast to sustain
A softened remembrance of sorrow and
    pain,
Is spotless, and holy, and gentle, and
    bright;   240
And glides o'er the earth like an angel of
    light.
    Pass, pass who will, yon chantry door;
And, through the chink in the fractured
    floor
Look down, and see a griesly sight;
A vault where the bodies are buried up-
    right !
There, face by face, and hand by hand,
The Claphams and Mauleverers stand;
And, in his place, among son and sire,
Is John de Clapham, that fierce Esquire,
A valiant man, and a name of dread   250
In the ruthless wars of the White and Red;
Who dragged Earl Pembroke from Ban-
    bury church
And smote off his head on the stones of
    the porch !
Look down among them, if you dare;
Oft does the White Doe loiter there,
Prying into the darksome rent;
Nor can it be with good intent:
So thinks that Dame of haughty air,
Who hath a Page her book to hold,
And wears a frontlet edged with gold.   260
Harsh thoughts with her high mood
    agree —
Who counts among her ancestry
Earl Pembroke, slain so impiously !
    That slender Youth, a scholar pale,
From Oxford come to his native vale,
He also hath his own conceit:
It is, thinks he, the gracious Fairy,
Who loved the Shepherd-lord to meet
In his wanderings solitary:
Wild notes she in his hearing sang,   270
A song of Nature's hidden powers;
That whistled like the wind, and rang
Among the rocks and holly bowers.
'T was said that She all shapes could wear;
And oftentimes before him stood,
Amid the trees of some thick wood,

In semblance of a lady fair;
And taught him signs, and showed him
    sights,
In Craven's dens, on Cumbrian heights;
When under cloud of fear he lay,   280
A shepherd clad in homely grey;
Nor left him at his later day.
And hence, when he, with spear and shield,
Rode full of years to Flodden-field,
His eye could see the hidden spring,
And how the current was to flow;
The fatal end of Scotland's King,
And all that hopeless overthrow.
But not in wars did he delight,
This Clifford wished for worthier might;
Nor in broad pomp, or courtly state;   291
Him his own thoughts did elevate, —
Most happy in the shy recess
Of Barden's lowly quietness.
And choice of studious friends had he
Of Bolton's dear fraternity;
Who, standing on this old church tower,
In many a calm propitious hour,
Perused, with him, the starry sky;
Or, in their cells, with him did pry   300
For other lore, — by keen desire
Urged to close toil with chemic fire;
In quest belike of transmutations
Rich as the mine's most bright creations.
But they and their good works are fled,
And all is now disquieted —
And peace is none, for living or dead !
    Ah, pensive Scholar, think not so,
But look again at the radiant Doe !
What quiet watch she seems to keep,   310
Alone, beside that grassy heap !
Why mention other thoughts unmeet
For vision so composed and sweet ?
While stand the people in a ring,
Gazing, doubting, questioning;
Yea, many overcome in spite
Of recollections clear and bright;
Which yet do unto some impart
An undisturbed repose of heart.
And all the assembly own a law   320
Of orderly respect and awe;
But see — they vanish one by one,
And last, the Doe herself is gone.
    Harp ! we have been full long beguiled
By vague thoughts, lured by fancies wild;
To which, with no reluctant strings,
Thou hast attuned thy murmurings;
And now before this Pile we stand
In solitude, and utter peace:
But, Harp ! thy murmurs may not cease —

A Spirit, with his angelic wings,　331
In soft and breeze-like visitings,
Has touched thee — and a Spirit's hand:
A voice is with us — a command
To chant, in strains of heavenly glory,
A tale of tears, a mortal story !

CANTO SECOND

THE Harp in lowliness obeyed;
And first we sang of the greenwood shade
And a solitary Maid;
Beginning, where the song must end,
With her, and with her sylvan Friend;
The Friend who stood before her sight,
Her only unextinguished light;
Her last companion in a dearth
Of love, upon a hopeless earth.

For She it was — this Maid, who wrought
Meekly, with foreboding thought,　11
In vermeil colours and in gold
An unblest work; which, standing by,
Her Father did with joy behold, —
Exulting in its imagery;
A Banner, fashioned to fulfil
Too perfectly his headstrong will:
For on this Banner had her hand
Embroidered (such her Sire's command)
The sacred Cross; and figured there　20
The five dear wounds our Lord did bear;
Full soon to be uplifted high,
And float in rueful company !

It was the time when England's Queen
Twelve years had reigned, a Sovereign
　　dread;
Nor yet the restless crown had been
Disturbed upon her virgin head;
But now the inly-working North
Was ripe to send its thousands forth,
A potent vassalage, to fight　30
In Percy's and in Neville's right,
Two Earls fast leagued in discontent,
Who gave their wishes open vent;
And boldly urged a general plea,
The rites of ancient piety
To be triumphantly restored,
By the stern justice of the sword !
And that same Banner, on whose breast
The blameless Lady had exprest
Memorials chosen to give life　40
And sunshine to a dangerous strife;
That Banner, waiting for the Call,
Stood quietly in Rylstone-hall.

It came; and Francis Norton said,
" O Father ! rise not in this fray —

The hairs are white upon your head;
Dear Father, hear me when I say
It is for you too late a day !
Bethink you of your own good name:
A just and gracious Queen have we,　50
A pure religion, and the claim
Of peace on our humanity. —
'T is meet that I endure your scorn;
I am your son, your eldest born;
But not for lordship or for land,
My Father, do I clasp your knees;
The Banner touch not, stay your hand,
This multitude of men disband,
And live at home in blameless ease;
For these my brethren's sake, for me;　60
And, most of all, for Emily ! "

Tumultuous noises filled the hall;
And scarcely could the Father hear
That name — pronounced with a dying
　　fall —
The name of his only Daughter dear,
As on the banner which stood near
He glanced a look of holy pride,
And his moist eyes were glorified;
Then did he seize the staff, and say:
" Thou, Richard, bear'st thy father's name,
Keep thou this ensign till the day　71
When I of thee require the same:
Thy place be on my better hand; —
And seven as true as thou, I see,
Will cleave to this good cause and me."
He spake, and eight brave sons straightway
All followed him, a gallant band !

Thus, with his sons, when forth he came
The sight was hailed with loud acclaim
And din of arms and minstrelsy,　80
From all his warlike tenantry,
All horsed and harnessed with him to
　　ride, —
A voice to which the hills replied !

But Francis, in the vacant hall,
Stood silent under dreary weight, —
A phantasm, in which roof and wall
Shook, tottered, swam before his sight;
A phantasm like a dream of night !
Thus overwhelmed, and desolate,
He found his way to a postern-gate;　90
And, when he waked, his languid eye
Was on the calm and silent sky;
With air about him breathing sweet,
And earth's green grass beneath his feet;
Nor did he fail ere long to hear
A sound of military cheer,
Faint — but it reached that sheltered spot;
He heard, and it disturbed him not.

There stood he, leaning on a lance
Which he had grasped unknowingly,   100
Had blindly grasped in that strong trance,
That dimness of heart-agony;
There stood he, cleansed from the despair
And sorrow of his fruitless prayer.
The past he calmly hath reviewed:
But where will be the fortitude
Of this brave man, when he shall see
That Form beneath the spreading tree,
And know that it is Emily ?
He saw her where in open view   110
She sate beneath the spreading yew —
Her head upon her lap, concealing
In solitude her bitter feeling:
" Might ever son *command* a sire,
The act were justified to-day."
This to himself — and to the Maid,
Whom now he had approached, he said —
" Gone are they, — they have their desire;
And I with thee one hour will stay,
To give thee comfort if I may."   120
She heard, but looked not up, nor spake;
And sorrow moved him to partake
Her silence;   then his thoughts turned round,
And fervent words a passage found.
" Gone are they, bravely, though mis-led;
With a dear Father at their head !
The Sons obey a natural lord;
The Father had given solemn word
To noble Percy; and a force
Still stronger, bends him to his course.   130
This said, our tears to-day may fall
As at an innocent funeral.
In deep and awful channel runs
This sympathy of Sire and Sons;
Untried our Brothers have been loved
With heart by simple nature moved;
And now their faithfulness is proved:
For faithful we must call them, bearing
That soul of conscientious daring.
— There were they all in circle — there   140
Stood Richard, Ambrose, Christopher,
John with a sword that will not fail,
And Marmaduke in fearless mail,
And those bright Twins were side by side;
And there, by fresh hopes beautified,
Stood He, whose arm yet lacks the power
Of man, our youngest, fairest flower !
I, by the right of eldest born,
And in a second father's place,
Presumed to grapple with their scorn,   150
And meet their pity face to face;

Yea, trusting in God's holy aid,
I to my Father knelt and prayed;
And one, the pensive Marmaduke,
Methought, was yielding inwardly,
And would have laid his purpose by,
But for a glance of his Father's eye,
Which I myself could scarcely brook.
Then be we, each and all, forgiven !
Thou, chiefly thou, my Sister dear,   160
Whose pangs are registered in heaven —
The stifled sigh, the hidden tear,
And smiles, that dared to take their place,
Meek filial smiles, upon thy face,
As that unhallowed Banner grew
Beneath a loving old Man's view.
Thy part is done — thy painful part;
Be thou then satisfied in heart !
A further, though far easier, task
Than thine hath been, my duties ask;   170
With theirs my efforts cannot blend,
I cannot for such cause contend;
Their aims I utterly forswear;
But I in body will be there.
Unarmed and naked will I go,
Be at their side, come weal or woe:
On kind occasions I may wait,
See, hear, obstruct, or mitigate.
Bare breast I take and an empty hand."
Therewith he threw away the lance,   180
Which he had grasped in that strong trance,
Spurned it, like something that would stand
Between him and the pure intent
Of love on which his soul was bent.
" For thee, for thee, is left the sense
Of trial past without offence
To God or man; such innocence,
Such consolation, and the excess
Of an unmerited distress;
In that thy very strength must lie.   190
— O Sister, I could prophesy !
The time is come that rings the knell
Of all we loved, and loved so well:
Hope nothing, if I thus may speak
To thee, a woman, and thence weak:
Hope nothing, I repeat; for we
Are doomed to perish utterly:
'T is meet that thou with me divide
The thought while I am by thy side,
Acknowledging a grace in this,   200
A comfort in the dark abyss.
But look not for me when I am gone,
And be no farther wrought upon:
Farewell all wishes, all debate,

All prayers for this cause, or for that !
Weep, if that aid thee; but depend
Upon no help of outward friend;
Espouse thy doom at once, and cleave
To fortitude without reprieve.
For we must fall, both we and ours —   210
This Mansion and these pleasant bowers,
Walks, pools, and arbours, homestead,
        hall —
Our fate is theirs, will reach them all;
The young horse must forsake his manger,
And learn to glory in a Stranger;
The hawk forget his perch; the hound
Be parted from his ancient ground:
The blast will sweep us all away —
One desolation, one decay !
And even this Creature !" which words say-
        ing,   220
He pointed to a lovely Doe,
A few steps distant, feeding, straying;
Fair creature, and more white than snow !
" Even she will to her peaceful woods
Return, and to her murmuring floods,
And be in heart and soul the same
She was before she hither came;
Ere she had learned to love us all,
Herself beloved in Rylstone-hall.
— But thou, my Sister, doomed to be   230
The last leaf on a blasted tree;
If not in vain we breathed the breath
Together of a purer faith;
If hand in hand we have been led,
And thou, (O happy thought this day!)
Not seldom foremost in the way;
If on one thought our minds have fed,
And we have in one meaning read;
If, when at home our private weal
Hath suffered from the shock of zeal,   240
Together we have learned to prize
Forbearance and self-sacrifice;
If we like combatants have fared,
And for this issue been prepared;
If thou art beautiful, and youth
And thought endue thee with all truth —
Be strong; — be worthy of the grace
Of God, and fill thy destined place:
A Soul, by force of sorrows high,
Uplifted to the purest sky   250
Of undisturbed humanity ! "
        He ended, — or she heard no more;
He led her from the yew-tree shade,
And at the mansion's silent door,
He kissed the consecrated Maid;
And down the valley then pursued,
Alone, the armèd Multitude.

CANTO THIRD

Now joy for you who from the towers
Of Brancepeth look in doubt and fear,
Telling melancholy hours !
Proclaim it, let your Masters hear
That Norton with his band is near !
The watchmen from their station high
Pronounced the word, — and the Earls de-
        scry,
Well-pleased, the armèd Company
Marching down the banks of Were.
        Said fearless Norton to the pair   10
Gone forth to greet him on the plain —
" This meeting, noble Lords ! looks fair,
I bring with me a goodly train;
Their hearts are with you: hill and dale
Have helped us: Ure we crossed, and Swale,
And horse and harness followed — see
The best part of their Yeomanry !
— Stand forth, my Sons ! — these eight are
        mine,
Whom to this service I commend;
Which way soe'er our fate incline,   20
These will be faithful to the end;
They are my all " — voice failed him
        here —
" My all save one, a Daughter dear !
Whom I have left, Love's mildest birth,
The meekest Child on this blessed earth.
I had — but these are by my side,
These Eight, and this is a day of pride !
The time is ripe. With festive din
Lo ! how the people are flocking in, —
Like hungry fowl to the feeder's hand   30
When snow lies heavy upon the land."
        He spake bare truth; for far and near
From every side came noisy swarms
Of Peasants in their homely gear;
And, mixed with these, to Brancepeth came
Grave Gentry of estate and name,
And Captains known for worth in arms
And prayed the Earls in self-defence
To rise, and prove their innocence. —
" Rise, noble Earls, put forth your might   40
For holy Church, and the People's right ! "
        The Norton fixed, at this demand,
His eye upon Northumberland,
And said; " The Minds of Men will own
No loyal rest while England's Crown
Remains without an Heir, the bait
Of strife and factions desperate;
Who, paying deadly hate in kind
Through all things else, in this can find
A mutual hope, a common mind;   50

And plot, and pant to overwhelm
All ancient honour in the realm.
— Brave Earls ! to whose heroic veins
Our noblest blood is given in trust,
To you a suffering State complains,
And ye must raise her from the dust.
With wishes of still bolder scope
On you we look, with dearest hope;
Even for our Altars — for the prize
In Heaven, of life that never dies;   60
For the old and holy Church we mourn,
And must in joy to her return.
Behold ! " — and from his Son whose stand
Was on his right, from that guardian hand
He took the Banner, and unfurled
The precious folds — " behold," said he,
" The ransom of a sinful world;
Let this your preservation be;
The wounds of hands and feet and side,
And the sacred Cross on which Jesus died.
— This bring I from an ancient hearth,   71
These Records wrought in pledge of love
By hands of no ignoble birth,
A Maid o'er whom the blessed Dove
Vouchsafed in gentleness to brood
While she the holy work pursued."
" Uplift the Standard ! " was the cry
From all the listeners that stood round,
" Plant it, — by this we live or die."
The Norton ceased not for that sound,   80
But said; " The prayer which ye have
       heard,
Much-injured Earls ! by these preferred,
Is offered to the Saints, the sigh
Of tens of thousands, secretly."
" Uplift it ! " cried once more the Band,
And then a thoughtful pause ensued:
" Uplift it ! " said Northumberland —
Whereat, from all the multitude
Who saw the Banner reared on high
In all its dread emblazonry,   90
A voice of uttermost joy brake out:
The transport was rolled down the river of
       Were,
And Durham, the time-honoured Durham,
       did hear,
And the towers of Saint Cuthbert were
       stirred by the shout !
   Now was the North in arms: — they shine
In warlike trim from Tweed to Tyne,
At Percy's voice: and Neville sees
His Followers gathering in from Tees,
From Were, and all the little rills
Concealed among the forked hills —   100
Seven hundred Knights, Retainers all

Of Neville, at their Master's call
Had sate together in Raby Hall !
Such strength that Earldom held of yore;
Nor wanted at this time rich store
Of well-appointed chivalry.
— Not loth the sleepy lance to wield,
And greet the old paternal shield,
They heard the summons; — and, further-
       more,
Horsemen and Foot of each degree,   110
Unbound by pledge of fealty,
Appeared, with free and open hate
Of novelties in Church and State;
Knight, burgher, yeoman, and esquire;
And Romish priest, in priest's attire.
And thus, in arms, a zealous Band
Proceeding under joint command,
To Durham first their course they bear;
And in Saint Cuthbert's ancient seat
Sang mass, — and tore the book of prayer, —
And trod the bible beneath their feet.   121
   Thence marching southward smooth and
       free
" They mustered their host at Wetherby,
Full sixteen thousand fair to see,"
The Choicest Warriors of the North !
But none for beauty and for worth
Like those eight Sons — who, in a ring,
(Ripe men, or blooming in life's spring)
Each with a lance, erect and tall,
A falchion, and a buckler small,   130
Stood by their Sire, on Clifford-moor,
To guard the Standard which he bore.
On foot they girt their Father round;
And so will keep the appointed ground
Where'er their march: no steed will he
Henceforth bestride; — triumphantly
He stands upon the grassy sod,
Trusting himself to the earth, and God.
Rare sight to embolden and inspire !
Proud was the field of Sons and Sire;   140
Of him the most; and, sooth to say,
No shape of man in all the array
So graced the sunshine of that day.
The monumental pomp of age
Was with this goodly Personage;
A stature undepressed in size,
Unbent, which rather seemed to rise,
In open victory o'er the weight
Of seventy years, to loftier height;
Magnific limbs of withered state;   150
A face to fear and venerate;
Eyes dark and strong; and on his head
Bright locks of silver hair, thick spread,
Which a brown morion half-concealed,

Light as a hunter's of the field;
And thus, with girdle round his waist,
Whereon the Banner-staff might rest
At need, he stood, advancing high
The glittering, floating Pageantry.
Who sees him? — thousands see, and One
With unparticipated gaze;   161
Who, 'mong those thousands, friend hath
    none,
And treads in solitary ways.
He, following wheresoe'er he might,
Hath watched the Banner from afar,
As shepherds watch a lonely star,
Or mariners the distant light
That guides them through a stormy night.
And now, upon a chosen plot
Of rising ground, yon heathy spot !   170
He takes alone his far-off stand,
With breast unmailed, unweaponed hand.
Bold is his aspect; but his eye
Is pregnant with anxiety,
While, like a tutelary Power,
He there stands fixed from hour to hour:
Yet sometimes in more humble guise,
Upon the turf-clad height he lies
Stretched, herdsman-like, as if to bask
In sunshine were his only task,   180
Or by his mantle's help to find
A shelter from the nipping wind:
And thus, with short oblivion blest,
His weary spirits gather rest.
Again he lifts his eyes; and lo !
The pageant glancing to and fro;
And hope is wakened by the sight,
He thence may learn, ere fall of night,
Which way the tide is doomed to flow.
    To London were the Chieftains bent; 190
But what avails the bold intent ?
A Royal army is gone forth
To quell the RISING OF THE NORTH;
They march with Dudley at their head,
And, in seven days' space, will to York be
    led ! —
Can such a mighty Host be raised
Thus suddenly, and brought so near ?
The Earls upon each other gazed,
And Neville's cheek grew pale with fear;
For, with a high and valiant name,   200
He bore a heart of timid frame;
And bold if both had been, yet they
"Against so many may not stay."
Back therefore will they hie to seize
A strong Hold on the banks of Tees;
There wait a favourable hour,
Until Lord Dacre with his power

From Naworth come; and Howard's aid
Be with them openly displayed.
    While through the Host, from man to
        man,   210
A rumour of this purpose ran,
The Standard trusting to the care
Of him who heretofore did bear
That charge, impatient Norton sought
The Chieftains to unfold his thought,
And thus abruptly spake; — "We yield
(And can it be ?) an unfought field ! —
How oft has strength, the strength of
    heaven,
To few triumphantly been given !
Still do our very children boast   220
Of mitred Thurston — what a Host
He conquered ! — Saw we not the Plain
(And flying shall behold again)
Where faith was proved ? —while to battle
    moved
The Standard, on the Sacred Wain
That bore it, compassed round by a bold
Fraternity of Barons old;
And with those grey-haired champions
    stood,
Under the saintly ensigns three,
The infant Heir of Mowbray's blood —   230
All confident of victory ! —
Shall Percy blush, then, for his name ?
Must Westmoreland be asked with shame
Whose were the numbers, where the loss,
In that other day of Neville's Cross ?
When the Prior of Durham with holy hand
Raised, as the Vision gave command,
Saint Cuthbert's Relic — far and near
Kenned on the point of a lofty spear;
While the Monks prayed in Maiden's
    Bower   240
To God descending in his power.
Less would not at our need be due
To us, who war against the Untrue; —
The delegates of Heaven we rise,
Convoked the impious to chastise:
We, we, the sanctities of old
Would re-establish and uphold:
Be warned " — His zeal the Chiefs con-
    founded,
But word was given, and the trumpet
    sounded:
Back through the melancholy Host   250
Went Norton, and resumed his post.
Alas ! thought he, and have I borne
This Banner raised with joyful pride,
This hope of all posterity,
By those dread symbols sanctified;

Thus to become at once the scorn
Of babbling winds as they go by,
A spot of shame to the sun's bright eye,
To the light clouds a mockery!
— ''Even these poor eight of mine would
                                stem — ''   260
Half to himself, and half to them
He spake — '' would stem, or quell, a force
Ten times their number, man and horse:
This by their own unaided might,
Without their father in their sight,
Without the Cause for which they fight;
A Cause, which on a needful day
Would breed us thousands brave as they.''
— So speaking, he his reverend head
Raised towards that Imagery once more:
But the familiar prospect shed   271
Despondency unfelt before:
A shock of intimations vain,
Dismay, and superstitious pain,
Fell on him, with the sudden thought
Of her by whom the work was wrought: —
Oh wherefore was her countenance bright
With love divine and gentle light ?
She would not, could not, disobey,
But her Faith leaned another way.   280
Ill tears she wept; I saw them fall,
I overheard her as she spake
Sad words to that mute Animal,
The White Doe, in the hawthorn brake;
She steeped, but not for Jesu's sake,
This Cross in tears: by her, and One
Unworthier far we are undone —
Her recreant Brother — he prevailed
Over that tender Spirit — assailed
Too oft, alas ! by her whose head   290
In the cold grave hath long been laid:
She first, in reason's dawn beguiled
Her docile, unsuspecting Child:
Far back — far back my mind must go
To reach the well-spring of this woe !
    While thus he brooded, music sweet
Of border tunes was played to cheer
The footsteps of a quick retreat;
But Norton lingered in the rear,
Stung with sharp thoughts; and ere the
                                last   300
From his distracted brain was cast,
Before his Father, Francis stood,
And spake in firm and earnest mood.
    '' Though here I bend a suppliant knee
In reverence, and unarmed, I bear
In your indignant thoughts my share;
Am grieved this backward march to see
So careless and disorderly.

I scorn your Chiefs — men who would lead,
And yet want courage at their need: 310
Then look at them with open eyes !
Deserve they further sacrifice ? —
If — when they shrink, nor dare oppose
In open field their gathering foes,
(And fast, from this decisive day,
Yon multitude must melt away;)
If now I ask a grace not claimed
While ground was left for hope; unblamed
Be an endeavour that can do
No injury to them or you.   320
My Father ! I would help to find
A place of shelter, till the rage
Of cruel men do like the wind
Exhaust itself and sink to rest;
Be Brother now to Brother joined !
Admit me in the equipage
Of your misfortunes, that at least,
Whatever fate remain behind,
I may bear witness in my breast
To your nobility of mind ! ''   330
    ''Thou Enemy, my bane and blight !
Oh ! bold to fight the Coward's fight
Against all good '' — but why declare,
At length, the issue of a prayer
Which love had prompted, yielding scope
Too free to one bright moment's hope ?
Suffice it that the Son, who strove
With fruitless effort to allay
That passion, prudently gave way;
Nor did he turn aside to prove   340
His Brothers' wisdom or their love —
But calmly from the spot withdrew;
His best endeavours to renew,
Should e'er a kindlier time ensue.

CANTO FOURTH

'T IS night: in silence looking down,
The Moon from cloudless ether sees
A Camp, and a beleaguered Town,
And Castle like a stately crown
On the steep rocks of winding Tees; —
And southward far, with moor between,
Hill-top, and flood, and forest green,
The bright Moon sees that valley small
Where Rylstone's old sequestered Hall
A venerable image yields   10
Of quiet to the neighbouring fields;
While from one pillared chimney breathes
The smoke, and mounts in silver wreaths.
— The courts are hushed; — for timely
                                sleep
The greyhounds to their kennel creep;

The peacock in the broad ash tree
Aloft is roosted for the night,
He who in proud prosperity
Of colours manifold and bright
Walked round, affronting the daylight; 20
And higher still, above the bower
Where he is perched, from yon lone Tower
The hall-clock in the clear moonshine
With glittering finger points at nine.
　Ah ! who could think that sadness here
Hath any sway ? or pain, or fear ?
A soft and lulling sound is heard
Of streams inaudible by day;
The garden pool's dark surface, stirred
By the night insects in their play, 30
Breaks into dimples small and bright;
A thousand, thousand rings of light
That shape themselves and disappear
Almost as soon as seen: — and lo !
Not distant far, the milk-white Doe —
The same who quietly was feeding
On the green herb, and nothing heeding,
When Francis, uttering to the Maid
His last words in the yew-tree shade,
Involved whate'er by love was brought 40
Out of his heart, or crossed his thought,
Or chance presented to his eye,
In one sad sweep of destiny —
The same fair Creature, who hath found
Her way into forbidden ground;
Where now — within this spacious plot
For pleasure made, a goodly spot,
With lawns and beds of flowers, and shades
Of trellis-work in long arcades,
And cirque and crescent framed by wall 50
Of close-clipt foliage green and tall,
Converging walks, and fountains gay,
And terraces in trim array —
Beneath yon cypress spiring high,
With pine and cedar spreading wide
Their darksome boughs on either side,
In open moonlight doth she lie;
Happy as others of her kind,
That, far from human neighbourhood,
Range unrestricted as the wind, 60
Through park, or chase, or savage wood.
　But see the consecrated Maid
Emerging from a cedar shade
To open moonshine, where the Doe
Beneath the cypress-spire is laid;
Like a patch of April snow —
Upon a bed of herbage green,
Lingering in a woody glade
Or behind a rocky screen —
Lonely relic ! which, if seen 70

By the shepherd, is passed by
With an inattentive eye.
Nor more regard doth She bestow
Upon the uncomplaining Doe
Now couched at ease, though oft this day
Not unperplexed nor free from pain,
When she had tried, and tried in vain,
Approaching in her gentle way,
To win some look of love, or gain
Encouragement to sport or play — 80
Attempts which still the heart-sick Maid
Rejected, or with slight repaid.
　Yet Emily is soothed; — the breeze
Came fraught with kindly sympathies.
As she approached yon rustic Shed
Hung with late-flowering woodbine, spread
Along the walls and overhead,
The fragrance of the breathing flowers
Revived a memory of those hours
When here, in this remote alcove, 90
(While from the pendent woodbine came
Like odours, sweet as if the same)
A fondly-anxious Mother strove
To teach her salutary fears
And mysteries above her years.
Yes, she is soothed: an Image faint,
And yet not faint — a presence bright
Returns to her — that blessed Saint
Who with mild looks and language mild
Instructed here her darling Child, 100
While yet a prattler on the knee,
To worship in simplicity
The invisible God, and take for guide
The faith reformed and purified.
　'T is flown — the Vision, and the sense
Of that beguiling influence,
" But oh ! thou Angel from above,
Mute Spirit of maternal love,
That stood'st before my eyes, more clear
Than ghosts are fabled to appear 110
Sent upon embassies of fear;
As thou thy presence hast to me
Vouchsafed, in radiant ministry
Descend on Francis; nor forbear
To greet him with a voice, and say; —
　If hope be a rejected stay,
' Do thou, my christian Son, beware
' Of that most lamentable snare,
' The self-reliance of despair ! ' "
　Then from within the embowered retreat
Where she had found a grateful seat 121
Perturbed she issues. She will go !
Herself will follow to the war,
And clasp her Father's knees; — ah, no !
She meets the insuperable bar,

The injunction by her Brother laid;
His parting charge — but ill obeyed —
That interdicted all debate,
All prayer for this cause or for that;
All efforts that would turn aside   130
The headstrong current of their fate:
Her duty is to stand and wait ;
In resignation to abide
The shock, AND FINALLY SECURE
O'ER PAIN AND GRIEF A TRIUMPH PURE.
— She feels it, and her pangs are checked.
But now, as silently she paced
The turf, and thought by thought was
    chased,
Came One who, with sedate respect,
Approached, and, greeting her, thus spake;
"An old man's privilege I take: 141
Dark is the time — a woeful day !
Dear daughter of affliction, say
How can I serve you ? point the way."
    "Rights have you, and may well be
    bold;
You with my Father have grown old
In friendship — strive — for his sake go —
Turn from us all the coming woe:
This would I beg; but on my mind
A passive stillness is enjoined.   150
On you, if room for mortal aid
Be left, is no restriction laid;
You not forbidden to recline
With hope upon the Will divine."
    "Hope," said the old Man, " must abide
With all of us, whate'er betide.
In Craven's Wilds is many a den,
To shelter persecuted men:
Far under ground is many a cave,
Where they might lie as in the grave,   160
Until this storm hath ceased to rave:
Or let them cross the River Tweed,
And be at once from peril freed ! "
    "Ah tempt me not ! " she faintly sighed;
" I will not counsel nor exhort,
With my condition satisfied;
But you, at least, may make report
Of what befalls; — be this your task —
This may be done; — 't is all I ask ! "
    She spake — and from the Lady's sight
The Sire, unconscious of his age,   171
Departed promptly as a Page
Bound on some errand of delight.
— The noble Francis — wise as brave,
Thought he, may want not skill to save.
With hopes in tenderness concealed,
Unarmed he followed to the field;
Him will I seek: the insurgent Powers

Are now besieging Barnard's Towers, —
" Grant that the Moon which shines this
    night   180
May guide them in a prudent flight ! "
    But quick the turns of chance and change,
And knowledge has a narrow range;
Whence idle fears, and needless pain,
And wishes blind, and efforts vain. —
The Moon may shine, but cannot be
Their guide in flight — already she
Hath witnessed their captivity.
She saw the desperate assault
Upon that hostile castle made; —   190
But dark and dismal is the vault
Where Norton and his sons are laid !
Disastrous issue ! — he had said
"This night yon faithless Towers must
    yield,
Or we for ever quit the field.
— Neville is utterly dismayed,
For promise fails of Howard's aid;
And Dacre to our call replies
That *he* is unprepared to rise.
My heart is sick; — this weary pause   200
Must needs be fatal to our cause.
The breach is open — on the wall,
This night, the Banner shall be planted ! "
— 'T was done: his Sons were with him —
    all;
They belt him round with hearts undaunted
And others follow; — Sire and Son
Leap down into the court; — " 'T is won " —
They shout aloud — but Heaven decreed
That with their joyful shout should close
The triumph of a desperate deed   210
Which struck with terror friends and foes !
The friend shrinks back — the foe recoils
From Norton and his filial band;
But they, now caught within the toils,
Against a thousand cannot stand; —
The foe from numbers courage drew,
And overpowered that gallant few.
" A rescue for the Standard ! " cried
The Father from within the walls;
But, see, the sacred Standard falls ! —   220
Confusion through the Camp spread wide:
Some fled; and some their fears detained:
But ere the Moon had sunk to rest
In her pale chambers of the west,
Of that rash levy nought remained.

CANTO FIFTH

HIGH on a point of rugged ground
Among the wastes of Rylstone Fell,

Above the loftiest ridge or mound
Where foresters or shepherds dwell,
An edifice of warlike frame
Stands single — Norton Tower its name —
It fronts all quarters, and looks round
O'er path and road, and plain and dell,
Dark moor, and gleam of pool and stream,
Upon a prospect without bound.   10
   The summit of this bold ascent —
Though bleak and bare, and seldom free
As Pendle-hill or Pennygent
From wind, or frost, or vapours wet —
Had often heard the sound of glee
When there the youthful Nortons met,
To practise games and archery:
How proud and happy they ! the crowd
Of Lookers-on how pleased and proud !
And from the scorching noon-tide sun,   20
From showers, or when the prize was won,
They to the Tower withdrew, and there
Would mirth run round, with generous
       fare;
And the stern old Lord of Rylstone-hall
Was happiest, proudest, of them all !
   But now, his Child, with anguish pale,
Upon the height walks to and fro;
'T is well that she hath heard the tale,
Received the bitterness of woe:
For she *had* hoped, had hoped and feared,
Such rights did feeble nature claim;   31
And oft her steps had hither steered,
Though not unconscious of self-blame;
For she her brother's charge revered,
His farewell words; and by the same,
Yea by her brother's very name,
Had, in her solitude, been cheered.
   Beside the lonely watch-tower stood
That grey-haired Man of gentle blood,
Who with her Father had grown old   40
In friendship; rival hunters they,
And fellow warriors in their day;
To Rylstone he the tidings brought;
Then on this height the Maid had sought,
And, gently as he could, had told
The end of that dire Tragedy,
Which it had been his lot to see.
   To him the Lady turned; " You said
That Francis lives, *he* is not dead ? "
" Your noble brother hath been spared;   50
To take his life they have not dared;
On him and on his high endeavour
The light of praise shall shine for ever !
Nor did he (such Heaven's will) in vain
His solitary course maintain;
Not vainly struggled in the might

Of duty, seeing with clear sight;
He was their comfort to the last,
Their joy till every pang was past.
   I witnessed when to York they came —
What, Lady, if their feet were tied;   61
They might deserve a good Man's blame;
But marks of infamy and shame —
These were their triumph, these their pride;
Nor wanted 'mid the pressing crowd
Deep feeling, that found utterance loud,
' Lo, Francis comes,' there were who cried,
' A Prisoner once, but now set free !
'T is well, for he the worst defied
Through force of natural piety;   70
He rose not in this quarrel; he,
For concord's sake and England's good,
Suit to his Brothers often made
With tears, and of his Father prayed —
And when he had in vain withstood
Their purpose — then did he divide,
He parted from them; but at their side
Now walks in unanimity.
Then peace to cruelty and scorn,
While to the prison they are borne,   80
Peace, peace to all indignity !'
   And so in Prison were they laid —
Oh hear me, hear me, gentle Maid,
For I am come with power to bless,
By scattering gleams, through your dis-
       tress,
Of a redeeming happiness.
Me did a reverent pity move
And privilege of ancient love;
And, in your service, making bold,
Entrance I gained to that stronghold.   90
   Your Father gave me cordial greeting;
But to his purposes, that burned
Within him, instantly returned:
He was commanding and entreating,
And said — ' We need not stop, my Son !
Thoughts press, and time is hurrying
       on ' —
And so to Francis he renewed
His words, more calmly thus pursued.
   ' Might this our enterprise have sped,
Change wide and deep the Land had seen,   100
A renovation from the dead,
A spring-tide of immortal green:
The darksome altars would have blazed
Like stars when clouds are rolled away;
Salvation to all eyes that gazed,
Once more the Rood had been upraised
To spread its arms, and stand for aye.
Then, then — had I survived to see
New life in Bolton Priory;

The voice restored, the eye of Truth   110
Re-opened that inspired my youth;
To see her in her pomp arrayed —
This Banner (for such vow I made)
Should on the consecrated breast
Of that same Temple have found rest:
I would myself have hung it high,
Fit offering of glad victory !
　　A shadow of such thought remains
To cheer this sad and pensive time;
A solemn fancy yet sustains   120
One feeble Being — bids me climb
Even to the last — one effort more
To attest my Faith, if not restore.
　　Hear then,' said he, 'while I impart,
My Son, the last wish of my heart.
The Banner strive thou to regain;
And, if the endeavour prove not vain,
Bear it — to whom if not to thee
Shall I this lonely thought consign ? —
Bear it to Bolton Priory,   130
And lay it on Saint Mary's shrine;
To wither in the sun and breeze
'Mid those decaying sanctities.
There let at least the gift be laid,
The testimony there displayed;
Bold proof that with no selfish aim,
But for lost Faith and Christ's dear name,
I helmeted a brow though white,
And took a place in all men's sight;
Yea offered up this noble Brood,   140
This fair unrivalled Brotherhood,
And turned away from thee, my Son !
And left — but be the rest unsaid,
The name untouched, the tear unshed; —
My wish is known, and I have done:
Now promise, grant this one request,
This dying prayer, and be thou blest !'
　　Then Francis answered — 'Trust thy Son,
For, with God's will, it shall be done !' --
　　The pledge obtained, the solemn word
Thus scarcely given, a noise was heard,   151
And Officers appeared in state
To lead the prisoners to their fate.
They rose, oh ! wherefore should I fear
To tell, or, Lady, you to hear ?
They rose — embraces none were given —
They stood like trees when earth and heaven
Are calm; they knew each other's worth,
And reverently the Band went forth.
They met, when they had reached the door,
One with profane and harsh intent   161
Placed there — that he might go before

And, with that rueful Banner borne
Aloft in sign of taunting scorn,
Conduct them to their punishment:
So cruel Sussex, unrestrained
By human feeling, had ordained.
The unhappy Banner Francis saw,
And, with a look of calm command
Inspiring universal awe,   170
He took it from the soldier's hand;
And all the people that stood round
Confirmed the deed in peace profound.
— High transport did the Father shed
Upon his Son — and they were led,
Led on, and yielded up their breath;
Together died, a happy death ! —
But Francis, soon as he had braved
That insult, and the Banner saved,
Athwart the unresisting tide   180
Of the spectators occupied
In admiration or dismay,
Bore instantly his Charge away."
　　These things, which thus had in the sight
And hearing passed of Him who stood
With Emily, on the Watch-tower height,
In Rylstone's woeful neighbourhood,
He told; and oftentimes with voice
Of power to comfort or rejoice;
For deepest sorrows that aspire,   190
Go high, no transport ever higher.
" Yes — God is rich in mercy," said
The old Man to the silent Maid,
" Yet, Lady ! shines, through this black night,
One star of aspect heavenly bright;
Your Brother lives — he lives — is come
Perhaps already to his home;
Then let us leave this dreary place."
She yielded, and with gentle pace,
Though without one uplifted look,   200
To Rylstone-hall her way she took.

CANTO SIXTH

WHY comes not Francis ? — From the doleful City
He fled, — and, in his flight, could hear
The death-sounds of the Minster-bell:
That sullen stroke pronounced farewell
To Marmaduke, cut off from pity !
To Ambrose that ! and then a knell
For him, the sweet half-opened Flower !
For all — all dying in one hour !
— Why comes not Francis ?　Thoughts of love
Should bear him to his Sister dear   10

With the fleet motion of a dove;
Yea, like a heavenly messenger
Of speediest wing, should he appear.
Why comes he not ? — for westward fast
Along the plain of York he past;
Reckless of what impels or leads,
Unchecked he hurries on; — nor heeds
The sorrow, through the Villages,
Spread by triumphant cruelties
Of vengeful military force,   20
And punishment without remorse.
He marked not, heard not, as he fled;
All but the suffering heart was dead
For him abandoned to blank awe,
To vacancy, and horror strong:
And the first object which he saw,
With conscious sight, as he swept along —
It was the Banner in his hand !
He felt — and made a sudden stand.
He looked about like one betrayed: 30
What hath he done ? what promise made ?
Oh weak, weak moment ! to what end
Can such a vain oblation tend,
And he the Bearer ? — Can he go
Carrying this instrument of woe,
And find, find anywhere, a right
To excuse him in his Country's sight ?
No; will not all men deem the change
A downward course, perverse and strange ?
Here is it; — but how ? when ? must she,   40
The unoffending Emily,
Again this piteous object see ?
Such conflict long did he maintain,
Nor liberty nor rest could gain:
His own life into danger brought
By this sad burden — even that thought,
Exciting self-suspicion strong,
Swayed the brave man to his wrong.
And how — unless it were the sense
Of all-disposing Providence,   50
Its will unquestionably shown —
How has the Banner clung so fast
To a palsied, and unconscious hand;
Clung to the hand to which it passed
Without impediment ? And why,
But that Heaven's purpose might be known,
Doth now no hindrance meet his eye,
No intervention, to withstand
Fulfilment of a Father's prayer
Breathed to a Son forgiven, and blest   60
When all resentments were at rest,
And life in death laid the heart bare ? —
Then, like a spectre sweeping by,
Rushed through his mind the prophecy
Of utter desolation made

To Emily in the yew-tree shade:
He sighed, submitting will and power
To the stern embrace of that grasping hour.
" No choice is left, the deed is mine —
Dead are they, dead ! — and I will go,   70
And, for their sakes, come weal or woe,
Will lay the Relic on the shrine."
So forward with a steady will
He went, and traversed plain and hill;
And up the vale of Wharf his way
Pursued; — and, at the dawn of day,
Attained a summit whence his eyes
Could see the Tower of Bolton rise.
There Francis for a moment's space
Made halt — but hark ! a noise behind   80
Of horsemen at an eager pace !
He heard, and with misgiving mind.
— 'T is Sir George Bowes who leads the
        Band:
They come, by cruel Sussex sent;
Who, when the Nortons from the hand
Of death had drunk their punishment,
Bethought him, angry and ashamed,
How Francis, with the Banner claimed
As his own charge, had disappeared,
By all the standers-by revered.   90
His whole bold carriage (which had quelled
Thus far the Opposer, and repelled
All censure, enterprise so bright
That even bad men had vainly striven
Against that overcoming light)
Was then reviewed, and prompt word given
That to what place so ever fled
He should be seized, alive or dead.
The troop of horse have gained the height
Where Francis stood in open sight.   100
They hem him round — " Behold the proof,"
They cried, " the Ensign in his hand !
He did not arm, he walked aloof !
For why ? — to save his Father's land; —
Worst Traitor of them all is he,
A Traitor dark and cowardly ! "
" I am no Traitor," Francis said,
" Though this unhappy freight I bear;
And must not part with. But beware; —
Err not, by hasty zeal misled,   110
Nor do a suffering Spirit wrong,
Whose self-reproaches are too strong ! "
At this he from the beaten road
Retreated towards a brake of thorn,
That like a place of vantage showed;
And there stood bravely, though forlorn.
In self-defence with warlike brow
He stood, — nor weaponless was now;
He from a Soldier's hand had snatched

A spear, — and, so protected, watched   120
The Assailants, turning round and round;
But from behind with treacherous wound
A Spearman brought him to the ground.
The guardian lance, as Francis fell,
Dropped from him; but his other hand
The Banner clenched; till, from out the
    Band,
One, the most eager for the prize,
Rushed in; and — while, O grief to tell!
A glimmering sense still left, with eyes
Unclosed the noble Francis lay —   130
Seized it, as hunters seize their prey;
But not before the warm life-blood
Had tinged more deeply, as it flowed,
The wounds the broidered Banner showed,
Thy fatal work, O Maiden, innocent as good!

Proudly the Horsemen bore away
The Standard; and where Francis lay
There was he left alone, unwept,
And for two days unnoticed slept.
For at that time bewildering fear   140
Possessed the country, far and near;
But, on the third day, passing by
One of the Norton Tenantry
Espied the uncovered Corse; the Man
Shrunk as he recognised the face,
And to the nearest homesteads ran
And called the people to the place.
— How desolate is Rylstone-hall!
This was the instant thought of all;
And if the lonely Lady there   150
Should be; to her they cannot bear
This weight of anguish and despair.
So, when upon sad thoughts had prest
Thoughts sadder still, they deemed it best
That, if the Priest should yield assent
And no one hinder their intent,
Then, they, for Christian pity's sake,
In holy ground a grave would make;
And straightway buried he should be
In the Churchyard of the Priory.   160

Apart, some little space, was made
The grave where Francis must be laid
In no confusion or neglect
This did they, — but in pure respect
That he was born of gentle blood;
And that there was no neighbourhood
Of kindred for him in that ground:
So to the Churchyard they are bound,
Bearing the body on a bier;
And psalms they sing — a holy sound   170
That hill and vale with sadness hear.

But Emily hath raised her head,
And is again disquieted;

She must behold! — so many gone,
Where is the solitary One?
And forth from Rylstone-hall stepped she, —
To seek her Brother forth she went,
And tremblingly her course she bent
Toward Bolton's ruined Priory.
She comes, and in the vale hath heard   180
The funeral dirge; — she sees the knot
Of people, sees them in one spot —
And darting like a wounded bird
She reached the grave, and with her breast
Upon the ground received the rest, —
The consummation, the whole ruth
And sorrow of this final truth!

CANTO SEVENTH

> "Powers there are
> That touch each other to the quick — in modes
> Which the gross world no sense hath to perceive,
> No soul to dream of."

THOU Spirit, whose angelic hand
Was to the harp a strong command,
Called the submissive strings to wake
In glory for this Maiden's sake,
Say, Spirit! whither hath she fled
To hide her poor afflicted head?
What mighty forest in its gloom
Enfolds her? — is a rifted tomb
Within the wilderness her seat?
Some island which the wild waves beat —   10
Is that the Sufferer's last retreat?
Or some aspiring rock, that shrouds
Its perilous front in mists and clouds?
High-climbing rock, low sunless dale,
Sea, desert, what do these avail?
Oh take her anguish and her fears
Into a deep recess of years!

'T is done; — despoil and desolation
O'er Rylstone's fair domain have blown;
Pools, terraces, and walks are sown   20
With weeds; the bowers are overthrown,
Or have given way to slow mutation,
While, in their ancient habitation
The Norton name hath been unknown.
The lordly Mansion of its pride
Is stripped; the ravage hath spread wide
Through park and field, a perishing
That mocks the gladness of the Spring!
And, with this silent gloom agreeing,
Appears a joyless human Being,   30
Of aspect such as if the waste
Were under her dominion placed.
Upon a primrose bank, her throne
Of quietness, she sits alone;

Among the ruins of a wood,
Erewhile a covert bright and green,
And where full many a brave tree stood,
That used to spread its boughs, and ring
With the sweet bird's carolling.
Behold her, like a virgin Queen,   40
Neglecting in imperial state
These outward images of fate,
And carrying inward a serene
And perfect sway, through many a thought
Of chance and change, that hath been
        brought
To the subjection of a holy,
Though stern and rigorous, melancholy !
The like authority, with grace
Of awfulness, is in her face, —
There hath she fixed it; yet it seems   50
To o'ershadow by no native right
That face, which cannot lose the gleams,
Lose utterly the tender gleams,
Of gentleness and meek delight,
And loving-kindness ever bright:
Such is her sovereign mien: — her dress
(A vest with woollen cincture tied,
A hood of mountain-wool undyed)
Is homely, — fashioned to express
A wandering Pilgrim's humbleness.   60
    And she *hath* wandered, long and far,
Beneath the light of sun and star;
Hath roamed in trouble and in grief,
Driven forward like a withered leaf,
Yea like a ship at random blown
To distant places and unknown.
But now she dares to seek a haven
Among her native wilds of Craven;
Hath seen again her Father's roof,
And put her fortitude to proof;   70
The mighty sorrow hath been borne,
And she is thoroughly forlorn:
Her soul doth in itself stand fast,
Sustained by memory of the past
And strength of Reason; held above
The infirmities of mortal love;
Undaunted, lofty, calm, and stable,
And awfully impenetrable.
    And so — beneath a mouldered tree,
A self-surviving leafless oak   80
By unregarded age from stroke
Of ravage saved — sate Emily.
There did she rest, with head reclined,
Herself most like a stately flower,
(Such have I seen) whom chance of birth
Hath separated from its kind,
To live and die in a shady bower,
Single on the gladsome earth.

When, with a noise like distant thunder,
A troop of deer came sweeping by;   90
And, suddenly, behold a wonder !
For One, among those rushing deer,
A single One, in mid career
Hath stopped, and fixed her large full
        eye
Upon the Lady Emily;
A Doe most beautiful, clear-white,
A radiant creature, silver-bright !
    Thus checked, a little while it stayed;
A little thoughtful pause it made;
And then advanced with stealth-like pace,
Drew softly near her, and more near —   101
Looked round — but saw no cause for
        fear;
So to her feet the Creature came,
And laid its head upon her knee,
And looked into the Lady's face,
A look of pure benignity,
And fond unclouded memory.
It is, thought Emily, the same,
The very Doe of other years ! —
The pleading look the Lady viewed,   110
And, by her gushing thoughts subdued,
She melted into tears —
A flood of tears that flowed apace,
Upon the happy Creature's face.
    Oh, moment ever blest ! O Pair
Beloved of Heaven, Heaven's chosen care,
This was for you a precious greeting;
And may it prove a fruitful meeting !
Joined are they, and the sylvan Doe
Can she depart ? can she forego   120
The Lady, once her playful peer,
And now her sainted Mistress dear ?
And will not Emily receive
This lovely chronicler of things
Long past, delights and sorrowings ?
Lone Sufferer ! will not she believe
The promise in that speaking face;
And welcome, as a gift of grace,
The saddest thought the Creature brings ?
    That day, the first of a re-union   130
Which was to teem with high communion,
That day of balmy April weather,
They tarried in the wood together.
And when, ere fall of evening dew,
She from her sylvan haunt withdrew,
The White Doe tracked with faithful pace
The Lady to her dwelling-place;
That nook where, on paternal ground,
A habitation she had found,
The Master of whose humble board   140
Once owned her Father for his Lord;

A hut, by tufted trees defended,
Where Rylstone brook with Wharf is
  blended.
  When Emily by morning light
Went forth, the Doe stood there in sight.
She shrunk: — with one frail shock of pain
Received and followed by a prayer,
She saw the Creature once again;
Shun will she not, she feels, will bear; —
But, wheresoever she looked round,   150
All now was trouble-haunted ground;
And therefore now she deems it good
Once more this restless neighbourhood
To leave. — Unwooed, yet unforbidden,
The White Doe followed up the vale,
Up to another cottage, hidden
In the deep fork of Amerdale;
And there may Emily restore
Herself, in spots unseen before.
— Why tell of mossy rock, or tree,   160
By lurking Dernbrook's pathless side,
Haunts of a strengthening amity
That calmed her, cheered, and fortified ?
For she hath ventured now to read
Of time, and place, and thought, and
  deed —
Endless history that lies
In her silent Follower's eyes;
Who with a power like human reason
Discerns the favourable season,
Skilled to approach or to retire, —   170
From looks conceiving her desire;
From look, deportment, voice, or mien,
That vary to the heart within.
If she too passionately wreathed
Her arms, or over-deeply breathed,
Walked quick or slowly, every mood
In its degree was understood;
Then well may their accord be true,
And kindliest intercourse ensue.
— Oh ! surely 't was a gentle rousing   180
When she by sudden glimpse espied
The White Doe on the mountain browsing,
Or in the meadow wandered wide !
How pleased, when down the Straggler sank
Beside her, on some sunny bank !
How soothed, when in thick bower enclosed,
They, like a nested pair, reposed !
Fair Vision ! when it crossed the Maid
Within some rocky cavern laid,
The dark cave's portal gliding by,   190
White as whitest cloud on high
Floating through the azure sky.
— What now is left for pain or fear ?
That Presence, dearer and more dear,

While they, side by side, were straying,
And the shepherd's pipe was playing,
Did now a very gladness yield
At morning to the dewy field,
And with a deeper peace endued
The hour of moonlight solitude.   200
  With her Companion, in such frame
Of mind, to Rylstone back she came;
And, ranging through the wasted groves,
Received the memory of old loves,
Undisturbed and undistrest,
Into a soul which now was blest
With a soft spring-day of holy,
Mild, and grateful, melancholy:
Not sunless gloom or unenlightened,
But by tender fancies brightened.   210
  When the bells of Rylstone played
Their sabbath music — " God us ayde ! "
That was the sound they seemed to speak;
Inscriptive legend which I ween
May on these holy bells be seen,
That legend and her Grandsire 's name ;
And oftentimes the Lady meek
Had in her childhood read the same;
Words which she slighted at that day;
But now, when such sad change was
  wrought,   220
And of that lonely name she thought —
The bells of Rylstone seemed to say,
While she sate listening in the shade,
With vocal music, " God us ayde ; "
And all the hills were glad to bear
Their part in this effectual prayer.
  Nor lacked she Reason's firmest power;
But with the White Doe at her side
Up would she climb to Norton Tower,
And thence look round her far and wide,   230
Her fate there measuring; — all is stilled, —
The weak One hath subdued her heart;
Behold the prophecy fulfilled,
Fulfilled, and she sustains her part !
But here her Brother's words have failed;
Here hath a milder doom prevailed;
That she, of him and all bereft,
Hath yet this faithful Partner left;
This one Associate that disproves
His words, remains for her, and loves.   240
If tears are shed, they do not fall
For loss of him — for one, or all;
Yet, sometimes, sometimes doth she weep
Moved gently in her soul's soft sleep;
A few tears down her cheek descend
For this her last and living Friend.
  Bless, tender Hearts, their mutual lot,
And bless for both this savage spot;

Which Emily doth sacred hold
For reasons dear and manifold —   250
Here hath she, here before her sight,
Close to the summit of this height,
The grassy rock-encircled Pound
In which the Creature first was found.
So beautiful the timid Thrall
(A spotless Youngling white as foam)
Her youngest Brother brought it home;
The youngest, then a lusty boy,
Bore it, or led, to Rylstone-hall
With heart brimful of pride and joy !   260
    But most to Bolton's sacred Pile,
On favouring nights, she loved to go;
There ranged through cloister, court, and
    aisle,
Attended by the soft-paced Doe;
Nor feared she in the still moonshine
To look upon Saint Mary's shrine;
Nor on the lonely turf that showed
Where Francis slept in his last abode.
For that she came; there oft she sate
Forlorn, but not disconsolate: 270
And, when she from the abyss returned
Of thought, she neither shrunk nor
    mourned;
Was happy that she lived to greet
Her mute Companion as it lay
In love and pity at her feet;
How happy in its turn to meet
The recognition ! the mild glance
Beamed from that gracious countenance;
Communication, like the ray
Of a new morning, to the nature   280
And prospects of the inferior Creature !
    A mortal Song we sing, by dower
Encouraged of celestial power;
Power which the viewless Spirit shed
By whom we were first visited;
Whose voice we heard, whose hand and
    wings
Swept like a breeze the conscious strings,
When, left in solitude, erewhile
We stood before this ruined Pile,
And, quitting unsubstantial dreams,   290
Sang in this Presence kindred themes;
Distress and desolation spread
Through human hearts, and pleasure
    dead, —
Dead — but to live again on earth,
A second and yet nobler birth;
Dire overthrow, and yet how high
The re-ascent in sanctity !
From fair to fairer; day by day
A more divine and loftier way !

Even such this blessèd Pilgrim trod,   300
By sorrow lifted towards her God;
Uplifted to the purest sky
Of undisturbed mortality.
Her own thoughts loved she; and could
    bend
A dear look to her lowly Friend;
There stopped; her thirst was satisfied
With what this innocent spring supplied:
Her sanction inwardly she bore,
And stood apart from human cares:
But to the world returned no more,   310
Although with no unwilling mind
Help did she give at need, and joined
The Wharfdale peasants in their prayers.
At length, thus faintly, faintly tied
To earth, she was set free, and died.
Thy soul, exalted Emily,
Maid of the blasted family,
Rose to the God from whom it came !
— In Rylstone Church her mortal frame
Was buried by her Mother's side.   320
    Most glorious sunset ! and a ray
Survives — the twilight of this day —
In that fair Creature whom the fields
Support, and whom the forest shields;
Who, having filled a holy place,
Partakes, in her degree, Heaven's grace;
And bears a memory and a mind
Raised far above the law of kind;
Haunting the spots with lonely cheer
Which her dear Mistress once held dear:
Loves most what Emily loved most —   331
The enclosure of this churchyard ground;
Here wanders like a gliding ghost,
And every sabbath here is found;
Comes with the people when the bells
Are heard among the moorland dells,
Finds entrance through yon arch, where
    way
Lies open on the sabbath-day;
Here walks amid the mournful waste
Of prostrate altars, shrines defaced,   340
And floors encumbered with rich show
Of fret-work imagery laid low;
Paces softly, or makes halt,
By fractured cell, or tomb, or vault;
By plate of monumental brass
Dim-gleaming among weeds and grass,
And sculptured Forms of Warriors brave:
But chiefly by that single grave,
That one sequestered hillock green,
The pensive visitant is seen.   350
There doth the gentle Creature lie
With those adversities unmoved:

Calm spectacle, by earth and sky
In their benignity approved !
And aye, methinks, this hoary Pile,
Subdued by outrage and decay,

Looks down upon her with a smile,
A gracious smile, that seems to say —
"Thou, thou art not a Child of Time,
But Daughter of the Eternal Prime !" 360

THE FORCE OF PRAYER

OR, THE FOUNDING OF BOLTON PRIORY

A TRADITION

1807. 1815

An Appendage to the "White Doe." My friend, Mr. Rogers, has also written on the subject. The story is preserved in Dr. Whitaker's *History of Craven* — a topographical writer of first-rate merit in all that concerns the past; but such was his aversion from the modern spirit, as shown in the spread of manufactories in those districts of which he treats, that his readers are left entirely ignorant both of the progress of these arts and their real bearing upon the comfort, virtues, and happiness of the inhabitants. While wandering on foot through the fertile valleys and over the moorlands of the Apennine that divides Yorkshire from Lancashire, I used to be delighted with observing the number of substantial cottages that had sprung up on every side, each having its little plot of fertile ground won from the surrounding waste. A bright and warm fire, if needed, was always to be found in these dwellings. The father was at his loom ; the children looked healthy and happy. Is it not to be feared that the increase of mechanic power has done away with many of these blessings, and substituted many evils ? Alas! if these evils grow, how are they to be checked, and where is the remedy to be found ? Political economy will not supply it; that is certain, we must look to something deeper, and purer, and higher.

" What is good for a bootless bene ? "
With these dark words begins my Tale;
And their meaning is, whence can comfort
   spring
When Prayer is of no avail ?

" What is good for a bootless bene ? "
The Falconer to the Lady said;
And she made answer "ENDLESS SORROW!"
For she knew that her Son was dead.

She knew it by the Falconer's words,
And from the look of the Falconer's eye ; 10

And from the love which was in her soul
For her youthful Romilly.

— Young Romilly through Barden woods
Is ranging high and low;
And holds a greyhound in a leash,
To let slip upon buck or doe.

The pair have reached that fearful chasm,
How tempting to bestride !
For lordly Wharf is there pent in
With rocks on either side. 20

This striding-place is called THE STRID,
A name which it took of yore:
A thousand years hath it borne that name,
And shall a thousand more.

And hither is young Romilly come,
And what may now forbid
That he, perhaps for the hundredth time,
Shall bound across THE STRID ?

He sprang in glee, — for what cared he
That the river was strong, and the rocks
   were steep ? — 30
But the greyhound in the leash hung back,
And checked him in his leap.

The Boy is in the arms of Wharf,
And strangled by a merciless force;
For never more was young Romilly seen
Till he rose a lifeless corse.

Now there is stillness in the vale,
And long, unspeaking, sorrow:
Wharf shall be to pitying hearts
A name more sad than Yarrow. 40

If for a lover the Lady wept,
A solace she might borrow
From death, and from the passion of
   death ; —
Old Wharf might heal her sorrow.

She weeps not for the wedding-day
Which was to be to-morrow :
Her hope was a further-looking hope,
And hers is a mother's sorrow.

He was a tree that stood alone,
And proudly did its branches wave; 50
And the root of this delightful tree
Was in her husband's grave !

Long, long in darkness did she sit,
And her first words were, " Let there be
In Bolton, on the field of Wharf,
A stately Priory ! "

The stately Priory was reared;
And Wharf, as he moved along,
To matins joined a mournful voice,
Nor failed at evensong. 60

And the Lady prayed in heaviness
That looked not for relief !
But slowly did her succour come,
And a patience to her grief.

Oh ! there is never sorrow of heart
That shall lack a timely end,
If but to God we turn, and ask
Of Him to be our friend !

COMPOSED WHILE THE AUTHOR WAS ENGAGED IN WRITING A TRACT OCCASIONED BY THE CONVENTION OF CINTRA

1808. 1815

NOT 'mid the world's vain objects that enslave
The free-born Soul — that World whose vaunted skill
In selfish interest perverts the will,
Whose factions lead astray the wise and brave —
Not there; but in dark wood and rocky cave,
And hollow vale which foaming torrents fill
With omnipresent murmur as they rave
Down their steep beds, that never shall be still:
Here, mighty Nature ! in this school sublime
I weigh the hopes and fears of suffering Spain;
For her consult the auguries of time,
And through the human heart explore my way;
And look and listen — gathering, whence I may,
Triumph, and thoughts no bondage can restrain.

COMPOSED AT THE SAME TIME AND ON THE SAME OCCASION

1808. 1815

I DROPPED my pen; and listened to the Wind
That sang of trees uptorn and vessels tost —
A midnight harmony; and wholly lost
To the general sense of men by chains confined
Of business, care, or pleasure; or resigned
To timely sleep. Thought I, the impassioned strain,
Which, without aid of numbers, I sustain,
Like acceptation from the World will find.
Yet some with apprehensive ear shall drink
A dirge devoutly breathed o'er sorrows past;
And to the attendant promise will give heed —
The prophecy, — like that of this wild blast,
Which, while it makes the heart with sadness shrink,
Tells also of bright calms that shall succeed.

GEORGE AND SARAH GREEN

1808. 1839

WHO weeps for strangers ? Many wept
For George and Sarah Green;
Wept for that pair's unhappy fate,
Whose grave may here be seen.

By night, upon these stormy fells,
Did wife and husband roam;
Six little ones at home had left,
And could not find that home.

For *any* dwelling-place of man
As vainly did they seek. 10
He perish'd; and a voice was heard —
The widow's lonely shriek.

Not many steps, and she was left
A body without life —
A few short steps were the chain that bound
The husband to the wife.

Now do those sternly-featured hills
Look gently on this grave;
And quiet *now* are the depths of air,
As a sea without a wave. 20

But deeper lies the heart of peace
　　In quiet more profound;
The heart of quietness is here
　　Within this churchyard bound.

And from all agony of mind
　　It keeps them safe, and far
From fear and grief, and from all need
　　Of sun or guiding star.

O darkness of the grave! how deep,
　　After that living night —　　　　　　30
That last and dreary living one
　　Of sorrow and affright!

O sacred marriage-bed of death,
　　That keeps them side by side
In bond of peace, in bond of love,
　　That may not be untied!

HOFER

1809. 1809

OF mortal parents is the Hero born
By whom the undaunted Tyrolese are led?
Or is it Tell's great Spirit, from the dead
Returned to animate an age forlorn?
He comes like Phœbus through the gates
　　of morn
When dreary darkness is discomfited,
Yet mark his modest state! upon his head,
That simple crest, a heron's plume, is worn.
O Liberty! they stagger at the shock
From van to rear — and with one mind
　　would flee,
But half their host is buried: — rock on rock
Descends: — beneath this godlike Warrior,
　　see!
Hills, torrents, woods, embodied to bemock
The Tyrant, and confound his cruelty.

"ADVANCE — COME FORTH FROM THY TYROLEAN GROUND"

1809. 1809

ADVANCE — come forth from thy Tyrolean
　　ground,
Dear Liberty! stern Nymph of soul un-
　　tamed;
Sweet Nymph, O rightly of the mountains
　　named!
Through the long chain of Alps from mound
　　to mound

And o'er the eternal snows, like Echo,
　　bound;
Like Echo, when the hunter train at dawn
Have roused her from her sleep: and for-
　　est-lawn,
Cliffs, woods and caves, her viewless steps
　　resound
And babble of her pastime! — On, dread
　　Power!
With such invisible motion speed thy flight,
Through hanging clouds, from craggy height
　　to height,
Through the green vales and through the
　　herdsman's bower —
That all the Alps may gladden in thy might,
Here, there, and in all places at one hour.

FEELINGS OF THE TYROLESE

1809. 1809

THE Land we from our fathers had in trust,
And to our children will transmit, or die:
This is our maxim, this our piety;
And God and Nature say that it is just.
That which we *would* perform in arms — we
　　must!
We read the dictate in the infant's eye;
In the wife's smile; and in the placid sky;
And, at our feet, amid the silent dust
Of them that were before us. — Sing aloud
Old songs, the precious music of the heart!
Give, herds and flocks, your voices to the
　　wind!
While we go forth, a self-devoted crowd,
With weapons grasped in fearless hands, to
　　assert
Our virtue, and to vindicate mankind.

"ALAS! WHAT BOOTS THE LONG LABORIOUS QUEST"

1809. 1809

ALAS! what boots the long laborious quest
Of moral prudence, sought through good
　　and ill;
Or pains abstruse — to elevate the will,
And lead us on to that transcendent rest
Where every passion shall the sway attest
Of Reason, seated on her sovereign hill;
What is it but a vain and curious skill,
If sapient Germany must lie deprest,
Beneath the brutal sword? — Her haughty
　　Schools

Shall blush; and may not we with sorrow
say —
A few strong instincts and a few plain
rules,
Among the herdsmen of the Alps, have
wrought
More for mankind at this unhappy day
Than all the pride of intellect and thought ?

"AND IS IT AMONG RUDE UNTUTORED DALES"

1809. 1809

AND is it among rude untutored Dales,
There, and there only, that the heart is
true ?
And, rising to repel or to subdue,
Is it by rocks and woods that man prevails ?
Ah no ! though Nature's dread protection
fails,
There is a bulwark in the soul. This knew
Iberian Burghers when the sword they drew
In Zaragoza, naked to the gales
Of fiercely-breathing war. The truth was
felt
By Palafox, and many a brave compeer,
Like him of noble birth and noble mind;
By ladies, meek-eyed women without fear;
And wanderers of the street, to whom is
dealt
The bread which without industry they
find.

"O'ER THE WIDE EARTH, ON MOUNTAIN AND ON PLAIN"

1809. 1809

O'ER the wide earth, on mountain and on
plain,
Dwells in the affections and the soul of man
A Godhead, like the universal PAN;
But more exalted, with a brighter train:
And shall his bounty be dispensed in vain,
Showered equally on city and on field,
And neither hope nor steadfast promise
yield
In these usurping times of fear and pain ?
Such doom awaits us. Nay, forbid it
Heaven !
We know the arduous strife, the eternal
laws
To which the triumph of all good is given,
High sacrifice, and labour without pause,

Even to the death: — else wherefore should
the eye
Of man converse with immortality ?

ON THE FINAL SUBMISSION OF THE TYROLESE

1809. 1809

IT was a *moral* end for which they fought;
Else how, when mighty Thrones were put to
shame,
Could they, poor Shepherds, have preserved
an aim,
A resolution, or enlivening thought ?
Nor hath that moral good been *vainly*
sought;
For in their magnanimity and fame
Powers have they left, an impulse, and a
claim
Which neither can be overturned nor
bought.
Sleep, Warriors, sleep ! among your hills
repose !
We know that ye, beneath the stern control
Of awful prudence, keep the unvanquished
soul:
And when, impatient of her guilt and woes,
Europe breaks forth; then, Shepherds ! shall
ye rise
For perfect triumph o'er your Enemies.

"HAIL, ZARAGOZA ! IF WITH UNWET EYE"

1809. 1815

HAIL, Zaragoza ! If with unwet eye
We can approach, thy sorrow to behold,
Yet is the heart not pitiless nor cold;
Such spectacle demands not tear or sigh.
These desolate remains are trophies high
Of more than martial courage in the breast
Of peaceful civic virtue: they attest
Thy matchless worth to all posterity.
Blood flowed before thy sight without
remorse;
Disease consumed thy vitals; War up-
heaved
The ground beneath thee with volcanic
force:
Dread trials ! yet encountered and sus-
tained
Till not a wreck of help or hope remained,
And law was from necessity received.

"SAY, WHAT IS HONOUR?—'T IS THE FINEST SENSE"

1809. 1815

SAY, what is Honour?—'T is the finest
sense
Of *justice* which the human mind can
frame,
Intent each lurking frailty to disclaim,
And guard the way of life from all offence
Suffered or done. When lawless violence
Invades a Realm, so pressed that in the
scale
Of perilous war her weightiest armies fail,
Honour is hopeful elevation,—whence
Glory, and triumph. Yet with politic skill
Endangered States may yield to terms
unjust;
Stoop their proud heads, but not unto the
dust—
A Foe's most favourite purpose to fulfil:
Happy occasions oft by self-mistrust
Are forfeited; but infamy doth kill.

"THE MARTIAL COURAGE OF A DAY IS VAIN"

1810. 1815

THE martial courage of a day is vain,
An empty noise of death the battle's roar,
If vital hope be wanting to restore,
Or fortitude be wanting to sustain,
Armies or kingdoms. We have heard a
strain
Of triumph, how the labouring Danube bore
A weight of hostile corses; drenched with
gore
Were the wide fields, the hamlets heaped
with slain.
Yet see (the mighty tumult overpast)
Austria a daughter of her Throne hath sold!
And her Tyrolean Champion we behold
Murdered, like one ashore by shipwreck cast,
Murdered without relief. Oh! blind as bold,
To think that such assurance can stand fast!

"BRAVE SCHILL! BY DEATH DELIVERED"

1809. 1815

BRAVE Schill! by death delivered, take
thy flight
From Prussia's timid region. Go, and rest

With heroes, 'mid the islands of the Blest,
Or in the fields of empyrean light.
A meteor wert thou crossing a dark night:
Yet shall thy name, conspicuous and sub-
lime,
Stand in the spacious firmament of time,
Fixed as a star: such glory is thy right.
Alas! it may not be: for earthly fame
Is Fortune's frail dependant; yet there lives
A Judge, who, as man claims by merit,
gives;
To whose all-pondering mind a noble aim,
Faithfully kept, is as a noble deed;
In whose pure sight all virtue doth suc-
ceed.

"CALL NOT THE ROYAL SWEDE UNFORTUNATE"

1809. 1815

CALL not the royal Swede unfortunate,
Who never did to Fortune bend the knee;
Who slighted fear; rejected steadfastly
Temptation; and whose kingly name and
state
Have "perished by his choice, and not his
fate!"
Hence lives He, to his inner self endeared;
And hence, wherever virtue is revered,
He sits a more exalted Potentate,
Throned in the hearts of men. Should
Heaven ordain
That this great Servant of a righteous cause
Must still have sad or vexing thoughts to
endure,
Yet may a sympathising spirit pause,
Admonished by these truths, and quench
all pain
In thankful joy and gratulation pure.

"LOOK NOW ON THAT ADVEN-TURER WHO HATH PAID"

1809. 1815

LOOK now on that Adventurer who hath
paid
His vows to Fortune; who, in cruel slight
Of virtuous hope, of liberty, and right,
Hath followed wheresoe'er a way was made
By the blind Goddess,—ruthless, undis-
mayed;
And so hath gained at length a prosperous
height,

Round which the elements of worldly might
Beneath his haughty feet, like clouds, are laid.
O joyless power that stands by lawless force !
Curses are *his* dire portion, scorn, and hate,
Internal darkness and unquiet breath;
And, if old judgments keep their sacred course,
Him from that height shall Heaven precipitate
By violent and ignominious death.

"IS THERE A POWER THAT CAN SUSTAIN AND CHEER"

1809. 1815

Is there a power that can sustain and cheer
The captive chieftain, by a tyrant's doom,
Forced to descend into his destined tomb —
A dungeon dark ! where he must waste the year,
And lie cut off from all his heart holds dear;
What time his injured country is a stage
Whereon deliberate Valour and the rage
Of righteous Vengeance side by side appear,
Filling from morn to night the heroic scene
With deeds of hope and everlasting praise: —
Say can he think of this with mind serene
And silent fetters ? Yes, if visions bright
Shine on his soul, reflected from the days
When he himself was tried in open light.

"AH ! WHERE IS PALAFOX? NOR TONGUE NOR PEN"

1809. 1815

Ah ! where is Palafox ? Nor tongue nor pen
Reports of him, his dwelling or his grave !
Does yet the unheard-of vessel ride the wave ?
Or is she swallowed up, remote from ken
Of pitying human nature ? Once again
Methinks that we shall hail thee, Champion brave,
Redeemed to baffle that imperial Slave,
And through all Europe cheer desponding men

With new-born hope. Unbounded is the might
Of martyrdom, and fortitude, and right.
Hark, how thy Country triumphs ! — Smilingly
The Eternal looks upon her sword that gleams,
Like his own lightning, over mountains high,
On rampart, and the banks of all her streams.

"IN DUE OBSERVANCE OF AN ANCIENT RITE"

1810. 1815

In due observance of an ancient rite,
The rude Biscayans, when their children lie
Dead in the sinless time of infancy,
Attire the peaceful corse in vestments white;
And, in like sign of cloudless triumph bright,
They bind the unoffending creature's brows
With happy garlands of the pure white rose:
Then do a festal company unite
In choral song; and, while the uplifted cross
Of Jesus goes before, the child is borne
Uncovered to his grave: 't is closed, — her loss
The Mother *then* mourns, as she needs must mourn;
But soon, through Christian faith, is grief subdued;
And joy returns, to brighten fortitude.

FEELINGS OF A NOBLE BISCAYAN AT ONE OF THOSE FUNERALS

1810. 1815

Yet, yet, Biscayans ! we must meet our Foes
With firmer soul, yet labour to regain
Our ancient freedom; else 't were worse than vain
To gather round the bier these festal shows.
A garland fashioned of the pure white rose
Becomes not one whose father is a slave:
Oh, bear the infant covered to his grave !
These venerable mountains now enclose

A people sunk in apathy and fear.
If this endure, farewell, for us, all good !
The awful light of heavenly innocence
Will fail to illuminate the infant's bier;
And guilt and shame, from which is no
defence,
Descend on all that issues from our blood.

ON A CELEBRATED EVENT IN ANCIENT HISTORY

1811. 1815

A ROMAN Master stands on Grecian
ground,
And to the people at the Isthmian Games
Assembled, He, by a herald's voice, pro-
claims
THE LIBERTY OF GREECE: — the words
rebound
Until all voices in one voice are drowned;
Glad acclamation by which air was rent !
And birds, high-flying in the element,
Dropped to the earth, astonished at the
sound !
Yet were the thoughtful grieved; and still
that voice
Haunts, with sad echoes, musing Fancy's
ear:
Ah ! that a *Conqueror's* words should be so
dear:
Ah ! that a *boon* could shed such rapturous
joys !
A gift of that which is not to be given
By all the blended powers of Earth and
Heaven.

UPON THE SAME EVENT

1811. 1815

WHEN, far and wide, swift as the beams
of morn
The tidings past of servitude repealed,
And of that joy which shook the Isthmian
Field,
The rough Ætolians smiled with bitter
scorn.
" 'T is known," cried they, " that he, who
would adorn
His envied temples with the Isthmian
crown,
Must either win, through effort of his
own,
The prize, or be content to see it worn

By more deserving brows. — Yet so ye
prop,
Sons of the brave who fought at Marathon,
Your feeble spirits ! Greece her head hath
bowed,
As if the wreath of liberty thereon
Would fix itself as smoothly as a cloud,
Which, at Jove's will, descends on Pelion's
top."

THE OAK OF GUERNICA

1810. 1815

The ancient oak of Guernica, says Laborde
in his account of Biscay, is a most venerable
natural monument. Ferdinand and Isabella,
in the year 1476, after hearing mass in the
church of Santa Maria de la Antigua, repaired
to this tree, under which they swore to the
Biscayans to maintain their *fueros* (privileges).
What other interest belongs to it in the minds
of this people will appear from the following

SUPPOSED ADDRESS TO THE SAME

OAK of Guernica ! Tree of holier power
Than that which in Dodona did enshrine
(So faith too fondly deemed) a voice divine
Heard from the depths of its aërial
bower —
How canst thou flourish at this blighting
hour ?
What hope, what joy can sunshine bring to
thee,
Or the soft breezes from the Atlantic sea,
The dews of morn, or April's tender
shower ?
Stroke merciful and welcome would that be
Which should extend thy branches on the
ground,
If never more within their shady round
Those lofty-minded Lawgivers shall meet,
Peasant and lord, in their appointed seat,
Guardians of Biscay's ancient liberty.

INDIGNATION OF A HIGH-MINDED SPANIARD

1810. 1815

WE can endure that He should waste our
lands,
Despoil our temples, and by sword and
flame
Return us to the dust from which we came;

Such food a Tyrant's appetite demands:
And we can brook the thought that by his
hands
Spain may be overpowered, and he possess,
For his delight, a solemn wilderness
Where all the brave lie dead. But, when
of bands
Which he will break for us he dares to
speak,
Of benefits, and of a future day
When our enlightened minds shall bless his
sway;
Then, the strained heart of fortitude proves
weak;
Our groans, our blushes, our pale cheeks
declare
That he has power to inflict what we lack
strength to bear.

"AVAUNT ALL SPECIOUS PLIANCY OF MIND"

1809. 1815

AVAUNT all specious pliancy of mind
In men of low degree, all smooth pretence !
I better like a blunt indifference,
And self-respecting slowness, disinclined
To win me at first sight: and be there
joined
Patience and temperance with this high
reserve,
Honour that knows the path and will not
swerve,
Affections, which, if put to proof, are kind;
And piety towards God. Such men of old
Were England's native growth; and,
throughout Spain
(Thanks to high God) forests of such re-
main:
Then for that Country let our hopes be bold;
For matched with these shall policy prove
vain,
Her arts, her strength, her iron, and her
gold.

"O'ERWEENING STATESMEN HAVE FULL LONG RELIED"

1810. 1815

O'ERWEENING Statesmen have full long
relied
On fleets and armies, and external wealth:
But from *within* proceeds a Nation's health;

Which shall not fail, though poor men
cleave with pride
To the paternal floor; or turn aside,
In the thronged city, from the walks of
gain,
As being all unworthy to detain
A Soul by contemplation sanctified.
There are who cannot languish in this strife,
Spaniards of every rank, by whom the good
Of such high course was felt and under-
stood;
Who to their Country's cause have bound a
life
Erewhile, by solemn consecration, given
To labour and to prayer, to nature, and to
heaven.

THE FRENCH AND THE SPANISH GUERILLAS

1809. 1815

HUNGER, and sultry heat, and nipping blast
From bleak hill-top, and length of march
by night
Through heavy swamp, or over snow-clad
height —
These hardships ill-sustained, these dangers
past,
The roving Spanish Bands are reached at
last,
Charged, and dispersed like foam: but as
a flight
Of scattered quails by signs do reunite,
So these, — and, heard of once again, are
chased
With combinations of long-practised art
And newly-kindled hope; but they are
fled —
Gone are they, viewless as the buried dead:
Where now ? — Their sword is at the Foe-
man's heart;
And thus from year to year his walk they
thwart,
And hang like dreams around his guilty bed.

EPITAPHS

TRANSLATED FROM CHIABRERA

1809(?)

Those from Chiabrera were chiefly trans-
lated when Mr. Coleridge was writing his
Friend, in which periodical my " Essay on
Epitaphs," written about that time, was first

published. For further notice of Chiabrera, in connection with his Epitàphs, see "Musings at Aquapendente."

I

1809(?). 1836

WEEP not, belovèd Friends ! nor let the air
For me with sighs be troubled. Not from
  life
Have I been taken; this is genuine life
And this alone — the life which now I live
In peace eternal; where desire and joy
Together move in fellowship without end.—
Francesco Ceni willed that, after death,
His tombstone thus should. speak for him.
  And surely
Small cause there is for that fond wish of
  ours
Long to continue in this world; a world
That keeps not faith, nor yet can point a
  hope
To good, whereof itself is destitute.

II

1809(?). 1810

PERHAPS some needful service of the State
Drew TITUS from the depth of studious
  bowers,
And doomed him to contend in faithless
  courts,
Where gold determines between right and
  wrong.
Yet did at length his loyalty of heart,
And his pure native genius, lead him back
To wait upon the bright and gracious
  Muses,
Whom he had early loved. And not in
  vain
Such course he held ! Bologna's learned
  schools
Were gladdened by the Sage's voice, and
  hung
With fondness on those sweet Nestorian
  strains.
There pleasure crowned his days; and all
  his thoughts
A roseate fragrance breathed. — O human
  life,
That never art secure from dolorous change !
Behold a high injunction suddenly
To Arno's side hath brought him, and he
  charmed
A Tuscan audience: but full soon was
  called

To the perpetual silence of the grave.
Mourn, Italy, the loss of him who stood
A Champion stedfast and invincible,
To quell the rage of literary War !

III

1809(?). 1810

O THOU who movest onward with a mind
Intent upon thy way, pause, though in
  haste !
'T will be no fruitless moment. I was born
Within Savona's walls, of gentle blood.
On Tiber's banks my youth was dedicate
To sacred studies; and the Roman Shep-
  herd
Gave to my charge Urbino's numerous
  flock.
Well did I watch, much laboured, nor had
  power
To escape from many and strange indigni-
  ties;
Was smitten by the great ones of the
  world,
But did not fall; for Virtue braves all
  shocks,
Upon herself resting immoveably.
Me did a kindlier fortune then invite
To serve the glorious Henry, King of
  France,
And in his hands I saw a high reward
Stretched out for my acceptance, — but
  Death came.
Now, Reader, learn from this my fate, how
  false,
How treacherous to her promise, is the
  world;
And trust in God — to whose eternal doom
Must bend the sceptred Potentates of earth.

IV

1809. 1809

THERE never breathed a man who, when
  his life
Was closing, might not of that life relate
Toils long and hard. — The warrior will
  report
Of wounds, and bright swords flashing in
  the field,
And blast of trumpets. He who hath been
  doomed
To bow his forehead in the courts of kings,
Will tell of fraud and never-ceasing hate,
Envy and heart-inquietude, derived

From intricate cabals of treacherous friends.
I, who on shipboard lived from earliest
youth,
Could represent the countenance horrible
Of the vexed waters, and the indignant
rage
Of Auster and Boötes. Fifty years
Over the well-steered galleys did I rule: —
From huge Pelorus to the Atlantic pillars,
Rises no mountain to mine eyes unknown;
And the broad gulfs I traversed oft and
oft.
Of every cloud which in the heavens might
stir
I knew the force; and hence the rough
sea's pride
Availed not to my Vessel's overthrow.
What noble pomp and frequent have not I
On regal decks beheld ! yet in the end
I learned that one poor moment can suffice
To equalise the lofty and the low.
We sail the sea of life — a *Calm* One finds,
And One a *Tempest* — and, the voyage o'er,
Death is the quiet haven of us all.
If more of my condition ye would know,
Savona was my birth-place, and I sprang
Of noble parents; seventy years and three
Lived I — then yielded to a slow disease.

V

1809(?). 1836

TRUE is it that Ambrosio Salinero
With an untoward fate was long involved
In odious litigation; and full long,
Fate harder still ! had he to endure assaults
Of racking malady. And true it is
That not the less a frank courageous heart
And buoyant spirit triumphed over pain;
And he was strong to follow in the steps
Of the fair Muses. Not a covert path
Leads to the dear Parnassian forest's shade,
That might from him be hidden; not a
track
Mounts to pellucid Hippocrene, but he
Had traced its windings. — This Savona
knows,
Yet no sepulchral honours to her Son
She paid, for in our age the heart is ruled
Only by gold. And now a simple stone
Inscribed with this memorial here is raised
By his bereft, his lonely, Chiabrera.
Think not, O Passenger ! who read'st the
lines,
That an exceeding love hath dazzled me;

No — he was One whose memory ought to
spread
Where'er Permessus bears an honoured
name,
And live as long as its pure stream shall
flow.

VI

1809. 1809

DESTINED to war from very infancy
Was I, Roberto Dati, and I took
In Malta the white symbol of the Cross:
Nor in life's vigorous season did I shun
Hazard or toil; among the sands was
seen
Of Libya; and not seldom, on the banks
Of wide Hungarian Danube, 't was my lot
To hear the sanguinary trumpet sounded.
So lived I, and repined not at such fate:
This only grieves me, for it seems a wrong,
That stripped of arms I to my end am
brought
On the soft down of my paternal home.
Yet haply Arno shall be spared all cause
To blush for me. Thou, loiter not nor
halt
In thy appointed way, and bear in mind
How fleeting and how frail is human life !

VII

1809(?). 1836

O FLOWER of all that springs from gentle
blood,
And all that generous nurture breeds to
make
Youth amiable; O friend so true of soul
To fair Aglaia; by what envy moved,
Lelius ! has death cut short thy brilliant
day
In its sweet opening ? and what dire mis-
hap
Has from Savona torn her best delight ?
For thee she mourns, nor e'er will cease to
mourn;
And, should the out-pourings of her eyes
suffice not
For her heart's grief, she will entreat Se-
beto
Not to withhold his bounteous aid, Sebetò
Who saw thee, on his margin, yield to
death,
In the chaste arms of thy belovèd Love !
What profit riches? what does youth avail?
Dust are our hopes; — I, weeping bitterly,

Penned these sad lines, nor can forbear to
	pray
That every gentle Spirit hither led
May read them, not without some bitter
	tears.

VIII

1809. 1810

NOT without heavy grief of heart did He
On whom the duty fell (for at that time
The father sojourned in a distant land)
Deposit in the hollow of this tomb
A brother's Child, most tenderly beloved !
FRANCESCO was the name the Youth had
	borne,
POZZOBONNELLI his illustrious house;
And, when beneath this stone the Corse
	was laid,
The eyes of all Savona streamed with tears.
Alas ! the twentieth April of his life
Had scarcely flowered: and at this early
	time,
By genuine virtue he inspired a hope
That greatly cheered his country: to his
	kin
He promised comfort; and the flattering
	thoughts
His friends had in their fondness enter-
	tained,
He suffered not to languish or decay.
Now is there not good reason to break
	forth
Into a passionate lament ? — O Soul !
Short while a Pilgrim in our nether world,
Do thou enjoy the calm empyreal air;
And round this earthly tomb let roses rise,
An everlasting spring ! in memory
Of that delightful fragrance which was
	once
From thy mild manners quietly exhaled.

IX

1809. 1810

PAUSE, courteous Spirit ! — Balbi suppli-
	cates
That Thou, with no reluctant voice, for
	him
Here laid in mortal darkness, wouldst pre-
	fer
A prayer to the Redeemer of the world.
This to the dead by sacred right belongs;
All else is nothing. — Did occasion suit
To tell his worth, the marble of this tomb
Would ill suffice: for Plato's lore sublime,

And all the wisdom of the Stagyrite,
Enriched and beautified his studious mind:
With Archimedes also he conversed
As with a chosen friend; nor did he leave
Those laureat wreaths ungathered which
	the Nymphs
Twine near their loved Permessus. —
	Finally,
Himself above each lower thought uplift-
	ing,
His ears he closed to listen to the songs
Which Sion's Kings did consecrate of old;
And his Permessus found on Lebanon.
A blessèd Man ! who of protracted days
Made not, as thousands do, a vulgar sleep;
But truly did *He* live his life. Urbino,
Take pride in him ! — O Passenger, fare-
	well !

MATERNAL GRIEF

1813–14. 1842

This was in part an overflow from the Soli-
tary's description of his own and his wife's feel-
ings upon the decease of their children. (See
" Excursion," book III.)

DEPARTED Child ! I could forget thee
	once
Though at my bosom nursed; this woeful
	gain
Thy dissolution brings, that in my soul
Is present and perpetually abides
A shadow, never, never to be displaced
By the returning substance, seen or touched,
Seen by mine eyes, or clasped in my em-
	brace.
Absence and death how differ they ! and
	how
Shall I admit that nothing can restore
What one short sigh so easily re-
	moved ? — 10
Death, life, and sleep, reality and thought,
Assist me, God, their boundaries to know,
O teach me calm submission to thy Will !
	The Child she mourned had overstepped
		the pale
Of Infancy, but still did breathe the air
That sanctifies its confines, and partook
Reflected beams of that celestial light
To all the Little-ones on sinful earth
Not unvouchsafed — a light that warmed
	and cheered
Those several qualities of heart and mind 20

Which, in her own blest nature, rooted
deep,
Daily before the Mother's watchful eye,
And not hers only, their peculiar charms
Unfolded, — beauty, for its present self,
And for its promises to future years,
With not unfrequent rapture fondly hailed.
    Have you espied upon a dewy lawn
A pair of Leverets each provoking each
To a continuance of their fearless sport,
Two separate Creatures in their several
gifts   30
Abounding, but so fashioned that, in all
That Nature prompts them to display,
their looks,
Their starts of motion and their fits of
rest,
An undistinguishable style appears
And character of gladness, as if Spring
Lodged in their innocent bosoms, and the
spirit
Of the rejoicing morning were their own?
    Such union, in the lovely Girl maintained
And her twin Brother, had the parent
seen,
Ere, pouncing like a ravenous bird of
prey,   40
Death in a moment parted them, and left
The Mother, in her turns of anguish, worse
Than desolate; for oft-times from the
sound
Of the survivor's sweetest voice (dear child,
He knew it not) and from his happiest
looks,
Did she extract the food of self-reproach,
As one that lived ungrateful for the stay
By Heaven afforded to uphold her maimed
And tottering spirit. And full oft the Boy,
Now first acquainted with distress and
grief,   50
Shrunk from his Mother's presence, shunned
with fear
Her sad approach, and stole away to find,
In his known haunts of joy where'er he
might,
A more congenial object. But, as time
Softened her pangs and reconciled the child
To what he saw, he gradually returned,
Like a scared Bird encouraged to renew
A broken intercourse; and, while his eyes
Were yet with pensive fear and gentle awe
Turned upon her who bore him, she would
stoop   60
To imprint a kiss that lacked not power to
spread

Faint colour over both their pallid cheeks,
And stilled his tremulous lip. Thus they
were calmed
And cheered; and now together breathe
fresh air
In open fields; and when the glare of day
Is gone, and twilight to the Mother's wish
Befriends the observance, readily they join
In walks whose boundary is the lost One's
grave,
Which he with flowers hath planted, find-
ing there
Amusement, where the Mother does not
miss   70
Dear consolation, kneeling on the turf
In prayer, yet blending with that solemn
rite
Of pious faith the vanities of grief;
For such, by pitying Angels and by Spirits
Transferred to regions upon which the
clouds
Of our weak nature rest not, must be
deemed
Those willing tears, and unforbidden sighs,
And all those tokens of a cherished sorrow,
Which, soothed and sweetened by the
grace of Heaven
As now it is, seems to her own fond heart,
Immortal as the love that gave it being.   81

CHARACTERISTICS OF A CHILD THREE YEARS OLD

1813(?). 1815

Written at Allanbank, Grasmere. Picture
of my Daughter Catharine, who died the year
after.

Loving she is, and tractable, though wild;
And Innocence hath privilege in her
To dignify arch looks and laughing eyes;
And feats of cunning; and the pretty round
Of trespasses, affected to provoke
Mock-chastisement and partnership in play.
And, as a faggot sparkles on the hearth,
Not less if unattended and alone
Than when both young and old sit gathered
round
And take delight in its activity;
Even so this happy Creature of herself
Is all-sufficient; solitude to her
Is blithe society, who fills the air
With gladness and involuntary songs.
Light are her sallies as the tripping fawn's

Forth-startled from the fern where she lay
   couched;
Unthought-of, unexpected, as the stir
Of the soft breeze ruffling the meadow-
   flowers,
Or from before it chasing wantonly
The many-coloured images imprest
Upon the bosom of a placid lake.

SPANISH GUERILLAS

1811. 1815

THEY seek, are sought; to daily battle led,
Shrink not, though far outnumbered by
   their Foes,
For they have learnt to open and to close
The ridges of grim war; and at their head
Are captains such as erst their country
   bred
Or fostered, self-supported chiefs, — like
   those
Whom hardy Rome was fearful to oppose;
Whose desperate shock the Carthaginian
   fled.
In One who lived unknown a shepherd's
   life
Redoubted Viriatus breathes again;
And Mina, nourished in the studious shade,
With that great Leader vies, who, sick of
   strife
And bloodshed, longed in quiet to be laid
In some green island of the western main.

"THE POWER OF ARMIES IS A VISIBLE THING"

1811. 1815

THE power of Armies is a visible thing,
Formal, and circumscribed in time and
   space;
But who the limits of that power shall
   trace
Which a brave People into light can bring
Or hide, at will, — for freedom combating
By just revenge inflamed? No foot may
   chase,
No eye can follow, to a fatal place
That power, that spirit, whether on the
   wing
Like the strong wind, or sleeping like the
   wind
Within its awful caves. — From year to
   year

Springs this indigenous produce far and near;
No craft this subtle element can bind,
Rising like water from the soil, to find
In every nook a lip that it may cheer.

"HERE PAUSE: THE POET CLAIMS AT LEAST THIS PRAISE"

1811. 1815

HERE pause: the poet claims at least this
   praise,
That virtuous Liberty hath been the scope
Of his pure song, which did not shrink from
   hope
In the worst moment of these evil days;
From hope, the paramount *duty* that
   Heaven lays,
For its own honour, on man's suffering heart.
Never may from our souls one truth de-
   part —
That an accursed thing it is to gaze
On prosperous tyrants with a dazzled eye;
Nor — touched with due abhorrence of *their*
   guilt
For whose dire ends tears flow, and blood
   is spilt,
And justice labours in extremity —
Forget thy weakness, upon which is built,
O wretched man, the throne of tyranny!

EPISTLE

TO SIR GEORGE HOWLAND BEAUMONT, BART.

FROM THE SOUTH-WEST COAST OF CUMBERLAND

1811. 1842

This poem opened, when first written, with a
paragraph that has been transferred as an in-
troduction to the first series of my Scotch
Memorials. The journey, of which the first
part is here described, was from Grasmere to
Bootle on the south-west coast of Cumberland,
the whole among mountain roads through a
beautiful country; and we had fine weather.
The verses end with our breakfast at the head
of Yewdale in a yeoman's house, which, like all
the other property in that sequestered vale, has
passed or is passing into the hands of Mr.
James Marshall of Monk Coniston, — in Mr.
Knott's, the late owner's, time called Water-
head. Our hostess married a Mr. Oldfield, a lieu-
tenant in the Navy: they lived together for
some time at Hacket, where she still resides as

his widow. It was in front of that house, on the mountain side, near which stood the peasant who, while we were passing at a distance, saluted us, waving a kerchief in her hand as described in the poem. (This matron and her husband were then residing at the Hacket. The house and its inmates are referred to in the fifth book of the " Excursion," in the passage beginning —

" You behold,
High on the breast of yon dark mountain, dark
With stony barrenness, a shining speck." — J. C.)

The dog which we met with soon after our starting belonged to Mr. Rowlandson, who for forty years was curate of Grasmere in place of the rector, who lived to extreme old age in a state of insanity. Of this Mr. R. much might be said both with reference to his character, and the way in which he was regarded by his parishioners. He was a man of robust frame, had a firm voice and authoritative manner, of strong natural talents, of which he was himself conscious, for he has been heard to say (it grieves me to add with an oath) — "If I had been brought up at college by —— I should have been a bishop.'' Two vices used to struggle in him for mastery, avarice and the love of strong drink: but avarice, as is common in like cases, always got the better of its opponent; for, though he was often intoxicated, it was never, I believe, at his own expense. As has been said of one in a more exalted station, he would take any *given* quantity. I have heard a story of him which is worth the telling. One summer's morning, our Grasmere curate, after a night's carouse in the vale of Langdale, on his return home, having reached a point near which the whole of the vale of Grasmere might be seen with the lake immediately below him, stepped aside and sat down on the turf. After looking for some time at the landscape, then in the perfection of its morning beauty, he exclaimed — ''Good God, that I should have led so long a life in such a place!'' — This no doubt was deeply felt by him at the time, but I am not authorised to say that any noticeable amendment followed. Penuriousness strengthened upon him as his body grew feebler with age. He had purchased property and kept some land in his own hands, but he could not find in his heart to lay out the necessary hire for labourers at the proper season, and consequently he has often been seen in half-dotage working his hay in the month of November by moonlight, a melancholy sight which I myself have witnessed. Notwithstanding all that has been said, this man, on account of his talents and superior education, was looked up to by his parishioners, who, without a single exception, lived at that time (and most of them upon

their own small inheritances) in a state of republican equality, a condition favourable to the growth of kindly feelings among them, and in a striking degree exclusive to temptations to gross vice and scandalous behaviour. As a pastor their curate did little or nothing for them ; but what could more strikingly set forth the efficacy of the Church of England through its Ordinances and Liturgy than that, in spite of the unworthiness of the minister, his church was regularly attended ; and, though there was not much appearance in his flock of what might be called animated piety, intoxication was rare, and dissolute morals unknown ? With the Bible they were for the most part well acquainted ; and, as was strikingly shown when they were under affliction, must have been supported and comforted by habitual belief in those truths which it is the aim of the Church to inculcate. — *Loughrigg Tarn.* This beautiful pool and the surrounding scene are minutely described in my little Book on the Lakes. Sir G. H. Beaumont, in the earlier part of his life, was induced, by his love of nature and the art of painting, to take up his abode at Old Brathay, about three miles from this spot, so that he must have seen it under many aspects ; and he was so much pleased with it that he purchased the Tarn with a view to build, near it, such a residence as is alluded to in this Epistle. Baronets and knights were not so common in that day as now, and Sir Michael le Fleming, not liking to have a rival in that kind of distinction so near him, claimed a sort of lordship over the territory, and showed dispositions little in unison with those of Sir G. Beaumont, who was eminently a lover of peace. The project of building was in consequence given up, Sir George retaining possession of the Tarn. Many years afterwards a Kendal tradesman born upon its banks applied to me for the purchase of it, and accordingly it was sold for the sum that had been given for it, and the money was laid out under my direction upon a substantial oak fence for a certain number of yew trees to be planted in Grasmere churchyard ; two were planted in each enclosure, with a view to remove, after a certain time, the one which throve the least. After several years, the stouter plant being left, the others were taken up and placed in other parts of the same churchyard, and were adequately fenced at the expense and under the care of the late Mr. Barber, Mr. Greenwood, and myself : the whole eight are now thriving, and are already an ornament to a place which, during late years, has lost much of its rustic simplicity by the introduction of iron palisades to fence off family burying-grounds, and by numerous monuments, some of them in very bad taste ; from which this place of burial was in my memory quite free. See the lines in the sixth book of the " Excursion " beginning — " Green is the churchyard, beautiful and green." The " Epistle " to which these notes refer, though written so far back as 1804, was carefully revised so late as 1842, previous to its publication. I am loth to add, that it was never seen by the person to whom it is addressed. So sensible am I of the deficiencies in all that I write, and so far does everything that I attempt fall short of what I wish it to be, that even private publication, if such a term may be allowed, requires more resolution than I can command. I have written to give vent to my own mind, and not without hope that, some time or other, kindred minds might benefit by my labours : but I am inclined to believe I should never have ventured to send forth any verses of mine to the world if it had not been done on the pressure of personal occasions. Had I been a rich man, my productions, like this " Epistle," the tragedy of the " Borderers," etc., would most likely have been confined to manuscript.

FAR from our home by Grasmere's quiet Lake,
From the Vale's peace which all her fields partake,
Here on the bleakest point of Cumbria's shore
We sojourn stunned by Ocean's ceaseless roar;
While, day by day, grim neighbour ! huge Black Comb
Frowns deepening visibly his native gloom,
Unless, perchance rejecting in despite
What on the Plain *we* have of warmth and light,
In his own storms he hides himself from sight.
Rough is the time; and thoughts, that would be free   10
From heaviness, oft fly, dear Friend, to thee;
Turn from a spot where neither sheltered road
Nor hedge-row screen invites my steps abroad;
Where one poor Plane-tree, having as it might
Attained a stature twice a tall man's height,
Hopeless of further growth, and brown and sere
Through half the summer, stands with top cut sheer,

Like an unshifting weathercock which proves
How cold the quarter that the wind best loves,
Or like a Centinel that, evermore   20
Darkening the window, ill defends the door
Of this unfinished house — a Fortress bare,
Where strength has been the Builder's only care;
Whose rugged walls may still for years demand
The final polish of the Plasterer's hand.
— This Dwelling's Inmate more than three weeks space
And oft a Prisoner in the cheerless place,
I — of whose touch the fiddle would complain,
Whose breath would labour at the flute in vain,
In music all unversed, nor blessed with skill   30
A bridge to copy, or to paint a mill,
Tired of my books, a scanty company !
And tired of listening to the boisterous sea —
Pace between door and window muttering rhyme,
An old resource to cheat a froward time !
Though these dull hours (mine is it, or their shame ?)
Would tempt me to renounce that humble aim.
— But if there be a Muse who, free to take
Her seat upon Olympus, doth forsake
Those heights (like Phœbus when his golden locks   40
He veiled, attendant on Thessalian flocks)
And, in disguise, a Milkmaid with her pail
Trips down the pathways of some winding dale;
Or, like a Mermaid, warbles on the shores
To fishers mending nets beside their doors;
Or, Pilgrim-like, on forest moss reclined,
Gives plaintive ditties to the heedless wind,
Or listens to its play among the boughs
Above her head and so forgets her vows —
If such a Visitant of Earth there be   50
And she would deign this day to smile on me
And aid my verse, content with local bounds
Of natural beauty and life's daily rounds,
Thoughts, chances, sights, or doings, which we tell
Without reserve to those whom we love well —

Then haply, Beaumont! words in current
    clear
Will flow, and on a welcome page appear
Duly before thy sight, unless they perish
    here.
    What shall I treat of? News from Mona's
      Isle?
Such have we, but unvaried in its style; 60
No tales of Runagates fresh landed, whence
And wherefore fugitive or on what pre-
    tence;
Of feasts, or scandal, eddying like the wind
Most restlessly alive when most confined.
Ask not of me, whose tongue can best
    appease
The mighty tumults of the HOUSE OF KEYS;
The last year's cup whose Ram or Heifer
    gained,
What slopes are planted, or what mosses
    drained:
An eye of fancy only can I cast
On that proud pageant now at hand or
    past,   70
When full five hundred boats in trim array,
With nets and sails outspread and streamers
    gay,
And chanted hymns and stiller voice of
    prayer,
For the old Manx-harvest to the Deep re-
    pair,
Soon as the herring-shoals at distance shine
Like beds of moonlight shifting on the brine.
    Mona from our Abode is daily seen,
But with a wilderness of waves between;
And by conjecture only can we speak
Of aught transacted there in bay or creek;
No tidings reach us thence from town or
    field,   81
Only faint news her mountain sunbeams
    yield,
And some we gather from the misty air,
And some the hovering clouds, our telegraph,
    declare.
But these poetic mysteries I withhold;
For Fancy hath her fits both hot and cold,
And should the colder fit with You be on
When You might read, my credit would be
    gone.
    Let more substantial themes the pen
    engage,
And nearer interests culled from the open-
    ing stage   90
Of our migration. — Ere the welcome dawn
Had from the east her silver star with-
    drawn,

The Wain stood ready, at our Cottage-door,
Thoughtfully freighted with a various store;
And long or ere the uprising of the Sun
O'er dew-damped dust our journey was
    begun,
A needful journey, under favouring skies,
Through peopled Vales; yet something in
    the guise
Of those old Patriarchs when from well to
    well
They roamed through Wastes where now
    the tented Arabs dwell.   100
    Say first, to whom did we the charge
    confide,
Who promptly undertook the Wain to guide
Up many a sharply-twining road and down,
And over many a wide hill's craggy crown,
Through the quick turns of many a hollow
    nook,
And the rough bed of many an unbridged
    brook?
A blooming Lass — who in her better hand
Bore a light switch, her sceptre of command
When, yet a slender Girl, she often led,
Skilful and bold, the horse and burthened
    sled   110
From the peat-yielding Moss on Gowdar's
    head.
What could go wrong with such a Charioteer
For goods and chattels, or those Infants
    dear,
A Pair who smilingly sat side by side,
Our hope confirming that the salt-sea tide
Whose free embraces we were bound to seek,
Would their lost strength restore and
    freshen the pale cheek?
Such hope did either Parent entertain
Pacing behind along the silent lane.
    Blithe hopes and happy musings soon
    took flight,   120
For lo! an uncouth melancholy sight —
On a green bank a creature stood forlorn
Just half protruded to the light of morn,
Its hinder part concealed by hedge-row
    thorn
The Figure called to mind a beast of prey
Stript of its frightful powers by slow decay,
And, though no longer upon rapine bent,
Dim memory keeping of its old intent.
We started, looked again with anxious eyes,
And in that griesly object recognise   130
The Curate's Dog — his long-tried friend,
    for they,
As well we knew, together had grown
    grey.

The Master died, his drooping servant's
grief
Found at the Widow's feet some sad relief;
Yet still he lived in pining discontent,
Sadness which no indulgence could prevent;
Hence whole day wanderings, broken
nightly sleeps
And lonesome watch that out of doors he
keeps;
Not oftentimes, I trust, as we, poor brute !
Espied him on his legs sustained, blank,
mute,   140
And of all visible motion destitute,
So that the very heaving of his breath
Seemed stopt, though by some other power
than death.
Long as we gazed upon the form and face,
A mild domestic pity kept its place,
Unscared by thronging fancies of strange
hue
That haunted us in spite of what we knew.
Even now I sometimes think of him as lost
In second-sight appearances, or crost
By spectral shapes of guilt, or to the ground,
On which he stood, by spells unnatural
bound,   151
Like a gaunt shaggy Porter forced to
wait
In days of old romance at Archimago's
gate.
    Advancing Summer, Nature's law ful-
filled,
The choristers in every grove had stilled;
But we, we lacked not music of our own,
For lightsome Fanny had thus early thrown,
Mid the gay prattle of those infant tongues,
Some notes prelusive, from the round of
songs
With which, more zealous than the liveliest
bird   160
That in wild Arden's brakes was ever heard,
Her work and her work's partners she can
cheer,
The whole day long, and all days of the
year.
    Thus gladdened from our own dear Vale
we pass
And soon approach Diana's Looking-glass !
To Loughrigg-tarn, round clear and bright
as heaven,
Such name Italian fancy would have given,
Ere on its banks the few grey cabins rose
That yet disturb not its concealed repose
More than the feeblest wind that idly
blows.   170

Ah, Beaumont ! when an opening in the
road
Stopped me at once by charm of what it
showed,
The encircling region vividly exprest
Within the mirror's depth, a world at rest —
Sky streaked with purple, grove and craggy
bield,
And the smooth green of many a pendent
field,
And, quieted and soothed, a torrent small,
A little daring would-be waterfall.
One chimney smoking and its azure wreath,
Associate all in the calm Pool beneath,   180
With here and there a faint imperfect
gleam
Of water-lilies veiled in misty steam —
What wonder at this hour of stillness deep,
A shadowy link 'tween wakefulness and
sleep,
When Nature's self, amid such blending,
seems
To render visible her own soft dreams,
If, mixed with what appeared of rock,
lawn, wood,
Fondly embosomed in the tranquil flood,
A glimpse I caught of that Abode, by
Thee
Designed to rise in humble privacy,   190
A lowly Dwelling, here to be outspread,
Like a small Hamlet, with its bashful head
Half hid in native trees. Alas 't is not,
Nor ever was; I sighed, and left the spot
Unconscious of its own untoward lot,
And thought in silence, with regret too keen,
Of unexperienced joys that might have
been;
Of neighbourhood and intermingling arts,
And golden summer days uniting cheerful
hearts.
But time, irrevocable time, is flown.   200
And let us utter thanks for blessings sown
And reaped — what hath been, and what is,
our own.
    Not far we travelled ere a shout of glee,
Startling us all, dispersed my reverie;
Such shout as many a sportive echo meeting
Oft-times from Alpine *chalets* sends a
greeting.
Whence the blithe hail ? behold a Peasant
stand
On high, a kerchief waving in her hand !
Not unexpectant that by early day
Our little Band would thrid this mountain
way,   210

Before her cottage on the bright hill side
She hath advanced with hope to be descried.
Right gladly answering signals we displayed,
Moving along a tract of morning shade,
And vocal wishes sent of like good will
To our kind Friend high on the sunny hill —
Luminous region, fair as if the prime
Were tempting all astir to look aloft or
    climb;
Only the centre of the shining cot
With door left open makes a gloomy spot,
Emblem of those dark corners sometimes
    found   221
Within the happiest breast on earthly
    ground.
    Rich prospect left behind of stream and
    vale,
And mountain-tops, a barren ridge we scale;
Descend, and reach, in Yewdale's depths,
    a plain
With haycocks studded, striped with
    yellowing grain —
An area level as a Lake and spread
Under a rock too steep for man to tread,
Where sheltered from the north and bleak
    northwest
Aloft the Raven hangs a visible nest,   230
Fearless of all assaults that would her
    brood molest.
Hot sunbeams fill the steaming vale; but
    hark,
At our approach, a jealous watch-dog's
    bark,
Noise that brings forth no liveried Page of
    state,
But the whole household, that our coming
    wait.
With Young and Old warm greetings we
    exchange,
And jocund smiles, and toward the lowly
    Grange
Press forward by the teasing dogs unscared.
Entering, we find the morning meal pre-
    pared: 239
So down we sit, though not till each had cast
Pleased looks around the delicate repast —
Rich cream, and snow-white eggs fresh from
    the nest,
With amber honey from the mountain's
    breast;
Strawberries from lane or woodland, offer-
    ing wild
Of children's industry, in hillocks piled;
Cakes for the nonce, and butter fit to lie
Upon a lordly dish; frank hospitality

Where simple art with bounteous nature
    vied,
And cottage comfort shunned not seemly
    pride.
    Kind Hostess ! Handmaid also of the
    feast,   250
If thou be lovelier than the kindling East,
Words by thy presence unrestrained may
    speak
Of a perpetual dawn from brow and cheek
Instinct with light whose sweetest promise
    lies,
Never retiring, in thy large dark eyes,
Dark but to every gentle feeling true,
As if their lustre flowed from ether's purest
    blue.
    Let me not ask what tears may have been
    wept
By those bright eyes, what weary vigils kept,
Beside that hearth what sighs may have
    been heaved   260
For wounds inflicted, nor what toil relieved
By fortitude and patience, and the grace
Of heaven in pity visiting the place.
Not unadvisedly those secret springs
I leave unsearched: enough that memory
    clings,
Here as elsewhere, to notices that make
Their own significance for hearts awake,
To rural incidents, whose genial powers
Filled with delight three summer morning
    hours.
    More could my pen report of grave or gay
That through our gipsy travel cheered the
    way;   271
But, bursting forth above the waves, the Sun
Laughs at my pains, and seems to say, " Be
    done."
Yet, Beaumont, thou wilt not, I trust, re-
    prove
This humble offering made by Truth to
    Love,
Nor chide the Muse that stooped to break
    a spell
Which might have else been on me yet: —
        FAREWELL.

UPON PERUSING THE FOREGOING EPIS-
TLE THIRTY YEARS AFTER ITS COM-
POSITION

1841. 1842

SOON did the Almighty Giver of all rest
Take those dear young Ones to a fearless
    nest:

And in Death's arms has long reposed the Friend
For whom this simple Register was penned.
Thanks to the moth that spared it for our eyes;
And Strangers even the slighted Scroll may prize,
Moved by the touch of kindred sympathies.
For — save the calm, repentance sheds o'er strife
Raised by remembrances of misused life,
The light from past endeavours purely willed
And by Heaven's favour happily fulfilled;
Save hope that we, yet bound to Earth, may share
The joys of the Departed — what so fair
As blameless pleasure, not without some tears,
Reviewed through Love's transparent veil of years ?

UPON THE SIGHT OF A BEAUTIFUL PICTURE

PAINTED BY SIR G. H. BEAUMONT, BART.

1811. 1815

This was written when we dwelt in the Parsonage at Grasmere. The principal features of the picture are Bredon Hill and Cloud Hill near Coleorton. I shall never forget the happy feeling with which my heart was filled when I was impelled to compose this Sonnet. We resided only two years in this house; and during the last half of the time, which was after this poem had been written, we lost our two children, Thomas and Catharine. Our sorrow upon these events often brought it to my mind, and cast me upon the support to which the last line of it gives expression —

" The appropriate calm of blest eternity."

It is scarcely necessary to add that we still possess the Picture.

PRAISED be the Art whose subtle power could stay
Yon cloud, and fix it in that glorious shape;
Nor would permit the thin smoke to escape,
Nor those bright sunbeams to forsake the day;
Which stopped that band of travellers on their way,
Ere they were lost within the shady wood;
And showed the Bark upon the glassy flood
For ever anchored in her sheltering bay.

Soul-soothing Art ! whom Morning, Noontide, Even,
Do serve with all their changeful pageantry;
Thou, with ambition modest yet sublime,
Here, for the sight of mortal man, hast given
To one brief moment caught from fleeting time
The appropriate calm of blest eternity.

INSCRIPTIONS

IN THE GROUNDS OF COLEORTON, THE SEAT OF SIR GEORGE BEAUMONT, BART., LEICESTERSHIRE

1811. 1815

In the grounds of Coleorton these verses are engraved on a stone placed near the Tree, which was thriving and spreading when I saw it in the summer of 1841.

THE embowering rose, the acacia, and the pine,
Will not unwillingly their place resign;
If but the Cedar thrive that near them stands,
Planted by Beaumont's and by Wordsworth's hands.
One wooed the silent Art with studious pains:
These groves have heard the Other's pensive strains;
Devoted thus, their spirits did unite
By interchange of knowledge and delight.
May Nature's kindliest powers sustain the Tree,
And Love protect it from all injury !
And when its potent branches, wide outthrown,
Darken the brow of this memorial Stone,
Here may some Painter sit in future days,
Some future Poet meditate his lays;
Not mindless of that distant age renowned
When Inspiration hovered o'er this ground,
The haunt of him who sang how spear and shield
In civil conflict met on Bosworth-field;
And of that famous Youth, full soon removed
From earth, perhaps by Shakspeare's self approved,
Fletcher's Associate, Jonson's Friend beloved.

IN A GARDEN OF SIR GEORGE BEAU-
MONT, BART.

1811. 1815

This Niche is in the sandstone-rock in the winter-garden at Coleorton, which garden, as has been elsewhere said, was made under our direction out of an old unsightly quarry. While the labourers were at work, Mrs. Wordsworth, my Sister, and I used to amuse ourselves occasionally in scooping this seat out of the soft stone. It is of the size, with something of the appearance, of a Stall in a Cathedral. This inscription is not engraven, as the former and the two following are, in the grounds.

OFT is the medal faithful to its trust
When temples, columns, towers, are laid in
    dust;
And 't is a common ordinance of fate
That things obscure and small outlive the
    great:
Hence, when yon mansion and the flowery
    trim
Of this fair garden, and its alleys dim,
And all its stately trees, are passed away,
This little Niche, unconscious of decay,
Perchance may still survive. And be it
    known
That it was scooped within the living
    stone, —
Not by the sluggish and ungrateful pains
Of labourer plodding for his daily gains,
But by an industry that wrought in love;
With help from female hands, that proudly
    strove
To aid the work, what time these walks
    and bowers
Were shaped to cheer dark winter's lonely
    hours.

WRITTEN AT THE REQUEST OF SIR GEORGE
BEAUMONT, BART., AND IN HIS NAME,
FOR AN URN, PLACED BY HIM AT THE
TERMINATION OF A NEWLY-PLANTED
AVENUE, IN THE SAME GROUNDS

1811. 1815

YE Lime-trees, ranged before this hallowed
    Urn,
Shoot forth with lively power at Spring's
    return;
And be not slow a stately growth to rear
Of pillars, branching off from year to year,

Till they have learned to frame a darksome
    aisle; —
That may recall to mind that awful Pile
Where Reynolds, 'mid our country's noblest
    dead,
In the last sanctity of fame is laid.
— There, though by right the excelling
    Painter sleep
Where Death and Glory a joint sabbath
    keep,
Yet not the less his Spirit would hold
    dear
Self-hidden praise, and Friendship's private
    vate tear:
Hence, on my patrimonial grounds, have I
Raised this frail tribute to his memory;
From youth a zealous follower of the Art
That he professed; attached to him in
    heart;
Admiring, loving, and with grief and pride
Feeling what England lost when Reynolds
    died.

FOR A SEAT IN THE GROVES OF
COLEORTON

1811. 1815

BENEATH yon eastern ridge, the craggy
    bound,
Rugged and high, of Charnwood's forest
    ground
Stand yet, but, Stranger ! hidden from thy
    view,
The ivied Ruins of forlorn GRACE DIEU;
Erst a religious House, which day and night
With hymns resounded, and the chanted
    rite:
And when those rites had ceased, the Spot
    gave birth
To honourable Men of various worth:
There, on the margin of a streamlet wild,
Did Francis Beaumont sport, an eager
    child;
There, under shadow of the neighbouring
    rocks,
Sang youthful tales of shepherds and their
    flocks;
Unconscious prelude to heroic themes,
Heart - breaking tears, and melancholy
    dreams
Of slighted love, and scorn, and jealous
    rage,
With which his genius shook the buskined
    stage.

Communities are lost, and Empires die,
And things of holy use unhallowed lie;
They perish; — but the Intellect can raise,
From airy words alone, a Pile that ne'er
decays.

SONG FOR THE SPINNING WHEEL

FOUNDED UPON A BELIEF PREVALENT
AMONG THE PASTORAL VALES OF
WESTMORELAND

1812. 1820

The belief on which this is founded I have
often heard expressed by an old neighbour of
Grasmere.

SWIFTLY turn the murmuring wheel !
Night has brought the welcome hour,
When the weary fingers feel
Help, as if from faery power;
Dewy night o'ershades the ground;
Turn the swift wheel round and round !

Now, beneath the starry sky,
Couch the widely-scattered sheep; —
Ply the pleasant labour, ply !
For the spindle, while they sleep,
Runs with speed more smooth and fine,
Gathering up a trustier line.

Short-lived likings may be bred
By a glance from fickle eyes;
But true love is like the thread
Which the kindly wool supplies,
When the flocks are all at rest
Sleeping on the mountain's breast.

COMPOSED ON THE EVE OF THE MARRIAGE OF A FRIEND IN THE VALE OF GRASMERE

1812. 1815

WHAT need of clamorous bells, or ribands
gay,
These humble nuptials to proclaim or
grace ?
Angels of love, look down upon the place;
Shed on the chosen vale a sun-bright day !
Yet no proud gladness would the Bride
display
Even for such promise: — serious is her
face,

Modest her mien; and she, whose thoughts
keep pace
With gentleness, in that becoming way
Will thank you. Faultless does the Maid
appear;
No disproportion in her soul, no strife:
But, when the closer view of wedded life
Hath shown that nothing human can be
clear
From frailty, for that insight may the Wife
To her indulgent Lord become more dear.

WATER–FOWL

OBSERVED FREQUENTLY OVER THE
LAKES OF RYDAL AND GRASMERE

1800–1806(?). 1823

" Let me be allowed the aid of verse to de-
scribe the evolutions which these visitants
sometimes perform, on a fine day towards the
close of winter." — *Extract from the Author's
Book on the Lakes.*

MARK how the feathered tenants of the
flood,
With grace of motion that might scarcely
seem
Inferior to angelical, prolong
Their curious pastime ! shaping in mid air
(And sometimes with ambitious wing that
soars
High as the level of the mountain-tops)
A circuit ampler than the lake beneath —
Their own domain; but ever, while intent
On tracing and retracing that large round,
Their jubilant activity evolves
Hundreds of curves and circlets, to and fro,
Upward and downward, progress intricate
Yet unperplexed, as if one spirit swayed
Their indefatigable flight.   'T is, done —
Ten times, or more, I fancied it had
ceased;
But lo ! the vanished company again
Ascending; they approach — I hear their
wings,
Faint, faint at first; and then an eager
sound,
Past in a moment — and as faint again !
They tempt the sun to sport amid their
plumes;
They tempt the water, or the gleaming ice,
To show them a fair image; 't is themselves,
Their own fair forms, upon the glimmering
plain,

Painted more soft and fair as they descend
Almost to touch; — then up again aloft,
Up with a sally and a flash of speed,
As if they scorned both resting-place and
    rest !

VIEW FROM THE TOP OF BLACK COMB

1811(?). 1815

Mrs. Wordsworth and I, as mentioned in the
" Epistle to Sir G. Beaumont," lived some time
under its shadow.

THIS Height a ministering Angel might
    select:
For from the summit of BLACK COMB
    (dread name
Derived from clouds and storms !) the
    amplest range
Of unobstructed prospect may be seen
That British ground commands: — low
    dusty tracts,
Where Trent is nursed, far southward !
    Cambrian hills
To the south-west, a multitudinous show;
And, in a line of eye-sight linked with
    these,
The hoary peaks of Scotland that give birth
To Tiviot's stream, to Annan, Tweed, and
    Clyde: —   10
Crowding the quarter whence the sun comes
    forth
Gigantic mountains rough with crags; be-
    neath,
Right at the imperial station's western base
Main ocean, breaking audibly, and stretched
Far into silent regions blue and pale; —
And visibly engirding Mona's Isle
That, as we left the plain, before our sight
Stood like a lofty mount, uplifting slowly
(Above the convex of the watery globe)
Into clear view the cultured fields that
    streak   20
Her habitable shores, but now appears
A dwindled object, and submits to lie
At the spectator's feet. — Yon azure ridge,
Is it a perishable cloud ? Or there
Do we behold the line of Erin's coast ?
Land sometimes by the roving shepherd-
    swain
(Like the bright confines of another world)
Not doubtfully perceived. — Look home-
    ward now !

In depth, in height, in circuit, how serene
The spectacle, how pure ! — Of Nature's
    works,   30
In earth, and air, and earth-embracing sea,
A revelation infinite it seems;
Display august of man's inheritance,
Of Britain's calm felicity and power !

WRITTEN WITH A SLATE PENCIL ON A STONE, ON THE SIDE OF THE MOUNTAIN OF BLACK COMB

1811(?). 1815

The circumstance alluded to at the conclu-
sion of these verses was told me by Dr. Sat-
terthwaite, who was Incumbent of Bootle, a
small town at the foot of Black Comb. He had
the particulars from one of the engineers who
was employed in making trigonometrical sur-
veys of that region.

STAY, bold Adventurer; rest awhile thy
    limbs
On this commodious Seat ! for much re-
    mains
Of hard ascent before thou reach the top
Of this huge Eminence, — from blackness
    named,
And, to far-travelled storms of sea and
    land,
A favourite spot of tournament and war !
But thee may no such boisterous visitants
Molest; may gentle breezes fan thy brow;
And neither cloud conceal, nor misty air
Bedim, the grand terraqueous spectacle,
From centre to circumference, unveiled !
Know, if thou grudge not to prolong thy
    rest,
That on the summit whither thou art bound,
A geographic Labourer pitched his tent,
With books supplied and instruments of
    art,
To measure height and distance; lonely
    task,
Week after week pursued ! — To him was
    given
Full many a glimpse (but sparingly be-
    stowed
On timid man) of Nature's processes
Upon the exalted hills. He made report
That once, while there he plied his studious
    work
Within that canvas Dwelling, colours,
    lines,

And the whole surface of the out-spread
  map,
Became invisible: for all around
Had darkness fallen — unthreatened, un-
  proclaimed —
As if the golden day itself had been
Extinguished in a moment; total gloom,
In which he sate alone, with unclosed eyes,
Upon the blinded mountain's silent top !

NOVEMBER 1813

1813. 1814

Now that all hearts are glad, all faces
  bright,
Our aged Sovereign sits, to the ebb and flow

Of states and kingdoms, to their joy or
  woe,
Insensible. He sits deprived of sight,
And lamentably wrapt in twofold night,
Whom no weak hopes deceived; whose
  mind ensued,
Through perilous war, with regal fortitude,
Peace that should claim respect from law-
  less Might.
Dread King of Kings, vouchsafe a ray
  divine
To his forlorn condition ! let thy grace
Upon his inner soul in mercy shine;
Permit his heart to kindle, and to embrace
(Though it were only for a moment's space)
The triumphs of this hour; for they are
  THINE !

THE EXCURSION

1797–1814. 1814

Something must now be said of this poem, but chiefly, as has been done through the whole of these notes, with reference to my personal friends, and especially to her who has perseveringly taken them down from my dictation. Towards the close of the first book stand the lines that were first written, beginning, "Nine tedious years," and ending, "Last human tenant of these ruined walls." These were composed in '95 at Racedown; and for several passages describing the employment and demeanour of Margaret during her affliction, I was indebted to observations made in Dorsetshire, and afterwards at Alfoxden in Somersetshire, where I resided in '97 and '98. The lines towards the conclusion of the fourth book — beginning, "For, the man, who, in this spirit," to the words "intellectual soul" — were in order of time composed the next, either at Racedown or Alfoxden, I do not remember which. The rest of the poem was written in the vale of Grasmere, chiefly during our residence at Allan Bank. The long poem on my own education was, together with many minor poems, composed while we lived at the cottage at Town-end. Perhaps my purpose of giving an additional interest to these my poems in the eyes of my nearest and dearest friends may be promoted by saying a few words upon the character of the Wanderer, the Solitary, and the Pastor, and some other of the persons introduced. And first, of the principal one, the Wanderer. My lamented friend Southey (for this is written a month after his decease) used to say that had he been born a papist, the course of life which would in all probability have been his was the one for which he was most fitted and most to his mind, — that of a Benedictine monk in a convent, furnished, as many once were and some still are, with an in-exhaustible library. *Books*, as appears from many passages in his writings, and as was evident to those who had opportunities of observing his daily life, were in fact *his passion;* and *wander-ing*, I can with truth affirm, was *mine;* but this propensity in me was happily counteracted by inability from want of fortune to fulfil my wishes. But, had I been born in a class which would have deprived me of what is called a liberal education, it is not unlikely that, being strong in body, I should have taken to a way of life such as that in which my Pedlar passed the greater part of his days. At all events, I am here called upon freely to acknowledge that the character I have represented in his person is chiefly an idea of what I fancied my own character might have become in his circumstances. Nevertheless, much of what he says and does had an external existence that fell under my own youthful and subsequent observation. An individual named Patrick, by birth and education a Scotchman, followed this humble occupation for many years, and afterwards settled in the town of Kendal. He married a kinswoman of my wife's, and her sister Sarah was brought up from early childhood under this good man's roof. My own imagina-tions I was happy to find clothed in reality, and fresh ones suggested, by what she reported of this man's tenderness of heart, his strong and pure imagination, and his solid attainments in liter-ature, chiefly religious whether in prose or verse. At Hawkshead also, while I was a schoolboy, there occasionally resided a Packman (the name then generally given to persons of this calling) with whom I had frequent conversations upon what had befallen him, and what he had observed, during his wandering life; and, as was natural, we took much to each other: and, upon the subject of *Pedlarism* in general, as *then* followed, and its favourableness to an intimate knowledge of human concerns, not merely among the humbler classes of society, I need say nothing here in addition to what is to be found in the "Excursion," and a note attached to it. Now for the Solitary. Of him I have much less to say. Not long after we took up our abode at Grasmere, came to reside there, from what motive I either never knew or have forgotten, a Scotchman a little past the middle of life, who had for many years been chaplain to a Highland regiment. He was in no respect, as far as I know, an interesting character, though in his appearance there was a good deal that attracted attention, as if he had been shattered in fortune and not happy in mind. Of his quondam position I availed myself, to connect with the Wanderer, also a Scotchman, a character suitable to my purpose, the elements of which I drew from several persons with whom I had been connected, and who fell under my observation during frequent residences in London at the beginning of the French Revolution. The chief of these was, one may *now* say, a Mr. Fawcett, a preacher at a dissenting meeting-house at the Old Jewry. It happened to me several times to be one of his congregation through my connection with Mr. Nicholson of Cateaton Street, who at that time, when I had not many acquaintances in London, used often to invite me to dine with him on Sundays; and I took that opportunity (Mr. N. being a dissenter) of going to hear Fawcett, who was an able and eloquent man. He published a poem on war, which had a good deal of merit, and made me think more about him than I should otherwise have done. But his Christianity was probably never very deeply rooted; and, like many others in those times of like showy talents, he had not strength of character to withstand the effects of the French Revolution, and of the wild and lax opinions which had done so much towards producing it, and far more in carrying it forward in its extremes. Poor Fawcett, I have been told, became pretty much such a person as I have described; and early disappeared from the stage, having fallen into habits of intemperance, which I have heard (though I will not answer for the fact) hastened his death. Of him I need say no more: there were many like him at that time, which the world will never be without, but which were more numerous then for reasons too obvious to be dwelt upon.

To what is said of the Pastor in the poem I have little to add, but what may be deemed superfluous. It has ever appeared to me highly favourable to the beneficial influence of the Church of England upon all gradations and classes of society, that the patronage of its benefices is in numerous instances attached to the estates of noble families of ancient gentry; and accordingly I am gratified by the opportunity afforded me in the "Excursion," to pourtray the character of a country clergyman of more than ordinary talents, born and bred in the upper ranks of society so as to partake of their refinements, and at the same time brought by his pastoral office and his love of rural life into intimate connection with the peasantry of his native district. To illustrate the relation which in my mind this Pastor bore to the Wanderer, and the resemblance between them, or rather the points of community in their nature, I likened one to an oak and the other to a sycamore; and, having here referred to this comparison, I need only add, I had no one individual in my mind, wishing rather to embody this idea than to break in upon the simplicity of it, by traits of individual character or of any peculiarity of opinion.

And now for a few words upon the scene where these interviews and conversations are supposed to occur. The scene of the first book of the poem is, I must own, laid in a tract of country not sufficiently near to that which soon comes into view in the second book, to agree with the fact. All that relates to Margaret and the ruined cottage, etc., was taken from observations made in the south-west of England, and certainly it would require more than seven-league boots to stretch in one morning from a common in Somersetshire or Dorsetshire to the heights of Furness Fells and the deep valleys they embosom. For thus dealing with space I need make, I trust, no apology, but my friends may be amused by the truth. In the poem, I suppose that the Pedlar and I ascended from a plain country up the vale of Langdale, and struck off a good way above the chapel to the western side of the vale. We ascended the hill and thence looked down upon the circular recess in which lies Blea-Tarn, chosen by the Solitary for his retreat. After we quit his cottage, passing over a low ridge we descend into another vale, that of Little Langdale, towards the head of which stands, embowered or partly shaded by yews and other trees, something between a cottage and a mansion or gentleman's house such as they once were in this country. This I convert into the Parsonage, and at the same time, and as by the waving of a magic wand, I turn the comparatively confined vale of Langdale, its Tarn, and the rude chapel which once adorned the valley, into the stately and comparatively spacious vale of Grasmere, its Lake, and its ancient Parish Church; and upon the side of Loughrigg Fell, at the foot of the Lake, and looking down upon it and the whole vale and its encompassing mountains, the

Pastor is supposed by me to stand, when at sunset he addresses his companions in words which I hope my readers will remember, or I should not have taken the trouble of giving so much in detail the materials on which my mind actually worked. Now for a few particulars of *fact* respecting the persons whose stories are told or characters are described by the different speakers. To Margaret I have already alluded. I will add here, that the lines beginning, "She was a woman of a steady mind," faithfully delineate, as far as they go, the character possessed in common by many women whom it has been my happiness to know in humble life; and that several of the most touching things which she is represented as saying and doing are taken from actual observation of the distresses and trials under which different persons were suffering, some of them strangers to me, and others daily under my notice. I was born too late to have a distinct remembrance of the origin of the American war, but the state in which I represent Robert's mind to be I had frequent opportunities of observing at the commencement of our rupture with France in '93, opportunities of which I availed myself in the story of the Female Vagrant as told in the poem on "Guilt and Sorrow." The account given by the Solitary towards the close of the second book, in all that belongs to the character of the Old Man, was taken from a Grasmere pauper, who was boarded in the last house quitting the vale on the road to Ambleside: the character of his hostess, and all that befell the poor man upon the mountain, belong to Patterdale: the woman I knew well; her name was Ruth Jackson, and she was exactly such a person as I describe. The ruins of the old chapel, among which the old man was found lying, may yet be traced, and stood upon the ridge that divides Patterdale from Boardale and Martindale, having been placed there for the convenience of both districts. The glorious appearance disclosed above and among the mountains was described partly from what my friend Mr. Luff, who then lived in Patterdale, witnessed upon that melancholy occasion, and partly from what Mrs. Wordsworth and I had seen in company with Sir George and Lady Beaumont above Hartshope Hall on our way from Patterdale to Ambleside.

And now for a few words upon the Church, its Monuments, and the Deceased who are spoken of as lying in the surrounding churchyard. But first for the one picture, given by the Pastor and the Wanderer, of the Living. In this nothing is introduced but what was taken from nature and real life. The cottage is called Hackett, and stands as described on the southern extremity of the ridge which separates the two Langdales: the pair who inhabited it were called Jonathan and Betty Yewdale. Once when our children were ill, of whooping-cough I think, we took them for change of air to this cottage, and were in the habit of going there to drink tea upon fine summer afternoons, so that we became intimately acquainted with the characters, habits, and lives of these good, and, let me say, in the main, wise people. The matron had, in her early youth, been a servant in a house at Hawkshead, where several boys boarded, while I was a schoolboy there. I did not remember her as having served in that capacity; but we had many little anecdotes to tell to each other of remarkable boys, incidents and adventures which had made a noise in their day in that small town. These two persons afterwards settled at Rydal, where they both died.

The church, as already noticed, is that of Grasmere. The interior of it has been improved lately — made warmer by under-drawing the roof and raising the floor — but the rude and antique majesty of its former appearance has been impaired by painting the rafters; and the oak benches, with a simple rail at the back dividing them from each other, have given way to seats that have more the appearance of pews. It is remarkable that, excepting only the pew belonging to Rydal Hall, that to Rydal Mount, the one to the Parsonage, and I believe another, the men and women still continue, as used to be the custom in Wales, to sit separate from each other. Is this practice as old as the Reformation? and when and how did it originate? In the Jewish synagogues and in Lady Huntingdon's chapels the sexes are divided in the same way. In the adjoining churchyard greater changes have taken place. It is now not a little crowded with tombstones; and near the school-house which stands in the churchyard is an ugly structure, built to receive the hearse, which is recently come into use. It would not be worth while to allude to this building or the hearse-vehicle it contains, but that the latter has been the means of introducing a change much to be lamented in the mode of conducting funerals among the mountains. Now, the coffin is lodged in the hearse at the door of the house of the deceased, and the corpse is so conveyed to the churchyard gate: all the solemnity which formerly attended its progress, as described in the poem, is put an end to. So much do I regret this, that I beg to be excused for giving utterance here to a wish that, should it befall me to die at Rydal Mount, my own body may be carried to Grasmere church after the manner in which, till lately, that of every one was borne to that place of sepulture, namely, on the shoulders of neighbours, no house being passed without some words of a funeral psalm being sung at the time by the attendants. When I put into the mouth of the Wanderer, "Many precious rites and customs of our rural ancestry are gone or stealing from us; this I hope will last for ever,'' and what follows, little did I foresee that the observance and mode of proceeding, which had often affected me so much, would so soon be superseded. Having said much of the injury done to this churchyard, let me add that one is at liberty to look forward to a time when, by the growth of the yew-trees, thriving there, a solemnity will be spread over the place that will in some degree make amends for the old simple character which has already been so much encroached upon, and will be still more every year. I will here set down by way of memorial, that my friend Sir George Beaumont, having long ago purchased the beautiful piece of water called Loughrigg Tarn, on the Banks of which he intended to build, I told him that a person in Kendal who was attached to the place wished to purchase it. Sir George, finding the possession of no use to him, consented to part with it, and placed the purchase-money — twenty pounds — at my disposal for any local use which I thought proper. Accordingly I resolved to plant yew-trees in the churchyard, and had four pretty strong large oak enclosures made, in each of which was planted, under my own eye, and principally if not entirely by my own hand, two young trees, with the intention of leaving the one that throve best to stand. Many years after, Mr. Barber, who will long be remembered in Grasmere; Mr. Greenwood, the chief landed proprietor; and myself, had four other enclosures made in the churchyard at our own expense, in each of which was planted a tree taken from its neighbour, and they all stand thriving admirably, the fences having been removed as no longer necessary. May the trees be taken care of hereafter when we are all gone, and some of them will perhaps at some far distant time rival in majesty the yew of Lorton and those which I have described as growing in Borrowdale, where they are still to be seen in grand assemblage.

And now for the persons that are selected as lying in the churchyard. But first for the individual whose grave is prepared to receive him. His story is here truly related: he was a schoolfellow of mine for some years. He came to us when he was at least seventeen years of age, very tall, robust, and full-grown. This prevented him from falling into the amusements and games of the school: consequently he gave more time to books. He was not remarkably bright or quick, but by industry he made a progress more than respectable. His parents not being wealthy enough to send him to college, when he left Hawkshead he became a schoolmaster, with a view to prepare himself for holy orders. About this time he fell in love as related in the poem, and everything followed as there described, except that I do not know exactly when and where he died. The number of youths that came to Hawkshead school, from the famalies of the humble yeomanry, to be educated to a certain degree of scholarship as a preparation for the church, was considerable, and the fortunes of these persons in after life various of course, and of some not a little remarkable. I have now one of this class in my eye who became an usher in a preparatory school and ended in making a large fortune. His manners when he came to Hawkshead were as uncouth as well could be; but he had good abilities, with skill to turn them to account; and when the master of the school, to which he was usher, died, he stept into his place and became proprietor of the establishment. He contrived to manage it with such address, and so much to the taste of what is called high society and the fashionable world, that no school of the kind, even till he retired, was in such high request. Ministers of state, the wealthiest gentry, and nobility of the first rank, vied with each other in bespeaking a place for their sons in the seminary of this fortunate teacher. In the solitude of Grasmere, while living as a married man in a cottage of eight pounds per annum rent, I often used to smile at the tales which reached me of the brilliant career of this quondam clown, for such in reality he was in manner and appearance before he was polished a little by attrition with *gentlemen's* sons trained at Hawkshead, rough and rude as many of our families were. Not two hundred yards from the cottage in Grasmere, just mentioned, to which I retired, this gentleman, who many years afterwards purchased a small estate in the neighbourhood, is now erecting a boat-house, with an upper story, to be resorted to as an entertaining-room when he and his associates may feel inclined to take their pastime on the lake. Every passenger will be disgusted with the sight of this edifice, not merely as a tasteless thing in itself, but as utterly out of place, and peculiarly fitted, as far as it is observed (and it obtrudes itself on notice at every point of view), to mar the beauty and destroy the pastoral simplicity of the vale. For my own part and that of my household it is our utter detestation, standing by a shore to which, before the highroad was made to pass that way, we used daily and hourly to repair for seclusion and for the shelter of a grove under which I composed many of my poems, the ''Brothers'' especially, and for this reason we gave the grove that name.

> ''That which each man loved
> And prized in his peculiar nook of earth
> Dies with him, or is changed.''

So much for my old school-fellow and his exploits. I will only add that as the foundation has twice failed, from the lake no doubt being intolerant of the intrusion, there is some ground for hoping that this impertinent structure will not stand. (It has been rebuilt in somewhat better taste and much as one wishes it away it is not now so very unsightly. The structure is an emblem of the man, — perseverance has conquered difficulties and given something of form and polish to rudeness [*added in pencil*]).

The Miner, next described as having found his treasure after twice ten years of labour, lived in Patterdale, and the story is true to the letter. It seems to me, however, rather remarkable that the strength of mind which had supported him through this long unrewarded labour did not enable him to bear its successful issue. Several times in the course of my life I have heard of sudden influxes of great wealth being followed by derangement, and in one instance the shock of good fortune was so great as to produce absolute idiocy: but these all happened where there had been little or no previous effort to acquire the riches, and therefore such a consequence might the more naturally be expected than in the case of the solitary Miner. In reviewing his story, one cannot but regret that such perseverance was not sustained by a worthier object. Archimedes leapt out of his bath and ran about the streets proclaiming his discovery in a transport of joy, but we are not told that he lost either his life or his senses in consequence. The next character, to whom the Priest is led by contrast with the resoluteness displayed by the foregoing, is taken from a person born and bred in Grasmere, by name Dawson; and whose talents, disposition, and way of life were such as are here delineated. I did not know him, but all was fresh in memory when we settled at Grasmere in the beginning of the century. From this point, the conversation leads to the mention of two individuals who, by their several fortunes, were, at different times, driven to take refuge at the small and obscure town of Hawkshead on the skirt of these mountains. Their stories I had from the dear old dame with whom, as a schoolboy and afterwards, I lodged for nearly the space of ten years. The elder, the Jacobite, was named Drummond, and was of a high family in Scotland: the Hanoverian Whig bore the name of Vandeput, and might perhaps be a descendant of some Dutchman who had come over in the train of King William. At all events his zeal was such that he ruined himself by a contest for the representation of London or Westminster, undertaken to support his party; and retired to this corner of the world, selected, as it had been by Drummond, for that obscurity which, since visiting the Lakes became fashionable, it has no longer retained. So much was this region considered out of the way till a late period, that persons who had fled from justice used often to resort hither for concealment; and some were so bold as to, not unfrequently, make excursions from the place of their retreat, for the purpose of committing fresh offences. Such was particularly the case with two brothers of the name of Weston who took up their abode at Old Brathay, I think about seventy years ago. They were highwaymen, and lived there some time without being discovered, though it was known that they often disappeared in a way and upon errands which could not be accounted for. Their horses were noticed as being of a choice breed, and I have heard from the Relph family, one of whom was a saddler in the town of Kendal, that they were curious in their saddles and housings and accoutrements of their horses. They, as I have heard, and as was universally believed, were in the end both taken and hanged.

> "Tall was her stature; her complexion dark
> And saturnine."

This person lived at Town-end, and was almost our next neighbour. I have little to notice concerning her beyond what is said in the poem. She was a most striking instance how far a woman may surpass in talent, in knowledge, and culture of mind, those with and among whom she lives, and yet fall below them in Christian virtues of the heart and spirit. It seemed almost, and I say it with grief, that in proportion as she excelled in the one, she failed in the other. How frequently has one to observe in both sexes the same thing, and how mortifying is the reflection!

> "As, on a sunny bank, a tender lamb
> Lurks in safe shelter from the winds of March."

The story that follows was told to Mrs. Wordsworth and my sister by the sister of this unhappy young woman; and every particular was exactly as I have related. The party was not known to me, though she lived at Hawkshead, but it was after I left school. The clergyman, who administered comfort to her in her distress, I knew well. Her sister who told the story was the wife of a leading yeoman in the vale of Grasmere, and they were an affectionate pair and greatly respected by every one who knew them. Neither lived to be old; and their estate — which was perhaps the most considerable then in the vale, and was endeared to them by many remembrances of a salutary character not easily understood, or sympathised with, by those who are born to great affluence — passed to their eldest son, according to the practice of these vales, who died soon after he came into possession. He was an amiable and promising youth, but was succeeded by an only brother, a good-natured man, who fell into habits of drinking, by which he gradually reduced his property; and the other day the last acre of it was sold, and his wife and children and he himself, still surviving, have very little left to live upon, which it would not perhaps have been worth while to record here but that, through all trials, this woman has proved a model of patience, meekness, affectionate forbearance, and forgiveness. Their eldest son, who, through the vices of his father, has thus been robbed of an ancient family inheritance, was never heard to murmur or complain against the cause of their distress, and is now (1843) deservedly the chief prop of his mother's hopes.

The clergyman and his family described at the beginning of the seventh book were, during many years, our principal associates in the vale of Grasmere, unless I were to except our very nearest neighbours. I have entered so particularly into the main points of their history, that I will barely testify in prose that — with the single exception of the particulars of their journey to Grasmere, which, however, was exactly copied from in another instance — the whole that I have said of them is as faithful to the truth as words can make it. There was much talent in the family : the eldest son was distinguished for poetical talent, of which a specimen is given in my notes to the sonnets to the Duddon. Once, when in our cottage at Town-end I was talking with him about poetry, in the course of conversation I presumed to find fault with the versification of Pope, of whom he was an enthusiastic admirer : he defended him with a warmth that indicated much irritation : nevertheless I would not abandon my point, and said, " In compass and variety of sound your own versification surpasses his." Never shall I forget the change in his countenance and tone of voice : the storm was laid in a moment ; he no longer disputed my judgment, and I passed immediately in his mind, no doubt, for as great a critic as ever lived. I ought to add, he was a clergyman and a well-educated man, and his verbal memory was the most remarkable of any individual I have known, except a Mr. Archer, an Irishman, who lived several years in this neighbourhood, and who, in this faculty, was a prodigy ; he afterwards became deranged, and I fear continues so, if alive. Then follows the character of Robert Walker, for which see notes to the Duddon. Then that of the deaf man, whose epitaph may be seen in the churchyard at the head of Haweswater, and whose qualities of mind and heart, and their benign influence in conjunction with his privation, I had from his relatives on the spot. The blind man, next commemorated, was John Gough, of Kendal, a man known, far beyond his neighbourhood, for his talents and attainments in natural history and science. Of the Infant's grave, next noticed, I will only say, it is an exact picture of what fell under my own observation ; and all persons who are intimately acquainted with cottage life must often have observed like instances of the workings of the domestic affections.

> " A volley thrice repeated o'er the corse
> Let down into the hollow of that grave."

This young volunteer bore the name of Dawson, and was younger brother, if I am not mistaken, to the prodigal of whose character and fortunes an account is given towards the beginning of the preceding book. The father of the family I knew well ; he was a man of literary education and of experience in society much beyond what was common among the inhabitants of the vale. He had lived a good while in the Highlands of Scotland, as a manager of iron-works at Bunaw, and had acted as clerk to one of my predecessors in the office of Distributor of Stamps, when he used to travel round the country collecting and bringing home the money due to Government, in gold, which, it may be worth while to mention for the sake of my friends, was deposited in the cell or iron closet under the west window of the long room at Rydal Mount, which still exists with the iron doors that guarded the property. This of course was before the time of Bills and Notes. The two sons of this person had no doubt been led by the knowledge of their father to take more delight in scholarship, and had been accustomed in their own minds to take a wider view of social interests than was usual among their associates. The premature death of this gallant young man was much lamented, and, as an attendant at the funeral, I myself witnessed the ceremony and the effect of it as described in the poem.

> " Tradition tells
> That, in Eliza's golden days, a Knight
> Came on a war-horse."
> " The house is gone."

The pillars of the gateway in front of the mansion remained when we first took up our abode at Grasmere. Two or three cottages still remain, which are called Knott-houses from the name of the gentleman (I have called him a knight) concerning whom these traditions survive. He was the ancestor of the Knott family, formerly considerable proprietors in the district. What follows in the discourse of the Wanderer upon the changes he had witnessed in rural life, by the introduction of machinery, is truly described from what I myself saw during my boyhood and early youth, and from what was often told me by persons of this humble calling. Happily, most happily, for these mountains, the mischief was diverted from the banks of their beautiful streams, and transferred to open and flat countries abounding in coal, where the agency of steam was found much more effectual for carrying on those demoralising works. Had it not been for this invention, long before the present time every torrent and river in this district would have had its factory, large and populous in proportion to the power of the water that could there have been commanded. Parliament has interfered to prevent the night-work which was once carried on in these mills as actively as during the daytime, and by necessity still more perniciously — a sad disgrace to the proprietors, and to the nation which could so long tolerate such unnatural proceedings. Reviewing at this late period, 1843, what I put into the mouths of my interlocutors a few years after the commencement of the century, I grieve that so little progress has been made in diminishing the evils deplored, or promoting the benefits of education which the Wanderer anticipates. The results of Lord Ashley's labours to defer the time when children might legally be allowed to work in factories, and his endeavours to limit still farther the hours of permitted labour, have fallen far short of his own humane wishes, and those of every benevolent and right-minded man who has carefully attended to this subject: and in the present session of Parliament (1843) Sir James Graham's attempt to establish a course of religious education among the children employed in factories has been abandoned, in consequence of what might easily have been foreseen, the vehement and turbulent opposition of the Dissenters: so that, for many years to come, it may be thought expedient to leave the religious instruction of children entirely in the hands of the several denominations of Christians in the island, each body to work according to its own means and in its own way. Such is my own confidence, a confidence I share with many others of my most valued friends, in the superior advantages, both religious and social, which attend a course of instruction presided over and guided by the clergy of the Church of England, that I have no doubt that, if but once its members, lay and clerical, were duly sensible of those benefits, their church would daily gain ground, and rapidly, upon every shape and fashion of Dissent: and in that case, a great majority in Parliament being sensible of these benefits, the Ministers of the country might be emboldened, were it necessary, to apply funds of the State to the support of education on Church principles. Before I conclude, I cannot forbear noticing the strenuous efforts made at this time in Parliament, by so many persons, to extend manufacturing and commercial industry at the expense of agricultural, though we have recently had abundant proofs that the apprehensions expressed by the Wanderer were not groundless.

> " I spake of mischief by the wise diffused
> With gladness, thinking that the more it spreads
> The healthier, the securer, we become —
> Delusion which a moment may destroy ! "

The Chartists are well aware of this possibility, and cling to it with an ardour and perseverance which nothing but wiser and more brotherly feeling towards the many, on the part of the wealthy few, can moderate or remove.

> " While, from the grassy mountain's open side,
> We gazed, in silence hushed."

The point here fixed upon in my imagination is half-way up the northern side of Loughrigg Fell, from which the Pastor and his companions are supposed to look upwards to the sky and mountain-tops, and round the vale, with the lake lying immediately beneath them.

> " But turned not without welcome promise made,
> That he would share the pleasures and pursuits
> Of yet another summer's day, consumed
> In wandering with us."

When I reported this promise of the Solitary, and long after, it was my wish, and I might say intention, that we should resume our wanderings, and pass the Borders into his native country, where, as I hoped, he might witness, in the society of the Wanderer, some religious ceremony — a sacrament, say, in the open fields, or a preaching among the mountains — which, by recalling to his mind the days of his early childhood, when he had been present on such occasions in company with his parents and nearest kindred, might have dissolved his heart into tenderness, and so have done more towards restoring the Christian faith in which he had been educated, and, with that, contentedness and even cheerfulness of mind, than all that the Wanderer and Pastor, by their several effusions and addresses, had been able to effect. An issue like this was in my intentions. But, alas !

> " 'Mid the wreck of is and was,
> Things incomplete and purposes betrayed
> Make sadder transits o'er thought's optic glass
> Than noblest objects utterly decayed ! "

To the Right Hon.
WILLIAM, EARL OF LONSDALE, K. G.
ETC. ETC.

OFT, through thy fair domains, illustrious Peer !
In youth I roamed, on youthful pleasures bent ;
And mused in rocky cell or sylvan tent,
Beside swift-flowing Lowther's current clear.
— Now, by thy care befriended, I appear
Before thee, LONSDALE, and this Work present,
A token (may it prove a monument !)
Of high respect and gratitude sincere.
Gladly would I have waited till my task
Had reached its close , but Life is insecure,
And Hope full oft fallacious as a dream :
Therefore, for what is here produced, I ask
Thy favour ; trusting that thou wilt not deem
The offering, though imperfect, premature.
WILLIAM WORDSWORTH.
RYDAL MOUNT, WESTMORELAND,
July 29, 1814.

PREFACE TO THE EDITION OF 1814

THE Title-page announces that this is only a portion of a poem; and the Reader must be here apprised that it belongs to the second part of a long and laborious Work, which is to consist of three parts. — The Author will candidly acknowledge that, if the first of these had been completed, and in such a manner as to satisfy his own mind, he should have preferred the natural order of publication, and have given that to the world first ; but, as the second division of the Work was designed to refer more to passing events, and to an existing state of things, than the others were meant to do, more continuous exertion was naturally bestowed upon it, and greater progress made here than in the rest of the poem ; and as this part does not depend upon the preceding to a degree which will materially injure its own peculiar interest, the Author, complying with the earnest entreaties of some valued Friends, presents the following pages to the Public.

It may be proper to state whence the poem, of which "The Excursion" is a part, derives its Title of "The Recluse."—Several years ago, when the Author retired to his native mountains, with the hope of being enabled to construct a literary Work that might live, it was a reasonable thing that he should take a review of his own mind, and examine how far Nature and Education had qualified him for such employment. As subsidiary to this preparation, he undertook to record, in verse. the origin and progress of his own powers, as far as he was acquainted with them. That Work, addressed to a dear Friend, most distinguished for his knowledge and genius, and to whom the Author's Intellect is deeply indebted, has been long finished ; and the result of the investigation which gave rise to it was a determination to compose a philosophical poem, containing views of Man, Nature, and Society ; and to be entitled, "The Recluse"; as having for its principal subject the sensations and opinions of a poet living in retirement. — The preparatory poem is biographical, and conducts the history of the Author's mind to the point when he was emboldened to hope that his faculties were sufficiently matured for entering upon the arduous labour which he had proposed to himself ; and the two Works have the same kind of relation to each other, if he may so express himself, as the ante-chapel has to the body of a Gothic church. Continuing this allusion, he may be permitted to add, that his minor Pieces, which have been long before the Public, when they shall be properly arranged, will be found by the attentive Reader to have such connection with the main Work as may give them claim to be likened to the little cells, oratories, and sepulchral recesses, ordinarily included in those edifices.

The Author would not have deemed himself justified in saying, upon this occasion, so much of performances either unfinished or unpublished, if he had not thought that the labour bestowed by him upon what he has heretofore and now laid before the Public entitled him to candid attention for such a statement as he thinks necessary to throw light upon his endeavours to please and, he would hope, to benefit his countrymen. — Nothing further need be added, than that the first and third parts of "The Recluse" will consist chiefly of meditations in the Author's own person ; and that in the intermediate part ("The Excursion") the intervention of characters speaking is employed, and something of a dramatic form adopted.

It is not the Author's intention formally to announce a system ; it is more animating to him to proceed in a different course ; and if he shall succeed in conveying to the mind clear thoughts, lively images, and strong feelings, the Reader will have no difficulty in extracting the system for himself. And in the meantime the following passage, taken from the conclusion of the first book of "The Recluse," may be acceptable as a kind of *Prospectus* of the design and scope of the whole Poem.

[See "The Recluse," page 231, lines 754–860, for the *Prospectus.*]

BOOK FIRST

THE WANDERER

ARGUMENT

A summer forenoon — The Author reaches a ruined Cottage upon a Common, and there meets with a revered Friend, the Wanderer, of whose education and course of life he gives an account — The Wanderer, while resting under the shade of the Trees that surround the Cottage, relates the History of its last Inhabitant.

'T WAS summer, and the sun had mounted high:
Southward the landscape indistinctly glared
Through a pale steam; but all the northern downs,
In clearest air ascending, showed far off
A surface dappled o'er with shadows flung
From brooding clouds; shadows that lay in spots
Determined and unmoved, with steady beams
Of bright and pleasant sunshine interposed;
To him most pleasant who on soft cool moss
Extends his careless limbs along the front　　10
Of some huge cave, whose rocky ceiling casts
A twilight of its own, an ample shade,
Where the wren warbles, while the dreaming man,
Half conscious of the soothing melody,
With side-long eye looks out upon the scene,
By power of that impending covert thrown
To finer distance. Mine was at that hour
Far other lot, yet with good hope that soon
Under a shade as grateful I should find
Rest, and be welcomed there to livelier joy.　　20
Across a bare wide Common I was toiling
With languid steps that by the slippery turf
Were baffled; nor could my weak arm disperse
The host of insects gathering round my face,
And ever with me as I paced along.

Upon that open moorland stood a grove,
The wished-for port to which my course was bound.
Thither I came, and there, amid the gloom
Spread by a brotherhood of lofty elms,
Appeared a roofless Hut; four naked walls
That stared upon each other ! — I looked round,　　31
And to my wish and to my hope espied
The Friend I sought; a Man of reverend age,

But stout and hale, for travel unimpaired.
There was he seen upon the cottage-bench,
Recumbent in the shade, as if asleep;
An iron-pointed staff lay at his side.

Him had I marked the day before — alone
And stationed in the public way, with face
Turned toward the sun then setting, while that staff　　40
Afforded, to the figure of the man
Detained for contemplation or repose,
Graceful support; his countenance as he stood
Was hidden from my view, and he remained
Unrecognised; but, stricken by the sight,
With slackened footsteps I advanced, and soon
A glad congratulation we exchanged
At such unthought-of meeting. — For the night
We parted, nothing willingly; and now
He by appointment waited for me here,　　50
Under the covert of these clustering elms.

We were tried Friends: amid a pleasant vale,
In the antique market-village where was passed
My school-time, an apartment he had owned,
To which at intervals the Wanderer drew,
And found a kind of home or harbour there.
He loved me; from a swarm of rosy boys
Singled out me, as he in sport would say,
For my grave looks, too thoughtful for my years.
As I grew up, it was my best delight　　60
To be his chosen comrade. Many a time,
On holidays, we rambled through the woods:
We sate — we walked; he pleased me with report
Of things which he had seen; and often touched
Abstrusest matter, reasonings of the mind
Turned inward; or at my request would sing
Old songs, the product of his native hills;
A skilful distribution of sweet sounds,
Feeding the soul, and eagerly imbibed
As cool refreshing water, by the care　　70
Of the industrious husbandman, diffused

Through a parched meadow-ground, in
    time of drought.
Still deeper welcome found his pure dis-
    course;
How precious, when in riper days I learned
To weigh with care his words, and to re-
    joice
In the plain presence of his dignity !

Oh ! many are the Poets that are sown
By Nature; men endowed with highest
    gifts,
The vision and the faculty divine;   79
Yet wanting the accomplishment of verse,
(Which, in the docile season of their youth,
It was denied them to acquire, through
    lack
Of culture and the inspiring aid of books,
Or haply by a temper too severe,
Or a nice backwardness afraid of shame)
Nor having e'er, as life advanced, been led
By circumstance to take unto the height
The measure of themselves, these favoured
    Beings,
All but a scattered few, live out their time,
Husbanding that which they possess within,
And go to the grave, unthought of. Strong-
    est minds   91
Are often those of whom the noisy world
Hears least; else surely this Man had not
    left
His graces unrevealed and unproclaimed.
But, as the mind was filled with inward
    light,
So not without distinction had he lived,
Beloved and honoured — far as he was
    known.
And some small portion of his eloquent
    speech,
And something that may serve to set in
    view
The feeling pleasures of his loneliness,   100
His observations, and the thoughts his
    mind
Had dealt with — I will here record in verse;
Which, if with truth it correspond, and sink
Or rise as venerable Nature leads,
The high and tender Muses shall accept
With gracious smile, deliberately pleased,
And listening Time reward with sacred
    praise.

Among the hills of Athol he was born;
Where, on a small hereditary farm,
An unproductive slip of rugged ground,   110

His Parents, with their numerous offspring,
    dwelt;
A virtuous household, though exceeding
    poor !
Pure livers were they all, austere and grave,
And fearing God; the very children taught
Stern self-respect, a reverence for God's
    word,
And an habitual piety, maintained
With strictness scarcely known on English
    ground.

From his sixth year, the Boy of whom I
    speak,
In summer, tended cattle on the hills;
But, through the inclement and the perilous
    days   120
Of long-continuing winter, he repaired,
Equipped with satchel, to a school, that
    stood
Sole building on a mountain's dreary edge,
Remote from view of city spire, or sound
Of minster clock ! From that bleak tene-
    ment
He, many an evening, to his distant home
In solitude returning, saw the hills
Grow larger in the darkness; all alone
Beheld the stars come out above his head,
And travelled through the wood, with no
    one near   130
To whom he might confess the things he
    saw.

So the foundations of his mind were laid.
In such communion, not from terror free,
While yet a child, and long before his time,
Had he perceived the presence and the
    power
Of greatness; and deep feelings had im-
    pressed
So vividly great objects that they lay
Upon his mind like substances, whose
    presence
Perplexed the bodily sense. He had re-
    ceived
A precious gift; for, as he grew in years,
With these impressions would he still
    compare   141
All his remembrances, thoughts, shapes,
    and forms;
And, being still unsatisfied with aught
Of dimmer character, he thence attained
An active power to fasten images
Upon his brain; and on their pictured lines
Intensely brooded, even till they acquired

The liveliness of dreams. Nor did he fail,
While yet a child, with a child's eagerness
Incessantly to turn his ear and eye   150
On all things which the moving seasons
          brought
To feed such appetite — nor this alone
Appeased his yearning : — in the after-day
Of boyhood, many an hour in caves forlorn,
And 'mid the hollow depths of naked
          crags
He sate, and even in their fixed lineaments,
Or from the power of a peculiar eye,
Or by creative feeling overborne,
Or by predominance of thought oppressed,
Even in their fixed and steady lineaments
He traced an ebbing and a flowing mind, 161
Expression ever varying !
                    Thus informed,
He had small need of books; for many a
          tale
Traditionary, round the mountains hung,
And many a legend, peopling the dark
          woods,
Nourished Imagination in her growth,
And gave the Mind that apprehensive
          power
By which she is made quick to recognise
The moral properties and scope of things.
But eagerly he read, and read again,   170
Whate'er the minister's old shelf supplied;
The life and death of martyrs, who sus-
          tained,
With will inflexible, those fearful pangs
Triumphantly displayed in records left
Of persecution, and the Covenant — times
Whose echo rings through Scotland to this
          hour !
And there, by lucky hap, had been preserved
A straggling volume, torn and incomplete,
That left half-told the preternatural tale,
Romance of giants, chronicle of fiends, 180
Profuse in garniture of wooden cuts
Strange and uncouth ; dire faces, figures
          dire,
Sharp-kneed, sharp-elbowed, and lean-
          ankled too,
With long and ghostly shanks—forms which
          once seen
Could never be forgotten !
                    In his heart,
Where Fear sate thus, a cherished visitant,
Was wanting yet the pure delight of love
By sound diffused, or by the breathing air,
Or by the silent looks of happy things,
Or flowing from the universal face   190

Of earth and sky. But he had felt the
          power
Of Nature, and already was prepared,
By his intense conceptions, to receive
Deeply the lesson deep of love which he,
Whom Nature, by whatever means, has
          taught
To feel intensely, cannot but receive.

Such was the Boy — but for the growing
          Youth
What soul was his, when, from the naked
          top
Of some bold headland, he beheld the sun
Rise up, and bathe the world in light ! He
          looked —   200
Ocean and earth, the solid frame of earth
And ocean's liquid mass, in gladness lay
Beneath him : — Far and wide the clouds
          were touched,
And in their silent faces could he read
Unutterable love. Sound needed none,
Nor any voice of joy; his spirit drank
The spectacle : sensation, soul, and form,
All melted into him; they swallowed up
His animal being; in them did he live, 209
And by them did he live; they were his life.
In such access of mind, in such high hour
Of visitation from the living God,
Thought was not; in enjoyment it expired.
No thanks he breathed, he proffered no
          request;
Rapt into still communion that transcends
The imperfect offices of prayer and praise,
His mind was a thanksgiving to the power
That made him; it was blessedness and
          love !

A Herdsman on the lonely mountain
          tops,   219
Such intercourse was his, and in this sort
Was his existence oftentimes *possessed*.
O then how beautiful, how bright, appeared
The written promise ! Early had he learned
To reverence the volume that displays
The mystery, the life which cannot die;
But in the mountains did he *feel* his faith.
All things, responsive to the writing, there
Breathed immortality, revolving life,
And greatness still revolving; infinite : 229
There littleness was not; the least of things
Seemed infinite; and there his spirit shaped
Her prospects, nor did he believe, — he *saw*.
What wonder if his being thus became
Sublime and comprehensive ! Low desires,

Low thoughts had there no place; yet was
    his heart
Lowly; for he was meek in gratitude,
Oft as he called those ecstasies to mind,
And whence they flowed; and from them
    he acquired
Wisdom, which works through patience;
    thence he learned
In oft-recurring hours of sober thought 240
To look on Nature with a humble heart,
Self-questioned where it did not understand,
And with a superstitious eye of love.

    So passed the time; yet to the nearest
    town
He duly went with what small overplus
His earnings might supply, and brought
    away
The book that most had tempted his desires
While at the stall he read. Among the hills
He gazed upon that mighty orb of song,
The divine Milton. Lore of different kind,
The annual savings of a toilsome life, 251
His Schoolmaster supplied; books that ex-
    plain
The purer elements of truth involved
In lines and numbers, and, by charm severe,
(Especially perceived where nature droops
And feeling is suppressed) preserve the
    mind
Busy in solitude and poverty.
These occupations oftentimes deceived
The listless hours, while in the hollow vale,
Hollow and green, he lay on the green turf
In pensive idleness. What could he do, 261
Thus daily thirsting, in that lonesome life,
With blind endeavours? Yet, still upper-
    most,
Nature was at his heart as if he felt,
Though yet he knew not how, a wasting
    power
In all things that from her sweet influence
Might tend to wean him. Therefore with
    her hues,
Her forms, and with the spirit of her forms,
He clothed the nakedness of austere truth.
While yet he lingered in the rudiments 270
Of science, and among her simplest laws,
His triangles — they were the stars of
    heaven,
The silent stars ! Oft did he take delight
To measure the altitude of some tall crag
That is the eagle's birth-place, or some
    peak
Familiar with forgotten years, that shows

Inscribed upon its visionary sides,
The history of many a winter storm,
Or obscure records of the path of fire.

    And thus before his eighteenth year was
    told, 280
Accumulated feelings pressed his heart
With still increasing weight; he was o'er-
    powered
By Nature; by the turbulence subdued
Of his own mind; by mystery and hope,
And the first virgin passion of a soul
Communing with the glorious universe.
Full often wished he that the winds might
    rage
When they were silent: far more fondly
    now
Than in his earlier season did he love
Tempestuous nights — the conflict and the
    sounds 290
That live in darkness. From his intellect
And from the stillness of abstracted thought
He asked repose; and, failing oft to win
The peace required, he scanned the laws of
    light
Amid the roar of torrents, where they send
From hollow clefts up to the clearer air
A cloud of mist that, smitten by the sun,
Varies its rainbow hues. But vainly thus,
And vainly by all other means, he strove
To mitigate the fever of his heart. 300

    In dreams, in study, and in ardent
    thought,
Thus was he reared; much wanting to assist
The growth of intellect, yet gaining more,
And every moral feeling of his soul
Strengthened and braced, by breathing in
    content
The keen, the wholesome, air of poverty,
And drinking from the well of homely life.
— But, from past liberty, and tried re-
    straints,
He now was summoned to select the course
Of humble industry that promised best 310
To yield him no unworthy maintenance.
Urged by his Mother, he essayed to teach
A village-school — but wandering thoughts
    were then
A misery to him; and the Youth resigned
A task he was unable to perform.

    That stern yet kindly Spirit, who con-
    strains
The Savoyard to quit his naked rocks,

The free-born Swiss to leave his narrow
      vales,
(Spirit attached to regions mountainous
Like their own stedfast clouds) did now
      impel   320
His restless mind to look abroad with hope.
— An irksome drudgery seems it to plod
      on,
Through hot and dusty ways, or pelting
      storm,
A vagrant Merchant under a heavy load
Bent as he moves, and needing frequent
      rest;
Yet do such travellers find their own de-
      light;
And their hard service, deemed debasing
      now,
Gained merited respect in simpler times;
When squire, and priest, and they who
      round them dwelt
In rustic sequestration — all dependent 330
Upon the PEDLAR'S toil — supplied their
      wants,
Or pleased their fancies, with the wares he
      brought.
Not ignorant was the Youth that still no
      few
Of his adventurous countrymen were led
By perseverance in this track of life
To competence and ease: — to him it offered
Attractions manifold; — and this he chose.
— His Parents on the enterprise bestowed
Their farewell benediction, but with hearts
Foreboding evil.   From his native hills 340
He wandered far; much did he see of men,
Their manners, their enjoyments, and pur-
      suits,
Their passions and their feelings; chiefly
      those
Essential and eternal in the heart,
That, 'mid the simpler forms of rural life,
Exist more simple in their elements,
And speak a plainer language.   In the
      woods,
A lone Enthusiast, and among the fields,
Itinerant in this labour, he had passed 349
The better portion of his time; and there
Spontaneously had his affections thriven
Amid the bounties of the year, the peace
And liberty of nature; there he kept
In solitude and solitary thought
His mind in a just equipoise of love.
Serene it was, unclouded by the cares
Of ordinary life; unvexed, unwarped
By partial bondage.   In his steady course,

No piteous revolutions had he felt,
No wild varieties of joy and grief.   360
Unoccupied by sorrow of its own,
His heart lay open; and, by nature tuned
And constant disposition of his thoughts
To sympathy with man, he was alive
To all that was enjoyed where'er he went,
And all that was endured; for, in himself
Happy, and quiet in his cheerfulness,
He had no painful pressure from within
That made him turn aside from wretched-
      ness
With coward fears.   He could *afford* to
      suffer   370
With those whom he saw suffer.   Hence it
      came
That in our best experience he was rich,
And in the wisdom of our daily life.
For hence, minutely, in his various rounds,
He had observed the progress and decay
Of many minds, of minds and bodies too;
The history of many families;
How they had prospered; how they were
      o'erthrown
By passion or mischance, or such misrule 379
Among the unthinking masters of the earth
As makes the nations groan.
                              This active course
He followed till provision for his wants
Had been obtained; — the Wanderer then
      resolved
To pass the remnant of his days, untasked
With needless services, from hardship free.
His calling laid aside, he lived at ease:
But still he loved to pace the public roads
And the wild paths; and, by the summer's
      warmth
Invited, often would he leave his home
And journey far, revisiting the scenes   390
That to his memory were most endeared.
— Vigorous in health, of hopeful spirits,
      undamped
By worldly-mindedness or anxious care;
Observant, studious, thoughtful, and re-
      freshed
By knowledge gathered up from day to
      day;
Thus had he lived a long and innocent life.

   The Scottish Church, both on himself and
      those
With whom from childhood he grew up,
      had held
The strong hand of her purity; and still
Had watched him with an unrelenting eye.

This he remembered in his riper age   401
With gratitude, and reverential thoughts.
But by the native vigour of his mind,
By his habitual wanderings out of doors,
By loneliness, and goodness, and kind
     works,
Whate'er, in docile childhood or in youth,
He had imbibed of fear or darker thought
Was melted all away; so true was this,
That sometimes his religion seemed to me
Self-taught, as of a dreamer in the woods;
Who to the model of his own pure heart 411
Shaped his belief, as grace divine inspired,
And human reason dictated with awe.
— And surely never did there live on earth
A man of kindlier nature. The rough
     sports
And teasing ways of children vexed not
     him;
Indulgent listener was he to the tongue
Of garrulous age; nor did the sick man's
     tale,
To his fraternal sympathy addressed,   419
Obtain reluctant hearing.
                         Plain his garb;
Such as might suit a rustic Sire, prepared
For sabbath duties; yet he was a man
Whom no one could have passed without
     remark.
Active and nervous was his gait; his limbs
And his whole figure breathed intelligence.
Time had compressed the freshness of his
     cheek
Into a narrower circle of deep red,
But had not tamed his eye; that, under
     brows
Shaggy and grey, had meanings which it
     brought
From years of youth; which, like a Being
     made   430
Of many Beings, he had wondrous skill
To blend with knowledge of the years to
     come,
Human, or such as lie beyond the grave.

So was He framed; and such his course
     of life
Who now, with no appendage but a staff,
The prized memorial of relinquished toils,
Upon that cottage-bench reposed his limbs,
Screened from the sun. Supine the Wan-
     derer lay,
His eyes as if in drowsiness half shut,
The shadows of the breezy elms above   440

Dappling his face. He had not heard the
     sound
Of my approaching steps, and in the shade
Unnoticed did I stand some minutes' space.
At length I hailed him, seeing that his hat
Was moist with water-drops, as if the brim
Had newly scooped a running stream. He
     rose,
And ere our lively greeting into peace
Had settled, " 'T is," said I, " a burning
     day:
My lips are parched with thirst, but you, it
     seems
Have somewhere found relief." He, at the
     word,   450
Pointing towards a sweet-briar, bade me
     climb
The fence where that aspiring shrub looked
     out
Upon the public way. It was a plot
Of garden ground run wild, its matted
     weeds
Marked with the steps of those, whom, as
     they passed,
The gooseberry trees that shot in long lank
     slips,
Or currants, hanging from their leafless
     stems,
In scanty strings, had tempted to o'erleap
The broken wall. I looked around, and
     there,
Where two tall hedge-rows of thick alder
     boughs   460
Joined in a cold damp nook, espied a well
Shrouded with willow-flowers and plumy
     fern.
My thirst I slaked, and, from the cheerless
     spot
Withdrawing, straightway to the shade re-
     turned
Where sate the old Man on the cottage-
     bench;
And, while, beside him, with uncovered
     head,
I yet was standing, freely to respire,
And cool my temples in the fanning air,
Thus did he speak. " I see around me
     here
Things which you cannot see: we die, my
     Friend,   470
Nor we alone, but that which each man
     loved
And prized in his peculiar nook of earth
Dies with him, or is changed; and very
     soon

Even of the good is no memorial left.
— The Poets, in their elegies and songs
Lamenting the departed, call the groves,
They call upon the hills and streams to
    mourn,
And senseless rocks; nor idly; for they
    speak,
In these their invocations, with a voice
Obedient to the strong creative power   480
Of human passion. Sympathies there are
More tranquil, yet perhaps of kindred
    birth,
That steal upon the meditative mind,
And grow with thought. Beside yon spring
    I stood,
And eyed its waters till we seemed to feel
One sadness, they and I.   For them a
    bond
Of brotherhood is broken: time has been
When, every day, the touch of human hand
Dislodged the natural sleep that binds them
    up
In mortal stillness; and they ministered   490
To human comfort. Stooping down to
    drink,
Upon the slimy foot-stone I espied
The useless fragment of a wooden bowl,
Green with the moss of years, and subject
    only
To the soft handling of the elements:
There let it lie — how foolish are such
    thoughts !
Forgive them; — never — never did my
    steps
Approach this door but she who dwelt
    within
A daughter's welcome gave me, and I loved
    her
As my own child. Oh, Sir ! the good die
    first,   500
And they whose hearts are dry as sum-
    mer dust
Burn to the socket. Many a passenger
Hath blessed poor Margaret for her gentle
    looks,
When she upheld the cool refreshment
    drawn
From that forsaken spring; and no one
    came
But he was welcome; no one went away
But that it seemed she loved him. She is
    dead,
The light extinguished of her lonely hut,
The hut itself abandoned to decay,
And she forgotten in the quiet grave.   510

I speak," continued he, " of One whose
    stock
Of virtues bloomed beneath this lowly
    roof.
She was a Woman of a steady mind,
Tender and deep in her excess of love;
Not speaking much, pleased rather with
    the joy
Of her own thoughts: by some especial care
Her temper had been framed, as if to make
A Being, who by adding love to peace
Might live on earth a life of happiness.
Her wedded Partner lacked not on his
    side   520
The humble worth that satisfied her heart:
Frugal, affectionate, sober, and withal
Keenly industrious. She with pride would
    tell
That he was often seated at his loom,
In summer, ere the mower was abroad
Among the dewy grass, — in early spring,
Ere the last star had vanished. — They
    who passed
At evening, from behind the garden fence
Might hear his busy spade, which he would
    ply,
After his daily work, until the light   530
Had failed, and every leaf and flower were
    lost
In the dark hedges. So their days were
    spent
In peace and comfort; and a pretty boy
Was their best hope, next to the God in
    heaven.

Not twenty years ago, but you I think
Can scarcely bear it now in mind, there
    came
Two blighting seasons, when the fields were
    left
With half a harvest. It pleased Heaven to
    add
A worse affliction in the plague of war:
This happy Land was stricken to the
    heart !   540
A Wanderer then among the cottages,
I, with my freight of winter raiment, saw
The hardships of that season: many rich
Sank down, as in a dream, among the
    poor;
And of the poor did many cease to be,
And their place knew them not. Mean-
    while, abridged
Of daily comforts, gladly reconciled
To numerous self-denials, Margaret

Went struggling on through those calami-
   tous years
With cheerful hope, until the second au-
   tumn,   550
When her life's Helpmate on a sick-bed
   lay,
Smitten with perilous fever. In disease
He lingered long; and, when his strength
   returned,
He found the little he had stored, to meet
The hour of accident or crippling age,
Was all consumed. A second infant now
Was added to the troubles of a time
Laden, for them and all of their degree,
With care and sorrow; shoals of artisans
From ill-requited labour turned adrift 560
Sought daily bread from public charity,
They, and their wives and children — hap-
   pier far
Could they have lived as do the little birds
That peck along the hedge-rows, or the
   kite
That makes her dwelling on the mountain
   rocks !

A sad reverse it was for him who long
Had filled with plenty, and possessed in
   peace,
This lonely Cottage. At the door he stood,
And whistled many a snatch of merry tunes
That had no mirth in them; or with his
   knife   570
Carved uncouth figures on the heads of
   sticks —
Then, not less idly, sought, through every
   nook
In house or garden, any casual work
Of use or ornament; and with a strange,
Amusing, yet uneasy, novelty,
He mingled, where he might, the various
   tasks
Of summer, autumn, winter, and of spring.
But this endured not; his good humour
   soon
Became a weight in which no pleasure was:
And poverty brought on a petted mood 580
And a sore temper: day by day he drooped,
And he would leave his work — and to the
   town
Would turn without an errand his slack
   steps;
Or wander here and there among the fields.
One while he would speak lightly of his
   babes,
And with a cruel tongue: at other times

He tossed them with a false unnatural joy:
And 't was a rueful thing to see the looks
Of the poor innocent children. ' Every
   smile,'
Said Margaret to me, here beneath these
   trees,   590
' Made my heart bleed.' "
            At this the Wanderer paused;
And, looking up to those enormous elms,
He said, " 'T is now the hour of deepest
   noon.
At this still season of repose and peace,
This hour when all things which are not at
   rest
Are cheerful; while this multitude of flies
With tuneful hum is filling all the air;
Why should a tear be on an old Man's
   cheek ?
Why should we thus, with an untoward
   mind,
And in the weakness of humanity,   600
From natural wisdom turn our hearts away;
To natural comfort shut our eyes and ears;
And, feeding on disquiet, thus disturb
The calm of nature with our restless
   thoughts ? "

HE spake with somewhat of a solemn tone:
But, when he ended, there was in his face
Such easy cheerfulness, a look so mild,
That for a little time it stole away
All recollection; and that simple tale
Passed from my mind like a forgotten
   sound.   610
A while on trivial things we held discourse,
To me soon tasteless. In my own despite,
I thought of that poor Woman as of one
Whom I had known and loved. He had
   rehearsed
Her homely tale with such familiar power,
With such an active countenance, an eye
So busy, that the things of which he spake
Seemed present; and, attention now re-
   laxed,
A heart-felt chillness crept along my veins;
I rose; and, having left the breezy shade,
Stood drinking comfort from the warmer
   sun,   621
That had not cheered me long — ere, look-
   ing round
Upon that tranquil Ruin, I returned,
And begged of the old Man that, for my
   sake,
He would resume his story.

He replied,
" It were a wantonness, and would demand
Severe reproof, if we were men whose
    hearts
Could hold vain dalliance with the misery
Even of the dead; contented thence to
    draw
A momentary pleasure, never marked   630
By reason, barren of all future good.
But we have known that there is often
    found
In mournful thoughts, and always might
    be found,
A power to virtue friendly; were 't not so,
I am a dreamer among men, indeed
An idle dreamer ! 'T is a common tale,
An ordinary sorrow of man's life,
A tale of silent suffering, hardly clothed
In bodily form. — But without further
    bidding   639
I will proceed.
            While thus it fared with them,
To whom this cottage, till those hapless
    years,
Had been a blessèd home, it was my chance
To travel in a country far remote;
And when these lofty elms once more ap-
    peared,
What pleasant expectations lured me on
O'er the flat Common ! — With quick step
    I reached
The threshold, lifted with light hand the
    latch;
But, when I entered, Margaret looked at
    me
A little while; then turned her head away
Speechless, — and, sitting down upon a
    chair,   650
Wept bitterly. I wist not what to do,
Nor how to speak to her. Poor Wretch !
    at last
She rose from off her seat, and then, — O
    Sir !
I cannot *tell* how she pronounced my
    name: —
With fervent love, and with a face of grief
Unutterably helpless, and a look
That seemed to cling upon me, she en-
    quired
If I had seen her husband. As she spake
A strange surprise and fear came to my
    heart,
Nor had I power to answer ere she told   660
That he had disappeared — not two months
    gone.

He left his house: two wretched days had
    past,
And on the third, as wistfully she raised
Her head from off her pillow, to look forth,
Like one in trouble, for returning light,
Within her chamber-casement she espied
A folded paper, lying as if placed
To meet her waking eyes. This trem-
    blingly
She opened — found no writing, but beheld
Pieces of money carefully enclosed,   670
Silver and gold. ' I shuddered at the
    sight,'
Said Margaret, ' for I knew it was his hand
That must have placed it there; and ere
    that day
Was ended, that long anxious day, I
    learned,
From one who by my husband had been
    sent
With the sad news, that he had joined a
    troop
Of soldiers, going to a distant land.
— He left me thus — he could not gather
    heart
To take a farewell of me; for he feared
That I should follow with my babes, and
    sink   680
Beneath the misery of that wandering life.'

This tale did Margaret tell with many
    tears:
And, when she ended, I had little power
To give her comfort, and was glad to take
Such words of hope from her own mouth
    as served
To cheer us both. But long we had not
    talked
Ere we built up a pile of better thoughts,
And with a brighter eye she looked around
As if she had been shedding tears of joy.
We parted. — 'T was the time of early
    spring;   690
I left her busy with her garden tools;
And well remember, o'er that fence she
    looked,
And, while I paced along the foot-way path,
Called out, and sent a blessing after me,
With tender cheerfulness, and with a voice
That seemed the very sound of happy
    thoughts.

I roved o'er many a hill and many a dale,
With my accustomed load; in heat and
    cold,

Through many a wood and many an open
    ground,   699
In sunshine and in shade, in wet and fair,
Drooping or blithe of heart, as might be-
    fall;
My best companions now the driving winds,
And now the 'trotting brooks' and whis-
    pering trees,
And now the music of my own sad steps,
With many a short-lived thought that
    passed between,
And disappeared.
           I journeyed back this way,
When, in the warmth of midsummer, the
    wheat
Was yellow; and the soft and bladed grass,
Springing afresh, had o'er the hay-field
    spread
Its tender verdure. At the door arrived, 710
I found that she was absent. In the shade,
Where now we sit, I waited her return.
Her cottage, then a cheerful object, wore
Its customary look, — only, it seemed,
The honeysuckle, crowding round the porch,
Hung down in heavier tufts; and that
    bright weed,
The yellow stone-crop, suffered to take
    root
Along the window's edge, profusely grew,
Blinding the lower panes. I turned aside,
And strolled into her garden. It appeared
To lag behind the season, and had lost 721
Its pride of neatness. Daisy-flowers and
    thrift
Had broken their trim border-lines, and
    straggled
O'er paths they used to deck: carnations,
    once
Prized for surpassing beauty, and no less
For the peculiar pains they had required,
Declined their languid heads, wanting
    support.
The cumbrous bind-weed, with its wreaths
    and bells,
Had twined about her two small rows of
    peas,
And dragged them to the earth.
               Ere this an hour
Was wasted. — Back I turned my restless
    steps;   731
A stranger passed; and, guessing whom I
    sought,
He said that she was used to ramble far. —
The sun was sinking in the west; and
    now

I sate with sad impatience. From within
Her solitary infant cried aloud;
Then, like a blast that dies away self-
    stilled,
The voice was silent. From the bench I
    rose;
But neither could divert nor soothe my
    thoughts.
The spot, though fair, was very desolate —
The longer I remained, more desolate: 741
And, looking round me, now I first observed
The corner stones, on either side the porch,
With dull red stains discoloured, and stuck
    o'er
With tufts and hairs of wool, as if the
    sheep,
That fed upon the Common, thither came
Familiarly, and found a couching-place
Even at her threshold. Deeper shadows
    fell
From these tall elms; the cottage-clock
    struck eight;—
I turned, and saw her distant a few steps.
Her face was pale and thin — her figure,
    too,   751
Was changed. As she unlocked the door,
    she said,
'It grieves me you have waited here so
    long,
But, in good truth, I've wandered much of
    late;
And sometimes — to my shame I speak —
    have need
Of my best prayers to bring me back again.'
While on the board she spread our evening
    meal,
She told me — interrupting not the work
Which gave employment to her listless
    hands —
That she had parted with her elder child,
To a kind master on a distant farm   761
Now happily apprenticed. — 'I perceive
You look at me, and you have cause; to-
    day
I have been travelling far; and many days
About the fields I wander, knowing this
Only, that what I seek I cannot find;
And so I waste my time: for I am changed;
And to myself,' said she, 'have done much
    wrong
And to this helpless infant. I have slept
Weeping, and weeping have I waked; my
    tears   770
Have flowed as if my body were not such
As others are; and I could never die.

But I am now in mind and in my heart
More easy; and I hope,' said she, ' that
God
Will give me patience to endure the things
Which I behold at home.'
     It would have grieved
Your very soul to see her. Sir, I feel
The story linger in my heart; I fear
'T is long and tedious; but my spirit clings
To that poor Woman: — so familiarly 780
Do I perceive her manner, and her look,
And presence; and so deeply do I feel
Her goodness, that, not seldom, in my
  walks
A momentary trance comes over me;
And to myself I seem to muse on One
By sorrow laid asleep; or borne away,
A human being destined to awake
To human life, or something very near
To human life, when he shall come again
For whom she suffered. Yes, it would
  have grieved 790
Your very soul to see her: evermore
Her eyelids drooped, her eyes downward
  were cast;
And, when she at her table gave me food,
She did not look at me. Her voice was
  low,
Her body was subdued. In every act
Pertaining to her house-affairs, appeared
The careless stillness of a thinking mind
Self-occupied; to which all outward things
Are like an idle matter. Still she sighed,
But yet no motion of the breast was seen,
No heaving of the heart. While by the
  fire 801
We sate together, sighs came on my ear,
I knew not how, and hardly whence they
  came.

Ere my departure, to her care I gave,
For her son's use, some tokens of regard,
Which with a look of welcome she received;
And I exhorted her to place her trust
In God's good love, and seek his help by
  prayer.
I took my staff, and, when I kissed her
  babe,
The tears stood in her eyes. I left her
  then 810
With the best hope and comfort I could
  give:
She thanked me for my wish; — but for
  my hope
It seemed she did not thank me.

       I returned,
And took my rounds along this road again
When on its sunny bank the primrose
  flower
Peeped forth, to give an earnest of the
  Spring.
I found her sad and drooping: she had
  learned
No tidings of her husband; if he lived,
She knew not that he lived; if he were
  dead,
She knew not he was dead. She seemed
  the same 820
In person and appearance; but her house
Bespake a sleepy hand of negligence;
The floor was neither dry nor neat, the
  hearth
Was comfortless, and her small lot of
  books,
Which, in the cottage-window, heretofore
Had been piled up against the corner
  panes
In seemly order, now, with straggling
  leaves
Lay scattered here and there, open or shut,
As they had chanced to fall. Her infant
  Babe
Had from its Mother caught the trick of
  grief, 830
And sighed among its playthings. I with-
  drew,
And once again entering the garden saw,
More plainly still, that poverty and grief
Were now come nearer to her: weeds de-
  faced
The hardened soil, and knots of withered
  grass:
No ridges there appeared of clear black
  mould,
No winter greenness; of her herbs and
  flowers,
It seemed the better part were gnawed away
Or trampled into earth; a chain of straw,
Which had been twined about the slender
  stem 840
Of a young apple-tree, lay at its root;
The bark was nibbled round by truant
  sheep.
— Margaret stood near, her infant in her
  arms,
And, noting that my eye was on the tree,
She said, ' I fear it will be dead and gone
Ere Robert come again.' When to the
  House
We had returned together, she enquired

If I had any hope: — but for her babe
And for her little orphan boy, she said,
She had no wish to live, that she must die
Of sorrow. Yet I saw the idle loom   851
Still in its place; his Sunday garments hung
Upon the self-same nail; his very staff
Stood undisturbed behind the door.
                    And when,
In bleak December, I retraced this way,
She told me that her little babe was dead,
And she was left alone. She now, released
From her maternal cares, had taken up
The employment common through these wilds, and gained,
By spinning hemp, a pittance for herself;
And for this end had hired a neighbour's boy   861
To give her needful help. That very time
Most willingly she put her work aside,
And walked with me along the miry road,
Heedless how far; and, in such piteous sort
That any heart had ached to hear her, begged
That, wheresoe'er I went, I still would ask
For him whom she had lost. We parted then —
Our final parting; for from that time forth
Did many seasons pass ere I returned   870
Into this tract again.
                    Nine tedious years;
From their first separation, nine long years,
She lingered in unquiet widowhood;
A Wife and Widow. Needs must it have been
A sore heart-wasting ! I have heard, my Friend,
That in yon arbour oftentimes she sate
Alone, through half the vacant sabbath day;
And, if a dog passed by, she still would quit
The shade, and look abroad. On this old bench   879
For hours she sate; and evermore her eye
Was busy in the distance, shaping things
That made her heart beat quick. You see that path,
Now faint, — the grass has crept o'er its grey line;
There, to and fro, she paced through many a day
Of the warm summer, from a belt of hemp

That girt her waist, spinning the long-drawn thread
With backward steps. Yet ever as there passed
A man whose garments showed the soldier's red,
Or crippled mendicant in sailor's garb,
The little child who sate to turn the wheel
Ceased from his task; and she with faltering voice   891
Made many a fond enquiry; and when they,
Whose presence gave no comfort, were gone by,
Her heart was still more sad. And by yon gate,
That bars the traveller's road, she often stood,
And when a stranger horseman came, the latch
Would lift, and in his face look wistfully;
Most happy, if, from aught discovered there
Of tender feeling, she might dare repeat
The same sad question. Meanwhile her poor Hut   900
Sank to decay; for he was gone, whose hand,
At the first nipping of October frost,
Closed up each chink, and with fresh bands of straw
Chequered the green-grown thatch. And so she lived
Through the long winter, reckless and alone;
Until her house by frost, and thaw, and rain,
Was sapped; and while she slept, the nightly damps
Did chill her breast; and in the stormy day
Her tattered clothes were ruffled by the wind,
Even at the side of her own fire. Yet still   910
She loved this wretched spot, nor would for worlds
Have parted hence; and still that length of road,
And this rude bench, one torturing hope endeared,
Fast rooted at her heart: and here, my Friend, —
In sickness she remained; and here she died;
Last human tenant of these ruined walls ! "

The old Man ceased: he saw that I was
    moved;
From that low bench, rising instinctively
I turned aside in weakness, nor had power
To thank him for the tale which he had
    told. 920
I stood, and leaning o'er the garden wall
Reviewed that Woman's sufferings; and it
    seemed
To comfort me while with a brother's love
I blessed her in the impotence of grief.
Then towards the cottage I returned; and
    traced
Fondly, though with an interest more mild,
That secret spirit of humanity
Which, 'mid the calm oblivious tendencies
Of nature, 'mid her plants, and weeds, and
    flowers,
And silent overgrowings, still survived. 930
The old Man, noting this, resumed, and
    said,
" My Friend! enough to sorrow you have
    given,
The purposes of wisdom ask no more:
Nor more would she have craved as due to
    One
Who, in her worst distress, had ofttimes
    felt
The unbounded might of prayer; and
    learned, with soul
Fixed on the Cross, that consolation springs,
From sources deeper far than deepest pain,
For the meek Sufferer. Why then should
    we read
The forms of things with an unworthy eye?
She sleeps in the calm earth, and peace is
    here. 941
I well remember that those very plumes,
Those weeds, and the high spear-grass on
    that wall,
By mist and silent rain-drops silvered o'er,
As once I passed, into my heart conveyed
So still an image of tranquillity,
So calm and still, and looked so beautiful
Amid the uneasy thoughts which filled my
    mind,
That what we feel of sorrow and despair
From ruin and from change, and all the
    grief 950
That passing shows of Being leave behind,
Appeared an idle dream, that could main-
    tain,
Nowhere, dominion o'er the enlightened
    spirit
Whose meditative sympathies repose

Upon the breast of Faith. I turned away,
And walked along my road in happiness."

He ceased. Ere long the sun declining
    shot
A slant and mellow radiance, which began
To fall upon us, while, beneath the trees,
We sate on that low bench: and now we
    felt, 960
Admonished thus, the sweet hour coming
    on.
A linnet warbled from those lofty elms,
A thrush sang loud, and other melodies,
At distance heard, peopled the milder air.
The old Man rose, and, with a sprightly
    mien
Of hopeful preparation, grasped his staff;
Together casting then a farewell look
Upon those silent walls, we left the shade;
And, ere the stars were visible, had reached
A village-inn, — our evening resting-place.

BOOK SECOND

THE SOLITARY

ARGUMENT

The Author describes his travels with the
Wanderer, whose character is further illus-
trated — Morning scene, and View of a Village
Wake — Wanderer's account of a Friend whom
he purposes to visit — View, from an eminence,
of the Valley which his Friend had chosen for
his retreat — Sound of singing from below — A
funeral procession — Descent into the Valley
— Observations drawn from the Wanderer
at sight of a book accidentally discovered in
a recess in the Valley — Meeting with the
Wanderer's friend, the Solitary — Wanderer's
description of the mode of burial in this moun-
tainous district — Solitary contrasts with this,
that of the individual carried a few minutes be-
fore from the cottage — The cottage entered —
Description of the Solitary's apartment — Re-
past there — View, from the window, of two
mountain summits; and the Solitary's descrip-
tion of the companionship they afford him —
Account of the departed inmate of the cottage
— Description of a grand spectacle upon the
mountains, with its effect upon the Solitary's
mind — Leave the house.

In days of yore how fortunately fared
The Minstrel! wandering on from hall to
    hall,
Baronial court or royal; cheered with gifts

Munificent, and love, and ladies' praise;
Now meeting on his road an armèd knight,
Now resting with a pilgrim by the side
Of a clear brook;—beneath an abbey's
    roof
One evening sumptuously lodged; the next,
Humbly in a religious hospital;
Or with some merry outlaws of the wood;
Or haply shrouded in a hermit's cell.   11
Him, sleeping or awake, the robber spared;
He walked — protected from the sword of
    war
By virtue of that sacred instrument
His harp, suspended at the traveller's side;
His dear companion wheresoe'er he went,
Opening from land to land an easy way
By melody, and by the charm of verse.
Yet not the noblest of that honoured Race
Drew happier, loftier, more empassioned,
    thoughts   20
From his long journeyings and eventful life,
Than this obscure Itinerant had skill
To gather, ranging through the tamer
    ground
Of these our unimaginative days;
Both while he trod the earth in humblest
    guise
Accoutred with his burthen and his staff;
And now, when free to move with lighter
    pace.

    What wonder, then, if I, whose favourite
    school
Hath been the fields, the roads, and rural
    lanes,
Looked on this guide with reverential love ?
Each with the other pleased, we now pur-
    sued   31
Our journey, under favourable skies.
Turn wheresoe'er we would, he was a light
Unfailing: not a hamlet could we pass,
Rarely a house, that did not yield to him
Remembrances; or from his tongue call
    forth
Some way-beguiling tale. Nor less regard
Accompanied those strains of apt discourse,
Which nature's various objects might in-
    spire;
And in the silence of his face I read   40
His overflowing spirit. Birds and beasts,
And the mute fish that glances in the stream,
And harmless reptile coiling in the sun,
And gorgeous insect hovering in the air,
The fowl domestic, and the household dog —
In his capacious mind, he loved them all:

Their rights acknowledging he felt for all.
Oft was occasion given me to perceive
How the calm pleasures of the pasturing
    herd
To happy contemplation soothed his walk;
How the poor brute's condition, forced to
    run   51
Its course of suffering in the public road,
Sad contrast ! all too often smote his heart
With unavailing pity. Rich in love
And sweet humanity, he was, himself,
To the degree that he desired, beloved.
Smiles of good-will from faces that he knew
Greeted us all day long; we took our seats
By many a cottage-hearth, where he re-
    ceived
The welcome of an Inmate from afar,   60
And I at once forgot, I was a Stranger.
— Nor was he loth to enter ragged huts,
Huts where his charity was blest; his voice
Heard as the voice of an experienced friend.
And, sometimes — where the poor man held
    dispute
With his own mind, unable to subdue
Impatience through inaptness to perceive
General distress in his particular lot;
Or cherishing resentment, or in vain
Struggling against it; with a soul perplexed,
And finding in herself no steady power   71
To draw the line of comfort that divides
Calamity, the chastisement of Heaven,
From the injustice of our brother men —
To him appeal was made as to a judge;
Who, with an understanding heart, allayed
The perturbation; listened to the plea;
Resolved the dubious point; and sentence
    gave
So grounded, so applied, that it was heard
With softened spirit, even when it con-
    demned.   80

    Such intercourse I witnessed, while we
    roved,
Now as his choice directed, now as mine;
Or both, with equal readiness of will,
Our course submitting to the changeful
    breeze
Of accident. But when the rising sun
Had three times called us to renew our walk,
My Fellow-traveller, with earnest voice,
As if the thought were but a moment old,
Claimed absolute dominion for the day.
We started — and he led me toward the
    hills,   90
Up through an ample vale, with higher hills

Before us, mountains stern and desolate;
But, in the majesty of distance, now
Set off, and to our ken appearing fair
Of aspect, with aërial softness clad,
And beautified with morning's purple beams.

  The wealthy, the luxurious, by the stress
Of business roused, or pleasure, ere their
    time,
May roll in chariots, or provoke the hoofs
Of the fleet coursers they bestride, to raise
From earth the dust of morning, slow to
    rise;   101
And they, if blest with health and hearts at
    ease,
Shall lack not their enjoyment: — but how
    faint
Compared with ours! who, pacing side by
    side,
Could, with an eye of leisure, look on all
That we beheld; and lend the listening
    sense
To every grateful sound of earth and air;
Pausing at will — our spirits braced, our
    thoughts
Pleasant as roses in the thickets blown,
And pure as dew bathing their crimson
    leaves.   110

  Mount slowly, sun! that we may journey
    long,
By this dark hill protected from thy beams!
Such is the summer pilgrim's frequent
    wish;
But quickly from among our morning
    thoughts
'T was chased away: for, toward the west-
    ern side
Of the broad vale, casting a casual glance,
We saw a throng of people; wherefore met?
Blithe notes of music, suddenly let loose
On the thrilled ear, and flags uprising, yield
Prompt answer; they proclaim the annual
    Wake,   120
Which the bright season favours. — Tabor
    and pipe
In purpose join to hasten or reprove
The laggard Rustic; and repay with boons
Of merriment a party-coloured knot,
Already formed upon the village-green.
— Beyond the limits of the shadow cast
By the broad hill, glistened upon our sight
That gay assemblage. Round them and
    above,
Glitter, with dark recesses interposed,

Casement, and cottage-roof, and stems of
    trees   130
Half-veiled in vapoury cloud, the silver
    steam
Of dews fast melting on their leafy boughs
By the strong sunbeams smitten. Like a
    mast
Of gold, the Maypole shines; as if the rays
Of morning, aided by exhaling dew,
With gladsome influence could re-animate
The faded garlands dangling from its sides.

  Said I, "The music and the sprightly
    scene
Invite us; shall we quit our road, and join
These festive matins?"—He replied, "Not
    loth   140
To linger I would here with you partake,
Not one hour merely, but till evening's
    close,
The simple pastimes of the day and place.
By the fleet Racers, ere the sun be set,
The turf of yon large pasture will be
    skimmed;
There, too, the lusty Wrestlers shall con-
    tend:
But know we not that he, who intermits
The appointed task and duties of the day,
Untunes full oft the pleasures of the day;
Checking the finer spirits that refuse   150
To flow when purposes are lightly changed?
A length of journey yet remains untraced:
Let us proceed." Then, pointing with his
    staff
Raised toward those craggy summits, his
    intent
He thus imparted: —
             "In a spot that lies
Among yon mountain fastnesses concealed,
You will receive, before the hour of noon,
Good recompense, I hope, for this day's toil,
From sight of One who lives secluded there,
Lonesome and lost: of whom, and whose
    past life,   160
(Not to forestall such knowledge as may be
More faithfully collected from himself)
This brief communication shall suffice.

  Though now sojourning there, he, like
    myself,
Sprang from a stock of lowly parentage
Among the wilds of Scotland, in a tract
Where many a sheltered and well-tended
    plant
Bears, on the humblest ground of social life,

Blossoms of piety and innocence. 169
Such grateful promises his youth displayed:
And, having shown in study forward zeal,
He to the Ministry was duly called;
And straight, incited by a curious mind
Filled with vague hopes, he undertook the charge
Of Chaplain to a military troop
Cheered by the Highland bagpipe, as they marched
In plaided vest, — his fellow-countrymen.
This office filling, yet by native power
And force of native inclination made
An intellectual ruler in the haunts 180
Of social vanity, he walked the world,
Gay, and affecting graceful gaiety;
Lax, buoyant — less a pastor with his flock
Than a soldier among soldiers — lived and roamed
Where Fortune led: — and Fortune, who oft proves
The careless wanderer's friend, to him made known
A blooming Lady — a conspicuous flower,
Admired for beauty, for her sweetness praised;
Whom he had sensibility to love,
Ambition to attempt, and skill to win. 190

For this fair Bride, most rich in gifts of mind,
Nor sparingly endowed with worldly wealth,
His office he relinquished; and retired
From the world's notice to a rural home.
Youth's season yet with him was scarcely past,
And she was in youth's prime. How free their love,
How full their joy ! 'Till, pitiable doom !
In the short course of one undreaded year
Death blasted all. Death suddenly o'erthrew
Two lovely Children — all that they possessed ! 200
The Mother followed: — miserably bare
The one Survivor stood; he wept, he prayed
For his dismissal, day and night, compelled
To hold communion with the grave, and face
With pain the regions of eternity.
An uncomplaining apathy displaced
This anguish; and, indifferent to delight,
To aim and purpose, he consumed his days,
To private interest dead, and public care. 209

So lived he; so he might have died.
                                    But now,
To the wide world's astonishment, appeared
A glorious opening, the unlooked-for dawn,
That promised everlasting joy to France !
Her voice of social transport reached even him !
He broke from his contracted bounds, repaired
To the great City, an emporium then
Of golden expectations, and receiving
Freights every day from a new world of hope.
Thither his popular talents he transferred;
And, from the pulpit, zealously maintained 220
The cause of Christ and civil liberty,
As one, and moving to one glorious end.
Intoxicating service ! I might say
A happy service; for he was sincere
As vanity and fondness for applause,
And new and shapeless wishes, would allow.

That righteous cause (such power hath freedom) bound,
For one hostility, in friendly league,
Ethereal natures and the worst of slaves;
Was served by rival advocates that came 230
From regions opposite as heaven and hell.
One courage seemed to animate them all:
And, from the dazzling conquests daily gained
By their united efforts, there arose
A proud and most presumptuous confidence
In the transcendent wisdom of the age,
And her discernment; not alone in rights,
And in the origin and bounds of power
Social and temporal; but in laws divine,
Deduced by reason, or to faith revealed. 240
An overweening trust was raised; and fear
Cast out, alike of person and of thing.
Plague from this union spread, whose subtle bane
The strongest did not easily escape;
And He, what wonder ! took a mortal taint.
How shall I trace the change, how bear to tell
That he broke faith with them whom he had laid
In earth's dark chambers, with a Christian's hope !
An infidel contempt of holy writ 249
Stole by degrees upon his mind; and hence
Life, like that Roman Janus, double-faced;

Vilest hypocrisy — the laughing, gay
Hypocrisy, not leagued with fear, but pride.
Smooth words he had to wheedle simple
souls;
But, for disciples of the inner school,
Old freedom was old servitude, and they
The wisest whose opinions stooped the
least
To known restraints; and who most boldly
drew
Hopeful prognostications from a creed,
That, in the light of false philosophy,   260
Spread like a halo round a misty moon,
Widening its circle as the storms advance.

His sacred function was at length re-
nounced;
And every day and every place enjoyed
The unshackled layman's natural liberty;
Speech, manners, morals, all without dis-
guise.
I do not wish to wrong him; though the
course
Of private life licentiously displayed
Unhallowed actions — planted like a crown
Upon the insolent aspiring brow   270
Of spurious notions — worn as open signs
Of prejudice subdued — still he retained,
'Mid much abasement, what he had received
From nature, an intense and glowing mind.
Wherefore, when humbled Liberty grew
weak,
And mortal sickness on her face appeared,
He coloured objects to his own desire
As with a lover's passion.   Yet his moods
Of pain were keen as those of better men,
Nay keener, as his fortitude was less: 280
And he continued, when worse days were
come,
To deal about his sparkling eloquence,
Struggling against the strange reverse with
zeal
That showed like happiness.   But, in de-
spite
Of all this outside bravery, within,
He neither felt encouragement nor hope:
For moral dignity, and strength of mind,
Were wanting; and simplicity of life;
And reverence for himself; and, last and
best,
Confiding thoughts, through love and fear
of Him   290
Before whose sight the troubles of this
world
Are vain, as billows in a tossing sea.

The glory of the times fading away —
The splendour, which had given a festal air
To self-importance, hallowed it, and veiled
From his own sight — this gone, he for-
feited
All joy in human nature; was consumed,
And vexed, and chafed, by levity and
scorn,
And fruitless indignation; galled by pride;
Made desperate by contempt of men who
throve   300
Before his sight in power or fame, and won,
Without desert, what he desired; weak
men,
Too weak even for his envy or his hate!
Tormented thus, after a wandering course
Of discontent, and inwardly opprest
With malady — in part, I fear, provoked
By weariness of life — he fixed his home,
Or, rather say, sate down by very chance,
Among these rugged hills; where now he
dwells,
And wastes the sad remainder of his hours,
Steeped in a self-indulging spleen, that
wants not   311
Its own voluptuousness; — on this resolved,
With this content, that he will live and die
Forgotten, — at safe distance from 'a world
Not moving to his mind.'"
                          These serious words
Closed the preparatory notices
That served my Fellow-traveller to beguile
The way, while we advanced up that wide
vale.
Diverging now (as if his quest had been
Some secret of the mountains, cavern, fall
Of water, or some lofty eminence,   321
Renowned for splendid prospect far and
wide)
We scaled, without a track to ease our
steps,
A steep ascent; and reached a dreary plain,
With a tumultuous waste of huge hill tops
Before us; savage region! which I paced
Dispirited: when, all at once, behold!
Beneath our feet, a little lowly vale,
A lowly vale, and yet uplifted high
Among the mountains; even as if the spot
Had been from eldest time by wish of
theirs   331
So placed, to be shut out from all the
world!
Urn-like it was in shape, deep as an urn;
With rocks encompassed, save that to the
south

Was one small opening, where a heath-clad
    ridge
Supplied a boundary less abrupt and close;
A quiet treeless nook, with two green fields,
A liquid pool that glittered in the sun,
And one bare dwelling; one abode, no more !
It seemed the home of poverty and toil, 340
Though not of want: the little fields, made
    green
By husbandry of many thrifty years,
Paid cheerful tribute to the moorland
    house.
— There crows the cock, single in his
    domain:
The small birds find in spring no thicket
    there
To shroud them; only from the neighbour-
    ing vales
The cuckoo, straggling up to the hill tops,
Shouteth faint tidings of some gladder
    place.

Ah ! what a sweet Recess, thought I, is
    here !   349
Instantly throwing down my limbs at ease
Upon a bed of heath; — full many a spot
Of hidden beauty have I chanced to espy
Among the mountains; never one like this;
So lonesome, and so perfectly secure;
Not melancholy — no, for it is green,
And bright, and fertile, furnished in itself
With the few needful things that life re-
    quires.
— In rugged arms how softly does it lie,
How tenderly protected ! Far and near
We have an image of the pristine earth,
The planet in its nakedness: were this 361
Man's only dwelling, sole appointed seat,
First, last, and single, in the breathing
    world,
It could not be more quiet; peace is here
Or nowhere; days unruffled by the gale
Of public news or private; years that pass
Forgetfully; uncalled upon to pay
The common penalties of mortal life,
Sickness, or accident, or grief, or pain.

On these and kindred thoughts intent I
    lay   370
In silence musing by my Comrade's side,
He also silent; when from out the heart
Of that profound abyss a solemn voice,
Or several voices in one solemn sound,
Was heard ascending; mournful, deep, and
    slow

The cadence, as of psalms — a funeral
    dirge !
We listened, looking down upon the hut,
But seeing no one: meanwhile from below
The strain continued, spiritual as before;
And now distinctly could I recognise   380
These words: — " *Shall in the grave thy
    love be known,*
In death thy faithfulness ? " — " God rest
    his soul ! "
Said the old man, abruptly breaking si-
    lence, —
" He is departed, and finds peace at last ! "

This scarcely spoken, and those holy
    strains
Not ceasing, forth appeared in view a band
Of rustic persons, from behind the hut
Bearing a coffin in the midst, with which
They shaped their course along the sloping
    side
Of that small valley, singing as they moved;
A sober company and few, the men   391
Bare-headed, and all decently attired !
Some steps when they had thus advanced,
    the dirge
Ended; and, from the stillness that ensued
Recovering, to my Friend I said, " You
    spake,
Methought, with apprehension that these
    rites
Are paid to Him upon whose shy retreat
This day we purposed to intrude." — " I did
    so,
But let us hence, that we may learn the
    truth:
Perhaps it is not he but some one else   400
For whom this pious service is performed;
Some other tenant of the solitude."

So, to a steep and difficult descent
Trusting ourselves, we wound from crag to
    crag,
Where passage could be won; and, as the
    last
Of the mute train, behind the heathy top
Of that off-sloping outlet, disappeared,
I, more impatient in my downward course,
Had landed upon easy ground; and there
Stood waiting for my Comrade. When
    behold   410
An object that enticed my steps aside !
A narrow, winding entry opened out
Into a platform — that lay, sheepfold-wise,
Enclosed between an upright mass of rock

And one old moss-grown wall; — a cool
recess,
And fanciful! For where the rock and
wall
Met in an angle, hung a penthouse, framed
By thrusting two rude staves into the wall
And overlaying them with mountain sods;
To weather-fend a little turf-built seat 420
Whereon a full-grown man might rest, nor
dread
The burning sunshine, or a transient shower;
But the whole plainly wrought by children's
hands!
Whose skill had thronged the floor with a
proud show
Of baby-houses, curiously arranged;
Nor wanting ornament of walks between,
With mimic trees inserted in the turf,
And gardens interposed. Pleased with the
sight,
I could not choose but beckon to my Guide,
Who, entering, round him threw a careless
glance, 430
Impatient to pass on, when I exclaimed,
" Lo! what is here?" and, stooping down,
drew forth
A book, that, in the midst of stones and
moss
And wreck of party-coloured earthen-ware,
Aptly disposed, had lent its help to raise
One of those petty structures. " His it
must be!"
Exclaimed the Wanderer, "cannot but be
his,
And he is gone!" The book, which in my
hand
Had opened of itself (for it was swoln
With searching damp, and seemingly had
lain 440
To the injurious elements exposed
From week to week,) I found to be a
work
In the French tongue, a Novel of Voltaire,
His famous Optimist. " Unhappy Man!"
Exclaimed my Friend: " here then has been
to him
Retreat within retreat, a sheltering-place
Within how deep a shelter! He had fits,
Even to the last, of genuine tenderness,
And loved the haunts of children: here, no
doubt,
Pleasing and pleased, he shared their simple
sports, 450
Or sate companionless; and here the book,
Left and forgotten in his careless way,

Must by the cottage-children have been
found:
Heaven bless them, and their inconsiderate
work!
To what odd purpose have the darlings
turned
This sad memorial of their hapless friend!"

" Me," said I, " most doth it surprise, to
find
Such book in such a place!" — " A book it
is,"
He answered, " to the Person suited well,
Though little suited to surrounding things:
'T is strange, I grant; and stranger still had
been 461
To see the Man who owned it, dwelling
here,
With one poor shepherd, far from all the
world! —
Now, if our errand hath been thrown away,
As from these intimations I forebode,
Grieved shall I be — less for my sake than
yours,
And least of all for him who is no more."

By this, the book was in the old Man's
hand;
And he continued, glancing on the leaves
An eye of scorn: — " The lover," said he,
" doomed 470
To love when hope hath failed him — whom
no depth
Of privacy is deep enough to hide,
Hath yet his bracelet or his lock of hair,
And that is joy to him. When change of
times
Hath summoned kings to scaffolds, do but
give
The faithful servant, who must hide his
head
Henceforth in whatsoever nook he may,
A kerchief sprinkled with his master's
blood,
And he too hath his comforter. How poor,
Beyond all poverty how destitute, 480
Must that Man have been left, who, hither
driven,
Flying or seeking, could yet bring with him
No dearer relique, and no better stay,
Than this dull product of a scoffer's pen,
Impure conceits discharging from a heart
Hardened by impious pride! —I did not fear
To tax you with this journey;" — mildly
said

My venerable Friend, as forth we stepped
Into the presence of the cheerful light —
" For I have knowledge that you do not
　　shrink　　　　　　　　　　　　　490
From moving spectacles; — but let us on."

　So speaking, on he went, and at the word
I followed, till he made a sudden stand:
For full in view, approaching through a
　　gate
That opened from the enclosure of green
　　fields
Into the rough uncultivated ground,
Behold the Man whom he had fancied dead!
I knew from his deportment, mien, and
　　dress,
That it could be no other; a pale face,
A meagre person, tall, and in a garb　　500
Not rustic — dull and faded like himself!
He saw us not, though distant but few
　　steps;
For he was busy, dealing, from a store
Upon a broad leaf carried, choicest strings
Of red ripe currants; gift by which he
　　strove,
With intermixture of endearing words,
To soothe a Child, who walked beside him,
　　weeping
As if disconsolate. — " They to the grave
Are bearing him, my Little-one," he said,
" To the dark pit; but he will feel no pain;
His body is at rest, his soul in heaven."　511

　More might have followed — but my
　　honoured Friend
Broke in upon the Speaker with a frank
And cordial greeting. — Vivid was the light
That flashed and sparkled from the other's
　　eyes;
He was all fire: no shadow on his brow
Remained, nor sign of sickness on his face.
Hands joined he with his Visitant, — a grasp,
An eager grasp; and many moments'
　　space —
When the first glow of pleasure was no
　　more,　　　　　　　　　　　　520
And, of the sad appearance which at once
Had vanished, much was come and
　　coming back —
An amicable smile retained the life
Which it had unexpectedly received,
Upon his hollow cheek. " How kind," he
　　said,
" Nor could your coming have been better
　　timed;

For this, you see, is in our narrow world
A day of sorrow. I have here a charge " —
And, speaking thus, he patted tenderly
The sun-burnt forehead of the weeping
　　child —　　　　　　　　　　　　530
" A little mourner, whom it is my task
To comfort; — but how came ye ? — if yon
　　track
(Which doth at once befriend us and be-
　　tray)
Conducted hither your most welcome feet,
Ye could not miss the funeral train — they
　　yet
Have scarcely disappeared." " This bloom-
　　ing Child,"
Said the old Man, " is of an age to weep
At any grave or solemn spectacle,
Inly distressed or overpowered with awe,
He knows not wherefore ; — but the boy to-
　　day,　　　　　　　　　　　　540
Perhaps is shedding orphan's tears; you
　　also
Must have sustained a loss." — " The hand
　　of Death,"
He answered, " has been here; but could
　　not well
Have fallen more lightly, if it had not fallen
Upon myself." — The other left these words
Unnoticed, thus continuing —
　　　　　　　　　" From yon crag,
Down whose steep sides we dropped into
　　the vale,
We heard the hymn they sang — a solemn
　　sound
Heard anywhere; but in a place like this
'T is more than human ! Many precious rites
And customs of our rural ancestry　　551
Are gone, or stealing from us; this, I hope,
Will last for ever. Oft on my way have I
Stood still, though but a casual passenger,
So much I felt the awfulness of life,
In that one moment when the corse is
　　lifted
In silence, with a hush of decency;
Then from the threshold moves with song
　　of peace,
And confidential yearnings, towards its
　　home,
Its final home on earth. What traveller —
　　who —　　　　　　　　　　　560
(How far soe'er a stranger) does not own
The bond of brotherhood, when he sees
　　them go,
A mute procession on the houseless road;
Or passing by some single tenement

Or clustered dwellings, where again they
    raise
The monitory voice ? But most of all
It touches, it confirms, and elevates,
Then, when the body, soon to be consigned
Ashes to ashes, dust bequeathed to dust,
Is raised from the church-aisle, and forward
    borne   570
Upon the shoulders of the next in love,
The nearest in affection or in blood;
Yea, by the very mourners who had knelt
Beside the coffin, resting on its lid
In silent grief their unuplifted heads,
And heard meanwhile the Psalmist's
    mournful plaint,
And that most awful scripture which de-
    clares
We shall not sleep, but we shall all be
    changed !
— Have I not seen — ye likewise may have
    seen —
Son, husband, brothers — brothers side by
    side,   580
And son and father also side by side,
Rise from that posture: — and in concert
    move,
On the green turf following the vested
    Priest,
Four dear supporters of one senseless
    weight,
From which they do not shrink, and under
    which
They faint not, but advance towards the
    open grave
Step after step — together, with their firm
Unhidden faces: he that suffers most,
He outwardly, and inwardly perhaps,
The most serene, with most undaunted
    eye ! —   590
Oh ! blest are they who live and die like
    these,
Loved with such love, and with such
    sorrow mourned ! "

"That poor Man taken hence to-day,"
    replied
The Solitary, with a faint sarcastic smile
Which did not please me, "must be
    deemed, I fear,
Of the unblest; for he will surely sink
Into his mother earth without such pomp
Of grief, depart without occasion given
By him for such array of fortitude.
Full seventy winters hath he lived, and
    mark !   600

This simple Child will mourn his one short
    hour,
And I shall miss him: scanty tribute ! yet,
This wanting, he would leave the sight of
    men,
If love were his sole claim upon their care,
Like a ripe date which in the desert falls
Without a hand to gather it."
                          At this
I interposed, though loth to speak, and
    said,
" Can it be thus among so small a band
As ye must needs be here ? in such a place
I would not willingly, methinks, lose sight
Of a departing cloud." — " 'T was not for
    love " —   611
Answered the sick Man with a careless
    voice —
" That I came hither; neither have I found
Among associates who have power of speech,
Nor in such other converse as is here,
Temptation so prevailing as to change
That mood, or undermine my first resolve."
Then, speaking in like careless sort, he
    said
To my benign Companion, — " Pity 't is
That fortune did not guide you to this
    house   620
A few days earlier; then would you have
    seen
What stuff the Dwellers in a solitude,
That seems by Nature hollowed out to be
The seat and bosom of pure innocence,
Are made of; an ungracious matter this !
Which, for truth's sake, yet in remem-
    brance too
Of past discussions with this zealous friend
And advocate of humble life, I now
Will force upon his notice; undeterred
By the example of his own pure course, 630
And that respect and deference which a
    soul
May fairly claim, by niggard age enriched
In what she most doth value, love of God
And his frail creature Man; — but ye shall
    hear.
I talk — and ye are standing in the sun
Without refreshment ! "
                    Quickly had he spoken,
And, with light steps still quicker than his
    words,
Led toward the Cottage. Homely was the
    spot;
And, to my feeling, ere we reached the
    door,

Had almost a forbidding nakedness; 640
Less fair, I grant, even painfully less fair,
Than it appeared when from the beetling
  rock
We had looked down upon it.   All within,
As left by the departed company,
Was silent; save the solitary clock
That on mine ear ticked with a mournful
  sound. —
Following our Guide, we clomb the cottage-
  stairs
And reached a small apartment dark and
  low,
Which was no sooner entered than our Host
Said gaily, " This is my domain, my cell, 650
My hermitage, my cabin, what you will —
I love it better than a snail his house.
But now ye shall be feasted with our best."

So, with more ardour than an unripe girl
Left one day mistress of her mother's
  stores,
He went about his hospitable task.
My eyes were busy, and my thoughts no
  less,
And pleased I looked upon my grey-haired
  Friend,
As if to thank him; he returned that look,
Cheered, plainly, and yet serious.   What a
  wreck   660
Had we about us ! scattered was the floor,
And, in like sort, chair, window-seat, and
  shelf,
With books, maps, fossils, withered plants
  and flowers,
And tufts of mountain moss.   Mechanic
  tools
Lay intermixed with scraps of paper, some
Scribbled with verse: a broken angling-
  rod
And shattered telescope, together linked
By cobwebs, stood within a dusty nook;
And instruments of music, some half-made,
Some in disgrace, hung dangling from the
  walls.   670
But speedily the promise was fulfilled;
A feast before us, and a courteous Host
Inviting us in glee to sit and eat.
A napkin, white as foam of that rough
  brook
By which it had been bleached, o'erspread
  the board;
And was itself half-covered with a store
Of dainties, — oaten bread, curd, cheese,
  and cream;

And cakes of butter curiously embossed,
Butter that had imbibed from meadow-
  flowers
A golden hue, delicate as their own   680
Faintly reflected in a lingering stream.
Nor lacked, for more delight on that warm
  day,
Our table, small parade of garden fruits,
And whortle-berries from the mountain
  side.
The Child, who long ere this had stilled
  his sobs,
Was now a help to his late comforter,
And moved, a willing Page, as he was bid,
Ministering to our need.
                          In genial mood,
While at our pastoral banquet thus we sate
Fronting the window of that little cell, 690
I could not, ever and anon, forbear
To glance an upward look on two huge
  Peaks
That from some other vale peered into this.
" Those lusty twins," exclaimed our host,
  " if here
It were your lot to dwell, would soon be-
  come
Your prized companions. — Many are the
  notes
Which, in his tuneful course, the wind
  draws forth
From rocks, woods, caverns, heaths, and
  dashing shores;
And well those lofty brethren bear their
  part
In the wild concert — chiefly when the
  storm   700
Rides high; then all the upper air they fill
With roaring sound, that ceases not to flow,
Like smoke, along the level of the blast,
In mighty current; theirs, too, is the song
Of stream and headlong flood that seldom
  fails;
And, in the grim and breathless hour of
  noon,
Methinks that I have heard them echo back
The thunder's greeting.   Nor have nature's
  laws
Left them ungifted with a power to yield
Music of finer tone; a harmony,   710
So do I call it, though it be the hand
Of silence, though there be no voice; — the
  clouds,
The mist, the shadows, light of golden suns,
Motions of moonlight, all come thither —
  touch,

And have an answer — thither come, and
    shape
A language not unwelcome to sick hearts
And idle spirits: — there the sun himself,
At the calm close of summer's longest day,
Rests his substantial orb; — between those
    heights
And on the top of either pinnacle,   720
More keenly than elsewhere in night's blue
    vault,
Sparkle the stars, as of their station proud.
Thoughts are not busier in the mind of man
Than the mute agents stirring there: —
    alone
Here do I sit and watch —— "
               A fall of voice,
Regretted like the nightingale's last note,
Had scarcely closed this high-wrought strain
    of rapture
Ere with inviting smile the Wanderer
    said:
" Now for the tale with which you threat-
    ened us ! "
" In truth the threat escaped me unawares:
Should the tale tire you, let this challenge
    stand   731
For my excuse. Dissevered from mankind,
As to your eyes and thoughts we must have
    seemed
When ye looked down upon us from the
    crag,
Islanders 'mid a stormy mountain sea,
We are not so; — perpetually we touch
Upon the vulgar ordinances of the world;
And he, whom this our cottage hath to-day
Relinquished, lived dependent for his bread
Upon the laws of public charity.   740
The Housewife, tempted by such slender
    gains
As might from that occasion be distilled,
Opened, as she before had done for me,
Her doors to admit this homeless Pen-
    sioner;
The portion gave of coarse but wholesome
    fare
Which appetite required — a blind dull
    nook,
Such as she had, the *kennel* of his rest !
This, in itself not ill, would yet have been
Ill borne in earlier life; but his was now
The still contentedness of seventy years.
Calm did he sit under the wide-spread
    tree   751
Of his old age: and yet less calm and
    meek,

Winningly meek or venerably calm,
Than slow and torpid; paying in this wise
A penalty, if penalty it were,
For spendthrift feats, excesses of his prime.
I loved the old Man, for I pitied him !
A task it was, I own, to hold discourse
With one so slow in gathering up his
    thoughts,
But he was a cheap pleasure to my eyes;
Mild, inoffensive, ready in *his* way,   761
And helpful to his utmost power: and there
Our housewife knew full well what she
    possessed !
He was her vassal of all labour, tilled
Her garden, from the pasture fetched her
    kine;
And, one among the orderly array
Of hay-makers, beneath the burning sun
Maintained his place; or heedfully pur-
    sued
His course, on errands bound, to other
    vales,
Leading sometimes an inexperienced child
Too young for any profitable task.   771
So moved he like a shadow that performed
Substantial service. Mark me now, and
    learn
For what reward ! — The moon her monthly
    round
Hath not completed since our dame, the
    queen
Of this one cottage and this lonely dale,
Into my little sanctuary rushed —
Voice to a rueful treble humanized,
And features in deplorable dismay.
I treat the matter lightly, but, alas !   780
It is most serious: persevering rain
Had fallen in torrents; all the mountain
    tops
Were hidden, and black vapours coursed
    their sides;
This had I seen, and saw; but, till she
    spake,
Was wholly ignorant that my ancient
    Friend —
Who at her bidding, early and alone,
Had clomb aloft to delve the moorland turf
For winter fuel — to his noontide meal
Returned not, and now, haply, on the
    heights
Lay at the mercy of this raging storm.   790
' Inhuman ! ' — said I, ' was an old Man's
    life
Not worth the trouble of a thought ? —
    alas !

This notice comes too late.' With joy I saw
Her husband enter — from a distant vale.
We sallied forth together; found the tools
Which the neglected veteran had dropped,
But through all quarters looked for him in
    vain.
We shouted — but no answer ! Darkness
    fell
Without remission of the blast or shower,
And fears for our own safety drove us
    home.   800

I, who weep little, did, I will confess,
The moment I was seated here alone,
Honour my little cell with some few tears
Which anger and resentment could not dry.
All night the storm endured; and, soon as
    help
Had been collected from the neighbouring
    vale,
With morning we renewed our quest: the
    wind
Was fallen, the rain abated, but the hills
Lay shrouded in impenetrable mist;   809
And long and hopelessly we sought in vain:
Till chancing on that lofty ridge to pass
A heap of ruin — almost without walls
And wholly without roof (the bleached re-
    mains
Of a small chapel, where, in ancient time,
The peasants of these lonely valleys used
To meet for worship on that central
    height) —
We there espied the object of our search,
Lying full three parts buried among tufts
Of heath-plant, under and above him
    strewn,
To baffle, as he might, the watery storm:
And there we found him breathing peace-
    ably,   821
Snug as a child that hides itself in sport
'Mid a green hay-cock in a sunny field.
We spake — he made reply, but would not
    stir
At our entreaty; less from want of power
Than   apprehension   and   bewildering
    thoughts.

So was he lifted gently from the ground,
And with their freight homeward the
    shepherds moved
Through the dull mist, I following — when
    a step,
A single step, that freed me from the skirts
Of the blind vapour, opened to my view   831

Glory beyond all glory ever seen
By waking sense or by the dreaming soul !
The appearance, instantaneously disclosed,
Was of a mighty city — boldly say
A wilderness of building, sinking far
And self-withdrawn into a boundless depth,
Far sinking into splendour — without end !
Fabric it seemed of diamond and of gold,
With alabaster domes, and silver spires,
And blazing terrace upon terrace, high   841
Uplifted; here, serene pavilions bright,
In avenues disposed; there, towers begirt
With   battlements   that   on   their   restless
    fronts
Bore stars — illumination of all gems !
By earthly nature had the effect been
    wrought
Upon the dark materials of the storm
Now pacified; on them, and on the coves
And mountain-steeps and summits, where-
    unto
The vapours had receded, taking there   850
Their station under a cerulean sky.
Oh, 't was an unimaginable sight !
Clouds, mists, streams, watery rocks and
    emerald turf,
Clouds of all tincture, rocks and sapphire
    sky,
Confused, commingled, mutually inflamed,
Molten together, and composing thus,
Each lost in each, that marvellous array
Of temple, palace, citadel, and huge
Fantastic pomp of structure without name,
In fleecy folds voluminous, enwrapped.   860
Right in the midst, where interspace ap-
    peared
Of open court, an object like a throne
Under a shining canopy of state
Stood fixed; and fixed resemblances were
    seen
To implements of ordinary use,
But vast in size, in substance glorified;
Such as by Hebrew Prophets were beheld
In vision — forms uncouth of mightiest
    power
For admiration and mysterious awe.   869
This little Vale, a dwelling-place of Man,
Lay low beneath my feet; 't was visible —
I saw not, but I felt that it was there.
That which I *saw* was the revealed abode
Of Spirits in beatitude: my heart
Swelled in my breast — ' I have been dead,'
    I cried,
' And now I live !   Oh ! wherefore *do* I
    live ? '

And with that pang I prayed to be no
   more ! —
— But I forget our Charge, as utterly
I then forgot him: — there I stood and
   gazed:
The apparition faded not away,   880
And I descended.
              Having reached the house,
I found its rescued inmate safely lodged,
And in serene possession of himself,
Beside a fire whose genial warmth seemed
   met
By a faint shining from the heart, a gleam,
Of comfort, spread over his pallid face.
Great show of joy the housewife made, and
   truly
Was glad to find her conscience set at ease;
And not less glad, for sake of her good
   name,
That the poor Sufferer had escaped with
   life.   890
But, though he seemed at first to have re-
   ceived
No harm, and uncomplaining as before
Went through his usual tasks, a silent
   change
Soon showed itself: he lingered three
   short weeks;
And from the cottage hath been borne to-
   day.

   So ends my dolorous tale, and glad I am
That it is ended." At these words he
   turned —
And, with blithe air of open fellowship,
Brought from the cupboard wine and
   stouter cheer,
Like one who would be merry. Seeing
   this,   900
My grey-haired Friend said courteously —
   " Nay, nay,
You have regaled us as a hermit ought;
Now let us forth into the sun ! " — Our
   Host
Rose, though reluctantly, and forth we
   went.

BOOK THIRD

DESPONDENCY

ARGUMENT

   Images in the Valley — Another Recess in
it entered and described — Wanderer's sensa-
tions — Solitary's excited by the same objects
— Contrast between these — Despondency of
the Solitary gently reproved — Conversation
exhibiting the Solitary's past and present opin-
ions and feelings, till he enters upon his own
History at length — His domestic felicity —
Afflictions—Dejection—Roused by the French
Revolution — Disappointment and disgust —
·Voyage to America — Disappointment and dis-
gust pursue him — His return — His languor
and depression of mind, from want of faith in
the great truths of Religion, and want of con-
fidence in the virtue of Mankind.

A HUMMING BEE — a little tinkling rill —
A pair of falcons wheeling on the wing,
In clamorous agitation, round the crest
Of a tall rock, their airy citadel —
By each and all of these the pensive ear
Was greeted, in the silence that ensued,
When through the cottage-threshold we had
   passed,
And, deep within that lonesome valley,
   stood
Once more beneath the concave of a blue
And cloudless sky. — Anon exclaimed our
   Host —   10
Triumphantly dispersing with the taunt
The shade of discontent which on his brow
Had gathered, — " Ye have left my cell, —
   but see
How Nature hems you in with friendly
   arms !
And by her help ye are my prisoners still.
But which way shall I lead you ? — how
   contrive,
In spot so parsimoniously endowed,
That the brief hours, which yet remain,
   may reap
Some recompense of knowledge or de-
   light ? "
So saying, round he looked, as if per-
   plexed;   20
And, to remove those doubts, my grey-
   haired Friend
Said — " Shall we take this pathway for our
   guide ? —
Upward it winds, as if, in summer heats,
Its line had first been fashioned by the
   flock
Seeking a place of refuge at the root
Of yon black Yew-tree, whose protruded
   boughs
Darken the silver bosom of the crag,
From which she draws her meagre suste-
   nance.
There in commodious shelter may we rest.

Or let us trace this streamlet to its
    source;   30
Feebly it tinkles with an earthy sound,
And a few steps may bring us to the spot
Where, haply, crowned with flowerets and
    green herbs,
The mountain infant to the sun comes
    forth,
Like human life from darkness."—A quick
    turn
Through a strait passage of encumbered
    ground,
Proved that such hope was vain:—for now
    we stood
Shut out from prospect of the open vale,
And saw the water, that composed this
    rill,
Descending, disembodied, and diffused   40
O'er the smooth surface of an ample crag,
Lofty, and steep, and naked as a tower.
All further progress here was barred;—
    And who,
Thought I, if master of a vacant hour,
Here would not linger, willingly de-
    tained?
Whether to such wild objects he were led
When copious rains have magnified the
    stream
Into a loud and white-robed waterfall,
Or introduced at this more quiet time.

Upon a semicirque of turf-clad ground, 50
The hidden nook discovered to our view
A mass of rock, resembling, as it lay
Right at the foot of that moist precipice,
A stranded ship, with keel upturned, that
    rests
Fearless of winds and waves.   Three
    several stones
Stood near, of smaller size, and not unlike
To monumental pillars: and, from these
Some little space disjoined a pair were
    seen,
That with united shoulders bore aloft
A fragment, like an altar, flat and smooth:
Barren the tablet, yet thereon appeared 61
A tall and shining holly, that had found
A hospitable chink, and stood upright,
As if inserted by some human hand
In mockery, to wither in the sun,
Or lay its beauty flat before a breeze,
The first that entered.   But no breeze did
    now
Find entrance;—high or low appeared no
    trace

Of motion, save the water that descended,
Diffused adown that barrier of steep rock,
And softly creeping, like a breath of air, 71
Such as is sometimes seen, and hardly seen,
To brush the still breast of a crystal lake.

" Behold a cabinet for sages built,
Which kings might envy ! " — Praise to
    this effect
Broke from the happy old Man's reverend
    lip;
Who to the Solitary turned, and said,
" In sooth, with love's familiar privilege,
You have decried the wealth which is your
    own.
Among these rocks and stones, methinks, I
    see   80
More than the heedless impress that be-
    longs
To lonely nature's casual work: they bear
A semblance strange of power intelligent,
And of design not wholly worn away.
Boldest of plants that ever faced the wind,
How gracefully that slender shrub looks
    forth
From its fantastic birth-place ! And I own,
Some shadowy intimations haunt me here,
That in these shows a chronicle survives
Of purposes akin to those of Man,   90
But wrought with mightier arm than now
    prevails.
— Voiceless the stream descends into the
    gulf
With timid lapse;—and lo ! while in this
    strait
I stand—the chasm of sky above my head
Is heaven's profoundest azure; no domain
For fickle, short-lived clouds to occupy,
Or to pass through; but rather an abyss
In which the everlasting stars abide;
And whose soft gloom, and boundless depth,
    might tempt
The curious eye to look for them by day. 100
— Hail Contemplation ! from the stately
    towers,
Reared by the industrious hand of human
    art
To lift thee high above the misty air
And turbulence of murmuring cities vast;
From academic groves, that have for thee
Been planted, hither come and find a lodge
To which thou mayst resort for holier
    peace, —
From whose calm centre thou, through
    height or depth,

Mayst penetrate, wherever truth shall lead;
Measuring through all degrees, until the
    scale   110
Of time and conscious nature disappear,
Lost in unsearchable eternity ! "

A pause ensued; and with minuter care
We scanned the various features of the
    scene:
And soon the Tenant of that lonely vale
With courteous voice thus spake —
             "I should have grieved
Hereafter, not escaping self-reproach,
If from my poor retirement ye had gone
Leaving this nook unvisited: but, in sooth,
Your unexpected presence had so roused 120
My spirits, that they were bent on enter-
    prise;
And, like an ardent hunter, I forgot,
Or, shall I say ? — disdained, the game that
    lurks
At my own door. The shapes before our
    eyes
And their arrangement, doubtless must be
    deemed
The sport of Nature, aided by blind Chance
Rudely to mock the works of toiling Man.
And hence, this upright shaft of unhewn
    stone,
From Fancy, willing to set off her stores
By sounding titles, hath acquired the name
Of Pompey's pillar; that I gravely style 131
My Theban obelisk; and, there, behold
A Druid cromlech ! — thus I entertain
The antiquarian humour, and am pleased
To skim along the surfaces of things,
Beguiling harmlessly the listless hours.
But if the spirit be oppressed by sense
Of instability, revolt, decay,
And change, and emptiness, these freaks of
    Nature
And her blind helper Chance, do *then*
    suffice   140
To quicken, and to aggravate — to feed
Pity and scorn, and melancholy pride,
Not less than that huge Pile (from some
    abyss
Of mortal power unquestionably sprung)
Whose hoary diadem of pendent rocks
Confines the shrill-voiced whirlwind, round
    and round
Eddying within its vast circumference,
On Sarum's naked plain — than pyramid
Of Egypt, unsubverted, undissolved —
Or Syria's marble ruins towering high 150

Above the sandy desert, in the light
Of sun or moon. — Forgive me, if I say
That an appearance which hath raised your
    minds
To an exalted pitch (the self-same cause
Different effect producing) is for me
Fraught rather with depression than delight,
Though shame it were, could I not look
    around,
By the reflection of your pleasure, pleased.
Yet happier in my judgment, even than you
With your bright transports fairly may be
    deemed,   160
The wandering Herbalist, — who, clear
    alike
From vain, and, that worse evil, vexing
    thoughts,
Casts, if he ever chance to enter here,
Upon these uncouth Forms a slight regard
Of transitory interest, and peeps round
For some rare floweret of the hills, or
    plant
Of craggy fountain; what he hopes for wins,
Or learns, at least, that 't is not to be won:
Then, keen and eager, as a fine-nosed
    hound
By soul-engrossing instinct driven along 170
Through wood or open field, the harmless
    Man
Departs, intent upon his onward quest ! —
Nor is that Fellow-wanderer, so deem I,
Less to be envied, (you may trace him oft
By scars which his activity has left
Beside our roads and pathways, though,
    thank Heaven !
This covert nook reports not of his hand)
He who with pocket-hammer smites the
    edge
Of luckless rock or prominent stone, dis-
    guised
In weather-stains or crusted o'er by Na-
    ture   180
With her first growths, detaching by the
    stroke
A chip or splinter — to resolve his doubts;
And, with that ready answer satisfied,
The substance classes by some barbarous
    name,
And hurries on; or from the fragments
    picks
His specimen, if but haply interveined
With sparkling mineral, or should crystal
    cube
Lurk in its cells — and thinks himself en-
    riched,

Wealthier, and doubtless wiser, than before!
Intrusted safely each to his pursuit,　　190
Earnest alike, let both from hill to hill
Range; if it please them, speed from clime
　　to clime;
The mind is full — and free from pain their
　　pastime."

"Then," said I, interposing, "One is near,
Who cannot but possess in your esteem
Place worthier still of envy.　May I name,
Without offence, that fair-faced cottage-
　　boy ?
Dame Nature's pupil of the lowest form,
Youngest apprentice in the school of art!
Him, as we entered from the open glen,　200
You might have noticed, busily engaged,
Heart, soul, and hands, — in mending the
　　defects
Left in the fabric of a leaky dam
Raised for enabling this penurious stream
To turn a slender mill (that new-made
　　plaything)
For his delight — the happiest he of all!"

"Far happiest," answered the despond-
　　ing Man,
"If, such as now he is, he might remain!
Ah! what avails imagination high
Or question deep? what profits all that
　　earth,　　210
Or heaven's blue vault, is suffered to put
　　forth
Of impulse or allurement, for the Soul
To quit the beaten track of life, and soar
Far as she finds a yielding element
In past or future; far as she can go
Through time or space — if neither in the
　　one,
Nor in the other region, nor in aught
That Fancy, dreaming o'er the map of
　　things,
Hath placed beyond these penetrable
　　bounds,
Words of assurance can be heard; if no-
　　where　　220
A habitation, for consummate good,
Or for progressive virtue, by the search
Can be attained, — a better sanctuary
From doubt and sorrow, than the senseless
　　grave?"

"Is this," the grey-haired Wanderer
　　mildly said,
"The voice, which we so lately overheard,

To that same child, addressing tenderly
The consolations of a hopeful mind?
'His body is at rest, his soul in heaven.'
These were your words; and, verily, me-
　　thinks　　230
Wisdom is oft-times nearer when we stoop
Than when we soar." —
　　　　　　The Other, not displeased,
Promptly replied — "My notion is the
　　same.
And I, without reluctance, could decline
All act of inquisition whence we rise,
And what, when breath hath ceased, we
　　may become.
Here are we, in a bright and breathing
　　world.
Our origin, what matters it?　In lack
Of worthier explanation, say at once
With the American (a thought which suits
The place where now we stand) that certain
　　men　　241
Leapt out together from a rocky cave;
And these were the first parents of man-
　　kind:
Or, if a different image be recalled
By the warm sunshine, and the jocund
　　voice
Of insects chirping out their careless lives
On these soft beds of thyme-besprinkled
　　turf,
Choose, with the gay Athenian, a conceit
As sound — blithe race! whose mantles
　　were bedecked
With golden grasshoppers, in sign that they
Had sprung, like those bright creatures,
　　from the soil　　251
Whereon their endless generations dwelt.
But stop! — these theoretic fancies jar
On serious minds: then, as the Hindoos
　　draw
Their holy Ganges from a skiey fount,
Even so deduce the stream of human life
From seats of power divine; and hope, or
　　trust,
That our existence winds her stately course
Beneath the sun, like Ganges, to make part
Of a living ocean; or, to sink engulfed, 260
Like Niger, in impenetrable sands
And utter darkness: thought which may be
　　faced,
Though comfortless! —
　　　　　　Not of myself I speak:
Such acquiescence neither doth imply,
In me, a meekly-bending spirit soothed
By natural piety; nor a lofty mind,

By philosophic discipline prepared
For calm subjection to acknowledged law;
Pleased to have been, contented not to be.
Such palms I boast not; — no! to me, who
    find,   270
Reviewing my past way, much to condemn,
Little to praise, and nothing to regret,
(Save some remembrances of dream-like
    joys
That scarcely seem to have belonged to
    me)
If I must take my choice between the pair
That rule alternately the weary hours,
Night is than day more acceptable; sleep
Doth, in my estimate of good, appear
A better state than waking; death than
    sleep:
Feelingly sweet is stillness after storm, 280
Though under covert of the wormy ground !

    Yet be it said, in justice to myself,
That in more genial times, when I was free
To explore the destiny of human kind
(Not as an intellectual game pursued
With curious subtilty, from wish to cheat
Irksome sensations; but by love of truth
Urged on, or haply by intense delight
In feeding thought, wherever thought could
    feed)
I did not rank with those (too dull or nice,
For to my judgment such they then ap-
    peared,   291
Or too aspiring, thankless at the best)
Who, in this frame of human life, perceive
An object whereunto their souls are tied
In discontented wedlock; nor did e'er,
From me, those dark impervious shades,
    that hang
Upon the region whither we are bound,
Exclude a power to enjoy the vital beams
Of present sunshine. — Deities that float
On wings, angelic Spirits ! I could muse 300
O'er what from eldest time we have been
    told
Of your bright forms and glorious faculties,
And with the imagination rest content,
Not wishing more; repining not to tread
The little sinuous path of earthly care,
By flowers embellished, and by springs re-
    freshed.
— 'Blow winds of autumn ! — let your
    chilling breath
'Take the live herbage from the mead, and
    strip
'The shady forest of its green attire, —

' And let the bursting clouds to fury rouse
' The gentle brooks ! — Your desolating
    sway,   311
' Sheds,' I exclaimed, 'no sadness upon me,
' And no disorder in your rage I find.
' What dignity, what beauty, in this change
' From mild to angry, and from sad to
    gay,
' Alternate and revolving !   How benign,
' How rich in animation and delight,
' How bountiful these elements — compared
' With aught, as more desirable and fair,
' Devised by fancy for the golden age; 320
' Or the perpetual warbling that prevails
' In Arcady, beneath unaltered skies,
' Through the long year in constant quiet
    bound,
' Night hushed as night, the day serene as
    day !'
— But why this tedious record? — Age, we
    know
Is garrulous; and solitude is apt
To anticipate the privilege of Age.
From far ye come; and surely with a hope
Of better entertainment: — let us hence ! "

    Loth to forsake the spot, and still more
    loth   330
To be diverted from our present theme,
I said, " My thoughts, agreeing, Sir, with
    yours,
Would push this censure farther; — for, if
    smiles
Of scornful pity be the just reward
Of Poesy thus courteously employed
In framing models to improve the scheme
Of Man's existence, and recast the world,
Why should not grave Philosophy be styled,
Herself, a dreamer of a kindred stock,
A dreamer yet more spiritless and dull ? 340
Yes, shall the fine immunities she boasts
Establish sounder titles of esteem
For her, who (all too timid and reserved
For onset, for resistance too inert,
Too weak for suffering, and for hope too
    tame)
Placed, among flowery gardens curtained
    round
With world-excluding groves, the brother-
    hood
Of soft Epicureans, taught — if they
The ends of being would secure, and win
The crown of wisdom — to yield up their
    souls   350
To a voluptuous unconcern, preferring

Tranquillity to all things. Or is she,"
I cried, "more worthy of regard, the
Power,
Who, for the sake of sterner quiet, closed
The Stoic's heart against the vain approach
Of admiration, and all sense of joy ? "

His countenance gave notice that my zeal
Accorded little with his present mind;
I ceased, and he resumed. — " Ah! gentle
Sir,
Slight, if you will, the *means ;* but spare to
slight   360
The *end* of those, who did, by system, rank,
As the prime object of a wise man's aim,
Security from shock of accident,
Release from fear; and cherished peaceful
days
For their own sakes, as mortal life's chief
good,
And only reasonable felicity.
What motive drew, what impulse, I would
ask,
Through a long course of later ages, drove,
The hermit to his cell in forest wide;
Or what detained him, till his closing eyes
Took their last farewell of the sun and
stars,   371
Fast anchored in the desert ? — Not alone
Dread of the persecuting sword, remorse,
Wrongs unredressed, or insults unavenged
And unavengeable, defeated pride,
Prosperity subverted, maddening want,
Friendship betrayed, affection unreturned,
Love with despair, or grief in agony; —
Not always from intolerable pangs
He fled; but, compassed round by pleasure,
sighed   380
For independent happiness; craving peace,
The central feeling of all happiness,
Not as a refuge from distress or pain,
A breathing-time, vacation, or a truce,
But for its absolute self; a life of peace,
Stability without regret or fear;
That hath been, is, and shall be ever-
more ! —
Such the reward he sought; and wore out
life,
There, where on few external things his
heart
Was set, and those his own; or, if not his,
Subsisting under nature's stedfast law.   391

What other yearning was the master tie
Of the monastic brotherhood, upon rock

Aërial, or in green secluded vale,
One after one, collected from afar,
An undissolving fellowship ? — What but
this,
The universal instinct of repose,
The longing for confirmed tranquillity,
Inward and outward; humble, yet sublime:
The life where hope and memory are as
one;   400
Where earth is quiet and her face un-
changed
Save by the simplest toil of human hands
Or seasons' difference; the immortal Soul
Consistent in self-rule; and heaven revealed
To meditation in that quietness ! —
Such was their scheme: and though the
wished-for end
By multitudes was missed, perhaps attained
By none, they for the attempt, and pains
employed,
Do, in my present censure, stand redeemed
From the unqualified disdain, that once   410
Would have been cast upon them by my
voice
Delivering her decisions from the seat
Of forward youth — that scruples not to
solve
Doubts, and determine questions, by the
rules
Of inexperienced judgment, ever prone
To overweening faith; and is inflamed,
By courage, to demand from real life
The test of act and suffering, to provoke
Hostility — how dreadful when it comes,
Whether affliction be the foe, or guilt !   420

A child of earth, I rested, in that stage
Of my past course to which these thoughts
advert,
Upon earth's native energies; forgetting
That mine was a condition which required
Nor energy, nor fortitude — a calm
Without vicissitude; which, if the like
Had been presented to my view elsewhere,
I might have even been tempted to despise.
But no — for the serene was always bright;
Enlivened happiness with joy o'erflowing,
With joy, and — oh ! that memory should
survive   431
To speak the word —with rapture ! Nature's
boon,
Life's genuine inspiration, happiness
Above what rules can teach, or fancy feign;
Abused, as all possessions *are* abused
That are not prized according to their worth.

And yet, what worth? what good is given
    to men,
More solid than the gilded clouds of
    heaven?
What joy more lasting than a vernal
    flower? —
None! 't is the general plaint of human kind
In solitude : and mutually addressed   441
From each to all, for wisdom's sake: —
    This truth
The priest announces from his holy seat:
And, crowned with garlands in the summer
    grove,
The poet fits it to his pensive lyre.
Yet, ere that final resting-place be gained,
Sharp contradictions may arise, by doom
Of this same life, compelling us to grieve
That the prosperities of love and joy   449
Should be permitted, oft-times, to endure
So long, and be at once cast down for ever.
Oh! tremble, ye, to whom hath been assigned
A course of days composing happy months,
And they as happy years; the present still
So like the past, and both so firm a pledge
Of a congenial future, that the wheels
Of pleasure move without the aid of hope:
For Mutability is Nature's bane;
And slighted Hope *will* be avenged; and,
    when
Ye need her favours, ye shall find her not;
But in her stead — fear — doubt — and
    agony!"   461

This was the bitter language of the heart:
But, while he spake, look, gesture, tone of
    voice,
Though discomposed and vehement, were
    such
As skill and graceful nature might suggest
To a proficient of the tragic scene
Standing before the multitude, beset
With dark events. Desirous to divert
Or stem the current of the speaker's
    thoughts,
We signified a wish to leave that place   470
Of stillness and close privacy, a nook
That seemed for self-examination made;
Or, for confession, in the sinner's need,
Hidden from all men's view. To our at-
    tempt
He yielded not; but, pointing to a slope
Of mossy turf defended from the sun,
And on that couch inviting us to rest,
Full on that tender-hearted Man he turned
A serious eye, and his speech thus renewed.

" You never saw, your eyes did never look
On the bright form of Her whom once I
    loved: —   481
Her silver voice was heard upon the earth,
A sound unknown to you; else, honoured
    Friend!
Your heart had borne a pitiable share
Of what I suffered, when I wept that loss,
And suffer now, not seldom, from the
    thought
That I remember, and can weep no more. —
Stripped as I am of all the golden fruit
Of self-esteem; and by the cutting blasts
Of self-reproach familiarly assailed;   490
Yet would I not be of such wintry bareness
But that some leaf of your regard should
    hang
Upon my naked branches: — lively thoughts
Give birth, full often, to unguarded words;
I grieve that, in your presence, from my
    tongue
Too much of frailty hath already dropped;
But that too much demands still more.
                You know,
Revered Compatriot — and to you, kind Sir,
(Not to be deemed a stranger, as you come
Following the guidance of these welcome
    feet   500
To our secluded vale) it may be told —
That my demerits did not sue in vain
To One on whose mild radiance many gazed
With hope, and all with pleasure. This fair
    Bride —
In the devotedness of youthful love,
Preferring me to parents, and the choir
Of gay companions, to the natal roof,
And all known places and familiar sights
(Resigned with sadness gently weighing
    down
Her trembling expectations, but no more   510
Than did to her due honour, and to me
Yielded, that day, a confidence sublime
In what I had to build upon) — this Bride,
Young, modest, meek, and beautiful, I led
To a low cottage in a sunny bay,
Where the salt sea innocuously breaks,
And the sea breeze as innocently breathes,
On Devon's leafy shores; — a sheltered hold,
In a soft clime encouraging the soil
To a luxuriant bounty! — As our steps   520
Approach the embowered abode — our
    chosen seat —
See, rooted in the earth, her kindly bed,
The unendangered myrtle, decked with
    flowers,

Before the threshold stands to welcome us !
While, in the flowering myrtle's neighbour-
hood,
Not overlooked but courting no regard,
Those native plants, the holly and the yew,
Gave modest intimation to the mind
How willingly their aid they would unite 529
With the green myrtle, to endear the hours
Of winter, and protect that pleasant place.
— Wild were the walks upon those lonely
Downs,
Track leading into track; how marked, how
worn
Into bright verdure, between fern and gorse
Winding away its never-ending line
On their smooth surface, evidence was none;
But, there, lay open to our daily haunt,
A range of unappropriated earth,
Where youth's ambitious feet might move
at large;
Whence, unmolested wanderers, we beheld
The shining giver of the day diffuse 541
His brightness o'er a tract of sea and land
Gay as our spirits, free as our desires;
As our enjoyments, boundless. — From
those heights
We dropped, at pleasure, into sylvan
combs;
Where arbours of impenetrable shade,
And mossy seats, detained us side by side,
With hearts at ease, and knowledge in our
hearts
'That all the grove and all the day was
ours.'

O happy time ! still happier was at hand;
For Nature called my Partner to resign 551
Her share in the pure freedom of that life,
Enjoyed by us in common. — To my hope,
To my heart's wish, my tender Mate be-
came
The thankful captive of maternal bonds;
And those wild paths were left to me alone.
There could I meditate on follies past;
And, like a weary voyager escaped
From risk and hardship, inwardly retrace
A course of vain delights and thoughtless
guilt, 560
And self-indulgence — without shame pur-
sued.
There, undisturbed, could think of and
could thank
Her whose submissive spirit was to me
Rule and restraint — my guardian — shall I
say

That earthly Providence, whose guiding
love
Within a port of rest had lodged me safe;
Safe from temptation, and from danger far ?
Strains followed of acknowledgment ad-
dressed
To an authority enthroned above
The reach of sight; from whom, as from
their source 570
Proceed all visible ministers of good
That walk the earth — Father of heaven
and earth,
Father, and king, and judge, adored and
feared !
These acts of mind, and memory, and
heart,
And spirit — interrupted and relieved
By observations transient as the glance
Of flying sunbeams, or to the outward form
Cleaving with power inherent and intense,
As the mute insect fixed upon the plant
On whose soft leaves it hangs, and from
whose cup 580
It draws its nourishment imperceptibly —
Endeared my wanderings; and the mo-
ther's kiss
And infant's smile awaited my return.

In privacy we dwelt, a wedded pair,
Companions daily, often all day long;
Not placed by fortune within easy reach
Of various intercourse, nor wishing aught
Beyond the allowance of our own fire-side,
The twain within our happy cottage born,
Inmates, and heirs of our united love; 590
Graced mutually by difference of sex,
And with no wider interval of time
Between their several births than served
for one
To establish something of a leader's sway;
Yet left them joined by sympathy in age;
Equals in pleasure, fellows in pursuit.
On these two pillars rested as in air
Our solitude.
                It soothes me to perceive,
Your courtesy withholds not from my
words
Attentive audience. But, oh ! gentle
Friends, 600
As times of quiet and unbroken peace,
Though, for a nation, times of blessedness,
Give back faint echoes from the historian's
page;
So, in the imperfect sounds of this dis-
course,

Depressed I hear, how faithless is the voice
Which those most blissful days reverberate.
What special record can, or need, be given
To rules and habits, whereby much was
    done,
But all within the sphere of little things;
Of humble, though, to us, important cares,
And precious interests ? Smoothly did our
    life   611
Advance, swerving not from the path pre-
    scribed;
Her annual, her diurnal, round alike
Maintained with faithful care. And you
    divine
The worst effects that our condition saw
If you imagine changes slowly wrought,
And in their progress unperceivable;
Not wished for; sometimes noticed with a
    sigh,
(Whate'er of good or lovely they might
    bring)
Sighs of regret, for the familiar good   620
And loveliness endeared which they re-
    moved.

Seven years of occupation undisturbed
Established seemingly a right to hold
That happiness; and use and habit gave
To what an alien spirit had acquired
A patrimonial sanctity. And thus,
With thoughts and wishes bounded to this
    world,
I lived and breathed; most grateful — if to
    enjoy
Without repining or desire for more,
For different lot, or change to higher sphere,
(Only except some impulses of pride   631
With no determined object, though upheld
By theories with suitable support) —
Most grateful, if in such wise to enjoy
Be proof of gratitude for what we have;
Else, I allow, most thankless. — But, at
    once,
From some dark seat of fatal power was
    urged
A claim that shattered all. — Our bloom-
    ing girl,
Caught in the gripe of death, with such
    brief time
To struggle in as scarcely would allow   640
Her cheek to change its colour, was con-
    veyed
From us to inaccessible worlds, to regions
Where height, or depth, admits not the
    approach

Of living man, though longing to pursue.
— With even as brief a warning — and how
    soon,
With what short interval of time between,
I tremble yet to think of — our last prop,
Our happy life's only remaining stay —
The brother followed; and was seen no
    more !

Calm as a frozen lake when ruthless
    winds   650
Blow fiercely, agitating earth and sky,
The Mother now remained; as if in her,
Who, to the lowest region of the soul,
Had been erewhile unsettled and disturbed,
This second visitation had no power
To shake; but only to bind up and seal;
And to establish thankfulness of heart
In Heaven's determinations, ever just.
The eminence whereon her spirit stood,
Mine was unable to attain. Immense   660
The space that severed us ! But, as the
    sight
Communicates with heaven's ethereal orbs
Incalculably distant; so, I felt
That consolation may descend from far
(And that is intercourse, and union, too,)
While, overcome with speechless gratitude,
And, with a holier love inspired, I looked
On her — at once superior to my woes
And partner of my loss. — O heavy change !
Dimness o'er this clear luminary crept   670
Insensibly; — the immortal and divine
Yielded to mortal reflux; her pure glory,
As from the pinnacle of worldly state
Wretched ambition drops astounded, fell
Into a gulf obscure of silent grief,
And keen heart-anguish — of itself ashamed,
Yet obstinately cherishing itself:
And, so consumed, she melted from my
    arms;
And left me, on this earth, disconsolate !

What followed cannot be reviewed in
    thought;   680
Much less, retraced in words. If she, of
    life
Blameless, so intimate with love and joy
And all the tender motions of the soul,
Had been supplanted, could I hope to
    stand —
Infirm, dependent, and now destitute ?
I called on dreams and visions, to disclose
That which is veiled from waking thought;
    conjured

Eternity, as men constrain a ghost
To appear and answer; to the grave I spake
Imploringly; — looked up, and asked the
   Heavens   690
If Angels traversed their cerulean floors,
If fixed or wandering star could tidings yield
Of the departed spirit — what abode
It occupies — what consciousness retains
Of former loves and interests. Then my
   soul
Turned inward, — to examine of what stuff
Time's fetters are composed; and life was
   put
To inquisition, long and profitless !
By pain of heart — now checked — and now
   impelled —
The intellectual power, through words and
   things,   700
Went sounding on, a dim and perilous way !
And from those transports, and these toils
   abstruse,
Some trace am I enabled to retain
Of time, else lost; — existing unto me
Only by records in myself not found.

From that abstraction I was roused, —
   and how ?
Even as a thoughtful shepherd by a flash
Of lightning startled in a gloomy cave
Of these wild hills. For, lo! the dread
   Bastille,
With all the chambers in its horrid towers,
Fell to the ground: — by violence over-
   thrown   711
Of indignation; and with shouts that
   drowned
The crash it made in falling ! From the
   wreck
A golden palace rose, or seemed to rise,
The appointed seat of equitable law
And mild paternal sway. The potent shock
I felt; the transformation I perceived,
As marvellously seized as in that moment
When, from the blind mist issuing, I beheld
Glory — beyond all glory ever seen,   720
Confusion infinite of heaven and earth,
Dazzling the soul. Meanwhile, prophetic
   harps
In every grove were ringing, 'War shall
   cease;
' Did ye not hear that conquest is abjured ?
' Bring garlands, bring forth choicest flowers,
   to deck
'The tree of Liberty.' — My heart re-
   bounded;

My melancholy voice the chorus joined;
— ' Be joyful all ye nations; in all lands,
' Ye that are capable of joy be glad !
' Henceforth, whate'er is wanting to your-
   selves   730
' In others ye shall promptly find; — and all,
' Enriched by mutual and reflected wealth,
' Shall with one heart honour their common
   kind.'

Thus was I reconverted to the world;
Society became my glittering bride,
And airy hopes my children. — From the
   depths
Of natural passion, seemingly escaped,
My soul diffused herself in wide embrace
Of institutions, and the forms of things;
As they exist, in mutable array,   740
Upon life's surface. What, though in my
   veins
There flowed no Gallic blood, nor had I
   breathed
The air of France, not less than Gallic zeal
Kindled and burnt among the sapless twigs
Of my exhausted heart. If busy men
In sober conclave met, to weave a web
Of amity, whose living threads should
   stretch
Beyond the seas, and to the farthest pole,
There did I sit, assisting. If, with noise
And acclamation, crowds in open air   750
Expressed the tumult of their minds, my
   voice
There mingled, heard or not. The powers
   of song
I left not uninvoked; and, in still groves,
Where mild enthusiasts tuned a pensive lay
Of thanks and expectation, in accord
With their belief, I sang Saturnian rule
Returned, — a progeny of golden years
Permitted to descend, and bless mankind.
— With promises the Hebrew Scriptures
   teem:
I felt their invitation; and resumed   760
A long-suspended office in the House
Of public worship, where, the glowing
   phrase
Of ancient inspiration serving me,
I promised also, — with undaunted trust
Foretold, and added prayer to prophecy;
The admiration winning of the crowd;
The help desiring of the pure devout.

Scorn and contempt forbid me to proceed!
But History, time's slavish scribe, will tell

How rapidly the zealots of the cause   770
Disbanded — or in hostile ranks appeared;
Some, tired of honest service; these, out-
   done,
Disgusted therefore, or appalled, by aims
Of fiercer zealots — so confusion reigned,
And the more faithful were compelled to
   exclaim,
As Brutus did to Virtue, 'Liberty,
'I worshipped thee, and find thee but a
   Shade!'

Such recantation had for me no charm,
Nor would I bend to it; who should have
   grieved
At aught, however fair, that bore the mien
Of a conclusion, or catastrophe.   781
Why then conceal, that, when the simply
   good
In timid selfishness withdrew, I sought
Other support, not scrupulous whence it
   came;
And, by what compromise it stood, not
   nice?
Enough if notions seemed to be high-
   pitched,
And qualities determined. — Among men
So charactered did I maintain a strife
Hopeless, and still more hopeless every
   hour;
But, in the process, I began to feel   790
That, if the emancipation of the world
Were missed, I should at least secure my
   own,
And be in part compensated. For rights,
Widely — inveterately usurped upon,
I spake with vehemence; and promptly
   seized
All that Abstraction furnished for my needs
Or purposes; nor scrupled to proclaim,
And propagate, by liberty of life,
Those new persuasions. Not that I re-
   joiced,
Or even found pleasure, in such vagrant
   course,   800
For its own sake; but farthest from the
   walk
Which I had trod in happiness and peace,
Was most inviting to a troubled mind,
That, in a struggling and distempered
   world,
Saw a seductive image of herself.
Yet, mark the contradictions of which Man
Is still the sport! Here Nature was my
   guide,

The Nature of the dissolute; but thee,
O fostering Nature! I rejected — smiled
At others' tears in pity; and in scorn   810
At those, which thy soft influence some-
   times drew
From my unguarded heart. — The tranquil
   shores
Of Britain circumscribed me; else, perhaps
I might have been entangled among deeds,
Which, now, as infamous, I should abhor —
Despise, as senseless: for my spirit relished
Strangely the exasperation of that Land,
Which turned an angry beak against the
   down
Of her own breast; confounded into hope
Of disencumbering thus her fretful wings.

But all was quieted by iron bonds   821
Of military sway. The shifting aims,
The moral interests, the creative might,
The varied functions and high attributes
Of civil action, yielded to a power
Formal, and odious, and contemptible.
— In Britain, ruled a panic dread of change;
The weak were praised, rewarded, and ad-
   vanced;
And, from the impulse of a just disdain,
Once more did I retire into myself.   830
There feeling no contentment, I resolved
To fly, for safeguard, to some foreign shore,
Remote from Europe; from her blasted
   hopes;
Her fields of carnage, and polluted air.

Fresh blew the wind, when o'er the At-
   lantic Main
The ship went gliding with her thoughtless
   crew;
And who among them but an Exile, freed
From discontent, indifferent, pleased to sit
Among the busily-employed, not more   839
With obligation charged, with service taxed,
Than the loose pendant — to the idle wind
Upon the tall mast streaming. But, ye
   Powers
Of soul and sense mysteriously allied,
Oh, never let the Wretched, if a choice
Be left him, trust the freight of his dis-
   tress
To a long voyage on the silent deep!
For, like a plague, will memory break out;
And, in the blank and solitude of things,
Upon his spirit, with a fever's strength,
Will conscience prey. — Feebly must they
   have felt   850

Who, in old time, attired with snakes and
　　whips
The vengeful Furies. *Beautiful* regards
Were turned on me — the face of her I
　　loved;
The Wife and Mother pitifully fixing
Tender reproaches, insupportable !
Where now that boasted liberty ?　No wel-
　　come
From unknown objects I received; and
　　those,
Known and familiar, which the vaulted sky
Did, in the placid clearness of the night,
Disclose, had accusations to prefer　　860
Against my peace.　Within the cabin stood
That volume — as a compass for the soul —
Revered among the nations.　I implored
Its guidance; but the infallible support
Of faith was wanting.　Tell me, why re-
　　fused
To One by storms annoyed and adverse
　　winds;
Perplexed with currents; of his weakness
　　sick;
Of vain endeavours tired; and by his own,
And by his nature's, ignorance, dismayed !

　　Long-wished-for　sight,　the　Western
　　　World appeared;　　　　　　870
And, when the ship was moored, I leaped
　　ashore
Indignantly — resolved to be a man,
Who, having o'er the past no power, would
　　live
No longer in subjection to the past,
With abject mind — from a tyrannic lord
Inviting penance, fruitlessly endured:
So, like a fugitive, whose feet have cleared
Some boundary, which his followers may
　　not cross
In prosecution of their deadly chase,
Respiring I looked round. — How bright
　　the sun,　　　　　　　　880
The breeze how soft !　Can anything pro-
　　duced
In the old World compare, thought I, for
　　power
And majesty with this gigantic stream,
Sprung from the desert ?　And behold a
　　city
Fresh, youthful, and aspiring !　What are
　　these
To me, or I to them ?　As much, at least
As he desires that they should be, whom
　　winds

And waves have wafted to this distant
　　shore,
In the condition of a damaged seed,
Whose fibres cannot, if they would, take
　　root.　　　　　　　　　　　890
Here may I roam at large; — my business
　　is,
Roaming at large, to observe, and not to
　　feel,
And, therefore, not to act — convinced that
　　all
Which bears the name of action, howsoe'er
Beginning, ends in servitude — still painful,
And mostly profitless.　And, sooth to say,
On nearer view, a motley spectacle
Appeared, of high pretensions, — unre-
　　proved
But by the obstreperous voice of higher
　　still;
Big passions strutting on a petty stage;　900
Which a detached spectator may regard
Not unamused. — But ridicule demands
Quick change of objects; and, to laugh
　　alone,
At a composing distance from the haunts
Of strife and folly, though it be a treat
As choice as musing Leisure can bestow;
Yet, in the very centre of the crowd,
To keep the secret of a poignant scorn,
Howe'er to airy Demons suitable,
Of all unsocial courses, is least fit　　910
For the gross spirit of mankind, — the one
That soonest fails to please, and quickliest
　　turns
Into vexation.
　　　　　　　　Let us, then, I said,
Leave this unknit Republic to the scourge
Of her own passions; and to regions haste,
Whose shades have never felt the encroach-
　　ing axe,
Or soil endured a transfer in the mart
Of dire rapacity.　There, Man abides,
Primeval Nature's child.　A creature weak
In combination, (wherefore else driven
　　back　　　　　　　　　　920
So far, and of his old inheritance
So easily deprived ?) but, for that cause,
More dignified, and stronger in himself;
Whether to act, judge, suffer, or enjoy.
True, the intelligence of social art
Hath overpowered his forefathers, and soon
Will sweep the remnant of his line away;
But contemplations, worthier, nobler far
Than her destructive energies, attend
His independence, when along the side　930

Of Mississippi, or that northern stream
That spreads into successive seas, he walks;
Pleased to perceive his own unshackled life,
And his innate capacities of soul,
There imaged: or when, having gained the
    top
Of some commanding eminence, which yet
Intruder ne'er beheld, he thence surveys
Regions of wood and wide savannah, vast
Expanse of unappropriated earth,
With mind that sheds a light on what he
    sees;   940
Free as the sun, and lonely as the sun,
Pouring above his head its radiance down
Upon a living and rejoicing world !

    So, westward, tow'rd the unviolated
        woods
I bent my way; and, roaming far and wide,
Failed not to greet the merry Mocking-bird;
And, while the melancholy Muccawiss
(The sportive bird's companion in the grove)
Repeated o'er and o'er his plaintive cry,
I sympathised at leisure with the sound;   950
But that pure archetype of human great-
    ness,
I found him not.   There, in his stead, ap-
    peared
A creature, squalid, vengeful, and impure;
Remorseless, and submissive to no law
But superstitious fear, and abject sloth.

    Enough is told !   Here am I — ye have
        heard
What evidence I seek, and vainly seek;
What from my fellow-beings I require,
And either they have not to give, or I
Lack virtue to receive; what I myself,   960
Too oft by wilful forfeiture, have lost
Nor can regain.   How languidly I look
Upon this visible fabric of the world,
May be divined — perhaps it hath been
    said: —
But spare your pity, if there be in me
Aught that deserves respect: for I exist,
Within myself, not comfortless. — The
    tenor
Which my life holds, he readily may con-
    ceive
Whoe'er hath stood to watch a mountain
    brook
In some still passage of its course, and
    seen,   970
Within the depths of its capacious breast,
Inverted trees, rocks, clouds, and azure sky;

And, on its glassy surface, specks of foam,
And conglobated bubbles undissolved,
Numerous as stars; that, by their onward
    lapse,
Betray to sight the motion of the stream,
Else imperceptible.   Meanwhile, is heard
A softened roar, or murmur; and the sound
Though soothing, and the little floating isles
Though beautiful, are both by Nature
    charged   980
With the same pensive office; and make
    known
Through what perplexing labyrinths, abrupt
Precipitations and untoward straits,
The earth-born wanderer hath passed; and
    quickly,
That respite o'er, like traverses and toils
Must he again encounter. — Such a stream
Is human Life; and so the Spirit fares
In the best quiet to her course allowed;
And such is mine, — save only for a hope   989
That my particular current soon will reach
The unfathomable gulf, where all is still ! "

BOOK FOURTH

DESPONDENCY CORRECTED

ARGUMENT

State of feeling produced by the foregoing
Narrative — A belief in a superintending Pro-
vidence the only adequate support under afflic-
tion — Wanderer's ejaculation — Acknowledges
the difficulty of a lively faith — Hence immod-
erate sorrow — Exhortations — How received
— Wanderer applies his discourse to that other
cause of dejection in the Solitary's mind — Dis-
appointment from the French Revolution —
States grounds of hope, and insists on the ne-
cessity of patience and fortitude with respect
to the course of great revolutions — Knowledge
the source of tranquillity — Rural Solitude
favourable to knowledge of the inferior Crea-
tures; Study of their habits and ways recom-
mended; exhortation to bodily exertion and
communion with Nature — Morbid Solitude
pitiable — Superstition better than apathy —
Apathy and destitution unknown in the infancy
of society — The various modes of Religion
prevented it — Illustrated in the Jewish, Per-
sian, Babylonian, Chaldean, and Grecian modes
of belief — Solitary interposes — Wanderer
points out the influence of religious and imagi-
native feeling in the humble ranks of society,
illustrated from present and past times —
These principles tend to recall exploded super-

stitions and popery — Wanderer rebuts this
charge, and contrasts the dignities of the Imag-
ination with the presumptuous littleness of
certain modern Philosophers — Recommends
other lights and guides — Asserts the power of
the soul to regenerate herself; Solitary asks
how — Reply — Personal appeal — Exhorta-
tion to activity of body renewed — How to com-
mune with Nature — Wanderer concludes with
a legitimate union of the imagination, affec-
tions, understanding, and reason — Effect of
his discourse — Evening; Return to the Cot-
tage.

HERE closed the Tenant of that lonely vale
His mournful narrative — commenced in
    pain,
In pain commenced, and ended without
    peace:
Yet tempered, not unfrequently, with
    strains
Of native feeling, grateful to our minds;
And yielding surely some relief to his,
While we sate listening with compassion due.
A pause of silence followed; then, with
    voice
That did not falter though the heart was
    moved,
The Wanderer said: —
                    "One adequate support
For the calamities of mortal life   11
Exists — one only; an assured belief
That the procession of our fate, howe'er
Sad or disturbed, is ordered by a Being
Of infinite benevolence and power;
Whose everlasting purposes embrace
All accidents, converting them to good.
— The darts of anguish *fix* not where the
    seat
Of suffering hath been thoroughly fortified
By acquiescence in the Will supreme   20
For time and for eternity; by faith,
Faith absolute in God, including hope,
And the defence that lies in boundless love
Of his perfections; with habitual dread
Of aught unworthily conceived, endured
Impatiently, ill-done, or left undone,
To the dishonour of his holy name.
Soul of our Souls, and safeguard of the
    world!
Sustain, thou only canst, the sick of heart;
Restore their languid spirits, and recall   30
Their lost affections unto thee and thine!"

Then, as we issued from that covert nook,
He thus continued, lifting up his eyes

To heaven: — "How beautiful this dome of
    sky;
And the vast hills, in fluctuation fixed
At thy command, how awful! Shall the
    Soul,
Human and rational, report of thee
Even less than these? — Be mute who will,
    who can,
Yet I will praise thee with impassioned
    voice:
My lips, that may forget thee in the crowd,
Cannot forget thee here; where thou hast
    built,   41
For thy own glory, in the wilderness!
Me didst thou constitute a priest of thine,
In such a temple as we now behold
Reared for thy presence: therefore, am I
    bound
To worship, here, and everywhere — as one
Not doomed to ignorance, though forced to
    tread,
From childhood up, the ways of poverty;
From unreflecting ignorance preserved,
And from debasement rescued. — By thy
    grace   50
The particle divine remained unquenched;
And, 'mid the wild weeds of a rugged soil,
Thy bounty caused to flourish deathless
    flowers,
From paradise transplanted: wintry age
Impends; the frost will gather round my
    heart;
If the flowers wither, I am worse than dead!
— Come, labour, when the worn-out frame
    requires
Perpetual sabbath; come, disease and want;
And sad exclusion through decay of sense;
But leave me unabated trust in thee —   60
And let thy favour, to the end of life,
Inspire me with ability to seek
Repose and hope among eternal things —
Father of heaven and earth! and I am rich,
And will possess my portion in content!

And what are things eternal? — powers
    depart,"
The grey-haired Wanderer stedfastly re-
    plied,
Answering the question which himself had
    asked,
"Possessions vanish, and opinions change,
And passions hold a fluctuating seat: 70
But, by the storms of circumstance un-
    shaken,
And subject neither to eclipse nor wane,

Duty exists; — immutably survive,
For our support, the measures and the forms,
Which an abstract intelligence supplies;
Whose kingdom is, where time and space
    are not.
Of other converse which mind, soul, and
    heart,
Do, with united urgency, require,
What more that may not perish? — Thou,
    dread source,
Prime, self-existing cause and end of all 80
That in the scale of being fill their place;
Above our human region, or below,
Set and sustained; — thou, who didst wrap
    the cloud
Of infancy around us, that thyself,
Therein, with our simplicity awhile
Might'st hold, on earth, communion undis-
    turbed;
Who from the anarchy of dreaming sleep,
Or from its death-like void, with punctual
    care,
And touch as gentle as the morning light,
Restor'st us, daily, to the powers of sense
And reason's stedfast rule — thou, thou
    alone   91
Art everlasting, and the blessèd Spirits,
Which thou includest, as the sea her waves:
For adoration thou endur'st; endure
For consciousness the motions of thy will;
For apprehension those transcendent truths
Of the pure intellect, that stand as laws
(Submission constituting strength and
    power)
Even to thy Being's infinite majesty!
This universe shall pass away — a work 100
Glorious! because the shadow of thy might,
A step, or link, for intercourse with thee.
Ah! if the time must come, in which my feet
No more shall stray where meditation leads,
By flowing stream, through wood, or craggy
    wild,
Loved haunts like these; the unimprisoned
    Mind
May yet have scope to range among her own,
Her thoughts, her images, her high desires.
If the dear faculty of sight should fail,
Still, it may be allowed me to remember
What visionary powers of eye and soul 111
In youth were mine; when, stationed on the
    top
Of some huge hill — expectant, I beheld
The sun rise up, from distant climes returned
Darkness to chase, and sleep; and bring the
    day

His bounteous gift! or saw him toward the
    deep
Sink, with a retinue of flaming clouds
Attended; then, my spirit was entranced
With joy exalted to beatitude;
The measure of my soul was filled with bliss,
And holiest love; as earth, sea, air, with
    light,   121
With pomp, with glory, with magnificence!

Those fervent raptures are for ever flown;
And, since their date, my soul hath under-
    gone
Change manifold, for better or for worse:
Yet cease I not to struggle, and aspire
Heavenward; and chide the part of me that
    flags,
Through sinful choice; or dread necessity
On human nature from above imposed.
'T is, by comparison, an easy task   130
Earth to despise; but, to converse with
    heaven —
This is not easy: — to relinquish all
We have, or hope, of happiness and joy,
And stand in freedom loosened from this
    world,
I deem not arduous; but must needs confess
That 't is a thing impossible to frame
Conceptions equal to the soul's desires;
And the most difficult of tasks to *keep*
Heights which the soul is competent to
    gain.
— Man is of dust: ethereal hopes are his,
Which, when they should sustain themselves
    aloft,   141
Want due consistence; like a pillar of smoke,
That with majestic energy from earth
Rises; but, having reached the thinner air,
Melts, and dissolves, and is no longer seen.
From this infirmity of mortal kind
Sorrow proceeds, which else were not; at
    least,
If grief be something hallowed and ordained,
If, in proportion, it be just and meet,
Yet, through this weakness of the general
    heart,   150
Is it enabled to maintain its hold
In that excess which conscience disapproves.
For who could sink and settle to that point
Of selfishness; so senseless who could be
As long and perseveringly to mourn
For any object of his love, removed
From this unstable world, if he could fix
A satisfying view upon that state
Of pure, imperishable, blessedness,

Which reason promises, and holy writ 160
Ensures to all believers ? — Yet mistrust
Is of such incapacity, methinks,
No natural branch; despondency far less;
And, least of all, is absolute despair.
— And, if there be whose tender frames
    have drooped
Even to the dust; apparently, through
    weight
Of anguish unrelieved, and lack of power
An agonizing sorrow to transmute;
Deem not that proof is here of hope with-
    held
When wanted most; a confidence impaired
So pitiably, that, having ceased to see 171
With bodily eyes, they are borne down by
    love
Of what is lost, and perish through regret.
Oh ! no, the innocent Sufferer often sees
Too clearly; feels too vividly; and longs
To realize the vision, with intense
And over-constant yearning; — there —
    there lies
The excess, by which the balance is de-
    stroyed.
Too, too contracted are these walls of flesh,
This vital warmth too cold, these visual
    orbs,   180
Though inconceivably endowed, too dim
For any passion of the soul that leads
To ecstasy; and, all the crooked paths
Of time and change disdaining, takes its
    course
Along the line of limitless desires.
I, speaking now from such disorder free,
Nor rapt, nor craving, but in settled peace,
I cannot doubt that they whom you deplore
Are glorified; or, if they sleep, shall wake
From sleep, and dwell with God in endless
    love.   190
Hope, below this, consists not with belief
In mercy, carried infinite degrees
Beyond the tenderness of human hearts:
Hope, below this, consists not with belief
In perfect wisdom, guiding mightiest power,
That finds no limits but her own pure will.

Here then we rest; not fearing for our
    creed
The worst that human reasoning can
    achieve,
To unsettle or perplex it: yet with pain
Acknowledging, and grievous self-reproach,
That, though immovably convinced, we
    want   201

Zeal, and the virtue to exist by faith
As soldiers live by courage; as, by strength
Of heart, the sailor fights with roaring seas.
Alas ! the endowment of immortal power
Is matched unequally with custom, time,
And domineering faculties of sense
In *all;* in most, with superadded foes,
Idle temptations; open vanities,
Ephemeral offspring of the unblushing
    world;   210
And, in the private regions of the mind,
Ill-governed passions, ranklings of despite,
Immoderate wishes, pining discontent,
Distress and care. What then remains ? —
    To seek
Those helps for his occasions ever near
Who lacks not will to use them; vows, re-
    newed
On the first motion of a holy thought;
Vigils of contemplation; praise; and
    prayer —
A stream, which, from the fountain of the
    heart
Issuing, however feebly, nowhere flows 220
Without access of unexpected strength.
But, above all, the victory is most sure
For him, who, seeking faith by virtue,
    strives
To yield entire submission to the law
Of conscience — conscience reverenced and
    obeyed,
As God's most intimate presence in the
    soul,
And his most perfect image in the world.
— Endeavour thus to live; these rules re-
    gard;
These helps solicit; and a stedfast seat
Shall then be yours among the happy few
Who dwell on earth, yet breathe empyreal
    air,   231
Sons of the morning. For your nobler
    part,
Ere disencumbered of her mortal chains,
Doubt shall be quelled and trouble chased
    away;
With only such degree of sadness left
As may support longings of pure desire;
And strengthen love, rejoicing secretly
In the sublime attractions of the grave."

While, in this strain, the venerable Sage
Poured forth his aspirations, and announced
His judgments, near that lonely house we
    paced   241
A plot of greensward, seemingly preserved

By nature's care from wreck of scattered
  stones,
And from encroachment of encircling heath:
Small space ! but, for reiterated steps,
Smooth and commodious; as a stately deck
Which to and fro the mariner is used
To tread for pastime, talking with his
  mates,
Or haply thinking of far-distant friends, 249
While the ship glides before a steady breeze.
Stillness prevailed around us: and the voice
That spake was capable to lift the soul
Toward regions yet more tranquil. But,
  methought,
That he, whose fixed despondency had
  given
Impulse and motive to that strong dis-
  course,
Was less upraised in spirit than abashed;
Shrinking from admonition, like a man
Who feels that to exhort is to reproach.
Yet not to be diverted from his aim,
The Sage continued: —
                    " For that other loss,
The loss of confidence in social man,   261
By the unexpected transports of our age
Carried so high, that every thought, which
  looked
Beyond the temporal destiny of the Kind,
To many seemed superfluous — as, no cause
Could e'er for such exalted confidence
Exist; so, none is now for fixed despair:
The two extremes are equally disowned
By reason: if, with sharp recoil, from one
You have been driven far as its opposite,
Between them seek the point whereon to
  build   271
Sound expectations.   So doth he advise
Who shared at first the illusion; but was
  soon
Cast from the pedestal of pride by shocks
Which Nature gently gave, in woods and
  fields;
Nor unreproved by Providence, thus speak-
  ing
To the inattentive children of the world:
' Vainglorious Generation ! what new powers
' On you have been conferred ? what gifts,
  withheld   279
' From your progenitors, have ye received,
' Fit recompense of new desert ? what claim
' Are ye prepared to urge, that my decrees
' For you should undergo a sudden change;
' And the weak functions of one busy day,
' Reclaiming and extirpating, perform

' What all the slowly-moving years of time,
' With their united force, have left undone ?
' By nature's gradual processes be taught;
' By story be confounded ! Ye aspire
' Rashly, to fall once more; and that false
  fruit,   290
' Which, to your overweening spirits, yields
' Hope of a flight celestial, will produce
' Misery and shame.   But Wisdom of her
  sons
' Shall not the less, though late, be justified.'

Such timely warning," said the Wanderer,
  " gave
That visionary voice; and, at this day,
When a Tartarean darkness overspreads
The groaning nations; when the impious
  rule,
By will or by established ordinance,
Their own dire agents, and constrain the
  good   300
To acts which they abhor; though I bewail
This triumph, yet the pity of my heart
Prevents me not from owning, that the
  law,
By which mankind now suffers, is most
  just.
For by superior energies; more strict
Affiance in each other; faith more firm
In their unhallowed principles; the bad
Have fairly earned a victory o'er the weak,
The vacillating, inconsistent good.
Therefore, not unconsoled, I wait — in hope
To see the moment, when the righteous
  cause   311
Shall gain defenders zealous and devout
As they who have opposed her; in which
  Virtue
Will, to her efforts, tolerate no bounds
That are not lofty as her rights; aspiring
By impulse of her own ethereal zeal.
That spirit only can redeem mankind;
And when that sacred spirit shall appear,
Then shall our triumph be complete as
  theirs.
Yet, should this confidence prove vain, the
  wise   320
Have still the keeping of their proper
  peace;
Are guardians of their own tranquillity.
They act, or they recede, observe, and
  feel;
' Knowing the heart of man is set to be
The centre of this world, about the which
Those revolutions of disturbances

Still roll; where all the aspècts of misery
Predominate; whose strong effects are such
As he must bear, being powerless to re-
 dress;
And that unless above himself he can 330
Erect himself, how poor a thing is Man!'

Happy is he who lives to understand,
Not human nature only, but explores
All natures, — to the end that he may find
The law that governs each; and where be-
 gins
The union, the partition where, that makes
Kind and degree, among all visible Beings;
The constitutions, powers, and faculties,
Which they inherit, — cannot step be-
 yond, —
And cannot fall beneath; that do assign 340
To every class its station and its office,
Through all the mighty commonwealth of
 things
Up from the creeping plant to sovereign
 Man.
Such converse, if directed by a meek,
Sincere, and humble spirit, teaches love:
For knowledge is delight; and such delight
Breeds love: yet, suited as it rather is
To thought and to the climbing intellect,
It teaches less to love, than to adore;
If that be not indeed the highest love !" 350

"Yet," said I, tempted here to interpose,
"The dignity of life is not impaired
By aught that innocently satisfies
The humbler cravings of the heart; and he
Is a still happier man, who, for those heights
Of speculation not unfit, descends;
And such benign affections cultivates
Among the inferior kinds; not merely those
That he may call his own, and which de-
 pend,
As individual objects of regard, 360
Upon his care, from whom he also looks
For signs and tokens of a mutual bond;
But others, far beyond this narrow sphere,
Whom, for the very sake of love, he loves.
Nor is it a mean praise of rural life
And solitude, that they do favour most,
Most frequently call forth, and best sustain,
These pure sensations; that can penetrate
The obstreperous city; on the barren seas
Are not unfelt; and much might recom-
 mend, 370
How much they might inspirit and endear,
The loneliness of this sublime retreat !"

"Yes," said the Sage, resuming the dis-
 course
Again directed to his downcast Friend,
"If, with the froward will and grovelling
 soul
Of man, offended, liberty is here,
And invitation every hour renewed,
To mark *their* placid state, who never heard
Of a command which they have power to
 break,
Or rule which they are tempted to trans-
 gress: 380
These, with a soothed or elevated heart,
May we behold; their knowledge register;
Observe their ways; and, free from envy,
 find
Complacence there: — but wherefore this to
 you ?
I guess that, welcome to your lonely hearth,
The redbreast, ruffled up by winter's cold
Into a 'feathery bunch,' feeds at your hand:
A box, perchance, is from your casement
 hung
For the small wren to build in; — not in
 vain,
The barriers disregarding that surround 390
This deep abiding place, before your sight
Mounts on the breeze the butterfly; and
 soars,
Small creature as she is, from earth's bright
 flowers,
Into the dewy clouds. Ambition reigns
In the waste wilderness: the Soul ascends
Drawn towards her native firmament of
 heaven,
When the fresh eagle, in the month of May,
Upborne, at evening, on replenished wing,
This shaded valley leaves; and leaves the
 dark
Empurpled hills, conspicuously renewing
A proud communication with the sun 401
Low sunk beneath the horizon ! — List ! —
 I heard,
From yon huge breast of rock, a voice sent
 forth
As if the visible mountain made the cry.
Again ! " — The effect upon the soul was
 such
As he expressed: from out the mountain's
 heart
The solemn voice appeared to issue, star-
 tling
The blank air — for the region all around
Stood empty of all shape of life, and si-
 lent 409

Save for that single cry, the unanswered
     bleat
Of a poor lamb — left somewhere to itself,
The plaintive spirit of the solitude !
He paused, as if unwilling to proceed,
Through consciousness that silence in such
     place
Was best, the most affecting eloquence.
But soon his thoughts returned upon them-
     selves,
And, in soft tone of speech, thus he re-
     sumed.

" Ah ! if the heart, too confidently raised,
Perchance too lightly occupied, or lulled
Too easily, despise or overlook   420
The vassalage that binds her to the earth,
Her sad dependence upon time, and all
The trepidations of mortality,
What place so destitute and void — but
     there
The little flower her vanity shall check;
The trailing worm reprove her thoughtless
     pride ?

These craggy regions, these chaotic wilds,
Does that benignity pervade, that warms
The mole contented with her darksome
     walk   429
In the cold ground; and to the emmet gives
Her foresight, and intelligence that makes
The tiny creatures strong by social league;
Supports the generations, multiplies
Their tribes, till we behold a spacious plain
Or grassy bottom, all, with little hills —
Their labour, covered, as a lake with waves;
Thousands of cities, in the desert place
Built up of life, and food, and means of
     life !
Nor wanting here, to entertain the thought,
Creatures that in communities exist   440
Less, as might seem, for general guardian-
     ship
Or through dependence upon mutual aid,
Than by participation of delight
And a strict love of fellowship, combined.
What other spirit can it be that prompts
The gilded summer flies to mix and weave
Their sports together in the solar beam,
Or in the gloom of twilight hum their joy ?
More obviously the self-same influence rules
The feathered kinds; the fieldfare's pensive
     flock,   450
The cawing rooks, and sea-mews from afar,
Hovering above these inland solitudes,

By the rough wind unscattered, at whose
     call
Up through the trenches of the long-drawn
     vales
Their voyage was begun: nor is its power
Unfelt among the sedentary fowl
That seek yon pool, and there prolong their
     stay
In silent congress; or together roused
Take flight; while with their clang the air
     resounds
And, over all, in that ethereal vault,   460
Is the mute company of changeful clouds;
Bright apparition, suddenly put forth,
The rainbow smiling on the faded storm;
The mild assemblage of the starry heavens;
And the great sun, earth's universal lord !

How bountiful is Nature ! he shall find
Who seeks not; and to him, who hath not
     asked,
Large measure shall be dealt.   Three sab-
     bath-days
Are scarcely told, since, on a service bent
Of mere humanity, you clomb those heights;
And what a marvellous and heavenly show
Was suddenly revealed ! — the swains
     moved on,   472
And heeded not: you lingered, you per-
     ceived
And felt, deeply as living man could feel.
There is a luxury in self-dispraise;
And inward self-disparagement affords
To meditative spleen a grateful feast.
Trust me, pronouncing on your own desert,
You judge unthankfully: distempered
     nerves
Infect the thoughts: the languor of the
     frame   480
Depresses the soul's vigour.   Quit your
     couch —
Cleave not so fondly to your moody cell;
Nor let the hallowed powers, that shed
     from heaven
Stillness and rest, with disapproving eye
Look down upon your taper, through a
     watch
Of midnight hours, unseasonably twinkling
In this deep Hollow, like a sullen star
Dimly reflected in a lonely pool.
Take courage, and withdraw yourself from
     ways
That run not parallel to nature's course. 490
Rise with the lark ! your matins shall obtain
Grace, be their composition what it may,

If but with hers performed; climb once
again,
Climb every day, those ramparts; meet the
breeze
Upon their tops, adventurous as a bee
That from your garden thither soars, to feed
On new-blown heath; let yon commanding
rock
Be your frequented watch-tower; roll the
stone
In thunder down the mountains; with all
your might
Chase the wild goat; and if the bold red
deer   500
Fly to those harbours, driven by hound
and horn
Loud echoing, add your speed to the pur-
suit;
So, wearied to your hut shall you return,
And sink at evening into sound repose."

The Solitary lifted toward the hills
A kindling eye: — accordant feelings rushed
Into my bosom, whence these words broke
forth:
"Oh! what a joy it were, in vigorous health,
To have a body (this our vital frame
With shrinking sensibility endued,   510
And all the nice regards of flesh and blood)
And to the elements surrender it
As if it were a spirit! — How divine,
The liberty, for frail, for mortal, man
To roam at large among unpeopled glens
And mountainous retirements, only trod
By devious footsteps; regions consecrate
To oldest time! and, reckless of the storm
That keeps the raven quiet in her nest,
Be as a presence or a motion — one   520
Among the many there; and while the mists
Flying, and rainy vapours, call out shapes
And phantoms from the crags and solid earth
As fast as a musician scatters sounds
Out of an instrument; and while the streams
(As at a first creation and in haste
To exercise their untried faculties)
Descending from the region of the clouds,
And starting from the hollows of the
earth   529
More multitudinous every moment, rend
Their way before them — what a joy to roam
An equal among mightiest energies;
And haply sometimes with articulate voice,
Amid the deafening tumult, scarcely heard
By him that utters it, exclaim aloud,
'Rage on ye elements! let moon and stars

Their aspects lend, and mingle in their turn
With this commotion (ruinous though it be)
From day to night, from night to day, pro-
longed!'"

"Yes," said the Wanderer, taking from
my lips   540
The strain of transport, "whosoe'er in youth
Has, through ambition of his soul, given
way
To such desires, and grasped at such de-
light,
Shall feel congenial stirrings late and long,
In spite of all the weakness that life brings,
Its cares and sorrows; he, though taught to
own
The tranquillizing power of time, shall wake,
Wake sometimes to a noble restlessness —
Loving the sports which once he gloried
in.

Compatriot, Friend, remote are Garry's
hills,   550
The streams far distant of your native glen;
Yet is their form and image here expressed
With brotherly resemblance. Turn your
steps
Wherever fancy leads; by day, by night,
Are various engines working, not the same
As those with which your soul in youth was
moved,
But by the great Artificer endowed
With no inferior power. You dwell alone;
You walk, you live, you speculate alone;
Yet doth remembrance, like a sovereign
prince,   560
For you a stately gallery maintain
Of gay or tragic pictures. You have seen,
Have acted, suffered, travelled far, observed
With no incurious eye; and books are yours,
Within whose silent chambers treasure lies
Preserved from age to age; more precious
far
Than that accumulated store of gold
And orient gems, which, for a day of need,
The Sultan hides deep in ancestral tombs.
These hoards of truth you can unlock at
will: 570
And music waits upon your skilful touch,
Sounds which the wandering shepherd from
these heights
Hears, and forgets his purpose; — furnished
thus,
How can you droop, if willing to be up-
raised?

A piteous lot it were to flee from Man —
Yet not rejoice in Nature. He, whose hours
Are by domestic pleasure uncaressed
And unenlivened; who exists whole years
Apart from benefits received or done   579
'Mid the transactions of the bustling crowd;
Who neither hears, nor feels a wish to hear,
Of the world's interests — such a one hath
    need
Of a quick fancy and an active heart,
That, for the day's consumption, books
    may yield
Food not unwholesome; earth and air correct
His morbid humour, with delight supplied
Or solace, varying as the seasons change.
— Truth has her pleasure-grounds, her
    haunts of ease
And easy contemplation; gay parterres,
And labyrinthine walks, her sunny glades
And shady groves in studied contrast —
    each,   591
For recreation, leading into each:
These may he range, if willing to partake
Their soft indulgences, and in due time
May issue thence, recruited for the tasks
And course of service Truth requires from
    those
Who tend her altars, wait upon her
    throne,
And guard her fortresses. Who thinks, and
    feels,
And recognises ever and anon   599
The breeze of nature stirring in his soul,
Why need such man go desperately astray,
And nurse 'the dreadful appetite of death?'
If tired with systems, each in its degree
Substantial, and all crumbling in their turn,
Let him build systems of his own, and smile
At the fond work, demolished with a touch;
If unreligious, let him be at once,
Among ten thousand innocents, enrolled
A pupil in the many-chambered school,
Where superstition weaves her airy dreams.

Life's autumn past, I stand on winter's
    verge;   611
And daily lose what I desire to keep:
Yet rather would I instantly decline
To the traditionary sympathies
Of a most rustic ignorance, and take
A fearful apprehension from the owl
Or death-watch: and as readily rejoice,
If two auspicious magpies crossed my
    way; —
To this would rather bend than see and hear

The repetitions wearisome of sense,   620
Where soul is dead, and feeling hath no
    place;
Where knowledge, ill begun in cold remark
On outward things, with formal inference
    ends;
Or, if the mind turn inward, she recoils
At once — or, not recoiling, is perplexed —
Lost in a gloom of uninspired research;
Meanwhile, the heart within the heart, the
    seat
Where peace and happy consciousness
    should dwell,
On its own axis restlessly revolving,
Seeks, yet can nowhere find, the light of
    truth.   630

Upon the breast of new-created earth
Man walked; and when and whereso'er he
    moved,
Alone or mated, solitude was not.
He heard, borne on the wind, the articulate
    voice
Of God; and Angels to his sight appeared
Crowning the glorious hills of paradise;
Or through the groves gliding like morning
    mist
Enkindled by the sun. He sate — and talked
With winged Messengers; who daily
    brought
To his small island in the ethereal deep   640
Tidings of joy and love. — From those pure
    heights
(Whether of actual vision, sensible
To sight and feeling, or that in this sort
Have condescendingly been shadowed forth
Communications spiritually maintained,
And intuitions moral and divine)
Fell Human-kind — to banishment con-
    demned
That flowing years repealed not: and dis-
    tress
And grief spread wide; but Man escaped
    the doom
Of destitution; — solitude was not.   650
— Jehovah — shapeless Power above all
    Powers,
Single and one, the omnipresent God,
By vocal utterance, or blaze of light,
Or cloud of darkness, localised in heaven;
On earth, enshrined within the wandering
    ark;
Or, out of Sion, thundering from his throne
Between the Cherubim — on the chosen
    Race

Showered miracles, and ceased not to dis-
pense
Judgments, that filled the land from age
to age
With hope, and love, and gratitude, and
fear;   660
And with amazement smote; — thereby to
assert
His scorned, or unacknowledged, sover-
eignty.
And when the One, ineffable of name,
Of nature indivisible, withdrew
From mortal adoration or regard,
Not then was Deity engulphed; nor Man,
The rational creature, left, to feel the
weight
Of his own reason, without sense or thought
Of higher reason and a purer will,
To benefit and bless, through mightier
power; —   670
Whether the Persian — zealous to reject
Altar and image, and the inclusive walls
And roofs of temples built by human
hands —
To loftiest heights ascending, from their
tops,
With myrtle-wreathed tiara on his brow,
Presented sacrifice to moon and stars,
And to the winds and mother elements,
And the whole circle of the heavens, for
him
A sensitive existence, and a God,
With lifted hands invoked, and songs of
praise: 680
Or, less reluctantly to bonds of sense
Yielding his soul, and Babylonian framed
For influence undefined a personal shape;
And, from the plain, with toil immense,
upreared
Tower eight times planted on the top of
tower,
That Belus, nightly to his splendid couch
Descending, there might rest; upon that
height
Pure and serene, diffused — to overlook
Winding Euphrates, and the city vast
Of his devoted worshippers, far-stretched,
With grove and field and garden inter-
spersed;   691
Their town, and foodful region for support
Against the pressure of beleaguering war.

Chaldean Shepherds, ranging trackless
fields,
Beneath the concave of unclouded skies

Spread like a sea, in boundless solitude,
Looked on the polar star, as on a guide
And guardian of their course, that never
closed
His stedfast eye. The planetary Five
With a submissive reverence they beheld;
Watched, from the centre of their sleeping
flocks,   701
Those radiant Mercuries, that seemed to
move
Carrying through ether, in perpetual round,
Decrees and resolutions of the Gods;
And, by their aspects, signifying works
Of dim futurity, to Man revealed.
— The imaginative faculty was lord
Of observations natural; and, thus
Led on, those shepherds made report of
stars
In set rotation passing to and fro,   710
Between the orbs of our apparent sphere
And its invisible counterpart, adorned
With answering constellations, under earth,
Removed from all approach of living sight
But present to the dead; who, so they
deemed,
Like those celestial messengers beheld
All accidents, and judges were of all.

The lively Grecian, in a land of hills,
Rivers and fertile plains, and sounding
shores, —
Under a cope of sky more variable,   720
Could find commodious place for every God,
Promptly received, as prodigally brought,
From the surrounding countries, at the
choice
Of all adventurers. With unrivalled skill,
As nicest observation furnished hints
For studious fancy, his quick hand bestowed
On fluent operations a fixed shape;
Metal or stone, idolatrously served.
And yet — triumphant o'er this pompous
show
Of art, this palpable array of sense,   730
On every side encountered; in despite
Of the gross fictions chanted in the streets
By wandering Rhapsodists; and in contempt
Of doubt and bold denial hourly urged
Amid the wrangling schools — a SPIRIT
hung,
Beautiful region! o'er thy towns and farms,
Statues and temples, and memorial tombs;
And emanations were perceived; and acts
Of immortality, in Nature's course,   739
Exemplified by mysteries, that were felt

As bonds, on grave philosopher imposed
And armèd warrior; and in every grove
A gay or pensive tenderness prevailed,
When piety more awful had relaxed.
— 'Take, running river, take these locks of
    mine ' —
Thus would the Votary say — ' this severed
    hair,
' My vow fulfilling, do I here present,
' Thankful for my belovèd child's return.
' Thy banks, Cephisus, he again hath trod,
' Thy murmurs heard; and drunk the crystal
    lymph   750
' With which thou dost refresh the thirsty
    lip,
' And, all day long, moisten these flowery
    fields ! '
And doubtless, sometimes, when the hair
    was shed
Upon the flowing stream, a thought arose
Of Life continuous, Being unimpaired;
That hath been, is, and where it was and is
There shall endure, — existence unexposed
To the blind walk of mortal accident;
From diminution safe and weakening age;
While man grows old, and dwindles, and
    decays;   760
And countless generations of mankind
Depart; and leave no vestige where they
    trod.

We live by Admiration, Hope and Love;
And, even as these are well and wisely
    fixed,
In dignity of being we ascend.
But what is error ? " — " Answer he who
    can ! "
The Sceptic somewhat haughtily exclaimed:
" Love, Hope, and Admiration, — are they
    not
Mad Fancy's favourite vassals ? Does not
    life
Use them, full oft, as pioneers to ruin, 770
Guides to destruction ? Is it well to trust
Imagination's light when reason's fails,
The unguarded taper where the guarded
    faints ?
— Stoop from those heights, and soberly
    declare
What error is; and, of our errors, which
Doth most debase the mind; the genuine
    seats
Of power, where are they ? Who shall
    regulate,
With truth, the scale of intellectual rank ? "

" Methinks," persuasively the Sage re-
    plied,   779
" That for this arduous office you possess
Some rare advantages. Your early days
A grateful recollection must supply
Of much exalted good by Heaven vouch-
    safed
To dignify the humblest state. — Your voice
Hath, in my hearing, often testified
That poor men's children, they, and they
    alone,
By their condition taught, can understand
The wisdom of the prayer that daily asks
For daily bread. A consciousness is yours
How feelingly religion may be learned 790
In smoky cabins, from a mother's tongue —
Heard while the dwelling vibrates to the
    din
Of the contiguous torrent, gathering
    strength
At every moment — and, with strength, in-
    crease
Of fury; or, while snow is at the door,
Assaulting and defending, and the wind,
A sightless labourer, whistles at his work —
Fearful; but resignation tempers fear,
And piety is sweet to infant minds.
— The Shepherd-lad, that in the sunshine
    carves,   800
On the green turf, a dial — to divide
The silent hours; and who to that report
Can portion out his pleasures, and adapt,
Throughout a long and lonely summer's
    day
His round of pastoral duties, is not left
With less intelligence for *moral* things
Of gravest import. Early he perceives,
Within himself, a measure and a rule,
Which to the sun of truth he can apply,
That shines for him, and shines for all
    mankind.   810
Experience daily fixing his regards
On nature's wants, he knows how few they
    are,
And where they lie, how answered and ap-
    peased.
This knowledge ample recompense affords
For manifold privations; he refers
His notions to this standard; on this rock
Rests his desires; and hence, in after life,
Soul-strengthening patience, and sublime
    content.
Imagination — not permitted here
To waste her powers, as in the worldling's
    mind,   820

On fickle pleasures, and superfluous cares,
And trivial ostentation — is left free
And puissant to range the solemn walks
Of time and nature, girded by a zone
That, while it binds, invigorates and sup-
ports.
Acknowledge, then, that whether by the
side
Of his poor hut, or on the mountain top,
Or in the cultured field, a Man so bred
(Take from him what you will upon the
score
Of ignorance or illusion) lives and breathes
For noble purposes of mind: his heart   831
Beats to the heroic song of ancient days;
His eye distinguishes, his soul creates.
And those illusions, which excite the scorn
Or move the pity of unthinking minds,
Are they not mainly outward ministers
Of inward conscience ? with whose service
charged
They came and go, appeared and disappear,
Diverting evil purposes, remorse
Awakening, chastening an intemperate
grief,   840
Or pride of heart abating: and, whene'er
For less important ends those phantoms
move,
Who would forbid them, if their presence
serve —
On thinly-peopled mountains and wild
heaths,
Filling a space, else vacant — to exalt
The forms of Nature, and enlarge her
powers ?

Once more to distant ages of the world
Let us revert, and place before our
thoughts
The face which rural solitude might wear
To the unenlightened swains of pagan
Greece.   850
— In that fair clime, the lonely herdsman,
stretched
On the soft grass through half a summer's
day,
With music lulled his indolent repose:
And, in some fit of weariness, if he,
When his own breath was silent, chanced to
hear
A distant strain, far sweeter than the
sounds
Which his poor skill could make, his fancy
fetched,
Even from the blazing chariot of the sun,

A beardless Youth, who touched a golden
lute,
And filled the illumined groves with ravish-
ment.   860
The nightly hunter, lifting a bright eye
Up towards the crescent moon, with grate-
ful heart
Called on the lovely wanderer who bestowed
That timely light, to share his joyous sport:
And hence, a beaming Goddess with her
Nymphs,
Across the lawn and through the darksome
grove,
Not unaccompanied with tuneful notes
By echo multiplied from rock or cave,
Swept in the storm of chase; as moon and
stars
Glance rapidly along the clouded heaven,
When winds are blowing strong. The trav-
eller slaked   871
His thirst from rill or gushing fount, and
thanked
The Naiad. Sunbeams, upon distant hills
Gliding apace, with shadows in their train,
Might, with small help from fancy, be
transformed
Into fleet Oreads sporting visibly.
The Zephyrs fanning, as they passed, their
wings,
Lacked not, for love, fair objects whom
they wooed
With gentle whisper. Withered boughs
grotesque,
Stripped of their leaves and twigs by hoary
age,   880
From depth of shaggy covert peeping forth
In the low vale, or on steep mountain side;
And, sometimes, intermixed with stirring
horns
Of the live deer, or goat's depending
beard, —
These were the lurking Satyrs, a wild brood
Of gamesome Deities; or Pan himself,
The simple shepherd's awe-inspiring
God ! "

The strain was aptly chosen; and I
could mark
Its kindly influence, o'er the yielding brow
Of our Companion, gradually diffused;   890
While listening, he had paced the noiseless
turf,
Like one whose untired ear a murmuring
stream
Detains; but tempted now to interpose,

He with a smile exclaimed: —
     " 'T is well you speak
At a safe distance from our native land,
And from the mansions where our youth
   was taught.
The true descendants of those godly men
Who swept from Scotland, in a flame of
   zeal,
Shrine, altar, image, and the massy piles
That harboured them, — the souls retaining
   yet   900
The churlish features of that after-race
Who fled to woods, caverns, and jutting
   rocks,
In deadly scorn of superstitious rites,
Or what their scruples construed to be
   such —
How, think you, would they tolerate this
   scheme
Of fine propensities, that tends, if urged
Far as it might be urged, to sow afresh
The weeds of Romish phantasy, in vain
Uprooted; would re-consecrate our wells
To good Saint Fillan and to fair Saint Anne;
And from long banishment recall Saint
   Giles,   911
To watch again with tutelary love
O'er stately Edinborough throned on crags?
A blessed restoration, to behold
The patron, on the shoulders of his priests,
Once more parading through her crowded
   streets,
Now simply guarded by the sober powers
Of science, and philosophy, and sense ! "

  This answer followed. — " You have
   turned my thoughts
Upon our brave Progenitors, who rose 920
Against idolatry with warlike mind,
And shrunk from vain observances, to lurk
In woods, and dwell under impending rocks
Ill-sheltered, and oft wanting fire and food;
Why ? — for this very reason that they felt,
And did acknowledge, wheresoe'er they
   moved,
A spiritual presence, oft-times miscon-
   ceived,
But still a high dependence, a divine
Bounty and government, that filled their
   hearts
With joy, and gratitude, and fear, and love;
And from their fervent lips drew hymns of
   praise,   931
That through the desert rang. Though
   favoured less,

Far less, than these, yet such, in their de-
   gree,
Were those bewildered Pagans of old time.
Beyond their own poor natures and above
They looked; were humbly thankful for
   the good
Which the warm sun solicited, and earth
Bestowed; were gladsome, — and their
   moral sense
They fortified with reverence for the Gods;
And they had hopes that overstepped the
   Grave.   940

  Now, shall our great Discoverers," he
   exclaimed,
Raising his voice triumphantly, " obtain
From sense and reason, less than these
   obtained,
Though far misled ?   Shall men for whom
   our age
Unbaffled powers of vision hath prepared,
To explore the world without and world
   within,
Be joyless as the blind ? Ambitious spirits—
Whom earth, at this late season, hath
   produced
To regulate the moving spheres, and weigh
The planets in the hollow of their hand;
And they who rather dive than soar, whose
   pains   951
Have solved the elements, or analysed
The thinking principle — shall they in fact
Prove a degraded Race ? and what avails
Renown, if their presumption make them
   such ?
Oh ! there is laughter at their work in
   heaven !
Inquire of ancient Wisdom; go, demand
Of mighty Nature, if 't was ever meant
That we should pry far off yet be un-
   raised;
That we should pore, and dwindle as we
   pore,   960
Viewing all objects unremittingly
In disconnection dead and spiritless;
And still dividing, and dividing still,
Break down all grandeur, still unsatisfied
With the perverse attempt, while littleness
May yet become more little; waging thus
An impious warfare with the very life
Of our own souls !
       And if indeed there be
An all-pervading Spirit, upon whom
Our dark foundations rest, could he design
That this magnificent effect of power, 971

The earth we tread, the sky that we behold
By day, and all the pomp which night re-
     veals;
That these — and that superior mystery
Our vital frame, so fearfully devised,
And the dread soul within it — should exist
Only to be examined, pondered, searched,
Probed, vexed, and criticised ?   Accuse me
     not
Of arrogance, unknown Wanderer as I am,
If, having walked with Nature threescore
     years,   980
And offered, far as frailty would allow,
My heart a daily sacrifice to Truth,
I now affirm of Nature and of Truth,
Whom I have served, that their DIVINITY
Revolts, offended at the ways of men
Swayed by such motives, to such ends em-
     ployed;
Philosophers, who, though the human soul
Be of a thousand faculties composed,
And twice ten thousand interests, do yet
     prize
This soul, and the transcendent universe,
No more than as a mirror that reflects   991
To proud Self-love her own intelligence;
That one, poor, finite object, in the abyss
Of infinite Being, twinkling restlessly !

Nor higher place can be assigned to him
And his compeers — the laughing Sage of
     France. —
Crowned was he, if my memory do not
     err,
With laurel planted upon hoary hairs,
In sign of conquest by his wit achieved
And benefits his wisdom had conferred;
His stooping body tottered with wreaths of
     flowers   1001
Opprest, far less becoming ornaments
Than Spring oft twines about a moulder-
     ing tree;
Yet so it pleased a fond, a vain, old Man,
And a most frivolous people.   Him I mean
Who penned, to ridicule confiding faith,
This sorry Legend; which by chance we
     found
Piled in a nook, through malice, as might
     seem,
Among more innocent rubbish." — Speak-
     ing thus,
With a brief notice when, and how, and
     where,   1010
We had espied the book, he drew it forth;
And courteously, as if the act removed,

At once, all traces from the good Man's
     heart
Of unbenign aversion or contempt,
Restored it to its owner.   "Gentle Friend,"
Herewith he grasped the Solitary's hand,
" You have known lights and guides better
     than these.
Ah ! let not aught amiss within dispose
A noble mind to practise on herself,   1019
And tempt opinion to support the wrongs
Of passion: whatsoe'er be felt or feared,
From higher judgment-seats make no ap-
     peal
To lower: can you question that the soul
Inherits an allegiance, not by choice
To be cast off, upon an oath proposed
By each new upstart notion ?   In the ports
Of levity no refuge can be found,
No shelter, for a spirit in distress.
He, who by wilful disesteem of life
And proud insensibility to hope,   1030
Affronts the eye of Solitude, shall learn
That her mild nature can be terrible;
That neither she nor Silence lack the power
To avenge their own insulted majesty.

O blest seclusion ! when the mind admits
The law of duty; and can therefore move
Through each vicissitude of loss and gain,
Linked in entire complacence with her
     choice;
When youth's presumptuousness is mellowed
     down,
And manhood's vain anxiety dismissed; 1040
When wisdom shows her seasonable fruit,
Upon the boughs of sheltering leisure hung
In sober plenty; when the spirit stoops
To drink with gratitude the crystal stream
Of unreproved enjoyment; and is pleased
To muse, and be saluted by the air
Of meek repentance, wafting wall-flower
     scents
From out the crumbling ruins of fallen
     pride
And chambers of transgression, now for-
     lorn.
O, calm contented days, and peaceful
     nights !   1050
Who, when such good can be obtained,
     would strive
To reconcile his manhood to a couch
Soft, as may seem, but, under that disguise,
Stuffed with the thorny substance of the
     past
For fixed annoyance; and full oft beset

With floating dreams, black and disconso-
    late,
The vapoury phantoms of futurity ?

Within the soul a faculty abides,   1058
That with interpositions, which would hide
And darken, so can deal that they become
Contingencies of pomp; and serve to exalt
Her native brightness. As the ample moon,
In the deep stillness of a summer even
Rising behind a thick and lofty grove,
Burns, like an unconsuming fire of light,
In the green trees; and, kindling on all sides
Their leafy umbrage, turns the dusky veil
Into a substance glorious as her own,
Yea, with her own incorporated, by power
Capacious and serene. Like power abides
In man's celestial spirit; virtue thus   1071
Sets forth and magnifies herself; thus feeds
A calm, a beautiful, and silent fire,
From the encumbrances of mortal life,
From error, disappointment — nay, from
    guilt;
And sometimes, so relenting justice wills,
From palpable oppressions of despair."

The Solitary by these words was touched
With manifest emotion, and exclaimed;
" But how begin ? and whence ? — ' The
    Mind is free —   1080
Resolve,' the haughty Moralist would say,
' This single act is all that we demand.'
Alas ! such wisdom bids a creature fly
Whose very sorrow is, that time hath shorn
His natural wings ! — To friendship let
    him turn
For succour; but perhaps he sits alone
On stormy waters, tossed in a little boat
That holds but him, and can contain no
    more !
Religion tells of amity sublime
Which no condition can preclude; of One
Who sees all suffering, comprehends all
    wants,   1091
All weakness fathoms, can supply all needs:
But is that bounty absolute ? — His gifts,
Are they not, still, in some degree, rewards
For acts of service ? Can his love extend
To hearts that own not him ? Will showers
    of grace,
When in the sky no promise may be seen,
Fall to refresh a parched and withered
    land ?
Or shall the groaning Spirit cast her load
At the Redeemer's feet ? "

                In rueful tone,
With some impatience in his mien, he spake:
Back to my mind rushed all that had been
    urged   1102
To calm the Sufferer when his story closed;
I looked for counsel as unbending now;
But a discriminating sympathy
Stooped to this apt reply: —
             " As men from men
Do, in the constitution of their souls,
Differ, by mystery not to be explained;
And as we fall by various ways, and sink
One deeper than another, self-condemned
Through manifold degrees of guilt and
    shame;   1111
So manifold and various are the ways
Of restoration, fashioned to the steps
Of all infirmity, and tending all
To the same point, attainable by all —
Peace in ourselves, and union with our God.
For you, assuredly, a hopeful road
Lies open: we have heard from you a voice
At every moment softened in its course
By tenderness of heart ; have seen your
    eye,   1120
Even like an altar lit by fire from heaven,
Kindle before us. — Your discourse this day,
That, like the fabled Lethe, wished to flow
In creeping sadness, through oblivious
    shades
Of death and night, has caught at every
    turn
The colours of the sun. Access for you
Is yet preserved to principles of truth,
Which the imaginative Will upholds
In seats of wisdom, not to be approached
By the inferior Faculty that moulds,   1130
With her minute and speculative pains,
Opinion, ever changing !
                I have seen
A curious child, who dwelt upon a tract
Of inland ground, applying to his ear
The convolutions of a smooth-lipped shell;
To which, in silence hushed, his very soul
Listened intensely; and his countenance
    soon
Brightened with joy; for from within were
    heard
Murmurings, whereby the monitor ex-
    pressed
Mysterious union with its native sea.   1140
Even such a shell the universe itself
Is to the ear of Faith; and there are times,
I doubt not, when to you it doth impart
Authentic tidings of invisible things;

Of ebb and flow, and ever-during power;
And central peace, subsisting at the heart
Of endless agitation. Here you stand,
Adore, and worship, when you know it not;
Pious beyond the intention of your thought;
Devout above the meaning of your will. 1150
— Yes, you have felt, and may not cease to
    feel.
The estate of man would be indeed for-
    lorn
If false conclusions of the reasoning power
Made the eye blind, and closed the passages
Through which the ear converses with the
    heart.
Has not the soul, the being of your life,
Received a shock of awful consciousness,
In some calm season, when these lofty rocks
At night's approach bring down the un-
    clouded sky,
To rest upon their circumambient walls;
A temple framing of dimensions vast, 1161
And yet not too enormous for the sound
Of human anthems, — choral song, or burst
Sublime of instrumental harmony,
To glorify the Eternal ! What if these
Did never break the stillness that prevails
Here, — if the solemn nightingale be
    mute,
And the soft woodlark here did never chant
Her vespers, — Nature fails not to provide
Impulse and utterance. The whispering
    air   1170
Sends inspiration from the shadowy heights,
And blind recesses of the caverned rocks;
The little rills, and waters numberless,
Inaudible by daylight, blend their notes
With the loud streams: and often, at the
    hour
When issue forth the first pale stars, is
    heard,
Within the circuit of this fabric huge,
One voice — the solitary raven, flying
Athwart the concave of the dark blue dome,
Unseen, perchance above all power of
    sight —   1180
An iron knell ! with echoes from afar
Faint — and still fainter — as the cry, with
    which
The wanderer accompanies her flight
Through the calm region, fades upon the
    ear,
Diminishing by distance till it seemed
To expire; yet from the abyss is caught
    again,
And yet again recovered !

                              But descending
From these imaginative heights, that yield
Far-stretching views into eternity,
Acknowledge that to Nature's humbler
    power   1190
Your cherished sullenness is forced to bend
Even here, where her amenities are sown
With sparing hand. Then trust yourself
    abroad
To range her blooming bowers, and spa-
    cious fields,
Where on the labours of the happy throng
She smiles, including in her wide embrace
City, and town, and tower, — and sea with
    ships
Sprinkled; — be our Companion while we
    track
Her rivers populous with gliding life;
While, free as air, o'er printless sands we
    march,   1200
Or pierce the gloom of her majestic woods;
Roaming, or resting under grateful shade
In peace and meditative cheerfulness;
Where living things, and things inanimate,
Do speak, at Heaven's command, to eye
    and ear,
And speak to social reason's inner sense,
With inarticulate language.
                              For, the Man —
Who, in this spirit, communes with the
    Forms
Of nature, who with understanding heart
Both knows and loves such objects as excite
No morbid passions, no disquietude,   1211
No vengeance, and no hatred — needs must
    feel
The joy of that pure principle of love
So deeply, that, unsatisfied with aught
Less pure and exquisite, he cannot choose
But seek for objects of a kindred love
In fellow-natures and a kindred joy.
Accordingly he by degrees perceives
His feelings of aversion softened down;
A holy tenderness pervade his frame.   1220
His sanity of reason not impaired,
Say rather, all his thoughts now flowing
    clear,
From a clear fountain flowing, he looks
    round
And seeks for good; and finds the good he
    seeks:
Until abhorrence and contempt are things
He only knows by name; and, if he hear,
From other mouths, the language which
    they speak,

He is compassionate; and has no thought,
No feeling, which can overcome his love.

And further; by contemplating these
  Forms   1230
In the relations which they bear to man,
He shall discern, how, through the various
  means
Which silently they yield, are multiplied
The spiritual presences of absent things.
Trust me, that for the instructed, time will
  come
When they shall meet no object but may
  teach
Some acceptable lesson to their minds
Of human suffering, or of human joy.
So shall they learn, while all things speak
  of man,
Their duties from all forms; and general
  laws,   1240
And local accidents, shall tend alike
To rouse, to urge; and, with the will,
  confer
The ability to spread the blessings wide
Of true philanthropy. The light of love
Not failing, perseverance from their steps
Departing not, for them shall be con-
  firmed
The glorious habit by which sense is made
Subservient still to moral purposes,
Auxiliar to divine. That change shall
  clothe
The naked spirit, ceasing to deplore 1250
The burthen of existence. Science then
Shall be a precious visitant; and then,
And only then, be worthy of her name:
For then her heart shall kindle; her dull
  eye,
Dull and inanimate, no more shall hang
Chained to its object in brute slavery;
But taught with patient interest to watch
The processes of things, and serve the cause
Of order and distinctness, not for this
Shall it forget that its most noble use, 1260
Its most illustrious province, must be found
In furnishing clear guidance, a support
Not treacherous, to the mind's *excursive*
  power.
— So build we up the Being that we are;
Thus deeply drinking-in the soul of things
We shall be wise perforce; and, while in-
  spired
By choice, and conscious that the Will is
  free,
Shall move unswerving, even as if impelled

By strict necessity, along the path 1269
Of order and of good. Whate'er we see,
Or feel, shall tend to quicken and refine
The humblest functions of corporeal sense;
Shall fix, in calmer seats of moral strength,
Earthly desires; and raise, to loftier heights
Of divine love, our intellectual soul."

Here closed the Sage that eloquent ha-
  rangue,
Poured forth with fervour in continuous
  stream,
Such as, remote, 'mid savage wilderness,
An Indian Chief discharges from his breast
Into the hearing of assembled tribes, 1280
In open circle seated round, and hushed
As the unbreathing air, when not a leaf
Stirs in the mighty woods. — So did he
  speak:
The words he uttered shall not pass away
Dispersed, like music that the wind takes up
By snatches, and lets fall, to be forgotten;
No — they sank into me, the bounteous gift
Of one whom time and nature had made
  wise,
Gracing his doctrine with authority
Which hostile spirits silently allow; 1290
Of one accustomed to desires that feed
On fruitage gathered from the tree of life;
To hopes on knowledge and experience
  built;
Of one in whom persuasion and belief
Had ripened into faith, and faith become
A passionate intuition; whence the Soul,
Though bound to earth by ties of pity and
  love,
From all injurious servitude was free.

The Sun, before his place of rest were
  reached,
Had yet to travel far, but unto us, 1300
To us who stood low in that hollow dell,
He had become invisible, — a pomp
Leaving behind of yellow radiance spread
Over the mountain sides, in contrast bold
With ample shadows, seemingly, no less
Than those resplendent lights, his rich be-
  quest;
A dispensation of his evening power.
— Adown the path that from the glen had
  led
The funeral train, the Shepherd and his
  Mate
Were seen descending: — forth to greet
  them ran 1310

Our little Page: the rustic pair approach;
And in the Matron's countenance may be
  read
Plain indication that the words, which told
How that neglected Pensioner was sent
Before his time into a quiet grave,
Had done to her humanity no wrong:
But we are kindly welcomed — promptly
  served
With ostentatious zeal. — Along the floor
Of the small Cottage in the lonely Dell
A grateful couch was spread for our repose;
Where, in the guise of mountaineers, we lay,
Stretched upon fragrant heath, and lulled
  by sound   1322
Of far-off torrents charming the still night,
And, to tired limbs and over-busy thoughts,
Inviting sleep and soft forgetfulness.

BOOK FIFTH

THE PASTOR

ARGUMENT

Farewell to the Valley — Reflections — A
large and populous Vale described — The Pas-
tor's Dwelling, and some account of him —
Church and Monuments — The Solitary musing,
and where — Roused — In the Churchyard the
Solitary communicates the thoughts which had
recently passed through his mind — Lofty tone
of the Wanderer's discourse of yesterday ad-
verted to — Rite of Baptism, and the profes-
sions accompanying it, contrasted with the real
state of human life — Apology for the Rite —
Inconsistency of the best men — Acknowledg-
ment that practice falls far below the injunc-
tions of duty as existing in the mind — General
complaint of a falling-off in the value of life
after the time of youth — Outward appearances
of content and happiness in degree illusive —
Pastor approaches — Appeal made to him —
His answer — Wanderer in sympathy with him
— Suggestion that the least ambitious enquirers
may be most free from error — The Pastor is
desired to give some portraits of the living or
dead from his own observation of life among
these Mountains — And for what purpose —
Pastor consents — Mountain cottage — Excel-
lent qualities of its Inhabitants — Solitary ex-
presses his pleasure; but denies the praise of
virtue to worth of this kind — Feelings of the
Priest before he enters upon his account of per-
sons interred in the Churchyard — Graves of
unbaptized Infants — Funeral and sepulchral
observances, whence — Ecclesiastical Estab-
lishments, whence derived — Profession of be-
lief in the doctrine of Immortality.

"FAREWELL, deep Valley, with thy one
  rude House,
And its small lot of life-supporting fields,
And guardian rocks ! — Farewell, attractive
  seat !
To the still influx of the morning light
Open, and day's pure cheerfulness, but
  veiled
From human observation, as if yet
Primeval forests wrapped thee round with
  dark
Impenetrable shade; once more farewell,
Majestic circuit, beautiful abyss,   9
By Nature destined from the birth of things
For quietness profound !"

                Upon the side
Of that brown ridge, sole outlet of the vale
Which foot of boldest stranger would at-
  tempt,
Lingering behind my comrades, thus I
  breathed
A parting tribute to a spot that seemed
Like the fixed centre of a troubled world.
Again I halted with reverted eyes;
The chain that would not slacken, was at
  length
Snapt, — and, pursuing leisurely my way,
How vain, thought I, is it by change of place
To seek that comfort which the mind
  denies;   21
Yet trial and temptation oft are shunned
Wisely; and by such tenure do we hold
Frail life's possessions, that even they whose
  fate
Yields no peculiar reason of complaint
Might, by the promise that is here, be won
To steal from active duties, and embrace
Obscurity, and undisturbed repose.
— Knowledge, methinks, in these disor-
  dered times,
Should be allowed a privilege to have   30
Her anchorites, like piety of old;
Men, who, from faction sacred, and un-
  stained
By war, might, if so minded, turn aside
Uncensured, and subsist, a scattered few
Living to God and nature, and content
With that communion. Consecrated be
The spots where such abide ! But happier
  still
The Man, whom, furthermore, a hope at-
  tends
That meditation and research may guide
His privacy to principles and powers   40
Discovered or invented; or set forth,

Through his acquaintance with the ways of
   truth,
In lucid order; so that, when his course
Is run, some faithful eulogist may say,
He sought not praise, and praise did over-
   look
His unobtrusive merit; but his life,
Sweet to himself, was exercised in good
That shall survive his name and memory.

Acknowledgments of gratitude sincere 49
Accompanied these musings; fervent thanks
For my own peaceful lot and happy choice;
A choice that from the passions of the
   world
Withdrew, and fixed me in a still retreat;
Sheltered, but not to social duties lost,
Secluded, but not buried; and with song
Cheering my days, and with industrious
   thought;
With the ever-welcome company of books;
With virtuous friendship's soul-sustaining
   aid,
And with the blessings of domestic love.

Thus occupied in mind I paced along, 60
Following the rugged road, by sledge or
   wheel
Worn in the moorland, till I overtook
My two Associates, in the morning sunshine
Halting together on a rocky knoll,
Whence the bare road descended rapidly
To the green meadows of·another vale.

Here did our pensive Host put forth his
   hand
In sign of farewell. "Nay," the old Man
   said,
"The fragrant air its coolness still retains;
The herds and flocks are yet abroad to crop
The dewy grass; you cannot leave us now, 71
We must not part at this inviting hour."
He yielded, though reluctant; for his mind
Instinctively disposed him to retire
To his own covert; as a billow, heaved
Upon the beach, rolls back into the sea.
— So we descend: and winding round a
   rock
Attain a point that showed the valley —
   stretched
In length before us; and, not distant far,
Upon a rising ground a grey church-tower,
Whose battlements were screened by tufted
   trees.   81
And towards a crystal Mere, that lay beyond

Among steep hills and woods embosomed,
   flowed
A copious stream with boldly-winding
   course;
Here traceable, there hidden — there again
To sight restored, and glittering in the sun.
On the stream's bank, and everywhere, ap-
   peared
Fair dwellings, single, or in social knots;
Some scattered o'er the level, others perched
On the hill sides, a cheerful quiet scene, 90
Now in its morning purity arrayed.

"As 'mid some happy valley of the
   Alps,"
Said I, "once happy, ere tyrannic power,
Wantonly breaking in upon the Swiss,
Destroyed their unoffending commonwealth,
A popular equality reigns here,
Save for yon stately House beneath whose
   roof
A rural lord might dwell." — "No feudal
   pomp,
Or power," replied the Wanderer, "to that
   House
Belongs, but there in his allotted Home 100
Abides, from year to year, a genuine
   Priest,
The shepherd of his flock; or, as a king
Is styled, when most affectionately praised,
The father of his people. Such is he;
And rich and poor, and young and old,
   rejoice
Under his spiritual sway. He hath vouch-
   safed
To me some portion of a kind regard;
And something also of his inner mind
Hath he imparted — but I speak of him
As he is known to all.
             The calm delights
Of unambitious piety he chose,   111
And learning's solid dignity; though born
Of knightly race, nor wanting powerful
   friends.
Hither, in prime of manhood, he withdrew
From academic bowers. He loved the spot—
Who does not love his native soil? — he
   prized
The ancient rural character, composed
Of simple manners, feelings unsupprest
And undisguised, and strong and serious
   thought,
A character reflected in himself,   120
With such embellishment as well be-
   seems

His rank and sacred function. This deep
vale
Winds far in reaches hidden from our sight,
And one a turreted manorial hall
Adorns, in which the good Man's ancestors
Have dwelt through ages, Patrons of this
Cure.
To them, and to his own judicious pains,
The Vicar's dwelling, and the whole do-
main,
Owes that presiding aspect which might
well
Attract your notice; statelier than could else
Have been bestowed, through course of
common chance,   131
On an unwealthy mountain Benefice."

This said, oft pausing, we pursued our
way;
Nor reached the village-churchyard till the
sun
Travelling at steadier pace than ours, had
risen
Above the summits of the highest hills,
And round our path darted oppressive
beams.

As chanced, the portals of the sacred
Pile
Stood open; and we entered. On my
frame,
At such transition from the fervid air,   140
A grateful coolness fell, that seemed to
strike
The heart, in concert with that temperate
awe
And natural reverence which the place in-
spired.
Not raised in nice proportions was the pile,
But large and massy; for duration built;
With pillars crowded, and the roof upheld
By naked rafters intricately crossed,
Like leafless underboughs, in some thick
wood,
All withered by the depth of shade above.
Admonitory texts inscribed the walls,   150
Each, in its ornamental scroll, enclosed;
Each also crowned with wingèd heads — a
pair
Of rudely-painted Cherubim. The floor
Of nave and aisle, in unpretending guise,
Was occupied by oaken benches ranged
In seemly rows; the chancel only showed
Some vain distinctions, marks of earthly
state

By immemorial privilege allowed;
Though with the Encincture's special
sanctity
But ill according. An heraldic shield,   160
Varying its tincture with the changeful
light,
Imbued the altar-window; fixed aloft
A faded hatchment hung, and one by time
Yet undiscoloured. A capacious pew
Of sculptured oak stood here, with drapery
lined;
And marble monuments were here displayed
Thronging the walls; and on the floor be-
neath
Sepulchral stones appeared, with emblems
graven
And foot-worn epitaphs, and some with
small
And shining effigies of brass inlaid.   170

The tribute by these various records
claimed,
Duly we paid, each after each, and read
The ordinary chronicle of birth,
Office, alliance, and promotion — all
Ending in dust; of upright magistrates,
Grave doctors strenuous for the mother-
church,
And uncorrupted senators, alike
To king and people true. A brazen plate,
Not easily deciphered, told of one
Whose course of earthly honour was begun
In quality of page among the train   181
Of the eighth Henry, when he crossed the
seas
His royal state to show, and prove his
strength
In tournament, upon the fields of France.
Another tablet registered the death,
And praised the gallant bearing, of a Knight
Tried in the sea-fights of the second
Charles.
Near this brave Knight his Father lay en-
tombed;
And, to the silent language giving voice,
I read, — how in his manhood's earlier day
He, 'mid the afflictions of intestine war   191
And rightful government subverted, found
One only solace — that he had espoused
A virtuous Lady tenderly beloved
For her benign perfections; and yet more
Endeared to him, for this, that, in her state
Of wedlock richly crowned with Heaven's
regard,
She with a numerous issue filled his house,

Who throve, like plants, uninjured by the
storm
That laid their country waste. No need to
speak   200
Of less particular notices assigned
To Youth or Maiden gone before their time,
And Matrons and unwedded Sisters old;
Whose charity and goodness were rehearsed
In modest panegyric.
                              " These dim lines,
What would they tell? " said I, — but, from
the task
Of puzzling out that faded narrative,
With whisper soft my venerable Friend
Called me; and, looking down the dark-
some aisle,
I saw the Tenant of the lonely vale   210
Standing apart; with curvèd arm re-
clined
On the baptismal font; his pallid face
Upturned, as if his mind were rapt, or lost
In some abstraction; — gracefully he stood,
The semblance bearing of a sculptured form
That leans upon a monumental urn
In peace, from morn to night, from year to
year.

Him from that posture did the Sexton
rouse;
Who entered, humming carelessly a tune,
Continuation haply of the notes   220
That had beguiled the work from which he
came,
With spade and mattock o'er his shoulder
hung;
To be deposited, for future need,
In their appointed place. The pale Recluse
Withdrew; and straight we followed, — to
a spot
Where sun and shade were intermixed; for
there
A broad oak, stretching forth its leafy arms
From an adjoining pasture, overhung
Small space of that green churchyard with
a light
And pleasant awning. On the moss-grown
wall   230
My ancient Friend and I together took
Our seats; and thus the Solitary spake,
Standing before us: —
                       " Did you note the mien
Of that self-solaced, easy-hearted churl,
Death's hireling, who scoops out his neigh-
bour's grave,
Or wraps an old acquaintance up in clay,

All unconcerned as he would bind a sheaf,
Or plant a tree? And did you hear his
voice?
I was abruptly summoned by the sound
From some affecting images and thoughts,
Which then were silent; but crave utter-
ance now.   241

Much," he continued, with dejected look,
" Much, yesterday, was said in glowing
phrase
Of our sublime dependencies, and hopes
For future states of being; and the wings
Of speculation, joyfully outspread,
Hovered above our destiny on earth:
But stoop, and place the prospect of the
soul
In sober contrast with reality,
And man's substantial life. If this mute
earth   250
Of what it holds could speak, and every
grave
Were as a volume, shut, yet capable
Of yielding its contents to eye and ear,
We should recoil, stricken with sorrow and
shame,
To see disclosed, by such dread proof, how
ill
That which is done accords with what is
known
To reason, and by conscience is enjoined;
How idly, how perversely, life's whole
course,
To this conclusion, deviates from the line,
Or of the end stops short, proposed to all
At her aspiring outset.
                         Mark the babe   261
Not long accustomed to this breathing
world;
One that hath barely learned to shape a
smile,
Though yet irrational of soul, to grasp
With tiny finger — to let fall a tear;
And, as the heavy cloud of sleep dissolves,
To stretch his limbs, bemocking, as might
seem,
The outward functions of intelligent man;
A grave proficient in amusive feats
Of puppetry, that from the lap declare   270
His expectations, and announce his claims
To that inheritance which millions rue
That they were ever born to! In due time
A day of solemn ceremonial comes;
When they, who for this Minor hold in
trust

Rights that transcend the loftiest heritage
Of mere humanity, present their Charge,
For this occasion daintily adorned,
At the baptismal font. And when the pure
And consecrating element hath cleansed
The original stain, the child is there re-
ceived   281
Into the second ark, Christ's church, with
trust
That he, from wrath redeemed, therein
shall float
Over the billows of this troublesome world
To the fair land of everlasting life.
Corrupt affections, covetous desires,
Are all renounced; high as the thought of
man
Can carry virtue, virtue is professed;
A dedication made, a promise given
For due provision to control and guide, 290
And unremitting progress to ensure
In holiness and truth."
                          " You cannot blame,"
Here interposing fervently I said,
" Rites which attest that Man by nature lies
Bedded for good and evil in a gulf
Fearfully low; nor will your judgment scorn
Those services, whereby attempt is made
To lift the creature toward that eminence
On which, now fallen, erewhile in majesty
He stood; or if not so, whose top serene
At least he feels 't is given him to de-
scry;   301
Not without aspirations, evermore
Returning, and injunctions from within
Doubt to cast off and weariness; in trust
That what the Soul perceives, if glory lost,
May be, through pains and persevering
hope,
Recovered; or, if hitherto unknown,
Lies within reach, and one day shall be
gained."

" I blame them not," he calmly answered
— " no;
The outward ritual and established forms
With which communities of men invest 311
These inward feelings, and the aspiring vows
To which the lips give public utterance
Are both a natural process; and by me
Shall pass uncensured; though the issue
prove,
Bringing from age to age its own reproach,
Incongruous, impotent, and blank. — But,
oh !
If to be weak is to be wretched — miserable,

As the lost Angel by a human voice
Hath mournfully pronounced, then, in my
mind,   320
Far better not to move at all than move
By impulse sent from such illusive power, —
That finds and cannot fasten down; that
grasps
And is rejoiced, and loses while it grasps;
That tempts, emboldens — for a time sus-
tains,
And then betrays; accuses and inflicts
Remorseless punishment; and so retreads
The inevitable circle: better far
Than this, to graze the herb in thoughtless
peace,
By foresight or remembrance, undisturbed !

Philosophy ! and thou more vaunted
name   331
Religion ! with thy statelier retinue,
Faith, Hope, and Charity — from the visible
world
Choose for your emblems whatsoe'er ye find
Of safest guidance or of firmest trust —
The torch, the star, the anchor; nor except
The cross itself, at whose unconscious feet
The generations of mankind have knelt
Ruefully seized, and shedding bitter tears,
And through that conflict seeking rest — of
you,   340
High-titled Powers, am I constrained to
ask,
Here standing, with the unvoyageable sky
In faint reflection of infinitude
Stretched overhead, and at my pensive feet
A subterraneous magazine of bones,
In whose dark vaults my own shall soon be
laid,
Where are your triumphs ? your dominion
where ?
And in what age admitted and confirmed ?
— Not for a happy land do I enquire,
Island or grove, that hides a blessed few
Who, with obedience willing and sincere, 351
To your serene authorities conform;
But whom, I ask, of individual Souls,
Have ye withdrawn from passion's crooked
ways,
Inspired, and thoroughly fortified ? — If the
heart
Could be inspected to its inmost folds
By sight undazzled with the glare of praise,
Who shall be named — in the resplendent
line
Of sages, martyrs, confessors — the man

Whom the best might of faith, wherever
 fixed,   360
For one day's little compass, has pre-
 served
From painful and discreditable shocks
Of contradiction, from some vague desire
Culpably cherished, or corrupt relapse
To some unsanctioned fear ? "
    " If this be so,
And Man," said I, " be in his noblest shape
Thus pitiably infirm; then, he who made,
And who shall judge the creature, will for-
 give.
— Yet, in its general tenor, your complaint
Is all too true; and surely not misplaced:
For, from this pregnant spot of ground,
 such thoughts   371
Rise to the notice of a serious mind
By natural exhalation. With the dead
In their repose, the living in their mirth,
Who can reflect, unmoved, upon the round
Of smooth and solemnized complacencies,
By which, on Christian lands, from age to
 age
Profession mocks performance? Earth is
 sick,
And Heaven is weary, of the hollow words
Which States and Kingdoms utter when
 they talk   380
Of truth and justice. Turn to private life
And social neighbourhood; look we to our-
 selves;
A light of duty shines on every day
For all; and yet how few are warmed or
 cheered !
How few who mingle with their fellow-men
And still remain self-governed, and apart,
Like this our honoured Friend; and thence
 acquire
Right to expect his vigorous decline,
That promises to the end a blest old age ! "

" Yet," with a smile of triumph thus
 exclaimed   390
The Solitary, " in the life of man,
If to the poetry of common speech
Faith may be given, we see as in a glass
A true reflection of the circling year,
With all its seasons. Grant that Spring is
 there,
In spite of many a rough untoward blast,
Hopeful and promising with buds and
 flowers;
Yet where is glowing Summer's long rich
 day,

That *ought* to follow faithfully expressed ?
And mellow Autumn, charged with boun-
 teous fruit,   400
Where is she imaged ? in what favoured
 clime
Her lavish pomp, and ripe magnificence ?
— Yet, while the better part is missed, the
 worse
In man's autumnal season is set forth
With a resemblance not to be denied,
And that contents him; bowers that hear
 no more
The voice of gladness, less and less supply
Of outward sunshine and internal warmth;
And, with this change, sharp air and falling
 leaves,
Foretelling aged Winter's desolate sway.

How gay the habitations that bedeck 411
This fertile valley ! Not a house but seems
To give assurance of content within;
Embosomed happiness, and placid love;
As if the sunshine of the day were met
With answering brightness in the hearts of
 all
Who walk this favoured ground. But
 chance-regards,
And notice forced upon incurious ears;
These, if these only, acting in despite
Of the encomiums by my Friend pronounced
On humble life, forbid the judging mind 421
To trust the smiling aspect of this fair
And noiseless commonwealth. The simple
 race
Of mountaineers (by nature's self removed
From foul temptations, and by constant
 care
Of a good shepherd tended, as themselves
Do tend their flocks) partake man's general
 lot
With little mitigation. They escape,
Perchance, the heavier woes of guilt; feel
 not
The tedium of fantastic idleness: 430
Yet life, as with the multitude, with them
Is fashioned like an ill-constructed tale;
That on the outset wastes its gay desires,
Its fair adventures, its enlivening hopes,
And pleasant interests — for the sequel
 leaving
Old things repeated with diminished grace;
And all the laboured novelties at best
Imperfect substitutes, whose use and power
Evince the want and weakness whence they
 spring."

While in this serious mood we held dis-
course,   440
The reverend Pastor toward the churchyard
gate
Approached; and, with a mild respectful air
Of native cordiality, our Friend
Advanced to greet him. With a gracious
mien
Was he received, and mutual joy prevailed.
Awhile they stood in conference, and I guess
That he, who now upon the mossy wall
Sate by my side, had vanished, if a wish
Could have transferred him to the flying
clouds,
Or the least penetrable hiding-place   450
In his own valley's rocky guardianship.
— For me, I looked upon the pair, well
pleased:
Nature had framed them both, and both
were marked
By circumstance, with intermixture fine
Of contrast and resemblance. To an oak
Hardy and grand, a weather-beaten oak,
Fresh in the strength and majesty of age,
One might be likened: flourishing appeared,
Though somewhat past the fulness of his
prime,
The other — like a stately sycamore,   460
That spreads, in gentle pomp, its honied
shade.

A general greeting was exchanged; and
soon
The Pastor learned that his approach had
given
A welcome interruption to discourse
Grave, and in truth too often sad. — "Is
Man
A child of hope ? Do generations press
On generations, without progress made ?
Halts the individual, ere his hairs be grey,
Perforce ? Are we a creature in whom
good
Preponderates, or evil ? Doth the will   470
Acknowledge reason's law ? A living
power
Is virtue, or no better than a name,
Fleeting as health or beauty, and unsound ?
So that the only substance which remains,
(For thus the tenor of complaint hath run)
Among so many shadows, are the pains
And penalties of miserable life,
Doomed to decay, and then expire in dust !
— Our cogitations this way have been
drawn.

These are the points," the Wanderer said,
" on which   480
Our inquest turns. — Accord, good Sir !
the light
Of your experience to dispel this gloom:
By your persuasive wisdom shall the heart
That frets, or languishes, be stilled and
cheered."

" Our nature," said the Priest, in mild
reply,
" Angels may weigh and fathom: they per-
ceive,
With undistempered and unclouded spirit,
The object as it is; but, for ourselves,
That speculative height we may not reach.
The good and evil are our own; and we   490
Are that which we would contemplate from
far.
Knowledge, for us, is difficult to gain —
Is difficult to gain, and hard to keep —
As virtue's self; like virtue is beset
With snares; tried, tempted, subject to de-
cay.
Love, admiration, fear, desire, and hate,
Blind were we without these: through these
alone
Are capable to notice or discern
Or to record; we judge, but cannot be
Indifferent judges. 'Spite of proudest
boast,   500
Reason, best reason, is to imperfect man
An effort only, and a noble aim;
A crown, an attribute of sovereign power,
Still to be courted — never to be won.
— Look forth, or each man dive into him-
self;
What sees he but a creature too perturbed;
That is transported to excess; that yearns,
Regrets, or trembles, wrongly, or too much;
Hopes rashly, in disgust as rash recoils;
Battens on spleen, or moulders in despair ?
Thus comprehension fails, and truth is
missed;   511
Thus darkness and delusion round our path
Spread, from disease, whose subtle injury
lurks
Within the very faculty of sight.

Yet for the general purposes of faith
In Providence, for solace and support,
We may not doubt that who can best sub-
ject
The will to reason's law, can strictliest live
And act in that obedience, he shall gain

The clearest apprehension of those truths,
Which unassisted reason's utmost power 521
Is too infirm to reach. But, waiving this,
And our regards confining within bounds
Of less exalted consciousness, through
   which
The very multitude are free to range,
We safely may affirm that human life
Is either fair and tempting, a soft scene
Grateful to sight, refreshing to the soul,
Or a forbidding tract of cheerless view;
Even as the same is looked at, or ap-
   proached.   530
Thus, when in changeful April fields are
   white
With new-fallen snow, if from the sullen
   north
Your walk conduct you hither, ere the sun
Hath gained his noontide height, this
   churchyard, filled
With mounds transversely lying side by
   side
From east to west, before you will appear
An unillumined, blank, and dreary plain,
With more than wintry cheerlessness and
   gloom
Saddening the heart. Go forward, and
   look back;
Look, from the quarter whence the lord of
   light,   540
Of life, of love, and gladness doth dispense
His beams; which, unexcluded in their fall,
Upon the southern side of every grave
Have gently exercised a melting power;
Then will a vernal prospect greet your eye,
All fresh and beautiful, and green and
   bright,
Hopeful and cheerful: — vanished is the pall
That overspread and chilled the sacred turf,
Vanished or hidden; and the whole domain,
To some, too lightly minded, might appear
A meadow carpet for the dancing hours. 551
— This contrast, not unsuitable to life,
Is to that other state more apposite,
Death and its two-fold aspect! wintry —
   one,
Cold, sullen, blank, from hope and joy shut
   out;
The other, which the ray divine hath
   touched,
Replete with vivid promise, bright as
   spring."

  "We see, then, as we feel," the Wan-
   derer thus

With a complacent animation spake,
"And in your judgment, Sir! the mind's
   repose   560
On evidence is not to be ensured
By act of naked reason. Moral truth
Is no mechanic structure, built by rule;
And which, once built, retains a stedfast
   shape
And undisturbed proportions; but a thing
Subject, you deem, to vital accidents;
And, like the water-lily, lives and thrives,
Whose root is fixed in stable earth, whose
   head
Floats on the tossing waves. With joy sin-
   cere
I re-salute these sentiments confirmed 570
By your authority. But how acquire
The inward principle that gives effect
To outward argument; the passive will
Meek to admit; the active energy,
Strong and unbounded to embrace, and firm
To keep and cherish? how shall man unite
With self-forgetting tenderness of heart
An earth-despising dignity of soul? •
Wise in that union, and without it blind!"

  "The way," said I, "to court, if not ob-
   tain   580
The ingenuous mind, apt to be set aright;
This, in the lonely dell discoursing, you
Declared at large; and by what exercise
From visible nature, or the inner self
Power may be trained, and renovation
   brought
To those who need the gift. But, after all,
Is aught so certain as that man is doomed
To breathe beneath a vault of ignorance?
The natural roof of that dark house in
   which
His soul is pent! How little can be
   known —   590
This is the wise man's sigh; how far we
   err —
This is the good man's not unfrequent pang!
And they perhaps err least, the lowly class
Whom a benign necessity compels
To follow reason's least ambitious course;
Such do I mean who, unperplexed by
   doubt,
And unincited by a wish to look
Into high objects farther than they may,
Pace to and fro, from morn till eventide,
The narrow avenue of daily toil   600
For daily bread."

         "Yes," buoyantly exclaimed

The pale Recluse — " praise to the sturdy
    plough,
And patient spade; praise to the simple
    crook,
And ponderous loom — resounding while it
    holds
Body and mind in one captivity;
And let the light mechanic tool be hailed
With honour; which, encasing by the power
Of long companionship, the artist's hand,
Cuts off that hand, with all its world of
    nerves,   609
From a too busy commerce with the heart !
— Inglorious implements of craft and toil,
Both ye that shape and build, and ye that
    force,
By slow solicitation, earth to yield
Her annual bounty, sparingly dealt forth
With wise reluctance; you would I extol,
Not for gross good alone which ye produce,
But for the impertinent and ceaseless strife
Of proofs and reasons ye preclude — in
    those
Who to your dull society are born,
And with their humble birthright rest con-
    tent.   620
— Would I had ne'er renounced it ! "
                            A slight flush
Of moral anger previously had tinged
The old Man's cheek; but, at this closing
    turn
Of self-reproach, it passed away. Said he,
" That which we feel we utter; as we think
So have we argued; reaping for our pains
No visible recompense. For our relief
You," to the Pastor turning thus he spake,
" Have kindly interposed. May I entreat
Your further help ? The mine of real life
Dig for us; and present us, in the shape 631
Of virgin ore, that gold which we, by pains
Fruitless as those of aëry alchemists,
Seek from the torturing crucible. There lies
Around us a domain where you have long
Watched both the outward course and inner
    heart:
Give us, for our abstractions, solid facts;
For our disputes, plain pictures. Say what
    man
He is who cultivates yon hanging field;
What qualities of mind she bears, who
    comes,   640
For morn and evening service, with her
    pail,
To that green pasture; place before our
    sight

The family who dwell within yon house
Fenced round with glittering laurel; or in
    that
Below, from which the curling smoke as-
    scends.
Or rather, as we stand on holy earth,
And have the dead around us, take from
    them
Your instances; for they are both best
    known,
And by frail man most equitably judged.
Epitomise the life; pronounce, you can, 650
Authentic epitaphs on some of these
Who, from their lowly mansions hither
    brought,
Beneath this turf lie mouldering at our
    feet:
So, by your records, may our doubts be
    solved;
And so, not searching higher we may learn
*To prize the breath we share with human
    kind;*
And look upon the dust of man with awe."

The Priest replied — " An office you im-
    pose
For which peculiar requisites are mine;
Yet much, I feel, is wanting — else the
    task   660
Would be most grateful. True indeed it
    is
That they whom death has hidden from our
    sight
Are worthiest of the mind's regard; with
    these
The future cannot contradict the past:
Mortality's last exercise and proof
Is undergone; the transit made that shows
The very Soul, revealed as she departs.
Yet, on your first suggestion, will I give,
Ere we descend into these silent vaults,
One picture from the living.
                            You behold,
High on the breast of yon dark mountain,
    dark   671
With stony barrenness, a shining speck
Bright as a sunbeam sleeping till a shower
Brush it away, or cloud pass over it;
And such it might be deemed — a sleeping
    sunbeam;
But 't is a plot of cultivated ground,
Cut off, an island in the dusky waste:
And that attractive brightness is its own.
The lofty site, by nature framed to tempt
Amid a wilderness of rocks and stones 68●

The tiller's hand, a hermit might have
chosen,
For opportunity presented, thence
Far forth to send his wandering eye o'er
land
And ocean, and look down upon the works,
The habitations, and the ways of men,
Himself unseen! But no tradition tells
That ever hermit dipped his maple dish
In the sweet spring that lurks 'mid yon
green fields;
And no such visionary views belong
To those who occupy and till the ground,
High on that mountain where they long
have dwelt   691
A wedded pair in childless solitude.
A house of stones collected on the spot,
By rude hands built, with rocky knolls in
front,
Backed also by a ledge of rock, whose
crest
Of birch-trees waves over the chimney top;
A rough abode — in colour, shape, and size,
Such as in unsafe times of border-war
Might have been wished for and contrived,
to elude
The eye of roving plunderer — for their
need   700
Suffices; and unshaken bears the assault
Of their most dreaded foe, the strong South-
west
In anger blowing from the distant sea.
— Alone within her solitary hut;
There, or within the compass of her fields,
At any moment may the Dame be found,
True as the stock-dove to her shallow nest
And to the grove that holds it. She be-
guiles
By intermingled work of house and field
The summer's day, and winter's; with suc-
cess   710
Not equal, but sufficient to maintain,
Even at the worst, a smooth stream of con-
tent,
Until the expected hour at which her Mate
From the far-distant quarry's vault re-
turns;
And by his converse crowns a silent day
With evening cheerfulness. In powers of
mind,
In scale of culture, few among my flock
Hold lower rank than this sequestered pair:
But true humility descends from heaven;
And that best gift of heaven hath fallen on
them;   720

Abundant recompense for every want.
— Stoop from your height, ye proud, and
copy these!
Who, in their noiseless dwelling-place, can
hear
The voice of wisdom whispering scripture
texts
For the mind's government, or temper's
peace;
And recommending for their mutual need,
Forgiveness, patience, hope, and charity!"

" Much was I pleased," the grey-haired
Wanderer said,
" When to those shining fields our notice
first
You turned; and yet more pleased have
from your lips   730
Gathered this fair report of them who
dwell
In that retirement; whither, by such course
Of evil hap and good as oft awaits
A tired way-faring man, once ˉwas brought
While traversing alone yon mountain pass.
Dark on my road the autumnal evening fell,
And night succeeded with unusual gloom,
So hazardous that feet and hands became
Guides better than mine eyes — until a
light
High in the gloom appeared, too high,
methought,   740
For human habitation; but I longed
To reach it, destitute of other hope.
I looked with steadiness as sailors look
On the north star, or watch-tower's distant
lamp,
And saw the light — now fixed —and shift-
ing now —
Not like a dancing meteor, but in line
Of never-varying motion, to and fro.
It is no night-fire of the naked hills,
Thought I — some friendly covert must be
near.
With this persuasion thitherward my steps
I turn, and reach at last the guiding
light;   751
Joy to myself! but to the heart of her
Who there was standing on the open hill,
(The same kind Matron whom your tongue
hath praised)
Alarm and disappointment! The alarm
Ceased, when she learned through what
mishap I came,
And by what help had gained those distant
fields.

Drawn from her cottage, on that aëry
      height,
Bearing a lantern in her hand she stood,
Or paced the ground — to guide her Hus-
      band home,   760
By that unwearied signal, kenned afar;
An anxious duty ! which the lofty site,
Traversed but by a few irregular paths,
Imposes, whensoe'er untoward chance
Detains him after his accustomed hour
Till night lies black upon the ground. ' But
      come,
Come,' said the Matron, 'to our poor abode;
Those dark rocks hide it !' Entering, I
      beheld
A blazing fire — beside a cleanly hearth
Sate down; and to her office, with leave
      asked,   770
The Dame returned.
                  Or ere that glowing pile
Of mountain turf required the builder's
      hand
Its wasted splendour to repair, the door
Opened, and she re-entered with glad looks,
Her Helpmate following. Hospitable fare,
Frank conversation, made the evening's
      treat:
Need a bewildered traveller wish for more?
But more was given; I studied as we sate
By the bright fire, the good Man's form,
      and face
Not less than beautiful; an open brow   780
Of undisturbed humanity; a cheek
Suffused with something of a feminine
      hue;
Eyes beaming courtesy and mild regard;
But, in the quicker turns of the discourse,
Expression slowly varying, that evinced
A tardy apprehension. From a fount
Lost, thought I, in the obscurities of time,
But honoured once, those features and that
      mien
May have descended, though I see them
      here.
In such a man, so gentle and subdued,   790
Withal so graceful in his gentleness,
A race illustrious for heroic deeds,
Humbled, but not degraded, may expire.
This pleasing fancy (cherished and upheld
By sundry recollections of such fall
From high to low, ascent from low to high,
As books record, and even the careless
      mind
Cannot but notice among men and things)
Went with me to the place of my repose.

Roused by the crowing cock at dawn of
      day,   800
I yet had risen too late to interchange
A morning salutation with my Host,
Gone forth already to the far-off seat
Of his day's work. ' Three dark mid-winter
      months
Pass,' said the Matron, ' and I never see,
Save when the sabbath brings its kind re-
      lease,
My Helpmate's face by light of day. He
      quits
His door in darkness, nor till dusk returns.
And, through Heaven's blessing, thus we
      gain the bread
For which we pray; and for the wants pro-
      vide   810
Of sickness, accident, and helpless age.
Companions have I many; many friends,
Dependants, comforters — my wheel, my
      fire,
All day the house-clock ticking in mine
      ear,
The cackling hen, the tender chicken
      brood,
And the wild birds that gather round my
      porch.
This honest sheep-dog's countenance I
      read;
With him can talk; nor blush to waste a
      word
On creatures less intelligent and shrewd.
And if the blustering wind that drives the
      clouds   820
Care not for me, he lingers round my
      door,
And makes me pastime when our tempers
      suit; —
But, above all, my thoughts are my sup-
      port,
My comfort: — would that they were
      oftener fixed
On what, for guidance in the way that
      leads
To heaven, I know, by my Redeemer
      taught.'
The Matron ended — nor could I forbear
To exclaim — ' O happy ! yielding to the
      law
Of these privations, richer in the main ! —
While thankless thousands are opprest and
      clogged   830
By ease and leisure; by the very wealth
And pride of opportunity made poor;
While tens of thousands falter in their path,

And sink, through utter want of cheering
    light;
For you the hours of labour do not flag;
For you each evening hath its shining star,
And every sabbath-day its golden sun.'"

"Yes!" said the Solitary with a smile
That seemed to break from an expanding
    heart,
"The untutored bird may found, and so
    construct,   840
And with such soft materials line, her
    nest
Fixed in the centre of a prickly brake,
That the thorns wound her not; they only
    guard.
Powers not unjustly likened to those gifts
Of happy instinct which the woodland bird
Shares with her species, nature's grace
    sometimes
Upon the individual doth confer,
Among her higher creatures born and
    trained
To use of reason. And, I own that, tired
Of the ostentatious world — a swelling stage
With empty actions and vain passions
    stuffed,   851
And from the private struggles of mankind
Hoping far less than I could wish to hope,
Far less than once I trusted and believed —
I love to hear of those, who, not contending
Nor summoned to contend for virtue's
    prize,
Miss not the humbler good at which they
    aim,
Blest with a kindly faculty to blunt
The edge of adverse circumstance, and turn
Into their contraries the petty plagues   860
And hindrances with which they stand
    beset.
In early youth, among my native hills,
I knew a Scottish Peasant who possessed
A few small crofts of stone-encumbered
    ground;
Masses of every shape and size, that lay
Scattered about under the mouldering
    walls
Of a rough precipice; and some, apart,
In quarters unobnoxious to such chance,
As if the moon had showered them down
    in spite.
But he repined not. Though the plough
    was scared   870
By these obstructions, 'round the shady
    stones

' A fertilising moisture,' said the Swain,
'Gathers, and is preserved; and feeding
    dews
' And damps, through all the droughty
    summer day
' From out their substance issuing, maintain
' Herbage that never fails; no grass springs
    up
' So green, so fresh, so plentiful, as mine!'
But thinly sown these natures; rare, at
    least,
The mutual aptitude of seed and soil
That yields such kindly product. He, whose
    bed   880
Perhaps yon loose sods cover, the poor
    Pensioner
Brought yesterday from our sequestered
    dell
Here to lie down in lasting quiet, he,
If living now, could otherwise report
Of rustic loneliness: that grey-haired Or-
    phan —
So call him, for humanity to him
No parent was — feelingly could have told,
In life, in death, what solitude can breed
Of selfishness, and cruelty, and vice;
Or, if it breed not, hath not power to cure.
— But your compliance, Sir! with our re-
    quest   891
My words too long have hindered."
                            Undeterred,
Perhaps incited rather, by these shocks,
In no ungracious opposition, given
To the confiding spirit of his own
Experienced faith, the Reverend Pastor
    said,
Around him looking; "Where shall I be-
    gin?
Who shall be first selected from my flock
Gathered together in their peaceful fold?"
He paused — and having lifted up his eyes
To the pure heaven, he cast them down
    again   901
Upon the earth beneath his feet; and
    spake: —

" To a mysteriously-united pair
This place is consecrate; to Death and Life,
And to the best affections that proceed
From their conjunction; consecrate to faith
In him who bled for man upon the cross;
Hallowed to revelation; and no less
To reason's mandates: and the hopes di-
    vine
Of pure imagination; — above all,   910

To charity, and love, that have provided,
Within these precincts, a capacious bed
And receptacle, open to the good
And evil, to the just and the unjust;
In which they find an equal resting-place:
Even as the multitude of kindred brooks
And streams, whose murmur fills this hol-
low vale,
Whether their course be turbulent or
smooth,
Their waters clear or sullied, all are lost
Within the bosom of yon crystal Lake, 920
And end their journey in the same repose!

And blest are they who sleep; and we
that know,
While in a spot like this we breathe and
walk,
That all beneath us by the wings are cov-
ered
Of motherly humanity, outspread
And gathering all within their tender shade,
Though loth and slow to come ! A battle-
field,
In stillness left when slaughter is no more,
With this compared, makes a strange spec-
tacle !
A dismal prospect yields the wild shore
strewn 930
With wrecks, and trod by feet of young
and old
Wandering about in miserable search
Of friends or kindred, whom the angry
sea
Restores not to their prayer ! Ah ! who
would think
That all the scattered subjects which com-
pose
Earth's melancholy vision through the space
Of all her climes — these wretched, these
depraved,
To virtue lost, insensible of peace,
From the delights of charity cut off,
To pity dead, the oppressor and the op-
prest; 940
Tyrants who utter the destroying word,
And slaves who will consent to be de-
stroyed —
Were of one species with the sheltered few,
Who, with a dutiful and tender hand,
Lodged, in a dear appropriated spot,
This file of infants; some that never
breathed
The vital air; others, which, though al-
lowed

That privilege, did yet expire too soon,
Or with too brief a warning, to admit
Administration of the holy rite 950
That lovingly consigns the babe to the
arms
Of Jesus, and his everlasting care.
These that in trembling hope are laid apart;
And the besprinkled nursling, unrequired
Till he begins to smile upon the breast
That feeds him; and the tottering little-one
Taken from air and sunshine when the
rose
Of infancy first blooms upon his cheek;
The thinking, thoughtless, school-boy; the
bold youth
Of soul impetuous, and the bashful maid
Smitten while all the promises of life 961
Are opening round her; those of middle
age,
Cast down while confident in strength they
stand,
Like pillars fixed more firmly, as might
seem,
And more secure, by very weight of all
That, for support, rests on them; the de-
cayed
And burthensome; and lastly, that poor few
Whose light of reason is with age extinct;
The hopeful and the hopeless, first and
last,
The earliest summoned and the longest
spared — 970
Are here deposited, with tribute paid
Various, but unto each some tribute paid;
As if, amid these peaceful hills and groves,
Society were touched with kind concern,
And gentle 'Nature grieved, that one
should die;'
Or, if the change demanded no regret,
Observed the liberating stroke — and
blessed.

And whence that tribute ? wherefore
these regards ?
Not from the naked *Heart* alone of Man
(Though claiming high distinction upon
earth 980
As the sole spring and fountain-head of
tears,
His own peculiar utterance for distress
Or gladness) — No," the philosophic Priest
Continued, " 't is not in the vital seat
Of feeling to produce them, without aid
From the pure soul, the soul sublime and
pure;

With her two faculties of eye and ear,
The one by which a creature, whom his
    sins
Have rendered prone, can upward look to
    heaven;   98_
The other that empowers him to perceive
The voice of Deity, on height and plain,
Whispering those truths in stillness, which
    the WORD,
To the four quarters of the winds, pro-
    claims.
Not without such assistance could the use
Of these benign observances prevail:
Thus are they born, thus fostered, thus
    maintained;
And by the care prospective of our wise
Forefathers, who, to guard against the
    shocks,
The fluctuation and decay of things,   999
Embodied and established these high truths
In solemn institutions: — men convinced
That life is love and immortality,
The being one, and one the element.
There lies the channel, and original bed,
From the beginning, hollowed out and
    scooped
For Man's affections — else betrayed and
    lost,
And swallowed up 'mid deserts infinite !
This is the genuine course, the aim, and end
Of prescient reason; all conclusions else
Are abject, vain, presumptuous, and per-
    verse.   1010
The faith partaking of those holy times,
Life, I repeat, is energy of love
Divine or human; exercised in pain,
In strife, and tribulation; and ordained,
If so approved and sanctified, to pass,
Through shades and silent rest, to endless
    joy."

BOOK SIXTH

THE CHURCHYARD AMONG THE MOUNTAINS

ARGUMENT

Poet's Address to the State and Church of
England — The Pastor not inferior to the an-
cient Worthies of the Church — He begins his
Narratives with an instance of unrequited Love
— Anguish of mind subdued, and how — The
lonely Miner — An instance of perseverance —
Which leads by contrast to an example of
abused talents, irresolution, and weakness —

Solitary, applying this covertly to his own case,
asks for an instance of some Stranger, whose
dispositions may have led him to end his days
here — Pastor, in answer, gives an account of
the harmonising influence of Solitude upon two
men of opposite principles, who had encoun-
tered agitations in public life — The rule by
which Peace may be obtained expressed, and
where — Solitary hints at an overpowering Fa-
tality — Answer of the Pastor — What subjects
he will exclude from his Narratives — Conversa-
tion upon this — Instance of an unamiable char-
acter, a Female, and why given — Contrasted
with this, a meek sufferer, from unguarded and
betrayed love — Instance of heavier guilt, and
its consequences to the Offender — With this
instance of a Marriage Contract broken is con-
trasted one of a Widower, evidencing his faith-
ful affection towards his deceased wife by his
care of their female Children.

HAIL to the crown by Freedom shaped —·
    to gird
An English Sovereign's brow ! and to the
    throne
Whereon he sits ! Whose deep foundations
    lie
In veneration and the people's love;
Whose steps are equity, whose seat is law.
— Hail to the State of England ! And con-
    join
With this a salutation as devout,
Made to the spiritual fabric of her Church;
Founded in truth; by blood of Martyrdom
Cemented;   by the hands of Wisdom
    reared   10
In beauty of holiness, with ordered pomp,
Decent and unreproved.   The voices that
    greets
The majesty of both, shall pray for both;
That, mutually protected and sustained,
They may endure long as the sea surrounds
This favoured Land, or sunshine warms her
    soil.

And O, ye swelling hills, and spacious
    plains
Besprent from shore to shore with steeple-
    towers,
And spires whose 'silent finger points to
    heaven;'
Nor wanting, at wide intervals, the bulk   20
Of ancient minster lifted above the cloud
Of the dense air, which town or city breeds
To intercept the sun's glad beams — may
    ne'er
That true succession fail of English hearts,

Who, with ancestral feeling, can perceive
What in those holy structures ye possess
Of ornamental interest, and the charm
Of pious sentiment diffused afar,
And human charity, and social love.
— Thus never shall the indignities of time
Approach their reverend graces, unop-
    posed;   31
Nor shall the elements be free to hurt
Their fair proportions; nor the blinder rage
Of bigot zeal madly to overturn;
And, if the desolating hand of war
Spare them, they shall continue to bestow
Upon the thronged abodes of busy men
(Depraved, and ever prone to fill the mind
Exclusively with transitory things)
An air and mien of dignified pursuit;   40
Of sweet civility, on rustic wilds.

The Poet, fostering for his native land
Such hope, entreats that servants may
    abound
Of those pure altars worthy; ministers
Detached from pleasure, to the love of gain
Superior, insusceptible of pride,
And by ambitious longings undisturbed;
Men, whose delight is where their duty
    leads
Or fixes them; whose least distinguished
    day
Shines with some portion of that heavenly
    lustre   50
Which makes the sabbath lovely in the
    sight
Of blessed angels, pitying human cares.
— And, as on earth it is the doom of truth
To be perpetually attacked by foes
Open or covert, be that priesthood still,
For her defence, replenished with a band
Of strenuous champions, in scholastic arts
Thoroughly disciplined; nor (if in course
Of the revolving world's disturbances
Cause should recur, which righteous Heaven
    avert!   60
To meet such trial) from their spiritual
    sires
Degenerate; who, constrained to wield the
    sword
Of disputation, shrunk not, though assailed
With hostile din, and combating in sight
Of angry umpires, partial and unjust;
And did, thereafter, bathe their hands in
    fire,
So to declare the conscience satisfied:
Nor for their bodies would accept release;

But, blessing God and praising him, be-
    queathed
With their last breath, from out the smoul-
    dering flame,   70
The faith which they by diligence had
    earned,
Or, through illuminating grace, received,
For their dear countrymen, and all man-
    kind.
O high example, constancy divine!

Even such a Man (inheriting the zeal
And from the sanctity of elder times
Not deviating, — a priest, the like of whom
If multiplied, and in their stations set,
Would o'er the bosom of a joyful land   79
Spread true religion and her genuine fruits)
Before me stood that day; on holy ground
Fraught with the relics of mortality,
Exalting tender themes, by just degrees
To lofty raised; and to the highest, last;
The head and mighty paramount of
    truths, —
Immortal life, in never-fading worlds,
For mortal creatures, conquered and se-
    cured.

That basis laid, those principles of faith
Announced, as a preparatory act   89
Of reverence done to the spirit of the place,
The Pastor cast his eyes upon the ground;
Not, as before, like one oppressed with awe
But with a mild and social cheerfulness;
Then to the Solitary turned, and spake.

"At morn or eve, in your retired domain,
Perchance you not unfrequently have
    marked
A Visitor — in quest of herbs and flowers;
Too delicate employ, as would appear,
For one, who, though of drooping mien, had
    yet
From nature's kindliness received a frame
Robust as ever rural labour bred."   101

The Solitary answered: "Such a Form
Full well I recollect. We often crossed
Each other's path; but, as the Intruder
    seemed
Fondly to prize the silence which he kept,
And as I willingly did cherish mine,
We met, and passed, like shadows. I have
    heard,
From my good Host, that being crazed in
    brain

By unrequited love, he scaled the rocks,
Dived into caves, and pierced the matted
   woods,   110
In hope to find some virtuous herb of
   power
To cure his malady!"
                  The Vicar smiled, —
"Alas! before to-morrow's sun goes down
His habitation will be here: for him
That open grave is destined."
                 "Died he then
Of pain and grief?" the Solitary asked,
"Do not believe it; never could that be!"

  "He loved," the Vicar answered, "deeply
   loved,
Loved fondly, truly, fervently; and dared
At length to tell his love, but sued in
   vain;   120
Rejected, yea repelled; and, if with scorn
Upon the haughty maiden's brow, 't is but
A high-prized plume which female Beauty
   wears
In wantonness of conquest, or puts on
To cheat the world, or from herself to hide
Humiliation, when no longer free.
That he could brook, and glory in; — but
   when
The tidings came that she whom he had
   wooed
Was wedded to another, and his heart
Was forced to rend away its only hope; 130
Then, Pity could have scarcely found on
   earth
An object worthier of regard than he,
In the transition of that bitter hour!
Lost was she, lost; nor could the Sufferer
   say
That in the act of preference he had been
Unjustly dealt with; but the Maid was
   gone!
Had vanished from his prospects and de-
   sires;
Not by translation to the heavenly choir
Who have put off their mortal spoils — ah
   no!   139
She lives another's wishes to complete, —
'Joy be their lot, and happiness,' he cried,
'His lot and hers, as misery must be mine!'

  Such was that strong concussion; but the
   Man,
Who trembled, trunk and limbs, like some
   huge oak
By a fierce tempest shaken, soon resumed

The stedfast quiet natural to a mind
Of composition gentle and sedate,
And, in its movements, circumspect and
   slow.
To books, and to the long-forsaken desk,
O'er which enchained by science he had
   loved   150
To bend, he stoutly re-addressed himself,
Resolved to quell his pain, and search for
   truth
With keener appetite (if that might be)
And closer industry. Of what ensued
Within the heart no outward sign appeared
Till a betraying sickliness was seen
To tinge his cheek; and through his frame
   it crept
With slow mutation unconcealable;
Such universal change as autumn makes
In the fair body of a leafy grove,   160
Discoloured, then divested.
                 'T is affirmed
By poets skilled in nature's secret ways
That Love will not submit to be con-
   trolled
By mastery: — and the good Man lacked
   not friends
Who strove to instil this truth into his
   mind,
A mind in all heart-mysteries unversed.
'Go to the hills,' said one, 'remit a while
'This baneful diligence: — at early morn
'Court the fresh air, explore the heaths and
   woods;
'And, leaving it to others to foretell,   170
'By calculations sage, the ebb and flow
'Of tides, and when the moon will be
   eclipsed,
'Do you, for your own benefit, construct
'A calendar of flowers, plucked as they
   blow
'Where health abides, and cheerfulness,
   and peace.'
The attempt was made; — 't is needless to
   report
How hopelessly; but innocence is strong,
And an entire simplicity of mind
A thing most sacred in the eye of Heaven;
That opens, for such sufferers, relief   180
Within the soul, fountains of grace divine;
And doth commend their weakness and
   disease
To Nature's care, assisted in her office
By all the elements that round her wait
To generate, to preserve, and to restore;
And by her beautiful array of forms

Shedding sweet influence from above; or
    pure
Delight exhaling from the ground they
    tread."

"Impute it not to impatience, if," ex-
    claimed   189
The Wanderer, "I infer that he was healed
By perseverance in the course prescribed."

"You do not err: the powers, that had
    been lost
By slow degrees, were gradually regained;
The fluttering nerves composed; the beat-
    ing heart
In rest established; and the jarring
    thoughts
To harmony restored. — But yon dark
    mould
Will cover him, in the fulness of his
    strength,
Hastily smitten by a fever's force;
Yet not with stroke so sudden as refused
Time to look back with tenderness on her
Whom he had loved in passion; and to
    send   201
Some farewell words — with one, but one,
    request;
That, from his dying hand, she would ac-
    cept
Of his possessions that which most he
    prized;
A book, upon whose leaves some chosen
    plants,
By his own hand disposed with nicest care,
In undecaying beauty were preserved;
Mute register, to him, of time and place,
And various fluctuations in the breast;
To her, a monument of faithful love   210
Conquered, and in tranquillity retained!

Close to his destined habitation, lies
One who achieved a humbler victory,
Though marvellous in its kind. A place
    there is
High in these mountains, that allured a
    band
Of keen adventurers to unite their pains
In search of precious ore: they tried, were
    foiled —
And all desisted, all, save him alone.
He, taking counsel of his own clear
    thoughts,   219
And trusting only to his own weak hands,
Urged unremittingly the stubborn work,

Unseconded, uncountenanced; then, as
    time
Passed on, while still his lonely efforts
    found
No recompense, derided; and at length,
By many pitied, as insane of mind;
By others dreaded as the luckless thrall
Of subterranean Spirits feeding hope
By various mockery of sight and sound;
Hope after hope, encouraged and destroyed.
— But when the lord of seasons had ma-
    tured   230
The fruits of earth through space of twice
    ten years,
The mountain's entrails offered to his view
And trembling grasp the long-deferred
    reward.
Not with more transport did Columbus
    greet
A world, his rich discovery! But our
    Swain,
A very hero till his point was gained,
Proved all unable to support the weight
Of prosperous fortune. On the fields he
    looked
With an unsettled liberty of thought,
Wishes and endless schemes; by daylight
    walked   240
Giddy and restless; ever and anon
Quaffed in his gratitude immoderate cups;
And truly might be said to die of joy!
He vanished; but conspicuous to this day
The path remains that linked his cottage-
    door
To the mine's mouth; a long and slanting
    track,
Upon the rugged mountain's stony side,
Worn by his daily visits to and from
The darksome centre of a constant hope.
This vestige, neither force of beating rain,
Nor the vicissitudes of frost and thaw   251
Shall cause to fade, till ages pass away;
And it is named, in memory of the event,
The PATH OF PERSEVERANCE."
                "Thou from whom
Man has his strength," exclaimed the
    Wanderer, "oh!
Do thou direct it! To the virtuous grant
The penetrative eye which can perceive
In this blind world the guiding vein of
    hope;
That, like this Labourer, such may dig their
    way
'Unshaken, unseduced, unterrified;'   260
Grant to the wise *his* firmness of resolve!"

"That prayer were not superfluous,"
    said the Priest,
"Amid the noblest relics, proudest dust,
That Westminster, for Britain's glory,
    holds
Within the bosom of her awful pile,
Ambitiously collected. Yet the sigh,
Which wafts that prayer to heaven, is due
    to all,
Wherever laid, who living fell below
Their virtue's humbler mark; a sigh of
    pain
If to the opposite extreme they sank.   270
How would you pity her who yonder rests;
Him, farther off; the pair, who here are
    laid;
But, above all, that mixture of earth's
    mould
Whom sight of this green hillock to my
    mind
Recalls !
    He lived not till his locks were nipped
By seasonable frost of age; nor died
Before his temples, prematurely forced
To mix the manly brown with silver grey,
Gave obvious instance of the sad effect
Produced, when thoughtless Folly hath
    usurped   280
The natural crown that sage Experience
    wears.
Gay, volatile, ingenious, quick to learn,
And prompt to exhibit all that he possessed
Or could perform; a zealous actor, hired
Into the troop of mirth, a soldier, sworn
Into the lists of giddy enterprise —
Such was he; yet, as if within his frame
Two several souls alternately had lodged,
Two sets of manners could the Youth put
    on;   289
And, fraught with antics as the Indian bird
That writhes and chatters in her wiry cage,
Was graceful, when it pleased him, smooth
    and still
As the mute swan that floats adown the
    stream,
Or, on the waters of the unruffled lake,
Anchors her placid beauty. Not a leaf,
That flutters on the bough, lighter than he;
And not a flower, that droops in the green
    shade,
More winningly reserved ! If ye enquire
How such consummate elegance was bred
Amid these wilds, this answer may suffice;
'T was Nature's will; who sometimes un-
    dertakes,   301

For the reproof of human vanity,
Art to outstrip in her peculiar walk.
Hence, for this Favourite — lavishly en-
    dowed
With personal gifts, and bright instinctive
    wit,
While both, embellishing each other, stood
Yet farther recommended by the charm
Of fine demeanour, and by dance and song,
And skill in letters — every fancy shaped
Fair expectations; nor, when to the world's
Capacious field forth went the Adventurer,
    there   311
Were he and his attainments overlooked,
Or scantily rewarded; but all hopes,
Cherished for him, he suffered to depart,
Like blighted buds; or clouds that mim-
    icked land
Before the sailor's eye; or diamond drops
That sparkling decked the morning grass;
    or aught
That *was* attractive, and hath ceased to be !

Yet, when this Prodigal returned, the
    rites
Of joyful greeting were on him bestowed,
Who, by humiliation undeterred,   321
Sought for his weariness a place of rest
Within his Father's gates. — Whence came
    he ? — clothed
In tattered garb, from hovels where abides
Necessity, the stationary host
Of vagrant poverty; from rifted barns
Where no one dwells but the wide-staring
    owl
And the owl's prey; from these bare haunts,
    to which
He had descended from the proud saloon,
He came, the ghost of beauty and of health,
The wreck of gaiety ! But soon revived   331
In strength, in power refitted, he renewed
His suit to Fortune; and she smiled again
Upon a fickle Ingrate. Thrice he rose,
Thrice sank as willingly. For he — whose
    nerves
Were used to thrill with pleasure, while his
    voice
Softly accompanied the tuneful harp,
By the nice finger of fair ladies touched
In glittering halls — was able to derive
No less enjoyment from an abject choice.
Who happier for the moment — who more
    blithe   341
Than this fallen Spirit ? in those dreary
    holds

His talents lending to exalt the freaks
Of merry-making beggars, — now provoked
To laughter multiplied in louder peals
By his malicious wit; then, all enchained
With mute astonishment, themselves to see
In their own arts outdone, their fame
    eclipsed,
As by the very presence of the Fiend
Who dictates and inspires illusive feats, 350
For knavish purposes ! The city, too,
(With shame I speak it) to her guilty bowers
Allured him, sunk so low in self-respect
As there to linger, there to eat his bread,
Hired minstrel of voluptuous blandishment;
Charming the air with skill of hand or voice,
Listen who would, be wrought upon who
    might,
Sincerely wretched hearts, or falsely gay.
— Such the too frequent tenor of his boast
In ears that relished the report; — but all
Was from his Parents happily concealed; 361
Who saw enough for blame and pitying
    love.
They also were permitted to receive
His last repentant breath; and closed his
    eyes,
No more to open on that irksome world
Where he had long existed in the state
Of a young fowl beneath one mother
    hatched,
Though from another sprung, different in
    kind:
Where he had lived, and could not cease to
    live,
Distracted in propensity; content   370
With neither element of good or ill;
And yet in both rejoicing; man unblest;
Of contradictions infinite the slave,
Till his deliverance, when Mercy made him
One with himself, and one with them that
    sleep."

"'T is strange," observed the Solitary,
    " strange
It seems, and scarcely less than pitiful,
That in a land where charity provides
For all that can no longer feed themselves,
A man like this should choose to bring his
    shame   380
To the parental door; and with his sighs
Infect the air which he had freely breathed
In happy infancy. He could not pine,
Through lack of converse; no — he must
    have found
Abundant exercise for thought and speech,

In his dividual being, self-reviewed,
Self-catechised, self-punished. — Some
    there are
Who, drawing near their final home, and
    much
And daily longing that the same were
    reached,
Would rather shun than seek the fellowship
Of kindred mould. — Such haply here are
    laid ? "   391

"Yes," said the Priest, "the Genius of
    our hills —
Who seems, by these stupendous barriers
    cast
Round his domain, desirous not alone
To keep his own, but also to exclude
All other progeny — doth sometimes lure,
Even by his studied depth of privacy,
The unhappy alien hoping to obtain
Concealment, or seduced by wish to find,
In place from outward molestation free, 400
Helps to internal ease. Of many such
Could I discourse; but as their stay was
    brief,
So their departure only left behind
Fancies, and loose conjectures. Other trace
Survives, for worthy mention, of a pair
Who, from the pressure of their several
    fates,
Meeting as strangers, in a petty town
Whose blue roofs ornament a distant reach
Of this far-winding vale, remained as friends
True to their choice; and gave their bones
    in trust   410
To this loved cemetery, here to lodge
With unescutcheoned privacy interred
Far from the family vault. — A Chieftain
    one
By right of birth; within whose spotless
    breast
The fire of ancient Caledonia burned:
He, with the foremost whose impatience
    hailed
The Stuart, landing to resume, by force
Of arms, the crown which bigotry had lost,
Aroused his clan; and, fighting at their
    head,
With his brave sword endeavoured to pre-
    vent   420
Culloden's fatal overthrow. Escaped
From that disastrous rout, to foreign shores
He fled; and when the lenient hand of time
Those troubles had appeased, he sought
    and gained,

For his obscured condition, an obscure
Retreat, within this nook of English ground.

The other, born in Britain's southern
    tract,
Had fixed his milder loyalty, and placed
His gentler sentiments of love and hate,
There, where *they* placed them who in con-
    science prized   430
The new succession, as a line of kings
Whose oath had virtue to protect the land
Against the dire assaults of papacy
And arbitrary rule. But launch thy bark
On the distempered flood of public life,
And cause for most rare triumph will be
    thine
If, spite of keenest eye and steadiest hand,
The stream, that bears thee forward, prove
    not, soon
Or late, a perilous master. He — who oft,
Beneath the battlements and stately trees
That round his mansion cast a sober gloom,
Had moralised on this, and other truths 442
Of kindred import, pleased and satisfied —
Was forced to vent his wisdom with a
    sigh
Heaved from the heart in fortune's bitter-
    ness,
When he had crushed a plentiful estate
By ruinous contest, to obtain a seat
In Britain's senate. Fruitless was the at-
    tempt:
And while the uproar of that desperate strife
Continued yet to vibrate on his ear,   450
The vanquished Whig, under a borrowed
    name,
(For the mere sound and echo of his own
Haunted him with sensations of disgust
That he was glad to lose) slunk from the
    world
To the deep shade of those untravelled
    Wilds;
In which the Scottish Laird had long pos-
    sessed
An undisturbed abode. Here, then, they
    met,
Two doughty champions; flaming Jacobite
And sullen Hanoverian! You might think
That losses and vexations, less severe   460
Than those which they had severally sus-
    tained,
Would have inclined each to abate his zeal
For his ungrateful cause; no, — I have
    heard
My reverend Father tell that, 'mid the calm

Of that small town encountering thus, they
    filled,
Daily, its bowling-green with harmless
    strife;
Plagued with uncharitable thoughts the
    church;
And vexed the market-place. But in the
    breasts
Of these opponents gradually was wrought,
With little change of general sentiment,
Such leaning towards each other, that their
    days   471
By choice were spent in constant fellowship;
And if, at times, they fretted with the yoke,
Those very bickerings made them love it
    more.

A favourite boundary to their lengthened
    walks
This Churchyard was. And, whether they
    had come
Treading their path in sympathy and linked
In social converse, or by some short space
Discreetly parted to preserve the peace,
One spirit seldom failed to extend its sway
Over both minds, when they awhile had
    marked   481
The visible quiet of this holy ground,
And breathed its soothing air: — the spirit
    of hope
And saintly magnanimity; that — spurning
The field of selfish difference and dispute,
And every care which transitory things,
Earth and the kingdoms of the earth,
    create —
Doth, by a rapture of forgetfulness,
Preclude forgiveness, from the praise de-
    barred,
Which else the Christian virtue might have
    claimed.   490

There live who yet remember here to
    have seen
Their courtly figures, seated on the stump
Of an old yew, their favourite resting-place.
But as the remnant of the long-lived tree
Was disappearing by a swift decay,
They, with joint care, determined to erect,
Upon its site, a dial, that might stand
For public use preserved, and thus survive
As their own private monument: for this
Was the particular spot, in which they
    wished   500
(And Heaven was pleased to accomplish
    the desire)

That, undivided, their remains should lie.
So, where the mouldered tree had stood,
          was raised
Yon structure, framing, with the ascent of
          steps
That to the decorated pillar lead,
A work of art more sumptuous than might
          seem
To suit this place; yet built in no proud
          scorn
Of rustic homeliness; they only aimed
To ensure for it respectful guardianship.
Around the margin of the plate, whereon
The shadow falls to note the stealthy
          hours,   511
Winds an inscriptive legend." — At these
          words
Thither we turned; and gathered, as we
          read,
The appropriate sense, in Latin numbers
          couched:
" *Time flies; it is his melancholy task,*
To bring, and bear away, delusive hopes,
And re-produce the troubles he destroys.
But, while his blindness thus is occupied,
Discerning Mortal! do thou serve the will
Of Time's eternal Master, and that peace, 520
Which the world wants, shall be for thee con-
          firmed!"

" Smooth verse, inspired by no unlettered
          Muse,"
Exclaimed the Sceptic, " and the strain of
          thought
Accords with nature's language; — the soft
          voice
Of yon white torrent falling down the rocks
Speaks, less distinctly, to the same effect.
If, then, their blended influence be not lost
Upon our hearts, not wholly lost, I grant,
Even upon mine, the more are we required
To feel for those among our fellow-men, 530
Who, offering no obeisance to the world,
Are yet made desperate by 'too quick a
          sense
Of constant infelicity,' cut off
From peace like exiles on some barren rock,
Their life's appointed prison; not more free
Than sentinels, between two armies, set,
With nothing better, in the chill night air,
Than their own thoughts to comfort them.
          Say why
That ancient story of Prometheus chained
To the bare rock, on frozen Caucasus; 540
The vulture, the inexhaustible repast

Drawn from his vitals? Say what meant
          the woes
By Tantalus entailed upon his race,
And the dark sorrows of the line of Thebes?
Fictions in form, but in their substance
          truths,
Tremendous truths! familiar to the men
Of long-past times, nor obsolete in ours.
Exchange the shepherd's frock of native
          grey
For robes with regal purple tinged; convert
The crook into a sceptre; give the pomp 550
Of circumstance; and here the tragic
          Muse
Shall find apt subjects for her highest art.
Amid the groves, under the shadowy hills,
The generations are prepared; the pangs,
The internal pangs, are ready; the dread
          strife
Of poor humanity's afflicted will
Struggling in vain with ruthless destiny."

" Though," said the Priest in answer,
          " these be terms
Which a divine philosophy rejects,
We, whose established and unfailing trust
Is in controlling Providence, admit   561
That, through all stations, human life
          abounds
With mysteries; — for, if Faith were left
          untried,
How could the might, that lurks within her,
          then
Be shown? her glorious excellence — that
          ranks
Among the first of Powers and Virtues —
          proved?
Our system is not fashioned to preclude
That sympathy which you for others ask;
And I could tell, not travelling for my
          theme
Beyond these humble graves, of grievous
          crimes   570
And strange disasters; but I pass them
          by,
Loth to disturb what Heaven hath hushed
          in peace.
— Still less, far less, am I inclined to treat
Of Man degraded in his Maker's sight
By the deformities of brutish vice:
For, in such portraits, though a vulgar face
And a coarse outside of repulsive life
And unaffecting manners might at once
Be recognised by all " — " Ah! do not
          think,"

The Wanderer somewhat eagerly ex-
claimed,   500
"Wish could be ours that you, for such
poor gain,
(Gain shall I call it ? — gain of what ? —
for whom ?)
Should breathe a word tending to violate
Your own pure spirit.   Not a step we look
for
In slight of that forbearance and reserve
Which common human-heartedness inspires,
And mortal ignorance and frailty claim,
Upon this sacred ground, if nowhere else."

"True," said the Solitary, "be it far
From us to infringe the laws of charity.   590
Let judgment here in mercy be pro-
nounced;
This, self-respecting Nature prompts, and
this
Wisdom enjoins; but if the thing we seek
Be genuine knowledge, bear we then in mind
How, from his lofty throne, the sun can
fling
Colours as bright on exhalations bred
By weedy pool or pestilential swamp,
As by the rivulet sparkling where it runs,
Or the pellucid lake."
                    "Small risk," said I,
"Of such illusion do we here incur;   600
Temptation here is none to exceed the
truth;
No evidence appears that they who rest
Within this ground, were covetous of praise,
Or of remembrance even, deserved or not.
Green is the Churchyard, beautiful and
green,
Ridge rising gently by the side of ridge,
A heaving surface, almost wholly free
From interruption of sepulchral stones,
And mantled o'er with aboriginal turf
And everlasting flowers.   These Dalesmen
trust   610
The lingering gleam of their departed
lives
To oral record, and the silent heart;
Depositories faithful and more kind
Than fondest epitaph: for, if those fail,
What boots the sculptured tomb ?   And
who can blame,
Who rather would not envy, men that feel
This mutual confidence; if, from such
source,
The practice flow, — if thence, or from a
deep

And general humility in death ?
Nor should I much condemn it, if it spring
From disregard of time's destructive
power,   621
As only capable to prey on things
Of earth, and human nature's mortal part.

Yet — in less simple districts, where we
see
Stone lift its forehead emulous of stone
In courting notice; and the ground all
paved
With commendations of departed worth;
Reading, where'er we turn, of innocent
lives,
Of each domestic charity fulfilled,
And sufferings meekly borne — I, for my
part,   630
Though with the silence pleased that here
prevails,
Among those fair recitals also range,
Soothed by the natural spirit which they
breathe.
And, in the centre of a world whose soil
Is rank with all unkindness, compassed
round
With such memorials, I have sometimes
felt,
It was no momentary happiness
To have one Enclosure where the voice that
speaks
In envy or detraction is not heard;
Which malice may not enter; where the
traces   640
Of evil inclinations are unknown;
Where love and pity tenderly unite
With resignation; and no jarring tone
Intrudes, the peaceful concert to disturb
Of amity and gratitude."
                    "Thus sanctioned,"
The Pastor said, "I willingly confine
My narratives to subjects that excite
Feelings with these accordant; love, es-
teem,
And admiration; lifting up a veil,
A sunbeam introducing among hearts   650
Retired and covert; so that ye shall have
Clear images before your gladdened eyes
Of nature's unambitious underwood,
And flowers that prosper in the shade.
And when
I speak of such among my flock as swerved
Or fell, those only shall be singled out
Upon whose lapse, or error, something
more

Than brotherly forgiveness may attend;
To such will we restrict our notice, else
Better my tongue were mute.
                    And yet there are,
I feel, good reasons why we should not
    leave   661
Wholly untraced a more forbidding way.
For, strength to persevere and to support,
And energy to conquer and repel —
These elements of virtue, that declare
The native grandeur of the human soul —
Are oft-times not unprofitably shown
In the perverseness of a selfish course:
Truth every day exemplified, no less
In the grey cottage by the murmuring
    stream   670
Than in fantastic conqueror's roving camp,
Or 'mid the factious senate, unappalled
Whoe'er may sink, or rise — to sink again,
As merciless proscription ebbs and flows.

    There," said the Vicar, pointing as he
        spake,
" A woman rests in peace; surpassed by few
In power of mind, and eloquent discourse.
Tall was her stature; her complexion dark
And saturnine; her head not raised to hold
Converse with heaven, nor yet deprest to-
        wards earth,   680
But in projection carried, as she walked
For ever musing. Sunken were her eyes;
Wrinkled and furrowed with habitual
        thought
Was her broad forehead; like the brow of
        one
Whose visual nerve shrinks from a painful
        glare
Of overpowering light. — While yet a child,
She, 'mid the humble flowerets of the vale,
Towered like the imperial thistle, not un-
        furnished
With its appropriate grace, yet rather
        seeking
To be admired, than coveted and loved. 690
Even at that age she ruled, a sovereign
        queen,
Over her comrades; else their simple sports,
Wanting all relish for her strenuous mind,
Had crossed her only to be shunned with
        scorn.
— Oh ! pang of sorrowful regret for those
Whom, in their youth, sweet study has
        enthralled,
That they have lived for harsher servitude,
Whether in soul, in body, or estate !

Such doom was hers; yet nothing could
        subdue
Her keen desire of knowledge, nor efface
Those brighter images by books imprest 701
Upon her memory, faithfully as stars
That occupy their places, and, though oft
Hidden by clouds, and oft bedimmed by
        haze,
Are not to be extinguished, nor impaired.

    Two passions, both degenerate, for they
        both
Began in honour, gradually obtained
Rule over her, and vexed her daily life;
An unremitting, avaricious thrift;
And a strange thraldom of maternal love,
That held her spirit, in its own despite, 711
Bound — by vexation, and regret, and scorn,
Constrained forgiveness, and relenting vows,
And tears, in pride suppressed, in shame
        concealed —
To a poor dissolute Son, her only child.
— Her wedded days had opened with mis-
        hap,
Whence dire dependence. What could she
        perform
To shake the burthen off ? Ah ! there was
        felt,
Indignantly, the weakness of her sex.
She mused, resolved, adhered to her re-
        solve;   720
The hand grew slack in alms-giving, the
        heart
Closed by degrees to charity; heaven's
        blessing
Not seeking from that source, she placed
        her trust
In ceaseless pains — and strictest parsimony
Which sternly hoarded all that could be
        spared,
From each day's need, out of each day's
        least gain.

    Thus all was re-established, and a pile
Constructed, that sufficed for every end,
Save the contentment of the builder's mind;
A mind by nature indisposed to aught 730
So placid, so inactive, as content;
A mind intolerant of lasting peace,
And cherishing the pang her heart deplored.
Dread life of conflict ! which I oft compared
To the agitation of a brook that runs
Down a rocky mountain, buried now and lost
In silent pools, now in strong eddies
        chained;

But never to be charmed to gentleness:
Its best attainment fits of such repose
As timid eyes might shrink from fathoming.

A sudden illness seized her in the strength   741
Of life's autumnal season. — Shall I tell
How on her bed of death the Matron lay,
To Providence submissive, so she thought;
But fretted, vexed, and wrought upon, almost
To anger, by the malady that griped
Her prostrate frame with unrelaxing power,
As the fierce eagle fastens on the lamb ?
She prayed, she moaned; — her husband's sister watched
Her dreary pillow, waited on her needs;   750
And yet the very sound of that kind foot
Was anguish to her ears ! ' And must she rule,'
This was the death-doomed Woman heard to say
In bitterness, ' and must she rule and reign,
Sole Mistress of this house, when I am gone ?
Tend what I tended, calling it her own !'
Enough; — I fear, too much. — One vernal evening,
While she was yet in prime of health and strength,
I well remember, while I passed her door
Alone, with loitering step, and upward eye
Turned towards the planet Jupiter that hung   761
Above the centre of the Vale, a voice
Roused me, her voice; it said, ' That glorious star
In its untroubled element will shine
As now it shines, when we are laid in earth
And safe from all our sorrows.' With a sigh
She spake, yet, I believe, not unsustained
By faith in glory that shall far transcend
Aught by these perishable heavens disclosed
To sight or mind. Nor less than care divine   770
Is divine mercy. She, who had rebelled,
Was into meekness softened and subdued;
Did, after trials not in vain prolonged,
With resignation sink into the grave;
And her uncharitable acts, I trust,
And harsh unkindnesses are all forgiven,
Tho', in this Vale, remembered with deep awe."

THE Vicar paused; and toward a seat advanced,
A long stone-seat, fixed in the Churchyard wall;
Part shaded by cool sycamore, and part   780
Offering a sunny resting-place to them
Who seek the House of worship, while the bells
Yet ring with all their voices, or before
The last hath ceased its solitary knoll.
Beneath the shade we all sate down; and there
His office, uninvited, he resumed.

" As on a sunny bank, a tender lamb
Lurks in safe shelter from the winds of March,
Screened by its parent, so that little mound
Lies guarded by its neighbour; the small heap   790
Speaks for itself; an Infant there doth rest;
The sheltering hillock is the Mother's grave.
If mild discourse, and manners that conferred
A natural dignity on humblest rank;
If gladsome spirits, and benignant looks,
That for a face not beautiful did more
Than beauty for the fairest face can do;
And if religious tenderness of heart,
Grieving for sin, and penitential tears
Shed when the clouds had gathered and distained   800
The spotless ether of a maiden life;
If these may make a hallowed spot of earth
More holy in the sight of God or Man;
Then, o'er that mould, a sanctity shall brood
Till the stars sicken at the day of doom.

Ah ! what a warning for a thoughtless man,
Could field or grove, could any spot of earth,
Show to his eye an image of the pangs
Which it hath witnessed; render back an echo
Of the sad steps by which it hath been trod !   810
There, by her innocent Baby's precious grave,
And on the very turf that roofs her own,
The Mother oft was seen to stand, or kneel

In the broad day, a weeping Magdalene.
Now she is not; the swelling turf reports
Of the fresh shower, but of poor Ellen's
     tears
Is silent; nor is any vestige left
Of the path worn by mournful tread of
     her
Who, at her heart's light bidding, once had
     moved
In virgin fearlessness, with step that
     seemed   820
Caught from the pressure of elastic turf
Upon the mountains gemmed with morning
     dew,
In the prime hour of sweetest scents and
     airs.
— Serious and thoughtful was her mind;
     and yet,
By reconcilement exquisite and rare,
The form, port, motions, of this Cottage-
     girl
Were such as might have quickened and
     inspired
A Titian's hand, addrest to picture forth
Oread or Dryad glancing through the shade
What time the hunter's earliest horn is
     heard   830
Startling the golden hills.
                         A wide-spread elm
Stands in our valley, named THE JOYFUL
     TREE;
From dateless usage which our peasants
     hold
Of giving welcome to the first of May
By dances round its trunk. — And if the
     sky
Permit, like honours, dance and song, are
     paid
To the Twelfth Night, beneath the frosty
     stars
Or the clear moon. The queen of these
     gay sports,
If not in beauty yet in sprightly air,
Was hapless Ellen. — No one touched the
     ground   840
So deftly, and the nicest maiden's locks
Less gracefully were braided; — but this
     praise,
Methinks, would better suit another place.

     She loved, and fondly deemed herself
          beloved.
— The road is dim, the current unper-
     ceived,
The weakness painful and most pitiful,

By which a virtuous woman, in pure youth,
May be delivered to distress and shame.
Such fate was hers. — The last time Ellen
     danced,
Among her equals, round THE JOYFUL
     TREE,   850
She bore a secret burthen; and full soon
Was left to tremble for a breaking vow, —
Then, to bewail a sternly-broken vow,
Alone, within her widowed Mother's house.
It was the season of unfolding leaves,
Of days advancing toward their utmost
     length,
And small birds singing happily to mates
Happy as they. With spirit-saddening
     power
Winds pipe through fading woods; but
     those blithe notes   859
Strike the deserted to the heart; I speak
Of what I know, and what we feel within.
— Beside the cottage in which Ellen dwelt
Stands a tall ash-tree; to whose topmost
     twig
A thrush resorts, and annually chants,
At morn and evening from that naked
     perch,
While all the undergrove is thick with
     leaves,
A time-beguiling ditty, for delight
Of his fond partner, silent in the nest.
— 'Ah why,' said Ellen, sighing to herself,
' Why do not words, and kiss, and solemn
     pledge;   870
And nature that is kind in woman's
     breast,
And reason that in man is wise and good,
And fear of him who is a righteous judge;
Why do not these prevail for human life,
To keep two hearts together, that began
Their spring-time with one love, and that
     have need
Of mutual pity and forgiveness, sweet
To grant, or be received; while that poor
     bird —
O come and hear him ! Thou who hast to
     me
Been faithless, hear him, though a lowly
     creature,   880
One of God's simple children that yet know
     not
The universal Parent, how he sings
As if he wished the firmament of heaven
Should listen, and give back to him the
     voice
Of his triumphant constancy and love;

The proclamation that he makes, how far
His darkness doth transcend our fickle
    light ! '

Such was the tender passage, not by me
Repeated without loss of simple phrase,
Which I perused, even as the words had
    been   890
Committed by forsaken Ellen's hand
To the blank margin of a Valentine,
Bedropped with tears. 'T will please you
    to be told
That, studiously withdrawing from the eye
Of all companionship, the Sufferer yet
In lonely reading found a meek resource:
How thankful for the warmth of summer
    days,
When she could slip into the cottage-barn,
And find a secret oratory there;
Or, in the garden, under friendly veil   900
Of their long twilight, pore upon her book
By the last lingering help of the open sky
Until dark night dismissed her to her bed !
Thus did a waking fancy sometimes lose
The unconquerable pang of despised love.

A kindlier passion opened on her soul
When that poor Child was born. Upon its
    face
She gazed as on a pure and spotless gift
Of unexpected promise, where a grief
Or dread was all that had been thought of,
    — joy   910
Far livelier than bewildered traveller feels,
Amid a perilous waste that all night long
Hath harassed him toiling through fearful
    storm,
When he beholds the first pale speck se-
    rene
Of day-spring, in the gloomy east, revealed,
And greets it with thanksgiving. ' Till
    this hour,'
Thus, in her Mother's hearing Ellen spake,
' There was a stony region in my heart;
But He, at whose command the parchèd
    rock
Was smitten, and poured forth a quenching
    stream,   920
Hath softened that obduracy, and made
Unlooked-for gladness in the desert place,
To save the perishing; and, henceforth, I
    breathe
The air with cheerful spirit, for thy sake
My infant ! and for that good Mother
    dear,

Who bore me; and hath prayed for me in
    vain; —
Yet not in vain; it shall not be in vain.'
She spake, nor was the assurance unful-
    filled;
And if heart-rending thoughts would oft
    return,
They stayed not long. — The blameless
    Infant grew;   930
The Child whom Ellen and her Mother
    loved
They soon were proud of; tended it and
    nursed;
A soothing comforter, although forlorn;
Like a poor singing-bird from distant
    lands;
Or a choice shrub, which he, who passes by
With vacant mind, not seldom may ob-
    serve
Fair-flowering in a thinly-peopled house,
Whose window, somewhat sadly, it adorns.

Through four months' space the Infant
    drew its food
From the maternal breast; then scruples
    rose;   940
Thoughts, which the rich are free from,
    came and crossed
The fond affection. She no more could
    bear
By her offence to lay a twofold weight
On a kind parent willing to forget
Their slender means: so, to that parent's
    care
Trusting her child, she left their common
    home,
And undertook with dutiful content
A Foster-mother's office.
            'T is, perchance,
Unknown to you that in these simple vales
The natural feeling of equality   950
Is by domestic service unimpaired;
Yet, though such service be, with us, re-
    moved
From sense of degradation, not the less
The ungentle mind can easily find means
To impose severe restraints and laws un-
    just,
Which hapless Ellen now was doomed to
    feel:
For (blinded by an over-anxious dread
Of such excitement and divided thought
As with her office would but ill accord)
The pair, whose infant she was bound to
    nurse,   960

Forbade her all communion with her own.
Week after week, the mandate they en-
    forced.
— So near ! yet not allowed, upon that
    sight
To fix her eyes — alas ! 't was hard to bear !
But worse affliction must be borne — far
    worse;
For 't is Heaven's will — that, after a dis-
    ease
Begun and ended within three days' space,
Her child should die; as Ellen now ex-
    claimed,
Her own — deserted child ! — Once, only
    once,
She saw it in that mortal malady;   970
And, on the burial-day, could scarcely
    gain
Permission to attend its obsequies.
She reached the house, last of the funeral
    train;
And some one, as she entered, having
    chanced
To urge unthinkingly their prompt depar-
    ture,
'Nay,' said she, with commanding look,
    a spirit
Of anger never seen in her before,
'Nay, ye must wait my time !' and down
    she sate,
And by the unclosed coffin kept her seat
Weeping and looking, looking on and
    weeping,   980
Upon the last sweet slumber of her Child,
Until at length her soul was satisfied.

You see the Infant's Grave; and to this
    spot,
The Mother, oft as she was sent abroad,
On whatsoever errand, urged her steps:
Hither she came; here stood, and some-
    times knelt
In the broad day, a rueful Magdalene !
So call her; for not only she bewailed
A mother's loss, but mourned in bitterness
Her own transgression; penitent sincere 990
As ever raised to heaven a streaming eye.
— At length the parents of the foster-child,
Noting that in despite of their commands
She still renewed and could not but renew
Those visitations, ceased to send her forth;
Or, to the garden's narrow bounds, con-
    fined.
I failed not to remind them that they erred;
For holy Nature might not thus be crossed,

Thus wronged in woman's breast: in vain
    I pleaded —
But the green stalk of Ellen's life was
    snapped,   1000
And the flower drooped; as every eye
    could see,
It hung its head in mortal languishment.
— Aided by this appearance, I at length
Prevailed; and, from those bonds released,
    she went
Home to her mother's house.
               The Youth was fled;
The rash betrayer could not face the shame
Or sorrow which his senseless guilt had
    caused;
And little would his presence, or proof
    given
Of a relenting soul, have now availed;
For, like a shadow, he was passed away
From Ellen's thoughts; had perished to
    her mind   1011
For all concerns of fear, or hope, or love,
Save only those which to their common
    shame,
And to his moral being appertained:
Hope from that quarter would, I know,
    have brought
A heavenly comfort; there she recognised
An unrelaxing bond, a mutual need;
There, and, as seemed, there only.
                  She had built,
Her fond maternal heart had built, a nest
In blindness all too near the river's edge;
That work a summer flood with hasty
    swell   1021
Had swept away; and now her Spirit
    longed
For its last flight to heaven's security.
— The bodily frame wasted from day to
    day;
Meanwhile, relinquishing all other cares,
Her mind she strictly tutored to find peace
And pleasure in endurance. Much she
    thought,
And much she read; and brooded feelingly
Upon her own unworthiness. To me,
As to a spiritual comforter and friend, 1030
Her heart she opened; and no pains were
    spared
To mitigate, as gently as I could,
The sting of self-reproach, with healing
    words.
Meek Saint ! through patience glorified on
    earth !
In whom, as by her lonely hearth she sate,

The ghastly face of cold decay put on
A sun-like beauty, and appeared divine !
May I not mention — that, within those walls,
In due observance of her pious wish,
The congregation joined with me in prayer
For her soul's good ? Nor was that office
    vain.   1041
— Much did she suffer: but, if any friend,
Beholding her condition, at the sight
Gave way to words of pity or complaint,
She stilled them with a prompt reproof,
    and said,
' He who afflicts me knows what I can
    bear;
And, when I fail, and can endure no more,
Will mercifully take me to himself.'
So, through the cloud of death, her Spirit
    passed
Into that pure and unknown world of love
Where injury cannot come: — and here is
    laid   1051
The mortal Body by her Infant's side."

    The Vicar ceased; and downcast looks
    made known
That each had listened with his inmost
    heart.
For me, the emotion scarcely was less
    strong
Or less benign than that which I had felt
When seated near my venerable Friend,
Under those shady elms, from him I heard
The story that retraced the slow decline
Of Margaret, sinking on the lonely heath
With the neglected house to which she
    clung.   1061
— I noted that the Solitary's cheek
Confessed the power of nature. — Pleased
    though sad,
More pleased than sad, the grey-haired
    Wanderer sate;
Thanks to his pure imaginative soul
Capacious and serene; his blameless life,
His knowledge, wisdom, love of truth, and
    love
Of human kind ! He was it who first broke
The pensive silence, saying: —
        " Blest are they
Whose sorrow rather is to suffer wrong 1070
Than to do wrong, albeit themselves have
    erred.
This tale gives proof that Heaven most
    gently deals
With such, in their affliction. — Ellen's fate,

Her tender spirit, and her contrite heart,
Call to my mind dark hints which I have
    heard
Of one who died within this vale, by doom
Heavier, as his offence was heavier far.
Where, Sir, I pray you, where are laid the
    bones
Of Wilfrid Armathwaite ? "
            The Vicar answered,
" In that green nook, close by the Church-
    yard wall,   1080
Beneath yon hawthorn, planted by myself
In memory and for warning, and in sign
Of sweetness where dire anguish had been
    known,
Of reconcilement after deep offence —
There doth he rest. No theme his fate
    supplies
For the smooth glozings of the indulgent
    world;
Nor need the windings of his devious course
Be here retraced; — enough that, by mishap
And venial error, robbed of competence,
And her obsequious shadow, peace of mind,
He craved a substitute in troubled joy; 1091
Against his conscience rose in arms, and,
    braving
Divine displeasure, broke the marriage-
    vow.
That which he had been weak enough to do
Was misery in remembrance; he was stung,
Stung by his inward thoughts, and by the
    smiles
Of wife and children stung to agony.
Wretched at home, he gained no peace
    abroad;
Ranged through the mountains, slept upon
    the earth,
Asked comfort of the open air, and found
No quiet in the darkness of the night, 1101
No pleasure in the beauty of the day.
His flock he slighted: his paternal fields
Became a clog to him, whose spirit wished
To fly — but whither ! And this gracious
    Church,
That wears a look so full of peace and hope
And love, benignant mother of the vale,
How fair amid her brood of cottages !
She was to him a sickness and reproach.
Much to the last remained unknown: but
    this   1110
Is sure, that through remorse and grief he
    died;
Though pitied among men, absolved by
    God,

He could not find forgiveness in himself;
Nor could endure the weight of his own
    shame.

Here rests a Mother. But from her I turn
And from her grave. — Behold — upon that
    ridge,
That, stretching boldly from the mountain
    side,
Carries into the centre of the vale
Its rocks and woods — the Cottage where
    she dwelt
And where yet dwells her faithful Partner,
    left   1120
(Full eight years past) the solitary prop
Of many helpless Children.   I begin
With words that might be prelude to a tale
Of sorrow and dejection; but I feel
No sadness, when I think of what mine eyes
See daily in that happy family.
— Bright garland form they for the pensive
    brow
Of their undrooping Father's widowhood,
Those six fair Daughters, budding yet —
    not one,
Not one of all the band, a full-blown flower.
Deprest, and desolate of soul, as once 1131
That Father was, and filled with anxious
    fear,
Now, by experience taught, he stands as-
    sured,
That God, who takes away, yet takes not
    half
Of what he seems to take; or gives it back,
Not to our prayer, but far beyond our
    prayer;
He gives it — the boon produce of a soil
Which our endeavours have refused to till,
And hope hath never watered.   The Abode,
Whose grateful owner can attest these
    truths,   1140
Even were the object nearer to our sight,
Would seem in no distinction to surpass
The rudest habitations.   Ye might think
That it had sprung self-raised from earth,
    or grown
Out of the living rock, to be adorned
By nature only; but, if thither led,
Ye would discover, then, a studious work
Of many fancies, prompting many hands.

Brought from the woods the honeysuckle
    twines
Around the porch, and seems, in that trim
    place,   1150

A plant no longer wild; the cultured rose
There blossoms, strong in health, and will
    be soon
Roof-high; the wild pink crowns the gar-
    den-wall,
And with the flowers are intermingled
    stones
Sparry and bright, rough scatterings of
    the hills.
These ornaments, that fade not with the
    year,
A hardy Girl continues to provide;
Who, mounting fearlessly the rocky heights,
Her Father's prompt attendant, does for
    him
All that a boy could do, but with delight
More keen and prouder daring; yet hath
    she,   1161
Within the garden, like the rest, a bed
For her own flowers and favourite herbs,
    a space,
By sacred charter, holden for her use.
— These, and whatever else the garden
    bears
Of fruit or flower, permission asked or not,
I freely gather; and my leisure draws
A not unfrequent pastime from the hum
Of bees around their range of sheltered
    hives
Busy in that enclosure; while the rill, 1170
That sparkling thrids the rocks, attunes
    his voice
To the pure course of human life which
    there
Flows on in solitude.   But, when the gloom
Of night is falling round my steps, then
    most
This Dwelling charms me; often I stop
    short,
(Who could refrain?) and feed by stealth
    my sight
With prospect of the company within,
Laid open through the blazing window: —
    there
I see the eldest Daughter at her wheel
Spinning amain, as if to overtake 1180
The never-halting time; or, in her turn,
Teaching some Novice of the sisterhood
That skill in this or other household work,
Which, from her Father's honoured hand,
    herself,
While she was yet a little-one, had learned.
Mild Man! he is not gay, but they are gay;
And the whole house seems filled with
    gaiety.

— Thrice happy, then, the Mother may be
     deemed,
The Wife, from whose consolatory grave
I turned, that ye in mind might witness
     where,   1190
And how, her Spirit yet survives on earth!"

BOOK SEVENTH

THE CHURCHYARD AMONG THE
MOUNTAINS — *(continued)*

ARGUMENT

Impression of these Narratives upon the
Author's mind — Pastor invited to give account
of certain Graves that lie apart — Clergyman
and his Family — Fortunate influence of change
of situation — Activity in extreme old age —
Another Clergyman, a character of resolute
Virtue — Lamentations over misdirected ap-
plause — Instance of less exalted excellence in
a deaf man — Elevated character of a blind
man — Reflection upon Blindness — Inter-
rupted by a Peasant who passes — His animal
cheerfulness and careless vivacity — He occa-
sions a digression on the fall of beautiful and in-
teresting Trees — A female Infant's Grave —
Joy at her Birth — Sorrow at her Departure — A
youthful Peasant — His patriotic enthusiasm
and distinguished qualities — His untimely
death — Exultation of the Wanderer, as a pa-
triot, in this Picture — Solitary how affected —
Monument of a Knight — Traditions concerning
him — Peroration of the Wanderer on the
transitoriness of things and the revolutions of
society — Hints at his own past Calling —
Thanks the Pastor.

WHILE thus from theme to theme the
     Historian passed,
The words he uttered, and the scene that
     lay
Before our eyes, awakened in my mind
Vivid remembrance of those long-past hours,
When, in the hollow of some shadowy vale,
(What time the splendour of the setting sun
Lay beautiful on Snowdon's sovereign brow,
On Cader Idris, or huge Penmanmaur)
A wandering Youth, I listened with delight
To pastoral melody or warlike air,   10
Drawn from the chords of the ancient British
     harp
By some accomplished Master, while he sate
Amid the quiet of the green recess,
And there did inexhaustibly dispense
An interchange of soft or solemn tunes,

Tender or blithe ; now, as the varying
     mood
Of his own spirit urged, — now, as a voice
From youth or maiden, or some honoured
     chief
Of his compatriot villagers (that hung
Around him, drinking in the impassioned
     notes   20
Of the time-hallowed minstrelsy) required
For their heart's ease or pleasure. Strains
     of power
Were they, to seize and occupy the sense;
But to a higher mark than song can reach
Rose this pure eloquence. And, when the
     stream
Which overflowed the soul was passed away,
A consciousness remained that it had left,
Deposited upon the silent shore
Of memory, images and precious thoughts,
That shall not die, and cannot be de-
     stroyed.   30

" These grassy heaps lie amicably close,"
Said I, " like surges heaving in the wind
Along the surface of a mountain pool:
Whence comes it, then, that yonder we
     behold
Five graves, and only five, that rise to-
     gether
Unsociably sequestered, and encroaching
On the smooth playground of the village-
     school ? "

The Vicar answered, — " No disdainful
     pride
In them who rest beneath, nor any course
Of strange or tragic accident, hath helped
To place those hillocks in that lonely guise.
— Once more look forth, and follow with
     your sight   42
The length of road that from yon moun-
     tain's base
Through bare enclosures stretches, 'till its
     line
Is lost within a little tuft of trees;
Then, reappearing in a moment, quits
The cultured fields; and up the heathy
     waste,
Mounts, as you see, in mazes serpentine,
Led towards an easy outlet of the vale,
That little shady spot, that sylvan tuft,   50
By which the road is hidden, also hides
A cottage from our view; though I discern
(Ye scarcely can) amid its sheltering trees
The smokeless chimney-top. —

All unembowered
And naked stood that lowly Parsonage
(For such in truth it is, and appertains
To a small Chapel in the vale beyond)
When hither came its last Inhabitant.
Rough and forbidding were the choicest
   roads
By which our northern wilds could then be
   crossed;   60
And into most of these secluded vales
Was no access for wain, heavy or light.
So, at his dwelling-place the Priest arrived
With store of household goods, in panniers
   slung
On sturdy horses graced with jingling bells,
And on the back of more ignoble beast;
That, with like burthen of effects most
   prized
Or easiest carried, closed the motley train.
Young was I then, a schoolboy of eight
   years;
But still, methinks, I see them as they
   passed   70
In order, drawing toward their wished-for
   home.
— Rocked by the motion of a trusty ass
Two ruddy children hung, a well-poised
   freight,
Each in his basket nodding drowsily;
Their bonnets, I remember, wreathed with
   flowers,
Which told it was the pleasant month of
   June;
And, close behind, the comely Matron rode,
A woman of soft speech and gracious
   smile,
And with a lady's mien. — From far they
   came,
Even from Northumbrian hills; yet theirs
   had been   80
A merry journey, rich in pastime, cheered
By music, prank, and laughter-stirring jest;
And freak put on, and arch word dropped
   — to swell
The cloud of fancy and uncouth surmise
That gathered round the slowly-moving
   train.
— ' Whence do they come ? and with what
   errand charged ?
Belong they to the fortune-telling tribe
Who pitch their tents under the greenwood
   tree ?
Or Strollers are they, furnished to enact
Fair Rosamond, and the Children of the
   Wood,   90

And, by that whiskered tabby's aid, set
   forth
The lucky venture of sage Whittington,
When the next village hears the show an-
   nounced
By blast of trumpet ? ' Plenteous was the
   growth
Of such conjectures, overheard, or seen
On many a staring countenance portrayed
Of boor or burgher, as they marched along.
And more than once their steadiness of face
Was put to proof, and exercise supplied
To their inventive humour, by stern looks,
And questions in authoritative tone,   101
From some staid guardian of the public
   peace,
Checking the sober steed on which he rode,
In his suspicious wisdom; oftener still,
By notice indirect, or blunt demand
From traveller halting in his own despite,
A simple curiosity to ease:
Of which adventures, that beguiled and
   cheered
Their grave migration, the good pair would
   tell,
With undiminished glee, in hoary age.   110

   A Priest he was by function; but his
   course
From his youth up, and high as manhood's
   noon,
(The hour of life to which he then was
   brought)
Had been irregular, I might say, wild;
By books unsteadied, by his pastoral care
Too little checked. An active, ardent mind;
A fancy pregnant with resource and scheme
To cheat the sadness of a rainy day;
Hands apt for all ingenious arts and games;
A generous spirit, and a body strong   120
To cope with stoutest champions of the
   bowl —
Had earned for him sure welcome, and the
   rights
Of a prized visitant, in the jolly hall
Of country 'squire; or at the statelier board
Of duke or earl, from scenes of courtly
   pomp
Withdrawn, — to while away the summer
   hours
In condescension among rural guests.

   With these high comrades he had revelled
   long,
Frolicked industriously, a simple Clerk

By hopes of coming patronage beguiled 130
Till the heart sickened. So, each loftier
    aim
Abandoning and all his showy friends,
For a life's stay (slender it was, but sure)
He turned to this secluded chapelry;
That had been offered to his doubtful
    choice
By an unthought-of patron. Bleak and
    bare
They found the cottage, their allotted
    home;
Naked without, and rude within; a spot
With which the Cure not long had been en-
    dowed: 139
And far remote the chapel stood, — remote,
And, from his Dwelling, unapproachable,
Save through a gap high in the hills, an
    opening
Shadeless and   shelterless, by driving
    showers
Frequented, and beset with howling winds.
Yet cause was none, whate'er regret might
    hang
On his own mind, to quarrel with the
    choice
Or the necessity that fixed him here;
Apart from old temptations, and con-
    strained   148
To punctual labour in his sacred charge.
See him a constant preacher to the poor !
And visiting, though not with saintly zeal,
Yet, when need was, with no reluctant will,
The sick in body, or distrest in mind;
And, by a salutary change, compelled
To rise from timely sleep, and meet the day
With no engagement, in his thoughts, more
    proud
Or splendid than his garden could afford,
His fields, or mountains by the heath-cock
    ranged
Or the wild brooks; from which he now
    returned
Contented to partake the quiet meal   160
Of his own board, where sat his gentle
    Mate
And three fair Children, plentifully fed
Though simply, from their little household
    farm;
Nor wanted timely treat of fish or fowl
By nature yielded to his practised hand; —
To help the small but certain comings-in
Of that spare benefice. Yet not the less
Theirs was a hospitable board, and theirs
A charitable door.

                    So days and years
Passed on; — the inside of that rugged
    house   170
Was trimmed and brightened by the Ma-
    tron's care,
And gradually enriched with things of price,
Which might be lacked for use or ornament.
What, though no soft and costly sofa there
Insidiously stretched out its lazy length,
And no vain mirror glittered upon the walls,
Yet were the windows of the low abode
By shutters weather-fended, which at once
Repelled the storm and deadened its loud
    roar.
There snow-white curtains hung in decent
    folds;   180
Tough moss, and long-enduring mountain
    plants,
That creep along the ground with sinuous
    trail,
Were nicely braided; and composed a work
Like Indian mats, that with appropriate
    grace
Lay at the threshold and the inner doors;
And a fair carpet, woven of homespun
    wool
But tinctured daintily with florid hues,
For seemliness and warmth, on festal days,
Covered the smooth blue slabs of mountain-
    stone
With which the parlour-floor, in simplest
    guise   190
Of pastoral homesteads, had been long in-
    laid.

Those pleasing works the Housewife's
    skill produced:
Meanwhile the unsedentary Master's hand
Was busier with his task — to rid, to plant,
To rear for food, for shelter, and delight;
A thriving covert ! And when wishes,
    formed
In youth, and sanctioned by the riper mind,
Restored me to my native valley, here
To end my days; well pleased was I to see
The once-bare cottage, on the mountain-
    side,   200
Screened from assault of every bitter
    blast;
While the dark shadows of the summer
    leaves
Danced in the breeze, chequering its mossy
    roof.
Time, which had thus afforded willing
    help

To beautify with nature's fairest growths
This rustic tenement, had gently shed,
Upon its Master's frame, a wintry grace;
The comeliness of unenfeebled age.

But how could I say, gently ? for he still
Retained a flashing eye, a burning palm, 210
A stirring foot, a head which beat at nights
Upon its pillow with a thousand schemes.
Few likings had he dropped, few pleasures
　　lost;
Generous and charitable, prompt to serve;
And still his harsher passions kept their
　　hold —
Anger and indignation.　Still he loved
The sound of titled names, and talked in
　　glee
Of long-past banquetings with high-born
　　friends:
Then, from those lulling fits of vain delight
Uproused by recollected injury, railed 220
At their false ways disdainfully, — and oft
In bitterness, and with a threatening eye
Of fire, incensed beneath its hoary brow.
— Those transports, with staid looks of
　　pure good-will,
And with soft smile, his consort would re-
　　prove.
She, far behind him in the race of years,
Yet keeping her first mildness, was ad-
　　vanced
Far nearer, in the habit of her soul,
To that still region whither all are bound;
Him might we liken to the setting sun 230
As seen not seldom on some gusty day,
Struggling and bold, and shining from the
　　west
With an inconstant and unmellowed light;
She was a soft attendant cloud, that hung
As if with wish to veil the restless orb;
From which it did itself imbibe a ray
Of pleasing lustre. — But no more of this;
I better love to sprinkle on the sod
That now divides the pair, or rather say,
That still unites them, praises, like heaven's
　　dew,　　　　　　　　　　　　　　240
Without reserve descending upon both.

Our very first in eminence of years
This old Man stood, the patriarch of the
　　Vale !
And, to his unmolested mansion, death
Had never come, through space of forty
　　years;
Sparing both old and young in that abode.

Suddenly then they disappeared: not twice
Had summer scorched the fields; not twice
　　had fallen,
On those high peaks, the first autumnal
　　snow,
Before the greedy visiting was closed, 250
And the long-privileged house left empty
　　— swept
As by a plague.　Yet no rapacious plague
Had been among them; all was gentle
　　death,
One after one, with intervals of peace.
A happy consummation ! an accord
Sweet, perfect, to be wished for ! save that
　　here
Was something which to mortal sense
　　might sound
Like harshness, — that the old grey-headed
　　Sire,
The oldest, he was taken last; survived
When the meek Partner of his age, his Son,
His Daughter, and that late and high-prized
　　gift,　　　　　　　　　　　　　261
His little smiling Grandchild, were no
　　more.

' All gone; all vanished ! he deprived and
　　bare,
How will he face the remnant of his life ?
What will become of him ? ' we said, and
　　mused
In sad conjectures — ' Shall we meet him
　　now
Haunting with rod and line the craggy
　　brooks ?
Or shall we overhear him, as we pass,
Striving to entertain the lonely hours
With music ? ' (for he had not ceased to
　　touch　　　　　　　　　　　　270
The harp or viol which himself had framed,
For their sweet purposes, with perfect
　　skill.)
' What titles will he keep ? will he remain
Musician, gardener, builder, mechanist,
A planter, and a rearer from the seed ?
A man of hope and forward-looking mind
Even to the last ! ' — Such was he, unsub-
　　dued.
But Heaven was gracious; yet a little while,
And this Survivor, with his cheerful throng
Of open projects, and his inward hoard 280
Of unsunned griefs, too many and too keen,
Was overcome by unexpected sleep,
In one blest moment. Like a shadow
　　thrown

Softly and lightly from a passing cloud,
Death fell upon him, while reclined he lay
For noontide solace on the summer grass,
The warm lap of his mother earth: and so,
Their lenient term of separation past,
That family (whose graves you there be-
    hold)
By yet a higher privilege once more   290
Were gathered to each other."
                    Calm of mind
And silence waited on these closing words;
Until the Wanderer (whether moved by
    fear
Lest in those passages of life were some
That might have touched the sick heart of
    his Friend
Too nearly, or intent to reinforce
His own firm spirit in degree deprest
By tender sorrow for our mortal state)
Thus silence broke: — " Behold a thought-
    less Man
From vice and premature decay preserved
By useful habits, to a fitter soil   301
Transplanted ere too late. — The hermit,
    lodged
Amid the untrodden desert, tells his beads,
With each repeating its allotted prayer,
And thus divides and thus relieves the
    time;
Smooth task, with *his* compared, whose
    mind could string,
Not scantily, bright minutes on the thread
Of keen domestic anguish; and beguile
A solitude, unchosen, unprofessed;
Till gentlest death released him.
                    Far from us
Be the desire — too curiously to ask   311
How much of this is but the blind result
Of cordial spirits and vital temperament,
And what to higher powers is justly due.
But you, Sir, know that in a neighbouring
    vale
A Priest abides before whose life such
    doubts
Fall to the ground; whose gifts of nature
    lie
Retired from notice, lost in attributes
Of reason, honourably effaced by debts
Which her poor treasure-house is content to
    owe,   320
And conquest over her dominion gained,
To which her frowardness must needs sub-
    mit.
In this one Man is shown a temperance —
    proof

Against all trials; industry severe
And constant as the motion of the day;
Stern self-denial round him spread, with
    shade
That might be deemed forbidding, did not
    there
All generous feelings flourish and rejoice;
Forbearance, charity in deed and thought,
And resolution competent to take   330
Out of the bosom of simplicity
All that her holy customs recommend,
And the best ages of the world prescribe.
— Preaching, administering, in every work
Of his sublime vocation, in the walks
Of worldly intercourse between man and
    man,
And in his humble dwelling, he appears
A labourer, with moral virtue girt,
With spiritual graces, like a glory,
    crowned."

" Doubt can be none," the Pastor said,
    " for whom   340
This portraiture is sketched. The great,
    the good,
The well-beloved, the fortunate, the wise, —
These titles emperors and chiefs have
    held,
Honour assumed or given: and him, the
    WONDERFUL,
Our simple shepherds, speaking from the
    heart,
Deservedly have styled. — From his abode
In a dependent chapelry that lies
Behind yon hill, a poor and rugged wild,
Which in his soul he lovingly embraced,
And, having once espoused, would never
    quit;   350
Into its graveyard will ere long be borne
That lowly, great, good Man. A simple
    stone
May cover him; and by its help, perchance,
A century shall hear his name pronounced,
With images attendant on the sound;
Then, shall the slowly-gathering twilight
    close
In utter night; and of his course remain
No cognizable vestiges, no more
Than of this breath, which shapes itself in
    words
To speak of him, and instantly dissolves."

The Pastor, pressed by thoughts which
    round his theme   361
Still lingered, after a brief pause, resumed;

" Noise is there not enough in doleful war,
But that the heaven-born poet must stand
    forth,
And lend the echoes of his sacred shell,
To multiply and aggravate the din ?
Pangs are there not enough in hopeless
    love —
And, in requited passion, all too much
Of turbulence, anxiety, and fear —
But that the minstrel of the rural shade   370
Must tune his pipe, insidiously to nurse
The perturbation in the suffering breast,
And propagate its kind, far as he may ?
— Ah who (and with such rapture as befits
The hallowed theme) will rise and celebrate
The good man's purposes and deeds; re-
    trace
His struggles, his discomfitures deplore,
His triumphs hail, and glorify his end;
That virtue, like the fumes and vapoury
    clouds
Through fancy's heat redounding in the
    brain,   380
And like the soft infections of the heart,
By charm of measured words may spread
    o'er field,
Hamlet, and town; and piety survive
Upon the lips of men in hall or bower;
Not for reproof, but high and warm delight,
And grave encouragement, by song in-
    spired ?
—Vain thought ! but wherefore murmur or
    repine ?
The memory of the just survives in heaven:
And, without sorrow, will the ground re-
    ceive
That venerable clay.   Meanwhile the best
Of what lies here confines us to degrees   391
In excellence less difficult to reach,
And milder worth: nor need we travel far
From those to whom our last regards were
    paid,
For such example.   Almost at the root
Of that tall pine, the shadow of whose bare
And slender stem, while here I sit at eve,
Oft stretches towards me, like a long
    straight path
Traced faintly in the greensward; there,
    beneath
A plain blue stone, a gentle Dalesman lies,
From whom, in early childhood, was with-
    drawn   401
The precious gift of hearing.   He grew up
From year to year in loneliness of soul;

And this deep mountain-valley was to him
Soundless, with all its streams.   The bird
    of dawn
Did never rouse this Cottager from sleep
With startling summons; not for his delight
The vernal cuckoo shouted; not for him
Murmured the labouring bee.   When
    stormy winds   409
Were working the broad bosom of the lake
Into a thousand thousand sparkling waves,
Rocking the trees, or driving cloud on
    cloud
Along the sharp edge of yon lofty crags,
The agitated scene before his eye
Was silent as a picture: evermore
Were all things silent, wheresoe'er he
    moved.
Yet, by the solace of his own pure thoughts
Upheld, he duteously pursued the round
Of rural labours; the steep mountain-side
Ascended, with his staff and faithful dog;
The plough he guided, and the scythe he
    swayed;   421
And the ripe corn before his sickle fell
Among the jocund reapers.   For himself,
All watchful and industrious as he was,
He wrought not: neither field nor flock he
    owned:
No wish for wealth had place within his
    mind;
Nor husband's love, nor father's hope or
    care.

    Though born a younger brother, need
        was none
That from the floor of his paternal home
He should depart, to plant himself anew.
And when, mature in manhood, he be-
    held   431
His parents laid in earth, no loss ensued
Of rights to him; but he remained well
    pleased,
By the pure bond of independent love,
An inmate of a second family;
The fellow-labourer and friend of him
To whom the small inheritance had fallen.
— Nor deem that his mild presence was a
    weight
That pressed upon his brother's house; for
    books
Were ready comrades whom he could not
    tire;   440
Of whose society the blameless Man
Was never satiate.   Their familiar voice,
Even to old age, with unabated charm

Beguiled his leisure hours; refreshed his
    thoughts;
Beyond its natural elevation raised
His introverted spirit; and bestowed
Upon his life an outward dignity
Which all acknowledged. The dark winter
    night,
The stormy day, each had its own re-
    source;
Song of the muses, sage historic tale,   450
Science severe, or word of holy Writ
Announcing immortality and joy
To the assembled spirits of just men
Made perfect, and from injury secure.
— Thus soothed at home, thus busy in the
    field,
To no perverse suspicion he gave way,
No languor, peevishness, nor vain com-
    plaint:
And they, who were about him, did not
    fail
In reverence, or in courtesy; they prized
His gentle manners: and his peaceful
    smiles,   460
The gleams of his slow-varying counte-
    nance,
Were met with answering sympathy and
    love.

At length, when sixty years and five were
    told,
A slow disease insensibly consumed
The powers of nature: and a few short
    steps
Of friends and kindred bore him from his
    home
(Yon cottage shaded by the woody crags)
To the profounder stillness of the grave.
— Nor was his funeral denied the grace
Of many tears, virtuous and thoughtful
    grief;   470
Heart-sorrow rendered sweet by gratitude.
And now that monumental stone preserves
His name, and unambitiously relates
How long, and by what kindly outward
    aids,
And in what pure contentedness of mind,
The sad privation was by him endured.
— And yon tall pine-tree, whose composing
    sound
Was wasted on the good Man's living ear,
Hath now its own peculiar sanctity;
And, at the touch of every wandering
    breeze,   480
Murmurs, not idly, o'er his peaceful grave.

Soul-cheering Light, most bountiful of
    things !
Guide of our way, mysterious comforter !
Whose sacred influence, spread through
    earth and heaven,
We all too thanklessly participate,
Thy gifts were utterly withheld from him
Whose place of rest is near yon ivied porch,
Yet, of the wild brooks ask if he com-
    plained;
Ask of the channelled rivers if they held
A safer, easier, more determined course.   490
What terror doth it strike into the mind
To think of one, blind and alone, advancing
Straight toward some precipice's airy brink !
But, timely warned, *He* would have stayed
    his steps,
Protected, say enlightened, by his ear;
And on the very edge of vacancy
Not more endangered than a man whose
    eye
Beholds the gulf beneath. — No floweret
    blooms
Throughout the lofty range of these rough
    hills,
Nor in the woods, that could from him
    conceal   500
Its birth-place; none whose figure did not
    live
Upon his touch. The bowels of the earth
Enriched with knowledge his industrious
    mind;
The ocean paid him tribute from the stores
Lodged in her bosom; and, by science led,
His genius mounted to the plains of heaven.
— Methinks I see him — how his eye-balls
    rolled,
Beneath his ample brow, in darkness
    paired, —
But each instinct with spirit; and the frame
Of the whole countenance alive with
    thought,   510
Fancy, and understanding; while the voice
Discoursed of natural or moral truth
With eloquence, and such authentic power,
That, in his presence, humbler knowledge
    stood
Abashed, and tender pity overawed."

" A noble — and, to unreflecting minds,
A marvellous spectacle," the Wanderer
    said,
" Beings like these present ! But proof
    abounds
Upon the earth that faculties, which seem

Extinguished, do not, *therefore*, cease to
be. 520
And to the mind among her powers of
sense
This transfer is permitted, — not alone
That the bereft their recompense may win;
But for remoter purposes of love
And charity; nor last nor least for this,
That to the imagination may be given
A type and shadow of an awful truth;
How, likewise, under sufferance divine,
Darkness is banished from the realms of
death,
By man's imperishable spirit quelled. 530
Unto the men who see not as we see
Futurity was thought, in ancient times,
To be laid open, and they prophesied.
And know we not that from the blind have
flowed
The highest, holiest, raptures of the lyre;
And wisdom married to immortal verse ? "

Among the humbler Worthies, at our feet
Lying insensible to human praise,
Love, or regret, — *whose* lineaments would
next
Have been portrayed, I guess not; but it
chanced 540
That, near the quiet churchyard where we
sate,
A team of horses, with a ponderous freight
Pressing behind, adown a rugged slope,
Whose sharp descent confounded their
array,
Came at that moment, ringing noisily.

"Here," said the Pastor, "do we muse,
and mourn
The waste of death; and lo ! the giant oak
Stretched on his bier — that massy timber
wain;
Nor fail to note the Man who guides the
team."

He was a peasant of the lowest class: 550
Grey locks profusely round his temples hung
In clustering curls, like ivy, which the bite
Of winter cannot thin; the fresh air lodged
Within his cheek, as light within a cloud;
And he returned our greeting with a smile.
When he had passed, the Solitary spake;
" A Man he seems of cheerful yesterdays
And confident to-morrows; with a face
Not worldly-minded, for it bears too much
Of Nature's impress, — gaiety and health,

Freedom and hope; but keen, withal, and
shrewd. 561
His gestures note, — and hark ! his tones of
voice
Are all vivacious as his mien and looks."

The Pastor answered: " You have read
him well.
Year after year is added to his store
With *silent* increase: summers, winters —
past,
Past or to come; yea, boldly might I say,
Ten summers and ten winters of a space
That lies beyond life's ordinary bounds,
Upon his sprightly vigour cannot fix 570
The obligation of an anxious mind,
A pride in having, or a fear to lose;
Possessed like outskirts of some large
domain,
By any one more thought of than by him
Who holds the land in fee, its careless
lord !
Yet is the creature rational, endowed
With foresight; hears, too, every sabbath
day,
The christian promise with attentive ear;
Nor will, I trust, the Majesty of Heaven
Reject the incense offered up by him, 580
Though of the kind which beasts and birds
present
In grove or pasture; cheerfulness of soul,
From trepidation and repining free.
How many scrupulous worshippers fall down
Upon their knees, and daily homage pay
Less worthy, less religious even, than his !

This qualified respect, the old Man's due,
Is paid without reluctance; but in truth,"
(Said the good Vicar with a fond half-smile)
" I feel at times a motion of despite 590
Towards one, whose bold contrivances and
skill,
As you have seen, bear such conspicuous
part
In works of havoc; taking from these vales,
One after one, their proudest ornaments.
Full oft his doings leave me to deplore
Tall ash-tree, sown by winds, by vapours
nursed,
In the dry crannies of the pendent rocks;
Light birch, aloft upon the horizon's edge,
A veil of glory for the ascending moon;
And oak whose roots by noontide dew were
damped, 600
And on whose forehead inaccessible

The raven lodged in safety. — Many a ship
Launched into Morecamb-bay to *him* hath
   owed
Her strong knee-timbers, and the mast that
   bears
The loftiest of her pendants; he, from
   park
Or forest, fetched the enormous axle-tree
That whirls (how slow itself !) ten thousand
   spindles:
And the vast engine labouring in the mine,
Content with meaner prowess, must have
   lacked
The trunk and body of its marvellous
   strength,   610
If his undaunted enterprise had failed
Among the mountain coves.
             Yon household fir,
A guardian planted to fence off the blast,
But towering high the roof above, as if
Its humble destination were forgot —
That sycamore, which annually holds
Within its shade, as in a stately tent
On all sides open to the fanning breeze,
A grave assemblage, seated while they shear
The fleece-encumbered flock — the JOYFUL
   ELM,   620
Around whose trunk the maidens dance in
   May —
And the LORD'S OAK — would plead their
   several rights
In vain, if he were master of their fate;
His sentence to the axe would doom them
   all.
But, green in age and lusty as he is,
And promising to keep his hold on earth
Less, as might seem, in rivalship with men
Than with the forest's more enduring
   growth,
His own appointed hour will come at last;
And, like the haughty Spoilers of the
   world,   630
This keen Destroyer, in his turn, must fall.

   Now from the living pass we once again:
From Age," the Priest continued, " turn
   your thoughts;
From Age, that often unlamented drops,
And mark that daisied hillock, three spans
   long !
— Seven lusty Sons sate daily round the
   board
Of Gold-rill side; and, when the hope had
   ceased
Of other progeny, a Daughter then

Was given, the crowning bounty of the
   whole;
And so acknowledged with a tremulous joy
Felt to the centre of that heavenly calm   641
With which by nature every mother's soul
Is stricken in the moment when her throes
Are ended, and her ears have heard the cry
Which tells her that a living child is born;
And she lies conscious, in a blissful rest,
That the dread storm is weathered by them
   both.

   The Father — him at this unlooked-for
   gift
A bolder transport seizes. From the side
Of his bright hearth, and from his open
   door,   650
Day after day the gladness is diffused
To all that come, almost to all that pass;
Invited, summoned, to partake the cheer
Spread on the never-empty board, and drink
Health and good wishes to his new-born
   girl,
From cups replenished by his joyous hand.
— Those seven fair brothers variously were
   moved
Each by the thoughts best suited to his
   years:
But most of all and with most thankful
   mind   659
The hoary grandsire felt himself enriched;
A happiness that ebbed not, but remained
To fill the total measure of his soul !
— From the low tenement, his own abode,
Whither, as to a little private cell,
He had withdrawn from bustle, care, and
   noise,
To spend the sabbath of old age in peace,
Once every day he duteously repaired
To rock the cradle of the slumbering babe:
For in that female infant's name he heard
The silent name of his departed wife;   670
Heart-stirring music ! hourly heard that
   name;
Full blest he was, 'Another Margaret
   Green,'
Oft did he say, ' was come to Gold-rill side.'

   Oh ! pang unthought of, as the precious
   boon
Itself had been unlooked-for; oh ! dire
   stroke
Of desolating anguish for them all !
— Just as the Child could totter on the
   floor,

And, by some friendly finger's help up-
stayed,
Range round the garden walk, while she
perchance
Was catching at some novelty of spring, 680
Ground-flower, or glossy insect from its
cell
Drawn by the sunshine — at that hopeful
season
The winds of March, smiting insidiously,
Raised in the tender passage of the throat
Viewless obstruction; whence, all unfore-
warned,
The household lost their pride and soul's
delight.
— But time hath power to soften all re-
grets,
And prayer and thought can bring to worst
distress
Due resignation. Therefore, though some
tears 689
Fail not to spring from either Parent's eye
Oft as they hear of sorrow like their own,
Yet this departed Little-one, too long
The innocent troubler of their quiet, sleeps
In what may now be called a peaceful bed.

On a bright day — so calm and bright, it
seemed
To us, with our sad spirits, heavenly-fair —
These mountains echoed to an unknown
sound;
A volley, thrice repeated o'er the Corse
Let down into the hollow of that grave,
Whose shelving sides are red with naked
mould. 700
Ye rains of April, duly wet this earth !
Spare, burning sun of midsummer, these
sods,
That they may knit together, and therewith
Our thoughts unite in kindred quietness !
Nor so the Valley shall forget her loss.
Dear Youth, by young and old alike be-
loved,
To me as precious as my own ! — Green
herbs
May creep (I wish that they would softly
creep)
Over thy last abode, and we may pass
Reminded less imperiously of thee; — 710
The ridge itself may sink into the breast
Of earth, the great abyss, and be no more;
Yet shall not thy remembrance leave our
hearts,
Thy image disappear !

The Mountain-ash
No eye can overlook, when 'mid a grove
Of yet unfaded trees she lifts her head
Decked with autumnal berries, that out-
shine
Spring's richest blossoms; and ye may have
marked,
By a brook-side or solitary tarn, 719
How she her station doth adorn: the pool
Glows at her feet, and all the gloomy rocks
Are brightened round her. In his native
vale
Such and so glorious did this Youth appear;
A sight that kindled pleasure in all hearts
By his ingenuous beauty, by the gleam
Of his fair eyes, by his capacious brow,
By all the graces with which nature's hand
Had lavishly arrayed him. As old bards
Tell in their idle songs of wandering gods,
Pan or Apollo, veiled in human form: 730
Yet, like the sweet-breathed violet of the
shade,
Discovered in their own despite to sense
Of mortals (if such fables without blame
May find chance-mention on this sacred
ground)
So, through a simple rustic garb's disguise,
And through the impediment of rural cares,
In him revealed a scholar's genius shone;
And so, not wholly hidden from men's sight,
In him the spirit of a hero walked
Our unpretending valley. — How the quoit
Whizzed from the Stripling's arm ! If
touched by him, 741
The inglorious foot-ball mounted to the
pitch
Of the lark's flight, — or shaped a rainbow
curve,
Aloft, in prospect of the shouting field !
The indefatigable fox had learned
To dread his perseverance in the chase.
With admiration would he lift his eyes
To the wide-ruling eagle, and his hand
Was loth to assault the majesty he loved:
Else had the strongest fastnesses proved
weak 750
To guard the royal brood. The sailing
glead,
The wheeling swallow, and the darting
snipe;
The sportive sea-gull dancing with the
waves,
And cautious water-fowl, from distant
climes,
Fixed at their seat, the centre of the Mere;

Were subject to young Oswald's steady
    aim,
And lived by his forbearance.
               From the coast
Of France a boastful Tyrant hurled his
    threats;
Our Country marked the preparation vast
Of hostile forces; and she called — with
    voice   760
That filled her plains, that reached her ut-
    most shores,
And in remotest vales was heard — to
    arms !
— Then, for the first time, here you might
    have seen
The shepherd's grey to martial scarlet
    changed,
That flashed uncouthly through the woods
    and fields.
Ten hardy Striplings, all in bright attire,
And graced with shining weapons, weekly
    marched,
From this lone valley, to a central spot
Where, in assemblage with the flower and
    choice
Of the surrounding district, they might
    learn   770
The rudiments of war; ten — hardy, strong,
And valiant; but young Oswald, like a
    chief
And yet a modest comrade, led them forth
From their shy solitude, to face the world,
With a gay confidence and seemly pride;
Measuring the soil beneath their happy feet
Like Youths released from labour, and yet
    bound
To most laborious service, though to them
A festival of unencumbered ease;
The inner spirit keeping holiday,   780
Like vernal ground to sabbath sunshine left.

Oft have I marked him, at some leisure
    hour,
Stretched on the grass, or seated in the
    shade,
Among his fellows, while an ample map
Before their eyes lay carefully outspread,
From which the gallant teacher would dis-
    course,
Now pointing this way, and now that, —
    ' Here flows,'
Thus would he say, ' the Rhine, that famous
    stream !
Eastward, the Danube toward this inland
    sea,

A mightier river, winds from realm to
    realm;   790
And, like a serpent, shows his glittering
    back
Bespotted — with innumerable isles:
Here reigns the Russian, there the Turk;
    observe
His capital city !' Thence, along a tract
Of livelier interest to his hopes and fears,
His finger moved, distinguishing the spots
Where wide-spread conflict then most
    fiercely raged;
Nor left unstigmatized those fatal fields
On which the sons of mighty Germany
Were taught a base submission. — ' Here
    behold   800
A nobler race, the Switzers, and their
    land,
Vales deeper far than these of ours, huge
    woods,
And mountains white with everlasting
    snow !'
— And, surely, he, that spake with kindling
    brow,
Was a true patriot, hopeful as the best
Of that young peasantry, who, in our days,
Have fought and perished for Helvetia's
    rights —
Ah, not in vain ! — or those who, in old
    time,
For work of happier issue, to the side
Of Tell came trooping from a thousand
    huts,   810
When he had risen alone ! No braver
    Youth
Descended from Judean heights, to march
With righteous Joshua; nor appeared in
    arms
When grove was felled, and altar was cast
    down,
And Gideon blew the trumpet, soul-in-
    flamed,
And strong in hatred of idolatry."

The Pastor, even as if by these last words
Raised from his seat within the chosen
    shade,
Moved toward the grave; — instinctively his
    steps
We followed; and my voice with joy ex-
    claimed: 820
" Power to the Oppressors of the world is
    given,
A might of which they dream not. Oh !
    the curse,

To be the awakener of divinest thoughts,
Father and founder of exalted deeds;
And, to whole nations bound in servile
    straits,
The liberal donor of capacities
More than heroic ! this to be, nor yet
Have sense of one connatural wish, nor
    yet
Deserve the least return of human thanks;
Winning no recompense but deadly hate 830
With pity mixed, astonishment with scorn !"

When this involuntary strain had ceased,
The Pastor said: " So Providence is served;
The forkèd weapon of the skies can send
Illumination into deep, dark holds,
Which the mild sunbeam hath not power
    to pierce.
Ye Thrones that have defied remorse, and
    cast
Pity away, soon shall ye quake with *fear !*
For, not unconscious of the mighty debt
Which to outrageous wrong the sufferer
    owes, 840
Europe, through all her habitable bounds,
Is thirsting for *their* overthrow, who yet
Survive, as pagan temples stood of yore,
By horror of their impious rites, preserved;
Are still permitted to extend their pride,
Like cedars on the top of Lebanon
Darkening the sun.
           But less impatient thoughts,
And love ' all hoping and expecting all,'
This hallowed grave demands, where rests
    in peace
A humble champion of the better cause, 850
A Peasant-youth, so call him, for he asked
No higher name; in whom our country
    showed,
As in a favourite son, most beautiful.
In spite of vice, and misery, and disease,
Spread with the spreading of her wealthy
    arts,
England, the ancient and the free, appeared
In him to stand before my swimming eyes,
Unconquerably virtuous and secure.
— No more of this, lest I offend his dust:
Short was his life, and a brief tale re-
    mains. 860

One day — a summer's day of annual
    pomp
And solemn chase — from morn to sultry
    noon
His steps had followed, fleetest of the fleet,

The red-deer driven along its native heights
With cry of hound and horn; and, from
    that toil
Returned with sinews weakened and re-
    laxed,
This generous Youth, too negligent of self,
Plunged — 'mid a gay and busy throng con-
    vened
To wash the fleeces of his Father's flock —
Into the chilling flood. Convulsions dire
Seized him, that self-same night; and
    through the space 871
Of twelve ensuing days his frame was
    wrenched,
Till nature rested from her work in death.
To him, thus snatched away, his comrades
    paid
A soldier's honours. At his funeral hour
Bright was the sun, the sky a cloudless
    blue —
A golden lustre slept upon the hills;
And if by chance a stranger, wandering
    there,
From some commanding eminence had
    looked
Down on this spot, well pleased would he
    have seen 880
A glittering spectacle; but every face
Was pallid: seldom hath that eye been
    moist
With tears, that wept not then; nor were
    the few,
Who from their dwellings came not forth
    to join
In this sad service, less disturbed than we.
They started at the tributary peal
Of instantaneous thunder, which announced,
Through the still air, the closing of the
    Grave;
And distant mountains echoed with a sound
Of lamentation, never heard before ! " 890

The Pastor ceased. — My venerable
    Friend
Victoriously upraised his clear bright eye;
And, when that eulogy was ended, stood
Enrapt, as if his inward sense perceived
The prolongation of some still response,
Sent by the ancient Soul of this wide land,
The Spirit of its mountains and its seas,
Its cities, temples, fields, its awful power,
Its rights and virtues — by that Deity
Descending, and supporting his pure
    heart 900
With patriotic confidence and joy.

And, at the last of those memorial words,
The pining Solitary turned aside;
Whether through manly instinct to conceal
Tender emotions spreading from the heart
To his worn cheek; or with uneasy shame
For those cold humours of habitual spleen
That, fondly seeking in dispraise of man
Solace and self-excuse, had sometimes
    urged
To self-abuse a not ineloquent tongue.   910
— Right toward the sacred Edifice his steps
Had been directed; and we saw him now
Intent upon a monumental stone,
Whose uncouth form was grafted on the
    wall,
Or rather seemed to have grown into the
    side
Of the rude pile; as oft-times trunks of
    trees,
Where nature works in wild and craggy
    spots,
Are seen incorporate with the living rock —
To endure for aye. The Vicar, taking note
Of his employment, with a courteous
    smile   920
Exclaimed —
           " The sagest Antiquarian's eye
That task would foil; " then, letting fall his
    voice
While he advanced, thus spake: " Tradi-
    tion tells
That, in Eliza's golden days, a Knight
Came on a war-horse sumptuously attired,
And fixed his home in this sequestered
    vale.
'T is left untold if here he first drew breath,
Or as a stranger reached this deep recess,
Unknowing and unknown. A pleasing
    thought
I sometimes entertain, that haply bound   930
To Scotland's court in service of his Queen,
Or sent on mission to some northern Chief
Of England's realm, this vale he might
    have seen
With transient observation; and thence
    caught
An image fair, which, brightening in his
    soul
When joy of war and pride of chivalry
Languished beneath accumulated years,
Had power to draw him from the world,
    resolved
To make that paradise his chosen home
To which his peaceful fancy oft had
    turned.   940

Vague thoughts are these; but, if belief
    may rest
Upon unwritten story fondly traced
From sire to son, in this obscure retreat
The Knight arrived, with spear and shield,
    and borne
Upon a Charger gorgeously bedecked
With broidered housings. And the lofty
    Steed —
His sole companion, and his faithful friend,
Whom he, in gratitude, let loose to range
In fertile pastures — was beheld with eyes
Of admiration and delightful awe,   950
By those untravelled Dalesmen. With less
    pride,
Yet free from touch of envious discontent,
They saw a mansion at his bidding rise,
Like a bright star, amid the lowly band
Of their rude homesteads. Here the
    Warrior dwelt;
And, in that mansion, children of his own,
Or kindred, gathered round him. As a
    tree
That falls and disappears, the house is
    gone;
And, through improvidence or want of love
For ancient worth and honourable things, 960
The spear and shield are vanished, which
    the Knight
Hung in his rustic hall. One ivied arch
Myself have seen, a gateway, last remains
Of that foundation in domestic care
Raised by his hands. And now no trace is
    left
Of the mild-hearted Champion, save this
    stone,
Faithless memorial ! and his family name
Borne by yon clustering cottages, that
    sprang
From out the ruins of his stately lodge:
These, and the name and title at full
    length, —   970
Sir Alfred Irthing, with appropriate words
Accompanied, still extant, in a wreath
Or posy, girding round the several fronts
Of three clear-sounding and harmonious
    bells,
That in the steeple hang, his pious gift."

" So fails, so languishes, grows dim, and
    dies,"
The grey-haired Wanderer pensively ex-
    claimed,
" All that this world is proud of. From
    their spheres

The stars of human glory are cast down;
Perish the roses and the flowers of kings,
Princes, and emperors, and the crowns and
　　palms　　　　　　　　　　　　　981
Of all the mighty, withered and consumed !
Nor is power given to lowliest innocence
Long to protect her own. The man him-
　　self
Departs; and soon is spent the line of
　　those
Who, in the bodily image, in the mind,
In heart or soul, in station or pursuit,
Did most resemble him. Degrees and
　　ranks,
Fraternities and orders — heaping high
New wealth upon the burthen of the old, 990
And placing trust in privilege confirmed
And re-confirmed — are scoffed at with a
　　smile
Of greedy foretaste, from the secret stand
Of Desolation, aimed: to slow decline
These yield, and these to sudden over-
　　throw:
Their virtue, service, happiness, and state
Expire; and nature's pleasant robe of
　　green,
Humanity's appointed shroud, enwraps
Their monuments and their memory. The
　　vast Frame
Of social nature changes evermore　　1000
Her organs and her members, with decay
Restless, and restless generation, powers
And functions dying and produced at
　　need, —
And by this law the mighty whole subsists:
With an ascent and progress in the main;
Yet, oh ! how disproportioned to the hopes
And expectations of self-flattering minds !

　　The courteous Knight, whose bones are
　　here interred,
Lived in an age conspicuous as our own
For strife and ferment in the minds of
　　men;　　　　　　　　　　　　1010
Whence alteration in the forms of things,
Various and vast. A memorable age !
Which did to him assign a pensive lot —
To linger 'mid the last of those bright
　　clouds
That, on the steady breeze of honour,
　　sailed
In long procession calm and beautiful.
He who had seen his own bright order
　　fade,
And its devotion gradually decline,

(While war, relinquishing the lance and
　　shield,
Her temper changed, and bowed to other
　　laws)　　　　　　　　　　　1020
Had also witnessed, in his morn of life,
That violent commotion, which o'erthrew,
In town and city and sequestered glen,
Altar, and cross, and church of solemn
　　roof,
And old religious house — pile after pile;
And shook their tenants out into the fields,
Like wild beasts without home ! Their hour
　　was come;
But why no softening thought of grati-
　　tude,
No just remembrance, scruple, or wise
　　doubt ?
Benevolence is mild; nor borrows help, 1030
Save at worst need, from bold impetuous
　　force,
Fitliest allied to anger and revenge.
But Human-kind rejoices in the might
Of mutability; and airy hopes,
Dancing around her, hinder and disturb
Those meditations of the soul that feed
The retrospective virtues. Festive songs
Break from the maddened nations at the
　　sight
Of sudden overthrow; and cold neglect
Is the sure consequence of slow decay. 1040

　　Even," said the Wanderer, " as that
　　courteous Knight,
Bound by his vow to labour for redress
Of all who suffer wrong, and to enact
By sword and lance the law of gentleness,
(If I may venture of myself to speak,
Trusting that not incongruously I blend
Low things with lofty) I too shall be
　　doomed
To outlive the kindly use and fair esteem
Of the poor calling which my youth em-
　　braced
With no unworthy prospect. But enough;
— Thoughts crowd upon me — and 't were
　　seemlier now　　　　　　　　1051
To stop, and yield our gracious Teacher
　　thanks
For the pathetic records which his voice
Hath here delivered; words of heartfelt
　　truth,
Tending to patience when affliction strikes;
To hope and love; to confident repose
In God; and reverence for the dust of
　　Man."

BOOK EIGHTH

THE PARSONAGE

ARGUMENT

Pastor's apology and apprehensions that he might have detained his Auditors too long, with the Pastor's invitation to his house — Solitary disinclined to comply — Rallies the Wanderer — And playfully draws a comparison between his itinerant profession and that of the Knight-errant — Which leads to Wanderer's giving an account of changes in the Country from the manufacturing spirit — Favourable effects — The other side of the picture, and chiefly as it has affected the humbler classes — Wanderer asserts the hollowness of all national grandeur if unsupported by moral worth — Physical science unable to support itself — Lamentations over an excess of manufacturing industry among the humbler Classes of Society — Picture of a Child employed in a Cotton-mill — Ignorance and degradation of Children among the agricultural Population reviewed — Conversation broken off by a renewed Invitation from the Pastor — Path leading to his House — Its appearance described — His Daughter — His Wife — His Son (a Boy) enters with his Companion — Their happy appearance — The Wanderer how affected by the sight of them.

THE pensive Sceptic of the lonely vale
To those acknowledgments subscribed his
    own,
With a sedate compliance, which the Priest
Failed not to notice, inly pleased, and
    said: —
" If ye, by whom invited I began
These narratives of calm and humble life,
Be satisfied, 't is well, — the end is gained;
And, in return for sympathy bestowed
And patient listening, thanks accept from
    me.
— Life, death, eternity! momentous themes
Are they — and might demand a seraph's
    tongue,   11
Were they not equal to their own support;
And therefore no incompetence of mine
Could do them wrong. The universal
    forms
Of human nature, in a spot like this,
Present themselves at once to all men's
    view:
Ye wished for act and circumstance, that
    make
The individual known and understood;
And such as my best judgment could se-
    lect

From what the place afforded, have been
    given;   20
Though apprehensions crossed me that my
    zeal
To his might well be likened, who unlocks
A cabinet stored with gems and pictures —
    draws
His treasures forth, soliciting regard
To this, and this, as worthier than the last,
Till the spectator, who awhile was pleased
More than the exhibitor himself, becomes
Weary and faint, and longs to be released.
— But let us hence ! my dwelling is in
    sight,
And there — "
          At this the Solitary shrunk
With backward will; but, wanting not ad-
    dress   31
That inward motion to disguise, he said
To his Compatriot, smiling as he spake;
— " The peaceable remains of this good
    Knight
Would be disturbed, I fear, with wrathful
    scorn,
If consciousness could reach him where he
    lies
That one, albeit of these degenerate times,
Deploring changes past, or dreading change
Foreseen, had dared to couple, even in
    thought,
The fine vocation of the sword and lance   40
With the gross aims and body-bending toil
Of a poor brotherhood who walk the earth
Pitied, and, where they are not known,
    despised.

Yet, by the good Knight's leave, the two
    estates
Are graced with some resemblance. Errant
    those,
Exiles and wanderers — and the like are
    these;
Who, with their burthen, traverse hill and
    dale,
Carrying relief for nature's simple wants.
— What though no higher recompense be
    sought
Than honest maintenance, by irksome toil   50
Full oft procured, yet may they claim re-
    spect,
Among the intelligent, for what this course
Enables them to be and to perform.
Their tardy steps give leisure to observe,
While solitude permits the mind to feel;
Instructs, and prompts her to supply defects

By the division of her inward self
For grateful converse: and to these poor
    men
Nature (I but repeat your favourite boast)
Is bountiful — go wheresoe'er they may; 60
Kind nature's various wealth is all their own.
Versed in the characters of men; and bound,
By ties of daily interest, to maintain
Conciliatory manners and smooth speech;
Such have been, and still are in their degree,
Examples efficacious to refine
Rude intercourse; apt agents to expel,
By importation of unlooked-for arts,
Barbarian torpor, and blind prejudice;
Raising, through just gradation, savage life
To rustic, and the rustic to urbane.   71
— Within their moving magazines is lodged
Power that comes forth to quicken and ex-
    alt
Affections seated in the mother's breast,
And in the lover's fancy; and to feed
The sober sympathies of long-tried friends.
— By these Itinerants, as experienced men,
Counsel is given; contention they appease
With gentle language; in remotest wilds,
Tears wipe away, and pleasant tidings
    bring;   80
Could the proud quest of chivalry do more? "

  "Happy," rejoined the Wanderer, "they
    who gain
A panegyric from your generous tongue !
But, if to these Wayfarers once pertained
Aught of romantic interest, it is gone.
Their purer service, in this realm at least,
Is past for ever. — An inventive Age
Has wrought, if not with speed of magic,
    yet
To most strange issues.   I have lived to
    mark
A new and unforeseen creation rise   90
From out the labours of a peaceful Land
Wielding her potent enginery to frame
And to produce, with appetite as keen
As that of war, which rests not night or day,
Industrious to destroy ! With fruitless
    pains
Might one like me now visit many a tract
Which, in his youth, he trod, and trod again,
A lone pedestrian with a scanty freight,
Wished-for, or welcome, wheresoe'er he
    came —
Among the tenantry of thorpe and vill; 100
Or straggling burgh, of ancient charter
    proud,

And dignified by battlements and towers
Of some stern castle, mouldering on the
    brow
Of a green hill or bank of rugged stream.
The foot-path faintly marked, the horse-
    track wild,
And formidable length of plashy lane,
(Prized avenues ere others had been shaped
Or easier links connecting place with place)
Have vanished — swallowed up by stately
    roads
Easy and bold, that penetrate the gloom 110
Of Britain's farthest glens.   The Earth has
    lent
Her waters, Air her breezes; and the sail
Of traffic glides with ceaseless intercourse,
Glistening along the low and woody dale;
Or, in its progress, on the lofty side,
Of some bare hill, with wonder kenned from
    far.

  Meanwhile, at social Industry's com-
    mand,
How quick, how vast an increase ! From
    the germ
Of some poor hamlet, rapidly produced
Here a huge town, continuous and compact,
Hiding the face of earth for leagues — and
    there,   121
Where not a habitation stood before,
Abodes of men irregularly massed
Like trees in forests, — spread through
    spacious tracts,
O'er which the smoke of unremitting fires
Hangs permanent, and plentiful as wreaths
Of vapour glittering in the morning sun.
And, wheresoe'er the traveller turns his
    steps,
He sees the barren wilderness erased,
Or disappearing; triumph that proclaims 130
How much the mild Directress of the plough
Owes to alliance with these new-born arts !
— Hence is the wide sea peopled, — hence
    the shores
Of Britain are resorted to by ships
Freighted from every climate of the world
With the world's choicest produce.   Hence
    that sum
Of keels that rest within her crowded ports,
Or ride at anchor in her sounds and bays;
That animating spectacle of sails
That, through her inland regions, to and
    fro   140
Pass with the respirations of the tide,
Perpetual, multitudinous !   Finally,

Hence a dread arm of floating power, a voice
Of thunder daunting those who would ap-
        proach
With hostile purposes the blessèd Isle,
Truth's consecrated residence, the seat
Impregnable of Liberty and Peace.

    And yet, O happy Pastor of a flock
Faithfully watched, and, by that loving care
And Heaven's good providence, preserved
        from taint!   150
With you I grieve, when on the darker side
Of this great change I look; and there be-
        hold
Such outrage done to nature as compels
The indignant power to justify herself;
Yea, to avenge her violated rights,
For England's bane. — When soothing dark-
        ness spreads
O'er hill and vale," the Wanderer thus ex-
        pressed
His recollections, " and the punctual stars,
While all things else are gathering to their
        homes,
Advance, and in the firmament of heaven 160
Glitter — but undisturbing, undisturbed;
As if their silent company were charged
With peaceful admonitions for the heart
Of all-beholding Man, earth's thoughtful
        lord;
Then, in full many a region, once like this
The assured domain of calm simplicity
And pensive quiet, an unnatural light
Prepared for never-resting Labour's eyes
Breaks from a many-windowed fabric huge;
And at the appointed hour a bell is heard —
Of harsher import than the curfew-knoll 171
That spake the Norman Conqueror's stern
        behest —
A local summons to unceasing toil!
Disgorged are now the ministers of day;
And, as they issue from the illumined pile,
A fresh band meets them, at the crowded
        door —
And in the courts — and where the rumbling
        stream,
That turns the multitude of dizzy wheels,
Glares, like a troubled spirit, in its bed
Among the rocks below. Men, maidens,
        youths,   180
Mother and little children, boys and girls,
Enter, and each the wonted task resumes
Within this temple, where is offered up
To Gain, the master idol of the realm,
Perpetual sacrifice.   Even thus of old

Our ancestors, within the still domain
Of vast cathedral or conventual church,
Their vigils kept; where tapers day and
        night
On the dim altar burned continually,
In token that the House was evermore   190
Watching to God. Religious men were
        they;
Nor would their reason, tutored to aspire
Above this transitory world, allow
That there should pass a moment of the
        year,
When in their land the Almighty's service
        ceased.

    Triumph who will in these profaner rites
Which we, a generation self-extolled,
As zealously perform! I cannot share
His proud complacency: — yet do I exult,
Casting reserve away, exult to see   200
An intellectual mastery exercised
O'er the blind elements; a purpose given,
A perseverance fed; almost a soul
Imparted — to brute matter. I rejoice,
Measuring the force of those gigantic
        powers
That, by the thinking mind, have been com-
        pelled
To serve the will of feeble-bodied Man.
For with the sense of admiration blends
The animating hope that time may come
When, strengthened, yet not dazzled, by
        the might   210
Of this dominion over nature gained,
Men of all lands shall exercise the same
In due proportion to their country's need;
Learning, though late, that all true glory
        rests,
All praise, all safety, and all happiness,
Upon the moral law. Egyptian Thebes,
Tyre, by the margin of the sounding waves,
Palmyra, central in the desert, fell;
And the Arts died by which they had been
        raised.
— Call Archimedes from his buried tomb
Upon the grave of vanished Syracuse,   221
And feelingly the Sage shall make report
How insecure, how baseless in itself,
Is the Philosophy whose sway depends
On mere material instruments; — how weak
Those arts, and high inventions, if un-
        propped
By virtue. — He, sighing with pensive
        grief,
Amid his calm abstractions, would admit

That not the slender privilege is theirs
To save themselves from blank forgetful-
   ness !"   230

When from the Wanderer's lips these
   words had fallen,
I said, "And, did in truth those vaunted
   Arts
Possess such privilege, how could we escape
Sadness and keen regret, we who revere,
And would preserve as things above all
   price,
The old domestic morals of the land,
Her simple manners, and the stable worth
That dignified and cheered a low estate ?
Oh ! where is now the character of peace,
Sobriety, and order, and chaste love,   240
And honest dealing, and untainted speech,
And pure good-will, and hospitable cheer;
That made the very thought of country-
   life
A thought of refuge, for a mind detained
Reluctantly amid the bustling crowd ?
Where now the beauty of the sabbath kept
With conscientious reverence, as a day
By the almighty Lawgiver pronounced
Holy and blest ? and where the winning
   grace
Of all the lighter ornaments attached   250
To time and season, as the year rolled
   round ?"

"Fled !" was the Wanderer's passionate
   response,
"Fled utterly ! or only to be traced
In a few fortunate retreats like this;
Which I behold with trembling, when I
   think
What lamentable change, a year — a
   month —
May bring; that brook converting as it
   runs
Into an instrument of deadly bane
For those, who, yet untempted to forsake
The simple occupations of their sires,   260
Drink the pure water of its innocent stream
With lip almost as pure. — Domestic bliss
(Or call it comfort, by a humbler name,)
How art thou blighted for the poor Man's
   heart !
Lo ! in such neighbourhood, from morn to
   eve,
The habitations empty ! or perchance
The Mother left alone, — no helping hand
To rock the cradle of her peevish babe;

No daughters round her, busy at the
   wheel,
Or in dispatch of each day's little growth
Of household occupation; no nice arts   271
Of needle-work; no bustle at the fire,
Where once the dinner was prepared with
   pride;
Nothing to speed the day, or cheer the
   mind;
Nothing to praise, to teach, or to com-
   mand !

The Father, if perchance he still retain
His old employments, goes to field or
   wood,
No longer led or followed by the Sons;
Idlers perchance they were, — but in *his*
   sight;
Breathing fresh air, and treading the green
   earth: 280
'Till their short holiday of childhood
   ceased,
Ne'er to return ! That birthright now is
   lost.
Economists will tell you that the State
Thrives by the forfeiture — unfeeling
   thought,
And false as monstrous ! Can the mother
   thrive
By the destruction of her innocent sons
In whom a premature necessity
Blocks out the forms of nature, precon-
   sumes
The reason, famishes the heart, shuts up
The infant Being in itself, and makes   290
Its very spring a season of decay !
The lot is wretched, the condition sad,
Whether a pining discontent survive,
And thirst for change; or habit hath sub-
   dued
The soul deprest, dejected — even to love
Of her close tasks, and long captivity.

Oh, banish far such wisdom as condemns
A native Briton to these inward chains,
Fixed in his soul, so early and so deep;
Without his own consent, or knowledge,
   fixed !   300
He is a slave to whom release comes not,
And cannot come. The boy, where'er he
   turns,
Is still a prisoner; when the wind is up
Among the clouds, and roars through the
   ancient woods;
Or when the sun is shining in the east,

Quiet and calm. Behold him — in the school
Of his attainments ? no; but with the air
Fanning his temples under heaven's blue arch.
His raiment, whitened o'er with cotton-flakes
Or locks of wool, announces whence he comes.   310
Creeping his gait and cowering, his lip pale,
His respiration quick and audible;
And scarcely could you fancy that a gleam
Could break from out those languid eyes, or a blush
Mantle upon his cheek. Is this the form,
Is that the countenance, and such the port,
Of no mean Being ? One who should be clothed
With dignity befitting his proud hope;
Who, in his very childhood, should appear
Sublime from present purity and joy !   320
The limbs increase; but liberty of mind
Is gone for ever; and this organic frame,
So joyful in its motions, is become
Dull, to the joy of her own motions dead;
And even the touch, so exquisitely poured
Through the whole body, with a languid will
Performs its functions; rarely competent
To impress a vivid feeling on·the mind
Of what there is delightful in the breeze,
The gentle visitations of the sun,   330
Or lapse of liquid element — by hand,
Or foot, or lip, in summer's warmth — perceived.
— Can hope look forward to a manhood raised
On such foundations ? "
          " Hope is none for him ! "
The pale Recluse indignantly exclaimed,
" And tens of thousands suffer wrong as deep.
Yet be it asked, in justice to our age,
If there were not, before those arts appeared,
These structures rose, commingling old and young,
And unripe sex with sex, for mutual taint;
If there were not, then, in our far-famed Isle,   341
Multitudes, who from infancy had breathed
Air unimprisoned, and had lived at large;
Yet walked beneath the sun, in human shape,

As abject, as degraded ? At this day,
Who shall enumerate the crazy huts
And tottering hovels, whence do issue forth
A ragged Offspring, with their upright hair
Crowned like the image of fantastic Fear;
Or wearing, (shall we say ?) in that white growth   350
An ill-adjusted turban, for defence
Or fierceness, wreathed around their sun-burnt brows,
By savage Nature ? Shrivelled are their lips,
Naked, and coloured like the soil, the feet
On which they stand; as if thereby they drew
Some nourishment, as trees do by their roots,
From earth, the common mother of us all.
Figure and mien, complexion and attire,
Are leagued to strike dismay; but out-stretched hand
And whining voice denote them supplicants
For the least boon that pity can bestow.   361
Such on the breast of darksome heaths are found;
And with their parents occupy the skirts
Of furze-clad commons; such are born and reared
At the mine's mouth under impending rocks;
Or dwell in chambers of some natural cave;
Or where their ancestors erected huts,
For the convenience of unlawful gain,
In forest purlieus; and the like are bred,
All England through, where nooks and slips of ground   370
Purloined, in times less jealous than our own,
From the green margin of the public way,
A residence afford them, 'mid the bloom
And gaiety of cultivated fields.
Such (we will hope the lowest in the scale)
Do I remember oft-times to have seen
'Mid Buxton's dreary heights. In earnest watch,
Till the swift vehicle approach, they stand;
Then, following closely with the cloud of dust,
An uncouth feat exhibit, and are gone   380
Heels over head, like tumblers on a stage.
— Up from the ground they snatch the copper coin,
And, on the freight of merry passengers
Fixing a steady eye, maintain their speed;
And spin — and pant — and overhead again,

Wild pursuivants ! until their breath is lost,
Or bounty tires — and every face, that
   smiled
Encouragement, hath ceased to look that
   way.
— But, like the vagrants of the gipsy tribe,
These, bred to little pleasure in them-
   selves,   390
Are profitless to others.

            Turn we then
To Britons born and bred within the pale
Of civil polity, and early trained
To earn, by wholesome labour in the field,
The bread they eat. A sample should I
   give
Of what this stock hath long produced to
   enrich
The tender age of life, ye would exclaim,
'Is this the whistling plough-boy whose
   shrill notes
Impart new gladness to the morning air !'
Forgive me if I venture to suspect   400
That many, sweet to hear of in soft verse,
Are of no finer frame. Stiff are his joints;
Beneath a cumbrous frock, that to the knees
Invests the thriving churl, his legs appear,
Fellows to those that lustily upheld
The wooden stools for everlasting use,
Whereon our fathers sate. And mark his
   brow
Under whose shaggy canopy are set
Two eyes — not dim, but of a healthy
   stare —
Wide, sluggish, blank, and ignorant, and
   strange —   410
Proclaiming boldly that they never drew
A look or motion of intelligence
From infant-conning of the Christ-cross-
   row,
Or puzzling through a primer, line by line,
Till perfect mastery crown the pains at
   last.
— What kindly warmth from touch of
   fostering hand,
What penetrating power of sun or breeze,
Shall e'er dissolve the crust wherein his
   soul
Sleeps, like a caterpillar sheathed in ice ?
This torpor is no pitiable work   420
Of modern ingenuity; no town
Nor crowded city can be taxed with aught
Of sottish vice or desperate breach of
   law,
To which (and who can tell where or how
   soon ?)

He may be roused. This Boy the fields
   produce:
His spade and hoe, mattock and glittering
   scythe,
The carter's whip that on his shoulder rests
In air high-towering with a boorish pomp,
The sceptre of his sway; his country's
   name,
Her equal rights, her churches and her
   schools —   430
What have they done for him ? And, let
   me ask,
For tens of thousands uninformed as he ?
In brief, what liberty of *mind* is here ? "

   This ardent sally pleased the mild good
   Man,
To whom the appeal couched in its closing
   words
Was pointedly addressed; and to the
   thoughts
That, in assent or opposition, rose
Within his mind, he seemed prepared to
   give
Prompt utterance; but the Vicar interposed
With invitation urgently renewed.   440
— We followed, taking as he led, a path
Along a hedge of hollies dark and tall,
Whose flexile boughs low bending with a
   weight
Of leafy spray, concealed the stems and
   roots
That gave them nourishment. When frosty
   winds
Howl from the north, what kindly warmth,
   methought,
Is here — how grateful this impervious
   screen !
— Not shaped by simple wearing of the
   foot
On rural business passing to and fro
Was the commodious walk: a careful
   hand   450
Had marked the line, and strewn its sur-
   face o'er
With pure cerulean gravel, from the heights
Fetched by a neighbouring brook. — Across
   the vale
The stately fence accompanied our steps;
And thus the pathway, by perennial green
Guarded and graced, seemed fashioned to
   unite,
As by a beautiful yet solemn chain,
The Pastor's mansion with the house of
   prayer.

Like image of solemnity, conjoined
With feminine allurement soft and fair, 460
The mansion's self displayed; — a reverend
    pile
With bold projections and recesses deep;
Shadowy, yet gay and lightsome as it stood
Fronting the noontide sun. We paused to
    admire
The pillared porch, elaborately embossed;
The low wide windows with their mullions
    old;
The cornice, richly fretted, of grey stone;
And that smooth slope from which the
    dwelling rose,
By beds and banks Arcadian of gay flowers
And flowering shrubs, protected and
    adorned: 470
Profusion bright ! and every flower assum-
    ing
A more than natural vividness of hue,
From unaffected contrast with the gloom
Of sober cypress, and the darker foil
Of yew, in which survived some traces,
    here
Not unbecoming, of grotesque device
And uncouth fancy. From behind the roof
Rose the slim ash and massy sycamore,
Blending their diverse foliage with the
    green
Of ivy, flourishing and thick, that clasped
The huge round chimneys, harbour of
    delight   481
For wren and redbreast, — where they sit
    and sing
Their slender ditties when the trees are bare.
Nor must I leave untouched (the picture
    else
Were incomplete) a relique of old times
Happily spared, a little Gothic niche
Of nicest workmanship; that once had held
The sculptured image of some patron-saint,
Or of the blessed Virgin, looking down
On all who entered those religious doors. 490

But lo ! where from the rocky garden-
    mount
Crowned by its antique summer-house —
    descends,
Light as the silver fawn, a radiant Girl;
For she hath recognised her honoured
    friend,
The Wanderer ever welcome ! A prompt
    kiss
The gladsome Child bestows at his request;
And, up the flowery lawn as we advance,

Hangs on the old Man with a happy look,
And with a pretty restless hand of love.
— We enter — by the Lady of the place 500
Cordially greeted. Graceful was her port:
A lofty stature undepressed by time,
Whose visitation had not wholly spared
The finer lineaments of form and face;
To that complexion brought which prudence
    trusts in
And wisdom loves. — But when a stately
    ship
Sails in smooth weather by the placid coast
On homeward voyage, — what if wind and
    wave,
And hardship undergone in various climes,
Have caused her to abate the virgin pride,
And that full trim of inexperienced hope 511
With which she left her haven — not for
    this,
Should the sun strike her, and the impartial
    breeze
Play on her streamers, fails she to assume
Brightness and touching beauty of her own,
That charm all eyes. So bright, so fair,
    appeared
This goodly Matron, shining in the beams
Of unexpected pleasure. — Soon the board
Was spread, and we partook a plain repast.

Here, resting in cool shelter, we be-
    guiled   520
The mid-day hours with desultory talk;
From trivial themes to general argument
Passing, as accident or fancy led,
Or courtesy prescribed. While question
    rose
And answer flowed, the fetters of reserve
Dropping from every mind, the Solitary
Resumed the manners of his happier days;
And in the various conversation bore
A willing, nay, at times, a forward part;
Yet with the grace of one who in the
    world   530
Had learned the art of pleasing, and had
    now
Occasion given him to display his skill,
Upon the stedfast 'vantage-ground of truth.
He gazed, with admiration unsuppressed,
Upon the landscape of the sun-bright vale,
Seen, from the shady room in which we
    sate,
In softened perspective; and more than
    once
Praised the consummate harmony serene
Of gravity and elegance, diffused

Around the mansion and its whole do-
　　main;　　　　　　　　　　　　540
Not, doubtless, without help of female taste
And female care.— "A blessed lot is yours!"
The words escaped his lip, with a tender
　　sigh
Breathed over them: but suddenly the door
Flew open, and a pair of lusty Boys
Appeared, confusion checking their delight.
— Not brothers they in feature or attire,
But fond companions, so I guessed, in field,
And by the river's margin — whence they
　　come,
Keen anglers with unusual spoil elated. 550
One bears a willow-pannier on his back,
The boy of plainer garb, whose blush sur-
　　vives
More deeply tinged.　Twin might the other
　　be
To that fair girl who from the garden-mount
Bounded: — triumphant entry this for him!
Between his hands he holds a smooth blue
　　stone,
On whose capacious surface see outspread
Large store of gleaming crimson-spotted
　　trouts;
Ranged side by side, and lessening by
　　degrees
Up to the dwarf that tops the pinnacle. 560
Upon the board he lays the sky-blue stone
With its rich freight; their number he pro-
　　claims;
Tells from what pool the noblest had been
　　dragged;
And where the very monarch of the brook,
After long struggle, had escaped at last —
Stealing alternately at them and us
(As doth his comrade too) a look of pride:
And, verily, the silent creatures made
A splendid sight, together thus exposed;
Dead — but not sullied or deformed by
　　death,　　　　　　　　　　　　570
That seemed to pity what he could not spare.

But oh, the animation in the mien
Of those two boys! yea in the very words
With which the young narrator was in-
　　spired,
When, as our questions led, he told at large
Of that day's prowess!　Him might I com-
　　pare,
His looks, tones, gestures, eager eloquence,
To a bold brook that splits for better speed,
And at the self-same moment, works its way
Through many channels, ever and anon 580

Parted and re-united: his compeer
To the still lake, whose stillness is to sight
As beautiful — as grateful to the mind.
— But to what object shall the lovely Girl
Be likened?　She whose countenance and
　　air
Unite the graceful qualities of both,
Even as she shares the pride and joy of
　　both.

My grey-haired Friend was moved; his
　　vivid eye
Glistened with tenderness; his mind, I
　　knew,
Was full; and had, I doubted not, re-
　　turned,　　　　　　　　　　　　590
Upon this impulse, to the theme — erewhile
Abruptly broken off.　The ruddy boys
Withdrew, on summons to their well-earned
　　meal;
And He — to whom all tongues resigned
　　their rights
With willingness, to whom the general ear
Listened with readier patience than to
　　strain
Of music, lute or harp, a long delight
That ceased not when his voice had ceased
　　— as One
Who from truth's central point serenely
　　views
The compass of his argument — began 600
Mildly, and with a clear and steady tone.

BOOK NINTH

DISCOURSE OF THE WANDERER, AND AN EVENING VISIT TO THE LAKE

ARGUMENT

Wanderer asserts that an active principle
pervades the Universe, its noblest seat the
human soul — How lively this principle is in
Childhood — Hence the delight in old Age of
looking back upon Childhood — The dignity,
powers, and privileges of Age asserted — These
not to be looked for generally but under a just
government — Right of a human Creature to
be exempt from being considered as a mere
Instrument — The condition of multitudes de-
plored — Former conversation recurred to, and
the Wanderer's opinions set in a clearer light
— Truth placed within reach of the humblest
— Equality — Happy state of the two Boys
again adverted to — Earnest wish expressed for
a System of National Education established

universally by Government — Glorious effects of this foretold — Walk to the Lake — Grand spectacle from the side of a hill — Address of Priest to the Supreme Being — In the course of which he contrasts with ancient Barbarism the present appearance of the scene before him — The change ascribed to Christianity — Apostrophe to his flock, living and dead — Gratitude to the Almighty — Return over the Lake — Parting with the Solitary — Under what circumstances.

"To every Form of being is assigned,"
Thus calmly spake the venerable Sage,
" An *active* Principle: — howe'er removed
From sense and observation, it subsists
In all things, in all natures; in the stars
Of azure heaven, the unenduring clouds,
In flower and tree, in every pebbly stone
That paves the brooks, the stationary rocks,
The moving waters, and the invisible air.
Whate'er exists hath properties that spread
Beyond itself, communicating good,   11
A simple blessing, or with evil mixed;
Spirit that knows no insulated spot,
No chasm, no solitude; from link to link
It circulates, the Soul of all the worlds.
This is the freedom of the universe;
Unfolded still the more, more visible,
The more we know; and yet is reverenced least,
And least respected in the human Mind,
Its most apparent home. The food of hope
Is meditated action; robbed of this   21
Her sole support, she languishes and dies.
We perish also; for we live by hope
And by desire; we see by the glad light
And breathe the sweet air of futurity;
And so we live, or else we have no life.
To-morrow — nay perchance this very hour
(For every moment hath its own to-mor-
          row !)
Those blooming Boys, whose hearts are almost sick
With present triumph, will be sure to find   30
A field before them freshened with the dew
Of other expectations; — in which course
Their happy year spins round. The youth obeys
A like glad impulse; and so moves the man
'Mid all his apprehensions, cares, and fears, —
Or so he ought to move. Ah ! why in age
Do we revert so fondly to the walks
Of childhood — but that there the Soul dis-
          cerns

The dear memorial footsteps unimpaired
Of her own native vigour; thence can hear
Reverberations; and a choral song,   41
Commingling with the incense that ascends,
Undaunted,   toward   the   imperishable
          heavens,
From her own lonely altar ?
                          Do not think
That good and wise ever will be allowed,
Though strength decay, to breathe in such estate
As shall divide them wholly from the stir
Of hopeful nature. Rightly it is said
That Man descends into the VALE of years;
Yet have I thought that we might also speak,   50
And not presumptuously, I trust, of Age,
As of a final EMINENCE; though bare
In aspect and forbidding, yet a point
On which 't is not impossible to sit
In awful sovereignty; a place of power,
A throne, that may be likened unto his,
Who, in some placid day of summer, looks
Down from a mountain-top, — say one of those
High peaks, that bound the vale where now we are.
Faint, and diminished to the gazing eye,   60
Forest and field, and hill and dale appear,
With all the shapes over their surface spread:
But, while the gross and visible frame of things
Relinquishes its hold upon the sense,
Yea almost on the Mind herself, and seems
All unsubstantialized, — how   loud   the voice
Of waters, with invigorated peal
From the full river in the vale below,
Ascending ! For on that superior height
Who sits, is disencumbered from the press
Of near obstructions, and is privileged   71
To breathe in solitude, above the host
Of ever-humming insects, 'mid thin air
That suits not them. The murmur of the leaves
Many and idle, visits not his ear:
This he is freed from, and from thousand notes
(Not less unceasing, not less vain than these,)
By which the finer passages of sense
Are occupied; and the Soul, that would in-
          cline
To listen, is prevented or deterred.   80

And may it not be hoped, that, placed by
    age
In like removal, tranquil though severe,
We are not so removed for utter loss;
But for some favour, suited to our need ?
What more than that the severing should
    confer
Fresh power to commune with the invisible
    world,
And hear the mighty stream of tendency
Uttering, for elevation of our thought,
A clear sonorous voice, inaudible
To the vast multitude; whose doom it is 90
To run the giddy round of vain delight,
Or fret and labour on the Plain below.

But, if to such sublime ascent the hopes
Of Man may rise, as to a welcome close
And termination of his mortal course;
Them only can such hope inspire whose
    minds
Have not been starved by absolute neglect;
Nor bodies crushed by unremitting toil;
To whom kind Nature, therefore, may af-
    ford
Proof of the sacred love she bears for all;
Whose birthright Reason, therefore, may
    ensure.   101
For me, consulting what I feel within
In times when most existence with herself
Is satisfied, I cannot but believe,
That, far as kindly Nature hath free
    scope
And Reason's sway predominates; even so
    far,
Country, society, and time itself,
That saps the individual's bodily frame,
And lays the generations low in dust,
Do, by the almighty Ruler's grace, par-
    take   110
Of one maternal spirit, bringing forth
And cherishing with ever-constant love,
That tires not, nor betrays. Our life is
    turned
Out of her course, wherever man is made
An offering, or a sacrifice, a tool
Or implement, a passive thing employed
As a brute mean, without acknowledgment
Of common right or interest in the end;
Used or abused, as selfishness may prompt,
Say, what can follow for a rational soul 120
Perverted thus, but weakness in all good,
And strength in evil ? Hence an after-call
For chastisement, and custody, and bonds,
And oft-times Death, avenger of the past,

And the sole guardian in whose hands we
    dare
Entrust the future. — Not for these sad is-
    sues
Was Man created; but to obey the law
Of life, and hope, and action. And 't is
    known
That when we stand upon our native soil,
Unelbowed by such objects as oppress 130
Our active powers, those powers themselves
    become
Strong to subvert our noxious qualities:
They sweep distemper from the busy day,
And make the chalice of the big round
    year
Run o'er with gladness; whence the Being
    moves
In beauty through the world; and all who
    see
Bless him, rejoicing in his neighbourhood."

" Then," said the Solitary, " by what
    force
Of language shall a feeling heart express
Her sorrow for that multitude in whom 140
We look for health from seeds that have
    been sown
In sickness, and for increase in a power
That works but by extinction ? On them-
    selves
They cannot lean, nor turn to their own
    hearts
To know what they must do; their wisdom
    is
To look into the eyes of others, thence
To be instructed what they must avoid:
Or rather, let us say, how least observed,
How with most quiet and most silent
    death,
With the least taint and injury to the air 150
The oppressor breathes, their human form
    divine,
And their immortal soul, may waste away."

The Sage rejoined, " I thank you — you
    have spared
My voice the utterance of a keen regret,
A wide compassion which with you I share.
When, heretofore, I placed before your
    sight
A Little-one, subjected to the arts
Of modern ingenuity, and made
The senseless member of a vast machine,
Serving as doth a spindle or a wheel; 160
Think not, that, pitying him, I could forget

The rustic Boy, who walks the fields, un-
taught;
The slave of ignorance, and oft of want,
And miserable hunger.   Much, too much,
Of this unhappy lot, in early youth
We both have witnessed, lot which I my-
self
Shared, though in mild and merciful de-
gree:
Yet was the mind to hindrances exposed,
Through which I struggled, not without
distress
And sometimes injury, like a lamb en-
thralled   170
'Mid thorns and brambles; or a bird that
breaks
Through a strong net, and mounts upon the
wind,
Though with her plumes impaired.   If
they, whose souls
Should open while they range the richer
fields
Of merry England, are obstructed less
By indigence, their ignorance is not less,
Nor less to be deplored.   For who can
doubt
That tens of thousands at this day exist
Such as the boy you painted, lineal heirs
Of those who once were vassals of her soil,
Following its fortunes like the beasts or
trees   181
Which it sustained.   But no one takes de-
light
In this oppression; none are proud of it;
It bears no sounding name, nor ever bore;
A standing grievance, an indigenous vice
Of every country under heaven.   My
thoughts
Were turned to evils that are new and
chosen,
A bondage lurking under shape of good, —
Arts, in themselves beneficent and kind,
But all too fondly followed and too far; —
To victims, which the merciful can see   191
Nor think that they are victims — turned
to wrongs,
By women, who have children of their
own,
Beheld without compassion, yea with
praise !
I spake of mischief by the wise diffused
With gladness, thinking that the more it
spreads
The healthier, the securer, we become;
Delusion which a moment may destroy !

Lastly, I mourned for those whom I had
seen
Corrupted and cast down, on favoured
ground,   200
Where circumstance and nature had com-
bined
To shelter innocence, and cherish love;
Who, but for this intrusion, would have
lived,
Possessed of health, and strength, and
peace of mind;
Thus would have lived, or never have been
born.

Alas ! what differs more than man from
man !
And whence that difference ? whence but
from himself ?
For see the universal Race endowed
With the same upright form ! — The sun is
fixed,
And the infinite magnificence of heaven   210
Fixed, within reach of every human eye;
The sleepless ocean murmurs for all ears;
The vernal field infuses fresh delight
Into all hearts.   Throughout the world of
sense,
Even as an object is sublime or fair,
That object is laid open to the view
Without reserve or veil; and as a power
Is salutary, or an influence sweet,
Are each and all enabled to perceive
That power, that influence, by impartial
law.   220
Gifts nobler are vouchsafed alike to all;
Reason, and, with that reason, smiles and
tears;
Imagination, freedom in the will;
Conscience to guide and check; and death
to be
Foretasted, immortality conceived
By all, — a blissful immortality,
To them whose holiness on earth shall make
The Spirit capable of heaven, assured.
Strange, then, nor less than monstrous,
might be deemed
The failure, if the Almighty, to this point 230
Liberal and undistinguishing, should hide
The excellence of moral qualities
From common understanding; leaving
truth
And virtue, difficult, abstruse, and dark;
Hard to be won, and only by a few;
Strange, should He deal herein with nice
respects,

And frustrate all the rest ! Believe it not:
The primal duties shine aloft — like stars;
The charities that soothe, and heal, and
bless,
Are scattered at the feet of Man — like
flowers. 240
The generous inclination, the just rule,
Kind wishes, and good actions, and pure
thoughts —
No mystery is here ! Here is no boon
For high — yet not for low; for proudly
graced —
Yet not for meek of heart. The smoke
ascends
To heaven as lightly from the cottage hearth
As from the haughtiest palace. He, whose
soul
Ponders this true equality, may walk
The fields of earth with gratitude and hope;
Yet, in that meditation, will he find 250
Motive to sadder grief, as we have found;
Lamenting ancient virtues overthrown,
And for the injustice grieving, that hath
made
So wide a difference between man and man.

Then let us rather fix our gladdened
thoughts
Upon the brighter scene. How blest that
pair
Of blooming Boys (whom we beheld even
now)
Blest in their several and their common
lot !
A few short hours of each returning day
The thriving prisoners of their village
school: 260
And thence let loose, to seek their pleasant
homes
Or range the grassy lawn in vacancy:
To breathe and to be happy, run and shout,
Idle, — but no delay, no harm, no loss;
For every genial power of heaven and
earth,
Through all the seasons of the changeful
year,
Obsequiously doth take upon herself
To labour for them; bringing each in turn
The tribute of enjoyment, knowledge,
health,
Beauty, or strength ! Such privilege is
theirs, 270
Granted alike in the outset of their course
To both; and, if that partnership must
cease,

I grieve not," to the Pastor here he turned,
" Much as I glory in that child of yours,
Repine not for his cottage-comrade, whom
Belike no higher destiny awaits
Than the old hereditary wish fulfilled;
The wish for liberty to live — content
With what Heaven grants, and die — in
peace of mind,
Within the bosom of his native vale. 280
At least, whatever fate the noon of life
Reserves for either, sure it is that both
Have been permitted to enjoy the dawn;
Whether regarded as a jocund time,
That in itself may terminate, or lead
In course of nature to a sober eve.
Both have been fairly dealt with; looking
back
They will allow that justice has in them
Been shown, alike to body and to mind."

He paused, as if revolving in his soul 290
Some weighty matter; then, with fervent
voice
And an impassioned majesty, exclaimed —

" O for the coming of that glorious time
When, prizing knowledge as her noblest
wealth
And best protection, this imperial Realm,
While she exacts allegiance, shall admit
An obligation, on her part, to *teach*
Them who are born to serve her and obey;
Binding herself by statute to secure
For all the children whom her soil maintains
The rudiments of letters, and inform 301
The mind with moral and religious truth,
Both understood and practised, — so that
none,
However destitute, be left to droop
By timely culture unsustained; or run
Into a wild disorder; or be forced
To drudge through a weary life without the
help
Of intellectual implements and tools;
A savage horde among the civilised,
A servile band among the lordly free ! 310
This sacred right, the lisping babe pro-
claims
To be inherent in him, by Heaven's will,
For the protection of his innocence;
And the rude boy — who, having overpast
The sinless age, by conscience is enrolled,
Yet mutinously knits his angry brow,
And lifts his wilful hand on mischief bent,
Or turns the godlike faculty of speech

To impious use — by process indirect
Declares his due, while he makes known
   his need.   320
— This sacred right is fruitlessly an-
   nounced,
This universal plea in vain addressed,
To eyes and ears of parents who themselves
Did, in the time of their necessity,
Urge it in vain; and, therefore, like a
   prayer
That from the humblest floor ascends to
   heaven,
It mounts to reach the State's parental ear ;
Who, if indeed she own a mother's heart,
And be not most unfeelingly devoid
Of gratitude to Providence, will grant   330
The unquestionable good — which, England,
   safe
From interference of external force,
May grant at leisure; without risk incurred
That what in wisdom for herself she doth,
Others shall e'er be able to undo.

Look ! and behold, from Calpe's sun-
   burnt cliffs
To the flat margin of the Baltic sea,
Long-reverenced titles cast away as weeds;
Laws overturned; and territory split,
Like fields of ice rent by the polar wind,   340
And forced to join in less obnoxious shapes
Which, ere they gain consistence, by a gust
Of the same breath are shattered and de-
   stroyed,
Meantime the sovereignty of these fair
   Isles
Remains entire and indivisible:
And, if that ignorance were removed, which
   breeds
Within the compass of their several shores
Dark discontent, or loud commotion, each
Might still preserve the beautiful repose
Of heavenly bodies shining in their spheres.
— The discipline of slavery is unknown   351
Among us, — hence the more do we require
The discipline of virtue; order else
Cannot subsist, nor confidence, nor peace.
Thus, duties rising out of good possest,
And prudent caution needful to avert
Impending evil, equally require
That the whole people should be taught and
   trained.
So shall licentiousness and black resolve
Be rooted out, and virtuous habits take   360
Their place; and genuine piety descend,
Like an inheritance, from age to age.

With such foundations laid, avaunt the
   fear
Of numbers crowded on their native soil,
To the prevention of all healthful growth
Through mutual injury ! Rather in the law
Of increase and the mandate from above
Rejoice ! — and ye have special cause for
   joy.
— For, as the element of air affords
An easy passage to the industrious bees   370
Fraught with their burthens; and a way as
   smooth
For those ordained to take their sounding
   flight
From the thronged hive, and settle where
   they list
In fresh abodes — their labour to renew;
So the wide waters, open to the power,
The will, the instincts, and appointed needs
Of Britain, do invite her to cast off
Her swarms, and in succession send them
   forth;
Bound to establish new communities
On every shore whose aspect favours hope
Or bold adventure; promising to skill   381
And perseverance their deserved reward.

Yes," he continued, kindling as he
   spake,
" Change wide, and deep, and silently per-
   formed,
This Land shall witness; and as days roll
   on,
Earth's universal frame shall feel the effect;
Even till the smallest habitable rock,
Beaten by lonely billows, hear the songs
Of humanised society; and bloom
With civil arts, that shall breathe forth
   their fragrance,   390
A grateful tribute to all-ruling Heaven.
From culture, unexclusively bestowed
On Albion's noble Race in freedom born,
Expect these mighty issues: from the pains
And faithful care of unambitious schools
Instructing simple childhood's ready ear:
Thence look for these magnificent results !
— Vast the circumference of hope — and
   ye
Are at its centre, British Lawgivers;
Ah ! sleep not there in shame ! Shall
   Wisdom's voice   400
From out the bosom of these troubled times
Repeat the dictates of her calmer mind,
And shall the venerable halls ye fill
Refuse to echo the sublime decree ?

Trust not to partial care a general good;
Transfer not to futurity a work
Of urgent need. — Your Country must complete
　　plete
Her glorious destiny. Begin even now,
Now, when oppression, like the Egyptian
　　plague
Of darkness, stretched o'er guilty Europe,
　　makes　　　　　　　　　　　　　410
The brightness more conspicuous that invests
　　vests
The happy Island where ye think and act;
Now, when destruction is a prime pursuit,
Show to the wretched nations for what
　　end
The powers of civil polity were given."

　　Abruptly here, but with a graceful air,
The Sage broke off. No sooner had he
　　ceased
Than, looking forth, the gentle Lady said,
" Behold the shades of afternoon have fallen
Upon this flowery slope; and see — beyond —
　　yond —　　　　　　　　　　　　420
The silvery lake is streaked with placid
　　blue;
As if preparing for the peace of evening.
How temptingly the landscape shines !
　　The air
Breathes invitation; easy is the walk
To the lake's margin, where a boat lies
　　moored
Under a sheltering tree." — Upon this hint
We rose together; all were pleased; but
　　most
The beauteous girl, whose cheek was flushed
　　with joy.
Light as a sunbeam glides along the hills
She vanished — eager to impart the scheme
To her loved brother and his shy compeer.
— Now was there bustle in the Vicar's
　　house　　　　　　　　　　　　432
And earnest preparation. — Forth we went,
And down the vale along the streamlet's
　　edge
Pursued our way, a broken company,
Mute or conversing, single or in pairs.
Thus having reached a bridge, that overarched
　　arched
The hasty rivulet where it lay becalmed
In a deep pool, by happy chance we saw
A twofold image; on a grassy bank　　440
A snow-white ram, and in the crystal flood
Another and the same ! Most beautiful,
On the green turf, with his imperial front

Shaggy and bold, and wreathèd horns superb,
　　perb,
The breathing creature stood; as beautiful,
Beneath him, showed his shadowy counterpart.
　　part.
Each had his glowing mountains, each his
　　sky,
And each seemed centre of his own fair
　　world:
Antipodes unconscious of each other,　　449
Yet, in partition, with their several spheres,
Blended in perfect stillness, to our sight !

　　" Ah ! what a pity were it to disperse,
Or to disturb, so fair a spectacle,
And yet a breath can do it !"
　　　　　　　　　　　　These few words
The Lady whispered, while we stood and
　　gazed
Gathered together, all in still delight,
Not without awe. Thence passing on, she
　　said
In like low voice to my particular ear,
" I love to hear that eloquent old Man
Pour forth his meditations, and descant　460
On human life from infancy to age.
How pure his spirit ! in what vivid hues
His mind gives back the various forms of
　　things,
Caught in their fairest, happiest, attitude !
While he is speaking, I have power to see
Even as he sees; but when his voice hath
　　ceased,
Then, with a sigh, sometimes I feel, as now,
That combinations so serene and bright
Cannot be lasting in a world like ours,
Whose highest beauty, beautiful as it is,　470
Like that reflected in yon quiet pool,
Seems but a fleeting sunbeam's gift, whose
　　peace
The sufferance only of a breath of air !"

　　More had she said — but sportive shouts
　　were heard
Sent from the jocund hearts of those two
　　Boys,
Who, bearing each a basket on his arm,
Down the green field came tripping after
　　us.
With caution we embarked; and now the
　　pair
For prouder service were addrest; but each,
Wishful to leave an opening for my choice,
Dropped the light oar his eager hand had
　　seized.　　　　　　　　　　　481

Thanks given for that becoming courtesy,
Their place I took — and for a grateful
   office
Pregnant with recollections of the time
When, on thy bosom, spacious Winder-
   mere !
A Youth, I practised this delightful art;
Tossed on the waves alone, or 'mid a crew
Of joyous comrades. Soon as the reedy
   marge
Was cleared, I dipped, with arms accord-
   ant, oars
Free from obstruction; and the boat ad-
   vanced   490
Through crystal water, smoothly as a hawk,
That, disentangled from the shady boughs
Of some thick wood, her place of covert,
   cleaves
With correspondent wings the abyss of air.
— " Observe," the Vicar said, " yon rocky
   isle
With birch-trees fringed; my hand shall
   guide the helm,
While thitherward we shape our course; or
   while
We seek that other, on the western shore;
Where the bare columns of those lofty firs,
Supporting gracefully a massy dome   500
Of sombre foliage, seem to imitate
A Grecian temple rising from the Deep."

   " Turn where we may," said I, " we can-
   not err
In this delicious region."— Cultured slopes,
Wild tracts of forest-ground, and scattered
   groves,
And mountains bare, or clothed with an-
   cient woods,
Surrounded us; and, as we held our way
Along the level of the glassy flood,
They ceased not to surround us; change of
   place
From kindred features diversely combined,
Producing change of beauty ever new.   511
— Ah ! that such beauty, varying in the
   light
Of living nature, cannot be portrayed
By words, nor by the pencil's silent skill;
But is the property of him alone
Who hath beheld it, noted it with care,
And in his mind recorded it with love !
Suffice it, therefore, if the rural Muse
Vouchsafe sweet influence, while her Poet
   speaks
Of trivial occupations well devised,   520

And unsought pleasures springing up by
   chance;
As if some friendly Genius had ordained
That, as the day thus far had been enriched
By acquisition of sincere delight,
The same should be continued to its close.

   One spirit animating old and young,
A gipsy-fire we kindled on the shore
Of the fair Isle with birch-trees fringed —
   and there,
Merrily seated in a ring, partook
A choice repast — served by our young
   companions   530
With rival earnestness and kindred glee.
Launched from our hands the smooth stone
   skimmed the lake;
With shouts we raised the echoes: — stiller
   sounds
The lovely Girl supplied — a simple song,
Whose low tones reached not to the distant
   rocks
To be repeated thence, but gently sank
Into our hearts; and charmed the peaceful
   flood.
Rapaciously we gathered flowery spoils
From land and water; lilies of each hue —
Golden and white, that float upon the
   waves,   540
And court the wind; and leaves of that shy
   plant,
(Her flowers were shed) the lily of the
   vale,
That loves the ground, and from the sun
   withholds
Her pensive beauty; from the breeze her
   sweets.

   Such product, and such pastime, did the
   place
And season yield; but, as we re-embarked,
Leaving, in quest of other scenes, the shore
Of that wild spot, the Solitary said
In a low voice, yet careless who might hear,
" The fire, that burned so brightly to our
   wish,   550
Where is it now ? — Deserted on the
   beach —
Dying, or dead ! Nor shall the fanning
   breeze
Revive its ashes. What care we for this,
Whose ends are gained ? Behold an em-
   blem here
Of one day's pleasure, and all mortal joys !
And, in this unpremeditated slight

Of that which is no longer needed, see
The common course of human gratitude !"

This plaintive note disturbed not the re-
    pose
Of the still evening. Right across the
    lake   560
Our pinnace moves; then, coasting creek
    and bay,
Glades we behold, and into thickets peep,
Where couch the spotted deer; or raised
    our eyes
To shaggy steeps on which the careless
    goat
Browsed by the side of dashing waterfalls;
And thus the bark, meandering with the
    shore,
Pursued her voyage, till a natural pier
Of jutting rock invited us to land.

Alert to follow as the Pastor led,
We clomb a green hill's side; and, as we
    clomb,   570
The Valley, opening out her bosom, gave
Fair prospect, intercepted less and less,
O'er the flat meadows and indented coast
Of the smooth lake, in compass seen: —
    far off,
And yet conspicuous, stood the old Church-
    tower,
In majesty presiding over fields
And habitations seemingly preserved
From all intrusion of the restless world
By rocks impassable and mountains huge.

Soft heath this elevated spot supplied, 580
And choice of moss-clad stones, whereon
    we couched
Or sate reclined; admiring quietly
The general aspect of the scene; but each
Not seldom over anxious to make known
His own discoveries; or to favourite points
Directing notice, merely from a wish
To impart a joy, imperfect while unshared.
That rapturous moment never shall I forget
When these particular interests were ef-
    faced
From every mind ! — Already had the sun,
Sinking with less than ordinary state,   591
Attained his western bound; but rays of
    light —
Now suddenly diverging from the orb
Retired behind the mountain tops or veiled
By the dense air — shot upwards to the
    crown

Of the blue firmament — aloft, and wide:
And multitudes of little floating clouds,
Through their ethereal texture pierced —
    ere we,
Who saw, of change were conscious — had
    become
Vivid as fire; clouds separately poised, —
Innumerable multitude of forms   601
Scattered through half the circle of the
    sky;
And giving back, and shedding each on
    each,
With prodigal communion, the bright hues
Which from the unapparent fount of glory
They had imbibed, and ceased not to re-
    ceive.
That which the heavens displayed, the
    liquid deep
Repeated; but with unity sublime !

While from the grassy mountain's open
    side
We gazed, in silence hushed, with eyes in-
    tent   610
On the refulgent spectacle, diffused
Through earth, sky, water, and all visible
    space,
The Priest in holy transport thus ex-
    claimed:
" Eternal Spirit ! universal God !
Power inaccessible to human thought,
Save by degrees and steps which thou hast
    deigned
To furnish; for this effluence of thyself,
To the infirmity of mortal sense
Vouchsafed; this local transitory type
Of thy paternal splendours, and the pomp
Of those who fill thy courts in highest
    heaven,   621
The radiant Cherubim; — accept the thanks
Which we, thy humble Creatures, here con-
    vened,
Presume to offer; we, who — from the
    breast
Of the frail earth, permitted to behold
The faint reflections only of thy face —
Are yet exalted, and in soul adore !
Such as they are who in thy presence stand
Unsullied, incorruptible, and drink
Imperishable majesty streamed forth   630
From thy empyreal throne, the elect of
    earth
Shall be — divested at the appointed hour
Of all dishonour, cleansed from mortal
    stain.

— Accomplish, then, their number; and
    conclude
Time's weary course ! Or if, by thy decree,
The consummation that will come by
    stealth
Be yet far distant, let thy Word prevail,
Oh ! let thy Word prevail, to take away
The sting of human nature. Spread the law,
As it is written in thy holy book,   640
Throughout all lands; let every nation hear
The high behest, and every heart obey;
Both for the love of purity, and hope
Which it affords, to such as do thy will
And persevere in good, that they shall rise,
To have a nearer view of thee, in heaven.
— Father of good ! this prayer in bounty
    grant,
In mercy grant it, to thy wretched sons.
Then, nor till then, shall persecution cease,
And cruel wars expire. The way is
    marked,   650
The guide appointed, and the ransom paid.
Alas ! the nations, who of yore received
These tidings, and in Christian temples meet
The sacred truth to acknowledge, linger
    still ;
Preferring bonds and darkness to a state
Of holy freedom, by redeeming love
Proffered to all, while yet on earth de-
    tained.

So fare the many; and the thoughtful few,
Who in the anguish of their souls bewail
This dire perverseness, cannot choose but
    ask,   660
Shall it endure ? — Shall enmity and strife,
Falsehood and guile, be left to sow their
    seed;
And the kind never perish ? Is the hope
Fallacious, or shall righteousness obtain
A peaceable dominion, wide as earth,
And ne'er to fail ? Shall that blest day
    arrive
When they, whose choice or lot it is to dwell
In crowded cities, without fear shall live
Studious of mutual benefit; and he,
Whom Morn awakens, among dews and
    flowers   670
Of every clime, to till the lonely field,
Be happy in himself ? — The law of faith
Working through love, such conquest shall
    it gain,
Such triumph over sin and guilt achieve ?
Almighty Lord, thy further grace impart !
And with that help the wonder shall be seen

Fulfilled, the hope accomplished; and thy
    praise
Be sung with transport and unceasing joy.

    Once," and with mild demeanour, as he
        spake,
On us the venerable Pastor turned   680
His beaming eye that had been raised to
    Heaven,
" Once, while the Name, Jehovah, was a
    sound
Within the circuit of this sea-girt isle
Unheard, the savage nations bowed the
    head
To Gods delighting in remorseless deeds;
Gods which themselves had fashioned, to
    promote
Ill purposes, and flatter foul desires.
Then, in the bosom of yon mountain-cove,
To those inventions of corrupted man
Mysterious rites were solemnised; and
    there —   690
Amid impending rocks and gloomy woods —
Of those terrific Idols some received
Such dismal service, that the loudest voice
Of the swoln cataracts (which now are
    heard
Soft murmuring) was too weak to over-
    come,
Though aided by wild winds, the groans
    and shrieks
Of human victims, offered up to appease
Or to propitiate. And, if living eyes
Had visionary faculties to see
The thing that hath been as the thing that
    is,   700
Aghast we might behold this crystal Mere
Bedimmed with smoke, in wreaths volumi-
    nous,
Flung from the body of devouring fires,
To Taranis erected on the heights
By priestly hands, for sacrifice performed
Exultingly, in view of open day
And full assemblage of a barbarous host;
Or to Andates, female Power ! who gave
(For so they fancied) glorious victory.
— A few rude monuments of mountain-
    stone   710
Survive; all else is swept away. — How
    bright
The appearances of things ! From such,
    how changed
The existing worship; and with those com-
    pared,
The worshippers how innocent and blest !

So wide the difference, a willing mind
Might almost think, at this affecting hour,
That paradise, the lost abode of man,
Was raised again: and to a happy few,
In its original beauty, here restored.

Whence but from thee, the true and only
   God,   720
And from the faith derived through Him
   who bled
Upon the cross, this marvellous advance
Of good from evil; as if one extreme
Were left, the other gained. — O ye, who
   come
To kneel devoutly in yon reverend Pile,
Called to such office by the peaceful sound
Of sabbath bells; and ye, who sleep in
   earth,
All cares forgotten, round its hallowed
   walls !
For you, in presence of this little band
Gathered together on the green hill-side, 730
Your Pastor is emboldened to prefer
Vocal thanksgivings to the eternal King;
Whose love, whose counsel, whose com-
   mands, have made
Your very poorest rich in peace of thought
And in good works; and him, who is en-
   dowed
With scantiest knowledge, master of all
   truth
Which the salvation of his soul requires.
Conscious of that abundant favour showered
On you, the children of my humble care,
And this dear land, our country, while on
   earth   740
We sojourn, have I lifted up my soul,
Joy giving voice to fervent gratitude.
These barren rocks, your stern inheritance;
These fertile fields, that recompense your
   pains;
The shadowy vale, the sunny mountain-top;
Woods waving in the wind their lofty heads,
Or hushed; the roaring waters and the
   still —
They see the offering of my lifted hands,
They hear my lips present their sacrifice,
They know if I be silent, morn or even: 750
For, though in whispers speaking, the full
   heart
Will find a vent; and thought is praise to
   him,
Audible praise, to thee, omniscient Mind,
From whom all gifts descend, all blessings
   flow !"

This vesper-service closed, without delay,
From that exalted station to the plain
Descending, we pursued our homeward
   course,
In mute composure, o'er the shadowy lake,
Under a faded sky. No trace remained
Of those celestial splendours; grey the
   vault —   760
Pure, cloudless, ether; and the star of eve
Was wanting; but inferior lights appeared
Faintly, too faint almost for sight; and
   some
Above the darkened hills stood boldly forth
In twinkling lustre, ere the boat attained
Her mooring-place; where, to the shelter-
   ing tree,
Our youthful Voyagers bound fast her prow,
With prompt yet careful hands. This
   done, we paced
The dewy fields; but ere the Vicar's door
Was reached, the Solitary checked his
   steps;   770
Then, intermingling thanks, on each be-
   stowed
A farewell salutation; and, the like
Receiving, took the slender path that leads
To the one cottage in the lonely dell:
But turned not without welcome promise
   made
That he would share the pleasures and
   pursuits
Of yet another summer's day, not loth
To wander with us through the fertile vales,
And o'er the mountain-wastes. "Another
   sun,"
Said he, "shall shine upon us, ere we part;
Another sun, and peradventure more; 781
If time, with free consent, be yours to give,
And season favours."

                 To enfeebled Power,
From this communion with uninjured Minds,
What renovation had been brought; and
   what
Degree of healing to a wounded spirit,
Dejected, and habitually disposed
To seek, in degradation of the Kind,
Excuse and solace for her own defects;
How far those erring notions were re-
   formed;   790
And whether aught, of tendency as good
And pure, from further intercourse ensued;
This — if delightful hopes, as heretofore,
Inspire the serious song, and gentle Hearts
Cherish, and lofty Minds approve the past —
My future labours may not leave untold.

LAODAMIA

1814. 1815

Written at Rydal Mount. The incident of the trees growing and withering put the subject into my thoughts, and I wrote with the hope of giving it a loftier tone than, so far as I know, has been given to it by any of the Ancients who have treated of it. It cost me more trouble than almost anything of equal length I have ever written.

"WITH sacrifice before the rising morn
Vows have I made by fruitless hope inspired;
And from the infernal Gods, 'mid shades forlorn
Of night, my slaughtered Lord have I required:
Celestial pity I again implore; —
Restore him to my sight — great Jove, restore!"

So speaking, and by fervent love endowed
With faith, the Suppliant heavenward lifts her hands;
While, like the sun emerging from a cloud,
Her countenance brightens — and her eye expands;   10
Her bosom heaves and spreads, her stature grows;
And she expects the issue in repose.

O terror! what hath she perceived? — O joy!
What doth she look on? — whom doth she behold?
Her Hero slain upon the beach of Troy?
His vital presence? his corporeal mould?
It is — if sense deceive her not — 't is He!
And a God leads him, wingèd Mercury!

Mild Hermes spake — and touched her with his wand
That calms all fear; "Such grace hath crowned thy prayer,   20
Laodamía! that at Jove's command
Thy Husband walks the paths of upper air:
He comes to tarry with thee three hours' space;
Accept the gift, behold him face to face!"

Forth sprang the impassioned Queen her Lord to clasp;
Again that consummation she essayed;
But unsubstantial Form eludes her grasp
As often as that eager grasp was made.
The Phantom parts — but parts to re-unite,
And re-assume his place before her sight.   30

"Protesiláus, lo! thy guide is gone!
Confirm, I pray, the vision with thy voice:
This is our palace, — yonder is thy throne;
Speak, and the floor thou tread'st on will rejoice.
Not to appal me have the gods bestowed
This precious boon; and blest a sad abode."

"Great Jove, Laodamía! doth not leave
His gifts imperfect: — Spectre though I be,
I am not sent to scare thee or deceive;
But in reward of thy fidelity.   40
And something also did my worth obtain;
For fearless virtue bringeth boundless gain.

"Thou knowest, the Delphic oracle foretold
That the first Greek who touched the Trojan strand
Should die; but me the threat could not withhold:
A generous cause a victim did demand;
And forth I leapt upon the sandy plain;
A self-devoted chief — by Hector slain."

"Supreme of Heroes — bravest, noblest, best!
Thy matchless courage I bewail no more,   50
Which then, when tens of thousands were deprest
By doubt, propelled thee to the fatal shore;
Thou found'st — and I forgive thee — here thou art —
A nobler counsellor than my poor heart.

"But thou, though capable of sternest deed,
Wert kind as resolute, and good as brave;
And he, whose power restores thee, hath decreed
Thou should'st elude the malice of the grave:
Redundant are thy locks, thy lips as fair
As when their breath enriched Thessalian air.   60

"No Spectre greets me, — no vain Shadow this;
Come, blooming Hero, place thee by my side!
Give, on this well-known couch, one nuptial kiss
To me, this day, a second time thy bride!"

Jove frowned in heaven: the conscious Parcæ threw
Upon those roseate lips a Stygian hue.

" This visage tells thee that my doom is past:
Nor should the change be mourned, even if the joys
Of sense were able to return as fast
And surely as they vanish.   Earth destroys
Those raptures duly — Erebus disdains: 71
Calm pleasures there abide — majestic pains.

" Be taught, O faithful Consort, to control
Rebellious passion: for the Gods approve
The depth, and not the tumult, of the soul;
A fervent, not ungovernable, love.
Thy transports moderate; and meekly mourn
When I depart, for brief is my sojourn — "

" Ah, wherefore ? — Did not Hercules by force
Wrest from the guardian Monster of the tomb   80
Alcestis, a reanimated corse,
Given back to dwell on earth in vernal bloom?
Medea's spells dispersed the weight of years,
And Æson stood a youth 'mid youthful peers.

" The Gods to us are merciful — and they
Yet further may relent: for mightier far
Than strength of nerve and sinew, or the sway
Of magic potent over sun and star,
Is love, though oft to agony distrest,
And though his favourite seat be feeble woman's breast.   90

" But if thou goest, I follow — " " Peace ! " he said, —
She looked upon him and was calmed and cheered;
The ghastly colour from his lips had fled;
In his deportment, shape, and mien, appeared
Elysian beauty, melancholy grace,
Brought from a pensive though a happy place.

He spake of love, such love as Spirits feel
In worlds whose course is equable and pure;
No fears to beat away — no strife to heal —
The past unsighed for, and the future sure;
Spake of heroic arts in graver mood   101
Revived, with finer harmony pursued;

Of all that is most beauteous — imaged there
In happier beauty; more pellucid streams,
An ampler ether, a diviner air,
And fields invested with purpureal gleams;
Climes which the sun, who sheds the brightest day
Earth knows, is all unworthy to survey.

Yet there the Soul shall enter which hath earned   109
That privilege by virtue. — " Ill," said he,
" The end of man's existence I discerned,
Who from ignoble games and revelry
Could draw, when we had parted, vain delight,
While tears were thy best pastime, day and night;

" And while my youthful peers before my eyes
(Each hero following his peculiar bent)
Prepared themselves for glorious enterprise
By martial sports, — or, seated in the tent,
Chieftains and kings in council were detained;   119
What time the fleet at Aulis lay enchained,

" The wished-for wind was given: — I then revolved
The oracle, upon the silent sea;
And, if no worthier led the way, resolved
That, of a thousand vessels, mine should be
The foremost prow in pressing to the strand, —
Mine the first blood that tinged the Trojan sand.

" Yet bitter, oft-times bitter, was the pang
When of thy loss I thought, belovèd Wife !
On thee too fondly did my memory hang,
And on the joys we shared in mortal life, —
The paths which we had trod — these fountains, flowers,   131
My new-planned cities, and unfinished towers.

" But should suspense permit the Foe to cry,
' Behold they tremble ! — haughty their array,
Yet of their number no one dares to die ? '
In soul I swept the indignity away:
Old frailties then recurred: — but lofty thought,
In act embodied, my deliverance wrought.

"And Thou, though strong in love, art all
    too weak
In reason, in self-government too slow; 140
I counsel thee by fortitude to seek
Our blest re-union in the shades below.
The invisible world with thee hath sym-
    pathised;
Be thy affections raised and solemnised.

"Learn, by a mortal yearning, to ascend —
Seeking a higher object.   Love was given,
Encouraged, sanctioned, chiefly for that end;
For this the passion to excess was driven —
That self might be annulled: her bondage
    prove
The fetters of a dream opposed to
    love.''—— 150

Aloud she shrieked! for Hermes re-ap-
    pears!
Round the dear Shade she would have clung
    — 't is vain:
The hours are past — too brief had they
    been years;
And him no mortal effort can detain:
Swift, toward the realms that know not
    earthly day,
He through the portal takes his silent way,
And on the palace-floor a lifeless corse She
    lay.

Thus, all in vain exhorted and reproved,
She perished; and, as for a wilful crime,
By the just Gods whom no weak pity moved,
Was doomed to wear out her appointed
    time, 161
Apart from happy Ghosts, that gather flowers
Of blissful quiet 'mid unfading bowers.

— Yet tears to human suffering are due;
And mortal hopes defeated and o'erthrown
Are mourned by man, and not by man alone,
As fondly he believes. — Upon the side
Of Hellespont (such faith was entertained)
A knot of spiry trees for ages grew
From out the tomb of him for whom she
    died; 170
And ever, when such stature they had
    gained
That Ilium's walls were subject to their
    view,
The trees' tall summits withered at the
    sight;
A constant interchange of growth and
    blight!

DION

(SEE PLUTARCH)

1816(?). 1820

This poem was first introduced by a stanza
that I have since transferred to the Notes, for
reasons there given, and I cannot comply with
the request expressed by some of my friends
that the rejected stanza should be restored. I
hope they will be content if it be, hereafter, im-
mediately attached to the poem, instead of its
being degraded to a place in the Notes.

I

SERENE, and fitted to embrace,
Where'er he turned, a swan-like grace
Of haughtiness without pretence,
And to unfold a still magnificence,
Was princely Dion, in the power
And beauty of his happier hour.
And what pure homage *then* did wait
On Dion's virtues, while the lunar beam
Of Plato's genius, from its lofty sphere,
Fell round him in the grove of Academe, 10
Softening their inbred dignity austere —
    That he, not too elate
    With self-sufficing solitude,
But with majestic lowliness endued,
    Might in the universal bosom reign,
And from affectionate observance gain
Help, under every change of adverse fate.

II

Five thousand warriors — O the rapturous
    day!
Each crowned with flowers, and armed
    with spear and shield,
Or ruder weapon which their course might
    yield, 20
To Syracuse advance in bright array.
Who leads them on? — The anxious people
    see
Long-exiled Dion marching at their head,
He also crowned with flowers of Sicily,
And in a white, far-beaming, corselet clad!
Pure transport undisturbed by doubt or fear
The gazers feel; and, rushing to the plain,
Salute those strangers as a holy train
Or blest procession (to the Immortals dear)
That brought their precious liberty again.
Lo! when the gates are entered, on each
    hand, 31
Down the long street, rich goblets filled
    with wine

In seemly order stand,
On tables set, as if for rites divine; —
And, as the great Deliverer marches by,
　He looks on festal ground with fruits
　　bestrown;
And flowers are on his person thrown
　In boundless prodigality;
Nor doth the general voice abstain from
　prayer,
Invoking Dion's tutelary care,　　　　40
As if a very Deity he were!

III

Mourn, hills and groves of Attica! and
　mourn
Ilissus, bending o'er thy classic urn!
Mourn, and lament for him whose spirit
　dreads
Your once sweet memory, studious walks
　and shades!
For him who to divinity aspired,
Not on the breath of popular applause,
But through dependence on the sacred laws
Framed in the schools where Wisdom dwelt
　retired,
Intent to trace the ideal path of right　50
(More fair than heaven's broad causeway
　paved with stars)
Which Dion learned to measure with sub-
　lime delight; —
But He hath overleaped the eternal bars;
And, following guides whose craft holds no
　consent
With aught that breathes the ethereal ele-
　ment,
Hath stained the robes of civil power with
　blood,
Unjustly shed, though for the public good.
Whence doubts that came too late, and
　wishes vain,
Hollow excuses, and triumphant pain;
And oft his cogitations sink as low　　60
As, through the abysses of a joyless heart,
The heaviest plummet of despair can go —
But whence that sudden check? that fear-
　ful start!
He hears an uncouth sound —
　Anon his lifted eyes
Saw, at a long-drawn gallery's dusky bound,
A Shape of more than mortal size
And hideous aspect, stalking round and
　round!
　A woman's garb the Phantom wore,
　And fiercely swept the marble floor, —
　Like Auster whirling to and fro,　71

His force on Caspian foam to try;
Or Boreas when he scours the snow
That skins the plains of Thessaly,
Or when aloft on Mænalus he stops
His flight, 'mid eddying pine-tree tops!

IV

So, but from toil less sign of profit reaping,
The sullen Spectre to her purpose bowed,
　Sweeping — vehemently sweeping —
No pause admitted, no design avowed!　80
" Avaunt, inexplicable Guest! — avaunt,"
Exclaimed the Chieftain — " let me rather
　see
The coronal that coiling vipers make;
The torch that flames with many a lurid
　flake,
And the long train of doleful pageantry
Which they behold, whom vengeful Furies
　haunt;
Who, while they struggle from the scourge
　to flee,
Move where the blasted soil is not unworn,
And, in their anguish, bear what other
　minds have borne! "

V

But Shapes that come not at an earthly call,
Will not depart when mortal voices bid;　91
Lords of the visionary eye whose lid,
Once raised, remains aghast, and will not
　fall!
Ye Gods, thought He, that servile Implement
Obeys a mystical intent!
Your Minister would brush away
The spots that to my soul adhere;
But should she labour night and day,
They will not, cannot disappear;
Whence angry perturbations, — and that look
Which no Philosophy can brook!　　101

VI

Ill-fated Chief! there are whose hopes are
　built
Upon the ruins of thy glorious name;
Who, through the portal of one moment's
　guilt,
Pursue thee with their deadly aim!
O matchless perfidy! portentous lust
Of monstrous crime! — that horror-striking
　blade,
Drawn in defiance of the Gods, hath laid
The noble Syracusan low in dust!
Shuddered the walls — the marble city
　wept —　　　　　　　　　　　　110

And sylvan places heaved a pensive sigh;
But in calm peace the appointed Victim
   slept,
As he had fallen in magnanimity;
Of spirit too capacious to require
That Destiny her course should change;
   too just
To his own native greatness to desire
That wretched boon, days lengthened by
   mistrust.

So were the hopeless troubles, that involved
The soul of Dion, instantly dissolved.
Released from life and cares of princely
   state,   120
He left this moral grafted on his Fate;
" Him only pleasure leads, and peace at-
   tends,
Him, only him, the shield of Jove defends,
Whose means are fair and spotless as his
   ends."

MEMORIALS OF A TOUR IN SCOTLAND

1814

In this tour, my wife and her sister Sara were my companions. The account of the " Brownie's Cell " and the Brownies was given me by a man we met with on the banks of Loch Lomond, a little above Tarbert, and in front of a huge mass of rock, by the side of which, we were told, preachings were often held in the open air. The place is quite a solitude, and the surrounding scenery very striking. How much is it to be regretted that, instead of writing such Poems as the " Holy Fair " and others, in which the religious observances of his country are treated with so much levity and too often with indecency, Burns had not employed his genius in describing religion under the serious and affecting aspects it must so frequently take.

I

SUGGESTED BY A BEAUTIFUL RUIN UPON ONE OF THE ISLANDS OF LOCH LOMOND, A PLACE CHOSEN FOR THE RETREAT OF A SOLITARY INDIVIDUAL, FROM WHOM THIS HABITATION ACQUIRED THE NAME OF

THE BROWNIE'S CELL

1814. 1820

I

To barren heath, bleak moor, and quaking
   fen,
Or depth of labyrinthine glen;
Or into trackless forest set
With trees, whose lofty umbrage met,
World-wearied Men withdrew of yore;
(Penance their trust, and prayer their
   store;)
And in the wilderness were bound
To such apartments as they found,
Or with a new ambition raised;
That God might suitably be praised.   10

II

High lodged the *Warrior*, like a bird of prey;
Or where broad waters round him lay:
But this wild Ruin is no ghost
Of his devices — buried, lost !

Within this little lonely isle
There stood a consecrated Pile;
Where tapers burned, and mass was sung,
For them whose timid Spirits clung
To mortal succour, though the tomb
Had fixed, for ever fixed, their doom !   20

III

Upon those servants of another world
When madding Power her bolts had hurled,
Their habitation shook — it fell,
And perished, save one narrow cell;
Whither, at length, a Wretch retired
Who neither grovelled nor aspired;
He, struggling in the net of pride,
The future scorned, the past defied;
Still tempering, from the unguilty forge
Of vain conceit, an iron scourge !   30

IV

Proud Remnant was he of a fearless Race,
Who stood and flourished face to face
With their perennial hills; — but Crime,
Hastening the stern decrees of Time,
Brought low a Power, which from its home
Burst, when repose grew wearisome;
And, taking impulse from the sword,
And, mocking its own plighted word,
Had found, in ravage widely dealt,
Its warfare's bourn, its travel's belt !   40

V

All, all were dispossessed, save him whose smile
Shot lightning through this lonely Isle !
No right had he but what he made
To this small spot, his leafy shade;
But the ground lay within that ring
To which he only dared to cling;
Renouncing here, as worse than dead,
The craven few who bowed the head
Beneath the change; who heard a claim
How loud ! yet lived in peace with shame. 50

VI

From year to year this shaggy Mortal went
(So seemed it) down a strange descent:
Till they, who saw his outward frame,
Fixed on him an unhallowed name;
Him, free from all malicious taint,
And guiding, like the Patmos Saint,
A pen unwearied — to indite,
In his lone Isle, the dreams of night;
Impassioned dreams, that strove to span
The faded glories of his Clan ! 60

VII

Suns that through blood their western harbour sought,
And stars that in their courses fought;
Towers rent, winds combating with woods,
Lands deluged by unbridled floods;
And beast and bird that from the spell
Of sleep took import terrible; —
These types mysterious (if the show
Of battle and the routed foe
Had failed) would furnish an array
Of matter for the dawning day ! 70

VIII

How disappeared He ? — ask the newt and toad,
Inheritors of his abode;
The otter crouching undisturbed,
In her dank cleft; — but be thou curbed,
O froward Fancy ! 'mid a scene
Of aspect winning and serene;
For those offensive creatures shun
The inquisition of the sun !
And in this region flowers delight,
And all is lovely to the sight. 80

IX

Spring finds not here a melancholy breast,
When she applies her annual test
To dead and living; when her breath
Quickens, as now, the withered heath; —
Nor flaunting Summer — when he throws
His soul into the briar-rose;
Or calls the lily from her sle
Prolonged beneath the bord   p;
Nor Autumn, when the view   en
Is warbling near the Brown   a. 90

X

Wild Relique ! beauteous as the chosen spot
In Nysa's isle, the embellished grot;
Whither, by care of Libyan Jove,
(High Servant of paternal Love)
Young Bacchus was conveyed — to lie
Safe from his step-dame Rhea's eye;
Where bud, and bloom, and fruitage, glowed,
Close-crowding round the infant-god;
All colours, — and the liveliest streak
A foil to his celestial cheek ! 100

II

COMPOSED AT CORA LINN,

IN SIGHT OF WALLACE'S TOWER

1814. 1820

I had seen this celebrated Waterfall twice before; but the feelings, to which it had given birth, were not expressed till they recurred in presence of the object on this occasion.

" — How Wallace fought for Scotland, left the name
Of Wallace to be found, like a wild flower,
All over his dear Country ; left the deeds
Of Wallace, like a family of ghosts,
To people the steep rocks and river banks,
Her natural sanctuaries, with a local soul
Of independence and stern liberty." — See p. 127.

Lord of the vale ! astounding Flood;
The dullest leaf in this thick wood
Quakes — conscious of thy power;
The caves reply with hollow moan;
And vibrates, to its central stone,
You time-cemented Tower !

And yet how fair the rural scene !
For thou, O Clyde, hast ever been
Beneficent as strong;
Pleased in refreshing dews to steep   10
The little trembling flowers that peep
Thy shelving rocks among.

Hence all who love their country, love
To look on thee — delight to rove

Where they thy voice can hear;
⌐ to the patriot-warrior's Shade,
     ⁀ ᵗʰᵉ vale ! to Heroes laid
     ʰat voice is dear !

     y banks, at dead of night
ᵢ   visibly the Wallace Wight;   20
Or   ᵤᵤds, in warlike vest,
Aloft, beneath the moon's pale beam,
A Champion worthy of the stream,
Yon grey tower's living crest !

But clouds and envious darkness hide
A Form not doubtfully descried: —
Their transient mission o'er,
O say to what blind region flee
These Shapes of awful phantasy ?
To what untrodden shore ?   30

Less than divine command they spurn;
But this we from the mountains learn,
And this the valleys show;
That never will they deign to hold
Communion where the heart is cold
To human weal and woe.

The man of abject soul in vain
Shall walk the Marathonian plain;
Or thrid the shadowy gloom,
That still invests the guardian Pass,   40
Where stood, sublime, Leonidas
Devoted to the tomb.

And let no Slave his head incline,
Or kneel, before the votive shrine
By Uri's lake, where Tell
Leapt, from his storm-vext boat, to land,
Heaven's Instrument, for by his hand
That day the Tyrant fell.

III

EFFUSION

**IN THE PLEASURE-GROUND ON THE
BANKS OF THE BRAN, NEAR DUNKELD**

1814. 1827

I am not aware that this condemnatory effu-
sion was ever seen by the owner of the place.
He might be disposed to pay little attention to
it ; but were it to prove otherwise I should be
glad, for the whole exhibition is distressingly
puerile.

" The waterfall, by a loud roaring, warned us
when we must expect it. We were first, how-
ever, conducted into a small apartment, where
the Gardener desired us to look at a picture of
Ossian, which, while he was telling the history
of the young Artist who executed the work,
disappeared, parting in the middle — flying
asunder as by the touch of magic — and lo !
we are at the entrance of a splendid apartment,
which was almost dizzy and alive with water-
falls, that tumbled in all directions ; the great
cascade, opposite the window, which faced us,
being reflected in innumerable mirrors upon
the ceiling and against the walls." — *Extract
from the Journal of my Fellow-Traveller.*

WHAT He — who, 'mid the kindred throng
Of Heroes that inspired his song,
Doth yet frequent the hill of storms,
The stars dim-twinkling through their
     forms !
What ! Ossian here — a painted Thrall,
Mute fixture on a stuccoed wall;
To serve — an unsuspected screen
For show that must not yet be seen;
And, when the moment comes, to part
And vanish by mysterious art;   10
Head, harp, and body, split asunder,
For ingress to a world of wonder;
A gay saloon, with waters dancing
Upon the sight wherever glancing;
One loud cascade in front, and lo !
A thousand like it, white as snow —
Streams on the walls, and torrent-foam
As active round the hollow dome,
Illusive cataracts ! of their terrors
Not stripped, nor voiceless in the mirrors, 20
That catch the pageant from the flood
Thundering adown a rocky wood.
What pains to dazzle and confound !
What strife of colour, shape and sound
In this quaint medley, that might seem
Devised out of a sick man's dream !
Strange scene, fantastic and uneasy
As ever made a maniac dizzy,
When disenchanted from the mood
That loves on sullen thoughts to brood ! 30
O Nature — in thy changeful visions,
Through all thy most abrupt transitions
Smooth, graceful, tender, or sublime —
Ever averse to pantomime,
Thee neither do they know nor us
Thy servants, who can trifle thus;
Else verily the sober powers
Of rock that frowns, and stream that roars,
Exalted by congenial sway
Of Spirits, and the undying Lay,   40

And Names that moulder not away,
Had wakened some redeeming thought
More worthy of this favoured Spot;
Recalled some feeling — to set free
The Bard from such indignity !
　　The Effigies of a valiant Wight
I once beheld, a Templar Knight;
Not prostrate, not like those that rest
On tombs, with palms together prest,
But sculptured out of living stone,　　50
And standing upright and alone,
Both hands with rival energy
Employed in setting his sword free
From its dull sheath — stern sentinel
Intent to guard St. Robert's cell;
As if with memory of the affray
Far distant, when, as legends say,
The Monks of Fountain's thronged to force
From its dear home the Hermit's corse,
That in their keeping it might lie,　　60
To crown their abbey's sanctity.
So had they rushed into the grot
Of sense despised, a world forgot,
And torn him from his loved retreat,
Where altar-stone and rock-hewn seat
Still hint that quiet best is found,
Even by the *Living*, under ground;
But a bold Knight, the selfish aim
Defeating, put the monks to shame,
There where you see his Image stand　　70
Bare to the sky, with threatening brand
Which lingering NID is proud to show
Reflected in the pool below.
　　Thus, like the men of earliest days,
Our sires set forth their grateful praise:
Uncouth the workmanship, and rude !
But, nursed in mountain solitude,
Might some aspiring artist dare
To seize whate'er, through misty air,
A ghost, by glimpses, may present　　80
Of imitable lineament,
And give the phantom an array
That less should scorn the abandoned clay;
Then let him hew with patient stroke
An Ossian out of mural rock,
And leave the figurative Man —
Upon thy margin, roaring Bran ! —
Fixed, like the Templar of the steep,
An everlasting watch to keep;
With local sanctities in trust,　　90
More precious than a hermit's dust;
And virtues through the mass infused,
Which old idolatry abused.
　　What though the Granite would deny
All fervour to the sightless eye;

And touch from rising suns in vain
Solicit a Memnonian strain;
Yet, in some fit of anger sharp,
The wind might force the **deep-grooved**
　　harp
To utter melancholy moans　　100
Not unconnected with the tones
Of soul-sick flesh and weary bones;
While grove and river notes would lend,
Less deeply sad, with these to blend !
　　Vain pleasures of luxurious life,
For ever with yourselves at strife;
Through town and country both deranged
By affectations interchanged,
And all the perishable gauds
That heaven-deserted man applauds;　　110
When will your hapless patrons learn
To watch and ponder — to discern
The freshness, the everlasting youth,
Of admiration sprung from truth;
From beauty infinitely growing
Upon a mind with love o'erflowing —
To sound the depths of every Art
That seeks its wisdom through the heart ?
　　Thus (where the intrusive Pile, ill-graced
With baubles of theatric taste,　　120
O'erlooks the torrent breathing showers
On motley banks of alien flowers
In stiff confusion set or sown,
Till Nature cannot find her own,
Or keep a remnant of the sod
Which Caledonian Heroes trod)
I mused; and, thirsting for redress,
Recoiled into the wilderness.

IV

YARROW VISITED

SEPTEMBER 1814

1814. 1815

As mentioned in my verses on the death of
the Ettrick Shepherd, my first visit to Yarrow
was in his company. We had lodged the night
before at Traquhair, where Hogg had joined
us and also Dr. Anderson, the Editor of the
British Poets, who was on a visit at the Manse.
Dr. A. walked with us till we came in view of
the Vale of Yarrow, and, being advanced in
life, he then turned back. The old **Man** was
passionately fond of poetry, though with not
much of a discriminating judgment, as the
Volumes he edited sufficiently show. But I
was much pleased to meet with him, and to
acknowledge my obligation to his collection,

which had been my brother John's companion in more than one voyage to India, and which he gave me before his departure from Grasmere, never to return. Through these Volumes I became first familiar with Chaucer, and so little money had I then to spare for books, that, in all probability, but for this same work, I should have known little of Drayton, Daniel, and other distinguished poets of the Elizabethan age, and their immediate successors, till a much later period of my life. I am glad to record this. not from any importance of its own, but as a tribute of gratitude to this simple-hearted old man, whom I never again had the pleasure of meeting. I seldom read or think of this poem without regretting that my dear Sister was not of the party, as she would have had so much delight in recalling the time when, travelling together in Scotland, we declined going in search of this celebrated stream, not altogether, I will frankly confess, for the reasons assigned in the poem on the occasion.

AND is this — Yarrow ? — *This* the Stream
Of which my fancy cherished,
So faithfully, a waking dream ?
An image that hath perished !
O that some Minstrel's harp were near,
To utter notes of gladness,
And chase this silence from the air,
That fills my heart with sadness !

Yet why ? — a silvery current flows
With uncontrolled meanderings;   10
Nor have these eyes by greener hills
Been soothed, in all my wanderings.
And, through her depths, Saint Mary's Lake
Is visibly delighted;
For not a feature of those hills
Is in the mirror slighted.

A blue sky bends o'er Yarrow vale,
Save where that pearly whiteness
Is round the rising sun diffused,
A tender hazy brightness;   20
Mild dawn of promise ! that excludes
All profitless dejection;
Though not unwilling here to admit
A pensive recollection.

Where was it that the famous Flower
Of Yarrow Vale lay bleeding ?
His bed perchance was yon smooth mound
On which the herd is feeding:
And haply from this crystal pool,
Now peaceful as the morning,   30

The Water-wraith ascended thrice —
And gave his doleful warning.

Delicious is the Lay that sings
The haunts of happy Lovers,
The path that leads them to the grove,
The leafy grove that covers:
And Pity sanctifies the Verse
That paints, by strength of sorrow,
The unconquerable strength of love;
Bear witness, rueful Yarrow !   40

But thou, that didst appear so fair
To fond imagination,
Dost rival in the light of day
Her delicate creation:
Meek loveliness is round thee spread,
A softness still and holy;
The grace of forest charms decayed,
And pastoral melancholy.

That region left, the vale unfolds
Rich groves of lofty stature,   50
With Yarrow winding through the pomp
Of cultivated nature;
And, rising from those lofty groves,
Behold a Ruin hoary !
The shattered front of Newark's Towers,
Renowned in Border story.

Fair scenes for childhood's opening bloom,
For sportive youth to stray in;
For manhood to enjoy his strength;
And age to wear away in !   60
Yon cottage seems a bower of bliss,
A covert for protection
Of tender thoughts, that nestle there —
The brood of chaste affection.

How sweet, on this autumnal day,
The wild-wood fruits to gather,
And on my True-love's forehead plant
A crest of blooming heather !
And what if I enwreathed my own !
'T were no offence to reason;   70
The sober Hills thus deck their brows
To meet the wintry season.

I see — but not by sight alone,
Loved Yarrow, have I won thee;
A ray of fancy still survives —
Her sunshine plays upon thee !
Thy ever-youthful waters keep
A course of lively pleasure;
And gladsome notes my lips can breathe,
Accordant to the measure.   80

The vapours linger round the Heights,
They melt, and soon must vanish;
One hour is theirs, nor more is mine —
Sad thought, which I would banish,

But that I know, where'er I go,
Thy genuine image, Yarrow !
Will dwell with me — to heighten joy,
And cheer my mind in sorrow.

"FROM THE DARK CHAMBERS OF DEJECTION FREED"

1814. 1815

Composed in Edinburgh, during my Scotch tour with Mrs. Wordsworth and my sister Miss Hutchinson, in the year 1814. Poor Gillies never rose above that course of extravagance in which he was at that time living, and which soon reduced him to poverty and all its degrading shifts, mendicity being far from the worst. I grieve whenever I think of him, for he was far from being without genius, and had a generous heart, not always to be found in men given up to profusion. He was nephew of Lord Gillies the Scotch judge, and also of the historian of Greece. He was cousin to Miss Margaret Gillies, who painted so many portraits with success in our house.

FROM the dark chambers of dejection freed,
Spurning the unprofitable yoke of care,
Rise, GILLIES, rise; the gales of youth shall bear
Thy genius forward like a wingèd steed.
Though bold Bellerophon (so Jove decreed
In wrath) fell headlong from the fields of air,
Yet a rich guerdon waits on minds that dare,
If aught be in them of immortal seed,
And reason govern that audacious flight
Which heavenward they direct. — Then droop not thou,
Erroneously renewing a sad vow
In the low dell 'mid Roslin's faded grove:
A cheerful life is what the Muses love,
A soaring spirit is their prime delight.

LINES

WRITTEN ON A BLANK LEAF IN A COPY OF THE AUTHOR'S POEM "THE EXCURSION," UPON HEARING OF THE DEATH OF THE LATE VICAR OF KENDAL

1814. 1815

To public notice, with reluctance strong,
Did I deliver this unfinished Song;

Yet for one happy issue; — and I look
With self-congratulation on the Book
Which pious, learned, MURFITT saw and read; —
Upon my thoughts his saintly Spirit fed;
He conned the new-born Lay with grateful heart —
Foreboding not how soon he must depart;
Unweeting that to him the joy was given
Which good men take with them from earth to heaven.

TO B. R. HAYDON

1815. 1816

HIGH is our calling, Friend ! — Creative Art
(Whether the instrument of words she use,
Or pencil pregnant with ethereal hues,)
Demands the service of a mind and heart,
Though sensitive, yet, in their weakest part,
Heroically fashioned — to infuse
Faith in the whispers of the lonely Muse,
While the whole world seems adverse to desert.
And, oh! when Nature sinks, as oft she may,
Through long-lived pressure of obscure distress,
Still to be strenuous for the bright reward,
And in the soul admit of no decay,
Brook no continuance of weak-mindedness —
Great is the glory, for the strife is hard !

ARTEGAL AND ELIDURE

1815. 1820

(SEE THE CHRONICLE OF GEOFFREY OF MONMOUTH AND MILTON'S HISTORY OF ENGLAND)

This was written at Rydal Mount, as a token of affectionate respect for the memory of Milton. " I have determined," says he, in his preface to his *History of England*, " to bestow the telling over even of these reputed tales, be it for nothing else but in favour of our English Poets and Rhetoricians, who by their wit will know how to use them judiciously."

WHERE be the temples which, in Britain's Isle,
For his paternal Gods, the Trojan raised ?
Gone like a morning dream, or like a pile
Of clouds that in cerulean ether blazed !
Ere Julius landed on her white-cliffed shore,
    They sank, delivered o'er
To fatal dissolution: and, I ween,
No vestige then was left that such had ever been.

Nathless, a British record (long concealed
In old Armorica, whose secret springs   10
No Gothic conqueror ever drank) revealed
The marvellous current of forgotten things;
How Brutus came, by oracles impelled,
    And Albion's giants quelled,
A brood whom no civility could melt,
" Who never tasted grace, and goodness ne'er had felt."

By brave Corineus aided, he subdued,
And rooted out the intolerable kind;
And this too-long-polluted land imbued
With goodly arts and usages refined;   20
Whence golden harvests, cities, warlike towers,
    And pleasure's sumptuous bowers;
Whence all the fixed delights of house and home,
Friendships that will not break, and love that cannot roam.

O, happy Britain ! region all too fair
For self-delighting fancy to endure
That silence only should inhabit there,
Wild beasts, or uncouth savages impure !
But, intermingled with the generous seed,
    Grew many a poisonous weed;   30
Thus fares it still with all that takes its birth
From human care, or grows upon the breast of earth.

Hence, and how soon ! that war of vengeance waged
By Guendolen against her faithless lord;
Till she, in jealous fury unassuaged
Had slain his paramour with ruthless sword:
Then, into Severn hideously defiled,
    She flung her blameless child,

Sabrina, — vowing that the stream should bear
That name through every age, her hatred to declare.   40

So speaks the Chronicle, and tells of Lear
By his ungrateful daughters turned adrift.
Ye lightnings, hear his voice ! — they cannot hear,
Nor can the winds restore his simple gift.
But One there is, a Child of nature meek,
    Who comes her Sire to seek;
And he, recovering sense, upon her breast
Leans smilingly, and sinks into a perfect rest.

There too we read of Spenser's fairy themes,
And those that Milton loved in youthful years;   50
The sage enchanter Merlin's subtle schemes;
The feats of Arthur and his knightly peers;
Of Arthur, — who, to upper light restored,
    With that terrific sword
Which yet he brandishes for future war,
Shall lift his country's fame above the polar star !

What wonder, then, if in such ample field
Of old tradition, one particular flower
Doth seemingly in vain its fragrance yield,
And bloom unnoticed even to this late hour ?   60
Now, gentle Muses, your assistance grant,
    While I this flower transplant
Into a garden stored with Poesy;
Where flowers and herbs unite, and haply some weeds be,
That, wanting not wild grace, are from all mischief free!

A KING more worthy of respect and love
Than wise Gorbonian ruled not in his day;
And grateful Britain prospered far above
All neighbouring countries through his righteous sway;
He poured rewards and honours on the good;   70
    The oppressor he withstood:
And while he served the Gods with reverence due
Fields smiled, and temples rose, and towns and cities grew.

He died, whom Artegal succeeds — his son;
But how unworthy of that sire was he !

A hopeful reign, auspiciously begun,
Was darkened soon by foul iniquity.
From crime to crime he mounted, till at
    length
    The nobles leagued their strength
With a vexed people, and the tyrant
    chased;   80
And, on the vacant throne, his worthier
    Brother placed.

From realm to realm the humbled Exile
    went,
Suppliant for aid his kingdom to regain;
In many a court, and many a warrior's tent,
He urged his persevering suit in vain.
Him, in whose wretched heart ambition
    failed,
    Dire poverty assailed;
And, tired with slights his pride no more
    could brook,
He towards his native country cast a long-
    ing look.

Fair blew the wished-for wind — the voy-
    age sped;   90
He landed; and, by many dangers scared,
" Poorly provided, poorly followèd,"
To Calaterium's forest he repaired.
How changed from him who, born to high-
    est place,
    Had swayed the royal mace,
Flattered and feared, despised yet deified,
In Troynovant, his seat by silver Thames's
    side !

From that wild region where the crownless
    King
Lay in concealment with his scanty train,
Supporting life by water from the spring,
And such chance food as outlaws can ob-
    tain,   101
Unto the few whom he esteems his friends
    A messenger he sends;
And from their secret loyalty requires
Shelter and daily bread, — the sum of his
    desires.

While he the issue waits, at early morn
Wandering by stealth abroad, he chanced
    to hear
A startling outcry made by hound and
    horn,
From which the tusky wild boar flies in fear;
And, scouring toward him o'er the grassy
    plain,   110

Behold the hunter train !
He bids his little company advance
With seeming unconcern and steady coun-
    tenance.

The royal Elidure, who leads the chase,
Hath checked his foaming courser: — can
    it be !
Methinks that I should recognise that face,
Though much disguised by long adversity !
He gazed rejoicing, and again he gazed,
    Confounded and amazed —
" It is the king, my brother ! " and, by
    sound   120
Of his own voice confirmed, he leaps upon
    the ground.

Long, strict, and tender was the embrace
    he gave,
Feebly returned by daunted Artegal;
Whose natural affection doubts enslave,
And apprehensions dark and criminal.
Loth to restrain the moving interview,
    The attendant lords withdrew;
And, while they stood upon the plain apart,
Thus Elidure, by words, relieved his strug-
    gling heart.

" By heavenly Powers conducted, we have
    met;   130
— O Brother ! to my knowledge lost so
    long,
But neither lost to love, nor to regret,
Nor to my wishes lost; — forgive the wrong,
(Such it may seem) if I thy crown have
    borne,
    Thy royal mantle worn:
I was their natural guardian; and 't is just
That now I should restore what hath been
    held in trust."

A while the astonished Artegal stood mute,
Then thus exclaimed: " To me, of titles
    shorn,
And stripped of power ! me, feeble, de-
    stitute,   140
To me a kingdom ! spare the bitter scorn:
If justice ruled the breast of foreign kings,
    Then, on the wide-spread wings
Of war, had I returned to claim my right;
This will I here avow, not dreading thy de-
    spite."

" I do not blame thee," Elidure replied;
" But, if my looks did with my words agree,

I should at once be trusted, not defied,
And thou from all disquietude be free.
May the unsullied Goddess of the chase, 150
  Who to this blessed place
At this blest moment led me, if I speak
With insincere intent, on me her vengeance
  wreak !

"Were this same spear, which in my hand
  I grasp,
The British sceptre, here would I to thee
The symbol yield; and would undo this clasp,
If it confined the robe of sovereignty.
Odious to me the pomp of regal court,
  And joyless sylvan sport,
While thou art roving, wretched and for-
  lorn, 160
Thy couch the dewy earth, thy roof the
  forest thorn ! "

Then Artegal thus spake: " I only sought
Within this realm a place of safe retreat;
Beware of rousing an ambitious thought;
Beware of kindling hopes, for me unmeet !
Thou art reputed wise, but in my mind
  Art pitiably blind:
Full soon this generous purpose thou may'st
  rue,
When that which has been done no wishes
  can undo.

"Who, when a crown is fixed upon his
  head, 170
Would balance claim with claim, and right
  with right ?
But thou — I know not how inspired, how
  led —
Wouldst change the course of things in all
  men's sight !
And this for one who cannot imitate
  Thy virtue, who may hate:
For, if, by such strange sacrifice restored,
He reign, thou still must be his king, and
  sovereign lord;

"Lifted in magnanimity above
Aught that my feeble nature could per-
  form,
Or even conceive; surpassing me in love 180
Far as in power the eagle doth the worm.
I, Brother ! only should be king in name,
  And govern to my shame;
A shadow in a hated land, while all
Of glad or willing service to thy share
  would fall."

"Believe it not," said Elidure ; " respect
Awaits on virtuous life, and ever most
Attends on goodness with dominion decked,
Which stands the universal empire's boast;
This can thy own experience testify: 190
  Nor shall thy foes deny
That, in the gracious opening of thy reign,
Our father's spirit seemed in thee to
  breathe again.

"And what if o'er that bright unbosoming
Clouds of disgrace and envious fortune
  past!
Have we not seen the glories of the spring
By veil of noontide darkness overcast ?
The frith that glittered like a warrior's
  shield,
  The sky, the gay green field,
Are vanished; gladness ceases in the
  groves, 200
And trepidation strikes the blackened
  mountain-coves.

"But is that gloom dissolved ? how passing
  clear
Seems the wide world, far brighter than
  before !
Even so thy latent worth will re-appear,
Gladdening the people's heart from shore
  to shore;
For youthful faults ripe virtues shall atone;
  Re-seated on thy throne,
Proof shalt thou furnish that misfortune,
  pain,
And sorrow, have confirmed thy native
  right to reign.

"But, not to overlook what thou may'st
  know, 210
Thy enemies are neither weak nor few;
And circumspect must be our course, and
  slow,
Or from my purpose ruin may ensue.
Dismiss thy followers; — let them calmly
  wait
  Such change in thy estate
As I already have in thought devised;
And which, with caution due, may soon be
  realised."

The Story tells what courses were pursued,
Until king Elidure, with full consent
Of all his peers, before the multitude, 220
Rose, — and, to consummate this just in-
  tent,

Did place upon his brother's head the
   crown,
   Relinquished by his own;
Then to his people cried, "Receive your
   lord,
Gorbonian's first-born son, your rightful
   king restored!"

The people answered with a loud acclaim:
Yet more; — heart-smitten by the heroic
   deed,
The reinstated Artegal became
Earth's noblest penitent; from bondage
   freed
Of vice — thenceforth unable to subvert 230
   Or shake his high desert.
Long did he reign; and, when he died, the
   tear
Of universal grief bedewed his honoured
   bier.

Thus was a Brother by a Brother saved;
With whom a crown (temptation that hath
   set
Discord in hearts of men till they have
   braved
Their nearest kin with deadly purpose met)
'Gainst duty weighed, and faithful love,
   did seem
   A thing of no esteem;
And, from this triumph of affection pure,
He bore the lasting name of "pious Eli-
   dure."   241

SEPTEMBER 1815

1815. 1816

"For me who under kindlier laws." This
conclusion has more than once, to my great
regret, excited painfully sad feelings in the
hearts of young persons fond of poetry and
poetic composition, by contrast of their feeble
and declining health with that state of robust
constitution which prompted me to rejoice in
a season of frost and snow as more favourable
to the Muses than summer itself.

WHILE not a leaf seems faded; while the
   fields,
With ripening harvest prodigally fair,
In brightest sunshine bask; this nipping
   air,
Sent from some distant clime where Win-
   ter wields
His icy scimitar, a foretaste yields

Of bitter change, and bids the flowers be-
   ware;
And whispers to the silent birds, "Prepare
Against the threatening foe your trustiest
   shields."
For me, who under kindlier laws belong
To Nature's tuneful quire, this rustling dry
Through leaves yet green, and yon crystal-
   line sky,
Announce a season potent to renew,
'Mid frost and snow, the instinctive joys of
   song,
And nobler cares than listless summer knew.

NOVEMBER 1

1815. 1816

Suggested on the banks of the Brathay by
the sight of Langdale Pikes. It is delightful
to remember these moments of far-distant
days, which probably would have been forgot-
ten if the impression had not been transferred
to verse. The same observation applies to the
next.

How clear, how keen, how marvellously
   bright
The effluence from yon distant mountain's
   head,
Which, strewn with snow smooth as the
   sky can shed,
Shines like another sun — on mortal sight
Uprisen, as if to check approaching Night,
And all her twinkling stars. Who now
   would tread,
If so he might, yon mountain's glittering
   head —
Terrestrial, but a surface, by the flight
Of sad mortality's earth-sullying wing,
Unswept, unstained? Nor shall the aërial
   Powers
Dissolve that beauty, destined to endure,
White, radiant, spotless, exquisitely pure,
Through all vicissitudes, till genial Spring
Has filled the laughing vales with welcome
   flowers.

"THE FAIREST, BRIGHTEST, HUES OF ETHER FADE"

1812. 1815

Suggested at Hackett, which is on the craggy
ridge that rises between the two Langdales
and looks towards Windermere. The Cottage

of Hackett was often visited by us, and at the time when this Sonnet was written, and long after, was occupied by the husband and wife described in the "Excursion," where it is mentioned that she was in the habit of walking in the front of the dwelling with a light to guide her husband home at night. The same cottage is alluded to in the "Epistle to Sir George Beaumont" as that from which the female peasant hailed us on our morning journey. The musician mentioned in the Sonnet was the Rev. Samuel Tillbrook of Peter-house, Cambridge, who remodelled the Ivy Cottage at Rydal after he had purchased it.

The fairest, brightest, hues of ether fade;
The sweetest notes must terminate and die;
O Friend! thy flute has breathed a harmony
Softly resounded through this rocky glade;
Such strains of rapture as the Genius played
In his still haunt on Bagdad's summit high;
He who stood visible to Mirza's eye,
Never before to human sight betrayed.
Lo, in the vale, the mists of evening spread!
The visionary Arches are not there,
Nor the green Islands, nor the shining Seas:
Yet sacred is to me this Mountain's head,
Whence I have risen, uplifted on the breeze
Of harmony, above all earthly care.

"WEAK IS THE WILL OF MAN, HIS JUDGMENT BLIND"

1807–14(?). 1815

"Weak is the will of Man, his judgment blind;
Remembrance persecutes, and Hope betrays;
Heavy is woe; — and joy, for human-kind,
A mournful thing, so transient is the blaze!"
Thus might *he* paint our lot of mortal days
Who wants the glorious faculty assigned
To elevate the more-than-reasoning Mind,
And colour life's dark cloud with orient rays.
Imagination is that sacred power,
Imagination lofty and refined;

'T is hers to pluck the amaranthine flower
Of Faith, and round the Sufferer's temples bind
Wreaths that endure affliction's heaviest shower,
And do not shrink from sorrow's keenest wind.

"HAIL, TWILIGHT, SOVEREIGN OF ONE PEACEFUL HOUR"

1812. 1815

Hail, Twilight, sovereign of one peaceful hour!
Not dull art Thou as undiscerning Night;
But studious only to remove from sight
Day's mutable distinctions. — Ancient Power!
Thus did the waters gleam, the mountains lower,
To the rude Briton, when, in wolf-skin vest
Here roving wild, he laid him down to rest
On the bare rock, or through a leafy bower
Looked ere his eyes were closed. By him was seen
The self-same Vision which we now behold,
At thy meek bidding, shadowy Power! brought forth;
These mighty barriers, and the gulf between;
The flood, the stars, — a spectacle as old
As the beginning of the heavens and earth!

"THE SHEPHERD, LOOKING EASTWARD, SOFTLY SAID"

1807–14(?). 1815

The Shepherd, looking eastward, softly said,
"Bright is thy veil, O Moon, as thou art bright!"
Forthwith, that little cloud, in ether spread
And penetrated all with tender light,
She cast away, and showed her fulgent head
Uncovered; dazzling the Beholder's sight
As if to vindicate her beauty's right,
Her beauty thoughtlessly disparaged.
Meanwhile that veil, removed or thrown aside,
Went floating from her, darkening as it went;

And a huge mass, to bury or to hide,
Approached this glory of the firmament;
Who meekly yields, and is obscured — content
With one calm triumph of a modest pride.

"EVEN AS A DRAGON'S EYE THAT FEELS THE STRESS"

1812. 1815

Even as a dragon's eye that feels the stress
Of a bedimming sleep, or as a lamp
Sullenly glaring through sepulchral damp,
So burns yon Taper 'mid a black recess
Of mountains, silent, dreary, motionless:
The lake below reflects it not; the sky,
Muffled in clouds, affords no company
To mitigate and cheer its loneliness.
Yet, round the body of that joyless Thing
Which sends so far its melancholy light,
Perhaps are seated in domestic ring
A gay society with faces bright,
Conversing, reading, laughing; — or they sing,
While hearts and voices in the song unite.

"MARK THE CONCENTRED HAZELS THAT ENCLOSE"

1807–14(?). 1815

Suggested in the wild hazel wood at the foot of Helm-crag, where the stone still lies, with others of like form and character, though much of the wood that veiled it from the glare of day has been felled. This beautiful ground was lately purchased by our friend Mrs. Fletcher, the ancient owners, most respected persons, being obliged to part with it in consequence of the imprudence, if not misconduct, of a son. It is gratifying to mention that, instead of murmuring and repining at this change of fortune, they offered their services to Mrs. Fletcher, the husband as an outdoor labourer, and the wife as a domestic servant. I have witnessed the pride and pleasure with which the man worked at improvements of the ground round the house. Indeed he expressed those feelings to me himself, and the countenance and manner of his wife always denoted feelings of the same character. I believe a similar disposition to contentment under change of fortune is common among the class to which these good people belong. Yet, in proof that to part with their patrimony is most painful to them, I may refer to those stanzas entitled "Repentance," no inconsiderable part of which was taken verbatim from the language of the speaker herself.

Mark the concentred hazels that enclose
Yon old gray Stone, protected from the ray
Of noontide suns : — and even the beams that play
And glance, while wantonly the rough wind blows,
Are seldom free to touch the moss that grows
Upon that roof, amid embowering gloom,
The very image framing of a Tomb,
In which some ancient Chieftain finds repose
Among the lonely mountains. — Live, ye trees !
And thou, grey Stone, the pensive likeness keep
Of a dark chamber where the Mighty sleep:
For more than Fancy to the influence bends
When solitary Nature condescends
To mimic Time's forlorn humanities.

TO THE POET, JOHN DYER

1807–11(?). 1815

Bard of the Fleece, whose skilful genius made
That work a living landscape fair and bright;
Nor hallowed less with musical delight
Than those soft scenes through which thy childhood strayed,
Those southern tracts of Cambria, " deep embayed,
With green hills fenced, with ocean's murmur lulled; "
Though hasty Fame hath many a chaplet culled
For worthless brows, while in the pensive shade
Of cold neglect she leaves thy head ungraced,
Yet pure and powerful minds, hearts meek and still,
A grateful few, shall love thy modest Lay,
Long as the shepherd's bleating flock shall stray
O'er naked Snowdon's wide aërial waste;
Long as the thrush shall pipe on Grongar Hill !

"BROOK! WHOSE SOCIETY THE POET SEEKS"

1802(?). 1815

BROOK! whose society the Poet seeks,
Intent his wasted spirits to renew;
And whom the curious Painter doth pursue
Through rocky passes, among flowery
    creeks,
And tracks thee dancing down thy water-
    breaks;
If wish were mine some type of thee to
    view,
Thee, and not thee thyself, I would not do
Like Grecian Artists, give thee human
    cheeks,
Channels for tears; no Naiad should'st thou
    be, —
Have neither limbs, feet, feathers, joints nor
    hairs:
It seems the Eternal Soul is clothed in
    thee
With purer robes than those of flesh and
    blood,
And hath bestowed on thee a safer good;
Unwearied joy, and life without its cares.

"SURPRISED BY JOY — IMPA-TIENT AS THE WIND"

1813–14. 1815

This was in fact suggested by my daughter Catharine long after her death.

SURPRISED by joy — impatient as the Wind
I turned to share the transport — Oh! with
    whom
But Thee, deep buried in the silent tomb,
That spot which no vicissitude can find?
Love, faithful love, recalled thee to my
    mind —
But how could I forget thee? Through
    what power,
Even for the least division of an hour,
Have I been so beguiled as to be blind
To my most grievous loss! — That thought's
    return
Was the worst pang that sorrow ever bore,
Save one, one only, when I stood forlorn,
Knowing my heart's best treasure was no
    more;
That neither present time, nor years unborn
Could to my sight that heavenly face re-
    store.

ODE

THE MORNING OF THE DAY APPOINTED FOR A GENERAL THANKSGIVING. JANUARY 18, 1816

1816. 1816

The first stanza of this Ode was composed almost extempore, in front of Rydal Mount, before church-time, and on such a morning and precisely with such objects before my eyes as are here described. The view taken of Napoleon's character and proceedings is little in accordance with that taken by some historians and critical philosophers. I am glad and proud of the difference, and trust that this series of poems, infinitely below the subject as they are, will survive to counteract, in unsophisticated minds, the pernicious and degrading tendency of those views and doctrines that lead to the idolatry of power, as power, and, in that false splendour to lose sight of its real nature and constitution as it often acts for the gratification of its possessor without reference to a beneficial end — an infirmity that has characterised men of all ages, classes, and employments, since Nimrod became a mighty hunter before the Lord.

I

HAIL, orient Conqueror of gloomy Night!
Thou that canst shed the bliss of gratitude
On hearts howe'er insensible or rude;
Whether thy punctual visitations smite
The haughty towers where monarchs dwell;
Or thou, impartial Sun, with presence bright
Cheer'st the low threshold of the peasant's
    cell!
Not unrejoiced I see thee climb the sky
In naked splendour, clear from mist or
    haze,
Or cloud approaching to divert the rays, 10
Which even in deepest winter testify
    Thy power and majesty,
Dazzling the vision that presumes to gaze.
— Well does thine aspect usher in this Day;
As aptly suits therewith that modest pace
    Submitted to the chains
That bind thee to the path which God or-
    dains
    That thou shalt trace,
Till, with the heavens and earth, thou pass
    away!
Nor less, the stillness of these frosty plains,
Their utter stillness, and the silent grace 21
Of yon ethereal summits white with snow,
(Whose tranquil pomp and spotless purity

Report of storms gone by
To us who tread below)
Do with the service of this Day accord.
— Divinest Object which the uplifted eye
Of mortal man is suffered to behold;
Thou, who upon those snow-clad Heights
  has poured
Meek lustre, nor forget'st the humble
  Vale;   30
Thou who dost warm Earth's universal
  mould,
And for thy bounty wert not unadored
  By pious men of old;
Once more, heart-cheering Sun, I bid thee
  hail !
Bright be thy course to-day, let not this
  promise fail !

II

'Mid the deep quiet of this morning hour,
All nature seems to hear me while I speak,
By feelings urged that do not vainly seek
Apt language, ready as the tuneful notes
That stream in blithe succession from the
  throats   40
Of birds, in leafy bower,
Warbling a farewell to a vernal shower.
— There is a radiant though a short-lived
  flame,
That burns for Poets in the dawning east;
And oft my soul hath kindled at the same,
When the captivity of sleep had ceased;
But He who fixed immoveably the frame
Of the round world, and built, by laws as
  strong,
  A solid refuge for distress —
  The towers of righteousness;   50
He knows that from a holier altar came
The quickening spark of this day's sacrifice;
Knows that the source is nobler whence
  doth rise
  The current of this matin song;
  That deeper far it lies
Than aught dependent on the fickle skies.

III

Have we not conquered ? — by the venge-
  ful sword ?
Ah no, by dint of Magnanimity;
That curbed the baser passions, and left free
A loyal band to follow their liege Lord   60
Clear-sighted Honour, and his staid Com-
  peers,
Along a track of most unnatural years;
In execution of heroic deeds

Whose memory, spotless as the crystal
  beads
Of morning dew upon the untrodden meads,
Shall live enrolled above the starry spheres.
He, who in concert with an earthly string
  Of Britain's acts would sing,
  He with enraptured voice will tell
Of One whose spirit no reverse could
  quell;   70
Of One that 'mid the failing never failed —
Who paints how Britain struggled and pre-
  vailed
Shall represent her labouring with an eye
  Of circumspect humanity;
Shall show her clothed with strength and
  skill,
  All martial duties to fulfil;
Firm as a rock in stationary fight;
In motion rapid as the lightning's gleam;
Fierce as a flood-gate bursting at midnight
To rouse the wicked from their giddy
  dream —   80
Woe, woe to all that face her in the field !
Appalled she may not be, and cannot yield.

IV

And thus is *missed* the sole true glory
That can belong to human story !
At which they only shall arrive
Who through the abyss of weakness dive.
The very humblest are too proud of heart;
And one brief day is rightly set apart
For Him who lifteth up and layeth low;
For that Almighty God to whom we owe,   90
Say not that we have vanquished — but that
  we survive.

V

How dreadful the dominion of the im-
  pure !
Why should the Song be tardy to proclaim
That less than power unbounded could not
  tame
That soul of Evil — which, from hell let
  loose,
Had filled the astonished world with such
  abuse
As boundless patience only could endure ?
— Wide-wasted regions — cities wrapt in
  flame —
Who sees, may lift a streaming eye
To Heaven; — who never saw, may heave a
  sigh;   100
But the foundation of our nature shakes,
And with an infinite pain the spirit aches,

When desolated countries, towns on fire,
 Are but the avowed attire
Of warfare waged with desperate mind
Against the life of virtue in mankind;
  Assaulting without ruth
  The citadels of truth;
While the fair gardens of civility,
 By ignorance defaced,   110
 By violence laid waste,
Perish without reprieve for flower or
 tree !

VI

A crouching purpose — a distracted will —
Opposed to hopes that battened upon scorn,
And to desires whose ever-waxing horn
Not all the light of earthly power could
 fill ;
Opposed to dark, deep plots of patient
 skill,
And to celerities of lawless force;
Which, spurning God, had flung away re-
 morse —
What could they gain but shadows of re-
 dress ?   120
— So bad proceeded propagating worse;
And discipline was passion's dire excess.
Widens the fatal web, its lines extend,
And deadlier poisons in the chalice blend.
When will your trials teach you to be
 wise ?
— O prostrate Lands, consult your agonies !

VII

No more — the guilt is banished,
 And, with the guilt, the shame is fled;
And, with the guilt and shame, the Woe
 hath vanished,
Shaking the dust and ashes from her
 head !   130
— No more — these lingerings of distress
Sully the limpid stream of thankfulness.
What robe can Gratitude employ
So seemly as the radiant vest of Joy ?
What steps so suitable as those that move
In prompt obedience to spontaneous mea-
 sures
Of glory, and felicity, and love,
Surrendering the whole heart to sacred
 pleasures ?

VIII

O Britain ! dearer far than life is dear,
 If one there be   140
 Of all thy progeny

Who can forget thy prowess, never more
Be that ungrateful Son allowed to hear
Thy green leaves rustle or thy torrents
 roar.
As springs the lion from his den,
  As from a forest-brake
  Upstarts a glistering snake,
The bold Arch-despot re-appeared ; — again
Wide Europe heaves, impatient to be cast,
 With all her armèd Powers, 150
 On that offensive soil, like waves upon
 a thousand shores.
The trumpet blew a universal blast !
But Thou art foremost in the field : — there
 stand :
Receive the triumph destined to thy hand !
All States have glorified themselves ; — their
 claims
Are weighed by Providence, in balance
 even;
And now, in preference to the mightiest
 names,
To Thee the exterminating sword is given.
Dread mark of approbation, justly gained !
Exalted office, worthily sustained ! 160

IX

Preserve, O Lord ! within our hearts
The memory of thy favour,
That else insensibly departs,
And loses its sweet savour !
Lodge it within us ! — as the power of
 light
Lives inexhaustibly in precious gems,
Fixed on the front of Eastern diadems,
So shine our thankfulness for ever bright !
What offering, what transcendent monu-
 ment
Shall our sincerity to Thee present ? 170
— Not work of hands; but trophies that
 may reach
To highest Heaven — the labour of the
 Soul;
That builds, as thy unerring precepts teach,
Upon the internal conquests made by each,
Her hope of lasting glory for the whole.
Yet will not heaven disown nor earth gain-
 say
The outward service of this day;
Whether the worshippers entreat
Forgiveness from God's mercy-seat;
Or thanks and praises to His throne ascend
That He has brought our warfare to an
 end,   181
And that we need no second victory ! ——

Ha! what a ghastly sight for man to
    see;
And to the heavenly saints in peace who
    dwell,
For a brief moment, terrible;
But, to thy sovereign penetration, fair,
Before whom all things are, that were,
All judgments that have been, or e'er shall
    be;
Links in the chain of thy tranquillity!
Along the bosom of this favoured Na-
    tion,   190
Breathe Thou, this day, a vital undulation!
Let all who do this land inherit
Be conscious of thy moving spirit!
Oh, 't is a goodly Ordinance, — the sight,
Though sprung from bleeding war, is one
    of pure delight;
Bless Thou the hour, or ere the hour ar-
    rive,
When a whole people shall kneel down in
    prayer,
And, at one moment, in one rapture, strive
With lip and heart to tell their gratitude
    For thy protecting care,   200
Their solemn joy — praising the Eternal
    Lord
For tyranny subdued,
And for the sway of equity renewed,
For liberty confirmed, and peace restored!

X

But hark — the summons! — down the
    placid lake
Floats the soft cadence of the church-tower
    bells;
Bright shines the Sun, as if his beams
    would wake
The tender insects sleeping in their cells;
Bright shines the Sun — and not a breeze to
    shake
The drops that tip the melting icicles.   210
    O, enter now his temple gate!
Inviting words — perchance already flung
(As the crowd press devoutly down the
    aisle
Of some old Minster's venerable pile)
From voices into zealous passion stung,
While the tubed engine feels the inspiring
    blast,
And has begun — its clouds of sound to
    cast
    Forth towards empyreal Heaven,
    As if the fretted roof were riven.
Us, humbler ceremonies now await;   220

But in the bosom, with devout respect
The banner of our joy we will erect,
And strength of love our souls shall ele-
    vate:
For to a few collected in his name,
Their heavenly Father will incline an ear
Gracious to service hallowed by its aim; —
Awake! the majesty of God revere!
    Go — and with foreheads meekly bowed
Present your prayers — go — and rejoice
    aloud —
    The Holy One will hear!   230
And what, 'mid silence deep, with faith sin-
    cere,
Ye, in your low and undisturbed estate,
Shall simply feel and purely meditate —
Of warnings — from the unprecedented
    might,
Which, in our time, the impious have dis-
    closed;
And of more arduous duties thence imposed
Upon the future advocates of right;
    Of mysteries revealed,
    And judgments unrepealed,
    Of earthly revolution,   240
    And final retribution, —
To his omniscience will appear
An offering not unworthy to find place,
On this high DAY of THANKS, before the
    Throne of Grace!

ODE

1816.   1816

I

IMAGINATION — ne'er before content,
But aye ascending, restless in her pride
From all that martial feats could yield
To her desires, or to her hopes present —
Stooped to the Victory, on that Belgic field
Achieved, this closing deed magnificent,
    And with the embrace was satisfied.
    — Fly, ministers of Fame,
With every help that ye from earth and
    heaven may claim!
Bear through the world these tidings of de-
    light!   10
— Hours, Days, and Months, *have* borne
    them in the sight
Of mortals, hurrying like a sudden shower
    That landward stretches from the sea,
    The morning's splendours to devour;
But this swift travel scorns the company

Of irksome change, or threats from sadden-
    ing power.
      —The shock is given — the Adversaries
      bleed —
      Lo, Justice triumphs ! Earth is freed !
Joyful annunciation ! — it went forth —
It pierced the caverns of the sluggish
    North —   20
    It found no barrier on the ridge
Of Andes — frozen gulphs became its
    bridge —
The vast Pacific gladdens with the freight —
Upon the Lakes of Asia 't is bestowed —
The Arabian desert shapes a willing road
    Across her burning breast,
For this refreshing incense from the West! —
— Where snakes and lions breed,
Where towns and cities thick as stars ap-
    pear,
Wherever fruits are gathered, and where'er
The upturned soil receives the hopeful
    seed —   31
While the Sun rules, and cross the shades
    of night —
The unwearied arrow hath pursued its
    flight !
The eyes of good men thankfully give
    heed,
    And in its sparkling progress read
Of virtue crowned with glory's deathless
    meed:
Tyrants exult to hear of kingdoms won,
And slaves are pleased to learn that mighty
    feats are done;
Even the proud Realm, from whose dis-
    tracted borders
This messenger of good was launched in air,
France, humbled France, amid her wild
    disorders,   41
Feels, and hereafter shall the truth de-
    clare,
That she too lacks not reason to rejoice,
And utter England's name with sadly-
    plausive voice.

II

O genuine glory, pure renown !
And well might it beseem that mighty
    Town
Into whose bosom earth's best treasures
    flow,
To whom all persecuted men retreat;
If a new Temple lift her votive brow
High on the shore of silver Thames — to
    greet   50

The peaceful guest advancing from afar.
Bright be the Fabric, as a star
Fresh risen, and beautiful within ! — there
    meet
Dependence infinite, proportion just;
A Pile that Grace approves, and Time can
    trust
With his most sacred wealth, heroic dust.

III

    But if the valiant of this land
In reverential modesty demand,
That all observance, due to them, be
    paid
Where their serene progenitors are laid; 60
Kings, warriors, high-souled poets, saint-
    like sages,
England's illustrious sons of long, long
    ages;
Be it not unordained that solemn rites,
Within the circuit of those Gothic walls,
Shall be performed at pregnant inter-
    vals;
Commemoration holy that unites
The living generations with the dead;
    By the deep soul-moving sense
    Of religious eloquence, —
    By visual pomp, and by the tie   70
    Of sweet and threatening harmony;
    Soft notes, awful as the omen
    Of destructive tempests coming,
    And escaping from that sadness
    Into elevated gladness;
    While the white-robed choir attendant,
    Under mouldering banners pendant,
Provoke all potent symphonies to raise
    Songs of victory and praise,
For them who bravely stood unhurt, or
    bled   80
With medicable wounds, or found their
    graves
Upon the battle field, or under ocean's
    waves;
Or were conducted home in single state,
And long procession — there to lie,
Where their sons' sons, and all posterity,
Unheard by them, their deeds shall cele-
    brate !

IV

    Nor will the God of peace and love
    Such martial service disapprove.
    He guides the Pestilence — the cloud
    Of locusts travels on his breath;   90
    The region that in hope was ploughed

His drought consumes, his mildew taints
with death;
He springs the hushed Volcano's mine,
He puts the Earthquake on her still de-
sign,
Darkens the sun, hath bade the forest
sink,
And, drinking towns and cities, still can
drink
Cities and towns — 't is Thou — the work
is Thine ! —
The fierce tornado sleeps within thy
courts —
He hears the word — he flies —
And navies perish in their ports;   100
For Thou art angry with thine enemies !
For these, and mourning for our errors,
And sins, that point their terrors,
We bow our heads before Thee, and we
laud
And magnify thy name, Almighty God !
But Man is thy most awful instru-
ment,
In working out a pure intent;
Thou cloth'st the wicked in their dazzling
mail,
And for thy righteous purpose they pre-
vail;
Thine arm from peril guards the coasts
Of them who in thy laws delight: 111
Thy presence turns the scale of doubtful
fight,
Tremendous God of battles, Lord of Hosts !

V

Forbear: — to Thee —
Father and Judge of all, with fervent
tongue
But in a gentler strain
Of contemplation, by no sense of wrong,
(Too quick and keen) incited to disdain
Of pity pleading from the heart in vain —
To THEE — To THEE —   120
Just God of christianised Humanity,
Shall praises be poured forth, and thanks
ascend,
That thou hast brought our warfare to an
end,
And that we need no second victory .
Blest, above measure blest,
If on thy love our Land her hopes shall
rest,
And all the Nations labour to fulfil
Thy law, and live henceforth in peace, in
pure good will.

INVOCATION TO THE EARTH

FEBRUARY 1816

1816. 1816

Composed immediately after the "Thanks-
giving Ode," to which it may be considered as
a second part.

I

" REST, rest, perturbèd Earth !
O rest, thou doleful Mother of Man-
kind ! "
A Spirit sang in tones more plaintive than
the wind:
" From regions where no evil thing has
birth
I come — thy stains to wash away,
Thy cherished fetters to unbind,
And open thy sad eyes upon a milder day.
The Heavens are thronged with martyrs
that have risen
From out thy noisome prison;
The penal caverns groan   10
With tens of thousands rent from off the
tree
Of hopeful life, — by battle's whirlwind
blown
Into the deserts of Eternity.
Unpitied havoc ! Victims unlamented !
But not on high, where madness is resented,
And murder causes some sad tears to flow,
Though, from the widely-sweeping blow,
The choirs of Angels spread, triumphantly
augmented.

II

" False Parent of Mankind !
Obdurate, proud, and blind,   20
I sprinkle thee with soft celestial dews,
Thy lost, maternal heart to re-infuse !
Scattering this far-fetched moisture from
my wings,
Upon the act a blessing I implore,
Of which the rivers in their secret springs,
The rivers stained so oft with human gore,
Are conscious; — may the like return no
more !
May Discord — for a Seraph's care
Shall be attended with a bolder prayer —
May she, who once disturbed the seats of
bliss   30
These mortal spheres above,
Be chained for ever to the black abyss.
And thou, O rescued Earth, by peace and
love,

And merciful desires, thy sanctity ap-
    prove ! "
The Spirit ended his mysterious rite,
And the pure vision closed in darkness in-
    finite.

ODE

1816. 1816

    —— Carmina possumus
Donare, et pretium dicere muneri.
Non incisa notis marmora publicis,
Per quæ spiritus et vita redit bonis
Post mortem ducibus
      —— clarius indicant
Laudes, quam —— Pierides ; neque,
Si chartæ sileant quod bene feceris,
Mercedem tuleris. — HOR. CAR. 8, Lib. 4.

I

WHEN the soft hand of sleep had closed
    the latch
On the tired household of corporeal sense,
And Fancy, keeping unreluctant watch,
Was free her choicest favours to dispense;
I saw, in wondrous pérspective displayed,
A landscape more august than happiest skill
Of pencil ever clothed with light and shade;
An intermingled pomp of vale and hill,
City, and naval stream, suburban grove, 9
And stately forest where the wild deer rove;
Nor wanted lurking hamlet, dusky towns,
And scattered rural farms of aspect bright;
And, here and there, between the pastoral
    downs,
The azure sea upswelled upon the sight.
Fair prospect, such as Britain only shows !
But not a living creature could be seen
Through its wide circuit, that, in deep repose,
And, even to sadness, lonely and serene,
Lay hushed; till — through a portal in the
    sky 19
Brighter than brightest loop-hole, in a storm,
Opening before the sun's triumphant eye —
Issued, to sudden view, a glorious Form !
Earthward it glided with a swift descent:
Saint George himself this Visitant must be;
And, ere a thought could ask on what intent
He sought the regions of Humanity,
A thrilling voice was heard, that vivified
City and field and flood; — aloud it cried —
    " Though from my celestial home,
      Like a Champion, armed I come; 30
    On my helm the dragon crest,
    And the red cross on my breast;
    I, the Guardian of this Land,
    Speak not now of toilsome duty;

    Well obeyed was that command —
    Whence bright days of festive beauty;
Haste, Virgins, haste ! — the flowers which
    summer gave
Have perished in the field;
But the green thickets plenteously shall yield
    Fit garlands for the brave, 40
That will be welcome, if by you entwined;
Haste, Virgins, haste; and you, ye Matrons
    grave,
Go forth with rival youthfulness of mind,
    And gather what ye find
Of hardy laurel and wild holly boughs —
To deck your stern Defenders' modest brows !
    Such simple gifts prepare,
Though they have gained a worthier meed;
    And in due time shall share
Those palms and amaranthine wreaths 50
Unto their martyred Countrymen decreed,
In realms where everlasting freshness
    breathes ! "

II

    And lo ! with crimson banners proudly
      streaming,
And upright weapons innocently gleaming,
Along the surface of a spacious plain
Advance in order the redoubted Bands,
And there receive green chaplets from the
    hands
    Of a fair female train —
    Maids and Matrons, dight
    In robes of dazzling white; 60
While from the crowd bursts forth a rap-
    turous noise
    By the cloud-capt hills retorted;
    And a throng of rosy boys
    In loose fashion tell their joys;
And grey-haired sires, on staffs supported,
Look round, and by their smiling seem to
    say,
'' Thus strives a grateful Country to display
The mighty debt which nothing can repay ! ''

III

    Anon before my sight a palace rose
Built of all precious substances, — so pure
And exquisite, that sleep alone bestows 71
    Ability like splendour to endure:
Entered, with streaming thousands, through
    the gate,
I saw the banquet spread beneath a Dome
    of state,
A lofty Dome, that dared to emulate
The heaven of sable night

With starry lustre; yet had power to
throw
Solemn effulgence, clear as solar light,
Upon a princely company below,
While the vault rang with choral harmony,
Like some Nymph-haunted grot beneath
the roaring sea.   81
— No sooner ceased that peal, than on the
verge
Of exultation hung a dirge
Breathed from a soft and lonely instru-
ment,
That kindled recollections
Of agonised affections;
And, though some tears the strain at-
tended,
The mournful passion ended
In peace of spirit, and sublime content !

IV

But garlands wither; festal shows de-
part,   90
Like dreams themselves; and sweetest
sound —
(Albeit of effect profound)
It was — and it is gone !
Victorious England ! bid the silent Art
Reflect, in glowing hues that shall not fade,
Those high achievements; even as she ar-
rayed
With second life the deed of Marathon
Upon Athenian walls;
So may she labour for thy civic halls:
And be the guardian spaces   100
Of consecrated places,
As nobly graced by Sculpture's patient toil;
And let imperishable Columns rise
Fixed in the depths of this courageous soil;
Expressive signals of a glorious strife,
And competent to shed a spark divine
Into the torpid breast of daily life; —
Records on which, for pleasure of all eyes,
The morning sun may shine
With gratulation thoroughly benign !   110

V

And ye, Pierian Sisters, sprung from Jove
And sage Mnemosyne, — full long de-
barred
From your first mansions, exiled all too
long
From many a hallowed stream and grove,
Dear native regions where ye wont to rove,
Chanting for patriot heroes the reward
Of never-dying song !

Now (for, though Truth descending from
above
The Olympian summit hath destroyed for
aye
Your kindred Deities, *Ye* live and move, 120
Spared for obeisance from perpetual love
For privilege redeemed of godlike sway)
Now, on the margin of some spotless foun-
tain,
Or top serene of unmolested mountain,
Strike audibly the noblest of your lyres,
And for a moment meet the soul's desires !
That I, or some more favoured Bard, may
hear
What ye, celestial Maids ! have often sung
Of Britain's acts, — may catch it with rapt
ear,   129
And give the treasure to our British tongue!
So shall the characters of that proud page
Support their mighty theme from age to
age;
And, in the desert places of the earth,
When they to future empires have given
birth,
So shall the people gather and believe
The bold report, transferred to every
clime;
And the whole world, not envious but ad-
miring,
And to the like aspiring,
Own — that the progeny of this fair Isle
Had power as lofty actions to achieve   140
As were performed in man's heroic prime;
Nor wanted, when their fortitude had held
Its even tenor, and the foe was quelled,
A corresponding virtue to beguile
The hostile purpose of wide-wasting
Time —
That not in vain they laboured to secure,
For their great deeds, perpetual memory,
And fame as largely spread as land and sea,
By Works of spirit high and passion pure !

ODE

1816. 1816

I

Who rises on the banks of Seine,
And binds her temples with the civic
wreath ?
What joy to read the promise of her mien !
How sweet to rest her wide-spread wings
beneath !

But they are ever playing,
And twinkling in the light,
And, if a breeze be straying,
That breeze she will invite;
And stands on tiptoe, conscious she is fair,   10
And calls a look of love into her face,
And spreads her arms, as if the general air
Alone could satisfy her wide embrace.
— Melt, Principalities, before her melt!
Her love ye hailed — her wrath have felt!
But She through many a change of form
        hath gone,
And stands amidst you now an arm√®d crea-
        ture,
Whose panoply is not a thing put on,
But the live scales of a portentous nature;
That, having forced its way from birth to
        birth,
Stalks round — abhorred by Heaven, a ter-
        ror to the Earth!   20

II

I marked the breathings of her dragon
        crest;
My Soul, a sorrowful interpreter,
In many a midnight vision bowed
Before the ominous aspect of her spear;
Whether the mighty beam, in scorn upheld,
Threatened her foes, — or, pompously at
        rest,
Seemed to bisect her orb√®d shield,
As stretches a blue bar of solid cloud
Across the setting sun and all the fiery
        west.

III

So did she daunt the Earth, and God
        defy!   30
And, wheresoe'er she spread her sove-
        reignty,
Pollution tainted all that was most pure.
— Have we not known — and live we not
        to tell —
That Justice seemed to hear her final
        knell?
Faith buried deeper in her own deep breast
Her stores, and sighed to find them inse-
        cure!
And Hope was maddened by the drops that
        fell
From shades, her chosen place of short-
        lived rest.
Shame followed shame, and woe supplanted
        woe —
Is this the only change that time can show?

How long shall vengeance sleep? Ye pa-
        tient Heavens, how long?   41
— Infirm ejaculation! from the tongue
Of Nations wanting virtue to be strong
Up to the measure of accorded might,
And daring not to feel the majesty of
        right!

IV

Weak Spirits are there — who would ask,
Upon the pressure of a painful thing,
The lion's sinews, or the eagle's wing;
Or let their wishes loose, in forest-glade,
        Among the lurking powers   50
        Of herbs and lowly flowers,
Or seek, from saints above, miraculous aid —
That Man may be accomplished for a task
Which his own nature hath enjoined; —
        and why?
If, when that interference hath relieved
        him,
        He must sink down to languish
In worse than former helplessness — and lie
        Till the caves roar, — and, imbe-
        cility
        Again engendering anguish,
The same weak wish returns, that had be-
        fore deceived him.   60

V

But Thou, supreme Disposer! may'st not
        speed
The course of things, and change the creed
Which hath been held aloft before men's
        sight
Since the first framing of societies,
Whether, as bards have told in ancient song,
Built up by soft seducing harmonies;
Or prest together by the appetite,
        And by the power, of wrong.

THE FRENCH ARMY IN RUSSIA

1812-13

1816. 1816

HUMANITY, delighting to behold
A fond reflection of her own decay,
Hath painted Winter like a traveller old,
Propped on a staff, and, through the sullen
        day,
In hooded mantle, limping o'er the plain,
As though his weakness were disturbed by
        pain:
Or, if a juster fancy should allow

An undisputed symbol of command,
The chosen sceptre is a withered bough,
Infirmly grasped within a palsied hand.   10
These emblems suit the helpless and for-
    lorn;
But mighty Winter the device shall scorn.

For he it was — dread Winter ! who beset,
Flinging round van and rear his ghastly net,
That host, when from the regions of the
    Pole
They shrunk, insane ambition's barren
    goal —
That host, as huge and strong as e'er defied
Their God, and placed their trust in human
    pride !
As fathers persecute rebellious sons,
He smote the blossoms of their warrior
    youth;   20
He called on Frost's inexorable tooth
Life to consume in Manhood's firmest hold;
Nor spared the reverend blood that feebly
    runs;
For why — unless for liberty enrolled
And sacred home — ah ! why should hoary
    Age be bold ?

Fleet the Tartar's reinless steed,
But fleeter far the pinions of the Wind,
Which from Siberian caves the Monarch
    freed,
And sent him forth, with squadrons of his
    kind,
And bade the Snow their ample backs be-
    stride,   30
    And to the battle ride.
No pitying voice commands a halt,
No courage can repel the dire assault;
Distracted, spiritless, benumbed, and blind,
Whole legions sink, and, in one instant, find
Burial and death: look for them — and
    descry,
When morn returns, beneath the clear blue
    sky,
A soundless waste, a trackless vacancy !

ON THE SAME OCCASION

1816. 1816

Ye Storms, resound the praises of your
    King !
And ye mild Seasons — in a sunny clime,
Midway on some high hill, while father
    Time

Looks on delighted — meet in festal ring,
And loud and long of Winter's triumph sing!
Sing ye, with blossoms crowned, and fruits,
    and flowers,
Of Winter's breath surcharged with sleety
    showers,
And the dire flapping of his hoary wing !
Knit the blithe dance upon the soft green
    grass;
With feet, hands, eyes, looks, lips, report
    your gain;
Whisper it to the billows of the main,
And to the aërial zephyrs as they pass,
That old decrepit Winter — *He* hath slain
That Host, which rendered all your boun-
    ties vain !

"BY MOSCOW SELF-DEVOTED TO A BLAZE"

1822. 1827

By Moscow self-devoted to a blaze
Of dreadful sacrifice; by Russian blood
Lavished in fight with desperate hardihood;
The unfeeling Elements no claim shall raise
To rob our Human-nature of just praise
For what she did and suffered. Pledges
    sure
Of a deliverance absolute and pure
She gave, if Faith might tread the beaten
    ways
Of Providence. But now did the Most
    High
Exalt his still small voice; — to quell that
    Host
Gathered his power, a manifest ally;
He, whose heaped waves confounded the
    proud boast
Of Pharaoh, said to Famine, Snow, and
    Frost,
" Finish the strife by deadliest victory ! "

THE GERMANS ON THE HEIGHTS OF HOCHHEIM

1820. 1822

Abruptly paused the strife; — the field
    throughout
Resting upon his arms each warrior stood,
Checked in the very act and deed of blood,
With breath suspended, like a listening scout.
O Silence ! thou wert mother of a shout

That through the texture of yon azure dome
Cleaves its glad way, a cry of harvest home
Uttered to Heaven in ecstasy devout !
The barrier Rhine hath flashed, through
    battle-smoke,
On men who gaze heart-smitten by the
    view,
As if all Germany had felt the shock !
—Fly, wretched Gauls ! ere they the charge
    renew
Who have seen — themselves now casting
    off the yoke —
The unconquerable Stream his course pur-
    sue.

SIEGE OF VIENNA RAISED BY JOHN SOBIESKI

FEBRUARY 1816

1816. 1816

OH, for a kindling touch from that pure
    flame
Which ministered, erewhile, to a sacrifice
Of gratitude, beneath Italian skies,
In words like these: " Up, Voice of song !
    proclaim
Thy saintly rapture with celestial aim:
For lo ! the Imperial City stands released
From bondage threatened by the embattled
    East,
And Christendom respires; from guilt and
    shame
Redeemed, from miserable fear set free
By one day's feat, one mighty victory.
—Chant the Deliverer's praise in every
    tongue !
The cross shall spread, the crescent hath
    waxed dim;
He conquering, as in joyful Heaven is
    sung,
HE CONQUERING THROUGH GOD, AND GOD
BY HIM."

OCCASIONED BY THE BATTLE OF WATERLOO

FEBRUARY 1816

1816. 1816

(The last six lines intended for an Inscription.)

INTREPID sons of Albion ! not by you
Is life despised; ah no, the spacious earth

Ne'er saw a race who held, by right of
    birth,
So many objects to which love is due:
Ye slight not life — to God and Nature true;
But death, becoming death, is dearer far,
When duty bids you bleed in open war:
Hence hath your prowess quelled that im-
    pious crew.
Heroes ! — for instant sacrifice prepared;
Yet filled with ardour and on triumph bent
'Mid direst shocks of mortal accident —
To you who fell, and you whom slaughter
    spared
To guard the fallen, and consummate the
    event,
Your Country rears this sacred Monument !

OCCASIONED BY THE BATTLE OF WATERLOO

FEBRUARY 1816

1816. 1816

THE Bard — whose soul is meek as dawn-
    ing day,
Yet trained to judgments righteously severe,
Fervid, yet conversànt with holy fear,
As recognising one Almighty sway:
He — whose experienced eye can pierce the
    array
Of past events; to whom, in vision clear,
The aspiring heads of future things appear,
Like mountain-tops whose mists have rolled
    away —
Assoiled from all encumbrance of our time,
He only, if such breathe, in strains devout
Shall comprehend this victory sublime;
Shall worthily rehearse the hideous rout,
The triumph hail, which from their peace-
    ful clime
Angels might welcome with a choral shout !

"EMPERORS AND KINGS, HOW OFT HAVE TEMPLES RUNG"

1816. 1827

EMPERORS and Kings, how oft have temples
    rung
With impious thanksgiving, the Almighty's
    scorn !
How oft above their altars have been hung
Trophies that led the good and wise to
    mourn

Triumphant wrong, battle of battle born,
And sorrow that to fruitless sorrow clung !
Now, from Heaven-sanctioned victory,
  Peace is sprung;
In this firm hour Salvation lifts her horn.
Glory to arms ! But, conscious that the
  nerve
Of popular reason, long mistrusted, freed
Your thrones, ye Powers, from duty fear
  to swerve !
Be just, be grateful; nor, the oppressor's
  creed
Reviving, heavier chastisement deserve
Than ever forced unpitied hearts to bleed.

FEELINGS OF A FRENCH ROY-
  ALIST, ON THE DISINTER-
  MENT OF THE REMAINS OF
  THE DUKE D'ENGHIEN

1816. 1816

DEAR Reliques ! from a pit of vilest mould
Uprisen — to lodge among ancestral kings;
And to inflict shame's salutary stings
On the remorseless hearts of men grown old
In a blind worship; men perversely bold
Even to this hour, — yet, some shall now
  forsake
Their monstrous Idol if the dead e'er
  spake,
To warn the living; if truth were ever told
By aught redeemed out of the hollow grave:
O murdered Prince ! meek, loyal, pious,
  brave !
The power of retribution once was given:
But 't is a rueful thought that willow bands
So often tie the thunder-wielding hands
Of Justice sent to earth from highest
  Heaven !

TRANSLATION OF PART OF THE
FIRST BOOK OF THE ÆNEID

1823(?)–24. 1832

TO THE EDITORS OF THE "PHILOLOGICAL
MUSEUM"

Your letter, reminding me of an expectation
I some time since held out to you of allowing
some specimens of my translation from the
Æneid to be printed in the Philological Mu-
seum, was not very acceptable; for I had aban-
doned the thought of ever sending into the
world any part of that experiment — for it
was nothing more — an experiment begun for
amusement, and I now think a less fortunate
one than when I first named it to you. Hav-
ing been displeased in modern translations
with the additions of incongruous matter, I be-
gan to translate with a resolve to keep clear of
that fault, by adding nothing; but I became
convinced that a spirited translation can
scarcely be accomplished in the English lan-
guage without admitting a principle of com-
pensation. On this point, however, I do not
wish to insist, and merely send the following
passage, taken at random, from a wish to com-
ply with your request.   W. W.

BUT Cytherea, studious to invent
Arts yet untried, upon new counsels bent,
Resolves that Cupid, changed in form and
  face
To young Ascanius, should assume his
  place;
Present the maddening gifts, and kindle
  heat
Of passion at the bosom's inmost seat.
She dreads the treacherous house, the
  double tongue;
She burns, she frets — by Juno's rancour
  stung;
The calm of night is powerless to remove
These cares, and thus she speaks to wingèd
  Love: 10

" O son, my strength, my power ! who
  dost despise
(What, save thyself, none dares through
  earth and skies)
The giant-quelling bolts of Jove, I flee,
O son, a suppliant to thy deity !
What perils meet Æneas in his course,
How Juno's hate with unrelenting force
Pursues thy brother — this to thee is
  known;
And oft-times hast thou made my griefs
  thine own.
Him now the generous Dido by soft chains
Of bland entreaty at her court detains; 20
Junonian hospitalities prepare
Such apt occasion that I dread a snare.
Hence, ere some hostile God can intervene,
Would I, by previous wiles, inflame the
  queen
With passion for Æneas, such strong love
That at my beck, mine only, she shall
  move.
Hear, and assist; — the father's mandate
  calls

His young Ascanius to the Tyrian walls;
He comes, my dear delight, — and costliest
    things
Preserved from fire and flood for presents
    brings.   30
Him will I take, and in close covert keep,
'Mid groves Idalian, lulled to gentle sleep,
Or on Cythera's far-sequestered steep,
That he may neither know what hope is
    mine,
Nor by his presence traverse the design.
Do thou, but for a single night's brief space,
Dissemble; be that boy in form and face !
And when enraptured Dido shall receive
Thee to her arms, and kisses interweave
With many a fond embrace, while joy runs
    high,   40
And goblets crown the proud festivity,
Instil thy subtle poison, and inspire,
At every touch, an unsuspected fire."

Love, at the word, before his mother's
    sight
Puts off his wings, and walks, with proud
    delight,
Like young Iulus; but the gentlest dews
Of slumber Venus sheds, to circumfuse
The true Ascanius steeped in placid rest;
Then wafts him, cherished on her careful
    breast,
Through upper air to an Idalian glade,   50
Where he on soft *amaracus* is laid,
With breathing flowers embraced, and fra-
    grant shade.
But Cupid, following cheerily his guide
Achates, with the gifts to Carthage hied;
And, as the hall he entered, there, between
The sharers of her golden couch, was seen
Reclined in festal pomp the Tyrian queen.
The Trojans, too (Æneas at their head),
On couches lie, with purple overspread:
Meantime in canisters is heaped the bread,
Pellucid water for the hands is borne,   61
And napkins of smooth texture, finely
    shorn.
Within are fifty handmaids, who prepare,
As they in order stand, the dainty fare;
And fume the household deities with store
Of odorous incense; while a hundred more
Matched with an equal number of like
    age,
But each of manly sex, a docile page,
Marshal the banquet, giving with due grace
To cup or viand its appointed place.   70
The Tyrians rushing in, an eager band,

Their painted couches seek, obedient to
    command.
They look with wonder on the gifts — they
    gaze
Upon Iulus, dazzled with the rays
That from his ardent countenance are
    flung,
And charmed to hear his simulating
    tongue;
Nor pass unpraised the robe and veil
    divine,
Round which the yellow flowers and wan-
    dering foliage twine.

But chiefly Dido, to the coming ill
Devoted, strives in vain her vast desires to
    fill;   80
She views the gifts; upon the child then
    turns
Insatiable looks, and gazing burns.
To ease a father's cheated love he hung
Upon Æneas, and around him clung;
Then seeks the queen; with her his arts he
    tries;
She fastens on the boy enamoured eyes,
Clasps in her arms, nor weens (O lot un-
    blest !)
How great a God, incumbent o'er her
    breast,
Would fill it with his spirit. He, to
    please
His Acidalian mother, by degrees   90
Blots out Sichaeus, studious to remove
The dead, by influx of a living love,
By stealthy entrance of a perilous guest,
Troubling a heart that had been long at
    rest.

Now when the viands were withdrawn,
    and ceased
The first division of the splendid feast,
While round a vacant board the chiefs re-
    cline,
Huge goblets are brought forth; they crown
    the wine;
Voices of gladness roll the walls around;
Those gladsome voices from the courts re-
    bound;   100
From gilded rafters many a blazing light
Depends, and torches overcome the night.
The minutes fly — till, at the queen's com-
    mand,
A bowl of state is offered to her hand:
Then she, as Belus wont, and all the line
From Belus, filled it to the brim with wine;

Silence ensued. " O Jupiter, whose care
Is hospitable dealing, grant my prayer !
Productive day be this of lasting joy
To Tyrians, and these exiles driven from
   Troy;   110
A day to future generations dear !
Let Bacchus, donor of soul-quick'ning
   cheer,
Be present; kindly Juno, be thou near !
And, Tyrians, may your choicest favours
   wait
Upon this hour, the bond to celebrate ! "
She spake and shed an offering on the
   board;
Then sipped the bowl whence she the wine
   had poured
And gave to Bitias, urging the prompt lord;
He raised the bowl, and took a long deep
   draught;
Then every chief in turn the beverage
   quaffed.   120

   Graced with redundant hair, Iopas sings
The lore of Atlas, to resounding strings,
The labours of the Sun, the lunar wander-
   ings;
Whence human kind, and brute; what
   natural .powers
Engender lightning, whence are falling
   showers.
He chaunts Arcturus, — that fraternal
   twain,
The glittering Bears, — the Pleiads fraught
   with rain;
— Why suns in winter, shunning heaven's
   steep heights
Post seaward, — what impedes the tardy
   nights.
The learnèd song from Tyrian hearers
   draws   130
Loud shouts, — the Trojans echo the ap-
   plause.
— But, lengthening out the night with con-
   verse new,
Large draughts of love unhappy Dido drew;
Of Priam asked, of Hector — o'er and o'er —
What arms the son of bright Aurora
   wore; —
What steeds the car of Diomed could boast;
Among the leaders of the Grecian host
How looked Achilles, their dread para-
   mount —
" But nay — the fatal wiles, O guest, re-
   count,
Retrace the Grecian cunning from its source,

Your own grief and your friends' — your
   wandering course;   141
For now, till this seventh summer have ye
   ranged
The sea, or trod the earth, to peace es-
   tranged."

A FACT, AND AN IMAGINATION

OR, CANUTE AND ALFRED, ON THE SEASHORE

1816. 1820

The first and last fourteen lines of this poem
each make a sonnet, and were composed as such ;
but I thought that by intermediate lines they
might be connected so as to make a whole.
One or two expressions are taken from Milton's
History of England.

THE Danish Conqueror, on his royal chair,
Mustering a face of haughty sovereignty,
To aid a covert purpose, cried — " O ye
Approaching Waters of the deep, that
   share
With this green isle my fortunes, come not
   where
Your Master's throne is set." — Deaf was
   the Sea;
Her waves rolled on, respecting his decree
Less than they heed a breath of wanton
   air.
— Then Canute, rising from the invaded
   throne,
Said to his servile Courtiers, — " Poor the
   reach,   10
The undisguised extent, of mortal sway !
He only is a King, and he alone
Deserves the name (this truth the billows
   preach)
Whose everlasting laws, sea, earth, and
   heaven obey. ''
   This just reproof the prosperous Dane
Drew from the influx of the main,
For some whose rugged northern mouths
   would strain
At oriental flattery;
And Canute (fact more worthy to be
   known)
From that time forth did for his brows
   disown   20
The ostentatious symbol of a crown;
Esteeming earthly royalty
Contemptible as vain.
   Now hear what one of elder days,

Rich theme of England's fondest praise,
Her darling Alfred, *might* have spoken;
To cheer the remnant of his host
When he was driven from coast to coast,
Distressed and harassed, but with mind
    unbroken:
" My faithful followers, lo ! the tide is
    spent   30
That rose, and steadily advanced to fill
The shores and channels, working Nature's
    will
Among the mazy streams that backward
    went,
And in the sluggish pools where ships are
    pent:
And now, his task performed, the flood
    stands still,
At the green base of many an inland hill,
In placid beauty and sublime content !
Such the repose that sage and hero find;
Such measured rest the sedulous and good
Of humbler name; whose souls do, like
    the flood   40
Of Ocean, press right on; or gently wind,
Neither to be diverted nor withstood,
Until they reach the bounds by Heaven
    assigned."

TO DORA

1816. 1820

The complaint in my eyes which gave occasion to this address to my daughter first showed itself as a consequence of inflammation, caught at the top of Kirkstone, when I was over-heated by having carried up the ascent my eldest son, a lusty infant. Frequently has the disease recurred since, leaving my eyes in a state which has often prevented my reading for months, and makes me at this day incapable of bearing without injury any strong light by day or night. My acquaintance with books has therefore been far short of my wishes ; and on this account, to acknowledge the services daily and hourly done me by my family and friends, this note is written.

" *A LITTLE onward lend thy guiding hand*
To these dark steps, a little further on ! "
— What trick of memory to *my* voice hath
    brought
This mournful iteration ? For though
    Time,
The Conqueror, crowns the Conquered, on
    this brow

Planting his favourite silver diadem,
Nor he, nor minister of his — intent
To run before him — hath enrolled me yet,
Though not unmenaced, among those who
    lean
Upon a living staff, with borrowed sight. 10
— O my own Dora, my belovèd child !
Should that day come — but hark ! the
    birds salute
The cheerful dawn, brightening for me the
    east;
For me, thy natural leader, once again
Impatient to conduct thee, not as erst
A tottering infant, with compliant stoop
From flower to flower supported; but to
    curb
Thy nymph-like step swift-bounding o'er
    the lawn,
Along the loose rocks, or the slippery verge
Of foaming torrents. — From thy orisons 20
Come forth; and, while the morning air is
    yet
Transparent as the soul of innocent youth,
Let me, thy happy guide, now point thy
    way,
And now precede thee, winding to and fro,
Till we by perseverance gain the top
Of some smooth ridge, whose brink precipitous
Kindles intense desire for powers withheld
From this corporeal frame; whereon who
    stands,
Is seized with strong incitement to push
    forth
His arms, as swimmers use, and plunge —
    dread thought,   30
For pastime plunge — into the " abrupt
    abyss," —
Where ravens spread their plumy vans, at
    ease !
    And yet more gladly thee would I conduct
Through woods and spacious forests, — to
    behold
There, how the Original of human art,
Heaven-prompted Nature, measures and
    erects
Her temples, fearless for the stately work,
Though waves, to every breeze, its high-
    arched roof,
And storms the pillars rock. But we such
    schools
Of reverential awe will chiefly seek   40
In the still summer noon, while beams of
    light,

Reposing here, and in the aisles beyond
Traceably gliding through the dusk, re-
     call
To mind the living presences of nuns;
A gentle, pensive, white-robed sisterhood,
Whose saintly radiance mitigates the gloom
Of those terrestrial fabrics, where they
     serve,
To Christ, the Sun of righteousness, es-
     poused.
   Now also shall the page of classic lore,
To these glad eyes from bondage freed,
     again   50
Lie open; and the book of Holy Writ,
Again unfolded, passage clear shall yield
To heights more glorious still, and into
     shades
More awful, where, advancing hand in
     hand,
We may be taught, O Darling of my care !
To calm the affections, elevate the soul,
And consecrate our lives to truth and love.

TO ——

ON HER FIRST ASCENT TO THE SUMMIT OF HELVELLYN

1816. 1820

   Written at Rydal Mount. The lady was
Miss Blackett, then residing with Mr. Montagu
Burgoyne at Fox-Ghyll. We were tempted to
remain too long upon the mountain ; and I, im-
prudently, with the hope of shortening the way,
led her among the crags and down a steep
slope which entangled us in difficulties that
were met by her with much spirit and courage.

INMATE of a mountain-dwelling,
Thou hast clomb aloft, and gazed
From the watch-towers of Helvellyn;
Awed, delighted, and amazed !

Potent was the spell that bound thee,
Not unwilling to obey;
For blue Ether's arms, flung round thee,
Stilled the pantings of dismay.

Lo ! the dwindled woods and meadows;
What a vast abyss is there !   10
Lo ! the clouds, the solemn shadows,
And the glistenings — heavenly fair !

And a record of commotion
Which a thousand ridges yield;

Ridge, and gulf, and distant ocean
Gleaming like a silver shield !

Maiden ! now take flight; — inherit
Alps or Andes — they are thine !
With the morning's roseate Spirit,
Sweep their length of snowy line;   20

Or survey their bright dominions
In the gorgeous colours drest,
Flung from off the purple pinions,
Evening spreads throughout the west !

Thine are all the choral fountains
Warbling in each sparry vault
Of the untrodden lunar mountains;
Listen to their songs ! — or halt,

To Niphates' top invited,
Whither spiteful Satan steered;   30
Or descend where the ark alighted,
When the green earth re-appeared;

For the power of hills is on thee,
As was witnessed through thine eye
Then, when old Helvellyn won thee
To confess their majesty !

VERNAL ODE

1817. 1820

   Composed at Rydal Mount, to place in view
the immortality of succession where immor-
tality is denied, as far as we know, to the indi-
vidual creature.
   Rerum Natura tota est nusquam magis quam
minimis. — PLIN. Nat. Hist.

I

BENEATH the concave of an April sky,
When all the fields with freshest green
     were dight,
Appeared, in presence of the spiritual eye
That aids or supersedes our grosser sight,
The form and rich habiliments of One
Whose countenance bore resemblance to
     the sun,
When it reveals, in evening majesty,
Features half lost amid their own pure
     light.
Poised like a weary cloud, in middle air
He hung, — then floated with angelic ease
(Softening that bright effulgence by de-
     grees)   15

Till he had reached a summit sharp and
    bare,
Where oft the venturous heifer drinks the
    noontide breeze.
Upon the apex of that lofty cone
Alighted, there the Stranger stood alone;
Fair as a gorgeous Fabric of the east
Suddenly raised by some enchanter's power,
Where nothing was; and firm as some old
    Tower
Of Britain's realm, whose leafy crest
Waves high, embellished by a gleaming
    shower !   20

II

Beneath the shadow of his purple wings
Rested a golden harp; — he touched the
    strings;
And, after prelude of unearthly sound
Poured through the echoing hills around,
He sang —
        " No wintry desolations,
Scorching blight or noxious dew,
Affect my native habitations;
Buried in glory, far beyond the scope
Of man's inquiring gaze, but to his hope
Imaged, though faintly, in the hue   30
Profound of night's ethereal blue;
And in the aspect of each radiant orb; —
Some fixed, some wandering with no timid
    curb:
But wandering star and fixed, to mortal
    eye,
Blended in absolute serenity,
And free from semblance of decline; —
Fresh as if Evening brought their natal
    hour,
Her darkness splendour gave, her silence
    power
To testify of Love and Grace divine.

III

" What if those bright fires   40
Shine subject to decay,
Sons hapiy of extinguished sires,
Themselves to lose their light, or pass away
Like clouds before the wind,
Be thanks poured out to Him whose hand
    bestows,
Nightly, on human kind
That vision of endurance and repose.
— And though to every draught of vital
    breath
Renewed throughout the bounds of earth or
    ocean,

The melancholy gates of Death   50
Respond with sympathetic motion;
Though all that feeds on nether air,
Howe'er magnificent or fair,
Grows but to perish, and entrust
Its ruins to their kindred dust;
Yet, by the Almighty's ever-during care,
Her procreant vigils Nature keeps
Amid the unfathomable deeps;
And saves the peopled fields of earth
From dread of emptiness or dearth.   60
Thus, in their stations, lifting tow'rd the
    sky
The foliaged head in cloud-like majesty,
The shadow-casting race of trees survive:
Thus, in the train of Spring, arrive
Sweet flowers; — what living eye hath
    viewed
Their myriads ? — endlessly renewed,
Wherever strikes the sun's glad ray;
Where'er the subtle waters stray;
Wherever sportive breezes bend
Their course, or genial showers descend !
Mortals, rejoice ! the very Angels quit   71
Their mansions unsusceptible of change,
Amid your pleasant bowers to sit,
And through your sweet vicissitudes to
    range ! "

IV

Oh, nursed at happy distance from the cares
Of a too-anxious world, mild pastoral
    Muse !
That, to the sparkling crown Urania wears,
And to her sister Clio's laurel wreath,
Prefer'st a garland culled from purple
    heath,
Or blooming thicket moist with morning
    dews;   80
Was such bright Spectacle vouchsafed to
    me ?
And was it granted to the simple ear
Of thy contented Votary
Such melody to hear !
Him rather suits it, side by side with thee,
Wrapped in a fit of pleasing indolence,
While thy tired lute hangs on the hawthorn-
    tree,
To lie and listen — till o'er-drowsèd sense
Sinks, hardly conscious of the influence —
To the soft murmur of the vagrant Bee.   90
— A slender sound ! yet hoary Time
Doth to the *Soul* exalt it with the chime
Of all his years; — a company
Of ages coming, ages gone;

(Nations from before them sweeping,
Regions in destruction steeping,)
But every awful note in unison
With that faint utterance, which tells
Of treasure sucked from buds and bells,
For the pure keeping of those waxen
    cells;   100
Where She — a statist prudent to confer
Upon the common weal; a warrior bold,
Radiant all over with unburnished gold,
And armed with living spear for mortal
    fight;
    A cunning forager
That spreads no waste; a social builder;
    one
In whom all busy offices unite
With all fine functions that afford de-
    light —
Safe through the winter storm in quiet
    dwells !

V

And is She brought within the power   110
Of vision ? — o'er this tempting flower
Hovering until the petals stay
Her flight, and take its voice away ! —
Observe each wing ! — a tiny van !
The structure of her laden thigh,
How fragile ! yet of ancestry
Mysteriously remote and high;
High as the imperial front of man;
The roseate bloom on woman's cheek;
The soaring eagle's curvèd beak;   120
The white plumes of the floating swan;
Old as the tiger's paw, the lion's mane
Ere shaken by that mood of stern disdain
At which the desert trembles. — Humming
    Bee !
Thy sting was needless then, perchance un-
    known,
The seeds of malice were not sown;
All creatures met in peace, from fierceness
    free,
And no pride blended with their dignity.
— Tears had not broken from their source;
Nor Anguish strayed from her Tartarean
    den;   130
The golden years maintained a course
Not undiversified though smooth and even;
We were not mocked with glimpse and
    shadow then,
Bright Seraphs mixed familiarly with
    men;
And earth and stars composed a universal
    heaven !

ODE TO LYCORIS. MAY 1817

1817. 1820

The discerning reader, who is aware that in the poem of Ellen Irwin I was desirous of throwing the reader at once out of the old ballad, so as, if possible, to preclude a comparison between that mode of dealing with the subject and the mode I meant to adopt — may here perhaps perceive that this poem originated in the last four lines of the first stanza. Those specks of snow, reflected in the lake and so transferred, as it were, to the subaqueous sky, reminded me of the swans which the fancy of the ancient classic poets yoked to the car of Venus. Hence the tenor of the whole first stanza, and the name of Lycoris, which — with some readers who think my theology and classical allusion too far-fetched and therefore more or less unnatural and affected — will tend to unrealise the sentiment that pervades these verses. But surely one who has written so much in verse as I have done may be allowed to retrace his steps in the regions of fancy which delighted him in his boyhood, when he first became acquainted with the Greek and Roman Poets. Before I read Virgil I was so strongly attached to Ovid, whose Metamorphoses I read at school, that I was quite in a passion whenever I found him, in books of criticism, placed below Virgil. As to Homer, I was never weary of travelling over the scenes through which he led me. Classical literature affected me by its own beauty. But the truths of scripture having been entrusted to the dead languages, and these fountains having been recently laid open at the Reformation, an importance and a sanctity were at that period attached to classical literature that extended, as is obvious in Milton's Lycidas, for example, both to its spirit and form in a degree that can never be revived. No doubt the hackneyed and lifeless use into which mythology fell towards the close of the 17th century, and which continued through the 18th, disgusted the general reader with all allusion to it in modern verse ; and though, in deference to this disgust, and also in a measure participating in it, I abstained in my earlier writings from all introduction of pagan fable, surely, even in its humble form, it may ally itself with real sentiment, as I can truly affirm it did in the present case.

I

AN age hath been when Earth was proud
Of lustre too intense
To be sustained; and Mortals bowed
The front in self-defence.
Who *then*, if Dian's crescent gleamed,

Or Cupid's sparkling arrow streamed,
While on the wing the Urchin played,
Could fearlessly approach the shade ?
— Enough for one soft vernal day,
If I, a bard of ebbing time,   10
And nurtured in a fickle clime,
May haunt this hornèd bay;
Whose amorous water multiplies
The flitting halcyon's vivid dyes;
And smooths her liquid breast — to show
These swan-like specks of mountain snow,
White as the pair that slid along the
        plains
Of heaven, when Venus held the reins !

II

In youth we love the darksome lawn
Brushed by the owlet's wing;   20
Then, Twilight is preferred to Dawn,
And Autumn to the Spring.
Sad fancies do we then affect,
In luxury of disrespect
To our own prodigal excess
Of too familiar happiness.
Lycoris (if such name befit
Thee, thee my life's celestial sign !)
When Nature marks the year's decline,
Be ours to welcome it;   30
Pleased with the harvest hope that runs
Before the path of milder suns;
Pleased while the sylvan world displays
Its ripeness to the feeding gaze;
Pleased when the sullen winds resound the
        knell
Of the resplendent miracle.

III

But something whispers to my heart
That, as we downward tend,
Lycoris ! life requires an *art*
To which our souls must bend;   40
A skill — to balance and supply;
And, ere the flowing fount be dry,
As soon it must, a sense to sip,
Or drink, with no fastidious lip.
Then welcome, above all, the Guest
Whose smiles, diffused o'er land and sea,
Seem to recall the Deity
Of youth into the breast:
May pensive Autumn ne'er present
A claim to her disparagement !   50
While blossoms and the budding spray
Inspire us in our own decay;
Still, as we nearer draw to life's dark goal
Be hopeful Spring the favourite of the Soul !

TO THE SAME

1817. 1820

This as well as the preceding . . . were composed in front of Rydal Mount and during my walks in the neighbourhood.. Nine-tenths of my verses have been murmured out in the open air: and here let me repeat what I believe has already appeared in print. One day a stranger having walked round the garden and grounds of Rydal Mount asked one of the female servants, who happened to be at the door, permission to see her master's study. ''This,'' said she, leading him forward, ''is my master's library where he keeps his books, but his study is out of doors.'' After a long absence from home it has more than once happened that some one of my cottage neighbours has said — ''Well, there he is; we are glad to hear him *booing* about again.'' Once more, in excuse for so much egotism, let me say, these notes are written for my familiar friends, and at their earnest request. Another time a gentleman whom James had conducted through the grounds asked him what kind of plants throve best there: after a little consideration he answered — ''Laurels.'' ''That is,'' said the stranger, ''as it should be; don't you know that the laurel is the emblem of poetry, and that poets used on public occasions to be crowned with it ?'' James stared when the question was first put, but was doubtless much pleased with the information.

ENOUGH of climbing toil ! — Ambition treads
Here, as 'mid busier scenes, ground steep
        and rough,
Or slippery even to peril ! and each step,
As we for most uncertain recompence
Mount toward the empire of the fickle clouds,
Each weary step, dwarfing the world below,
Induces, for its old familiar sights,
Unacceptable feelings of contempt,
With wonder mixed — that Man could e'er
        be tied,
In anxious bondage, to such nice array   10
And formal fellowship of petty things !
— Oh ! 't is the *heart* that magnifies this
        life,
Making a truth and beauty of her own;
And moss-grown alleys, circumscribing
        shades,
And gurgling rills, assist her in the work
More efficaciously than realms outspread,
As in a map, before the adventurer's gaze —
Ocean and Earth contending for regard.
    The umbrageous woods are left — how
        far beneath !

But lo ! where darkness seems to guard the
    mouth   20
Of yon wild cave, whose jaggèd brows are
    fringed
With flaccid threads of ivy, in the still
And sultry air, depending motionless.
Yet cool the space within, and not uncheered
(As whoso enters shall ere long perceive)
By stealthy influx of the timid day
Mingling with night, such twilight to compose
As Numa loved ; when, in the Egerian grot,
From the sage Nymph appearing at his wish,
He gained whate'er a regal mind might ask,
Or need, of counsel breathed through lips
    divine.   31
    Long as the heat shall rage, let that dim
    cave
Protect us, there deciphering as we may
Diluvian records; or the sighs of Earth
Interpreting; or counting for old Time
His minutes, by reiterated drops,
Audible tears, from some invisible source
That deepens upon fancy — more and more
Drawn toward the centre whence those
    sighs creep forth
To awe the lightness of humanity: 40
Or, shutting up thyself within thyself,
There let me see thee sink into a mood
Of gentler thought, protracted till thine eye
Be calm as water when the winds are
    gone,
And no one can tell whither. Dearest
    Friend !
We two have known such happy hours
    together
That, were power granted to replace them
    (fetched
From out the pensive shadows where they
    lie)
In the first warmth of their original sun-
    shine,
Loth should I be to use it: passing sweet 50
Are the domains of tender memory !

THE LONGEST DAY

ADDRESSED TO MY DAUGHTER

1817. 1820

Suggested by the sight of my daughter
(Dora) playing in front of Rydal Mount; and
composed in a great measure the same after-
noon. I have often wished to pair this poem
upon the *longest* with one upon the *shortest*, day,
and regret even now that it has not been done.

LET us quit the leafy arbour,
And the torrent murmuring by;
For the sun is in his harbour,
Weary of the open sky.

Evening now unbinds the fetters
Fashioned by the glowing light;
All that breathe are thankful debtors
To the harbinger of night.

Yet by some grave thoughts attended
Eve renews her calm career: 10
For the day that now is ended,
Is the longest of the year.

Dora ! sport, as now thou sportest,
On this platform, light and free;
Take thy bliss, while longest, shortest,
Are indifferent to thee !

Who would check the happy feeling
That inspires the linnet's song ?
Who would stop the swallow, wheeling
On her pinions swift and strong ?   20

Yet at this impressive season,
Words which tenderness can speak
From the truths of homely reason,
Might exalt the loveliest cheek;

And, while shades to shades succeeding
Steal the landscape from the sight,
I would urge this moral pleading,
Last forerunner of " Good night ! "

SUMMER ebbs; — each day that follows
Is a reflux from on high,   30
Tending to the darksome hollows
Where the frosts of winter lie.

He who governs the creation,
In his providence, assigned
Such a gradual declination
To the life of human kind.

Yet we mark it not; — fruits redden,
Fresh flowers blow, as flowers have blown,
And the heart is loth to deaden
Hopes that she so long hath known.   40

Be thou wiser, youthful Maiden !
And when thy decline shall come,
Let not flowers, or boughs fruit-laden,
Hide the knowledge of thy doom.

Now, even now, ere wrapped in slumber,
Fix thine eyes upon the sea
That absorbs time, space, and number;
Look thou to Eternity !

Follow thou the flowing river
On whose breast are thither borne   50
All deceived, and each deceiver,
Through the gates of night and morn;

Through the year's successive portals;
Through the bounds which many a star
Marks, not mindless of frail mortals
When his light returns from far.

Thus when thou with Time hast travelled
Toward the mighty gulf of things,
And the mazy stream unravelled
With thy best imaginings;   60

Think, if thou on beauty leanest,
Think how pitiful that stay,
Did not virtue give the meanest
Charms superior to decay.

Duty, like a strict preceptor,
Sometimes frowns, or seems to frown;
Choose her thistle for thy sceptre,
While youth's roses are thy crown.

Grasp it, — if thou shrink and tremble,
Fairest damsel of the green,   70
Thou wilt lack the only symbol
That proclaims a genuine queen;

And ensures those palms of honour
Which selected spirits wear,
Bending low before the Donor,
Lord of heaven's unchanging year !

HINT FROM THE MOUNTAINS

FOR CERTAIN POLITICAL PRETENDERS

1817. 1820

Bunches of fern may often be seen wheeling
about in the wind as here described. The par-
ticular bunch that suggested these verses was
noticed in the Pass of Dunmail Raise. The
verses were composed in 1817, but the applica-
tion is for all times and places.

" WHO but hails the sight with pleasure
When the wings of genius rise,

Their ability to measure
With great enterprise;
But in man was ne'er such daring
As yon Hawk exhibits, pairing
His brave spirit with the war in
The stormy skies !

" Mark him, how his power he uses,
Lays it by, at will resumes !   10
Mark, ere for his haunt he chooses
Clouds and utter glooms !
There, he wheels in downward mazes;
Sunward now his flight he raises,
Catches fire, as seems, and blazes
With uninjured plumes ! " —

ANSWER

" Stranger, 't is no act of courage
Which aloft thou dost discern;
No bold *bird* gone forth to forage
'Mid the tempest stern;   20
But such mockery as the nations
See, when public perturbations
Lift men from their native stations
Like yon TUFT OF FERN;

" Such it is; the aspiring creature
Soaring on undaunted wing,
(So you fancied) is by nature
A dull helpless thing,
Dry and withered, light and yellow; —
That to be the tempest's fellow !   30
Wait — and you shall see how hollow
Its endeavouring ! "

THE PASS OF KIRKSTONE

1817. 1820

Written at Rydal Mount. Thoughts and
feelings of many walks in all weathers, by day
and night, over this Pass, alone and with be-
loved friends.

I

WITHIN the mind strong fancies work,
A deep delight the bosom thrills
Oft as I pass along the fork
Of these fraternal hills:
Where, save the rugged road, we find
No appanage of human kind,
Nor hint of man; if stone or rock
Seem not his handywork to mock
By something cognizably shaped;
Mockery — or model roughly hewn,   10

And left as if by earthquake strewn,
Or from the Flood escaped:
Altars for Druid service fit
(But where no fire was ever lit,
Unless the glow-worm to the skies
Thence offer nightly sacrifice);
Wrinkled Egyptian monument;
Green moss-grown tower; or hoary tent;
Tents of a camp that never shall be razed —
On which four thousand years have gazed!

II

Ye plough-shares sparkling on the slopes! 21
Ye snow-white lambs that trip
Imprisoned 'mid the formal props
Of restless ownership!
Ye trees, that may to-morrow fall
To feed the insatiate Prodigal!
Lawns, houses, chattels, groves, and fields,
All that the fertile valley shields;
Wages of folly — baits of crime,
Of life's uneasy game the stake, 30
Playthings that keep the eyes awake
Of drowsy, dotard Time; —
O care! O guilt! — O vales and plains,
Here, 'mid his own unvexed domains,
A Genius dwells, that can subdue
At once all memory of You, —
Most potent when mists veil the sky,
Mists that distort and magnify;
While the coarse rushes, to the sweeping
    breeze,
Sigh forth their ancient melodies! 40

III

List to those shriller notes! — *that* march
Perchance was on the blast,
When, through this Height's inverted arch,
Rome's earliest legion passed!
— They saw, adventurously impelled,
And older eyes than theirs beheld,
This block — and yon, whose church-like
    frame
Gives to this savage Pass its name.
Aspiring Road! that lov'st to hide
Thy daring in a vapoury bourn, 50
Not seldom may the hour return
When thou shalt be my guide:
And I (as all men may find cause,
When life is at a weary pause,
And they have panted up the hill
Of duty with reluctant will)
Be thankful, even though tired and faint,
For the rich bounties of constraint;

Whence oft invigorating transports flow
That choice lacked courage to bestow! 60

IV

My Soul was grateful for delight
That wore a threatening brow;
A veil is lifted — can she slight
The scene that opens now?
Though habitation none appear,
The greenness tells, man must be there;
The shelter — that the pérspective
Is of the clime in which we live;
Where Toil pursues his daily round;
Where Pity sheds sweet tears — and Love,
In woodbine bower or birchen grove, 71
Inflicts his tender wound.
— Who comes not hither ne'er shall know
How beautiful the world below;
Nor can he guess how lightly leaps
The brook adown the rocky steeps.
Farewell, thou desolate Domain!
Hope, pointing to the cultured plain,
Carols like a shepherd-boy;
And who is she? — Can that be Joy! 80
Who, with a sunbeam for her guide,
Smoothly skims the meadows wide;
While Faith, from yonder opening cloud,
To hill and vale proclaims aloud,
"Whate'er the weak may dread, the wicked
    dare,
Thy lot, O Man, is good, thy portion, fair!"

LAMENT OF MARY QUEEN OF SCOTS

ON THE EVE OF A NEW YEAR

1817. 1820

This arose out of a flash of moonlight that
struck the ground when I was approaching
the steps that lead from the garden at Rydal
Mount to the front of the house. "From her
sunk eye a stagnant tear stole forth" is taken,
with some loss, from a discarded poem, "The
Convict," in which occurred, when he was dis-
covered lying in the cell, these lines: —

"But now he upraises the deep-sunken eye,
  The motion unsettles a tear;
The silence of sorrow it seems to supply
  And asks of me — why I am here."

I

SMILE of the Moon! — for so I name
That silent greeting from above;
A gentle flash of light that came
From her whom drooping captives love;

Or art thou of still higher birth ?
Thou that didst part the clouds of earth,
My torpor to reprove !

II

Bright boon of pitying Heaven ! — alas,
I may not trust thy placid cheer !
Pondering that Time to-night will pass   10
The threshold of another year;
For years to me are sad and dull;
My very moments are too full
Of hopelessness and fear.

III

And yet, the soul-awakening gleam,
That struck perchance the farthest cone
Of Scotland's rocky wilds, did seem
To visit me, and me alone;
Me, unapproached by any friend,
Save those who to my sorrows lend   20
Tears due unto their own.

IV

To-night the church-tower bells will ring
Through these wide realms a festive peal;
To the new year a welcoming;
A tuneful offering for the weal
Of happy millions lulled in sleep;
While I am forced to watch and weep,
By wounds that may not heal.

V

Born all too high, by wedlock raised
Still higher — to be cast thus low !   30
Would that mine eyes had never gazed
On aught of more ambitious show
Than the sweet flowerets of the fields!
— It is my royal state that yields
This bitterness of woe.

VI

Yet how ? — for I, if there be truth
In the world's voice, was passing fair;
And beauty, for confiding youth,
Those shocks of passion can prepare
That kill the bloom before its time;   40
And blanch, without the owner's crime,
The most resplendent hair.

VII

Unblest distinction ! showered on me
To bind a lingering life in chains:
All that could quit my grasp, or flee,
Is gone; — but not the subtle stains
Fixed in the spirit; for even here

Can I be proud that jealous fear
Of what I was remains.

VIII

A Woman rules my prison's key;   50
A sister Queen, against the bent
Of law and holiest sympathy,
Detains me, doubtful of the event;
Great God, who feel'st for my distress,
My thoughts are all that I possess,
O keep them innocent !

IX

Farewell desire of human aid,
Which abject mortals vainly court !
By friends deceived, by foes betrayed,
Of fears the prey, of hopes the sport;   60
Nought but the world-redeeming Cross
Is able to supply my loss,
My burthen to support.

X

Hark ! the death-note of the year
Sounded by the castle-clock !
From her sunk eyes a stagnant tear
Stole forth, unsettled by the shock;
But oft the woods renewed their green,
Ere the tired head of Scotland's Queen
Reposed upon the block !   70

SEQUEL TO THE "BEGGARS," 1802

COMPOSED MANY YEARS AFTER

1817. 1827

WHERE are they now, those wanton Boys ?
For whose free range the dædal earth
Was filled with animated toys,
And implements of frolic mirth;
With tools for ready wit to guide;
And ornaments of seemlier pride,
More fresh, more bright, than princes wear;
For what one moment flung aside,
Another could repair;
What good or evil have they seen   10
Since I their pastime witnessed here,
Their daring wiles, their sportive cheer ?
I ask — but all is dark between !
    They met me in a genial hour,
When universal nature breathed
As with the breath of one sweet flower, —
A time to overrule the power
Of discontent, and check the birth
Of thoughts with better thoughts at strife,

The most familiar bane of life   20
Since parting Innocence bequeathed
Mortality to Earth !
Soft clouds, the whitest of the year,
Sailed through the sky—the brooks ran clear;
The lambs from rock to rock were bounding;
With songs the budded groves resounding;
And to my heart are still endeared
The thoughts with which it then was cheered;
The faith which saw that gladsome pair
Walk through the fire with unsinged hair.
Or, if such faith must needs deceive —   31
Then, Spirits of beauty and of grace,
Associates in that eager chase;
Ye, who within the blameless mind
Your favourite seat of empire find —
Kind Spirits ! may we not believe
That they, so happy and so fair
Through your sweet influence, and the care
Of pitying Heaven, at least were free
From touch of *deadly* injury ?   40
Destined, whate'er their earthly doom,
For mercy and immortal bloom?

THE PILGRIM'S DREAM

OR, THE STAR AND THE GLOW-WORM

1818. 1820

I distinctly recollect the evening when these
verses were suggested in 1818. I was on the
road between Rydal and Grasmere, where Glow-
worms abound. A Star was shining above the
ridge of Loughrigg Fell, just opposite. I re-
member a blockhead of a critic, in some review
or other, crying out against this piece. ''What
so monstrous,'' said he, ''as to make a star
talk to a glow-worm !'' Poor fellow, we know
well from this sage observation what the prim-
rose on the river's brim was to him.

A PILGRIM, when the summer day
Had closed upon his weary way,
A lodging begged beneath a castle's roof;
But him the haughty Warder spurned;
And from the gate the Pilgrim turned,
To seek such covert as the field
Or heath-besprinkled copse might yield,
Or lofty wood, shower-proof.

He paced along; and, pensively,
Halting beneath a shady tree,   10
Whose moss-grown root might serve for
    couch or seat,
Fixed on a Star his upward eye;
Then, from the tenant of the sky

He turned, and watched with kindred look.
A Glow-worm, in a dusky nook,
Apparent at his feet.

The murmur of a neighbouring stream
Induced a soft and slumbrous dream,
A pregnant dream, within whose shadowy
    bounds
He recognised the earth-born Star,   20
And *That* which glittered from afar;
And (strange to witness !) from the frame
Of the ethereal Orb, there came
Intelligible sounds.

Much did it taunt the humble Light
That now, when day was fled, and night
Hushed the dark earth, fast closing weary
    eyes,
A very reptile could presume
To show her taper in the gloom,
As if in rivalship with One   30
Who sate a ruler on his throne
Erected in the skies.

" Exalted Star ! " the Worm replied,
" Abate this unbecoming pride,
Or with a less uneasy lustre shine;
Thou shrink'st as momently thy rays
Are mastered by the breathing haze;
While neither mist, nor thickest cloud
That shapes in heaven its murky shroud,
Hath power to injure mine.   40

But not for this do I aspire
To match the spark of local fire,
That at my will burns on the dewy lawn,
With thy acknowledged glories;— No !
Yet, thus upbraided, I may show
What favours do attend me here,
Till, like thyself, I disappear
Before the purple dawn."

When this in modest guise was said,
Across the welkin seemed to spread   50
A boding sound—for aught but sleep unfit !
Hills quaked, the rivers backward ran;
That Star, so proud of late, looked wan;
And reeled with visionary stir
In the blue depth, like Lucifer
Cast headlong to the pit !

Fire raged: and, when the spangled floor
Of ancient ether was no more,
New heavens succeeded, by the dream
    brought forth:

And all the happy Souls that rode 60
Transfigured through that fresh abode,
Had heretofore, in humble trust,
Shone meekly 'mid their native dust,
The Glow-worms of the earth !

This knowledge, from an Angel's voice
Proceeding, made the heart rejoice
Of Him who slept upon the open lea:
Waking at morn he murmured not;
And, till life's journey closed, the spot
Was to the Pilgrim's soul endeared, 70
Where by that dream he had been cheered
Beneath the shady tree.

INSCRIPTIONS

SUPPOSED TO BE FOUND IN AND NEAR A
HERMIT'S CELL

1818. 1820

I

HOPES, what are they ? — Beads of morning
Strung on slender blades of grass;
Or a spider's web adorning
In a strait and treacherous pass.

What are fears but voices airy ?
Whispering harm where harm is not;
And deluding the unwary
Till the fatal bolt is shot !

What is glory ? — in the socket
See how dying tapers fare ! 10
What is pride ? — a whizzing rocket
That would emulate a star.

What is friendship ? — do not trust her,
Nor the vows which she has made;
Diamonds dart their brightest lustre
From a palsy-shaken head.

What is truth ? — a staff rejected;
Duty ? — an unwelcome clog;
Joy ? — a moon by fits reflected
In a swamp or watery bog; 20

Bright, as if through ether steering,
To the Traveller's eye it shone:
He hath hailed it re-appearing —
And as quickly it is gone;

Such is Joy — as quickly hidden,
Or mis-shapen to the sight,

And by sullen weeds forbidden
To resume its native light.

What is youth ? — a dancing billow,
(Winds behind, and rocks before !) 30
Age ? — a drooping, tottering willow
On a flat and lazy shore.

What is peace ? — when pain is over,
And love ceases to rebel,
Let the last faint sigh discover
That precedes the passing knell !

II

INSCRIBED UPON A ROCK

The monument of ice here spoken of I ob-
served while ascending the middle road of the
three ways that lead from Rydal to Grasmere.
It was on my right hand, and my eyes were
upon it when it fell, as told in these lines.

PAUSE, Traveller ! whosoe'er thou be
Whom chance may lead to this retreat,
Where silence yields reluctantly
Even to the fleecy straggler's bleat;

Give voice to what my hand shall trace,
And fear not lest an idle sound
Of words unsuited to the place
Disturb its solitude profound.

I saw this Rock, while vernal air
Blew softly o'er the russet heath,
Uphold a Monument as fair
As church or abbey furnisheth.

Unsullied did it meet the day,
Like marble, white, like ether, pure;
As if, beneath, some hero lay,
Honoured with costliest sepulture.

My fancy kindled as I gazed;
And, ever as the sun shone forth,
The flattered structure glistened, blazed,
And seemed the proudest thing on earth.

But frost had reared the gorgeous Pile
Unsound as those which Fortune builds -
To undermine with secret guile,
Sapped by the very beam that gilds.

And, while I gazed, with sudden shock
Fell the whole Fabric to the ground;
And naked left this dripping Rock,
With shapeless ruin spread around !

III

Where the second quarry now is, as you pass from Rydal to Grasmere, there was formerly a length of smooth rock that sloped towards the road, on the right hand. I used to call it Tadpole Slope, from having frequently observed there the water-bubbles gliding under the ice, exactly in the shape of that creature.

HAST thou seen, with flash incessant,
Bubbles gliding under ice,
Bodied forth and evanescent,
No one knows by what device ?

Such are thoughts ! — A wind-swept meadow
Mimicking a troubled sea,
Such is life; and death a shadow
From the rock eternity !

IV

NEAR THE SPRING OF THE HERMITAGE

TROUBLED long with warring notions,
Long impatient of thy rod,
I resign my soul's emotions
Unto Thee, mysterious God !

What avails the kindly shelter
Yielded by this craggy rent,
If my spirit toss and welter
On the waves of discontent ?

Parching Summer hath no warrant
To consume this crystal Well;
Rains, that make each rill a torrent,
Neither sully it nor swell.

Thus, dishonouring not her station,
Would my Life present to Thee,
Gracious God, the pure oblation
Of divine tranquillity !

V

NOT seldom, clad in radiant vest,
Deceitfully goes forth the Morn;
Not seldom Evening in the west
Sinks smilingly forsworn.

The smoothest seas will sometimes prove,
To the confiding Bark, untrue;
And, if she trust the stars above,
They can be treacherous too.

The umbrageous Oak, in pomp outspread
Full oft, when storms the welkin rend,

Draws lightning down upon the head
It promised to defend.

But Thou art true, incarnate Lord,
Who didst vouchsafe for man to die;
Thy smile is sure, thy plighted word
No change can falsify !

I bent before thy gracious throne,
And asked for peace on suppliant knee;
And peace was given, — nor peace alone,
But faith sublimed to ecstasy !

COMPOSED UPON AN EVENING OF EXTRAORDINARY SPLENDOUR AND BEAUTY

1817. 1820

Felt, and in a great measure composed upon the little mount in front of our abode at Rydal. In concluding my notices of this class of poems it may be as well to observe that among the "Miscellaneous Sonnets" are a few alluding to morning impressions which might be read with mutual benefit in connection with these "Evening Voluntaries." See, for example, that one on Westminster Bridge, that composed on a May morning, the one on the song of the Thrush, and that beginning — "While beams of orient light shoot wide and high."

I

HAD this effulgence disappeared
With flying haste, I might have sent,
Among the speechless clouds, a look
Of blank astonishment;
But 't is endued with power to stay,
And sanctify one closing day,
That frail Mortality may see —
What is ? — ah no, but what *can* be !
Time was when field and watery cove
With modulated echoes rang,   10
While choirs of fervent Angels sang
Their vespers in the grove;
Or, crowning, star-like, each some sovereign height,
Warbled, for heaven above and earth below,
Strains suitable to both. — Such holy rite,
Methinks, if audibly repeated now
From hill or valley, could not move
Sublimer transport, purer love,
Than doth this silent spectacle — the gleam —
The shadow — and the peace supreme !   20

II

No sound is uttered, — but a deep
And solemn harmony pervades
The hollow vale from steep to steep,
And penetrates the glades.
Far-distant images draw nigh,
Called forth by wondrous potency
Of beamy radiance, that imbues,
Whate'er it strikes, with gem-like hues !
In vision exquisitely clear,
Herds range along the mountain side;   30
And glistening antlers are descried;
And gilded flocks appear.
Thine is the tranquil hour, purpureal Eve !
But long as god-like wish, or hope divine,
Informs my spirit, ne'er can I believe
That this magnificence is wholly thine !
— From worlds not quickened by the sun
A portion of the gift is won;
An intermingling of Heaven's pomp is
    spread
On ground which British shepherds tread !

III

And, if there be whom broken ties   41
Afflict, or injuries assail,
Yon hazy ridges to their eyes
Present a glorious scale,
Climbing suffused with sunny air,
To stop — no record hath told where !
And tempting Fancy to ascend,
And with immortal Spirits blend !
— Wings at my shoulders seem to play;
But, rooted here, I stand and gaze   50
On those bright steps that heavenward raise
Their practicable way.
Come forth, ye drooping old men, look
    abroad,
And see to what fair countries ye are bound !
And if some traveller, weary of his road,
Hath slept since noon-tide on the grassy
    ground,
Ye Genii ! to his covert speed;
And wake him with such gentle heed
As may attune his soul to meet the dower
Bestowed on this transcendent hour !   60

IV

Such hues from their celestial Urn
Were wont to stream before mine eye,
Where'er it wandered in the morn
Of blissful infancy.
This glimpse of glory, why renewed ?
Nay, rather speak with gratitude;

For, if a vestige of those gleams
Survived, 't was only in my dreams.
Dread Power ! whom peace and calmness
    serve
No less than Nature's threatening voice,   70
If aught unworthy be my choice,
From THEE if I would swerve;
Oh, let thy grace remind me of the light
Full early lost, and fruitlessly deplored;
Which, at this moment, on my waking sight
Appears to shine, by miracle restored;
My soul, though yet confined to earth,
Rejoices in a second birth !
— 'T is past, the visionary splendour fades;
And night approaches with her shades.   80

COMPOSED DURING A STORM

1819. 1819

Written in Rydal Woods, by the side of a
torrent.

ONE who was suffering tumult in his soul,
Yet failed to seek the sure relief of prayer,
Went forth — his course surrendering to the
    care
Of the fierce wind, while mid-day lightnings
    prowl
Insidiously, untimely thunders growl;
While trees, dim-seen, in frenzied numbers,
    tear
The lingering remnant of their yellow hair,
And shivering wolves, surprised with dark-
    ness, howl
As if the sun were not. He raised his eye
Soul-smitten; for, that instant, did appear
Large space ('mid dreadful clouds) of pur-
    est sky,
An azure disc — shield of Tranquillity;
Invisible, unlooked-for, minister
Of providential goodness ever nigh !

THIS, AND THE TWO FOLLOW-ING, WERE SUGGESTED BY MR. W. WESTALL'S VIEWS OF THE CAVES, ETC., IN YORKSHIRE

1818. 1819

PURE element of waters ! wheresoe'er
Thou dost forsake thy subterranean haunts,
Green herbs, bright flowers, and berry-
    bearing plants,

Rise into life and in thy train appear:
And, through the sunny portion of the year,
Swift insects shine, thy hovering pursui-
    vants:
And, if thy bounty fail, the forest pants;
And hart and hind and hunter with his
    spear,
Languish and droop together.   Nor unfelt
In man's perturbèd soul thy sway benign;
And, haply, far within the marble belt
Of central earth, where tortured Spirits
    pine
For grace and goodness lost, thy murmurs
    melt
Their anguish, — and they blend sweet
    songs with thine.

MALHAM COVE

1818. 1819

WAS the aim frustrated by force or guile,
When giants scooped from out the rocky
    ground,
Tier under tier, this semicirque profound ?
(Giants — the same who built in Erin's isle
That Causeway with incomparable toil !) —
Oh, had this vast theatric structure wound
With finished sweep into a perfect round,
No mightier work had gained the plausive
    smile
Of all-beholding Phœbus !   But, alas,
Vain earth ! false world !   Foundations
    must be laid
In Heaven; for, 'mid the wreck of IS and
    WAS,
Things incomplete and purposes betrayed
Make sadder transits o'er thought's optic
    glass
Than noblest objects utterly decayed.

GORDALE

1818. 1819

AT early dawn, or rather when the air
Glimmers with fading light, and shadowy
    Eve
Is busiest to confer and to bereave;
Then, pensive Votary ! let thy feet repair
To Gordale-chasm, terrific as the lair
Where the young lions couch; for so, by
    leave
Of the propitious hour, thou may'st per-
    ceive
The local Deity, with oozy hair
And mineral crown, beside his jaggèd urn,

Recumbent: him thou may'st behold, who
    hides
His lineaments by day, yet there presides,
Teaching the docile waters how to turn,
Or (if need be) impediment to spurn,
And force their passage to the salt-sea
    tides !

"AËRIAL ROCK — WHOSE SOLITARY BROW "

(?). 1819

A projecting point of Loughrigg, nearly in
front of Rydal Mount. Thence looking at it,
you are struck with the boldness of its aspect ;
but walking under it, you admire the beauty of
its details. It is vulgarly called Holme-scar,
probably from the insulated pasture by the
waterside below it.

AËRIAL Rock — whose solitary brow
From this low threshold daily meets my
    sight,
When I step forth to hail the morning light,
Or quit the stars with a lingering farewell
    — how
Shall Fancy pay to thee a grateful vow ?
How, with the Muse's aid, her love attest ?
— By planting on thy naked head the crest
Of an imperial Castle, which the plough
Of ruin shall not touch.   Innocent scheme !
That doth presume no more than to supply
A grace the sinuous vale and roaring stream
Want, through neglect of hoar Antiquity.
Rise, then, ye votive Towers ! and catch a
    gleam
Of golden sunset, ere it fade and die.

THE WILD DUCK'S NEST

(?). 1819

I observed this beautiful nest on the largest
island of Rydal Water.

THE imperial Consort of the Fairy-king
Owns not a sylvan bower; or gorgeous cell
With emerald floored, and with purpureal
    shell
Ceilinged and roofed; that is so fair a thing
As this low structure, for the tasks of
    Spring,
Prepared by one who loves the buoyant
    swell
Of the brisk waves, yet here consents to
    dwell;

And spreads in steadfast peace her brooding wing.
Words cannot paint the o'ershadowing yew-tree bough,
And dimly-gleaming Nest, — a hollow crown
Of golden leaves inlaid with silver down,
Fine as the mother's softest plumes allow:
I gazed — and, self-accused while gazing, sighed
For human-kind, weak slaves of cumbrous pride !

WRITTEN UPON A BLANK LEAF IN "THE COMPLETE ANGLER"

(?). 1819

WHILE flowing rivers yield a blameless sport,
Shall live the name of Walton: Sage benign !
Whose pen, the mysteries of the rod and line
Unfolding, did not fruitlessly exhort
To reverend watching of each still report
That Nature utters from her rural shrine.
Meek, nobly versed in simple discipline,
He found the longest summer day too short,
To his loved pastime given by sedgy Lee,
Or down the tempting maze of Shawford brook —
Fairer than life itself, in this sweet Book,
The cowslip-bank and shady willow-tree;
And the fresh meads — where flowed, from every nook
Of his full bosom, gladsome Piety !

CAPTIVITY — MARY QUEEN OF SCOTS

(?). 1819

" As the cold aspect of a sunless way
Strikes through the Traveller's frame with deadlier chill,
Oft as appears a grove, or obvious hill,
Glistening with unparticipated ray,
Or shining slope where he must never stray;
So joys, remembered without wish or will
Sharpen the keenest edge of present ill, —
On the crushed heart a heavier burthen lay.
Just Heaven, contract the compass of my mind

To fit proportion with my altered state !
Quench those felicities whose light I find
Reflected in my bosom all too late ! —
O be my spirit, like my thraldom, strait;
And, like mine eyes that stream with sorrow, blind ! "

TO A SNOWDROP

(?). 1819

LONE Flower, hemmed in with snows and white as they
But hardier far, once more I see thee bend
Thy forehead, as if fearful to offend,
Like an unbidden guest. Though day by day,
Storms, sallying from the mountain-tops, waylay
The rising sun, and on the plains descend;
Yet art thou welcome, welcome as a friend
Whose zeal outruns his promise ! Blue-eyed May
Shall soon behold this border thickly set
With bright jonquils, their odours lavishing
On the soft west-wind and his frolic peers;
Nor will I then thy modest grace forget,
Chaste Snowdrop, venturous harbinger of Spring,
And pensive monitor of fleeting years !

ON SEEING A TUFT OF SNOW-DROPS IN A STORM

(?). 1820

WHEN haughty expectations prostrate lie,
And grandeur crouches like a guilty thing,
Oft shall the lowly weak, till nature bring
Mature release, in fair society
Survive, and Fortune's utmost anger try;
Like these frail snowdrops that together cling,
And nod their helmets, smitten by the wing
Of many a furious whirl-blast sweeping by.
Observe the faithful flowers ! if small to great
May lead the thoughts, thus struggling used to stand
The Emathian phalanx, nobly obstinate;
And so the bright immortal Theban band,
Whom onset, fiercely urged at Jove's command,
Might overwhelm, but could not separate !

TO THE RIVER DERWENT

(?). 1819

AMONG the mountains were we nursed,
    loved Stream,
Thou near the eagle's nest — within brief
    sail,
I, of his bold wing floating on the gale,
Where thy deep voice could lull me ! Faint
    the beam
Of human life when first allowed to gleam
On mortal notice. — Glory of the vale,
Such thy meek outset, with a crown, though
    frail,
Kept in perpetual verdure by the steam
Of thy soft breath ! — Less vivid wreath
    entwined
Nemæan victor's brow; less bright was
    worn,
Meed of some Roman chief — in triumph
    borne
With captives chained; and shedding from
    his car
The sunset splendours of a finished war
Upon the proud enslavers of mankind !

COMPOSED IN ONE OF THE VALLEYS OF WESTMORE-LAND, ON EASTER SUNDAY

1814(?). 1819

WITH each recurrence of this glorious
    morn
That saw the Saviour in his human frame
Rise from the dead, erewhile the Cottage-
    dame
Put on fresh raiment — till that hour un-
    worn:
Domestic hands the home-bred wool had
    shorn,
And she who span it culled the daintiest
    fleece,
In thoughtful reverence to the Prince of
    Peace,
Whose temples bled beneath the platted
    thorn.
A blest estate when piety sublime
These humble props disdained not ! O
    green dales !
Sad may *I* be who heard your sabbath
    chime
When Art's abused inventions were un-
    known;

Kind Nature's various wealth was all your
    own;
And benefits were weighed in Reason's
    scales !

"GRIEF, THOU HAST LOST AN EVER-READY FRIEND"

1807(?). 1819

I could write a treatise of lamentation upon
the changes brought about among the cottages
of Westmoreland by the silence of the spinning-
wheel. During long winter nights and wet
days, the wheel upon which wool was spun
gave employment to a great part of a family.
The old man, however infirm, was able to card
the wool, as he sate in the corner by the fire-
side ; and often, when a boy, have I admired
the cylinders of carded wool which were softly
laid upon each other by his side. Two wheels
were often at work on the same floor; and
others of the family, chiefly little children,
were occupied in teasing and cleaning the wool
to fit it for the hand of the carder. So that all,
except the smallest infants, were contributing
to mutual support. Such was the employment
that prevailed in the pastoral vales. Where
wool was not at hand, in the small rural towns,
the wheel for spinning flax was almost in as
constant use, if knitting was not preferred ;
which latter occupation has the advantage (in
some cases disadvantage) that, not being of
necessity stationary, it allowed of gossiping
about from house to house, which good house-
wives reckoned an idle thing.

GRIEF, thou hast lost an ever-ready friend
Now that the cottage Spinning-wheel is
    mute;
And Care — a comforter that best could
    suit
Her froward mood, and softliest reprehend;
And Love — a charmer's voice, that used to
    lend,
More efficaciously than aught that flows
From harp or lute, kind influence to com-
    pose
The throbbing pulse — else troubled with-
    out end:
Even Joy could tell, Joy craving truce and
    rest
From her own overflow, what power sedate
On those revolving motions did await
Assiduously — to soothe her aching breast;
And, to a point of just relief, abate
The mantling triumphs of a day too blest.

"I WATCH, AND LONG HAVE WATCHED, WITH CALM RE-GRET"

(?). 1819

Suggested in front of Rydal Mount, the rocky parapet being the summit of Loughrigg Fell opposite. Not once only, but a hundred times, have the feelings of this Sonnet been awakened by the same objects seen from the same place.

I WATCH, and long have watched, with
    calm regret
Yon slowly-sinking star — immortal Sire
(So might he seem) of all the glittering
    quire !
Blue ether still surrounds him — yet — and
    yet;
But now the horizon's rocky parapet
Is reached, where, forfeiting his bright
    attire,
He burns — transmuted to a dusky fire —
Then pays submissively the appointed debt
To the flying moments, and is seen no
    more.
Angels and gods ! We struggle with our
    fate,
While health, power, glory, from their
    height decline,
Depressed; and then extinguished; and
    our state,
In this, how different, lost Star, from thine,
That no to-morrow shall our beams restore !

"I HEARD (ALAS ! 'T WAS ONLY IN A DREAM)"

1818. 1819

I HEARD (alas ! 't was only in a dream)
Strains — which, as sage Antiquity believed,
By waking ears have sometimes been re-
    ceived
Wafted adown the wind from lake or
    stream;
A most melodious requiem, a supreme
And perfect harmony of notes, achieved
By a fair Swan on drowsy billows heaved,
O'er which her pinions shed a silver gleam.
For is she not the votary of Apollo ?
And knows she not, singing as he inspires,
That bliss awaits her which the ungenial
    Hollow
Of the dull earth partakes not, nor desires ?

Mount, tuneful Bird, and join the immortal
    quires !
She soared — and I awoke, struggling in
    vain to follow.

THE HAUNTED TREE

TO ——

1819. 1820

This tree grew in the park of Rydal, and I have often listened to its creaking as described.

THOSE silver clouds collected round the sun
His mid-day warmth abate not, seeming
    less
To overshade than multiply his beams
By soft reflection — grateful to the sky,
To rocks, fields, woods. Nor doth our hu-
    man sense
Ask, for its pleasure, screen or canopy
More ample than the time-dismantled Oak
Spreads o'er this tuft of heath, which now,
    attired
In the whole fulness of its bloom, affords
Couch beautiful as e'er for earthly use   10
Was fashioned; whether, by the hand of
    Art,
That eastern Sultan, amid flowers en-
    wrought
On silken tissue, might diffuse his limbs
In languor; or, by Nature, for repose
Of panting Wood-nymph, wearied with the
    chase.
O Lady ! fairer in thy Poet's sight
Than fairest spiritual creature of the
    groves,
Approach; — and, thus invited, crown with
    rest
The noon-tide hour: though truly some
    there are
Whose footsteps superstitiously avoid   20
This venerable Tree; for, when the wind
Blows keenly, it sends forth a creaking
    sound
(Above the general roar of woods and
    crags)
Distinctly heard from far — a doleful note !
As if (so Grecian shepherds would have
    deemed)
The Hamadryad, pent within, bewailed
Some bitter wrong. Nor is it unbelieved,
By ruder fancy, that a troubled ghost
Haunts the old trunk; lamenting deeds of
    which

The flowery ground is conscious. But no
wind   30
Sweeps now along this elevated ridge;
Not even a zephyr stirs; — the obnoxious
Tree
Is mute; and, in his silence, would look
down,
O lovely Wanderer of the trackless hills,
On thy reclining form with more delight
Than his coevals in the sheltered vale
Seem to participate, the while they view
Their own far-stretching arms and leafy
heads
Vividly pictured in some glassy pool,
That, for a brief space, checks the hurry-
ing stream !   40

SEPTEMBER 1819

1819. 1820

THE sylvan slopes with corn-clad fields
Are hung, as if with golden shields,
Bright trophies of the sun !
Like a fair sister of the sky,
Unruffled doth the blue lake lie,
The mountains looking on.

And, sooth to say, yon vocal grove,
Albeit uninspired by love,
By love untaught to ring,
May well afford to mortal ear   10
An impulse more profoundly dear
Than music of the Spring.

For *that* from turbulence and heat
Proceeds, from some uneasy seat
In nature's struggling frame,
Some region of impatient life:
And jealousy, and quivering strife,
Therein a portion claim.

This, this is holy; — while I hear
These vespers of another year,   20
This hymn of thanks and praise,
My spirit seems to mount above
The anxieties of human love,
And earth's precarious days.

But list ! — though winter storms be nigh,
Unchecked is that soft harmony:
There lives Who can provide
For all his creatures; and in Him,
Even like the radiant Seraphim,
These choristers confide.   30

UPON THE SAME OCCASION

1819. 1820

DEPARTING summer hath assumed
An aspect tenderly illumed,
The gentlest look of spring;
That calls from yonder leafy shade
Unfaded, yet prepared to fade,
A timely carolling.

No faint and hesitating trill,
Such tribute as to winter chill
The lonely redbreast pays !
Clear, loud, and lively is the din,   10
From social warblers gathering in
Their harvest of sweet lays.

Nor doth the example fail to cheer
Me, conscious that my leaf is sere,
And yellow on the bough: —
Fall, rosy garlands, from my head !
Ye myrtle wreaths, your fragrance shed
Around a younger brow !

Yet will I temperately rejoice;
Wide is the range, and free the choice   20
Of undiscordant themes;
Which, haply, kindred souls may prize
Not less than vernal ecstasies,
And passion's feverish dreams.

For deathless powers to verse belong,
And they like Demi-gods are strong
On whom the Muses smile;
But some their function have disclaimed,
Best pleased with what is aptliest framed
To enervate and defile.   30

Not such the initiatory strains
Committed to the silent plains
In Britain's earliest dawn:
Trembled the groves, the stars grew pale,
While all-too-daringly the veil
Of nature was withdrawn !

Nor such the spirit-stirring note
When the live chords Alcæus smote,
Inflamed by sense of wrong;
Woe ! woe to Tyrants ! from the lyre   40
Broke threateningly, in sparkles dire
Of fierce vindictive song.

And not unhallowed was the page
By wingèd Love inscribed, to assuage
The pangs of vain pursuit;

Love listening while the Lesbian Maid
With finest touch of passion swayed
Her own Æolian lute.

O ye, who patiently explore
The wreck of Herculanean lore,   50
What rapture ! could ye seize
Some Theban fragment, or unroll
One precious, tender-hearted, scroll
Of pure Simonides.

That were, indeed, a genuine birth
Of poesy; a bursting forth
Of genius from the dust:
What Horace gloried to behold,
What Maro loved, shall we enfold ?
Can haughty Time be just !

"THERE IS A LITTLE UNPRE-TENDING RILL"

1802(?). 1820

This Rill trickles down the hill-side into
Windermere, near Lowwood. My sister and
I, on our first visit together to this part of the
country, walked from Kendal, and we rested
to refresh ourselves by the side of the lake
where the streamlet falls into it. This sonnet
was written some years after in recollection of
that happy ramble, that most happy day and
hour.

THERE is a little unpretending Rill
Of limpid water, humbler far than aught
That ever among Men or Naiads sought
Notice or name ! — It quivers down the
     hill,
Furrowing its shallow way with dubious
     will;
Yet to my mind this scanty Stream is
     brought
Oftener than Ganges or the Nile; a
     thought
Of private recollection sweet and still !
Months perish with their moons; year
     treads on year !
But, faithful Emma ! thou with me canst
     say
That, while ten thousand pleasures disap-
     pear,
And flies their memory fast almost as
     they;
The immortal Spirit of one happy day
Lingers beside that Rill, in vision clear.

COMPOSED ON THE BANKS OF A ROCKY STREAM

(?). 1820

DOGMATIC Teachers, of the snow-white
     fur !
Ye wrangling Schoolmen, of the scarlet
     hood !
Who, with a keenness not to be withstood,
Press the point home, or falter and demur,
Checked in your course by many a teasing
     burr;
These natural council-seats your acrid blood
Might cool; — and, as the Genius of the
     flood
Stoops willingly to animate and spur
Each lighter function slumbering in the
     brain,
Yon eddying balls of foam, these arrowy
     gleams
That o'er the pavement of the surging
     streams
Welter and flash, a synod might detain
With subtle speculations, haply vain,
But surely less so than your far-fetched
     themes !

ON THE DEATH OF HIS MAJESTY (GEORGE THE THIRD)

1820. 1820

WARD of the LAW ! — dread Shadow of a
     King !
Whose realm had dwindled to one stately
     room;
Whose universe was gloom immersed in
     gloom,
Darkness as thick as life o'er life could fling,
Save haply for some feeble glimmering
Of Faith and Hope — if thou, by nature's
     doom,
Gently hast sunk into the quiet tomb,
Why should we bend in grief, to sorrow
     cling,
When thankfulness were best ? — Fresh-
     flowing tears,
Or, where tears flow not, sigh succeeding
     sigh,
Yield to such after-thought the sole reply
Which justly it can claim. The Nation
     hears
In this deep knell, silent for threescore
     years,
An unexampled voice of awful memory !

"THE STARS ARE MANSIONS BUILT BY NATURE'S HAND"

(?). 1820

THE stars are mansions built by Nature's
    hand,
And, haply, there the spirits of the blest
Dwell, clothed in radiance, their immortal
    vest;
Huge Ocean shows, within his yellow strand,
A habitation marvellously planned,
For life to occupy in love and rest;
All that we see — is dome, or vault, or nest,
Or fortress, reared at Nature's sage com-
    mand.
Glad thought for every season! but the
    Spring
Gave it while cares were weighing on my
    heart,
'Mid song of birds, and insects murmur-
    ing;
And while the youthful year's prolific art —
Of bud, leaf, blade, and flower — was
    fashioning
Abodes where self-disturbance hath no part.

TO THE LADY MARY LOWTHER

1819. 1820

With a selection from the Poems of Anne,
Countess of Winchilsea; and extracts of similar
character from other Writers; transcribed by
a female friend.

LADY! I rifled a Parnassian Cave
(But seldom trod) of mildly-gleaming ore;
And culled, from sundry beds, a lucid
    store
Of genuine crystals, pure as those that pave
The azure brooks, where Dian joys to lave
Her spotless limbs; and ventured to explore
Dim shades — for reliques, upon Lethe's
    shore,
Cast up at random by the sullen wave.
To female hands the treasures were re-
    signed;
And lo this Work! — a grotto bright and
    clear
From stain or taint; in which thy blameless
    mind
May feed on thoughts though pensive not
    austere;
Or, if thy deeper spirit be inclined
To holy musing, it may enter here.

ON THE DETRACTION WHICH FOLLOWED THE PUBLICATION OF A CERTAIN POEM

1820. 1820

See Milton's Sonnet, beginning, "A Book
was writ of late called 'Tetrachordon.'"

A BOOK came forth of late, called PETER
    BELL;
Not negligent the style; — the matter? —
    good
As aught that song records of Robin Hood;
Or Roy, renowned through many a Scottish
    dell;
But some (who brook those hackneyed
    themes full well,
Nor heat, at Tam o' Shanter's name, their
    blood)
Waxed wroth, and with foul claws, a harpy
    brood,
On Bard and Hero clamorously fell.
Heed not, wild Rover once through heath
    and glen,
Who mad'st at length the better life thy
    choice,
Heed not such onset! nay, if praise of men
To thee appear not an unmeaning voice,
Lift up that grey-haired forehead, and rejoice
In the just tribute of thy Poet's pen!

OXFORD, MAY 30, 1820

1820. 1820

YE sacred Nurseries of blooming Youth!
In whose collegiate shelter England's
    Flowers
Expand, enjoying through their vernal hours
The air of liberty, the light of truth;
Much have ye suffered from Time's gnaw-
    ing tooth:
Yet, O ye spires of Oxford! domes and
    towers!
Gardens and groves! your presence over-
    powers
The soberness of reason; till, in sooth,
Transformed, and rushing on a bold ex-
    change,
I slight my own beloved Cam, to range
Where silver Isis leads my stripling feet;
Pace the long avenue, or glide adown
The stream-like windings of that glorious
    street —
An eager Novice robed in fluttering gown!

OXFORD, MAY 30, 1820

1820. 1820

SHAME on this faithless heart! that could
    allow
Such transport, though but for a moment's
    space;
Not while — to aid the spirit of the place —
The crescent moon clove with its glittering
    prow
The clouds, or night-bird sang from shady
    bough;
But in plain daylight: — She, too, at my
    side,
Who, with her heart's experience satisfied,
Maintains inviolate its slightest vow!
Sweet Fancy! other gifts must I receive;
Proofs of a higher sovereignty I claim;
Take from *her* brow the withering flowers
    of eve,
And to that brow life's morning wreath
    restore;
Let *her* be comprehended in the frame
Of these illusions, or they please no more.

JUNE 1820

1820. 1820

FAME tells of groves — from England far
    away —
Groves that inspire the Nightingale to trill
And modulate, with subtle reach of skill
Elsewhere unmatched, her ever-varying
    lay;
Such bold report I venture to gainsay:
For I have heard the quire of Richmond
    hill
Chanting, with indefatigable bill,
Strains that recalled to mind a distant
    day;
When, haply under shade of that same
    wood,
And scarcely conscious of the dashing oars
Plied steadily between those willowy shores,
The sweet-souled Poet of the Seasons
    stood —
Listening, and listening long, in rapturous
    mood,
Ye heavenly Birds! to your Progenitors.

MEMORIALS OF A TOUR ON THE CONTINENT

1820. 1822

I set out in company with my Wife and Sister, and Mr. and Mrs. Monkhouse, then just married, and Miss Horrocks. These two ladies, sisters, we left at Berne, while Mr. Monkhouse took the opportunity of making an excursion with us among the Alps as far as Milan. Mr. H. C. Robinson joined us at Lucerne, and when this ramble was completed we rejoined at Geneva the two ladies we had left at Berne and proceeded to Paris, where Mr. Monkhouse and H. C. R. left us, and where we spent five weeks, of which there is not a record in these poems.

DEDICATION

(SENT WITH THESE POEMS, IN MS.,
TO ——)

1820. 1821

DEAR Fellow-travellers! think not that the Muse,
To You presenting these memorial Lays,
Can hope the general eye thereon would gaze,
As on a mirror that gives back the hues
Of living Nature; no — though free to choose
The greenest bowers, the most inviting ways,
The fairest landscapes and the brightest days —
Her skill she tried with less ambitious views.
For You she wrought: Ye only can supply
The life, the truth, the beauty: she confides
In that enjoyment which with You abides,
Trusts to your love and vivid memory;
Thus far contented, that for You her verse
Shall lack not power the " meeting soul to pierce! "

            W. WORDSWORTH.

RYDAL MOUNT, *Nov.* 1821.

I

FISH-WOMEN — ON LANDING AT CALAIS

1820. 1822

'T IS said, fantastic ocean doth enfold
The likeness of whate'er on land is seen;
But, if the Nereid Sisters and their Queen,
Above whose heads the tide so long hath
    rolled,
The Dames resemble whom we here behold,
How fearful were it down through opening
    waves
To sink, and meet them in their fretted
    caves,
Withered, grotesque, immeasurably old,
And shrill and fierce in accent! — Fear it not:

For they Earth's fairest daughters do excel;
Pure undecaying beauty is their lot;
Their voices into liquid music swell,
Thrilling each pearly cleft and sparry grot,
The undisturbed abodes where Sea-nymphs
   dwell !

II

BRUGÈS

1820. 1822

BRUGÈS I saw attired with golden light
(Streamed from the west) as with a robe of
   power:
The splendour fled; and now the sunless
   hour,
That, slowly making way for peaceful night,
Best suits with fallen grandeur, to my sight
Offers the beauty, the magnificence,
And sober graces, left her for defence
Against the injuries of time, the spite
Of fortune, and the desolating storms
Of future war. Advance not — spare to
   hide,
O gentle Power of darkness ! these mild
   hues;
Obscure not yet these silent avenues
Of stateliest architecture, where the Forms
Of nun-like females, with soft motion,
   glide !

III

BRUGÈS

1820. 1822

THE Spirit of Antiquity — enshrined
In sumptuous buildings, vocal in sweet song,
In picture, speaking with heroic tongue,
And with devout solemnities entwined —
Mounts to the seat of grace within the
   mind:
Hence Forms that glide with swan-like ease
   along,
Hence motions, even amid the vulgar
   throng,
To an harmonious decency confined:
As if the streets were consecrated ground,
The city one vast temple, dedicate
To mutual respect in thought and deed;
To leisure, to forbearances sedate;
To social cares from jarring passions freed;
A deeper peace than that in deserts found !

IV

AFTER VISITING THE FIELD OF
WATERLOO

1820. 1822

A WINGÈD Goddess — clothed in vesture
   wrought
Of rainbow colours; One whose port was
   bold,
Whose overburthened hand could scarcely
   hold
The glittering crowns and garlands which
   it brought —
Hovered in air above the far-famed Spot.
She vanished; leaving prospect blank and
   cold
Of wind-swept corn that wide around us
   rolled
In dreary billows; wood, and meagre cot,
And monuments that soon must disappear:
Yet a dread local recompence we found;
While glory seemed betrayed, while patriot-
   zeal
Sank in our hearts, we felt as men *should*
   feel
With such vast hoards of hidden carnage
   near,
And horror breathing from the silent
   ground !

V

BETWEEN NAMUR AND LIEGE

1820. 1822

The scenery on the Meuse pleases me more,
upon the whole, than that of the Rhine, though
the river itself is much inferior in grandeur.
The rocks both in form and colour, especially
between Namur and Liege, surpass any upon
the Rhine, though they are in several places
disfigured by quarries, whence stones were
taken for the new fortifications. This is much
to be regretted, for they are useless, and the
scars will remain perhaps for thousands of
years. A like injury to a still greater degree
has been inflicted, in my memory, upon the
beautiful rocks of Clifton on the banks of the
Avon. There is probably in existence a very
long letter of mine to Sir Uvedale Price, in
which was given a description of the land-
scapes on the Meuse as compared with those
on the Rhine.
Details in the spirit of these sonnets are
given both in Mrs. Wordsworth's Journals and
my Sister's, and the re-perusal of them has

strengthened a wish long entertained that
somebody would put together, as in one work,
the notices contained in them, omitting particu-
lars that were written down merely to aid our
memory, and bringing the whole into as small
a compass as is consistent with the general in-
terests belonging to the scenes, circumstances,
and objects touched on by each writer.

WHAT lovelier home could gentle Fancy
    choose ?
Is this the stream, whose cities, heights, and
    plains,
War's favourite playground, are with crim-
    son stains
Familiar, as the Morn with pearly dews ?
The Morn, that now, along the silver
    MEUSE,
Spreading her peaceful ensigns, calls the
    swains
To tend their silent boats and ringing wains,
Or strip the bough whose mellow fruit be-
    strews
The ripening corn beneath it. As mine eyes
Turn from the fortified and threatening hill,
How sweet the prospect of yon watery glade,
With its grey rocks clustering in pensive
    shade —
That, shaped like old monastic turrets, rise
From the smooth meadow-ground, serene
    and still !

VI

AIX-LA-CHAPELLE

1820. 1822

WAS it to disenchant, and to undo,
That we approached the Seat of Charle-
    maine ?
To sweep from many an old romantic strain
That faith which no devotion may renew !
Why does this puny Church present to view
Her feeble columns ? and that scanty chair !
This sword that one of our weak times
    might wear !
Objects of false pretence, or meanly true !
If from a traveller's fortune I might claim
A palpable memorial of that day,
Then would I seek the Pyrenean Breach
That ROLAND clove with huge two-handed
    sway,
And to the enormous labour left his name,
Where unremitting frosts the rocky crescent
    bleach.

VII

IN THE CATHEDRAL AT COLOGNE

1820. 1822

O FOR the help of Angels to complete
This Temple — Angels governed by a plan
Thus far pursued (how gloriously !) by
    Man,
Studious that HE might not disdain the
    seat
Who dwells in heaven ! But that aspiring
    heat
Hath failed; and now, ye Powers ! whose
    gorgeous wings
And splendid aspect yon emblazonings
But faintly picture, 't were an office meet
For you, on these unfinished shafts to try
The midnight virtues of your harmony: —
This vast design might tempt you to re-
    peat
Strains that call forth upon empyreal
    ground
Immortal Fabrics, rising to the sound
Of penetrating harps and voices sweet !

VIII

IN A CARRIAGE, UPON THE BANKS OF THE RHINE

1820. 1822

AMID this dance of objects sadness steals
O'er the defrauded heart — while sweeping
    by,
As in a fit of Thespian jollity,
Beneath her vine-leaf crown the green
    Earth reels:
Backward, in rapid evanescence, wheels
The venerable pageantry of Time,
Each beetling rampart, and each tower
    sublime,
And what the Dell unwillingly reveals
Of lurking cloistral arch, through trees es-
    pied
Near the bright River's edge. Yet why
    repine ?
To muse, to creep, to halt at will, to gaze —
Such sweet wayfaring — of life's spring
    the pride,
Her summer's faithful joy — *that* still is
    mine,
And in fit measure cheers autumnal days.

IX

HYMN

FOR THE BOATMEN, AS THEY APPROACH
THE RAPIDS UNDER THE CASTLE OF
HEIDELBERG

1820. 1822

JESU! bless our slender Boat,
  By the current swept along;
Loud its threatenings — let them not
  Drown the music of a song
Breathed thy mercy to implore,
Where these troubled waters roar!

Saviour, for our warning, seen
  Bleeding on that precious Rood;
If, while through the meadows green
  Gently wound the peaceful flood,
We forgot Thee, do not Thou
Disregard thy Suppliants now!

Hither, like yon ancient Tower
  Watching o'er the River's bed,
Fling the shadow of thy power,
  Else we sleep among the dead;
Thou who trod'st the billowy sea,
Shield us in our jeopardy!

Guide our Bark among the waves;
  Through the rocks our passage smooth;
Where the whirlpool frets and raves
  Let thy love its anger soothe:
All our hope is placed in Thee;
Miserere Domine!

X

THE SOURCE OF THE DANUBE

1820. 1822

NOT, like his great Compeers, indignantly
Doth DANUBE spring to life! The wan-
    dering Stream
(Who loves the Cross, yet to the Crescent's
    gleam
Unfolds a willing breast) with infant glee
Slips from his prison walls: and Fancy,
    free
To follow in his track of silver light,
Mounts on rapt wing, and with a moment's
    flight
Hath reached the encincture of that gloomy
    sea

Whose waves the Orphean lyre forbade to
    meet
In conflict; whose rough winds forgot their
    jars
To waft the heroic progeny of Greece;
When the first Ship sailed for the Golden
    Fleece —
ARGO — exalted for that daring feat
To fix in heaven her shape distinct with
    stars.

XI

ON APPROACHING THE STAUB-
BACH, LAUTERBRUNNEN

1820. 1822

UTTERED by whom, or how inspired — de-
    signed
For what strange service, does this concert
    reach
Our ears, and near the dwellings of man-
    kind!
'Mid fields familiarized to human speech? —
No Mermaid's warble — to allay the wind
Driving some vessel toward a dangerous
    beach —
More thrilling melodies; Witch answering
    Witch,
To chant a love-spell, never intertwined
Notes shrill and wild with art more musi-
    cal:
Alas! that from the lips of abject Want
Or Idleness in tatters mendicant
The strain should flow — free Fancy to en-
    thral,
And with regret and useless pity haunt
This bold, this bright, this sky-born,
    WATERFALL!

XII

THE FALL OF THE AAR —
HANDEC

1820. 1822

FROM the fierce aspect of this River, throw-
    ing
His giant body o'er the steep rock's brink,
Back in astonishment and fear we shrink:
But, gradually a calmer look bestowing,
Flowers we espy beside the torrent grow-
    ing;

Flowers that peep forth from many a cleft
    and chink,
And, from the whirlwind of his anger,
    drink
Hues ever fresh, in rocky fortress blow-
    ing:
They suck — from breath that, threatening
    to destroy,
Is more benignant than the dewy eve —
Beauty, and life, and motions as of joy:
Nor doubt but HE to whom yon Pine-trees
    nod
Their heads in sign of worship, Nature's
    God,
These humbler adorations will receive.

XII

MEMORIAL

NEAR THE OUTLET OF THE LAKE OF THUN

*" DEM
ANDENKEN
MEINES FREUNDES
ALOYS REDING
MDCCCXVIII."*

1820. 1822

Aloys Reding, it will be remembered, was
Captain-General of the Swiss forces, which,
with a courage and perseverance worthy of
the cause, opposed the flagitious and too suc-
cessful attempt of Buonaparte to subjugate
their country.

AROUND a wild and woody hill
A gravelled pathway treading,
We reached a votive Stone that bears
The name of Aloys Reding.

Well judged the Friend who placed it
    there
For silence and protection;
And haply with a finer care
Of dutiful affection.

The Sun regards it from the West;
And, while in summer glory
He sets, his sinking yields a type
Of that pathetic story:

And oft he tempts the patriot Swiss
Amid the grove to linger;
Till all is dim, save this bright Stone
Touched by his golden finger.

XIV

COMPOSED IN ONE OF THE CATHOLIC CANTONS

1820. 1822

DOOMED as we are our native dust
To wet with many a bitter shower,
It ill befits us to disdain
The altar, to deride the fane,
Where simple Sufferers bend, in trust
To win a happier hour.

I love, where spreads the village lawn,
Upon some knee-worn cell to gaze:
Hail to the firm unmoving cross,
Aloft, where pines their branches toss !
And to the chapel far withdrawn,
That lurks by lonely ways !

Where'er we roam — along the brink
Of Rhine — or by the sweeping Po,
Through Alpine vale, or champain wide,
Whate'er we look on, at our side
Be Charity ! — to bid us think,
And feel, if we would know.

XV

AFTER-THOUGHT

1832–37. 1832–37

O LIFE ! without thy chequered scene
Of right and wrong, of weal and woe,
Success and failure, could a ground
For magnanimity be found;
For faith, 'mid ruined hopes, serene ?
Or whence could virtue flow ?

Pain entered through a ghastly breach —
Nor while sin lasts must effort cease;
Heaven upon earth 's an empty boast;
But, for the bowers of Eden lost,
Mercy has placed within our reach
A portion of God's peace.

XVI

SCENE ON THE LAKE OF BRIENTZ

1820. 1822

" WHAT know we of the Blest above
But that they sing and that they love ? "

Yet, if they ever did inspire
A mortal hymn, or shaped the choir,
Now, where those harvest Damsels float
Homeward in their rugged Boat,
(While all the ruffling winds are fled —
Each slumbering on some mountain's head)
Now, surely, hath that gracious aid
Been felt, that influence is displayed.
Pupils of Heaven, in order stand
The rustic Maidens, every hand
Upon a Sister's shoulder laid, —
To chant, as glides the boat along,
A simple, but a touching, song;
To chant, as Angels do above,
The melodies of Peace in love !

XVII

ENGELBERG, THE HILL OF ANGELS

1820. 1822

For gentlest uses, oft-times Nature takes
The work of Fancy from her willing hands;
And such a beautiful creation makes
As renders needless spells and magic wands,
And for the boldest tale belief commands.
When first mine eyes beheld that famous Hill,
The sacred ENGELBERG, celestial Bands,
With intermingling motions soft and still,
Hung round its top, on wings that changed
    their hues at will.

Clouds do not name those Visitants; they were
The very Angels whose authentic lays,
Sung from that heavenly ground in middle
    air,
Made known the spot where piety should
    raise
A holy Structure to the Almighty's praise.
Resplendent Apparition ! if in vain
My ears did listen, 't was enough to gaze;
And watch the slow departure of the train,
Whose skirts the glowing Mountain thirsted
    to detain.

XVIII

OUR LADY OF THE SNOW

1820. 1822

Meek Virgin Mother, more benign
Than fairest Star, upon the height
Of thy own mountain, set to keep
Lone vigils through the hours of sleep,

What eye can look upon thy shrine
Untroubled at the sight ?

These crowded offerings as they hang
In sign of misery relieved,
Even these, without intent of theirs,
Report of comfortless despairs,   10
Of many a deep and cureless pang
And confidence deceived.

To Thee, in this aërial cleft,
As to a common centre, tend
All sufferers that no more rely
On mortal succour — all who sigh
And pine, of human hope bereft,
Nor wish for earthly friend.

And hence, O Virgin Mother mild !
Though plenteous flowers around thee blow
Not only from the dreary strife   21
Of Winter, but the storms of life,
Thee have thy Votaries aptly styled,
OUR LADY OF THE SNOW.

Even for the Man who stops not here,
But down the irriguous valley hies,
Thy very name, O Lady ! flings,
O'er blooming fields and gushing springs,
A tender sense of shadowy fear,
And chastening sympathies !   30

Nor falls that intermingling shade
To summer-gladsomeness unkind:
It chastens only to requite
With gleams of fresher, purer, light;
While, o'er the flower-enamelled glade,
More sweetly breathes the wind.

But on ! — a tempting downward way,
A verdant path before us lies;
Clear shines the glorious sun above;
Then give free course to joy and love,   40
Deeming the evil of the day
Sufficient for the wise.

XIX

EFFUSION

IN PRESENCE OF THE PAINTED TOWER OF TELL, AT ALTORF

1822. 1822

This Tower stands upon the spot where grew
the Linden Tree against which his Son is said

to have been placed, when the Father's archery
was put to proof under circumstances so famous
in Swiss Story.

WHAT though the Italian pencil wrought
    not here,
Nor such fine skill as did the meed bestow
On Marathonian valour, yet the tear
Springs forth in presence of this gaudy show,
While narrow cares their limits overflow.
Thrice happy, burghers, peasants, warriors
    old,
Infants in arms, and ye, that as ye go
Homeward or schoolward, ape what ye
    behold !
Heroes before your time, in frolic fancy
    bold !

And when that calm Spectatress from on
    high
Looks down — the bright and solitary Moon,
Who never gazes but to beautify;
And snow-fed torrents, which the blaze of
    noon
Roused into fury, murmur a soft tune
That fosters peace, and gentleness recalls;
Then might the passing Monk receive a boon
Of saintly pleasure from these pictured
    walls,
While, on the warlike groups, the mellow-
    ing lustre falls.

How blest the souls who when their trials
    come
Yield not to terror or despondency,
But face like that sweet Boy their mortal
    doom,
Whose head the ruddy apple tops, while he
Expectant stands beneath the linden tree:
He quakes not like the timid forest game,
But smiles — the hesitating shaft to free;
Assured that Heaven its justice will pro-
    claim,
And to his Father give its own unerring aim.

XX

THE TOWN OF SCHWYTZ

1820. 1822

BY antique Fancy trimmed — though lowly,
    bred
To dignity — in thee, O SCHWYTZ ! are seen
The genuine features of the golden mean;
Equality by Prudence governèd,

Or jealous Nature ruling in her stead;
And, therefore, art thou blest with peace,
    serene
As that of the sweet fields and meadows
    green
In unambitious compass round thee spread.
Majestic BERNE, high on her guardian
    steep,
Holding a central station of command,
Might well be styled this noble body's
    HEAD;
Thou, lodged 'mid mountainous entrench-
    ments deep,
Its HEART; and ever may the heroic Land
Thy name, O SCHWYTZ, in happy freedom
    keep !

XXI

ON HEARING THE "RANZ DES VACHES" ON THE TOP OF THE PASS OF ST. GOTHARD

1820. 1822

I LISTEN — but no faculty of mine
Avails those modulations to detect,
Which, heard in foreign lands, the Swiss
    affect
With tenderest passion; leaving him to pine
(So fame reports) and die, — his sweet-
    breathed kine
Remembering, and green Alpine pastures
    decked
With vernal flowers. Yet may we not re-
    ject
The tale as fabulous. — Here while I re-
    cline,
Mindful how others by this simple Strain
Are moved, for me — upon this Mountain
    named
Of God himself from dread pre-eminence —
Aspiring thoughts, by memory reclaimed,
Yield to the Music's touching influence;
And joys of distant home my heart enchain.

XXII

FORT FUENTES

1820. 1822

The Ruins of Fort Fuentes form the crest of
a rocky eminence that rises from the plain at
the head of the Lake of Como, commanding
views up the Valteline, and toward the town of
Chiavenna. The prospect in the latter direc-

tion is characterised by melancholy sublimity. We rejoiced at being favoured with a distinct view of those Alpine heights; not, as we had expected from the breaking up of the storm, steeped in celestial glory, yet in communion with clouds floating or stationary — scatterings from heaven. The Ruin is interesting both in mass and in detail. An Inscription, upon elaborately sculptured marble lying on the ground, records that the Fort had been erected by Count Fuentes in the year 1600, during the reign of Philip the Third; and the Chapel, about twenty years after, by one of his Descendants. Marble pillars of gateways are yet standing, and a considerable part of the Chapel walls: a smooth green turf has taken place of the pavement, and we could see no trace of altar or image; but everywhere something to remind one of former splendour, and of devastation and tumult. In our ascent we had passed abundance of wild vines intermingled with bushes: near the ruins were some ill tended, but growing willingly; and rock, turf, and fragments of the pile, are alike covered or adorned with a variety of flowers, among which the rose-coloured pink was growing in great beauty. While descending, we discovered on the ground, apart from the path, and at a considerable distance from the ruined Chapel, a statue of a Child in pure white marble, uninjured by the explosion that had driven it so far down the hill. " How little," we exclaimed, " are these things valued here! Could we but transport this pretty Image to our own garden! " — Yet it seemed it would have been a pity any one should remove it from its couch in the wilderness, which may be its own for hundreds of years. — *Extract from Journal.*

DREAD hour! when, upheaved by war's
    sulphurous blast,
  This sweet-visaged Cherub of Parian
    stone
So far from the holy enclosure was cast,
  To couch in this thicket of brambles
    alone,

To rest where the lizard may bask in the
    palm
  Of his half-open hand pure from blemish
    or speck;
And the green, gilded snake, without troubling the calm
  Of the beautiful countenance, twine
    round his neck;

Where haply (kind service to Piety due!)
  When winter the grove of its mantle
    bereaves,

Some bird (like our own honoured redbreast) may strew
  The desolate Slumberer with moss and
    with leaves.

FUENTES once harboured the good and the
    brave,
  Nor to her was the dance of soft pleasure
    unknown;
Her banners for festal enjoyment did wave
  While the thrill of her fifes thro' the
    mountains was blown:

Now gads the wild vine o'er the pathless
    ascent; —
O silence of Nature, how deep is thy sway,
When the whirlwind of human destruction
    is spent,
  Our tumults appeased, and our strifes
    passed away!

XXIII

THE CHURCH OF SAN SALVADOR

SEEN FROM THE LAKE OF LUGANO

1820. 1822

This Church was almost destroyed by lightning a few years ago, but the altar and the image of the Patron Saint were untouched. The Mount, upon the summit of which the Church is built, stands amid the intricacies of the Lake of Lugano; and is, from a hundred points of view, its principal ornament, rising to the height of 2000 feet, and on one side nearly perpendicular. The ascent is toilsome; but the traveller who performs it will be amply rewarded. Splendid fertility, rich woods and dazzling waters, seclusion and confinement of view contrasted with sealike extent of plain fading into the sky; and this again, in an opposite quarter, with an horizon of the loftiest and boldest Alps — unite in composing a prospect more diversified by magnificence, beauty, and sublimity, than perhaps any other point in Europe, of so inconsiderable an elevation, commands.

THOU sacred Pile! whose turrets rise
From yon steep mountain's loftiest stage,
Guarded by lone San Salvador;
Sink (if thou must) as heretofore,
To sulphurous bolts a sacrifice,
But ne'er to human rage!

On Horeb's top, on Sinai, deigned
To rest the universal Lord:

Why leap the fountains from their cells
Where everlasting Bounty dwells ? —   10
That, while the Creature is sustained,
His God may be adored.

Cliffs, fountains, rivers, seasons, times —
Let all remind the soul of heaven;
Our slack devotion needs them all;
And Faith — so oft of sense the thrall,
While she, by aid of Nature, climbs —
May hope to be forgiven.

Glory, and patriotic Love,
And all the Pomps of this frail " spot   20
Which men call Earth,"have yearned to seek,
Associate with the simply meek,
Religion in the sainted grove,
And in the hallowed grot.

Thither, in time of adverse shocks,
Of fainting hopes and backward wills,
Did mighty Tell repair of old —
A Hero cast in Nature's mould,
Deliverer of the stedfast rocks
And of the ancient hills !   30

He, too, of battle-martyrs chief !
Who, to recall his daunted peers,
For victory shaped an open space,
By gathering with a wide embrace,
Into his single breast, a sheaf
Of fatal Austrian spears.

XXIV

THE ITALIAN ITINERANT AND THE SWISS GOATHERD

1820. 1822

PART I

I

Now that the farewell tear is dried,
Heaven prosper thee, be hope thy guide,
Hope be thy guide, adventurous Boy;
The wages of thy travel, joy !
Whether for London bound — to trill
Thy mountain notes with simple skill;
Or on thy head to poise a show
Of Images in seemly row;
The graceful form of milk-white Steed,
Or Bird that soared with Ganymede;   10
Or through our hamlets thou wilt bear
The sightless Milton, with his hair
Around his placid temples curled;

And Shakspeare at his side — a freight,
If clay could think and mind were weight,
For him who bore the world !
Hope be thy guide, adventurous Boy;
The wages of thy travel, joy !

II

But thou, perhaps, (alert as free
Though serving sage philosophy)   20
Wilt ramble over hill and dale,
A Vender of the well-wrought Scale,
Whose sentient tube instructs to time
A purpose to a fickle clime:
Whether thou choose this useful part,
Or minister to finer art,
Tnough robbed of many a cherished dream,
And crossed by many a shattered scheme,
What stirring wonders wilt thou see
In the proud Isle of liberty !   30
Yet will the Wanderer sometimes pine
With thoughts which no delights can chase,
Recall a Sister's last embrace,
His Mother's neck entwine;
Nor shall forget the Maiden coy
That *would* have loved the bright-haired Boy !

III

My Song, encouraged by the grace
That beams from his ingenuous face,
For this Adventurer scruples not
To prophesy a golden lot;   40
Due recompence, and safe return
To COMO's steeps — his happy bourne !
Where he, aloft in garden glade,
Shall tend, with his own dark-eyed Maid,
The towering maize, and prop the twig
That ill supports the luscious fig;
Or feed his eye in paths sun-proof
With purple of the trellis-roof,
That through the jealous leaves escapes
From Cadenabbia's pendent grapes.   50
— Oh might he tempt that Goatherd-child
To share his wanderings ! him whose look
Even yet my heart can scarcely brook,
So touchingly he smiled —
As with a rapture caught from heaven —
For unasked alms in pity given.

PART II

I

WITH nodding plumes, and lightly drest
Like foresters in leaf-green vest,
The Helvetian Mountaineers, on ground

For Tell's dread archery renowned,   60
Before the target stood — to claim
The guerdon of the steadiest aim.
Loud was the rifle-gun's report —
A startling thunder quick and short !
But, flying through the heights around,
Echo prolonged a tell-tale sound
Of hearts and hands alike " prepared
The treasures they enjoy to guard ! "
And, if there be a favoured hour
When Heroes are allowed to quit   70
The tomb, and on the clouds to sit
With tutelary power,
On their Descendants shedding grace —
This was the hour, and that the place.

II

But Truth inspired the Bards of old
When of an iron age they told,
Which to unequal laws gave birth,
And drove Astræa from the earth.
— A gentle Boy (perchance with blood
As noble as the best endued,   80
But seemingly a Thing despised;
Even by the sun and air unprized;
For not a tinge or flowery streak
Appeared upon his tender cheek)
Heart-deaf to those rebounding notes,
Apart, beside his silent goats,
Sate watching in a forest shed,
Pale, raggèd, with bare feet and head;
Mute as the snow upon the hill,
And, as the saint he prays to, still.   90
Ah, what avails heroic deed ?
What liberty ? if no defence
Be won for feeble Innocence.
Father of all ! though wilful Manhood read
His punishment in soul-distress,
Grant to the morn of life its natural blessed-
    ness !

XXV

THE LAST SUPPER

BY LEONARDO DA VINCI, IN THE REFEC-
TORY OF THE CONVENT OF MARIA
DELLA GRAZIA — MILAN

1820. 1822

Tho' searching damps and many an envi-
    ous flaw
Have marred this Work; the calm ethereal
    grace,

The love deep-seated in the Saviour's face,
The mercy, goodness, have not failed to awe
The Elements; as they do melt and thaw
The heart of the Beholder — and erase
(At least for one rapt moment) every trace
Of disobedience to the primal law.
The annunciation of the dreadful truth
Made to the Twelve, survives: lip, fore-
    head, cheek,
And hand reposing on the board in ruth
Of what it utters, while the unguilty seek
Unquestionable meanings — still bespeak
A labour worthy of eternal youth !

XXVI

THE ECLIPSE OF THE SUN, 1820

1820. 1822

HIGH on her speculative tower
Stood Science waiting for the hour
When Sol was destined to endure
That darkening of his radiant face
Which Superstition strove to chase,
Erewhile, with rites impure.

Afloat beneath Italian skies,
Through regions fair as Paradise
We gaily passed, — till Nature wrought
A silent and unlooked-for change,   10
That checked the desultory range
Of joy and sprightly thought.

Where'er was dipped the toiling oar,
The waves danced round us as before,
As lightly, though of altered hue,
'Mid recent coolness, such as falls
At noontide from umbrageous walls
That screen the morning dew.

No vapour stretched its wings; no cloud
Cast far or near a murky shroud;   20
The sky an azure field displayed;
'T was   sunlight   sheathed and   gently
    charmed,
Of all its sparkling rays disarmed,
And as in slumber laid, —

Or something night and day between,
Like moonshine — but the hue was green;
Still moonshine, without shadow, spread
On jutting rock, and curvèd shore,
Where gazed the peasant from his door
And on the mountain's head.   30

It tinged the Julian steeps — it lay,
Lugano ! on thy ample bay;
The solemnizing veil was drawn
O'er villas, terraces, and towers;
To Albogasio's olive bowers,
Porlezza's verdant lawn.

But Fancy with the speed of fire
Hath passed to Milan's loftiest spire,
And there alights 'mid that aërial host
Of Figures human and divine,   40
White as the snows of Apennine
Indúrated by frost.

Awe-stricken she beholds the array
That guards the Temple night and day;
Angels she sees — that might from heaven
          have flown,
And Virgin-saints, who not in vain
Have striven by purity to gain
The beatific crown —

Sees long-drawn files, concentric rings
Each narrowing above each; — the wings, 50
The uplifted palms, the silent marble lips,
The starry zone of sovereign height —
All steeped in this portentous light !
All suffering dim eclipse !

Thus after Man had fallen (if aught
These perishable spheres have wrought
May with that issue be compared)
Throngs of celestial visages,
Darkening like water in the breeze,
A holy sadness shared.   60

Lo ! while I speak, the labouring Sun
His glad deliverance has begun:
The cypress waves her sombre plume
More cheerily; and town and tower,
The vineyard and the olive-bower,
Their lustre re-assume !

O Ye, who guard and grace my home
While in far-distant lands we roam,
What countenance hath this Day put on for
          you ?
While we looked round with favoured eyes,
Did sullen mists hide lake and skies   71
And mountains from your view ?

Or was it given you to behold
Like vision, pensive though not cold,
From the smooth breast of gay Winander-
          mere ?

Saw ye the soft yet awful veil
Spread over Grasmere's lovely dale,
Helvellyn's brow severe ?

I ask in vain — and know far less
If sickness, sorrow, or distress   80
Have spared my Dwelling to this hour;
Sad blindness ! but ordained to prove
Our faith in Heaven's unfailing love
And all-controlling power.

XXVII

THE THREE COTTAGE GIRLS

1820. 1822

I

How blest the Maid whose heart — yet free
From Love's uneasy sovereignty —
Beats with a fancy running high,
Her simple cares to magnify;
Whom Labour, never urged to toil,
Hath cherished on a healthful soil;
Who knows not pomp, who heeds not pelf;
Whose heaviest sin it is to look
Askance upon her pretty Self
Reflected in some crystal brook;   10
Whom grief hath spared — who sheds no
          tear
But in sweet pity; and can hear
Another's praise from envy clear.

II

Such (but O lavish Nature ! why
That dark unfathomable eye,
Where lurks a Spirit that replies
To stillest mood of softest skies,
Yet hints at peace to be o'erthrown,
Another's first, and then her own ?)
Such, haply, yon ITALIAN Maid,   20
Our Lady's laggard Votaress,
Halting beneath the chestnut shade
To accomplish there her loveliness:
Nice aid maternal fingers lend;
A Sister serves with slacker hand;
Then, glittering like a star, she joins the
          festal band.

III

How blest (if truth may entertain
Coy fancy with a bolder strain)
The HELVETIAN Girl — who daily braves,
In her light skiff, the tossing waves,   30
And quits the bosom of the deep

Only to climb the rugged steep !
— Say whence that modulated shout !
From Wood-nymph of Diana's throng ?
Or does the greeting to a rout
Of giddy Bacchanals belong ?
Jubilant outcry ! rock and glade
Resounded — but the voice obeyed
The breath of an Helvetian Maid.

IV

Her beauty dazzles the thick wood;   40
Her courage animates the flood;
Her steps the elastic greensward meets
Returning unreluctant sweets;
The mountains (as ye heard) rejoice
Aloud, saluted by her voice !
Blithe Paragon of Alpine grace,
Be as thou art — for through thy veins
The blood of Heroes runs its race !
And nobly wilt thou brook the chains
That, for the virtuous, Life prepares;   50
The fetters which the Matron wears;
The patriot Mother's weight of anxious
   cares !

V

"Sweet HIGHLAND Girl ! a very shower
Of beauty was thy earthly dower,"
When thou didst flit before mine eyes,
Gay Vision under sullen skies,
While Hope and Love around thee played,
Near the rough falls of Inversneyd !
Have they, who nursed the blossom, seen
No breach of promise in the fruit ?   60
Was joy, in following joy, as keen
As grief can be in grief's pursuit ?
When youth had flown did hope still bless
Thy goings — or the cheerfulness
Of innocence survive to mitigate distress ?

VI

But from our course why turn — to tread
A way with shadows overspread;
Where what we gladliest would believe
Is feared as what may most deceive ?
Bright Spirit, not with amaranth crowned
But heath-bells from thy native ground,   71
Time cannot thin thy flowing hair,
Nor take one ray of light from Thee;
For in my Fancy thou dost share
The gift of immortality;
And there shall bloom, with Thee allied,
The Votaress by Lugano's side;
And that intrepid Nymph, on Uri's steep
   descried !

XXVIII

THE COLUMN INTENDED BY
BUONAPARTE FOR A TRI-
UMPHAL EDIFICE IN MILAN,
NOW LYING BY THE WAY-SIDE
IN THE SIMPLON PASS

1820. 1822

AMBITION — following down this far-famed
   slope
Her Pioneer, the snow-dissolving Sun,
While clarions prate of kingdoms to be
   won —
Perchance, in future ages, here may stop;
Taught to mistrust her flattering horoscope
By admonition from this prostrate Stone !
Memento uninscribed of Pride o'erthrown;
Vanity's hieroglyphic; a choice trope
In Fortune's rhetoric. Daughter of the
   Rock,
Rest where thy course was stayed by Power
   divine !
The Soul transported sees, from hint of
   thine,
Crimes which the great Avenger's hand pro-
   voke,
Hears combats whistling o'er the ensan-
   guined heath:
What groans ! what shrieks ! what quiet-
   ness in death.

XXIX

STANZAS

COMPOSED IN THE SIMPLON PASS

1820. 1822

VALLOMBROSA ! I longed in thy shadiest
   wood
To slumber, reclined on the moss-covered
   floor,
To listen to ANIO's precipitous flood,
When the stillness of evening hath deep-
   ened its roar;
To range through the Temples of PÆSTUM,
   to muse
In POMPEII preserved by her burial in
   earth;
On pictures to gaze where they drank in
   their hues;
And murmur sweet songs on the ground of
   their birth.

The beauty of Florence, the grandeur of
  Rome,
Could I leave them unseen, and not yield to
  regret?   10
With a hope (and no more) for a season to
  come,
Which ne'er may discharge the magnificent
  debt?
Thou fortunate Region! whose Greatness
  inurned
Awoke to new life from its ashes and dust;
Twice-glorified fields! if in sadness I turned
From your infinite marvels, the sadness
  was just.

Now, risen ere the light-footed Chamois
  retires
From dew-sprinkled grass to heights
  guarded with snow,
Toward the mists that hang over the land
  of my Sires,   19
From the climate of myrtles contented I go.
My thoughts become bright like yon edg-
  ing of Pines
On the steep's lofty verge: how it blackened
  the air!
But, touched from behind by the Sun, it
  now shines
With threads that seem part of his own
  silver hair.

Though the toil of the way with dear
  Friends we divide,
Though by the same zephyr our temples be
  fanned
As we rest in the cool orange-bower side
  by side,
A yearning survives which few hearts shall
  withstand:
Each step hath its value while homeward
  we move; —   29
O joy when the girdle of England appears!
What moment in life is so conscious of love,
Of love in the heart made more happy by
  tears?

XXX

ECHO, UPON THE GEMMI

1820. 1822

WHAT beast of chase hath broken from the
  cover?
Stern GEMMI listens to as full a cry,
As multitudinous a harmony

Of sounds as rang the heights of Latmos
  over,
When, from the soft couch of her sleeping
  Lover,
Up-starting, Cynthia skimmed the moun-
  tain dew
In keen pursuit — and gave, where'er she
  flew,
Impetuous motion to the Stars above her.
A solitary Wolf-dog, ranging on
Through the bleak concave, wakes this
  wondrous chime
Of aëry voices locked in unison, —
Faint — far-off — near — deep — solemn
  and sublime! —
So, from the body of one guilty deed,
A thousand ghostly fears, and haunting
  thoughts, proceed!

XXXI

PROCESSIONS

SUGGESTED ON A SABBATH MORNING IN
THE VALE OF CHAMOUNY

1820. 1822

To appease the Gods; or public thanks to
  yield;
Or to solicit knowledge of events,
Which in her breast Futurity concealed;
And that the past might have its true
  intents
Feelingly told by living monuments —
Mankind of yore were prompted to devise
Rites such as yet Persepolis presents
Graven on her cankered walls, solemnities
That moved in long array before admiring
  eyes.

The Hebrews thus, carrying in joyful state
Thick boughs of palm, and willows from
  the brook,   11
Marched round the altar — to commemo-
  rate
How, when their course they through the
  desert took,
Guided by signs which ne'er the sky for-
  sook,
They lodged in leafy tents and cabins low;
Green boughs were borne, while, for the
  blast that shook
Down to the earth the walls of Jericho,
Shouts rise, and storms of sound from
  lifted trumpets blow!

And thus, in order, 'mid the sacred grove
Fed in the Libyan waste by gushing wells, 20
The priests and damsels of Ammonian Jove
Provoked responses with shrill canticles;
While, in a ship begirt with silver bells,
They round his altar bore the hornèd God,
Old Cham, the solar Deity, who dwells
Aloft, yet in a tilting vessel rode,
When universal sea the mountains over-
    flowed.

Why speak of Roman Pomps ? the haughty
    claims
Of Chiefs triumphant after ruthless wars;
The feast of Neptune — and the Cereal
    Games,   30
With images, and crowns, and empty cars;
The dancing Salii — on the shields of Mars
Smiting with fury; and a deeper dread
Scattered on all sides by the hideous jars
Of Corybantian cymbals, while the head
Of Cybelè was seen, sublimely turreted !

At length a Spirit more subdued and soft
Appeared — to govern Christian pageant-
    ries:
The Cross, in calm procession, borne aloft
Moved to the chant of sober litanies.   40
Even such, this day, came wafted on the
    breeze
From a long train — in hooded vestments
    fair
Enwrapt — and winding, between Alpine
    trees
Spiry and dark, around their House of
    prayer,
Below the icy bed of bright ARGENTIERE.

Still in the vivid freshness of a dream,
The pageant haunts me as it met our
    eyes !
Still, with those white-robed Shapes — a
    living Stream,
The glacier Pillars join in solemn guise
For the same service, by mysterious ties; 50
Numbers exceeding credible account
Of number, pure and silent Votaries
Issuing or issued from a wintry fount;
The impenetrable heart of that exalted
    Mount !

They, too, who send so far a holy gleam
While they the Church engird with motion
    slow,
A product of that awful Mountain seem,

Poured from his vaults of everlasting
    snow;
Not virgin lilies marshalled in bright row,
Not swans descending with the stealthy
    tide,   60
A livelier sisterly resemblance show
Than the fair Forms, that in long order
    glide,
Bear to the glacier band — those Shapes
    aloft descried.

Trembling, I look upon the secret springs
Of that licentious craving in the mind
To act the God among external things,
To bind, on apt suggestion, or unbind;
And marvel not that antique Faith inclined
To crowd the world with metamorphosis,
Vouchsafed in pity or in wrath assigned; 70
Such insolent temptations wouldst thou
    miss,
Avoid these sights; nor brood o'er Fable's
    dark abyss !

XXXII

ELEGIAC STANZAS

1820. 1822

The lamented Youth whose untimely death
gave occasion to these elegiac verses, was Fred-
erick William Goddard, from Boston in North
America. He was in his twentieth year, and
had resided for some time with a clergyman in
the neighbourhood of Geneva for the completion
of his education. Accompanied by a fellow-
pupil, a native of Scotland, he had just set out
on a Swiss tour when it was his misfortune to
fall in with a Friend of mine who was hasten-
ing to join our party. The travellers, after
spending a day together on the road from
Berne and at Soleure, took leave of each other
at night, the young men having intended to
proceed directly to Zurich. But early in the
morning my friend found his new acquaint-
ances, who were informed of the object of his
journey, and the friends he was in pursuit of,
equipped to accompany him. We met at
Lucerne the succeeding evening, and Mr. G.
and his fellow-student became in consequence
our travelling companions for a couple of days.
We ascended the Righi together; and, after
contemplating the sunrise from that noble
mountain, we separated at an hour and on a
spot well suited to the parting of those who
were to meet no more. Our party descended
through the valley of our Lady of the Snow,
and our late companions, to Art. We had
hoped to meet in a few weeks at Geneva; but

on the third succeeding day (on the 21st of
August) Mr. Goddard perished, being overset
in a boat while crossing the lake of Zurich.
His companion saved himself by swimming,
and was hospitably received in the mansion of
a Swiss gentleman (M. Keller) situated on the
eastern coast of the lake. The corpse of poor
Goddard was cast ashore on the estate of the
same gentleman, who generously performed all
the rites of hospitality which could be ren-
dered to the dead as well as to the living. He
caused a handsome mural monument to be
erected in the Church of Küsnacht, which
records the premature fate of the young Amer-
ican, and on the shores too of the lake the
traveller may read an inscription pointing out
the spot where the body was deposited by the
waves.

LULLED by the sound of pastorai bells,
Rude Nature's Pilgrims did we go,
From the dread summit of the Queen
Of mountains, through a deep ravine,
Where, in her holy chapel, dwells
" Our Lady of the Snow."

The sky was blue, the air was mild;
Free were the streams and green the
        bowers;
As if, to rough assaults unknown,
The genial spot had *ever* shown   10
A countenance that as sweetly smiled —
The face of summer-hours.

And we were gay, our hearts at ease;
With pleasure dancing through the frame
We journeyed; all we knew of care —
Our path that straggled here and there;
Of trouble — but the fluttering breeze;
Of Winter — but a name.

If foresight could have rent the veil
Of three short days — but hush — no more !
Calm is the grave, and calmer none   21
Than that to which thy cares are gone,
Thou Victim of the stormy gale;
Asleep on ZURICH'S shore !

O GODDARD ! what art thou ? — a name —
A sunbeam followed by a shade !
Nor more, for aught that time supplies,
The great, the experienced, and the wise:
Too much from this frail earth we claim,
And therefore are betrayed.   30

We met, while festive mirth ran wild,
Where, from a deep lake's mighty urn,

Forth slips, like an enfranchised slave,
A sea-green river, proud to lave,
With current swift and undefiled,
The towers of old LUCERNE.

We parted upon solemn ground
Far-lifted towards the unfading sky;
But all our thoughts were *then* of Earth,
That gives to common pleasures birth;   40
And nothing in our hearts we found
That prompted even a sigh.

Fetch, sympathising Powers of air,
Fetch, ye that post o'er seas and lands,
Herbs, moistened by Virginian dew,
A most untimely grave to strew,
Whose turf may never know the care
Of *kindred* human hands !

Beloved by every gentle Muse
He left his Transatlantic home: 50
Europe, a realised romance,
Had opened on his eager glance;
What present bliss ! — what golden views !
What stores for years to come !

Though lodged within no vigorous frame,
His soul her daily tasks renewed,
Blithe as the lark on sun-gilt wings
High poised — or as the wren that sings
In shady places, to proclaim
Her modest gratitude.   6c

Not vain in sadly-uttered praise;
The words of truth's memorial vow
Are sweet as morning fragrance shed
From flowers 'mid GOLDAU'S ruins bred;
As evening's fondly-lingering rays,
On RIGHI'S silent brow.

Lamented Youth ! to thy cold clay
Fit obsequies the Stranger paid;
And piety shall guard the Stone
Which hath not left the spot unknown   70
Where the wild waves resigned their
        prey —
And *that* which marks thy bed.

And, when thy Mother weeps for Thee,
Lost Youth ! a solitary Mother;
This tribute from a casual Friend
A not unwelcome aid may lend,
To feed the tender luxury,
The rising pang to smother.

XXXIII

SKY-PROSPECT — FROM THE PLAIN OF FRANCE

1820. 1822

Lo ! in the burning west, the craggy nape
Of a proud Ararat ! and, thereupon,
The Ark, her melancholy voyage done !
Yon rampant cloud mimics a lion's shape;
There, combats a huge crocodile — agape
A golden spear to swallow ! and that brown
And massy grove, so near yon blazing town,
Stirs and recedes — destruction to 'escape !
Yet all is harmless — as the Elysian shades
Where Spirits dwell in undisturbed repose —
Silently disappears, or quickly fades:
Meek Nature's evening comment on the shows
That for oblivion take their daily birth
From all the fuming vanities of Earth !

XXXIV

ON BEING STRANDED NEAR THE HARBOUR OF BOULOGNE

1820. 1822

WHY cast ye back upon the Gallic shore,
Ye furious waves ! a patriotic Son
Of England — who in hope her coast had won,
His project crowned, his pleasant travel o'er ?
Well — let him pace this noted beach once more,
That gave the Roman his triumphal shells;
That saw the Corsican his cap and bells
Haughtily shake, a dreaming Conqueror ! —
Enough: my Country's cliffs I can behold,
And proudly think, beside the chafing sea,
Of checked ambition, tyranny controlled,
And folly cursed with endless memory:
These local recollections ne'er can cloy;
Such ground I from my very heart enjoy !

XXXV

AFTER LANDING — THE VALLEY OF DOVER

Nov. 1820

1820. 1822

WHERE be the noisy followers of the game
Which faction breeds; the turmoil where?
that passed

Through Europe, echoing from the news-man's blast,
And filled our hearts with grief for England's shame.
Peace greets us; — rambling on without an aim
We mark majestic herds of cattle, free
To ruminate, couched on the grassy lea;
And hear far-off the mellow horn proclaim
The Season's harmless pastime. Ruder sound
Stirs not; enrapt I gaze with strange delight,
While consciousnesses, not to be disowned,
Here only serve a feeling to invite
That lifts the spirit to a calmer height,
And makes this rural stillness more profound.

XXXVI

AT DOVER

1837. 1838

For the impressions on which this sonnet turns, I am indebted to the experience of my daughter, during her residence at Dover with our dear friend, Miss Fenwick.

FROM the Pier's head, musing, and with increase
Of wonder, I have watched this sea-side Town,
Under the white cliff's battlemented crown,
Hushed to a depth of more than Sabbath peace:
The streets and quays are thronged, but why disown
Their natural utterance: whence this strange release
From social noise — silence elsewhere unknown ? —
A Spirit whispered, " Let all wonder cease ;
Ocean's o'erpowering murmurs have set free
Thy sense from pressure of life's common din;
As the dread Voice that speaks from out the sea
Of God's eternal Word, the Voice of Time
Doth deaden, shocks of tumult, shrieks of crime,
The shouts of folly, and the groans of sin."

XXXVII

DESULTORY STANZAS

UPON RECEIVING THE PRECEDING
SHEETS FROM THE PRESS

1822. 1822

Is then the final page before me spread,
Nor further outlet left to mind or heart?
Presumptuous Book! too forward to be read,
How can I give thee licence to depart?
One tribute more: unbidden feelings start
Forth from their coverts; slighted objects
    rise;
My spirit is the scene of such wild art
As on Parnassus rules, when lightning flies,
Visibly leading on the thunder's harmonies.

All that I saw returns upon my view,   10
All that I heard comes back upon my ear,
All that I felt this moment doth renew;
And where the foot with no unmanly fear
Recoiled — and wings alone could travel —
    there
I move at ease; and meet contending
    themes
That press upon me, crossing the career
Of recollections vivid as the dreams
Of midnight, — cities, plains, forests, and
    mighty streams.

Where Mortal never breathed I dare to sit
Among the interior Alps, gigantic crew, 20
Who triumphed o'er diluvian power! —
    and yet
What are they but a wreck and residue,
Whose only business is to perish? — true
To which sad course, these wrinkled Sons
    of Time
Labour their proper greatness to subdue;
Speaking of death alone, beneath a clime
Where life and rapture flow in plenitude
    sublime.

Fancy hath flung for me an airy bridge
Across thy long deep Valley, furious Rhone!
Arch that *here* rests upon the granite ridge
Of Monte Rosa — *there* on frailer stone 31
Of secondary birth, the Jung-frau's cone;
And, from that arch, down-looking on the
    Vale
The aspect I behold of every zone;
A sea of foliage, tossing with the gale,
Blithe Autumn's purple crown, and Win-
    ter's icy mail!

Far as ST. MAURICE, from yon eastern
    FORKS,
Down the main avenue my sight can range:
And all its branchy vales, and all that lurks
Within them, church, and town, and hut,
    and grange,   40
For my enjoyment meet in vision strange;
Snows, torrents; — to the region's utmost
    bound,
Life, Death, in amicable interchange; —
But list! the avalanche — the hush pro-
    found
That follows — yet more awful than that
    awful sound!

Is not the chamois suited to his place?
The eagle worthy of her ancestry?
— Let Empires fall; but ne'er shall Ye dis-
    grace
Your noble birthright, ye that occupy
Your council-seats beneath the open sky, 50
On Sarnen's Mount, there judge of fit and
    right,
In simple democratic majesty;
Soft breezes fanning your rough brows —
    the might
And purity of nature spread before your
    sight!

From this appropriate Court, renowned
    LUCERNE
Calls me to pace her honoured Bridge —
    that cheers
The Patriot's heart with pictures rude and
    stern,
An uncouth Chronicle of glorious years.
Like portraiture, from loftier source, en-
    dears
That work of kindred frame, which spans
    the lake   60
Just at the point of issue, where it fears
The form and motion of a stream to take;
Where it begins to stir, *yet* voiceless as a
    snake.

Volumes of sound, from the Cathedral
    rolled,
This long-roofed Vista penetrate — but see,
One after one, its tablets, that unfold
The whole design of Scripture history;
From the first tasting of the fatal Tree,
Till the bright Star appeared in eastern skies,
Announcing, ONE was born mankind to free:
His acts, his wrongs, his final sacrifice; 71
Lessons for every heart, a Bible for all eyes.

Our pride misleads, our timid likings
   kill.
— Long may these homely Works devised
   of old,
These simple efforts of Helvetian skill,
Aid, with congenial influence, to uphold
The State, — the Country's destiny to
   mould;
Turning, for them who pass, the common
   dust
Of servile opportunity to gold;
Filling the soul with sentiments august —
The beautiful, the brave, the holy, and the
   just !   81

No more; Time halts not in his noiseless
   march —
Nor turns, nor winds, as doth the liquid
   flood;
Life slips from underneath us, like that arch
Of airy workmanship whereon we stood,
Earth stretched below, heaven in our neigh-
   bourhood.
Go forth, my little Book ! pursue thy way;
Go forth, and please the gentle and the
   good;
Nor be a whisper stifled, if it say
That treasures, yet untouched, may grace
   some future Lay.   90

THE RIVER DUDDON

A SERIES OF SONNETS

1802(?)–1820. 1820

It is with the little river Duddon as it is with most other rivers, Ganges and Nile not excepted, — many springs might claim the honour of being its head. In my own fancy I have fixed its rise near the noted Shire-stones placed at the meeting-point of the counties, Westmoreland, Cumberland, and Lancashire. They stand by the wayside on the top of the Wrynose Pass, and it used to be reckoned a proud thing to say that, by touching them at the same time with feet and hands, one had been in the three counties at once. At what point of its course the stream takes the name of Duddon I do not know. I first became acquainted with the Duddon, as I have good reason to remember, in early boyhood. Upon the banks of the Derwent I had learnt to be very fond of angling. Fish abound in that large river; not so in the small streams in the neighbourhood of Hawkshead ; and I fell into the common delusion that the farther from home the better sport would be had. Accordingly, one day I attached myself to a person living in the neighbourhood of Hawkshead, who was going to try his fortune as an angler near the source of the Duddon. We fished a great part of the day with very sorry success, the rain pouring torrents, and long before we got home I was worn out with fatigue ; and, if the good man had not carried me on his back, I must have lain down under the best shelter I could find. Little did I think then it would be my lot to celebrate, in a strain of love and admiration, the stream which for many years I never thought of without recollections of disappointment and distress.

During my college vacation, and two or three years afterwards, before taking my Bachelor's degree, I was several times resident in the house of a near relative who lived in the small town of Broughton. I passed many delightful hours upon the banks of this river, which becomes an estuary about a mile from that place. The remembrances of that period are the subject of the 21st Sonnet. The subject of the 27th is in fact taken from a tradition belonging to Rydal Hall, which once stood, as is believed, upon a rocky and woody hill on the right hand as you go from Rydal to Ambleside, and was deserted from the superstitious fear here described, and the present site fortunately chosen instead. The present Hall was erected by Sir Michael le Fleming, and it may be hoped that at some future time there will be an edifice more worthy of so beautiful a position. With regard to the 30th Sonnet it is odd enough that this imagination was realised in the year 1840, when I made a tour through that district with my wife and daughter, Miss Fenwick and her niece, and Mr. and Miss Quillinan. Before our return from Seathwaite chapel the party separated. Mrs. Wordsworth, while most of us went further up the stream, chose an opposite direction, having told us that we should overtake her on our way to Ulpha. But she was tempted out of the main road to ascend a rocky eminence near it, thinking it impossible we should pass without seeing her. This, however, unfortunately happened, and then ensued vexation and distress, especially to me, which I should be ashamed to have recorded, for I lost my temper entirely. Neither I nor those that were with me saw her again till we reached the Inn at Broughton, seven miles. This may perhaps in some degree excuse my irritability on the occasion, for I could not but think she had been much to blame. It appeared, however, on explanation, that she had remained on the rock, calling out and waving her handkerchief as we were passing, in order that we also might ascend and enjoy a prospect which had much charmed her. " But on we went, her signals proving vain." How then could she reach Broughton before us ? When we found she had not gone on before to Ulpha Kirk, Mr. Quillinan went back in one of the carriages in search of her. He met her on the road, took her up, and by a shorter way conveyed her to Broughton, where we were all reunited and spent a happy evening.

I have many affecting remembrances connected with this stream. Those I forbear to mention ; especially things that occurred on its banks during the later part of that visit to the seaside of which the former part is detailed in my " Epistle to Sir George Beaumont."

The River Duddon rises upon Wrynose Fell, on the confines of Westmoreland, Cumberland, and Lancashire ; and, having served as a boundary to the two last counties for the space of about twenty-five miles, enters the Irish Sea, between the Isle of Walney and the Lordship of Millum.

TO

THE REV. DR. WORDSWORTH

(WITH THE SONNETS TO THE RIVER DUDDON,
AND OTHER POEMS IN THIS COLLECTION, 1820)

1819. 1820

THE Minstrels played their Christmas tune
To-night beneath my cottage-eaves ;
While, smitten by a lofty moon,
The encircling laurels, thick with leaves,
Gave back a rich and dazzling sheen,
That overpowered their natural green.

Through hill and valley every breeze
Had sunk to rest with folded wings :
Keen was the air, but could not freeze,
Nor check, the music of the strings ;   10
So stout and hardy were the band
That scraped the chords with strenuous hand ;

And who but listened ? — till was paid
Respect to every Inmate's claim :
The greeting given, the music played,
In honour of each household name,
Duly pronounced with lusty call,
And " merry Christmas " wished to all !

O Brother ! I revere the choice
That took thee from thy native hills ;   20
And it is given thee to rejoice :
Though public care full often tills
(Heaven only witness of the toil)
A barren and ungrateful soil.

Yet, would that Thou, with me and mine,
Hadst heard this never-failing rite ;
And seen on other faces shine
A true revival of the light
Which Nature and these rustic Powers,
In simple childhood, spread through ours.   30

For pleasure hath not ceased to wait
On these expected annual rounds ;
Whether the rich man's sumptuous gate
Call forth the unelaborate sounds,
Or they are offered at the door
That guards the lowliest of the poor.

How touching, when, at midnight, sweep
Snow-muffled winds, and all is dark,
To hear — and sink again to sleep !
Or, at an earlier call, to mark,   40
By blazing fire, the still suspense
Of self-complacent innocence ;

The mutual nod, — the grave disguise
Of hearts with gladness brimming o'er ;
And some unbidden tears that rise
For names once heard, and heard no more ;
Tears brightened by the serenade
For infant in the cradle laid.

Ah ! not for emerald fields alone,
With ambient streams more pure and bright   50
Than fabled Cytherea's zone
Glittering before the Thunderer's sight,
Is to my heart of hearts endeared
The ground where we were born and reared !

Hail, ancient Manners ! sure defence,
Where they survive, of wholesome laws ;
Remnants of love whose modest sense
Thus into narrow room withdraws ;
Hail, Usages of pristine mould,
And ye that guard them, Mountains old !   60

Bear with me, Brother ! quench the thought
That slights this passion, or condemns ;
If thee fond Fancy ever brought
From the proud margin of the Thames,
And Lambeth's venerable towers,
To humbler streams, and greener bowers.

Yes, they can make, who fail to find,
Short leisure even in busiest days ;
Moments, to cast a look behind,
And profit by those kindly rays   70
That through the clouds do sometimes steal,
And all the far-off past reveal.

Hence, while the imperial City's din
Beats frequent on thy satiate ear,
A pleased attention I may win
To agitations less severe,
That neither overwhelm nor cloy,
But fill the hollow vale with joy !

I

(?). 1820

NOT envying Latian shades — if yet they
throw
A grateful coolness round that crystal
Spring,
Blandusia, prattling as when long ago
The Sabine Bard was moved her praise to
sing;

Careless of flowers that in perennial blow
Round the moist marge of Persian fountains
    cling;
Heedless of Alpine torrents thundering
Through ice-built arches radiant as heaven's
    bow;
I seek the birthplace of a native Stream. —
All hail, ye mountains! hail, thou morning
    light!
Better to breathe at large on this clear
    height
Than toil in needless sleep from dream to
    dream:
Pure flow the verse, pure, vigorous, free,
    and bright,
For Duddon, long-loved Duddon, is my
    theme!

II

(?). 1820

CHILD of the clouds! remote from every
    taint
Of sordid industry thy lot is cast;
Thine are the honours of the lofty waste;
Not seldom, when with heat the valleys
    faint,
Thy handmaid Frost with spangled tissue
    quaint
Thy cradle decks; — to chant thy birth, thou
    hast
No meaner Poet than the whistling Blast,
And Desolation is thy Patron-saint!
She guards thee, ruthless Power! who
    would not spare
Those mighty forests, once the bison's
    screen,
Where stalked the huge deer to his shaggy
    lair
Through paths and alleys roofed with
    darkest green;
Thousands of years before the silent air
Was pierced by whizzing shaft of hunter
    keen!

III

(?). 1820

How shall I paint thee? — Be this naked
    stone
My seat, while I give way to such intent;
Pleased could my verse, a speaking monu-
    ment,
Make to the eyes of men thy features known.

But as of all those tripping lambs not one
Outruns his fellows, so hath Nature lent
To thy beginning nought that doth present
Peculiar ground for hope to build upon.
To dignify the spot that gives thee birth,
No sign of hoar Antiquity's esteem
Appears, and none of modern Fortune's
    care;
Yet thou thyself hast round thee shed a
    gleam
Of brilliant moss, instinct with freshness
    rare;
Prompt offering to thy Foster-mother
    Earth!

IV

(?). 1820

TAKE, cradled Nursling of the mountain,
    take
This parting glance, no negligent adieu!
A Protean change seems wrought while I
    pursue
The curves, a loosely-scattered chain doth
    make;
Or rather thou appear'st a glistering snake,
Silent, and to the gazer's eye untrue,
Thridding with sinuous lapse the rushes,
    through
Dwarf willows gliding, and by ferny brake.
Starts from a dizzy steep the undaunted Rill
Robed instantly in garb of snow-white foam;
And laughing dares the Adventurer, who
    hath clomb
So high, a rival purpose to fulfil;
Else let the dastard backward wend, and
    roam,
Seeking less bold achievement, where he
    will!

V

(?). 1820

SOLE listener, Duddon! to the breeze that
    played
With thy clear voice, I caught the fitful
    sound
Wafted o'er sullen moss and craggy
    mound —
Unfruitful solitudes, that seemed to upbraid
The sun in heaven! — but now, to form a
    shade
For Thee, green alders have together wound
Their foliage; ashes flung their arms around;
And birch-trees risen in silver colonnade.

And thou hast also tempted here to rise,
'Mid sheltering pines, this Cottage rude
  and grey;
Whose ruddy children, by the mother's
  eyes
Carelessly watched, sport through the sum-
  mer day,
Thy pleased associates: — light as endless
  May
On infant bosoms lonely Nature lies.

VI

FLOWERS

(?). 1820

ERE yet our course was graced with social
  trees
It lacked not old remains of hawthorn
  bowers,
Where small birds warbled to their para-
  mours;
And, earlier still, was heard the hum of
  bees;
I saw them ply their harmless robberies,
And caught the fragrance which the sundry
  flowers,
Fed by the stream with soft perpetual
  showers,
Plenteously yielded to the vagrant breeze.
There bloomed the strawberry of the wilder-
  ness;
The trembling eyebright showed her
  sapphire blue,
The thyme her purple, like the blush of
  Even;
And if the breath of some to no caress
Invited, forth they peeped so fair to view,
All kinds alike seemed favourites of Heaven.

VII

(?). 1820

" CHANGE me, some God, into that breath-
  ing rose ! "
The love-sick Stripling fancifully sighs,
The envied flower beholding, as it lies
On Laura's breast, in exquisite repose;
Or he would pass into her bird, that throws
The darts of song from out its wiry cage;
Enraptured, — could he for himself engage
The thousandth part of what the Nymph
  bestows;

And what the little careless innocent
Ungraciously receives. Too daring choice !
There are whose calmer mind it would
  content
To be an unculled floweret of the glen,
Fearless of plough and scythe; or darkling
  wren
That tunes on Duddon's banks her slender
  voice.

VIII

(?). 1820

WHAT aspect bore the Man who roved or fled,
First of his tribe, to this dark dell — who first
In this pellucid Current slaked his thirst ?
What hopes came with him ? what designs
  were spread
Along his path ? His unprotected bed
What dreams encompassed ? Was the in-
  truder nursed
In hideous usages, and rites accursed,
That thinned the living and disturbed the
  dead ?
No voice replies; — both air and earth are
  mute;
And Thou, blue Streamlet, murmuring
  yield'st no more
Than a soft record, that, whatever fruit
Of ignorance thou might'st witness hereto-
  fore,
Thy function was to heal and to restore,
To soothe and cleanse, not madden and
  pollute !

IX

THE STEPPING-STONES

(?). 1820

THE struggling Rill insensibly is grown
Into a Brook of loud and stately march,
Crossed ever and anon by plank or arch;
And, for like use, lo ! what might seem a
  zone
Chosen for ornament — stone matched with
  stone
In studied symmetry, with interspace
For the clear waters to pursue their race
Without restraint. How swiftly have they
  flown,
Succeeding — still succeeding ! Here the
  Child
Puts, when the high-swoln Flood runs fierce
  and wild,

His budding courage to the proof; and
    here
Declining Manhood learns to note the sly
And sure encroachments of infirmity,
Thinking how fast time runs, life's end
    how near!

X

THE SAME SUBJECT

(?). 1820

NOT so that Pair whose youthful spirits
    dance
With prompt emotion, urging them to
    pass;
A sweet confusion checks the Shepherd-
    lass;
Blushing she eyes the dizzy flood askance;
To stop ashamed — too timid to advance;
She ventures once again — another pause!
His outstretched hand He tauntingly with-
    draws —
She sues for help with piteous utterance!
Chidden she chides again; the thrilling
    touch
Both feel, when he renews the wished-for
    aid:
Ah! if their fluttering hearts should stir
    too much,
Should beat too strongly, both may be be-
    trayed.
The frolic Loves, who, from yon high rock,
    see
The struggle, clap their wings for victory!

XI

THE FAËRY CHASM

(?). 1820

No fiction was it of the antique age:
A sky-blue stone, within this sunless cleft,
Is of the very footmarks unbereft
Which tiny Elves impressed; — on that
    smooth stage
Dancing with all their brilliant equipage
In secret revels — haply after theft
Of some sweet Babe — Flower stolen, and
    coarse Weed left
For the distracted Mother to assuage
Her grief with, as she might! — But,
    where, oh! where
Is traceable a vestige of the notes

That ruled those dances wild in char-
    acter? —
Deep underground? Or in the upper air,
On the shrill wind of midnight? or where
    floats
O'er twilight fields the autumnal gossamer?

XII

HINTS FOR THE FANCY

(?). 1820

ON, loitering Muse — the swift Stream
    chides us — on!
Albeit his deep-worn channel doth immure
Objects immense portrayed in miniature,
Wild shapes for many a strange compari-
    son!
Niagaras, Alpine passes, and anon
Abodes of Naiads, calm abysses pure,
Bright liquid mansions, fashioned to en-
    dure
When the broad oak drops, a leafless
    skeleton,
And the solidities of mortal pride,
Palace and tower, are crumbled into
    dust! —
The Bard who walks with Duddon for his
    guide,
Shall find such toys of fancy thickly set:
Turn from the sight, enamoured Muse —
    we must;
And, if thou canst, leave them without
    regret!

XIII

OPEN PROSPECT

(?). 1820

HAIL to the fields — with Dwellings sprin-
    kled o'er,
And one small hamlet, under a green hill
Clustering, with barn and byre, and spout-
    ing mill!
A glance suffices; — should we wish for
    more,
Gay June would scorn us. But when bleak
    winds roar
Through the stiff lance-like shoots of pollard
    ash,
Dread swell of sound! loud as the gusts
    that lash
The matted forests of Ontario's shore

By wasteful steel unsmitten — then would I
Turn into port; and, reckless of the gale,
Reckless of angry Duddon sweeping by,
While the warm hearth exalts the mantling
ale,
Laugh with the generous household heartily
At all the merry pranks of Donnerdale !

XIV

1806(?). 1807

O MOUNTAIN Stream ! the Shepherd and
his Cot
Are privileged Inmates of deep solitude;
Nor would the nicest Anchorite exclude
A field or two of brighter green, or plot
Of tillage-ground, that seemeth like a spot
Of stationary sunshine: — thou hast viewed
These only, Duddon ! with their paths re-
newed
By fits and starts, yet this contents thee not.
Thee hath some awful Spirit impelled to
leave,
Utterly to desert, the haunts of men,
Though simple thy companions were and
few;
And through this wilderness a passage
cleave
Attended but by thy own voice, save when
The clouds and fowls of the air thy way
pursue !

XV

(?). 1820

FROM this deep chasm, where quivering
sunbeams play
Upon its loftiest crags, mine eyes behold
A gloomy NICHE, capacious, blank, and
cold;
A concave free from shrubs and mosses
grey;
In semblance fresh, as if, with dire affray,
Some Statue, placed amid these regions old
For tutelary service, thence had rolled,
Startling the flight of timid Yesterday !
Was it by mortals sculptured ? — weary
slaves
Of slow endeavour ! or abruptly cast
Into rude shape by fire, with roaring blast
Tempestuously let loose from central caves?
Or fashioned by the turbulence of waves,
Then, when o'er highest hills the Deluge
passed ?

XVI

AMERICAN TRADITION

(?). 1820

SUCH fruitless questions may not long be-
guile
Or plague the fancy 'mid the sculptured
shows
Conspicuous yet where Oroonoko flows;
There would the Indian answer with a smile
Aimed at the White Man's ignorance, the
while,
Of the GREAT WATERS telling how they
rose,
Covered the plains, and, wandering where
they chose,
Mounted through every intricate defile,
Triumphant — Inundation wide and deep,
O'er which his Fathers urged, to ridge and
steep
Else unapproachable, their buoyant way;
And carved, on mural cliff's undreaded side,
Sun, moon, and stars, and beast of chase
or prey;
Whate'er they sought, shunned, loved, or
deified !

XVII

RETURN

(?). 1820

A DARK plume fetch me from yon blasted
yew,
Perched on whose top the Danish Raven
croaks;
Aloft, the imperial Bird of Rome invokes
Departed ages, shedding where he flew
Loose fragments of wild wailing, that be-
strew
The clouds and thrill the chambers of the
rocks;
And into silence hush the timorous flocks,
That, calmly couching while the nightly dew
Moistened each fleece, beneath the twin-
kling stars
Slept amid that lone Camp on Hardknot's
height,
Whose Guardians bent the knee to Jove
and Mars:
Or, near that mystic Round of Druid frame
Tardily sinking by its proper weight
Deep into patient Earth, from whose smooth
breast it came !

XVIII

SEATHWAITE CHAPEL

(?). 1820

SACRED Religion ! " mother of form and
fear,"
Dread arbitress of mutable respect,
New rites ordaining when the old are
wrecked,
Or cease to please the fickle worshipper;
Mother of Love ! (that name best suits
thee here)
Mother of Love ! for this deep vale, pro-
tect
Truth's holy lamp, pure source of bright
effect,
Gifted to purge the vapoury atmosphere
That seeks to stifle it; — as in those days
When this low Pile a Gospel Teacher
knew,
Whose good works formed an endless re-
tinue:
A Pastor such as Chaucer's verse por-
trays;
Such as the heaven-taught skill of Herbert
drew;
And tender Goldsmith crowned with death-
less praise !

XIX

TRIBUTARY STREAM

(?). 1820

MY frame hath often trembled with de-
light
When hope presented some far-distant good,
That seemed from heaven descending, like
the flood
Of yon pure waters, from their aëry height
Hurrying, with lordly Duddon to unite;
Who, 'mid a world of images imprest
On the calm depth of his transparent
breast,
Appears to cherish most that Torrent
white,
The fairest, softest, liveliest of them all !
And seldom hath ear listened to a tune
More lulling than the busy hum of Noon,
Swoln by that voice — whose murmur
musical
Announces to the thirsty fields a boon
Dewy and fresh, till showers again shall
fall.

XX

THE PLAIN OF DONNERDALE

1807(?). 1820

THE old inventive Poets, had they seen,
Or rather felt, the entrancement that detains
Thy waters, Duddon ! 'mid these flowery
plains —
The still repose, the liquid lapse serene,
Transferred to bowers imperishably green,
Had beautified Elysium ! But these chains
Will soon be broken; — a rough course re-
mains,
Rough as the past; where Thou, of placid
mien,
Innocuous as a firstling of the flock,
And countenanced like a soft cerulean sky,
Shalt change thy temper; and, with many
a shock
Given and received in mutual jeopardy,
Dance, like a Bacchanal, from rock to rock,
Tossing her frantic thyrsus wide and high !

XXI

(?). 1820

WHENCE that low voice ? — A whisper
from the heart,
That told of days long past, when here I
roved
With friends and kindred tenderly beloved;
Some who had early mandates to depart,
Yet are allowed to steal my path athwart
By Duddon's side; once more do we unite,
Once more, beneath the kind Earth's tran-
quil light;
And smothered joys into new being start.
From her unworthy seat, the cloudy stall
Of Time, breaks forth triumphant Memory;
Her glistening tresses bound, yet light and
free
As golden locks of birch, that rise and fall
On gales that breathe too gently to recall
Aught of the fading year's inclemency !

XXII

TRADITION

(?). 1820

A LOVE-LORN Maid, at some far-distant time,
Came to this hidden pool, whose depths
surpass

In crystal clearness Dian's looking-glass;
And, gazing, saw that Rose, which from the
    prime
Derives its name, reflected, as the chime ·
Of echo doth reverberate some sweet sound:
The starry treasure from the blue profound
She longed to ravish; — shall she plunge, or
    climb
The humid precipice, and seize the guest
Of April, smiling high in upper air ?
Desperate alternative ! what fiend could
    dare
To prompt the thought ? — Upon the steep
    rock's breast
The lonely Primrose yet renews its bloom,
Untouched memento of her hapless doom !

XXIII

SHEEP-WASHING

(?). 1820

SAD thoughts, avaunt ! — partake we their
    blithe cheer
Who gathered in betimes the unshorn flock
To wash the fleece, where haply bands of
    rock,
Checking the stream, make a pool smooth
    and clear
As this we look on. Distant Mountains hear,
Hear and repeat, the turmoil that unites
Clamour of boys with innocent despites
Of barking dogs, and bleatings from strange
    fear.
And what if Duddon's spotless flood receive
Unwelcome mixtures as the uncouth noise
Thickens, the pastoral River will forgive
Such wrong; nor need *we* blame the li-
    censed joys,
Though false to Nature's quiet equipoise:
Frank are the sports, the stains are fugitive.

XXIV

THE RESTING-PLACE

(?). 1820

MID-NOON is past; — upon the sultry mead
No zephyr breathes, no cloud its shadow
    throws:
If we advance unstrengthened by repose,
Farewell the solace of the vagrant reed !
This Nook — with woodbine hung and
    straggling weed

Tempting recess as ever pilgrim chose,
Half grot, half arbour — proffers to en-
    close
Body and mind, from molestation freed,
In narrow compass — narrow as itself:
Or if the Fancy, too industrious Elf,
Be loth that we should breathe awhile ex-
    empt
From new incitements friendly to our task,
Here wants not stealthy prospect, that may
    tempt
Loose Idless to forego her wily mask.

XXV

(?). 1820

METHINKS 't were no unprecedented feat
Should some benignant Minister of air
Lift, and encircle with a cloudy chair,
The One for whom my heart shall ever
    beat
With tenderest love; — or, if a safer seat
Atween his downy wings be furnished,
    there
Would lodge her, and the cherished burden
    bear
O'er hill and valley to this dim retreat !
Rough ways my steps have trod; — too
    rough and long
For her companionship; here dwells soft
    ease:
With sweets that she partakes not, some
    distaste
Mingles, and lurking consciousness of
    wrong;
Languish the flowers; the waters seem to
    waste
Their vocal charm; their sparklings cease
    to please.

XXVI

1802(?). 1820

RETURN, Content ! for fondly I pursued,
Even when a child, the Streams — un-
    heard, unseen;
Through tangled woods, impending rocks
    between;
Or, free as air, with flying inquest viewed
The sullen reservoirs whence their bold
    brood —
Pure as the morning, fretful, boisterous,
    keen,

Green as the salt-sea billows, white and
   green —
Poured down the hills, a choral multitude !
Nor have I tracked their course for scanty
   gains;
They taught me random cares and truant
   joys,
That shield from mischief and preserve
   from stains
Vague minds, while men are growing out
   of boys;
Maturer Fancy owes to their rough noise
Impetuous thoughts that brook not servile
   reins.

XXVII

1819(?). 1819

FALLEN, and diffused into a shapeless heap,
Or quietly self-buried in earth's mould,
Is that embattled House, whose massy
   Keep,
Flung from yon cliff a shadow large and
   cold.
There dwelt the gay, the bountiful, the
   bold;
Till nightly lamentations, like the sweep
Of winds — though winds were silent —
   struck a deep
And lasting terror through that ancient
   Hold.
Its line of Warriors fled; — they shrunk
   when tried
By ghostly power: — but Time's unsparing
   hand
Hath plucked such foes, like weeds, from
   out the land;
And now, if men with men in peace abide,
All other strength the weakest may with-
   stand,
All worse assaults may safely be defied.

XXVIII

JOURNEY RENEWED

(?). 1820

I ROSE while yet the cattle, heat-opprest,
Crowded together under rustling trees
Brushed by the current of the water-
   breeze;
And for *their* sakes, and love of all that
   rest,

On Duddon's margin, in the sheltering
   nest;
For all the startled scaly tribes that slink
Into his coverts, and each fearless link
Of dancing insects forged upon his breast;
For these, and hopes and recollections worn
Close to the vital seat of human clay;
Glad meetings, tender partings, that up-
   stay
The drooping mind of absence, by vows
   sworn
In his pure presence near the trysting
   thorn —
I thanked the Leader of my onward way.

XXIX

(?). 1820

No record tells of lance opposed to lance,
Horse charging horse, 'mid these retired
   domains;
Tells that their turf drank purple from the
   veins
Of heroes, fallen, or struggling to advance,
Till doubtful combat issued in a trance
Of victory, that struck through heart and
   reins
Even to the inmost seat of mortal pains,
And lightened o'er the pallid countenance.
Yet, to the loyal and the brave, who lie
In the blank earth, neglected and forlorn,
The passing Winds memorial tribute pay;
The Torrents chant their praise, inspiring
   scorn
Of power usurped; with proclamation high,
And glad acknowledgment, of lawful sway.

XXX

(?). 1820

WHO swerves from innocence, who makes
   divorce
Of that serene companion — a good name,
Recovers not his loss; but walks with
   shame,
With doubt, with fear, and haply with re-
   morse:
And oft-times he — who, yielding to the
   force
Of chance-temptation, ere his journey end,
From chosen comrade turns, or faithful
   friend —
In vain shall rue the broken intercourse.

Not so with such as loosely wear the
    chain
That binds them, pleasant River! to thy
    side: —
Through the rough copse wheel thou with
    hasty stride;
I choose to saunter o'er the grassy plain,
Sure, when the separation has been tried,
That we, who part in love, shall meet
    again.

XXXI

(?). 1820

THE KIRK of ULPHA to the pilgrim's eye
Is welcome as a star, that doth present
Its shining forehead through the peaceful
    rent
Of a black cloud diffused o'er half the
    sky:
Or as a fruitful palm-tree towering high
O'er the parched waste beside an Arab's
    tent;
Or the Indian tree whose branches, down-
    ward bent,
Take root again, a boundless canopy.
How sweet were leisure! could it yield no
    more
Than 'mid that wave-washed Churchyard
    to recline,
From pastoral graves extracting thoughts
    divine;
Or there to pace, and mark the summits
    hoar
Of distant moonlit mountains faintly shine,
Soothed by the unseen River's gentle roar.

XXXII

(?). 1820

NOT hurled precipitous from steep to steep;
Lingering no more 'mid flower-enamelled
    lands
And blooming thickets; nor by rocky bands
Held; but in radiant progress toward the
    Deep
Where mightiest rivers into powerless sleep
Sink, and forget their nature — now expands
Majestic Duddon, over smooth flat sands
Gliding in silence with unfettered sweep!
Beneath an ampler sky a region wide
Is opened round him: — hamlets, towers,
    and towns,

And blue-topped hills, behold him from
    afar;
In stately mien to sovereign Thames allied,
Spreading his bosom under Kentish downs,
With commerce freighted, or triumphant
    war.

XXXIII

CONCLUSION

(?). 1820

BUT here no cannon thunders to the gale;
Upon the wave no haughty pendants cast
A crimson splendour: lowly is the mast
That rises here, and humbly spread, the
    sail;
While, less disturbed than in the narrow
    Vale
Through which with strange vicissitudes he
    passed,
The Wanderer seeks that receptacle vast
Where all his unambitious functions fail
And may thy Poet, cloud-born Stream! be
    free —
The sweets of earth contentedly resigned,
And each tumultuous working left behind
At seemly distance — to advance like Thee;
Prepared, in peace of heart, in calm of mind
And soul, to mingle with Eternity!

XXXIV

AFTER–THOUGHT

(?). 1820

I THOUGHT of Thee, my partner and my guide,
As being past away. — Vain sympathies!
For, backward, Duddon, as I cast my eyes,
I see what was, and is, and will abide;
Still glides the Stream, and shall for ever
    glide;
The Form remains, the Function never dies;
While we, the brave, the mighty, and the wise,
We Men, who in our morn of youth defied
The elements, must vanish; — be it so!
Enough, if something from our hands have
    power
To live, and act, and serve the future hour;
And if, as toward the silent tomb we go,
Through love, through hope, and faith's tran-
    scendent dower,
We feel that we are greater than we know.

A PARSONAGE IN OXFORD-SHIRE

1820. 1822

This Parsonage was the residence of my friend Jones, and is particularly described in another note.

WHERE holy ground begins, unhallowed ends,
Is marked by no distinguishable line;
The turf unites, the pathways intertwine;
And, wheresoe'er the stealing footstep tends,
Garden, and that domain where kindred, friends,
And neighbours rest together, here confound
Their several features, mingled like the sound
Of many waters, or as evening blends
With shady night. Soft airs, from shrub and flower,
Waft fragrant greetings to each silent grave;
And while those lofty poplars gently wave
Their tops, between them comes and goes a sky
Bright as the glimpses of eternity,
To saints accorded in their mortal hour.

TO ENTERPRISE

1821. 1822

KEEP for the Young the impassioned smile
Shed from thy countenance, as I see thee stand
High on that chalky cliff of Britain's Isle,
A slender volume grasping in thy hand —
(Perchance the pages that relate
The various turns of Crusoe's fate) —
Ah, spare the exulting smile,
And drop thy pointing finger bright
As the first flash of beacon light;
But neither veil thy head in shadows dim, 10
Nor turn thy face away
From One who, in the evening of his day,
To thee would offer no presumptuous hymn!

I

Bold Spirit ! who art free to rove
Among the starry courts of Jove,

And oft in splendour dost appear
Embodied to poetic eyes,
While traversing this nether sphere,
Where Mortals call thee ENTERPRISE.
Daughter of Hope ! her favourite Child, 20
Whom she to young Ambition bore,
When hunter's arrow first defiled
The grove, and stained the turf with gore;
Thee wingèd Fancy took, and nursed
On broad Euphrates' palmy shore,
And where the mightier Waters burst
From caves of Indian mountains hoar !
She wrapped thee in a panther's skin;
And Thou, thy favourite food to win,
The flame-eyed eagle oft wouldst scare 30
From her rock-fortress in mid air,
With infant shout; and often sweep,
Paired with the ostrich, o'er the plain;
Or, tired with sport, wouldst sink asleep
Upon the couchant lion's mane !
With rolling years thy strength increased
And, far beyond thy native East,
To thee, by varying titles known
As variously thy power was shown,
Did incense-bearing altars rise, 40
Which caught the blaze of sacrifice,
From suppliants panting for the skies !

II

What though this ancient Earth be trod
No more by step of Demi-god
Mounting from glorious deed to deed
As thou from clime to clime didst lead;
Yet still, the bosom beating high,
And the hushed farewell of an eye
Where no procrastinating gaze
A last infirmity betrays, 50
Prove that thy heaven-descended sway
Shall ne'er submit to cold decay.
By thy divinity impelled,
The Stripling seeks the tented field;
The aspiring Virgin kneels; and, pale
With awe, receives the hallowed veil,
A soft and tender Heroine
Vowed to severer discipline;
Inflamed by thee, the blooming Boy
Makes of the whistling shrouds a toy, 60
And of the ocean's dismal breast
A play-ground, — or a couch of rest;
'Mid the blank world of snow and ice,
Thou to his dangers dost enchain
The Chamois-chaser awed in vain
By chasm or dizzy precipice;
And hast Thou not with triumph seen
How soaring Mortals glide between

Or through the clouds, and brave the light
With bolder than Icarian flight ?   70
How they, in bells of crystal, dive —
Where winds and waters cease to strive —
For no unholy visitings,
Among the monsters of the Deep;
And all the sad and precious things
Which there in ghastly silence sleep ?
Or, adverse tides and currents headed,
And breathless calms no longer dreaded,
In never-slackening voyage go
Straight as an arrow from the bow;   80
And, slighting sails and scorning oars,
Keep faith with Time on distant shores ?
— Within our fearless reach are placed
The secrets of the burning Waste;
Egyptian tombs unlock their dead,
Nile trembles at his fountain head;
Thou speak'st — and lo ! the polar Seas
Unbosom their last mysteries.
— But oh ! what transports, what sublime
        reward,
Won from the world of mind, dost thou
        prepare   90
For philosophic Sage; or high-souled Bard
Who, for thy service trained in lonely
        woods,
Hath fed on pageants floating through the
        air,
Or calentured in depth of limpid floods;
Nor grieves — tho' doomed thro' silent
        night to bear
The domination of his glorious themes,
Or struggle in the net-work of thy dreams !

III

If there be movements in the Patriot's
        soul,
From source still deeper, and of higher
        worth,
'T is thine the quickening impulse to con-
        trol,   100
And in due season send the mandate
        forth;
Thy call a prostrate Nation can restore,
When but a single Mind resolves to crouch
        no more.

IV

Dread Minister of wrath !
Who to their destined punishment dost
        urge
The Pharaohs of the earth, the men of hard-
        ened heart !
Not unassisted by the flattering stars,

Thou strew'st temptation o'er the path
When they in pomp depart   109
With trampling horses and refulgent cars —
Soon to be swallowed by the briny surge;
Or cast, for lingering death, on unknown
        strands;
Or caught amid a whirl of desert sands —
An Army now, and now a living hill
That a brief while heaves with convulsive
        throes —
Then all is still;
Or, to forget their madness and their
        woes,
Wrapt in a winding-sheet of spotless snows !

V

Back flows the willing current of my
        Song:
If to provoke such doom the Impious
        dare,   120
Why should it daunt a blameless prayer ?
— Bold Goddess ! range our Youth among;
Nor let thy genuine impulse fail to beat
In hearts no longer young;
Still may a veteran Few have pride
In thoughts whose sternness makes them
        sweet;
In fixed resolves by Reason justified;
That to their object cleave like sleet
Whitening a pine tree's northern side,
When fields are naked far and wide,   130
And withered leaves, from earth's cold
        breast
Up-caught in whirlwinds, nowhere can find
        rest.

VI

But, if such homage thou disdain
As doth with mellowing years agree,
One rarely absent from thy train
More humble favours may obtain
For thy contented Votary.
She, who incites the frolic lambs
In presence of their heedless dams,
And to the solitary fawn   140
Vouchsafes her lessons, bounteous Nymph
That wakes the breeze, the sparkling lymph
Doth hurry to the lawn;
She, who inspires that strain of joyance holy
Which the sweet Bird, misnamed the mel-
        ancholy,
Pours forth in shady groves, shall plead for
        me;
And vernal mornings opening bright
With views of undefined delight,

And cheerful songs, and suns that shine
On busy days, with thankful nights, be
    mine.   150

VII

But thou, O Goddess ! in thy favourite Isle
(Freedom's impregnable redoubt,
The wide earth's store-house fenced about

With breakers roaring to the gales
That stretch a thousand thousand sails)
Quicken the slothful, and exalt the vile ! —
Thy impulse is the life of Fame;
Glad Hope would almost cease to be
If torn from thy society;
And Love, when worthiest of his name, 160
Is proud to walk the earth with Thee !

ECCLESIASTICAL SONNETS

IN SERIES

1821. 1822

My purpose in writing this Series was, as much as possible, to confine my view to the introduction, progress, and operation of the Church in England, both previous and subsequent to the Reformation. The Sonnets were written long before ecclesiastical history and points of doctrine had excited the interest with which they have been recently enquired into and discussed. The former particular is mentioned as an excuse for my having fallen into error in respect to an incident which had been selected as setting forth the height to which the power of the Popedom over temporal sovereignty had attained, and the arrogance with which it was displayed. I allude to the last Sonnet but one in the first series, where Pope Alexander the third at Venice is described as setting his foot on the neck of the Emperor Barbarossa. Though this is related as a fact in history, I am told it is a mere legend of no authority. Substitute for it an undeniable truth not less fitted for my purpose, namely, the penance inflicted by Gregory the Seventh upon the Emperor Henry the Fourth.

Before I conclude my notice of these Sonnets, let me observe that the opinion I pronounced in favour of Laud (long before the Oxford Tract movement) and which had brought censure upon me from several quarters, is not in the least changed. Omitting here to examine into his conduct in respect to the persecuting spirit with which he has been charged, I am persuaded that most of his aims to restore ritual practices which had been abandoned were good and wise, whatever errors he might commit in the manner he sometimes attempted to enforce them. I further believe that, had not he, and others who shared his opinions and felt as he did, stood up in opposition to the reformers of that period, it is questionable whether the Church would ever have recovered its lost ground and become the blessing it now is, and will, I trust, become in a still greater degree, both to those of its communion and to those who unfortunately are separated from it.

PART I

FROM THE INTRODUCTION OF CHRISTIANITY INTO BRITAIN, TO THE CONSUMMATION OF THE PAPAL DOMINION

" A verse may catch a wandering Soul, that flies
Profounder Tracts, and by a blest surprise
Convert delight into a Sacrifice."

I

INTRODUCTION

1821. 1822

I, WHO accompanied with faithful pace
Cerulean Duddon from its cloud-fed spring,
And loved with spirit ruled by his to sing
Of mountain quiet and boon nature's grace:

I, who essayed the nobler Stream to trace
Of Liberty, and smote the plausive string
Till the checked torrent, proudly triumphing,
Won for herself a lasting resting-place;
Now seek upon the heights of Time the source
Of a HOLY RIVER, on whose banks are found
Sweet pastoral flowers, and laurels that have crowned
Full oft the unworthy brow of lawless force;
And, for delight of him who tracks its course,
Immortal amaranth and palms abound.

II
CONJECTURES
1821. 1822

IF there be prophets on whose spirits rest
Past things, revealed like future, they can
tell
What Powers, presiding o'er the sacred well
Of Christian Faith, this savage Island
blessed
With its first bounty. Wandering through
the west,
Did holy Paul a while in Britain dwell,
And call the Fountain forth by miracle,
And with dread signs the nascent Stream
invest ?
Or He, whose bonds dropped off, whose
prison doors
Flew open, by an Angel's voice unbarred ?
Or some of humbler name, to these wild
shores
Storm-driven; who, having seen the cup of
woe
Pass from their Master, sojourned here to
guard
The precious Current they had taught to
flow ?

III
TREPIDATION OF THE DRUIDS
1821. 1822

SCREAMS round the Arch-druid's brow the
seamew — white
As Menai's foam; and toward the mystic
ring
Where Augurs stand, the Future question-
ing,
Slowly the cormorant aims her heavy flight,
Portending ruin to each baleful rite,
That, in the lapse of ages, hath crept o'er
Diluvian truths, and patriarchal lore.
Haughty the Bard: can these meek doctrines
blight
His transports ? wither his heroic strains ?
But all shall be fulfilled; — the Julian
spear
A way first opened; and, with Roman
chains,
The tidings come of Jesus crucified;
They come — they spread — the weak, the
suffering, hear;
Receive the faith, and in the hope abide.

IV
DRUIDICAL EXCOMMUNICATION
1821. 1822

MERCY and Love have met thee on thy road,
Thou wretched Outcast, from the gift of
fire
And food cut off by sacerdotal ire,
From every sympathy that Man bestowed !
Yet shall it claim our reverence, that to God,
Ancient of days ! that to the eternal Sire,
These jealous Ministers of law aspire,
As to the one sole fount whence wisdom
flowed,
Justice, and order. Tremblingly escaped,
As if with prescience of the coming storm,
That intimation when the stars were shaped;
And still, 'mid yon thick woods, the primal
truth
Glimmers through many a superstitious
form
That fills the Soul with unavailing ruth.

V
UNCERTAINTY
1821. 1822

DARKNESS surrounds us; seeking, we are
lost
On Snowdon's wilds, amid Brigantian coves,
Or where the solitary shepherd roves
Along the plain of Sarum, by the ghost
Of Time and shadows of Tradition, crost;
And where the boatman of the Western
Isles
Slackens his course — to mark those holy
piles
Which yet survive on bleak Iona's coast.
Nor these, nor monuments of eldest name,
Nor Taliesin's unforgotten lays,
Nor characters of Greek or Roman fame,
To an unquestionable Source have led;
Enough — if eyes, that sought the fountain-
head
In vain, upon the growing Rill may gaze.

VI
PERSECUTION
1821. 1822

LAMENT ! for Diocletian's fiery sword
Works busy as the lightning; but instinct

With malice ne'er to deadliest weapon
    linked
Which God's ethereal store-houses afford:
Against the Followers of the incarnate Lord
It rages; some are smitten in the field —
Some pierced to the heart through the in-
    effectual shield
Of sacred home; — with pomp are others
    gored
And dreadful respite. Thus was Alban
    tried,
England's first Martyr, whom no threats
    could shake;
Self-offered victim, for his friend he died,
And for the faith; nor shall his name for-
    sake
That Hill, whose flowery platform seems
    to rise
By Nature decked for holiest sacrifice.

VII

RECOVERY

1821. 1822

As, when a storm hath ceased, the birds
    regain
Their cheerfulness, and busily retrim
Their nests, or chant a gratulating hymn
To the blue ether and bespangled plain;
Even so, in many a re-constructed fane,
Have the survivors of this Storm renewed
Their holy rites with vocal gratitude:
And solemn ceremonials they ordain
To celebrate their great deliverance;
Most feelingly instructed 'mid their fear —
That persecution, blind with rage extreme,
May not the less, through Heaven's mild
    countenance,
Even in her own despite, both feed and
    cheer;
For all things are less dreadful than they
    seem.

VIII

TEMPTATIONS FROM ROMAN REFINE-
MENTS

1821. 1822

Watch, and be firm! for soul-subduing
    vice,
Heart-killing luxury, on your steps await.
Fair houses, baths, and banquets delicate,
And temples flashing, bright as polar ice,

Their radiance through the woods — may
    yet suffice
To sap your hardy virtue, and abate
Your love of Him upon whose forehead sate
The crown of thorns; whose life-blood
    flowed, the price
Of your redemption. Shun the insidious arts
That Rome provides, less dreading from
    her frown
Than from her wily praise, her peaceful
    gown,
Language, and letters; — these, though
    fondly viewed
As humanising graces, are but parts
And instruments of deadliest servitude !

IX

DISSENSIONS

1821. 1822

That heresies should strike (if truth be
    scanned
Presumptuously) their roots both wide and
    deep,
Is natural as dreams to feverish sleep.
Lo ! Discord at the altar dares to stand
Uplifting toward high Heaven her fiery
    brand,
A cherished Priestess of the new-baptized !
But chastisement shall follow peace de-
    spised.
The Pictish cloud darkens the enervate land
By Rome abandoned; vain are suppliant
    cries,
And prayers that would undo her forced
    farewell;
For she returns not. — Awed by her own
    knell,
She casts the Britons upon strange Allies
Soon to become more dreaded enemies
Than heartless misery called them to repel.

X

STRUGGLE OF THE BRITONS AGAINST
THE BARBARIANS

1821. 1822

Rise ! — they *have* risen: of brave Aneurin
    ask
How they have scourged old foes, perfidious
    friends:
The Spirit of Caractacus descends
Upon the Patriots, animates their task; —

Amazement runs before the towering casque
Of Arthur, bearing through the stormy field
The virgin sculptured on his Christian
    shield: —
Stretched in the sunny light of victory
    bask
The Host that followed Urien as he strode
O'er heaps of slain; — from Cambrian wood
    and moss
Druids descend, auxiliars of the Cross;
Bards, nursed on blue Plinlimmon's still
    abode,
Rush on the fight, to harps preferring
    swords,
And everlasting deeds to burning words !

XI

SAXON CONQUEST

1821. 1822

NOR wants the cause the panic-striking aid
Of hallelujahs tost from hill to hill —
For instant victory. But Heaven's high
    will
Permits a second and a darker shade
Of Pagan night. Afflicted and dismayed,
The Relics of the sword flee to the moun-
    tains:
O wretched Land ! whose tears have flowed
    like fountains;
Whose arts and honours in the dust are laid
By men yet scarcely conscious of a care
For other monuments than those of Earth;
Who, as the fields and woods have given
    them birth,
Will build their savage fortunes only there;
Content, if foss, and barrow, and the girth
Of long-drawn rampart, witness what they
    were.

XII

MONASTERY OF OLD BANGOR

1821. 1822

*THE oppression of the tumult — wrath and
    scorn —*
The tribulation — and the gleaming blades —
Such is the impetuous spirit that pervades
The song of Taliesin; — Ours shall mourn
The *unarmed* Host who by their prayers
    would turn
The sword from Bangor's walls, and guard
    the store
Of Aboriginal and Roman lore,

And Christian monuments, that now must
    burn
To senseless ashes. Mark ! how all things
    swerve
From their known course, or vanish like a
    dream;
Another language spreads from coast to
    coast;
Only perchance some melancholy Stream
And some indignant Hills old names pre-
    serve,
When laws, and creeds, and people all are
    lost !

XIII

CASUAL INCITEMENT

1821. 1822

A BRIGHT-HAIRED company of youthful
    slaves,
Beautiful strangers, stand within the pale
Of a sad market, ranged for public sale,
Where Tiber's stream the immortal City
    laves:
ANGLI by name; and not an ANGEL waves
His wing who could seem lovelier to man's
    eye
Than they appear to holy Gregory;
Who, having learnt that name, salvation
    craves
For Them, and for their Land. The ear-
    nest Sire,
His questions urging, feels, in slender ties
Of chiming sound, commanding sympathies;
DE-IRIANS — he would save them from
    God's IRE;
Subjects of Saxon ÆLLA — they shall sing
Glad HALLE-lujahs to the eternal King !

XIV

GLAD TIDINGS

1821. 1822

FOR ever hallowed be this morning fair,
Blest be the unconscious shore on which
    ye tread,
And blest the silver Cross, which ye, instead
Of martial banner, in procession bear;
The Cross preceding Him who floats in air,
The pictured Saviour ! — By Augustin led,
They come — and onward travel without
    dread,
Chanting in barbarous ears a tuneful
    prayer —

Sung for themselves, and those whom they
    would free !
Rich conquest waits them: — the tempestu-
    ous sea
Of Ignorance, that ran so rough and high
And heeded not the voice of clashing
    swords,
These good men humble by a few bare
    words,
And calm with fear of God's divinity.

XV

PAULINUS

1821. 1822

BUT, to remote Northumbria's royal Hall,
Where thoughtful Edwin, tutored in the
    school
Of sorrow, still maintains a heathen rule,
Who comes with functions apostolical ?
Mark him, of shoulders curved, and stature
    tall,
Black hair, and vivid eye, and meagre
    cheek,
His prominent feature like an eagle's beak;
A Man whose aspect doth at once appal
And strike with reverence. The Monarch
    leans
Toward the pure truths this Delegate pro-
    pounds,
Repeatedly his own deep mind he sounds
With careful hesitation, — then convenes
A synod of his Councillors: — give ear,
And what a pensive Sage doth utter, hear !

XVI

PERSUASION

1821. 1822

" MAN'S life is like a Sparrow, mighty
    King !
That — while at banquet with your Chiefs
    you sit
Housed near a blazing fire — is seen to flit
Safe from the wintry tempest. Fluttering,
Here did it enter; there, on hasty wing,
Flies out, and passes on from cold to cold;
But whence it came we know not, nor be-
    hold
Whither it goes. Even such, that transient
    Thing,
The human Soul; not utterly unknown
While in the Body lodged, her warm abode;

But from what world She came, what woe
    or weal
On her departure waits, no tongue hath
    shown;
This mystery if the Stranger can reveal,
His be a welcome cordially bestowed ! "

XVII

CONVERSION

1821. 1822

PROMPT transformation works the novel
    Lore;
The Council closed, the Priest in full career
Rides forth, an armèd man, and hurls a
    spear
To desecrate the Fane which heretofore
He served in folly. Woden falls, and Thor
Is overturned; the mace, in battle heaved
(So might they dream) till victory was
    achieved,
Drops, and the God himself is seen no
    more.
Temple and Altar sink, to hide their shame
Amid oblivious weeds. " *O come to me,*
Ye heavy laden ! " such the inviting voice
Heard near fresh streams; and thousands,
    who rejoice
In the new Rite, the pledge of sanctity,
Shall, by regenerate life, the promise claim.

XVIII

APOLOGY

1821. 1822

NOR scorn the aid which Fancy oft doth
    lend
The Soul's eternal interests to promote:
Death, darkness, danger, are our natural
    lot;
And evil Spirits *may* our walk attend
For aught the wisest know or comprehend;
Then be *good* Spirits free to breathe a note
Of elevation; let their odours float
Around these Converts; and their glories
    blend,
The midnight stars outshining, or the blaze
Of the noon-day. Nor doubt that golden
    cords
Of good works, mingling with the visions,
    raise
The Soul to purer worlds: and *who* the
    line

Shall draw, the limits of the power define,
That even imperfect faith to man affords?

XIX

PRIMITIVE SAXON CLERGY

1821. 1822

How beautiful your presence, how benign,
Servants of God! who not a thought will
share
With the vain world; who, outwardly as
bare
As winter trees, yield no fallacious sign
That the firm soul is clothed with fruit
divine!
Such Priest, when service worthy of his
care
Has called him forth to breathe the com-
mon air,
Might seem a saintly Image from its shrine
Descended: — happy are the eyes that
meet
The Apparition; evil thoughts are stayed
At his approach, and low-bowed necks
entreat
A benediction from his voice or hand;
Whence grace, through which the heart
can understand,
And vows, that bind the will, in silence
made.

XX

OTHER INFLUENCES

1821. 1822

AH, when the Body, round which in love
we clung,
Is chilled by death, does mutual service
fail?
Is tender pity then of no avail?
Are intercessions of the fervent tongue
A waste of hope? — From this sad source
have sprung
Rites that console the Spirit, under grief
Which ill can brook more rational relief:
Hence, prayers are shaped amiss, and
dirges sung
For Souls whose doom is fixed! The way
is smooth
For Power that travels with the human
heart:
Confession ministers the pang to soothe
In him who at the ghost of guilt doth
start.

Ye holy Men, so earnest in your care,
Of your own mighty instruments beware!

XXI

SECLUSION

1821. 1822

LANCE, shield, and sword relinquished, at
his side
A bead-roll, in his hand a claspèd book,
Or staff more harmless than a shepherd's
crook,
The war-worn Chieftain quits the world —
to hide
His thin autumnal locks where Monks abide
In cloistered privacy. But not to dwell
In soft repose he comes: within his cell,
Round the decaying trunk of human pride,
At morn, and eve, and midnight's silent
hour,
Do penitential cogitations cling;
Like ivy, round some ancient elm, they
twine
In grisly folds and strictures serpentine;
Yet, while they strangle, a fair growth they
bring,
For recompence — their own perennial
bower.

XXII

CONTINUED

1821. 1822

METHINKS that to some vacant hermitage
My feet would rather turn — to some dry
nook
Scooped out of living rock, and near a brook
Hurled down a mountain-cove from stage
to stage,
Yet tempering, for my sight, its bustling
rage
In the soft heaven of a translucent pool;
Thence creeping under sylvan arches cool,
Fit haunt of shapes whose glorious equipage
Would elevate my dreams. A beechen bowl,
A maple dish, my furniture should be;
Crisp, yellow leaves my bed; the hooting
owl
My night-watch: nor should e'er the crested
fowl
From thorp or vill his matins sound for
me,
Tired of the world and all its industry.

XXIII

REPROOF

1821. 1822

But what if One, through grove or flowery
mead,
Indulging thus at will the creeping feet
Of a voluptuous indolence, should meet
Thy hovering Shade, O venerable Bede !
The saint, the scholar, from a circle freed
Of toil stupendous, in a hallowed seat
Of learning, where thou heard'st the billows
beat
On a wild coast, rough monitors to feed
Perpetual industry.   Sublime Recluse !
The recreant soul, that dares to shun the
debt
Imposed on human kind, must first forget
Thy diligence, thy unrelaxing use
Of a long life; and, in the hour of death,
The last dear service of thy passing breath !

XXIV

SAXON MONASTERIES, AND LIGHTS AND SHADES OF THE RELIGION

1821. 1822

By such examples moved to unbought pains,
The people work like congregated bees;
Eager to build the quiet Fortresses
Where Piety, as they believe, obtains
From Heaven a *general* blessing; timely rains
Or needful sunshine; prosperous enterprise,
Justice and peace: — bold faith ! yet also
rise
The sacred Structures for less doubtful
gains.
The Sensual think with reverence of the
palms
Which the chaste Votaries seek, beyond the
grave
If penance be redeemable, thence alms
Flow to the poor, and freedom to the slave;
And if full oft the Sanctuary save
Lives black with guilt, ferocity it calms.

XXV

MISSIONS AND TRAVELS

1821. 1822

Not sedentary all: there are who roam
To scatter seeds of life on barbarous shores;
Or quit with zealous step their knee-worn
floors
To seek the general mart of Christendom;
Whence they, like richly-laden merchants,
come
To their belovèd cells: — or shall we say
That, like the Red-cross Knight, they urge
their way,
To lead in memorable triumph home
Truth, their immortal Una ?   Babylon,
Learnèd and wise, hath perished utterly,
Nor leaves her Speech one word to aid the
sigh
That would lament her; — Memphis, Tyre,
are gone
With all their Arts, — but classic lore glides
on
By these Religious saved for all posterity.

XXVI

ALFRED

1821. 1822

Behold a pupil of the monkish gown,
The pious Alfred, King to Justice dear !
Lord of the harp and liberating spear;
Mirror of Princes !   Indigent Renown
Might range the starry ether for a crown
Equal to *his* deserts, who, like the year,
Pours forth his bounty, like the day doth
cheer,
And awes like night with mercy-tempered
frown.
Ease from this noble miser of his time
No moment steals; pain narrows not his
cares.
Though small his kingdom as a spark or
gem,
Of Alfred boasts remote Jerusalem,
And Christian India, through her wide-
spread clime,
In sacred converse gifts with Alfred shares.

XXVII

HIS DESCENDANTS

1821. 1822

When thy great soul was freed from mortal
chains,
Darling of England ! many a bitter shower
Fell on thy tomb; but emulative power
Flowed in thy line through undegenerate
veins.

The Race of Alfred covet glorious pains
When dangers threaten, dangers ever new !
Black tempests bursting, blacker still in view !
But manly sovereignty its hold retains;
The root sincere, the branches bold to strive
With the fierce tempest, while, within the round
Of their protection, gentle virtues thrive;
As oft, 'mid some green plot of open ground,
Wide as the oak extends its dewy gloom,
The fostered hyacinths spread their purple bloom.

XXVIII

INFLUENCE ABUSED

1821. 1822

URGED by Ambition, who with subtlest skill
Changes her means, the Enthusiast as a dupe
Shall soar, and as a hypocrite can stoop,
And turn the instruments of good to ill,
Moulding the credulous people to his will.
Such DUNSTAN :—from its Benedictine coop
Issues the master Mind, at whose fell swoop
The chaste affections tremble to fulfil
Their purposes. Behold, pre-signified,
The Might of spiritual sway ! his thoughts, his dreams,
Do in the supernatural world abide:
So vaunt a throng of Followers, filled with pride
In what they see of virtues pushed to extremes,
And sorceries of talent misapplied.

XXIX

DANISH CONQUESTS

1821. 1822

WOE to the Crown that doth the Cowl obey !
Dissension, checking arms that would re-strain
The incessant Rovers of the northern main,
Helps to restore and spread a Pagan sway:
But Gospel-truth is potent to allay
Fierceness and rage; and soon the cruel Dane
Feels, through the influence of her gentle reign,
His native superstitions melt away.

Thus, often, when thick gloom the east o'ershrouds,
The full-orbed Moon, slow climbing, doth appear
Silently to consume the heavy clouds;
How no one can resolve; but every eye
Around her sees, while air is hushed, a clear
And widening circuit of ethereal sky.

XXX

CANUTE

1821. 1822

A PLEASANT music floats along the Mere,
From Monks in Ely chanting service high,
While-as Canùte the King is rowing by:
" My Oarsmen," quoth the mighty King, " draw near,
That we the sweet song of the Monks may hear ! "
He listens (all past conquests, and all schemes
Of future, vanishing like empty dreams)
Heart-touched, and haply not without a tear.
The Royal Minstrel, ere the choir is still,
While his free Barge skims the smooth flood along,
Gives to that rapture an accordant Rhyme.
O suffering Earth ! be thankful: sternest clime
And rudest age are subject to the thrill
Of heaven-descended Piety and Song.

XXXI

THE NORMAN CONQUEST

1821. 1822

THE woman-hearted Confessor prepares
The evanescence of the Saxon line.
Hark ! 't is the tolling Curfew ! — the stars shine;
But of the lights that cherish household cares
And festive gladness, burns not one that dares
To twinkle after that dull stroke of thine,
Emblem and instrument, from Thames to Tyne,
Of force that daunts, and cunning that en-snares !

Yet as the terrors of the lordly bell,
That quench, from hut to palace, lamps and
fires,
Touch not the tapers of the sacred quires;
Even so a thraldom, studious to expel
Old laws, and ancient customs to derange,
To Creed or Ritual brings no fatal change.

XXXII
(?). 1837

COLDLY we spake. The Saxons, over-
powered
By wrong triumphant through its own ex-
cess,
From fields laid waste, from house and
home devoured
By flames, look up to heaven and crave re-
dress
From God's eternal justice. Pitiless
Though men be, there are angels that can feel
For wounds that death alone has power to
heal,
For penitent guilt, and innocent distress.
And has a Champion risen in arms to try
His Country's virtue, fought, and breathes
no more;
Him in their hearts the people canonize;
And far above the mine's most precious ore
The least small pittance of bare mould they
prize
Scooped from the sacred earth where his
dear relics lie.

XXXIII
THE COUNCIL OF CLERMONT
1821. 1822

"AND shall," the Pontiff asks, "profane-
ness flow
From Nazareth — source of Christian piety,
From Bethlehem, from the Mounts of
Agony
And glorified Ascension? Warriors, go,
With prayers and blessings we your path
will sow;
Like Moses hold our hands erect, till ye
Have chased far off by righteous victory
These sons of Amalek, or laid them
low!" —
"GOD WILLETH IT," the whole assembly
cry;
Shout which the enraptured multitude as-
tounds!

The Council-roof and Clermont's towers
reply; —
"God willeth it," from hill to hill rebounds,
And, in awe-stricken Countries far and nigh,
Through "Nature's hollow arch" that voice
resounds.

XXXIV
CRUSADES
1821. 1822

THE turbaned Race are poured in thicken-
ing swarms
Along the west; though driven from Aqui-
taine,
The Crescent glitters on the towers of Spain;
And soft Italia feels renewed alarms;
The scimitar, that yields not to the charms
Of ease, the narrow Bosphorus will disdain;
Nor long (that crossed) would Grecian hills
detain
Their tents, and check the current of their
arms.
Then blame not those who, by the mightiest
lever
Known to the moral world, Imagination,
Upheave, so seems it, from her natural sta-
tion
All Christendom: — they sweep along (was
never
So huge a host!) — to tear from the Un-
believer
The precious Tomb, their haven of salvation.

XXXV
RICHARD I
1821. 1822

REDOUBTED King, of courage leonine,
I mark thee, Richard! urgent to equip
Thy warlike person with the staff and scrip;
I watch thee sailing o'er the midland brine;
In conquered Cyprus see thy Bride decline
Her blushing cheek, love-vows upon her lip,
And see love-emblems streaming from thy
ship,
As thence she holds her way to Palestine.
My Song, a fearless homager, would attend
Thy thundering battle-axe as it cleaves the
press
Of war, but duty summons her away
To tell — how, finding in the rash distress
Of those Enthusiasts a subservient friend,
To giddier heights hath clomb the Papal
sway.

XXXVI

AN INTERDICT

1821. 1822

REALMS quake by turns: proud Arbitress
      of grace,
The Church, by mandate shadowing forth
      the power
She arrogates o'er heaven's eternal door,
Closes the gates of every sacred place.
Straight from the sun and tainted air's em-
      brace
All sacred things are covered: cheerful morn
Grows sad as night—no seemly garb is worn,
Nor is a face allowed to meet a face
With natural smiles of greeting.   Bells are
      dumb;
Ditches are graves — funereal rites denied;
And in the churchyard he must take his bride
Who dares be wedded! Fancies thickly come
Into the pensive heart ill fortified,
And comfortless despairs the soul benumb.

XXXVII

PAPAL ABUSES

1821. 1822

As with the Stream our voyage we pursue,
The gross materials of this world present
A marvellous study of wild accident;
Uncouth proximities of old and new;
And bold transfigurations, more untrue
(As might be deemed) to disciplined intent
Than aught the sky's fantastic element,
When most fantastic, offers to the view.
Saw we not Henry scourged at Becket's
      shrine ?
Lo ! John self-stripped of his insignia: —
      crown,
Sceptre and mantle, sword and ring, laid down
At a proud Legate's feet !   The spears that
      line
Baronial halls, the opprobrious insult feel;
And angry Ocean roars a vain appeal.

XXXVIII

SCENE IN VENICE

1821. 1822

BLACK Demons hovering o'er his mitred
      head,
To Cæsar's Successor the Pontiff spake;

" Ere I absolve thee, stoop ! that on thy
      neck
Levelled with earth this foot of mine may
      tread."
Then he, who to the altar had been led,
He, whose strong arm the Orient could not
      check,
He, who had held the Soldan at his beck,
Stooped, of all glory disinherited,
And even the common dignity of man ! —
Amazement strikes the crowd: while many
      turn
Their eyes away in sorrow, others burn
With scorn, invoking a vindictive ban
From outraged Nature; but the sense of
      most
In abject sympathy with power is lost.

XXXIX

PAPAL DOMINION

1821. 1822

UNLESS to Peter's Chair the viewless wind
Must come and ask permission when to
      blow,
What further empire would it have ? for
      now
A ghostly Domination, unconfined
As that by dreaming Bards to Love as-
      signed,
Sits there in sober truth — to raise the low,
Perplex the wise, the strong to overthrow;
Through earth and heaven to bind and to
      unbind ! —
Resist — the thunder quails thee ! — crouch
      — rebuff
Shall be thy recompence ! from land to land
The ancient thrones of Christendom are stuff
For occupation of a magic wand,
And 't is the Pope that wields it: — whether
      rough
Or smooth his front, our world is in his
      hand !

PART II

TO THE CLOSE OF THE TROUBLES IN
THE REIGN OF CHARLES I

I

(?). 1845

How soon — alas ! did Man, created pure —
By Angels guarded, deviate from the line

Prescribed to duty: — woeful forfeiture
He made by wilful breach of law divine.
With like perverseness did the Church
    abjure
Obedience to her Lord, and haste to twine,
'Mid Heaven-born flowers that shall for aye
    endure,
Weeds on whose front the world had fixed
    her sign.
O Man, — if with thy trials thus it fares,
If good can smooth the way to evil choice,
From all rash censure be the mind kept
    free;
He only judges right who weighs, compares,
And in the sternest sentence which his
    voice
Pronounces, ne'er abandons Charity.

II

1842(?). 1845

FROM false assumption rose, and, fondly
    hailed
By superstition, spread the Papal power;
Yet do not deem the Autocracy prevailed
Thus only, even in error's darkest hour.
She daunts, forth-thundering from her
    spiritual tower,
Brute rapine, or with gentle lure she tames.
Justice and Peace through Her uphold their
    claims;
And Chastity finds many a sheltering
    bower.
Realm there is none that if controlled or
    swayed
By her commands partakes not, in degree,
Of good, o'er manners, arts and arms,
    diffused:
Yes, to thy domination, Roman See,
Tho' miserably, oft monstrously, abused
By blind ambition, be this tribute paid.

III

CISTERTIAN MONASTERY

1821. 1822

"HERE Man more purely lives, less oft
    doth fall,
More promptly rises, walks with stricter
    heed,
More safely rests, dies happier, is freed
Earlier from cleansing fires, and gains
    withal

A brighter crown." — On yon Cistertian
    wall
That confident assurance may be read;
And, to like shelter, from the world have
    fled
Increasing multitudes. The potent call
Doubtless shall cheat full oft the heart's
    desires;
Yet, while the rugged Age on pliant knee
Vows to rapt Fancy humble fealty,
A gentler life spreads round the holy spires;
Where'er they rise, the sylvan waste re-
    tires,
And aëry harvests crown the fertile lea.

IV

(?). 1835

DEPLORABLE his lot who tills the ground,
His whole life long tills it, with heartless
    toil
Of villain-service, passing with the soil
To each new Master, like a steer or hound,
Or like a rooted tree, or stone earth-bound;
But mark how gladly, through their own
    domains,
The Monks relax or break these iron chains;
While Mercy, uttering, through their voice,
    a sound
Echoed in Heaven, cries out, " Ye Chiefs,
    abate
These legalized oppressions ! Man — whose
    name
And nature God disdained not; Man —
    whose soul
Christ died for — cannot forfeit his high
    claim
To live and move exempt from all control
Which fellow-feeling doth not mitigate ! "

V

MONKS AND SCHOOLMEN

1821. 1822

RECORD we too, with just and faithful
    pen,
That many hooded Cenobites there are,
Who in their private cells have yet a care
Of public quiet; unambitious Men,
Counsellors for the world, of piercing ken;
Whose fervent exhortations from afar
Move Princes to their duty, peace or war;
And oft-times in the most forbidding den

Of solitude, with love of science strong,
How patiently the yoke of thought they bear,
How subtly glide its finest threads along !
Spirits that crowd the intellectual sphere
With mazy boundaries, as the astronomer
With orb and cycle girds the starry throng.

VI

OTHER BENEFITS

1821. 1822

AND, not in vain embodied to the sight,
Religion finds even in the stern retreat
Of feudal sway her own appropriate seat;
From the collegiate pomps on Windsor's
height
Down to the humbler altar, which the
Knight
And his retainers of the embattled hall
Seek in domestic oratory small,
For prayer in stillness, or the chanted rite;
Then chiefly dear, when foes are planted
round,
Who teach the intrepid guardians of the
place —
Hourly exposed to death, with famine worn,
And suffering under many a perilous
wound —
How sad would be their durance, if forlorn
Of offices dispensing heavenly grace !

VII

CONTINUED

1821. 1822

AND what melodious sounds at times pre-
vail !
And, ever and anon, how bright a gleam
Pours on the surface of the turbid Stream !
What heartfelt fragrance mingles with the
gale
That swells the bosom of our passing sail !
For where, but on *this* River's margin, blow
Those flowers of chivalry, to bind the brow
Of hardihood with wreaths that shall not
fail ? —
Fair Court of Edward ! wonder of the
world !
I see a matchless blazonry unfurled
Of wisdom, magnanimity, and love;
And meekness tempering honourable pride;
The lamb is couching by the lion's side,
And near the flame-eyed eagle sits the dove.

VIII

CRUSADERS

1821. 1822

FURL we the sails, and pass with tardy oars
Through these bright regions, casting many
a glance
Upon the dream-like issues — the romance
Of many-coloured life that Fortune pours
Round the Crusaders, till on distant shores
Their labours end; or they return to lie,
The vow performed, in cross-legged effigy,
Devoutly stretched upon their chancel floors.
Am I deceived ? Or is their requiem
chanted
By voices never mute when Heaven unties
Her inmost, softest, tenderest harmonies;
Requiem which Earth takes up with voice
undaunted,
When she would tell how Brave, and Good,
and Wise,
For their high guerdon not in vain have
panted !

IX

1842. 1845

As faith thus sanctified the warrior's crest
While from the Papal Unity there came,
What feebler means had failed to give, one
aim
Diffused thro' all the regions of the West;
So does her Unity its power attest
By works of Art, that shed, on the out-
ward frame
Of worship, glory and grace, which who
shall blame
That ever looked to heaven for final rest ?
Hail countless Temples ! that so well befit
Your ministry; that, as ye rise and take
Form, spirit and character from holy writ,
Give to devotion, wheresoe'er awake,
Pinions of high and higher sweep, and make
The unconverted soul with awe submit.

X

(?). 1845

WHERE long and deeply hath been fixed
the root
In the blest soil of gospel truth, the Tree
(Blighted or scathed tho' many branches be,
Put forth to wither, many a hopeful shoot)

Can never cease to bear celestial fruit.
Witness the Church that oft-times, with effect
Dear to the saints, strives earnestly to eject
Her bane, her vital energies recruit.
Lamenting, do not hopelessly repine,
When such good work is doomed to be undone,
The conquests lost that were so hardly won: —
All promises vouchsafed by Heaven will shine
In light confirmed while years their course shall run,
Confirmed alike in progress and decline.

XI

TRANSUBSTANTIATION

1821. 1822

ENOUGH ! for see, with dim association
The tapers burn; the odorous incense feeds
A greedy flame; the pompous mass proceeds;
The Priest bestows the appointed consecration;
And, while the HOST is raised, its elevation
An awe and supernatural horror breeds;
And all the people bow their heads, like reeds
To a soft breeze, in lowly adoration.
This Valdo brooks not. On the banks of Rhone
He taught, till persecution chased him thence,
To adore the Invisible, and Him alone.
Nor are his Followers loth to seek defence,
'Mid woods and wilds, on Nature's craggy throne,
From rites that trample upon soul and sense.

XII

THE VAUDOIS

(?). 1835

BUT whence came they who for the Saviour Lord
Have long borne witness as the Scriptures teach ? —
Ages ere Valdo raised his voice to preach
In Gallic ears the unadulterate Word,
Their fugitive Progenitors explored
Subalpine vales, in quest of safe retreats

Where that pure Church survives, though summer heats
Open a passage to the Romish sword,
Far as it dares to follow. Herbs self-sown,
And fruitage gathered from the chestnut wood,
Nourish the sufferers then; and mists, that brood
O'er chasms with new-fallen obstacles bestrown,
Protect them; and the eternal snow that daunts
Aliens, is God's good winter for their haunts.

XIII

(?). 1835

PRAISED be the Rivers, from their mountain springs
Shouting to Freedom, " Plant thy banners here ! "
To harassed Piety, " Dismiss thy fear,
And in our caverns smooth thy ruffled wings ! "
Nor be unthanked their final lingerings —
Silent, but not to high-souled Passion's ear —
'Mid reedy fens wide-spread and marshes drear,
Their own creation. Such glad welcomings
As Po was heard to give where Venice rose
Hailed from aloft those Heirs of truth divine
Who near his fountains sought obscure repose,
Yet came prepared as glorious lights to shine,
Should that be needed for their sacred Charge;
Blest Prisoners They, whose spirits were at large !

XIV

WALDENSES

1821. 1822

THOSE had given earliest notice, as the lark
Springs from the ground the morn to gratulate;
Or rather rose the day to antedate,
By striking out a solitary spark,

When all the world with midnight gloom
was dark. —
Then followed the Waldensian bands, whom
Hate
In vain endeavours to exterminate,
Whom Obloquy pursues with hideous
bark:
But they desist not; — and the sacred fire,
Rekindled thus, from dens and savage
woods
Moves, handed on with never-ceasing care,
Through courts, through camps, o'er limit-
ary floods;
Nor lacks this sea-girt Isle a timely share
Of the new Flame, not suffered to expire.

XV

ARCHBISHOP CHICHELEY TO HENRY V

1821. 1822

"WHAT beast in wilderness or cultured
field
The lively beauty of the leopard shows ?
What flower in meadow-ground or garden
grows
That to the towering lily doth not yield ?
Let both meet only on thy royal shield !
Go forth, great King ! claim what thy
birth bestows;
Conquer the Gallic lily which thy foes
Dare to usurp; — thou hast a sword to
wield,
And Heaven will crown the right." — The
mitred Sire
Thus spake — and lo ! a Fleet, for Gaul
addrest,
Ploughs her bold course across the wonder-
ing seas;
For, sooth to say, ambition, in the breast
Of youthful heroes, is no sullen fire,
But one that leaps to meet the fanning
breeze.

XVI

WARS OF YORK AND LANCASTER

1821. 1822

THUS is the storm abated by the craft
Of a shrewd Counsellor, eager to protect
The Church, whose power hath recently
been checked,
Whose monstrous riches threatened. So
the shaft

Of victory mounts high, and blood is quaffed
In fields that rival Cressy and Poictiers —
Pride to be washed away by bitter tears !
For deep as Hell itself, the avenging draught
Of civil slaughter. Yet, while temporal
power
Is by these shocks exhausted, spiritual
truth
Maintains the else endangered gift of life;
Proceeds from infancy to lusty youth;
And, under cover of this woeful strife,
Gathers unblighted strength from hour to
hour.

XVII

WICLIFFE

1821. 1822

ONCE more the Church is seized with sud-
den fear,
And at her call is Wicliffe disinhumed:
Yea, his dry bones to ashes are consumed
And flung into the brook that travels near;
Forthwith, that ancient Voice which Streams
can hear
Thus speaks (that Voice which walks upon
the wind,
Though seldom heard by busy human
kind) —
"As thou these ashes, little Brook! wilt bear
Into the Avon, Avon to the tide
Of Severn, Severn to the narrow seas,
Into main Ocean they, this deed accurst
An emblem yields to friends and enemies
How the bold Teacher's Doctrine, sanctified
By truth, shall spread, throughout the
world dispersed."

XVIII

CORRUPTIONS OF THE HIGHER CLERGY

1821. 1822

"WOE to you, Prelates ! rioting in ease
And cumbrous wealth — the shame of your
estate;
You, on whose progress dazzling trains
await
Of pompous horses; whom vain titles please;
Who will be served by others on their
knees,
Yet will yourselves to God no service pay;
Pastors who neither take nor point the
way
To Heaven; for, either lost in vanities

Ye have no skill to teach, or if ye know
And speak the word —— " Alas ! of fear-
        ful things
'T is the most fearful when the people's
        eye
Abuse hath cleared from vain imaginings;
And taught the general voice to prophesy
Of Justice armed, and Pride to be laid low.

XIX

ABUSE OF MONASTIC POWER

1821. 1822

AND what is Penance with her knotted
        thong;
Mortification with the shirt of hair,
Wan cheek, and knees indúrated with
        prayer,
Vigils, and fastings rigorous as long;
If cloistered Avarice scruple not to wrong
The pious, humble, useful Secular,
And rob the people of his daily care,
Scorning that world whose blindness makes
        her strong ?
Inversion strange ! that, unto One who
        lives
For self, and struggles with himself alone,
The amplest share of heavenly favour
        gives;
That to a Monk allots, both in the esteem
Of God and man, place higher than to
        him
Who on the good of others builds his own !

XX

MONASTIC VOLUPTUOUSNESS

1821. 1822

YET more, — round many a Convent's blaz-
        ing fire
Unhallowed threads of revelry are spun;
There Venus sits disguisèd like a Nun, —
While Bacchus, clothed in semblance of a
        Friar,
Pours out his choicest beverage high and
        higher
Sparkling, until it cannot choose but run
Over the bowl, whose silver lip hath won
An instant kiss of masterful desire —
To stay the precious waste. Through
        every brain
The domination of the sprightly juice

Spreads high conceits to madding Fancy
        dear,
Till the arched roof, with resolute abuse
Of its grave echoes, swells a choral strain,
Whose votive burthen is — " OUR KING-
DOM 'S HERE ! "

XXI

DISSOLUTION OF THE MONASTERIES

1821. 1822

THREATS come which no submission may
        assuage,
No sacrifice avert, no power dispute;
The tapers shall be quenched, the belfries
        mute,
And, 'mid their choirs unroofed by selfish
        rage,
The warbling wren shall find a leafy cage;
The gadding bramble hang her purple fruit;
And the green lizard and the gilded newt
Lead unmolested lives, and die of age.
The owl of evening and the woodland fox
For their abode the shrines of Waltham
        choose:
Proud Glastonbury can no more refuse
To stoop her head before these desperate
        shocks —
She whose high pomp displaced, as story tells,
Arimathean Joseph's wattled cells.

XXII

THE SAME SUBJECT

1821. 1822

THE lovely Nun (submissive, but more meek
Through saintly habit than from effort due
To unrelenting mandates that pursue
With equal wrath the steps of strong and
        weak)
Goes forth — unveiling timidly a cheek
Suffused with blushes of celestial hue,
While through the Convent's gate to open
        view
Softly she glides, another home to seek.
Not Iris, issuing from her cloudy shrine,
An Apparition more divinely bright !
Not more attractive to the dazzled sight
Those watery glories, on the stormy brine
Poured forth, while summer suns at dis-
        tance shine,
And the green vales lie hushed in sober
        light !

XXIII

CONTINUED

1821. 1822

YET many a Novice of the cloistral shade,
And many chained by vows, with eager glee
The warrant hail, exulting to be free;
Like ships before whose keels, full long embayed
In polar ice, propitious winds have made
Unlooked-for outlet to an open sea,
Their liquid world, for bold discovery,
In all her quarters temptingly displayed!
Hope guides the young; but when the old must pass
The threshold, whither shall they turn to find
The hospitality — the alms (alas!
Alms may be needed) which that House bestowed?
Can they, in faith and worship, train the mind
To keep this new and questionable road?

XXIV

SAINTS

1821. 1822

YE, too, must fly before a chasing hand,
Angels and Saints, in every hamlet mourned!
Ah! if the old idolatry be spurned,
Let not your radiant Shapes desert the Land:
Her adoration was not your demand,
The fond heart proffered it — the servile heart;
And therefore are ye summoned to depart,
Michael, and thou, St. George, whose flaming brand
The Dragon quelled; and valiant Margaret
Whose rival sword a like Opponent slew:
And rapt Cecilia, seraph-haunted Queen
Of harmony; and weeping Magdalene,
Who in the penitential desert met
Gales sweet as those that over Eden blew!

XXV

THE VIRGIN

1821. 1822

MOTHER! whose virgin bosom was uncrost
With the least shade of thought to sin allied;
Woman! above all women glorified,
Our tainted nature's solitary boast;
Purer than foam on central ocean tost;
Brighter than eastern skies at daybreak strewn
With fancied roses, than the unblemished moon
Before her wane begins on heaven's blue coast;
Thy Image falls to earth. Yet some, I ween,
Not unforgiven the suppliant knee might bend,
As to a visible Power, in which did blend
All that was mixed and reconciled in Thee
Of mother's love with maiden purity,
Of high with low, celestial with terrene!

XXVI

APOLOGY

1821. 1822

NOT utterly unworthy to endure
Was the supremacy of crafty Rome;
Age after age to the arch of Christendom
Aërial keystone haughtily secure;
Supremacy from Heaven transmitted pure,
As many hold; and, therefore, to the tomb
Pass, some through fire — and by the scaffold some —
Like saintly Fisher, and unbending More.
" Lightly for both the bosom's lord did sit
Upon his throne;" unsoftened, undismayed
By aught that mingled with the tragic scene
Of pity or fear: and More's gay genius played
With the inoffensive sword of native wit,
Than the bare axe more luminous and keen.

XXVII

IMAGINATIVE REGRETS

1821. 1822

DEEP is the lamentation! Not alone
From Sages justly honoured by mankind;
But from the ghostly tenants of the wind,
Demons and Spirits, many a dolorous groan
Issues for that dominion overthrown:
Proud Tiber grieves, and far-off Ganges, blind
As his own worshippers: and Nile, reclined
Upon his monstrous urn, the farewell moan

Renews. Through every forest, cave, and den,
Where frauds were hatched of old, hath sorrow past —
Hangs o'er the Arabian Prophet's native Waste,
Where once his airy helpers schemed and planned
'Mid spectral lakes bemocking thirsty men,
And stalking pillars built of fiery sand.

XXVIII

REFLECTIONS

1821. 1822

GRANT, that by this unsparing hurricane
Green leaves with yellow mixed are torn away,
And goodly fruitage with the mother spray;
'T were madness — wished we, therefore, to detain,
With hands stretched forth in mollified disdain,
The " trumpery " that ascends in bare display —
Bulls, pardons, relics, cowls black, white, and grey —
Upwhirled, and flying o'er the ethereal plain
Fast bound for Limbo Lake. And yet not choice
But habit rules the unreflecting herd,
And airy bonds are hardest to disown;
Hence, with the spiritual sovereignty transferred
Unto itself, the Crown assumes a voice
Of reckless mastery, hitherto unknown.

XXIX

TRANSLATION OF THE BIBLE

1821. 1822

BUT, to outweigh all harm, the sacred Book,
In dusty sequestration wrapt too long,
Assumes the accents of our native tongue;
And he who guides the plough, or wields the crook,
With understanding spirit now may look
Upon her records, listen to her song,
And sift her laws — much wondering that the wrong,
Which Faith has suffered, Heaven could calmly brook.

Transcendent boon ! noblest that earthly King
Ever bestowed to equalize and bless
Under the weight of mortal wretchedness !
But passions spread like plagues, and thousands wild
With bigotry shall tread the Offering
Beneath their feet, detested and defiled.

XXX

THE POINT AT ISSUE

(?). 1827

FOR what contend the wise ? — for nothing less
Than that the Soul, freed from the bonds of Sense,
And to her God restored by evidence
Of things not seen, drawn forth from their recess,
Root there, and not in forms, her holiness ; —
For Faith, which to the Patriarchs did dispense
Sure guidance, ere a ceremonial fence
Was needful round men thirsting to transgress ; —
For Faith, more perfect still, with which the Lord
Of all, himself a Spirit, in the youth
Of Christian aspiration, deigned to fill
The temples of their hearts who, with his word
Informed, were resolute to do his will,
And worship him in spirit and in truth.

XXXI

EDWARD VI

1821. 1822

" SWEET is the holiness of Youth " — so felt
Time-honoured Chaucer speaking through that Lay
By which the Prioress beguiled the way,
And many a Pilgrim's rugged heart did melt.
Hadst thou, loved Bard ! whose spirit often dwelt
In the clear land of vision, but foreseen
King, child, and seraph, blended in the mien
Of pious Edward kneeling as he knelt
In meek and simple infancy, what joy
For universal Christendom had thrilled

Thy heart! what hopes inspired thy genius,
    skilled
(O great Precursor, genuine morning Star)
The lucid shafts of reason to employ,
Piercing the Papal darkness from afar!

XXXII

EDWARD SIGNING THE WARRANT FOR THE EXECUTION OF JOAN OF KENT

1821. 1822

THE tears of man in various measure gush
From various sources; gently overflow
From blissful transport some — from clefts
    of woe
Some with ungovernable impulse rush;
And some, coëval with the earliest blush
Of infant passion, scarcely dare to show
Their pearly lustre — coming but to go;
And some break forth when others' sorrows
    crush
The sympathising heart. Nor these, nor yet
The noblest drops to admiration known,
To gratitude, to injuries forgiven —
Claim Heaven's regard like waters that have
    wet
The innocent eyes of youthful Monarchs
    driven
To pen the mandates nature doth disown.

XXXIII

REVIVAL OF POPERY

(?). 1827

THE saintly Youth has ceased to rule, dis-
    crowned
By unrelenting Death. O People keen
For change, to whom the new looks always
    green!
Rejoicing did they cast upon the ground
Their Gods of wood and stone; and, at the
    sound
Of counter-proclamation, now are seen
(Proud triumph is it for a sullen Queen!)
Lifting them up, the worship to confound
Of the Most High. Again do they invoke
The Creature, to the Creature glory give;
Again with frankincense the altars smoke
Like those the Heathen served; and mass
    is sung;
And prayer, man's rational prerogative,
Runs through blind channels of an unknown
    tongue.

XXXIV

LATIMER AND RIDLEY

(?). 1827

How fast the Marian death-list is unrolled!
See Latimer and Ridley in the might
Of Faith stand coupled for a common flight!
One (like those prophets whom God sent of
    old)
Transfigured, from this kindling hath fore-
    told
A torch of inextinguishable light;
The Other gains a confidence as bold;
And thus they foil their enemy's despite.
The penal instruments, the shows of crime,
Are glorified while this once-mitred pair
Of saintly Friends the "murtherer's chain
    partake,
Corded, and burning at the social stake:"
Earth never witnessed object more sublime
In constancy, in fellowship more fair!

XXXV

CRANMER

1821. 1822

OUTSTRETCHING flameward his upbraided
    hand
(O God of mercy, may no earthly Seat
Of judgment such presumptuous doom re-
    peat!)
Amid the shuddering throng doth Cranmer
    stand;
Firm as the stake to which with iron band
His frame is tied; firm from the naked feet
To the bare head. The victory is complete;
The shrouded Body to the Soul's command
Answers with more than Indian fortitude,
Through all her nerves with finer sense en-
    dued,
Till breath departs in blissful aspiration:
Then, 'mid the ghastly ruins of the fire,
Behold the unalterable heart entire,
Emblem of faith untouched, miraculous
    attestation!

XXXVI

GENERAL VIEW OF THE TROUBLES OF THE REFORMATION

1821. 1822

AID, glorious Martyrs, from your fields of
    light,
Our mortal ken! Inspire a perfect trust

(While we look round) that Heaven's de-
crees are just:
Which few can hold committed to a fight
That shows, ev'n on its better side, the might
Of proud Self-will, Rapacity, and Lust,
'Mid clouds enveloped of polemic dust,
Which showers of blood seem rather to incite
Than to allay. Anathemas are hurled
From both sides; veteran thunders (the
brute test
Of truth) are met by fulminations new —
Tartarean flags are caught at, and unfurled —
Friends strike at friends — the flying shall
pursue —
And Victory sickens, ignorant where to rest!

XXXVII

ENGLISH REFORMERS IN EXILE

1821. 1822

SCATTERING, like birds escaped the fowler's
net,
Some seek with timely flight a foreign
strand;
Most happy, re-assembled in a land
By dauntless Luther freed, could they forget
Their Country's woes. But scarcely have
they met,
Partners in faith, and brothers in distress,
Free to pour forth their common thankful-
ness,
Ere hope declines: — their union is beset
With speculative notions rashly sown,
Whence thickly-sprouting growth of poison-
ous weeds;
Their forms are broken staves; their pas-
sions, steeds
That master them. How enviably blest
Is he who can, by help of grace, enthrone
The peace of God within his single breast !

XXXVIII

ELIZABETH

1821. 1822

HAIL, Virgin Queen ! o'er many an envious
bar
Triumphant, snatched from many a
treacherous wile !
All hail, sage Lady, whom a grateful Isle
Hath blest, respiring from that dismal war
Stilled by thy voice ! But quickly from
afar

Defiance breathes with more malignant aim;
And alien storms with home-bred ferments
claim
Portentous fellowship. Her silver car,
By sleepless prudence ruled, glides slowly
on;
Unhurt by violence, from menaced taint
Emerging pure, and seemingly more bright:
Ah ! wherefore yields it to a foul constraint
Black as the clouds its beams dispersed,
while shone,
By men and angels blest, the glorious light ?

XXXIX

EMINENT REFORMERS

1821. 1822

METHINKS that I could trip o'er heaviest
soil,
Light as a buoyant bark from wave to wave,
Were mine the trusty staff that JEWEL gave
To youthful HOOKER, in familiar style
The gift exalting, and with playful smile:
For thus equipped, and bearing on his head
The Donor's farewell blessing, can he dread
Tempest, or length of way, or weight of
toil ? —
More sweet than odours caught by him who
sails
Near spicy shores of Araby the blest,
A thousand times more exquisitely sweet,
The freight of holy feeling which we meet,
In thoughtful moments, wafted by the gales
From fields where good men walk, or bowers
wherein they rest.

XL

THE SAME

1821. 1822

HOLY and heavenly Spirits as they are,
Spotless in life, and eloquent as wise,
With what entire affection do they prize
Their Church reformed ! labouring with
earnest care
To baffle all that may her strength impair;
That Church, the unperverted Gospel's seat;
In their afflictions a divine retreat;
Source of their liveliest hope, and tenderest
prayer ! —
The truth exploring with an equal mind,
In doctrine and communion they have
sought

Firmly between the two extremes to steer;
But theirs the wise man's ordinary lot —
To trace right courses for the stubborn
blind,
And prophesy to ears that will not hear.

XLI

DISTRACTIONS

1821. 1822

MEN, who have ceased to reverence, soon
defy,
Their forefathers; lo! sects are formed,
and split
With morbid restlessness; — the ecstatic fit
Spreads wide; though special mysteries
multiply,
The Saints must govern, is their common cry;
And so they labour, deeming Holy Writ
Disgraced by aught that seems content to
sit
Beneath the roof of settled Modesty.
The Romanist exults; fresh hope he draws
From the confusion, craftily incites
The overweening, personates the mad —
To heap disgust upon the worthier Cause:
Totters the Throne; the new-born Church
is sad,
For every wave against her peace unites.

XLII

GUNPOWDER PLOT

1821. 1822

FEAR hath a hundred eyes that all agree
To plague her beating heart; and there is
one
(Nor idlest that!) which holds communion
With things that were not, yet were *meant*
to be.
Aghast within its gloomy cavity
That eye (which sees as if fulfilled and done
Crimes that might stop the motion of the
sun)
Beholds the horrible catastrophe
Of an assembled Senate unredeemed
From subterraneous Treason's darkling
power:
Merciless act of sorrow infinite!
Worse than the product of that dismal night,
When gushing, copious as a thunder-shower,
The blood of Huguenots through Paris
streamed.

XLIII

ILLUSTRATION

THE JUNG-FRAU AND THE FALL OF
THE RHINE NEAR SCHAFFHAUSEN

1821. 1822

THE Virgin Mountain, wearing like a Queen
A brilliant crown of everlasting snow,
Sheds ruin from her sides; and men below
Wonder that aught of aspect so serene
Can link with desolation. Smooth and
green,
And seeming, at a little distance, slow,
The waters of the Rhine; but on they go
Fretting and whitening, keener and more
keen;
Till madness seizes on the whole wide Flood,
Turned to a fearful Thing whose nostrils
breathe
Blasts of tempestuous smoke — wherewith
he tries
To hide himself, but only magnifies;
And doth in more conspicuous torment
writhe,
Deafening the region in his ireful mood.

XLIV

TROUBLES OF CHARLES THE FIRST

1821. 1822

EVEN such the contrast that, where'er we
move,
To the mind's eye Religion doth present;
Now with her own deep quietness con-
tent;
Then, like the mountain, thundering from
above
Against the ancient pine-trees of the grove
And the Land's humblest comforts. Now
her mood
Recalls the transformation of the flood,
Whose rage the gentle skies in vain re-
prove;
Earth cannot check. O terrible excess
Of headstrong will! Can this be Piety?
No — some fierce Maniac hath usurped her
name;
And scourges England struggling to be
free:
Her peace destroyed! her hopes a wilder-
ness!
Her blessings cursed — her glory turned to
shame!

XLV

LAUD

1821. 1822

Prejudged by foes determined not to spare,
An old weak Man for vengeance thrown
     aside,
Laud, " in the painful art of dying " tried,
(Like a poor bird entangled in a snare
Whose heart still flutters, though his wings
     forbear
To stir in useless struggle) hath relied
On hope that conscious innocence sup-
     plied,
And in his prison breathes celestial air.
Why tarries then thy chariot ?   Wherefore
     stay,
O Death ! the ensanguined yet triumphant
     wheels,
Which thou prepar'st, full often, to con-
     vey
(What time a State with madding faction
     reels)
The Saint or Patriot to the world that
     heals
All wounds, all perturbations doth allay ?

XLVI

AFFLICTIONS OF ENGLAND

1821. 1822

Harp ! could'st thou venture, on thy bold-
     est string,
The faintest note to echo which the blast
Caught from the hand of Moses as it passed
O'er Sinai's top, or from the Shepherd
     king,
Early awake, by Siloa's brook, to sing
Of dread Jehovah; then, should wood and
     waste
Hear also of that name, and mercy cast
Off to the mountains, like a covering
Of which the Lord was weary.   Weep, oh !
     weep,
Weep with the good, beholding King and
     Priest
Despised by that stern God to whom they
     raise
Their suppliant hands; but holy is the
     feast
He keepeth; like the firmament his ways:
His statutes like the chambers of the
     deep.

PART III

FROM THE RESTORATION TO THE PRESENT TIMES

1821. 1822

When I came to this part of the series I had
the dream described in this Sonnet. The figure
was that of my daughter, and the whole passed
exactly as here represented. The Sonnet was
composed on the middle road leading from
Grasmere to Ambleside : it was begun as I left
the last house of the vale, and finished, word
for word as it now stands, before I came in
view of Rydal. I wish I could say the same of
the five or six hundred I have written : most
of them were frequently retouched in the course
of composition, and, not a few, laboriously.

I have only further to observe that the in-
tended Church which prompted these Sonnets
was erected on Coleorton Moor towards the
centre of a very populous parish between three
and four miles from Ashby-de-la-Zouch, on the
road to Loughborough, and has proved, I be-
lieve, a great benefit to the neighbourhood.

I

I saw the figure of a lovely Maid
Seated alone beneath a darksome tree,
Whose fondly-overhanging canopy
Set off her brightness with a pleasing shade.
No Spirit was she; *that* my heart betrayed,
For she was one I loved exceedingly;
But while I gazed in tender reverie
(Or was it sleep that with my Fancy
     played ?)
The bright corporeal presence — form and
     face —
Remaining still distinct grew thin and rare,
Like sunny mist;— at length the golden hair,
Shape, limbs, and heavenly features, keep-
     ing pace
Each with the other in a lingering race
Of dissolution, melted into air.

II

PATRIOTIC SYMPATHIES

1821. 1822

Last night, without a voice, that Vision spake
Fear to my Soul, and sadness which might
     seem
Wholly dissevered from our present theme;
Yet, my belovèd Country ! I partake
Of kindred agitations for thy sake;

Thou, too, dost visit oft my midnight dream;
Thy glory meets me with the earliest beam
Of light, which tells that Morning is awake.
If aught impair thy beauty or destroy,
Or but forebode destruction, I deplore
With filial love the sad vicissitude;
If thou hast fallen, and righteous Heaven
    restore
The prostrate, then my spring-time is re-
    newed,
And sorrow bartered for exceeding joy.

III

CHARLES THE SECOND

1821. 1822

WHO comes — with rapture greeted, and
    caressed
With frantic love — his kingdom to regain ?
Him Virtue's Nurse, Adversity, in vain
Received, and fostered in her iron breast:
For all she taught of hardiest and of best,
Or would have taught, by discipline of pain
And long privation, now dissolves amain,
Or is remembered only to give zest
To wantonness. — Away, Circean revels !
But for what gain ? if England soon must
    sink
Into a gulf which all distinction levels —
That bigotry may swallow the good name,
And, with that draught, the life-blood:
    misery, shame,
By Poets loathed; from which Historians
    shrink !

IV

LATITUDINARIANISM

1821. 1822

YET Truth is keenly sought for, and the
    wind
Charged with rich words poured out in
    thought's defence;
Whether the Church inspire that eloquence,
Or a Platonic Piety confined
To the sole temple of the inward mind;
And One there is who builds immortal lays,
Though doomed to tread in solitary ways,
Darkness before and danger's voice behind;
Yet not alone, nor helpless to repel
Sad thoughts; for from above the starry
    sphere
Come secrets, whispered nightly to his ear;
And the pure spirit of celestial light

Shines through his soul — " that he may see
    and tell
Of things invisible to mortal sight."

V

WALTON'S BOOK OF LIVES

1821. 1822

THERE are no colours in the fairest sky
So fair as these. The feather, whence the
    pen
Was shaped that traced the lives of these
    good men,
Dropped from an Angel's wing. With
    moistened eye
We read of faith and purest charity
In Statesman, Priest, and humble Citizen:
Oh could we copy their mild virtues, then
What joy to live, what blessedness to die !
Methinks their very names shine still and
    bright;
Apart — like glow-worms on a summer
    night;
Or lonely tapers when from far they fling
A guiding ray; or seen — like stars on high,
Satellites burning in a lucid ring
Around meek Walton's heavenly memory.

VI

CLERICAL INTEGRITY

1821. 1822

NOR shall the eternal roll of praise reject
Those Unconforming; whom one rigorous
    day
Drives from their Cures, a voluntary prey
To poverty, and grief, and disrespect.
And some to want — as if by tempests
    wrecked
On a wild coast — how destitute ! did They
Feel not that Conscience never can be-
    tray,
That peace of mind is Virtue's sure effect.
Their altars they forego, their homes they
    quit,
Fields which they love, and paths they
    daily trod,
And cast the future upon Providence;
As men the dictate of whose inward sense
Outweighs the world; whom self-deceiving
    wit
Lures not from what they deem the cause
    of God.

VII

PERSECUTION OF THE SCOTTISH COVENANTERS

(?). 1827

WHEN Alpine Vales threw forth a suppliant
  cry,
The Majesty of England interposed
And the sword stopped; the bleeding
  wounds were closed;
And Faith preserved her ancient purity.
How little boots that precedent of good,
Scorned or forgotten, Thou canst testify,
For England's shame, O Sister Realm !
  from wood,
Mountain, and moor, and crowded street,
  where lie
The headless martyrs of the Covenant,
Slain by Compatriot-protestants that draw
From councils senseless as intolerant
Their warrant.   Bodies fall by wild sword-
  law;
But who would force the Soul, tilts with a
  straw
Against a Champion cased in adamant.

VIII

ACQUITTAL OF THE BISHOPS

1821. 1822

A VOICE, from long-expecting thousands sent,
Shatters the air, and troubles tower and
  spire;
For Justice hath absolved the innocent,
And Tyranny is balked of her desire:
Up, down, the busy Thames — rapid as fire
Coursing a train of gunpowder — it went,
And transport finds in every street a vent,
Till the whole City rings like one vast quire.
The Fathers urge the People to be still,
With outstretched hands and earnest speech
  — in vain !
Yea, many, haply wont to entertain
Small reverence for the mitre's offices,
And to Religion's self no friendly will,
A Prelate's blessing ask on bended knees.

IX

WILLIAM THE THIRD

1821. 1822

CALM as an under-current, strong to draw
Millions of waves into itself, and run,
From sea to sea, impervious to the sun
And ploughing storm, the spirit of Nassau
Swerves not, (how blest if by religious awe
Swayed, and thereby enabled to contend
With the wide world's commotions) from
  its end
Swerves not — diverted by a casual law.
Had mortal action e'er a nobler scope ?
The Hero comes to liberate, not defy;
And, while he marches on with stedfast
  hope,
Conqueror beloved ! expected anxiously !
The vacillating Bondman of the Pope
Shrinks from the verdict of his stedfast
  eye.

X

OBLIGATIONS OF CIVIL TO RELIGIOUS LIBERTY

1821. 1822

UNGRATEFUL Country, if thou e'er forget
The sons who for thy civil rights have bled !
How, like a Roman, Sidney bowed his
  head,
And Russel's milder blood the scaffold wet;
But these had fallen for profitless regret
Had not thy holy Church her champions
  bred,
And claims from other worlds inspirited
The star of Liberty to rise.   Nor yet
(Grave this within thy heart !) if spiritual
  things
Be lost, through apathy, or scorn, or fear,
Shalt thou thy humbler franchises support,
However hardly won or justly dear:
What came from heaven to heaven by
  nature clings,
And, if dissevered thence, its course is
  short.

XI

SACHEVEREL

(?). 1827

A SUDDEN conflict rises from the swell
Of a proud slavery met by tenets strained
In Liberty's behalf.   Fears, true or feigned,
Spread through all ranks; and lo ! the
  Sentinel
Who loudest rang his pulpit 'larum bell,
Stands at the Bar, absolved by female eyes
Mingling their glances with grave flatteries
Lavished on *Him* — that England may
  rebel

Against her ancient virtue. HIGH and
    Low,
Watchwords of Party, on all tongues are
    rife;
As if a Church, though sprung from heaven,
    must owe
To opposites and fierce extremes her life, —
Not to the golden mean, and quiet flow
Of truths that soften hatred, temper strife.

XII

1820. 1822

DOWN a swift Stream, thus far, a bold
    design
Have we pursued, with livelier stir of heart
Than his who sees, borne forward by the
    Rhine,
The living landscapes greet him, and de-
    part;
Sees spires fast sinking — up again to start !
And strives the towers to number, that
    recline
O'er the dark steeps, or on the horizon
    line
Striding with shattered crests his eye
    athwart,
So have we hurried on with troubled plea-
    sure:
Henceforth, as on the bosom of a stream
That slackens, and spreads wide a watery
    gleam,
We, nothing loth a lingering course to
    measure,
May gather up our thoughts, and mark at
    leisure
How widely spread the interests of our
    theme.

XIII

ASPECTS OF CHRISTIANITY IN AMERICA

I. THE PILGRIM FATHERS

1842. 1842

WELL worthy to be magnified are they
Who, with sad hearts, of friends and
    country took
A last farewell, their loved abodes forsook,
And hallowed ground in which their fathers
    lay;
Then to the new-found World explored
    their way,

That so a Church, unforced, uncalled to
    brook
Ritual restraints, within some sheltering
    nook
Her Lord might worship and his word obey
In freedom. Men they were who could not
    bend;
Blest Pilgrims, surely, as they took for
    guide
A will by sovereign Conscience sanctified;
Blest while their Spirits from the woods
    ascend
Along a Galaxy that knows no end,
But in His glory who for Sinners died.

XIV

II. CONTINUED

1842. 1842

FROM Rite and Ordinance abused they fled
To Wilds where both were utterly unknown;
But not to them had Providence foreshown
What benefits are missed, what evils bred,
In worship neither raised nor limited
Save by Self-will. Lo ! from that distant
    shore,
For Rite and Ordinance, Piety is led
Back to the Land those Pilgrims left of
    yore,
Led by her own free choice. So Truth
    and Love
By Conscience governed do their steps re-
    trace. —
Fathers ! your Virtues, such the power of
    grace,
Their spirit, in your Children, thus approve.
Transcendent over time, unbound by place,
Concord and Charity in circles move.

XV

III. CONCLUDED. — AMERICAN EPISCOPACY

1842. 1842

PATRIOTS informed with Apostolic light
Were they, who, when their Country had
    been freed,
Bowing with reverence to the ancient creed,
Fixed on the frame of England's Church
    their sight,
And strove in filial love to reunite
What force had severed. Thence they
    fetched the seed

Of Christian unity, and won a meed
Of praise from Heaven. To Thee, O
　saintly White,
Patriarch of a wide-spreading family,
Remotest lands and unborn times shall turn,
Whether they would restore or build — to
　Thee,
As one who rightly taught how zeal should
　burn,
As one who drew from out Faith's holiest
　urn
The purest stream of patient Energy.

XVI

(?). 1845

Bishops and Priests, blessèd are ye, if deep
(As yours above all offices is high),
Deep in your hearts the sense of duty lie;
Charged as ye are by Christ to feed and
　keep
From wolves your portion of his chosen
　sheep:
Labouring as ever in your Master's sight,
Making your hardest task your best de-
　light,
What perfect glory ye in Heaven shall
　reap ! —
But, in the solemn Office which ye sought
And undertook premonished, if unsound
Your practice prove, faithless though but in
　thought,
Bishops and Priests, think what a gulf pro-
　found
Awaits you then, if they were rightly taught
Who framed the Ordinance by your lives
　disowned !

XVII

PLACES OF WORSHIP

1821. 1822

As star that shines dependent upon star
Is to the sky while we look up and love;
As to the deep fair ships which though they
　move
Seem fixed, to eyes that watch them from
　afar;
As to the sandy desert fountains are,
With palm-groves shaded at wide inter-
　vals,
Whose fruit around the sun-burnt Native
　falls,

Of roving tired or desultory war —
Such to this British Isle her christian
　Fanes,
Each linked to each for kindred services;
Her Spires, her Steeple-towers with glitter-
　ing vanes
Far-kenned, her Chapels lurking among
　trees,
Where a few villagers on bended knees
Find solace which a busy world disdains.

XVIII

PASTORAL CHARACTER

1821. 1822

A genial hearth, a hospitable board,
And a refined rusticity, belong
To the neat mansion, where, his flock among,
The learned Pastor dwells, their watchful
　Lord.
Though meek and patient as a sheathèd
　sword;
Though pride's least lurking thought appear
　a wrong
To human kind; though peace be on his
　tongue,
Gentleness in his heart — can earth afford
Such genuine state, pre-eminence so free,
As when, arrayed in Christ's authority,
He from the pulpit lifts his awful hand;
Conjures, implores, and labours all he
　can
For re-subjecting to divine command
The stubborn spirit of rebellious man ?

XIX

THE LITURGY

1821. 1822

Yes, if the intensities of hope and fear
Attract us still, and passionate exercise
Of lofty thoughts, the way before us lies
Distinct with signs, through which in set
　career,
As through a zodiac, moves the ritual
　year
Of England's Church; stupendous mys-
　teries !
Which whoso travels in her bosom eyes,
As he approaches them, with solemn
　cheer.
Upon that circle traced from sacred story
We only dare to cast a transient glance,

Trusting in hope that Others may ad-
vance
With mind intent upon the King of Glory,
From his mild advent till his countenance
Shall dissipate the seas and mountains
hoary.

XX

BAPTISM

(?). 1827

DEAR be the Church, that, watching o'er
the needs
Of Infancy, provides a timely shower
Whose virtue changes to a christian Flower
A Growth from sinful Nature's bed of
weeds ! —
Fitliest beneath the sacred roof proceeds
The ministration; while parental Love
Looks on, and Grace descendeth from
above
As the high service pledges now, now
pleads.
There, should vain thoughts outspread their
wings and fly
To meet the coming hours of festal mirth,
The tombs — which hear and answer that
brief cry,
The Infant's notice of his second birth —
Recall the wandering Soul to sympathy
With what man hopes from Heaven, yet
fears from Earth.

XXI

SPONSORS

1827. 1832

FATHER ! — to God himself we cannot give
A holier name ! then lightly do not bear
Both names conjoined, but of thy spiritual
care
Be duly mindful: still more sensitive
Do Thou, in truth a second Mother, strive
Against disheartening custom, that by Thee
Watched, and with love and pious industry
Tended at need, the adopted Plant may
thrive
For everlasting bloom. Benign and pure
This Ordinance, whether loss it would sup-
ply,
Prevent omission, help deficiency,
Or seek to make assurance doubly sure.
Shame if the consecrated Vow be found
An idle form, the Word an empty sound !

XXII

CATECHISING

1821. 1822

FROM Little down to Least, in due degree,
Around the Pastor, each in new-wrought vest,
Each with a vernal posy at his breast,
We stood, a trembling, earnest Company !
With low soft murmur, like a distant bee,
Some spake, by thought-perplexing fears
betrayed;
And some a bold unerring answer made:
How fluttered then thy anxious heart for me,
Belovèd Mother ! Thou whose happy hand
Had bound the flowers I wore, with faithful
tie:
Sweet flowers ! at whose inaudible command
Her countenance, phantom-like, doth re-ap-
pear:
O lost too early for the frequent tear,
And ill requited by this heartfelt sigh !

XXIII

CONFIRMATION

(?). 1827

THE Young-ones gathered in from hill and
dale,
With holiday delight on every brow:
'T is passed away; far other thoughts pre-
vail;
For they are taking the baptismal Vow
Upon their conscious selves; their own lips
speak
The solemn promise. Strongest sinews fail,
And many a blooming, many a lovely, cheek
Under the holy fear of God turns pale;
While on each head his lawn-robed Servant
lays
An apostolic hand, and with prayer seals
The Covenant. The Omnipotent will raise
Their feeble Souls; and bear with *his* regrets,
Who, looking round the fair assemblage,
feels
That ere the Sun goes down their childhood
sets.

XXIV

CONFIRMATION CONTINUED

(?). 1827

I SAW a Mother's eye intensely bent
Upon a Maiden trembling as she knelt;

In and for whom the pious Mother felt
Things that we judge of by a light too
     faint:
Tell, if ye may, some star-crowned Muse,
     or Saint !
Tell what rushed in, from what she was re-
     lieved —
Then, when her Child the hallowing touch
     received,
And such vibration through the Mother
     went
That tears burst forth amain.   Did gleams
     appear ?
Opened a vision of that blissful place
Where dwells a Sister-child ?   And was
     power given
Part of her lost One's glory back to trace
Even to this Rite ?   For thus *She* knelt,
     and, ere
The summer-leaf had faded, passed to
     Heaven.

XXV

SACRAMENT

(?). 1827

By chain yet stronger must the Soul be
     tied;
One duty more, last stage of this ascent,
Brings to thy food, mysterious Sacrament !
The Offspring, haply, at the Parent's side;
But not till They, with all that do abide
In Heaven, have lifted up their hearts to
     laud
And magnify the glorious name of God,
Fountain of grace, whose Son for sinners
     died.
Ye, who have duly weighed the summons,
     pause
No longer; ye, whom to the saving rite
The Altar calls, come early under laws
That can secure for you a path of light
Through gloomiest shade; put on (nor dread
     its weight)
Armour divine, and conquer in your cause !

XXVI

THE MARRIAGE CEREMONY

1842. 1845

The Vested Priest before the Altar stands;
Approach, come gladly, ye prepared, in
     sight

Of God and chosen friends, your troth to
     plight
With the symbolic ring, and willing hands
Solemnly joined.   Now sanctify the bands
O Father ! — to the Espoused thy blessing
     give,
That mutually assisted they may live
Obedient, as here taught, to thy commands.
So prays the Church, to consecrate a Vow
" The which would endless matrimony
     make; "
Union that shadows forth and doth partake
A mystery potent human love to endow
With heavenly, each more prized for the
     other's sake;
Weep not, meek Bride ! uplift thy timid
     brow.

XXVII

THANKSGIVING AFTER CHILDBIRTH

1842(?). 1845

Woman ! the Power who left his throne on
     high,
And deigned to wear the robe of flesh we
     wear,
The Power that thro' the straits of Infancy
Did pass dependent on maternal care,
His own humanity with Thee will share,
Pleased with the thanks that in his People's
     eye
Thou offerest up for safe Delivery
From Childbirth's perilous throes.   And
     should the Heir
Of thy fond hopes hereafter walk inclined
To courses fit to make a mother rue
That ever he was born, a glance of mind
Cast upon this observance may renew
A better will; and, in the imagined view
Of thee thus kneeling, safety he may find.

XXVIII

VISITATION OF THE SICK

1842(?). 1845

The Sabbath bells renew the inviting peal;
Glad music ! yet there be that, worn with
     pain
And sickness, listen where they long have
     lain,
In sadness listen.   With maternal zeal
Inspired, the Church sends ministers to
     kneel
Beside the afflicted; to sustain with prayer,

And soothe the heart confession hath laid
  bare —
That pardon, from God's throne, may set its
  seal
On a true Penitent. When breath departs
From one disburthened so, so comforted,
His Spirit Angels greet; and ours be hope
That, if the Sufferer rise from his sick-bed,
Hence he will gain a firmer mind, to cope
With a bad world, and foil the Tempter's
  arts.

XXIX

THE COMMINATION SERVICE

1842(?). 1845

SHUN not this Rite, neglected, yea abhorred,
By some of unreflecting mind, as calling
Man to curse man, (thought monstrous and
  appalling.)
Go thou and hear the threatenings of the
  LORD;
Listening within his Temple see his sword
Unsheathed in wrath to strike the offender's
  head,
Thy own, if sorrow for thy sin be dead,
Guilt unrepented, pardon unimplored.
Two aspects bears Truth needful for salva-
  tion;
Who knows not *that ?* — yet would this
  delicate age
Look only on the Gospel's brighter page:
Let light and dark duly our thoughts em-
  ploy;
So shall the fearful words of Commination
Yield timely fruit of peace and love and
  joy.

XXX

FORMS OF PRAYER AT SEA

1842(?). 1845

To kneeling Worshippers no earthly floor
Gives holier invitation than the deck
Of a storm-shattered Vessel saved from
  Wreck
(When all that Man could do availed no
  more)
By him who raised the Tempest and re-
  strains:
Happy the crew who this have felt, and pour
Forth for his mercy, as the Church ordains,
Solemn thanksgiving. Nor will *they* im-
  plore
In vain who, for a rightful cause, give breath

To words the Church prescribes, aiding the
  lip
For the heart's sake, ere ship with hostile
  ship
Encounters, armed for work of pain and
  death.
Suppliants ! the God to whom your cause
  ye trust
Will listen, and ye know that He is just.

XXXI

FUNERAL SERVICE

1842(?). 1845

FROM the Baptismal hour, thro weal and
  woe,
The Church extends her care to thought
  and deed;
Nor quits the Body when the Soul is freed,
The mortal weight cast off to be laid low.
Blest Rite for him who hears in faith, " I
  know
That my Redeemer liveth," — hears each
  word
That follows — striking on some kindred
  chord
Deep in the thankful heart; — yet tears will
  flow.
Man is as grass that springeth up at morn,
Grows green, and is cut down and wither-
  eth
Ere nightfall — truth that well may claim
  a sigh,
Its natural echo; but hope comes reborn
At Jesu's bidding. We rejoice, " O Death,
Where is thy Sting ? — O Grave, where is
  thy Victory ? "

XXXII

RURAL CEREMONY

1821. 1822

CLOSING the sacred Book which long has
  fed
Our meditations, give we to a day
Of annual joy one tributary lay;
This day, when, forth by rustic music led,
The village Children, while the sky is red
With evening lights, advance in long array
Through the still churchyard, each with
  garland gay,
That, carried sceptre-like, o'ertops the
  head

Of the proud Bearer. To the wide church-
 door,
Charged with these offerings which their
 fathers bore
For decoration in the Papal time,
The innocent procession softly moves: —
The spirit of Laud is pleased in heaven's
 pure clime,
And Hooker's voice the spectacle approves !

XXXIII

REGRETS

1821. 1822

Would that our scrupulous Sires had dared
 to leave
Less scanty measure of those graceful rites
And usages, whose due return invites
A stir of mind too natural to deceive;
Giving to Memory help when she would
 weave
A crown for Hope ! — I dread the boasted
 lights
That all too often are but fiery blights,
Killing the bud o'er which in vain we grieve.
Go, seek, when Christmas snows discomfort
 bring,
The counter Spirit found in some gay
 church
Green with fresh holly, every pew a perch
In which the linnet or the thrush might
 sing,
Merry and loud and safe from prying search,
Strains offered only to the genial Spring.

XXXIV

MUTABILITY

1821. 1822

From low to high doth dissolution climb,
And sink from high to low, along a scale
Of awful notes, whose concord shall not
 fail;
A musical but melancholy chime,
Which they can hear who meddle not with
 crime,
Nor avarice, nor over-anxious care.
Truth fails not; but her outward forms that
 bear
The longest date do melt like frosty rime,
That in the morning whitened hill and plain
And is no more; drop like the tower sub-
 lime

Of yesterday, which royally did wear
His crown of weeds, but could not even
 sustain
Some casual shout that broke the silent
 air,
Or the unimaginable touch of Time.

XXXV

OLD ABBEYS

1821. 1822

Monastic Domes ! following my down-
 ward way,
Untouched by due regret I marked your
 fall !
Now, ruin, beauty, ancient stillness, all
Dispose to judgments temperate as we
 lay
On our past selves in life's declining day:
For as, by discipline of Time made wise,
We learn to tolerate the infirmities
And faults of others — gently as he may,
So with our own the mild Instructor deals,
Teaching us to forget them or forgive.
Perversely curious, then, for hidden ill
Why should we break Time's charitable
 seals ?
Once ye were holy, ye are holy still;
Your spirit freely let me drink, and live !

XXXVI

EMIGRANT FRENCH CLERGY

(?). 1827

Even while I speak, the sacred roofs of
 France
Are shattered into dust; and self-exiled
From altars threatened, levelled, or defiled,
Wander the Ministers of God, as chance
Opens a way for life, or consonance
Of faith invites.   More welcome to no land
The fugitives than to the British strand,
Where priest and layman with the vigilance
Of true compassion greet them.   Creed and
 test
Vanish before the unreserved embrace
Of catholic humanity: — distrest
They came, — and, while the moral tempest
 roars
Throughout the Country they have left, our
 shores
Give to their Faith a fearless resting-
 place.

XXXVII

CONGRATULATION

1821. 1822

THUS all things lead to Charity secured
By THEM who blessed the soft and happy
    gale
That landward urged the great Deliverer's
    sail,
Till in the sunny bay his fleet was moored !
Propitious hour ! — had we, like them, en-
    dured
Sore stress of apprehension, with a mind
Sickened by injuries, dreading worse de-
    signed,
From month to month trembling and un-
    assured,
How had we then rejoiced ! But we have
    felt,
As a loved substance, their futurity:
Good, which they dared not hope for, we
    have seen;
A State whose generous will through earth
    is dealt;
A State — which, balancing herself be-
    tween
Licence and slavish order, dares be free.

XXXVIII

NEW CHURCHES

1821. 1822

BUT liberty, and triumphs on the Main,
And laurelled armies, not to be withstood —
What serve they ? if, on transitory good
Intent, and sedulous of abject gain,
The State (ah, surely not preserved in
    vain !)
Forbear to shape due channels which the
    Flood
Of sacred truth may enter — till it brood
O'er the wide realm, as o'er the Egyptian
    plain
The all-sustaining Nile. No more — the
    time
Is conscious of her want; through England's
    bounds,
In rival haste, the wished-for Temples rise !
I hear their sabbath bells' harmonious
    chime
Float on the breeze — the heavenliest of all
    sounds
That vale or hill prolongs or multiplies !

XXXIX

CHURCH TO BE ERECTED

1821. 1822

BE this the chosen site; the virgin sod,
Moistened from age to age by dewy eve,
Shall disappear, and grateful earth receive
The corner-stone from hands that build to
    God.
Yon reverend hawthorns, hardened to the rod
Of winter storms, yet budding cheerfully;
Those forest oaks of Druid memory,
Shall long survive, to shelter the Abode
Of genuine Faith. Where, haply, 'mid
    this band
Of daisies, shepherds sate of yore and wove
May-garlands, there let the holy altar stand
For kneeling adoration; — while — above,
Broods, visibly portrayed, the mystic Dove,
That shall protect from blasphemy the
    Land.

XL

CONTINUED

1821. 1822

MINE ear has rung, my spirit sunk subdued,
Sharing the strong emotion of the crowd,
When each pale brow to dread hosannas
    bowed
While clouds of incense mounting veiled
    the rood,
That glimmered like a pine-tree dimly
    viewed
Through Alpine vapours. Such appalling rite
Our Church prepares not, trusting to the
    might
Of simple truth with grace divine imbued;
Yet will we not conceal the precious Cross,
Like men ashamed: the Sun with his first
    smile
Shall greet that symbol crowning the low
    Pile:
And the fresh air of incense-breathing morn
Shall wooingly embrace it; and green moss
Creep round its arms through centuries un-
    born.

XLI

NEW CHURCHYARD

1821. 1822

THE encircling ground, in native turf ar-
    rayed,
Is now by solemn consecration given

To social interests, and to favouring
  Heaven;
And where the rugged colts their gambols
  played,
And wild deer bounded through the forest
  glade,
Unchecked as when by merry Outlaw driven,
Shall hymns of praise resound at morn and
  even;
And soon, full soon, the lonely Sexton's spade
Shall wound the tender sod. Encincture
  small,
But infinite its grasp of weal and woe!
Hopes, fears, in never-ending ebb and
  flow; —
The spousal trembling, and the " dust to
  dust,"
The prayers, the contrite struggle, and the
  trust
That to the Almighty Father looks through
  all.

XLII

CATHEDRALS, ETC.

1821. 1822

OPEN your gates, ye everlasting Piles!
Types of the spiritual Church which God
  hath reared;
Not loth we quit the newly-hallowed sward
And humble altar, 'mid your sumptuous
  aisles
To kneel, or thrid your intricate defiles,
Or down the nave to pace in motion slow;
Watching, with upward eye, the tall tower
  grow
And mount, at every step, with living wiles
Instinct — to rouse the heart and lead the
  will
By a bright ladder to the world above.
Open your gates, ye Monuments of love
Divine! thou Lincoln, on thy sovereign hill!
Thou, stately York! and Ye, whose splen-
  dours cheer
Isis and Cam, to patient Science dear!

XLIII

INSIDE OF KING'S COLLEGE CHAPEL,
CAMBRIDGE

1820(?). 1822

TAX not the royal Saint with vain expense,
With ill-matched aims the Architect who
  planned —
Albeit labouring for a scanty band

Of white robed Scholars only — this im-
  mense
And glorious Work of fine intelligence!
Give all thou canst; high Heaven rejects
  the lore
Of nicely-calculated less or more;
So deemed the man who fashioned for the
  sense
These lofty pillars, spread that branching
  roof
Self-poised, and scooped into ten thousand
  cells,
Where light and shade repose, where music
  dwells
Lingering — and wandering on as loth to
  die;
Like thoughts whose very sweetness yield-
  eth proof
That they were born for immortality.

XLIV

THE SAME

1820(?). 1822

WHAT awful pérspective! while from our
  sight
With gradual stealth the lateral windows
  hide
Their Portraitures, their stone-work glim-
  mers, dyed
In the soft chequerings of a sleepy light.
Martyr, or King, or sainted Eremite,
Whoe'er ye be, that thus, yourselves unseen,
Imbue your prison-bars with solemn sheen,
Shine on, until ye fade with coming Night! —
But, from the arms of silence — list! O list!
The music bursteth into second life;
The notes luxuriate, every stone is kissed
By sound, or ghost of sound, in mazy strife;
Heart-thrilling strains, that cast, before the
  eye
Of the devout, a veil of ecstasy!

XLV

CONTINUED

1820(?). 1822

THEY dreamt not of a perishable home
Who thus could build. Be mine, in hours
  of fear
Or grovelling thought, to seek a refuge here;
Or through the aisles of Westminster to
  roam:

Where bubbles burst, and folly's dancing
    foam
Melts, if it cross the threshold; where the
    wreath
Of awe-struck wisdom droops: or let my path
Lead to that younger Pile, whose sky-like
    dome
Hath typified by reach of daring art
Infinity's embrace; whose guardian crest,
The silent Cross, among the stars shall
    spread
As now, when She hath also seen her breast
Filled with mementos, satiate with its part
Of grateful England's overflowing Dead.

XLVI

EJACULATION

1821. 1822

GLORY to God ! and to the Power who came
In filial duty, clothed with love divine,
That made his human tabernacle shine
Like Ocean burning with purpureal flame;
Or like the Alpine Mount, that takes its
    name
From roseate hues, far kenned at morn and
    even
In hours of peace, or when the storm is
    driven
Along the nether region's rugged frame !
Earth prompts — Heaven urges; let us seek
    the light,

Studious of that pure intercourse begun
When first our infant brows their lustre won;
So, like the Mountain, may we grow more
    bright
From unimpeded commerce with the Sun,
At the approach of all-involving night.

XLVII

CONCLUSION

1821. 1822

WHY sleeps the future, as a snake enrolled,
Coil within coil, at noon-tide ? For the
    WORD
Yields, if with unpresumptuous faith ex-
    plored,
Power at whose touch the sluggard shall
    unfold
His drowsy rings. Look forth ! — that
    Stream behold,
THAT STREAM upon whose bosom we have
    passed
Floating at ease while nations have effaced
Nations, and Death has gathered to his fold
Long lines of mighty Kings — look forth,
    my Soul !
(Nor in this vision be thou slow to trust)
The living Waters, less and less by guilt
Stained and polluted, brighten as they roll,
Till they have reached the eternal City —
    built
For the perféated Spirit of the just !

MEMORY

1823. 1827

A PEN — to register; a key —
That winds through secret wards,
Are well assigned to Memory
By allegoric Bards.

As aptly, also, might be given
A Pencil to her hand;
That, softening objects, sometimes even
Outstrips the heart's demand;

That smooths foregone distress, the
    lines
Of lingering care subdues,
Long-vanished happiness refines,
And clothes in brighter hues;

Yet, like a tool of Fancy, works
Those Spectres to dilate
That startle Conscience, as she lurks
Within her lonely seat.

Oh! that our lives, which flee so fast,
In purity were such,
That not an image of the past
Should fear that pencil's touch !

Retirement then might hourly look
Upon a soothing scene,
Age steal to his allotted nook
Contented and serene;

With heart as calm as lakes that sleep,
In frosty moonlight glistening;
Or mountain rivers, where they creep
Along a channel smooth and deep,
To their own far-off murmurs listening.

TO THE LADY FLEMING

ON SEEING THE FOUNDATION PREPARING
FOR THE ERECTION OF RYDAL CHAPEL,
WESTMORELAND

1823. 1827

After thanking Lady Fleming in prose for
the service she had done to her neighbourhood
by erecting this Chapel, I have nothing to say
beyond the expression of regret that the archi-
tect did not furnish an elevation better suited
to the site in a narrow mountain-pass, and,
what is of more consequence, better constructed
in the interior for the purposes of worship. It
has no chancel; the altar is unbecomingly con-
fined; the pews are so narrow as to preclude
the possibility of kneeling with comfort; there
is no vestry; and what ought to have been first
mentioned, the font, instead of standing at its
proper place at the entrance, is thrust into the
farther end of a pew. When these defects shall
be pointed out to the munificent Patroness, they
will, it is hoped, be corrected.

I

Blest is this Isle — our native Land;
Where battlement and moated gate
Are objects only for the hand
Of hoary Time to decorate;
Where shady hamlet, town that breathes
Its busy smoke in social wreaths,
No rampart's stern defence require,
Nought but the heaven-directed spire,
And steeple tower (with pealing bells
Far-heard) — our only citadels.   10

II

O Lady! from a noble line
Of chieftains sprung, who stoutly bore
The spear, yet gave to works divine
A bounteous help in days of yore
(As records mouldering in the Dell
Of Nightshade haply yet may tell);
Thee kindred aspirations moved
To build, within a vale beloved,
For Him upon whose high behests
All peace depends, all safety rests.   20

III

How fondly will the woods embrace
This daughter of thy pious care,
Lifting her front with modest grace
To make a fair recess more fair;
And to exalt the passing hour;
Or soothe it with a healing power

Drawn from the Sacrifice fulfilled,
Before this rugged soil was tilled,
Or human habitation rose
To interrupt the deep repose!   30

IV

Well may the villagers rejoice!
Nor heat, nor cold, nor weary ways,
Will be a hindrance to the voice
That would unite in prayer and praise;
More duly shall wild wandering Youth
Receive the curb of sacred truth,
Shall tottering Age, bent earthward, hear
The Promise, with uplifted ear;
And all shall welcome the new ray
Imparted to their sabbath-day.   40

V

Nor deem the Poet's hope misplaced,
His fancy cheated — that can see
A shade upon the future cast,
Of time's pathetic sanctity;
Can hear the monitory clock
Sound o'er the lake with gentle shock
At evening, when the ground beneath
Is ruffled o'er with cells of death;
Where happy generations lie,
Here tutored for eternity.   50

VI

Lives there a man whose sole delights
Are trivial pomp and city noise,
Hardening a heart that loathes or slights
What every natural heart enjoys?
Who never caught a noon-tide dream
From murmur of a running stream;
Could strip, for aught the prospect
          yields
To him, their verdure from the fields;
And take the radiance from the clouds
In which the sun his setting shrouds.   60

VII

A soul so pitiably forlorn,
If such do on this earth abide,
May season apathy with scorn,
May turn indifference to pride;
And still be not unblest — compared
With him who grovels, self-debarred
From all that lies within the scope
Of holy faith and christian hope;
Or, shipwrecked, kindles on the coast
False fires, that others may be lost.   70

VIII

Alas ! that such perverted zeal
Should spread on Britain's favoured ground !
That public order, private weal,
Should e'er have felt or feared a wound
From champions of the desperate law
Which from their own blind hearts they
    draw;
Who tempt their reason to deny
God, whom their passions dare defy,
And boast that they alone are free
Who reach this dire extremity !   80

IX

But turn we from these "bold bad" men;
The way, mild Lady ! that hath led
Down to their "dark opprobrious den,"
Is all too rough for Thee to tread.
Softly as morning vapours glide
Down Rydal-cove from Fairfield's side,
Should move the tenor of *his* song
Who means to charity no wrong;
Whose offering gladly would accord   89
With this day's work, in thought and word.

X

Heaven prosper it ! may peace, and love,
And hope, and consolation, fall,
Through its meek influence, from above,
And penetrate the hearts of all;
All who, around the hallowed Fane,
Shall sojourn in this fair domain;
Grateful to Thee, while service pure,
And ancient ordinance, shall endure,
For opportunity bestowed
To kneel together, and adore their God! 100

ON THE SAME OCCASION

1823. 1827

Oh ! gather whencesoe'er ye safely may
The help which slackening Piety requires;
Nor deem that he perforce must go astray
Who treads upon the footmarks of his sires.

Our churches, invariably perhaps, stand east
and west, but *why* is by few persons *exactly*
known ; nor, that the degree of deviation from
due east often noticeable in the ancient ones
was determined, in each particular case, by the
point in the horizon, at which the sun rose upon
the day of the saint to whom the church was
dedicated. These observances of our ancestors,
and the causes of them, are the subject of the
following stanzas.

WHEN in the antique age of bow and spear
And feudal rapine clothed with iron mail,
Came ministers of peace, intent to rear
The Mother Church in yon sequestered vale;

Then, to her Patron Saint a previous rite
Resounded with deep swell and solemn close,
Through unremitting vigils of the night,
Till from his couch the wished-for Sun up-
    rose.

He rose, and straight — as by divine com
    mand,
They, who had waited for that sign to trace
Their work's foundation, gave with careful
    hand
To the high altar its determined place;

Mindful of Him who in the Orient born
There lived, and on the cross his life re-
    signed,
And who, from out the regions of the
    morn,
Issuing in pomp, shall come to judge man-
    kind.

So taught *their* creed; — nor failed the east-
    ern sky,
'Mid these more awful feelings, to infuse
The sweet and natural hopes that shall not
    die,
Long as the sun his gladsome course renews.

For us hath such prelusive vigil ceased;
Yet still we plant, like men of elder days,
Our christian altar faithful to the east,
Whence the tall window drinks the morn-
    ing rays;

That obvious emblem giving to the eye
Of meek devotion, which erewhile it gave,
That symbol of the dayspring from on high,
Triumphant o'er the darkness of the grave.

"A VOLANT TRIBE OF BARDS ON EARTH ARE FOUND"

(?). 1823

A VOLANT Tribe of Bards on earth are
    found,
Who, while the flattering Zephyrs round
    them play,
On "coignes of vantage" hang their nests
    of clay;
How quickly from that aëry hold unbound,
Dust for oblivion ! To the solid ground

Of nature trusts the Mind that builds for aye;
Convinced that there, there only, she can lay
Secure foundations. As the year runs
    round,
Apart she toils within the chosen ring;
While the stars shine, or while day's purple
    eye
Is gently closing with the flowers of spring;
Where even the motion of an Angel's wing
Would interrupt the intense tranquillity
Of silent hills, and more than silent sky.

"NOT LOVE, NOT WAR, NOR THE TUMULTUOUS SWELL"

(?). 1823

Not Love, not War, nor the tumultuous swell
Of civil conflict, nor the wrecks of change,
Nor Duty struggling with afflictions
    strange —
Not these *alone* inspire the tuneful shell;
But where untroubled peace and concord
    dwell,
There also is the Muse not loth to range,
Watching the twilight smoke of cot or
    grange,
Skyward ascending from a woody dell.
Meek aspirations please her, lone endeavour,
And sage content, and placid melancholy;
She loves to gaze upon a crystal river —
Diaphanous because it travels slowly;
Soft is the music that would charm for ever;
The flower of sweetest smell is shy and
    lowly.

TO ——

1824. 1827

Written at Rydal Mount. On Mary Words-
worth.

Let other bards of angels sing,
  Bright suns without a spot;
But thou art no such perfect thing:
  Rejoice that thou art not !

Heed not tho' none should call thee fair;
  So, Mary, let it be
If nought in loveliness compare
  With what thou art to me.

True beauty dwells in deep retreats,
  Whose veil is unremoved
Till heart with heart in concord beats,
  And the lover is beloved.

TO ——

1824. 1827

Written at Rydal Mount. To M. W.

O dearer far than light and life are dear,
Full oft our human foresight I deplore;
Trembling, through my unworthiness, with
    fear
That friends, by death disjoined, may meet
    no more !

Misgivings, hard to vanquish or control,
Mix with the day, and cross the hour of rest;
While all the future, for thy purer soul,
With " sober certainties " of love is blest.

That sigh of thine, not meant for human ear,
Tells that these words thy humbleness of-
    fend;
Yet bear me up — else faltering in the rear
Of a steep march: support me to the end.

Peace settles where the intellect is meek,
And Love is dutiful in thought and deed;
Through Thee communion with that Love
    I seek:
The faith Heaven strengthens where *he*
    moulds the Creed.

" HOW RICH THAT FOREHEAD'S CALM EXPANSE "

1824. 1827

Written at Rydal Mount. Mrs. Words-
worth's impression is that the Poem was writ-
ten at Coleorton : it was certainly suggested by
a Print at Coleorton Hall.

How rich that forehead's calm expanse !
How bright that heaven-directed glance !
— Waft her to glory, wingèd Powers,
Ere sorrow be renewed,
And intercourse with mortal hours
Bring back a humbler mood !
So looked Cecilia when she drew
An Angel from his station;
So looked; not ceasing to pursue
Her tuneful adoration !
But hand and voice alike are still;
No sound *here* sweeps away the will
That gave it birth: in service meek
One upright arm sustains the cheek,
And one across the bosom lies —
That rose, and now forgets to rise,
Subdued by breathless harmonies

Of meditative feeling;
Mute strains from worlds beyond the skies,
Through the pure light of female eyes,
Their sanctity revealing!

TO —

1824. 1827

Written at Rydal Mount. Prompted by the undue importance attached to personal beauty by some dear friends of mine.

LOOK at the fate of summer flowers,
Which blow at daybreak, droop e'er even-
song;
And, grieved for their brief date, confess
that ours,
Measured by what we are and ought to be,
Measured by all that, trembling, we foresee,
Is not so long!

If human Life do pass away,
Perishing yet more swiftly than the flower,
If we are creatures of a *winter's* day;
What space hath Virgin's beauty to disclose
Her sweets, and triumph o'er the breathing
rose?
Not even an hour!

The deepest grove whose foliage hid
The happiest lovers Arcady might boast,
Could not the entrance of this thought for-
bid:
O be thou wise as they, soul-gifted Maid!
Nor rate too high what must so quickly fade,
So soon be lost.

Then shall love teach some virtuous Youth
" To draw, out of the object of his eyes,"
The while on thee they gaze in simple truth,
Hues more exalted, " a refinèd Form,"
That dreads not age, nor suffers from the
worm,
And never dies.

A FLOWER GARDEN

AT COLEORTON HALL, LEICESTERSHIRE
1824. 1827

Planned by my friend, Lady Beaumont, in connection with the garden at Coleorton.

TELL me, ye Zephyrs! that unfold,
While fluttering o'er this gay Recess,

Pinions that fanned the teeming mould
Of Eden's blissful wilderness,
Did only softly-stealing hours
There close the peaceful lives of flowers?

Say, when the *moving* creatures saw
All kinds commingled without fear,
Prevailed a like indulgent law
For the still growths that prosper here? 10
Did wanton fawn and kid forbear
The half-blown rose, the lily spare?

Or peeped they often from their beds
And prematurely disappeared,
Devoured like pleasure ere it spreads
A bosom to the sun endeared?
If such their harsh untimely doom,
It falls not *here* on bud or bloom.

All summer long the happy Eve
Of this fair Spot her flowers may bind, 20
Nor e'er, with ruffled fancy, grieve,
From the next glance she casts, to find
That love for little things by Fate
Is rendered vain as love for great.

Yet, where the guardian fence is wound,
So subtly are our eyes beguiled
We see not nor suspect a bound,
No more than in some forest wild;
The sight is free as air — or crost
Only by art in nature lost. 30

And, though the jealous turf refuse
By random footsteps to be prest,
And feed on never-sullied dews,
Ye, gentle breezes from the west,
With all the ministers of hope
Are tempted to this sunny slope!

And hither throngs of birds resort;
Some, inmates lodged in shady nests,
Some, perched on stems of stately port
That nod to welcome transient guests; 40
While hare and leveret, seen at play,
Appear not more shut out than they.

Apt emblem (for reproof of pride)
This delicate Enclosure shows
Of modest kindness, that would hide
The firm protection she bestows;
Of manners, like its viewless fence,
Ensuring peace to innocence.

Thus spake the moral Muse — her wing
Abruptly spreading to depart, 50

She left that farewell offering,
Memento for some docile heart;
That may respect the good old age
When Fancy was Truth's willing Page;
And Truth would skim the flowery glade,
Though entering but as Fancy's Shade.

TO THE LADY E. B. AND THE HON. MISS P.

1824. 1827

Composed in the Grounds of Plass Newidd, near Llangollen, 1824.

In this Vale of Meditation my friend Jones resided, having been allowed by his diocesan to fix himself there without resigning his Living in Oxfordshire. He was with my wife and daughter and me when we visited these celebrated ladies who had retired, as one may say, into notice in this vale. Their cottage lay directly in the road between London and Dublin, and they were of course visited by their Irish friends as well as innumerable strangers. They took much delight in passing jokes on our friend Jones's plumpness, ruddy cheeks, and smiling countenance, as little suited to a hermit living in the Vale of Meditation. We all thought there was ample room for retort on his part, so curious was the appearance of these ladies, so elaborately sentimental about themselves and their *Caro Albergo*, as they named it in an inscription on a tree that stood opposite, the endearing epithet being preceded by the word Ecco! calling upon the saunterer to look about him. So oddly was one of these ladies attired that we took her, at a little distance, for a Roman Catholic priest, with a crucifix and relics hung at his neck. They were without caps, their hair bushy and white as snow, which contributed to the mistake.

A Stream, to mingle with your favourite
    Dee,
Along the Vale of Meditation flows;
So styled by those fierce Britons, pleased to
    see
In Nature's face the expression of repose;
Or haply there some pious hermit chose
To live and die, the peace of heaven his aim;
To whom the wild sequestered region owes
At this late day, its sanctifying name.
Glyn Cafaillgaroch, in the Cambrian
    tongue,
In ours, the Vale of Friendship, let *this*
    spot
Be named; where, faithful to a low-roofed
    Cot,

On Deva's banks, ye have abode so long;
Sisters in love, a love allowed to climb,
Even on this earth, above the reach of
    Time!

TO THE TORRENT AT THE DEVIL'S BRIDGE, NORTH WALES, 1824

1824. 1827

How art thou named? In search of what
    strange land,
From what huge height descending? Can
    such force
Of waters issue from a British source,
Or hath not Pindus fed thee, where the
    band
Of Patriots scoop their freedom out, with
    hand
Desperate as thine? Or come the inces-
    sant shocks
From that young Stream, that smites the
    throbbing rocks
Of Viamala? There I seem to stand,
As in life's morn; permitted to behold,
From the dread chasm, woods climbing
    above woods,
In pomp that fades not; everlasting snows;
And skies that ne'er relinquish their repose;
Such power possess the family of floods
Over the minds of Poets, young or old!

COMPOSED AMONG THE RUINS OF A CASTLE IN NORTH WALES

1824. 1827

Through shattered galleries, 'mid roofless
    halls,
Wandering with timid footsteps oft be-
    trayed,
The Stranger sighs, nor scruples to upbraid
Old Time, though he, gentlest among the
    Thralls
Of Destiny, upon these wounds hath laid
His lenient touches, soft as light that falls,
From the wan Moon, upon the towers and
    walls,
Light deepening the profoundest sleep of
    shade.
Relic of Kings! Wreck of forgotten wars,
To winds abandoned and the prying stars,
Time *loves* Thee! at his call the Seasons
    twine

Luxuriant wreaths around thy forehead
 hoar;
And, though past pomp no changes can
 restore,
A soothing recompence, his gift, is thine!

ELEGIAC STANZAS

ADDRESSED TO SIR G. H. B. UPON THE
DEATH OF HIS SISTER-IN-LAW

1824. 1827

On Mrs. Fermor. This lady had been a
widow long before I knew her. Her husband
was of the family of the lady celebrated in the
"Rape of the Lock," and was, I believe, a
Roman Catholic. The sorrow which his death
caused her was fearful in its character as de-
scribed in this poem, but was subdued in
course of time by the strength of her religious
faith. I have been, for many weeks at a time,
an inmate with her at Coleorton Hall, as were
also Mrs. Wordsworth and my Sister. The
truth in the sketch of her character here given
was acknowledged with gratitude by her near-
est relatives. She was eloquent in conversa-
tion, energetic upon public matters, open in
respect to those, but slow to communicate her
personal feelings; upon these she never touched
in her intercourse with me, so that I could not
regard myself as her confidential friend, and
was accordingly surprised when I learnt she
had left me a legacy of £100, as a token of
her esteem. See, in further illustration, the
second stanza inscribed upon her Cenotaph in
Coleorton church.

O FOR a dirge! But why complain?
Ask rather a triumphal strain
When FERMOR'S race is run;
A garland of immortal boughs
To twine around the Christian's brows,
Whose glorious work is done.

We pay a high and holy debt;
No tears of passionate regret
Shall stain this votive lay;
Ill-worthy, Beaumont! were the grief 10
That flings itself on wild relief
When Saints have passed away.

Sad doom, at Sorrow's shrine to kneel,
For ever covetous to feel,
And impotent to bear!
Such once was hers — to think and think
On severed love, and only sink
From anguish to despair!

But nature to its inmost part
Faith had refined; and to her heart 20
A peaceful cradle given:
Calm as the dew-drop's, free to rest
Within a breeze-fanned rose's breast
Till it exhales to Heaven.

Was ever Spirit that could bend
So graciously? — that could descend,
Another's need to suit,
So promptly from her lofty throne? —
In works of love, in these alone,
How restless, how minute! 30

Pale was her hue; yet mortal cheek
Ne'er kindled with a livelier streak
When aught had suffered wrong, —
When aught that breathes had felt a wound;
Such look the Oppressor might confound,
However proud and strong.

But hushed be every thought that springs
From out the bitterness of things;
Her quiet is secure;
No thorns can pierce her tender feet, 40
Whose life was, like the violet, sweet,
As climbing jasmine, pure —

As snowdrop on an infant's grave,
Or lily heaving with the wave
That feeds it and defends;
As Vesper, ere the star hath kissed
The mountain top, or breathed the mist
That from the vale ascends.

Thou takest not away, O Death!
Thou strikest — absence perisheth, 50
Indifference is no more;
The future brightens on our sight;
For on the past hath fallen a light
That tempts us to adore.

CENOTAPH

1824. 1842

See "Elegiac Stanzas. Addressed to Sir G.
H. B. upon the death of his Sister-in-Law."

In affectionate remembrance of Frances Fer-
mor, whose remains are deposited in the church
of Claines, near Worcester, this stone is erected
by her sister, Dame Margaret, wife of Sir George
Beaumont, Bart., who, feeling not less than the
love of a brother for the deceased, commends
this memorial to the care of his heirs and suc-
cessors in the possession of this place.

By vain affections unenthralled,
Though resolute when duty called
To meet the world's broad eye,
Pure as the holiest cloistered nun
That ever feared the tempting sun,

Did Fermor live and die.
This Tablet, hallowed by her name,
One heart-relieving tear may claim;
But if the pensive gloom
Of fond regret be still thy choice,
Exalt thy spirit, hear the voice
Of Jesus from her tomb!

"I AM THE WAY, THE TRUTH, AND THE
LIFE"

EPITAPH

IN THE CHAPEL-YARD OF LANGDALE, WESTMORELAND

1841. 1842

Owen Lloyd, the subject of this epitaph, was born at Old Brathay, near Ambleside, and was the son of Charles Lloyd and his wife Sophia (née Pemberton), both of Birmingham, who came to reside in this part of the country soon after their marriage. They had many children, both sons and daughters, of whom the most remarkable was the subject of this epitaph. He was educated under Mr. Dawes, at Ambleside, Dr. Butler, of Shrewsbury, and lastly at Trinity College, Cambridge, where he would have been greatly distinguished as a scholar but for inherited infirmities of bodily constitution, which, from early childhood, affected his mind. His love for the neighbourhood in which he was born, and his sympathy with the habits and characters of the mountain yeomanry, in conjunction with irregular spirits, that unfitted him for facing duties in situations to which he was unaccustomed, induced him to accept the retired curacy of Langdale. How much he was beloved and honoured there, and with what feelings he discharged his duty under the oppression of severe malady, is set forth, though imperfectly, in the epitaph.

By playful smiles (alas! too oft
A sad heart's sunshine), by a soft
And gentle nature, and a free
Yet modest hand of charity,
Through life was OWEN LLOYD endeared
To young and old; and how revered
Had been that pious spirit, a tide
Of humble mourners testified,
When, after pains dispensed to prove

The measure of God's chastening love,
Here, brought from far, his corse found
    rest, —
Fulfilment of his own request; —
Urged less for this Yew's shade, though he
Planted with such fond hope the tree;
Less for the love of stream and rock,
Dear as they were, than that his Flock,
When they no more their Pastor's voice
Could hear to guide them in their choice
Through good and evil, help might have,
Admonished, from his silent grave,
Of righteousness, of sins forgiven,
For peace on earth and bliss in heaven.

THE CONTRAST

THE PARROT AND THE WREN

1825. 1827

The Parrot belonged to Mrs. Luff while living at Fox-Ghyll. The Wren was one that haunted for many years the summer-house between the two terraces at Rydal Mount.

I

WITHIN her gilded cage confined,
I saw a dazzling Belle,
A Parrot of that famous kind
Whose name is NON-PAREIL.

Like beads of glossy jet her eyes;
And, smoothed by Nature's skill,
With pearl or gleaming agate vies
Her finely-curvèd bill.

Her plumy mantle's living hues   10
In mass opposed to mass,
Outshine the splendour that imbues
The robes of pictured glass.

And, sooth to say, an apter Mate
Did never tempt the choice
Of feathered Thing most delicate
In figure and in voice.

But, exiled from Australian bowers,
And singleness her lot,
She trills her song with tutored powers,
Or mocks each casual note.   20

No more of pity for regrets
With which she may have striven!
Now but in wantonness she frets,
Or spite, if cause be given;

Arch, volatile, a sportive bird
By social glee inspired;
Ambitious to be seen or heard,
And pleased to be admired!

II

THIS moss-lined shed, green, soft, and dry,
Harbours a self-contented Wren,   30
Not shunning man's abode, though shy,
Almost as thought itself, of human ken.

Strange places, coverts unendeared,
She never tried; the very nest
In which this Child of Spring was reared
Is warmed, thro' winter, by her feathery
    breast.

To the bleak winds she sometimes gives
A slender unexpected strain;
Proof that the hermitess still lives,
Though she appear not, and be sought in
    vain.   40

Say, Dora! tell me, by yon placid moon,
If called to choose between the favoured
    pair,
Which would you be, — the bird of the
    saloon
By lady-fingers tended with nice care,
Caressed, applauded, upon dainties fed,
Or Nature's DARKLING of this mossy shed?

TO A SKY-LARK

1825. 1827

Written at Rydal Mount.

ETHEREAL minstrel! pilgrim of the sky!
Dost thou despise the earth where cares
    abound?
Or, while the wings aspire, are heart and eye
Both with thy nest upon the dewy ground?
Thy nest which thou canst drop into at will,
Those quivering wings composed, that mu-
    sic still!

Leave to the nightingale her shady wood;
A privacy of glorious light is thine;
Whence thou dost pour upon the world a
    flood
Of harmony, with instinct more divine;
Type of the wise who soar, but never roam;
True to the kindred points of Heaven and
    Home!

"ERE WITH COLD BEADS OF
MIDNIGHT DEW"

1826. 1827

Written at Rydal Mount. Suggested by the
condition of a friend.

ERE with cold beads of midnight dew
    Had mingled tears of thine,
I grieved, fond Youth! that thou shouldst
    sue
    To haughty Geraldine.

Immoveable by generous sighs,
    She glories in a train
Who drag, beneath our native skies,
    An oriental chain.

Pine not like them with arms across,
    Forgetting in thy care
How the fast-rooted trees can toss
    Their branches in mid air.

The humblest rivulet will take
    Its own wild liberties;
And, every day, the imprisoned lake
    Is flowing in the breeze.

Then, crouch no more on suppliant knee,
    But scorn with scorn outbrave;
A Briton, even in love, should be
    A subject, not a slave!

ODE

COMPOSED ON MAY MORNING

1826. 1835

This and the following poem originated in the
lines "How delicate the leafy veil," etc. — My
daughter and I left Rydal Mount upon a tour
through our mountains with Mr. and Mrs. Carr
in the month of May 1826, and as we were going
up the vale of Newlands I was struck with the
appearance of the little chapel gleaming through
the veil of half-opened leaves; and the feeling
which was then conveyed to my mind was ex-
pressed in the stanza referred to above. As in
the case of "Liberty" and "Humanity," my
first intention was to write only one poem, but
subsequently I broke it into two, making addi-
tions to each part so as to produce a consistent
and appropriate whole.

WHILE from the purpling east departs
    The star that led the dawn,

Blithe Flora from her couch upstarts,
   For May is on the lawn.
A quickening hope, a freshening glee,
   Foreran the expected Power,
Whose first-drawn breath, from bush and
     tree,
   Shakes off that pearly shower.

All Nature welcomes Her whose sway
   Tempers the year's extremes;   10
Who scattereth lustres o'er noon-day,
   Like morning's dewy gleams;
While mellow warble, sprightly trill,
   The tremulous heart excite;
And hums the balmy air to still
   The balance of delight.

Time was, blest Power! when youths and
     maids
   At peep of dawn would rise,
And wander forth, in forest glades
   Thy birth to solemnize.   20
Though mute the song — to grace the
     rite
   Untouched the hawthorn bough,
Thy Spirit triumphs o'er the slight;
   Man changes, but not Thou!

Thy feathered Lieges bill and wings
   In love's disport employ;
Warmed by thy influence, creeping things
   Awake to silent joy:
Queen art thou still for each gay plant
   Where the slim wild deer roves;   30
And   served   in   depths   where   fishes
     haunt
   Their own mysterious groves.

Cloud-piercing peak, and trackless heath,
   Instinctive homage pay;
Nor wants the dim-lit cave a wreath
   To honour thee, sweet May!
Where cities fanned by thy brisk airs
   Behold a smokeless sky,
Their puniest flower-pot-nursling dares
   To open a bright eye.   40

And if, on this thy natal morn,
   The pole, from which thy name
Hath not departed, stands forlorn
   Of song and dance and game;
Still from the village-green a vow
   Aspires to thee addrest,
Wherever peace is on the brow,
   Or love within the breast.

Yes! where Love nestles thou canst teach
   The soul to love the more;   50
Hearts also shall thy lessons reach
   That never loved before.
Stript is the haughty one of pride,
   The bashful freed from fear,
While rising, like the ocean-tide,
   In flows the joyous year.

Hush, feeble lyre! weak words refuse
   The service to prolong!
To yon exulting thrush the Muse
   Entrusts the imperfect song;   60
His voice shall chant, in accents clear,
   Throughout the live-long day,
Till the first silver star appear,
   The sovereignty of May.

TO MAY

1826–34. 1835

THOUGH many suns have risen and set
   Since thou, blithe May, wert born,
And Bards, who hailed thee, may forget
   Thy gifts, thy beauty scorn;
There are who to a birthday strain
   Confine not harp and voice,
But evermore throughout thy reign
   Are grateful and rejoice!

Delicious odours! music sweet,
   Too sweet to pass away!   10
Oh for a deathless song to meet
   The soul's desire — a lay
That, when a thousand years are told,
   Should praise thee, genial Power!
Through summer heat, autumnal cold,
   And winter's dreariest hour.

Earth, sea, thy presence feel — nor less,
   If yon ethereal blue
With its soft smile the truth express,
   The heavens have felt it too.   20
The inmost heart of man if glad
   Partakes a livelier cheer;
And eyes that cannot but be sad
   Let fall a brightened tear.

Since thy return, through days and weeks
   Of hope that grew by stealth,
How many wan and faded cheeks
   Have kindled into health!
The Old, by thee revived, have said,
   " Another year is ours;"   30

And wayworn Wanderers, poorly fed,
Have smiled upon thy flowers.

Who tripping lisps a merry song
Amid his playful peers ?
The tender Infant who was long
A prisoner of fond fears;
But now, when every sharp-edged blast
Is quiet in its sheath,
His Mother leaves him free to taste
Earth's sweetness in thy breath.   40

Thy help is with the weed that creeps
Along the humblest ground;
No cliff so bare but on its steeps
Thy favours may be found;
But most on some peculiar nook
That our own hands have drest,
Thou and thy train are proud to look,
And seem to love it best.

And yet how pleased we wander forth
When May is whispering, " Come !   50
Choose from the bowers of virgin earth
The happiest for your home;
Heaven's bounteous love through me is
    spread
From sunshine, clouds, winds, waves,
Drops on the mouldering turret's head,
And on your turf-clad graves ! "

Such greeting heard, away with sighs
For lilies that must fade,
Or " the rathe primrose as it dies
Forsaken " in the shade !   60
Vernal fruitions and desires
Are linked in endless chase;
While, as one kindly growth retires,
Another takes its place.

And what if thou, sweet May, hast known
Mishap by worm and blight;
If expectations newly blown
Have perished in thy sight;
If loves and joys, while up they sprung,
Were caught as in a snare;   70
Such is the lot of all the young,
However bright and fair.

Lo ! Streams that April could not check
Are patient of thy rule;
Gurgling in foamy water-break,
Loitering in glassy pool:
By thee, thee only, could be sent
Such gentle mists as glide,

Curling with unconfirmed intent,
On that green mountain's side.   80

How delicate the leafy veil
Through which yon house of God
Gleams, mid the peace of this deep dale
By few but shepherds trod !
And lowly huts, near beaten ways,
No sooner stand attired
In thy fresh wreaths, than they for praise
Peep forth, and are admired.

Season of fancy and of hope,
Permit not for one hour,   90
A blossom from thy crown to drop,
Nor add to it a flower !
Keep, lovely May, as if by touch
Of self-restraining art,
This modest charm of not too much,
Part seen, imagined part !

"ONCE I COULD HAIL (HOWE'ER SERENE THE SKY)"

1826. 1827

" No faculty yet given me to espy
The dusky Shape within her arms imbound."

Afterwards, when I could not avoid seeing it,
I wondered at this, and the more so because,
like most children, I had been in the habit of
watching the moon through all her changes,
and had often continued to gaze at it when at
the full, till half blinded.

" Late, late yestreen I saw the new moone
Wi' the auld moone in hir arme."

Ballad of Sir Patrick Spence,
Percy's Reliques.

ONCE I could hail (howe'er serene the sky)
The Moon re-entering her monthly round,
No faculty yet given me to espy
The dusky Shape within her arms imbound,
That thin memento of effulgence lost
Which some have named her Predecessor's
    ghost.

Young, like the Crescent that above me shone,
Nought I perceived within it dull or dim;
All that appeared was suitable to One
Whose fancy had a thousand fields to
    skim;   10
To expectations spreading with wild growth,
And hope that kept with me her plighted
    troth.

I saw (ambition quickening at the view)
A silver boat launched on a boundless flood;
A pearly crest, like Dian's when it threw
Its brightest splendour round a leafy wood;
But not a hint from under-ground, no sign
Fit for the glimmering brow of Proserpine.

Or was it Dian's self that seemed to move
Before me? — nothing blemished the fair
    sight;   20
On her I looked whom jocund Fairies love,
Cynthia, who puts the *little* stars to flight,
And by that thinning magnifies the great,
For exaltation of her sovereign state.

And when I learned to mark the spectral
    Shape
As each new Moon obeyed the call of Time,
If gloom fell on me, swift was my escape;
Such happy privilege hath life's gay Prime,
To see or not to see, as best may please
A buoyant Spirit, and a heart at ease.   30

Now, dazzling Stranger! when thou meet'st
    my glance,
Thy dark Associate ever I discern;
Emblem of thoughts too eager to advance
While I salute my joys, thoughts sad or
    stern;
Shades of past bliss, or phantoms that, to
    gain
Their fill of promised lustre, wait in vain.

So changes mortal Life with fleeting years;
A mournful change, should Reason fail to
    bring
The timely insight that can temper fears,
And from vicissitude remove its sting;   40
While Faith aspires to seats in that domain
Where joys are perfect — neither wax nor
    wane.

"THE MASSY WAYS, CARRIED ACROSS THESE HEIGHTS"

1826. 1835

The walk is what we call the *Far-terrace*,
beyond the summer-house at Rydal Mount.
The lines were written when we were afraid of
being obliged to quit the place to which we
were so much attached.

THE massy Ways, carried across these
    heights
By Roman perseverance, are destroyed,

Or hidden under ground, like sleeping
    worms.
How venture then to hope that Time will
    spare
This humble Walk? Yet on the moun-
    tain's side
A POET'S hand first shaped it; and the
    steps
Of that same Bard — repeated to and fro
At morn, at noon, and under moonlight
    skies
Through the vicissitudes of many a year —
Forbade the weeds to creep o'er its grey
    line.
No longer, scattering to the heedless winds
The vocal raptures of fresh poesy,
Shall he frequent these precincts; locked
    no more
In earnest converse with belovèd Friends,
Here will he gather stores of ready bliss,
As from the beds and borders of a garden
Choice flowers are gathered! But, if
    Power may spring
Out of a farewell yearning — favoured more
Than kindred wishes mated suitably
With vain regrets — the Exile would con-
    sign
This Walk, his loved possession, to the care
Of those pure Minds that reverence the
    Muse.

THE PILLAR OF TRAJAN

1826. 1827

These verses perhaps had better be trans-
ferred to the class of "Italian Poems." I had
observed in the Newspaper, that the Pillar of
Trajan was given as a subject for a prize-poem
in English verse. I had a wish perhaps that
my son, who was then an undergraduate at
Oxford, should try his fortune, and I told him
so; but he, not having been accustomed to
write verse, wisely declined to enter on the
task; whereupon I showed him these lines as a
proof of what might, without difficulty, be
done on such a subject.

WHERE towers are crushed, and unfor-
    bidden weeds
O'er mutilated arches shed their seeds;
And temples, doomed to milder change,
    unfold
A new magnificence that vies with old;
Firm in its pristine majesty hath stood
A votive Column, spared by fire and
    flood: —

And, though the passions of man's fretful
    race
Have never ceased to eddy round its base,
Not injured more by touch of meddling
    hands
Than a lone obelisk, 'mid Nubian sands, 10
Or aught in Syrian deserts left to save
From death the memory of the good and
    brave.
Historic figures round the shaft embost
Ascend, with lineaments in air not lost;
Still as he turns, the charmed spectator
    sees
Group winding after group with dream-like
    ease;
Triumphs in sunbright gratitude displayed,
Or softly stealing into modest shade.
— So, pleased with purple clusters to en-
    twine
Some lofty elm-tree, mounts the daring
    vine;   20
The woodbine so, with spiral grace, and
    breathes
Wide-spreading odours from her flowery
    wreaths.
    Borne by the Muse from rills in shep-
        herds' ears
Murmuring but one smooth story for all
    years,
I gladly commune with the mind and
    heart
Of him who thus survives by classic art,
His actions witness, venerate his mien,
And study Trajan as by Pliny seen;
Behold how fought the Chief whose con-
    quering sword
Stretched far as earth might own a single
    lord;   30
In the delight of moral prudence schooled,
How feelingly at home the Sovereign ruled;
Best of the good — in pagan faith allied
To more than Man, by virtue deified.
    Memorial Pillar ! 'mid the wrecks of
        Time
Preserve thy charge with confidence sub-
    lime —
The exultations, pomps, and cares of Rome,
Whence half the breathing world received
    its doom;
Things that recoil from language; that, if
    shown   39
By apter pencil, from the light had flown.
A Pontiff, Trajan *here* the Gods implores,
There greets an Embassy from Indian
    shores;

Lo ! he harangues his cohorts — *there* the
    storm
Of battle meets him in authentic form !
Unharnessed, naked, troops of Moorish
    horse
Sweep to the charge; more high, the
    Dacian force,
To hoof and finger mailed; — yet, high or
    low,
None bleed, and none lie prostrate but the
    foe.
In every Roman, through all turns of fate,
Is Roman dignity inviolate;   50
Spirit in him pre-eminent, who guides,
Supports, adorns, and over all presides;
Distinguished only by inherent state
From honoured Instruments that round
    him wait;
Rise as he may, his grandeur scorns the test
Of outward symbol, nor will deign to rest
On aught by which another is deprest.
— Alas ! that One thus disciplined could toil
To enslave whole nations on their native soil;
So emulous of Macedonian fame,   60
That, when his age was measured with his
    aim,
He drooped, 'mid else unclouded victories,
And turned his eagles back with deep-
    drawn sighs:
O weakness of the Great ! O folly of the
    Wise !
    Where now the haughty Empire that
        was spread
With such fond hope ? her very speech is
    dead;
Yet glorious Art the power of Time defies,
And Trajan still, through various enterprise,
Mounts, in this fine illusion, toward the
    skies:
Still are we present with the imperial Chief,
Nor cease to gaze upon the bold Relief   71
Till Rome, to silent marble unconfined,
Becomes with all her years a vision of the
    Mind.

FAREWELL LINES

1828(?). 1842

These lines were designed as a farewell to
Charles Lamb and his sister, who had retired
from the throngs of London to comparative
solitude in the village of Enfield.

" HIGH bliss is only for a higher state,"
But, surely, if severe afflictions borne

With patience merit the reward of peace,
Peace ye deserve; and may the solid good,
Sought by a wise though late exchange, and
   here
With bounteous hand beneath a cottage-roof
To you accorded, never be withdrawn,
Nor for the world's best promises re-
   nounced.
Most soothing was it for a welcome Friend,
Fresh from the crowded city, to behold
That lonely union, privacy so deep,
Such calm employments, such entire con-
   tent.
So when the rain is over, the storm laid,
A pair of herons oft-times have I seen,
Upon a rocky islet, side by side,
Drying their feathers in the sun, at ease;
And so, when night with grateful gloom
   had fallen,
Two glow-worms in such nearness that they
   shared,
As seemed, their soft self-satisfying light,
Each with the other, on the dewy ground,
Where He that made them blesses their
   repose. —
When wandering among lakes and hills I
   note,
Once more, those creatures thus by nature
   paired,
And guarded in their tranquil state of life,
Even, as your happy presence to my mind
Their union brought, will they repay the
   debt,
And send a thankful spirit back to you,
With hope that we, dear Friends! shall
   meet again.

ON SEEING A NEEDLECASE IN THE FORM OF A HARP

THE WORK OF E. M. S.

1827. 1827

FROWNS are on every Muse's face,
   Reproaches from their lips are sent,
That mimicry should thus disgrace
   The noble Instrument.

A very Harp in all but size!
   Needles for strings in apt gradation!
Minerva's self would stigmatize
   The unclassic profanation.

Even her *own* needle that subdued
   Arachne's rival spirit,   10

Though wrought in Vulcan's happiest
   mood,
   Such honour could not merit.

And this, too, from the Laureate's Child,
   A living lord of melody!
How will her Sire be reconciled
   To the refined indignity?

I spake, when whispered a low voice,
   " Bard! moderate your ire;
Spirits of all degrees rejoice
   In presence of the lyre.   20

The Minstrels of Pygmean bands,
   Dwarf Genii, moonlight-loving Fays,
Have shells to fit their tiny hands
   And suit their slender lays.

Some, still more delicate of ear,
   Have lutes (believe my words)
Whose framework is of gossamer,
   While sunbeams are the chords.

Gay Sylphs this miniature will court,
   Made vocal by their brushing wings, 30
And sullen Gnomes will learn to sport
   Around its polished strings;

Whence strains to love-sick maiden dear,
   While in her lonely bower she tries
To cheat the thought she cannot cheer,
   By fanciful embroideries.

Trust, angry Bard! a knowing Sprite,
   Nor think the Harp her lot deplores!
Though 'mid the stars the Lyre shine bright,
   Love *stoops* as fondly as he soars." 40

TO ——

1826(?). 1827

In the cottage, Town-end, Grasmere, one
afternoon in 1801, my sister read to me the
Sonnets of Milton. I had long been well ac-
quainted with them, but I was particularly
struck on that occasion by the dignified sim-
plicity and majestic harmony that runs through
most of them, — in character so totally differ-
ent from the Italian, and still more so from
Shakspeare's fine Sonnets. I took fire, if I
may be allowed to say so, and produced three
Sonnets the same afternoon, the first I ever
wrote except an irregular one at school. Of
these three, the only one I distinctly remember

is "I grieved for Buonaparté." One was never written down: the third, which was, I believe, preserved, I cannot particularise.

HAPPY the feeling from the bosom thrown
In perfect shape (whose beauty Time shall
    spare
Though a breath made it) like a bubble blown
For summer pastime into wanton air;
Happy the thought best likened to a stone
Of the sea-beach, when, polished with nice
    care,
Veins it discovers exquisite and rare,
Which for the loss of that moist gleam atone
That tempted first to gather it. That here,
O chief of Friends! such feelings I present,
To thy regard, with thoughts so fortunate,
Were a vain notion; but the hope is dear,
That thou, if not with partial joy elate,
Wilt smile upon this gift with more than
    mild content!

"HER ONLY PILOT THE SOFT BREEZE"
(?). 1827

HER only pilot the soft breeze, the boat
Lingers, but Fancy is well satisfied;
With keen-eyed Hope, with Memory, at
    her side,
And the glad Muse at liberty to note
All that to each is precious, as we float
Gently along; regardless who shall chide
If the heavens smile, and leave us free to
    glide,
Happy Associates breathing air remote
From trivial cares. But, Fancy and the
    Muse,
Why have I crowded this small bark with
    you
And others of your kind, ideal crew!
While here sits One whose brightness owes
    its hues
To flesh and blood; no Goddess from above,
No fleeting Spirit, but my own true love?

"WHY, MINSTREL, THESE UN-TUNEFUL MURMURINGS"
(?). 1827

"WHY, Minstrel, these untuneful mur-
    murings —
Dull, flagging notes that with each other
    jar?"

"Think, gentle Lady, of a Harp so far
From its own country, and forgive the
    strings."
A simple answer! but even so forth springs,
From the Castalian fountain of the heart,
The Poetry of Life, and all *that* Art
Divine of words quickening insensate things.
From the submissive necks of guiltless men
Stretched on the block, the glittering axe
    recoils;
Sun, moon, and stars, all struggle in the
    toils
Of mortal sympathy; what wonder then
That the poor Harp distempered music
    yields
To its sad Lord, far from his native fields?

TO S. H.
(?). 1827

EXCUSE is needless when with love sincere
Of occupation, not by fashion led,
Thou turn'st the Wheel that slept with
    dust o'erspread;
My nerves from no such murmur shrink, —
    tho' near,
Soft as the Dorhawk's to a distant ear,
When twilight shades darken the moun-
    tain's head.
Even She who toils to spin our vital thread
Might smile on work, O Lady, once so dear
To household virtues. Venerable Art,
Torn from the Poor! yet shall kind Heaven
    protect
Its own; though Rulers, with undue respect,
Trusting to crowded factory and mart
And proud discoveries of the intellect,
Heed not the pillage of man's ancient heart.

DECAY OF PIETY
1821-22. 1827

Attendance at church on prayer-days, Wednesdays and Fridays and Holidays, received a shock at the Revolution. It is now, however, happily reviving. The ancient people described in this Sonnet were among the last of that pious class. May we hope that the practice, now in some degree renewed, will continue to spread.

OFT have I seen, ere Time had ploughed
    my cheek,
Matrons and Sires — who, punctual to the
    call

Of their loved Church, on fast or festival
Through the long year the house of Prayer
      would seek:
By Christmas snows, by visitation bleak
Of Easter winds, unscared, from hut or hall
They came to lowly bench or sculptured
      stall,
But with one fervour of devotion meek.
I see the places where they once were known,
And ask, surrounded even by kneeling
      crowds,
Is ancient Piety for ever flown?
Alas! even then they seemed like fleecy
      clouds
That, struggling through the western sky,
      have won
Their pensive light from a departed sun!

"SCORN NOT THE SONNET"

(?). 1827

Composed, almost extempore, in a short walk
on the western side of Rydal Lake.

SCORN not the Sonnet; Critic, you have
      frowned,
Mindless of its just honours; with this key
Shakspeare unlocked his heart; the melody
Of this small lute gave ease to Petrarch's
      wound;
A thousand times this pipe did Tasso sound;
With it Camöens soothed an exile's grief;
The Sonnet glittered a gay myrtle leaf
Amid the cypress with which Dante crowned
His visionary brow: a glow-worm lamp,
It cheered mild Spenser, called from Faery-
      land
To struggle through dark ways; and, when
      a damp
Fell round the path of Milton, in his hand
The Thing became a trumpet; whence he
      blew
Soul-animating strains — alas, too few!

"FAIR PRIME OF LIFE! WERE IT ENOUGH TO GILD"

1826(?). 1827

Suggested by observation of the way in
which a young friend, whom I do not choose to
name, misspent his time and misapplied his
talents. He took afterwards a better course,
and became a useful member of society, re-
spected, I believe, wherever he has been known.

FAIR Prime of life! were it enough to gild
With ready sunbeams every straggling
      shower;
And, if an unexpected cloud should lower,
Swiftly thereon a rainbow arch to build
For Fancy's errands, — then, from fields
      half-tilled
Gathering green weeds to mix with poppy
      flower,
Thee might thy Minions crown, and chant
      thy power,
Unpitied by the wise, all censure stilled.
Ah! show that worthier honours are thy
      due;
Fair Prime of life! arouse the deeper heart;
Confirm the Spirit glorying to pursue
Some path of steep ascent and lofty aim;
And, if there be a joy that slights the claim
Of grateful memory, bid that joy depart.

RETIREMENT

1826(?). 1827

IF the whole weight of what we think and
      feel,
Save only far as thought and feeling blend
With action, were as nothing, patriot
      Friend!
From thy remonstrance would be no appeal;
But to promote and fortify the weal
Of our own Being is her paramount end;
A truth which they alone shall comprehend
Who shun the mischief which they cannot
      heal.
Peace in these feverish times is sovereign
      bliss:
Here, with no thirst but what the stream
      can slake,
And startled only by the rustling brake,
Cool air I breathe; while the unincumbered
      Mind
By some weak aims at services assigned
To gentle Natures, thanks not Heaven amiss.

"THERE IS A PLEASURE IN POETIC PAINS"

(?). 1827

THERE is a pleasure in poetic pains
Which only Poets know;—'t was rightly said;
Whom could the Muses else allure to tread
Their smoothest paths, to wear their light-
*   est chains?*

When happiest Fancy has inspired the strains,
How oft the malice of one luckless word
Pursues the Enthusiast to the social board,
Haunts him belated on the silent plains !
Yet he repines not, if his thought stand clear,
At last, of hindrance and obscurity,
Fresh as the star that crowns the brow of morn;
Bright, speckless, as a softly-moulded tear
The moment it has left the virgin's eye,
Or rain-drop lingering on the pointed thorn.

RECOLLECTION OF THE PORTRAIT OF KING HENRY EIGHTH, TRINITY LODGE, CAMBRIDGE

(?). 1827

THE imperial Stature, the colossal stride,
Are yet before me; yet do I behold
The broad full visage, chest of amplest mould,
The vestments 'broidered with barbaric pride:
And lo ! a poniard, at the Monarch's side,
Hangs ready to be grasped in sympathy
With the keen threatenings of that fulgent eye,
Below the white-rimmed bonnet, far-descried.
Who trembles now at thy capricious mood ?
'Mid those surrounding Worthies, haughty King,
We rather think, with grateful mind sedate,
How Providence educeth, from the spring
Of lawless will, unlooked-for streams of good,
Which neither force shall check nor time abate !

"WHEN PHILOCTETES IN THE LEMNIAN ISLE"

(?). 1827

WHEN Philoctetes in the Lemnian isle
Like a form sculptured on a monument
Lay couched; on him or his dread bow unbent
Some wild Bird oft might settle and beguile
The rigid features of a transient smile,

Disperse the tear, or to the sigh give vent,
Slackening the pains of ruthless banishment
From his loved home, and from heroic toil.
And trust that spiritual Creatures round us move,
Griefs to allay which Reason cannot heal;
Yea, veriest reptiles have sufficed to prove
To fettered wretchedness, that no Bastile
Is deep enough to exclude the light of love,
Though man for brother man has ceased to feel.

"WHILE ANNA'S PEERS AND EARLY PLAYMATES TREAD"

1825–26(?). 1827

This is taken from the account given by Miss Jewsbury of the pleasure she derived, when long confined to her bed by sickness, from the inanimate object on which this Sonnet turns.

WHILE Anna's peers and early playmates tread,
In freedom, mountain-turf and river's marge;
Or float with music in the festal barge;
Rein the proud steed, or through the dance are led;
Her doom it is to press a weary bed —
Till oft her guardian Angel, to some charge
More urgent called, will stretch his wings at large,
And friends too rarely prop the languid head.
Yet, helped by Genius — untired comforter,
The presence even of a stuffed Owl for her
Can cheat the time; sending her fancy out
To ivied castles and to moonlight skies,
Though he can neither stir a plume, nor shout;
Nor veil, with restless film, his staring eyes.

TO THE CUCKOO

(?). 1827

NOT the whole warbling grove in concert heard
When sunshine follows shower, the breast can thrill
Like the first summons, Cuckoo ! of thy bill,
With its twin notes inseparably paired.

The captive 'mid damp vaults unsunned,
      unaired,
Measuring the periods of his lonely doom,
That cry can reach; and to the sick man's
      room
Sends gladness, by no languid smile de-
      clared,
The lordly eagle-race through hostile
      search
May perish; time may come when never
      more
The wilderness shall hear the lion roar;
But, long as cock shall crow from house-
      hold perch
To rouse the dawn, soft gales shall speed
      thy wing,
And thy erratic voice be faithful to the
      Spring!

THE INFANT M—— M——

1824. 1827

The infant was Mary Monkhouse, the only
daughter of my friend and cousin Thomas
Monkhouse.

UNQUIET Childhood here by special grace
Forgets her nature, opening like a flower
That neither feeds nor wastes its vital power
In painful struggles. Months each other
      chase,
And nought untunes that Infant's voice; no
      trace
Of fretful temper sullies her pure cheek;
Prompt, lively, self-sufficing, yet so meek
That one enrapt with gazing on her face
(Which even the placid innocence of death
Could scarcely make more placid, heaven
      more bright)
Might learn to picture, for the eye of faith,
The Virgin, as she shone with kindred
      light;
A nursling couched upon her mother's knee,
Beneath some shady palm of Galilee.

TO ROTHA Q——

(?). 1827

Rotha, the daughter of my son-in-law Mr.
Quillinan.

ROTHA, my Spiritual Child! this head was
      grey
When at the sacred font for thee I stood;

Pledged till thou reach the verge of woman-
      hood,
And shalt become thy own sufficient stay:
Too late, I feel, sweet Orphan! was the day
For stedfast hope the contract to fulfil;
Yet shall my blessing hover o'er thee still,
Embodied in the music of this Lay,
Breathed forth beside the peaceful moun-
      tain Stream
Whose murmur soothed thy languid Mo-
      ther's ear
After her throes, this Stream of name more
      dear
Since thou dost bear it,—a memorial
      theme
For others; for thy future self, a spell
To summon fancies out of Time's dark cell.

TO ——, IN HER SEVENTIETH YEAR

1824. 1827

Lady Fitzgerald, as described to me by Lady
Beaumont.

SUCH age how beautiful! O Lady bright,
Whose mortal lineaments seem all refined
By favouring Nature and a saintly Mind
To something purer and more exquisite
Than flesh and blood; whene'er thou
      meet'st my sight,
When I behold thy blanched unwithered
      cheek,
Thy temples fringed with locks of gleam-
      ing white,
And head that droops because the soul is
      meek,
Thee with the welcome Snowdrop I com-
      pare;
That child of winter, prompting thoughts
      that climb
From desolation toward the genial prime;
Or with the Moon conquering earth's misty
      air,
And filling more and more with crystal
      light
As pensive Evening deepens into night.

"IN MY MIND'S EYE A TEMPLE, LIKE A CLOUD"

(?). 1827

IN my mind's eye a Temple, like a cloud
Slowly surmounting some invidious hill,

Rose out of darkness: the bright Work
    stood still:
And might of its own beauty have been
    proud,
But it was fashioned and to God was vowed
By Virtues that diffused, in every part,
Spirit divine through forms of human art:
Faith had her arch — her arch, when winds
    blow loud,
Into the consciousness of safety thrilled;
And Love her towers of dread foundation
    laid
Under the grave of things; Hope had her
    spire
Star-high, and pointing still to something
    higher;
Trembling I gazed, but heard a voice — it
    said,
" Hell-gates are powerless Phantoms when
    we build."

'GO BACK TO ANTIQUE AGES, IF THINE EYES "

1826(?). 1827

Go back to antique ages, if thine eyes
The genuine mien and character would
    trace
Of the rash Spirit that still holds her
    place,
Prompting the world's audacious vanities !
Go back, and see the Tower of Babel rise;
The pyramid extend its monstrous base,
For some Aspirant of our short-lived race,
Anxious an aery name to immortalize.
There, too, ere wiles and politic dispute
Gave specious colouring to aim and act,
See the first mighty Hunter leave the
    brute —
To chase mankind, with men in armies
    packed
For his field-pastime high and absolute,
While, to dislodge his game, cities are
    sacked !

IN THE WOODS OF RYDAL

(?). 1827

WILD Redbreast ! hadst thou at Jemima's
    lip
Pecked, as at mine, thus boldly, Love might
    say,

A half-blown rose had tempted thee to sip
Its glistening dews; but hallowed is the clay
Which the Muse warms; and I, whose head
    is grey,
Am not unworthy of thy fellowship;
Nor could I let one thought — one notion
    — slip
That might thy sylvan confidence betray.
For are we not all His without whose care
Vouchsafed no sparrow falleth to the
    ground ?
Who gives his Angels wings to speed
    through air,
And rolls the planets through the blue
    profound;
Then peck or perch, fond Flutterer ! nor
    forbear
To trust a Poet in still musings bound.

CONCLUSION

TO ——

1827. 1827

IF these brief Records, by the Muses' art
Produced as lonely Nature or the strife
That animates the scenes of public life
Inspired, may in thy leisure claim a part;
And if these Transcripts of the private
    heart
Have gained a sanction from thy falling
    tears;
Then I repent not. But my soul hath fears
Breathed from eternity; for, as a dart
Cleaves the blank air, Life flies: now every
    day
Is but a glimmering spoke in the swift
    wheel
Of the revolving week. Away, away,
All fitful cares, all transitory zeal !
So timely Grace the immortal wing may
    heal,
And honour rest upon the senseless clay.

A MORNING EXERCISE

1825(?). 1832

Written at Rydal Mount. I could wish the
last five stanzas of this to be read with the
poem addressed to the skylark.

FANCY, who leads the pastimes of the glad,
Full oft is pleased a wayward dart to throw;

Sending sad shadows after things not sad,
Peopling the harmless fields with signs of
    woe:
Beneath her sway, a simple forest cry
Becomes an echo of man's misery.

Blithe ravens croak of death; and when
    the owl
Tries his two voices for a favourite strain —
Tu-whit — Tu-whoo! the unsuspecting fowl
Forebodes mishap or seems but to com-
    plain;   10
Fancy, intent to harass and annoy,
Can thus pervert the evidence of joy.

Through border wilds where naked In-
    dians stray,
Myriads of notes attest her subtle skill;
A feathered task-master cries, " Work
    away!"
And, in thy iteration, " Whip poor
    Will!"
Is heard the spirit of a toil-worn slave,
Lashed out of life, not quiet in the grave.

What wonder? at her bidding, ancient
    lays   19
Steeped in dire grief the voice of Philomel;
And that fleet messenger of summer days,
The Swallow, twittered subject to like spell;
But ne'er could Fancy bend the buoyant
    Lark
To melancholy service — hark! O hark!

The daisy sleeps upon the dewy lawn,
Not lifting yet the head that evening bowed;
But *He* is risen, a later star of dawn,
Glittering and twinkling near yon rosy
    cloud;
Bright gem instinct with music, vocal spark;
The happiest bird that sprang out of the
    Ark!   30

Hail, blest above all kinds! — Supremely
    skilled,
Restless with fixed to balance, high with low,
Thou leav'st the halcyon free her hopes to
    build
On such forbearance as the deep may show;
Perpetual flight, unchecked by earthly ties,
Leav'st to the wandering bird of paradise.

Faithful, though swift as lightning, the
    meek dove;
Yet more hath Nature reconciled in thee;

So constant with thy downward eye of love,
Yet, in aërial singleness, so free;   40
So humble, yet so ready to rejoice
In power of wing and never-wearied voice.

To the last point of vision, and beyond,
Mount, daring warbler! — that love-
    prompted strain
('Twixt thee and thine a never-failing bond)
Thrills not the less the bosom of the plain:
Yet might'st thou seem, proud privilege!
    to sing
All independent of the leafy spring.

How would it please old Ocean to partake,
With sailors longing for a breeze in vain,   50
The harmony thy notes most gladly make
Where earth resembles most his own do-
    main!
Urania's self might welcome with pleased
    ear
These matins mounting towards her native
    sphere.

Chanter by heaven attracted, whom no
    bars
To day-light known deter from that pursuit,
'T is well that some sage instinct, when the
    stars
Come forth at evening, keeps Thee still and
    mute;
For not an eyelid could to sleep incline
Wert thou among them, singing as they
    shine!   60

THE TRIAD

1828. 1829

Written at Rydal Mount. The Girls, Edith
Southey, my daughter Dora, and Sara Cole-
ridge.

Show me the noblest Youth of present
    time,
Whose trembling fancy would to love give
    birth;
Some God or Hero, from the Olympian
    clime
Returned, to seek a Consort upon earth;
Or, in no doubtful prospect, let me see
The brightest star of ages yet to be,
And I will mate and match him blissfully.
I will not fetch a Naiad from a flood
Pure as herself — (song lacks not mightier
    power)

Nor leaf-crowned Dryad from a pathless
   wood,   10
Nor Sea-nymph glistening from her coral
   bower;
Mere Mortals bodied forth in vision still,
Shall with Mount Ida's triple lustre fill
The chaster coverts of a British hill.
   "Appear!—obey my lyre's command!
Come, like the Graces, hand in hand!
For ye, though not by birth allied,
Are Sisters in the bond of love;
Nor shall the tongue of envious pride
Presume those interweavings to reprove 20
In you, which that fair progeny of Jove,
Learned from the tuneful spheres that
   glide
In endless union, earth and sea above."
  —I sing in vain;—the pines have hushed
   their waving:
A peerless Youth expectant at my side,
Breathless as they, with unabated craving
Looks to the earth, and to the vacant air;
And, with a wandering eye that seems to
   chide,
Asks of the clouds what occupants they
   hide:—
But why solicit more than sight could bear,
By casting on a moment all we dare? 31
Invoke we those bright Beings one by one;
And what was boldly promised, truly shall
   be done.
   "Fear not a constraining measure!
  —Yielding to this gentle spell,
Lucida! from domes of pleasure,
Or from cottage-sprinkled dell,
Come to regions solitary,
Where the eagle builds her aery,
Above the hermit's long-forsaken cell!" 40
  —She comes!—behold
That Figure, like a ship with snow-white
   sail!
Nearer she draws; a breeze uplifts her veil;
Upon her coming wait
As pure a sunshine and as soft a gale
As e'er, on herbage covering earthly mould,
Tempted the bird of Juno to unfold
His richest splendour—when his veering
   gait
And every motion of his starry train
Seem governed by a strain   50
Of music, audible to him alone.
   "O Lady, worthy of earth's proudest
   throne!
Nor less, by excellence of nature, fit
Beside an unambitious hearth to sit

Domestic queen, where grandeur is un
   known;
What living man could fear
The worst of Fortune's malice, wert Thou
   near,
Humbling that lily-stem, thy sceptre meek,
That its fair flowers may from his cheek
Brush the too happy tear?   60
  ——Queen, and handmaid lowly!
Whose skill can speed the day with lively
   cares,
And banish melancholy
By all that mind invents or hand prepares;
O Thou, against whose lip, without its smile
And in its silence even, no heart is proof;
Whose goodness, sinking deep, would recon-
   cile
The softest Nursling of a gorgeous palace
To the bare life beneath the hawthorn-roof
Of Sherwood's Archer, or in caves of
   Wallace—   70
Who that hath seen thy beauty could con-
   tent
His soul with but a *glimpse* of heavenly
   day?
Who that hath loved thee, but would lay
His strong hand on the wind, if it were bent
To take thee in thy majesty away?
Pass onward (even the glancing deer
Till we depart intrude not here);
That mossy slope, o'er which the woodbine
   throws
A canopy, is smoothed for thy repose!"
  —Glad moment is it when the throng 80
Of warblers in full concert strong
Strive, and not vainly strive, to rout
The lagging shower, and force coy Phœbus
   out,
Met by the rainbow's form divine,
Issuing from her cloudy shrine;—
So may the thrillings of the lyre
Prevail to further our desire,
While to these shades a sister Nymph I
   call.
   "Come, if the notes thine ear may
   pierce,
Come, youngest of the lovely Three,
Submissive to the might of verse
And the dear voice of harmony,
By none more deeply felt than Thee!"
  —I sang; and lo! from pastimes virginal
She hastens to the tents
Of nature, and the lonely elements.
Air sparkles round her with a dazzling
   sheen;

But mark her glowing cheek, her vesture
    green !
And, as if wishful to disarm
Or to repay the potent Charm,   100
She bears the stringèd lute of old romance,
That cheered the trellised arbour's privacy,
And soothed war-wearied knights in raft-
    ered hall.
How vivid, yet how delicate, her glee !
So tripped the Muse, inventress of the
    dance;
So, truant in waste woods, the blithe Eu-
    phrosyne !
But the ringlets of that head
Why are they ungarlanded ?
Why bedeck her temples less
Than the simplest shepherdess ?   110
Is it not a brow inviting
Choicest flowers that ever breathed,
Which the myrtle would delight in
With Idalian rose enwreathed ?
But her humility is well content
With *one* wild floweret (call it not for-
    lorn),
FLOWER OF THE WINDS, beneath her bosom
    worn —
Yet more for love than ornament.
Open, ye thickets ! let her fly,
Swift as a Thracian Nymph o'er field and
    height !   120
For She, to all but those who love her, shy,
Would gladly vanish from a Stranger's
    sight;
Though where she is beloved and loves,
Light as the wheeling butterfly she moves;
Her happy spirit as a bird is free,
That rifles blossoms on a tree,
Turning them inside out with arch audacity.
Alas ! how little can a moment show
Of an eye where feeling plays
In ten thousand dewy rays;   130
A face o'er which a thousand shadows go !
— She stops — is fastened to that rivulet's
    side;
And there (while, with sedater mien,
O'er timid waters that have scarcely left
Their birthplace in the rocky cleft
She bends) at leisure may be seen
Features to old ideal grace allied,
Amid their smiles and dimples dignified —
Fit countenance for the soul of primal truth;
The bland composure of eternal youth !   140
What more changeful than the sea ?
But over his great tides
Fidelity presides;

And this light-hearted Maiden constant **is**
    as he.
High is her aim as heaven above,
And wide as ether her good-will;
And, like the lowly reed, her love
Can drink its nurture from the scantiest
    rill:
Insight as keen as frosty star
Is to *her* charity no bar,   150
Nor interrupts her frolic graces
When she is, far from these wild places,
Encircled by familiar faces.
O the charm that manners draw,
Nature, from thy genuine law !
If from what her hand would do,
Her voice would utter, aught ensue
Untoward or unfit;
She, in benign affections pure,
In self-forgetfulness secure,   160
Sheds round the transient harm or vague
    mischance
A light unknown to tutored elegance:
Hers is not a cheek shame-stricken,
But her blushes are joy-flushes;
And the fault (if fault it be)
Only ministers to quicken
Laughter-loving gaiety,
And kindle sportive wit —
Leaving this Daughter of the mountains free
As if she knew that Oberon king of Faery
Had crossed her purpose with some quaint
    vagary,   171
And heard his viewless bands
Over their mirthful triumph clapping hands.
  " Last of the Three, though eldest born,
Reveal thyself, like pensive Morn
Touched by the skylark's earliest note,
Ere humbler gladness be afloat.
But whether in the semblance drest
Of Dawn — or Eve, fair vision of the west,
Come with each anxious hope subdued   180
By woman's gentle fortitude,
Each grief, through meekness, settling into
    rest.
— Or I would hail thee when some high-
    wrought page
Of a closed volume lingering in thy hand
Has raised thy spirit to a peaceful stand
Among the glories of a happier age."
Her brow hath opened on me — see it there,
Brightening the umbrage of her hair;
So gleams the crescent moon, that loves
To be descried through shady groves.   190
Tenderest bloom is on her cheek;
Wish not for a richer streak;

Nor dread the depth of meditative eye;
But let thy love, upon that azure field
Of thoughtfulness and beauty, yield
Its homage offered up in purity.
What would'st thou more? In sunny glade,
Or under leaves of thickest shade,
Was such a stillness e'er diffused
Since earth grew calm while angels
    mused?   200
Softly she treads, as if her foot were loth
To crush the mountain dew-drops — soon
    to melt
On the flower's breast; as if she felt
That flowers themselves, whate'er their hue,
With all their fragrance, all their glistening,
Call to the heart for inward listening —
And though for bridal wreaths and tokens
    true
Welcomed wisely; though a growth
Which the careless shepherd sleeps on,
As fitly spring from turf the mourner weeps
    on —   210
And without wrong are cropped the marble
    tomb to strew.
The Charm is over; the mute Phantoms
    gone,
Nor will return — but droop not, favoured
    Youth;
The apparition that before thee shone
Obeyed a summons covetous of truth.
From these wild rocks thy footsteps I will
    guide
To bowers in which thy fortune may be
    tried,
And one of the bright Three become thy
    happy Bride.

THE WISHING–GATE

1828. 1829

Written at Rydal Mount. See also " Wish-
ing-gate Destroyed."
In the vale of Grasmere, by the side of the
old high-way leading to Ambleside, is a gate,
which, time out of mind, has been called the
Wishing-gate, from a belief that wishes formed
or indulged there have a favourable issue.

Hope rules a land for ever green:
All powers that serve the bright-eyed
    Queen
    Are confident and gay;
Clouds at her bidding disappear;
Points she to aught? — the bliss draws near,
    And Fancy smooths the way.

Not such the land of Wishes — there
Dwell fruitless day-dreams, lawless prayer,
    And thoughts with things at strife;
Yet how forlorn, should *ye* depart,   10
Ye superstitions of the *heart*,
    How poor, were human life!

When magic lore abjured its might,
Ye did not forfeit one dear right,
    One tender claim abate;
Witness this symbol of your sway,
Surviving near the public way,
    The rustic Wishing-gate!

Inquire not if the faery race
Shed kindly influence on the place,   20
    Ere northward they retired;
If here a warrior left a spell,
Panting for glory as he fell;
    Or here a saint expired.

Enough that all around is fair,
Composed with Nature's finest care,
    And in her fondest love —
Peace to embosom and content —
To overawe the turbulent,
    The selfish to reprove.   30

Yea! even the Stranger from afar,
Reclining on this moss-grown bar,
    Unknowing, and unknown,
The infection of the ground partakes,
Longing for his Beloved — who makes
    All happiness her own.

Then why should conscious Spirits fear
The mystic stirrings that are here,
    The ancient faith disclaim?
The local Genius ne'er befriends   40
Desires whose course in folly ends,
    Whose just reward is shame.

Smile if thou wilt, but not in scorn,
If some, by ceaseless pains outworn,
    Here crave an easier lot;
If some have thirsted to renew
A broken vow, or bind a true,
    With firmer, holier knot.

And not in vain, when thoughts are cast
Upon the irrevocable past,   50
    Some Penitent sincere
May for a worthier future sigh,
While trickles from his downcast eye
    No unavailing tear.

The Worldling, pining to be freed
From turmoil, who would turn or speed
    The current of his fate,
Might stop before this favoured scene,
At Nature's call, nor blush to lean
    Upon the Wishing-gate.   60

The Sage, who feels how blind, how weak
Is man, though loth such help to *seek*,
    Yet, passing, here might pause,
And thirst for insight to allay
Misgiving, while the crimson day
    In quietness withdraws;

Or when the church-clock's knell pro-
        found
To Time's first step across the bound
    Of midnight makes reply;
Time pressing on with starry crest,   70
To filial sleep upon the breast
    Of dread eternity.

THE WISHING-GATE
DESTROYED

(?). 1842

'T is gone — with old belief and dream
That round it clung, and tempting scheme
    Released from fear and doubt;
And the bright landscape too must lie,
By this blank wall, from every eye,
    Relentlessly shut out.

Bear witness ye who seldom passed
That opening — but a look ye cast
    Upon the lake below,
What spirit-stirring power it gained   10
From faith which here was entertained,
    Though reason might say no.

Blest is that ground, where, o'er the
        springs
Of history, Glory claps her wings,
    Fame sheds the exulting tear;
Yet earth is wide, and many a nook
Unheard of is, like this, a book
    For modest meanings dear.

It was in sooth a happy thought
That grafted, on so fair a spot,   20
    So confident a token
Of coming good; — the charm is fled,
Indulgent centuries spun a thread,
    Which one harsh day has broken.

Alas ! for him who gave the word;
Could he no sympathy afford,
    Derived from earth or heaven,
To hearts so oft by hope betrayed;
Their very wishes wanted aid
    Which here was freely given ?   30

Where, for the love-lorn maiden's wound,
Will now so readily be found
    A balm of expectation ?
Anxious for far-off children, where
Shall mothers breathe a like sweet air
    Of home-felt consolation ?

And not unfelt will prove the loss
'Mid trivial care and petty cross
    And each day's shallow grief;
Though the most easily beguiled   40
Were oft among the first that smiled
    At their own fond belief.

If still the reckless change we mourn,
A reconciling thought may turn
    To harm that might lurk here,
Ere judgment prompted from within
Fit aims, with courage to begin,
    And strength to persevere.

Not Fortune's slave is Man: our state
Enjoins, while firm resolves await   50
    On wishes just and wise.
That strenuous action follow both,
And life be one perpetual growth
    Of heaven-ward enterprise.

So taught, so trained, we boldly face
All accidents of time and place;
    Whatever props may fail,
Trust in that sovereign law can spread
New glory o'er the mountain's head,
    Fresh beauty through the vale.   60

That truth informing mind and heart,
The simplest cottager may part,
    Ungrieved, with charm and spell;
And yet, lost Wishing-gate, to thee
The voice of grateful memory
    Shall bid a kind farewell !

A JEWISH FAMILY

IN A SMALL VALLEY OPPOSITE ST. GOAR,
        UPON THE RHINE

1828. 1835

Coleridge, my daughter, and I, in 1828, passed
a fortnight upon the banks of the Rhine, prin-

cipally under the hospitable roof of Mr. Aders of Gotesburg, but two days of the time we spent at St. Goar in rambles among the neighbouring valleys. It was at St. Goar that I saw the Jewish family here described. Though exceedingly poor, and in rags, they were not less beautiful than I have endeavoured to make them appear. We had taken a little dinner with us in a basket, and invited them to partake of it, which the mother refused to do, both for herself and children, saying it was with them a fast-day; adding diffidently, that whether such observances were right or wrong, she felt it her duty to keep them strictly. The Jews, who are numerous on this part of the Rhine, greatly surpass the German peasantry in the beauty of their features and in the intelligence of their countenances. But the lower classes of the German peasantry have, here at least, the air of people grievously opprest. Nursing mothers, at the age of seven or eight and twenty, often look haggard and far more decayed and withered than women of Cumberland and Westmoreland twice their age. This comes from being underfed and overworked in their vineyards in a hot and glaring sun.

GENIUS of Raphael! if thy wings
  Might bear thee to this glen,
With faithful memory left of things
  To pencil dear and pen,
Thou would'st forego the neighbouring
    Rhine,
  And all his majesty —
A studious forehead to incline
  O'er this poor family.

The Mother — her thou must have seen,
  In spirit, ere she came   10
To dwell these rifted rocks between,
  Or found on earth a name;
An image, too, of that sweet Boy,
  Thy inspirations give —
Of playfulness, and love, and joy,
  Predestined here to live.

Downcast, or shooting glances far,
  How beautiful his eyes,
That blend the nature of the star
  With that of summer skies!   20
I speak as if of sense beguiled;
  Uncounted months are gone,
Yet am I with the Jewish Child,
  That exquisite Saint John.

I see the dark-brown curls, the brow,
  The smooth transparent skin,

Refined, as with intent to show
  The holiness within;
The grace of parting Infancy
  By blushes yet untamed;   30
Age faithful to the mother's knee,
  Nor of her arms ashamed.

Two lovely Sisters, still and sweet
  As flowers, stand side by side;
Their soul-subduing looks might cheat
  The Christian of his pride:
Such beauty hath the Eternal poured
  Upon them not forlorn,
Though of a lineage once abhorred,
  Nor yet redeemed from scorn.   40

Mysterious safeguard, that, in spite
  Of poverty and wrong,
Doth here preserve a living light,
  From Hebrew fountains sprung;
That gives this ragged group to cast
  Around the dell a gleam
Of Palestine, of glory past,
  And proud Jerusalem!

THE GLEANER

SUGGESTED BY A PICTURE

1828. 1829

This poem was first printed in the Annual called the *Keepsake*. The painter's name I am not sure of, but I think it was Holmes.

THAT happy gleam of vernal eyes,
Those locks from summer's golden skies,
  That o'er thy brow are shed;
That cheek — a kindling of the morn,
That lip — a rose-bud from the thorn,
  I saw; and Fancy sped
To scenes Arcadian, whispering, through
    soft air,
Of bliss that grows without a care,
And happiness that never flies —
(How can it where love never dies?)   10
Whispering of promise, where no blight
Can reach the innocent delight;
Where pity, to the mind conveyed
In pleasure, is the darkest shade
That Time, unwrinkled grandsire, flings
From his smoothly gliding wings.
  What mortal form, what earthly face
Inspired the pencil, lines to trace,
And mingle colours, that should breed
Such rapture, nor want power to feed;   20

For had thy charge been idle flowers,
Fair Damsel! o'er my captive mind,
To truth and sober reason blind,
'Mid that soft air, those long-lost bowers,
The sweet illusion might have hung, for
   hours.
Thanks to this tell-tale sheaf of corn,
That touchingly bespeaks thee born
Life's daily tasks with them to share
Who, whether from their lowly bed
They rise, or rest the weary head,   30
Ponder the blessing they entreat
From Heaven, and *feel* what they repeat,
While they give utterance to the prayer
That asks for daily bread.

ON THE POWER OF SOUND

1828. 1835

Written at Rydal Mount. I have often
regretted that my tour in Ireland, chiefly
performed in the short days of October in a
Carriage-and-four (I was with Mr. Marshall),
supplied my memory with so few images that
were new, and with so little motive to write.
The lines however in this poem, " Thou too
be heard, lone eagle! " were suggested near
the Giant's Causeway, or rather at the pro-
montory of Fairhead, where a pair of eagles
wheeled above our heads and darted off as if to
hide themselves in a blaze of sky made by the
setting sun.

ARGUMENT

The Ear addressed, as occupied by a spiritual
functionary, in communion with sounds, indi-
vidual, or combined in studied harmony —
Sources and effects of those sounds (to the
close of 6th Stanza) — The power of music,
whence proceeding, exemplified in the idiot —
Origin of music, and its effect in early ages —
How produced (to the middle of 10th Stanza)
— The mind recalled to sounds acting casually
and severally — Wish uttered (11th Stanza)
that these could be united into a scheme or
system for moral interests and intellectual
contemplation — (Stanza 12th) The Pytha-
gorean theory of numbers and music, with
their supposed power over the motions of the
universe — Imaginations consonant with such a
theory — Wish expressed (in 11th Stanza) real-
ised, in some degree, by the representation of all
sounds under the form of thanksgiving to the
Creator — (Last Stanza) The destruction of
earth and the planetary system — The survival
of audible harmony, and its support in the
Divine Nature, as revealed in Holy Writ.

I

THY functions are ethereal,
As if within thee dwelt a glancing mind,
Organ of vision! And a Spirit aërial
Informs the cell of Hearing, dark and blind;
Intricate labyrinth, more dread for thought
To enter than oracular cave;
Strict passage, through which sighs are
   brought,
And whispers for the heart, their slave;
And shrieks, that revel in abuse
Of shivering flesh; and warbled air,   10
Whose piercing sweetness can unloose
The chains of frenzy, or entice a smile
Into the ambush of despair;
Hosannas, pealing down the long-drawn
   aisle,
And requiems answered by the pulse that
   beats
Devoutly, in life's last retreats!

II

The headlong streams and fountains
Serve Thee, invisible Spirit, with untired
   powers;
Cheering the wakeful tent on Syrian moun-
   tains,
They lull perchance ten thousand thousand
   flowers.   20
That roar, the prowling lion's *Here I am,*
How fearful to the desert wide!
That bleat, how tender! of the dam
Calling a straggler to her side.
Shout, cuckoo! — let the vernal soul
Go with thee to the frozen zone;
Toll from thy loftiest perch, lone bell-bird,
   toll!
At the still hour to Mercy dear,
Mercy from her twilight throne
Listening to nun's faint throb of holy fear,
To sailor's prayer breathed from a darken-
   ing sea,   31
Or widow's cottage-lullaby.

III

Ye Voices, and ye Shadows
And Images of voice — to hound and horn
From rocky steep and rock-bestudded mea-
   dows
Flung back, and, in the sky's blue caves,
   reborn —
On with your pastime! till the church-tower
   bells
A greeting give of measured glee;
And milder echoes from their cells

Repeat the bridal symphony. 40
Then, or far earlier, let us rove
Where mists are breaking up or gone,
And from aloft look down into a cove
Besprinkled with a careless quire,
Happy milk-maids, one by one
Scattering a ditty each to her desire,
A liquid concert matchless by nice Art,
A stream as if from one full heart.

IV

Blest be the song that brightens
The blind man's gloom, exalts the veteran's
mirth; 50
Unscorned the peasant's whistling breath,
that lightens
His duteous toil of furrowing the green
earth.
For the tired slave, Song lifts the languid
oar,
And bids it aptly fall, with chime
That beautifies the fairest shore,
And mitigates the harshest clime.
Yon pilgrims see — in lagging file
They move; but soon the appointed way
A choral *Ave Marie* shall beguile,
And to their hope the distant shrine 60
Glisten with a livelier ray:
Nor friendless he, the prisoner of the
mine,
Who from the well-spring of his own clear
breast
Can draw, and sing his griefs to rest.

V

When civic renovation
Dawns on a kingdom, and for needful haste
Best eloquence avails not, Inspiration
Mounts with a tune, that travels like a
blast
Piping through cave and battlemented
tower;
Then starts the sluggard, pleased to meet
That voice of Freedom, in its power 71
Of promises, shrill, wild, and sweet!
Who, from a martial *pageant*, spreads
Incitements of a battle-day,
Thrilling the unweaponed crowd with
plumeless heads ? —
Even She whose Lydian airs inspire
Peaceful striving, gentle play
Of timid hope and innocent desire
Shot from the dancing Graces, as they
move,
Fanned by the plausive wings of Love. 80

VI

How oft along thy mazes,
Regent of sound, have dangerous Passions
trod!
O Thou, through whom the temple rings
with praises,
And blackening clouds in thunder speak of
God,
Betray not by the cozenage of sense
Thy votaries, wooingly resigned
To a voluptuous influence
That taints the purer, better, mind;
But lead sick Fancy to a harp
That hath in noble tasks been tried; 90
And, if the virtuous feel a pang too sharp,
Soothe it into patience, — stay
The uplifted arm of Suicide;
And let some mood of thine in firm array
Knit every thought the impending issue
needs,
Ere martyr burns, or patriot bleeds !

VII

As Conscience, to the centre
Of being, smites with irresistible pain
So shall a solemn cadence, if it enter
The mouldy vaults of the dull idiot's brain,
Transmute him to a wretch from quiet
hurled — 101
Convulsed as by a jarring din;
And then aghast, as at the world
Of reason partially let in
By concords winding with a sway
Terrible for sense and soul !
Or, awed he weeps, struggling to quell
dismay.
Point not these mysteries to an Art
Lodged above the starry pole;
Pure modulations flowing from the heart
Of divine Love, where Wisdom, Beauty,
Truth 111
With Order dwell, in endless youth?

VIII

Oblivion may not cover
All treasures hoarded by the miser, Time.
Orphean Insight ! truth's undaunted lover,
To the first leagues of tutored passion climb,
When Music deigned within this grosser
sphere
Her subtle essence to enfold,
And voice and shell drew forth a tear
Softer than Nature's self could mould. 120
Yet *strenuous* was the infant Age:
Art, daring because souls could feel,

Stirred nowhere but an urgent equipage
Of rapt imagination sped her march
Through the realms of woe and weal:
Hell to the lyre bowed low ; the upper
    arch
Rejoiced that clamorous spell and magic
    verse
Her wan disasters could disperse.

IX

The GIFT to king Amphion
That walled a city with its melody   130
Was for belief no dream: — thy skill,
    Arion !
Could humanise the creatures of the sea,
Where men were monsters.   A last grace
    he craves,
Leave for one chant; — the dulcet sound
Steals from the deck o'er willing waves,
And listening dolphins gather round.
Self-cast, as with a desperate course,
'Mid that strange audience, he bestrides
A proud One docile as a managed horse;
And singing, while the accordant hand 140
Sweeps his harp, the Master rides;
So shall he touch at length a friendly
    strand,
And he, with his preserver, shine star-
    bright
In memory, through silent night.

X

The pipe of Pan, to shepherds
Couched in the shadow of Mænalian pines,
Was passing sweet; the eyeballs of the
    leopards,
That in high triumph drew the Lord of
    vines,
How did they sparkle to the cymbal's
    clang !
While Fauns and Satyrs beat the ground 150
In cadence, — and Silenus swang
This way and that, with wild-flowers
    crowned.
To life, to *life* give back thine ear:
Ye who are longing to be rid
Of fable, though to truth subservient, hear
The little sprinkling of cold earth that
    fell
Echoed from the coffin-lid;
The convict's summons in the steeple's
    knell;
"The vain distress-gun," from a leeward
    shore,
Repeated — heard, and heard no more ! 160

XI

For terror, joy, or pity,
Vast is the compass and the swell of notes:
From the babe's first cry to voice of regal
    city,
Rolling a solemn sea-like bass, that floats
Far as the woodlands — with the trill to
    blend
Of that shy songstress, whose love-tale
Might tempt an angel to descend,
While hovering o'er the moonlight vale.
Ye wandering Utterances, has earth no
    scheme,
No scale of moral music — to unite 170
Powers that survive but in the faintest
    dream
Of memory ? — O that ye might stoop to
    bear
Chains, such precious chains of sight
As laboured minstrelsies through ages
    wear !
O for a balance fit the truth to tell
Of the Unsubstantial, pondered well !

XII

By one pervading spirit
Of tones and numbers all things are con-
    trolled,
As sages taught, where faith was found to
    merit
Initiation in that mystery old. 180
The heavens, whose aspect makes our minds
    as still
As they themselves appear to be,
Innumerable voices fill
With everlasting harmony;
The towering headlands, crowned with mist,
Their feet among the billows, know
That Ocean is a mighty harmonist;
Thy pinions, universal Air,
Ever waving to and fro,
Are delegates of harmony, and bear 190
Strains that support the Seasons in their
    round;
Stern Winter loves a dirge-like sound.

XIII

Break forth into thanksgiving,
Ye banded instruments of wind and chords
Unite, to magnify the Ever-living,
Your inarticulate notes with the voice of
    words !
Nor hushed be service from the lowing
    mead,
Nor mute the forest hum of noon;

Thou too be heard, lone eagle! freed
From snowy peak and cloud, attune   200
Thy hungry barkings to the hymn
Of joy, that from her utmost walls
The six-days' Work, by flaming Seraphim
Transmits to Heaven! As Deep to Deep
Shouting through one valley calls,
All worlds, all natures, mood and measure
  keep
For praise and ceaseless gratulation, poured
Into the ear of God, their Lord!

XIV

A Voice to Light gave Being;
To Time, and Man, his earth-born chroni-
  cler;   210
A Voice shall finish doubt and dim fore-
  seeing,
And sweep away life's visionary stir;
The trumpet (we, intoxicate with pride,
Arm at its blast for deadly wars)
To archangelic lips applied,
The grave shall open, quench the stars.
O Silence! are Man's noisy years
No more than moments of thy life?
Is Harmony, blest queen of smiles and
  tears,
With her smooth tones and discords just, 220
Tempered into rapturous strife,
Thy destined bond-slave? No! though
  earth be dust
And vanish, though the heavens dissolve,
  her stay
Is in the WORD, that shall not pass away.

INCIDENT AT BRUGÈS

(?). 1835

This occurred at Brugès in 1828. Mr. Cole-
ridge, my Daughter, and I made a tour together
in Flanders, upon the Rhine, and returned by
Holland. Dora and I, while taking a walk
along a retired part of the town, heard the
voice as here described, and were afterwards
informed it was a Convent in which were many
English. We were both much touched, I might
say affected, and Dora moved as appears in
the verses.

IN Brugès town is many a street
  Whence busy life hath fled;
Where, without hurry, noiseless feet
  The grass-grown pavement tread.
There heard we, halting in the shade
  Flung from a Convent-tower,

A harp that tuneful prelude made
  To a voice of thrilling power.

The measure, simple truth to tell,
  Was fit for some gay throng;   10
Though from the same grim turret fell
  The shadow and the song.
When silent were both voice and chords,
  The strain seemed doubly dear,
Yet sad as sweet, — for *English* words
  Had fallen upon the ear.

It was a breezy hour of eve;
  And pinnacle and spire
Quivered and seemed almost to heave,
  Clothed with innocuous fire;   20
But, where we stood, the setting sun
  Showed little of his state;
And, if the glory reached the Nun,
  'T was through an iron grate.

Not always is the heart unwise,
  Nor pity idly born,
If even a passing Stranger sighs
  For them who do not mourn.
Sad is thy doom, self-solaced dove,
  Captive, whoe'er thou be!   30
Oh! what is beauty, what is love,
  And opening life to thee?

Such feeling pressed upon my soul,
  A feeling sanctified
By one soft trickling tear that stole
  From the Maiden at my side;
Less tribute could she pay than this,
  Borne gaily o'er the sea,
Fresh from the beauty and the bliss
  Of English liberty?   40

GOLD AND SILVER FISHES IN A VASE

1829. 1835

They were a present from Miss Jewsbury, of
whom mention is made in the note at the end
of the next poem. The fish were healthy to
all appearance in their confinement for a long
time, but at last, for some cause we could not
make out, they languished, and, one of them
being all but dead, they were taken to the pool
under the old Pollard oak. The apparently
dying one lay on its side unable to move. I
used to watch it, and about the tenth day it be-
gan to right itself, and in a few days more was
able to swim about with its companions. For

many months they continued to prosper in their new place of abode ; but one night by an unusually great flood they were swept out of the pool, and perished to our great regret.

THE soaring lark is blest as proud
　When at heaven's gate she sings;
The roving bee proclaims aloud
　Her flight by vocal wings;
While Ye, in lasting durance pent,
　Your silent lives employ
For something more than dull content,
　Though haply less than joy.

Yet might your glassy prison seem
　A place where joy is known,　　　10
Where golden flash and silver gleam
　Have meanings of their own;
While, high and low, and all about,
　Your motions, glittering Elves !
Ye weave — no danger from without,
　And peace among yourselves.

Type of a sunny human breast
　Is your transparent cell;
Where Fear is but a transient guest,
　No sullen Humours dwell;　　　20
Where, sensitive of every ray
　That smites this tiny sea,
Your scaly panoplies repay
　The loan with usury.

How beautiful ! — Yet none knows why
　This ever-graceful change,
Renewed — renewed incessantly —
　Within your quiet range.
Is it that ye with conscious skill
　For mutual pleasure glide;　　　30
And sometimes, not without your will,
　Are dwarfed, or magnified ?

Fays, Genii of gigantic size !
　And now, in twilight dim,
Clustering like constellated eyes,
　In wings of Cherubim,
When the fierce orbs abate their glare; —
　Whate'er your forms express,
Whate'er ye seem, whate'er ye are —
　All leads to gentleness.　　　40

Cold though your nature be, 't is pure;
　Your birthright is a fence
From all that haughtier kinds endure
　Through tyranny of sense.
Ah ! not alone by colours bright
　Are ye to heaven allied,

When, like essential Forms of light,
　Ye mingle, or divide.

For day-dreams soft as e'er beguiled
　Day-thoughts while limbs repose;　　50
For moonlight fascinations mild,
　Your gift, ere shutters close —
Accept, mute Captives ! thanks and praise;
　And may this tribute prove
That gentle admirations raise
　Delight resembling love.

LIBERTY

(SEQUEL TO THE ABOVE)

ADDRESSED TO A FRIEND ; THE GOLD AND SILVER FISHES HAVING BEEN REMOVED TO A POOL IN THE PLEASURE-GROUND OF RYDAL MOUNT

1829. 1835

" The liberty of a people consists in being governed by laws which they have made for themselves, under whatever form it be of government. The liberty of a private man, in being master of his own time and actions, as far as may consist with the laws of God and of his country. Of this latter we are here to discourse." — COWLEY.

THOSE breathing Tokens of your kind regard,
(Suspect not, Anna, that their fate is hard;
Not soon does aught to which mild fancies cling
In lonely spots, become a slighted thing;)
Those silent Inmates now no longer share,
Nor do they need, our hospitable care,
Removed in kindness from their glassy Cell
To the fresh waters of a living Well —
An elfin pool so sheltered that its rest
No winds disturb; the mirror of whose breast　　　10
Is smooth as clear, save where with dimples small
A fly may settle, or a blossom fall.
— *There* swims, of blazing sun and beating shower
Fearless (but how obscured !) the golden Power,
That from his bauble prison used to cast
Gleams by the richest jewel unsurpast;
And near him, darkling like a sullen Gnome,
The silver Tenant of the crystal dome;
Dissevered both from all the mysteries

Of hue and altering shape that charmed all
    eyes.   20
Alas! they pined, they languished while
    they shone;
And, if not so, what matters beauty gone
And admiration lost, by change of place
That brings to the inward creature no dis-
    grace?
But if the change restore his birthright,
    then,
Whate'er the difference, boundless is the
    gain.
Who can divine what impulses from God
Reach the caged lark, within a town-abode,
From his poor inch or two of daisied sod?
O yield him back his privilege! — No sea
Swells like the bosom of a man set free; 31
A wilderness is rich with liberty.
Roll on, ye spouting whales, who die or keep
Your independence in the fathomless Deep!
Spread, tiny nautilus, the living sail;
Dive, at thy choice, or brave the freshening
    gale!
If unreproved the ambitious eagle mount
Sunward to seek the daylight in its fount,
Bays, gulfs, and ocean's Indian width, shall
    be,
Till the world perishes, a field for thee! 40
    While musing here I sit in shadow cool,
And watch these mute Companions, in the
    pool,
(Among reflected boughs of leafy trees)
By glimpses caught — disporting at their
    ease,
Enlivened, braced, by hardy luxuries,
I ask what warrant fixed them (like a spell
Of witchcraft fixed them) in the crystal
    cell;
To wheel with languid motion round and
    round,
Beautiful, yet in mournful durance bound.
Their peace, perhaps, our lightest footfall
    marred; 50
On their quick sense our sweetest music
    jarred;
And whither could they dart, if seized with
    fear?
No sheltering stone, no tangled root was
    near.
When fire or taper ceased to cheer the
    room,
They wore away the night in starless
    gloom;
And, when the sun first dawned upon the
    streams,

How faint their portion of his vital beams!
Thus, and unable to complain, they fared,
While not one joy of ours by them was
    shared.
    Is there a cherished bird (I venture now
To snatch a sprig from Chaucer's reverend
    brow) — 61
Is there a brilliant fondling of the cage,
Though sure of plaudits on his costly stage,
Though fed with dainties from the snow-
    white hand
Of a kind mistress, fairest of the land,
But gladly would escape; and, if need were,
Scatter the colours from the plumes that
    bear
The emancipated captive through blithe air
Into strange woods, where he at large may
    live
On best or worst which they and Nature
    give? 70
The beetle loves his unpretending track,
The snail the house he carries on his back;
The far-fetched worm with pleasure would
    disown
The bed we give him, though of softest
    down;
A noble instinct; in all kinds the same,
All ranks! What Sovereign, worthy of
    the name,
If doomed to breathe against his lawful will
An element that flatters him — to kill,
But would rejoice to barter outward show
For the least boon that freedom can be-
    stow? 80
    But most the Bard is true to inborn
    right,
Lark of the dawn, and Philomel of night,
Exults in freedom, can with rapture vouch
For the dear blessings of a lowly couch,
A natural meal — days, months, from Na-
    ture's hand;
Time, place, and business, all at his com-
    mand! —
Who bends to happier duties, who more wise
Than the industrious Poet, taught to prize,
Above all grandeur, a pure life uncrossed
By cares in which simplicity is lost? 90
That life — the flowery path that winds by
    stealth —
Which Horace needed for his spirit's health;
Sighed for, in heart and genius, overcome
By noise and strife, and questions weari-
    some,
And the vain splendours of Imperial
    Rome? —

Let easy mirth his social hours inspire
And fiction animate his sportive lyre,
Attuned to verse that, crowning light Dis-
　　tress
With garlands, cheats her into happiness;
Give *me* the humblest note of those sad
　　strains　　　　　　　　　　　　　100
Drawn forth by pressure of his gilded
　　chains,
As a chance-sunbeam from his memory
　　fell
Upon the Sabine farm he loved so well;
Or when the prattle of Blandusia's spring
Haunted his ear — he only listening —
He, proud to please, above all rivals, fit
To win the palm of gaiety and wit;
He, doubt not, with involuntary dread,
Shrinking from each new favour to be
　　shed,
By the world's Ruler, on his honoured
　　head !　　　　　　　　　　　　　110
　In a deep vision's intellectual scene,
Such earnest longings and regrets as keen
Depressed the melancholy Cowley, laid
Under a fancied yew-tree's luckless shade;
A doleful bower for penitential song,
Where Man and Muse complained of mu-
　　tual wrong;
While Cam's ideal current glided by,
And antique towers nodded their foreheads
　　high,
Citadels dear to studious privacy.
But Fortune, who had long been used to
　　sport　　　　　　　　　　　　　120
With this tried Servant of a thankless Court,
Relenting met his wishes; and to you
The remnant of his days at least was true;
You, whom, though long deserted, he loved
　　best;
You, Muses, books, fields, liberty, and rest !
　Far happier they who, fixing hope and
　　aim
On the humanities of peaceful fame,
Enter betimes with more than martial fire
The generous course, aspire, and still aspire;
Upheld by warnings heeded not too late　130
Stifle the contradictions of their fate,
And to one purpose cleave, their Being's
　　godlike mate !
　Thus, gifted Friend, but with the placid
　　brow
That woman ne'er should forfeit, keep *thy*
　　vow;
With modest scorn reject whate'er would
　　blind

The ethereal eyesight, cramp the wingèd
　　mind !
Then, with a blessing granted from above
To every act, word, thought, and look of
　　love,
Life's book for Thee may lie unclosed, till
　　age
Shall with a thankful tear bedrop its latest
　　page.　　　　　　　　　　　　　140

HUMANITY

1829. 1835

These verses and those entitled " Liberty "
were composed as one piece, which Mrs. Words-
worth complained of as unwieldy and ill-pro-
portioned; and accordingly it was divided into
two on her judicious recommendation.

The Rocking-stones, alluded to in the begin-
ning of the following verses, are supposed to
have been used, by our British ancestors, both
for judicial and religious purposes. Such
stones are not uncommonly found, at this day,
both in Great Britain and in Ireland.

WHAT though the Accused, upon his own
　　appeal
To righteous Gods when man has ceased to
　　feel,
Or at a doubting Judge's stern command,
Before the STONE OF POWER no longer
　　stand —
To take his sentence from the balanced
　　Block,
As, at his touch, it rocks, or seems to rock;
Though, in the depths of sunless groves, no
　　more
The Druid-priest the hallowed Oak adore;
Yet, for the Initiate, rocks and whispering
　　trees
Do still perform mysterious offices !　　10
And functions dwell in beast and bird that
　　sway
The reasoning mind, or with the fancy play,
Inviting, at all seasons, ears and eyes
To watch for undelusive auguries: —
Not uninspired appear their simplest ways;
Their voices mount symbolical of praise —
To mix with hymns that Spirits make and
　　hear;
And to fallen man their innocence is dear.
Enraptured Art draws from those sacred
　　springs
Streams that reflect the poetry of things !
Where christian Martyrs stand in hues
　　portrayed,　　　　　　　　　　　21

That, might a wish avail, would never fade;
Borne in their hands the lily and the palm
Shed round the altar a celestial calm;
There, too, behold the lamb and guileless
    dove
Prest in the tenderness of virgin love
To saintly bosoms ! — Glorious is the blend-
    ing
Of right affections climbing or descending
Along a scale of light and life, with cares
Alternate; carrying holy thoughts and
    prayers   30
Up to the sovereign seat of the Most High;
Descending to the worm in charity;
Like those good Angels whom a dream of
    night
Gave, in the field of Luz, to Jacob's sight,
All, while *he* slept, treading the pendent
    stairs
Earthward or heavenward, radiant mes-
    sengers,
That, with a perfect will in one accord
Of strict obedience, serve the Almighty
    Lord;
And with untired humility forbore
To speed their errand by the wings they
    wore.   40
    What a fair world were ours for verse to
        paint,
If Power could live at ease with self-re-
    straint !
Opinion bow before the naked sense
Of the great Vision, — faith in Providence;
Merciful over all his creatures, just
To the least particle of sentient dust:
But, fixing by immutable decrees,
Seedtime and harvest for his purposes !
Then would be closed the restless oblique
    eye
That looks for evil like a treacherous spy; 50
Disputes would then relax, like stormy winds
That into breezes sink; impetuous minds
By discipline endeavour to grow meek
As Truth herself, whom they profess to seek.
Then Genius, shunning fellowship with
    Pride,
Would braid his golden locks at Wisdom's
    side;
Love ebb and flow untroubled by caprice;
And not alone *harsh* tyranny would cease,
But unoffending creatures find release
From qualified oppression, whose defence 60
Rests on a hollow plea of recompence;
Thought-tempered wrongs, for each humane
    respect

Oft worse to bear, or deadlier in effect.
Witness those glances of indignant scorn
From some high-minded Slave, impelled to
    spurn
The kindness that would make him less
    forlorn;
Or, if the soul to bondage be subdued,
His look of pitiable gratitude !
    Alas for thee, bright Galaxy of Isles,
Whose day departs in pomp, returns with
    smiles —   70
To greet the flowers and fruitage of a land,
As the sun mounts, by sea-born breezes
    fanned;
A land whose azure mountain-tops are seats
For Gods in council, whose green vales,
    retreats
Fit for the shades of heroes, mingling there
To breathe Elysian peace in upper air.
    Though cold as winter, gloomy as the
        grave,
Stone-walls a prisoner make, but not a
    slave.
Shall man assume a property in man ?
Lay on the moral will a withering ban ? 80
Shame that our laws at distance still protect
Enormities, which they at home reject !
" Slaves cannot breathe in England " — yet
    that boast
Is but a mockery ! when from coast to coast,
Though *fettered* slave be none, her floors
    and soil
Groan underneath a weight of slavish toil,
For the poor Many, measured out by rules
Fetched with cupidity from heartless
    schools,
That to an Idol, falsely called " the Wealth
Of Nations," sacrifice a People's health, 90
Body and mind and soul; a thirst so keen
Is ever urging on the vast machine
Of sleepless Labour, 'mid whose dizzy
    wheels
The Power least prized is that which thinks
    and feels.
    Then, for the pastimes of this delicate age,
And all the heavy or light vassalage
Which for their sakes we fasten, as may
    suit
Our varying moods, on human kind or
    brute,
'T were well in little, as in great, to pause,
Lest Fancy trifle with eternal laws.   100
Not from his fellows only man may learn
Rights to compare and duties to discern !
All creatures and all objects, in degree,

Are friends and patrons of humanity.
There are to whom the garden, grove, and
    field,
Perpetual lessons of forbearance yield;
Who would not lightly violate the grace
The lowliest flower possesses in its place;
Nor shorten the sweet life, too fugitive,
Which nothing less than Infinite Power
    could give.   110

"THIS LAWN, A CARPET ALL ALIVE"

1829. 1835

This Lawn is the sloping one approaching the kitchen-garden, and was made out of it. Hundreds of times have I watched the dancing of shadows amid a press of sunshine, and other beautiful appearances of light and shade, flowers and shrubs. What a contrast between this and the cabbages and onions and carrots that used to grow there on a piece of ugly-shaped unsightly ground! No reflection, however, either upon cabbages or onions; the latter we know were worshipped by the Egyptians, and he must have a poor eye for beauty who has not observed how much of it there is in the form and colour which cabbages and plants of that genus exhibit through the various stages of their growth and decay. A richer display of colour in vegetable nature can scarcely be conceived than Coleridge, my Sister, and I saw in a bed of potato-plants in blossom near a hut upon the moor between Inversneyd and Loch Katrine. These blossoms were of such extraordinary beauty and richness that no one could have passed them without notice. But the sense must be cultivated through the mind before we can perceive these inexhaustible treasures of Nature, for such they really are, without the least necessary reference to the utility of her productions, or even to the laws whereupon, as we learn by research, they are dependent. Some are of opinion that the habit of analysing, decomposing, and anatomising is inevitably unfavourable to the perception of beauty. People are led into this mistake by overlooking the fact that, such processes being to a certain extent within the reach of a limited intellect, we are apt to ascribe to them that insensibility of which they are in truth the effect and not the cause. Admiration and love, to which all knowledge truly vital must tend, are felt by men of real genius in proportion as their discoveries in natural Philosophy are enlarged; and the beauty in form of a plant or an animal is not made less but more apparent as a whole by more accurate insight into its constituent

properties and powers. A *Savant* who is not also a poet in soul and a religionist in heart is a feeble and unhappy creature.

THIS Lawn, a carpet all alive
With shadows flung from leaves — to strive
    In dance, amid a press
Of sunshine, an apt emblem yields
Of Worldlings revelling in the fields
    Of strenuous idleness;

Less quick the stir when tide and breeze
Encounter, and to narrow seas
    Forbid a moment's rest;
The medley less when boreal Lights
Glance to and fro, like aery Sprites
    To feats of arms addrest!

Yet, spite of all this eager strife,
This ceaseless play, the genuine life
    That serves the stedfast hours,
Is in the grass beneath, that grows
Unheeded, and the mute repose
    Of sweetly-breathing flowers.

THOUGHTS ON THE SEASONS

1829. 1835

Written at Rydal Mount.

FLATTERED with promise of escape
    From every hurtful blast,
Spring takes, O sprightly May! thy shape,
    Her loveliest and her last.

Less fair is summer riding high
    In fierce solstitial power,
Less fair than when a lenient sky
    Brings on her parting hour.

When earth repays with golden sheaves
    The labours of the plough,
And ripening fruits and forest leaves
    All brighten on the bough;

What pensive beauty autumn shows,
    Before she hears the sound
Of winter rushing in, to close
    The emblematic round!

Such be our Spring, our Summer such;
    So may our Autumn blend
With hoary Winter, and Life touch,
    Through heaven-born hope, her end!

A GRAVESTONE UPON THE FLOOR IN THE CLOISTERS OF WORCESTER CATHEDRAL

1828(?). 1829

"Miserrimus." Many conjectures have been formed as to the person who lies under this stone. Nothing appears to be known for a certainty. Query — The Rev. Mr. Morris, a nonconformist, a sufferer for conscience-sake: a worthy man who, having been deprived of his benefice after the accession of William III., lived to an old age in extreme destitution, on the alms of charitable Jacobites?

" *MISERRIMUS,*" and neither name nor date,
Prayer, text, or symbol, graven upon the stone;
Nought but that word assigned to the unknown,
That solitary word — to separate
From all, and cast a cloud around the fate
Of him who lies beneath. Most wretched one,
Who chose his epitaph ? — Himself alone
Could thus have dared the grave to agitate,
And claim, among the dead, this awful crown;
Nor doubt that He marked also for his own
Close to these cloistral steps a burial-place,
That every foot might fall with heavier tread,
Trampling upon his vileness. Stranger, pass
Softly ! — To save the contrite, Jesus bled.

A TRADITION OF OKER HILL IN DARLEY DALE, DERBYSHIRE

1828. 1829

This pleasing tradition was told me by the coachman at whose side I sate while he drove down the dale, he pointing to the trees on the hill as he related the story.

'T is said that to the brow of yon fair hill
Two Brothers clomb, and, turning face from face,
Nor one look more exchanging, grief to still
Or feed, each planted on that lofty place
A chosen Tree; then, eager to fulfil
Their courses, like two new-born rivers, they
In opposite directions urged their way

Down from the far-seen mount. No blast might kill
Or blight that fond memorial; — the trees grew,
And now entwine their arms; but ne'er again
Embraced those Brothers upon earth's wide plain;
Nor aught of mutual joy or sorrow knew
Until their spirits mingled in the sea
That to itself takes all, Eternity.

THE ARMENIAN LADY'S LOVE

1830. 1835

Written at Rydal Mount.

The subject of the following poem is from the *Orlandus* of the author's friend, Kenelm Henry Digby : and the liberty is taken of inscribing it to him as an acknowledgment, however unworthy, of pleasure and instruction derived from his numerous and valuable writings, illustrative of the piety and chivalry of the olden time.

I

You have heard " a Spanish Lady
   How she wooed an English man; "
Hear now of a fair Armenian,
   Daughter of the proud Soldàn;
How she loved a Christian slave, and told her pain
By word, look, deed, with hope that he might love again.

II

" Pluck that rose, it moves my liking,"
   Said she, lifting up her veil;
" Pluck it for me, gentle gardener,
   Ere it wither and grow pale."   10
" Princess fair, I till the ground, but may not take
From twig or bed an humbler flower, even for your sake ! "

III

" Grieved am I, submissive Christian !
   To behold thy captive state;
Women, in your land, may pity
   (May they not ?) the unfortunate."
" Yes, kind Lady ! otherwise man could not bear
Life, which to every one that breathes is full of care."

IV

"Worse than idle is compassion
  If it ends in tears and sighs; 20
Thee from bondage would I rescue
  And from vile indignities;
Nurtured, as thy mien bespeaks, in high
  degree,
Look up — and help a hand that longs to
  set thee free."

V

"Lady! dread the wish, nor venture
  In such peril to engage;
Think how it would stir against you
  Your most loving father's rage:
Sad deliverance would it be, and yoked
  with shame,
Should troubles overflow on her from whom
  it came." 30

VI

"Generous Frank! the just in effort
  Are of inward peace secure:
Hardships for the brave encountered,
  Even the feeblest may endure:
If almighty grace through me thy chains
  unbind,
My father for slave's work may seek a slave
  in mind."

VII

"Princess, at this burst of goodness,
  My long-frozen heart grows warm!"
"Yet you make all courage fruitless,
  Me to save from chance of harm: 40
Leading such companion I that gilded dome,
Yon minarets, would gladly leave for his
  worst home."

VIII

"Feeling tunes your voice, fair Princess,
  And your brow is free from scorn,
Else these words would come like
  mockery,
  Sharper than the pointed thorn."
"Whence the undeserved mistrust? Too
  wide apart
Our faith hath been, — O would that eyes
  could see the heart!"

IX

"Tempt me not, I pray; my doom is
  These base implements to wield; 50
Rusty lance, I ne'er shall grasp thee,
  Ne'er assoil my cobwebbed shield!

Never see my native land, nor castle tow-
  ers,
Nor Her who thinking of me there counts
  widowed hours."

X

"Prisoner! pardon youthful fancies;
  Wedded? If you *can*, say no!
Blessèd is and be your consort;
  Hopes I cherished — let them go!
Handmaid's privilege would leave my pur-
  pose free,
Without another link to my felicity." 60

XI

"Wedded love with loyal Christians,
  Lady, is a mystery rare;
Body, heart, and soul in union,
  Make one being of a pair."
"Humble love in me would look for no re-
  turn,
Soft as a guiding star that cheers, but can-
  not burn."

XII

"Gracious Allah! by such title
  Do I dare to thank the God,
Him who thus exalts thy spirit,
  Flower of an unchristian sod! 70
Or hast thou put off wings which thou in
  heaven dost wear!
What have I seen, and heard, or dreamt?
  where am I? where?"

XIII

Here broke off the dangerous converse:
  Less impassioned words might tell
How the pair escaped together,
  Tears not wanting, nor a knell
Of sorrow in her heart while through her
  father's door,
And from her narrow world, she passed for
  evermore.

XIV

But affections higher, holier,
  Urged her steps; she shrunk from
  trust 80
In a sensual creed that trampled
  Woman's birthright into dust.
Little be the wonder then, the blame be
  none,
If she, a timid Maid, hath put such bold-
  ness on.

XV

Judge both Fugitives with knowledge:
   In those old romantic days
Mighty were the soul's commandments
   To support, restrain, or raise.
Foes might hang upon their path, snakes
      rustle near,
But nothing from their inward selves had
      they to fear.   90

XVI

Thought infirm ne'er came between
      them,
   Whether printing desert sands
With accordant steps, or gathering
   Forest-fruit with social hands;
Or whispering like two reeds that in the
      cold moonbeam
Bend with the breeze their heads, beside a
      crystal stream.

XVII

On a friendly deck reposing
   They at length for Venice steer;
There, when they had closed their
      voyage
   One, who daily on the pier   100
Watched for tidings from the East, beheld
      his Lord,
Fell down and clasped his knees for joy,
      not uttering word.

XVIII

Mutual was the sudden transport;
   Breathless questions followed fast,
Years contracting to a moment,
   Each word greedier than the last;
" Hie thee to the Countess, friend ! return
      with speed,
And of this Stranger speak, by whom her
      lord was freed

XIX

Say that I, who might have languished,
   Drooped and pined till life was spent,
Now before the gates of Stolberg   111
   My Deliverer would present
For a crowning recompence, the precious
      grace
Of her who in my heart still holds her an-
      cient place.

XX

Make it known that my Companion
   Is of royal eastern blood,

Thirsting after all perfection,
   Innocent, and meek, and good,
Though with misbelievers bred; but that
      dark night
Will holy Church disperse by beams of
      gospel-light.''   120

XXI

Swiftly went that grey-haired Servant,
   Soon returned a trusty Page
Charged with greetings, benedictions,
   Thanks and praises, each a gage
For a sunny thought to cheer the Stranger's
      way,
Her virtuous scruples to remove, her fears
      allay.

XXII

And how blest the Reunited,
   While beneath their castle-walls,
Runs a deafening noise of welcome ! —
   Blest, though every tear that falls   130
Doth in its silence of past sorrow tell,
And makes a meeting seem most like a
      dear farewell.

XXIII

Through a haze of human nature,
   Glorified by heavenly light,
Looked the beautiful Deliverer
   On that overpowering sight,
While across her virgin cheek pure blushes
      strayed,
For every tender sacrifice her heart had
      made.

XXIV

On the ground the weeping Countess
   Knelt, and kissed the Stranger's hand;
Act of soul-devoted homage,   141
   Pledge of an eternal band:
Nor did aught of future days that kiss
      belie,
Which, with a generous shout, the crowd
      did ratify.

XXV

Constant to the fair Armenian,
   Gentle pleasures round her moved,
Like a tutelary spirit
   Reverenced, like a sister, loved,
Christian meekness smoothed for all the
      path of life,
Who, loving most, should wiseliest love,
      their only strife.   150

XXVI

Mute memento of that union
    In a Saxon church survives,
Where a cross-legged Knight lies sculp-
        tured
    As between two wedded wives —
Figures with armorial signs of race and
        birth,
And the vain rank the pilgrims bore while
    yet on earth.

THE RUSSIAN FUGITIVE

1828. 1835

Early in life this story had interested me,
and I often thought it would make a pleasing
subject for an opera or musical drama.

PART I

ENOUGH of rose-bud lips, and eyes
    Like harebells bathed in dew,
Of cheek that with carnation vies,
    And veins of violet hue;
Earth wants not beauty that may scorn
    A likening to frail flowers;
Yea, to the stars, if they were born
    For seasons and for hours.

Through Moscow's gates, with gold un-
        barred,
    Stepped One at dead of night,   10
Whom such high beauty could not guard
    From meditated blight;
By stealth she passed, and fled as fast
    As doth the hunted fawn,
Nor stopped, till in the dappling east
    Appeared unwelcome dawn.

Seven days she lurked in brake and field,
    Seven nights her course renewed,
Sustained by what her scrip might yield,
    Or berries of the wood;   20
At length, in darkness travelling on,
    When lowly doors were shut,
The haven of her hope she won,
    Her Foster-mother's hut.

"To put your love to dangerous proof
    I come," said she, "from far;
For I have left my Father's roof,
    In terror of the Czar."
No answer did the Matron give,
    No second look she cast,   30

But hung upon the Fugitive,
    Embracing and embraced.

She led the Lady to a seat
    Beside the glimmering fire,
Bathed duteously her wayworn feet,
    Prevented each desire:
The cricket chirped, the house-dog dozed,
    And on that simple bed,
Where she in childhood had reposed,
    Now rests her weary head.   40

When she, whose couch had been the sod,
    Whose curtain, pine or thorn,
Had breathed a sigh of thanks to God,
    Who comforts the forlorn;
While over her the Matron bent
    Sleep sealed her eyes, and stole
Feeling from limbs with travel spent,
    And trouble from the soul.

Refreshed, the Wanderer rose at morn,
    And soon again was dight   50
In those unworthy vestments worn
    Through long and perilous flight;
And "O beloved Nurse," she said,
    "My thanks with silent tears
Have unto Heaven and You been paid:
    Now listen to my fears !

"Have you forgot" — and here she
        smiled —
    "The babbling flatteries
You lavished on me when a child
    Disporting round your knees ?   60
I was your lambkin, and your bird,
    Your star, your gem, your flower;
Light words, that were more lightly heard
    In many a cloudless hour !

"The blossom you so fondly praised
    Is come to bitter fruit;
A mighty One upon me gazed;
    I spurned his lawless suit,
And must be hidden from his wrath:
    You, Foster-father dear,   70
Will guide me in my forward path;
    I may not tarry here !

"I cannot bring to utter woe
    Your proved fidelity." —
"Dear Child, sweet Mistress, say not so !
    For you we both would die."
"Nay, nay, I come with semblance feigned
    And cheek embrowned by art;

Yet, being inwardly unstained,
  With courage will depart."   80

" But whither would you, could you, flee ?
  A poor Man's counsel take;
The Holy Virgin gives to me
  A thought for your dear sake;
Rest, shielded by our Lady's grace,
  And soon shall you be led
Forth to a safe abiding-place,
  Where never foot doth tread."

PART II

THE dwelling of this faithful pair
  In a straggling village stood,
For One who breathed unquiet air
  A dangerous neighbourhood;
But wide around lay forest ground
  With thickets rough and blind;
And pine-trees made a heavy shade
  Impervious to the wind.

And there, sequestered from the sight,
  Was spread a treacherous swamp,   10
On which the noonday sun shed light
  As from a lonely lamp;
And midway in the unsafe morass,
  A single Island rose
Of firm dry ground, with healthful grass
  Adorned, and shady boughs.

The Woodman knew, for such the craft
  This Russian vassal plied,
That never fowler's gun, nor shaft
  Of archer, there was tried;   20
A sanctuary seemed the spot
  From all intrusion free;
And there he planned an artful Cot
  For perfect secrecy.

With earnest pains unchecked by dread
  Of Power's far-stretching hand,
The bold good Man his labour sped
  At nature's pure command;
Heart-soothed, and busy as a wren,
  While, in a hollow nook,   30
She moulds her sight-eluding den
  Above a murmuring brook.

His task accomplished to his mind,
  The twain ere break of day
Creep forth, and through the forest wind
  Their solitary way;

Few words they speak, nor dare to slack
  Their pace from mile to mile,
Till they have crossed the quaking marsh
  And reached the lonely Isle.   40

The sun above the pine-trees showed
  A bright and cheerful face;
And Ina looked for her abode,
  The promised hiding-place;
She sought in vain, the Woodman smiled;
  No threshold could be seen,
Nor roof, nor window; — all seemed wild
  As it had ever been.

Advancing, you might guess an hour,
  The front with such nice care   50
Is masked, " if house it be or bower,"
  But in they entered are;
As shaggy as were wall and roof
  With branches intertwined,
So smooth was all within, air-proof,
  And delicately lined:

And hearth was there, and maple dish,
  And cups in seemly rows,
And couch — all ready to a wish
  For nurture or repose;   60
And Heaven doth to her virtue grant
  That here she may abide
In solitude, with every want
  By cautious love supplied.

No queen, before a shouting crowd,
  Led on in bridal state,
E'er struggled with a heart so proud,
  Entering her palace gate:
Rejoiced to bid the world farewell,
  No saintly anchoress   70
E'er took possession of her cell
  With deeper thankfulness.

" Father of all, upon thy care
  And mercy am I thrown;
Be thou my safeguard ! " — such her
    prayer
  When she was left alone,
Kneeling amid the wilderness
  When joy had passed away,
And smiles, fond efforts of distress
  To hide what they betray !   80

The prayer is heard, the Saints have seen,
  Diffused through form and face,
Resolves devotedly serene;
  That monumental grace

Of Faith, which doth all passions tame
  That Reason *should* control;
And shows in the untrembling frame
  A statue of the soul.

PART III

'T IS sung in ancient minstrelsy
  That Phœbus wont to wear
The leaves of any pleasant tree
  Around his golden hair;
Till Daphne, desperate with pursuit
  Of his imperious love,
At her own prayer transformed, took root,
  A laurel in the grove.

Then did the Penitent adorn
  His brow with laurel green;   10
And 'mid his bright locks never shorn
  No meaner leaf was seen;
And poets sage, through every age,
  About their temples wound
The bay; and conquerors thanked the Gods,
  With laurel chaplets crowned.

Into the mists of fabling Time
  So far runs back the praise
Of Beauty, that disdains to climb
  Along forbidden ways;   20
That scorns temptation; power defies
  Where mutual love is not;
And to the tomb for rescue flies
  When life would be a blot.

To this fair Votaress, a fate
  More mild doth Heaven ordain
Upon her Island desolate;
  And words, not breathed in vain,
Might tell what intercourse she found,
  Her silence to endear;   30
What birds she tamed, what flowers the ground
  Sent forth her peace to cheer.

To one mute Presence, above all,
  Her soothed affections clung,
A picture on the cabin wall
  By Russian usage hung —
The Mother-maid, whose countenance bright
  With love abridged the day;
And, communed with by taper light,
  Chased spectral fears away.   40

And oft, as either Guardian came,
  The joy in that retreat
Might any common friendship shame,
  So high their hearts would beat;
And to the lone Recluse, whate'er
  They brought, each visiting
Was like the crowding of the year
  With a new burst of spring.

But, when she of her Parents thought,
  The pang was hard to bear;   50
And, if with all things not enwrought,
  That trouble still is near.
Before her flight she had not dared
  Their constancy to prove,
Too much the heroic Daughter feared
  The weakness of their love.

Dark is the past to them, and dark
  The future still must be,
Till pitying Saints conduct her bark
  Into a safer sea —   60
Or gentle Nature close her eyes,
  And set her Spirit free
From the altar of this sacrifice,
  In vestal purity.

Yet, when above the forest-glooms
  The white swans southward passed,
High as the pitch of their swift plumes
  Her fancy rode the blast;
And bore her toward the fields of France
  Her Father's native land,   70
To mingle in the rustic dance,
  The happiest of the band !

Of those belovèd fields she oft
  Had heard her Father tell
In phrase that now with echoes soft
  Haunted her lonely cell;
She saw the hereditary bowers,
  She heard the ancestral stream;
The Kremlin and its haughty towers
  Forgotten like a dream !

PART IV

THE ever-changing Moon had traced
  Twelve times her monthly round,
When through the unfrequented Waste
  Was heard a startling sound;
A shout thrice sent from one who chased
  At speed a wounded deer,

Bounding through branches interlaced,
  And where the wood was clear.

The fainting creature took the marsh,
  And toward the Island fled,   10
While plovers screamed with tumult harsh
  Above his antlered head:
This, Ina saw; and, pale with fear,
  Shrunk to her citadel;
The desperate deer rushed on, and near
  The tangled covert fell.

Across the marsh, the game in view,
  The Hunter followed fast,
Nor paused, till o'er the stag he blew
  A death-proclaiming blast;   20
Then, resting on her upright mind,
  Came forth the Maid — "In me
Behold," she said, "a stricken Hind
  Pursued by destiny!

From your deportment, Sir! I deem
  That you have worn a sword,
And will not hold in light esteem
  A suffering woman's word;
There is my covert, there perchance
  I might have lain concealed,   30
My fortunes hid, my countenance
  Not even to you revealed.

Tears might be shed, and I might pray,
  Crouching and terrified,
That what has been unveiled to-day,
  You would in mystery hide;
But I will not defile with dust
  The knee that bends to adore
The God in heaven; — attend, be just;
  This ask I, and no more!   40

I speak not of the winter's cold,
  For summer's heat exchanged,
While I have lodged in this rough hold,
  From social life estranged;
Nor yet of trouble and alarms:
  High Heaven is my defence;
And every season has soft arms
  For injured Innocence.

From Moscow to the Wilderness
  It was my choice to come,   50
Lest virtue should be harbourless,
  And honour want a home;
And happy were I, if the Czar
  Retain his lawless will,

To end life here like this poor deer,
  Or a lamb on a green hill."

"Are you the Maid," the Stranger cried,
  "From Gallic parents sprung,
Whose vanishing was rumoured wide,
  Sad theme for every tongue;   60
Who foiled an Emperor's eager quest?
  You, Lady, forced to wear
These rude habiliments, and rest
  Your head in this dark lair!"

But wonder, pity, soon were quelled;
  And in her face and mien
The soul's pure brightness he beheld
  Without a veil between:
He loved, he hoped, — a holy flame
  Kindled 'mid rapturous tears;   70
The passion of a moment came
  As on the wings of years.

"Such bounty is no gift of chance,"
  Exclaimed he; "righteous Heaven,
Preparing your deliverance,
  To me the charge hath given.
The Czar full oft in words and deeds
  Is stormy and self-willed;
But, when the Lady Catherine pleads,
  His violence is stilled.   80

Leave open to my wish the course,
  And I to her will go;
From that humane and heavenly source,
  Good, only good, can flow."
Faint sanction given, the Cavalier
  Was eager to depart,
Though question followed question, dear,
  To the Maiden's filial heart.

Light was his step, — his hopes, more light,
  Kept pace with his desires;   90
And the fifth morning gave him sight
  Of Moscow's glittering spires.
He sued: — heart-smitten by the wrong,
  To the lorn Fugitive
The Emperor sent a pledge as strong
  As sovereign power could give.

O more than mighty change! If e'er
  Amazement rose to pain,
And joy's excess produced a fear
  Of something void and vain;   100
'T was when the Parents, who had mourned
  So long the lost as dead,

Beheld their only Child returned,
The household floor to tread.

Soon gratitude gave way to love
  Within the Maiden's breast;
Delivered and Deliverer move
  In bridal garments drest;
Meek Catherine had her own reward;
  The Czar bestowed a dower;   110
And universal Moscow shared
  The triumph of that hour.

Flowers strewed the ground; the nuptial
    feast
  Was held with costly state;
And there, 'mid many a noble guest,
  The Foster-parents sate;
Encouraged by the imperial eye,
  They shrank not into shade;
Great was their bliss, the honour high
  To them and nature paid!

THE EGYPTIAN MAID

OR, THE ROMANCE OF THE WATER LILY

1828. 1835

For the names and persons in the following poem, see the *History of the renowned Prince Arthur and his Knights of the Round Table;* for the rest the Author is answerable ; only it may be proper to add, that the Lotus, with the bust of the Goddess appearing to rise out of the full-blown flower, was suggested by the beautiful work of ancient art, once included among the Townley Marbles, and now in the British Museum.

In addition to the short notice prefixed to this poem it may be worth while here to say that it rose out of a few words casually used in conversation by my nephew Henry Hutchinson. He was describing with great spirit the appearance and movement of a vessel which he seemed to admire more than any other he had ever seen, and said her name was the *Water Lily.* This plant has been my delight from my boyhood, as I have seen it floating on the lake ; and that conversation put me upon constructing and composing the poem. Had I not heard those words it would never have been written. The form of the stanza is new, and is nothing but a repetition of the first five lines as, they were thrown off, and is not perhaps well suited to narrative, and certainly would not have been trusted to had I thought at the be-

ginning that the poem would have gone to such a length.

WHILE Merlin paced the Cornish sands,
Forth-looking toward the rocks of Scilly,
The pleased Enchanter was aware
Of a bright Ship that seemed to hang in air,
Yet was she work of mortal hands,
And took from men her name — THE
    WATER LILY.

Soft was the wind, that landward blew;
And, as the Moon, o'er some dark hill
    ascendant,
Grows from a little edge of light
To a full orb, this Pinnace bright   10
Became, as nearer to the coast she drew,
More glorious, with spread sail and stream-
    ing pendant.

Upon this wingèd Shape so fair
Sage Merlin gazed with admiration:
Her lineaments, thought he, surpass
Aught that was ever shown in magic
    glass;
Was ever built with patient care;
Or, at a touch, produced by happiest trans-
    formation.

Now, though a Mechanist, whose skill
Shames the degenerate grasp of modern
    science,   20
Grave Merlin (and belike the more
For practising occult and perilous lore)
Was subject to a freakish will
That sapped good thoughts, or scared them
    with defiance.

Provoked to envious spleen, he cast
An altered look upon the advancing
    Stranger
Whom he had hailed with joy, and cried,
" My Art shall help to tame her pride — "
Anon the breeze became a blast,
And the waves rose, and sky portended
    danger.   30

With thrilling word, and potent sign
Traced on the beach, his work the Sor-
    cerer urges;
The clouds in blacker clouds are lost,
Like spiteful Fiends that vanish, crossed
By Fiends of aspect more malign;
And the winds roused the Deep with fiercer
    scourges.

But worthy of the name she bore
Was this Sea-flower, this buoyant Galley;
Supreme in loveliness and grace
Of motion, whether in the embrace   40
Of trusty anchorage, or scudding o'er
The main flood roughened into hill and
  valley.

Behold,. how wantonly she laves
Her sides, the Wizard's craft confounding;
Like something out of Ocean sprung
To be for ever fresh and young,
Breasts the sea-flashes, and huge waves
Top-gallant high, rebounding and rebounding !

But Ocean under magic heaves,
And cannot spare the Thing he cherished:
Ah !. what avails that she was fair,   51
Luminous, blithe, and debonair ?
The storm has stripped her of her leaves;
The Lily floats no longer ! — She hath
  perished.

Grieve for her, — she deserves no less;
So like, yet so unlike, a living Creature !
No heart had she, no busy brain;
Though loved, she could not love again;
Though pitied, *feel* her own distress;
Nor aught that troubles us, the fools of
  Nature.   60

Yet is there cause for gushing tears;
So richly was this Galley laden,
A fairer than herself she bore,
And, in her struggles, cast ashore;
A lovely One, who nothing hears
Of wind or wave — a meek and guileless
  Maiden.

Into a cave had Merlin fled
From mischief, caused by spells himself
  had muttered;
And while, repentant all too late,
In moody posture there he sate,   70
He heard a voice, and saw, with half-
  raised head,
A Visitant by whom these words were
  uttered;

" On Christian service this frail Bark
Sailed " (hear me, Merlin !) " under
  high protection,

Though on her prow a sign of heathen
  power
Was carved — a Goddess with a Lily
  flower,
The old Egyptian's emblematic mark
Of joy immortal and of pure affection.

Her course was for the British strand;
Her freight, it was a Damsel peerless;   80
God reigns above, and Spirits strong
May gather to avenge this wrong
Done to the Princess, and her Land
Which she in duty left, sad but not cheerless.

And to Caerleon's loftiest tower
Soon will the Knights of Arthur's Table
A cry of lamentation send;
And all will weep who there attend,
To grace that Stranger's bridal hour,
For whom the sea was made unnavigable.

Shame ! should a Child of royal line   91
Die through the blindness of thy
  malice ? "
Thus to the Necromancer spake
Nina, the Lady of the Lake,
A gentle Sorceress, and benign,
Who ne'er embittered any good man's
  chalice.

" What boots," continued she, " to
  mourn ?
To expiate thy sin endeavour:
From the bleak isle where she is laid,
Fetched by our art, the Egyptian Maid
May yet to Arthur's court be borne   101
Cold as she is, ere life be fled for ever.

My pearly Boat, a shining Light,
That brought me down that sunless
  river,
Will bear me on from wave to wave,
And back with her to this sea-cave; —
Then Merlin ! for a rapid flight
Through air, to thee my Charge will I
  deliver.

The very swiftest of thy cars
Must, when my part is done, be ready;
Meanwhile, for further guidance, look   111
Into thy own prophetic book;
And, if that fail, consult the Stars
To learn thy course; farewell ! be prompt
  and steady."

This scarcely spoken, she again
Was seated in her gleaming shallop,
That, o'er the yet-distempered Deep,
Pursued its way with bird-like sweep,
Or like a steed, without a rein,
Urged o'er the wilderness in sportive
   gallop.   120

Soon did the gentle Nina reach
That Isle without a house or haven;
Landing, she found not what she sought,
Nor saw of wreck or ruin aught
But a carved Lotus cast upon the beach
By the fierce waves, a flower in marble
   graven.

Sad relique, but how fair the while !
For gently each from each retreating
With backward curve, the leaves revealed
The bosom half, and half concealed, 130
Of a Divinity, that seemed to smile
On Nina, as she passed, with hopeful
   greeting.

No quest was hers of vague desire,
Of tortured hope and purpose shaken;
Following the margin of a bay,
She spied the lonely Castaway,
Unmarred, unstripped of her attire,
But with closed eyes, — of breath and bloom
   forsaken.

Then Nina, stooping down, embraced,
With tenderness and mild emotion,   140
The Damsel, in that trance embound;
And, while she raised her from the
   ground,
And in the pearly shallop placed,
Sleep fell upon the air, and stilled the ocean.

The turmoil hushed, celestial springs
Of music opened, and there came a
   blending
Of fragrance, underived from earth,
With gleams that owed not to the sun
   their birth,
And that soft rustling of invisible wings
Which Angels make, on works of love de-
   scending.   150

And Nina heard a sweeter voice
Than if the Goddess of the flower had
   spoken:
" Thou hast achieved, fair Dame ! what
   none

Less pure in spirit could have done;
Go, in thy enterprise rejoice !
Air, earth, sea, sky, and heaven, success
   betoken."

So cheered, she left that Island bleak,
A bare rock of the Scilly cluster;
And, as they traversed the smooth brine,
The self-illumined Brigantine   160
Shed, on the Slumberer's cold wan cheek
And pallid brow, a melancholy lustre.

Fleet was their course, and when they
   came
To the dim cavern, whence the river
Issued into the salt-sea flood,
Merlin, as fixed in thought he stood,
Was thus accosted by the Dame;
" Behold to thee my Charge I now deliver !

But where attends thy chariot —
   where ? " —
Quoth Merlin, " Even as I was bidden, 170
So have I done; as trusty as thy barge
My vehicle shall prove — O precious
   Charge !
If this be sleep, how soft ! if death, how
   fair !
Much have my books disclosed, but the end
   is hidden."

He spake; and gliding into view
Forth from the grotto's dimmest chamber
Came two mute Swans, whose plumes of
   dusky white
Changed, as the pair approached the
   light,
Drawing an ebon car, their hue
(Like clouds of sunset) into lucid amber.

Once more did gentle Nina lift   181
The Princess, passive to all changes:
The car received her: — then up-went
Into the ethereal element
The Birds with progress smooth and swift
As thought, when through bright regions
   memory ranges.

Sage Merlin, at the Slumberer's side,
Instructs the Swans their way to measure;
And soon Caerleon's towers appeared,
And notes of minstrelsy were heard 190
From rich pavilions spreading wide,
For some high day of long-expected plea-
   sure.

Awe-stricken stood both Knights and
Dames
Ere on firm ground the car alighted;
Eftsoons astonishment was past,
For in that face they saw the last,
Last lingering look of clay, that tames
All pride; by which all happiness is blighted.

Said Merlin, "Mighty King, fair Lords,
Away with feast and tilt and tourney! 200
Ye saw, throughout this royal House,
Ye heard, a rocking marvellous
Of turrets, and a clash of swords
Self-shaken, as I closed my airy journey.

Lo! by a destiny well known
To mortals, joy is turned to sorrow;
This is the wished-for Bride, the Maid
Of Egypt, from a rock conveyed
Where she by shipwreck had been thrown,
Ill sight! but grief may vanish ere the
morrow." 210

"Though vast thy power, thy words are
weak,"
Exclaimed the King, "a mockery hateful;
Dutiful Child, her lot how hard!
Is this her piety's reward?
Those watery locks, that bloodless cheek!
O winds without remorse! O shore un-
grateful!

Rich robes are fretted by the moth;
Towers, temples, fall by stroke of thun-
der;
Will that, or deeper thoughts, abate
A Father's sorrow for her fate? 220
He will repent him of his troth;
His brain will burn, his stout heart split
asunder.

Alas! and I have caused this woe;
For, when my prowess from invading
Neighbours
Had freed his Realm, he plighted word
That he would turn to Christ our Lord,
And his dear Daughter on a Knight be-
stow
Whom I should choose for love and match-
less labours.

Her birth was heathen; but a fence
Of holy Angels round her hovered: 230
A Lady added to my court
So fair, of such divine report

And worship, seemed a recompence
For fifty kingdoms by my sword recovered

Ask not for whom, O Champions true!
She was reserved by me her life's be-
trayer;
She who was meant to be a bride
Is now a corse: then put aside
Vain thoughts, and speed ye, with observ-
ance due
Of Christian rites, in Christian ground to
lay her." 240

"The tomb," said Merlin, "may not close
Upon her yet, earth hide her beauty;
Not froward to thy sovereign will
Esteem me, Liege! if I, whose skill
Wafted her hither, interpose
To check this pious haste of erring duty.

My books command me to lay bare
The secret thou art bent on keeping:
Here must a high attest be given,
What Bridegroom was for her ordained
by Heaven. 250
And in my glass significants there are
Of things that may to gladness turn this
weeping.

For this, approaching, One by One,
Thy Knights must touch the cold hand
of the Virgin;
So, for the favoured One, the Flower
may bloom
Once more; but, if unchangeable her
doom,
If life departed be for ever gone,
Some blest assurance, from this cloud
emerging,

May teach him to bewail his loss;
Not with a grief that, like a vapour, rises
And melts; but grief devout that shall
endure, 261
And a perpetual growth secure
Of purposes which no false thought shall
cross,
A harvest of high hopes and noble enter-
prises."

"So be it," said the King; — "anon,
Here, where the Princess lies, begin the
trial;
Knights each in order as ye stand
Step forth." — To touch the pallid hand

Sir Agravaine advanced; no sign he won
From Heaven or earth; — Sir Kaye had like
   denial.   270

Abashed, Sir Dinas turned away;
Even for Sir Percival was no disclosure;
Though he, devoutest of all Champions,
   ere
He reached that ebon car, the bier
Whereon diffused like snow the Damsel
   lay,
Full thrice had crossed himself in meek
   composure.

Imagine (but ye Saints! who can?)
How in still air the balance trembled —
The wishes, peradventure the despites
That overcame some not ungenerous
   Knights;   280
And all the thoughts that lengthened out
   a span
Of time to Lords and Ladies thus assem-
   bled.

What patient confidence was here!
And there how many bosoms panted!
While drawing toward the car Sir Ga-
   waine, mailed
For tournament, his beaver vailed,
And softly touched; but, to his princely
   cheer
And high expectancy, no sign was granted.

Next, disencumbered of his harp,
Sir Tristram, dear to thousands as a
   brother,   290
Came to the proof, nor grieved that there
   ensued
No change; — the fair Izonda he had
   wooed
With love too true, a love with pangs too
   sharp,
From hope too distant, not to dread another.

Not so Sir Launcelot; — from Heaven's
   grace
A sign he craved, tired slave of vain con-
   trition;
The royal Guinever looked passing glad
When his touch failed. — Next came Sir
   Galahad;
He paused, and stood entranced by that
   still face
Whose features he had seen in noontide
   vision.   300

For late, as near a murmuring stream
He rested 'mid an arbour green and shady,
Nina, the good Enchantress, shed
A light around his mossy bed;
And, at her call, a waking dream
Prefigured to his sense the Egyptian Lady.

Now, while his bright-haired front he
   bowed,
And stood, far-kenned by mantle furred
   with ermine,
As o'er the insensate Body hung
The enrapt, the beautiful, the young,   310
Belief sank deep into the crowd
That he the solemn issue would determine.

Nor deem it strange; the Youth had worn
That very mantle on a day of glory,
The day when he achieved that matchless
   feat,
The marvel of the PERILOUS SEAT,
Which whosoe'er approached of strength
   was shorn,
Though King or Knight the most renowned
   in story.

He touched with hesitating hand —
And lo! those Birds, far-famed through
   Love's dominions,   320
The Swans, in triumph clap their wings;
And their necks play, involved in rings,
Like sinless snakes in Eden's happy
   land; —
"Mine is she," cried the Knight; — again
   they clapped their pinions.

"Mine was she — mine she is, though
   dead,
And to her name my soul shall cleave in
   sorrow;"
Whereat, a tender twilight streak
Of colour dawned upon the Damsel's
   cheek;
And her lips, quickening with uncertain
   red,
Seemed from each other a faint warmth to
   borrow.   330

Deep was the awe, the rapture high,
Of love emboldened, hope with dread
   entwining,
When, to the mouth, relenting Death
Allowed a soft and flower-like breath,
Precursor to a timid sigh,
To lifted eyelids, and a doubtful shining.

In silence did King Arthur gaze
Upon the signs that pass away or tarry;
In silence watched the gentle strife
Of Nature leading back to life;   340
Then eased his soul at length by praise
Of God, and Heaven's pure Queen — the
    blissful Mary.

Then said he, "Take her to thy heart,
Sir Galahad! a treasure, that God giv-
    eth,
Bound by indissoluble ties to thee
Through mortal change and immortal-
    ity;
Be happy and unenvied, thou who art
A goodly Knight that hath no peer that liv-
    eth!"

Not long the Nuptials were delayed;
And sage tradition still rehearses   350
The pomp, the glory of that hour
When toward the altar from her bower
King Arthur led the Egyptian Maid,
And Angels carolled these far-echoed
    verses; —

Who shrinks not from alliance
Of evil with good Powers,
To God proclaims defiance,
And mocks whom he adores.

A Ship to Christ devoted
From the Land of Nile did go;   360
Alas! the bright Ship floated,
An Idol at her prow.

By magic domination,
The Heaven-permitted vent
Of purblind mortal passion,
Was wrought her punishment.

The Flower the Form within it,
What served they in her need?
Her port she could not win it,
Nor from mishap be freed.   370

The tempest overcame her,
And she was seen no more;
But gently, gently blame her —
She cast a Pearl ashore.

The Maid to Jesu hearkened,
And kept to him her faith,
Till sense in death was darkened,
Or sleep akin to death.

But Angels round her pillow
Kept watch, a viewless band;   380
And, billow favouring billow,
She reached the destined strand.

Blest Pair! whate'er befall you,
Your faith in Him approve
Who from frail earth can call you
To bowers of endless love!

THE POET AND THE CAGED TURTLEDOVE

1830. 1835

Written at Rydal Mount. This dove was
one of a pair that had been given to my
daughter by our excellent friend, Miss Jews-
bury, who went to India with her husband, Mr.
Fletcher, where she died of cholera. The dove
survived its mate many years, and was killed,
to our great sorrow, by a neighbour's cat that
got in at the window and dragged it partly out
of the cage. These verses were composed ex-
tempore, to the letter, in the Terrace Summer-
house before spoken of. It was the habit of
the bird to begin cooing and murmuring when-
ever it heard me making my verses.

As often as I murmur here
    My half-formed melodies,
Straight from her osier mansion near,
    The Turtledove replies:
Though silent as a leaf before,
    The captive promptly coos;
Is it to teach her own soft lore,
    Or second my weak Muse?

I rather think, the gentle Dove
    Is murmuring a reproof,
Displeased that I from lays of love
    Have dared to keep aloof;
That I, a Bard of hill and dale,
    Have carolled, fancy free,
As if nor dove nor nightingale,
    Had heart or voice for me.

If such thy meaning, O forbear,
    Sweet Bird! to do me wrong;
Love, blessèd Love, is everywhere
    The spirit of my song:
'Mid grove, and by the calm fireside,
    Love animates my lyre —
That coo again! — 't is not to chide,
    I feel, but to inspire.

PRESENTIMENTS
1830. 1835
Written at Rydal Mount.

PRESENTIMENTS ! they judge not right
Who deem that ye from open light
　　Retire in fear of shame;
All *heaven-born* Instincts shun the touch
Of vulgar sense, — and, being such,
　　Such privilege ye claim.

The tear whose source I could not guess,
The deep sigh that seemed fatherless,
　　Were mine in early days;
And now, unforced by time to part　　10
With fancy, I obey my heart,
　　And venture on your praise.

What though some busy foes to good,
Too potent over nerve and blood,
　　Lurk near you — and combine
To taint the health which ye infuse;
This hides not from the moral Muse
　　Your origin divine.

How oft from you, derided Powers !
Comes Faith that in auspicious hours　　20
　　Builds castles, not of air:
Bodings unsanctioned by the will
Flow from your visionary skill,
　　And teach us to beware.

The bosom-weight, your stubborn gift,
That no philosophy can lift,
　　Shall vanish, if ye please,
Like morning mist: and, where it lay,
The spirits at your bidding play
　　In gaiety and ease.　　30

Star-guided contemplations move
Through space, though calm, not raised above
　　Prognostics that ye rule;
The naked Indian of the wild,
And haply, too, the cradled Child,
　　Are pupils of your school.

But who can fathom your intents,
Number their signs or instruments ?
　　A rainbow, a sunbeam,
A subtle smell that Spring unbinds,　　40
Dead pause abrupt of midnight winds,
　　An echo, or a dream.

The laughter of the Christmas hearth
With sighs of self-exhausted mirth
　　Ye feelingly reprove;

And daily, in the conscious breast,
Your visitations are a test
　　And exercise of love.

When some great change gives boundless
　　　scope
To an exulting Nation's hope,　　50
　　Oft, startled and made wise
By your low-breathed interpretings,
The simply-meek foretaste the springs
　　Of bitter contraries.

Ye daunt the proud array of war,
Pervade the lonely ocean far
　　As sail hath been unfurled;
For dancers in the festive hall
What ghastly partners hath your call
　　Fetched from the shadowy world.　　60

'T is said, that warnings ye dispense,
Emboldened by a keener sense;
　　That men have lived for whom,
With dread precision, ye made clear
The hour that in a distant year
　　Should knell them to the tomb.

Unwelcome insight ! Yet there are
Blest times when mystery is laid bare,
　　Truth shows a glorious face,
While on that isthmus which commands　　70
The councils of both worlds, she stands,
　　Sage Spirits ! by your grace.

God, who instructs the brutes to scent
All changes of the element,
　　Whose wisdom fixed the scale
Of natures, for our wants provides
By higher, sometimes humbler, guides,
　　When lights of reason fail.

"IN THESE FAIR VALES HATH MANY A TREE"
1830. 1835
Engraven, during my absence in Italy, upon a brass plate inserted in the Stone.

In these fair vales hath many a Tree
At Wordsworth's suit been spared;
And from the builder's hand this Stone,
For some rude beauty of its own,
　　Was rescued by the Bard:
So let it rest; and time will come
　　When here the tender-hearted
May heave a gentle sigh for him,
　　As one of the departed.

ELEGIAC MUSINGS

IN THE GROUNDS OF COLEORTON HALL,
THE SEAT OF THE LATE SIR G. H.
BEAUMONT, BART.

1830. 1835

These verses were in fact composed on horse-
back during a storm, while I was on my way
from Coleorton to Cambridge: they are alluded
to elsewhere.

In these grounds stands the Parish Church,
wherein is a mural monument bearing an In-
scription which, in deference to the earnest
request of the deceased, is confined to name,
dates, and these words: — "Enter not into
judgment with thy servant, O LORD!"

WITH copious eulogy in prose or rhyme
Graven on the tomb we struggle against
    Time,
Alas, how feebly! but our feelings rise
And still we struggle when a good man
    dies:
Such offering BEAUMONT dreaded and for-
    bade,
A spirit meek in self-abasement clad.
Yet *here* at least — though few have num-
    bered days
That shunned so modestly the light of
    praise —
His graceful manners, and the temperate ray
Of that arch fancy which would round him
    play,   10
Brightening a converse never known to
    swerve
From courtesy and delicate reserve;
That sense, the bland philosophy of life,
Which checked discussion ere it warmed to
    strife —
Those rare accomplishments, and varied
    powers,
Might have their record among sylvan
    bowers.
Oh, fled for ever! vanished like a blast
That shook the leaves in myriads as it
    passed; —
Gone from this world of earth, air, sea, and
    sky,
From all its spirit-moving imagery,   20
Intensely studied with a painter's eye,
A poet's heart; and, for congenial view,
Portrayed with happiest pencil, not untrue
To common recognitions while the line
Flowed in a course of sympathy divine, —
Oh! severed, too abruptly, from delights

That all the seasons shared with equal
    rights; —
Rapt in the grace of undismantled age,
From soul-felt music, and the treasured
    page
Lit by that evening lamp which loved to
    shed   30
Its mellow lustre round thy honoured head;
While Friends beheld thee give with eye,
    voice, mien,
More than theatric force to Shakspeare's
    scene; —
If thou hast heard me — if thy Spirit know
Aught of these bowers and whence their
    pleasures flow;
If things in our remembrance held so dear,
And thoughts and projects fondly cherished
    here,
To thy exalted nature only seem
Time's vanities, light fragments of earth's
    dream —
Rebuke us not! — The mandate is obeyed
That said, "Let praise be mute where I
    am laid;"   41
The holier deprecation, given in trust
To the cold marble, waits upon thy dust;
Yet have we found how slowly genuine
    grief
From *silent* admiration wins relief.
Too long abashed, thy Name is like a rose
That doth "within itself its sweetness
    close;"
A drooping daisy changed into a cup
In which her bright-eyed beauty is shut up.
Within these groves, where still are flitting
    by   50
Shades of the Past, oft noticed with a sigh,
Shall stand a votive Tablet, haply free,
When towers and temples fall, to speak of
    Thee!
If sculptured emblems of our mortal doom
Recall not there the wisdom of the Tomb,
Green ivy risen from out the cheerful earth,
Will fringe the lettered stone; and herbs
    spring forth,
Whose fragrance, by soft dews and rain
    unbound,
Shall penetrate the heart without a wound;
While truth and love their purposes fulfil,
Commemorating genius, talent, skill,   61
That could not lie concealed where Thou
    wert known;
Thy virtues *He* must judge, and He alone,
The God upon whose mercy they are
    thrown.

"CHATSWORTH! THY STATELY MANSION, AND THE PRIDE"

1830. 1835

I have reason to remember the day that gave rise to this Sonnet, the 6th of November 1830. Having undertaken, a great feat for me, to ride my daughter's pony from Westmoreland to Cambridge, that she might have the use of it while on a visit to her uncle at Trinity Lodge, on my way from Bakewell to Matlock I turned aside to Chatsworth, and had scarcely gratified my curiosity by the sight of that celebrated place before there came on a severe storm of wind and rain which continued till I reached Derby, both man and pony in a pitiable plight. For myself, I went to bed at noon-day. In the course of that journey I had to encounter a storm, worse if possible, in which the pony could (or would) only make his way slantwise. I mention this merely to add that notwithstanding this battering I composed, on horseback, the lines to the memory of Sir George Beaumont, suggested during my recent visit to Coleorton.

CHATSWORTH! thy stately mansion, and the pride
Of thy domain, strange contrast do present
To house and home in many a craggy rent
Of the wild Peak; where new-born waters glide
Through fields whose thrifty occupants abide
As in a dear and chosen banishment,
With every semblance of entire content;
So kind is simple Nature, fairly tried!
Yet He whose heart in childhood gave her troth
To pastoral dales, thin-set with modest farms,
May learn, if judgment strengthen with his growth,
That, not for Fancy only, pomp hath charms;
And, strenuous to protect from lawless harms
The extremes of favoured life, may honour both.

THE PRIMROSE OF THE ROCK

1831. 1835

Written at Rydal Mount. The Rock stands on the right hand a little way leading up the middle road from Rydal to Grasmere. We have been in the habit of calling it the glow-worm rock from the number of glow-worms we have often seen hanging on it as described. The tuft of primrose has, I fear, been washed away by the heavy rains.

A ROCK there is whose homely front
The passing traveller slights;
Yet there the glow-worms hang their lamps,
Like stars, at various heights;
And one coy Primrose to that Rock
The vernal breeze invites.

What hideous warfare hath been waged,
What kingdoms overthrown,
Since first I spied that Primrose-tuft
And marked it for my own;   10
A lasting link in Nature's chain
From highest heaven let down!

The flowers, still faithful to the stems,
Their fellowship renew;
The stems are faithful to the root,
That worketh out of view;
And to the rock the root adheres
In every fibre true.

Close clings to earth the living rock,
Though threatening still to fall;   20
The earth is constant to her sphere;
And God upholds them all:
So blooms this lonely Plant, nor dreads
Her annual funeral.

.   .   .   .

Here closed the meditative strain;
But air breathed soft that day,
The hoary mountain-heights were cheered,
The sunny vale looked gay;
And to the Primrose of the Rock
I gave this after-lay.   30

I sang — Let myriads of bright flowers,
Like Thee, in field and grove
Revive unenvied; — mightier far,
Than tremblings that reprove
Our vernal tendencies to hope,
Is God's redeeming love;

That love which changed — for wan disease,
For sorrow that had bent
O'er hopeless dust, for withered age —
Their moral element,   40
And turned the thistles of a curse
To types beneficent.

Sin-blighted though we are, we too,
  The reasoning Sons of Men,
From one oblivious winter called
  Shall rise, and breathe again;
And in eternal summer lose
  Our threescore years and ten.

To humbleness of heart descends
  This prescience from on high,   50
The faith that elevates the just,
  Before and when they die;
And makes each soul a separate heaven,
  A court for Deity.

YARROW REVISITED, AND OTHER POEMS

COMPOSED (TWO EXCEPTED) DURING A TOUR IN SCOTLAND AND ON THE ENGLISH BORDER, IN THE AUTUMN OF 1831

In the autumn of 1831, my daughter and I set off from Rydal to visit Sir Walter Scott before his departure for Italy. This journey had been delayed by an inflammation in my eyes till we found that the time appointed for his leaving home would be too near for him to receive us without considerable inconvenience. Nevertheless we proceeded and reached Abbotsford on Monday. I was then scarcely able to lift up my eyes to the light. How sadly changed did I find him from the man I had seen so healthy, gay, and hopeful, a few years before, when he said at the inn at Paterdale, in my presence, his daughter Anne also being there, with Mr. Lockhart, my own wife and daughter, and Mr. Quillinan, — "I mean to live till I am *eighty*, and shall write as long as I live." But to return to Abbotsford, the inmates and guests we found there were Sir Walter, Major Scott, Anne Scott, and Mr. and Mrs. Lockhart, Mr. Liddell, his Lady and Brother, and Mr. Allan the painter, and Mr. Laidlow, a very old friend of Sir Walter's. One of Burns's sons, an officer in the Indian service, had left the house a day or two before, and had kindly expressed his regret that he could not await my arrival, a regret that I may truly say was mutual. In the evening, Mr. and Mrs. Liddell sang, and Mrs. Lockhart chanted old ballads to her harp; and Mr. Allan, hanging over the back of a chair, told and acted odd stories in a humorous way. With this exhibition and his daughter's singing, Sir Walter was much amused, as indeed were we all as far as circumstances would allow. But what is most worthy of mention is the admirable demeanour of Major Scott during the following evening, when the Liddells were gone and only ourselves and Mr. Allan were present. He had much to suffer from the sight of his father's infirmities and from the great change that was about to take place at the residence he had built, and where he had long lived in so much prosperity and happiness. But what struck me most was the patient kindness with which he supported himself under the many fretful expressions that his sister Anne addressed to him or uttered in his hearing. She, poor thing, as mistress of that house, had been subject, after her mother's death, to a heavier load of care and responsibility and greater sacrifices of time than one of such a constitution of body and mind was able to bear. Of this, Dora and I were made so sensible, that, as soon as we had crossed the Tweed on our departure, we gave vent at the same moment to our apprehensions that her brain would fail and she would go out of her mind, or that she would sink under the trials she had passed and those which awaited her. On Tuesday morning Sir Walter Scott accompanied us and most of the party to Newark Castle on the Yarrow. When we alighted from the carriages he walked pretty stoutly, and had great pleasure in revisiting those his favourite haunts. Of that excursion the verses "Yarrow revisited" are a memorial. Notwithstanding the romance that pervades Sir Walter's works and attaches to many of his habits, there is too much pressure of fact for these verses to harmonise as much as I could wish with other poems. On our return in the afternoon we had to cross the Tweed directly opposite Abbotsford. The wheels of our carriage grated upon the pebbles in the bed of the stream, that there flows somewhat rapidly; a rich but sad light of rather a purple than a golden hue was spread over the Eildon hills at that moment; and, thinking it probable that it might be the last time Sir Walter would cross the stream, I was not a little moved, and expressed some of my feelings in the sonnet beginning — "A trouble, not of clouds, or weeping rain." At noon on Thursday we left Abbotsford, and in the morning of that day Sir Walter and I had a serious conversation *tête-à-tête*, when he spoke with gratitude of the happy life which upon the whole he had led. He had written in my daughter's Album, before he came into the breakfast-room that morning, a few stanzas addressed to her, and, while putting the book into her hand, in his own study, standing by his desk, he said to her in my presence — "I should not have done anything of this kind but for your father's sake: they are probably the last verses I shall ever write." They show how much his mind was impaired, not by the strain of thought but by the execution, some of the lines being imperfect, and one stanza wanting corresponding rhymes : one letter, the initial S, had been omitted in the spelling of his own name. In this interview also it was that, upon my expressing a hope of his health being benefited by the climate of the country to which he was going, and by the interest he would take in the classic remembrances of Italy, he made use of the quotation from " Yarrow unvisited " as recorded by me in the " Musings at Aquapendente " six years after-wards. Mr. Lockhart has mentioned in his Life of him what I heard from several quarters while abroad, both at Rome and elsewhere, that little seemed to interest him but what he could collect or heard of the fugitive Stuarts and their adherents who had followed them into exile. Both the " Yarrow revisited " and the " Sonnet " were sent him before his departure from England. Some further particulars of the conversations which occurred during this visit I should have set down had they not been already accurately recorded by Mr. Lockhart. I first became acquainted with this great and amiable man — Sir Walter Scott — in the year 1803, when my sister and I, making a tour in Scotland, were hospitably received by him in Lasswade upon the banks of the Esk, where he was then living. We saw a good deal of him in the course of the following week : the particulars are given in my sister's Journal of that tour.

TO

SAMUEL ROGERS, Esq.,

AS A TESTIMONY OF FRIENDSHIP,
AND ACKNOWLEDGMENT
OF INTELLECTUAL OBLIGATIONS,
THESE MEMORIALS ARE AFFECTIONATELY INSCRIBED

RYDAL MOUNT, *Dec.* 11, 1834.

I

1831. 1835

The following Stanzas are a memorial of a day passed with Sir Walter Scott and other Friends visiting the Banks of the Yarrow under his guidance, immediately before his departure from Abbotsford, for Naples.

The title " Yarrow Revisited " will stand in no need of explanation for Readers acquainted with the Author's previous poems suggested by that celebrated Stream.

THE gallant Youth, who may have gained,
  Or seeks, a " winsome Marrow,"
Was but an Infant in the lap
  When first I looked on Yarrow;
Once more, by Newark's Castle-gate
  Long left without a warder,
I stood, looked, listened, and with Thee,
  Great Minstrel of the Border !

Grave thoughts ruled wide on that sweet day,
  Their dignity installing   10
In gentle bosoms, while sere leaves
  Were on the bough, or falling;
But breezes played, and sunshine gleamed —
  The forest to embolden;
Reddened the fiery hues, and shot
  Transparence through the golden.

For busy thoughts the Stream flowed on
  In foamy agitation;

And slept in many a crystal pool
  For quiet contemplation: 20
No public and no private care
  The freeborn mind enthralling,
We made a day of happy hours,
  Our happy days recalling.

Brisk Youth appeared, the Morn of youth,
  With freaks of graceful folly, —
Life's temperate Noon, her sober Eve,
  Her Night not melancholy;
Past, present, future, all appeared
  In harmony united,   30
Like guests that meet, and some from
    far,
  By cordial love invited.

And if, as Yarrow, through the woods
  And down the meadow ranging,
Did meet us with unaltered face,
  Though we were changed and changing;
If, *then*, some natural shadows spread
  Our inward prospect over,
The soul's deep valley was not slow
  Its brightness to recover.   40

Eternal blessings on the Muse,
  And her divine employment !
The blameless Muse, who trains her Sons
  For hope and calm enjoyment;
Albeit sickness, lingering yet,
  Has o'er their pillow brooded;

And Care waylays their steps — a Sprite
  Not easily eluded.

For thee, O SCOTT ! compelled to change
  Green Eildon-hill and Cheviot   50
For warm Vesuvio's vine-clad slopes;
  And leave thy Tweed and Tiviot
For mild Sorento's breezy waves;
  May classic Fancy, linking
With native Fancy her fresh aid,
  Preserve thy heart from sinking !

Oh ! while they minister to thee,
  Each vying with the other,
May Health return to mellow Age
  With Strength, her venturous brother; 60
And Tiber, and each brook and rill
  Renowned in song and story,
With unimagined beauty shine,
  Nor lose one ray of glory !

For Thou, upon a hundred streams,
  By tales of love and sorrow,
Of faithful love, undaunted truth,
  Hast shed the power of Yarrow;
And streams unknown, hills yet unseen,
  Wherever they invite Thee,   70
At parent Nature's grateful call,
  With gladness must requite Thee.

A gracious welcome shall be thine,
  Such looks of love and honour
As thy own Yarrow gave to me
  When first I gazed upon her;
Beheld what I had feared to see,
  Unwilling to surrender
Dreams treasured up from early days,
  The holy and the tender.   80

And what, for this frail world, were all
  That mortals do or suffer,
Did no responsive harp, no pen,
  Memorial tribute offer ?
Yea, what were mighty Nature's self ?
  Her features, could they win us,
Unhelped by the poetic voice
  That hourly speaks within us ?

Nor deem that localised Romance
  Plays false with our affections;   90
Unsanctifies our tears — made sport
  For fanciful dejections:
Ah, no ! the visions of the past
  Sustain the heart in feeling
Life as she is — our changeful Life,
  With friends and kindred dealing.

Bear witness, Ye, whose thoughts that day
  In Yarrow's groves were centred;
Who through the silent portal arch
  Of mouldering Newark entered;   100
And clomb the winding stair that once
  Too timidly was mounted
By the " last Minstrel," (not the last !)
  Ere he his Tale recounted.

Flow on for ever, Yarrow Stream !
  Fulfil thy pensive duty,
Well pleased that future Bards should chant
  For simple hearts thy beauty,
To dream-light dear while yet unseen,
  Dear to the common sunshine,   110
And dearer still, as now I feel,
  To memory's shadowy moonshine !

II

ON THE DEPARTURE OF SIR
  WALTER SCOTT FROM AB-
  BOTSFORD, FOR NAPLES

1831. 1833

A TROUBLE, not of clouds, or weeping rain,
Nor of the setting sun's pathetic light
Engendered, hangs o'er Eildon's triple
      height:
Spirits of Power, assembled there, complain
For kindred Power departing from their
      sight;
While Tweed, best pleased in chanting a
      blithe strain,
Saddens his voice again, and yet again.
Lift up your hearts, ye Mourners ! for the
      might
Of the whole world's good wishes with him
      goes;
Blessings and prayers, in nobler retinue
Than sceptred king or laurelled conqueror
      knows
Follow this wondrous Potentate. Be true,
Ye winds of ocean, and the midland sea,
Wafting your Charge to soft Parthenope !

III

A PLACE OF BURIAL IN THE
  SOUTH OF SCOTLAND

1831. 1835

Similar places for burial are not unfrequent
in Scotland. The one that suggested this Son-
net lies on the banks of a small stream called

the Wauchope that flows into the Esk near Langholme. Mickle, who, as it appears from his poem on Sir Martin, was not without genuine poetic feelings, was born and passed his boyhood in this neighbourhood, under his father, who was a minister of the Scotch Kirk. The Esk, both above and below Langholme, flows through a beautiful country, and the two streams of the Wauchope and the Ewes, which join it near that place, are such as a pastoral poet would delight in.

PART fenced by man, part by a rugged steep
That curbs a foaming brook, a Grave-yard lies;
The hare's best couching-place for fearless sleep;
Which moonlit elves, far seen by credulous eyes,
Enter in dance. Of church, or sabbath ties,
No vestige now remains; yet thither creep
Bereft Ones, and in lowly anguish weep
Their prayers out to the wind and naked skies.
Proud tomb is none; but rudely-sculptured knights,
By humble choice of plain old times, are seen
Level with earth, among the hillocks green:
Union not sad, when sunny daybreak smites
The spangled turf, and neighbouring thickets ring
With *jubilate* from the choirs of spring !

IV

ON THE SIGHT OF A MANSE IN THE SOUTH OF SCOTLAND

1833. 1835

The manses in Scotland and tne gardens and grounds about them have seldom that attractive appearance which is common about our English parsonages, even when the clergyman's income falls below the average of the Scotch minister's. This is not merely owing to the one country being poor in comparison with the other, but arises rather out of the equality of their benefices, so that no one has enough to spare for decorations that might serve as an example for others ; whereas, with us, the taste of the richer incumbent extends its influence more or less to the poorest. After all, in these observations the surface only of the matter is

touched. I once heard a conversation in which the Roman Catholic Religion was decried on account of its abuses. " You cannot deny, however," said a lady of the party, repeating an expression used by Charles II., " that it is the religion of a gentleman." It may be left to the Scotch themselves to determine how far this observation applies to their Kirk, while it cannot be denied, if it is wanting in that characteristic quality, the aspect of common life, so far as concerns its beauty, must suffer. Sincere christian piety may be thought not to stand in need of refinement or studied ornament ; but assuredly it is ever ready to adopt them, when they fall within its notice, as means allow ; and this observation applies not only to manners, but to everything a christian (truly so in spirit) cultivates and gathers round him, however humble his social condition.

SAY, ye far-travelled clouds, far-seeing hills —
Among the happiest-looking homes of men
Scattered all Britain over, through deep glen,
On airy upland, and by forest rills,
And o'er wide plains cheered by the lark that trills
His sky-born warblings — does aught meet your ken
More fit to animate the Poet's pen,
Aught that more surely by its aspect fills
Pure minds with sinless envy, than the Abode
Of the good Priest: who, faithful through all hours
To his high charge, and truly serving God,
Has yet a heart and hand for trees and flowers,
Enjoys the walks his predecessors trod,
Nor covets lineal rights in lands and towers.

V

COMPOSED IN ROSLIN CHAPEL DURING A STORM

1831. 1835

We were detained by incessant rain and storm at the small inn near Roslin Chapel, and I passed a great part of the day pacing to and fro in this beautiful structure, which, though not used for public service, is not allowed to go to ruin. Here this Sonnet was composed, and I shall be fully satisfied if it has at all done justice to the feeling which the place and the storm raging without inspired. I was as a prisoner : a painter delineating the interior of the chapel and its minute features under such circumstances would have, no doubt, found his time agreeably shortened. But the movements of the mind must be more free while dealing with words than with lines and colours; such at least was then and has been on many other occasions my belief, and, as it is allotted to few to follow both arts with success, I am grateful to my own calling for this and a thousand other recommendations which are denied to that of the painter.

THE wind is now thy organist; — a clank
(We know not whence) ministers for a bell
To mark some change of service. As the swell
Of music reached its height, and even when sank
The notes, in prelude, ROSLIN! to a blank
Of silence, how it thrilled thy sumptuous roof,
Pillars, and arches, — not in vain time-proof,
Though Christian rites be wanting! From what bank
Came those live herbs? by what hand were they sown
Where dew falls not, where rain-drops seem unknown?
Yet in the Temple they a friendly niche
Share with their sculptured fellows, that, green-grown,
Copy their beauty more and more, and preach,
Though mute, of all things blending into one.

VI

THE TROSACHS

1831. 1835

As recorded in my sister's Journal, I had first seen the Trosachs in her and Coleridge's company. The sentiment that runs through this Sonnet was natural to the season in which I again saw this beautiful spot; but this and some other sonnets that follow were coloured by the remembrance of my recent visit to Sir Walter Scott, and the melancholy errand on which he was going.

THERE's not a nook within this solemn Pass,
But were an apt confessional for One
Taught by his summer spent, his autumn gone,
That Life is but a tale of morning grass
Withered at eve. From scenes of art which chase
That thought away, turn, and with watchful eyes
Feed it 'mid Nature's old felicities,
Rocks, rivers, and smooth lakes more clear than glass
Untouched, unbreathed upon. Thrice happy quest,
If from a golden perch of aspen spray
(October's workmanship to rival May)
The pensive warbler of the ruddy breast
That moral sweeten by a heaven-taught lay,
Lulling the year, with all its cares, to rest!

VII

1831. 1835

THE pibroch's note, discountenanced or mute;
The Roman kilt, degraded to a toy
Of quaint apparel for a half-spoilt boy;
The target mouldering like ungathered fruit;
The smoking steam-boat eager in pursuit,
As eagerly pursued; the umbrella spread
To weather-fend the Celtic herdsman's head —
All speak of manners withering to the root,
And of old honours, too, and passions high:
Then may we ask, though pleased that thought should range
Among the conquests of civility,
Survives imagination — to the change
Superior? Help to virtue does she give?
If not, O Mortals, better cease to live!

VIII

COMPOSED AFTER READING A NEWSPAPER OF THE DAY

1831. 1835

"PEOPLE! your chains are severing link by link;
Soon shall the Rich be levelled down — the Poor
Meet them half way." Vain boast! for These, the more
They thus would rise, must low and lower sink

Till, by repentance stung, they fear to
    think;
While all lie prostrate, save the tyrant
    few
Bent in quick turns each other to undo,
And mix the poison, they themselves must
    drink.
Mistrust thyself, vain Country! cease to
    cry,
"Knowledge will save me from the threat-
    ened woe."
For, if than other rash ones more thou know,
Yet on presumptuous wing as far would
    fly
Above thy knowledge as they dared to
    go,
Thou wilt provoke a heavier penalty.

IX

COMPOSED IN THE GLEN OF LOCH ETIVE

1831. 1835

"That make the Patriot-spirit." It was mor-
tifying to have frequent occasions to observe the
bitter hatred of the lower orders of the High-
landers to their superiors; love of country
seemed to have passed into its opposite. Emi-
gration was the only relief looked to with
hope.

"THIS Land of Rainbows spanning glens
    whose walls,
Rock-built, are hung with rainbow-coloured
    mists —
Of far-stretched Meres whose salt flood
    never rests —
Of tuneful Caves and playful Waterfalls —
Of Mountains varying momently their
    crests —
Proud be this Land! whose poorest huts
    are halls
Where Fancy entertains becoming guests;
While native song the heroic Past re-
    calls."
Thus, in the net of her own wishes caught,
The Muse exclaimed; but Story now must
    hide
Her trophies, Fancy crouch; the course of
    pride
Has been diverted, other lessons taught,
That make the Patriot-spirit bow her head
Where the all-conquering Roman feared to
    tread.

X

EAGLES

COMPOSED AT DUNOLLIE CASTLE IN THE BAY OF OBAN

1831. 1835

"The last I saw was on the wing," off the
promontory of Fairhead, county of Antrim. I
mention this because, though my tour in Ire-
land with Mr. Marshall and his son was made
many years ago, this allusion to the eagle is the
only image supplied by it to the poetry I have
since written. We travelled through that coun-
try in October, and to the shortness of the days
and the speed with which we travelled (in a
carriage and four) may be ascribed this want
of notices, in my verse, of a country so interest-
ing. The deficiency I am somewhat ashamed
of, and it is the more remarkable as contrasted
with my Scotch and Continental tours, of which
are to be found in this volume so many memo-
rials.

DISHONOURED Rock and Ruin! that, by
    law
Tyrannic, keep the Bird of Jove embarred
Like a lone criminal whose life is spared.
Vexed is he, and screams loud. The last
    I saw
Was on the wing; stooping, he struck with
    awe
Man, bird, and beast; then, with a consort
    paired,
From a bold headland, their loved aery's
    guard,
Flew high above Atlantic waves, to draw
Light from the fountain of the setting sun.
Such was this Prisoner once; and, when his
    plumes
The sea-blast ruffles as the storm comes
    on,
Then, for a moment, he, in spirit, resumes
His rank 'mong freeborn creatures that live
    free,
His power, his beauty, and his majesty.

XI

IN THE SOUND OF MULL

1831. 1835

Touring late in the season in Scotland is an
uncertain speculation. We were detained a
week by rain at Bunaw on Loch Etive in a vain

hope that the weather would clear up and allow me to show my daughter the beauties of Glencoe. Two days we were at the isle of Mull, on a visit to Major Campbell ; but it rained incessantly, and we were obliged to give up our intention of going to Staffa. The rain pursued us to Tyndrum, where the Twelfth Sonnet was composed in a storm.

TRADITION, be thou mute ! Oblivion, throw
Thy veil in mercy o'er the records, hung
Round strath and mountain, stamped by
    the ancient tongue
On rock and ruin darkening as we go, —
Spots where a word, ghostlike, survives to
    show
What crimes from hate, or desperate love,
    have sprung;
From honour misconceived, or fancied
    wrong,
What feuds, not quenched but fed by mutual woe.
Yet, though a wild vindictive Race, untamed
By civil arts and labours of the pen,
Could gentleness be scorned by those fierce
    Men,
Who, to spread wide the reverence they
    claimed
For patriarchal occupations, named
Yon towering Peaks, " Shepherds of Etive
    Glen ? "

XII

SUGGESTED AT TYNDRUM IN A STORM

1831. 1835

ENOUGH of garlands, of the Arcadian crook,
And all that Greece and Italy have sung
Of Swains reposing myrtle groves among !
Ours couch on naked rocks, — will cross a
    brook
Swoln with chill rains, nor ever cast a look
This way or that, or give it even a thought
More than by smoothest pathway may be
    brought
Into a vacant mind. Can written book
Teach what *they* learn ? Up, hardy Mountaineer !
And guide the Bard, ambitious to be One
Of Nature's privy council, as thou art,
On cloud-sequestered heights, that see and
    hear

To what dread Powers He delegates his part
On earth, who works in the heaven of
    heavens, alone.

XIII

THE EARL OF BREADALBANE'S RUINED MANSION AND FAMILY BURIAL-PLACE, NEAR KILLIN

1831. 1835

WELL sang the Bard who called the grave,
    in strains
Thoughtful and sad, the " narrow house."
    No style
Of fond sepulchral flattery can beguile
Grief of her sting; nor cheat, where he
    detains
The sleeping dust, stern Death. How
    reconcile
With truth, or with each other, decked remains
Of a once warm Abode, and that *new* Pile,
For the departed, built with curious pains
And mausolean pomp ? Yet here they stand
Together, — 'mid trim walks and artful
    bowers,
To be looked down upon by ancient hills,
That, for the living and the dead, demand
And prompt a harmony of genuine powers;
Concord that elevates the mind, and stills.

XIV

"REST AND BE THANKFUL!"

AT THE HEAD OF GLENCROE

1831. 1835

DOUBLING and doubling with laborious walk,
Who, that has gained at length the wished-
    for Height,
This brief, this simple wayside Call can slight,
And rests not thankful ? Whether cheered
    by talk
With some loved friend, or by the unseen
    hawk
Whistling to clouds and sky-born streams
    that shine,
At the sun's outbreak, as with light divine,
Ere they descend to nourish root and stalk
Of valley flowers. Nor, while the limbs
    repose,
Will we forget that, as the fowl can keep

Absolute stillness, poised aloft in air,
And fishes front, unmoved, the torrent's
    sweep, —
So may the Soul, through powers that
    Faith bestows,
Win rest, and ease, and peace, with bliss
    that Angels share.

XV

HIGHLAND HUT

1831. 1835

SEE what gay wild flowers deck this earth-
    built Cot,
Whose smoke, forth-issuing whence and
    how it may,
Shines in the greeting of the sun's first ray
Like wreaths of vapour without stain or blot.
The limpid mountain rill avoids it not;
And why shouldst thou? — If rightly trained
    and bred,
Humanity is humble, finds no spot
Which her Heaven-guided feet refuse to
    tread.
The walls are cracked, sunk is the flowery
    roof,
Undressed the pathway leading to the door;
But love, as Nature loves, the lonely Poor;
Search, for their worth, some gentle heart
    wrong-proof,
Meek, patient, kind, and, were its trials
    fewer,
Belike less happy. — Stand no more aloof !

XVI

THE BROWNIE

1831. 1835

Upon a small island, not far from the head
of Loch Lomond, are some remains of an an-
cient building, which was for several years the
abode of a solitary Individual, one of the last
survivors of the clan of Macfarlane, once power-
ful in that neighbourhood. Passing along the
shore opposite this island in the year 1814,
the Author learned these particulars, and that
this person then living there had acquired the
appellation of "The Brownie." See "The
Brownie's Cell," p. 529, to which the following
is a sequel.

"How disappeared he?" Ask the newt
    and toad;
Ask of his fellow-men, and they will tell

How he was found, cold as an icicle,
Under an arch of that forlorn abode;
Where he, unpropped, and by the gathering
    flood
Of years hemmed round, had dwelt, pre-
    pared to try
Privation's worst extremities, and die
With no one near save the omnipresent God.
Verily so to live was an awful choice —
A choice that wears the aspect of a doom;
But in the mould of mercy all is cast
For Souls familiar with the eternal Voice;
And this forgotten Taper to the last
Drove from itself, we trust, all frightful
    gloom.

XVII

TO THE PLANET VENUS, AN EVENING STAR

COMPOSED AT LOCH LOMOND

1831. 1835

THOUGH joy attend Thee orient at the birth
Of dawn, it cheers the lofty spirit most
To watch thy course when Day-light, fled
    from earth,
In the grey sky hath left his lingering Ghost,
Perplexed as if between a splendour lost
And splendour slowly mustering. Since
    the Sun,
The absolute, the world-absorbing One,
Relinquished half his empire to the host
Emboldened by thy guidance, holy Star,
Holy as princely — who that looks on thee,
Touching, as now, in thy humility
The mountain borders of this seat of care,
Can question that thy countenance is bright,
Celestial Power, as much with love as
    light ?

XVIII

BOTHWELL CASTLE

PASSED UNSEEN, ON ACCOUNT OF STORMY WEATHER

1831. 1835

In my Sister's Journal is an account of Both-
well Castle as it appeared to us at that time.

IMMURED in Bothwell's towers, at times the
    Brave
(So beautiful is Clyde) forgot to mourn

The liberty they lost at Bannockburn.
Once on those steeps *I* roamed at large,
　　and have
In mind the landscape, as if still in sight;
The river glides, the woods before me wave;
Then why repine that now in vain I crave
Needless renewal of an old delight ?
Better to thank a dear and long-past day
For joy its sunny hours were free to give
Than blame the present, that our wish hath
　　crost.
Memory, like sleep, hath powers which
　　dreams obey,
Dreams, vivid dreams, that are not fugitive:
How little that she cherishes is lost !

XIX

PICTURE OF DANIEL IN THE LIONS' DEN, AT HAMILTON PALACE

1831. 1835

AMID a fertile region green with wood
And fresh with rivers, well did it become
The ducal Owner, in his palace-home
To naturalise this tawny Lion brood;
Children of Art, that claim strange brother-
　　hood
(Couched in their den) with those that
　　roam at large
Over the burning wilderness, and charge
The wind with terror while they roar for
　　food.
Satiate are *these;* and stilled to eye and ear;
Hence, while we gaze, a more enduring
　　fear !
Yet is the Prophet calm, nor would the cave
Daunt him — if his Companions, now be-
　　drowsed,
Outstretched and listless, were by hunger
　　roused,
Man placed him here, and God, he knows,
　　can save.

XX

THE AVON

A FEEDER OF THE ANNAN

1831. 1835

" Yet is it one that other rivulets bear."
There is the Shakspeare Avon. the Bristol
Avon; the one that flows by Salisbury, and a
small river in Wales, I believe, bear the name;
Avon being in the ancient tongue the general
name for river.

AVON — a precious, an immortal name !
Yet is it one that other rivulets bear
Like this unheard-of, and their channels
　　wear
Like this contented, though unknown to
　　Fame:
For great and sacred is the modest claim
Of Streams to Nature's love, where'er they
　　flow;
And ne'er did Genius slight them, as they
　　go,
Tree, flower, and green herb, feeding with-
　　out blame.
But Praise can waste her voice on work of
　　tears,
Anguish, and death: full oft where innocent
　　blood
Has mixed its current with the limpid
　　flood,
Her heaven-offending trophies Glory rears:
Never for like distinction may the good
Shrink from *thy* name, pure Rill, with un-
　　pleased ears.

XXI

SUGGESTED BY A VIEW FROM AN EMINENCE IN INGLEWOOD FOREST

1831. 1835

The extensive forest of Inglewood has been enclosed within my memory. I was well ac-quainted with it in its ancient state. The Hart's-horn tree mentioned in the next Sonnet was one of its remarkable objects, as well as another tree that grew upon an eminence not far from Penrith: it was single and conspicuous; and being of a round shape, though it was uni-versally known to be a Sycamore, it was always called the " *Round Thorn,*" so difficult is it to chain fancy down to fact.

THE forest huge of ancient Caledon
Is but a name, no more is Inglewood,
That swept from hill to hill, from flood to
　　flood:
On her last thorn the nightly moon has
　　shone;
Yet still, though unappropriate Wild be
　　none,

Fair parks spread wide where Adam Bell
    might deign
With Clym o' the Clough, were they alive
    again,
To kill for merry feast their venison.
Nor wants the holy Abbot's gliding Shade
His church with monumental wreck be-
    strown;
The feudal Warrior-chief, a Ghost unlaid,
Hath still his castle, though a skeleton,
That he may watch by night, and lessons con
Of power that perishes, and rights that
    fade.

XXII

HART'S-HORN TREE, NEAR PEN-RITH

1831. 1835

HERE stood an Oak, that long had borne
    affixed
To his huge trunk, or, with more subtle art,
Among its withering topmost branches
    mixed,
The palmy antlers of a hunted Hart,
Whom the Dog Hercules pursued — his
    part
Each desperately sustaining, till at last
Both sank and died, the life-veins of the
    chased
And chaser bursting here with one dire
    smart.
Mutual the victory, mutual the defeat !
High was the trophy hung with pitiless
    pride;
Say, rather, with that generous sympathy
That wants not, even in rudest breasts, a
    seat;
And, for this feeling's sake, let no one
    chide
Verse that would guard thy memory,
    HART'S-HORN TREE !

XXIII

FANCY AND TRADITION

1833. 1835

THE Lovers took within this ancient grove
Their last embrace; beside those crystal
    springs
The Hermit saw the Angel spread his
    wings

For instant flight; the Sage in yon alcove
Sate musing; on that hill the Bard would
    rove,
Not mute, where now the linnet only sings:
Thus everywhere to truth Tradition clings,
Or Fancy localises Powers we love.
Were only History licensed to take note
Of things gone by, her meagre monu-
    ments
Would ill suffice for persons and events:
There is an ampler page for man to quote,
A readier book of manifold contents,
Studied alike in palace and in cot.

XXIV

COUNTESS'S PILLAR

1831. 1835

Suggested by the recollection of Julian's
Bower and other traditions connected with this
ancient forest.

On the roadside between Penrith and
Appleby, there stands a pillar with the follow-
ing inscription : —

"This Pillar was erected, in the year 1656, by
Anne Countess Dowager of Pembroke, &c., for
a memorial of her last parting with her pious
mother, Margaret Countess Dowager of Cum-
berland, on the 2d of April, 1616; in memory
whereof she hath left an annuity of 4l. to be dis-
tributed to the poor of the parish of Brougham,
every 2d day of April for ever, upon the stone
table placed hard by. Laus Deo!"

WHILE the Poor gather round, till the end
    of time
May this bright flower of Charity display
Its bloom, unfolding at the appointed day;
Flower than the loveliest of the vernal
    prime
Lovelier — transplanted from heaven's
    purest clime !
"Charity never faileth:" on that creed,
More than on written testament or deed,
The pious Lady built with hope sublime.
Alms on this stone to be dealt out, *for ever !*
"LAUS DEO." Many a Stranger passing by
Has with that Parting mixed a filial sigh,
Blest its humane Memorial's fond en-
    deavour;
And, fastening on those lines an eye tear-
    glazed,
Has ended, though no Clerk, with "God
    be praised !"

XXV
ROMAN ANTIQUITIES

FROM THE ROMAN STATION AT OLD PENRITH

1831. 1835

How profitless the relics that we cull,
Troubling the last holds of ambitious Rome,
Unless they chasten fancies that presume
Too high, or idle agitations lull !
Of the world's flatteries if the brain be full,
To have no seat for thought were better doom,
Like this old helmet, or the eyeless skull
Of him who gloried in its nodding plume.
Heaven out of view, our wishes what are they ?
Our fond regrets tenacious in their grasp ?
The Sage's theory ? the Poet's lay ?
Mere Fibulæ without a robe to clasp;
Obsolete lamps, whose light no time recalls;
Urns without ashes, tearless lacrymals !

XXVI
APOLOGY FOR THE FOREGOING POEMS

1831. 1835

No more: the end is sudden and abrupt,
Abrupt — as without preconceived design
Was the beginning; yet the several Lays
Have moved in order, to each other bound
By a continuous and acknowledged tie
Though unapparent — like those Shapes distinct
That yet survive ensculptured on the walls
Of palaces, or temples, 'mid the wreck
Of famed Persepolis; each following each,
As might beseem a stately embassy,   10
In set array; these bearing in their hands
Ensign of civil power, weapon of war,
Or gift to be presented at the throne
Of the Great King; and others, as they go
In priestly vest, with holy offerings charged,
Or leading victims drest for sacrifice.
Nor will the Power we serve, that sacred Power,
The Spirit of humanity, disdain
A ministration humble but sincere,   19

That from a threshold loved by every Muse
Its impulse took — that sorrow-stricken door,
Whence, as a current from its fountain-head,
Our thoughts have issued, and our feelings flowed,
Receiving, willingly or not, fresh strength
From kindred sources; while around us sighed
(Life's three first seasons having passed away)
Leaf-scattering winds; and hoar-frost sprinklings fell
(Foretaste of winter) on the moorland heights;
And every day brought with it tidings new
Of rash change, ominous for the public weal.   30
Hence, if dejection has too oft encroached
Upon that sweet and tender melancholy
Which may itself be cherished and caressed
More than enough; a fault so natural
(Even with the young, the hopeful, or the gay)
For prompt forgiveness will not sue in vain.

XXVII
THE HIGHLAND BROACH

1831. 1835

On ascending a hill that leads from Loch Awe towards Inverary, I fell into conversation with a woman of the humbler class who wore one of those Highland Broaches. I talked with her about it; and upon parting with her, when I said with a kindness I truly felt — " May that Broach continue in your family through many generations to come, as you have already possessed it " — she thanked me most becomingly, and seemed not a little moved.

The exact resemblance which the old Broach (still in use, though rarely met with, among the Highlanders) bears to the Roman Fibula must strike every one, and concurs, with the plaid and kilt, to recall to mind the communication which the ancient Romans had with this remote country.

If to Tradition faith be due,
And echoes from old verse speak true,
Ere the meek Saint, Columba, bore
Glad tidings to Iona's shore,
No common light of nature blessed
The mountain region of the west,

A land where gentle manners ruled
O'er men in dauntless virtues schooled,
That raised, for centuries, a bar
Impervious to the tide of war:　10
Yet peaceful Arts did entrance gain
Where haughty Force had striven in vain;
And, 'mid the works of skilful hands,
By wanderers brought from foreign lands
And various climes, was not unknown
The clasp that fixed the Roman Gown;
The Fibula, whose shape, I ween,
Still in the Highland Broach is seen,
The silver Broach of massy frame,
Worn at the breast of some grave Dame　20
On road or path, or at the door
Of fern-thatched hut on heathy moor:
But delicate of yore its mould,
And the material finest gold;
As might beseem the fairest Fair,
Whether she graced a royal chair,
Or shed, within a vaulted hall,
No fancied lustre on the wall
Where shields of mighty heroes hung,
While Fingal heard what Ossian sung.　30
　The heroic Age expired — it slept
Deep in its tomb: — the bramble crept
O'er Fingal's hearth; the grassy sod
Grew on the floors his sons had trod:
Malvina ! where art thou ?　Their state
The noblest-born must abdicate;
The fairest, while with fire and sword
Come Spoilers — horde impelling horde,
Must walk the sorrowing mountains, drest
By ruder hands in homelier vest.　40
Yet still the female bosom lent,
And loved to borrow, ornament;
Still was its inner world a place
Reached by the dews of heavenly grace;
Still pity to this last retreat
Clove fondly; to his favourite seat
Love wound his way by soft approach,
Beneath a massier Highland Broach.

　When alternations came of rage
Yet fiercer, in a darker age;　50
And feuds, where, clan encountering clan,
The weaker perished to a man;
For maid and mother, when despair
Might else have triumphed, baffling prayer,
One small possession lacked not power,
Provided in a calmer hour,
To meet such need as might befall —
Roof, raiment, bread, or burial:
For woman, even of tears bereft,
The hidden silver Broach was left.　60
　As generations come and go
Their arts, their customs, ebb and flow;
Fate, fortune, sweep strong powers away,
And feeble, of themselves, decay;
What poor abodes the heir-loom hide,
In which the castle once took pride !
Tokens, once kept as boasted wealth,
If saved at all, are saved by stealth.
Lo ! ships, from seas by nature barred,
Mount along ways by man prepared;　70
And in far-stretching vales, whose streams
Seek other seas, their canvas gleams.
Lo ! busy towns spring up, on coasts
Thronged yesterday by airy ghosts;
Soon, like a lingering star forlorn
Among the novelties of morn,
While young delights on old encroach,
Will vanish the last Highland Broach.
　But when, from out their viewless bed,
Like vapours, years have rolled and spread;
And this poor verse, and worthier lays,　81
Shall yield no light of love or praise;
Then, by the spade, or cleaving plough,
Or torrent from the mountain's brow,
Or whirlwind, reckless what his might
Entombs, or forces into light;
Blind Chance, a volunteer ally,
That oft befriends Antiquity,
And clears Oblivion from reproach,
May render back the Highland Broach.　90

DEVOTIONAL INCITEMENTS

1832. 1835

Written at Rydal Mount.

" Not to the earth confined,
Ascend to heaven."

WHERE will they stop, those breathing Powers,
The Spirits of the new-born flowers ?

They wander with the breeze, they wind
Where'er the streams a passage find;
Up from their native ground they rise
In mute aërial harmonies;
From humble violet — modest thyme —
Exhaled, the essential odours climb,
As if no space below the sky
Their subtle flight could satisfy:　10
Heaven will not tax our thoughts with pride
If like ambition be *their* guide.

Roused by this kindliest of May-show-
ers,
The spirit-quickener of the flowers,
That with moist virtue softly cleaves
The buds, and freshens the young leaves,
The birds pour forth their souls in notes
Of rapture from a thousand throats —
Here checked by too impetuous haste,
While there the music runs to waste,   20
With bounty more and more enlarged,
Till the whole air is overcharged;
Give ear, O Man! to their appeal,
And thirst for no inferior zeal,
Thou, who canst *think*, as well as feel.
Mount from the earth; aspire! aspire!
So pleads the town's cathedral quire,
In strains that from their solemn height
Sink, to attain a loftier flight;
While incense from the altar breathes   30
Rich fragrance in embodied wreaths;
Or, flung from swinging censer, shrouds
The taper-lights, and curls in clouds
Around angelic Forms, the still
Creation of the painter's skill,
That on the service wait concealed
One moment, and the next revealed.
— Cast off your bonds, awake, arise,
And for no transient ecstasies!
What else can mean the visual plea   40
Of still or moving imagery —
The iterated summons loud,
Not wasted on the attendant crowd,
Nor wholly lost upon the throng
Hurrying the busy streets along?
Alas! the sanctities combined
By art to unsensualise the mind
Decay and languish; or, as creeds
And humours change, are spurned like
weeds:
The priests are from their altars thrust;   50
Temples are levelled with the dust;
And solemn rites and awful forms
Founder amid fanatic storms.
Yet evermore, through years renewed
In undisturbed vicissitude
Of seasons balancing their flight
On the swift wings of day and night,
Kind Nature keeps a heavenly door
Wide open for the scattered Poor.
Where flower-breathed incense to the skies
Is wafted in mute harmonies;   61
And ground fresh-cloven by the plough
Is fragrant with a humbler vow;
Where birds and brooks from leafy dells
Chime forth unwearied canticles,

And vapours magnify and spread
The glory of the sun's bright head —
Still constant in her worship, still
Conforming to the eternal Will,
Whether men sow or reap the fields,   70
Divine monition Nature yields,
That not by bread alone we live,
Or what a hand of flesh can give;
That every day should leave some part
Free for a sabbath of the heart:
So shall the seventh be truly blest,
From morn to eve, with hallowed rest.

"CALM IS THE FRAGRANT AIR"

1832. 1835

CALM is the fragrant air, and loth to
lose
Day's grateful warmth, tho' moist with fall-
ing dews.
Look for the stars, you 'll say that there are
none;
Look up a second time, and, one by one,
You mark them twinkling out with silvery
light,
And wonder how they could elude the
sight!
The birds, of late so noisy in their bowers,
Warbled a while with faint and fainter
powers,
But now are silent as the dim-seen flowers:
Nor does the village Church-clock's iron
tone   10
The time's and season's influence disown;
Nine beats distinctly to each other bound
In drowsy sequence — how unlike the sound
That, in rough winter, oft inflicts a fear
On fireside listeners, doubting what they
hear!
The shepherd, bent on rising with the
sun,
Had closed his door before the day was
done,
And now with thankful heart to bed doth
creep,
And joins his little children in their sleep.
The bat, lured forth where trees the lane
o'ershade,   20
Flits and reflits along the close arcade;
The busy dor-hawk chases the white moth
With burring note, which Industry and
Sloth
Might both be pleased with, for it suits
them both.

A stream is heard — I see it not, but know
By its soft music whence the waters flow:
Wheels and the tread of hoofs are heard no
  more;
One boat there was, but it will touch the
  shore
With the next dipping of its slackened oar;
Faint sound, that, for the gayest of the
  gay,   30
Might give to serious thought a moment's
  sway,
As a last token of man's toilsome day !

TO B. R. HAYDON, ON SEEING HIS PICTURE OF NAPOLEON BUONAPARTE ON THE ISLAND OF ST. HELENA

1831. 1832

This Sonnet, though said to be written on see-
ing the Portrait of Napoleon, was, in fact, com-
posed some time after, extempore, in the wood
at Rydal Mount.

HAYDON ! let worthier judges praise the
  skill
Here by thy pencil shown in truth of lines
And charm of colours; *I* applaud those
  signs
Of thought, that give the true poetic thrill;
That unencumbered whole of blank and still
Sky without cloud — ocean without a wave;
And the one Man that laboured to enslave
The World, sole-standing high on the bare
  hill —
Back turned, arms folded, the unapparent
  face
Tinged, we may fancy, in this dreary place,
With light reflected from the invisible sun
Set, like his fortunes; but not set for aye
Like them. The unguilty Power pursues
  his way,
And before *him* doth dawn perpetual run.

RURAL ILLUSIONS

1832. 1835

Written at Rydal Mount. Observed a hun-
dred times in the grounds there.

SYLPH was it ? or a Bird more bright
  Than those of fabulous stock ?
A second darted by; — and lo !
  Another of the flock,

Through sunshine flitting from the bough
  To nestle in the rock.
Transient deception ! a gay freak
  Of April's mimicries !
Those brilliant strangers, hailed with joy
  Among the budding trees,   10
Proved last year's leaves, pushed from the
  spray
  To frolic on the breeze.

Maternal Flora ! show thy face,
  And let thy hand be seen,
Thy hand here sprinkling tiny flowers,
  That, as they touch the green,
Take root (so seems it) and look up
  In honour of their Queen,
Yet, sooth, those little starry specks,
  That not in vain aspired   20
To be confounded with live growths,
  Most dainty, most admired,
Were only blossoms dropt from twigs
  Of their own offspring tired.

Not such the World's illusive shows;
  Her wingless flutterings,
Her blossoms which, though shed, outbrave
  The floweret as it springs,
For the undeceived, smile as they may,
  Are melancholy things: 30
But gentle Nature plays her part
  With ever-varying wiles,
And transient feignings with plain truth
  So well she reconciles,
That those fond Idlers most are pleased
  Whom oftenest she beguiles.

LOVING AND LIKING

IRREGULAR VERSES

ADDRESSED TO A CHILD

(BY MY SISTER)

1832. 1835

Written at Rydal Mount. It arose, I be-
lieve, out of a casual expression of one of Mr.
Swinburne's children.

THERE 's more in words than I can teach:
Yet listen, Child ! — I would not preach;
But only give some plain directions
To guide your speech and your affections.
Say not you *love* a roasted fowl,
But you may love a screaming owl.

And, if you can, the unwieldy toad
That crawls from his secure abode
Within the mossy garden wall
When evening dews begin to fall.   10
Oh mark the beauty of his eye:
What wonders in that circle lie !
So clear, so bright, our fathers said
He wears a jewel in his head !
And when, upon some showery day,
Into a path or public way
A frog leaps out from bordering grass,
Startling the timid as they pass,
Do you observe him, and endeavour
To take the intruder into favour;   20
Learning from him to find a reason
For a light heart in a dull season.
And you may love him in the pool,
That is for him a happy school,
In which he swims as taught by nature,
Fit pattern for a human creature,
Glancing amid the water bright,
And sending upward sparkling light.
    Nor blush if o'er your heart be stealing
A love for things that have no feeling: 30
The spring's first rose by you espied,
May fill your breast with joyful pride;
And you may love the strawberry-flower,
And love the strawberry in its bower;
But when the fruit, so often praised
For beauty, to your lip is raised,
Say not you *love* the delicate treat,
But *like* it, enjoy it, and thankfully eat.
    Long may you love your pensioner mouse,
Though one of a tribe that torment the
    house: 40
Nor dislike for her cruel sport the cat,
Deadly foe both of mouse and rat;
Remember she follows the law of her kind,
And Instinct is neither wayward nor blind.
Then think of her beautiful gliding form,
Her tread that would scarcely crush a
    worm,
And her soothing song by the winter fire,
Soft as the dying throb of the lyre.
    I would not circumscribe your love:
It may soar with the eagle and brood with
    the dove,   50
May pierce the earth with the patient
    mole,
Or track the hedgehog to his hole.
Loving and liking are the solace of life,
Rock the cradle of joy, smooth the death-
    bed of strife.
You love your father and your mother,
Your grown-up and your baby brother;

You love your sister, and your friends,
And countless blessings which God sends:
And while these right affections play,
You *live* each moment of your day;   60
They lead you on to full content,
And likings fresh and innocent,
That store the mind, the memory feed,
And prompt to many a gentle deed:
But *likings* come, and pass away;
'T is *love* that remains till our latest day:
Our heavenward guide is holy love,
And will be our bliss with saints above.

UPON THE LATE GENERAL FAST

MARCH 1832

1832. 1832

RELUCTANT call it was; the rite delayed;
And in the Senate some there were who
    doffed
The last of their humanity, and scoffed
At providential judgments, undismayed
By their own daring. But the People
    prayed
As with one voice; their flinty heart grew
    soft
With penitential sorrow, and aloft
Their spirit mounted, crying, "God us
    aid ! "
Oh that with aspirations more intense,
Chastised by self-abasement more pro-
    found,
This People, once so happy, so renowned
For liberty, would seek from God defence
Against far heavier ill, the pestilence
Of revolution, impiously unbound !

FILIAL PIETY

ON THE WAYSIDE BETWEEN PRESTON
AND LIVERPOOL

1828. 1829

This was communicated to me by a coach-
man at whose side I sat while he was driving.
In the course of my many coach rambles and
journeys, which, during the daytime always
and often in the night, were taken on the out-
side of the coach, I had good and frequent op-
portunities of learning the characteristics of
this class of men. One remark I made that is
worth recording ; that whenever I had occasion
especially to notice their well-ordered, respect-

ful, and kind behaviour to women, of whatever age, I found them, I may say almost always, to be married men.

UNTOUCHED through all severity of cold;
Inviolate, whate'er the cottage hearth
Might need for comfort, or for festal mirth;
That Pile of Turf is half a century old:
Yes, Traveller! fifty winters have been told
Since suddenly the dart of death went forth
'Gainst him who raised it, — his last work
　　on earth:
Thence has it, with the Son, so strong a
　　hold
Upon his Father's memory, that his hands,
Through reverence, touch it only to repair
Its waste. — Though crumbling with each
　　breath of air,
In annual renovation thus it stands —
Rude Mausoleum! but wrens nestle there,
And red-breasts warble when sweet sounds
　　are rare.

"IF THOU INDEED DERIVE THY LIGHT FROM HEAVEN"

(?). 1827

These verses were written some time after we had become residents at Rydal Mount, and I will take occasion from them to observe upon the beauty of that situation, as being backed and flanked by lofty fells, which bring the heavenly bodies to touch, as it were, the earth upon the mountain-tops, while the prospect in front lies open to a length of level valley, the extended lake, and a terminating ridge of low hills; so that it gives an opportunity to the inhabitants of the place of noticing the stars in both the positions here alluded to, namely, on the tops of the mountains, and as winter-lamps at a distance among the leafless trees.

IF thou indeed derive thy light from
　　Heaven,
Then, to the measure of that heaven-born
　　light,
Shine, Poet! in thy place, and be content: —
The stars pre-eminent in magnitude,
And they that from the zenith dart their
　　beams,
(Visible though they be to half the earth,
Though half a sphere be conscious of their
　　brightness)
Are yet of no diviner origin,
No purer essence, than the one that burns,

Like an untended watch-fire on the ridge
Of some dark mountain; or than those
　　which seem
Humbly to hang, like twinkling winter
　　lamps,
Among the branches of the leafless trees.
All are the undying offspring of one Sire:
Then, to the measure of the light vouch-
　　safed,
Shine, Poet! in thy place, and be content.

TO THE AUTHOR'S PORTRAIT

Painted at Rydal Mount, by W. Pickersgill, Esq., for St. John's College, Cambridge.

1832. 1835

The six last lines of this Sonnet are not written for poetical effect, but as a matter of fact, which, in more than one instance, could not escape my notice in the servants of the house.

Go, faithful Portrait! and where long hath
　　knelt
Margaret, the Saintly Foundress, take thy
　　place;
And, if Time spare the colours for the grace
Which to the work surpassing skill hath
　　dealt,
Thou, on thy rock reclined, though king-
　　doms melt
And states be torn up by the roots, wilt seem
To breathe in rural peace, to hear the
　　stream,
And think and feel as once the Poet felt.
Whate'er thy fate, those features have not
　　grown
Unrecognised through many a household
　　tear
More prompt, more glad, to fall than drops
　　of dew
By morning shed around a flower half-
　　blown;
Tears of delight, that testified how true
To life thou art, and, in thy truth, how
　　dear!

A WREN'S NEST

1833. 1835

Written at Rydal Mount. This nest was built, as described, in a tree that grows near the pool in Dora's field next the Rydal Mount garden.

AMONG the dwellings framed by birds
  In field or forest with nice care,
Is none that with the little Wren's
  In snugness may compare.

No door the tenement requires,
  And seldom needs a laboured roof:
Yet is it to the fiercest sun
  Impervious, and storm-proof.

So warm, so beautiful withal,
  In perfect fitness for its aim,   10
That to the Kind by special grace
  Their instinct surely came.

And when for their abodes they seek
  An opportune recess,
The hermit has no finer eye
  For shadowy quietness.

These find, 'mid ivied abbey-walls,
  A canopy in some still nook;
Others are pent-housed by a brae
  That overhangs a brook.   20

There to the brooding bird her mate
  Warbles by fits his low clear song;
And by the busy streamlet both
  Are sung to all day long.

Or in sequestered lanes they build,
  Where, till the flitting bird's return,
Her eggs within the nest repose,
  Like relics in an urn.

But still, where general choice is good,
  There is a better and a best;   30
And, among fairest objects, some
  Are fairer than the rest;

This, one of those small builders proved
  In a green covert, where, from out
The forehead of a pollard oak,
  The leafy antlers sprout;

For She who planned the mossy lodge,
  Mistrusting her evasive skill,
Had to a Primrose looked for aid
  Her wishes to fulfil.   40

High on the trunk's projecting brow,
  And fixed an infant's span above
The budding flowers, peeped forth the
    nest
  The prettiest of the grove !

The treasure proudly did I show
  To some whose minds without disdain
Can turn to little things; but once
  Looked up for it in vain:

'T is gone — a ruthless spoiler's prey,
  Who heeds not beauty, love, or song, 50
'T is gone ! (so seemed it) and we grieved
  Indignant at the wrong.

Just three days after, passing by
  In clearer light the moss-built cell
I saw, espied its shaded mouth;
  And felt that all was well.

The Primrose for a veil had spread
  The largest of her upright leaves;
And thus, for purposes benign,
  A simple flower deceives.   60

Concealed from friends who might disturb
  Thy quiet with no ill intent,
Secure from evil eyes and hands
  On barbarous plunder bent,

Rest, Mother-bird ! and when thy young
  Take flight, and thou art free to roam,
When withered is the guardian Flower,
  And empty thy late home,

Think how ye prospered, thou and thine,
  Amid the unviolated grove,   70
Housed near the growing Primrose-tuft
  In foresight, or in love.

TO ——

UPON THE BIRTH OF HER FIRST-BORN
CHILD, MARCH 1833

1833. 1835

Written at Moresby near Whitehaven, when
I was on a visit to my son, then Incumbent of
that small living. While I am dictating these
notes to my friend, Miss Fenwick, January 24,
1843, the child upon whose birth these verses
were written is under my roof, and is of a dispo-
sition so promising that the wishes and prayers
and prophecies which I then breathed forth in
verse are, through God's mercy, likely to be
realised.

"Tum porro puer, ut sævis projectus ab undis
  Navita, nudus humi jacet, etc." — LUCRETIUS.

LIKE a shipwrecked Sailor tost
By rough waves on a perilous coast,
Lies the Babe, in helplessness
And in tenderest nakedness,
Flung by labouring nature forth
Upon the mercies of the earth.
Can its eyes beseech ? — no more
Than the hands are free to implore:
Voice but serves for one brief cry;
Plaint was it ? or prophecy   10
Of sorrow that will surely come ?
Omen of man's grievous doom !
  But, O Mother ! by the close
Duly granted to thy throes;
By the silent thanks, now tending
Incense-like to Heaven, descending
Now to mingle and to move
With the gush of earthly love,
As a debt to that frail Creature,
Instrument of struggling Nature   20
For the blissful calm, the peace
Known but to this *one* release —
Can the pitying spirit doubt
That for human-kind springs out
From the penalty a sense
Of more than mortal recompence ?
  As a floating summer cloud,
Though of gorgeous drapery proud,
To the sun-burnt traveller,
Or the stooping labourer,   30
Oft-times makes its bounty known
By its shadow round him thrown;
So, by chequerings of sad cheer,
Heavenly Guardians, brooding near,
Of their presence tell — too bright
Haply for corporeal sight !
Ministers of grace divine
Feelingly their brows incline
O'er this seeming Castaway
Breathing, in the light of day,   40
Something like the faintest breath
That has power to baffle death —
Beautiful, while very weakness
Captivates like passive meekness.
  And, sweet Mother ! under warrant
Of the universal Parent,
Who repays in season due
Them who have, like thee, been true
To the filial chain let down
From his everlasting throne,   50
Angels hovering round thy couch,
With their softest whispers vouch,
That — whatever griefs may fret,
Cares entangle, sins beset,
This thy First-born, and with tears

Stain her cheek in future years —
Heavenly succour, not denied
To the babe, whate'er betide,
Will to the woman be supplied !
  Mother ! blest be thy calm ease;   60
Blest the starry promises, —
And the firmament benign
Hallowed be it, where they shine !
Yes, for them whose souls have scope
Ample for a wingèd hope,
And can earthward bend an ear
For needful listening, pledge is here,
That, if thy new-born Charge shall tread
In thy footsteps, and be led
By that other Guide, whose light   70
Of manly virtues, mildly bright,
Gave him first the wished-for part
In thy gentle virgin heart;
Then, amid the storms of life
Presignified by that dread strife
Whence ye have escaped together,
She may look for serene weather;
In all trials sure to find
Comfort for a faithful mind;
Kindlier issues, holier rest,   80
Than even now await her prest,
Conscious Nursling, to thy breast !

THE WARNING

A SEQUEL TO THE FOREGOING

1833. 1835

These lines were composed during the fever
spread through the Nation by the Reform Bill.
As the motives which led to this measure, and
the good or evil which has attended or has risen
from it, will be duly appreciated by future
historians, there is no call for dwelling on the
subject in this place. I will content myself
with saying that the then condition of the
people's mind is not, in these verses, exag-
gerated.

LIST, the winds of March are blowing;
Her ground-flowers shrink, afraid of show-
    ing
Their meek heads to the nipping air,
Which ye feel not, happy pair !
Sunk into a kindly sleep.
We, meanwhile, our hope will keep;
And if Time leagued with adverse Change
(Too busy fear !) shall cross its range,
Whatsoever check they bring,

Anxious duty hindering,   10
To like hope our prayers will cling.
   Thus, while the ruminating spirit feeds
Upon the events of home as life proceeds,
Affections pure and holy in their source
Gain a fresh impulse, run a livelier course;
Hopes that within the Father's heart pre-
   vail,
Are in the experienced Grandsire's slow to
   fail;
And if the harp pleased his gay youth, it
   rings
To his grave touch with no unready strings,
While thoughts press on, and feelings over-
   flow,   20
And quick words round him fall like flakes
   of snow.
   Thanks to the Powers that yet maintain
      their sway,
And have renewed the tributary Lay,
Truths of the heart flock in with eager
   pace,
And FANCY greets them with a fond em-
   brace;
Swift as the rising sun his beams extends
She shoots the tidings forth to distant
   friends;
Their gifts she hails (deemed precious, as
   they prove
For the unconscious Babe so prompt a
   love !).
But from this peaceful centre of delight 30
Vague sympathies have urged her to take
   flight:
Rapt into upper regions, like the bee
That sucks from mountain heath her honey
   fee;
Or, like the warbling lark intent to shroud
His head in sunbeams or a bowery cloud,
She soars — and here and there her pinions
   rest
On proud towers, like this humble cottage,
   blest
With a new visitant, an infant guest —
Towers where red streamers flout the breezy
   sky
In pomp foreseen by her creative eye,   40
When feasts shall crowd the hall, and
   steeple bells
Glad proclamation make, and heights and
   dells
Catch the blithe music as it sinks and
   swells,
And harboured ships, whose pride is on the
   sea,

Shall hoist their topmost flags in sign of
   glee,
Honouring the hope of noble ancestry.
   But who (though neither reckoning ills
      assigned
By Nature, nor reviewing in the mind
The track that was, and is, and must be,
   worn   49
With weary feet by all of woman born) —
Shall *now* by such a gift with joy be moved,
Nor feel the fulness of that joy reproved ?
Not He, whose last faint memory will
   command
The truth that Britain was his native land;
Whose infant soul was tutored to confide
In the cleansed faith for which her martyrs
   died;
Whose boyish ear the voice of her renown
With rapture thrilled; whose Youth re-
   vered the crown
Of Saxon liberty that Alfred wore,
Alfred, dear Babe, thy great Progenitor ! 60
— Not He, who from her mellowed practice
   drew
His social sense of just, and fair, and true;
And saw, thereafter, on the soil of France
Rash Polity begin her maniac dance,
Foundations broken up, the deeps run wild,
Nor grieved to see (himself not unbe-
   guiled) —
Woke from the dream, the dreamer to up-
   braid,
And learn how sanguine expectations fade
When novel trusts by folly are betrayed, —
To see Presumption, turning pale, refrain 70
From further havoc, but repent in vain, —
Good aims lie down, and perish in the road
Where guilt had urged them on with cease-
   less goad,
Proofs thickening round her that on public
   ends
Domestic virtue vitally depends,
That civic strife can turn the happiest
   hearth
Into a grievous sore of self-tormenting
   earth.
   Can such a One, dear Babe ! though
      glad and proud   78
To welcome thee, repel the fears that crowd
Into his English breast, and spare to quake
Less for his own than for thy innocent sake ?
Too late — or, should the providence of
   God
Lead, through dark ways by sin and sorrow
   trod,

Justice and peace to a secure abode,
Too soon — thou com'st into this breathing
    world;
Ensigns of mimic outrage are unfurled.
Who shall preserve or prop the tottering
    Realm ?
What hand suffice to govern the state-helm ?
If, in the aims of men, the surest test
Of good or bad (whate'er be sought for or
    profest)   90
Lie in the means required, or ways or-
    dained,
For compassing the end, else never gained;
Yet governors and governed both are blind
To this plain truth, or fling it to the wind;
If to expedience principle must bow;
Past, future, shrinking up beneath the in-
    cumbent Now;
If cowardly concession still must feed
The thirst for power in men who ne'er con-
    cede;
Nor turn aside, unless to shape a way
For domination at some riper day;   100
If generous Loyalty must stand in awe
Of subtle Treason, in his mask of law,
Or with bravado insolent and hard,
Provoking punishment, to win reward;
If office help the factious to conspire,
And they who *should* extinguish, fan the
    fire —
Then, will the sceptre be a straw, the crown
Sit loosely, like the thistle's crest of down;
To be blown off at will, by Power that
    spares it
In cunning patience, from the head that
    wears it.   110
    Lost people, trained to theoretic feud !
Lost above all, ye labouring multitude !
Bewildered whether ye, by slanderous
    tongues
Deceived, mistake calamities for wrongs;
And over fancied usurpations brood,
Oft snapping at revenge in sullen mood;
Or, from long stress of real injuries, fly
To desperation for a remedy;
In bursts of outrage spread your judgments
    wide,
And to your wrath cry out, " Be thou our
    guide; "   120
Or, bound by oaths, come forth to tread
    earth's floor
In marshalled thousands, darkening street
    and moor
With the worst shape mock-patience ever
    wore;

Or, to the giddy top of self-esteem
By Flatterers carried, mount into a dream
Of boundless suffrage, at whose sage be-
    hest
Justice shall rule, disorder be supprest,
And every man sit down as Plenty's Guest !
— Oh for a bridle bitted with remorse
To stop your Leaders in their headstrong
    course !   130
Oh may the Almighty scatter with his grace
These mists, and lead you to a safer place,
By paths no human wisdom can foretrace !
May He pour round you, from worlds far
    above
Man's feverish passions, his pure light of
    love,
That quietly restores the natural mien
To hope, and makes truth willing to be seen !
Else shall your blood-stained hands in
    frenzy reap
Fields gaily sown when promises were
    cheap. —
Why is the Past belied with wicked art,   140
The Future made to play so false a part,
Among a people famed for strength of
    mind,
Foremost in freedom, noblest of mankind ?
We act as if we joyed in the sad tune
Storms make in rising, valued in the moon
Nought but her changes. Thus, ungrate-
    ful Nation !
If thou persist, and scorning moderation,
Spread for thyself the snares of tribulation,
Whom, then, shall meekness guard ? What
    saving skill
Lie in forbearance, strength in standing
    still ?   150
— Soon shall the widow (for the speed of
    Time
Nought equals when the hours are winged
    with crime)
Widow, or wife, implore on tremulous knee,
From him who judged her lord, a like
    decree;
The skies will weep o'er old men desolate:
Ye little-ones ! Earth shudders at your
    fate,
Outcasts and homeless orphans ——
    But turn, my Soul, and from the sleeping
    pair
Learn thou the beauty of omniscient care !
Be strong in faith, bid anxious thoughts
    lie still;   160
Seek for the good and cherish it — the ill
Oppose, or bear with a submissive will.

"IF THIS GREAT WORLD OF JOY AND PAIN"

1832. 1835

If this great world of joy and pain
  Revolve in one sure track;
If freedom, set, will rise again,
  And virtue, flown, come back;
Woe to the purblind crew who fill
  The heart with each day's care;
Nor gain, from past or future, skill
  To bear, and to forbear!

ON A HIGH PART OF THE COAST OF CUMBERLAND

Easter Sunday, April 7

THE AUTHOR'S SIXTY-THIRD BIRTHDAY

1833. 1835

The lines were composed on the road between Moresby and Whitehaven while I was on a visit to my son, then rector of the former place. This and some other Voluntaries originated in the concluding lines of the last paragraph of this poem. With this coast I have been famil-iar from my earliest childhood, and remember being struck for the first time by the town and port of Whitehaven, and the white waves breaking against its quays and piers, as the whole came into view from the top of the high ground down which the road (it has since been altered) then descended abruptly. My sister, when she first heard the voice of the sea from this point, and beheld the scene spread before her, burst into tears. Our family then lived at Cockermouth, and this fact was often men-tioned among us as indicating the sensibility for which she was so remarkable.

The Sun, that seemed so mildly to retire,
Flung back from distant climes a streaming
    fire,
Whose blaze is now subdued to tender
    gleams,
Prelude of night's approach with soothing
    dreams.
Look round; — of all the clouds not one is
    moving;
'T is the still hour of thinking, feeling,
    loving.
Silent, and stedfast as the vaulted sky,
The boundless plain of waters seems to
    lie: —
Comes that low sound from breezes rustling
    o'er

The grass-crowned headland that conceals
    the shore?
No; 't is the earth-voice of the mighty sea,
Whispering how meek and gentle he *can* be!
  Thou Power supreme! who, arming to
    rebuke
Offenders, dost put off the gracious look,
And clothe thyself with terrors like the
    flood
Of ocean roused into its fiercest mood,
Whatever discipline thy Will ordain
For the brief course that must for me re-
    main;
Teach me with quick-eared spirit to rejoice
In admonitions of thy softest voice!
Whate'er the path these mortal feet may
    trace,
Breathe through my soul the blessing of
    thy grace,
Glad, through a perfect love, a faith sincere
Drawn from the wisdom that begins with
    fear,
Glad to expand; and, for a season, free
From finite cares, to rest absorbed in Thee!

(BY THE SEASIDE)

1833. 1835

The sun is couched, the sea-fowl gone to
    rest,
And the wild storm hath somewhere found
    a nest;
Air slumbers — wave with wave no longer
    strives,
Only a heaving of the deep survives,
A tell-tale motion! soon will it be laid,
And by the tide alone the water swayed.
Stealthy withdrawings, interminglings mild
Of light with shade in beauty reconciled —
Such is the prospect far as sight can range,
The soothing recompence, the welcome
    change.   10
Where, now, the ships that drove before
    the blast,
Threatened by angry breakers as they
    passed;
And by a train of flying clouds bemocked;
Or, in the hollow surge, at anchor rocked
As on a bed of death? Some lodge in
    peace,
Saved by His care who bade the tempest
    cease;
And some, too heedless of past danger,
    court

Fresh gales to waft them to the far-off port.
But near, or hanging sea and sky between,
Not one of all those wingèd powers is seen,
Seen in her course, nor 'mid this quiet
   heard;   21
Yet oh ! how gladly would the air be stirred
By some acknowledgment of thanks and
   praise,
Soft in its temper as those vesper lays
Sung to the Virgin while accordant oars
Urge the slow bark along Calabrian shores;
A sea-born service through the mountains
   felt
Till into one loved vision all things melt:

Or like those hymns that soothe with graver
   sound
The gulfy coast of Norway iron-bound; 30
And, from the wide and open Baltic, rise
With punctual care, Lutherian harmonies.
Hush, not a voice is here ! but why repine,
Now when the star of eve comes forth to
   shine
On British waters with that look benign ?
Ye mariners, that plough your onward way,
Or in the haven rest, or sheltering bay,
May silent thanks at least to God be given
With a full heart; " our thoughts are *heard*
   in heaven."

POEMS

COMPOSED OR SUGGESTED DURING A TOUR IN THE SUMMER OF 1833

My companions were H. C. Robinson and my son John.

Having been prevented by the lateness of the season, in 1831, from visiting Staffa and Iona, the author made these the principal objects of a short tour in the summer of 1833, of which the following series of poems is a Memorial. The course pursued was down the Cumberland river Derwent, and to Whitehaven ; thence (by the Isle of Man, where a few days were passed) up the Frith of Clyde to Greenock, then to Oban, Staffa, Iona; and back towards England, by Loch Awe, Inverary, Loch Goil-head, Greenock, and through parts of Renfrewshire, Ayrshire, and Dumfriesshire to Carlisle, and thence up the river Eden, and homewards by Ullswater.

I

1833. 1835

ADIEU, Rydalian Laurels ! that have grown
And spread as if ye knew that days might
   come
When ye would shelter in a happy home,
On this fair Mount, a Poet of your own,
One who ne'er ventured for a Delphic crown
To sue the God; but, haunting your green
   shade
All seasons through, is humbly pleased to
   braid
Ground-flowers, beneath your guardianship,
   self-sown.
Farewell ! no Minstrels now with harp new-
   strung
For summer wandering quit their house-
   hold bowers;
Yet not for this wants Poesy a tongue
To cheer the Itinerant on whom she pours
Her spirit, while he crosses lonely moors,
Or musing sits forsaken halls among.

II

1833. 1835

WHY should the Enthusiast, journeying
   through this Isle
Repine as if his hour were come too late ?
Not unprotected in her mouldering state,
Antiquity salutes him with a smile,
'Mid fruitful fields that ring with jocund
   toil,
And pleasure-grounds where Taste, refined
   Co-mate
Of Truth and Beauty, strives to imitate,
Far as she may, primeval Nature's style.
Fair land ! by Time's parental love made
   free,
By Social Order's watchful arms em-
   braced;
With unexampled union meet in thee,
For eye and mind, the present and the
   past;
With golden prospect for futurity,
If that be reverenced which ought to last.

III

1833. 1835

THEY called Thee MERRY ENGLAND, in
 old time;
A happy people won for thee that name
With envy heard in many a distant clime;
And, spite of change, for me thou keep'st
 the same
Endearing title, a responsive chime
To the heart's fond belief; though some
 there are
Whose sterner judgments deem that word
 a snare
For inattentive Fancy, like the lime
Which foolish birds are caught with. Can,
 I ask,
This face of rural beauty be a mask
For discontent, and poverty, and crime;
These spreading towns a cloak for lawless
 will ?
Forbid it, Heaven ! — and MERRY ENG-
 LAND still
Shall be thy rightful name, in prose and
 rhyme !

IV

TO THE RIVER GRETA, NEAR KESWICK

1833. 1835

GRETA, what fearful listening ! when huge
 stones
Rumble along thy bed, block after block:
Or, whirling with reiterated shock,
Combat, while darkness aggravates the
 groans:
But if thou (like Cocytus from the moans
Heard on his rueful margin) thence wert
 named
The Mourner, thy true nature was de-
 famed,
And the habitual murmur that atones
For thy worst rage, forgotten. Oft as
 Spring
Decks, on thy sinuous banks, her thousand
 thrones
Seats of glad instinct and love's carolling,
The concert, for the happy, then may vie
With liveliest peals of birth-day har-
 mony:
To a grieved heart, the notes are beni-
 sons.

V

IN SIGHT OF THE TOWN OF COCKERMOUTH

1833. 1835

Where the Author was born, and his Father's
remains are laid.

A POINT of life between my Parent's dust,
And yours, my buried Little-ones ! am I;
And to those graves looking habitually
In kindred quiet I repose my trust.
Death to the innocent is more than just,
And, to the sinner, mercifully bent;
So may I hope, if truly I repent
And meekly bear the ills which bear I
 must:
And You, my Offspring ! that do still re-
 main,
Yet may outstrip me in the appointed race,
If e'er, through fault of mine, in mutual
 pain
We breathed together for a moment's space,
The wrong, by love provoked, let love
 arraign,
And only love keep in your hearts a place.

VI

ADDRESS FROM THE SPIRIT OF COCKERMOUTH CASTLE

1833. 1835

" THOU look'st upon me, and dost fondly
 think,
Poet ! that, stricken as both are by years,
We, differing once so much, are now Com-
 peers,
Prepared, when each has stood his time, to
 sink
Into the dust. Erewhile a sterner link
United us; when thou, in boyish play,
Entering my dungeon, didst become a prey
To soul-appalling darkness. Not a blink
Of light was there; — and thus did I, thy
 Tutor,
Make thy young thoughts acquainted with
 the grave;
While thou wert chasing the winged but-
 terfly
Through my green courts; or climbing, a
 bold suitor,
Up to the flowers whose golden progeny
Still round my shattered brow in beauty
 wave."

VII

NUN'S WELL, BRIGHAM

1833. 1835

So named from the religious House which stood close by. I have rather an odd anecdote to relate of the Nun's Well. One day the landlady of a public-house, a field's length from the well, on the road side, said to me — " You have been to see the Nun's Well, Sir?"—"The Nun's Well! what is that?" said the Postman, who in his royal livery stopt his mail-car at the door. The landlady and I explained to him what the name meant, and what sort of people the nuns were. A countryman who was standing by, rather tipsy, stammered out — " Aye, those nuns were good people; they are gone; but we shall soon have them back again." The Reform mania was just then at its height.

THE cattle crowding round this beverage
    clear
To slake their thirst, with reckless hoofs
    have trod
The encircling turf into a barren clod;
Through which the waters creep, then dis-
    appear,
Born to be lost in Derwent flowing near;
Yet, o'er the brink, and round the lime-
    stone cell
Of the pure spring (they call it the " Nun's
    Well,"
Name that first struck by chance my startled
    ear)
A tender Spirit broods — the pensive Shade
Of ritual honours to this Fountain paid
By hooded Votaresses with saintly cheer;
Albeit oft the Virgin-mother mild
Looked down with pity upon eyes beguiled
Into the shedding of " too soft a tear."

VIII

TO A FRIEND

ON THE BANKS OF THE DERWENT

1834(?). 1835

My son John, who was then building a parsonage on his small living at Brigham.

PASTOR and Patriot!—at whose bidding
    rise
These modest walls, amid a flock that need,
For one who comes to watch them and to
    feed,

A fixed Abode — keep down presageful
    sighs.
Threats, which the unthinking only can de-
    spise,
Perplex the Church; but be thou firm, —
    be true
To thy first hope, and this good work pursue,
Poor as thou art. A welcome sacrifice
Dost Thou prepare, whose sign will be the
    smoke
Of thy new hearth; and sooner shall its
    wreaths,
Mounting while earth her morning incense
    breathes,
From wandering fiends of air receive a
    yoke,
And straightway cease to aspire, than God
    disdain
This humble tribute as ill-timed or vain.

IX

MARY QUEEN OF SCOTS

LANDING AT THE MOUTH OF THE DER-
WENT, WORKINGTON

1833. 1835

I will mention for the sake of the friend who is writing down these notes, that it was among the fine Scotch firs near Ambleside, and particularly those near Green Bank, that I have over and over again paused at the sight of this image. Long may they stand to afford a like gratification to others! — This wish is not uncalled for, several of their brethren having already disappeared.

DEAR to the Loves, and to the Graces
    vowed,
The Queen drew back the wimple that she
    wore;
And to the throng, that on the Cumbrian
    shore
Her landing hailed, how touchingly she
    bowed!
And like a Star (that, from a heavy cloud
Of pine-tree foliage poised in air, forth
    darts,
When a soft summer gale at evening parts
The gloom that did its loveliness enshroud)
She smiled; but Time, the old Saturnian
    seer,
Sighed on the wing as her foot pressed the
    strand,

With step prelusive to a long array
Of woes and degradations hand in hand —
Weeping captivity, and shuddering fear
Stilled by the ensanguined block of Fother-
ingay !

X

STANZAS SUGGESTED IN A
STEAMBOAT OFF SAINT BEES'
HEADS, ON THE COAST OF
CUMBERLAND

1833. 1835

IF Life were slumber on a bed of down,
Toil unimposed, vicissitude unknown,
Sad were our lot: no hunter of the hare
Exults like him whose javelin from the lair
Has roused the lion; no one plucks the rose,
Whose proffered beauty in safe shelter
blows
'Mid a trim garden's summer luxuries,
With joy like his who climbs, on hands and
knees,
For some rare plant, yon Headland of St.
Bees.

This independence upon oar and sail,   10
This new indifference to breeze or gale,
This straight-lined progress, furrowing a
flat lea,
And regular as if locked in certainty —
Depress the hours.   Up, Spirit of the
storm !
That Courage may find something to per-
form;
That Fortitude, whose blood disdains to
freeze
At Danger's bidding, may confront the
seas,
Firm as the towering Headlands of St.
Bees.

Dread cliff of Baruth ! *that* wild wish may
sleep,
Bold as if men and creatures of the Deep
Breathed the same element; too many
wrecks   21
Have struck thy sides, too many ghastly
decks
Hast thou looked down upon, that such a
thought
Should here be welcome, and in verse en-
wrought:

With thy stern aspect better far agrees
Utterance of thanks that we have past with
ease,
As millions thus shall do, the Headlands of
St. Bees.

Yet, while each useful Art augments her
store,
What boots the gain if Nature should lose
more ?
And Wisdom, as she holds a Christian
place   30
In man's intelligence sublimed by grace ?
When Bega sought of yore the Cumbrian
coast,
Tempestuous winds her holy errand crossed:
She knelt in prayer — the waves their wrath
appease;
And, from her vow well weighed in Hea-
ven's decrees,
Rose, where she touched the strand, the
Chantry of St. Bees.

"Cruel of heart were they, bloody of
hand,"
Who in these Wilds then struggled for
command;
The strong were merciless, without hope
the weak;
Till this bright Stranger came, fair as day-
break,   40
And as a cresset true that darts its length
Of beamy lustre from a tower of strength;
Guiding the mariner through troubled
seas,
And cheering oft his peaceful reveries,
Like the fixed Light that crowns yon Head-
land of St. Bees.

To aid the Votaress, miracles believed
Wrought in men's minds, like miracles
achieved;
So piety took root; and Song might tell
What humanizing virtues near her cell
Sprang up, and spread their fragrance wide
around;   50
How savage bosoms melted at the sound
Of gospel-truth enchained in harmonies
Wafted o'er waves, or creeping through
close trees,
From her religious Mansion of St. Bees.

When her sweet Voice, that instrument of
love,
Was glorified, and took its place, above

The silent stars, among the angelic quire,
Her chantry blazed with sacrilegious fire,
And perished utterly ; but her good
    deeds
Had ·sown the spot, that witnessed them,
    with seeds   60
Which lay in earth expectant, till a breeze
With quickening impulse answered their
    mute pleas,
And lo ! a *statelier* pile, the Abbey of St.
    Bees.

There are the naked clothed, the hungry
    fed;
And Charity extendeth to the dead
Her intercessions made for the soul's rest
Of tardy penitents; or for the best
Among the good (when love might else have
    slept,
Sickened, or died) in pious memory kept.
Thanks to the austere and simple Devo-
    tees,   70
Who, to that service bound by venial
    fees,
Keep watch before the altars of St. Bees.

Are not, in sooth, their Requiem's sacred
    ties
Woven out of passion's sharpest agonies,
Subdued, composed, and formalized by
    art,
To fix a wiser sorrow in the heart ?
The prayer for them whose hour is past
    away
Says to the Living, profit while ye may !
A little part, and that the worst, he sees
Who thinks that priestly cunning holds the
    keys   80
That best unlock the secrets of St. Bees.

Conscience, the timid being's inmost light,
Hope of the dawn and solace of the
    night,
Cheers these Recluses with a steady ray
In many an hour when judgment goes
    astray.
Ah ! scorn not hastily their rule who try
Earth to despise, and flesh to mortify;
Consume with zeal, in wingèd ectasies
Of prayer and praise forget their rosaries,
Nor hear the loudest surges of St. Bees. 90

Yet none so prompt to succour and pro-
    tect
The forlorn traveller, or sailor wrecked

On the bare coast; nor do they grudge the
    boon
Which staff and cockle hat and sandal
    shoon
Claim for the pilgrim: and, though chid-
    ings sharp
May sometimes greet the strolling min-
    strel's harp,
It is not then when, swept with sportive
    ease,
It charms a feast-day throng of all de-
    grees,
Brightening the archway of revered St.
    Bees.

How did the cliffs and echoing hills re-
    joice   100
What time the Benedictine Brethren's
    voice,
Imploring, or commanding with meet pride,
Summoned the Chiefs to lay their feuds
    aside,
And under one blest ensign serve the
    Lord
In Palestine. Advance, indignant Sword !
Flaming till thou from Panym hands re-
    lease
That Tomb, dread centre of all sanctities
Nursed in the quiet Abbey of St. Bees.

But look we now to them whose minds
    from far
Follow the fortunes which they may not
    share.   110
While in Judea Fancy loves to roam,
She helps to make a Holy-land at home:
The Star of Bethlehem from its sphere in-
    vites
To sound the crystal depth of maiden
    rights;
And wedded Life, through scriptural mys-
    teries,
Heavenward ascends with all her chari-
    ties,
Taught by the hooded Celibates of St.
    Bees.

Nor be it e'er forgotten how, by skill
Of cloistered Architects, free their souls to
    fill
With love of God, throughout the Land
    were raised   120
Churches, on whose symbolic beauty gazed
Peasant and mail-clad Chief with pious
    awe;

As at this day men seeing what they saw,
Or the bare wreck of faith's solemnities,
Aspire to more than earthly destinies;
Witness yon Pile that greets us from St.
  Bees.

Yet more; around those Churches, gathered
    Towns
Safe from the feudal Castle's haughty
    frowns;
Peaceful abodes, where Justice might up-
    hold
Her scales with even hand, and culture
    mould   130
The heart to pity, train the mind in care
For rules of life, sound as the Time could
    bear.
Nor dost thou fail, thro' abject love of
    ease,
Or hindrance raised by sordid purposes,
To bear thy part in this good work, St.
    Bees.

Who with the ploughshare clove the barren
    moors,
And to green meadows changed the swampy
    shores ?
Thinned the rank woods; and for the cheer-
    ful grange
Made room, where wolf and boar were used
    to range ?
Who taught, and showed by deeds, that
    gentler chains   140
Should bind the vassal to his lord's do-
    mains ? —
The thoughtful Monks, intent their God to
    please,
For Christ's dear sake, by human sympa-
    thies
Poured from the bosom of thy Church, St.
    Bees !

But all availed not; by a mandate given
Through lawless will the Brotherhood was
    driven
Forth from their cells; their ancient House
    laid low
In Reformation's sweeping overthrow.
But now once more the local Heart re-
    vives,
The inextinguishable Spirit strives.   150
Oh may that Power who hushed the stormy
    seas,
And cleared a way for the first Votaries,
Prosper the new-born College of St. Bees !

Alas ! the Genius of our age, from Schools
Less humble, draws her lessons, aims, and
    rules.
To Prowess guided by her insight keen
Matter and Spirit are as one Machine;
Boastful Idolatress of formal skill
She in her own would merge the eternal
    will:
Better, if Reason's triumphs match with
    these,   160
Her flight before the bold credulities
That furthered the first teaching of St.
    Bees.

XI

IN THE CHANNEL, BETWEEN THE COAST OF CUMBERLAND AND THE ISLE OF MAN

1833. 1835

RANGING the heights of Scawfell or Black-
    comb,
In his lone course the Shepherd oft will
    pause,
And strive to fathom the mysterious laws
By which the clouds, arrayed in light or
    gloom,
On Mona settle, and the shapes assume
Of all her peaks and ridges. What he
    draws
From sense, faith, reason, fancy, of the
    cause,
He will take with him to the silent tomb.
Or, by his fire, a child upon his knee,
Haply the untaught Philosopher may speak
Of the strange sight, nor hide his theory
That satisfies the simple and the meek,
Blest in their pious ignorance, though
    weak
To cope with Sages undevoutly free.

XII

AT SEA OFF THE ISLE OF MAN

1833. 1835

BOLD words affirmed, in days when faith
    was strong
And doubts and scruples seldom teased the
    brain,
That no adventurer's bark had power to gain
These shores if he approached them bent
    on wrong;

For, suddenly up-conjured from the Main,
Mists rose to hide the Land — that search,
though long
And eager, might be still pursued in vain.
O Fancy, what an age was *that* for song !
That age, when not by *laws* inanimate,
As men believed, the waters were impelled,
The air controlled, the stars their courses
held;
But element and orb on *acts* did wait
Of *Powers* endued with visible form, in-
stinct
With will, and to their work by passion
linked.

XIII

1833. 1835

DESIRE we past illusions to recall ?
To reinstate wild Fancy, would we hide
Truths whose thick veil Science has drawn
aside ?
No, — let this Age, high as she may, instal
In her esteem the thirst that wrought man's
fall,
The universe is infinitely wide;
And conquering Reason, if self-glorified,
Can nowhere move uncrossed by some new
wall
Or gulf of mystery, which thou alone,
Imaginative Faith ! canst overleap,
In progress toward the fount of Love, —
the throne
Of Power whose ministers the records keep
Of periods fixed, and laws established, less
Flesh to exalt than prove its nothingness.

XIV

ON ENTERING DOUGLAS BAY, ISLE OF MAN

1833. 1835

" Dignum laude virum Musa vetat mori."

THE feudal Keep, the bastions of Cohorn,
Even when they rose to check or to repel
Tides of aggressive war, oft served as
well
Greedy ambition, armed to treat with
scorn
Just limits; but yon Tower, whose smiles
adorn
This perilous bay, stands clear of all offence;

Blest work it is of love and innocence,
A Tower of refuge built for the else forlorn.
Spare it, ye waves, and lift the mariner,
Struggling for life, into its saving arms !
Spare, too, the human helpers ! Do they
stir
'Mid your fierce shock like men afraid to
die ?
No; their dread service nerves the heart it
warms,
And they are led by noble HILLARY.

XV

BY THE SEASHORE, ISLE OF MAN

1833. 1835

WHY stand we gazing on the sparkling
Brine,
With wonder smit by its transparency,
And all-enraptured with its purity ? —
Because the unstained, the clear, the crys-
talline,
Have ever in them something of benign;
Whether in gem, in water, or in sky,
A sleeping infant's brow, or wakeful eye
Of a young maiden, only not divine.
Scarcely the hand forbears to dip its palm
For beverage drawn as from a mountain-
well;
Temptation centres in the liquid Calm;
Our daily raiment seems no obstacle
To instantaneous plunging in, deep Sea !
And revelling in long embrace with thee.

XVI

ISLE OF MAN

1833. 1835

My son William is here the person alluded
to as saving the life of the youth, and the cir-
cumstances were as mentioned in the Sonnet.

A YOUTH too certain of his power to wade
On the smooth bottom of this clear bright
sea,
To sight so shallow, with a bather's glee
Leapt from this rock, and but for timely aid
He, by the alluring element betrayed,
Had perished. Then might Sea-nymphs
(and with sighs

Of self-reproach) have chanted elegies
Bewailing his sad fate, when he was laid
In peaceful earth: for, doubtless, he was
frank,
Utterly in himself devoid of guile;
Knew not the double-dealing of a smile;
Nor aught that makes men's promises a
blank,
Or deadly snare: and He survives to bless
The Power that saved him in his strange
distress.

XVII

ISLE OF MAN

1833. 1835

DID pangs of grief for lenient time too
keen,
Grief that devouring waves had caused, or
guilt
Which they had witnessed — sway the man
who built
This Homestead, placed where nothing
could be seen,
Nought heard, of ocean troubled or serene ?
A tired Ship-soldier on paternal land,
That o'er the channel holds august com-
mand,
The dwelling raised, — a veteran Marine.
He, in disgust, turned from the neighbour-
ing sea
To shun the memory of a listless life
That hung between two callings. May no
strife
More hurtful here beset him, doomed
though free,
Self-doomed, to worse inaction, till his eye
Shrink from the daily sight of earth and
sky !

XVIII

BY A RETIRED MARINER, H. H.

Mrs. Wordsworth's Brother Henry.

1833. 1835

FROM early youth I ploughed the restless
Main,
My mind as restless and as apt to change;
Through every clime and ocean did I range,
In hope at length a competence to gain;
For poor to Sea I went, and poor I still
remain.

Year after year I strove, but strove in vain,
And hardships manifold did I endure,
For Fortune on me never deigned to smile;
Yet I at last a resting-place have found,
With just enough life's comforts to procure,
In a snug Cove on this our favoured Isle,
A peaceful spot where Nature's gifts
abound;
Then sure I have no reason to complain,
Though poor to Sea I went, and poor I
still remain.

XIX

AT BALA-SALA, ISLE OF MAN

1833. 1835

Supposed to be written by a friend (Mr.
Cookson) who died there a few years after.

BROKEN in fortune, but in mind entire
And sound in principle, I seek repose
Where ancient trees this convent-pile en-
close,
In ruin beautiful.   When vain desire
Intrudes on peace, I pray the eternal Sire
To cast a soul-subduing shade on' me,
A grey-haired, pensive, thankful Refugee;
A shade — but with some sparks of hea-
venly fire
Once to these cells vouchsafed.   And when
I note
The old Tower's brow yellowed as with the
beams
Of sunset ever there, albeit streams
Of stormy weather-stains that semblance
wrought,
I thank the silent Monitor, and say
" Shine so, my aged brow, at all hours of
the day ! "

XX

TYNWALD HILL

1833. 1835

Mr. Robinson and I walked the greater part
of the way from Castle-town to Piel, and
stopped some time at Tynwald Hill. One of
my companions was an elderly man, who in a
muddy way (for he was tipsy) explained and
answered, as far as he could, my enquiries
about this place and the ceremonies held here.
I found more agreeable company in some little
children; one of whom, upon my request, re-

cited the Lord's Prayer to me, and I helped her to a clearer understanding of it as well as I could; but I was not at all satisfied with my own part; hers was much better done, and I am persuaded that, like other children, she knew more about it than she was able to express, especially to a stranger.

ONCE on the top of Tynwald's formal mound
(Still marked with green turf circles narrowing
Stage above stage) would sit this Island's King,
The laws to promulgate, enrobed and crowned:
While, compassing the little mount around,
Degrees and Orders stood, each under each:
Now, like to things within fate's easiest reach
The power is merged, the pomp a grave has found.
Off with yon cloud, old Snafell! that thine eye
Over three Realms may take its widest range;
And let, for them, thy fountains utter strange
Voices, thy winds break forth in prophecy,
If the whole State must suffer mortal change
Like Mona's miniature of sovereignty.

XXI

1833. 1835

DESPOND who will — *I* heard a voice exclaim,
" Though fierce the assault, and shattered the defence,
It cannot be that Britain's social frame,
The glorious work of time and providence,
Before a flying season's rash pretence,
Should fall; that She, whose virtue put to shame,
When Europe prostrate lay, the Conqueror's aim,
Should perish, self-subverted. Black and dense
The cloud is; but brings *that* a day of doom
To Liberty ? Her sun is up the while,
That orb whose beams round Saxon Alfred shone:
Then laugh, ye innocent Vales ! ye Streams, sweep on,
Nor let one billow of our heaven-blest Isle
Toss in the fanning wind a humbler plume."

XXII

IN THE FRITH OF CLYDE, AILSA CRAG

DURING AN ECLIPSE OF THE SUN, JULY 17

1833. 1835

The morning of the eclipse was exquisitely beautiful while we passed the Crag as described in the Sonnet. On the deck of the steamboat were several persons of the poor and labouring class, and I could not but be struck by their cheerful talk with each other, while not one of them seemed to notice the magnificent objects with which we were surrounded ; and even the phenomenon of the eclipse attracted but little of their attention. Was it right not to regret this ? They appeared to me, however, so much alive in their own minds to their own concerns that I could not look upon it as a misfortune that they had little perception for such pleasures as cannot be cultivated without ease and leisure. Yet if one surveys life in all its duties and relations, such ease and leisure will not be found so enviable a privilege as it may at first appear. Natural Philosophy, Painting, and Poetry, and refined taste, are no doubt great acquisitions to society ; but among those who dedicate themselves to such pursuits it is to be feared that few are as happy, and as consistent in the management of their lives, as the class of persons who at that time led me into this course of reflection. I do not mean by this to be understood to derogate from intellectual pursuits, for that would be monstrous : I say it in deep gratitude for this compensation to those whose cares are limited to the necessities of daily life. Among them, self-tormentors, so numerous in the higher classes of society, are rare.

SINCE risen from ocean, ocean to defy,
Appeared the crag of Ailsa, ne'er did morn
With gleaming lights more gracefully adorn
His sides, or wreathe with mist his forehead high:
Now, faintly darkening with the sun's eclipse,
Still is he seen, in lone sublimity,
Towering above the sea and little ships;
For dwarfs the tallest seem while sailing by,
Each for her haven; with her freight of Care,
Pleasure, or Grief, and Toil that seldom looks
Into the secret of to-morrow's fare;
Though poor, yet rich, without the wealth of books,

Or aught that watchful Love to Nature owes
For her mute Powers, fixed Forms, or
    transient Shows.

XXIII

ON THE FRITH OF CLYDE

IN A STEAMBOAT

1833. 1835

The mountain outline on the north of this
island, as seen from the Frith of Clyde, is much
the finest I have ever noticed in Scotland or
elsewhere.

ARRAN! a single-crested Teneriffe,
A St. Helena next — in shape and hue,
Varying her crowded peaks and ridges blue;
Who but must covet a cloud-seat, or skiff
Built for the air, or wingèd Hippogriff?
That he might fly, where no one could
    pursue,
From this dull Monster and her sooty crew;
And, as a God, light on thy topmost cliff.
Impotent wish! which reason would despise
If the mind knew no union of extremes,
No natural bond between the boldest
    schemes
Ambition frames, and heart-humilities.
Beneath stern mountains many a soft vale
    lies,
And lofty springs give birth to lowly
    streams.

XXIV

ON REVISITING DUNOLLY CASTLE

1833. 1835

See former series, "Yarrow Revisited," etc.,
p. 685.

THE captive Bird was gone; — to cliff or
    moor
Perchance had flown, delivered by the
    storm;
Or he had pined, and sunk to feed the
    worm:
Him found we not: but, climbing a tall
    tower,
There saw, impaved with rude fidelity
Of art mosaic, in a roofless floor,
An Eagle with stretched wings, but beam-
    less eye —

An Eagle that could neither wail nor soar.
Effigy of the Vanished — (shall I dare
To call thee so?) or symbol of fierce deeds
And of the towering courage which past
    times
Rejoiced in — take, whate'er thou be, a share,
Not undeserved, of the memorial rhymes
That animate my way where'er it leads!

XXV

THE DUNOLLY EAGLE

1833. 1835

NOT to the clouds, not to the cliff, he flew;
But when a storm, on sea or mountain bred,
Came and delivered him, alone he sped
Into the castle-dungeon's darkest mew.
Now, near his master's house in open view
He dwells, and hears indignant tempests
    howl,
Kennelled and chained. Ye tame domestic
    fowl,
Beware of him! Thou, saucy cockatoo,
Look to thy plumage and thy life! — The
    roe,
Fleet as the west wind, is for him no quarry;
Balanced in ether he will never tarry,
Eyeing the sea's blue depths. Poor Bird!
    even so
Doth man of brother man a creature make
That clings to slavery for its own sad sake.

XXVI

WRITTEN IN A BLANK LEAF OF MACPHERSON'S OSSIAN

1824. 1827

The verses —
            "Or strayed
    From hope and promise, self-betrayed,"

were, I am sorry to say, suggested from appre-
hensions of the fate of my friend, H. C., the
subject of the verses addressed to " H. C. when
six years old." The piece to " Memory " arose
out of similar feelings.

OFT have I caught, upon a fitful breeze,
Fragments of far-off melodies,
With ear not coveting the whole,
A part so charmed the pensive soul.
While a dark storm before my sight
Was yielding, on a mountain height

Loose vapours have I watched, that won
Prismatic colours from the sun;
Nor felt a wish that heaven would show
The image of its perfect bow.   10
What need, then, of these finished Strains ?
Away with counterfeit Remains !
An abbey in its lone recess,
A temple of the wilderness,
Wrecks though they be, announce with
    feeling
The majesty of honest dealing.
Spirit of Ossian ! if imbound
In language thou may'st yet be found,
If aught (intrusted to the pen
Or floating on the tongues of men,   20
Albeit shattered and impaired)
Subsist thy dignity to guard,
In concert with memorial claim
Of old grey stone, and high-born name
That cleaves to rock or pillared cave
Where moans the blast, or beats the wave,
Let Truth, stern arbitress of all,
Interpret that Original,
And for presumptuous wrongs atone; —
Authentic words be given, or none !   30
Time is not blind; — yet He, who spares
Pyramid pointing to the stars,
Hath preyed with ruthless appetite
On all that marked the primal flight
Of the poetic ecstasy
Into the land of mystery.
No tongue is able to rehearse
One measure, Orpheus ! of thy verse;
Musæus, stationed with his lyre
Supreme among the Elysian quire,   40
Is, for the dwellers upon earth,
Mute as a lark ere morning's birth.
Why grieve for these, though past away
The music, and extinct the lay ?
When thousands, by severer doom,
Full early to the silent tomb
Have sunk, at Nature's call; or strayed
From hope and promise, self-betrayed;
The garland withering on their brows;
Stung with remorse for broken vows;   50
Frantic — else how might they rejoice ?
And friendless, by their own sad choice !
Hail, Bards of mightier grasp ! on you
I chiefly call, the chosen Few,
Who cast not off the acknowledged guide,
Who faltered not, nor turned aside;
Whose lofty genius could survive
Privation, under sorrow thrive;
In whom the fiery Muse revered
The symbol of a snow-white beard,   60

Bedewed with meditative tears
Dropped from the lenient cloud of years.
    Brothers in soul ! though distant times
Produced you nursed in various climes,
Ye, when the orb of life had waned,
A plenitude of love retained:
Hence, while in you each sad regret
By corresponding hope was met,
Ye lingered among human kind,
Sweet voices for the passing wind,   70
Departing sunbeams, loth to stop,
Though smiling on the last hill top !
Such to the tender-hearted maid
Even ere her joys begin to fade;
Such, haply, to the rugged chief
By fortune crushed, or tamed by grief;
Appears, on Morven's lonely shore,
Dim-gleaming through imperfect lore,
The Son of Fingal; such was blind
Mæonides of ampler mind;   80
Such Milton, to the fountain head
Of glory by Urania led !

XXVII

CAVE OF STAFFA

1833. 1835

WE saw, but surely, in the motley crowd,
Not One of us has felt the far-famed sight;
How *could* we feel it ? each the other's blight,
Hurried and hurrying, volatile and loud.
O for those motions only that invite
The Ghost of Fingal to his tuneful Cave
By the breeze entered, and wave after wave
Softly embosoming the timid light !
And by *one* Votary who at will might stand
Gazing and take into his mind and heart,
With undistracted reverence, the effect
Of those proportions where the almighty
    hand
That made the worlds, the sovereign Archi-
    tect,
Has deigned to work as if with human Art !

XXVIII

CAVE. OF STAFFA

AFTER THE CROWD HAD DEPARTED

1833. 1835

THANKS for the lessons of this Spot — fit
    school
For the presumptuous thoughts that would
    assign

Mechanic laws to agency divine;
And, measuring heaven by earth, would
    overrule
Infinite Power.   The pillared vestibule,
Expanding yet precise, the roof embowed,
Might seem designed to humble man, when
    proud
Of his best workmanship by plan and tool.
Down-bearing with his whole Atlantic weight
Of tide and tempest on the Structure's base,
And flashing to that Structure's topmost
    height,
Ocean has proved its strength, and of its
    grace
In calms is conscious, finding for his freight
Of softest music some responsive place.

XXIX

CAVE OF STAFFA

1833. 1835

YE shadowy Beings, that have rights and
    claims
In every cell of Fingal's mystic Grot,
Where are ye ? Driven or venturing to the
    spot,
Our fathers glimpses caught of your thin
    Frames,
And, by your mien and bearing knew your
    names;
And they could hear *his* ghostly song who
    trod   •
Earth, till the flesh lay on him like a load,
While he struck his desolate harp without
    hopes or aims.
Vanished ye are, but subject to recall;
Why keep *we* else the instincts whose dread
    law
Ruled here of yore, till what men felt they
    saw,
Not by black arts but magic natural !
If eyes be still sworn vassals of belief,
Yon light shapes forth a Bard, that shade a
    Chief.

XXX

FLOWERS ON THE TOP OF THE PILLARS AT THE ENTRANCE OF THE CAVE

1833. 1835

HOPE smiled when your nativity was cast,
Children of Summer ! Ye fresh Flowers
    that brave

What Summer here escapes not, the fierce
    wave,
And whole artillery of the western blast,
Battering the Temple's front, its long-drawn
    nave
Smiting, as if each moment were their last.
But ye, bright Flowers on frieze and archi-
    trave
Survive, and once again the Pile stands fast:
Calm as the Universe, from specular towers
Of heaven contemplated by Spirits pure
With mute astonishment, it stands sus-
    tained
Through every part in symmetry, to endure,
Unhurt, the assault of Time with all his
    hours,
As the supreme Artificer ordained.

XXXI

IONA

1833. 1835

ON to Iona ! — What can she afford
To *us* save matter for a thoughtful sigh,
Heaved over ruin with stability
In urgent contrast ? To diffuse the WORD
(Thy Paramount, mighty Nature ! and
    Time's Lord)
Her Temples rose, 'mid pagan gloom; but
    why,
Even for a moment, has our verse deplored
Their wrongs, since they fulfilled their
    destiny ?
And when, subjected to a common doom
Of mutability, those far-famed Piles
Shall disappear from both the sister Isles,
Iona's Saints, forgetting not past days,
Garlands shall wear of amaranthine bloom,
While heaven's vast sea of voices chants
    their praise.

XXXII

IONA

UPON LANDING

1833. 1835

How sad a welcome ! To each voyager
Some raggèd child holds up for sale a store
Of wave-worn pebbles, pleading on the
    shore
Where once came monk and nun with gen-
    tle stir,

Blessings to give, news ask, or suit prefer.
Yet is yon neat trim church a grateful speck
Of novelty amid the sacred wreck
Strewn far and wide. Think, proud Philo-
    sopher!
Fallen though she be, this Glory of the
    west,
Still on her sons the beams of mercy shine;
And " hopes, perhaps more heavenly bright
    than thine,
A grace by thee unsought and unpossest,
A faith more fixed, a rapture more divine,
Shall gild their passage to eternal rest."

XXXIII

THE BLACK STONES OF IONA

1833. 1835

See Martin's *Voyage among the Western Isles.*

HERE on their knees men swore: the stones
    were black,
Black in the people's minds and words, yet
    they
Were at that time, as now, in colour grey.
But what is colour, if upon the rack
Of conscience souls are placed by deeds
    that lack
Concord with oaths? What differ night
    and day
Then, when before the Perjured ôn his way
Hell opens, and the heavens in vengeance
    crack
Above his head uplifted in vain prayer
To Saint, or Fiend, or to the Godhead
    whom
He had insulted — Peasant, King, or Thane?
Fly where the culprit may, guilt meets a
    doom;
And, from invisible worlds at need laid
    bare,
Come links for social order's awful chain.

XXXIV

1833. 1835

HOMEWARD we turn. Isle of Columba's
    Cell,
Where Christian piety's soul - cheering
    spark
(Kindled from Heaven between the light
    and dark

Of time) shone like the morning-star, fare-
    well ! —
And fare thee well, to Fancy visible,
Remote St. Kilda, lone and loved sea-
    mark
For many a voyage made in her swift
    bark,
When with more hues than in the rainbow
    dwell
Thou a mysterious intercourse dost hold,
Extracting from clear skies and air serene,
And out of sun-bright waves, a lucid veil,
That thickens, spreads, and, mingling fold
    .with fold,
Makes known, when thou no longer canst
    be seen,
Thy whereabout, to warn the approaching
    sail.

XXXV

GREENOCK

1833. 1835

Per me si va nella Città dolente.

WE have not passed into a doleful City,
We who were led to-day down a grim dell,
By some too boldly named " the Jaws of
    Hell:"
Where be the wretched ones, the sights for
    pity?
These crowded streets resound no plaintive
    ditty: —
As from the hive where bees in summer
    dwell,
Sorrow seems here excluded; and that
    knell,
It neither damps the gay, nor checks the
    witty.
Alas! too busy Rival of old Tyre,
Whose merchants Princes were, whose
    decks were thrones;
Soon may the punctual sea in vain respire
To serve thy need, in union with that
    Clyde
Whose nursling current brawls o'er mossy
    stones,
The poor, the lonely, herdsman's joy and
    pride.

XXXVI

1833. 1835

Mosgiel was thus pointed out to me by a
young man on the top of the coach on my way

from Glasgow to Kilmarnock. It is remarkable that, though Burns lived some time here, and during much the most productive period of his poetical life, he nowhere adverts to the splendid prospects stretching towards the sea and bounded by the peaks of Arran on one part, which in clear weather he must have had daily before his eyes. In one of his poetical effusions he speaks of describing " fair Nature's face " as a privilege on which he sets a high value ; nevertheless, natural appearances rarely take a lead in his poetry. It is as a human being, eminently sensitive and intelligent, and not as a poet, clad in his priestly robes and carrying the ensigns of sacerdotal office, that he interests and affects us. Whether he speaks of rivers, hills, and woods, it is not so much on account of the properties with which they are absolutely endowed, as relatively to local patriotic remembrances and associations, or as they ministered to personal feelings, especially those of love, whether happy or otherwise ; — yet it is not always so. Soon after we had passed Mosgiel Farm we crossed the Ayr, murmuring and winding through a narrow woody hollow. His line — " Auld hermit Ayr strays through his woods " — came at once to my mind with Irwin, Lugar, Ayr, and Doon, — Ayrshire streams over which he breathes a sigh as being unnamed in song ; and surely his own attempts to make them known were as successful as his heart could desire.

" THERE ! " said a Stripling, pointing with
    meet pride
Towards a low roof with green trees half
    concealed,
" Is Mosgiel Farm ; and that 's the very
    field
Where Burns ploughed up the Daisy." Far
    and wide
A plain below stretched seaward, while,
    descried
Above sea-clouds, the Peaks of Arran
    rose ;
And, by that simple notice, the repose
Of earth, sky, sea, and air, was vivified.
Beneath " the random *bield* of clod or
    stone "
Myriads of daisies have shone forth in
    flower
Near the lark's nest, and in their natural
    hour
Have passed away ; less happy than the
    One
That, by the unwilling ploughshare, died to
    prove
The tender charm of poetry and love.

XXXVII

THE RIVER EDEN, CUMBERLAND

1833. 1835

" Nature gives thee flowers that have no rivals among British bowers." This can scarcely be true to the letter ; but, without stretching the point at all, I can say that the soil and air appear more congenial with many upon the banks of this river than I have observed in any other parts of Great Britain.

EDEN ! till now thy beauty had I viewed
By glimpses only, and confess with shame
That verse of mine, whate'er its varying
    mood,
Repeats but once the sound of thy sweet
    name :
Yet fetched from Paradise that honour
    came,
Rightfully borne ; for Nature gives thee
    flowers
That have no rivals among British bowers ;
And thy bold rocks are worthy of their
    fame.
Measuring thy course, fair Stream ! at
    length I pay
To my life's neighbour dues of neighbour-
    hood ;
But I have traced thee on thy winding way
With pleasure sometimes by this thought
    restrained —
For things far off we toil, while many a
    good
Not sought, because too near, is never
    gained.

XXXVIII

MONUMENT OF MRS. HOWARD

by Nollekens

IN WETHERAL CHURCH, NEAR CORBY, ON THE BANKS OF THE EDEN

1833. 1835

Before this monument was put up in the Church at Wetheral, I saw it in the sculptor's studio. Nollekens, who, by the bye, was a strange and grotesque figure that interfered much with one's admiration of his works, showed me at the same time the various models in clay which he had made, one after another, of the Mother and her Infant : the improvement on each was surprising ; and how so much grace, beauty, and tenderness had come out of such a head I was sadly puzzled to conceive. Upon a window-seat in his parlour lay two casts of faces, one of the Duchess of Devonshire, so noted in her day; and the other of Mr. Pitt, taken after his death, a ghastly resemblance, as these things always are, even when taken from the living subject, and more ghastly in this instance from the peculiarity of the features. The heedless and apparently neglectful manner in which the faces of these two persons were left — the one so distinguished in London Society, and the other upon whose counsels and public conduct, during a most momentous period, depended the fate of this great Empire and perhaps of all Europe — afforded a lesson to which the dullest of casual visitors could scarcely be insensible. It touched me the more because I had so often seen Mr. Pitt upon his own ground at Cambridge and upon the floor of the House of Commons.

STRETCHED on the dying Mother's lap, lies dead
Her new-born Babe; dire ending of bright hope!
But Sculpture here, with the divinest scope
Of luminous faith, heavenward hath raised that head
So patiently; and through one hand has spread
A touch so tender for the insensate Child —
(Earth's lingering love to parting reconciled,
Brief parting, for the spirit is all but fled) —
That we, who contemplate the turns of life
Through this still medium, are consoled and cheered;
Feel with the Mother, think the severed Wife
Is less to be lamented than revered;
And own that Art, triumphant over strife
And pain, hath powers to Eternity endeared.

XXXIX

SUGGESTED BY THE FOREGOING

1833. 1835

TRANQUILLITY! the sovereign aim wert thou
In heathen schools of philosophic lore;
Heart-stricken by stern destiny of yore
The Tragic Muse thee served with thoughtful vow;

And what of hope Elysium could allow
Was fondly seized by Sculpture, to restore
Peace to the Mourner. But when He who wore
The crown of thorns around his bleeding brow
Warmed our sad being with celestial light,
Then Arts which still had drawn a softening grace
From shadowy fountains of the Infinite,
Communed with that Idea face to face:
And move around it now as planets run,
Each in its orbit round the central Sun.

XL

NUNNERY

1833. 1835

I became acquainted with the walks of Nunnery when a boy: they are within easy reach of a day's pleasant excursion from the town of Penrith, where I used to pass my summer holidays under the roof of my maternal Grandfather. The place is well worth visiting; though, within these few years, its privacy, and therefore the pleasure which the scene is so well fitted to give, has been injuriously affected by walks cut in the rocks on that side the stream which had been left in its natural state.

THE floods are roused, and will not soon be weary;
Down from the Pennine Alps how fiercely sweeps
CROGLIN, the stately Eden's tributary!
He raves, or through some moody passage creeps
Plotting new mischief — out again he leaps
Into broad light, and sends, through regions airy,
That voice which soothed the Nuns while on the steeps
They knelt in prayer, or sang to blissful Mary.
That union ceased: then, cleaving easy walks
Through crags, and smoothing paths beset with danger,
Came studious Taste; and many a pensive stranger
Dreams on the banks, and to the river talks.
What change shall happen next to Nunnery Dell?
Canal, and Viaduct, and Railway, tell!

XLI

STEAMBOATS, VIADUCTS, AND RAILWAYS

1833. 1835

MOTIONS and Means, on land and sea at
   war
With old poetic feeling, not for this,
Shall ye, by Poets even, be judged amiss !
Nor shall your presence, howsoe'er it mar
The loveliness of Nature, prove a bar
To the Mind's gaining that prophetic sense
Of future change, that point of vision,
   whence
May be discovered what in soul ye are.
In spite of all that beauty may disown
In your harsh features, Nature doth em-
   brace
Her lawful offspring in Man's art; and Time,
Pleased with your triumphs o'er his brother
   Space,
Accepts from your bold hands the proffered
   crown
Of hope, and smiles on you with cheer
   sublime.

XLII

THE MONUMENT COMMONLY CALLED LONG MEG AND HER DAUGHTERS, NEAR THE RIVER EDEN

1821. 1822

A WEIGHT of awe, not easy to be borne,
Fell suddenly upon my Spirit — cast
From the dread bosom of the unknown
   past,
When first I saw that family forlorn.
Speak Thou, whose massy strength and
   stature scorn
The power of years — pre-eminent, and
   placed
Apart, to overlook the circle vast —
Speak, Giant-mother ! tell it to the Morn
While she dispels the cumbrous shades of
   Night;
Let the Moon hear, emerging from a
   cloud;
At whose behest uprose on British ground
That Sisterhood, in hieroglyphic round
Forth-shadowing, some have deemed, the
   infinite
The inviolable God, that tames the proud !

XLIII

LOWTHER

1833. 1835

"Cathedral pomp." It may be questioned
whether this union was in the contemplation of
the artist when he planned the edifice. How-
ever this might be, a poet may be excused for
taking the view of the subject presented in this
Sonnet.

LOWTHER ! in thy majestic Pile are seen
Cathedral pomp and grace, in apt accord
With the baronial castle's sterner mien;
Union significant of God adored,
And charters won and guarded by the
   sword
Of ancient honour; whence that goodly
   state
Of polity which wise men venerate,
And will maintain, if God his help afford.
Hourly the democratic torrent swells;
For airy promises and hopes suborned
The strength of backward-looking thoughts
   is scorned.
Fall if ye must, ye Towers and Pinnacles,
With what ye symbolise; authentic Story
Will say, Ye disappeared with England's
   Glory !

XLIV

TO THE EARL OF LONSDALE

1833. 1835

"Magistratus indicat virum"

LONSDALE ! it were unworthy of a Guest,
Whose heart with gratitude to thee in-
   clines,
If he should speak, by fancy touched, of
   signs
On thy Abode harmoniously imprest,
Yet be unmoved with wishes to attest
How in thy mind and moral frame agree
Fortitude, and that Christian Charity
Which, filling, consecrates the human breast.
And if the Motto on thy 'scutcheon teach
With truth, "THE MAGISTRACY SHOWS
   THE MAN;"
That searching test thy public course has
   stood;
As will be owned alike by bad and good,
Soon as the measuring of life's little span
Shall place thy virtues out of Envy's
   reach.

XLV

THE SOMNAMBULIST

1828(?). 1835

This poem might be dedicated to my friends, Sir G. Beaumont and Mr. Rogers, jointly. While we were making an excursion together in this part of the Lake District we heard that Mr. Glover, the artist, while lodging at Lyulph's Tower, had been disturbed by a loud shriek, and upon rising he had learnt that it had come from a young woman in the house who was in the habit of walking in her sleep. In that state she had gone downstairs, and, while attempting to open the outer door, either from some difficulty or the effect of the cold stone upon her feet, had uttered the cry which alarmed him. It seemed to us all that this might serve as a hint for a poem, and the story here told was constructed and soon after put into verse by me as it now stands.

LIST, ye who pass by Lyulph's Tower
  At eve; how softly then
Doth Aira-force, that torrent hoarse,
  Speak from the woody glen !
Fit music for a solemn vale !
  And holier seems the ground
To him who catches on the gale
The spirit of a mournful tale,
  Embodied in the sound.

Not far from that fair site whereon   10
  The Pleasure-house is reared,
As story says, in antique days
  A stern-browed house appeared;
Foil to a Jewel rich in light
  There set, and guarded well;
Cage for a Bird of plumage bright,
Sweet-voiced, nor wishing for a flight
  Beyond her native dell.

To win this bright Bird from her cage,
  To make this Gem their own,   20
Came Barons bold, with store of gold,
  And Knights of high renown;
But one She prized, and only one;
  Sir Eglamore was he;
Full happy season, when was known,
Ye Dales and Hills ! to you alone
  Their mutual loyalty —

Known chiefly, Aira ! to thy glen,
  Thy brook, and bowers of holly;
Where Passion caught what Nature taught,
  That all but love is folly;   31

Where Fact with Fancy stooped to play;
  Doubt came not, nor regret —
To trouble hours that winged their way,
As if through an immortal day
  Whose sun could never set.

But in old times Love dwelt not long
  Sequestered with repose;
Best throve the fire of chaste desire,
  Fanned by the breath of foes.   40
" A conquering lance is beauty's test,
  And proves the Lover true; "
So spake Sir Eglamore, and pressed
  The drooping Emma to his breast,
  And looked a blind adieu.

They parted. — Well with him it fared
  Through wide-spread regions errant;
A knight of proof in love's behoof,
  The thirst of fame his warrant:
And She her happiness can build   50
  On woman's quiet hours;
Though faint, compared with spear and
    shield,
The solace beads and masses yield,
  And needlework and flowers.

Yet blest was Emma when she heard
  Her Champion's praise recounted;
Though brain would swim, and eyes grow
    dim,
  And high her blushes mounted;
Or when a bold heroic lay
  She warbled from full heart;   60
Delightful blossoms for the *May*
Of absence ! but they will not stay,
  Born only to depart.

Hope wanes with her, while lustre fills
  Whatever path he chooses;
As if his orb, that owns no curb,
  Received the light hers loses.
He comes not back; an ampler space
  Requires for nobler deeds;
He ranges on from place to place,   70
  Till of his doings is no trace,
  But what her fancy breeds.

His fame may spread, but in the past
  Her spirit finds its centre;
Clear sight She has of what he was,
  And that would now content her.
" Still is he my devoted Knight ? "
  The tear in answer flows;

Month falls on month with heavier weight;
Day sickens round her, and the night   80
  Is empty of repose.

In sleep She sometimes walked abroad,
  Deep sighs with quick words blending,
Like that pale Queen whose hands are
    seen
  With fancied spots contending;
But *she* is innocent of blood, —
  The moon is not more pure
That shines aloft, while through the wood
She thrids her way, the sounding Flood
  Her melancholy lure !   90

While 'mid the fern-brake sleeps the doe,
  And owls alone are waking,
In white arrayed, glides on the Maid
  The downward pathway taking,
That leads her to the torrent's side
  And to a holly bower;
By whom on this still night descried ?
By whom in that lone place espied ?
  By thee, Sir Eglamore !

A wandering Ghost, so thinks the Knight,
  His coming step has thwarted,   101
Beneath the boughs that heard their
    vows,
  Within whose shade they parted.
Hush, hush, the busy Sleeper see !
  Perplexed her fingers seem,
As if they from the holly tree
Green twigs would pluck, as rapidly
  Flung from her to the stream.

What means the Spectre ?   Why intent
  To violate the Tree,   110
Thought Eglamore, by which I swore
  Unfading constancy ?
Here am I, and to-morrow's sun,
  To her I left, shall prove
That bliss is ne'er so surely won
As when a circuit has been run
  Of valour, truth, and love.

So from the spot whereon he stood,
  He moved with stealthy pace;
And, drawing nigh, with his living eye,   120
  He recognised the face;
And whispers caught, and speeches small,
  Some to the green-leaved tree,
Some muttered to the torrent-fall; —
  " Roar on, and bring him with thy call;
  I heard, and so may He ! "

Soul-shattered was the Knight, nor knew
  If Emma's Ghost it were,
Or boding Shade, or if the Maid
  Her very self stood there.   130
He touched; what followed who shall
    tell ?
The soft touch snapped the thread
Of slumber — shrieking back she fell,
And the Stream whirled her down the
    dell
  Along its foaming bed.

In plunged the Knight ! — when on firm
    ground
  The rescued Maiden lay,
Her eyes grew bright with blissful light,
  Confusion passed away;
She heard, ere to the throne of grace   140
  Her faithful Spirit flew,
His voice — beheld his speaking face;
And, dying, from his own embrace,
  She felt that he was true.

So was he reconciled to life:
  Brief words may speak the rest;
Within the dell he built a cell,
  And there was Sorrow's guest;
In hermits' weeds repose he found,
  From vain temptations free;   150
Beside the torrent dwelling — bound
By one deep heart-controlling sound,
  And awed to piety.

Wild stream of Aira, hold thy course,
  Nor fear memorial lays,
Where clouds that spread in solemn shade,
  Are edged with golden rays !
Dear art thou to the light of heaven,
  Though minister of sorrow;
Sweet is thy voice at pensive even;   160
And thou, in lovers' hearts forgiven,
  Shalt take thy place with Yarrow !

XLVI

TO CORDELIA M——

HALLSTEADS, ULLSWATER

1833. 1835

NOT in the mines beyond the western main,
You say, Cordelia, was the metal sought,
Which a fine skill, of Indian growth, has
    wrought

Into this flexible yet faithful Chain;
Nor is it silver of romantic Spain
But from our loved Helvellyn's depths was
  brought,
Our own domestic mountain. Thing and
  thought
Mix strangely; trifles light, and partly
  vain,
Can prop, as you have learnt, our nobler
  being:
Yes, Lady, while about your neck is
  wound
(Your casual glance oft meeting) this bright
  cord,
What witchery, for pure gifts of inward
  seeing,
Lurks in it, Memory's Helper, Fancy's
  Lord,
For precious tremblings in your bosom
  found !

XLVII

1833. 1835

Most sweet it is with unuplifted eyes
To pace the ground, if path be there or none,
While a fair region round the traveller lies
Which he forbears again to look upon;
Pleased rather with some soft ideal scene,
The work of Fancy, or some happy tone
Of meditation, slipping in between
The beauty coming and the beauty gone.
If Thought and Love desert us, from that day
Let us break off all commerce with the
  Muse:
With Thought and Love companions of our
  way,
Whate'er the senses take or may refuse,
The Mind's internal heaven shall shed her
  dews
Of inspiration on the humblest lay.

COMPOSED BY THE SEASHORE

1833. 1842

These lines were suggested during my residence under my Son's roof at Moresby, on the coast near Whitehaven, at the time when I was composing those verses among the " Evening Voluntaries " that have reference to the sea. It was in that neighbourhood I first became acquainted with the ocean and its appearances and movements. My infancy and early childhood were passed at Cockermouth, about eight miles from the coast, and I well remember that mysterious awe with which I used to listen to anything said about storms and shipwrecks. Sea-shells of many descriptions were common in the town; and I was not a little surprised when I heard that Mr. Landor had denounced me as a plagiarist from himself for having described a boy applying a sea-shell to his ear and listening to it for intimations of what was going on in its native element. This I had done myself scores of times, and it was a belief among us that we could know from the sound whether the tide was ebbing or flowing.

What mischief cleaves to unsubdued regret,
How fancy sickens by vague hopes beset;
How baffled projects on the spirit prey,
And fruitless wishes eat the heart away,
The Sailor knows; he best, whose lot is cast
On the relentless sea that holds him fast

On chance dependent, and the fickle star
Of power, through long and melancholy war.
O sad it is, in sight of foreign shores,
Daily to think on old familiar doors,   10
Hearths loved in childhood, and ancestral
  floors;
Or, tossed about along a waste of foam,
To ruminate on that delightful home
Which with the dear Betrothèd was to
  come;
Or came and was and is, yet meets the eye
Never but in the world of memory;
Or in a dream recalled, whose smoothest
  range
Is crossed by knowledge, or by dread, of
  change,
And if not so, whose perfect joy makes
  sleep
A thing too bright for breathing man to
  keep.   20
Hail to the virtues which that perilous life
Extracts from Nature's elemental strife;
And welcome glory won in battles fought
As bravely as the foe is keenly sought.
But to each gallant Captain and his crew
A less imperious sympathy is due,
Such as my verse now yields, while moon-
  beams play
On the mute sea in this unruffled bay;
Such as will promptly flow from every
  breast,

Where good men, disappointed in the quest
Of wealth and power and honours, long for
   rest;   31
Or, having known the splendours of success,
Sigh for the obscurities of happiness.

"NOT IN THE LUCID INTER-VALS OF LIFE"

1834. 1835

The lines following "nor do words" were
written with Lord Byron's character, as a poet,
before me, and that of others, his contempo-
raries, who wrote under like influences.

Not in the lucid intervals of life
That come but as a curse to party-strife;
Not in some hour when Pleasure with a sigh
Of languor puts his rosy garland by;
Not in the breathing-times of that poor slave
Who daily piles up wealth in Mammon's
   cave —
Is Nature felt, or can be; nor do words,
Which practised talent readily affords,
Prove that her hand has touched responsive
   chords;
Nor has her gentle beauty power to move 10
With genuine rapture and with fervent love
The soul of Genius, if he dare to take
Life's rule from passion craved for passion's
   sake;
Untaught that meekness is the cherished
   bent
Of all the truly great and all the innocent.
  But who is innocent ? By grace divine,
Not otherwise, O Nature ! we are thine,
Through good and evil thine, in just degree
Of rational and manly sympathy.
To all that Earth from pensive hearts is
   stealing,   20
And Heaven is now to gladdened eyes re-
   vealing,
Add every charm the Universe can show
Through every change its aspects undergo —
Care may be respited, but not repealed;
No perfect cure grows on that bounded
   field.
Vain is the pleasure, a false calm the peace,
If He, through whom alone our conflicts
   cease,
Our virtuous hopes without relapse advance,
Come not to speed the Soul's deliverance;
To the distempered Intellect refuse   30
His gracious help, or give what we abuse.

BY THE SIDE OF RYDAL MERE

1834. 1835

The linnet's warble, sinking towards a
   close,
Hints to the thrush 't is time for their re-
   pose;
The shrill-voiced thrush is heedless, and
   again
The monitor revives his own sweet strain;
But both will soon be mastered, and the copse
Be left as silent as the mountain-tops,
Ere some commanding star dismiss to rest
The throng of rooks, that now, from twig
   or nest,
(After a steady flight on home-bound wings,
And a last game of mazy hoverings   10
Around their ancient grove) with cawing
   noise
Disturb the liquid music's equipoise.
  O Nightingale ! Who ever heard thy
   song
Might here be moved, till Fancy grows so
   strong
That listening sense is pardonably cheated
Where wood or stream by thee was never
   greeted.
Surely, from fairest spots of favoured lands,
Were not some gifts withheld by jealous
   hands,
This hour of deepening darkness here would
   be
As a fresh morning for new harmony;   20
And lays as prompt would hail the dawn of
   Night:
A *dawn* she has both beautiful and bright,
When the East kindles with the full moon's
   light;
Not like the rising sun's impatient glow
Dazzling the mountains, but an overflow
Of solemn splendour, in mutation slow.
  Wanderer by spring with gradual prog-
   ress led,
For sway profoundly felt as widely spread;
To king, to peasant, to rough sailor, dear,
And to the soldier's trumpet-wearied ear;
How welcome wouldst thou be to this green
   Vale   31
Fairer than Tempe ! Yet, sweet Nightin-
   gale !
From the warm breeze that bears thee on,
   alight
At will, and stay thy migratory flight;
Build, at thy choice, or sing, by pool or
   fount,

Who shall complain, or call thee to account?
The wisest, happiest, of our kind are they
That ever walk content with Nature's
way,
God's goodness — measuring bounty as it
may;
For whom the gravest thought of what
they miss,   40
Chastening the fulness of a present bliss,
Is with that wholesome office satisfied,
While unrepining sadness is allied
In thankful bosoms to a modest pride.

"SOFT AS A CLOUD IS YON BLUE RIDGE"

1834. 1835

SOFT as a cloud is yon blue Ridge — the
Mere
Seems firm as solid crystal, breathless,
clear,
And motionless; and, to the gazer's eye,
Deeper than ocean, in the immensity
Of its vague mountains and unreal sky!
But, from the process in that still retreat,
Turn to minuter changes at our feet;
Observe how dewy Twilight has with-
drawn
The crowd of daisies from the shaven lawn,
And has restored to view its tender green,
That, while the sun rode high, was lost
beneath their dazzling sheen.
— An emblem this of what the sober Hour
Can do for minds disposed to feel its power!
Thus oft, when we in vain have wished
away
The petty pleasures of the garish day,
Meek eve shuts up the whole usurping
host
(Unbashful dwarfs each glittering at his
post)
And leaves the disencumbered spirit free
To reassume a staid simplicity.
'T is well — but what are helps of time
and place,
When wisdom stands in need of nature's
grace;
Why do good thoughts, invoked or not,
descend,
Like Angels from their bowers, our virtues
to befriend;
If yet To-morrow, unbelied, may say,
"I come to open out, for fresh display,
The elastic vanities of yesterday"?

"THE LEAVES THAT RUSTLED ON THIS OAK-CROWNED HILL"

1834. 1835

Composed by the side of Grasmere lake. The
mountains that enclose the vale, especially to-
wards Easdale, are most favourable to the re-
verberation of sound. There is a passage in the
"Excursion," towards the close of the fourth
book, where the voice of the raven in flight is
traced through the modifications it undergoes,
as I have often heard it in that vale and others
of this district.

> "Often, at the hour
> When issue forth the first pale stars, is heard,
> Within the circuit of this fabric huge,
> One voice — the solitary raven."

THE leaves that rustled on this oak-crowned
hill,
And sky that danced among those leaves,
are still;
Rest smooths the way for sleep; in field and
bower
Soft shades and dews have shed their
blended power
On drooping eyelid and the closing flower;
Sound is there none at which the faintest
heart
Might leap, the weakest nerve of supersti-
tion start;
Save when the Owlet's unexpected scream
Pierces the ethereal vault; and ('mid the
gleam
Of unsubstantial imagery, the dream,   10
From the hushèd vale's realities, transferred
To the still lake) the imaginative Bird
Seems, 'mid inverted mountains, not un-
heard.
Grave Creature! — whether, while the
moon shines bright
On thy wings opened wide for smoothest
flight,
Thou art discovered in a roofless tower,
Rising from what may once have been a
lady's bower;
Or spied where thou sitt'st moping in thy
mew
At the dim centre of a churchyard yew;
Or, from a rifted crag or ivy tod   20
Deep in a forest, thy secure abode,
Thou giv'st, for pastime's sake, by shriek
or shout,
A puzzling notice of thy whereabout —
May the night never come, nor day be seen,
When I shall scorn thy voice or mock thy
mien!

In classic ages men perceived a soul
Of sapience in thy aspect, headless Owl!
Thee Athens reverenced in the studious
    grove;
And, near the golden sceptre grasped by Jove,
His Eagle's favourite perch, while round
    him sate   30
The Gods revolving the decrees of Fate,
Thou, too, wert present at Minerva's side:—
Hark to that second larum!—far and wide
The elements have heard, and rock and
    cave replied.

THE LABOURER'S NOON–DAY HYMN

1834. 1835

Bishop Ken's Morning and Evening Hymns are, as they deserve to be, familiarly known. Many other hymns have also been written on the same subject; but, not being aware of any being designed for noon-day, I was induced to compose these verses. Often one has occasion to observe cottage children carrying, in their baskets, dinner to their Fathers engaged with their daily labours in the fields and woods. How gratifying would it be to me could I be assured that any portion of these stanzas had been sung by such a domestic concert under such circumstances. A friend of mine has told me that she introduced this Hymn into a village-school which she superintended, and the stanzas in succession furnished her with texts to comment upon in a way which without difficulty was made intelligible to the children, and in which they obviously took delight, and they were taught to sing it to the tune of the old 100th Psalm.

UP to the throne of God is borne
The voice of praise at early morn,
And he accepts the punctual hymn
Sung as the light of day grows dim:

Nor will he turn his ear aside
From holy offerings at noontide:
Then here reposing let us raise
A song of gratitude and praise.

What though our burthen be not light,
We need not toil from morn to night;   10
The respite of the mid-day hour
Is in the thankful Creature's power.

Blest are the moments, doubly blest,
That, drawn from this one hour of rest,
Are with a ready heart bestowed
Upon the service of our God!

Each field is then a hallowed spot,
An altar is in each man's cot,
A church in every grove that spreads
Its living roof above our heads.   20

Look up to Heaven! the industrious Sun
Already half his race hath run;
He cannot halt nor go astray,
But our immortal Spirits may.

Lord! since his rising in the East,
If we have faltered or transgressed,
Guide, from thy love's abundant source,
What yet remains of this day's course:

Help with thy grace, through life's short
    day,
Our upward and our downward way;   30
And glorify for us the west,
When we shall sink to final rest.

THE REDBREAST

SUGGESTED IN A WESTMORELAND COTTAGE

1834. 1835

Written at Rydal Mount. All our cats having been banished the house, it was soon frequented by redbreasts. Two or three of them, when the window was open, would come in, particularly when Mary was breakfasting alone, and hop about the table picking up the crumbs. My sister being then confined to her room by sickness, as, dear creature, she still is, had one that, without being caged, took up its abode with her, and at night used to perch upon a nail from which a picture had hung. It used to sing and fan her face with its wings in a manner that was very touching.

DRIVEN in by Autumn's sharpening air
From half-stripped woods and pastures bare,
Brisk Robin seeks a kindlier home:
Not like a beggar is he come,
But enters as a looked-for guest,
Confiding in his ruddy breast,
As if it were a natural shield
Charged with a blazon on the field,
Due to that good and pious deed
Of which we in the Ballad read.   10

But pensive fancies putting by,
And wild-wood sorrows, speedily
He plays the expert ventriloquist;
And, caught by glimpses now — now missed,
Puzzles the listener with a doubt
If the soft voice he throws about
Comes from within doors or without !
Was ever such a sweet confusion,
Sustained by delicate illusion ?
He 's at your elbow — to your feeling   20
The notes are from the floor or ceiling;
And there 's a riddle to be guessed,
'Till you have marked his heaving chest,
And busy throat whose sink and swell,
Betray the Elf that loves to dwell
In Robin's bosom, as a chosen cell.

Heart-pleased we smile upon the Bird
If seen, and with like pleasure stirred
Commend him, when he 's only heard.
But small and fugitive our gain   30
Compared with *hers* who long hath lain,
With languid limbs and patient head
Reposing on a lone sick-bed;
Where now, she daily hears a strain
That cheats her of too busy cares,
Eases her pain, and helps her prayers.
And who but this dear Bird beguiled
The fever of that pale-faced Child;
Now cooling, with his passing wing,
Her forehead, like a breeze of Spring: 40
Recalling now, with descant soft
Shed round her pillow from aloft,
Sweet thoughts of angels hovering nigh,
And the invisible sympathy
Of " Matthew, Mark, and Luke, and John,
Blessing the bed she lies upon " ?
And sometimes, just as listening ends
In slumber, with the cadence blends
A dream of that low-warbled hymn
Which old folk, fondly pleased to trim   50
Lamps of faith, now burning dim,
Say that the Cherubs, carved in stone,
When clouds gave way at dead of night
And the ancient church was filled with
        light,
Used to sing in heavenly tone,
Above and round the sacred places
They guard, with wingèd baby-faces.
Thrice happy Creature ! in all lands
Nurtured by hospitable hands:
Free entrance to this cot has he,   60
Entrance and exit both *yet* free;
And, when the keen unruffled weather
That thus brings man and bird together,
Shall with its pleasantness be past,

And casement closed and door made fast,
To keep at bay the howling blast,
He needs not fear the season's rage,
For the whole house is Robin's cage.
Whether the bird flit here or there,
O'er table *lilt*, or perch on chair,   70
Though some may frown and make a stir,
To scare him as a trespasser,
And he belike will flinch or start,
Good friends he has to take his part;
One chiefly, who with voice and look
Pleads for him from the chimney-nook,
Where sits the Dame, and wears away
Her long and vacant holiday;
With images about her heart,
Reflected from the years gone by,   80
On human nature's second infancy.

LINES

SUGGESTED BY A PORTRAIT FROM THE PENCIL OF F. STONE

1834. 1835

This Portrait has hung for many years in our
principal sitting-room, and represents J. Q. as
she was when a girl. The picture, though it is
somewhat thinly painted, has much merit in
tone and general effect: it is chiefly valuable,
however, from the sentiment that pervades it.
The Anecdote of the saying of the Monk in
sight of Titian's picture was told in this house
by Mr. Wilkie, and was, I believe, first com-
municated to the public in this poem, the for-
mer portion of which I was composing at the
time. Southey heard the story from Miss
Hutchinson, and transferred it to the " Doctor ";
but it is not easy to explain how my friend Mr.
Rogers, in a note subsequently added to his
" Italy," was led to speak of the same remark-
able words having many years before been
spoken in his hearing by a monk or priest in
front of a picture of the Last Supper, placed
over a Refectory-table in a convent at Padua.

BEGUILED into forgetfulness of care
Due to the day's unfinished task; of pen
Or book regardless, and of that fair scene
In Nature's prodigality displayed
Before my window, oftentimes and long
I gaze upon a Portrait whose mild gleam
Of beauty never ceases to enrich
The common light; whose stillness charms
        the air,
Or seems to charm it, into like repose;   9
Whose silence, for the pleasure of the ear,

Surpasses sweetest music. There she sits
With emblematic purity attired
In a white vest, white as her marble neck
Is, and the pillar of the throat would be
But for the shadow by the drooping chin
Cast into that recess — the tender shade,
The shade and light, both there and every-
    where,
And through the very atmosphere she
    breathes,
Broad, clear, and toned harmoniously, with
    skill
That might from nature have been learnt
    in the hour   20
When the lone shepherd sees the morning
    spread
Upon the mountains.   Look at her, whoe'er
Thou be that, kindling with a poet's soul,
Hast loved the painter's true Promethean
    craft
Intensely — from Imagination take
The treasure, — what mine eyes behold,
    see thou,
Even though the Atlantic ocean roll be-
    tween.
  A silver line, that runs from brow to
    crown
And in the middle parts the braided hair,
Just serves to show how delicate a soil   30
The golden harvest grows in; and those
    eyes,
Soft and capacious as a cloudless sky
Whose azure depth their colour emulates,
Must needs be conversant with upward
    looks,
Prayer's voiceless service; but now, seeking
    nought
And shunning nought, their own peculiar
    life
Of motion they renounce, and with the head
Partake its inclination towards earth
In humble grace, and quiet pensiveness
Caught at the point where it stops short of
    sadness.   40
  Offspring of soul-bewitching Art, make
    me
Thy confidant ! say, whence derived that air
Of calm abstraction ? Can the ruling
    thought
Be with some lover far away, or one
Crossed by misfortune, or of doubted faith ?
Inapt conjecture ! Childhood here, a moon
Crescent in simple loveliness serene,
Has but approached the gates of woman-
    hood,

Not entered them; her heart is yet un-
    pierced
By the blind Archer-god; her fancy free: 50
The fount of feeling if unsought elsewhere,
Will not be found.
              Her right hand, as it lies
Across the slender wrist of the left arm
Upon her lap reposing, holds — but mark
How slackly, for the absent mind permits
No firmer grasp — a little wild-flower,
    joined
As in a posy, with a few pale ears
Of yellowing corn, the same that overtopped
And in their common birthplace sheltered
    it
'Till they were plucked together; a blue
    flower   60
Called by the thrifty husbandman a weed;
But Ceres, in her garland, might have worn
That ornament, unblamed. The floweret,
    held
In scarcely conscious fingers, was, she
    knows,
(Her Father told her so) in youth's gay
    dawn
Her Mother's favourite; and the orphan
    Girl,
In her own dawn — a dawn less gay and
    bright,
Loves it, while there in solitary peace
She sits, for that departed Mother's sake.
— Not from a source less sacred is derived
(Surely I do not err) that pensive air   71
Of calm abstraction through the face dif-
    fused
And the whole person.
           Words have something told
More than the pencil can, and verily
More than is needed, but the precious Art
Forgives their interference — Art divine,
That both creates and fixes, in despite
Of Death and Time, the marvels it hath
    wrought.
  Strange contrasts have we in this world
    of ours !
That posture, and the look of filial love 80
Thinking of past and gone, with what is
    left
Dearly united, might be swept away
From this fair Portrait's fleshly Archetype,
Even by an innocent fancy's slightest freak
Banished, nor ever, haply, be restored
To their lost place, or meet in harmony
So exquisite; but *here* do they abide,
Enshrined for ages. Is not then the Art

Godlike, a humble branch of the divine,
In visible quest of immortality,   90
Stretched forth with trembling hope ? — In
    every realm,
From high Gibraltar to Siberian plains,
Thousands, in each variety of tongue
That Europe knows, would echo this ap-
    peal;
One above all, a Monk who waits on God
In the magnific Convent built of yore
To sanctify the Escurial palace. He —
Guiding, from cell to cell and room to
    room,
A British Painter (eminent for truth
In character, and depth of feeling, shown
By labours that have touched the hearts of
    kings,   101
And are endeared to simple cottagers —
Came, in that service, to a glorious work,
Our Lord's Last Supper, beautiful as when
    first
The appropriate Picture, fresh from Titian's
    hand,
Graced the Refectory: and there, while
    both
Stood with eyes fixed upon that master-
    piece,
The hoary Father in the Stranger's ear
Breathed out these words: — " Here daily
    do' we sit,
Thanks given to God for daily bread, and
    here   110
Pondering the mischiefs of these restless
    times,
And thinking of my Brethren, dead, dis-
    persed,
Or changed and changing, I not seldom
    gaze
Upon this solemn Company unmoved
By shock of circumstance, or lapse of
    years,
Until I cannot but believe that they —
They are in truth the Substance, we the
    Shadows."
So spake the mild Jeronymite, his griefs
Melting away within him like a dream
Ere he had ceased to gaze, perhaps to
    speak: 120
And I, grown old, but in a happier land,
Domestic Portrait ! have to verse consigned
In thy calm presence those heart-moving
    words:
Words that can soothe, more than they
    agitate;
Whose spirit, like the angel that went down

Into Bethesda's pool, with healing virtue
Informs the fountain in the human breast
Which by the visitation was disturbed.
— But why this stealing tear ?   Companion
    mute,
On thee I look, not sorrowing; fare thee
    well,   130
My Song's Inspirer, once again farewell !

THE FOREGOING SUBJECT RESUMED

1834. 1835

AMONG a grave fraternity of Monks,
For One, but surely not for One alone,
Triumphs, in that great work, the Painter's
    skill,
Humbling the body, to exalt the soul;
Yet representing, amid wreck and wrong
And dissolution and decay, the warm
And breathing life of flesh, as if already
Clothed with impassive majesty, and graced
With no mean earnest of a heritage
Assigned to it in future worlds. Thou,
    too,   10
With thy memorial flower, meek Portrait-
    ure !
From whose serene companionship I passed
Pursued by thoughts that haunt me still;
    thou also —
Though but a simple object, into light
Called forth by those affections that en-
    dear
The private hearth; though keeping thy
    sole seat
In singleness, and little tried by time,
Creation, as it were, of yesterday —
With a congenial function art endued
For each and all of us, together joined   20
In course of nature under a low roof
By charities and duties that proceed
Out of the bosom of a wiser vow.
To a like salutary sense of awe
Or sacred wonder, growing with the power
Of meditation that attempts to weigh,
In faithful scales, things and their oppo-
    sites,
Can thy enduring quiet gently raise
A household small and sensitive, — whose
    love,
Dependent as in part its blessings are   30
Upon frail ties dissolving or dissolved
On earth, will be revived, we trust, in
    heaven.

TO A CHILD

WRITTEN IN HER ALBUM

1834. 1835

This quatrain was extempore on observing this image, as I had often done, on the lawn of Rydal Mount. It was first written down in the Album of my God-daughter, Rotha Quillinan.

SMALL service is true service while it lasts:
Of humblest Friends, bright Creature! scorn not one:
The Daisy, by the shadow that it casts,
Protects the lingering dew-drop from the Sun.

LINES

WRITTEN IN THE ALBUM OF THE COUNTESS OF LONSDALE. NOV. 5, 1834

1834. 1835

This is a faithful picture of that amiable Lady, as she then was. The youthfulness of figure and demeanour and habits, which she retained in almost unprecedented degree, departed a very few years after, and she died without violent disease by gradual decay before she reached the period of old age.

LADY! a Pen (perhaps with thy regard,
Among the Favoured, favoured not the least)
Left, 'mid the Records of this Book inscribed,
Deliberate traces, registers of thought
And feeling, suited to the place and time
That gave them birth: — months passed, and still this hand,
That had not been too timid to imprint
Words which the virtues of thy Lord inspired,
Was yet not bold enough to write of Thee.
And why that scrupulous reserve? In sooth   10
The blameless cause lay in the Theme itself.
Flowers are there many that delight to strive
With the sharp wind, and seem to court the shower,
Yet are by nature careless of the sun
Whether he shine on them or not; and some,
Where'er he moves along the unclouded sky,
Turn a broad front full on his flattering beams:

Others do rather from their notice shrink,
Loving the dewy shade, — a humble band,
Modest and sweet, a progeny of earth,   20
Congenial with thy mind and character,
High-born Augusta!
                Witness, Towers and Groves!
And Thou, wild Stream, that giv'st the honoured name
Of Lowther to this ancient Line, bear witness
From thy most secret haunts; and ye Parterres,
Which She is pleased and proud to call her own,
Witness how oft upon my noble Friend
Mute offerings, tribute from an inward sense
Of admiration and respectful love,
Have waited — till the affections could no more   30
Endure that silence, and broke out in song,
Snatches of music taken up and dropt
Like those self-solacing, those under, notes
Trilled by the redbreast, when autumnal leaves
Are thin upon the bough. Mine, only mine,
The pleasure was, and no one heard the praise,
Checked, in the moment of its issue, checked
And reprehended, by a fancied blush
From the pure qualities that called it forth.
    Thus Virtue lives debarred from Virtue's meed;   40
Thus, Lady, is retiredness a veil
That, while it only spreads a softening charm
O'er features looked at by discerning eyes,
Hides half their beauty from the common gaze;
And thus, even on the exposed and breezy hill
Of lofty station, female goodness walks,
When side by side with lunar gentleness,
As in a cloister. Yet the grateful Poor
(Such the immunities of low estate,
Plain Nature's enviable privilege,   50
Her sacred recompence for many wants)
Open their hearts before Thee, pouring out
All that they think and feel, with tears of joy;
And benedictions not unheard in heaven·
And friend in the ear of friend, where speech is free
To follow truth, is eloquent as they.

Then let the Book receive in these prompt
    lines
A just memorial; and thine eyes consent
To read that they, who mark thy course,
    behold
A life declining with the golden light   60
Of summer, in the season of sere leaves;
See cheerfulness undamped by stealing
    Time;
See studied kindness flow with easy stream,
Illustrated with inborn courtesy;
And an habitual disregard of self
Balanced by vigilance for others' weal.
    And shall the Verse not tell of lighter
    gifts
With these ennobling attributes conjoined
And blended, in peculiar harmony,
By Youth's surviving spirit? What agile
    grace!   70
A nymph-like liberty, in nymph-like form,
Beheld with wonder; whether floor or
    path
Thou tread; or sweep — borne on the
    managed steed —
Fleet as the shadows, over down or field,
Driven by strong winds at play among the
    clouds.
    Yet one word more — one farewell word
    — a wish
Which came, but it has passed into a
    prayer —
That, as thy sun in brightness is declining,
So — at an hour yet distant for *their* sakes
Whose tender love, here faltering on the
    way   80
Of a diviner love, will be forgiven —
So may it set in peace, to rise again
For everlasting glory won by faith.

TO THE MOON

COMPOSED BY THE SEASIDE, — ON THE
COAST OF CUMBERLAND

1835. 1837

WANDERER! that stoop'st so low, and
    com'st so near
To human life's unsettled atmosphere;
Who lov'st with Night and Silence to par-
    take,
So might it seem, the cares of them that
    wake;
And, through the cottage-lattice softly
    peeping,

Dost shield from harm the humblest of the
    sleeping;
What pleasure once encompassed those
    sweet names
Which yet in thy behalf the Poet claims,
An idolizing dreamer as of yore! —
I slight them all; and, on this sea-beat shore
Sole-sitting, only can to thoughts attend 11
That bid me hail thee as the SAILOR'S
    FRIEND;
So call thee for heaven's grace through thee
    made known
By confidence supplied and mercy shown,
When not a twinkling star or beacon's light
Abates the perils of a stormy night;
And for less obvious benefits, that find
Their way, with thy pure help, to heart
    and mind;
Both for the adventurer starting in life's
    prime;
And veteran ranging round from clime to
    clime,   20
Long-baffled hope's slow fever in his veins,
And wounds and weakness oft his labour's
    sole remains.
    The aspiring Mountains and the winding
    Streams,
Empress of Night! are gladdened by thy
    beams;
A look of thine the wilderness pervades,
And penetrates the forest's inmost shades;
Thou, chequering peaceably the minster's
    gloom,
Guid'st the pale Mourner to the lost one's
    tomb;
Canst reach the Prisoner — to his grated
    cell   29
Welcome, though silent and intangible! —
And lives there one, of all that come and go
On the great waters toiling to and fro,
One, who has watched thee at some quiet
    hour
Enthroned aloft in undisputed power,
Or crossed by vapoury streaks and clouds
    that move
Catching the lustre they in part reprove —
Nor sometimes felt a fitness in thy sway
To call up thoughts that shun the glare of
    day,
And make the serious happier than the gay?
    Yes, lovely Moon! if thou so mildly
    bright   40
Dost rouse, yet surely in thy own despite,
To fiercer mood the phrenzy-stricken brain,
Let me a compensating faith maintain;

That there's a sensitive, a tender, part
Which thou canst touch in every human
    heart,
For healing and composure. — But, as least
And mightiest billows ever have confessed
Thy domination; as the whole vast Sea
Feels through her lowest depths thy
    sovereignty;
So shines that countenance with especial
    grace   50
On them who urge the keel her *plains* to
    trace
Furrowing its way right onward. The most
    rude,
Cut off from home and country, may have
    stood —
Even till long gazing hath bedimmed his eye,
Or the mute rapture ended in a sigh —
Touched by accordance of thy placid cheer,
With some internal lights to memory dear,
Or fancies stealing forth to soothe the breast
Tired with its daily share of earth's unrest, —
Gentle awakenings, visitations meek;   60
A kindly influence whereof few will speak,
Though it can wet with tears the hardiest
    cheek.
    And when thy beauty in the shadowy
        cave
Is hidden, buried in its monthly grave;
Then, while the Sailor, 'mid an open sea
Swept by a favouring wind that leaves
    thought free,
Paces the deck — no star perhaps in sight,
And nothing save the moving ship's own
    light
To cheer the long dark hours of vacant
    night —   69
Oft with his musings does thy image blend,
In his mind's eye thy crescent horns ascend,
And thou art still, O Moon, that SAILOR'S
FRIEND !

TO THE MOON

RYDAL

1835. 1837

QUEEN of the stars ! — so gentle, so benign,
That ancient Fable did to thee assign,
When darkness creeping o'er thy silver brow
Warned thee these upper regions to forego,
Alternate empire in the shades below —
A Bard, who, lately near the wide-spread sea
Traversed by gleaming ships, looked up
    to thee

With grateful thoughts, doth now thy ris-
    ing hail
From the close confines of a shadowy vale.
Glory of night, conspicuous yet serene,   10
Nor less attractive when by glimpses seen
Through cloudy umbrage, well might that
    fair face,
And all those attributes of modest grace,
In days when Fancy wrought unchecked by
    fear,
Down to the green earth fetch thee from
    thy sphere,
To sit in leafy woods by fountains clear !
    O still beloved (for thine, meek Power,
        are charms
That fascinate the very Babe in arms,
While he, uplifted towards thee, laughs
    outright,
Spreading his little palms in his glad
    Mother's sight)   20
O still beloved, once worshipped ! Time,
    that frowns
In his destructive flight on earthly crowns,
Spares thy mild splendour; still those far-
    shot beams
Tremble on dancing waves and rippling
    streams
With stainless touch, as chaste as when thy
    praise
Was sung by Virgin-choirs in festal lays;
And through dark trials still dost thou
    explore
Thy way for increase punctual as of yore,
When teeming Matrons — yielding to rude
    faith
In mysteries of birth and life and death   30
And painful struggle and deliverance —
    prayed
Of thee to visit them with lenient aid.
What though the rites be swept away, the
    fanes
Extinct that echoed to the votive strains;
Yet thy mild aspect does not, cannot, cease
Love to promote and purity and peace;
And Fancy, unreproved, even yet may trace
Faint types of suffering in thy beamless
    face.
    Then, silent Monitress ! let us — not blind
To worlds unthought of till the searching
    mind   40
Of Science laid them open to mankind —
Told, also, how the voiceless heavens de-
    clare
God's glory; and acknowledging thy share
In that blest charge; let us — without offence

To aught of highest, holiest influence —
Receive whatever good 't is given thee to
    dispense.
May sage and simple, catching with one eye
The moral intimations of the sky,
Learn from thy course, where'er their own
    be taken,
" To look on tempests, and be never
    shaken;"   50
To keep with faithful step the appointed
    way,
Eclipsing or eclipsed, by night or day,
And from example of thy monthly range
Gently to brook decline and fatal change;
Meek, patient, stedfast, and with loftier
    scope,
Than thy revival yields, for gladsome hope!

WRITTEN AFTER THE DEATH
OF CHARLES LAMB

1835. 1835–37

Light will be thrown upon the tragic circum-
stance alluded to in this poem when, after the
death of Charles Lamb's Sister, his biographer,
Mr. Sergeant Talfourd, shall be at liberty to
relate particulars which could not, at the time
his Memoir was written, be given to the public.
Mary Lamb was ten years older than her
brother, and has survived him as long a time.
Were I to give way to my own feelings, I
should dwell not only on her genius and intel-
lectual powers, but upon the delicacy and re-
finement of manner which she maintained in-
violable under most trying circumstances. She
was loved and honoured by all her brother's
friends; and others, some of them strange
characters, whom his philanthropic peculiarities
induced him to countenance. The death of C.
Lamb himself was doubtless hastened by his
sorrow for that of Coleridge, to whom he had
been attached from the time of their being
school-fellows at Christ's Hospital. Lamb was
a good Latin scholar, and probably would have
gone to college upon one of the school founda-
tions but for the impediment in his speech.
Had such been his lot, he would most likely
have been preserved from the indulgences of
social humours and fancies which were often
injurious to himself, and causes of severe re-
gret to his friends, without really benefiting
the object of his misapplied kindness.

To a good Man of most dear memory
This Stone is sacred. Here he lies apart
From the great city where he first drew
    breath,
Was reared and taught; and humbly earned
    his bread,
To the strict labours of the merchant's desk
By duty chained. Not seldom did those
    tasks
Tease, and the thought of time so spent
    depress,
His spirit, but the recompence was high;
Firm Independence, Bounty's rightful sire;
Affections, warm as sunshine, free as air; 10
And when the precious hours of leisure
    came,
Knowledge and wisdom, gained from con-
    verse sweet
With books, or while he ranged the crowded
    streets
With a keen eye, and overflowing heart:
So genius triumphed over seeming wrong,
And poured out truth in works by thought-
    ful love
Inspired — works potent over smiles and
    tears.
And as round mountain-tops the lightning
    plays,
Thus innocently sported, breaking forth
As from a cloud of some grave sympathy, 20
Humour and wild instinctive wit, and all
The vivid flashes of his spoken words.
From the most gentle creature nursed in
    fields
Had been derived the name he bore — a
    name,
Wherever Christian altars have been raised,
Hallowed to meekness and to innocence;
And if in him meekness at times gave way,
Provoked out of herself by troubles strange,
Many and strange, that hung about his life;
Still, at the centre of his being, lodged   30
A soul by resignation sanctified:
And if too often, self-reproached, he felt
That innocence belongs not to our kind,
A power that never ceased to abide in
    him,
Charity, 'mid the multitude of sins
That she can cover, left not his exposed
To an unforgiving judgment from just
    Heaven.
Oh, he was good, if e'er a good Man lived !
. . . .
From a reflecting mind and sorrowing heart
Those simple lines flowed with an earnest
    wish,   40
Though but a doubting hope, that they
    might serve
Fitly to guard the precious dust of him

Whose virtues called them forth. That
aim is missed;
For much that truth most urgently required
Had from a faltering pen been asked in
vain:
Yet, haply, on the printed page received,
The imperfect record, there, may stand un-
blamed
As long as verse of mine shall breathe the
air
Of memory, or see the light of love.
    Thou wert a scorner of the fields, my
Friend,   50
But more in show than truth; and from the
fields,
And from the mountains, to thy rural grave
Transported, my soothed spirit hovers o'er
Its green untrodden turf, and blowing
flowers;
And taking up a voice shall speak (tho' still
Awed by the theme's peculiar sanctity
Which words less free presumed not even
to touch)
Of that fraternal love, whose heaven-lit
lamp
From infancy, through manhood, to the last
Of threescore years, and to thy latest hour,
Burnt on with ever-strengthening light,
enshrined   61
Within thy bosom.
                "Wonderful" hath been
The love established between man and man,
"Passing the love of women;" and between
Man and his help-mate in fast wedlock
joined
Through God, is raised a spirit and soul of
love
Without whose blissful influence Paradise
Had been no Paradise; and earth were now
A waste where creatures bearing human
form,
Direst of savage beasts, would roam in fear,
Joyless and comfortless. Our days glide
on;   71
And let him grieve who cannot choose but
grieve
That he hath been an Elm without his Vine,
And her bright dower of clustering char-
ities,
That, round his trunk and branches, might
have clung
Enriching and adorning. Unto thee,
Not so enriched, not so adorned, to thee
Was given (say rather, thou of later birth
Wert given to her) a Sister — 't is a word

Timidly uttered, for she *lives*, the meek, 80
The self-restraining, and the ever-kind;
In whom thy reason and intelligent heart
Found — for all interests, hopes, and tender
cares,
All   softening,   humanising,   hallowing
powers,
Whether withheld, or for her sake un-
sought —
More than sufficient recompence !
                            Her love
(What weakness prompts the voice to tell
it here ?)
Was as the love of mothers; and when
years,
Lifting the boy to man's estate, had called
The long-protected to assume the part   90
Of a protector, the first filial tie
Was undissolved; and, in or out of sight,
Remained imperishably interwoven
With life itself. Thus, 'mid a shifting
world,
Did they together testify of time
And season's difference — a double tree
With two collateral stems sprung from one
root;
Such were they — such thro' life they *might*
have been
In union, in partition only such;
Otherwise wrought the will of the Most
High;   100
Yet, thro' all visitations and all trials,
Still they were faithful; like two vessels
launched
From the same beach one ocean to explore
With mutual help, and sailing — to their
league
True, as inexorable winds, or bars
Floating or fixed of polar ice, allow.
    But turn we rather, let my spirit turn
With thine, O silent and invisible Friend !
To those dear intervals, nor rare nor brief,
When reunited, and by choice withdrawn
From miscellaneous converse, ye were
taught   111
That the remembrance of foregone distress,
And the worse fear of future ill (which oft
Doth hang around it, as a sickly child
Upon its mother) may be both alike
Disarmed of power to unsettle present good
So prized, and things inward and outward
held
In such an even balance, that the heart
Acknowledges God's grace, his mercy feels,
And in its depth of gratitude is still.   120

O gift divine of quiet sequestration !
The hermit, exercised in prayer and praise,
And feeding daily on the hope of heaven,
Is happy in his vow, and fondly cleaves
To life-long singleness; but happier far
Was to your souls, and, to the thoughts of
    others,
A thousand times more beautiful appeared,
Your *dual* loneliness. The sacred tie
Is broken; yet why grieve ? for Time but
    holds
His moiety in trust, till Joy shall lead   130
To the blest world where parting is un-
    known.

EXTEMPORE   EFFUSION   UPON
THE DEATH OF JAMES HOGG

1835. 1835

These verses were written extempore, imme-
diately after reading a notice of the Ettrick
Shepherd's death in the Newcastle paper, to the
Editor of which I sent a copy for publication.
The persons lamented in these verses were all
either of my friends or acquaintance.   In
Lockhart's *Life of Sir Walter Scott* an account
is given of my first meeting with him in 1803.
How the Ettrick Shepherd and I became known
to each other has already been mentioned in
these notes. He was undoubtedly a man of
original genius, but of coarse manners and low
and offensive opinions. Of Coleridge and
Lamb I need not speak here. Crabbe I have
met in London at Mr. Rogers's, but more fre-
quently and favourably at Mr. Hoare's upon
Hampstead Heath. Every spring he used to
pay that family a visit of some length, and was
upon terms of intimate friendship with Mrs.
Hoare, and still more with her daughter-in-
law, who has a large collection of his letters
addressed to herself. After the Poet's decease,
application was made to her to give up these
letters to his biographer, that they, or at least
part of them, might be given to the public.
She hesitated to comply, and asked my opinion
on the subject. " By no means," was my an-
swer, grounded not upon any objection there
might be to publishing a selection from these
letters, but from an aversion I have always felt
to meet idle curiosity by calling back the re-
cently departed to become the object of trivial
and familiar gossip. Crabbe obviously for the
most part preferred the company of women to
that of men, for this among other reasons, that
he did not like to be put upon the stretch in
general conversation: accordingly in miscel-

laneous society his *talk* was so much below
what might have been expected from a man so
deservedly celebrated, that to me it seemed
trifling. It must upon other occasions have
been of a different character, as I found in our
rambles together on Hampstead Heath, and
not so much from a readiness to communicate
his knowledge of life and manners as of natural
history in all its branches. His mind was in-
quisitive, and he seems to have taken refuge
from the remembrance of the distresses he had
gone through, in these studies and the employ-
ments to which they led. Moreover, such
contemplations might tend profitably to coun-
terbalance the painful truths which he had
collected from his intercourse with mankind.
Had I been more intimate with him, I should
have ventured to touch upon his office as a min-
ister of the Gospel, and how far his heart and
soul were in it so as to make him a zealous and
diligent labourer : in poetry, though he wrote
much, as we all know, he assuredly was not so.
I happened once to speak of pains as necessary
to produce merit of a certain kind which I
highly valued : his observation was — " It is
not worth while." You are quite right, thought
I, if the labour encroaches upon the time due
to teach truth as a steward of the mysteries of
God : if there be cause to fear *that*, write less:
but, if poetry is to be produced at all, make
what you do produce as good as you can. Mr.
Rogers once told me that he expressed his re-
gret to Crabbe that he wrote in his later works
so much less correctly than in his earlier.
" Yes," replied he, " but then I had a reputa-
tion to make ; now I can afford to relax."
Whether it was from a modest estimate of his
own qualifications, or from causes less credit-
able, his motives for writing verse and his hopes
and aims were not so high as is to be desired.
After being silent for more than twenty years,
he again applied himself to poetry, upon the
spur of applause he received from the periodi-
cal publications of the day, as he himself tells
us in one of his prefaces. Is it not to be
lamented that a man who was so conversant
with permanent truth, and whose writings are
so valuable an acquisition to our country's
literature, should have *required* an impulse from
such a quarter ? — Mrs. Hemans was unfor-
tunate as a poetess in being obliged by cir-
cumstances to write for money, and that so
frequently and so much, that she was compelled
to look out for subjects wherever she could
find them, and to write as expeditiously as
possible. As a woman, she was to a consider-
able degree a spoilt child of the world. She
had been early in life distinguished for talent,
and poems of hers were published while she
was a girl. She had also been handsome in

her youth, but her education had been most unfortunate. She was totally ignorant of housewifery, and could as easily have managed the spear of Minerva as her needle. It was from observing these deficiencies, that, one day while she was under my roof, I *purposely* directed her attention to household economy, and told her I had purchased *Scales*, which I intended to present to a young lady as a wedding present; pointed out their utility (for her especial benefit), and said that no *ménage* ought to be without them. Mrs. Hemans, not in the least suspecting my drift, reported this saying, in a letter to a friend at the time, as a proof of my simplicity. Being disposed to make large allowances for the faults of her education and the circumstances in which she was placed, I felt most kindly disposed towards her, and took her part upon all occasions, and I was not a little affected by learning that after she withdrew to Ireland, a long and severe sickness raised her spirit as it depressed her body. This I heard from her most intimate friends, and there is striking evidence of it in a poem written and published not long before her death. These notices of Mrs. Hemans would be very unsatisfactory to her intimate friends, as indeed they are to myself, not so much for what is said, but what for brevity's sake is left unsaid. Let it suffice to add, there was much sympathy between us, and, if opportunity had been allowed me to see more of her, I should have loved and valued her accordingly; as it is, I remember her with true affection for her amiable qualities, and, above all, for her delicate and irreproachable conduct during her long separation from an unfeeling husband, whom she had been led to marry from the romantic notions of inexperienced youth. Upon this husband I never heard her cast the least reproach, nor did I ever hear her even name him, though she did not wholly forbear to touch upon her domestic position; but never so as that any fault could be found with her manner of adverting to it.

WHEN first, descending from the moor-
    lands,
I saw the Stream of Yarrow glide
Along a bare and open valley,
The Ettrick Shepherd was my guide.

When last along its banks I wandered,
Through groves that had begun to shed
Their golden leaves upon the pathways,
My steps the Border-minstrel led.

The mighty Minstrel breathes no longer,
'Mid mouldering ruins low he lies;   10

And death upon the braes of Yarrow,
Has closed the Shepherd-poet's eyes:

Nor has the rolling year twice measured,
From sign to sign, its stedfast course,
Since every mortal power of Coleridge
Was frozen at its marvellous source;

The rapt One, of the godlike forehead,
The heaven-eyed creature sleeps in earth:
And Lamb, the frolic and the gentle,
Has vanished from his lonely hearth.   20

Like clouds that rake the mountain-sum-
    mits,
Or waves that own no curbing hand,
How fast has brother followed brother
From sunshine to the sunless land!

Yet I, whose lids from infant slumber
Were earlier raised, remain to hear
A timid voice, that asks in whispers,
"Who next will drop and disappear?"

Our haughty life is crowned with darkness,
Like London with its own black wreath,   30
On which with thee, O Crabbe! forth-
    looking,
I gazed from Hampstead's breezy heath.

As if but yesterday departed,
Thou too art gone before; but why,
O'er ripe fruit, seasonably gathered,
Should frail survivors heave a sigh?

Mourn rather for that holy Spirit,
Sweet as the spring, as ocean deep;
For Her who, ere her summer faded,
Has sunk into a breathless sleep.   40

No more of old romantic sorrows,
For slaughtered Youth or love-lorn Maid!
With sharper grief is Yarrow smitten,
And Ettrick mourns with her their Poet
    dead.

UPON SEEING A COLOURED DRAWING OF THE BIRD OF PARADISE IN AN ALBUM

1835–36. 1837

I cannot forbear to record that the last seven lines of this Poem were composed in bed during the night of the day on which my sister

Sara Hutchinson died about 6 P.M., and it was the thought of her innocent and beautiful life that, through faith, prompted the words —

" On wings that fear no glance of God's pure sight,
No tempest from his breath."

The reader will find two poems on pictures of this bird among my Poems. I will here observe that in a far greater number of instances than have been mentioned in these notes one poem has, as in this case, grown out of another, either because I felt the subject had been inadequately treated, or that the thoughts and images suggested in course of composition have been such as I found interfered with the unity indispensable to every work of art, however humble in character.

WHO rashly strove thy Image to portray ?
Thou buoyant minion of the tropic air;
How could he think of the live creature — gay
With a divinity of colours, drest
In all her brightness, from the dancing crest
Far as the last gleam of the filmy train
Extended and extending to sustain
The motions that it graces — and forbear
To drop his pencil ! Flowers of every clime
Depicted on these pages smile at time;   10
And gorgeous insects copied with nice care
Are here, and likenesses of many a shell
Tossed ashore by restless waves,
Or in the diver's grasp fetched up from caves
Where sea-nymphs might be proud to dwell:
But whose rash hand (again I ask) could dare,
'Mid casual tokens and promiscuous shows,
To circumscribe this Shape in fixed repose;
Could imitate for indolent survey,
Perhaps for touch profane,   20
Plumes that might catch, but cannot keep, a stain;
And, with cloud-streaks lightest and loftiest, share
The sun's first greeting, his last farewell ray !
    Resplendent Wanderer ! followed with glad eyes
Where'er her course; mysterious Bird !
To whom, by wondering Fancy stirred,
Eastern Islanders have given
A holy name — the Bird of Heaven !
And even a title higher still,
The Bird of God ! whose blessed will   30
She seems performing as she flies

Over the earth and through the skies
In never-wearied search of Paradise —
Region that crowns her beauty with the name
She bears for *us* — for us how blest,
How happy at all seasons, could like aim
Uphold our Spirits urged to kindred flight
On wings that fear no glance of God's pure sight,
No tempest from his breath, their promised rest
Seeking with indefatigable quest   4•
Above a world that deems itself most wise
When most enslaved by gross realities !

"BY A BLEST HUSBAND GUIDED, MARY CAME"

(?). 1835

This lady was named Carleton; she, along with a sister, was brought up in the neighbourhood of Ambleside. The epitaph, a part of it at least, is in the church at Bromsgrove, where she resided after her marriage.

BY a blest Husband guided, Mary came
From nearest kindred, Vernon her new name;
She came, though meek of soul, in seemly pride
Of happiness and hope, a youthful Bride.
O dread reverse ! if aught *be* so, which proves
That God will chasten whom he dearly loves.
Faith bore her up through pains in mercy given,
And troubles that were each a step to Heaven:
Two Babes were laid in earth before she died;
A third now slumbers at the Mother's side;
Its Sister-twin survives, whose smiles afford
A trembling solace to her widowed Lord.
    Reader ! if to thy bosom cling the pain
Of recent sorrow combated in vain;
Or if thy cherished grief have failed to thwart
Time still intent on his insidious part,
Lulling the mourner's best good thoughts asleep,
Pilfering regrets we would, but cannot keep;

Bear with Him — judge *Him* gently who
  makes known
His bitter loss by this memorial Stone;
And pray that in his faithful breast the
  grace
Of resignation find a hallowed place.

SONNETS

I

(?). 1835

DESPONDING Father! mark this altered
  bough,
So beautiful of late, with sunshine warmed,
Or moist with dews; what more unsightly
  now,
Its blossoms shrivelled, and its fruit, if
  formed,
Invisible? yet Spring her genial brow
Knits not o'er that discolouring and decay
As false to expectation. Nor fret thou
At like unlovely process in the May
Of human life: a Stripling's graces blow,
Fade and are shed, that from their timely
  fall
(Misdeem it not a cankerous change) may
  grow
Rich mellow bearings, that for thanks shall
  call:
In all men, sinful is it to be slow
To hope — in Parents, sinful above all.

II

ROMAN ANTIQUITIES DISCOVERED AT BISHOPSTONE, HEREFORDSHIRE

(?). 1835

My attention to these antiquities was directed
by Mr. Walker, son to the itinerant Eidouranian
Philosopher. The beautiful pavement was dis-
covered within a few yards of the front door of
his parsonage, and appeared from the site (in
full view of several hills upon which there had
formerly been Roman encampments) as if it
might have been the villa of the commander of
the forces, at least such was Mr. Walker's con-
jecture.

WHILE poring Antiquarians search the
  ground
Upturned with curious pains, the Bard, a
  Seer,
Takes fire: — The men that have been re-
  appear;

Romans for travel girt, for business gowned;
And some recline on couches, myrtle-
  crowned,
In festal glee: why not? For fresh and
  clear,
As if its hues were of the passing year,
Dawns this time-buried pavement. From
  that mound
Hoards may come forth of Trajans, Maxi-
  mins,
Shrunk into coins with all their warlike
  toil:
Or a fierce impress issues with its foil
Of tenderness — the Wolf, whose suckling
  Twins
The unlettered ploughboy pities when he
  wins
The casual treasure from the furrowed soil.

III

ST. CATHERINE OF LEDBURY

(?). 1835

Written on a journey from Brinsop Court,
Herefordshire.

WHEN human touch (as monkish books
  attest)
Nor was applied nor could be, Ledbury
  bells
Broke forth in concert flung adown the
  dells,
And upward, high as Malvern's cloudy
  crest;
Sweet tones, and caught by a noble Lady
  blest
To rapture! Mabel listened at the side
Of her loved mistress: soon the music died,
And Catherine said, *Here I set up my rest.*
Warned in a dream, the Wanderer long
  had sought
A home that by such miracle of sound
Must be revealed: — she heard it now, or
  felt
The deep, deep joy of a confiding thought;
And there, a saintly Anchoress, she dwelt
Till she exchanged for heaven that happy
  ground.

IV

1830. 1835

In the month of January, when Dora and I
were walking from Town-end, Grasmere, across
the vale, snow being on the ground, she espied,

in the thick though leafless hedge, a bird's nest half filled with snow. Out of this comfortless appearance arose this Sonnet, which was, in fact, written without the least reference to any individual object, but merely to prove to myself that I could, if I thought fit, write in a strain that Poets have been fond of. On the 14th of February in the same year, my daughter, in a sportive mood, sent it as a Valentine, under a fictitious name, to her cousin C. W.

WHY art thou silent! Is thy love a plant
Of such weak fibre that the treacherous air
Of absence withers what was once so fair?
Is there no debt to pay, no boon to grant?
Yet have my thoughts for thee been vigilant —
Bound to thy service with unceasing care,
The mind's least generous wish a mendicant
For nought but what thy happiness could spare.
Speak — though this soft warm heart, once free to hold
A thousand tender pleasures, thine and mine,
Be left more desolate, more dreary cold
Than a forsaken bird's-nest filled with snow
'Mid its own bush of leafless eglantine —
Speak, that my torturing doubts their end may know!

V

(?). 1835

Suggested on the road between Preston and Lancaster where it first gives a view of the Lake country, and composed on the same day, on the roof of the coach.

FOUR fiery steeds impatient of the rein
Whirled us o'er sunless ground beneath a sky
As void of sunshine, when, from that wide plain,
Clear tops of far-off mountains we descry,
Like a Sierra of cerulean Spain,
All light and lustre. Did no heart reply?
Yes, there was One; — for One, asunder fly
The thousand links of that ethereal chain;
And green vales open out, with grove and field,
And the fair front of many a happy Home;
Such tempting spots as into vision come
While Soldiers, weary of the arms they wield
And sick at heart of strifeful Christendom,
Gaze on the moon by parting clouds revealed.

VI

TO ——

(?). 1835

The fate of this poor Dove, as described, was told to me at Brinsop Court, by the young lady to whom I have given the name of Lesbia.

"Miss not the occasion: by the forelock take
That subtile Power, the never-halting Time,
Lest a mere moment's putting-off should make
Mischance almost as heavy as a crime."

"WAIT, prithee, wait!" this answer Lesbia threw
Forth to her Dove, and took no further heed;
Her eye was busy, while her fingers flew
Across the harp, with soul-engrossing speed;
But from that bondage when her thoughts were freed
She rose, and toward the close-shut casement drew,
Whence the poor unregarded Favourite, true
To old affections, had been heard to plead
With flapping wing for entrance. What a shriek!
Forced from that voice so lately tuned to a strain
Of harmony! — a shriek of terror, pain,
And self-reproach! for, from aloft, a Kite
Pounced, — and the Dove, which from its ruthless beak
She could not rescue, perished in her sight!

VII

1838. 1838

SAID Secrecy to Cowardice and Fraud,
Falsehood and Treachery, in close council met,
Deep under ground, in Pluto's cabinet,
"The frost of England's pride will soon be thawed;
Hooded the open brow that overawed
Our schemes: the faith and honour, never yet
By us with hope encountered, be upset; —
For once I burst my bands, and cry, applaud!"
Then whispered she, "The Bill is carrying out!"
They heard, and, starting up, the Brood of Night
Clapped hands, and shook with glee their matted locks;
All Powers and Places that abhor the light

Joined in the transport, echoed back their
    shout,
Hurrah for ——, hugging his Ballot-box!

NOVEMBER 1836

1836. 1837

EVEN so for me a Vision sanctified
The sway of Death; long ere mine eyes had
    seen
Thy countenance — the still rapture of thy
    mien —
When thou, dear Sister! wert become
    Death's Bride:
No trace of pain or languor could abide
That change: — age on thy brow was
    smoothed — thy cold
Wan cheek at once was privileged to unfold
A loveliness to living youth denied.
Oh! if within me hope should e'er decline,

The lamp of faith, lost Friend! too faintly
    burn;
Then may that heaven-revealing smile of
    thine,
The bright assurance, visibly return:
And let my spirit in that power divine
Rejoice, as, through that power, it ceased
    to mourn.

"SIX MONTHS TO SIX YEARS ADDED HE REMAINED"

(?). 1837

SIX months to six years added he remained
Upon this sinful earth, by sin unstained:
O blessed Lord! whose mercy then removed
A Child whom every eye that looked on
    loved;
Support us, teach us calmly to resign
What we possessed, and now is wholly thine!

MEMORIALS OF A TOUR IN ITALY

1837-42. 1842

During my whole life I had felt a strong desire to visit Rome and the other celebrated cities and regions of Italy, but did not think myself justified in incurring the necessary expense till I received from Mr. Moxon, the publisher of a large edition of my poems, a sum sufficient to enable me to gratify my wish without encroaching upon what I considered due to my family. My excellent friend H. C. Robinson readily consented to accompany me, and in March 1837, we set off from London, to which we returned in August, earlier than my companion wished or I should myself have desired had I been, like him, a bachelor. These Memorials of that tour touch upon but a very few of the places and objects that interested me, and, in what they do advert to, are for the most part much slighter than I could wish. More particularly do I regret that there is no notice in them of the South of France, nor of the Roman antiquities abounding in that district, especially of the Pont de Degard, which, together with its situation, impressed me full as much as any remains of Roman architecture to be found in Italy. Then there was Vaucluse, with its Fountain, its Petrarch, its rocks of all seasons, its small plots of lawn in their first vernal freshness, and the blossoms of the peach and other trees embellishing the scene on every side. The beauty of the stream also called forcibly for the expression of sympathy from one who from his childhood had studied the brooks and torrents of his native mountains. Between two and three hours did I run about climbing the steep and rugged crags from whose base the water of Vaucluse breaks forth. "Has Laura's Lover," often said I to myself, "ever sat down upon this stone? or has his foot ever pressed that turf?" Some, especially of the female sex, would have felt sure of it: my answer was (impute it to my years), "I fear not." Is it not in fact obvious that many of his love verses must have flowed, I do not say from a wish to display his own talent, but from a habit of exercising his intellect in that way rather than from an impulse of his heart? It is otherwise with his Lyrical poems, and particularly with the one upon the degradation of his country: there he pours out his reproaches, lamentations, and aspirations like an ardent and sincere patriot. But enough: it is time to turn to my own effusions, such as they are.

TO

HENRY CRABB ROBINSON

COMPANION! by whose buoyant Spirit cheered,
In whose experience trusting, day by day
Treasures I gained with zeal that neither feared
The toils nor felt the crosses of the way,

These records take, and happy should I be
Were but the Gift a meet Return to thee
For kindnesses that never ceased to flow,
And prompt self-sacrifice to which I owe
Far more than any heart but mine can know.

                       W. WORDSWORTH.

RYDAL MOUNT, *Feb.* 14*th*, 1842.

The Tour of which the following Poems are very inadequate remembrances was shortened by report, too well founded, of the prevalence of Cholera at Naples. To make some amends for what was reluctantly left unseen in the South of Italy, we visited the Tuscan Sanctuaries among the Apennines, and the principal Italian Lakes among the Alps. Neither of those lakes, nor of Venice, is there any notice in these Poems, chiefly because I have touched upon them elsewhere. See, in particular " Descriptive Sketches," " Memorials of a Tour on the Continent in 1820," and a Sonnet upon the extinction of the Venetian Republic.

I

MUSINGS NEAR AQUAPEN-DENTE APRIL 1837.

1841. 1842

" Not the less
Had his sunk eye kindled at those dear words
That spake of bards and minstrels."

His, Sir Walter Scott's eye, *did* in fact kindle at them, for the lines, " Places forsaken now," and the two that follow were adopted from a poem of mine which nearly forty years ago was in part read to him, and he never forgot them.

" Old Helvellyn's brow,
Where once together, in his day of strength,
We stood rejoicing."

Sir Humphrey Davy was with us at the time. We had ascended from Paterdale, and I could not but admire the vigour with which Scott scrambled along that horn of the mountain called " Striding Edge." Our progress was necessarily slow, and was beguiled by Scott's telling many stories and amusing anecdotes, as was his custom. Sir H. Davy would have probably been better pleased if other topics had occasionally been interspersed, and some discussion entered upon: at all events he did not remain with us long at the top of the mountain, but left us to find our way down its steep side together into the vale of Grasmere, where, at my cottage, Mrs. Scott was to meet us at dinner.

" With faint smile
He said, — ' When I am there, although 't is fair,
'T will be another Yarrow.' "

See among these notes the one on " Yarrow Revisited."

" A few short steps (painful they were)."

This, though introduced here, I did not know till it was told me at Rome by Miss Mackenzie of Seaforth, a lady whose friendly attentions during my residence at Rome I have gratefully acknowledged, with expressions of sincere regret that she is no more. Miss M. told me that she accompanied Sir Walter to the Janicular Mount, and, after showing him the grave of Tasso in the church upon the top, and a mural monument there erected to his memory, they left the church and stood together on the brow of the hill overlooking the city of Rome : his daughter Anne was with them, and she, naturally desirous, for the sake of Miss Mackenzie especially, to have some expression of pleasure from her father, half reproached him for showing nothing of that kind either by his looks or voice : " How can I," replied he, " having only one leg to stand upon, and that in extreme pain ! " so that the prophecy was more than fulfilled.

" Over waves rough and deep."

We took boat near the lighthouse at the point of the right horn of the bay which makes a sort of natural port for Genoa ; but the wind was high, and the waves long and rough, so that I did not feel quite recompensed by the view of the city, splendid as it was, for the danger apparently incurred. The boatman (I had only one) encouraged me, saying we were quite safe, but I was not a little glad when we gained the shore, though Shelley and Byron — one of them at least, who seemed to have courted agitation from any quarter — would have probably rejoiced in such a situation: more than once I believe were they both in extreme danger even on the Lake of Geneva. Every man however has his fears of some kind or other ; and no doubt they had theirs : of all men whom I have ever known, Coleridge had the most of passive courage in bodily peril, but no one was so easily cowed when moral firmness was required in miscellaneous conversation or in the daily intercourse of social life.

" How lovely robed in forenoon light and shade,
Each ministering to each, didst thou appear,
Savona."

There is not a single bay along this beautiful coast that might not raise in a traveller a wish to take up his abode there, each as it succeeds seems more inviting than the other ; but the desolated convent on the cliff in the bay of Savona struck my fancy most ; and had I, for the sake of my own health or that of a dear friend, or any other cause, been desirous of a residence abroad, I should have let my thoughts loose upon a scheme of turning some part of this building into a habitation provided as far as might be with English comforts. There is close by it a row or avenue, I forget which, of tall cypresses. I could not forbear saying to myself — " What a sweet family walk, or one for lonely musings, would be found under the shade ! " but there, probably, the trees remained little noticed and seldom enjoyed.

" This flowering broom's dear neighbourhood."

The broom is a great ornament through the months of March and April to the vales and hills of the Apennines, in the wild parts of which it blows in the utmost profusion, and of course successively at different elevations as the season advances. It surpasses ours in beauty and fragrance, but, speaking from my own limited observation only, I cannot affirm the same of several of their wild spring flowers, the primroses in particular, which I saw not unfrequently but thinly scattered and languishing compared to ours.

The note at the close of this poem, upon the Oxford movement, was intrusted to my friend Mr. Frederick Faber. I told him what I wished to be said, and begged that, as he was intimately acquainted with several of the Leaders of it, he would express my thought in the way least likely to be taken amiss by them. Much of the work they are undertaking was grievously wanted, and God grant their endeavours may continue to prosper as they have done.

YE Apennines ! with all your fertile vales
Deeply embosomed, and your winding shores
Of either sea — an Islander by birth,
A Mountaineer by habit, would resound
Your praise, in meet accordance with your
    claims
Bestowed by Nature, or from man's great
    deeds
Inherited : — presumptuous thought ! — it
    fled
Like vapour, like a towering cloud, dis-
    solved.
Not, therefore, shall my mind give way to
    sadness ; —
Yon snow-white torrent-fall, plumb down it
    drops   10
Yet ever hangs or seems to hang in air,
Lulling the leisure of that high perched
    town,
AQUAPENDENTE, in her lofty site
Its neighbour and its namesake — town, and
    flood
Forth flashing out of its own gloomy chasm
Bright sunbeams — the fresh verdure of
    this lawn
Strewn with grey rocks, and on the horizon's
    verge,

O'er intervenient waste, through glimmer-
    ing haze,
Unquestionably kenned, that cone-shaped
    hill
With fractured summit, no indifferent sight
To travellers, from such comforts as are
    thine,   21
Bleak Radicofani ! escaped with joy —
These are before me; and the varied scene
May well suffice, till noon-tide's sultry heat
Relax, to fix and satisfy the mind
Passive yet pleased. What ! with this
    Broom in flower
Close at my side ! She bids me fly to greet
Her sisters, soon like her to be attired
With golden blossoms opening at the feet
Of my own Fairfield. The glad greeting
    given,   30
Given with a voice and by a look returned
Of old companionship, Time counts not
    minutes
Ere, from accustomed paths, familiar fields,
The local Genius hurries me aloft,
Transported over that cloud-wooing hill,
Seat Sandal, a fond suitor of the clouds,
With dream-like smoothness, to Helvellyn's
    top,
There to alight upon crisp moss and range,
Obtaining ampler boon, at every step,
Of visual sovereignty — hills multitudinous,
(Not Apennine can boast of fairer) hills   41
Pride of two nations, wood and lake and
    plains,
And prospect right below of deep coves
    shaped
By skeleton arms, that, from the moun-
    tain's trunk
Extended, clasp the winds, with mutual
    moan
Struggling for liberty, while undismayed
The shepherd struggles with them. On-
    ward thence
And downward by the skirt of Greenside
    fell,
And by Glenridding-screes, and low Glen-
    coign,
Places forsaken now, though loving still   50
The muses, as they loved them in the days
Of the old minstrels and the border bards. —
But here am I fast bound; and let it pass,
The simple rapture ; — who that travels far
To feed his mind with watchful eyes could
    share
Or wish to share it ? — One there surely
    was,

"The Wizard of the North," with anxious hope
Brought to this genial climate, when disease
Preyed upon body and mind — yet not the less
Had his sunk eye kindled at those dear words 60
That spake of bards and minstrels; and his spirit
Had flown with mine to old Helvellyn's brow,
Where once together, in his day of strength,
We stood rejoicing, as if earth were free
From sorrow, like the sky above our heads.
Years followed years, and when, upon the eve
Of his last going from Tweed-side, thought turned,
Or by another's sympathy was led,
To this bright land, Hope was for him no friend,
Knowledge no help; Imagination shaped 70
No promise. Still, in more than ear-deep seats,
Survives for me, and cannot but survive
The tone of voice which wedded borrowed words
To sadness not their own, when, with faint smile
Forced by intent to take from speech its edge,
He said, "When I am there, although 't is fair,
'T will be another Yarrow." Prophecy
More than fulfilled, as gay Campania's shores
Soon witnessed, and the city of seven hills,
Her sparkling fountains and her mouldering tombs; 80
And more than all, that Eminence which showed
Her splendours, seen, not felt, the while he stood
A few short steps (painful they were) apart
From Tasso's Convent-haven, and retired grave.
Peace to their Spirits ! why should Poesy
Yield to the lure of vain regret, and hover
In gloom on wings with confidence outspread
To move in sunshine ? — Utter thanks, my Soul !
Tempered with awe, and sweetened by compassion

For them who in the shades of sorrow dwell, 90
That I — so near the term to human life
Appointed by man's common heritage,
Frail as the frailest, one withal (if that
Deserve a thought) but little known to fame —
Am free to rove where Nature's loveliest looks,
Art's noblest relics, history's rich bequests,
Failed to reanimate and but feebly cheered
The whole world's Darling — free to rove at will
O'er high and low, and if requiring rest,
Rest from enjoyment only.
　　　　　　　Thanks poured forth
For what thus far hath blessed my wanderings, thanks 101
Fervent but humble as the lips can breathe
Where gladness seems a duty — let me guard
Those seeds of expectation which the fruit
Already gathered in this favoured Land
Enfolds within its core. The faith be mine,
That He who guides and governs all, approves
When gratitude, though disciplined to look
Beyond these transient spheres, doth wear a crown
Of earthly hope put on with trembling hand; 110
Nor is least pleased, we trust, when golden beams,
Reflected through the mists of age, from hours
Of innocent delight, remote or recent,
Shoot but a little way — 't is all they can —
Into the doubtful future. Who would keep
Power must resolve to cleave to it through life,
Else it deserts him, surely as he lives.
Saints would not grieve nor guardian angels frown
If one — while tossed, as was my lot to be,
In a frail bark urged by two slender oars 120
Over waves rough and deep, that, when they broke,
Dashed their white foam against the palace walls
Of Genoa the superb — should there be led
To meditate upon his own appointed tasks,
However humble in themselves, with thoughts
Raised and sustained by memory of Him

Who oftentimes within those narrow bounds
Rocked on the surge, there tried his spirit's
    strength
And grasp of purpose, long ere sailed his
    ship
To lay a new world open.
                    Nor less prized
Be those impressions which incline the
    heart   131
To mild, to lowly, and to seeming weak,
Bend that way her desires. The dew, the
    storm —
The dew whose moisture fell in gentle
    drops
On the small hyssop destined to become,
By Hebrew ordinance devoutly kept,
A purifying instrument — the storm
That shook on Lebanon the cedar's top,
And as it shook, enabling the blind roots
Further to force their way, endowed its
    trunk   140
With magnitude and strength fit to uphold
The glorious temple — did alike proceed
From the same gracious will, were both an
    offspring
Of bounty infinite.
                    Between Powers that aim
Higher to lift their lofty heads, impelled
By no profane ambition, Powers that thrive
By conflict, and their opposites, that trust
In lowliness — a midway tract there lies
Of thoughtful sentiment for every mind
Pregnant with good. Young, Middle-aged,
    and Old,   150
From century on to century, must have
    known
The emotion — nay, more fitly were it said —
The blest tranquillity that sunk so deep
Into my spirit, when I paced, enclosed
In Pisa's Campo Santo, the smooth floor
Of its Arcades paved with sepulchral slabs,
And through each window's open fretwork
    looked
O'er the blank Area of sacred earth
Fetched from Mount Calvary, or haply
    delved
In precincts nearer tó the Saviour's tomb, 160
By hands of men, humble as brave, who
    fought
For its deliverance — a capacious field
That to descendants of the dead it holds
And to all living mute memento breathes,
More touching far than aught which on the
    walls
Is pictured, or their epitaphs can speak,

Of the changed City's long-departed power,
Glory, and wealth, which, perilous as they
    are,
Here did not kill, but nourished, Piety.
And, high above that length of cloistral
    roof,   170
Peering in air and backed by azure sky,
To kindred contemplations ministers
The Baptistery's dome, and that which
    swells
From the Cathedral pile; and with the
    twain
Conjoined in prospect mutable or fixed
(As hurry on in eagerness the feet,
Or pause) the summit of the Leaning-
    tower.
Nor less remuneration waits on him
Who having left the Cemetery stands
In the Tower's shadow, of decline and fall
Admonished not without some sense of
    fear,   181
Fear that soon vanishes before the sight
Of splendour unextinguished, pomp un-
    scathed,
And beauty unimpaired. Grand in itself,
And for itself, the assemblage, grand and
    fair
To view, and for the mind's consenting eye
A type of age in man, upon its front
Bearing the world-acknowledged evidence
Of past exploits, nor fondly after more
Struggling against the stream of destiny, 190
But with its peaceful majesty content.
— Oh what a spectacle at every turn
The Place unfolds, from pavement skinned
    with moss
Or grass-grown spaces, where the heaviest
    foot
Provokes no echoes, but must softly tread;
Where Solitude with Silence paired stops
    short
Of Desolation, and to Ruin's scythe
Decay submits not.
                    But where'er my steps
Shall wander, chiefly let me cull with care
Those images of genial beauty, oft   200
Too lovely to be pensive in themselves
But by reflection made so, which do best
And fitliest serve to crown with fragrant
    wreaths
Life's cup when almost filled with years,
    like mine.
— How lovely robed in forenoon light and
    shade,
Each ministering to each, didst thou appear

Savona, Queen of territory fair
As aught that marvellous coast thro' all its
 length
Yields to the Stranger's eye. Remembrance
 holds
As a selected treasure thy one cliff,   210
That, while it wore for melancholy crest
A shattered Convent, yet rose proud to have
Clinging to its steep sides a thousand herbs
And shrubs, whose pleasant looks gave
 proof how kind
The breath of air can be where earth had
 else
Seemed churlish. And behold, both far
 and near,
Garden and field all decked with orange
 bloom,
And peach and citron, in Spring's mildest
 breeze
Expanding; and, along the smooth shore
 curved
Into a natural port, a tideless sea,   220
To that mild breeze with motion and with
 voice
Softly responsive; and, attuned to all
Those vernal charms of sight and sound,
 appeared
Smooth space of turf which from the guard-
 ian fort
Sloped seaward, turf whose tender April
 green,
In coolest climes too fugitive, might even
 here
Plead with the sovereign Sun for longer
 stay
Than his unmitigated beams allow,
Nor plead in vain, if beauty could preserve,
From mortal change, aught that is born on
 earth   230
Or doth on time depend.
            While on the brink
Of that high Convent-crested cliff I stood,
Modest Savona ! over all did brood
A pure poetic Spirit — as the breeze,
Mild — as the verdure, fresh — the sun-
 shine, bright —
Thy gentle Chiabrera ! — not a stone,
Mural or level with the trodden floor,
In Church or Chapel, if my curious quest
Missed not the truth, retains a single name
Of young or old, warrior, or saint, or sage,
To whose dear memories his sepulchral
 verse   241
Paid simple tribute, such as might have
 flowed

From the clear spring of a plain English
 heart,
Say rather, one in native fellowship
With all who want not skill to couple grief
With praise, as genuine admiration prompts.
The grief, the praise, are severed from their
 dust,
Yet in his page the records of that worth
Survive, uninjured; — glory then to words,
Honour to word-preserving Arts, and hail
Ye kindred local influences that still,   251
If Hope's familiar whispers merit faith,
Await my steps when they the breezy height
Shall range of philosophic Tusculum;
Or Sabine vales explored inspire a wish
To meet the shade of Horace by the side
Of his Bandusian fount; or I invoke
His presence to point out the spot where
 once
He sate, and eulogized with earnest pen
Peace, leisure, freedom, moderate desires;
And all the immunities of rural life   261
Extolled, behind Vacuna's crumbling fane.
Or let me loiter, soothed with what is
 given
Nor asking more, on that delicious Bay,
Parthenope's Domain — Virgilian haunt,
Illustrated with never-dying verse,
And, by the Poet's laurel-shaded tomb,
Age after age to Pilgrims from all lands
Endeared.
            And who — if not a man as cold
In heart as dull in brain — while pacing
 ground   270
Chosen by Rome's legendary Bards, high
 minds
Out of her early struggles well inspired
To localize heroic acts — could look
Upon the spots with undelighted eye,
Though even to their last syllable the
 Lays
And very names of those who gave them
 birth
Have perished ? — Verily, to her utmost
 depth,
Imagination feels what Reason fears not
To recognize, the lasting virtue lodged
In those bold fictions that, by deeds assigned
To the Valerian, Fabian, Curian Race,   281
And others like in fame, created Powers
With attributes from History derived,
By Poesy irradiate, and yet graced,
Through marvellous felicity of skill,
With something more propitious to high
 aims

Than either, pent within her separate
sphere,
Can oft with justice claim.
                    And not disdaining
Union with those primeval energies
To virtue consecrate, stoop ye from your
height   290
Christian Traditions ! at my Spirit's call
Descend, and, on the brow of ancient Rome
As she survives in ruin, manifest
Your glories mingled with the brightest
hues
Of her memorial halo, fading, fading,
But never to be extinct while Earth endures.
O come, if undishonoured by the prayer,
From all her Sanctuaries ! — Open for my
feet
Ye Catacombs, give to mine eyes a glimpse
Of the Devout, as, 'mid your glooms con-
vened   300
For safety, they of yore enclasped the
Cross
On knees that ceased from trembling, or
intoned
Their orisons with voices half-suppressed,
But sometimes heard, or fancied to be
heard,
Even at this hour.
                    And thou Mamertine prison,
Into that vault receive me from whose
depth
Issues, revealed in no presumptuous vision,
Albeit lifting human to divine,
A Saint, the Church's Rock, the mystic
Keys
Grasped in his hand; and lo ! with upright
sword   310
Prefiguring his own impendent doom,
The Apostle of the Gentiles; both prepared
To suffer pains with heathen scorn and
hate
Inflicted; — blessèd Men, for so to Heaven
They follow their dear Lord !
                    Time flows — nor winds,
Nor stagnates, nor precipitates his course,
But many a benefit borne upon his breast
For human-kind sinks out of sight, is gone,
No one knows how; nor seldom is put forth
An angry arm that snatches good away,   320
Never perhaps to reappear.   The Stream
Has to our generation brought and brings
Innumerable gains; yet we, who now
Walk in the light of day, pertain full surely
To a chilled age, most pitiably shut out
From that which *is* and actuates, by forms,

Abstractions, and by lifeless fact to fact
Minutely linked with diligence uninspired,
Unrectified, unguided, unsustained,
By godlike insight.   To this fate is doomed
Science, wide-spread and spreading still as
be   331
Her conquests, in the world of sense made
known,
So with the internal mind it fares; and so
With morals, trusting, in contempt or fear
Of vital principle's controlling law,
To her purblind guide Expediency; and so
Suffers religious faith.   Elate with view
Of what is won, we overlook or scorn
The best that should keep pace with it, and
must,
Else more and more the general mind will
droop,   340
Even as if bent on perishing.   There lives
No faculty within us which the Soul
Can spare, and humblest earthly Weal de-
mands,
For dignity not placed beyond her reach,
Zealous co-operation of all means
Given or acquired, to raise us from the
mire,
And liberate our hearts from low pursuits.
By gross Utilities enslaved, we need
More of ennobling impulse from the past,
If to the future aught of good must come
Sounder and therefore holier than the ends
Which, in the giddiness of self-applause, 352
We covet as supreme.   O grant the crown
That Wisdom wears, or take his treacher-
ous staff
From Knowledge ! — If the Muse, whom I
have served
This day, be mistress of a single pearl
Fit to be placed in that pure diadem;
Then, not in vain, under these chestnut
boughs
Reclined, shall I have yielded up my soul
To transports from the secondary founts
Flowing of time and place, and paid to
both   361
Due homage; nor shall fruitlessly have
striven,
By love of beauty moved, to enshrine in
verse
Accordant meditations, which in times
Vexed and disordered, as our own, may
shed
Influence, at least among a scattered few,
To soberness of mind and peace of heart
Friendly; as here to my repose hath been

This flowering broom's dear neighbourhood,
     the light
And murmur issuing from yon pendent
     flood,   370
And all the varied landscape.   Let us now
Rise, and to-morrow greet magnificent
     Rome.

II

THE PINE OF MONTE MARIO
AT ROME

1837. 1842

Sir George Beaumont told me that, when he
first visited Italy, pine-trees of this species
abounded, but that on his return thither, which
was more than thirty years after, they had dis-
appeared from many places where he had been
accustomed to admire them, and had become
rare all over the country, especially in and
about Rome.   Several Roman villas have
within these few years passed into the hands of
foreigners, who, I observed with pleasure, have
taken care to plant this tree, which in course
of years will become a great ornament to the
city and to the general landscape.   May I ven-
ture to add here, that having ascended the
Monte Mario, I could not resist embracing the
trunk of this interesting monument of my de-
parted friend's feelings for the beauties of na-
ture, and the power of that art which he loved
so much, and in the practice of which he was
so distinguished.

I saw far off the dark top of a Pine
Look like a cloud — a slender stem the tie
That bound it to its native earth — poised
     high
'Mid evening hues, along the horizon line,
Striving in peace each other to outshine.
But when I learned the Tree was living
     there,
Saved from the sordid axe by Beaumont's
     care,
Oh, what a gush of tenderness was mine !
The rescued Pine-Tree, with its sky so
     bright
And cloud-like beauty, rich in thoughts of
     home,
Death-parted friends, and days too swift in
     flight,
Supplanted the whole majesty of Rome
(Then first apparent from the Pincian
     Height)
Crowned with St. Peter's everlasting Dome.

III

AT ROME

1837. 1842

Sight is at first a sad enemy to imagination
and to those pleasures belonging to old times
with which some exertions of that power will
always mingle : nothing perhaps brings this
truth home to the feelings more than the city
of Rome ; not so much in respect to the impres-
sion made at the moment when it is first seen
and looked at as a whole, for then the imagi-
nation may be invigorated and the mind's eye
quickened ; but when particular spots or ob-
jects are sought out, disappointment is I believe
invariably felt.   Ability to recover from this
disappointment will exist in proportion to know-
ledge, and the power of the mind to reconstruct
out of fragments and parts, and to make details
in the present subservient to more adequate
comprehension of the past.

Is this, ye Gods, the Capitolian Hill ?
Yon petty Steep in truth the fearful Rock,
Tarpeian named of yore, and keeping still
That name, a local Phantom proud to mock
The Traveller's expectation ? — Could our
     Will
Destroy the ideal Power within, 't were done
Thro' what men see and touch, — slaves
     wandering on,
Impelled by thirst of all but Heaven-taught
     skill.
Full oft, our wish obtained, deeply we sigh ;
Yet not unrecompensed are they who learn,
From that depression raised, to mount on
     high
With stronger wing, more clearly to discern
Eternal things ; and, if need be, defy
Change, with a brow not insolent, though
     stern.

IV

AT ROME — REGRETS — IN AL-
LUSION TO NIEBUHR AND
OTHER MODERN HISTORIANS

1837. 1842

Those old credulities, to nature dear,
Shall they no longer bloom upon the stock
Of History, stript naked as a rock
'Mid a dry desert ?   What is it we hear ?
The glory of Infant Rome must disappear,
Her morning splendours vanish, and their
     place

Know them no more.   If Truth, who veiled
  her face
With those bright beams yet hid it not,
  must steer
Henceforth a humbler course perplexed and
  slow;
One solace yet remains for us who came
Into this world in days when story lacked
Severe research, that in our hearts we know
How, for exciting youth's heroic flame,
Assent is power, belief the soul of fact.

V

CONTINUED

1837–42. 1842

COMPLACENT Fictions were they, yet the
  same
Involved a history of no doubtful sense,
History that proves by inward evidence
From what a precious source of truth it
  came.
Ne'er could the boldest Eulogist have dared
Such deeds to paint, such characters to
  frame,
But for coeval sympathy prepared
To greet with instant faith their loftiest
  claim.
None but a noble people could have loved
Flattery in Ancient Rome's pure-minded
  style:
Not in like sort the Runic Scald was moved;
He, nursed 'mid savage passions that de-
  file
Humanity, sang feats that well might call
For the blood-thirsty mead of Odin's riot-
  ous Hall.

VI

PLEA FOR THE HISTORIAN

1837–42. 1842

FORBEAR to deem the Chronicler unwise,
Ungentle, or untouched by seemly ruth,
Who, gathering up all that Time's envious
  tooth
Has spared of sound and grave realities,
Firmly rejects those dazzling flatteries,
Dear as they are to unsuspecting Youth,
That might have drawn down Clio from the
  skies
To vindicate the majesty of truth.

Such was her office while she walked with
  men,
A Muse, who, not unmindful of her Sire
All-ruling Jove, whate'er the theme might
  be,
Revered her Mother, sage Mnemosyne,
And taught her faithful servants how the
  lyre
Should animate, but not mislead, the pen.

VII

AT ROME

1837–42. 1842

I have a private interest in this Sonnet, for
I doubt whether it would ever have been writ-
ten but for the lively picture given me by
Anna Ricketts of what they had witnessed of
the indignation and sorrow expressed by some
Italian noblemen of their acquaintance upon
the surrender, which circumstances had obliged
them to make, of the best portion of their fam-
ily mansions to strangers.

THEY — who have seen the noble Roman's
  scorn
Break forth at thought of laying down his
  head,
When the blank day is over, garreted
In his ancestral palace, where, from morn
To night, the desecrated floors are worn
By feet of purse-proud strangers; they —
  who have read
In one meek smile, beneath a peasant's shed,
How patiently the weight of wrong is borne;
They — who have heard some learned
  Patriot treat
Of freedom, with mind grasping the whole
  theme
From ancient Rome, downwards through
  that bright dream
Of Commonwealths, each city a starlike seat
Of rival glory; they — fallen Italy —
Nor must, nor will, nor can, despair of
  Thee !

VIII

NEAR ROME, IN SIGHT OF ST. PETER'S

1837–42. 1842

LONG has the dew been dried on tree and
  lawn:
O'er man and beast a not unwelcome boon

Is shed, the languor of approaching noon;
To shady rest withdrawing or withdrawn
Mute are all creatures, as this couchant
   fawn,
Save insect-swarms that hum in air afloat,
Save that the Cock is crowing, a shrill note,
Startling and shrill as that which roused the
   dawn.
— Heard in that hour, or when, as now, the
   nerve
Shrinks from the note as from a mistimed
   thing,
Oft for a holy warning may it serve,
Charged with remembrance of *his* sudden
   sting,
His bitter tears, whose name the Papal
   Chair
And yon resplendent Church are proud to
   bear.

IX

AT ALBANO

1837–42. 1842

   This Sonnet is founded on simple fact, and
was written to enlarge, if possible, the views
of those who can see nothing but evil in the in-
tercessions countenanced by the Church of Rome.
That they are in many respects lamentably
pernicious must be acknowledged; but, on the
other hand, they who reflect, while they see
and observe, cannot but be struck with instances
which will prove that it is a great error to con-
demn in all cases such mediation as purely
idolatrous. This remark bears with especial
force upon addresses to the Virgin.

Days passed — and Monte Calvo would not
   clear
His head from mist; and, as the wind
   sobbed through
Albano's dripping Ilex avenue,
My dull forebodings in a Peasant's ear
Found casual vent. She said, " Be of
   good cheer;
Our yesterday's procession did not sue
In vain; the sky will change to sunny blue,
Thanks to our Lady's grace." I smiled to
   hear,
But not in scorn: — the Matron's Faith may
   lack
The heavenly sanction needed to ensure
Fulfilment; but, we trust, her upward track
Stops not at this low point, nor wants the
   lure

Of flowers the Virgin without fear may
   own,
For by her Son's blest hand the seed was
   sown.

X

1837–42. 1842

Near Anio's stream, I spied a gentle Dove
Perched on an olive branch, and heard her
   cooing
'Mid new-born blossoms that soft airs were
   wooing,
While all things present told of joy and
   love.
But restless Fancy left that olive grove
To hail the exploratory Bird renewing
Hope for the few, who, at the world's un-
   doing,
On the great flood were spared to live and
   move.
O bounteous Heaven! signs true as dove
   and bough
Brought to the ark are coming evermore,
Given though we seek them not, but, while
   we plough
This sea of life without a visible shore,
Do neither promise ask nor grace implore
In what alone is ours, the living Now.

XI

FROM THE ALBAN HILLS, LOOKING TOWARDS ROME

1837–42. 1842

Forgive, illustrious Country! these deep
   sighs,
Heaved less for thy bright plains and hills
   bestrown
With monuments decayed or overthrown,
For all that tottering stands or prostrate
   lies,
Than for like scenes in moral vision shown,
Ruin perceived for keener sympathies;
Faith crushed, yet proud of weeds, her
   gaudy crown;
Virtues laid low, and mouldering energies.
Yet why prolong this mournful strain? —
   Fallen Power,
Thy fortunes, twice exalted, might provoke
Verse to glad notes prophetic of the hour
When thou, uprisen, shalt break thy double
   yoke,

And enter, with prompt aid from the Most
High,
On the third stage of thy great destiny.

XII

NEAR THE LAKE OF THRASY-
MENE

1837-42. 1842

WHEN here with Carthage Rome to conflict
came,
An earthquake, mingling with the battle's
shock,
Checked not its rage; unfelt the ground
did rock,
Sword dropped not, javelin kept its deadly
aim. —
Now all is sun-bright peace. Of that day's
shame,
Or glory, not a vestige seems to endure,
Save in this Rill that took from blood the
name
Which yet it bears, sweet Stream! as
crystal pure.
So may all trace and sign of deeds aloof
From the true guidance of humanity,
Thro' Time and Nature's influence, purify
Their spirit; or, unless they for reproof
Or warning serve, thus let them all, on
ground
That gave them being, vanish to a sound.

XIII

NEAR THE SAME LAKE

1837-42. 1842

FOR action born, existing to be tried,
Powers manifold we have that intervene
To stir the heart that would too closely
screen
Her peace from images to pain allied.
What wonder if at midnight, by the side
Of Sanguinetto, or broad Thrasymene,
The clang of arms is heard, and phantoms
glide,
Unhappy ghosts in troops by moonlight seen;
And singly thine, O vanquished Chief!
whose corse,
Unburied, lay hid under heaps of slain:
But who is He? — the Conqueror. Would
he force

His way to Rome? Ah, no, — round hill
and plain
Wandering, he haunts, at fancy's strong
command,
This spot — his shadowy death-cup in his
hand.

XIV

THE CUCKOO AT LAVERNA

MAY 25, 1837

1837. 1842

Among a thousand delightful feelings con-
nected in my mind with the voice of the cuckoo,
there is a personal one which is rather mel-
ancholy. I was first convinced that age had
rather dulled my hearing, by not being able to
catch the sound at the same distance as the
younger companions of my walks; and of this
failure I had a proof upon the occasion that
suggested these verses. I did not hear the
sound till Mr. Robinson had twice or thrice
directed my attention to it.

LIST — 't was the Cuckoo. — O with what
delight
Heard I that voice! and catch it now, though
faint,
Far off and faint, and melting into air,
Yet not to be mistaken. Hark again!
Those louder cries give notice that the Bird,
Although invisible as Echo's self,
Is wheeling hitherward. Thanks, happy
Creature,
For this unthought-of greeting!
While allured
From vale to hill, from hill to vale led on,
We have pursued, through various lands,
a long   10
And pleasant course; flower after flower
has blown,
Embellishing the ground that gave them
birth
With aspects novel to my sight; but still
Most fair, most welcome, when they drank
the dew
In a sweet fellowship with kinds beloved,
For old remembrance sake. And oft —
where Spring
Displayed her richest blossoms among files
Of orange-trees bedecked with glowing
fruit
Ripe for the hand, or under a thick shade
Of Ilex, or, if better suited to the hour, 20
The lightsome Olive's twinkling canopy —

Oft have I heard the Nightingale and Thrush
Blending as in a common English grove
Their love-songs; but, where'er my feet might roam,
Whate'er assemblages of new and old,
Strange and familiar, might beguile the way,
A gratulation from that vagrant Voice
Was wanting, — and most happily till now.
  For see, Laverna! mark the far-famed Pile,
High on the brink of that precipitous rock,
Implanted like a Fortress, as in truth   31
It is, a Christian Fortress, garrisoned
In faith and hope, and dutiful obedience,
By a few Monks, a stern society,
Dead to the world and scorning earth-born joys.
Nay — though the hopes that drew, the fears that drove,
St. Francis, far from Man's resort, to abide
Among these sterile heights of Apennine,
Bound him, nor, since he raised yon House, have ceased
To bind his spiritual Progeny, with rules   40
Stringent as flesh can tolerate and live;
His milder Genius (thanks to the good God
That made us) over those severe restraints
Of mind, that dread heart-freezing discipline,
Doth sometimes here predominate, and works
By unsought means for gracious purposes;
For earth through heaven, for heaven, by changeful earth,
Illustrated, and mutually endeared.
  Rapt though He were above the power of sense,
Familiarly, yet out of the cleansed heart
Of that once sinful Being overflowed   51
On sun, moon, stars, the nether elements,
And every shape of creature they sustain,
Divine affections; and with beast and bird
(Stilled from afar — such marvel story tells —
By casual outbreak of his passionate words,
And from their own pursuits in field or grove
Drawn to his side by look or act of love
Humane, and virtue of his innocent life)
He wont to hold companionship so free,   60
So pure, so fraught with knowledge and delight,
As to be likened in his Followers' minds

To that which our first Parents, ere the fall
From their high state darkened the Earth with fear,
Held with all kinds in Eden's blissful bowers.
  Then question not that, 'mid the austere Band,
Who breathe the air he breathed, tread where he trod,
Some true Partakers of his loving spirit
Do still survive, and, with those gentle hearts
Consorted, Others, in the power, the faith,
Of a baptized imagination, prompt   71
To catch from Nature's humblest monitors
Whate'er they bring of impulses sublime.
  Thus sensitive must be the Monk, though pale
With fasts, with vigils worn, depressed by years,
Whom in a sunny glade I chanced to see,
Upon a pine-tree's storm-uprooted trunk,
Seated alone, with forehead sky-ward raised,
Hands clasped above the crucifix he wore
Appended to his bosom, and lips closed   80
By the joint pressure of his musing mood
And habit of his vow. That ancient Man —
Nor haply less the Brother whom I marked,
As we approached the Convent gate, aloft
Looking far forth from his aerial cell,
A young Ascetic — Poet, Hero, Sage,
He might have been, Lover belike he was —
If they received into a conscious ear
The notes whose first faint greeting startled me,
Whose sedulous iteration thrilled with joy
My heart — may have been moved like me to think,   91
Ah! not like me who walk in the world's ways,
On the great Prophet, styled *the Voice of One*
Crying amid the wilderness, and given,
Now that their snows must melt, their herbs and flowers
Revive, their obstinate winter pass away,
That awful name to Thee, thee, simple Cuckoo,
Wandering in solitude, and evermore
Foretelling and proclaiming, ere thou leave
This thy last haunt beneath Italian skies   100
To carry thy glad tidings over heights
Still loftier, and to climes more near the Pole.

Voice of the Desert, fare-thee-well; sweet
    Bird !
If that substantial title please thee more,
Farewell ! — but go thy way, no need hast
    thou
Of a good wish sent after thee; from bower
To bower as green, from sky to sky as clear,
Thee gentle breezes waft — or airs, that
    meet
Thy course and sport around thee, softly
    fan —
Till Night, descending upon hill and vale,
Grants to thy mission a brief term of
    silence,   III
And folds thy pinions up in blest repose.

XV

AT THE CONVENT OF CAMAL-DOLI

1837–42. 1842

GRIEVE for the Man who hither came be-
    reft,
And seeking consolation from above;
Nor grieve the less that skill to him was
    left
To paint this picture of his lady-love:
Can she, a blessed saint, the work approve ?
And oh, good Brethren of the cowl, a thing
So fair, to which with peril he must cling,
Destroy in pity, or with care remove.
That bloom — those eyes — can they assist
    to bind
Thoughts that would stray from Heaven ?
    The dream must cease
To be; by Faith, not sight, his soul must
    live;
Else will the enamoured Monk too surely
    find
How wide a space can part from inward
    peace
The most profound repose his cell can
    give.

XVI

CONTINUED

1837–42. 1842

THE world forsaken, all its busy cares
And stirring interests shunned with desper-
    ate flight,
All trust abandoned in the healing might

Of virtuous action; all that courage dares,
Labour accomplishes, or patience bears —
Those helps rejected, they, whose minds
    perceive
How subtly works man's weakness, sighs
    may heave
For such a One beset with cloistral snares.
Father of Mercy ! rectify his view,
If with his vows this object ill agree;
Shed over it thy grace, and thus subdue
Imperious passion in a heart set free: —
That earthly love may to herself be true,
Give him a soul that cleaveth unto thee.

XVII

AT THE EREMITE OR UPPER CONVENT OF CAMALDOLI

1837–42. 1842

WHAT aim had they, the Pair of Monks,
    in size
Enormous, dragged, while side by side
    they sate,
By panting steers up to this convent gate ?
How, with empurpled cheeks and pampered
    eyes,
Dare they confront the lean austerities
Of Brethren who, here fixed, on Jesu wait
In sackcloth, and God's anger deprecate
Through all that humbles flesh and morti-
    fies ?
Strange contrast ! — verily the world of
    dreams,
Where mingle, as for mockery combined,
Things in their very essences at strife,
Shows not a sight incongruous as the ex-
    tremes
That everywhere, before the thoughtful
    mind,
Meet on the solid ground of waking life.

XVIII

AT VALLOMBROSA

1837–42. 1842

" Thick as autumnal leaves that strew the brooks
In Vallombrosa, where Etrurian shades
High over-arch'd embower."
                  Paradise Lost.

I must confess, though of course I did not
acknowledge it in the few lines I wrote in the
Strangers' book kept at the convent, that I was

somewhat disappointed at Vallombrosa. I had expected, as the name implies, a deep and narrow valley overshadowed by enclosing hills; but the spot where the convent stands is in fact not a valley at all, but a cove or crescent open to an extensive prospect. In the book before mentioned, I read the notice in the English language that if any one would ascend the steep ground above the convent, and wander over it. he would be abundantly rewarded by magnificent views. I had not time to act upon this recommendation, and only went with my young guide to a point, nearly on a level with the site of the convent, that overlooks the vale of Arno for some leagues. To praise great and good men has ever been deemed one of the worthiest employments of poetry, but the objects of admiration vary so much with time and circumstances, and the noblest of mankind have been found, when intimately known, to be of characters so imperfect, that no eulogist can find a subject which he will venture upon with the animation necessary to create sympathy, unless he confines himself to a particular art or he takes something of a one-sided view of the person he is disposed to celebrate. This is a melancholy truth, and affords a strong reason for the poetic mind being chiefly exercised in works of fiction : the poet can then follow wherever the spirit of admiration leads him, unchecked by such suggestions as will be too apt to cross his way if all that he is prompted to utter is to be tested by fact. Something in this spirit I have written in the note attached to the sonnet on the king of Sweden ; and many will think that in this poem and elsewhere I have spoken of the author of " Paradise Lost " in a strain of panegyric scarcely justifiable by the tenor of some of his opinions, whether theological or political, and by the temper he carried into public affairs in which, unfortunately for his genius, he was so much concerned.

" VALLOMBROSA — I longed in thy shadiest wood
To slumber, reclined on the moss-covered floor ! "
Fond wish that was granted at last, and the Flood,
That lulled me asleep bids me listen once more.
Its murmur how soft ! as it falls down the steep,
Near that Cell — yon sequestered Retreat high in air —
Where our Milton was wont lonely vigils to keep
For converse with God, sought through study and prayer.

The Monks still repeat the tradition with pride,
And its truth who shall doubt ? for his Spirit is here;　　10
In the cloud-piercing rocks doth her grandeur abide,
In the pines pointing heavenward her beauty austere;
In the flower-besprent meadows his genius we trace
Turned to humbler delights, in which youth might confide,
That would yield him fit help while prefiguring that Place
Where, if Sin had not entered, Love never had died.

When with life lengthened out came a desolate time,
And darkness and danger had compassed him round,
With a thought he would flee to these haunts of his prime
And here once again a kind shelter be found.　　20
And let me believe that when nightly the Muse
Did waft him to Sion, the glorified hill,
Here also, on some favoured height, he would choose
To wander, and drink inspiration at will.

Vallombrosa ! of thee I first heard in the page
Of that holiest of Bards, and the name for my mind
Had a musical charm, which the winter of age
And the changes it brings had no power to unbind.
And now, ye Miltonian shades ! under you
I repose, nor am forced from sweet fancy to part,　　30
While your leaves I behold and the brooks they will strew,
And the realised vision is clasped to my heart.

Even so, and unblamed, we rejoice as we may
In Forms that must perish, frail objects of sense;
Unblamed — if the Soul be intent on the day
When the Being of Beings shall summon her hence.

For he and he only with wisdom is blest
Who, gathering true pleasures wherever
    they grow,
Looks up in all places, for joy or for rest,
To the Fountain whence Time and Eternity
    flow.   40

XIX

AT FLORENCE

1837–42. 1842

Upon what evidence the belief rests that this
stone was a favourite seat of Dante, I do not
know ; but a man would little consult his own
interest as a traveller, if he should busy himself
with doubts as to the fact. The readiness with
which traditions of this character are received,
and the fidelity with which they are preserved
from generation to generation, are an evidence
of feelings honourable to our nature. I re-
member how, during one of my rambles in the
course of a college vacation, I was pleased on
being shown a seat near a kind of rocky cell
at the source of the river, on which it was said
that Congreve wrote his " Old Bachelor." One
can scarcely hit on any performance less in
harmony with the scene ; but it was a local
tribute paid to intellect by those who had not
troubled themselves to estimate the moral worth
of that author's comedies ; and why should
they ? He was a man distinguished in his day ;
and the sequestered neighbourhood in which he
often resided was perhaps as proud of him as
Florence of her Dante : it is the same feeling,
though proceeding from persons one cannot
bring together in this way without offering some
apology to the Shade of the great Visionary.

UNDER the shadow of a stately Pile,
The dome of Florence, pensive and alone,
Nor giving heed to aught that passed the
    while,
I stood, and gazed upon a marble stone,
The laurelled Dante's favourite seat. A
    throne,
In just esteem, it rivals ; though no style
Be there of decoration to beguile
The mind, depressed by thought of great-
    ness flown.
As a true man, who long had served the lyre,
I gazed with earnestness, and dared no more.
But in his breast the mighty Poet bore
A Patriot's heart, warm with undying fire.
Bold with the thought, in reverence I sate
    down,
And, for a moment, filled that empty
    Throne.

XX

BEFORE THE PICTURE OF THE BAPTIST, BY RAPHAEL, IN THE GALLERY AT FLORENCE

1840. 1842

It was very hot weather during the week we
stayed at Florence ; and, never having been there
before, I went through much hard service, and
am not therefore *ashamed* to confess I fell asleep
before this picture and sitting with my back to-
wards the Venus de Medicis. Buonaparte —
in answer to one who had spoken of his being
in a sound sleep up to the moment when one of
his great battles was to be fought, as a proof
of the calmness of his mind and command over
anxious thoughts — said frankly, that he slept
because from bodily exhaustion he could not
help it. In like manner it is noticed that
criminals on the night previous to their execution
seldom awake before they are called, a proof
that the body is the master of us far more than
we need be willing to allow. Should this note
by any possible chance be seen by any of my
countrymen who might have been in the gallery
at the time (and several persons were there)
and witnessed such an indecorum, I hope he will
give up the opinion which he might naturally
have formed to my prejudice.

THE Baptist might have been ordained to cry
Forth from the towers of that huge Pile,
    wherein
His Father served Jehovah ; but how win
Due audience, how for aught but scorn defy
The obstinate pride and wanton revelry
Of the Jerusalem below, her sin
And folly, if they with united din
Drown not at once mandate and prophecy ?
Therefore the Voice spake from the Desert,
    thence
To Her, as to her opposite in peace,
Silence, and holiness, and innocence,
To Her and to all Lands its warning sent,
Crying with earnestness that might not
    cease,
" Make straight a highway for the Lord —
    repent ! "

XXI

AT FLORENCE — FROM MICHAEL ANGELO

1839. 1842

However at first these two sonnets from
Michael Angelo may seem in their spirit some-

what inconsistent with each other, I have not scrupled to place them side by side as characteristic of their great author, and others with whom he lived. I feel nevertheless a wish to know at what periods of his life they were respectively composed. The latter, as it expresses, was written in his advanced years when it was natural that the Platonism that pervades the one should give way to the Christian feeling that inspired the other: between both there is more than poetic affinity.

RAPT above earth by power of one fair face,
Hers in whose sway alone my heart delights,
I mingle with the blest on those pure heights
Where Man, yet mortal, rarely finds a place.
With Him who made the Work that Work accords
So well, that by its help and through his grace
I raise my thoughts, inform my deeds and words,
Clasping her beauty in my soul's embrace.
Thus, if from two fair eyes mine cannot turn,
I feel how in their presence doth abide
Light which to God is both the way and guide;
And, kindling at their lustre, if I burn,
My noble fire emits the joyful ray
That through the realms of glory shines for aye.

XXII

AT FLORENCE — FROM M. ANGELO

1805(?)–1840. 1842

ETERNAL Lord! eased of a cumbrous load,
And loosened from the world, I turn to Thee;
Shun, like a shattered bark, the storm, and flee
To thy protection for a safe abode.
The crown of thorns, hands pierced upon the tree,
The meek, benign, and lacerated face,
To a sincere repentance promise grace,
To the sad soul give hope of pardon free.
With justice mark not Thou, O Light divine,
My fault, nor hear it with thy sacred ear;

Neither put forth that way thy arm severe;
Wash with thy blood my sins; thereto incline
More readily the more my years require
Help, and forgiveness speedy and entire.

XXIII

AMONG THE RUINS OF A CONVENT IN THE APENNINES

1837–42. 1842

The political revolutions of our time have multiplied, on the Continent, objects that unavoidably call forth reflections such as are expressed in these verses, but the Ruins in those countries are too recent to exhibit, in anything like an equal degree, the beauty with which time and nature have invested the remains of our Convents and Abbeys. These verses it will be observed take up the beauty long before it is matured, as one cannot but wish it may be among some of the desolations of Italy, France, and Germany.

YE Trees! whose slender roots entwine
Altars that piety neglects;
Whose infant arms enclasp the shrine
Which no devotion now respects;
If not a straggler from the herd
Here ruminate, nor shrouded bird,
Chanting her low-voiced hymn, take pride
In aught that ye would grace or hide —
How sadly is your love misplaced,
Fair Trees, your bounty run to waste!

Ye, too, wild Flowers! that no one heeds,
And ye — full often spurned as weeds —
In beauty clothed, or breathing sweetness
From fractured arch and mouldering wall —
Do but more touchingly recall
Man's headstrong violence and Time's fleetness,
Making the precincts ye adorn
Appear to sight still more forlorn.

XXIV

IN LOMBARDY

1837–42. 1842

SEE, where his difficult way that Old Man wins
Bent by a load of Mulberry leaves! — most hard

Appears *his* lot, to the small Worm's com-
pared,
For whom his toil with early day begins.
Acknowledging no task-master, at will
(As if her labour and her ease were twins)
She seems to work, at pleasure to lie still; —
And softly sleeps within the thread she
spins.
So fare they — the Man serving as her Slave.
Ere long their fates do each to each con-
form:
Both pass into new being, — but the Worm,
Transfigured, sinks into a hopeless grave;
His volant Spirit will, he trusts, ascend
To bliss unbounded, glory without end.

XXV

AFTER LEAVING ITALY

1837–42. 1842

I had proof in several instances that the
Carbonari, if I may still call them so, and their
favourers, are opening their eyes to the neces-
sity of patience, and are intent upon spreading
knowledge actively but quietly as they can.
May they have resolution to continue in this
course! for it is the only one by which they
can truly benefit their country. We left Italy
by the way which is called the "Nuova Strada
de Allmagna," to the east of the high passes of
the Alps, which take you at once from Italy
into Switzerland. This road leads across sev-
eral smaller heights, and winds down different
vales in succession, so that it was only by the
accidental sound of a few German words that
I was aware we had quitted Italy, and hence
the unwelcome shock alluded to in the two or
three last lines of the latter sonnet.

FAIR Land! Thee all men greet with joy;
how few,
Whose souls take pride in freedom, virtue,
fame,

Part from thee without pity dyed in shame:
I could not — while from Venice we with-
drew,
Led on till an Alpine strait confined our
view
Within its depths, and to the shore we came
Of Lago Morto, dreary sight and name,
Which o'er sad thoughts a sadder colouring
threw.
Italia! on the surface of thy spirit,
(Too aptly emblemed by that torpid lake)
Shall a few partial breezes only creep? —
Be its depths quickened; what thou dost
inherit
Of the world's hopes, dare to fulfil; awake,
Mother of Heroes, from thy death-like
sleep!

XXVI

CONTINUED

1837. 1842

As indignation mastered grief, my tongue
Spake bitter words; words that did ill
agree
With those rich stores of Nature's imagery,
And divine Art, that fast to memory
clung —
Thy gifts, magnificent Region, ever young
In the sun's eye, and in his sister's sight
How beautiful! how worthy to be sung
In strains of rapture, or subdued delight!
I feign not; witness that unwelcome shock
That followed the first sound of German
speech,
Caught the far-winding barrier Alps among.
In that announcement, greeting seemed to
mock
Parting; the casual word had power to
reach
My heart, and filled that heart with conflict
strong.

AT BOLOGNA, IN REMEMBRANCE OF THE LATE INSURREC-TIONS, 1837

1837. 1842

I

AH why deceive ourselves! by no mere fit
Of sudden passion roused shall men attain
True freedom where for ages they have lain
Bound in a dark abominable pit,

With life's best sinews more and more un-
knit.
Here, there, a banded few who loathe the
chain
May rise to break it; effort worse than vain
For thee, O great Italian nation, split
Into those jarring fractions. — Let thy scope
Be one fixed mind for all; thy rights approve
To thy own conscience gradually renewed;
Learn to make Time the father of wise Hope;

Then trust thy cause to the arm of Fortitude,
The light of Knowledge, and the warmth of
Love.

CONTINUED

II

HARD task ! exclaim the undisciplined, to
lean
On Patience coupled with such slow en-
deavour,
That long-lived servitude must last for ever.
Perish the grovelling few, who, prest be-
tween
Wrongs and the terror of redress, would
wean
Millions from glorious aims.   Our chains to
sever
Let us break forth in tempest now or
never ! —
What, is there then no space for golden
mean
And gradual progress ? — Twilight leads to
day,
And, even within the burning zones of earth,
The hastiest sunrise yields a temperate
ray;
The softest breeze to fairest flowers gives
birth:
Think not that Prudence dwells in dark
abodes,
She scans the future with the eye of gods.

CONCLUDED

III

As leaves are to the tree whereon they grow
And wither, every human generation
Is, to the Being of a mighty nation,
Locked in our world's embrace through
weal and woe;
Thought that should teach the zealot to
forego
Rash schemes, to abjure all selfish agitation,
And seek through noiseless pains and mod-
eration
The unblemished good they only can bestow.
Alas ! with most, who weigh futurity
Against time present, passion holds the
scales:
Hence equal ignorance of both prevails,
And nations sink ; or, struggling to be
free,
Are doomed to flounder on, like wounded
whales
Tossed on the bosom of a stormy sea.

"WHAT IF OUR NUMBERS BARELY COULD DEFY"

1802(?). 1837

WHAT if our numbers barely could defy
The arithmetic of babes, must foreign
hordes,
Slaves, vile as ever were befooled by words,
Striking through English breasts the an-
archy
Of Terror, bear us to the ground, and tie
Our hands behind our backs with felon
cords ?
Yields every thing to discipline of swords ?
Is man as good as man, none low, none
high ? —
Nor discipline nor valour can withstand
The shock, nor quell the inevitable rout,
When in some great extremity breaks out
A people, on their own beloved Land
Risen, like one man, to combat in the sight
Of a just God for liberty and right.

A NIGHT THOUGHT

(?). 1837

These verses were thrown off extempore
upon leaving Mrs. Luff's house at Fox-Ghyll,
one evening.   The good woman is not disposed
to look at the bright side of things, and there
happened to be present certain ladies who had
reached the point of life where *youth* is ended,
and who seemed to contend with each other in
expressing their dislike of the country and cli-
mate.   One of them had been heard to say she
could not endure a country where there was
" neither sunshine nor cavaliers."

Lo ! where the Moon along the sky
Sails with her happy destiny;
Oft is she hid from mortal eye
        Or dimly seen,
But when the clouds asunder fly
        How bright her mien !

Far different we — a froward race,
Thousands though rich in Fortune's grace
With cherished sullenness of pace
        Their way pursue,
Ingrates who wear a smileless face
        The whole year through.

If kindred humours e'er would make
My spirit droop for drooping's sake,

From Fancy following in thy wake,
Bright ship of heaven!
A counter impulse let me take
And be forgiven.

TO THE PLANET VENUS

Upon its approximation (as an Evening Star) to the Earth, Jan. 1838.

1838. 1838

WHAT strong allurement draws, what
spirit guides,
Thee, Vesper! brightening still, as if the
nearer
Thou com'st to man's abode the spot grew
dearer
Night after night? True is it Nature hides
Her treasures less and less.—Man now
presides
In power, where once he trembled in his
weakness;
Science advances with gigantic strides;
But are we aught enriched in love and
meekness?
Aught dost thou see, bright Star! of pure
and wise
More than in humbler times graced human
story;
That makes our hearts more apt to sym-
pathise
With heaven, our souls more fit for future
glory,
When earth shall vanish from our closing
eyes,
Ere we lie down in our last dormitory?

COMPOSED AT RYDAL ON MAY MORNING, 1838

1838. 1838

This and the sonnet entitled "The Pillar
of Trajan," p. 646, were composed on what
we call the "Far Terrace" at Rydal Mount,
where I have murmured out many thousands
of verses.

IF with old love of you, dear Hills! I
share
New love of many a rival image brought
From far, forgive the wanderings of my
thought:
Nor art thou wronged, sweet May! when I
compare

Thy present birth-morn with thy last, so
fair,
So rich to me in favours. For my lot
Then was, within the famed Egerian Grot
To sit and muse, fanned by its dewy air
Mingling with thy soft breath! That morn-
ing too,
Warblers I heard their joy unbosoming
Amid the sunny, shadowy, Colyseum;
Heard them, unchecked by aught of sadden-
ing hue,
For victories there won by flower-crowned
Spring,
Chant in full choir their innocent Te Deum.

COMPOSED ON A MAY MORNING, 1838

1838. 1838

LIFE with yon Lambs, like day, is just be-
gun,
Yet Nature seems to them a heavenly guide.
Does joy approach? they meet the coming
tide;
And sullenness avoid, as now they shun
Pale twilight's lingering glooms,—and in
the sun
Couch near their dams, with quiet satis-
fied;
Or gambol—each with his shadow at his
side,
Varying its shape wherever he may run.
As they from turf yet hoar with sleepy
dew
All turn, and court the shining and the
green,
Where herbs look up, and opening flowers
are seen;
Why to God's goodness cannot We be
true,
And so, His gifts and promises between,
Feed to the last on pleasures ever new?

"HARK! 'T IS THE THRUSH, UN-DAUNTED, UNDEPREST"

1838. 1838

HARK! 't is the Thrush, undaunted, unde-
prest,
By twilight premature of cloud and rain;
Nor does that roaring wind deaden his
strain

Who carols thinking of his Love and nest,
And seems, as more incited, still more blest.
Thanks; thou hast snapped a fireside
Prisoner's chain,
Exulting Warbler! eased a fretted brain,
And in a moment charmed my cares to
rest.
Yes, I will forth, bold Bird! and front the
blast,
That we may sing together, if thou wilt,
So loud, so clear, my Partner through life's
day,
Mute in her nest love-chosen, if not love-
built
Like thine, shall gladden, as in seasons past,
Thrilled by loose snatches of the social Lay.

"'T IS HE WHOSE YESTER-EVENING'S HIGH DISDAIN"

1838. 1838

'T IS He whose yester-evening's high dis-
dain
Beat back the roaring storm — but how
subdued
His day-break note, a sad vicissitude!
Does the hour's drowsy weight his glee
restrain?
Or, like the nightingale, her joyous vein
Pleased to renounce, does this dear Thrush
attune
His voice to suit the temper of yon Moon
Doubly depressed, setting, and in her wane?
Rise, tardy Sun! and let the Songster prove
(The balance trembling between night and
morn
No longer) with what ecstasy upborne
He can pour forth his spirit. In heaven
above,
And earth below, they best can serve true
gladness
Who meet most feelingly the calls of sad-
ness.

"OH WHAT A WRECK! HOW CHANGED IN MIEN AND SPEECH!"

1837. 1838

The sad condition of poor Mrs. Southey put
me upon writing this. It has afforded comfort
to many persons whose friends have been simi-
larly affected.

OH what a Wreck! how changed in mien
and speech!
Yet — though dread Powers, that work in
mystery, spin
Entanglings of the brain; though shadows
stretch
O'er the chilled heart — reflect; far, far
within
Hers is a holy Being, freed from Sin.
She is not what she seems, a forlorn wretch;
But delegated Spirits comfort fetch
To Her from heights that Reason may not
win.
Like Children, She is privileged to hold
Divine communion; both do live and move,
Whate'er to shallow Faith their ways unfold,
Inly illumined by Heaven's pitying love;
Love pitying innocence not long to last,
In them — in Her our sins and sorrows past.

A PLEA FOR AUTHORS, MAY 1838

1838. 1838

FAILING impartial measure to dispense
To every suitor, Equity is lame;
And social Justice, stript of reverence
For natural rights, a mockery and a shame;
Law but a servile dupe of false pretence,
If, guarding grossest things from common
claim
Now and for ever, She, to works that came
From mind and spirit, grudge a short-lived
fence.
"What! lengthened privilege, a lineal tie,
For *Books!*" Yes, heartless Ones, or be it
proved
That 't is a fault in Us to have lived and
loved
Like others, with like temporal hopes to
die;
No public harm that Genius from her course
Be turned; and streams of truth dried up,
even at their source!

A POET TO HIS GRANDCHILD

SEQUEL TO THE FOREGOING

1838. 1838

"SON of my buried Son, while thus thy
hand
Is clasping mine, it saddens me to think

How Want may press thee down, and with
    thee sink
Thy children left unfit, through vain demand
Of culture, even to feel or understand
My simplest Lay that to their memory
May cling; — hard fate! which haply need
    not be
Did Justice mould the statutes of the Land.
A Book time-cherished and an honoured
    name
Are high rewards; but bound they Nature's
    claim
Or Reason's? No — hopes spun in timid
    line
From out the bosom of a modest home
Extend through unambitious years to come,
My careless Little-one, for thee and thine!"

"BLEST STATESMAN HE, WHOSE MIND'S UNSELFISH WILL"

1838. 1838

BLEST Statesman He, whose Mind's unself-
    ish will
Leaves him at ease among grand thoughts:
    whose eye
Sees that, apart from magnanimity,
Wisdom exists not; nor the humbler skill
Of Prudence, disentangling good and ill
With patient care. What tho' assaults run
    high,
They daunt not him who holds his ministry,
Resolute, at all hazards, to fulfil
Its duties; — prompt to move, but firm to
    wait, —
Knowing, things rashly sought are rarely
    found;
That, for the functions of an ancient State —
Strong by her charters, free because im-
    bound,
Servant of Providence, not slave of Fate —
Perilous is sweeping change, all chance un-
    sound.

VALEDICTORY SONNET

1838. 1838

Closing the Volume of Sonnets published in
1838.

SERVING no haughty Muse, my hands have
    here
Disposed some cultured Flowerets (drawn
    from spots

Where they bloomed singly, or in scattered
    knots),
Each kind in several beds of one parterre;
Both to allure the casual Loiterer,
And that, so placed, my Nurslings may
    requite
Studious regard with opportune delight,
Nor be unthanked, unless I fondly err.
But metaphor dismissed, and thanks apart,
Reader, farewell! My last words let them
    be —
If in this book Fancy and Truth agree;
If simple Nature trained by careful Art
Through It have won a passage to thy heart;
Grant me thy love, I crave no other fee!

PROTEST AGAINST THE BALLOT

1838. 1838

FORTH rushed from Envy sprung and Self-
    conceit,
A Power misnamed the SPIRIT of REFORM,
And through the astonished Island swept
    in storm,
Threatening to lay all orders at her feet
That crossed her way. Now stoops she to
    entreat
Licence to hide at intervals her head
Where she may work, safe, undisquieted,
In a close Box, covert for Justice meet.
St. George of England! keep a watchful
    eye
Fixed on the Suitor; frustrate her request —
Stifle her hope; for, if the State comply,
From such Pandorian gift may come a Pest
Worse than the Dragon that bowed low his
    crest,
Pierced by thy spear in glorious victory.

SONNETS

UPON THE PUNISHMENT OF DEATH

IN SERIES

1839–40. 1841

I

SUGGESTED BY THE VIEW OF LANCAS-TER CASTLE (ON THE ROAD FROM THE SOUTH)

THIS Spot — at once unfolding sight so fair
Of sea and land, with yon grey towers that
    still

Rise up as if to lord it over air —
Might soothe in human breasts the sense of
    ill,
Or charm it out of memory; yea, might fill
The heart with joy and gratitude to God
For all his bounties upon man bestowed:
Why bears it then the name of "Weeping
    Hill"?
Thousands, as toward yon old Lancastrian
    Towers,
A prison's crown, along this way they past
For lingering durance or quick death with
    shame,
From this bare eminence thereon have cast
Their first look — blinded as tears fell in
    showers
Shed on their chains; and hence that dole-
    ful name.

II

TENDERLY do we feel by Nature's law
For worst offenders: though the heart will
    heave
With indignation, deeply moved we grieve,
In after thought, for Him who stood in
    awe
Neither of God nor man, and only saw,
Lost wretch, a horrible device enthroned
On proud temptations, till the victim
    groaned
Under the steel his hand had dared to
    draw.
But oh, restrain compassion, if its course,
As oft befalls, prevent or turn aside
Judgments and aims and acts whose higher
    source
Is sympathy with the unforewarned, who
    died
Blameless — with them that shuddered o'er
    his grave,
And all who from the law firm safety crave.

III

THE Roman Consul doomed his sons to die
Who had betrayed their country. The
    stern word
Afforded (may it through all time afford)
A theme for praise and admiration high.
Upon the surface of humanity
He rested not; its depths his mind explored;
He felt; but his parental bosom's lord
Was Duty, — Duty calmed his agony.
And some, we know, when they by wilful
    act
A single human life have wrongly taken,

Pass sentence on themselves, confess the
    fact,
And, to atone for it, with soul unshaken
Kneel at the feet of Justice, and, for faith
Broken with all mankind, solicit death.

IV

Is *Death*, when evil against good has fought
With such fell mastery that a man may dare
By deeds the blackest purpose to lay bare;
Is Death, for one to that condition brought,
For him, or any one, the thing that ought
To be *most* dreaded?   Lawgivers, beware,
Lest, capital pains remitting till ye spare
The murderer, ye, by sanction to that
    thought
Seemingly given, debase the general mind;
Tempt the vague will tried standards to
    disown,
Nor only palpable restraints unbind,
But upon Honour's head disturb the crown,
Whose absolute rule permits not to with-
    stand
In the weak love of life his least command.

V

NOT to the object specially designed,
Howe'er momentous in itself it be,
Good to promote or curb depravity,
Is the wise Legislator's view confined.
His Spirit, when most severe, is oft most
    kind;
As all Authority in earth depends
On Love and Fear, their several powers he
    blends,
Copying with awe the one Paternal mind.
Uncaught by processes in show humane,
He feels how far the act would derogate
From even the humblest functions of the
    State;
If she, self-shorn of Majesty, ordain
That never more shall hang upon her breath
The last alternative of Life or Death.

VI

YE brood of conscience — Spectres! that
    frequent
The bad Man's restless walk, and haunt
    his bed —
Fiends in your aspect, yet beneficent
In act, as hovering Angels when they spread
Their wings to guard the unconscious
    Innocent —
Slow be the Statutes of the land to share
A laxity that could not but impair

Your power to punish crime, and so pre-
vent.
And ye, Beliefs ! coiled serpent-like about
The adage on all tongues, "Murder will
out,"
How shall your ancient warnings work for
good
In the full might they hitherto have shown,
If for deliberate shedder of man's blood
Survive not Judgment that requires his
own ?

VII

BEFORE the world had past her time of
youth
While polity and discipline were weak,
The precept eye for eye, and tooth for tooth,
Came forth — a light, though but as of day-
break,
Strong as could then be borne. A Master
meek
Proscribed the spirit fostered by that rule,
Patience *his* law, long-suffering *his* school,
And love the end, which all through peace
must seek.
But lamentably do they err who strain
His mandates, given rash impulse to con-
trol
And keep vindictive thirstings from the
soul,
So far that, if consistent in their scheme,
They must forbid the State to inflict a pain,
Making of social order a mere dream.

VIII

FIT retribution, by the moral code
Determined, lies beyond the State's em-
brace,
Yet, as she may, for each peculiar case
She plants well-measured terrors in the road
Of wrongful acts. Downward it is and
broad,
And, the main fear once doomed to banish-
ment,
Far oftener then, bad ushering worse event,
Blood would be spilt that in his dark abode
Crime might lie better hid. And, should
the change
Take from the horror due to a foul deed,
Pursuit and evidence so far must fail,
And, guilt escaping, passion then might
plead
In angry spirits for her old free range,
And the " wild justice of revenge " pre-
vail.

IX

THOUGH to give timely warning and deter
Is one great aim of penalty, extend
Thy mental vision further and ascend
Far higher, else full surely shalt thou err.
What is a State ? The wise behold in her
A creature born of time, that keeps one
eye
Fixed on the statutes of Eternity,
To which her judgments reverently defer.
Speaking through Law's dispassionate voice
the State
Endues her conscience with external life
And being, to preclude or quell the strife
Of individual will, to elevate
The grovelling mind, the erring to recall,
And fortify the moral sense of all.

X

OUR bodily life, some plead, that life the
shrine
Of an immortal spirit, is a gift
So sacred, so informed with light divine,
That no tribunal, though most wise to sift
Deed and intent, should turn the Being
adrift
Into that world where penitential tear
May not avail, nor prayer have for God's
ear
A voice — that world whose veil no hand
can lift
For earthly sight. " Eternity and Time,"
They urge, " have interwoven claims and
rights
Not to be jeopardised through foulest
crime:
The sentence rule by mercy's heaven-born
lights."
Even so; but measuring not by finite sense
Infinite Power, perfect Intelligence.

XI

AH, think how one compelled for life to
abide
Locked in a dungeon needs must eat the
heart
Out of his own humanity, and part
With every hope that mutual cares provide;
And, should a less unnatural doom confide
In life-long exile on a savage coast,
Soon the relapsing penitent may boast
Of yet more heinous guilt, with fiercer pride.
Hence thoughtful Mercy, Mercy sage and
pure,
Sanctions the forfeiture that Law demands,

Leaving the final issue in *His* hands
Whose goodness knows no change, whose
love is sure,
Who sees, foresees; who cannot judge amiss,
And wafts at will the contrite soul to bliss.

XII

SEE the Condemned alone within his cell
And prostrate at some moment when re-
morse
Stings to the quick, and, with resistless force,
Assaults the pride she strove in vain to
quell.
Then mark him, him who could so long rebel,
The crime confessed, a kneeling Penitent
Before the Altar, where the Sacrament
Softens his heart, till from his eyes outwell
Tears of salvation. Welcome death ! while
Heaven
Does in this change exceedingly rejoice;
While yet the solemn heed the State hath
given
Helps him to meet the last Tribunal's voice
In faith, which fresh offences, were he cast
On old temptations, might for ever blast.

XIII

CONCLUSION

YES, though He well may tremble at the
sound
Of his own voice, who from the judgment-
seat
Sends the pale Convict to his last retreat
In death; though Listeners shudder all
around,
They know the dread requital's source pro-
found;
Nor is, they feel, its wisdom obsolete —
(Would that it were !) the sacrifice unmeet
For Christian Faith. But hopeful signs
abound;
The social rights of man breathe purer air,
Religion deepens her preventive care;
Then, moved by needless fear of past abuse,
Strike not from Law's firm hand that awful
rod,
But leave it thence to drop for lack of use:
Oh, speed the blessèd hour, Almighty God !

XIV

APOLOGY

THE formal World relaxes her cold chain
For One who speaks in numbers; ampler
scope

His utterance finds; and, conscious of the
gain,
Imagination works with bolder hope
The cause of grateful reason to sustain;
And, serving Truth, the heart more strongly
beats
Against all barriers which his labour meets
In lofty place, or humble Life's domain.
Enough;— before us lay a painful road,
And guidance have I sought in duteous love
From Wisdom's heavenly Father. Hence
hath flowed
Patience, with trust that, whatsoe'er the way
Each takes in this high matter, all may
move
Cheered with the prospect of a brighter
day.

ON A PORTRAIT OF I. F.,
PAINTED BY MARGARET GIL-
LIES

1840. 1851

WE gaze — nor grieve to think that we
must die,
But that the precious love this friend hath
sown
Within our hearts, the love whose flower
hath blown
Bright as if heaven were ever in its eye,
Will pass so soon from human memory;
And not by strangers to our blood alone,
But by our best descendants be unknown,
Unthought of — this may surely claim a
sigh.
Yet, blessed Art, we yield not to dejection;
Thou against Time so feelingly dost strive.
Where'er, preserved in this most true re-
flection,
An image of her soul is kept alive,
Some lingering fragrance of the pure affec-
tion,
Whose flower with us will vanish, must
survive.

TO I. F.

1840. 1851

THE star which comes at close of day to
shine
More heavenly bright than when it leads
the morn,
Is friendship's emblem, whether the forlorn
She visiteth, or, shedding light benign

Through shades that solemnize Life's calm
  decline,
Doth make the happy happier. This have we
Learnt, Isabel, from thy society,
Which now we too unwillingly resign
Though for brief absence. But farewell!
  the page
Glimmers before my sight through thankful
  tears,
Such as start forth, not seldom, to approve
Our truth, when we, old yet unchilled by age,
Call thee, though known but for a few fleet
  years,
The heart-affianced sister of our love!

POOR ROBIN

1840. 1842

I often ask myself what will become of Rydal Mount after our day. Will the old walls and steps remain in front of the house and about the grounds, or will they be swept away with all the beautiful mosses and ferns and wild geraniums and other flowers which their rude construction suffered and encouraged to grow among them? — This little wild flower — "Poor Robin" — is here constantly courting my attention, and exciting what may be called a domestic interest with the varying aspects of its stalks and leaves and flowers. Strangely do the tastes of men differ according to their employment and habits of life. "What a nice well would that be," said a labouring man to me one day, "if all that rubbish was cleared off." The "rubbish" was some of the most beautiful mosses and lichens and ferns and other wild growths that could possibly be seen. Defend us from the tyranny of trimness and neatness showing itself in this way! Chatterton says of freedom — "Upon her head wild weeds were spread;" and depend upon it if "the marvellous boy" had undertaken to give Flora a garland, he would have preferred what we are apt to call weeds to garden-flowers. True taste has an eye for both. Weeds have been called flowers out of place. I fear the place most people would assign to them is too limited. Let them come near to our abodes, as surely they may without impropriety or disorder.

Now when the primrose makes a splendid
  show,
And lilies face the March-winds in full blow,
And humbler growths as moved with one
  desire
Put on, to welcome spring, their best attire,
Poor Robin is yet flowerless; but how gay

With his red stalks upon this sunny day!
And, as his tufts of leaves he spreads, content
With a hard bed and scanty nourishment,
Mixed with the green, some shine not lacking power
To rival summer's brightest scarlet flower;
And flowers they well might seem to
  passers-by   11
If looked at only with a careless eye;
Flowers — or a richer produce (did it suit
The season) sprinklings of ripe strawberry
  fruit.
But while a thousand pleasures come unsought,
Why fix upon his wealth or want a thought?
Is the string touched in prelude to a lay
Of pretty fancies that would round him play
When all the world acknowledged elfin
  sway?
Or does it suit our humour to commend   20
Poor Robin as a sure and crafty friend,
Whose practice teaches, spite of names, to
  show
Bright colours whether they deceive or
  no? —
Nay, we would simply praise the free goodwill
With which, though slighted, he, on naked
  hill
Or in warm valley, seeks his part to fill;
Cheerful alike if bare of flowers as now,
Or when his tiny gems shall deck his brow:
Yet more, we wish that men by men despised,
And such as lift their foreheads overprized,   30
Should sometimes think, where'er they
  chance to spy
This child of Nature's own humility,
What recompence is kept in store or left
For all that seem neglected or bereft;
With what nice care equivalents are given,
How just, how bountiful, the hand of
  Heaven.

ON A PORTRAIT OF THE DUKE OF WELLINGTON UPON THE FIELD OF WATERLOO, BY HAYDON

1840. 1842

This was composed while I was ascending Helvellyn in company with my daughter and her husband. She was on horseback and rode to the top of the hill without once dismounting, a feat which it was scarcely possible to perform except during a season of dry weather; and a guide, with whom we fell in on the mountain, told us he believed it had never been accomplished before by any one.

By Art's bold privilege Warrior and War-
    horse stand
On ground yet strewn with their last battle's
    wreck;
Let the Steed glory while his Master's hand
Lies fixed for ages on his conscious neck;
But by the Chieftain's look, though at his
    side
Hangs that day's treasured sword, how firm
    a check
Is given to triumph and all human pride !
Yon trophied Mound shrinks to a shadowy
    speck
In his calm presence ! Him the mighty
    deed
Elates not, brought far nearer the grave's
    rest,
As shows that time-worn face, for he such
    seed
Has sown as yields, we trust, the fruit of
    fame
In Heaven; hence no one blushes for thy
    name,
Conqueror, 'mid some sad thoughts, divinely
    blest!

TO A PAINTER

1840. 1842

The picture which gave occasion to this and the following Sonnet was from the pencil of Miss M. Gillies, who resided for several weeks under our roof at Rydal Mount.

All praise the Likeness by thy skill por-
    trayed;
But 't is a fruitless task to paint for me,
Who, yielding not to changes Time has
    made,
By the habitual light of memory see
Eyes unbedimmed, see bloom that cannot
    fade,
And smiles that from their birth-place ne'er
    shall flee
Into the land where ghosts and phantoms
    be;
And, seeing this, own nothing in its stead.
Couldst thou go back into far-distant years,

Or share with me, fond thought ! that in-
    ward eye,
Then, and then only, Painter ! could thy Art
The visual powers of Nature satisfy,
Which hold, whate'er to common sight
    appears,
Their sovereign empire in a faithful heart.

ON THE SAME SUBJECT

1840. 1842

Though I beheld at first with blank sur-
    prise
This Work, I now have gazed on it so long
I see its truth with unreluctant eyes;
O, my Belovèd ! I have done thee wrong,
Conscious of blessedness, but, whence it
    sprung,
Ever too heedless, as I now perceive:
Morn into noon did pass, noon into eve,
And the old day was welcome as the young
As welcome, and as beautiful — in sooth
More beautiful, as being a thing more holy:
Thanks to thy virtues, to the eternal youth
Of all thy goodness, never melancholy;
To thy large heart and humble mind, that
    cast
Into one vision, future, present, past.

"WHEN SEVERN'S SWEEPING FLOOD HAD OVERTHROWN"

1842. 1842

When Severn's sweeping flood had over-
    thrown
St. Mary's Church, the preacher then
    would cry: —
"Thus, Christian people, God his might
    hath shown
That ye to him your love may testify;
Haste, and rebuild the pile." — But not a
    stone
Resumed its place.   Age after age went by,
And Heaven still lacked its due, though
    piety
In secret did, we trust, her loss bemoan.
But now her Spirit hath put forth its claim
In Power, and Poesy would lend her voice;
Let the new Church be worthy of its aim,
That in its beauty Cardiff may rejoice !
Oh ! in the past if cause there was for
    shame,
Let not our times halt in their better choice.

"INTENT ON GATHERING WOOL FROM HEDGE AND BRAKE"

1842. 1842

Suggested by a conversation with Miss Fenwick, who along with her sister had, during their childhood, found much delight in such gatherings for the purposes here alluded to.

INTENT on gathering wool from hedge and
    brake
Yon busy Little-ones rejoice that soon
A poor old Dame will bless them for the
    boon:
Great is their glee while flake they add to
    flake
With rival earnestness; far other strife
Than will hereafter move them, if they
    make
Pastime their idol, give their day of life
To pleasure snatched for reckless pleasure's
    sake.
Can pomp and show allay one heart-born
    grief?
Pains which the World inflicts can she
    requite?
Not for an interval however brief;
The silent thoughts that search for stedfast
    light,
Love from her depths, and Duty in her
    might,
And Faith — these only yield secure relief.

PRELUDE

PREFIXED TO THE VOLUME ENTITLED "POEMS CHIEFLY OF EARLY AND LATE YEARS"

1842. 1842

These verses were begun while I was on a visit to my son John at Brigham, and were finished at Rydal. As the contents of the volume, to which they are now prefixed, will be assigned to their respective classes when my poems shall be collected in one volume, I should be at a loss where with propriety to place this prelude, being too restricted in its bearing to serve for a preface for the whole. The lines towards the conclusion allude to the discontents then fomented through the country by the agitators of the Anti-Corn-Law League: the particular causes of such troubles are transitory, but disposition to excite and liability to be excited are nevertheless permanent, and therefore proper objects for the poet's regard.

IN desultory walk through orchard grounds,
Or some deep chestnut grove, oft have I
    paused
The while a Thrush, urged rather than
    restrained
By gusts of vernal storm, attuned his song
To his own genial instincts; and was heard
(Though not without some plaintive tónes
    between)
To utter, above showers of blossom swept
From tossing boughs, the promise of a calm,
Which the unsheltered traveller might re-
    ceive
With thankful spirit. The descant, and the
    wind   10
That seemed to play with it in love or scorn,
Encouraged and endeared the strain of
    words
That haply flowed from me, by fits of si-
    lence
Impelled to livelier pace. But now, my
    Book!
Charged with those lays, and others of like
    mood,
Or loftier pitch if higher rose the theme,
Go, single — yet aspiring to be joined
With thy Forerunners that through many
    a year
Have faithfully prepared each other's
    way —
Go forth upon a mission best fulfilled   20
When and wherever, in this changeful
    world,
Power hath been given to please for higher
    ends
Than pleasure only; gladdening to prepare
For wholesome sadness, troubling to refine,
Calming to raise; and, by a sapient Art
Diffused through all the mysteries of our
    Being,
Softening the toils and pains that have not
    ceased
To cast their shadows on our mother Earth
Since the primeval doom. Such is the
    grace
Which, though unsued for, fails not to de-
    scend   30
With heavenly inspiration; such the aim
That Reason dictates; and, as even the wish
Has virtue in it, why should hope to me
Be wanting that sometimes, where fancied
    ills
Harass the mind and strip from off the
    bowers
Of private life their natural pleasantness,

A Voice — devoted to the love whose seeds
Are sown in every human breast, to beauty
Lodged within compass of the humblest
    sight,
To cheerful intercourse with wood and
    field,   40
And sympathy with man's substantial
    griefs —
Will not be heard in vain? And in those
    days
When unforeseen distress spreads far and
    wide
Among a People mournfully cast down,
Or into anger roused by venal words
In recklessness flung out to overturn
The judgment, and divert the general heart
From mutual good — some strain of thine,
    my Book!
Caught at propitious intervals, may win
Listeners who not unwillingly admit   50
Kindly emotion tending to console
And reconcile; and both with young and
    old
Exalt the sense of thoughtful gratitude
For benefits that still survive, by faith
In progress, under laws divine, maintained.

FLOATING ISLAND

(?). 1842

My poor sister takes a pleasure in repeating
these verses, which she composed not long be-
fore the beginning of her sad illness.

These lines are by the author of the "Ad-
dress to the Wind," etc., published heretofore
along with my Poems.

HARMONIOUS Powers with Nature work
On sky, earth, river, lake and sea;
Sunshine and cloud, whirlwind and breeze,
All in one duteous task agree.

Once did I see a slip of earth
(By throbbing waves long undermined)
Loosed from its hold; how, no one knew,
But all might see it float, obedient to the
    wind;

Might see it, from the mossy shore
Dissevered, float upon the Lake,
Float with its crest of trees adorned
On which the warbling birds their pastime
    take.

Food, shelter, safety, there they find;
There berries ripen, flowerets bloom;
There insects live their lives, and die;
A peopled world it is; in size a tiny room.

And thus through many seasons' space
This little Island may survive;
But Nature, though we mark her not,
Will take away, may cease to give.

Perchance when you are wandering forth
Upon some vacant sunny day,
Without an object, hope, or fear,
Thither your eyes may turn — the Isle is
    passed away;

Buried beneath the glittering Lake!
Its place no longer to be found;
Yet the lost fragments shall remain
To fertilize some other ground.

"THE CRESCENT-MOON, THE STAR OF LOVE"

1841. 1842

THE Crescent-moon, the Star of Love,
    Glories of evening, as ye there are seen
With but a span of sky between —
    Speak one of you, my doubts remove,
Which is the attendant Page and which the
    Queen?

TO A REDBREAST — (IN SICK-NESS)

(?). 1842

Almost the only verses by our lamented Sis-
ter Sara Hutchinson.

STAY, little cheerful Robin! stay,
    And at my casement sing,
Though it should prove a farewell lay
    And this our parting spring.

Though I, alas! may ne'er enjoy
    The promise in thy song;
A charm, *that* thought can not destroy,
    Doth to thy strain belong.

Methinks that in my dying hour
    Thy song would still be dear,
And with a more than earthly power
    My passing Spirit cheer.

Then, little Bird, this boon confer,
  Come, and my requiem sing,
Nor fail to be the harbinger
  Of everlasting Spring.

MISCELLANEOUS SONNETS
(?). 1842

I

I was impelled to write this Sonnet by the disgusting frequency with which the word *artistical*, imported with other impertinences from the Germans, is employed by writers of the present day: for artistical let them substitute artificial, and the poetry written on this system, both at home and abroad, will be for the most part much better characterised.

A POET! — He hath put his heart to school,
Nor dares to move unpropped upon the staff
Which Art hath lodged within his hand —
    must laugh
By precept only, and shed tears by rule.
Thy Art be Nature; the live current quaff,
And let the groveller sip his stagnant pool,
In fear that else, when Critics grave and
    cool
Have killed him, Scorn should write his
    epitaph.
How does the Meadow-flower its bloom un-
    fold?
Because the lovely little flower is free
Down to its root, and, in that freedom,
    bold;
And so the grandeur of the Forest-tree
Comes not by casting in a formal mould,
But from its *own* divine vitality.

II

Hundreds of times have I seen, hanging about and above the vale of Rydal, clouds that might have given birth to this Sonnet, which was thrown off on the impulse of the moment one evening when I was returning home from the favourite walk of ours, along the Rotha, under Loughrigg.

THE most alluring clouds that mount the
    sky
Owe to a troubled element their forms,
Their hues to sunset.   If with raptured eye
We watch their splendour, shall we covet
    storms,
And wish the Lord of day his slow decline
Would hasten, that such pomp may float on
    high?
Behold, already they forget to shine,
Dissolve — and leave, to him who gazed, a
    sigh.
Not loth to thank each moment for its boon
Of pure delight, come whencesoe'er it may,
Peace let us seek, — to stedfast things
    attune
Calm expectations — leaving to the gay
And volatile their love of transient bowers,
The house that cannot pass away be ours.

III

This Sonnet is recommended to the perusal of all those who consider that the evils under which we groan are to be removed or palliated by measures ungoverned by moral and religious principles.

FEEL for the wrongs to universal ken
Daily exposed, woe that unshrouded lies;
And seek the Sufferer in his darkest den,
Whether conducted to the spot by sighs
And moanings, or he dwells (as if the wren
Taught him concealment) hidden from all
    eyes
In silence and the awful modesties
Of sorrow; — feel for all, as brother Men!
Rest not in hope want's icy chain to thaw
By casual boons and formal charities;
Learn to be just, just through impartial
    law;
Far as ye may, erect and equalise;
And, what ye cannot reach by statute, draw
Each from his fountain of self-sacrifice!

IV

IN ALLUSION TO VARIOUS RECENT HISTORIES AND NOTICES OF THE FRENCH REVOLUTION

PORTENTOUS change when History can ap-
    pear
As the cool Advocate of foul device;
Reckless audacity extol, and jeer
At consciences perplexed with scruples
    nice!
They who bewail not, must abhor, the
    sneer
Born of Conceit, Power's blind Idolater;
Or haply sprung from vaunting Cowardice
Betrayed by mockery of holy fear.
Hath it not long been said the wrath of
    Man

Works not the righteousness of God ?   Oh
  bend,
Bend, ye Perverse ! to judgments from on
  High,
Laws that lay under Heaven's perpetual ban,
All principles of action that transcend
The sacred limits of humanity.

V
CONTINUED

WHO ponders National events shall find
An awful balancing of loss and gain,
Joy based on sorrow, good with ill com-
  bined,
And proud deliverance issuing out of pain
And direful throes; as if the All-ruling Mind,
With whose perfection it consists to ordain
Volcanic burst, earthquake, and hurricane,
Dealt in like sort with feeble human kind
By laws immutable.   But woe for him
Who thus deceived shall lend an eager hand
To social havoc.   Is not Conscience ours,
And Truth, whose eye guilt only can make
  dim ;
And Will, whose office, by divine command,
Is to control and check disordered Powers ?

VI
CONCLUDED

LONG-FAVOURED England ! be not thou
  misled
By monstrous theories of alien growth,
Lest alien frenzy seize thee, waxing wroth,
Self-smitten till thy garments reek dyed red
With thy own blood, which tears in torrents
  shed
Fail to wash out, tears flowing ere thy troth
Be plighted, not to ease but sullen sloth,
Or wan despair — the ghost of false hope fled
Into a shameful grave.   Among thy youth,
My Country ! if such warning be held dear,
Then shall a Veteran's heart be thrilled
  with joy,
One who would gather from eternal truth,
For time and season, rules that work to
  cheer —
Not scourge, to save the People — not de-
  stroy.

VII
1839. 1842

MEN of the Western World ! in Fate's dark
  book
Whence these opprobrious leaves of dire
  portent ?

Think ye your British Ancestors forsook
Their native Land, for outrage provident ;
From unsubmissive necks the bridle shook
To give, in their Descendants, freer vent
And wider range to passions turbulent,
To mutual tyranny a deadlier look ?
Nay, said a voice, soft as the south wind's
  breath,
Dive through the stormy surface of the
  flood
To the great current flowing underneath ;
Explore the countless springs of silent
  good ;
So shall the truth be better understood,
And thy grieved Spirit brighten strong in
  faith.

VIII
(?). 1842

Lo ! where she stands fixed in a saint-like
  trance,
One upward hand, as if she needed rest
From rapture, lying softly on her breast !
Nor wants her eyeball an ethereal glance ;
But not the less — nay more — that counte-
  nance,
While thus illumined, tells of painful strife
For a sick heart made weary of this life
By love, long crossed with adverse circum-
  stance.
— Would She were now as when she hoped
  to pass
At God's appointed hour to them who tread
Heaven's sapphire pavement, yet breathed
  well content,
Well pleased, her foot should print earth's
  common grass,
Lived thankful for day's light, for daily
  bread,
For health, and time in obvious duty spent.

THE NORMAN BOY
(?). 1842

  The subject of this poem was sent me by Mrs.
Ogle, to whom I was personally unknown, with
a hope on her part that I might be induced to
relate the incident in verse ; and I do not regret
that I took the trouble ; for not improbably the
fact is illustrative of the boy's early piety, and
may concur with my other little pieces on
children to produce profitable reflection among
my youthful readers. This is said however
with an absolute conviction that children will
derive most benefit from books which are not
unworthy the perusal of persons of any age.   I

protest with my whole heart against those pro-
ductions, so abundant in the present day, in
which the doings of children are dwelt upon
as if they were incapable of being interested in
anything else. On this subject I have dwelt at
length in the poem on the growth of my own
mind.

HIGH on a broad unfertile tract of forest-
    skirted Down,
Nor kept by Nature for herself, nor made
    by man his own,
From home and company remote and every
    playful joy,
Served, tending a few sheep and goats, a
    raggèd Norman Boy.

Him never saw I, nor the spot; but from
    an English Dame,
Stranger to me and yet my friend, a simple
    notice came,
With suit that I would speak in verse of
    that sequestered child
Whom, one bleak winter's day, she met
    upon the dreary Wild.

His flock, along the woodland's edge with
    relics sprinkled o'er
Of last night's snow, beneath a sky threat-
    ening the fall of more,   10
Where tufts of herbage tempted each, were
    busy at their feed,
And the poor Boy was busier still, with
    work of anxious heed.

There *was* he, where of branches rent and
    withered and decayed,
For covert from the keen north wind, his
    hands a hut had made.
A tiny tenement, forsooth, and frail, as
    needs must be
A thing of such materials framed, by a
    builder such as he.

The hut stood finished by his pains, nor
    seemingly lacked aught
That skill or means of his could add, but
    the architect had wrought
Some limber twigs into a Cross, well-shaped
    with fingers nice,
To be engrafted on the top of his small
    edifice.   20

That Cross he now was fastening there, as
    the surest power and best
For supplying all deficiencies, all wants of
    the rude nest

In which, from burning heat, or tempest
    driving far and wide,
The innocent Boy, else shelterless, his lonely
    head must hide.

That Cross belike he also raised as a stand-
    ard for the true
And faithful service of his heart in the
    worst that might ensue
Of hardship and distressful fear, amid the
    houseless waste
Where he, in his poor self so weak, by
    Providence was placed.

—— Here, Lady ! might I cease; but nay,
    let *us* before we part
With this dear holy shepherd-boy breathe
    a prayer of earnest heart,   30
That unto him, where'er shall lie his life's
    appointed way,
The Cross, fixed in his soul, may prove an
    all-sufficing stay.

THE POET'S DREAM

SEQUEL TO THE NORMAN BOY

(?). 1842

JUST as those final words were penned, the
    sun broke out in power,
And gladdened all things; but, as chanced,
    within that very hour,
Air blackened, thunder growled, fire flashed
    from clouds that hid the sky,
And, for the Subject of my Verse, I heaved
    a pensive sigh.

Nor could my heart by second thoughts
    from heaviness be cleared,
For bodied forth before my eyes the cross-
    crowned hut appeared;
And, while around it storm as fierce seemed
    troubling earth and air,
I saw, within, the Norman Boy kneeling
    alone in prayer.

The Child, as if the thunder's voice spake
    with articulate call,
Bowed meekly in submissive fear, before
    the Lord of All;   10
His lips were moving; and his eyes, up-
    raised to sue for grace,
With soft illumination cheered the dimness
    of that place.

How beautiful is holiness ! — what wonder
　　if the sight,
Almost as vivid as a dream, produced a
　　dream at night ?
It came with sleep and showed the Boy, no
　　cherub, not transformed,
But the poor raggèd Thing whose ways my
　　human heart had warmed.

Me had the dream equipped with wings, so
　　I took him in my arms,
And lifted from the grassy floor, stilling his
　　faint alarms,
And bore him high through yielding air my
　　debt of love to pay,
By giving him, for both our sakes, an hour
　　of holiday.　　　　　　　20

I whispered, "Yet a little while, dear
　　Child ! thou art my own,
To show thee some delightful thing, in
　　country or in town.
What shall it be ? a mirthful throng ? or
　　that holy place and calm
St. Denis, filled with royal tombs, or the
　　Church of Notre Dame ?

St. Ouen's golden Shrine ? Or choose what
　　else would please thee most
Of any wonder Normandy, or all proud
　　France, can boast !"
"My Mother," said the Boy, "was born
　　near to a blessèd Tree,
The Chapel Oak of Allonville; good Angel,
　　show it me !"

On wings, from broad and stedfast poise
　　let loose by this reply,
For Allonville, o'er down and dale, away
　　then did we fly;　　　　　30
O'er town and tower we fled, and fields in
　　May's fresh verdure drest;
The wings they did not flag; the Child,
　　though grave, was not deprest.

But who shall show, to waking sense, the
　　gleam of light that broke
Forth from his eyes, when first the Boy
　　looked down on that huge oak,
For length of days so much revered, so
　　famous where it stands
For twofold hallowing — Nature's care, and
　　work of human hands ?

Strong as an Eagle with my charge I glided
　　round and round
The wide-spread boughs, for view of door,
　　window, and stair that wound
Gracefully up the gnarled trunk; nor left
　　we unsurveyed
The pointed steeple peering forth from the
　　centre of the shade.　　　　40

I lighted — opened with soft touch the
　　chapel's iron door,
Past softly, leading in the Boy; and, while
　　from roof to floor
From floor to roof all round his eyes the
　　Child with wonder cast,
Pleasure on pleasure crowded in, each live-
　　lier than the last.

For, deftly framed within the trunk, the
　　sanctuary showed,
By light of lamp and precious stones, that
　　glimmered here, there glowed,
Shrine, Altar, Image, Offerings hung in
　　sign of gratitude;
Sight that inspired accordant thoughts;
　　and speech I thus renewed:

"Hither the Afflicted come, as thou hast
　　heard thy Mother say,
And, kneeling, supplication make to our
　　Lady de la Paix;　　　　　50
What mournful sighs have here been heard,
　　and, when the voice was stopt
By sudden pangs; what bitter tears have
　　on this pavement dropt !

Poor Shepherd of the naked Down, a
　　favoured lot is thine,
Far happier lot, dear Boy, than brings full
　　many to this shrine;
From body pains and pains of soul thou
　　needest no release,
Thy hours as they flow on are spent, if not
　　in joy, in peace.

Then offer up thy heart to God in thank-
　　fulness and praise,
Give to Him prayers, and many thoughts,
　　in thy most busy days;
And in His sight the fragile Cross, on thy
　　small hut, will be
Holy as that which long hath crowned the
　　Chapel of this Tree;　　　　60

Holy as that far seen which crowns the
    sumptuous Church in Rome
Where thousands meet to worship God
    under a mighty Dome;
He sees the bending multitude, he hears
    the choral rites,
Yet not the less, in children's hymns and
    lonely prayer, delights.

God for his service needeth not proud work
    of human skill;
They please him best who labour most to
    do in peace his will:
So let us strive to live, and to our Spirits
    will be given
Such wings as, when our Saviour calls, shall
    bear us up to heaven."

The Boy no answer made by words, but,
    so earnest was his look,
Sleep fled, and with it fled the dream — re-
    corded in this book,   70
Lest all that passed should melt away in
    silence from my mind,
As visions still more bright have done, and
    left no trace behind.

But oh ! that Country-man of thine, whose
    eye, loved Child, can see
A pledge of endless bliss in acts of early
    piety,
In verse, which to thy ear might come,
    would treat this simple theme,
Nor leave untold our happy flight in that
    adventurous dream.

Alas the dream, to thee, poor Boy ! to thee
    from whom it flowed,
Was nothing, scarcely can be aught, yet
    't was bounteously bestowed,
If I may dare to cherish hope that gentle
    eyes will read
Not loth, and listening Little-ones, heart-
    touched, their fancies feed.   80

THE WIDOW ON WINDERMERE SIDE

1837(?). 1842

The facts recorded in this Poem were given
me, and the character of the person described,
by my friend the Rev. R. P. Graves, who has
long officiated as curate at Bowness, to the
great benefit of the parish and neighbourhood.

The individual was well known to him. She
died before these verses were composed. It is
scarcely worth while to notice that the stanzas
are written in the sonnet form, which was
adopted when I thought the matter might be
included in twenty-eight lines.

I

How beautiful when up a lofty height
Honour ascends among the humblest poor,
And feeling sinks as deep ! See there the
    door
Of One, a Widow, left beneath a weight
Of blameless debt. On evil Fortune's spite
She wasted no complaint, but strove to
    make
A just repayment, both for conscience-sake
And that herself and hers should stand
    upright
In the world's eye. Her work when day-
    light failed
Paused not, and through the depth of night
    she kept   10
Such earnest vigils, that belief prevailed
With some, the noble Creature never slept;
But, one by one, the hand of death assailed
Her children from her inmost heart be-
    wept.

II

The Mother mourned, nor ceased her tears
    to flow,
Till a winter's noonday placed her buried
    Son
Before her eyes, last child of many gone —
His raiment of angelic white, and lo !
His very feet bright as the dazzling snow
Which they are touching; yea far brighter,
    even   20
As that which comes, or seems to come,
    from heaven,
Surpasses aught these elements can show.
Much she rejoiced, trusting that from that
    hour
Whate'er befell she could not grieve or pine;
But the Transfigured, in and out of season,
Appeared, and spiritual presence gained a
    power
Over material forms that mastered reason.
Oh, gracious Heaven, in pity make her
    thine !

III

But why that prayer ? as if to her could
    come
No good but by the way that leads to bliss

Through Death, — so judging we should
　　judge amiss.　　　　　　　　31
Since reason failed want is her threatened
　　doom,
Yet frequent transports mitigate the gloom:
Nor of those maniacs is she one that kiss
The air or laugh upon a precipice;
No, passing through strange sufferings to-
　　wards the tomb
She smiles as if a martyr's crown were won:
Oft, when light breaks through clouds or
　　waving trees,
With outspread arms and fallen upon her
　　knees
The Mother hails in her descending Son　40
An Angel, and in earthly ecstasies
Her own angelic glory seems begun.

AIREY-FORCE VALLEY

1835(?). 1842

—— Not a breath of air
Ruffles the bosom of this leafy glen.
From the brook's margin, wide around, the
　　trees
Are stedfast as the rocks; the brook itself,
Old as the hills that feed it from afar,
Doth rather deepen than disturb the calm
Where all things else are still and motion-
　　less.
And yet, even now, a little breeze, perchance
Escaped from boisterous winds that rage
　　without,
Has entered, by the sturdy oaks unfelt,
But to its gentle touch how sensitive
Is the light ash! that, pendent from the
　　brow
Of yon dim cave, in seeming silence makes
A soft eye-music of slow-waving boughs,
Powerful almost as vocal harmony
To stay the wanderer's steps and soothe his
　　thoughts.

"LYRE! THOUGH SUCH POWER DO IN THY MAGIC LIVE"

(?). 1842

Lyre! though such power do in thy magic
　　live
　As might from India's farthest plain
　Recall the not unwilling Maid,
　　　Assist me to detain
　　　The lovely Fugitive:

Check with thy notes the impulse which,
　　betrayed
By her sweet farewell looks, I longed to
　　aid.
Here let me gaze enrapt upon that eye,
The impregnable and awe-inspiring fort
Of contemplation, the calm port　　　10
By reason fenced from winds that sigh
Among the restless sails of vanity.
But if no wish be hers that we should part,
A humbler bliss would satisfy my heart.
　　Where all things are so fair,
Enough by her dear side to breathe the air
　　Of this Elysian weather;
And on or in, or near, the brook, espy
　　Shade upon the sunshine lying
　　　Faint and somewhat pensively;　20
　　And downward Image gaily vying
　　　With its upright living tree
'Mid silver clouds, and openings of blue
　　sky
As soft almost and deep as her cerulean eye.

Nor less the joy with many a glance
Cast up the Stream or down at her be-
　　seeching,
To mark its eddying foam-balls prettily
　　distrest
By ever-changing shape and want of rest;
　　　Or watch, with mutual teaching,
　　　The current as it plays　　30
　　　In flashing leaps and stealthy
　　　　creeps
　　　Adown a rocky maze;
Or note (translucent summer's happiest
　　chance!)
In the slope-channel floored with pebbles
　　bright,
Stones of all hues, gem emulous of gem,
So vivid that they take from keenest sight
The liquid veil that seeks not to hide them.

TO THE CLOUDS

1808. 1842

These verses were suggested while I was
walking on the foot-road between Rydal Mount
and Grasmere. The clouds were driving over
the top of Nab-Scar across the vale: they set
my thoughts agoing, and the rest followed al-
most immediately.

Army of Clouds! ye wingèd Hosts in
　　troops
Ascending from behind the motionless brow

Of that tall rock, as from a hidden world,
Oh whither with such eagerness of speed?
What seek ye, or what shun ye? of the gale
Companions, fear ye to be left behind,
Or racing o'er your blue ethereal field
Contend ye with each other? of the sea
Children, thus post ye over vale and height
To sink upon your mother's lap — and rest?
Or were ye rightlier hailed, when first mine
   eyes   11
Beheld in your impetuous march the like-
   ness
Of a wide army pressing on to meet
Or overtake some unknown enemy? —
But your smooth motions suit a peaceful
   aim;
And Fancy, not less aptly pleased, compares
Your squadrons to an endless flight of birds
Aerial, upon due migration bound
To milder climes; or rather do ye urge
In caravan your hasty pilgrimage   20
To pause at last on more aspiring heights
Than these, and utter your devotion there
With thunderous voice? Or are ye jubi-
   lant,
And would ye, tracking your proud lord
   the Sun,
Be present at his setting; or the pomp
Of Persian mornings would ye fill, and
   stand
Poising your splendours high above the
   heads
Of worshippers kneeling to their up-risen
   God?
Whence, whence, ye Clouds! this eagerness
   of speed?
Speak, silent creatures. — They are gone,
   are fled,   30
Buried together in yon gloomy mass
That loads the middle heaven; and clear
   and bright
And vacant doth the region which they
   thronged
Appear; a calm descent of sky conducting
Down to the unapproachable abyss,
Down to that hidden gulf from which they
   rose
To vanish — fleet as days and months and
   years,
Fleet as the generations of mankind,
Power, glory, empire, as the world itself,
The lingering world, when time hath ceased
   to be.   40
But the winds roar, shaking the rooted
   trees,

And see! a bright precursor to a train
Perchance as numerous, overpeers the rock
That sullenly refuses to partake
Of the wild impulse. From a fount of life
Invisible, the long procession moves
Luminous or gloomy, welcome to the vale
Which they are entering, welcome to mine
   eye
That sees them, to my soul that owns in
   them,
And in the bosom of the firmament   50
O'er which they move, wherein they are
   contained,
A type of her capacious self and all
Her restless progeny.
               A humble walk
Here is my body doomed to tread, this
   path,
A little hoary line and faintly traced,
Work, shall we call it, of the shepherd's
   foot
Or of his flock? — joint vestige of them
   both.
I pace it unrepining, for my thoughts
Admit no bondage and my words have
   wings.
Where is the Orphean lyre, or Druid harp,
To accompany the verse? The mountain
   blast   61
Shall be our *hand* of music; he shall sweep
The rocks, and quivering trees, and billowy
   lake,
And search the fibres of the caves, and they
Shall answer, for our song is of the Clouds,
And the wind loves them; and the gentle
   gales —
Which by their aid re-clothe the naked
   lawn
With annual verdure, and revive the woods,
And moisten the parched lips of thirsty
   flowers —
Love them; and every idle breeze of air   70
Bends to the favourite burthen. Moon and
   stars
Keep their most solemn vigils when the
   Clouds
Watch also, shifting peaceably their place
Like bands of ministering Spirits, or when
   they lie,
As if some Protean art the change had
   wrought,
In listless quiet o'er the ethereal deep
Scattered, a Cyclades of various shapes
And all degrees of beauty. O ye Light-
   nings!

Ye are their perilous offspring; and the
Sun —
Source inexhaustible of life and joy,   80
And type of man's far-darting reason, there-
fore
In old time worshipped as the god of verse,
A blazing intellectual deity —
Loves his own glory in their looks, and
showers
Upon that unsubstantial brotherhood
Visions with all but beatific light
Enriched — too transient, were they not re-
newed
From age to age, and did not, while we gaze
In silent rapture, credulous desire
Nourish the hope that memory lacks not
power   90
To keep the treasure unimpaired. Vain
thought!
Yet why repine, created as we are
For joy and rest, albeit to find them only
Lodged in the bosom of eternal things ?

"WANSFELL! THIS HOUSEHOLD HAS A FAVOURED LOT "

1842. 1845

Wansfell ! this Household has a favoured
lot,
Living with liberty on thee to gaze,
To watch while Morn first crowns thee
with her rays,
Or when along thy breast serenely float
Evening's angelic clouds. Yet ne'er a note
Hath sounded (shame upon the Bard !) thy
praise
For all that thou, as if from heaven, hast
brought
Of glory lavished on our quiet days.
Bountiful Son of Earth ! when we are gone
From every object dear to mortal sight,
As soon we shall be, may these words attest
How oft, to elevate our spirits, shone
Thy visionary majesties of light,
How in thy pensive glooms our hearts found
rest.

THE EAGLE AND THE DOVE

1842. 1842

Shade of Caractacus, if spirits love
The cause they fought for in their earthly
home

To see the Eagle ruffled by the Dove
May soothe thy memory of the chains of
Rome.

These children claim thee for their sire; the
breath
Of thy renown, from Cambrian mountains,
fans
A flame within them that despises death
And glorifies the truant youth of Vannes.

With thy own scorn of tyrants they ad-
vance,
But truth divine has sanctified their rage,
A silver cross enchased with flowers of
France
Their badge, attests the holy fight they
wage.

The shrill defiance of the young crusade
Their veteran foes mock as an idle noise;
But unto Faith and Loyalty comes aid
From Heaven, gigantic force to beardless
boys.

GRACE DARLING

1843. 1843–45

Among the dwellers in the silent fields
The natural heart is touched, and public
way
And crowded street resound with ballad
strains,
Inspired by one whose very name bespeaks
Favour divine, exalting human love;
Whom, since her birth on bleak Northum-
bria's coast,
Known unto few but prized as far as known,
A single Act endears to high and low
Through the whole land — to Manhood,
moved in spite
Of the world's freezing cares — to generous
Youth —   10
To Infancy, that lisps her praise — to Age
Whose eye reflects it, glistening through a
tear
Of tremulous admiration. Such true fame
Awaits her now; but, verily, good deeds
Do not imperishable record find
Save in the rolls of heaven, where hers may
live
A theme for angels, when they celebrate
The high-souled virtues which forgetful
earth

Has witnessed. Oh! that winds and waves
  could speak
Of things which their united power called
  forth   20
From the pure depths of her humanity!
A Maiden gentle, yet, at duty's call,
Firm and unflinching, as the Lighthouse
  reared
On the Island-rock, her lonely dwelling-
  place;
Or like the invincible Rock itself that
  braves,
Age after age, the hostile elements,
As when it guarded holy Cuthbert's cell.
  All night the storm had raged, nor
  ceased, nor paused,
When, as day broke, the Maid, through
  misty air,
Espies far off a Wreck, amid the surf,   30
Beating on one of those disastrous isles —
Half of a Vessel, half — no more; the
  rest
Had vanished, swallowed up with all that
  there
Had for the common safety striven in vain,
Or thither thronged for refuge. With quick
  glance
Daughter and Sire through optic-glass
  discern,
Clinging about the remnant of this Ship,
Creatures — how precious in the Maiden's
  sight!
For whom, belike, the old Man grieves
  still more
Than for their fellow-sufferers engulfed 40
Where every parting agony is hushed,
And hope and fear mix not in further strife.
"But courage, Father! let us out to sea —
A few may yet be saved." The Daughter's
  words,
Her earnest tone, and look beaming with
  faith,
Dispel the Father's doubts: nor do they
  lack
The noble-minded Mother's helping hand
To launch the boat; and with her blessing
  cheered,
And inwardly sustained by silent prayer,
Together they put forth, Father and Child!
Each grasps an oar, and struggling on they
  go —   51
Rivals in effort; and, alike intent
Here to elude and there . surmount, they
  watch
The billows lengthening, mutually crossed

And shattered, and re-gathering their
  might;
As if the tumult, by the Almighty's will
Were, in the conscious sea, roused and
  prolonged
That woman's fortitude — so tried, so
  proved —
May brighten more and more!
                        True to the mark,
They stem the current of that perilous
  gorge,   60
Their arms still strengthening with the
  strengthening heart,
Though danger, as the Wreck is neared,
  becomes
More imminent. Not unseen do they
  approach;
And rapture, with varieties of fear
Incessantly conflicting, thrills the frames
Of those who, in that dauntless energy,
Foretaste deliverance; but the least per-
  turbed
Can scarcely trust his eyes, when he per-
  ceives
That of the pair — tossed on the waves to
  bring
Hope to the hopeless, to the dying, life — 70
One is a Woman, a poor earthly sister,
Or, be the Visitant other than she seems,
A guardian Spirit sent from pitying Heaven,
In woman's shape. But why prolong the
  tale,
Casting weak words amid a host of thoughts
Armed to repel them? Every hazard faced
And difficulty mastered, with resolve
That no one breathing should be left to
  perish,
This last remainder of the crew are all
Placed in the little boat, then o'er the
  deep   80
Are safely borne, landed upon the beach,
And, in fulfilment of God's mercy, lodged
Within the sheltering Lighthouse. — Shout,
  ye Waves,
Send forth a song of triumph. Waves and
  Winds,
Exult in this deliverance wrought through
  faith
In Him whose Providence your rage hath
  served!
Ye screaming Sea-mews, in the concert
  join!
And would that some immortal Voice — a
  Voice
Fitly attuned to all that gratitude

Breathes out from floor or couch, through
    pallid lips   90
Of the survivors — to the clouds might
    bear —
Blended with praise of that parental love,
Beneath whose watchful eye the Maiden
    grew
Pious and pure, modest and yet so brave,
Though young so wise, though meek so
    resolute —
Might carry to the clouds and to the stars,
Yea, to celestial Choirs, GRACE DARLING'S
    name !

"WHILE BEAMS OF ORIENT LIGHT SHOOT WIDE AND HIGH"

1843. 1845

WHILE beams of orient light shoot wide
    and high,
Deep in the vale a little rural Town
Breathes forth a cloud-like creature of its
    own,
That mounts not toward the radiant
    morning sky,
But, with a less ambitious sympathy,
Hangs o'er its Parent waking to the cares
Troubles and toils that every day prepares.
So Fancy, to the musing Poet's eye,
Endears that Lingerer. And how blest her
    sway
(Like influence never may my soul reject)
If the calm Heaven, now to its zenith decked
With glorious forms in numberless array,
To the lone shepherd on the hills disclose
Gleams from a world in which the saints
    repose.

TO THE REV. CHRISTOPHER WORDSWORTH, D. D., MASTER OF HARROW SCHOOL

After the perusal of his *Theophilus Anglicanus*, recently published.

1843. 1845

ENLIGHTENED Teacher, gladly from thy
    hand
Have I received this proof of pains bestowed
By Thee to guide thy Pupils on the road
That, in our native isle, and every land,
The Church, when trusting in divine com-
    mand
And in her Catholic attributes, hath trod:

O may these lessons be with profit scanned
To thy heart's wish, thy labour blest by
    God !
So the bright faces of the young and gay
Shall look more bright — the happy, happier
    still;
Catch, in the pauses of their keenest play,
Motions of thought which elevate the will
And, like the Spire that from your classic
    Hill
Points heavenward, indicate the end and
    way.

INSCRIPTION

FOR A MONUMENT IN CROSTHWAITE CHURCH, IN THE VALE OF KESWICK

1843. 1845

YE vales and hills whose beauty hither drew
The poet's steps, and fixed him here, on you
His eyes have closed ! And ye, loved books,
    no more
Shall Southey feed upon your precious lore,
To works that ne'er shall forfeit their re-
    nown,
Adding immortal labours of his own —
Whether he traced historic truth, with zeal
For the State's guidance, or the Church's
    weal,
Or Fancy, disciplined by studious art,
Informed his pen, or wisdom of the heart,
Or judgments sanctioned in the Patriot's
    mind
By reverence for the rights of all mankind.
Wide were his aims, yet in no human breast
Could private feelings meet for holier rest.
His joys, his griefs, have vanished like a
    cloud
From Skiddaw's top; but he to heaven was
    vowed
Through his industrious life, and Christian
    faith
Calmed in his soul the fear of change and
    death.

ON THE PROJECTED KENDAL AND WINDERMERE RAILWAY

1844. 1844

Is then no nook of English ground secure
From rash assault ? Schemes of retire-
    ment sown
In youth, and 'mid the busy world kept pure

As when their earliest flowers of hope were blown,
Must perish; — how can they this blight endure ?
And must he too the ruthless change bemoan
Who scorns a false utilitarian lure
'Mid his paternal fields at random thrown ?
Baffle the threat, bright Scene, from Orrest-head
Given to the pausing traveller's rapturous glance:
Plead for thy peace, thou beautiful romance
Of nature; and, if human hearts be dead,
Speak, passing winds; ye torrents, with your strong
And constant voice, protest against the wrong.

"PROUD WERE YE, MOUNTAINS, WHEN, IN TIMES OF OLD"

1844. 1844

PROUD were ye, Mountains, when, in times of old,
Your patriot sons, to stem invasive war,
Intrenched your brows; ye gloried in each scar:
Now, for your shame, a Power, the Thirst of Gold,
That rules o'er Britain like a baneful star,
Wills that your peace, your beauty, shall be sold,
And clear way made for her triumphal car
Through the beloved retreats your arms enfold !
Heard YE that Whistle ? As her long-linked Train
Swept onwards, did the vision cross your view ?
Yes, ye were startled; — and, in balance true,
Weighing the mischief with the promised gain,
Mountains, and Vales, and Floods, I call on you
To share the passion of a just disdain.

AT FURNESS ABBEY

1840. 1845

HERE, where, of havoc tired and rash un-doing,
Man left this Structure to become Time's prey

A soothing spirit follows in the way
That Nature takes, her counter-work pursuing,
See how her Ivy clasps the sacred Ruin
Fall to prevent or beautify decay;
And, on the mouldered walls, how bright, how gay,
The flowers in pearly dews their bloom renewing !
Thanks to the place, blessings upon the hour;
Even as I speak the rising Sun's first smile
Gleams on the grass-crowned top of yon tall Tower
Whose cawing occupants with joy proclaim
Prescriptive title to the shattered pile
Where, Cavendish, *thine* seems nothing but a name !

"FORTH FROM A JUTTING RIDGE, AROUND WHOSE BASE"

1845. 1845

FORTH from a jutting ridge, around whose base
Winds our deep Vale, two heath-clad Rocks ascend
In fellowship, the loftiest of the pair
Rising to no ambitious height; yet both,
O'er lake and stream, mountain and flowery mead,
Unfolding prospects fair as human eyes
Ever beheld. Up-led with mutual help,
To one or other brow of those twin Peaks
Were two adventurous Sisters wont to climb,
And took no note of the hour while thence they gazed,
The blooming heath their couch, gazed, side by side,
In speechless admiration. I, a witness
And frequent sharer of their calm delight
With thankful heart, to either Eminence
Gave the baptismal name each Sister bore.
Now are they parted, far as Death's cold hand
Hath power to part the Spirits of those who love
As they did love. Ye kindred Pinnacles —
That, while the generations of mankind
Follow each other to their hiding-place
In time's abyss, are privileged to endure
Beautiful in yourselves, and richly graced
With like command of beauty — grant your aid

For MARY's humble, SARAH's silent claim,
That their pure joy in nature may sur-
 vive
From age to age in blended memory.

THE WESTMORELAND GIRL

TO MY GRANDCHILDREN

1845. 1845

PART I

SEEK who will delight in fable,
I shall tell you truth.   A Lamb
Leapt from this steep bank to follow
'Cross the brook its thoughtless dam.

Far and wide on hill and valley
Rain had fallen, unceasing rain,
And the bleating mother's Young-one
Struggled with the flood in vain:

But, as chanced, a Cottage-maiden
(Ten years scarcely had she told)   10
Seeing, plunged into the torrent,
Clasped the Lamb and kept her hold.

Whirled adown the rocky channel,
Sinking, rising, on they go,
Peace and rest, as seems, before them
Only in the lake below.

Oh! it was a frightful current
Whose fierce wrath the Girl had braved;
Clap your hands with joy my Hearers,
Shout in triumph, both are saved;   20

Saved by courage that with danger
Grew, by strength the gift of love,
And belike a guardian angel
Came with succour from above.

PART II

Now, to a maturer Audience,
Let me speak of this brave Child
Left among her native mountains
With wild Nature to run wild.

So, unwatched by love maternal,
Mother's care no more her guide,
Fared this little bright-eyed Orphan
Even while at her father's side.

Spare your blame, — remembrance makes
 him
Loth to rule by strict command;   10
Still upon his cheek are living
Touches of her infant hand,

Dear caresses given in pity,
Sympathy that soothed his grief,
As the dying mother witnessed
To her thankful mind's relief.

Time passed on; the Child was happy,
Like a Spirit of air she moved,
Wayward, yet by all who knew her
For her tender heart beloved.   20

Scarcely less than sacred passions,
Bred in house, in grove, and field,
Link her with the inferior creatures,
Urge her powers their rights to shield.

Anglers, bent on reckless pastime,
Learn how she can feel alike
Both for tiny harmless minnow
And the fierce and sharp-toothed pike.

Merciful protectress, kindling
Into anger or disdain;   30
Many a captive hath she rescued,
Others saved from lingering pain.

Listen yet awhile; — with patience
Hear the homely truths I tell,
She in Grasmere's old church-steeple
Tolled this day the passing-bell.

Yes, the wild Girl of the mountains
To their echoes gave the sound,
Notice punctual as the minute,
Warning solemn and profound.   40

She, fulfilling her sire's office,
Rang alone the far-heard knell,
Tribute, by her hand, in sorrow,
Paid to One who loved her well.

When his spirit was departed,
On that service she went forth;
Nor will fail the like to render
When his corse is laid in earth.

What then wants the Child to temper,
In her breast, unruly fire,   50
To control the froward impulse
And restrain the vague desire ?

Easily a pious training
And a stedfast outward power
Would supplant the weeds and cherish,
In their stead, each opening flower.

Thus the fearless Lamb-deliv'rer,
Woman-grown, meek-hearted, sage,
May become a blest example
For her sex, of every age.   60

Watchful as a wheeling eagle,
Constant as a soaring lark,
Should the country need a heroine,
She might prove our Maid of Arc.

Leave that thought; and here be uttered
Prayer that Grace divine may raise
Her humane courageous spirit
Up to heaven, thro' peaceful ways.

AT FURNESS ABBEY

1845. 1845

WELL have yon Railway Labourers to THIS
    ground
Withdrawn for noontide rest. They sit,
    they walk
Among the Ruins, but no idle talk
Is heard; to grave demeanour all are bound;
And from one voice a Hymn with tuneful
    sound
Hallows once more the long-deserted Quire
And thrills the old sepulchral earth, around.
Others look up, and with fixed eyes ad-
    mire
That wide-spanned arch, wondering how it
    was raised,
To keep, so high in air, its strength and
    grace:
All seem to feel the spirit of the place,
And by the general reverence God is praised:
Profane Despoilers, stand ye not reproved,
While thus these simple-hearted men are
    moved ?

"YES! THOU ART FAIR, YET BE NOT MOVED"

(?). 1845

YES! thou art fair, yet be not moved
    To scorn the declaration,
That sometimes I in thee have loved
    My fancy's own creation.

Imagination needs must stir;
    Dear Maid, this truth believe,
Minds that have nothing to confer
    Find little to perceive.

Be pleased that nature made thee fit
    To feed my heart's devotion,
By laws to which all Forms submit
    In sky, air, earth, and ocean.

"WHAT HEAVENLY SMILES! O LADY MINE"

(?). 1845

WHAT heavenly smiles! O Lady mine
Through my very heart they shine;
And, if my brow gives back their light,
Do thou look gladly on the sight;
As the clear Moon with modest pride
    Beholds her own bright beams
Reflected from the mountain's side
And from the headlong streams.

TO A LADY

IN ANSWER TO A REQUEST THAT I
WOULD WRITE HER A POEM UPON
SOME DRAWINGS THAT SHE HAD MADE
OF FLOWERS IN THE ISLAND OF MA-
DEIRA

1843. 1845

FAIR Lady! can I sing of flowers
    That in Madeira bloom and fade,
I who ne'er sate within their bowers,
    Nor through their sunny lawns have
        strayed?
How they in sprightly dance are worn
    By Shepherd-groom or May-day queen,
Or holy festal pomps adorn,
    These eyes have never seen.

Yet tho' to me the pencil's art
    No like remembrances can give,   10
Your portraits still may reach the heart
    And there for gentle pleasure live;
While Fancy ranging with free scope
    Shall on some lovely Alien set
A name with us endeared to hope,
    To peace, or fond regret.

Still as we look with nicer care,
    Some new resemblance we may trace:

A *Heart's-ease* will perhaps be there,
A *Speedwell* may not want its place.   20
And so may we, with charmèd mind
Beholding what your skill has wrought,
Another *Star-of-Bethlehem* find,
A new *Forget-me-not.*

From earth to heaven with motion fleet
From heaven to earth our thoughts will
    pass,
A *Holy-thistle* here we meet
And there a *Shepherd's weather-glass;*
And haply some familiar name
Shall grace the fairest, sweetest, plant   30
Whose presence cheers the drooping frame
Of English Emigrant.

Gazing she feels its power beguile
Sad thoughts, and breathes with easier
    breath;
Alas ! that meek, that tender smile
Is but a harbinger of death:
And pointing with a feeble hand
She says, in faint words by sighs broken,
Bear for me to my native land
This precious Flower, true love's last
    token.   40

"GLAD SIGHT WHEREVER NEW WITH OLD"

1842. 1845

GLAD sight wherever new with old
Is joined through some dear homeborn tie;
The life of all that we behold
Depends upon that mystery.
Vain is the glory of the sky,
The beauty vain of field and grove,
Unless, while with admiring eye
We gaze, we also learn to love.

LOVE LIES BLEEDING

1842(?). 1842

It has been said that the English, though
their country has produced so many great poets,
is now the most unpoetical nation in Europe.
It is probably true; for they have more tempt-
ation to become so than any other European
people. Trade, commerce, and manufactures,
physical science, and mechanic arts, out of
which so much wealth has arisen, have made
our countrymen infinitely less sensible to move-
ments of imagination and fancy than were our

forefathers in their simple state of society.
How touching and beautiful were, in most in-
stances, the names they gave to our indigenous
flowers, or any other they were familiarly ac-
quainted with ! — Every month for many years
have we been importing plants and flowers
from all quarters of the globe, many of which
are spread through our gardens, and some per-
haps likely to be met with on the few Commons
which we have left. Will their botanical
names ever be displaced by plain English ap-
pellations, which will bring them home to our
hearts by connection with our joys and sorrows?
It can never be, unless society treads back her
steps towards those simplicities which have
been banished by the undue influence of towns
spreading and spreading in every direction, so
that city-life with every generation takes more
and more the lead of rural. Among the an-
cients, villages were reckoned the seats of bar-
barism. Refinement, for the most part false,
increases the desire to accumulate wealth; and
while theories of political economy are boast-
fully pleading for the practice, inhumanity
pervades all our dealings in buying and selling.
This selfishness wars against disinterested
imagination in all directions, and, evils coming
round in a circle, barbarism spreads in every
quarter of our island. Oh for the reign of jus-
tice, and then the humblest man among us
would have more power and dignity in and
about him than the highest have now !

YOU call it, " Love lies bleeding," — so you
    may,
Though the red Flower, not prostrate,
    only droops,
As we have seen it here from day to day,
From month to month, life passing not
    away:
A flower how rich in sadness !   Even thus
    stoops,
(Sentient by Grecian sculpture's marvellous
    power)
Thus leans, with hanging brow and body
    bent
Earthward in uncomplaining languishment
The dying Gladiator. So, sad Flower !
('T is Fancy guides me willing to be led,
Though by a slender thread)
So drooped Adonis, bathed in sanguine dew
Of his death-wound, when he from innocent
    air
The gentlest breath of resignation drew;
While Venus in a passion of despair
Rent, weeping over him, her golden hair
Spangled with drops of that celestial
    shower.

She suffered, as Immortals sometimes do;
But pangs more lasting far, *that* Lover
  knew
Who first, weighed down by scorn, in some
  lone bower
Did press this semblance of unpitied
  smart
Into the service of his constant heart,
His own dejection, downcast Flower ! could
  share
With thine, and gave the mournful name
  which thou wilt ever bear.

COMPANION TO THE FORE-GOING

1842(?). 1842

NEVER enlivened with the liveliest ray
That fosters growth or checks or cheers
  decay,
Nor by the heaviest rain-drops more
  deprest,
This Flower, that first appeared as sum-
  mer's guest,
Preserves her beauty 'mid autumnal leaves
And to her mournful habits fondly cleaves.
When files of stateliest plants have ceased
  to bloom,
One after one submitting to their doom,
When her coevals each and all are fled,
What keeps her thus reclined upon her
  lonesome bed ?
  The old mythologists, more impressed
    than we
Of this late day by character in tree
Or herb, that claimed peculiar sympathy,
Or by the silent lapse of fountain clear,
Or with the language of the viewless air
By bird or beast made vocal, sought a cause
To solve the mystery, not in Nature's
  laws
But in Man's fortunes. Hence a thousand
  tales
Sung to the plaintive lyre in Grecian vales.
Nor doubt that something of their spirit
  swayed
The fancy-stricken Youth or heart-sick
  Maid,
Who, while each stood companionless and
  eyed
This undeparting Flower in crimson dyed,
Thought of a wound which death is slow to
  cure,
A fate that has endured and will endure,

And, patience coveting yet passion feeding,
Called the dejected Lingerer, *Loves lies
  bleeding*.

THE CUCKOO–CLOCK

1840. 1842

Of this clock I have nothing further to say
than what the poem expresses, except that it
must be here recorded that it was a present
from the dear friend for whose sake these notes
were chiefly undertaken, and who has written
them from my dictation.

WOULDST thou be taught, when sleep has
  taken flight,
By a sure voice that can most sweetly tell,
How far off yet a glimpse of morning light,
And if to lure the truant back be well,
Forbear to covet a Repeater's stroke,
That, answering to thy touch, will sound
  the hour ;
Better provide thee with a Cuckoo-clock
For service hung behind thy chamber-door;
And in due time the soft spontaneous shock,
The double note, as if with living power,   10
Will to composure lead — or make thee
  blithe as bird in bower.

List, Cuckoo — Cuckoo ! — oft tho' tem-
  pests howl,
Or nipping frost remind thee trees are bare,
How cattle pine, and droop the shivering
  fowl,
Thy spirits will seem to feed on balmy air;
I speak with knowledge, — by that Voice
  beguiled,
Thou wilt salute old memories as they
  throng
Into thy heart; and fancies, running wild
Through fresh green fields, and budding
  groves among,
Will make thee happy, happy as a child: 20
Of sunshine wilt thou think, and flowers,
  and song,
And breathe as in a world where nothing
  can go wrong.

And know — that, even for him who shuns
  the day
And nightly tosses on a bed of pain;
Whose joys, from all but memory swept
  away,
Must come unhoped for, if they come again;

Know—that, for him whose waking
  thoughts, severe
As his distress is sharp, would scorn my
  theme,
The mimic notes, striking upon his ear
In sleep, and intermingling with his
  dream,   30
Could from sad regions send him to a dear
Delightful land of verdure, shower and
  gleam,
To mock the *wandering* Voice beside some
  haunted stream.

O bounty without measure ! while the grace
Of Heaven doth in such wise, from humblest
  springs,
Pour pleasure forth, and solaces that trace
A mazy course along familiar things,
Well may our hearts have faith that bless-
  ings come,
Streaming from founts above the starry sky,
With angels when their own untroubled
  home   40
They leave, and speed on nightly embassy
To visit earthly chambers, — and for whom?
Yea, both for souls who God's forbearance
  try,
And those that seek his help, and for his
  mercy sigh.

"SO FAIR, SO SWEET, WITHAL
  SO SENSITIVE"

1844. 1845

So fair, so sweet, withal so sensitive,
Would that the little Flowers were born to
  live,
Conscious of half the pleasure which they
  give;

That to this mountain-daisy's self were
  known
The beauty of its star - shaped shadow,
  thrown
On the smooth surface of this naked stone !

And what if hence a bold desire should mount
High as the Sun, that he could take account
Of all that issues from his glorious fount !

So might he ken how by his sovereign aid
These delicate companionships are made;
And how he rules the pomp of light and
  shade;

And were the Sister-power that shines by
  night
So privileged, what a countenance of delight
Would through the clouds break forth on
  human sight !

Fond fancies ! wheresoe'er shall turn thine
  eye
On earth, air, ocean, or the starry sky,
Converse with Nature in pure sympathy;

All vain desires, all lawless wishes quelled,
Be Thou to love and praise alike impelled,
Whatever boon is granted or withheld.

TO THE PENNSYLVANIANS

1845. 1845

DAYS undefiled by luxury or sloth,
Firm self-denial, manners grave and staid,
Rights equal, laws with cheerfulness obeyed,
Words that require no sanction from an
  oath,
And simple honesty a common growth —
This high repute, with bounteous Nature's
  aid,
Won confidence, now ruthlessly betrayed
At will, your power the measure of your
  troth ! —
All who revere the memory of Penn
Grieve for the land on whose wild woods
  his name
Was fondly grafted with a virtuous aim,
Renounced, abandoned by degenerate Men
For state-dishonour black as ever came
To upper air from Mammon's loathsome
  den.

"YOUNG ENGLAND — WHAT IS
  THEN BECOME OF OLD"

1845. 1845

YOUNG ENGLAND — what is then become of
  Old,
Of dear Old England ? Think they she is
  dead,
Dead to the very name ? Presumption fed
On empty air ! That name will keep its
  hold
In the true filial bosom's inmost fold
Forever. — The Spirit of Alfred, at the head
Of all who for her rights watched, toiled
  and bled,

Knows that this prophecy is not too bold.
What — how ! shall she submit in will and deed
To Beardless Boys — an imitative race,
The *servum pecus* of a Gallic breed ?
Dear Mother ! if thou *must* thy steps retrace,
Go where at least meek Innocency dwells;
Let Babes and Sucklings be thy oracles.

"THOUGH THE BOLD WINGS OF POESY AFFECT"

(?). 1842

THOUGH the bold wings of Poesy affect
The clouds, and wheel around the mountain tops
Rejoicing, from her loftiest height she drops
Well pleased to skim the plain with wild flowers deckt
Or muse in solemn grove whose shades protect
The lingering dew — there steals along, or stops
Watching the least small bird that round her hops,
Or creeping worm, with sensitive respect.
Her functions are they therefore less divine,
Her thoughts less deep, or void of grave intent
Her simplest fancies ? Should that fear be thine,
Aspiring Votary, ere thy hand present
One offering, kneel before her modest shrine,
With brow in penitential sorrow bent !

SUGGESTED BY A PICTURE OF THE BIRD OF PARADISE

(?). 1842

This subject has been treated of in another note. I will here only by way of comment direct attention to the fact that pictures of animals and other productions of nature as seen in conservatories, menageries, museums, etc., would do little for the national mind, nay they would be rather injurious to it, if the imagination were excluded by the presence of the object, more or less out of a state of nature. If it were not that we learn to talk and think of the lion and the eagle, the palm-tree and even the cedar, from the impassioned introduction of them so frequently into Holy Scripture and by great poets, and divines who write as poets, the spiritual part of our nature, and therefore the higher part of it, would derive no benefit from such intercourse with such objects.

THE gentlest Poet, with free thoughts endowed,
And a true master of the glowing strain,
Might scan the narrow province with disdain
That to the Painter's skill is here allowed.
This, this the Bird of Paradise ! disclaim
The daring thought, forget the name;
This the Sun's Bird, whom Glendoveers might own
As no unworthy Partner in their flight
Through seas of ether, where the ruffling sway
Of nether air's rude billows is unknown; 10
Whom Sylphs, if e'er for casual pastime they
Through India's spicy regions wing their way,
Might bow to as their Lord. What character,
O sovereign Nature ! I appeal to thee,
Of all thy feathered progeny
Is so unearthly, and what shape so fair ?
So richly decked in variegated down,
Green, sable, shining yellow, shadowy brown,
Tints softly with each other blended,
Hues doubtfully begun and ended; 20
Or intershooting, and to sight
Lost and recovered, as the rays of light
Glance on the conscious plumes touched here and there ?
Full surely, when with such proud gifts of life
Began the pencil's strife,
O'erweening Art was caught as in a snare.
 A sense of seemingly presumptuous wrong
Gave the first impulse to the Poet's song;
But, of his scorn repenting soon, he drew
A juster judgment from a calmer view; 30
And, with a spirit freed from discontent,
Thankfully took an effort that was meant
Not with God's bounty, Nature's love, to vie,
Or made with hope to please that inward eye
Which ever strives in vain itself to satisfy,
But to recall the truth by some faint trace
Of power ethereal and celestial grace,
That in the living Creature find on earth a place.

SONNET

1846. 1850

WHY should we weep or mourn, Angelic
　　boy,
For such thou wert ere from our sight
　　removed,
Holy, and ever dutiful — beloved
From day to day with never-ceasing joy,
And hopes as dear as could the heart em-
　　ploy
In aught to earth pertaining? Death has
　　proved
His might, nor less his mercy, as behoved —
Death conscious that he only could de-
　　stroy
The bodily frame. That beauty is laid
　　low
To moulder in a far-off field of Rome;
But Heaven is now, blest Child, thy Spirit's
　　home:
When such divine communion, which we
　　know,
Is felt, thy Roman burial place will be
Surely a sweet remembrancer of Thee.

"WHERE LIES THE TRUTH? HAS MAN, IN WISDOM'S CREED"

1846. 1850

WHERE lies the truth? has Man, in wisdom's
　　creed,
A pitiable doom; for respite brief
A care more anxious, or a heavier grief?
Is he ungrateful, and doth little heed
God's bounty, soon forgotten; or indeed,
Must Man, with labour born, awake to
　　sorrow
When Flowers rejoice and Larks with rival
　　speed
Spring from their nests to bid the Sun good
　　morrow?
They mount for rapture as their songs pro-
　　claim
Warbled in hearing both of earth and
　　sky;
But o'er the contrast wherefore heave a
　　sigh?
Like those aspirants let us soar — our
　　aim,
Through life's worst trials, whether shocks
　　or snares,
A happier, brighter, purer Heaven than
　　theirs.

"I KNOW AN AGED MAN CONSTRAINED TO DWELL"

1846. 1850

I KNOW an aged Man constrained to dwell
In a large house of public charity,
Where he abides, as in a Prisoner's cell,
With numbers near, alas! no company.

When he could creep about, at will, though
　　poor
And forced to live on alms, this old Man fed
A Redbreast, one that to his cottage door
Came not, but in a lane partook his bread.

There, at the root of one particular tree,
An easy seat this worn-out Labourer found
While Robin pecked the crumbs upon his
　　knee　　　　　　　　　　　　　　　　11
Laid one by one, or scattered on the ground.

Dear intercourse was theirs, day after day;
What signs of mutual gladness when they
　　met!
Think of their common peace, their simple
　　play,
The parting moment and its fond regret.

Months passed in love that failed not to
　　fulfil,
In spite of season's change, its own demand,
By fluttering pinions here and busy bill;
There by caresses from a tremulous hand. 20

Thus in the chosen spot a tie so strong
Was formed between the solitary pair,
That when his fate had housed him 'mid a
　　throng
The Captive shunned all converse proffered
　　there.

Wife, children, kindred, they were dead and
　　gone;
But, if no evil hap his wishes crossed,
One living Stay was left, and on that one
Some recompence for all that he had lost.

Oh that the good old Man had power to
　　prove,
By message sent through air or visible
　　token,　　　　　　　　　　　　　　　30
That still he loves the Bird, and still must
　　love;
That friendship lasts though fellowship is
　　broken!

"HOW BEAUTIFUL THE QUEEN OF NIGHT"

(?). 1850

How beautiful the Queen of Night, on high
Her way pursuing among scattered clouds,
Where, ever and anon, her head she shrouds
Hidden from view in dense obscurity.
But look, and to the watchful eye
A brightening edge will indicate that soon
We shall behold the struggling Moon
Break forth, — again to walk the clear blue
    sky.

EVENING VOLUNTARIES

TO LUCCA GIORDANO

1846. 1850

GIORDANO, verily thy Pencil's skill
Hath here portrayed with Nature's happiest
    grace
The fair Endymion couched on Latmos-hill;
And Dian gazing on the Shepherd's face
In rapture, — yet suspending her embrace,
As not unconscious with what power the
    thrill
Of her most timid touch his sleep would
    chase,
And, with his sleep, that beauty calm and
    still.
Oh may this work have found its last retreat
Here in a Mountain-bard's secure abode,
One to whom, yet a School-boy, Cynthia
    showed
A face of love which he in love would greet,
Fixed, by her smile, upon some rocky seat;
Or lured along where greenwood paths he
    trod.

"WHO BUT IS PLEASED TO WATCH THE MOON ON HIGH"

1846. 1850

WHO but is pleased to watch the moon on
    high
Travelling where she from time to time en-
    shrouds
Her head, and nothing loth her Majesty
Renounces, till among the scattered clouds
One with its kindling edge declares that
    soon
Will reappear before the uplifted eye
A Form as bright, as beautiful a moon,

To glide in open prospect through clear
    sky.
Pity that such a promise e'er should prove
False in the issue, that yon seeming space
Of sky should be in truth the stedfast face
Of a cloud flat and dense, through which
    must move
(By transit not unlike man's frequent doom)
The Wanderer lost in more determined
    gloom.

ILLUSTRATED BOOKS AND NEWSPAPERS

1846. 1850

DISCOURSE was deemed Man's noblest at-
    tribute,
And written words the glory of his hand;
Then followed Printing with enlarged com-
    mand
For thought — dominion vast and absolute
For spreading truth, and making love
    expand.
Now prose and verse sunk into disrepute
Must lacquey a dumb Art that best can
    suit
The taste of this once-intellectual Land.
A backward movement surely have we here,
From manhood, — back to childhood; for
    the age —
Back towards caverned life's first rude
    career.
Avaunt this vile abuse of pictured page !
Must eyes be all in all, the tongue and ear
Nothing ? Heaven keep us from a lower
    stage !

"THE UNREMITTING VOICE OF NIGHTLY STREAMS"

1846. 1850

THE unremitting voice of nightly streams
That wastes so oft, we think, its tuneful
    powers,
If neither soothing to the worm that gleams
Through dewy grass, nor small birds hushed
    in bowers,
Nor unto silent leaves and drowsy flowers, —
That voice of unpretending harmony
(For who what is shall measure by what
    seems
To be, or not to be,
Or tax high Heaven with prodigality ?)

Wants not a healing influence that can
    creep
Into the human breast, and mix with sleep
To regulate the motion of our dreams
For kindly issues — as through every clime
Was felt near murmuring brooks in earliest
    time;
As at this day, the rudest swains who dwell
Where torrents roar, or hear the tinkling
    knell
Of water-breaks, with grateful heart could
    tell.

SONNET

TO AN OCTOGENARIAN

1846. 1850

AFFECTIONS lose their object; Time brings
    forth
No successors; and, lodged in memory,
If love exist no longer, it must die, —
Wanting accustomed food, must pass from
    earth,
Or never hope to reach a second birth.
This sad belief, the happiest that is left
To thousands, share not Thou; howe'er
    bereft,
Scorned, or neglected, fear not such a
    dearth.
Though poor and destitute of friends thou
    art,
Perhaps the sole survivor of thy race,
One to whom Heaven assigns that mourn-
    ful part
The utmost solitude of age to face,
Still shall be left some corner of the heart
Where Love for living Thing can find a
    place.

ON THE BANKS OF A ROCKY STREAM

(?). 1850

BEHOLD an emblem of our human mind
Crowded with thoughts that need a settled
    home,
Yet, like to eddying balls of foam
Within this whirlpool, they each other
    chase
Round and round, and neither find
An outlet nor a resting-place !
Stranger, if such disquietude be thine,
Fall on thy knees and sue for help divine.

ODE ON THE INSTALLATION OF HIS ROYAL HIGHNESS PRINCE ALBERT AS CHANCELLOR OF THE UNIVERSITY OF CAMBRIDGE, JULY 1847

1847. 1847

INTRODUCTION AND CHORUS

FOR thirst of power that Heaven dis-
    owns,
For temples, towers, and thrones,
Too long insulted by the Spoiler's shock,
Indignant Europe cast
Her stormy foe at last
To reap the whirlwind on a Libyan rock.

SOLO — (TENOR)

War is passion's basest game
Madly played to win a name;
Up starts some tyrant, Earth and Heaven
    to dare,
The servile million bow;   10
But will the lightning glance aside to spare
The Despot's laurelled brow ?

CHORUS

War is mercy, glory, fame,
Waged in Freedom's holy cause;
Freedom, such as Man may claim
Under God's restraining laws.
Such is Albion's fame and glory:
Let rescued Europe tell the story.

RECIT. (*accompanied*) — (CONTRALTO)

But lo, what sudden cloud has darkened
    all
The land as with a funeral pall ?   20
The Rose of England suffers blight,
The flower has drooped, the Isle's delight,
Flower and bud together fall —
A Nation's hopes lie crushed in Claremont's
    desolate hall.

AIR — (SOPRANO)

Time a chequered mantle wears; —
    Earth awakes from wintry sleep;
Again the Tree a blossom bears —
    Cease, Britannia, cease to weep !
Hark to the peals on this bright May morn !
They tell that your future Queen is born. 30

SOPRANO SOLO AND CHORUS

A Guardian Angel fluttered
Above the Babe, unseen;

One word he softly uttered —
It named the future Queen:
And a joyful cry through the Island rang,
As clear and bold as the trumpet's clang,
As bland as the reed of peace —
" VICTORIA be her name ! "
For righteous triumphs are the base
Whereon Britannia rests her peaceful fame.

QUARTET

Time, in his mantle's sunniest fold, 41
Uplifted in his arms the child;
And, while the fearless Infant smiled,
Her happier destiny foretold: —
" Infancy, by Wisdom mild,
Trained to health and artless beauty;
Youth, by pleasure unbeguiled
From the lore of lofty duty;
Womanhood is pure renown,
Seated on her lineal throne: 50
Leaves of myrtle in her Crown,
Fresh with lustre all their own.
Love, the treasure worth possessing,
More than all the world beside,
This shall be her choicest blessing,
Oft to royal hearts denied."

RECIT. (*accompanied*) — (BASS)

That eve, the Star of Brunswick shone
With stedfast ray benign
On Gotha's ducal roof, and on
The softly flowing Leine; 60
Nor failed .to gild the spires of Bonn,
And glittered on the Rhine —
Old Camus, too, on that prophetic night
Was conscious of the ray;
And his willows whispered in its light,
Not to the Zephyr's sway,
But with a Delphic life, in sight
Of this auspicious day:

CHORUS

This day, when Granta hails her chosen Lord,
And proud of her award, 70
Confiding in the Star serene,
Welcomes the Consort of a happy Queen.

AIR — (CONTRALTO)

Prince, in these Collegiate bowers,
Where Science, leagued with holier truth,

Guards the sacred heart of youth,
Solemn monitors are ours.
These reverend aisles, these hallowed
towers,
Raised by many a hand august,
Are haunted by majestic Powers,
The memories of the Wise and Just, 8c
Who, faithful to a pious trust,
Here, in the Founder's spirit sought
To mould and stamp the ore of thought
In that bold form and impress high
That best betoken patriot loyalty.
Not in vain those Sages taught, —
True disciples, good as great,
Have pondered here their country's weal,
Weighed the Future by the Past,
Learned how social frames may last, 90
And how a Land may rule its fate
By constancy inviolate,
Though worlds to their foundations reel
The sport of factious Hate or godless Zeal.

AIR — (BASS)

Albert, in thy race we cherish
A Nation's strength that will not perish
While England's sceptred Line
True to the King of Kings is found;
Like that Wise ancestor of thine
Who threw the Saxon shield o'er Luther's
life, 100
When first above the yells of bigot strife
The trumpet of the Living Word
Assumed a voice of deep portentous sound,
From gladdened Elbe to startled Tiber
heard.

CHORUS

What shield more sublime
E'er was blazoned or sung ?
And the PRINCE whom we greet
From its Hero is sprung.
Resound, resound the strain,
That hails him for our own ! 110
Again, again, and yet again,
For the Church, the State, the Throne !
And that Presence fair and bright,
Ever blest wherever seen,
Who deigns to grace our festal rite,
The pride of the Islands, VICTORIA
THE QUEEN.

PREFACES, ETC.

MUCH the greatest part of the foregoing Poems has been so long before the Public that no prefatory matter, explanatory of any portion of them or of the arrangement which has been adopted, appears to be required; and had it not been for the observations contained in those Prefaces upon the principles of Poetry in general, they would not have been reprinted even as an Appendix in this Edition.

PREFACE

TO THE SECOND EDITION OF SEVERAL OF THE FOREGOING POEMS, PUBLISHED, WITH AN ADDITIONAL VOLUME, UNDER THE TITLE OF "LYRICAL BALLADS"

1800

Note. — In succeeding Editions, when the Collection was much enlarged and diversified, this Preface was transferred to the end of the Volumes as having little of a special application to their contents.

The first Volume of these Poems has already been submitted to general perusal. It was published as an experiment, which, I hoped, might be of some use to ascertain how far, by fitting to metrical arrangement a selection of the real language of men in a state of vivid sensation, that sort of pleasure and that quantity of pleasure may be imparted, which a Poet may rationally endeavour to impart.

I had formed no very inaccurate estimate of the probable effect of those Poems: I flattered myself that they who should be pleased with them would read them with more than common pleasure: and, on the other hand, I was well aware, that by those who should dislike them they would be read with more than common dislike. The result has differed from my expectation in this only, that a greater number have been pleased than I ventured to hope I should please.

. . . .

Several of my Friends are anxious for the success of these Poems, from a belief that, if the views with which they were composed were indeed realised, a class of Poetry would be produced, well adapted to interest mankind permanently, and not unimportant in the quality and in the multiplicity of its moral relations:

and on this account they have advised me to prefix a systematic defence of the theory upon which the Poems were written. But I was unwilling to undertake the task, knowing that on this occasion the Reader would look coldly upon my arguments, since I might be suspected of having been principally influenced by the selfish and foolish hope of *reasoning* him into an approbation of these particular Poems: and I was still more unwilling to undertake the task, because adequately to display the opinions, and fully to enforce the arguments, would require a space wholly disproportionate to a preface. For, to treat the subject with the clearness and coherence of which it is susceptible, it would be necessary to give a full account of the present state of the public taste in this country, and to determine how far this taste is healthy or depraved; which, again, could not be determined without pointing out in what manner language and the human mind act and re-act on each other, and without retracing the revolutions, not of literature alone, but likewise of society itself. I have therefore altogether declined to enter regularly upon this defence; yet I am sensible that there would be something like impropriety in abruptly obtruding upon the Public, without a few words of introduction, Poems so materially different from those upon which general approbation is at present bestowed.

It is supposed that by the act of writing in verse an Author makes a formal engagement that he will gratify certain known habits of association; that he not only thus apprises the Reader that certain classes of ideas and expressions will be found in his book, but that others will be carefully excluded. This exponent or symbol held forth by metrical language must in different eras of literature have excited very different expectations: for example, in the age of Catullus, Terence, and Lucretius, and that of Statius or Claudian; and in our own country, in the age of Shakspeare and Beaumont and Fletcher, and that of Donne and Cowley, or Dryden, or Pope. I will not take upon me to determine the exact import of the promise which, by the act of writing in verse, an Author in the present day makes to his reader; but it will undoubtedly appear to many persons that I have not fulfilled the terms of an engagement thus voluntarily contracted. They who have been accustomed to the gaudiness and inane phraseology of many modern writers, if they persist in reading this book to its conclusion, will, no doubt, frequently have to struggle with feelings of strangeness and awkwardness: they will look round for poetry, and will be induced to inquire by what species of courtesy these attempts can be permitted to assume that title. I hope, therefore, the reader will not censure me for attempting to state what I have proposed to myself to perform; and also (as far as the limits of a preface will permit) to explain some of the chief reasons which have determined me in the choice of my purpose: that at least he may be spared any unpleasant feeling of disappointment, and that I myself may be protected from one of the most dishonourable accusations which can be brought against an Author; namely, that of an indolence which prevents him from endeavouring to ascertain what is his duty, or, when his duty is ascertained, prevents him from performing it.

The principal object, then, proposed in these Poems, was to choose incidents and situations from common life, and to relate or describe them throughout, as far as was possible, in a selection of language really used by men, and, at the same time, to throw over them a certain colouring of imagination, whereby ordinary things should be presented to the mind in an unusual aspect; and further, and above all, to make these incidents and situations interesting by tracing in them, truly though not ostentatiously, the primary laws of our nature: chiefly, as far as regards the manner in which we associate ideas in a state of excitement. Humble and rustic life was generally chosen, because in that condition the essential passions of the heart find a better soil in which they can attain their maturity, are less under restraint, and speak a plainer and more emphatic language; because in that condition of life our elementary feelings co-exist in a state of greater simplicity, and, consequently, may be more accurately contemplated, and more forcibly communicated; because the manners of rural life germinate from those elementary feelings, and, from the necessary character of rural occupations, are more easily comprehended, and are more durable; and, lastly, because in that condition the passions of men are incorporated with the beautiful and permanent forms of nature. The language, too, of these men has been adopted (purified indeed from what appear to be its real defects, from all lasting and rational causes of dislike or disgust), because such men hourly communicate with the best objects from which the best part of language is originally derived; and because, from their rank in society and the sameness and narrow circle of their intercourse, being less under the influence of social vanity, they convey their feelings and notions in simple and unelaborated expressions. Accordingly, such a language, arising out of repeated experience and regular feelings, is a more permanent, and a far more philosophical language, than that which is frequently substituted for it by Poets, who think that they are conferring honour upon themselves and their art in proportion as they separate themselves from the

sympathies of men, and indulge in arbitrary and capricious habits of expression, in order to furnish food for fickle tastes and fickle appetites of their own creation.[1]

I cannot, however, be insensible to the present outcry against the triviality and meanness, both of thought and language, which some of my contemporaries have occasionally introduced into their metrical compositions; and I acknowledge that this defect, where it exists, is more dishonourable to the Writer's own character than false refinement or arbitrary innovation, though I should contend at the same time that it is far less pernicious in the sum of its consequences. From such verses the Poems in these volumes will be found distinguished at least by one mark of difference, that each of them has a worthy *purpose*. Not that I always began to write with a distinct purpose formally conceived; but habits of meditation have, I trust, so prompted and regulated my feelings, that my descriptions of such objects as strongly excite those feelings will be found to carry along with them a *purpose*. If this opinion be erroneous, I can have little right to the name of a Poet. For all good poetry is the spontaneous overflow of powerful feelings: and though this be true, Poems to which any value can be attached were never produced on any variety of subjects but by a man who, being possessed of more than usual organic sensibility, had also thought long and deeply. For our continued influxes of feeling are modified and directed by our thoughts, which are indeed the representatives of all our past feelings; and as, by contemplating the relation of these general representatives to each other, we discover what is really important to men, so, by the repetition and continuance of this act, our feelings will be connected with important subjects, till at length, if we be originally possessed of much sensibility, such habits of mind will be produced that, by obeying blindly and mechanically the impulses of those habits, we shall describe objects, and utter sentiments, of such a nature, and in such connection with each other, that the understanding of the Reader must necessarily be in some degree enlightened, and his affection strengthened and purified.

It has been said that each of these Poems has a purpose. Another circumstance must be mentioned which distinguishes these Poems from the popular Poetry of the day; it is this, that the feeling therein developed gives importance to the action and situation, and not the action and situation to the feeling.

A sense of false modesty shall not prevent me from asserting that the Reader's attention is pointed to this mark of distinction, far less for the sake of these particular Poems than from the general importance of the subject. The subject is indeed important! For the human mind is capable of being excited without

---

[1] It is worth while here to observe that the affecting parts of Chaucer are almost always expressed in language pure and universally intelligible even to this day.

the application of gross and violent stimulants; and he must have a very faint perception of its beauty and dignity who does not know this, and who does not further know, that one being is elevated above another in proportion as he possesses this capability. It has therefore appeared to me, that to endeavour to produce or enlarge this capability is one of the best services in which, at any period, a Writer can be engaged; but this service, excellent at all times, is especially so at the present day. For a multitude of causes, unknown to former times, are now acting with a combined force to blunt the discriminating powers of the mind, and, unfitting it for all voluntary exertion, to reduce it to a state of almost savage torpor. The most effective of these causes are the great national events which are daily taking place, and the increasing accumulation of men in cities, where the uniformity of their occupations produces a craving for extraordinary incident which the rapid communication of intelligence hourly gratifies. To this tendency of life and manners the literature and theatrical exhibitions of the country have conformed themselves. The invaluable works of our elder writers, I had almost said the works of Shakspeare and Milton, are driven into neglect by frantic novels, sickly and stupid German Tragedies, and deluges of idle and extravagant stories in verse. — When I think upon this degrading thirst after outrageous stimulation, I am almost ashamed to have spoken of the feeble endeavour made in these volumes to counteract it; and, reflecting upon the magnitude of the general evil, I should be oppressed with no dishonourable melancholy, had I not a deep impression of certain inherent and indestructible qualities of the human mind, and likewise of certain powers in the great and permanent objects that act upon it, which are equally inherent and indestructible; and were there not added to this impression a belief that the time is approaching when the evil will be systematically opposed by men of greater powers, and with far more distinguished success.

Having dwelt thus long on the subjects and aim of these Poems, I shall request the Reader's permission to apprise him of a few circumstances relating to their *style*, in order, among other reasons, that he may not censure me for not having performed what I never attempted. The Reader will find that personifications of abstract ideas rarely occur in these volumes, and are utterly rejected as an ordinary device to elevate the style and raise it above prose. My purpose was to imitate, and, as far as is possible, to adopt the very language of men; and assuredly such personifications do not make any natural or regular part of that language. They are, indeed, a figure of speech occasionally prompted by passion, and I have made use of them as such; but have endeavoured utterly to reject them as a mechanical device of style, or as a family language which Writers in metre seem to lay claim to by prescription. I have wished to keep the Reader in the company of

flesh and blood, persuaded that by so doing I shall interest him. Others who pursue a different track will interest him likewise; I do not interfere with their claim, but wish to prefer a claim of my own. There will also be found in these volumes little of what is usually called poetic diction; as much pains has been taken to avoid it as is ordinarily taken to produce it; this has been done for the reason already alleged, to bring my language near to the language of men; and further, because the pleasure which I have proposed to myself to impart is of a kind very different from that which is supposed by many persons to be the proper object of poetry. Without being culpably particular, I do not know how to give my Reader a more exact notion of the style in which it was my wish and intention to write, than by informing him that I have at all times endeavoured to look steadily at my subject; consequently there is, I hope, in these Poems little falsehood of description, and my ideas are expressed in language fitted to their respective importance. Something must have been gained by this practice, as it is friendly to one property of all good poetry, namely, good sense: but it has necessarily cut me off from a large portion of phrases and figures of speech which from father to son have long been regarded as the common inheritance of Poets. I have also thought it expedient to restrict myself still further, having abstained from the use of many expressions, in themselves proper and beautiful, but which have been foolishly repeated by bad Poets, till such feelings of disgust are connected with them as it is scarcely possible by any art of association to overpower.

If in a poem there should be found a series of lines, or even a single line, in which the language, though naturally arranged, and according to the strict laws of metre, does not differ from that of prose, there is a numerous class of critics, who, when they stumble upon these prosaisms, as they call them, imagine that they have made a notable discovery, and exult over the Poet as over a man ignorant of his own profession. Now these men would establish a canon of criticism which the Reader will conclude he must utterly reject, if he wishes to be pleased with these volumes. And it would be a most easy task to prove to him that not only the language of a large portion of every good poem, even of the most elevated character, must necessarily, except with reference to the metre, in no respect differ from that of good prose, but likewise that some of the most interesting parts of the best poems will be found to be strictly the language of prose when prose is well written. The truth of this assertion might be demonstrated by innumerable passages from almost all the poetical writings, even of Milton himself. To illustrate the subject in a general manner, I will here adduce a short composition of Gray, who was at the head of those who, by their reasonings, have attempted to widen the space of separation betwixt Prose and Metrical composition, and was more than any other man curiously elaborate in the structure of his own poetic diction.

> " In vain to me the smiling mornings shine,
> And reddening Phœbus lifts his golden fire ;
> The birds in vain their amorous descant join,
> Or cheerful fields resume their green attire.
> These ears, alas ! for other notes repine ;
> *A different object do these eyes require ;*
> *My lonely anguish melts no heart but mine ;*
> *And in my breast the imperfect joys expire ;*
> Yet morning smiles the busy race to cheer,
> And new-born pleasure brings to happier men ;
> The fields to all their wonted tribute bear ;
> To warm their little loves the birds complain.
> *I fruitless mourn to him that cannot hear,*
> *And weep t.e more because I weep in vain.*"

It will easily be perceived, that the only part of this Sonnet which is of any value is the lines printed in Italics ; it is equally obvious that, except in the rhyme and in the use of the single word "fruitless" for fruitlessly, which is so far a defect, the language of these lines does in no respect differ from that of prose.

By the foregoing quotation it has been shown that the language of Prose may yet be well adapted to Poetry ; and it was previously asserted that a large portion of the language of every good poem can in no respect differ from that of good Prose. We will go further. It may be safely affirmed that there neither is, nor can be, any *essential* difference between the language of prose and metrical composition. We are fond of tracing the resemblance between Poetry and Painting, and, accordingly, we call them Sisters : but where shall we find bonds of connection sufficiently strict to typify the affinity betwixt metrical and prose composition ? They both speak by and to the same organs ; the bodies in which both of them are clothed may be said to be of the same substance, their affections are kindred, and almost identical, not necessarily differing even in degree ; Poetry [1] sheds no tears "such as Angels weep," but natural and human tears ; she can boast of no celestial ichor that distinguishes her vital juices from those of Prose ; the same human blood circulates through the veins of them both.

If it be affirmed that rhyme and metrical arrangement of themselves constitute a distinction which overturns what has just been said on the strict affinity of metrical language with that of Prose, and paves the way for other artificial distinctions which the mind voluntarily admits, I answer that the language of such Poetry as is here recommended is, as

---

[1] I here use the word "Poetry" (though against my own judgment) as opposed to the word Prose, and synonymous with metrical composition. But much confusion has been introduced into criticism by this contradistinction of Poetry and Prose, instead of the more philosophical one of Poetry and Matter of Fact, or Science. The only strict antithesis to Prose is Metre ; nor is this, in truth, a *strict* antithesis, because lines and passages of metre so naturally occur in writing prose, that it would be scarcely possible to avoid them, even were it desirable.

far as is possible, a selection of the language really spoken by men ; that this selection, wherever it is made with true taste and feeling, will of itself form a distinction far greater than would at first be imagined, and will entirely separate the composition from the vulgarity and meanness of ordinary life ; and, if metre be superadded thereto, I believe that a dissimilitude will be produced altogether sufficient for the gratification of a rational mind. What other distinction would we have ? Whence is it to come ? And where is it to exist ? Not, surely, where the Poet speaks through the mouths of his characters : it cannot be necessary here, either for elevation of style, or any of its supposed ornaments ; for, if the Poet's subject be judiciously chosen, it will naturally, and upon fit occasion, lead him to passions, the language of which, if selected truly and judiciously, must necessarily be dignified and variegated, and alive with metaphors and figures. I forbear to speak of an incongruity which would shock the intelligent Reader, should the Poet interweave any foreign splendour of his own with that which the passion naturally suggests : it is sufficient to say that such addition is unnecessary. And, surely, it is more probable that those passages, which with propriety abound with metaphors and figures, will have their due effect if, upon other occasions where the passions are of a milder character, the style also be subdued and temperate.

But, as the pleasure which I hope to give by the Poems now presented to the Reader must depend entirely on just notions upon this subject, and as it is in itself of high importance to our taste and moral feelings, I cannot content myself with these detached remarks. And if, in what I am about to say, it shall appear to some that my labour is unnecessary, and that I am like a man fighting a battle without enemies, such persons may be reminded that, whatever be the language outwardly holden by men, a practical faith in the opinions which I am wishing to establish is almost unknown. If my conclusions are admitted, and carried as far as they must be carried if admitted at all, our judgments concerning the works of the greatest Poets, both ancient and modern, will be far different from what they are at present, both when we praise and when we censure : and our moral feelings influencing and influenced by these judgments will, I believe, be corrected and purified.

Taking up the subject, then, upon general grounds, let me ask, what is meant by the word Poet ? What is a Poet ? To whom does he address himself ? And what language is to be expected from him ? — He is a man speaking to men : a man, it is true, endowed with more lively sensibility, more enthusiasm and tenderness, who has a greater knowledge of human nature, and a more comprehensive soul, than are supposed to be common among mankind ; a man pleased with his own passions and volitions, and who rejoices more than other men in the spirit of life that is in him; delighting to contemplate similar volitions and passions as manifested in the goings-on of the Universe, and habitually impelled to create them where he does not find them. To these qualities he has added a disposition to be affected more than any other men by absent things as if they were present; an ability of conjuring up in himself passions, which are indeed far from being the same as those produced by real events, yet (especially in those parts of the general sympathy which are pleasing and delightful) do more near'y resemble the passions produced by real events than anything which, from the motions of their own minds merely, other men are accustomed to feel in themselves: — whence, and from practice, he has acquired a greater readiness and power in expressing what he thinks and feels, and especially those thoughts and feelings which, by his own choice, or from the structure of his own mind, arise in him without immediate external excitement.

But whatever portion of this faculty we may suppose even the greatest Poet to possess, there cannot be a doubt that the language which it will suggest to him must often, in liveliness and truth, fall short of that which is uttered by men in real life under the actual pressure of those passions, certain shadows of which the Poet thus produces, or feels to be produced, in himself.

However exalted a notion we would wish to cherish of the character of a Poet, it is obvious that, while he describes and imitates passions, his employment is in some degree mechanical compared with the freedom and power of real and substantial action and suffering. So that it will be the wish of the Poet to bring his feelings near to those of the persons whose feelings he describes, nay, for short spaces of time, perhaps, to let himself slip into an entire delusion, and even confound and identify his own feelings with theirs; modifying only the language which is thus suggested to him by a consideration that he describes for a particular purpose, that of giving pleasure. Here, then, he will apply the principle of selection which has been already insisted upon. He will depend upon this for removing what would otherwise be painful or disgusting in the passion; he will feel that there is no necessity to trick out or to elevate nature: and the more industriously he applies this principle the deeper will be his faith that no words, which *his* fancy or imagination can suggest, will be to be compared with those which are the emanations of reality and truth.

But it may be said by those who do not object to the general spirit of these remarks, that, as it is impossible for the Poet to produce upon all occasions language as exquisitely fitted for the passion as that which the real passion itself suggests, it is proper that he should consider himself as in the situation of a translator, who does not scruple to substitute excellences of another kind for those which are unattainable by him; and endeavours occasionally to surpass his original, in order to make some amends for the general inferiority to which he feels he must submit. But this would be to encourage idleness and unmanly despair. Further, it is the language of men who speak of what they do not understand; who talk of Poetry, as of a matter of amusement and idle pleasure; who will converse with us as gravely about a *taste* for Poetry, as they express it, as if it were a thing as indifferent as a taste for rope-dancing, or Frontiniac or Sherry. Aristotle, I have been told, has said, that Poetry is the most philosophic of all writing: it is so: its object is truth, not individual and local, but general and operative; not standing upon external testimony, but carried alive into the heart by passion; truth which is its own testimony, which gives competence and confidence to the tribunal to which it appeals, and receives them from the same tribunal. Poetry is the image of man and nature. The obstacles which stand in the way of the fidelity of the Biographer and Historian, and of their consequent utility, are incalculably greater than those which are to be encountered by the Poet who comprehends the dignity of his art. The Poet writes under one restriction only, namely, the necessity of giving immediate pleasure to a human Being possessed of that information which may be expected from him, not as a lawyer, a physician, a mariner, an astronomer, or a natural philosopher, but as a Man. Except this one restriction, there is no object standing between the Poet and the image of things; between this, and the Biographer and Historian, there are a thousand.

Nor let this necessity of producing immediate pleasure be considered as a degradation of the Poet's art. It is far otherwise. It is an acknowledgment of the beauty of the universe, an acknowledgment the more sincere because not formal, but indirect; it is a task light and easy to him who looks at the world in the spirit of love: further, it is a homage paid to the native and naked dignity of man, to the grand elementary principle of pleasure, by which he knows, and feels, and lives, and moves. We have no sympathy but what is propagated by pleasure: I would not be misunderstood; but wherever we sympathise with pain, it will be found that the sympathy is produced and carried on by subtle combinations with pleasure. We have no knowledge, that is, no general principles drawn from the contemplation of particular facts, but what has been built up by pleasure, and exists in us by pleasure alone. The Man of science, the Chemist and Mathematician, whatever difficulties and disgusts they may have had to struggle with, know and feel this. However painful may be the objects with which the Anatomist's knowledge is connected, he feels that his knowledge is pleasure; and where he has no pleasure he has no knowledge. What then does the Poet? He considers man and the objects that surround him as acting and re-acting upon each other, so as to produce an infinite complexity of pain and pleasure; he considers man in his own nature and in his ordinary life as contemplating this with a certain quantity of immediate knowledge, with certain convictions, intuitions, and deductions, which from habit acquire the quality of intuitions; he considers him as looking upon this complex scene of ideas and sensations, and finding everywhere objects that immediately excite in him sympathies which, from the necessities of his nature, are accompanied by an overbalance of enjoyment.

To this knowledge which all men carry about with them, and to these sympathies in which, without any other discipline than that of our daily life, we are fitted to take delight, the Poet principally directs his attention. He considers man and nature as essentially adapted to each other, and the mind of man as naturally the mirror of the fairest and most interesting properties of nature. And thus the Poet, prompted by this feeling of pleasure, which accompanies him through the whole course of his studies, converses with general nature, with affections akin to those which, through labour and length of time, the Man of science has raised up in himself, by conversing with those particular parts of nature which are the objects of his studies. The knowledge both of the Poet and the Man of science is pleasure; but the knowledge of the one cleaves to us as a necessary part of our existence, our natural and unalienable inheritance; the other is a personal and individual acquisition, slow to come to us, and by no habitual and direct sympathy connecting us with our fellow-beings. The Man of science seeks truth as a remote and unknown benefactor; he cherishes and loves it in his solitude: the Poet, singing a song in which all human beings join with him, rejoices in the presence of truth as our visible friend and hourly companion. Poetry is the breath and finer spirit of all knowledge; it is the impassioned expression which is in the countenance of all Science. Emphatically may it be said of the Poet, as Shakspeare hath said of man, "that he looks before and after." He is the rock of defence for human nature; an upholder and preserver, carrying everywhere with him relationship and love. In spite of difference of soil and climate, of language and manners, of laws and customs: in spite of things silently gone out of mind, and things violently destroyed; the Poet binds together by passion and knowledge the vast empire of human society, as it is spread over the whole earth and over all time. The objects of the Poet's thoughts are everywhere; though the eyes and senses of man are, it is true, his favourite guides, yet he will follow wheresoever he can find an atmosphere of sensation in which to move his wings. Poetry is the first and last of all knowledge — it is as immortal as the heart of man. If the labours of Men of science should ever create any material revolution, direct or indirect, in our condition, and in the impressions which we habitually receive, the Poet will sleep then no

more than at present; he will be ready to follow the steps of the Man of science, not only in those general indirect effects, but he will be at his side, carrying sensation into the midst of the objects of the science itself. The remotest discoveries of the Chemist, the Botanist, or Mineralogist, will be as proper objects of the Poet's art as any upon which it can be employed, if the time should ever come when these things shall be familiar to us, and the relations under which they are contemplated by the followers of these respective sciences shall be manifestly and palpably material to us as enjoying and suffering beings. If the time should ever come when what is now called science, thus familiarised to men, shall be ready to put on, as it were, a form of flesh and blood, the Poet will lend his divine spirit to aid the transfiguration, and will welcome the Being thus produced as a dear and genuine inmate of the household of man. — It is not, then, to be supposed that any one, who holds that sublime notion of Poetry which I have attempted to convey, will break in upon the sanctity and truth of his pictures by transitory and accidental ornaments, and endeavour to excite admiration of himself by arts, the necessity of which must manifestly depend upon the assumed meanness of his subject.

What has been thus far said applies to Poetry in general, but especially to those parts of compositions where the Poet speaks through the mouths of his characters; and upon this point it appears to authorise the conclusion that there are few persons of good sense who would not allow that the dramatic parts of composition are defective in proportion as they deviate from the real language of nature, and are coloured by a diction of the Poet's own, either peculiar to him as an individual Poet or belonging simply to Poets in general; to a body of men who, from the circumstance of their compositions being in metre, it is expected will employ a particular language.

It is not, then, in the dramatic parts of composition that we look for this distinction of language; but still it may be proper and necessary where the Poet speaks to us in his own person and character. To this I answer by referring the Reader to the description before given of a Poet. Among the qualities there enumerated as principally conducing to form a Poet, is implied nothing merely differing in kind from other men, but only in degree. The sum of what was said is, that the Poet is chiefly distinguished from other men by a greater promptness to think and feel without immediate external excitement, and a greater power in expressing such thoughts and feelings as are produced in him in that manner. But these passions and thoughts and feelings are the general passions and thoughts and feelings of men. And with what are they connected? Undoubtedly with our moral sentiments and animal sensations, and with the causes which excite these; with the operations of the elements, and the appearances of the visible universe; with storm and sunshine, with the revolutions of the seasons,

with cold and heat, with loss of friends and
kindred, with injuries and resentments, grati-
tude and hope, with fear and sorrow. These,
and the like, are the sensations and objects
which the Poet describes, as they are the sen-
sations of other men and the objects which
interest them. The Poet thinks and feels in
the spirit of human passions. How, then, can
his language differ in any material degree from
that of all other men who feel vividly and see
clearly? It might be *proved* that it is impos-
sible. But supposing that this were not the
case, the Poet might then be allowed to use
a peculiar language when expressing his feel-
ings for his own gratification, or that of men
like himself. But Poets do not write for Poets
alone, but for men. Unless, therefore, we are
advocates for that admiration which subsists
upon ignorance, and that pleasure which arises
from hearing what we do not understand, the
Poet must descend from this supposed height ;
and, in order to excite rational sympathy, he
must express himself as other men express
themselves. To this it may be added, that
while he is only selecting from the real language
of men, or, which amounts to the same thing,
composing accurately in the spirit of such se-
lection, he is treading upon safe ground, and
we know what we are to expect from him.
Our feelings are the same with respect to metre ;
for, as it may be proper to remind the Reader,
the distinction of metre is regular and uniform,
and not, like that which is produced by what
is usually called POETIC DICTION, arbitrary, and
subject to infinite caprices, upon which no cal-
culation whatever can be made. In the one
case, the Reader is utterly at the mercy of the
Poet, respecting what imagery or diction he may
choose to connect with the passion ; whereas,
in the other, the metre obeys certain laws, to
which the Poet and Reader both willingly sub-
mit because they are certain, and because no
interference is made by them with the passion
but such as the concurring testimony of ages
has shown to heighten and improve the pleasure
which co-exists with it.

It will now be proper to answer an obvious
question, namely, Why, professing these opin-
ions, have I written in verse ? To this, in ad-
dition to such answer as is included in what has
been already said, I reply, in the first place,
Because, however I may have restricted my-
self, there is still left open to me what confes-
sedly constitutes the most valuable object of
all writing, whether in prose or verse ; the great
and universal passions of men, the most general
and interesting of their occupations, and the
entire world of nature before me — to supply
endless combinations of forms and imagery.
Now, supposing for a moment that whatever is
interesting in these objects may be as vividly
described in prose, why should I be condemned
for attempting to superadd to such description
the charm which, by the consent of all nations,
is acknowledged to exist in metrical language ?
To this, by such as are yet unconvinced, it may
be answered that a very small part of the plea-

sure given by Poetry depends upon the metre,
and that it is injudicious to write in metre, un-
less it be accompanied with the other artificial
distinctions of style with which metre is usually
accompanied, and that, by such deviation, more
will be lost from the shock which will thereby
be given to the Reader's associations than will
be counterbalanced by any pleasure which he
can derive from the general power of numbers.
In answer to those who still contend for the
necessity of accompanying metre with certain
appropriate colours of style in order to the
accomplishment of its appropriate end, and who
also, in my opinion, greatly under-rate the
power of metre in itself, it might, perhaps, as
far as relates to these Volumes, have been almost
sufficient to observe, that poems are extant,
written upon more humble subjects, and in a
still more naked and simple style, which have
continued to give pleasure from generation to
generation. Now, if nakedness and simplicity
be a defect, the fact here mentioned affords a
strong presumption that poems somewhat less
naked and simple are capable of affording plea-
sure at the present day ; and, what I wished
chiefly to attempt, at present, was to justify my-
self for having written under the impression of
this belief.

But various causes might be pointed out why,
when the style is manly, and the subject of
some importance, words metrically arranged
will long continue to impart such a pleasure to
mankind as he who proves the extent of that
pleasure will be desirous to impart. The end
of poetry is to produce excitement in co-exist-
ence with an overbalance of pleasure ; but, by
the supposition, excitement is an unusual and
irregular state of the mind ; ideas and feelings
do not, in that state, succeed each other in ac-
customed order. If the words, however, by
which this excitement is produced be in them-
selves powerful, or the images and feelings have
an undue proportion of pain connected with
them, there is some danger that the excitement
may be carried beyond its proper bounds. Now
the co-presence of something regular, something
to which the mind has been accustomed in vari-
ous moods and in a less excited state, cannot but
have great efficacy in tempering and restraining
the passion by an intertexture of ordinary feel-
ing, and of feeling not strictly and necessarily
connected with the passion. This is unquestion-
ably true ; and hence, though the opinion will
at first appear paradoxical, from the tendency
of metre to divest language, in a certain degree,
of its reality, and thus to throw a sort of half-
consciousness of unsubstantial existence over
the whole composition, there can be little doubt
but that more pathetic situations and senti-
ments, that is, those which have a greater pro-
portion of pain connected with them, may be
endured in metrical composition, especially in
rhyme, than in prose. The metre of the old
ballads is very artless, yet they contain many
passages which would illustrate this opinion ;
and, I hope, if the following poems be atten-
tively perused, similar instances will be found

in them. This opinion may be further illustrated by appealing to the Reader's own experience of the reluctance with which he comes to the reperusal of the distressful parts of "Clarissa Harlowe," or the "Gamester"; while Shakspeare's writings, in the most pathetic scenes, never act upon us, as pathetic, beyond the bounds of pleasure—an effect which, in a much greater degree than might at first be imagined, is to be ascribed to small, but continual and regular impulses of pleasurable surprise from the metrical arrangement.—On the other hand (what it must be allowed will much more frequently happen), if the Poet's words should be incommensurate with the passion, and inadequate to raise the Reader to a height of desirable excitement, then (unless the Poet's choice of his metre has been grossly injudicious), in the feelings of pleasure which the Reader has been accustomed to connect with metre in general, and in the feeling, whether cheerful or melancholy, which he has been accustomed to connect with that particular movement of metre, there will be found something which will greatly contribute to impart passion to the words, and to effect the complex end which the Poet proposes to himself.

If I had undertaken a SYSTEMATIC defence of the theory here maintained, it would have been my duty to develop the various causes upon which the pleasure received from metrical language depends. Among the chief of these causes is to be reckoned a principle which must be well known to those who have made any of the Arts the object of accurate reflection; namely, the pleasure which the mind derives from the perception of similitude in dissimilitude. This principle is the great spring of the activity of our minds, and their chief feeder. From this principle the direction of the sexual appetite, and all the passions connected with it, take their origin: it is the life of our ordinary conversation; and upon the accuracy with which similitude in dissimilitude, and dissimilitude in similitude, are perceived, depend our taste and our moral feelings. It would not be a useless employment to apply this principle to the consideration of metre, and to show that metre is hence enabled to afford much pleasure, and to point out in what manner that pleasure is produced. But my limits will not permit me to enter upon this subject, and I must content myself with a general summary.

I have said that poetry is the spontaneous overflow of powerful feelings: it takes its origin from emotion recollected in tranquillity; the emotion is contemplated till, by a species of re-action, the tranquillity gradually disappears, and an emotion, kindred to that which was before the subject of contemplation, is gradually produced, and does itself actually exist in the mind. In this mood successful composition generally begins, and in a mood similar to this it is carried on; but the emotion, of whatever kind, and in whatever degree, from various causes, is qualified by various pleasures, so that in describing any passions whatsoever, which are voluntarily described, the mind will, upon the whole, be in a state of enjoyment. If Nature be thus cautious to preserve in a state of enjoyment a being so employed, the Poet ought to profit by the lesson held forth to him, and ought especially to take care that, whatever passions he communicates to his Reader, those passions, if his Reader's mind be sound and vigorous, should always be accompanied with an over-balance of pleasure. Now the music of harmonious metrical language, the sense of difficulty overcome, and the blind association of pleasure which has been previously received from works of rhyme or metre of the same or similar construction, an indistinct perception perpetually renewed of language closely resembling that of real life, and yet, in the circumstance of metre, differing from it so widely—all these imperceptibly make up a complex feeling of delight, which is of the most important use in tempering the painful feeling always found intermingled with powerful descriptions of the deeper passions. This effect is always produced in pathetic and impassioned poetry; while, in lighter compositions, the ease and gracefulness with which the Poet manages his numbers are themselves confessedly a principal source of the gratification of the Reader. All that it is *necessary* to say, however, upon this subject, may be effected by affirming, what few persons will deny, that of two descriptions, either of passions, manners, or characters, each of them equally well executed, the one in prose and the other in verse, the verse will be read a hundred times where the prose is read once.

Having thus explained a few of my reasons for writing in verse, and why I have chosen subjects from common life, and endeavoured to bring my language near to the real language of men, if I have been too minute in pleading my own cause, I have at the same time been treating a subject of general interest; and for this reason a few words shall be added with reference solely to these particular poems, and to some defects which will probably be found in them. I am sensible that my associations must have sometimes been particular instead of general, and that, consequently, giving to things a false importance, I may have sometimes written upon unworthy subjects; but I am less apprehensive on this account, than that my language may frequently have suffered from those arbitrary connections of feelings and ideas with particular words and phrases from which no man can altogether protect himself. Hence I have no doubt that, in some instances, feelings, even of the ludicrous, may be given to my Readers by expressions which appeared to me tender and pathetic. Such faulty expressions, were I convinced they were faulty at present, and that they must necessarily continue to be so, I would willingly take all reasonable pains to correct. But it is dangerous to make these alterations on the simple authority of a few individuals, or even of certain classes of men; for where the understanding of an author is not convinced, or his feelings altered, this cannot be done without great injury to himself: for his own feelings are his stay and support; and, if he set them aside in one instance, he may be induced to repeat this act till his mind shall lose all confidence in itself, and become utterly debilitated. To this it may be added, that the critic ought never to forget that he is himself exposed to the same errors as the Poet, and, perhaps, in a much greater degree: for there can be no presumption in saying of most readers, that it is not probable they will be so well acquainted with the various stages of meaning through which words have passed, or with the fickleness or stability of the relations of particular ideas to each other; and, above all, since they are so much less interested in the subject, they may decide lightly and carelessly.

Long as the reader has been detained, I hope he will permit me to caution him against a mode of false criticism which has been applied to poetry, in which the language closely resembles that of life and nature. Such verses have been triumphed over in parodies, of which Dr. Johnson's stanza is a fair specimen: —

> " I put my hat upon my head
> And walked into the Strand,
> And there I met another man
> Whose hat was in his hand."

Immediately under these lines let us place one of the most justly-admired stanzas of the "Babes in the Wood."

> " These pretty Babes with hand in hand
> Went wandering up and down;
> But never more they saw the Man
> Approaching from the Town."

In both these stanzas the words, and the order of the words, in no respect differ from the most unimpassioned conversation. There are words in both, for example, " the Strand," and " the Town," connected with none but the most familiar ideas; yet the one stanza we admit as admirable, and the other as a fair example of the superlatively contemptible. Whence arises this difference? Not from the metre, not from the language, not from the order of the words; but the *matter* expressed in Dr. Johnson's stanza is contemptible. The proper method of treating trivial and simple verses, to which Dr. Johnson's stanza would be a fair parallelism, is not to say, this is a bad kind of poetry, or, this is not poetry; but, this wants sense; it is neither interesting in itself, nor can *lead* to anything interesting; the images neither originate in that sane state of feeling which arises out of thought, nor can excite thought or feeling in the Reader. This is the only sensible manner of dealing with such verses. Why trouble yourself about the species till you have previously decided upon the genus? Why take pains to prove that an ape is not a Newton, when it is self-evident that he is not a man?

One request I must make of my Reader, which is, that in judging these Poems he would decide by his own feelings genuinely, and not by reflection upon what will probably be the judgment of others. How common is it to hear a person say, I myself do not object to this style of composition, or this or that expression, but to such and such classes of people it will appear mean or ludicrous! This mode of criticism, so destructive of all sound unadulterated judgment, is almost universal: let the Reader then abide, independently, by his own feelings, and, if he finds himself affected, let him not suffer such conjectures to interfere with his pleasure.

If an Author, by any single composition, has impressed us with respect for his talents, it is useful to consider this as affording a presumption that on other occasions where we have been displeased he, nevertheless, may not have written ill or absurdly; and further, to give him so much credit for this one composition as may induce us to review what has displeased us with more care than we should otherwise have bestowed upon it. This is not only an act of justice, but, in our decisions upon poetry especially, may conduce, in a high degree, to the improvement of our own taste: for an *accurate* taste in poetry, and in all the other arts, as Sir Joshua Reynolds has observed, is an *acquired* talent, which can only be produced by thought and a long-continued intercourse with the best models of composition. This is mentioned, not with so ridiculous a purpose as to prevent the most inexperienced Reader from judging for himself (I have already said that I wish him to judge for himself), but merely to temper the rashness of decision, and to suggest that, if Poetry be a subject on which much time has not been bestowed, the judgment may be erroneous; and that, in many cases, it necessarily will be so.

Nothing would, I know, have so effectually contributed to further the end which I have in view, as to have shown of what kind the pleasure is, and how that pleasure is produced, which is confessedly produced by metrical composition essentially different from that which I have here endeavoured to recommend: for the Reader will say that he has been pleased by such composition; and what more can be done for him? The power of any art is limited; and he will suspect that, if it be proposed to furnish him with new friends, that can be only upon condition of his abandoning his old friends. Besides, as I have said, the Reader is himself conscious of the pleasure which he has received from such composition, composition to which he has peculiarly attached the endearing name of Poetry; and all men feel an habitual gratitude, and something of an honourable bigotry, for the objects which have long continued to please them: we not only wish to be pleased, but to be pleased in that particular way in which we have been accustomed to be pleased. There is in these feelings enough to resist a host of arguments; and I should be the less able to combat them successfully, as I am willing to allow that, in order entirely to enjoy the Poetry which I am recommending, it would be necessary to give up much of what is ordinarily enjoyed. But would my limits have permitted me to point out how this pleasure is produced, many obstacles might have been removed, and the Reader assisted in perceiving that the powers of language are not so limited as he may suppose; and that it is possible for poetry to give other enjoyments, of a purer, more lasting, and more exquisite nature. This part of the subject has not been altogether neglected, but it has not been so much my present aim to prove, that the interest excited by some other kinds of poetry is less vivid, and less worthy of the nobler powers of the mind,

as to offer reasons for presuming that if my purpose were fulfilled, a species of poetry would be produced which is genuine poetry ; in its nature well adapted to interest mankind permanently, and likewise important in the multiplicity and quality of its moral relations.

From what has been said, and from a perusal of the Poems, the Reader will be able clearly to perceive the object which I had in view : he will determine how far it has been attained, and, what is a much more important question, whether it be worth attaining : and upon the decision of these two questions will rest my claim to the approbation of the Public.

APPENDIX

1802

See page 796 — " by what is usually called POETIC DICTION."

PERHAPS, as I have no right to expect that attentive perusal, without which, confined, as I have been, to the narrow limits of a preface, my meaning cannot be thoroughly understood, I am anxious to give an exact notion of the sense in which the phrase poetic diction has been used ; and for this purpose, a few words shall here be added, concerning the origin and characteristics of the phraseology which I have condemned under that name.

The earliest poets of all nations generally wrote from passion excited by real events ; they wrote naturally, and as men : feeling powerfully as they did, their language was daring, and figurative. In succeeding times, Poets, and Men ambitious of the fame of Poets, perceiving the influence of such language, and desirous of producing the same effect without being animated by the same passion, set themselves to a mechanical adoption of these figures of speech, and made use of them, sometimes with propriety, but much more frequently applied them to feelings and thoughts with which they had no natural connection whatsoever. A language was thus insensibly produced, differing materially from the real language of men in *any situation*. The Reader or Hearer of this distorted language found himself in a perturbed and unusual state of mind : when affected by the genuine language of passion he had been in a perturbed and unusual state of mind also : in both cases he was willing that his common judgment and understanding should be laid asleep, and he had no instinctive and infallible perception of the true to make him reject the false ; the one served as a passport for the other. The emotion was in both cases delightful, and no wonder if he confounded the one with the other, and believed them both to be produced by the same or similar causes. Besides, the Poet spake to him in the character of a man to be looked up to, a man of genius and authority. Thus, and from a variety of other causes, this distorted language

was received with admiration ; and Poets, it is probable, who had before contented themselves for the most part with misapplying only expressions which at first had been dictated by real passion, carried the abuse still further, and introduced phrases composed apparently in the spirit of the original figurative language of passion, yet altogether of their own invention, and characterised by various degrees of wanton deviation from good sense and nature.

It is indeed true that the language of the earliest Poets was felt to differ materially from ordinary language, because it was the language of extraordinary occasions ; but it was really spoken by men, language which the Poet himself had uttered when he had been affected by the events which he described, or which he had heard uttered by those around him. To this language it is probable that metre of some sort or other was early superadded. This separated the genuine language of Poetry still further from common life, so that whoever read or heard the poems of these earliest Poets felt himself moved in a way in which he had not been accustomed to be moved in real life, and by causes manifestly different from those which acted upon him in real life. This was the great temptation to all the corruptions which have followed : under the protection of this feeling succeeding Poets constructed a phraseology which had one thing, it is true, in common with the genuine language of poetry, namely, that it was not heard in ordinary conversation ; that it was unusual. But the first Poets, as I have said, spake a language which, though unusual, was still the language of men. This circumstance, however, was disregarded by their successors ; they found that they could please by easier means : they became proud of modes of expression which they themselves had invented, and which were uttered only by themselves. In process of time metre became a symbol or promise of this unusual language, and whoever took upon him to write in metre, according as he possessed more or less of true poetic genius, introduced less or more of this adulterated phraseology into his compositions, and the true and the false were inseparably interwoven until, the taste of men becoming gradually perverted, this language was received as a natural language, and at length, by the influence of books upon men, did to a certain degree really become so. Abuses of this kind were imported from one nation to another, and with the progress of refinement this diction became daily more and more corrupt, thrusting out of sight the plain humanities of nature by a motley masquerade of tricks, quaintnesses, hieroglyphics, and enigmas.

It would not be uninteresting to point out the causes of the pleasure given by this extravagant and absurd diction. It depends upon a great variety of causes, but upon none, perhaps, more than its influence in impressing a notion of the peculiarity and exaltation of the Poet's character, and in flattering the Reader's self-love by bringing him nearer to a sympathy with that character; an effect which is accomplished by unsettling ordinary habits of thinking, and thus assisting the Reader to approach to that perturbed and dizzy state of mind in which if he does not find himself, he imagines that he is *balked* of a peculiar enjoyment which poetry can and ought to bestow.

The sonnet quoted from Gray in the Preface, except the lines printed in Italics, consists of little else but this diction, though not of the worst kind; and indeed, if one may be permitted to say so, it is far too common in the best writers, both ancient and modern. Perhaps in no way, by positive example, could more easily be given a notion of what I mean by the phrase *poetic diction* than by referring to a comparison between the metrical paraphrase which we have of passages in the Old and New Testament, and those passages as they exist in our common Translation. See Pope's "Messiah" throughout; Prior's "Did sweeter sounds adorn my flowing tongue," etc. "Though I speak with the tongues of men and of angels," etc. 1st Corinthians, chap. xiii. By way of immediate example, take the following of Dr. Johnson:—

"Turn on the prudent Ant thy heedless eyes,
  Observe her labours, Sluggard, and be wise;
No stern command, no monitory voice,
  Prescribes her duties, or directs her choice;
Yet, timely provident, she hastes away
  To snatch the blessings of a plenteous day;
When fruitful Summer loads the teeming plain,
  She crops the harvest, and she stores the grain.
How long shall sloth usurp thy useless hours,
  Unnerve thy vigour, and enchain thy powers?
While artful shades thy downy couch enclose,
  And soft solicitation courts repose,
Amidst the drowsy charms of dull delight,
  Year chases year with unremitted flight,
Till Want now following, fraudulent and slow,
  Shall spring to seize thee, like an ambush'd foe."

From this hubbub of words pass to the original. "Go to the ant, thou sluggard; consider her ways, and be wise: which having no guide, overseer, or ruler, provideth her meat in the summer, and gathereth her food in the harvest. How long wilt thou sleep, O sluggard? when wilt thou arise out of thy sleep? Yet a little sleep, a little slumber, a little folding of the hands to sleep: so shall thy poverty come as one that travelleth, and thy want as an armed man." Proverbs, chap. vi.

One more quotation, and I have done. It is from Cowper's Verses supposed to be written by Alexander Selkirk:—

"Religion! what treasure untold
  Resides in that heavenly word!
More precious than silver and gold,
  Or all that this earth can afford.
But the sound of the church-going bell
  These valleys and rocks never heard,
Ne'er sighed at the sound of a knell,
  Or smiled when a sabbath appeared.

Ye winds, that have made me your sport,
  Convey to this desolate shore
Some cordial endearing report
  Of a land I must visit no more.
My Friends, do they now and then send
  A wish or a thought after me?
O tell me I yet have a friend,
  Though a friend I am never to see "

This passage is quoted as an instance of three different styles of composition. The first four lines are poorly expressed; some Critics would call the language prosaic; the fact is, it would be bad prose, so bad, that it is scarcely worse in metre. The epithet "church-going" applied to a bell, and that by so chaste a writer as Cowper, is an instance of the strange abuses which Poets have introduced into their language, till they and their Readers take them as matters of course, if they do not single them out expressly as objects of admiration. The two lines "Ne'er sighed at the sound," etc., are, in my opinion, an instance of the language of passion wrested from its proper use, and, from the mere circumstance of the composition being in metre, applied upon an occasion that does not justify such violent expressions; and I should condemn the passage, though perhaps few Readers will agree with me, as vicious poetic diction. The last stanza is throughout admirably expressed: it would be equally good whether in prose or verse, except that the Reader has an exquisite pleasure in seeing such natural language so naturally connected with metre. The beauty of this stanza tempts me to conclude with a principle which ought never to be lost sight of, and which has been my chief guide in all I have said, — namely, that in works *of imagination and sentiment*, for of these only have I been treating, in proportion as ideas and feelings are valuable, whether the composition be in prose or in verse, they require and exact one and the same language. Metre is but adventitious to composition, and the phraseology for which that passport is necessary, even where it may be graceful at all, will be little valued by the judicious.

DEDICATION
PREFIXED TO THE EDITION OF 1815

TO

SIR GEORGE HOWLAND BEAUMONT, BART.

My dear Sir George,

Accept my thanks for the permission given me to dedicate these Volumes to you. In addition to a lively pleasure derived from general considerations, I feel a particular satisfaction; for, by inscribing these Poems with your Name, I seem to myself in some degree to repay, by an appropriate honour, the great obligation which I owe to one part of the Collection — as having been the means of first making us personally known to each other. Upon much of the remainder, also, you have a peculiar claim, — for some of the best pieces were composed under the shade of your own groves, upon the classic ground of Coleorton; where I was animated by the recollection of those illustrious Poets of your name and family, who were born in that neighbourhood; and, we may be assured, did not wander with indifference by the dashing stream of Grace Dieu, and among the rocks that diversify the forest of Charnwood. — Nor is there any one to whom such parts of this Collection as have been inspired or coloured by the beautiful Country from which I now address you, could be presented with more propriety than to yourself — to whom it has suggested so many admirable pictures. Early in life, the sublimity and beauty of this region excited your admiration; and I know that you are bound to it in mind by a still strengthening attachment.

Wishing and hoping that this Work, with the embellishments it has received from your pencil,[1] may survive as a lasting memorial of a friendship, which I reckon among the blessings of my life,

I have the honour to be,
My dear Sir George,
Yours most affectionately and faithfully,
WILLIAM WORDSWORTH.

Rydal Mount, Westmoreland,
February 1, 1815.

PREFACE TO THE EDITION OF 1815

THE powers requisite for the production of poetry are: first, those of Observation and Description, — *i. e.* the ability to observe with accuracy things as they are in themselves, and with fidelity to describe them, unmodified by any passion or feeling existing in the mind of the describer: whether the things depicted be actually present to the senses, or have a place only in the memory. This power, though indispensable to a Poet, is one which he employs only in submission to necessity, and never for a continuance of time: as its exercise supposes all the higher qualities of the mind to be passive, and in a state of subjection to external objects, much in the same way as a translator or engraver ought to be to his original. 2dly, Sensibility, — which, the more exquisite it is, the wider will be the range of a poet's perceptions; and the more will he be incited to observe objects, both as they exist in themselves and as re-acted upon by his own mind. (The distinction between poetic and human sensibility has been marked in the character of the Poet delineated in the original preface.) 3dly, Reflection, — which makes the Poet acquainted with the value of actions, images, thoughts, and feelings; and assists the sensibility in perceiving their connection with each other. 4thly, Imagination and Fancy, — to modify, to create, and to associate. 5thly, Invention, — by which characters are composed out of materials supplied by observation; whether of the Poet's own heart and mind, or of external life and nature; and such incidents and situations produced as are most impressive to the imagination, and most fitted to do justice to the characters, sentiments, and passions, which the poet undertakes to illustrate. And, lastly, Judgment, — to decide how and where, and in what degree, each of these faculties ought to be exerted; so that the less shall not be sacrificed to the greater; nor the greater, slighting the less, arrogate, to its own injury, more than its due. By judgment, also, is determined what are the laws and appropriate graces of every species of composition.[2]

The materials of Poetry, by these powers collected and produced, are cast, by means of various moulds, into divers forms. The moulds may be enumerated, and the forms specified, in the following order. 1st, The Narrative, — including the Epopœia, the Historic Poem, the Tale, the Romance, the Mock-heroic, and, if the spirit of Homer will tolerate such neighbourhood, that dear production of our days, the metrical Novel. Of this Class, the distinguishing mark is, that the Narrator, however liberally his speaking agents be introduced, is himself the source from which everything primarily flows. Epic Poets, in order that their mode of composition may accord with the elevation of their subject, represent themselves as *singing* from the inspiration of the Muse, "Arma virumque *cano;*" but this is a fiction, in modern times, of slight value: the Iliad or the "Paradise

---

[1] The state of the plates has, for some time, not allowed them to be repeated.

[2] As sensibility to harmony of numbers, and the power of producing it, are invariably attendants upon the faculties above specified, nothing has been said upon those requisites.

Lost " would gain little in our estimation by being chanted. The other poets who belong to this class are commonly content to *tell* their tale ; — so that of the whole it may be affirmed that they neither require nor reject the accompaniment of music.

2dly, The Dramatic, — consisting of Tragedy, Historic Drama, Comedy, and Masque, in which the poet does not appear at all in his own person, and where the whole action is carried on by speech and dialogue of the agents ; music being admitted only incidentally and rarely. The Opera may be placed here, inasmuch as it proceeds by dialogue ; though depending, to the degree that it does, upon music, it has a strong claim to be ranked with the lyrical. The characteristic and impassioned Epistle, of which Ovid and Pope have given examples, considered as a species of monodrama, may, without impropriety, be placed in this class.

3dly, The Lyrical — containing the Hymn, the Ode, the Elegy, the Song, and the Ballad ; in all which, for the production of their *full* effect, an accompaniment of music is indispensable.

4thly, The Idyllium, — descriptive chiefly either of the processes and appearances of external nature, as the "Seasons" of Thomson ; or of characters, manners, and sentiments, as are Shenstone's "Schoolmistress," "The Cotter's Saturday Night" of Burns, the "Twa Dogs" of the same Author ; or of these in conjunction with the appearances of Nature, as most of the pieces of Theocritus, the "Allegro" and "Penseroso" of Milton, Beattie's "Minstrel," Goldsmith's "Deserted Village." The Epitaph, the Inscription, the Sonnet, most of the epistles of poets writing in their own persons, and all locodescriptive poetry, belong to this class.

5thly, Didactic, — the principal object of which is direct instruction ; as the Poem of Lucretius, the "Georgics" of Virgil, "The Fleece" of Dyer, Mason's "English Garden," etc.

And, lastly, philosophical Satire, like that of Horace and Juvenal ; personal and occasional Satire rarely comprehending sufficient of the general in the individual to be dignified with the name of poetry.

Out of the three last has been constructed a composite order, of which Young's "Night Thoughts," and Cowper's "Task," are excellent examples.

It is deducible from the above, that poems, apparently miscellaneous, may with propriety be arranged either with reference to the powers of mind *predominant* in the production of them ; or to the mould in which they are cast ; or, lastly, to the subjects to which they relate. From each of these considerations, the following Poems have been divided into classes ; which, that the work may more obviously correspond with the course of human life, and for the sake of exhibiting in it the three requisites of a legitimate whole, a beginning, a middle, and an end, have been also arranged, as far as it was possible, according to an order of time, commencing with Childhood, and terminating with Old Age, Death, and Immortality. My guiding wish was that the small pieces of which these volumes consist, thus discriminated, might be regarded under a two-fold view ; as composing an entire work within themselves, and as adjuncts to the philosophical Poem, "The Recluse." This arrangement has long presented itself habitually to my own mind. Nevertheless, I should have preferred to scatter the contents of these volumes at random, if I had been persuaded that, by the plan adopted, anything material would be taken from the natural effect of the pieces, individually, on the mind of the unreflecting Reader. I trust there is a sufficient variety in each class to prevent this ; while, for him who reads with reflection, the arrangement will serve as a commentary unostentatiously directing his attention to my purposes, both particular and general. But as I wish to guard against the possibility of misleading by this classification, it is proper first to remind the Reader that certain poems are placed according to the powers of mind, in the Author's conception, predominant in the production of them ; *predominant*, which implies the exertion of other faculties in less degree. Where there is more imagination than fancy in a poem, it is placed under the head of imagination, and *vice versâ*. Both the above classes might without impropriety have been enlarged from that consisting of "Poems founded on the Affections ;" as might this latter from those, and from the class "proceeding from Sentiment and Reflection." The most striking characteristics of each piece, mutual illustration, variety, and proportion, have governed me throughout.

None of the other Classes, except those of Fancy and Imagination, require any particular notice. But a remark of general application may be made. All Poets, except the dramatic, have been in the practice of feigning that their works were composed to the music of the harp or lyre : with what degree of affectation this has been done in modern times, I leave to the judicious to determine. For my own part, I have not been disposed to violate probability so far, or to make such a large demand upon the Reader's charity. Some of these pieces are essentially lyrical ; and, therefore, cannot have their due force without a supposed musical accompaniment ; but, in much the greatest part, as a substitute for the classic lyre or romantic harp, I require nothing more than an animated or impassioned recitation, adapted to the subject. Poems, however humble in their kind, if they be good in that kind, cannot read themselves ; the law of long syllable and short must not be so inflexible, — the letter of metre must not be so impassive to the spirit of versification, — as to deprive the Reader of all voluntary power to modulate, in subordination to the sense, the music of the poem ; — in the same manner as his mind is left at liberty, and even summoned, to act upon its thoughts and images. But, though the accompaniment of a musical instrument be frequently dispensed with, the true Poet does not therefore abandon his privilege distinct from that of the mere Proseman;

" He murmurs near the running brooks
A music sweeter than their own."

Let us come now to the consideration of the words Fancy and Imagination, as employed in the classification of the following Poems. " A man," says an intelligent author, " has imagination in proportion as he can distinctly copy in idea the impressions of sense: it is the faculty which *images* within the mind the phenomena of sensation. A man has fancy in proportion as he can call up, connect, or associate, at pleasure, those internal images (φαντάζειν is to cause to appear), so as to complete ideal representations of absent objects. Imagination is the power of depicting, and fancy of evoking and combining. The imagination is formed by patient observation; the fancy by a voluntary activity in shifting the scenery of the mind. The more accurate the imagination, the more safely may a painter, or a poet, undertake a delineation, or a description, without the presence of the objects to be ⌐haracterised. The more versatile the fancy, the more original and striking will be the decorations produced." — *British Synonyms discriminated, by W. Taylor.*

Is not this as if a man should undertake to supply an account of a building, and be so intent upon what he had discovered of the foundation, as to conclude his task without once looking up at the superstructure? Here, as in other instances throughout the volume, the judicious Author's mind is enthralled by Etymology; he takes up the original word as his guide and escort, and too often does not perceive how soon he becomes its prisoner, without liberty to tread in any path but that to which it confines him. It is not easy to find out how imagination, thus explained, differs from distinct remembrance of images; or fancy from quick and vivid recollection of them: each is nothing more than a mode of memory. If the two words bear the above meaning, and no other, what term is left to designate that faculty of which the Poet is " all compact; " he whose eye glances from earth to heaven, whose spiritual attributes body forth what his pen is prompt in turning to shape; or what is left to characterise Fancy, as insinuating herself into the heart of objects with creative activity? — Imagination, in the sense of the word as giving title to a class of the following Poems, has no reference to images that are merely a faithful copy, existing in the mind, of absent external objects; but is a word of higher import, denoting operations of the mind upon those objects, and processes of creation or of composition, governed by certain fixed laws. I proceed to illustrate my meaning by instances. A parrot *hangs* from the wires of his cage by his beak or by his claws; or a monkey from the bough of a tree by his paws or his tail. Each creature does so literally and actually. In the first Eclogue of Virgil, the shepherd, thinking of the time when he is to take leave of his farm, thus addresses his goats: —

" Non ego vos posthac viridi projectus in antro
Dumosa *pendere* procul de rupe videbo."

—— " half way down
Hangs one who gathers samphire,"

is the well-known expression of Shakspeare, delineating an ordinary image upon the cliffs of Dover. In these two instances is a slight exertion of the faculty which I denominate imagination, in the use of one word: neither the goats nor the samphire-gatherer do literally hang, as does the parrot or the monkey; but, presenting to the senses something of such an appearance, the mind in its activity, for its own gratification, contemplates them as hanging.

"As when far off at sea a fleet descried
Hangs in the clouds, by equinoctial winds
Close sailing from Bengala, or the isles
Of Ternate or Tidore, whence merchants bring
Their spicy drugs; they on the trading flood
Through the wide Ethiopian to the Cape
Ply, stemming nightly toward the Pole: so seemed
Far off the flying Fiend."

Here is the full strength of the imagination involved in the word *hangs*, and exerted upon the whole image: First, the fleet, an aggregate of many ships, is represented as one mighty person, whose track, we know and feel, is upon the waters; but, taking advantage of its appearance to the senses, the Poet dares to represent it as *hanging in the clouds*, both for the gratification of the mind in contemplating the image itself, and in reference to the motion and appearance of the sublime objects to which it is compared.

From impressions of sight we will pass to those of sound; which, as they must necessarily be of a less definite character, shall be selected from these volumes: —

" Over his own sweet voice the Stock-dove *broods*,"

of the same bird,

"His voice was *buried* among trees,
Yet to be come at by the breeze; "

" O, Cuckoo! shall I call thee *Bird*,
Or but a wandering *Voice?* "

The stock-dove is said to *coo*, a sound well imitating the note of the bird; but, by the intervention of the metaphor *broods*, the affections are called in by the imagination to assist in marking the manner in which the bird reiterates and prolongs her soft note, as if herself delighting to listen to it, and participating of a still and quiet satisfaction, like that which may be supposed inseparable from the continuous process of incubation. " His voice was buried among trees," a metaphor expressing the love of *seclusion* by which this Bird is marked; and characterising its note as not partaking of the shrill and the piercing, and therefore more easily deadened by the intervening shade; yet a note so peculiar and withal so pleasing, that the breeze, gifted with that love of the sound which the Poet feels, penetrates the shades in which it is entombed, and conveys it to the ear of the listener.

"Shall I call thee Bird,
Or but a wandering Voice?"

This concise interrogation characterises the seeming ubiquity of the voice of the cuckoo, and dispossesses the creature almost of a corporeal existence; the Imagination being tempted to this exertion of her power by a consciousness in the memory that the cuckoo is almost perpetually heard throughout the season of spring, but seldom becomes an object of sight.

Thus far of images independent of each other, and immediately endowed by the mind with properties that do not inhere in them, upon an incitement from properties and qualities the existence of which is inherent and obvious. These processes of imagination are carried on either by conferring additional properties upon an object, or abstracting from it some of those which it actually possesses, and thus enabling it to re-act upon the mind which hath performed the process like a new existence.

I pass from the Imagination acting upon an individual image to a consideration of the same faculty employed upon images in a conjunction by which they modify each other. The Reader has already had a fine instance before him in the passage quoted from Virgil, where the apparently perilous situation of the goat, hanging upon the shaggy precipice, is contrasted with that of the shepherd contemplating it from the seclusion of the cavern in which he lies stretched at ease and in security. Take these images separately, and how unaffecting the picture compared with that produced by their being thus connected with, and opposed to, each other!

"As a huge stone is sometimes seen to lie
Couched on the bald top of an eminence,
Wonder to all who do the same espy
By what means it could thither come, and whence,
So that it seems a thing endued with sense,
Like a sea-beast crawled forth, which on a shelf
Of rock or sand reposeth, there to sun himself.

Such seemed this Man; not all alive or dead,
Nor all asleep, in his extreme old age.
.   .   .   .
Motionless as a cloud the old Man stood,
That heareth not the loud winds when they call,
And moveth altogether if it move at all."

In these images, the conferring, the abstracting, and the modifying powers of the Imagination, immediately and mediately acting, are all brought into conjunction. The stone is endowed with something of the power of life to approximate it to the sea-beast; and the sea-beast stripped of some of its vital qualities to assimilate it to the stone; which intermediate image is thus treated for the purpose of bringing the original image, that of the stone, to a nearer resemblance to the figure and condition of the aged Man; who is divested of so much of the indications of life and motion as to bring him to the point where the two objects unite and coalesce in just comparison. After what has been said, the image of the cloud need not be commented upon.

Thus far of an endowing or modifying power; but the Imagination also shapes and *creates*; and how? By innumerable processes; and in none does it more delight than in that of consolidating numbers into unity, and dissolving and separating unity into number,—alternations proceeding from, and governed by, a sublime consciousness of the soul in her own mighty and almost divine powers. Recur to the passage already cited from Milton. When the compact Fleet, as one Person, has been introduced "Sailing from Bengala," "They," *i. e.* the "merchants," representing the fleet resolved into a multitude of ships, "ply" their voyage towards the extremities of the earth: "So" (referring to the word "As" in the commencement) "seemed the flying Fiend;" the image of his Person acting to recombine the multitude of ships into one body,—the point from which the comparison set out. "So seemed," and to whom seemed? To the heavenly Muse who dictates the poem, to the eye of the Poet's mind, and to that of the Reader, present at one moment in the wide Ethiopian, and the next in the solitudes, then first broken in upon, of the infernal regions!

"Modo me Thebis, modo ponit Athenis."

Hear again this mighty Poet,—speaking of the Messiah going forth to expel from heaven the rebellious angels,

"Attended by ten thousand thousand Saints
He onward came: far off his coming shone,"—

the retinue of Saints, and the Person of the Messiah himself, lost almost and merged in the splendour of that indefinite abstraction "His coming"!

As I do not mean here to treat this subject further than to throw some light upon the present Volumes, and especially upon one division of them, I shall spare myself and the Reader the trouble of considering the Imagination as it deals with thoughts and sentiments, as it regulates the composition of characters, and determines the course of actions: I will not consider it (more than I have already done by implication) as that power which, in the language of one of my most esteemed Friends, "draws all things to one; which makes things animate or inanimate, beings with their attributes, subjects with their accessories, take one colour and serve to one effect."[1] The grand storehouses of enthusiastic and meditative Imagination, of poetical, as contradistinguished from human and dramatic Imagination, are the prophetic and lyrical parts of the Holy Scriptures, and the works of Milton; to which I cannot forbear to add those of Spenser. I select these writers in preference to those of ancient Greece and Rome, because the anthropomorphism of the Pagan religion subjected the minds of the

[1] Charles Lamb upon the genius of Hogarth.

greatest poets in those countries too much to the bondage of definite form; from which the Hebrews were preserved by their abhorrence of idolatry. This abhorrence was almost as strong in our great epic Poet, both from circumstances of his life, and from the constitution of his mind. However imbued the surface might be with classical literature, he was a Hebrew in soul; and all things tended in him towards the sublime. Spenser, of a gentler nature, maintained his freedom by aid of his allegorical spirit, at one time inciting him to create persons out of abstractions; and, at another, by a superior effort of genius, to give the universality and permanence of abstractions to his human beings, by means of attributes and emblems that belong to the highest moral truths and the purest sensations, — of which his character of Una is a glorious example. Of the human and dramatic Imagination the works of Shakspeare are an inexhaustible source.

"I tax not you, ye Elements, with unkindness,
  I never gave you kingdoms, call'd you Daughters!"

And if, bearing in mind the many Poets distinguished by this prime quality, whose names I omit to mention, yet justified by recollection of the insults which the ignorant, the incapable, and the presumptuous, have heaped upon these and my other writings, I may be permitted to anticipate the judgment of posterity upon myself, I shall declare (censurable, I grant, if the notoriety of the fact above stated does not justify me) that I have given in these unfavourable times evidence of exertions of this faculty upon its worthiest objects, the external universe, the moral and religious sentiments of Man, his natural affections, and his acquired passions; which have the same ennobling tendency as the productions of men, in this kind, worthy to be holden in undying remembrance.

To the mode in which Fancy has already been characterised as the power of evoking and combining, or, as my friend Mr. Coleridge has styled it, "the aggregative and associative power," my objection is only that the definition is too general. To aggregate and to associate, to evoke and to combine, belong as well to the Imagination as to the Fancy; but either the materials evoked and combined are different, or they are brought together under a different law, and for a different purpose. Fancy does not require that the materials which she makes use of should be susceptible of change in their constitution from her touch; and, where they admit of modification, it is enough for her purpose if it be slight, limited, and evanescent. Directly the reverse of these are the desires and demands of the Imagination. She recoils from everything but the plastic, the pliant, and the indefinite. She leaves it to Fancy to describe Queen Mab as coming,

"In shape no bigger than an agate-stone
  On the fore-finger of an alderman."

Having to speak of stature, she does not tell you that her gigantic Angel was as tall as Pompey's Pillar; much less that he was twelve cubits or twelve hundred cubits high; or that his dimensions equalled those of Teneriffe or Atlas; — because these, and if they were a million times as high it would be the same, are bounded: The expression is, "His stature reached the sky!" the illimitable firmament! — When the Imagination frames a comparison, if it does not strike on the first presentation, a sense of the truth of the likeness, from the moment that it is perceived, grows — and continues to grow — upon the mind; the resemblance depending less upon outline of form and feature than upon expression and effect; less upon casual and outstanding than upon inherent and internal properties: moreover, the images invariably modify each other. — The law under which the processes of Fancy are carried on is as capricious as the accidents of things, and the effects are surprising, playful, ludicrous, amusing, tender, or pathetic, as the objects happen to be appositely produced or fortunately combined. Fancy depends upon the rapidity and profusion with which she scatters her thoughts and images; trusting that their number, and the felicity with which they are linked together, will make amends for the want of individual value: or she prides herself upon the curious subtilty and the successful elaboration with which she can detect their lurking affinities. If she can win you over to her purpose, and impart to you her feelings, she cares not how unstable or transitory may be her influence, knowing that it will not be out of her power to resume it upon an apt occasion. But the Imagination is conscious of an indestructible dominion; — the Soul may fall away from it, not being able to sustain its grandeur; but, if once felt and acknowledged, by no act of any other faculty of the mind can it be relaxed, impaired, or diminished. — Fancy is given to quicken and to beguile the temporal part of our nature, Imagination to incite and to support the eternal. — Yet it is not the less true that Fancy, as she is an active, is also, under her own laws and in her own spirit, a creative faculty. In what manner Fancy ambitiously aims at a rivalship with Imagination, and Imagination stoops to work with the materials of Fancy, might be illustrated from the compositions of all eloquent writers, whether in prose or verse; and chiefly from those of our own Country. Scarcely a page of the impassioned parts of Bishop Taylor's Works can be opened that shall not afford examples. — Referring the Reader to those inestimable volumes, I will content myself with placing a conceit (ascribed to Lord Chesterfield) in contrast with a passage from the "Paradise Lost:" —

"The dews of the evening most carefully shun,
  They are the tears of the sky for the loss of the sun."

After the transgression of Adam, Milton, with other appearances of sympathising Nature, thus marks the immediate consequence,

"Sky lowered, and, muttering thunder, some sad drops
    Wept at completing of the mortal sin."

The associating link is the same in each instance: Dew and rain, not distinguishable from the liquid substance of tears, are employed as indications of sorrow. A flash of surprise is the effect in the former case ; a flash of surprise, and nothing more ; for the nature of things does not sustain the combination. In the latter, the effects from the act, of which there is this immediate consequence and visible sign, are so momentous that the mind acknowledges the justice and reasonableness of the sympathy in nature so manifested ; and the sky weeps drops of water as if with human eyes, as "Earth had before trembled from her entrails, and Nature given a second groan."

Finally, I will refer to Cotton's "Ode upon Winter," an admirable composition, though stained with some peculiarities of the age in which he lived, for a general illustration of the characteristics of Fancy. The middle part of this ode contains a most lively description of the entrance of Winter, with his retinue, as "A palsied king," and yet a military monarch, — advancing for conquest with his army ; the several bodies of which, and their arms and equipments, are described with a rapidity of detail, and a profusion of *fanciful* comparisons, which indicate on the part of the poet extreme activity of intellect, and a correspondent hurry of delightful feeling. Winter retires from the foe into his fortress, where

———— "a magazine
Of sovereign juice is cellared in ;
Liquor that will the siege maintain
Should Phœbus ne'er return again."

Though myself a water-drinker, I cannot resist the pleasure of transcribing what follows, as an instance still more happy of Fancy employed in the treatment of feeling than, in its preceding passages, the Poem supplies of her management of forms.

" 'T is that, that gives the poet rage,
    And thaws the gelly'd blood of age;

Matures the young, restores the old,
And makes the fainting coward bold.

It lays the careful head to rest,
Calms palpitations in the breast,
Renders our lives' misfortune sweet ;
·   ·   ·   ·   ·   ·   ·   ·

Then let the chill Sirocco blow,
And gird us round with hills of snow,
Or else go whistle to the shore,
And make the hollow mountains roar,

Whilst we together jovial sit
Careless, and crowned with mirth and wit,
Where, though bleak winds confine us home,
Our fancies round the world shall roam.

We 'll think of all the Friends we know,
And drink to all worth drinking to ;
When having drunk all thine and mine,
We rather shall want healths than wine.

But where Friends fail us, we 'll supply
Our friendships with our charity ;
Men that remote in sorrows live,
Shall by our lusty brimmers thrive.

We 'll drink the wanting into wealth,
And those that languish into health,
The afflicted into joy ; th' opprest
Into security and rest.

The worthy in disgrace shall find
Favour return again more kind,
And in restraint who stifled lie,
Shall taste the air of liberty.

The brave shall triumph in success,
The lovers shall have mistresses,
Poor unregarded Virtue, praise,
And the neglected Poet, bays.

Thus shall our healths do others good,
Whilst we ourselves do all we would ;
For, freed from envy and from care,
What would we be but what we are ? "

When I sate down to write this Preface, it was my intention to have made it more comprehensive ; but, thinking that I ought rather to apologise for detaining the reader so long, I will here conclude.

ESSAY, SUPPLEMENTARY TO THE PREFACE

1815

WITH the young of both sexes, Poetry is, like love, a passion ; but, for much the greater part of those who have been proud of its power over their minds, a necessity soon arises of breaking the pleasing bondage ; or it relaxes of itself ; — the thoughts being occupied in domestic cares, or the time engrossed by business. Poetry then becomes only an occasional recreation, while to those whose existence passes away in a course of fashionable pleasure, it is a species of luxurious amusement. In middle and declining age, a scattered number of serious persons resort to poetry, as to religion, for a protection against the pressure of trivial employments, and as a consolation for the afflictions of life. And, lastly, there are many who, having been enamoured of this art in their youth, have found leisure, after youth was spent, to cultivate general literature ; in which poetry has continued to be comprehended *as a study*.

Into the above classes the Readers of poetry may be divided ; Critics abound in them all ; but from the last only can opinions be collected of absolute value, and worthy to be depended upon, as prophetic of the destiny of a new work. The young, who in nothing can escape delusion, are especially subject to it in their intercourse with Poetry. The cause, not so obvious as the fact is unquestionable, is the same as that from which erroneous judgments in this art, in the minds of men of all ages, chiefly proceed ; but upon Youth it operates with peculiar force. The appropriate business of poetry (which, nevertheless, if genuine, is as permanent as pure science), her appropriate employment, her privilege and her *duty*, is to treat of things not as they *are*, but as they *appear ;* not as they exist in themselves, but as they *seem* to exist to the *senses*, and to the *passions*. What a world of delusion does this acknowledged obligation prepare for the inexperienced ! what temptations to go astray are here held forth for them whose thoughts have been little disciplined by the understanding, and whose feelings revolt from the sway of reason ! — When a juvenile Reader is in the height of his rapture with some vicious passage, should experience throw in doubts, or common sense suggest suspicions, a lurking consciousness that the realities of the Muse are but shows, and that her liveliest excitements are raised by transient shocks of conflicting feeling and successive assemblages of contradictory thoughts — is ever at hand to justify extravagance, and to sanction absurdity. But, it may be asked, as these illusions are unavoidable, and, no doubt, eminently useful to the mind as a process, what good can be gained by making observations, the tendency of which is to diminish the confidence of youth in its feelings, and thus to abridge its innocent and even profitable pleasures ? The reproach implied in the question could not be warded off, if Youth were incapable of being delighted with what is truly excellent ; or if these errors always terminated of themselves in due season. But, with the majority, though their force be abated, they continue through life. Moreover, the fire of youth is too vivacious an element to be extinguished or damped by a philosophical remark ; and, while there is no danger that what has been said will be injurious or painful to the ardent and the confident, it may prove beneficial to those who, being enthusiastic, are, at the same time, modest and ingenuous. The intimation may unite with their own misgivings to regulate their sensibility, and to bring in, sooner than it would otherwise have arrived, a more discreet and sound judgment.

If it should excite wonder that men of ability, in later life, whose understandings have been rendered acute by practice in affairs, should be so easily and so far imposed upon when they happen to take up a new work in verse, this appears to be the cause ; — that, having discontinued their attention to poetry, whatever progress may have been made in other departments of knowledge, they have not, as to this art, advanced in true discernment beyond the age of youth. If, then, a new poem fall in their way, whose attractions are of that kind which would have enraptured them during the heat of youth, the judgment not being improved to a degree that they shall be disgusted, they are dazzled ; and prize and cherish the faults for having had power to make the present time vanish before them, and to throw the mind back, as by enchantment, into the happiest season of life. As they read, powers seem to be revived, passions are regenerated, and pleasures restored. The Book was probably taken up after an escape from the burden of business, and with a wish to forget the world, and all its vexations and anxieties. Having obtained this wish, and so much more, it is natural that they should make report as they have felt.

If Men of mature age, through want of practice, be thus easily beguiled into admiration of absurdities, extravagances, and misplaced ornaments, thinking it proper that their understandings should enjoy a holiday, while they are unbending their minds with verse, it may be expected that such Readers will resemble their former selves also in strength of prejudice, and an inaptitude to be moved by the unostentatious beauties of a pure style. In the higher poetry, an enlightened Critic chiefly looks for a reflection of the wisdom of the heart and the grandeur of the imagination. Wherever these appear, simplicity accompanies them ; Magnificence herself, when legitimate, depending upon a simplicity of her own, to regulate her ornaments. But it is a well-known property of human nature, that our estimates are ever governed by comparisons, of which we are conscious with various degrees of distinctness. Is it not, then, inevitable (confining these observations to the effects of style merely) that an eye, accustomed to the glaring hues of diction by which such Readers are caught and excited, will for the most part be rather repelled than attracted by an original Work, the colouring of which is disposed according to a pure and refined scheme of harmony ? It is in the fine arts as in the affairs of life, no man can *serve* (*i. e.* obey with zeal and fidelity) two Masters.

As Poetry is most just to its own divine origin when it administers the comforts and breathes the spirit of religion, they who have learned to perceive this truth, and who betake themselves to reading verse for sacred purposes, must be preserved from numerous illusions to which the two Classes of Readers, whom we have been considering, are liable. But as the mind grows serious from the weight of life, the range of its passions is contracted accordingly ; and its sympathies become so exclusive that many species of high excellence wholly escape, or but languidly excite, its notice. Besides, men who read from religious or moral inclinations, even when the subject is of that kind which they approve, are beset with misconceptions and mistakes peculiar to themselves. Attaching so much importance to the truths which interest them, they are prone to over-rate the Authors by whom those truths are expressed and enforced. They come prepared to impart so much passion to the Poet's language, that they remain unconscious how little, in fact, they received from it. And, on the other hand, religious faith is to him who holds it so momentous a thing, and error appears to be attended with such tremendous consequences, that, if opinions touching upon religion occur which the Reader condemns, he not only cannot sympathise with them, however animated the expression, but there is, for the most part, an end put to all satisfaction and enjoyment. Love, if it before existed, is converted into dislike; and the heart of the Reader is set against the Author and his book. — To these excesses they, who from their professions ought to be the most guarded against them, are perhaps the most liable; I mean those sects whose religion, being from the calculating understanding, is cold and formal. For when Christianity, the religion of humility, is founded upon the proudest faculty of our nature, what can be expected but contradictions? Accordingly, believers of this cast are at one time contemptuous; at another, being troubled, as they are and must be, with inward misgivings, they are jealous and suspicious; and at all seasons they are under temptation to supply, by the heat with which they defend their tenets, the animation which is wanting to the constitution of the religion itself.

Faith was given to man that his affections, detached from the treasures of time, might be inclined to settle upon those of eternity: — the elevation of his nature, which this habit produces on earth, being to him a presumptive evidence of a future state of existence, and giving him a title to partake of its holiness. The religious man values what he sees chiefly as an "imperfect shadowing forth" of what he is incapable of seeing. The concerns of religion refer to indefinite objects, and are too weighty for the mind to support them without relieving itself by resting a great part of the burthen upon words and symbols. The commerce between Man and his Maker cannot be carried on but by a process where much is represented in little, and the Infinite Being accommodates himself to a finite capacity. In all this may be perceived the affinity between religion and poetry; between religion — making up the deficiencies of reason by faith; and poetry — passionate for the instruction of reason; between religion — whose element is infinitude, and whose ultimate trust is the supreme of things, submitting herself to circumscription, and reconciled to substitutions; and poetry — ethereal and transcendent, yet incapable to sustain her existence without sensuous incarnation. In this community of nature may be perceived also the lurking incitements of kindred error; — so that we shall find that no poetry has been more subject to distortion than that species, the argument and scope of which is religious; and no lovers of the art have gone farther astray than the pious and the devout.

Whither then shall we turn for that union of qualifications which must necessarily exist before the decisions of a critic can be of absolute value? For a mind at once poetical and philosophical; for a critic whose affections are as free and kindly as the spirit of society, and whose understanding is severe as that of dispassionate government? Where are we to look for that initiatory composure of mind which no selfishness can disturb? For a natural sensibility that has been tutored into correctness without losing anything of its quickness; and for active faculties, capable of answering the demands which an Author of original imagination shall make upon them, associated with a judgment that cannot be duped into admiration by aught that is unworthy of it? — among those and those only, who, never having suffered their youthful love of poetry to remit much of its force, have applied to the consideration of the laws of this art the best power of their understandings. At the same time it must be observed that, as this Class comprehends the only judgments which are trustworthy, so does it include the most erroneous and perverse. For to be mistaught is worse than to be untaught; and no perverseness equals that which is supported by system, no errors are so difficult to root out as those which the understanding has pledged its credit to uphold. In this Class are contained censors, who, if they be pleased with what is good, are pleased with it only by imperfect glimpses, and upon false principles; who, should they generalise rightly to a certain point, are sure to suffer for it in the end; who, if they stumble upon a sound rule, are fettered by misapplying it, or by straining it too far; being incapable of perceiving when it ought to yield to one of higher order. In it are found critics too petulant to be passive to a genuine poet, and too feeble to grapple with him; men, who take upon them to report of the course which he holds whom they are utterly unable to accompany, — confounded if he turn quick upon the wing, dismayed if he soar steadily "into the region;" — men of palsied imaginations and indurated hearts; in whose minds all healthy action is languid, who therefore feed as the many direct them, or, with the many, are greedy after vicious provocatives; — judges, whose censure is auspicious, and whose praise ominous! In this class meet together the two extremes of best and worst.

The observations presented in the foregoing series are of too ungracious a nature to have been made without reluctance; and, were it only on this account, I would invite the reader to try them by the test of comprehensive experience. If the number of judges who can be confidently relied upon be in reality so small, it ought to follow that partial notice only, or neglect, perhaps long continued, or attention wholly inadequate to their merits, must have been the fate of most works in the higher departments of poetry; and that, on the other hand, numerous productions have blazed into popularity, and have passed away, leaving scarcely a trace behind them: it will be further found, that when Authors shall have at length raised themselves into general admiration and maintained their ground, errors and prejudices have prevailed concerning their genius and their works, which the few who are conscious of those errors and prejudices would deplore ; if they were not recompensed by perceiving that there are select Spirits for whom it is ordained that their fame shall be in the world an existence like that of Virtue, which owes its being to the struggles it makes, and its vigour to the enemies whom it provokes ; — a vivacious quality, ever doomed to meet with opposition, and still triumphing over it ; and, from the nature of its dominion, incapable of being brought to the sad conclusion of Alexander, when he wept that there were no more worlds for him to conquer.

Let us take a hasty retrospect of the poetical literature of this Country for the greater part of the last two centuries, and see if the facts support these inferences.

Who is there that now reads the "Creation" of Dubartas ? Yet all Europe once resounded with his praise ; he was caressed by kings ; and, when his Poem was translated into our language, the "Faery Queen" faded before it. The name of Spenser, whose genius is of a higher order than even that of Ariosto, is at this day scarcely known beyond the limits of the British Isles. And if the value of his works is to be estimated from the attention now paid to them by his countrymen, compared with that which they bestow on those of some other writers, it must be pronounced small indeed.

"The laurel, meed of mighty conquerors
And poets *sage*" —

are his own words ; but his wisdom has, in this particular, been his worst enemy : while its opposite, whether in the shape of folly or madness, has been *their* best friend. But he was a great power, and bears a high name : the laurel has been awarded to him.

A dramatic Author, if he write for the stage, must adapt himself to the taste of the audience, or they will not endure him ; accordingly the mighty genius of Shakspeare was listened to. The people were delighted ; but I am not sufficiently versed in stage antiquities to determine whether they did not flock as eagerly to the representation of many pieces of contemporary Authors, wholly undeserving to appear upon the same boards. Had there been a formal contest for superiority among dramatic writers, that Shakspeare, like his predecessors Sophocles and Euripides, would have often been subject to the mortification of seeing the prize adjudged to sorry competitors, becomes too probable, when we reflect that the admirers of Settle and Shadwell were, in a later age, as numerous, and reckoned as respectable in point of talent, as those of Dryden. At all events, that Shakspeare stooped to accommodate himself to the People, is sufficiently apparent ; and one of the most striking proofs of his almost omnipotent genius is, that he could turn to such glorious purpose those materials which the prepossessions of the age compelled him to make use of. Yet even this marvellous skill appears not to have been enough to prevent his rivals from having some advantage over him in public estimation ; else how can we account for passages and scenes that exist in his works, unless upon a supposition that some of the grossest of them, a fact which in my own mind I have no doubt of, were foisted in by the Players, for the gratification of the many ?

But that his Works, whatever might be their reception upon the stage, made but little impression upon the ruling Intellects of the time, may be inferred from the fact that Lord Bacon, in his multifarious writings, nowhere either quotes or alludes to him.[1] — His dramatic excellence enabled him to resume possession of the stage after the Restoration ; but Dryden tells us that in his time two of the plays of Beaumont and Fletcher were acted for one of Shakspeare's. And so faint and limited was the perception of the poetic beauties of his dramas in the time of Pope, that, in his Edition of the Plays, with a view of rendering to the general reader a necessary service, he printed between inverted commas those passages which he thought most worthy of notice.

At this day, the French Critics have abated nothing of their aversion to this darling of our Nation : "the English, with their bouffon de Shakspeare," is as familiar an expression among them as in the time of Voltaire. Baron Grimm is the only French writer who seems to have perceived his infinite superiority to the first names of the French Theatre ; an advantage which the Parisian critic owed to his German blood and German education. The most enlightened Italians, though well acquainted with our language, are wholly incompetent to measure the proportions of Shakspeare. The Germans only, of foreign nations, are approaching towards a knowledge and feeling of what he is. In some respects they have acquired a superiority over the fellow-countrymen of the Poet : for among us it is a current, I might say an established opinion, that Shakspeare is justly praised when he is pronounced to be "a wild irregular genius, in whom great faults are compensated by great beauties." How long may it be before this misconception passes away, and it becomes universally acknowledged that the judgment of Shakspeare in the selection of his materials, and in the manner in which he has made them, heterogeneous as they often are, constitute a unity of their own, and contribute all to one great end, is not less admirable than his imagination, his invention, and his intuitive knowledge of human Nature !

There is extant a small Volume of miscellaneous poems, in which Shakspeare expresses

[1] The learned Hakewill (a third edition of whose book bears date 1635), writing to refute the error "touching Nature's perpetual and universal decay," cites triumphantly the names of Ariosto, Tasso, Bartas, and Spenser, as instances that poetic genius had not degenerated ; but he makes no mention of Shakspeare.

his own feelings in his own person. It is not difficult to conceive that the Editor, George Steevens, should have been insensible to the beauties of one portion of that Volume, the Sonnets; though in no part of the writings of this Poet is found, in an equal compass, a greater number of exquisite feelings felicitously expressed. But, from regard to the Critic's own credit, he would not have ventured to talk of an[1] act of parliament not being strong enough to compel the perusal of those little pieces, if he had not known that the people of England were ignorant of the treasures contained in them: and if he had not, moreover, shared the too common propensity of human nature to exult over a supposed fall into the mire of a genius whom he had been compelled to regard with admiration, as an inmate of the celestial regions — "there sitting where he durst not soar."

Nine years before the death of Shakspeare, Milton was born; and early in life he published several small poems, which, though on their first appearance they were praised by a few of the judicious, were afterwards neglected to that degree, that Pope in his youth could borrow from them without risk of its being known. Whether these poems are at this day justly appreciated, I will not undertake to decide: nor would it imply a severe reflection upon the mass of readers to suppose the contrary; seeing that a man of the acknowledged genius of Voss, the German poet, could suffer their spirit to evaporate; and could change their character, as is done in the translation made by him of the most popular of those pieces. At all events, it is certain that these Poems of Milton are now much read, and loudly praised; yet were they little heard of till more than 150 years after their publication; and of the Sonnets, Dr. Johnson, as appears from Boswell's Life of him, was in the habit of thinking and speaking as contemptuously as Steevens wrote upon those of Shakspeare.

About the time when the Pindaric odes of Cowley and his imitators, and the productions of that class of curious thinkers whom Dr. Johnson has strangely styled metaphysical Poets, were beginning to lose something of that extravagant admiration which they had excited, the "Paradise Lost" made its appearance. "Fit audience find though few," was the petition addressed by the Poet to his inspiring Muse. I have said elsewhere that he gained more than he asked; this I believe to be true; but Dr. Johnson has fallen into a gross mistake when he attempts to prove, by the sale of the work, that Milton's Countrymen were "*just to it*" upon its first appearance. Thirteen hundred Copies were sold in two years; an uncom-

mon example, he asserts, of the prevalence of genius in opposition to so much recent enmity as Milton's public conduct had excited. But, be it remembered that, if Milton's political and religious opinions, and the manner in which he announced them, had raised him many enemies, they had procured him numerous friends; who, as all personal danger was passed away at the time of publication, would be eager to procure the master-work of a man whom they revered, and whom they would be proud of praising. Take, from the number of purchasers, persons of this class, and also those who wished to possess the Poem as a religious work, and but few, I fear, would be left who sought for it on account of its poetical merits. The demand did not immediately increase; "for," says Dr. Johnson, "many more readers" (he means persons in the habit of reading poetry) "than were supplied at first the Nation did not afford." How careless must a writer be who can make this assertion in the face of so many existing title-pages to belie it! Turning to my own shelves, I find the folio of Cowley, seventh edition, 1681. A book near it is Flatman's Poems, fourth edition, 1686; Waller, fifth edition, same date. The Poems of Norris of Bemerton not long after went, I believe, through nine editions. What further demand there might be for these works I do not know; but I well remember that, twenty-five years ago, the booksellers' stalls in London swarmed with the folios of Cowley. This is not mentioned in disparagement of that able writer and amiable man; but merely to show that, if Milton's work were not more read, it was not because readers did not exist at the time. The early editions of the "Paradise Lost" were printed in a shape which allowed them to be sold at a low price, yet only three thousand copies of the Work were sold in eleven years; and the Nation, says Dr. Johnson, had been satisfied from 1623 to 1664, that is, forty-one years, with only two editions of the Works of Shakspeare, which probably did not together make one thousand Copies; facts adduced by the critic to prove the "paucity of Readers." — There were readers in multitudes; but their money went for other purposes, as their admiration was fixed elsewhere. We are authorized, then, to affirm that the reception of the "Paradise Lost," and the slow progress of its fame, are proofs as striking as can be desired that the positions which I am attempting to establish are not erroneous.[1] — How amusing to shape to one's self such a critique as a Wit of Charles's days, or a Lord of the Miscellanies or trading Journalist of King William's time, would have brought forth, if he had set his faculties industriously to work upon this Poem, everywhere impregnated with *original* excellence.

---

[1] This flippant insensibility was publicly reprehended by Mr. Coleridge in a course of Lectures upon Poetry given by him at the Royal Institution. For the various merits of thought and language in Shakspeare's Sonnets see Numbers 27, 29, 30, 32, 33, 54, 64, 66, 68, 73, 76, 86, 91, 92, 93, 97, 98, 105, 107, 108, 109, 111, 113, 114, 116, 117, 129, and many others.

[1] Hughes is express upon this subject: in his dedication of Spenser's Works to Lord Somers, he writes thus: "It was your Lordship's encouraging a beautiful Edition of 'Paradise Lost' that first brought that incomparable Poem to be generally known and esteemed."

So strange indeed are the obliquities of admiration, that they whose opinions are much influenced by authority will often be tempted to think that there are no fixed principles[1] in human nature for this art to rest upon. I have been honoured by being permitted to peruse in MS. a tract composed between the period of the Revolution and the close of that century. It is the Work of an English Peer of high accomplishments, its object to form the character and direct the studies of his son. Perhaps nowhere does a more beautiful treatise of the kind exist. The good sense and wisdom of the thoughts, the delicacy of the feelings, and the charm of the style, are throughout equally conspicuous. Yet the Author, selecting among the Poets of his own country those whom he deems most worthy of his son's perusal, particularises only Lord Rochester, Sir John Denham, and Cowley. Writing about the same time, Shaftesbury, an author at present unjustly depreciated, describes the English Muses as only yet lisping in their cradles.

The arts by which Pope, soon afterwards, contrived to procure to himself a more general and a higher reputation than perhaps any English Poet ever attained during his life-time, are known to the judicious. And as well known is it to them, that the undue exertion of those arts is the cause why Pope has for some time held a rank in literature, to which, if he had not been seduced by an over-love of immediate popularity, and had confided more in his native genius, he never could have descended. He bewitched the nation by his melody, and dazzled it by his polished style, and was himself blinded by his own success. Having wandered from humanity in his Eclogues with boyish inexperience, the praise which these compositions obtained tempted him into a belief that Nature was not to be trusted, at least in pastoral Poetry. To prove this by example, he put his friend Gay upon writing those Eclogues, which their author intended to be burlesque. The instigator of the work, and his admirers, could perceive in them nothing but what was ridiculous. Nevertheless, though these Poems contain some detestable passages, the effect, as Dr. Johnson well observes, "of reality and truth became conspicuous even when the intention was to show them grovelling and degraded." The Pastorals, ludicrous to such as prided themselves upon their refinement, in spite of those disgusting passages, "became popular, and were read with delight, as just representations of rural manners and occupations."

Something less than sixty years after the publication of the "Paradise Lost" appeared Thomson's "Winter;" which was speedily followed by his other Seasons. It is a work of inspiration; much of it is written from himself, and nobly from himself. How was it received?

[1] This opinion seems actually to have been entertained by Adam Smith, the worst critic, David Hume not excepted, that Scotland, a soil to which this sort of weed seems natural, has produced.

"It was no sooner read," says o[f] temporary biographers, "than [t] mired: those only excepted who [...] used to feel, or to look for anything in poetry, beyond a *point* of satirical or epigrammatic wit, a smart *antithesis* richly trimmed with rhyme, or the softness of an *elegiac* complaint. To such his manly classical spirit could not readily commend itself; till, after a more attentive perusal, they had got the better of their prejudices, and either acquired or affected a truer taste. A few others stood aloof, merely because they had long before fixed the articles of their poetical creed, and resigned themselves to an absolute despair of ever seeing anything new and original. These were somewhat mortified to find their notions disturbed by the appearance of a poet, who seemed to owe nothing but to nature and his own genius. But, in a short time, the applause became unanimous; every one wondering how so many pictures, and pictures so familiar, should have moved them but faintly to what they felt in his descriptions. H[i]s digressions too, the overflowings of a tender benevolent heart, charmed the reader no less; leaving him in doubt, whether he should more admire the Poet or love the Man."

This case appears to bear strongly against us: — but we must distinguish between wonder and legitimate admiration. The subject of the work is the changes produced in the appearances of nature by the revolution of the year: and, by undertaking to write in verse, Thomson pledged himself to treat his subject as became a Poet. Now it is remarkable that, excepting the nocturnal "Reverie of Lady Winchilsea," and a passage or two in the "Windsor Forest" of Pope, the poetry of the period intervening between the publication of the "Paradise Lost" and the "Seasons" does not contain a single new image of external nature, and scarcely presents a familiar one from which it can be inferred that the eye of the Poet had been steadily fixed upon his object, much less that his feelings had urged him to work upon it in the spirit of genuine imagination. To what a low state knowledge of the most obvious and important phenomena had sunk, is evident from the style in which Dryden has executed a description of Night in one of his Tragedies, and Pope his translation of the celebrated moonlight scene in the Iliad. A blind man, in the habit of attending accurately to descriptions casually dropped from the lips of those around him, might easily depict these appearances with more truth. Dryden's lines are vague, bombastic, and senseless;[1] those of Pope, though he had Homer to guide him, are throughout false and contradictory. The verses of Dryden,

[1] CORTES *alone in a night-gown.*

All things are hush'd as Nature's self lay dead;
The mountains seem to nod their drowsy head.
The little Birds in dreams their songs repeat,
And sleeping Flowers beneath the Night-dew sweat:
Even Lust and Envy sleep; yet Love denies
Rest to my soul, and slumber to my eyes.
                    DRYDEN's *Indian Emperor*

once highly celebrated, are forgotten; those of Pope still retain their hold upon public estimation,—nay, there is not a passage of descriptive poetry, which at this day finds so many and such ardent admirers. Strange to think of an enthusiast, as may have been the case with thousands, reciting those verses under the cope of a moonlight sky, without having his raptures in the least disturbed by a suspicion of their absurdity!—If these two distinguished writers could habitually think that the visible universe was of so little consequence to a poet, that it was scarcely necessary for him to cast his eyes upon it, we may be assured that those passages of the elder poets which faithfully and poetically describe the phenomena of nature, were not at that time holden in much estimation, and that there was little accurate attention paid to those appearances.

Wonder is the natural product of Ignorance; and as the soil was *in such good condition* at the time of the publication of the "Seasons," the crop was doubtless abundant. Neither individuals nor nations become corrupt all at once, nor are they enlightened in a moment. Thomson was an inspired poet, but he could not work miracles; in cases where the art of seeing had in some degree been learned, the teacher would further the proficiency of his pupils, but he could do little *more;* though so far does vanity assist men in acts of self-deception, that many would often fancy they recognised a likeness when they knew nothing of the original. Having shown that much of what his biographer deemed genuine admiration must in fact have been blind wonderment—how is the rest to be accounted for?—Thomson was fortunate in the very title of his poem, which seemed to bring it home to the prepared sympathies of every one: in the next place, notwithstanding his high powers, he writes a vicious style; and his false ornaments are exactly of that kind which would be most likely to strike the undiscerning. He likewise abounds with sentimental commonplaces that, from the manner in which they were brought forward, bore an imposing air of novelty. In any well-used copy of the "Seasons" the book generally opens of itself with the rhapsody on love, or with one of the stories (perhaps Damon and Musidora); these also are prominent in our collections of Extracts, and are the parts of his Work which, after all, were probably most efficient in first recommending the author to general notice. Pope, repaying praises which he had received, and wishing to extol him to the highest, only styles him "an elegant and philosophical Poet;" nor are we able to collect any unquestionable proofs that the true characteristics of Thomson's genius as an imaginative poet[1] were perceived, till the elder Warton, nearly forty years after the

[1] Since these observations upon Thomson were written, I have perused the second edition of his "Seasons," and find that even that does not contain the most striking passages which Warton points out for admiration; these, with other improvements, throughout the whole work, must have been added at a later period.

publication of the "Seasons," pointed them out by a note in his *Essay on the Life and Writings of Pope.* In the "Castle of Indolence" (of which Gray speaks so coldly) these characteristics were almost as conspicuously displayed, and in verse more harmonious and diction more pure. Yet that fine poem was neglected on its appearance, and is at this day the delight only of a few!

When Thomson died, Collins breathed forth his regrets in an Elegiac Poem, in which he pronounces a poetical curse upon *him* who should regard with insensibility the place where the Poet's remains were deposited. The Poems of the mourner himself have now passed through innumerable editions, and are universally known; but if, when Collins died, the same kind of imprecation had been pronounced by a surviving admirer, small is the number whom it would not have comprehended. The notice which his poems attained during his life-time was so small, and of course the sale so insignificant, that not long before his death he deemed it right to repay to the bookseller the sum which he had advanced for them, and threw the edition into the fire.

Next in importance to the "Seasons" of Thomson, though at considerable distance from that work in order of time, come the *Reliques of Ancient English Poetry,* collected, new-modelled, and in many instances (if such a contradiction in terms may be used) composed by the Editor, Dr. Percy. This work did not steal silently into the world, as is evident from the number of legendary tales that appeared not long after its publication; and had been modelled, as the authors persuaded themselves, after the old Ballad. The Compilation was however ill suited to the then existing taste of city society; and Dr. Johnson, 'mid the little senate to which he gave laws, was not sparing in his exertions to make it an object of contempt. The critic triumphed, the legendary imitators were deservedly disregarded, and, as undeservedly, their ill-imitated models sank, in this country, into temporary neglect; while Bürger, and other able writers of Germany, were translating or imitating these Reliques, and composing, with the aid of inspiration thence derived, poems which are the delight of the German nation. Dr. Percy was so abashed by the ridicule flung upon his labours from the ignorance and insensibility of the persons with whom he lived, that, though while he was writing under a mask he had not wanted resolution to follow his genius into the regions of true simplicity and genuine pathos (as is evinced by the exquisite ballad of Sir Cauline and by many other pieces), yet when he appeared in his own person and character as a poetical writer, he adopted, as in the tale of the Hermit of Warkworth, a diction scarcely in any one of its features distinguishable from the vague, the glossy, and unfeeling language of his day. I mention this remarkable fact[1]

[1] Shenstone, in his "Schoolmistress," gives a still more remarkable instance of this timidity. On its first

with regret. esteeming the genius of Dr. Percy in this kind of writing superior to that of any other man by whom in modern times it has been cultivated. That even Bürger (to whom Klopstock gave in my hearing a commendation which he denied to Goethe and Schiller, pronouncing him to be a genuine poet, and one of the few among the Germans whose works would last) had not the fine sensibility of Percy, might be shown from many passages, in which he has deserted his original only to go astray. For example,

> " Now daye was gone, and night was come,
> And all were fast asleepe,
> All save the Lady Emeline,
> Who sate in her bowre to weepe :
> And soone she heard her true Love's voice
> Low whispering at the walle,
> Awake, awake, my dear Ladye,
> 'T is I thy true-love call."

Which is thus tricked out and dilated :

> " Als nun die Nacht Gebirg' und Thal
> Vermummt in Rabenschatten,
> Und Hochburgs Lampen überall
> Schon ausgeflimmert hatten,
> Und alles tief entschlafen war ;
> Doch nur das Fräulein immerdar,
> Voll Fieberängst, noch wachte,
> Und seinen Ritter dachte :
> Da horch ! Ein süsser Liebeston
> Kam leis' empor geflogen.
> ' Ho, Trudchen, ho ! Da bin ich schon !
> Frisch auf ! Dich angezogen ! ' "

But from humble ballads we must ascend to heroics.

All hail, Macpherson ! hail to thee, Sire of Ossian ! The Phantom was begotten by the snug embrace of an impudent Highlander upon a cloud of tradition — it travelled southward, where it was greeted with acclamation, and the thin Consistence took its course through Europe, upon the breath of popular applause. The Editor of the *Reliques* had indirectly preferred a claim to the praise of invention, by not concealing that his supplementary labours were considerable ! how selfish his conduct, contrasted with that of the disinterested Gael, who, like Lear, gives his kingdom away, and is content to become a pensioner upon his own issue for a beggarly pittance ! — Open this far-famed Book ! — I have done so at random, and the beginning of the " Epic Poem Temora," in eight Books, presents itself. " The blue waves of Ullin roll in light. The green hills are covered with day. Trees shake their dusky heads in the breeze. Grey torrents pour their noisy streams. Two green hills with aged oaks surround a narrow plain. The blue course of a

appearance (see D'Israeli's 2d series of the *Curiosities of Literature*) the Poem was accompanied with an absurd prose commentary, showing, as indeed some incongruous expressions in the text imply, that the whole was intended for burlesque. In subsequent editions the commentary was dropped, and the People have since continued to read in seriousness, doing for the Author what he had not courage openly to venture upon for himself.

stream is there. On its banks stood Cairbar of Atha. His spear supports the king ; the red eyes of his fear are sad. Cormac rises on his soul with all his ghastly wounds." Precious memorandums from the pocketbook of the blind Ossian !

If it be unbecoming, as I acknowledge that for the most part it is, to speak disrespectfully of Works that have enjoyed for a length of time a widely-spread reputation, without at the same time producing irrefragable proofs of their unworthiness, let me be forgiven upon this occasion. — Having had the good fortune to be born and reared in a mountainous country, from my very childhood I have felt the falsehood that pervades the volumes imposed upon the world under the name of Ossian. From what I saw with my own eyes, I knew that the imagery was spurious. In nature everything is distinct, yet nothing defined into absolute independent singleness. In Macpherson's work, it is exactly the reverse ; everything (that is not stolen) is in this manner defined, insulated, dislocated, deadened, — yet nothing distinct. It will always be so when words are substituted for things. To say that the characters never could exist, that the manners are impossible, and that a dream has more substance than the whole state of society, as there depicted, is doing nothing more than pronouncing a censure which Macpherson defied ; when, with the steeps of Morven before his eyes, he could talk so familiarly of his Car-borne heroes ; — of Morven, which, if one may judge from its appearance at the distance of a few miles, contains scarcely an acre of ground sufficiently accommodating for a sledge to be trailed along its surface. — Mr. Malcolm Laing has ably shown that the diction of this pretended translation is a motley assemblage from all quarters ; but he is so fond of making out parallel passages as to call poor Macpherson to account for his " *ands* " and his " *buts !* ", and he has weakened his argument by conducting it as if he thought that every striking resemblance was a *conscious* plagiarism. It is enough that the coincidences are too remarkable for its being probable or possible that they could arise in different minds without communication between them. Now as the Translators of the Bible, and Shakspeare, Milton, and Pope, could not be indebted to Macpherson, it follows that he must have owed his fine feathers to them ; unless we are prepared gravely to assert, with Madame de Staël, that many of the characteristic beauties of our most celebrated English Poets are derived from the ancient Fingallian ; in which case the modern translator would have been but giving back to Ossian his own. — It is consistent that Lucien Buonaparte, who could censure Milton for having surrounded Satan in the infernal regions with courtly and regal splendour, should pronounce the modern Ossian to be the glory of Scotland ; — a country that has produced a Dunbar, a Buchanan, a Thomson, and a Burns ! These opinions are of ill omen for the Epic ambition of him who has given them to the world.

Yet, much as those pretended treasures of antiquity have been admired, they have been wholly uninfluential upon the literature of the Country. No succeeding writer appears to have caught from them a ray of inspiration; no author, in the least distinguished, has ventured formally to imitate them — except the boy, Chatterton, on their first appearance. He had perceived, from the successful trials which he himself had made in literary forgery, how few critics were able to distinguish between a real ancient medal and a counterfeit of modern manufacture; and he set himself to the work of filling a magazine with *Saxon Poems,* — counterparts of those of Ossian, as like his as one of his misty stars is to another. This incapability to amalgamate with the literature of the Island is, in my estimation, a decisive proof that the book is essentially unnatural; nor should I require any other to demonstrate it to be a forgery, audacious as worthless. — Contrast, in this respect, the effect of Macpherson's publication with the *Reliques* of Percy, so unassuming, so modest in their pretensions! — I have already stated how much Germany is indebted to this latter work; and for our own country, its poetry has been absolutely redeemed by it. I do not think that there is an able writer in verse of the present day who would not be proud to acknowledge his obligations to the *Reliques;* I know that it is so with my friends; and, for myself, I am happy in this occasion to make a public avowal of my own. Dr. Johnson, more fortunate in his contempt of the labours of Macpherson than those of his modest friend, was solicited not long after to furnish Prefaces, biographical and critical, for the works of some of the most eminent English Poets. The booksellers took upon themselves to make the collection; they referred probably to the most popular miscellanies, and, unquestionably, to their books of accounts; and decided upon the claim of authors to be admitted into a body of the most eminent from the familiarity of their names with the readers of that day, and by the profits which, from the sale of his works, each had brought and was bringing to the Trade. The Editor was allowed a limited exercise of discretion, and the Authors whom he recommended are scarcely to be mentioned without a smile. We open the volume of Prefatory Lives, and to our astonishment the *first* name we find is that of Cowley! — What is become of the morning-star of English Poetry? Where is the bright Elizabethan constellation? Or, if names be more acceptable than images, where is the ever-to-be-honoured Chaucer? where is Spenser? where Sidney? and, lastly, where he, whose rights as a poet, contradistinguished from those which he is universally allowed to possess as a dramatist, we have vindicated, — where Shakspeare? — These, and a multitude of others not unworthy to be placed near them, their contemporaries and successors, we have *not*. But in their stead, we have (could better be expected when precedence was to be settled by an abstract of reputation at

any given period made, as in this case before us?) Roscommon, and Stepney, and Phillips, and Walsh, and Smith, and Duke, and King, and Spratt — Halifax, Granville, Sheffield, Congreve, Broome, and other reputed Magnates — metrical writers utterly worthless and useless, except for occasions like the present, when their productions are referred to as evidence what a small quantity of brain is necessary to procure a considerable stock of admiration, provided the aspirant will accommodate himself to the likings and fashions of his day.

As I do not mean to bring down this retrospect to our own times, it may with propriety be closed at the era of this distinguished event. From the literature of other ages and countries, proofs equally cogent might have been adduced, that the opinions announced in the former part of this Essay are founded upon truth. It was not an agreeable office, nor a prudent undertaking, to declare them; but their importance seemed to render it a duty. It may still be asked, where lies the particular relation of what has been said to these Volumes? — The question will be easily answered by the discerning Reader who is old enough to remember the taste that prevailed when some of these poems were first published, seventeen years ago; who has also observed to what degree the poetry of this Island has since that period been coloured by them; and who is further aware of the unremitting hostility with which, upon some principle or other, they have each and all been opposed. A sketch of my own notion of the constitution of Fame has been given; and as far as concerns myself, I have cause to be satisfied. The love, the admiration, the indifference, the slight, the aversion, and even the contempt, with which these Poems have been received, knowing, as I do, the source within my own mind from which they have proceeded, and the labour and pains which, when labour and pains appeared needful, have been bestowed upon them, must all, if I think consistently, be received as pledges and tokens, bearing the same general impression, though widely different in value; — they are all proofs that for the present time I have not laboured in vain; and afford assurances, more or less authentic, that the products of my industry will endure.

If there be one conclusion more forcibly pressed upon us than another by the review which has been given of the fortunes and fate of poetical Works, it is this, — that every author, as far as he is great and at the same time *original*, has had the task of *creating* the taste by which he is to be enjoyed: so has it been, so will it continue to be. This remark was long since made to me by the philosophical Friend for the separation of whose poems from my own I have previously expressed my regret. The predecessors of an original Genius of a high order will have smoothed the way for all that he has in common with them; — and much he will have in common; but, for what is peculiarly his own, he will be called upon to clear and often to shape his own road: — he will be in the condition of Hannibal among the Alps.

And where lies the real difficulty of creating that taste by which a truly original poet is to be relished? Is it in breaking the bonds of custom, in overcoming the prejudices of false refinement, and displacing the aversions of inexperience? Or, if he labour for an object which here and elsewhere I have proposed to myself, does it consist in divesting the reader of the pride that induces him to dwell upon those points wherein men differ from each other, to the exclusion of those in which all men are alike, or the same; and in making him ashamed of the vanity that renders him insensible of the appropriate excellence which civil arrangements, less unjust than might appear, and Nature illimitable in her bounty, have conferred on men who may stand below him in the scale of society? Finally, does it lie in establishing that dominion over the spirits of readers by which they are to be humbled and humanised, in order that they may be purified and exalted?

If these ends are to be attained by the mere communication of *knowledge*, it does *not* lie here. — TASTE, I would remind the reader, like IMAGINATION, is a word which has been forced to extend its services far beyond the point to which philosophy would have confined them. It is a metaphor, taken from a *passive* sense of the human body, and transferred to things which are in their essence *not* passive, — to intellectual *acts* and *operations*. The word Imagination has been overstrained, from impulses honourable to mankind, to meet the demands of the faculty which is perhaps the noblest of our nature. In the instance of Taste, the process has been reversed; and from the prevalence of dispositions at once injurious and discreditable, being no other than that selfishness which is the child of apathy, — which, as Nations decline in productive and creative power, makes them value themselves upon a presumed refinement of judging. Poverty of language is the primary cause of the use which we make of the word Imagination; but the word Taste has been stretched to the sense which it bears in modern Europe by habits of self-conceit, inducing that inversion in the order of things whereby a passive faculty is made paramount among the faculties conversant with the fine arts. Proportion and congruity, the requisite knowledge being supposed, are subjects upon which taste may be trusted; it is competent to this office; — for in its intercourse with these the mind is *passive*, and is affected painfully or pleasurably as by an instinct. But the profound and the exquisite in feeling, the lofty and universal in thought and imagination; or, in ordinary language, the pathetic and the sublime; — are neither of them, accurately speaking, objects of a faculty which could ever without a sinking in the spirit of Nations have been designated by the metaphor — *Taste*. And why? Because without the exertion of a co-operating *power* in the mind of the Reader, there can be no adequate sympathy with either of these emotions: without this auxiliary impulse, elevated or profound passion cannot exist.

Passion, it must be observed, is derived from a word which signifies *suffering*; but the connection which suffering has with effort, with exertion, and *action*, is immediate and inseparable. How strikingly is this property of human nature exhibited by the fact that, in popular language, to be in a passion is to be angry! — But,

> " Anger in hasty *words* or *blows*
> Itself discharges on its foes."

To be moved, then, by a passion, is to be excited, often to external, and always to internal, effort; whether for the continuance and strengthening of the passion, or for its suppression, accordingly as the course which it takes may be painful or pleasurable. If the latter, the soul must contribute to its support, or it never becomes vivid, — and soon languishes, and dies. And this brings us to the point. If every great poet with whose writings men are familiar, in the highest exercise of his genius, before he can be thoroughly enjoyed, has to call forth and to communicate *power*, this service, in a still greater degree, falls upon an original writer at his first appearance in the world. — Of genius the only proof is the act of doing well what is worthy to be done, and what was never done before: Of genius, in the fine arts, the only infallible sign is the widening the sphere of human sensibility for the delight, honour, and benefit of human nature. Genius is the introduction of a new element into the intellectual universe: or, if that be not allowed, it is the application of powers to objects on which they had not before been exercised, or the employment of them in such a manner as to produce effects hitherto unknown. What is all this but an advance, or a conquest, made by the soul of the poet? Is it to be supposed that the reader can make progress of this kind, like an Indian prince or general — stretched on his palanquin, and borne by slaves?· No; he is invigorated and inspirited by his leader, in order that he may exert himself; for he cannot proceed in quiescence, he cannot be carried like a dead weight. Therefore to create taste is to call forth and bestow power, of which knowledge is the effect; and *there* lies the true difficulty.

As the pathetic participates of an *animal* sensation, it might seem that, if the springs of this emotion were genuine, all men, possessed of competent knowledge of the facts and circumstances, would be instantaneously affected. And, doubtless, in the works of every true poet will be found passages of that species of excellence which is proved by effects immediate and universal. But there are emotions of the pathetic that are simple and direct, and others that are complex and revolutionary; some to which the heart yields with gentleness; others against which it struggles with pride; these varieties are infinite as the combinations of circumstance and the constitutions of character. Remember, also, that the medium through which, in poetry, the heart is to be affected is language; a thing subject to endless fluctuations and arbitrary associations. The genius of the poet melts these down for his purpose; but they retain their shape and quality to him who is not capable of exerting, within his own mind, a corresponding energy. There is also a meditative, as well as a human, pathos; an enthusiastic as well as an ordinary sorrow; a sadness that has its seat in the depths of reason, to which the mind cannot sink gently of itself — but to which it must descend by treading the steps of thought. And for the sublime, — if we consider what are the cares that occupy the passing day, and how remote is the practice and the course of life from the sources of sublimity in the soul of Man, can it be wondered that there is little existing preparation for a poet charged with a new mission to extend its kingdom, and to augment and spread its enjoyments?

Away, then, with the senseless iteration of the word *popular* applied to new works in poetry, as if there were no test of excellence in this first of the fine arts but that all men should run after its productions, as if urged by an appetite, or constrained by a spell! — The qualities of writing best fitted for eager reception are either such as startle the world into attention by their audacity and extravagance; or they are chiefly of a superficial kind, lying upon the surfaces of manners; or arising out of a selection and arrangement of incidents, by which the mind is kept upon the stretch of curiosity, and the fancy amused without the trouble of thought. But in everything which is to send the soul into herself, to be admonished of her weakness, or to be made conscious of her power; wherever life and nature are described as operated upon by the creative or abstracting virtue of the imagination; wherever the instinctive wisdom of antiquity and her heroic passions uniting, in the heart of the poet, with the meditative wisdom of later ages, have produced that accord of sublimated humanity, which is at once a history of the remote past and a prophetic enunciation of the remotest future; *there*, the poet must reconcile himself for a season to few and scattered hearers. — Grand thoughts (and Shakspeare must often have sighed over this truth), as they are most naturally and most fitly conceived in solitude, so can they not be brought forth in the midst of plaudits without some violation of their sanctity. Go to a silent exhibition of the productions of the sister Art, and be convinced that the qualities which dazzle at first sight, and kindle the admiration of the multitude, are essentially different from those by which permanent influence is secured. Let us not shrink from following up these principles as far as they will carry us, and conclude with observing that there never has been a period, and perhaps

never will be, in which vicious poetry, of some kind or other, has not excited more zealous admiration, and been far more generally read, than good; but this advantage attends the good, that the *individual*, as well as the species, survives from age to age; whereas, of the depraved, though the species be immortal, the individual quickly *perishes;* the object of present admiration vanishes, being supplanted by some other as easily produced; which, though no better, brings with it at least the irritation of novelty, — with adaptation, more or less skilful, to the changing humours of the majority of those who are most at leisure to regard poetical works when they first solicit their attention.

Is it the result of the whole that, in the opinion of the Writer, the judgment of the People is not to be respected? The thought is most injurious; and, could the charge be brought against him, he would repel it with indignation. The People have already been justified, and their eulogium pronounced by implication, when it was said above that, of *good* poetry, the *individual*, as well as the species, *survives*. And how does it survive but through the People? What preserves it but their intellect and their wisdom?

"—— Past and future, are the wings
On whose support, harmoniously conjoined,
Moves the great Spirit of human knowledge —— "
MS.

The voice that issues from this Spirit, is that Vox Populi which the Deity inspires. Foolish must he be who can mistake for this a local acclamation, or a transitory outcry — transitory though it be for years, local though from a Nation. Still more lamentable is his error who can believe that there is anything of divine infallibility in the clamour of that small though loud portion of the community, ever governed by factitious influence, which, under the name of the PUBLIC, passes itself, upon the unthinking, for the PEOPLE. Towards the Public, the Writer hopes that he feels as much deference as it is entitled to: but to the People, philosophically characterised, and to the embodied spirit of their knowledge, so far as it exists and moves, at the present, faithfully supported by its two wings, the past and the future, he devout respect, his reverence, is due. He offers it willingly and readily; and, this done, takes leave of his Readers, by assuring them that, if he were not persuaded that the contents of these Volumes, and the work to which they are subsidiary, evince something of the "Vision and the Faculty divine"; and that, both in words and things, they will operate in their degree to extend the domain of sensibility for the delight, the honour, and the benefit of human nature, notwithstanding the many happy hours which he has employed in their composition, and the manifold comforts and enjoyments they have procured to him, he would not, if a wish could do it, save them from immediate destruction — from becoming at this moment, to the world, as a thing that had never been.

POSTSCRIPT

1835

In the present Volume, as in those that have preceded it, the reader will have found occasionally opinions expressed upon the course of public affairs, and feelings given vent to as national interests excited them. Since nothing, I trust, has been uttered but in the spirit of reflective patriotism, those notices are left to produce their own effect; but, among the many objects of general concern, and the changes going forward, which I have glanced at in verse, are some especially affecting the lower orders of society: in reference to these, I wish here to add a few words in plain prose.

Were I conscious of being able to do justice to those important topics, I might avail myself of the periodical press for offering anonymously my thoughts, such as they are, to the world; but I feel that in procuring attention, they may derive some advantage, however small, from my name, in addition to that of being presented in a less fugitive shape. It is also not impossible that the state of mind which some of the foregoing poems may have produced in the reader, will dispose him to receive more readily the impression which I desire to make, and to admit the conclusions I would establish.

I. The first thing that presses upon my attention is the Poor-Law Amendment Act. I am aware of the magnitude and complexity of the subject, and the unwearied attention which it has received from men of far wider experience than my own; yet I cannot forbear touching upon one point of it, and to this I will confine myself, though not insensible to the objection which may reasonably be brought against treating a portion of this, or any other, great scheme of civil polity separately from the whole. The point to which I wish to draw the reader's attention is, that *all* persons who cannot find employment, or procure wages sufficient to support the body in health and strength, are entitled to a maintenance by law.

This dictate of humanity is acknowledged in the Report of the Commissioners: but is there not room for apprehension that some of the regulations of the new act have a tendency to render the principle nugatory by difficulties thrown in the way of applying it? If this be so, persons will not be wanting to show it, by examining the provisions of the act in detail, — an attempt which would be quite out of place here; but it will not, therefore, be deemed unbecoming in one who fears that the prudence of the head may, in framing some of those provisions, have supplanted the wisdom of the heart, to enforce a principle which cannot be violated without infringing upon one of the most precious rights of the English people, and opposing one of the most sacred claims of civilized humanity.

There can be no greater error, in this department of legislation, than the belief that this principle does by necessity operate for the degradation of those who claim, or are so circumstanced as to make it likely they may claim, through laws founded upon it, relief or assistance. The direct contrary is the truth: it may be unanswerably maintained that its tendency is to raise, not to depress; by stamping a value upon life, which can belong to it only where the laws have placed men who are willing to work, and yet cannot find employment, above the necessity of looking for protection against hunger and other natural evils, either to individual and casual charity, to despair and death, or to the breach of law by theft or violence.

And here, as in the Report of the Commissioners, the fundamental principle has been recognised, I am not at issue with them any farther than I am compelled to believe that their "remedial measures" obstruct the application of it more than the interests of society require.

And, calling to mind the doctrines of political economy which are now prevalent, I cannot forbear to enforce the justice of the principle, and to insist upon its salutary operation.

And first for its justice: If self-preservation be the first law of our nature, would not every one in a state of nature be morally justified in taking to himself that which is indispensable to such preservation, where, by so doing, he would not rob another of that which might be equally indispensable to *his* preservation? And if the value of life be regarded in a right point of view, may it not be questioned whether this right of preserving life, at any expense short of endangering the life of another, does not survive man's entering into the social state; whether this right can be surrendered or forfeited, except when it opposes the divine law, upon any supposition of a social compact, or of any convention for the protection of mere rights of property?

But if it be not safe to touch the abstract question of man's right in a social state to help himself even in the last extremity, may we not still contend for the duty of a christian government, standing *in loco parentis* towards all its subjects, to make such effectual provision, that no one shall be in danger of perishing either through the neglect or harshness of its legislation? Or, waiving this, is it not indisputable that the claim of the state to the allegiance involves the protection of the subject? And, as all rights in one party impose a correlative duty upon another, it follows that the right of the state to require the services of its members, even to the jeoparding of their lives in the common defence, establishes a right in the people (not to be gainsaid by utilitarians and economists) to public support when from any cause they may be unable to support themselves.

Let us now consider the salutary and benign operation of this principle. Here we must have recourse to elementary feelings of human nature, and to truths which from their very obviousness are apt to be slighted, till they are forced upon our notice by our own sufferings or those of others. In the "Paradise Lost," Milton represents Adam, after the Fall, as exclaiming, in the anguish of his soul —

> "Did I request Thee, Maker, from my clay
> To mould me man; did I solicit Thee
> From darkness to promote me ?
> . . . . My will
> Concurred not to my being."

Under how many various pressures of misery have men been driven thus, in a strain touching upon impiety, to expostulate with the Creator ! and under few so afflictive as when the source and origin of earthly existence have been brought back to the mind by its impending close in the pangs of destitution. But as long as, in our legislation, due weight shall be given to this principle, no man will be forced to bewail the gift of life in hopeless want of the necessaries of life.

Englishmen have, therefore, by the progress of civilisation among them, been placed in circumstances more favourable to piety and resignation to the divine will than the inhabitants of other countries, where a like provision has not been established. And as Providence, in this care of our countrymen, acts through a human medium, the objects of that care must, in like manner, be more inclined towards a grateful love of their fellow-men. Thus, also, do stronger ties attach the people to their country, whether while they tread its soil, or, at a distance, think of their native land as an indulgent parent, to whose arms even they who have been imprudent and undeserving may, like the prodigal son, betake themselves, without fear of being rejected.

Such is the view of the case that would first present itself to a reflective mind ; and it is in vain to show, by appeals to experience, in contrast with this view, that provisions founded upon the principle have promoted profaneness of life and dispositions the reverse of philanthropic, by spreading idleness, selfishness, and rapacity: for these evils have arisen, not as an inevitable consequence of the principle, but for want of judgment in framing laws based upon it ; and, above all, from faults in the mode of administering the law. The mischief that has grown to such a height from granting relief in cases where proper vigilance would have shown that it was not required, or in bestowing it in undue measure, will be urged by no truly enlightened statesman as a sufficient reason for banishing the principle itself from legislation.

Let us recur to the miserable states of consciousness that it precludes.

There is a story told, by a traveller in Spain, of a female who, by a sudden shock of domestic calamity, was driven out of her senses, and ever after looked up incessantly to the sky, feeling that her fellow-creatures could do nothing for her relief. Can there be Englishmen who, with a good end in view, would, upon system, expose their brother Englishmen to a like necessity of looking upwards only ; or downwards to the earth, after it shall contain no spot where the destitute can demand, by civil right, what by right of nature they are entitled to ?

Suppose the objects of our sympathy not sunk into this blank despair, but wandering about as strangers in streets and ways, with the hope of succour from casual charity ; what have we gained by such a change of scene ? Woful is the condition of the famished Northern Indian, dependent, among winter snows, upon the chance-passage of a herd of deer, from which one, if brought down by his rifle-gun, may be made the means of keeping him and his companions alive. As miserable is that of some savage Islander, who, when the land has ceased to afford him sustenance, watches for food which the waves may cast up, or in vain endeavours to extract it from the inexplorable deep. But neither of these is in a state of wretchedness comparable to that which is so often endured in civilised society : multitudes, in all ages, have known it, of whom may be said : —

> "Homeless, near a thousand homes they stood,
> And near a thousand tables pined, and wanted food."

Justly might I be accused of wasting time in an uncalled-for attempt to excite the feelings of the reader, if systems of political economy, widely spread, did not impugn the principle, and if the safeguards against such extremities were left unimpaired. It is broadly asserted by many, that every man who endeavours to find work *may* find it : were this assertion capable of being verified, there still would remain a question, what kind of work, and how far may the labourer be fit for it ? For if sedentary work is to be exchanged for standing, and some light and nice exercise of the fingers, to which an artisan has been accustomed all his life, for severe labour of the arms, the best efforts would turn to little account, and occasion would be given for the unthinking and the unfeeling unwarrantably to reproach those who are put upon such employment as idle, froward, and unworthy of relief, either by law or in any other way ! Were this statement correct, there would indeed be an end of the argument, the principle here maintained would be superseded. But, alas ! it is far otherwise. That principle, applicable to the benefit of all countries, is indispensable for England, upon whose coast families are perpetually deprived of their support by shipwreck, and where large masses of men are so liable to be thrown out of their ordinary means of gaining bread, by changes in commercial intercourse, subject mainly or solely to the will of foreign powers ; by new discoveries in arts and manufactures ; and by reckless laws in conformity with theories of political economy, which, whether right or wrong in the abstract, have proved a scourge to tens of thousands by the abruptness with which they have been carried into practice.

But it is urged, — refuse altogether compulsory relief to the able-bodied, and the number of those who stand in need of relief will steadily diminish through a conviction of an absolute necessity for greater forethought and more prudent care of a man's earnings. Undoubtedly it would, but so also would it, and in a much greater degree, if the legislative provisions were retained, and parochial relief administered under the care of the upper classes, as it ought to be. For it has been invariably found, that wherever the funds have been raised and applied under the superintendence of gentlemen and substantial proprietors, acting in vestries and as overseers, pauperism has diminished accordingly. Proper care in that quarter would effectually check what is felt in some districts to be one of the worst evils in the poor law system, viz. the readiness of small and needy proprietors to join in imposing rates that seemingly subject them to great hardships, while, in fact, this is done with a mutual understanding that the relief each is ready to bestow upon his still poorer neighbours will be granted to himself, or his relatives, should it hereafter be applied for.

But let us look to inner sentiments of a nobler quality, in order to know what we have to build upon. Affecting proofs occur in every one's experience, who is acquainted with the unfortunate and the indigent, of their unwillingness to derive their subsistence from aught but their own funds or labour, or to be indebted to parochial assistance for the attainment of any object, however dear to them. A case was reported, the other day, from a coroner's inquest, of a pair who, through the space of four years, had carried about their dead infant from house to house, and from lodging to lodging, as their necessities drove them, rather than ask the parish to bear the expense of its interment: — the poor creatures lived in the hope of one day being able to bury their child at their own cost. It must have been heart-rendering to see and hear the mother, who had been called upon to account for the state in which the body was found, make this deposition. By some, judging coldly, if not harshly, this conduct might be imputed to an unwarrantable pride, as she and her husband had, it is true, been once in prosperity. But examples, where the spirit of independence works with equal strength, though not with like miserable accompaniments, are frequently to be found even yet among the humblest peasantry and mechanics. There is not, then, sufficient cause for doubting that a like sense of honour may be revived among the people, and their ancient habits of independence restored, without resorting to those severities which the new Poor Law Act has introduced.

But even if the surfaces of things only are to be examined, we have a right to expect that lawgivers should take into account the various tempers and dispositions of mankind: while some are led, by the existence of a legislative provision, into idleness and extravagance, the economical virtues might be cherished in others by the knowledge that, if all their efforts fail, they have in the Poor Laws a "refuge from the storm and a shadow from the heat." Despondency and distraction are no friends to prudence: the springs of industry will relax, if cheerfulness be destroyed by anxiety; without hope men become reckless, and have a sullen pride in adding to the heap of their own wretchedness. He who feels that he is abandoned by his fellowmen will be almost irresistibly driven to care little for himself; will lose his self-respect accordingly, and with that loss what remains to him of virtue?

With all due deference to the particular experience and general intelligence of the individuals who framed the Act, and of those who in and out of parliament have approved of and supported it, it may be said that it proceeds too much upon the presumption that it is a labouring man's own fault if he be not, as the phrase is, beforehand with the world. But the most prudent are liable to be thrown back by sickness, cutting them off from labour, and causing to them expense: and who but has observed how distress creeps upon multitudes without misconduct of their own; and merely from a gradual fall in the price of labour, without a correspondent one in the price of provisions; so that men who may have ventured upon the marriage state with a fair prospect of maintaining their families in comfort and happiness, see them reduced to a pittance which no effort of theirs can increase? Let it be remembered, also, that there are thousands with whom vicious habits of expense are not the cause why they do not store up their gains; but they are generous and kind-hearted, and ready to help their kindred and friends; moreover, they have a faith in Providence that those who have been prompt to assist others, will not be left destitute, should they themselves come to need. By acting from these blended feelings, numbers have rendered themselves incapable of standing up against a sudden reverse. Nevertheless, these men, in common with all who have the misfortune to be in want, if many theorists had their wish, would be thrown upon one or other of those three sharp points of condition before adverted to, from which the intervention of law has hitherto saved them.

All that has been said tends to show how the principle contended for makes the gift of life more valuable, and has, it may be hoped, led to the conclusion that its legitimate operation is to make men worthier of that gift: in other words, not to degrade but to exalt human nature. But the subject must not be dismissed without adverting to the indirect influence of the same principle upon the moral sentiments of a people among whom it is embodied in law. In our criminal jurisprudence there is a maxim, deservedly eulogised, that it is better that ten guilty persons shall escape, than that one innocent man should suffer; so, also, might it be maintained, with regard to the Poor Laws, that it is better for the interests of humanity among the people at large, that ten undeserving should partake of the funds provided, than that one morally good man, through want of relief, should either have his principles corrupted or his energies destroyed; than that such a one should either be driven to do wrong or be cast to the earth in utter hopelessness. In France the English maxim of criminal jurisprudence is reversed; there, it is deemed better that ten innocent men should suffer than one guilty escape: in France there is no universal provision for the poor; and we may judge of the small value set upon human life in the metropolis of that country, by merely noticing the disrespect with which, after death, the body is treated, not by the thoughtless vulgar, but in schools of anatomy, presided over by men allowed to be, in their own art and in physical science, among the most enlightened in the world. In the East, where countries are overrun with population as with a weed, infinitely more respect is shown to the remains of the deceased; and what a bitter mockery is it, that this insensibility should be found where civil polity is so busy in minor regulations, and ostentatiously careful to gratify the luxurious propensities, whether social or intellectual, of the multitude! Irreligion is, no doubt, much concerned with this offensive disrespect shown to the bodies of the dead in France; but it is mainly attributable to the state in which so many of the living are left by the absence of compulsory provision for the indigent so humanely established by the law of England.

Sights of abject misery, perpetually recurring, harden the heart of the community. In the perusal of history and of works of fiction we are not, indeed, unwilling to have our commiseration excited by such objects of distress as they present to us; but, in the concerns of real life, men know that such emotions are not given to be indulged for their own sakes: there, the conscience declares to them that sympathy must be followed by action; and if there exist a previous conviction that the power to relieve is utterly inadequate to the demand, the eye shrinks from communication with wretchedness, and pity and compassion languish, like any other qualities that are deprived of their natural aliment. Let these considerations be duly weighed by those who trust to the hope that an increase of private charity, with all its advantages of superior discrimination, would more than compensate for the abandonment of those principles, the wisdom of which has been here insisted upon. How discouraging, also, would be the sense of injustice, which could not fail to arise in the minds of the well-disposed, if the burden of supporting the poor, a burden of which the selfish have hitherto by compulsion borne a share, should now, or hereafter, be thrown exclusively upon the benevolent.

By having put an end to the Slave Trade and Slavery, the British people are exalted in the scale of humanity; and they cannot but feel so, if they look into themselves, and duly consider their relation to God and their fellow-creatures. That was a noble advance; but a retrograde movement will assuredly be made, if ever the principle which has been here defended should be either avowedly abandoned or but ostensibly retained.

But, after all, there may be a little reason to apprehend permanent injury from any experiment that may be tried. On the one side will be human nature rising up in her own defence, and on the other prudential selfishness acting to the same purpose, from a conviction that, without a compulsory provision for the exigencies of the labouring multitude, that degree of ability to regulate the price of labour, which is indispensable for the reasonable interest of arts and manufactures, cannot, in Great Britain, be upheld.

II. In a poem of the foregoing collection allusion is made to the state of the workmen congregated in manufactories. In order to relieve many of the evils to which that class of society are subject, and to establish a better harmony between them and their employers, it would be well to repeal such laws as prevent the formation of joint-stock companies. There are, no doubt, many and great obstacles to the formation and salutary working of these societies, inherent in the mind of those whom they would obviously benefit. But the combinations of masters to keep down, unjustly, the price of labour would be fairly checked by them, as far as they were practicable; they would encourage economy, inasmuch as they would enable a man to draw profit from his savings, by investing them in buildings or machinery for processes of manufacture with which he was habitually connected. His little capital would then be working for him while he was at rest or asleep; he would more clearly perceive the necessity of capital for carrying on great works; he would better learn to respect the larger portions of it in the hands of others; he would be less tempted to join in unjust combinations; and, for the sake of his own property, if not for higher reasons, he would be slow to promote local disturbance or endanger public tranquillity; he would, at least, be loth to act in that way *knowingly:* for it is not to be denied that such societies might be nurseries of opinions unfavourable to a mixed constitution of government, like that of Great Britain. The democratic and republican spirit which they might be apt to foster would not, however, be dangerous in itself, but only as it might act without being sufficiently counterbalanced, either by landed proprietorship, or by a Church extending itself so as to embrace an ever-growing and ever-shifting population of mechanics and artisans. But if the tendencies of such societies would be to make the men prosper who might belong to them, rulers and legislators should rejoice in the result, and do their duty to the state by upholding and extending the influence of that Church to which it owes, in so great a measure, its safety, its prosperity, and its glory.

This, in the temper of the present times, may be difficult, but it is become indispensable, since large towns in great numbers have sprung up, and others have increased tenfold, with little or no dependence upon the gentry and the landed proprietors; and apart from those mitigated feudal institutions, which, till of late, have acted so powerfully upon the composition of the House of Commons. Now it may be affirmed that, in quarters where there is not an attachment to the Church, or the landed aristocracy, and a pride in supporting them, *there* the people will dislike both, and be ready, upon such incitements as are perpetually recurring, to join in attempts to overthrow them. There is no neutral ground here: from want of due attention to the state of society in large towns and manufacturing districts, and ignorance or disregard of these obvious truths, innumerable well-meaning persons became zealous supporters of a Reform Bill, the qualities and powers of which, whether destructive or constructive, they would otherwise have been afraid of; and even the framers of that bill, swayed as they might be by party resentments and personal ambition, could not have gone so far, had not they too been lamentably ignorant or neglectful of the same truths both of fact and philosophy.

But let that pass; and let no opponent of the bill be tempted to compliment his own foresight, by exaggerating the mischiefs and dangers that have sprung from it: let not time be wasted in profitless regrets; and let those party distinctions vanish to their very names that have separated men who, whatever course they may have pursued, have ever had a bond of union in the wish to save the limited monarchy and those other institutions that have, under Providence, rendered for so long a period of time this country the happiest and worthiest of which there is any record since the foundation of civil society.

III. A philosophic mind is best pleased when looking at religion in its spiritual bearing; as a guide of conduct, a solace under affliction, and a support amid the instabilities of mortal life: but the Church having been forcibly brought by political considerations to my notice, while treating of the labouring classes, I cannot forbear saying a few words upon that momentous topic.

There is a loud clamour for extensive change in that department. The clamour would be entitled to more respect if they who are the most eager to swell it with their voices were not generally the most ignorant of the real state of the Church and the service it renders to the community. *Reform* is the word employed. Let us pause and consider what sense it is apt to carry, and how things are confounded by a lax use of it. The great religious Reformation, in the sixteenth century, did not profess to be a new construction, but a restoration of some-thing fallen into decay, or put out of sight. That familiar and justifiable use of the word seems to have paved the way for fallacies with respect to the term reform, which it is difficult to escape from. Were we to speak of improvement and the correction of abuses, we should run less risk of being deceived ourselves or of misleading others. We should be less likely to fall blindly into the belief that the change demanded is a renewal of something that has existed before, and that, therefore, we have experience on our side; nor should we be equally tempted to beg the question that the change for which we are eager must be advantageous. From generation to generation, men are the dupes of words; and it is painful to observe that so many of our species are most tenacious of those opinions which they have formed with the least consideration. They who are the readiest to meddle with public affairs, whether in church or state, fly to generalities, that they may be eased from the trouble of thinking about particulars; and thus is deputed to mechanical instrumentality the work which vital knowledge only can do well.

"Abolish pluralities, have a resident incumbent in every parish," is a favourite cry; but, without adverting to other obstacles in the way of this specious scheme, it may be asked what benefit would accrue from its *indiscriminate* adoption to counterbalance the harm it would introduce, by nearly extinguishing the order of curates, unless the revenues of the church should grow with the population, and be greatly increased in many thinly-peopled districts, especially among the parishes of the North.

The order of curates is so beneficial, that some particular notice of it seems to be required in this place. For a church poor as, relatively to the numbers of people, that of England is, and probably will continue to be, it is no small advantage to have youthful servants, who will work upon the wages of hope and expectation. Still more advantageous is it to have, by means of this order, young men scattered over the country, who being more detached from the temporal concerns of the benefice, have more leisure for improvement and study, and are less subject to be brought into secular collision with those who are under their spiritual guardianship. The curate, if he reside at a distance from the incumbent, undertakes the requisite responsibilities of a temporal kind, in that modified way which prevents him, as a new-comer, from being charged with selfishness: while it prepares him for entering upon a benefice of his own with something of a suitable experience. If he should act under and in co-operation with a resident incumbent, the gain is mutual. His studies will probably be assisted; and his training, managed by a superior, will not be liable to relapse in matters of prudence, seemliness, or in any of the highest cares of his functions; and by way of return for these benefits to the pupil, it will often happen that the zeal of a middle-aged or declining incumbent will be revived, by being in near communion with the ardour of youth, when his own efforts may have languished through a melancholy consciousness that they have not produced as much good among his flock as, when he first entered upon the charge, he fondly hoped.

Let one remark, and that not the least important, be added. A curate, entering for the first time upon his office, comes from college after a course of expense, and with such inexperience in the use of money that in his new situation he is apt to fall unawares into pecuniary difficulties. If this happens to him, much more likely is it to happen to the youthful incumbent, whose relations, to his parishioners and to society, are more complicated; and, his income being larger and independent of another, a costlier style of living is required of him by public opinion. If embarrassment should ensue, and with that unavoidably some loss of respectability, his future usefulness will be proportionably impaired: not so with the curate, for he can easily remove and start afresh with a stock of experience and an unblemished reputation; whereas the early indiscretions of an incumbent being rarely forgotten, may be impediments to the efficacy of his ministry for the remainder of his life. The same observations would apply with equal force to doctrine. A young minister is liable to errors, from his notions being either too lax or overstrained. In both cases it would prove injurious that the error should be remembered, after study and reflection, with advancing years, shall have brought him to a clearer discernment of the truth, and better judgment in the application of it.

It must be acknowledged that, among the regulations of ecclesiastical polity, none at first view are more attractive than that which prescribes for every parish a resident incumbent. How agreeable to picture to one's self, as has been done by poets and romance-writers, from Chaucer down to Goldsmith, a man devoted to his ministerial office, with not a wish or a thought ranging beyond the circuit of its cares! Nor is it in poetry and fiction only that such characters are found; they are scattered, it is hoped not sparingly, over real life, especially in sequestered and rural districts, where there is but small influx of new inhabitants, and little change of occupation. The spirit of the Gospel, unaided by acquisitions of profane learning and experience in the world,—that spirit and the obligations of the sacred office may, in such situations, suffice to effect most of what is needful. But for the complex state of society that prevails in England much more is required, both in large towns and in many extensive districts of the country. A minister there should not only be irreproachable in manners and morals, but accomplished in learning, as far as is possible without sacrifice of the least of his pastoral duties. As necessary, perhaps more so, is it that he should be a citizen as well as a scholar; thoroughly acquainted with the structure of society and the constitution of civil government, and able to reason upon both with the most expert; all ultimately in order to support the truths of Christianity and to diffuse its blessings.

A young man coming fresh from the place of his education cannot have brought with him these accomplishments; and if the scheme of equalising church incomes, which many advisers are much bent upon, be realised, so that there should be little or no secular inducement for a clergyman to desire a removal from the spot where he may chance to have been first set down; surely not only opportunities for obtaining the requisite qualifications would be diminished, but the motives for desiring to obtain them would be proportionably weakened. And yet these qualifications are indispensable for the diffusion of that knowledge by which alone the political philosophy of the New Testament can be rightly expounded, and its precepts adequately enforced. In these times, when the press is daily exercising so great a power over the minds of the people, for wrong or for right as may happen, *that* preacher ranks among the first of benefactors who, without stooping to the direct treatment of current politics and passing events, can furnish infallible guidance through the delusions that surround them; and who, appealing to the sanctions of Scripture, may place the grounds of its injunctions in so clear a light that disaffection shall cease to be cultivated as a laudable propensity, and loyalty cleansed from the dishonour of a blind and prostrate obedience.

It is not, however, in regard to civic duties alone, that this knowledge in a minister of the Gospel is important; it is still more so for softening and subduing private and personal discontents. In all places, and at all times, men have gratuitously troubled themselves, because their survey of the dispensations of Providence has been partial and narrow; but now that readers are so greatly multiplied, men judge as they are *taught*, and repinings are engendered everywhere, by imputations being cast upon the government; and are prolonged or aggravated by being ascribed to misconduct or injustice in rulers, when the individual himself only is in fault. If a Christian pastor be competent to deal with these humours, as they may be dealt with, and by no members of society so successfully, both from more frequent and more favourable opportunities of intercourse, and by aid of the authority with which he speaks; he will be a teacher of moderation, a dispenser of the wisdom that blunts approaching distress by submission to God's will, and lightens, by patience, grievances which cannot be removed.

We live in times when nothing, of public good at least, is generally acceptable, but what we believe can be traced to preconceived intention and specific acts and formal contrivances of human understanding. A Christian instructor thoroughly accomplished would be a standing restraint upon such presumptuousness of judgment, by impressing the truth that

" In the unreasoning progress of the world
A wiser spirit is at work for us,
A better eye than ours." *MS.*

Revelation points to the purity and peace of a future world ; but our sphere of duty is upon earth ; and the relations of impure and conflicting things to each other must be understood, or we shall be perpetually going wrong, in all but goodness of intention; and goodness of intention will itself relax through frequent disappointment. How desirable, then, is it, that a minister of the Gospel should be versed in the knowledge of existing facts, and be accustomed to a wide range of social experience ! Nor is it less desirable for the purpose of counterbalancing and tempering in his own mind that ambition with which spiritual power is as apt to be tainted as any other species of power which men covet or possess.

It must be obvious that the scope of the argument is to discourage an attempt which would introduce into the Church of England an equality of income and station, upon the model of that of Scotland. The sounder part of the Scottish nation know what good their ancestors derived from their church, and feel how deeply the living generation is indebted to it. They respect and love it, as accommodated in so great a measure to a comparatively poor country, through the far greater portion of which prevails a uniformity of employment; but the acknowledged deficiency of theological learning among the clergy of that church is easily accounted for by this very equality. What else may be wanting there it would be unpleasant to inquire, and might prove invidious to determine : one thing, however, is clear ; that in all countries the temporalities of the Church Establishment should bear an analogy to the state of society, otherwise it cannot diffuse its influence through the whole community. In a country so rich and luxurious as England, the character of its clergy must unavoidably sink, and their influence be everywhere impaired, if individuals from the upper ranks, and men of leading talents, are to have no inducements to enter into that body but such as are purely spiritual. And this "tinge of secularity" is no reproach to the clergy, nor does it imply a deficiency of spiritual endowments. Parents and guardians, looking forward to sources of honourable maintenance for their children and wards, often direct their thoughts early towards the church, being determined partly by outward circumstances, and partly by indications of seriousness or intellectual fitness. It is natural that a boy or youth, with such a prospect before him, should turn his attention to those studies, and be led into those habits of reflection, which will in some degree tend to prepare him for the duties he is hereafter to undertake. As he draws nearer to the time when he will be called to these duties, he is both led and compelled to examine the Scriptures. He becomes more and more sensible of their truth. Devotion grows in him ; and what might begin in temporal considerations, will end (as in a majority of instances we trust it does) in a spiritual-mindedness not unworthy of that Gospel, the lessons of which he is to teach, and the faith of which he

is to inculcate. Not inappositely may be here repeated an observation which, from its obviousness and importance, must have been frequently made, viz. that the impoverishing of the clergy, and bringing their incomes much nearer to a level, would not cause them to become less worldly-minded : the emoluments, howsoever reduced, would be as eagerly sought for, but by men from lower classes in society ; men who, by their manners, habits, abilities, and the scanty measure of their attainments, would unavoidably be less fitted for their station, and less competent to discharge its duties.

Visionary notions have in all ages been afloat upon the subject of best providing for the clergy; notions which have been sincerely entertained by good men, with a view to the improvement of that order, and eagerly caught at and dwelt upon by the designing, for its degradation and disparagement. Some are beguiled by what they call the *voluntary system*, not seeing (what stares one in the face at the very threshold) that they who stand in most need of religious instruction are unconscious of the want, and therefore cannot reasonably be expected to make any sacrifices in order to supply it. Will the licentious, the sensual, and the depraved, take from the means of their gratifications and pursuits, to support a discipline that cannot advance without uprooting the trees that bear the fruit which they devour so greedily ? Will *they* pay the price of that seed whose harvest is to be reaped in an invisible world ? A voluntary system for the religious exigencies of a people numerous and circumstanced as we are ! Not more absurd would it be to expect that a knot of boys should draw upon the pittance of their pocket-money to build schools, or out of the abundance of their discretion be able to select fit masters to teach and keep them in order ! Some, who clearly perceive the incompetence and folly of such a scheme for the agricultural part of the people, nevertheless think it feasible in large towns, where the rich might subscribe for the religious instruction of the poor. Alas ! they know little of the thick darkness that spreads over the streets and alleys of our large towns. The parish of Lambeth, a few years since, contained not more than one church and three or four small proprietary chapels, while dissenting chapels of every denomination were still more scantily found there ; yet the inhabitants of the parish amounted at that time to upwards of 50,000. Were the parish church and the chapels of the Establishment existing there an *impediment* to the spread of the Gospel among that mass of people ? Who shall dare to say so ? But if any one, in the face of the fact which has just been stated, and in opposition to authentic reports to the same effect from various other quarters, should still contend that a voluntary system is sufficient for the spread and maintenance of religion, we would ask, what kind of religion ? wherein would it differ, among the many, from deplorable fanaticism ?

For the preservation of the Church Establishment, all men, whether they belong to it or not, could they perceive their true interest, would be strenuous; but how inadequate are its provisions for the needs of the country ! and how much is it to be regretted that, while its zealous friends yield to alarms on account of the hostility of dissent, they should so much overrate the danger to be apprehended from that quarter, and almost overlook the fact that hundreds of thousands of our fellow-countrymen, though formally and nominally of the Church of England, never enter her places of worship, neither have they communication with her ministers! This deplorable state of things was partly produced by a decay of zeal among the rich and influential, and partly by a want of due expansive power in the constitution of the Establishment as regulated by law. Private benefactors, in their efforts to build and endow churches, have been frustrated or too much impeded by legal obstacles : these, where they are unreasonable or unfitted for the times, ought to be removed; and, keeping clear of intolerance and injustice, means should be used to render the presence and powers of the church commensurate with the wants of a shifting and still-increasing population.

This cannot be effected, unless the English Government vindicate the truth that, as her church exists for the benefit of all (though not in equal degree), whether of her communion or not, all should be made to contribute to its support. If this ground be abandoned, cause will be given to fear that a moral wound may be inflicted upon the heart of the English people, for which a remedy cannot be speedily provided by the utmost efforts which the members of the Church will themselves be able to make.

But let the friends of the church be of good courage. Powers are at work, by which, under Divine Providence, she may be strengthened and the sphere of her usefulness extended ; not by alterations in her Liturgy, accommodated to this or that demand of finical taste, nor by cutting off this or that from her articles or Canons, to which the scrupulous or the overweening may object. Covert schism, and open nonconformity, would survive after alterations, however promising in the eyes of those whose subtilty had been exercised in making them. Latitudinarianism is the parhelion of liberty of conscience, and will ever successfully lay claim to a divided worship. Among Presbyterians, Socinians, Baptists, and Independents, there will always be found numbers who will tire of their several creeds, and some will come over to the Church. Conventicles may disappear, congregations in each denomination may fall into decay or be broken up, but the conquests which the National Church ought chiefly to aim at, lie among the thousands and tens of thousands of the unhappy outcasts who grow up with no religion at all. The wants of these cannot but be feelingly remembered. Whatever may be the disposition of the new constituencies under the reformed parliament, and the course which the men of their choice may be inclined or com-

pelled to follow, it may be confidently hoped that individuals, acting in their private capacities, will endeavour to make up for the deficiencies of the legislature. Is it too much to expect that proprietors of large estates, where the inhabitants are without religious instruction, or where it is sparingly supplied, will deem it their duty to take part in this good work ; and that thriving manufacturers and merchants will, in their several neighbourhoods, be sensible of the like obligation, and act upon it with generous rivalry ?

Moreover, the force of public opinion is rapidly increasing, and some may bend to it, who are not so happy as to be swayed by a higher motive; especially they who derive large incomes from lay-impropriations in tracts of country where ministers are few and meagrely provided for. A claim still stronger may be acknowledged by those who, round their superb habitations, or elsewhere, walk over vast estates which were lavished upon their ancestors by royal favouritism or purchased at insignificant prices after church-spoliation ; such proprietors, though not conscience-stricken (there is no call for that), may be prompted to make a return for which their tenantry and dependents will learn to bless their names. An impulse has been given ; an accession of means from these several sources, co-operating with a *well*-considered change in the distribution of some parts of the property at present possessed by the church, a change scrupulously founded upon due respect to law and justice, will, we trust, bring about so much of what her friends desire, that the rest may be calmly waited for, with thankfulness for what shall have been obtained.

Let it not be thought unbecoming in a layman to have treated at length a subject with which the clergy are more intimately conversant. All may, without impropriety, speak of what deeply concerns all ; nor need an apology be offered for going over ground which has been trod before so ably and so often : without pretending, however, to anything of novelty, either in matter or manner, something may have been offered to view which will save the writer from the imputation of having little to recommend his labour but goodness of intention.

It was with reference to thoughts and feelings expressed in verse, that I entered upon the above notices, and with verse I will conclude. The passage is extracted from my MSS. written above thirty years ago : it turns upon the individual dignity which humbleness of social condition does not preclude, but frequently promotes. It has no direct bearing upon clubs for the discussion of public affairs, nor upon political or trade-unions ; but if a single workman — who, being a member of one of those clubs, runs the risk of becoming an agitator, or who, being enrolled in a union, must be left without a will of his own, and therefore a slave — should read these lines, and be touched by them, I should indeed rejoice, and little would I care for losing credit as a poet with intemperate critics, who think differently from me upon political philosophy or public measures, if the sober-minded admit that, in general views, my affections have been moved, and my imagination exercised, under and *for* the guidance of reason.

" Here might I pause, and bend in reverence
To Nature, and the power of human minds;
To men as they are men within themselves.
How oft high service is performed within,
When all the external man is rude in show;
Not like a temple rich with pomp and gold,
But a mere mountain chapel that protects
Its simple worshippers from sun and shower !
Of these, said I, shall be my song ; of these,
If future years mature me for the task,
Will I record the praises, making verse
Deal boldly with substantial things — in truth
And sanctity of passion, speak of these,
That justice may be done, obeisance paid
Where it is due.   Thus haply shall I teach,
Inspire, through unadulterated ears
Pour rapture, tenderness, and hope ; my theme
No other than the very heart of man,
As found among the best of those who live,
Not unexalted by religious faith,
Nor uninformed by books, good books, though few,
In Nature's presence : thence may I select
Sorrow that is not sorrow, but delight,
And miserable love that is not pain
To hear of, for the glory that redounds

Therefrom to human kind, and what we are.
Be mine to follow with no timid step
Where knowledge leads me ; it shall be my pride
That I have dared to tread this holy ground,
Speaking no dream, but things oracular,
Matter not lightly to be heard by those
Who to the letter of the outward promise
Do read the invisible soul ; by men adroit
In speech, and for communion with the world
Accomplished, minds whose faculties are then
Most active when they are most eloquent,
And elevated most when most admired.
Men may be found of other mould than these ;
Who are their own upholders, to themselves
Encouragement and energy, and will ;
Expressing liveliest thoughts in lively words
As native passion dictates.   Others, too,
There are, among the walks of homely life,
Still higher, men for contemplation framed ;
Shy, and unpractised in the strife of phrase ;
Meek men, whose very souls perhaps would sink
Beneath them, summoned to such intercourse.
Theirs is the language of the heavens, the power,
The thought, the image, and the silent joy :
Words are but under-agents in their souls ;
When they are grasping with their greatest strength
They do not breathe among them ; this I speak
In gratitude to God, who feeds our hearts
For his own service, knoweth, loveth us,
When we are unregarded by the world."

NOTES

Page 1. Lines Written as a School Exercise at Hawkshead.

I was called upon, among other scholars, to write verses upon the completion of the second centenary of the school in 1585, by Archbishop Sandys. These verses were much admired, far more than they deserved, for they were but a tame imitation of Pope's versification, and a little in his style. This exercise, however, put it into my head to compose verses from the impulse of my own mind. . . W. W. ("Autobiographical Memoranda").

Page 2. Extract from the Conclusion of a Poem, Composed in Anticipation of Leaving School.

Composed at Hawkshead, probably before Wordsworth's departure for Cambridge in 1787. The poem which it concluded was "The Vale of Esthwaite," a long, rambling, often lurid account of the Gothic adventures of a young minstrel among the lakes. Like all Wordsworth's juvenile pieces, it was drastically revised before publication. In the schoolboy's poem these lines stood as follows:

> Yet if Heaven bear me far away
> To close the evening of my day,
>
> My soul shall cast the wistful view,
> The longing look, alone on you.
> As Phoebus, when he sinks to rest
> Far on the mountains in the west,
> While all the vale is dark between
> Ungilded by his golden sheen,
> A lingering lustre softly throws
> On the dear hills where first he rose.

Wordsworth recalls the composition of these lines in *The Prelude* (VIII.458–475).

Page 3. An Evening Walk.

This highly derivative topographical poem mingles tradition and innovation in complex ways. It was composed in 1788 and 1789, an enlargement and revision of parts of "The Vale of Esthwaite." "Huddled up" for publication in 1793, it was revised again in 1794 and 1815, when extracts appeared among Wordsworth's collected works. In later editions the poem was printed entire. "There are some glaring faults," Dorothy Wordsworth wrote a friend in 1793, "but I hope you will discover many beauties, which could only have been created by the imagination of a *poet*." The following notes include a few of the many allusions in the poem, to suggest the degree to which the young Wordsworth sought to imitate the poets he admired. The version here printed is that of 1849.

Lines 3 and 4. The cataract of Lodore flows into the lake of Derwentwater.

Line 9. *Winander sleeps.* These lines are only applicable to the middle part of that lake. W. W.

Line 20. *woodcocks roamed.* In the beginning of the winter, these mountains are frequented by woodcocks, which in dark nights retire into the woods. W. W.

Line 49. *intake.* The word *intake* is local, and signifies a mountain enclosure. W. W.

Line 54. *ghyll.* Ghyll is also, I believe, a term confined to this country: *ghyll* and *dingle* have the same meaning. W. W. I.e., a deep cleft or hollow.

Line 68. *secret bridge.* The reader who has made a tour of this country, will recognize, in this description, the features which characterize the lower waterfall in the grounds of Rydal. W. W.

Lines 72 and 73. See Horace's ode (III.xiii) praising the Bandusian (or Blandusian) spring.

Line 133. *'green rings.'* "Vivid rings of green." — Greenwood's *Poems on Shooting.* W. W.

Line 135. "Down the rough slope the pond'rous waggon rings." Beattie [James Beattie's *Minstrel*, I.xxxix]. W. W. Noted in the 1793 edition only.

Line 146. *Sweetly ferocious.* "Dolcemente feroce." — Tasso.

In this description of the cock, I remembered a spirited one of the same animal in *L'Agriculture, ou Les Georgiques François*, of M. Rossuet. W. W.

Line 191. *Gives one bright glance*, etc. From Thomson. W. W. James Thomson's *Seasons*, "Summer," lines 1628–29. The passage was discussed at length in John Scott's *Critical Essays* (1785), as Wordsworth pointed out in the note of 1793.

Line 207. *Winding in ordered pomp.* See a description of an appearance of this kind in Clark's *Survey of the Lakes*, accompanied by vouchers of its veracity, that may amuse the reader. W. W.

Line 230. This is a fact of which I have been an eyewitness. W. W. In 1793 edition only.

Line 237. *"By distance made more sweet."* William Collins, "The Passions: An Ode for Music," line 60.

Line 279. *Sweet are the sounds.* Goldsmith's "Deserted Village," line 113.

Line 280. *Folding star.* Collins, "Ode to Evening," line 21.

Line 291. In 1793 Wordsworth cites Spenser's *Faerie Queene*, I.iii.4.

Line 306. *Wreck.* A vestige or trace. See *The Tempest*, IV.i.155–56.

Lines 323 ff. This portrait of the owl preserves much of the stylistic complexity of the 1793 version, which Wordsworth later came to see as "inflated and obscure."

Page 9. REMEMBRANCE OF COLLINS.
Line 14. *Who murmuring here a later ditty.* Collins's "Ode on the Death of Thomson," the last written, I believe, of the poems which were published during his lifetime. This Ode is also alluded to in the next Stanza. W. W. Wordsworth alludes to lines 13–16 of the "Ode":

Remembrance oft shall haunt the shore
  When Thames in summer wreaths is drest,
And oft suspend the dashing oar
  To bid his gentle spirit rest.

Collins's poem is also set on the Thames near Richmond, where James Thomson (1700–48) is buried; Wordsworth eulogizes Collins where Collins had eulogized Thomson.

Page 10. DESCRIPTIVE SKETCHES.
Although the "sketches" of this poem were taken from the Alpine walking tour of 1790, Wordsworth's celebration of mountain liberty reflects his ardent commitment to the French Revolution (and perhaps Annette Vallon) in 1792, when much of the poem was composed. For certain descriptions Wordsworth relied heavily on literary sources, particularly Ramond de Carbonnières's notes (1782) to William Coxe's *Travels in Switzerland*. The poem was first published in 1793; the version here printed is that republished in later years.
Line 24. *"Calls it luxury."* See Joseph Addison's *Cato*, I.iv.71.
Line 32. *Memnon's lyre.* The lyre of Memnon is reported to have emitted melancholy or cheerful tones, as it was touched by the sun's evening or morning rays. W. W.
Line 70. *The Cross.* Alluding to the crosses seen on the tops of the spiry rocks of the Chartreuse, which have every appearance of being inaccessible. W. W.
Line 71. *"Parting Genius."* Milton, "On the Morning of Christ's Nativity," line 186.
Line 72. *streams of Life and Death.* Names of rivers at the Chartreuse. W. W.
Line 75. *Vallombre.* Name of one of the valleys of the Chartreuse. W. W.
Line 87. If any of my readers should ever visit the Lake of Como, I recommend it to him to take a stroll along this charming little pathway; he must chuse the evening, as it is on the western side of the Lake. We pursued it from the foot of the water to its head: it is once interrupted by a ferry. W. W. In 1793 edition only.
Line 137. *Slavery.* At the time of Wordsworth's visit to the Italian lakes, the region was part of the Austrian duchy of Milan.
Line 157. *her waters gleam.* The river along whose banks you descend in crossing the Alps by the Simplon Pass. W. W.
Line 200. *cells.* The Catholic religion prevails here; these cells are, as is well known, very com-

mon in the Catholic countries, planted, like the Roman tombs, along the roadside. W. W.
Line 202. *death-cross.* Crosses, commemorative of the deaths of travellers by the fall of snow, and other accidents, are very common along this dreadful road. W. W.
Line 214. *wood-cottages.* The houses in the more retired Swiss valleys are all built of wood. W. W.
Line 284. I had once given to these sketches the title of Picturesque; but the Alps are insulted in applying to them that term. Whoever, in attempting to describe their sublime features, should confine himself to the cold rules of painting would give his reader but a very imperfect idea of those emotions which they have the irresistible power of communicating to the most impassive imagination. The fact is, that controlling influence, which distinguishes the Alps from all other scenery, is derived from images which disdain the pencil. Had I wished to make a picture of this scene I had thrown much less light into it. But I consulted nature and my feelings. The ideas excited by the stormy sunset I am here describing owed their sublimity to that deluge of light, or rather of fire, in which nature had wrapped the immense forms around me; any intrusion of shade, by destroying the unity of the impression, had necessarily diminished it's [*sic*] grandeur. W. W. In 1793 edition only.
Lines 293–302. Wordsworth alludes to four famous battlegrounds, and the heroes who died there: the Plains of Abraham, outside Quebec, where the British general James Wolfe died in 1759; Aosta, Italy, where the French hero Bayard was killed in 1524; the battle of Zutphen, where Sir Philip Sidney was killed in 1586; and the battle of Killiecrankie, Scotland, where Graham of Claverhouse, Viscount Dundee, died in 1679.
Line 307. *Through vacant worlds,* etc. For most of the images in the next sixteen verses, I am indebted to M. Raymond's interesting observations annexed to his translation of Coxe's *Tour in Switzerland*. W. W.
Line 339. *pensive Underwalden's pastoral heights.* The people of this Canton are supposed to be of a more melancholy disposition than the other inhabitants of the Alps; this, if true, may proceed from their being more secluded. W. W.
Line 348. *chalets,* etc. This picture is from the middle region of the Alps. *Chalets* are summer huts for the Swiss herdsmen. W. W.
Line 359. *sugh.* Sugh, a Scotch word expressive of the sound of the wind through the trees. W. W.
Line 367. This wind, which announces the spring to the Swiss, is called in their language FOEN; and is according to M. Raymond the Syroco of the Italians. W. W. In 1793 edition only.
Line 387. This tradition of the golden age of the Alps, as M. Raymond observes, is highly interesting, interesting not less to the philosopher than to the poet. Here I cannot help remarking, that the superstitions of the Alps appear to be far from possessing that poetical char-

acter which so eminently distinguishes those of Scotland and the other mountainous northern countries. The Devil with his horns, etc., seems to be, in their idea, the principal agent that brings about the sublime natural revolutions that take place daily before their eyes. W. W. In 1793 edition only.

Line 452. *few in arms*, etc. Alluding to several battles which the Swiss in very small numbers have gained over their oppressors, the house of Austria; and in particular to one fought at Naeffels, near Glarus, where three hundred and fifty men are said to have defeated an army of between fifteen and twenty thousand Austrians. Scattered over the valley are to be found eleven stones, with this inscription, 1388, the year the battle was fought, marking out, as I was told upon the spot, the several places where the Austrians, attempting to make a stand, were repulsed anew. W. W.

Line 472. *Pikes, of darkness.* As Schreck-Horn, the pike of terror; Wetter-Horn, the pike of storms, etc., etc. W. W.

Line 527. *Bows his young head*, etc. The well-known effect of the famous air called in France "Ranz des Vaches," upon the Swiss troops. W. W.

Line 546. *Einsiedlen's wretched fane.* This shrine is resorted to, from a hope of relief, by multitudes from every corner of the Catholic world, labouring under mental or bodily afflications. W. W.

Line 560. *The fountains.* Rude fountains built and covered with sheds for the accommodation of the Pilgrims, in their ascent of the mountain. W. W.

Line 577. It is only from the higher part of the valley of Chamouny that Mont Blanc is visible. W. W. In 1793 edition only.

Line 588. It is scarce necessary to observe that these lines were written before the emancipation of Savoy. W. W. In 1793 edition only. Savoy was annexed by France in November 1792.

Line 619. *Sourd.* An insect so called, which emits a short, melancholy cry, heard at the close of the summer evenings, on the banks of the Loire. W. W.

Line 624. The river Loiret, which has the honour of giving name to a department, rises out ,of the earth at a place, called La Source, a league and a half south-east of Orleans, and taking at once the character of a considerable stream, winds under a most delicious bank on its left, with a flat country of meadows, woods, and vineyards on its right, till it falls into the Loire about three or four leagues below Orleans. The hand of false taste has committed on its banks those outrages which the Abbe de Lille so pathetically deprecates in those charming verses descriptive of the Seine, visiting in secret the retreat of his friend Watelet. Much as the Loiret, in its short course, suffers from injudicious ornament, yet are there spots to be found upon its banks as soothing as meditation could wish for: the curious traveller may meet with some of them where it loses itself among the mills in the neighbourhood of the villa called La Fontaine.

The walks of La Source, where it takes its rise, may, in the eyes of some people, derive an additional interest from the recollection that they were the retreat of Bolingbroke during his exile, and that here it was that his philosophical works were chiefly composed. The inscriptions of which he speaks in one of his letters to Swift descriptive of this spot, are not, I believe, now extant. The gardens have been modelled within these twenty years according to a plan evidently not dictated by the taste of the friend of Pope. W. W. In 1793 edition only.

Line 636. *majestic course*, etc. The duties upon many parts of the French rivers were so exorbitant that the poorer people, deprived of the benefit of water carriage, were obliged to transport their goods by land. W. W.

Line 655. *mighty stream.* Here Wordsworth compares the progress of the Revolution across Europe to the violent ebbing of the Biblical flood, which at the time was thought to have carved the topography of the Alps.

Page 19. GUILT AND SORROW.

Composed in 1793–94, under circumstances described in the headnote and Advertisement. See also the headnote to "We Are Seven" (p. 71). The poem was rewritten in 1795, and a version of stanzas XII–XXXIV and XXXVIII–L published in the *Lyrical Ballads* of 1798 under the title of "The Female Vagrant." The version here printed is that of 1842, when the poem was first published in its entirety.

Line 81. *And, hovering, round it often did a raven fly.* From a short MS. poem read to me when an undergraduate, by my schoolfellow and friend, Charles Farish, long since deceased. The verses were by a brother of his, a man of promising genius, who died young. W. W.

Line 122. *giant wicker.* See Caesar's description of the Druids in *The Gallic Wars*, VI, 16: "They have besides gigantic images, the limbs of which made of wickerwork they fill with living men and set on fire, and the victims perish, encompassed with the flames."

Line 199. *By Derwent's side.* The woman's story was separately published in the *Lyrical Ballads* of 1798 under the title of "The Female Vagrant."

Line 658. The far more somber tone of the 1795 poem may be judged by its concluding stanza:

They left him hung on high in iron case,
And dissolute men, unthinking and untaught,
Planted their festive booths beneath his face;
And to that spot, which idle thousands sought,
Women and children were by fathers brought;
And now some kindred sufferer driven, perchance,
That way, when into storm the sky is wrought,
Upon that swinging corpse his eye may glance
And drop, as he once dropp'd, in miserable trance.

Page 31. LINES LEFT UPON A SEAT IN A YEW-TREE.

Lines 1–4. Note the parody of eighteenth-century poetic diction, here used to suggest the pride of certain human expectations of nature.

Line 12. The individual spoken of was educated at the university, and was a man of talent and learning. W. W.

Page 33. THE BORDERERS.

Composed at Racedown and Alfoxden, in 1796 and 1797. The text here printed is that revised for publication in 1842. Wordsworth's intentions in this psychological drama are clarified by a prefatory essay on the main character, in which he sought to explain the "apparently *motiveless* actions of bad men": "If . . . I am asked what are [Oswald's] motives to the atrocity detailed in the drama? I answer: they are founded chiefly in the very constitution of his character; in his pride which borders even upon madness, in his restless disposition, in his disturbed mind, in his superstition, in irresistible propensities to embody in practical experiments his worst & most extravagant speculations, in his thoughts & in his feelings, in his general habits & his particular impulses, in his perverted reason justifying his perverted instincts. The general moral intended to be impressed by the delineation of such a character is obvious: it is to show the dangerous use which may be made of reason when a man has committed a great crime." Readers should compare Wordsworth's discussion of reason in Book X of *The Prelude*, lines 223 ff., which describes the state of mind that produced "The Borderers."

Wordsworth appended the following note to the play in 1842:

"This Dramatic Piece, as noticed in its title-page, was composed in 1795-96. It lay nearly from that time till within the last two or three months unregarded among my papers, without being mentioned even to my most intimate friends. Having, however, impressions upon my mind which made me unwilling to destroy the MS., I determined to undertake the responsibility of publishing it during my own life, rather than impose upon my successors the task of deciding its fate. Accordingly it has been revised with some care; but, as it was at first written, and is now published, without any view of its exhibition upon the stage, not the slightest alteration has been made in the conduct of the story, or the composition of the characters; above all, in respect to the two leading Persons of the Drama, I felt no inducement to make any change. The study of human nature suggests this awful truth; that as in the trials to which life subjects us, sin and crime are apt to start from their very opposite qualities, so are there no limits to the hardening of the heart and the perversion of the understanding to which they may carry their slaves. During my long residence in France, while the Revolution was rapidly advancing to its extreme of wickedness, I had frequent opportunities of being an eye-witness of this process, and it was while that knowledge was fresh upon my memory that the Tragedy of 'The Borderers' was composed." W. W.

The following motto preceded the play in its early version:

On human actions reason though you can,
It may be reason, but it is not man,
His principle of action once explore,
That instant 'tis his principle no more.
    Pope. ("Epistle to Cobham," lines 35-38)

Page 70. THE REVERIE OF POOR SUSAN.

Line 1. *Wood Street.* Like Cheapside and Lothbury (lines 7-8), a busy street in the heart of London's market district, east of St. Paul's. The thrush (line 2) "hangs" in a cage, and the "vapour" and "river" are in Susan's imagination.

Line 16. As first published in 1800, an additional stanza followed:

Poor Outcast! return — to receive thee once more
The house of thy Father will open its door,
And thou once again, in thy plain russet gown,
May'st hear the thrush sing from a tree of its own.

Page 70. THE BIRTH OF LOVE.

A translation of "L'Education de l'Amour," by the Vicomte de Segur (1756-1805).

Page 71. A NIGHT-PIECE.

One of the first poems Wordsworth composed at Alfoxden, in Somerset, where he and Dorothy moved to join Coleridge. Dorothy's journal for January 25, 1798, reproduces much of Wordsworth's language: "The sky spread over with one continuous cloud, whitened by the light of the moon, which, though her dim shape was seen, did not throw forth so strong a light as to chequer the earth with shadows. At once the clouds seemed to cleave asunder, left her in the centre of a black-blue vault. She sailed along, followed by multitudes of stars, small and bright, and sharp. Their brightness seemed concentrated (half-moon)." Wordsworth cited this poem, along with "Yew-trees," as among his best "for the imaginative power displayed."

Page 71. WE ARE SEVEN.

One of the original "Lyrical Ballads." In the Preface of 1800 Wordsworth stated that the poem sought to show "the perplexity and obscurity which in childhood attend our notion of death, or rather our utter inability to admit that notion."

Page 73. ANECDOTE FOR FATHERS.

A "Lyrical Ballad." Subtitled in 1798: "Shewing how the art of lying may be taught." In 1845 Wordsworth added the Latin motto, which records the reply of the Delphic oracle to over-eager inquisitors: "Restrain that eagerness of yours, for if you press me I shall speak falsehood." In a letter Wordsworth wrote that his intention was "to point out the injurious effects of putting inconsiderate questions to children, and urging them to give answers upon matters either uninteresting to them, or upon which they had no decided opinion."

Page 74. THE THORN.

A "Lyrical Ballad." In the Advertisement to the 1798 edition Wordsworth wrote that this poem, "as the reader will soon discover, is not supposed to be spoken in the author's own person: the character of the loquacious narrator will sufficiently shew itself in the course of the story." In 1800 he appended a much longer note:

"This Poem ought to have been preceded by an introductory Poem, which I have been prevented from writing by never having felt myself in a mood when it was probable that I should write it well. The character which I have here introduced speaking is sufficiently common. The Reader will perhaps have a general notion of it, if he has ever known a man, a Captain of a small trading vessel, for example, who being past the middle age of life, had retired upon an annuity or small independent income to some village or country town of which he was not a native, or in which he had not been accustomed to live. Such men, having little to do, become credulous and talkative from indolence; and from the same cause, and other predisposing causes by which it is probable that such men may have been affected, they are prone to superstition. On which account it appeared to me proper to select a character like this to exhibit some of the general laws by which superstition acts upon the mind. Superstitious men are almost always men of slow faculties and deep feelings; their minds are not loose, but adhesive; they have a reasonable share of imagination, by which word I mean the faculty which produces impressive effects out of simple elements; but they are utterly destitute of fancy, the power by which pleasure and surprise are excited by sudden varieties of situation and an accumulated imagery.

"It was my wish in this poem to show the manner in which such men cleave to the same ideas; and to follow the turns of passion, always different, yet not palpably different, by which their conversation is swayed. I had two objects to attain; first, to represent a picture which should not be unimpressive, yet consistent with the character that should describe it; secondly, while I adhered to the style in which such persons describe, to take care that words, which in their minds are impregnated with passion, should likewise convey passion to Readers who are not accustomed to sympathize with men feeling in that manner or using such language. It seemed to me that this might be done by calling in the assistance of Lyrical and rapid Metre. It was necessary that the Poem, to be natural, should in reality move slowly; yet I hoped that, by the aid of the metre, to those who should at all enter into the spirit of the Poem, it would appear to move quickly. The Reader will have the kindness to excuse this note, as I am sensible that an introductory Poem is necessary to give this Poem its full effect.

"Upon this occasion I will request permission to add a few words closely connected with 'The Thorn' and many other Poems in these volumes. There is a numerous class of readers who imagine that the same words cannot be repeated without tautology: this is a great error: virtual tautology is much oftener produced by using different words when the meaning is exactly the same.

Words, a Poet's words more particularly, ought to be weighed in the balance of feeling, and not measured by the space which they occupy upon paper. For the Reader cannot be too often reminded that Poetry is passion: it is the history or science of feelings; now every man must know that an attempt is rarely made to communicate impassioned feelings without something of an accompanying consciousness of the inadequateness of our own powers, or the deficiencies of language. During such efforts there will be a craving in the mind, and as long as it is unsatisfied the speaker will cling to the same words, or words of the same character. There are also various other reasons why repetition and apparent tautology are frequently beauties of the highest kind. Among the chief of these reasons is the interest which the mind attaches to words, not only as symbols of the passion, but as *things*, active and efficient, which are of themselves part of the passion. And further, from a spirit of fondness, exultation, and gratitude, the mind luxuriates in the repetition of words which appear successfully to communicate its feelings. The truth of these remarks might be shown by innumerable passages from the Bible, and from the impassioned poetry of every nation. 'Awake, awake, Deborah!' &c. Judges, chap. v, verses 12th, 27th, and part of 28th. See also the whole of that tumultuous and wonderful Poem."

Page 77. GOODY BLAKE AND HARRY GILL.
A "Lyrical Ballad." In the Advertisement of 1798, Wordsworth noted that the poem "is founded on a well-authenticated fact which happened in Warwickshire," and in the Preface of 1800 justified his use of meter in poetry by referring to it: "I wished to draw attention to the truth that the power of the human imagination is sufficient to produce such changes even in our physical nature as might almost appear miraculous. The truth is an important one; the fact (for it is a *fact*) is a valuable illustration of it. And I have the satisfaction of knowing that it has been communicated to many hundreds of people who would never have heard of it, had it not been narrated as a Ballad, and in a more impressive metre than is usual in Ballads."
Line 6. *duffle*. A coarse, thick woolen cloth. Also spelled *duffil*.
Line 39. *canty*. Cheerful, merry (Scottish dialect).

Page 79. HER EYES ARE WILD.
A "Lyrical Ballad," until 1815 entitled "The Mad Mother." In the Preface of 1800 Wordsworth described the poem as an attempt to trace "the maternal passion through many of its more subtle windings."

Page 80. SIMON LEE.
A "Lyrical Ballad," as are the two following. According to the Preface of 1800, the poem places the reader "in the way of receiving from ordinary moral sensations another and more salutary impression than we are accustomed to receive from them."

Page 83. EXPOSTULATION AND REPLY, THE TABLES TURNED.

Both "Lyrical Ballads," which arose, according to the Advertisement of 1798, "out of conversation with a friend who was somewhat unreasonably attached to modern books of moral philosophy." The friend may have been the critic William Hazlitt, who visited Wordsworth and Coleridge in the spring of 1798.

Page 84. THE COMPLAINT OF A FORSAKEN INDIAN WOMAN, THE LAST OF THE FLOCK.

Both "Lyrical Ballads." The former Wordsworth described in the Preface as an attempt to accompany "the last struggles of a human being at the approach of death, cleaving in solitude to life and society. . . ."

Page 86. THE IDIOT BOY.

A "Lyrical Ballad" that according to the Preface seeks, like "Her Eyes Are Wild," to trace the "more subtle windings" of the maternal passion. Although its humble subject attracted much criticism, Wordsworth refused to alter the poem, arguing in 1802 that "I have indeed often looked upon the conduct of fathers and mothers of the lower classes of society towards Idiots as the great triumph of the human heart. It is there that we see the strength, disinterestedness, and grandeur of love. . . .'"

Page 91. LINES . . . TINTERN ABBEY.

⸱⫯The final poem in the *Lyrical Ballads* of 1798. Wordsworth had visited the River Wye in the summer of 1793, after the solitary journey across Salisbury Plain that he recorded in "Guilt and Sorrow." His return five years later, with Dorothy at his side, provided the occasion for this poem, one of his greatest meditative lyrics. In the Preface he noted: "I have not ventured to call this Poem an Ode; but it was written with a hope that in the transitions, and the impassioned music of the versification, would be found the principal requisites of that species of composition."

Line 4. *inland murmur*. The river is not affected by the tides a few miles above Tintern. W. W.

Lines 5–8. Mary Moorman compares a passage in William Gilpin's *Observations on the River Wye* (1782): "Many of the furnaces, on the banks of the river, consume charcoal, . . . and the smoke, which is frequently seen issuing from the sides of the hills; and spreading it's [*sic*] thin veil over a part of them, beautifully breaks their lines, and unites them with the sky."

Lines 22–49. The three gifts enumerated in this passage — "sensations" (line 27), "feelings" (line 30), and a "blessed mood" (line 37) — suggest both a movement from external phenomena into profound inwardness and an ascent toward the highest functions of mind.

Lines 66–87. As Arthur Beatty was the first to emphasize, Wordsworth here assumes three stages of life: childhood (the "boyish days" of line 73), youth (recalled from his first visit to the Wye), and maturity (the present moment). In actual

fact he was not a "thoughtless" youth on his first visit, in 1793, but a young man of twenty-three.

Line 106. This line has a close resemblance to an admirable line of Young's, the exact expression of which I do not recollect. W. W. (1798). See Edward Young's *Night Thoughts* (1742–45), VI. 424–25: [The eyes] half create the wondrous world they see,/Our senses, as our reason, are divine."

Line 113. *Genial spirits*. "Genial" means "conducive to growth" as well as "native."

Line 152. *A worshipper of Nature*. To some readers this phrase has suggested that Wordsworth was a pantheist, which he himself stoutly denied. "She talks of my being a worshipper of Nature — a passionate expression uttered incautiously in the Poem upon the Wye has led her into this mistake — she reading in cold-heartedness and substituting the letter for the spirit" [from a letter of 1814].

Page 93. THE OLD CUMBERLAND BEGGAR.

Composed in February–March 1798, although the opening description (lines 1–66) dates from 1797 or earlier (and was originally linked to "Animal Tranquillity and Decay," p. 96). The poem attacks the institution of the workhouse (line 179), which by the later eighteenth century had become a common means of providing "support" to the vagrant poor. The headnote refers to the Amended Poor Law of 1834, which not only sanctioned the workhouses but sought to render them as unattractive as possible, in order to discourage pauperism. See Wordsworth's discussion in the Postscript of 1835, pp. 817–20.

Line 57. Cited by Wordsworth in the course of a discussion of metrical irregularity as "the most dislocated line I know of in my writings. . . . The words to which the passion is at[tached?] are 'white road' and 'same line,' and the verse dislocates [for the] sake of these. This will please or displease by the quantity of feeling excited by the image, to those in whom it excites [such? much?] feeling, as in one it will be musical, to others not." See his similar argument in the Preface of 1800, p. 796.

Page 96. PETER BELL.

Like "The Idiot Boy," this poem was much criticized on its publication in 1819 for the vulgarity of its subject; it was parodied by Shelley and John Hamilton Reynolds, the friend of Keats. See Wordsworth's sonnet in its defense, "On the Detraction which Followed the Publication of a certain Poem" (p. 574).

PART FIRST. Line 11. *A Potter*. In the dialect of the North, a hawker of earthenware is thus designated. W. W.

Page 109. THE SIMPLON PASS.

A recollection of the walking tour of 1790; also found in *The Prelude*, VI.621–640.

Pages 110, 111. INFLUENCE OF NATURAL OBJECTS, THERE WAS A BOY.

Also in *The Prelude*, I.401–463, and V.364–388. The last two lines of the latter, Coleridge wrote, "I should have recognized anywhere; and had I met these lines running wild in the deserts of Arabia, I should have instantly screamed out, 'Wordsworth'!" In the Preface of 1815, Wordsworth interpreted "There Was a Boy": ". . . in the series of Poems placed under the head of Imagination, I have begun with one of the earliest processes of Nature in the development of this faculty. Guided by one of my own primary consciousnesses, I have represented a commutation and transfer of internal feelings, co-operating with external accidents to plant, for immortality, images of sound and sight, in the celestial soil of the Imagination. The Boy, there introduced, is listening, with something of a feverish and restless anxiety, for the recurrence of the riotous sounds which he had previously excited; and, at the moment when the intenseness of his mind is beginning to remit, he is surprized into a perception of the solemn and tranquillizing images which the Poem describes."

Page 112. "Strange Fits of Passion Have I Known."
The first of the five "Lucy poems," all but one of which were composed in Germany in the winter of 1798–99. Lucy has never been satisfactorily identified; the name was common in the sentimental poetry of the later eighteenth century, and perhaps Coleridge was right in supposing that the "sublime epitaph" of "A Slumber Did My Spirit Seal" was written "in some gloomier moment [when] he had fancied the moment in which his Sister might die."
Line 28. In the earliest manuscript this final stanza follows:

I told her this: her laughter light
Is ringing in my ears:
And when I think upon that night
My eyes are dim with tears.

Page 112. "She Dwelt among the Untrodden Ways"
Line 1. In the earliest manuscript this stanza is preceded by:

My hope was one, from cities far,
Nursed on a lonesome heath;
Her lips were red as roses are,
Her hair a woodbine wreath.

Line 8. In the earliest manuscript this stanza is followed by:

And she was graceful as the broom
That flowers by Carron's side;
But slow distemper checked her bloom,
And on the Heath she died.

Line 9. This stanza ran as follows in the earliest manuscript:

Long time before her head lay low
Dead to the world was she:
But now she's in her grave, and, oh,
The difference to me!

Page 112. "I Travelled among Unknown Men."
Composed in 1801, two years after the other Lucy poems; the headnote is inaccurate.

Page 113. "Three Years She Grew in Sun and Shower."
Line 37. *The work was done.* Lucy becomes the woman Nature prophesied; she is not a child when she dies.

Page 114. Address to the Scholars of the Village School of _____.
This and the three following poems reflect Wordsworth's affectionate memory of William Taylor, his headmaster at the Hawkshead Grammar School. See *Prelude*, X.534.

Page 118. Lucy Gray.
The child of this poem should not be confused with the woman of the Lucy poems.

Page 123. "Bleak Season Was It."
This and the following extract from *The Recluse* were first published in 1851, in Christopher Wordsworth's *Memoirs* of his uncle. Where the 1851 text departs from the poet's manuscripts, I have followed the latter.

Page 124. The Prelude.
Begun in 1798 as a series of blank-verse "pictures" of Wordsworth's boyhood, the poem was composed during the next seven years and completed in May 1805. Wordsworth revised the poem repeatedly during the next forty-five years, altering its style more than its content. But he never published it, feeling perhaps that such a "prelude" required a greater work that might justify its apparent egotism. "An alarming length!" he wrote to his friend and patron Beaumont in 1805, "and a thing unprecedented in Literary history that a man should talk so much about himself. It is not self-conceit, as you will know well, that has induced [me] to do this, but real humility; I began the work because I was unprepared to treat any more arduous subject and diffident of my own powers. Here at least I hoped that to a certain degree I should be sure of succeeding, as I had nothing to do but describe what I had felt and thought. . . ." The title, subtitle, and advertisement were added by Mary Wordsworth when she published the poem in 1850, shortly after Wordsworth's death.
The Prelude may be read as a straightforward autobiography, a narrative of private and public events at a revolutionary moment in western history. But it is much more: in describing what he "felt and thought" Wordsworth traces and confirms the goodness that attends on the natural and yet mysterious growth of the human mind and spirit in time. He celebrates not only the contributions of external nature to this process, but the powers of the growing mind itself, which offer the hope of victory over loss and despair. As Stephen Gill has pointed out, the poem is also a "sensitive record of Wordsworth's growth during the years of the poem's composition,"

years in which he began to question and modify his dedication to nature, so evident in the early books, in order to proclaim the power of the mature imagination. Perhaps the finest comment on the poem was the first — Coleridge's response, in 1806, to his first hearing of the completed work. "That lay," he called it,

More than historic, that prophetic lay
Wherein (high theme by thee first sung aright)
Of the foundations and the building up
Of a Human Spirit thou hast dared to tell
What may be told . . .
                    An Orphic song indeed,
A song divine of high and passionate thoughts
To their own music chaunted!

The present text is that of 1850. In the following cases, however, I have followed Professor Stillinger in preferring late manuscript readings to the printed text: I.327, *Roved* for *moved*; I.371, *for* for *far*; IV.51, *froward* for *famous*; VI.31, *more* for *now*; VI.65, *admire* for *achieve*; VII.747, *Indian. On* for *Indian, on*; X.304, *wear* for *wean*; X.407, *forced* for *fond*; XI.107, *we* for *us*.

Advertisement. In quoting the Preface to *The Excursion*, Mary Wordsworth perpetuated the poet's somewhat misleading account of the genesis of this poem. As is evident from the first book of *The Prelude*, and from the letters and poems of 1798, Wordsworth's "determination to compose a philosophical Poem, . . . *The Recluse*," was not an outgrowth of his work on *The Prelude*. It was rather his high hopes for *The Recluse* and his inability to realize them in 1798 that inspired the more workable inventory of his poetic powers that became *The Prelude*.

Book First. Lines 1–45. As the late John Finch demonstrated, this "glad preamble" and the following account of Wordsworth's solitary journey to a "chosen Vale" describe his visit, in the fall of 1799, to the Vale of Grasmere, where he was shortly to settle with Dorothy. Details in the passage reflect earlier escapes from urban to pastoral life: from London to Dorset in 1795, and from Goslar, Germany, in the spring of 1799.

Line 14. *The earth is all before me.* Cf. *Paradise Lost* (XII.646): "The world was all before them, where to choose/Their place of rest." The first of many allusions to Milton's epic poem.

Line 46. *Friend.* Coleridge, who did not hear the completed poem until he returned from Malta in 1806.

Line 96. *Æolian visitations.* Wordsworth compares his soul (line 95) to a windharp, or Aeolian harp (from Aeolus, ancient god of the winds).

Line 187. *Mithridates.* King of Pontus, who warred on Rome until his defeat by Pompey in 66 B.C.

Line 189. *Odin.* De Selincourt cites Gibbon, who describes the flight of this supposed contemporary of Mithridates northward into Sweden, "with the great design of forming . . . a religion and a people which . . . might be subservient to his immortal revenge."

Line 191. *Sertorius*, democratic governor of Spain, who opposed the Roman dictator Sulla. After his murder in 72 B.C., according to legend, his followers escaped to the Canary Islands, where their descendants survived until a great plague in 1494. De Selincourt cites the account in Plutarch's *Lives*, where Wordsworth also found the story of Mithridates.

Line 206. *Frenchman.* "Dominique de Gourgues, a French gentleman who went in 1568 to Florida to avenge the massacre of the French by the Spaniards there" [Note, 1850].

Line 212. *Gustavus.* Gustavus I of Sweden (1496–1560), who in 1520 liberated his country from Danish rule.

Line 214. *Wallace.* William Wallace (ca. 1270–1305), who led Scottish opposition to English domination until he was executed in 1305.

Line 270. *the fairest of all rivers.* The River Derwent, which flows past the garden of the Wordsworth house in Cockermouth. The following scenes from Wordsworth's childhood were composed in late 1798, and mark the inception of the poem.

Line 283. *towers.* Cockermouth Castle, the ruins of which overlook the town of Cockermouth. See "Address from the Spirit of Cockermouth Castle," p. 707.

Line 295. *Skiddaw.* A prominent mountain in the north of the Lake District, near Keswick.

Line 304. *that beloved Vale.* The Vale of Esthwaite, where Wordsworth was sent, in 1787, to attend the Hawkshead Grammar School.

Line 310. *springes.* Snares.

Line 357. *One summer evening.* The following episode offers a memorable example of Wordsworth's theme: the joint contribution of mind and nature to the building of the mind.

Line 380. *Upreared its head.* The boy rows facing the stern of his skiff; as he moves out from shore, the more distant peak rises from behind the nearer ridge, and every stroke of his oars seems to bring it higher and closer.

Line 450. *reflex.* Reflection.

Line 437. *The pack loud chiming.* The game of "hare and hounds."

Line 511. *With crosses and with cyphers.* Tick-tack-toe.

Line 514. *Snow-white deal.* Norway spruce, from which one of the tables was made.

Line 516. *Loo or Whist.* Card games. The following description deliberately evokes memories of the game of Ombre in Pope's *Rape of the Lock* (III.27ff).

Line 539. *Knaves.* Jacks.

Line 545. *extrinsic passion.* Feelings, that is, which are extrinsic to the "forms" of nature but nevertheless associated with them by the growing mind. Throughout this book and part of the next Wordsworth is concerned with the unconscious and "collateral" impression made by nature on the mind of a boy conscious only of "boyish sport" (II.53).

Book Second. Line 56. *Windermere.* The largest of the lakes in the Lake District.

Line 103. *that large Abbey.* Furness Abbey, some twenty miles from Hawkshead.

Line 203. *For her own sake.* The boy's love of nature now becomes conscious.

Line 214. *succedaneum.* An inferior substitute.

Line 279. *props of my affections.* An obscure reference, perhaps to Wordsworth's parents, more probably to the sports and games that had hitherto provided the conscious motives of the boy's intercourse with nature.

Line 333. *a Friend.* John Fleming, Wordsworth's classmate at the Hawkshead School.

BOOK THIRD. Line 16. *Cam.* The river that winds through the town of Cambridge.

Line 46. *St. John.* Wordsworth entered St. John's College on October 30, 1787. Next to St. John's, and visible from his bedroom window, stands Trinity College (line 53).

Line 278. *Mill.* Near Cambridge, the scene of Chaucer's "Reeve's Tale."

Line 479. *Bucer . . . Melancthon.* Classical scholars of the Renaissance.

BOOK FOURTH. Line 13. *Ferryman.* A ferry still takes passengers across Windermere to the road that leads to Hawkshead.

Line 21. *snow-white church.* The Norman Church at Hawkshead, which dates from the twelfth century, was whitewashed in Wordsworth's day.

Line 28. *my old Dame.* Ann Tyson, with whom Wordsworth boarded while a student at Hawkshead School. Her cottage, in the hamlet of Colthouse, still stands.

Line 120. *talking to itself.* Wordsworth habitually composed aloud, while walking.

Line 245. *those fair Seven.* The Pleiades, or Seven Sisters.

Lines 323–338. Although often called the "dedication" episode, this famous passage describes a dedication that is neither conscious nor devoted, necessarily, to poetry.

Line 328. *Grain-tinctured.* Scarlet or crimson. De Selincourt compares Milton's "skie-tinctur'd grain" (*Paradise Lost*, V.285).

Line 373. *Winander.* Another name for Windermere.

Lines 379–469. The description of the meeting with the discharged soldier was composed in early 1798, and is thus one of the earliest parts of the poem.

BOOK FIFTH. Line 51. *studious friend.* Probably Coleridge.

Line 60. I read while at school all Fielding's works, *Don Quixote*, *Gil Blas*, *Gulliver's Travels*, and the *Tale of the Tub*. W. W.

Line 70. *a dream.* The following dream, as Janet Smyser pointed out, was derived from a dream dreamed by Descartes in 1619, and probably related to Wordsworth by Coleridge.

Line 166. A major division in the poem: Wordsworth here turns from the theme of Books I–IV, the shaping power of nature, to the complementary power of books and human culture.

Line 257. *My honoured Mother.* Wordsworth's mother died in 1778, when he was eight.

Line 364. *There was a boy.* See the notes to this episode, which was published separately, on p. 111 and pp. 831–32.

Line 561. *a dear friend.* John Fleming of Rayrigg.

BOOK SIXTH. Line 6. *Granta's cloisters.* Cambridge (Granta is a name for the River Cam).

Line 48. *this very week.* The first week of April 1804. "The Intimations ode, in which life's morning radiance *has* left the hills, was completed perhaps only a week or two earlier" (Stillinger).

Line 180. *Bard.* James Thomson, in *The Castle of Indolence* (1748).

Line 192. *That streamlet.* The River Dove in Derbyshire, which Wordsworth visited during the summer vacation of 1788.

Line 204. *Emont.* This river winds past the ruins of Brougham Castle, which Wordsworth visited with Dorothy and Mary Hutchinson (line 224) during his summer vacations.

Line 208. *Sidney.* Sir Philip Sidney, Elizabethan courtier and poet, who dedicated his *Arcadia* to his sister. Though appropriate to Wordsworth's subject, the tradition of Sidney's visit to Brougham Castle is (as de Selincourt points out) probably inaccurate.

Lines 208, 209. *Helvellyn, Cross-fell.* Mountains visible from the castle.

Line 240. Coleridge left the Lake District in January 1804 and sailed for Malta in April.

Line 251. *Etesian.* A north wind that cools the Mediterranean in summer.

Lines 266–274. A blue-coat-boy at Christ's Hospital, London. "Come back into memory as thou wert in the day-spring of thy fancies, Samuel Taylor Coleridge, logician, metaphysician, bard! How I have seen the casual passer through the cloisters stand still, entranced . . . while the walls of the old Grey Friars re-echoed to the accents of the *inspired charity boy!*" — Charles Lamb [G].

Line 271. *To shut thine eyes.* Wordsworth alludes to Coleridge's poems on his childhood, the "Sonnet to the River Otter" and "Frost at Midnight," and in the following lines to his friend's difficulties — financial, scholastic, and romantic — in his early life.

Lines 322 ff. In the following lines Wordsworth again describes the walking tour of 1790, but from a point of view far different from that in *Descriptive Sketches*.

Line 323. *Friend.* Robert Jones, a Cambridge classmate and lifelong friend.

Line 346. *That great federal day.* July 14, the first anniversary of the fall of the Bastille. "We went staff in hand, without knapsacks, and carrying each his needments tied up in a pocket handkerchief, with about twenty pounds apiece in our pockets. We crossed from Dover and landed at Calais on the eve of the day when the king was to swear fidelity to the new constitution. . . ." W. W. ("Autobiographical Memoranda").

Line 418. *Convent of the Chartreuse.* A Carthusian monastery high in the foothills of the French Alps. It was occupied by the Revolutionary Army in 1792.

Line 436. *St. Bruno's.* A forest near the monastery.

Line 439. *Streams of Life and Death.* "Names of rivers near the Chartreuse." W. W. (note to *Descriptive Sketches*).

Line 480. *Vallombre.* A valley near the monastery.

Line 484. *Cross of Jesus.* "Alluding to crosses seen on the tops of the spiry rocks of the Chartreuse which have every appearance of being inaccessible." W. W. (note to *Descriptive Sketches*).

Line 563. The Simplon Pass, which links Switzerland and Italy, was in 1790 crossed by a mule track.

Line 592. *Imagination — here the Power.* This impassioned interruption of the narrative, it should be noted, occurs during the writing of the poem, as the poet reflects on the significance of the disappointment of 1790.

Line 638. *Great Apocalypse.* The Revelation of St. John. In the desolate sublimity of this gorge Wordsworth may have seen geological evidence of the Flood, and thus of the power and wrath of God. "Among the more awful scenes of the Alps," he wrote to Dorothy in 1790, "I had not a thought of man, or a single created being; my whole soul was turned to him who produced the terrible majesty before me."

Line 655. *Locarno's Lake.* Wordsworth and Jones descended to the town of Locarno, on Lago Maggiore, then crossed to Lake Como, and the town of Gravedona (line 700).

Line 764. *Brabant armies.* Belgian revolutionary troops.

BOOK SEVENTH. Line 1. *Six . . . years.* Wordsworth is writing in the fall of 1804; he looks back to the fall of 1799, when he composed the "glad preamble" (in the 1804 version he writes, accurately, "five years").

Line 61. The following memories of London date not only from the months following Wordsworth's graduation from Cambridge, in 1791, but from earlier and later visits, especially that after he returned from France in 1793.

Line 81. *Alcairo.* Cairo.

Line 112. Dick Whittington (died 1423), hero of the folktale and thrice Lord Mayor of London.

Line 121. *Vauxhall and Ranelagh.* London pleasure gardens.

Lines 130 ff. Famous London landmarks: St. Paul's Cathedral, Westminster Abbey, Gog and Magog (giants of the Guildhall), Bedlam (or Bethlehem) Hospital for the insane, the Monument of the fire of 1666, and the Tower of London.

Line 174. *Raree-show.* A peepshow.

Line 193. *files of ballads.* Printed ballads hung on a string for sale.

Line 227. *Lascars.* East Indian sailors.

Line 267. *Sadler's Wells.* A popular theater in the suburbs.

Lines 283–4. From Milton's *Samson Agonistes*, lines 87–89.

Line 288. *Hamlet*, III.ii.23.

Line 297. *Buttermere.* A lake and town in the Lake District. The story of Mary, "Maid of Buttermere," was made into a popular play, but Wordsworth had seen her before her notoriety, probably in 1799. Mary's seducer, the "Spoiler," was hanged at Carlisle in 1803.

Line 406. Sarah Siddons, the famous actress (1755–1831).

Line 498. See *Henry V*, IV.iii.51–55.

Lines 512 ff. Edmund Burke, statesman and author (1729–1797). This appreciation of the conservative politician was added to *The Prelude* in 1820 or after.

Line 564. *The Death of Abel.* Salomon Gessner's popular poem, published in 1758. *The Bard.* Edward Young, author of *Night Thoughts* (1742–45).

Line 568. *Morven.* A Scottish mountain named in James MacPherson's forged Ossianic poems (1760–63).

Line 676. *the Fair.* Bartholomew's Fair, held in Wordsworth's time on the four days following September 3.

BOOK EIGHTH. Lines 48–52. From *Malvern Hills* by Joseph Cottle (1770–1853), the first publisher of the *Lyrical Ballads*.

Line 77. *Gehol.* Site of the garden of the Emperor of China.

Lines 129–44. To the actual rural life of Westmorland Wordsworth contrasts various examples of legendary and literary pastoral: the golden age of Saturn, the Arcadia of Hellenic literature, the romantic countryside of Shakespeare's Arden (in *As You Like It*) and Bohemia (in *The Winter's Tale*), and perhaps Book VI of Spenser's *Faerie Queene*.

Lines 175, 180, 182. *Galesus, Clitumnus, Lucretilus.* Two rivers and a hill in Italy, celebrated in Latin pastoral poetry.

Line 215. *Hercynian forest.* Roman name for vast forests in western Germany.

Lines 285–287. *Corin, Phyllis.* Types of shepherd and shepherdess in literary pastoral.

Line 459. *Thrustonmere.* A name for Coniston-water, a lake near Hawkshead.

Lines 562–64. *Antiparos; Yordas.* A Greek island; a cave near Ingleton in Yorkshire.

BOOK NINTH. Line 40. *a pleasant town.* Orleans.

Lines 45–48. Each of the places named, which span Paris from west to east and north to south, was associated with the Revolution.

Line 49. *National Synod, Jacobins.* The meeting places, respectively, of the National Assembly and the radical Jacobin Club.

Line 52. *Arcades.* The Palais Royale.

Line 77. *Magdalene.* A famous painting by Charles Le Brun (1616–90).

Line 123. *Patriot.* A supporter of the Revolutionary regime, a Republican.

Line 176. *Carra, Gorsas.* Journalists of Republican sympathies.

Line 183. *emigrants.* Supporters of the king who had fled the country.

Line 288. *one.* Michel Beaupuy.

Lines 392–93. *Rotha, Greta, Derwent.* Streams in the English Lake District.

Line 398. *nature.* Human nature, as Stillinger points out.

Line 409. *Dion.* Pupil of Plato and a model of the philosopher-king, who deposed Dionysis, tyrant of Syracuse, in 357 B.C. See "Dion," p. 527.

Lines 451, 453. *Angelica, Erminia.* Heroines of two famous Italian romantic epics: Ludovico

Ariosto's *Orlando Furioso* (1532) and Torquato Tasso's *Gerusalemme Liberata* (1581).

Line 547. *a tale.* In the version of 1805 Wordsworth continued this story of "youthful lovers"; in 1820 he published it separately (see p. 327).

BOOK TENTH. Line 1. Wordsworth left the Loire in late October 1792.

Lines 12 ff. The King was deposed and imprisoned on August 10; Royalist forces entered France shortly after, bent on his restoration, but were defeated by Republican troops at Valmy, on September 20.

Line 36. *the baffled League.* Austria and Prussia, allied against France.

Line 41. France assumed the title of Republic on September 21, 1792.

Line 73. *September massacres.* In the first week of September an angry crowd seized and murdered over a thousand Royalist suspects.

Line 87. *"Sleep no more."* See *Macbeth*, II.ii.34.

Line 111. On October 29 Jean Baptiste Louvet accused Robespierre, leader of the radical left, of crimes against the state, but a week later Robespierre's defense carried the day.

Lines 198, 199. *Harmodius, Aristogiton.* Athenian noblemen who died leading a rebellion against the tyrants of Athens in 514 B.C. As a schoolboy Wordsworth translated a song in their honor.

Line 247. *onset.* Unsuccessful attempts in 1788 and 1792 to pass a bill abolishing slavery.

Line 264. England declared war on France on February 11, 1793.

Line 315. *red-cross flag.* The Union Jack. Wordsworth spent a month during the summer of 1793 on the Isle of Wight, from which he could see the fleet anchored in the Solent Estuary. See his Advertisement to "Guilt and Sorrow," p. 20.

Line 356. *Domestic carnage.* The Reign of Terror (October 1793–July 1794).

Line 381. *wife of Roland.* Her last words before she was guillotined were addressed to a statue representing Liberty: "O Liberty, what crimes are committed in your name!"

Line 430. *second love.* His love of man, which in the following lines is contrasted with his first love, of nature.

Line 498. *Arras.* A reminiscence of Wordsworth's visit to the town during the walking tour of 1790. It was Robespierre's birthplace.

Line 512. *The day.* Robespierre was executed on July 28, 1794; the news reached Wordsworth as he crossed the Leven estuary in Cumberland, around August 20.

Line 534. *teacher.* William Taylor (1754–86), Wordsworth's headmaster at the Hawkshead Grammar School from 1781 to 1786.

BOOK ELEVENTH. Line 62. The following lines allude to repressive measures taken by the administration of William Pitt, such as the suspension of the Habeas Corpus Act (1794), which permitted the government to imprison political suspects without trial.

Lines 74 ff. Wordsworth now surveys the events of 1792–93 from a more personal and subjective standpoint.

Lines 105–144. This passage was first published in Coleridge's periodical, *The Friend*, on October 26, 1809, under the title "French Revolution, as it appeared to Enthusiasts at its Commencement" (p. 340).

Line 189. *wild theories.* Rationalistic schemes that "promised to abstract the hopes of Man/Out of his feelings" (lines 225–26), including perhaps those of William Godwin, whose *Enquiry Concerning Political Justice* was published in February 1793.

Line 206. By the fall of 1794 French aggression was evident in Spain, Italy, and Holland.

Line 283. *some dramatic tale.* What follows looks forward to the first four books of *The Excursion*, as Stillinger suggests, and also backward to the situation of Marmaduke in *The Borderers.*

Line 305. An important moment in the history of Wordsworth's growth, as he gives up, "in despair," a central assumption of classical and Enlightenment humanism — that the reason can ascertain human moral responsibility.

Line 328. *abstract science.* In 1805 Wordsworth specified "mathematics," probably thinking in particular of geometry.

Line 333. Wordsworth was briefly reunited with Dorothy in the spring of 1794, but he probably refers to their permanent reunion in the fall of 1795, when they settled in Dorset.

Line 359. *a Pope.* Napoleon crowned himself emperor, in the presence of Pope Pius VII, on December 2, 1804.

Lines 377 ff. Coleridge spent the fall of 1804 in Sicily.

Line 379. *Timoleon.* After deposing the tyrant Dionysius in 343 B.C., Timoleon established a democratic regime in Syracuse.

Line 420. *Enna.* See *Paradise Lost*, IV.268–71.

Lines 434–35. *Empedocles, Archimedes.* Philosopher and scientist, respectively, of classical Sicily.

Line 437. *Theocritus.* Sicilian pastoral poet, who flourished in the third century B.C. Comates (line 444) appears in his seventh *Idyll.*

Line 465. *Arethuse.* A legendary fountain in Sicily.

BOOK TWELFTH. Lines 106 ff. The following confession of transgressions against nature looks back not only to the effects of the French Revolution, and the suffering it caused Wordsworth, but to the fashionable cult of the picturesque (the "strong infection" of line 113) and to the psychological dominance of the eye (see "Tintern Abbey," lines 81–83).

Line 151. *a maid.* Probably Mary Hutchinson, Wordsworth's wife.

Lines 208–225. A passage of central significance, in which Wordsworth seeks to celebrate and explain the power of remembered experience to restore the mind in present time. The explanation given here — that remembered "spots of time" illustrate the mind's transcendence of "outward sense" — was added in 1804 to an earlier draft that conceded far more power to the external natural world. Compare lines 142–43 of the Immortality Ode, p. 355, which were also written in 1804.

Line 287. This incident occurred in December 1783, as Wordsworth waited for the horses that would carry him and his brothers from Hawkshead to Cockermouth for the Christmas vacation. His father died on December 30.

BOOK THIRTEENTH. Line 22. *right reason.* In reaffirming his faith in the human reason Wordsworth redefines it, drawing a distinction between the mathematical and demonstrative reason, the failure of which he traced in Book XI, and a higher reason that he here finds embodied in natural law, and later identifies with love and the imagination (XIV.198ff.).

Lines 64 ff. Wordsworth here turns from theoretical appraisals of human nature to experience: the men and women he saw and talked to in the English countryside.

Lines 232 ff. An eloquent statement of the faith and ambition that led to the composition of the *Lyrical Ballads.*

Line 314. *Sarum's Plain.* Salisbury Plain, across which Wordsworth had wandered alone in the summer of 1793.

Line 320. The following complementary visions of primitive barbarity and science appear as well in the first version of the poem Wordsworth composed at the time, "Guilt and Sorrow."

BOOK FOURTEENTH. Line 3. *Cambria.* Wales.

Line 4. *Bethgelert.* A village at the southern foot of Mt. Snowdon, which Wordsworth climbed in the summer of 1791.

Line 44. *this still ocean.* The "sea" of mist, by means of which nature transforms itself, elevating human response — as is suggested by the echo in the preceding line of Milton's account of the creation (*Paradise Lost,* VII.285–287). In the following passage Wordsworth will compare such natural self-transformation to the analogous power of the human imagination over nature.

Line 67. *a majestic intellect.* The human mind, ideally conceived.

Line 245. See *Paradise Lost,* IX.489–91.

Line 267. *One.* Mary Hutchinson.

Line 355. *Calvert.* Raisley Calvert, a youth who on his death in 1795 left Wordsworth a legacy of £900. "The act," Wordsworth later wrote, "was done entirely from a confidence on his part that I had powers and attainments which might be of use to mankind." The printer of the 1850 edition omitted the following two lines after 358:

Withdrawing, and from kindred whom he loved,
A part of no redundant patrimony, did

Line 395. *That summer.* The spring and summer of 1798, when both poets lived near the Quantock hills in Somerset.

Lines 400 ff. Wordsworth alludes to poems composed in 1798: Coleridge's "Ancient Mariner" and "Christabel" and his own "Idiot Boy" and "Thorn."

Line 419. *private grief.* The death of his brother John on February 5, 1805.

Page 222. THE RECLUSE.
Intended as the first book of Part I of Wordsworth's grand philosophical poem, *The Recluse,* "Home at Grasmere" was first published in 1888.

Although parts of the poem were probably composed in 1800, shortly after the retirement to Grasmere it describes, the late John Finch has demonstrated that the earliest surviving manuscripts very probably date from 1806.

Line 1. *barrier.* Probably Red Bank, a ridge from which a walker from Hawkshead would first look down on the vale of Grasmere.

Lines 71–97, 110–25, 152–67, 203–29. Published separately; see pp. 123, 401, and notes.

Lines 152 ff. Wordsworth recounts his and Dorothy's journey, in December 1799, to Grasmere from the Hutchinson's farm at Sockburn-on-Tees, Yorkshire.

Line 655. *Pilgrim of the Sea.* John, Wordsworth's brother.

Line 658. *Sisters.* The Hutchinson sisters, Mary and Sara.

Line 659. *Brother.* Coleridge.

Lines 754–860. Offered as a "Prospectus" to *The Excursion* in 1814, this passage is perhaps Wordsworth's most ambitious and eloquent discourse on poetry.

Line 776. *fit audience.* See *Paradise Lost,* VII.30–31.

Lines 799–824. Wordsworth claims a more lofty and inclusive subject matter than Milton. See *Paradise Lost,* I.14–16.

Line 819. The poet William Blake disagreed strongly with this line: "You shall not," he wrote in the margin, "bring me down to believe such fitting & fitted I know better & Please your Lordship."

Line 824. *high argument. Paradise Lost,* I.24.

Line 850. *The transitory Being.* Wordsworth himself.

Page 232. THE BROTHERS.
One of several "pastorals" Wordsworth composed for the volume of 1800. For Wordsworth's purpose in the poem, see the note to "Michael," below.

Line 16. *Ennerdale.* A vale in the Lake District.

Lines 143–45. The impressive circumstance here described, actually took place some years ago in this country, upon an eminence called Kidstow Pike, one of the highest of the mountains that surround Hawes-water. The summit of the Pike was stricken by lightning; and every trace of one of the fountains disappeared, while the other continued to flow as before. W. W. (note to 1800–1805 editions).

Lines 182–83. There is not anything more worthy of remark in the manners of the inhabitants of these mountains, than the tranquillity, I might say indifference, with which they think and talk upon the subject of death. Some of the country church-yards, as here described, do not contain a single tombstone, and most of them have a very small number. W. W. (note to 1800 edition).

Line 310, *the Great Gavel . . . Leeza.* The Great Gavel, so called, I imagine, from its resemblance to the gable end of a house, is one of the highest of the Cumberland Mountains. It stands at the head of the several vales of Ennerdale, Wastdale, and Borrowdale. The Leeza is a river which flows into the lake of Ennerdale: on issuing from the Lake, it changes its name, and is called the End, Eyne, or Enna. It falls into the Sea a little below Egremont. W. W.

Page 238. MICHAEL.

Wordsworth described the purpose of this poem and "The Brothers" in a letter of 1801 to Charles James Fox, the leader of the Whig party: "I have attempted to draw a picture of the domestic affections as I know they exist amongst a class of men who are now almost confined to the North of England. They are small independent proprietors of land here called statesmen, men of respectable education who daily labour on their own little properties." Noting that this class was rapidly disappearing, and that Fox had worked in Parliament to save it, Wordsworth continued: "The poems are faithful copies from nature; and I hope . . . you will at least be able to perceive that they may excite profitable sympathies in many kind and good hearts, and may in some small degree enlarge our feelings of reverence for our species, and our knowledge of human nature. . . . I thought, at a time when these feelings are sapped in so many ways that the two poems might co-operate, however feebly, with the illustrious efforts which you have made to stem this and other evils with which the country is labouring. . . ."

Line 2. *Greenhead Ghyll.* A desolate mountain valley to the east of Grasmere, in which a ruined sheepfold still stands.

Line 169. *Clipping Tree.* Clipping is the word used in the north of England for shearing. W. W.

Line 258. The story alluded to here is well known in the country. The chapel is called Ings Chapel; and is on the right-hand side of the road leading from Kendal to Ambleside. W. W. (note to 1800–1805 editions).

Line 324. *Sheep-fold.* It may be proper to inform some readers, that a sheep-fold in these mountains is an unroofed building of stone walls, with different divisions. It is generally placed by the side of a brook, for the convenience of washing the sheep; but it is also useful as a shelter for them, and as a place to drive them into, to enable the shepherds conveniently to single out one or more for any particular purpose. W. W. (note to 1800–1805 editions).

Page 244. THE IDLE SHEPHERD-BOYS.

Headnote. *Mrs. Barbauld.* Anna Letitia Barbauld (1743-1825), popular poet and essayist.

The poem is set below the Langdale Pikes; Dungeon-Ghyll Force is a mountain torrent that descends from them into Langdale.

Page 247. I. "IT WAS AN APRIL MORNING: FRESH AND CLEAR."

Line 39. *Emma.* Wordsworth's sister, Dorothy, as in several other poems.

Page 248. II. TO JOANNA.

Joanna was Mary Hutchinson's youngest sister. The poem is a study of the imagination, as Wordsworth suggests in a note recorded by de

Selincourt: "The poem supposes that at the Rock something had taken place in my mind either then, or afterwards in thinking upon what then took place which, if related, will cause the Vicar to smile. . . . I begin to relate the story, meaning in a certain degree to divert or partly play upon the Vicar. I begin — my mind partly forgets its purpose, being softened by the images of beauty in the description of the rock, and the delicious morning, and when I come to the 2 lines 'The Rock like something' *etc.*, I am caught in the trap of my own imagination. I entirely lose sight of my first purpose. I take fire in the lines 'that ancient woman.' I go on in that strain of fancy 'Old Skiddaw' and terminate the description in tumult 'And Kirkstone' *etc.* . . . When the description is closed, or perhaps partly before I waken from the dream and see that the Vicar thinks I have been exaggerating, as I intended he should, I then tell the story as it happened really; and as the recollection of it exists permanently and regularly in my mind. . . . The poem then concludes in a strain of deep tenderness."

Lines 56–65. *That ancient Woman.* From one angle there appears to be an old woman seated on this crag above Grasmere. The heights of Hammar-scar, Silver-how, Loughrigg, and Fairfield also overlook Grasmere. Helvellyn, Skiddaw, Glaramara, and Kirkstone stand at greater (and more improbable) distances.

Page 249. III. "THERE IS AN EMINENCE." The

"eminence" is Stone-Arthur, on the east of the road leading over Dunmail Raise, and is between Greenhead Ghyll and Tongue Ghyll [G].

Page 250. V. To M. H.

To Mary Hutchinson, two years before our marriage. W. W.

Page 251. THE WATERFALL AND THE EGLANTINE.

There are three roads from Grasmere to Rydal: one, a footpath under Nab Scar, which Dr. [Thomas] Arnold called "Old Corruption;" a second over White Moss Common, which he called "Bit by Bit Reform;" and a third, the coach road by the lake-side, "Radical Reform." It is by the first of these roads that the scene of this poem is laid. Eglantines still grow there, though not abundantly [G].

Page 253. HART-LEAP WELL.

Wordsworth mentions the visit to Hartleap Well in one version of "Home at Grasmere":

> And when the trance
> Came to us, as we stood by Hart-leap Well,
> The intimation of the milder day
> Which is to be, the fairer world than this,
> And rais'd us up, dejected as we were,
> Among the records of that doleful place,
> By sorrow for the hunted Beast who there
> Had yielded up his breath, the awful trance
> The vision of humanity, and of God
> The Mourner, God the Sufferer, when the heart
> Of his poor Creatures suffers wrongfully —.

Page 256. " 'TIS SAID, THAT SOME HAVE DIED FOR LOVE."
More distantly than the Lucy poems, this may contemplate the possibility of Dorothy's death.

Page 257. THE CHILDLESS FATHER.
Line 10. *funeral basin*. In several parts of the North of England, when a funeral takes place, a basin full of sprigs of boxwood is placed at the door of the house from which the coffin is taken up, and each person who attends the funeral ordinarily takes a sprig of this boxwood, and throws it into the grave of the deceased. W. W.
Line 17. In an early edition of the Preface of 1800, Wordsworth cited the last stanza of this poem as an example of "one other circumstance which distinguishes these Poems from the popular Poetry of the day; it is this, that the feeling therein developed gives importance to the action and situation and not the action and situation to the feeling."

Page 257. SONG FOR THE WANDERING JEW.
The text here printed is that of 1815, the last edition in which the poem appeared.

Page 258. ELLEN IRWIN.
Line 2. The Kirtle is a river in the southern part of Scotland, on the banks of which the events here related took place. W. W.

Page 259. ANDREW JONES.
Originally part of *Peter Bell*, which Wordsworth composed in 1798.

Page 262. "PELION AND OSSA FLOURISH SIDE BY SIDE."
Line 4. *that inspiring Hill*. Mount Parnassus, sacred to the Muses. De Selincourt cites Spenser's "Virgil's Gnat," lines 21-24.

Page 266. THE CUCKOO AND THE NIGHTINGALE.
Line 201. *With such a master*, etc. From a manuscript in the Bodleian, as are also Stanzas xliv. and xlv., which are necessary to complete the sense. W. W.

Page 274. ALICE FELL.
Line 57. *duffil*. Duffle, a coarse woolen cloth.

Page 275. BEGGARS.
Written in 1802, but the event described took place in 1800, when Dorothy described it in her journal. See "Sequel to the 'Beggars,'" p. 563.

Page 276. TO A BUTTERFLY.
Dorothy recorded the circumstances inspiring this poem in her journal for March 14, 1802: "While we were at breakfast, that is (for I had breakfasted) he with his basin of broth before him untouched, and a little plate of bread and butter, wrote the Poem To a Butterfly. He ate not a morsel, nor put on his stockings, but sate with his neck unbuttoned, and his waistcoat open while he did it. The thought first came upon him as we were talking about the pleasure we both always feel at the sight of a butterfly. I told him

that I was afraid of brushing the dust off their wings. He told me how they used to kill all the white ones when he went to school because they were Frenchmen."

Page 277. "AMONG ALL LOVELY THINGS MY LOVE HAD BEEN."
Called by Dorothy "The Glow-worm." "The incident of this Poem took Place about seven years ago between Dorothy and me." W. W., writing in 1802.

Page 278. WRITTEN IN MARCH.
In her journal for April 16, 1802, Dorothy wrote: "When we came to the foot of Brother's Water I left William sitting on the bridge. . . . When I returned I found William writing a poem descriptive of the sights and sounds we saw and heard. There was the gentle flowing of the stream, the glittering, lively lake, green fields without a living creature to be seen on them; behind us, a flat pasture with forty-two cattle feeding. . . . The people were at work ploughing, harrowing, and sowing; lasses working, a dog barking now and then; the snow in patches at the top of the highest hills."

Page 278. THE REDBREAST CHASING THE BUTTERFLY.
Line 12. *Father Adam*. See "Paradise Lost," book xi. W. W.

Page 279. FORESIGHT.
"William was in the Orchard. . . . I happened to say that when I was young I would not have pulled a strawberry blossom. . . . At dinner time he came in with the poem of Children gathering Flowers, but it was not quite finished, and it kept him long off his dinner." Dorothy's journal, April 28, 1802.

Page 279. TO THE SMALL CELANDINE.
Line 8. *Celandine*. Common pilewort. W. W.

Page 280. RESOLUTION AND INDEPENDENCE.
Although this poem was written in May–July 1802, the meeting with the old man took place on October 3, 1800, as Dorothy noted in her journal: "We met an old man almost double. He had on a coat, thrown over his shoulders above his waistcoat and coat. Under this he carried a bundle, and had an apron on and a nightcap. . . . His trade was to gather leeches, but now leeches are scarce, and he had not strength for it." In a letter of June 1802, Wordsworth defended a first version of this poem; several of his comments are quoted below.
Lines 1–49. "A young Poet in the midst of the happiness of Nature is described as overwhelmed by the thought of the miserable reverses which have befallen the happiest of all men, viz. Poets — I think of this till I am so deeply impressed by it, that I consider the manner in which I was rescued from my dejection and despair almost as an interposition of Providence." W. W.
Line 43. *Chatterton*. Thomas Chatterton (1752-

70) poisoned himself at the age of seventeen in a fit of despair.

Line 45. *Him.* Robert Burns (1759–96).

Lines 50–51. "A person reading this Poem with feelings like mine will have been awed and controlled, expecting almost something spiritual or supernatural." W. W.

Lines 57–63. In his Preface to the edition of 1815, Wordsworth cited this stanza as a preeminent example of "the conferring, the abstracting, and the modifying powers of the imagination."

Page 282. "I Grieved for Buonaparté."
See the headnote to "Nuns Fret Not at Their Convent's Narrow Room," p. 346.

Page 284. Composed upon Westminster Bridge.
Probably composed on July 31, 1802, as Dorothy and William left London on their way to Dover and France, where they planned to visit Annette and Caroline. Dorothy wrote in her journal: "We left London on Saturday morning at half past five or six, the [31st] of July. . . . It was a beautiful morning. The city, St. Paul's, with the river, and a multitude of little boats, made a most beautiful sight as we crossed Westminster Bridge. The houses were not overhung by their cloud of smoke, and they were spread out endlessly, yet the sun shone so brightly, with such a fierce light, that there was something like the purity of one of nature's own grand spectacles."

Page 284. Composed by the Sea-side, near Calais.
This and the following four sonnets were composed during Wordsworth's visit to France in July and August 1802. "Arrived at Calais at four in the morning . . . Delightful walks in the evenings: seeing far off in the West the coast of England, like a cloud, crested with Dover Castle, the Evening Star, and the glory of the sky" (Dorothy's journal).

Page 285. Composed near Calais, on the Road Leading to Ardres.
Line 1. *Jones! as from Calais southward.*
This excellent Person, one of my earliest and dearest friends, died in the year 1835. We were undergraduates together of the same year, at the same college; and companions in many a delightful ramble through his own romantic Country of North Wales. Much of the latter part of his life he passed in comparative solitude, which I know was often cheered by remembrance of our youthful adventures, and of the beautiful regions which, at home and abroad, we had visited together. Our long friendship was never subject to a moment's interruption, — and, while revising these volumes for the last time, I have been so often reminded of my loss, with a not unpleasing sadness, that I trust the Reader will excuse this passing mention of a Man who well deserves from me something more than so brief a notice. Let me only add, that during the middle part of his life he resided many years (as Incumbent of the Living) at a Parsonage in Oxfordshire, which is the subject of the sonnet entitled "A Parsonage in Oxfordshire," p. 602. W. W.

Line 3. *day.* Fourteenth of July, 1790. W. W. See "A Character," p. 260, and note.

Page 285. "It Is a Beauteous Evening, Calm and Free."
Line 9. *Dear Child.* Wordsworth's French daughter, Caroline.
Line 12. *Abraham's bosom.* See Luke 16:22.

Page 285. On the Extinction of the Venetian Republic.
Napoleon occupied Venice in May 1797.
Lines 7–8. "Referring to the ceremony, enacted on each Ascension Day, when the Doge used to wed the Adriatic by dropping a ring into it, as a symbol of the dependence of the greatness of Venice on sea power" [de Selincourt].

Page 286. The King of Sweden.
In this and a succeeding sonnet on the same subject, let me be understood as a Poet availing himself of the situation which the King of Sweden occupied, and of the principles avowed in his manifestos; as laying hold of these advantages for the purpose of embodying moral truths. This remark might, perhaps, as well have been suppressed; for to those who may be in sympathy with the course of these Poems, it will be superfluous, and will, I fear, be thrown away upon that other class, whose besotted admiration of the intoxicated despot hereafter placed in contrast with him, is the most melancholy evidence of degradation in British feeling and intellect which the times have furnished. W. W. Gustavus IV of Sweden was a steadfast opponent of Napoleon until his deposition in 1809.

Page 286. To Toussaint L'Ouverture.
A freed slave who led a rebellion against the French on Santo Domingo, Toussaint was arrested and imprisoned in Paris by Napoleon. He died in 1803.

Page 287. "Great Men Have Been among Us."
Lines 3–4. Algernon Sidney (1622–83), republican soldier and statesman in the English Civil War, executed by Charles II; Andrew Marvell (1621–78), poet and friend of Milton; James Harrington (1611–77), republican political theorist; Sir Henry Vane (1613–62), statesman executed by the royal party.

Page 288. Stanzas Written in My Pocket-copy of Thomson's "Castle of Indolence."
Line 1–36 describe Wordsworth; lines 37–72 describe Coleridge.

Page 290. To H. C.
Coleridge's eldest son, Hartley (1796–1849).

Page 290. To the Daisy.
This Poem, and two others to the same flower, were written in the year 1802; which is mentioned, because in some of the ideas, though not in the manner in which those ideas are con-

nected, and likewise even in some of the expressions, there is a resemblance to passages in a Poem (lately published) of Mr. Montgomery's, entitled, "A Field Flower." This being said, Mr. Montgomery will not think any apology due to him; I cannot, however, help addressing him in the words of the Father of English Poets: —

"Though it happe me to rehersin —
That ye han in your freshe songis saied,
Forberith me, and beth not ill apaied,
Sith that ye se I doe it in the honour
Of Love, and eke in service of the Flour."
W. W., 1807.

In a letter of 1808 Wordsworth corrected a reader who had referred to the poem "on *a* Daisy": "By the bye, it is on *the* Daisy, a mighty difference."
Line 80. *Art Nature's favorite.* See, in Chaucer and the elder Poets, the honours formerly paid to the flower. W. W.

Page 292. YEW-TREES.
Cited by Wordsworth, along with "A Night-piece," as being "among the best [of his poems] for the imaginative power displayed in them."
Line 5. *Umfraville, Percy.* English noblemen who warred against the Scots in the late middle ages.
Lines 7-8. *Azincour, Crecy, Poictiers.* Great English victories of the Hundred Years' War (1415, 1346, 1356).
Line 33. *Glaramara.* A mountain at the head of Borrowdale.

Page 294. I. DEPARTURE FROM THE VALE OF GRASMERE.
Probably written in 1811, although not published until 1827.

Page 294. II. AT THE GRAVE OF BURNS.
The party reached Dumfries on the evening of the 17th.

Page 295. III. THOUGHTS SUGGESTED THE DAY FOLLOWING, ON THE BANKS OF THE NITH.
The following is extracted from the journal of my fellow-traveller [Dorothy], to which, as persons acquainted with my poems will know, I have been obliged on other occasions: —
'Dumfries, August 1803.
"On our way to the churchyard where Burns is buried, we were accompanied by a bookseller, who showed us the outside of Burns's house, where he died. It has a mean appearance, and is in a bye situation; the front whitewashed; dirty about the doors, as most Scotch houses are; flowering plants in the window. Went to visit his grave; he lies in a corner of the churchyard, and his second son, Francis Wallace, beside him. There is no stone to mark the spot; but a hundred guineas have been collected to be expended upon some sort of monument. 'There,' said the bookseller, pointing to a pompous monument, 'lies Mr.' — (I have forgotten the name) — 'a remarkably clever man; he was an attorney, and scarcely ever lost a cause he undertook. Burns made many a lampoon upon him, and there they

rest as you see.' We looked at Burns's grave with melancholy and painful reflections, repeating to each other his own poet's epitaph: —

'Is there a man whose judgment clear
Can others teach the course to steer,
Yet runs himself life's mad career
Wild as the wave? —
Here let him pause and through a tear
Survey this grave.' "

"The churchyard is full of grave-stones and expensive monuments, in all sorts of fantastic shapes, obelisk-wise, pillar-wise, etc. When our guide had left us we turned again to Burns's grave, and afterwards went to his house, wishing to inquire after Mrs. Burns, who was gone to spend some time by the seashore with her children. We spoke to the maid-servant at the door, who invited us forward, and we sate down in the parlour. The walls were coloured with a blue wash; on one side of the fire was a mahogany desk; opposite the window a clock, which Burns mentions, in one of his letters, having received as a present. The house was cleanly and neat in the inside, the stairs of stone scoured white, the kitchen on the right side of the passage, the parlour on the left. In the room above the parlour the poet died, and his son, very lately, in the same room. The servant told us she had lived four years with Mrs. Burns, who was now in great sorrow for the death of Wallace. She said that Mrs. B.'s youngest son was now at Christ's Hospital. We were glad to leave Dumfries, where we could think of little but poor Burns, and his moving about on that unpoetic ground. In our road to Brownhill, the next stage, we passed Ellisland, at a little distance on our right — his farm-house. Our pleasure in looking round would have been still greater, if the road had led us nearer the spot.

"I cannot take leave of this country which we passed through to-day, without mentioning that we saw the Cumberland mountains within half-a-mile of Ellisland, Burns's house, the last view we had of them. Drayton has prettily described the connection which this neighbourhood has with ours, when he makes Skiddaw say, —

'Scruffel, from the sky
That Annandale doth crown, with a most amorous eye
Salutes me every day, or at my pride looks grim,
Oft threatening me with clouds, as I oft threaten him.'

"These lines came to my brother's memory, as well as the Cumberland saying, —

'If Skiddaw hath a cap
Scruffel was well of that.'

"We talked of Burns, and of the prospect he must have had, perhaps from his own door, of Skiddaw and his companions; indulging ourselves in the fancy that we might have been personally known to each other, and he have looked upon those objects with more pleasure for our sakes."
W. W.

Wordsworth added the following note to a manuscript of 1842:

"With the Poems of Burns I became acquainted almost immediately upon their first appearance in the volume printed at Kilmarnock in 1786. Their effect upon my mind has been sufficiently expressed above. Familiarity with the dialect of the border counties of Cumberland and Westmorland made it easy for me not only to understand but to feel them. It was not so with his contemporary or rather his predecessor Cowper, as appears from one of his letters. This is to be regretted; for the simplicity, the truth and the vigour of Burns would have strongly recommended him, notwithstanding occasional coarseness, to the sympathies of Cowper, and ensured the approval of his judgment. It gives me pleasure, venial I trust, to acknowledge at this late day my obligations to these two great authors, whose writings, in conjunction with Percy's *Reliques*, powerfully counteracted the mischievous influence of Darwin's dazzling manner, the extravagance of the earlier dramas of Schiller, and that of other German writers upon my taste and natural tendencies. May these few words serve as a warning to youthful Poets who are in danger of being carried away by the inundation of foreign literature, from which our own is at present suffering so much, both in style and points of far greater moment. True it is that in the poems of Burns, as now collected, are too many reprehensible passages; but their immorality is rather the ebullition of natural temperament and a humour of levity than a studied thing: whereas in these foreign Writers, and in some of our own country not long deceased (and in an eminent deceased Poet of our own age), the evil, whether of voluptuousness, impiety, or licentiousness, is courted upon system, and therefore is greater, and less pardonable."

Page 296. IV. To the Sons of Burns.
De Selincourt points out that stanzas ii, iii, iv, and viii were composed in 1805 and 1806; stanzas i, v, vi, vii were added in 1827.

Page 297. V. To a Highland Girl.
"When beginning to descend the hill toward Loch Lomond we overtook two girls, who told us we could not cross the ferry until evening, for the boat was gone with a number of people to church. One of the girls was exceedingly beautiful: and the figures of both of them, in gray plaids falling to their feet, their faces only being uncovered, excited our attention before we spoke to them" (Dorothy's journal).

Page 298. VI. Glen Almain.
Dorothy's journal records the occasion: "At the end of the long valley we ascended a hill to a great height, and reached the top, when the sun, on the point of setting, shed a soft yellow light upon every eminence. The prospect was very extensive; over hollows and plains, no towns, and few houses visible; — a prospect, extensive as it was, in harmony with the secluded dell, and fixing its own peculiar character of

removedness from the world, and the secure possession of the quiet of nature more deeply in our minds. The following poem was written by William on hearing of a tradition relating to it, which we did not know when we were there."

Page 298. VII. Stepping Westward.
Composed nearly two years after the event, which Dorothy described in her journal: "We met two neatly dressed women. One of them said to us in a friendly, soft tone of voice 'What! you are stepping westward?' I cannot describe how affecting this simple expression was in that remote place, with the western sky in front, yet glowing with the departed sun."

Page 298. VIII. The Solitary Reaper.
Composed in 1805, and suggested to Wordsworth by a sentence in the manuscript of Thomas Wilkinson's *Tours to the British Mountains* (published in 1824): "Passed by a Female who was reaping alone, she sung in Erse as she bended over her sickle, the sweetest human voice I ever heard. Her strains were tenderly melancholy, and felt delicious long after they were heard no more."

Page 299. IX. Address to Kilchurn Castle.
Line 43. *Lost on the aërial heights of the Crusades.* The tradition is that the Castle was built by a Lady during the absence of her Lord in Palestine. W. W.

Page 300. X. Rob Roy's Grave.
Robert MacGregor, or Rob Roy (1671–1734), highland outlaw and folk hero.
Line 10. The people of the neighbourhood of Loch Ketterine, in order to prove the extraordinary length of their Hero's arm, tell you that "he could garter his Tartan Stockings below the knee when standing upright." According to their account he was a tremendous Swordsman; after having sought all occasions of proving his prowess, he was never conquered but once, and this was not until he was an Old Man. W. W. (1807).

Page 301. XI. Sonnet Composed at _____ Castle.
Line 13. *gentle Tweed.* The River Tweed.

Page 301. XII. Yarrow Unvisited.
"We left the Tweed when we were within about a mile and a half or two miles of Clovenford, where we were to lodge. Turned up the side of a hill and went along the sheep-grounds till we reached the spot, — a single stone house. On our mentioning Mr. Scott's name the woman of the house showed us all possible civility. Mr. Scott is respected everywhere; I believe that by favour of his name one might be hospitably entertained throughout all the borders of Scotland. At Clovenford, being so near Yarrow, we could not but think of the possibility of going thither, but came to the conclusion of reserving the pleasure for some future time, in consequence of which, after our return, William wrote the poem

which I shall here transcribe" (Dorothy's journal).

Line 6. *Marrow.* Lass.

Line 20. *lintwhite.* Linnet.

Lines 43–44. Aubrey de Vere recollected Wordsworth's comment on these lines: ". . . Scott misquoted in one of his novels my lines on *Yarrow.* He makes me write,

"The swans on sweet St. Mary's lake
Float double, swans and shadow;"

but I wrote

"The *swan* on *still* St. Mary's lake."

Never could I have written "swans" in the plural. The scene when I saw it, with its still and dim lake, under the dusky hills, was one of utter loneliness: there was *one* swan, and one only, stemming the water, and the pathetic loneliness of the region gave importance to the one companion of that swan, its own white image in the water. It was for that reason that I recorded the Swan and the Shadow. Had there been many swans and many shadows, they would have implied nothing as regards the character of the scene; and I should have said nothing about them."

Page 303. XV. The Blind Highland Boy.

Line 116. *Turtle-shell.* "The 'shell' was substituted for the 'washing' tub on the suggestion of Coleridge." W. W., in a letter of 1828.

Page 306. October 1803.

This and the following eight poems were written in response to the threat of a French invasion.

Page 308. In the Pass of Killicranky.

At the battle of Killicrankie (1689) Scots forces under John Graham of Claverhouse, Viscount Dundee, defeated the English under General Mackay.

Page 308. Lines on the Expected Invasion.

Lines 3–7. Viscount Falkland (1610–43) and the first Marquis of Montrose (1612–50) were Royalists; John Pym (1584–1643), like Milton, was a Republican.

Page 308. The Farmer of Tilsbury Vale.

With this picture, which was taken from real life, compare the imaginative one of "The Reverie of Poor Susan," p. 70; and see (to make up the deficiencies of this class) "The Excursion," *passim.* W. W.

Page 311. "She Was a Phantom of Delight."

Written, said Wordsworth, "on my dear wife."

Page 311. "I Wandered Lonely as a Cloud."

Composed in 1804. The incident described occurred two years before, during a walk by the lake of Ullswater. "We saw a few daffodils close to the waterside. . . . But as we went along there were more and yet more; and at last, under the boughs of the trees, we saw that there was a long belt of them along the shore, about the breadth of a country turnpike road. I never

saw daffodils so beautiful. They grew among the mossy stones about and about them; some rested their heads upon these stones as on a pillow for weariness; and the rest tossed and reeled and danced, and seemed as if they verily laughed with the wind, that blew upon them over the lake; they looked so gay, ever glancing, ever changing" (Dorothy's journal). In 1815 Wordsworth described the subject of the poem as "an elementary feeling and simple impression (approaching to the nature of an ocular spectrum) upon the imaginative faculty, [rather] than an *exertion* of it." For an example of an "exertion" of the imagination, see "With Ships the Sea Was Sprinkled" (p. 349) and note.

Lines 7–12. This stanza was added in 1815.

Lines 13–14. Wordsworth objected strenuously, in a letter of 1808, to a reader's reference to "Daffodils reflected in the Water.": ". . . what shall we think of criticism or judgement founded upon and exemplified by a Poem which must have been so inattentively perused? My language is precise, and, therefore, it would be false modesty to charge myself with blame.

— Beneath the trees,
Ten thousand dancing in the *breeze.*
The *waves beside* them danced, but they
Outdid the *sparkling waves* in glee

Can expression be more distinct? And let me ask your Friend how it is possible for flowers to be *reflected* in water where there are *waves.* They may indeed in *still* water — but the very object of my poem is the trouble or agitation both of the flowers and the Water. . . . Sincerity compels me to say that my Poems must be more nearly looked at before they can give rise to any remarks of much value, even from the strongest minds."

Lines 21–22. "The two best lines" referred to in the headnote as being "by Mary."

Page 314. The Seven Sisters.

The story of this poem is from the German of Frederica Brun. W. W. (1807).

Page 318. At Applethwaite, Near Keswick.

Line 1. Sir George Beaumont (1753–1827), art patron and landscape painter, befriended the Wordsworths for many years.

Page 319. To the Supreme Being.

This sonnet, together with "Yes! Hope May with My Strong Desire Keep Pace" (p. 350) and "No Mortal Object Did These Eyes Require" (p. 351), was published in Richard Duppa's *Life of Michelangelo* (1806–07).

Page 319. Ode to Duty.

Composed in 1804. The Latin motto, added in 1837, is adapted from Seneca's description of the truly virtuous man (*Moral Epistles,* CXX.10). It may be translated: "Now I am not good by taking thought, but have been brought by habit to such a point that I am not so much able to act rightly as I am unable to act otherwise than rightly."

Line 40. In 1807 this line was followed by an additional stanza:

Yet not the less would I throughout
Still act according to the voice
Of my own wish; and feel past doubt
That my submissiveness was choice:
Not seeking in the school of pride
For 'precepts over dignified,''
Denial and restraint I prize
No farther than they breed a second Will more
    wise.

The quotation in line 6 is from Milton's tract on *The Doctrine and Discipline of Divorce*.
Lines 49-56. In the "Reply to Mathetes" (1809-10), Wordsworth describes the speaker of these lines: ". . . in his character of Philosophical Poet, having thought of Morality as implying in its essence voluntary obedience, and producing the effect of order, he transfers, in the transport of imagination, the law of Moral to physical natures, and, having contemplated, through the medium of that order, all modes of existence as subservient to one spirit, concludes his address to the power of Duty. . . ."
Line 53. *lowly wise.* A crucial injunction in *Paradise Lost* (VIII.173).

Page 320. FIDELITY.
Line 20. *tarn.* A small Mere or Lake, mostly high up in the mountains. W. W.
Lines 25-6. See headnote to "The Idle Shepherd-Boys," p. 244.

Page 322. TRIBUTE TO THE MEMORY OF THE SAME DOG.
The dog "Music" died, aged and blind, by falling into a draw-well at Gallow Hill. W. W.

Page 322. "WHEN TO THE ATTRACTIONS OF THE BUSY WORLD."
Included by Wordsworth among the Poems on the Naming of Places.
Line 110. This wish was not granted; the lamented Person not long after perished by shipwreck, in discharge of his duty as Commander of the Honourable East India Company's Vessel, the Earl of Abergavenny. W. W. John Wordsworth died on February 5, 1805.

Page 324. ELEGIAC VERSES.
This and the two following elegies were suggested by the death of John Wordsworth.
Line 52. *Meek Flower. Moss Campion (Silene acaulis).* This most beautiful plant is scarce in England, though it is found in great abundance upon the mountains of Scotland. The first specimen I ever saw of it, in its native bed, was singularly fine, the tuft or cushion being at least eight inches in diameter, and the root proportionably thick. I have only met with it in two places among our mountains, in both of which I have since sought for it in vain.
Botanists will not, I hope, take it ill, if I caution them against carrying off, inconsiderately, rare and beautiful plants. This has often been done, particularly from Ingleborough, and other mountains in Yorkshire, till the species have totally disappeared, to the great regret of lovers of nature living near the places where they grew. W. W.

Page 325. TO THE DAISY.
The following was written in remembrance of a beautiful letter of my Brother John, sent to us from Portsmouth, when he had left us at Grasmere, and first taken command of his unfortunate ship, more than four years ago. Some of the expressions in the poem are the very words he used in his letter. N.B. I have written two Poems to the same flower before — this is partly alluded to in the first stanza. W. W., in a letter of 1805.

Page 325. ELEGIAC STANZAS SUGGESTED BY A PICTURE OF PEELE CASTLE.
Line 1. Peele (or Piel) Castle stands on an island opposite Rampside, in Lancashire. Wordsworth visited the area for several months in the summer of 1794.
Lines 14-16. Altered in 1820 to:

a gleam

Of lustre, known to neither sea nor land
But borrowed from the youthful Poet's dream.

The original reading was restored in 1832 at the request of a friend, Barron Field, who wrote that the lines "have passed into a quotation; . . . I don't see what right you have to reclaim and clip the wings of the words and tame them thus."

Page 326. LOUISA.
In all editions before that of 1845 the following stanza stood between lines 6 and 7.

And she hath smiles to earth unknown,
Smiles, that with motion of their own
Do spread, and sink, and rise:
That come and go with endless play,
And ever, as they pass away,
Are hidden in her eyes.

Page 327. VAUDRACOUR AND JULIA.
This tale originally ended Book Nine of *The Prelude* in its 1805 version. It was published separately for the first time in 1820.

Page 331. THE WAGGONER.
"Several years after the event that forms the subject of the Poem, in company with my friend, the late Mr. Coleridge, I happened to fall in with the person to whom the name of Benjamin is given. Upon our expressing regret that we had not, for a long time, seen upon the road either him or his wagon, he said, 'They could not do without me; and as to the man who was put in my place, no good could come out of him; he was a man of no *ideas.*'
"The fact of my discarded hero's getting the horses out of a great difficulty with a word, as related in the poem, was told me by an eyewitness." W. W.
Charles Lamb was greatly pleased by the dedication. "We read it twice for once that we do the poem," he wrote in 1819, ". . . yet Benjamin is no common favorite — there is a spirit of

beautiful tolerance in it — it is as good as it was in 1806. . . ."

CANTO FIRST. Line 3. *The buzzing dor-hawk*, etc. When the Poem was first written the note of the bird was thus described: —

"The Night-hawk is singing his frog-like tune,
    Twirling his watchman's rattle about —"

but from unwillingness to startle the reader at the outset by so bold a mode of expression, the passage was altered as it now stands. W. W.

Line 53. *Dove and Olive-bough*. The sign which used to hang from Dove Cottage when it was a public house [G].

Line 88. *Swan*. An inn that still stands on the high-road near Grasmere.

Line 96. This rude piece of self-taught art (such as the progress of refinement) has been supplanted by a professional production. W. W.

Line 168. *Helm-crag*. A mountain of Grasmere, the broken summit of which presents two figures, full as distinctly shaped as that of the famous Cobbler near Arroquhar in Scotland. W. W.

Line 210. Dunmail, the last king of Cumberland, was supposed to be buried under a pile of stones by the road from Grasmere to Keswick.

CANTO SECOND. Line 30. *Merry-night*. A term well known in the North of England, as applied to rural festivals where young persons meet in the evening for the purpose of dancing. W. W.

Line 97. *fiddle's squeak*. At the close of each strathspey, or jig, a particular note from the fiddle summons the Rustic to the agreeable duty of saluting his partner. W. W.

CANTO THIRD. Line 28. *Can any mortal clog*, etc. After the line, "Can any mortal clog come to her," followed in the MS. an incident which has been kept back. Part of the suppressed verses shall here be given as a gratification of private feeling, which the well-disposed reader will find no difficulty in excusing. They are now printed for the first time.

"Can any mortal clog come to her?
It can: .   .   .   .   .   .

.   .   .   .
But Benjamin, in his vexation,
Possesses inward consolation;
He knows his ground, and hopes to find
A spot with all things to his mind,
An upright mural block of stone,
Moist with pure water trickling down.
A slender spring; but kind to man
It is, a true Samaritan;
Close to the highway, pouring out
Its offering from a chink or spout;
Whence all, howe'er athirst, or drooping
With toil, may drink, and without stooping.
    Cries Benjamin, 'Where is it, where?'
Voice it hath none, but must be near.'
— A star, declining towards the west,
Upon the watery surface threw
Its image tremulously imprest,
That just marked out the object and withdrew,
Right welcome service! .   .   .   .

.   .   .   .
                    ROCK OF NAMES!
Light is the strain, but not unjust
To Thee, and Thy memorial trust
That once seemed only to express

Love that was love in idleness;
Tokens, as year hath followed year
How changed, alas, in character!
For they were graven on thy smooth breast
By hands of those my soul loved best;
Meek women, men as true and brave
As ever went to a hopeful grave:
Their hands and mine, when side by side
With kindred zeal and mutual pride,
We worked until the Initials took
Shapes that defied a scornful look. —
Long as for us a genial feeling
Survives, or one in need of healing,
The power, dear Rock, around thee cast,
Thy monumental power, shall last
For me and mine! O thought of pain,
That would impair it or profane!
Take all in kindness then, as said
With a staid heart but playful head;
And fail not Thou, loved Rock! to keep
Thy charge when we are laid asleep." W. W.

The "Rock of Names" stood by the lake of Thirlmere, on Benjamin's route. On it stood the following initials: W.W., M.H., D.W., S.T.C., J.W., S.H. (Sara Hutchinson).

CANTO FOURTH. Line 21. *Ghimmer-crag*. The crag of the ewe lamb. W. W.

Page 340. FRENCH REVOLUTION.
From *The Prelude*, XI.105–44.

Page 342. THE HORN OF EGREMONT CASTLE.
This story is a Cumberland tradition. I have heard it also related of the Hall of Hutton John, an ancient residence of the Hudlestons, in a sequestered valley upon the river Dacor. W. W.

Page 343. A COMPLAINT.
The friend was probably Coleridge.

Page 345. "YES, IT WAS THE MOUNTAIN ECHO."
The headnote continues as follows: ". . . to Mary, who was then confined with her son Thomas, who died in his 7th year, as is recorded on his head-stone in Grasmere Church-yard." The following stanza stood between lines 4 and 5 in the edition of 1807:

Whence the Voice? from air or earth?
This the Cuckoo cannot tell;
But a startling sound had birth,
As the Bird must know full well.

Page 346. PERSONAL TALK.
Line 41. *The gentle Lady*. Desdemona, in Shakespeare's *Othello*.
Line 42. *Una*. Heroine of Spenser's *Faerie Queene*, Book I.
Lines 51–53. Cut upon the pedestal of the poet's statue in Westminster Abbey.

Page 347. " 'BELOVED VALE!' I SAID."
Probably a memory of Wordsworth's return to the Vale of Esthwaite, perhaps in 1799.

Page 348. "THOSE WORDS WERE UTTERED AS IN PENSIVE MOOD."
In Wordsworth's arrangement this sonnet fol-

lows (and refers to) "Composed after a Journey across the Hambleton Hills" (p. 288).

Page 348. "WITH HOW SAD STEPS, O MOON."
From a sonnet of Sir Philip Sidney. W. W. (*Astrophel and Stella*, xxxi).

Page 349. "THE WORLD IS TOO MUCH WITH US."
Lines 13-14. See *Paradise Lost*, III.603-604, and Spenser's *Colin Clouts Come Home Againe*, lines 245-51.

Page 349. "WITH SHIPS THE SEA WAS SPRINKLED FAR AND NIGH."
In a letter of 1807 Wordsworth cited this sonnet as evidence of the fact that "there is scarcely one of my Poems which does not aim to direct the attention to some moral sentiment, or to some general principle, or law of thought, or of our intellectual constitution. For instance in the present case, who is there that has not felt that the mind can have no rest among a multitude of objects, of which it either cannot make one whole, or from which it cannot single out one individual, whereupon may be concentrated the attention divided among or distracted by a multitude?" Further comments are given below.
Lines 1-3. "I am represented . . . as casting my eyes over the sea . . . my mind may be supposed to float up and down among them in a kind of dreamy indifference with respect either to this or that one, only in a pleasurable state of feeling with respect to the whole prospect."
Line 4. "That feeling [of pleasure] may be supposed to have passed away, and a kind of comparative listlessness or apathy to have succeeded."
Lines 7-8. "All at once, while I am in this state, comes forth an object, an individual, and my mind, sleepy and unfixed, is awakened and unfastened in a moment."
Lines 9-10. "This ship . . . may . . . be said to come upon a mission of the poetic Spirit, because in its own appearance and attributes it is barely sufficiently distinguish[ed] to rouse the creative faculty of the human mind. . . . The mind being once fixed and rouzed, all the rest comes from itself; it is merely a lordly Ship, nothing more."
Line 11. "My mind wantons with grateful joy in the exercise of its own powers, and, loving its own creation, . . . making her a sovereign or a regent."
Line 14. "Thus taking up again the Reader with whom I began, letting him know how long I must have watched this favorite Vessel, and inviting him to rest his mind as mine is resting."

Page 350. TWO TRANSLATIONS.
The first of these two versions of Michelangelo's famous quatrain was initialed "W. W."

Page 351. TO THE MEMORY OF RAISLEY CALVERT.
Wordsworth also paid tribute to Calvert in *The Prelude*, XIV.354-69.

Page 351. "METHOUGHT I SAW."
The sonnet referred to in the headnote is "November 1836" (p. 741).

Page 352. LINES COMPOSED AT GRASMERE.
Line 10. "Importuna e grave salma." — Michael Angelo. W. W.
Line 17. *A Power*. Charles James Fox, the leader of the Whig party and a statesman who earned Wordsworth's respect, died on September 13, 1806. See the note to "Michael," p. 838.

Page 352. NOVEMBER 1806.
Line 2. *Another mighty Empire*. Napoleon defeated the forces of Prussia at the Battle of Jena, October 14, 1806.

Page 353. ODE.
The importance of this poem to Wordsworth is suggested by his decision to place it at the end of every edition of his collected works. All or part of the first four stanzas were written in late March 1802, probably on the 27th, the day after he composed the poem quoted in the motto, "My Heart Leaps Up." The remainder of the poem was composed in 1804, probably in March. On its first appearance in 1807 the poem was entitled simply "Ode," with a Latin motto ("Paulo majora canamus," or "Let us sing a somewhat ampler strain," from Virgil's *Eclogue* IV, line 1). In 1814 Wordsworth wrote in a letter that the poem "rests entirely on two recollections of Childhood; one that of a splendour in the objects of Sense which is passed away, and the other an indisposition to bend to the law of death as applying to our own particular case — A Reader who has not a vivid recollection of these feelings having existed in his mind in Childhood cannot understand that poem."
Lines 1-9. An echo of Coleridge's "The Mad Monk," lines 9-16:

There was a time when earth, and sea, and skies,
    The bright green vale, and forest's dark recess,
With all things, lay beneath mine eyes
    In steady loveliness:
But now I feel, on earth's uneasy scene,
    Such sorrows as will never cease; —
    I only ask for peace;
If I must live to know that such a time has been!

Line 21. *tabor*. A small drum.
Line 23. *A timely utterance*. Often identified as "My Heart Leaps Up."
Lines 58 ff. As Wordsworth points out in the headnote, this "notion of pre-existence" is not advanced as a serious belief, but as a metaphorical and at times fanciful explanation of the loss perceived in Stanzas I-IV. It is the far more serious psychological and epistemological "explanation" of Stanza IX that permits the poise and hope with which the poem ends.
Line 104. *"humorous stage."* From Samuel Daniel's dedicatory sonnet to *Musophilus*.
Line 120. In the original version four lines followed:

To whom the grave
Is but a lonely bed without the sense of sight

Of day or the warm light,
A place of thought where we in waiting lie

These lines were probably deleted in response to
Coleridge, who found the notion of "lying *awake*"
in the grave "frightful."

Line 130. At this point the poet's attention
turns from speculative to empirical evidence for
the immortality of the soul, namely his memories
of the mind's power over the material world.

Line 132. *nature*. Human nature, as in line 147.

Line 144. *Fallings from us, vanishings*; De
Selincourt quotes a letter from Bonamy Price that
clarifies this difficult line: "The venerable old
man [Wordsworth] . . . was walking in the mid-
dle, and passed across me to a five-barred gate
in the wall which bounded the road. . . . He
clenched the top bar firmly with his right hand,
pushed strongly against it, and then uttered
these ever-memorable words: 'There was a time
in my life when I had to push against something
that resisted, to be sure that there was any-
thing outside me. I was sure of my own mind;
everything else fell away, and vanished into
thought.'"

Line 153. Wordsworth amplified this thought
in two lines which follow in one manuscript:

Throw off from us, or mitigate, the spell
Of that strong frame of sense in which we dwell;

Lines 203-4. An echo of Thomas Gray's "Ode
on the Pleasure Arising from Vicissitude," a
poem Wordsworth had imitated as a schoolboy:

> The meanest floweret of the vale,
> The simplest note that swells the gale,
> The common sun, the air, the skies
> To him are opening Paradise.

Page 356. A PROPHECY.
An appeal to the Germans to stand fast against
Napoleon.

Line 4. *Arminius*. Led Germany's successful
resistance to imperial Rome (17 B.C.–21 A.D.).

Line 10. *new-born Kings*. German monarchs
who confederated with Napoleon in 1806, under
the leadership of the "Bavarian," Frederick
Augustus, Elector of Saxony.

Page 356. THOUGHT OF A BRITON ON THE SUBJU-
GATION OF SWITZERLAND.
Napoleon invaded Switzerland for a second
time in 1802. Coleridge described this sonnet as
"one of the noblest sonnets in the language and
the happiest comment on the line of Milton,
'The mountain nymph, sweet Liberty'" (see
Milton's "L'Allegro," line 36).

Page 356. TO THOMAS CLARKSON.
An anti-slavery agitator since 1785, Thomas
Clarkson (1760–1846) was instrumental in securing
the passage, in 1807–1808, of a bill abolishing the
slave trade.

Page 357. THE MOTHER'S RETURN.
"Mrs. Wordsworth has a strong impression that
'The Mother's Return' was written at Coleorton,
where Miss Wordsworth was then staying with
the children, during the absence of the former."
W. W.

Page 357. GIPSIES.
The apologetic last four lines were added in
1820, in response to criticism of the poem.

Page 358. "Though Narrow Be That Old Man's
Cares."
The motto is from *A Midsummer Night's
Dream*, V.i.16–17.

Line 10. Both these superstitions are prevalent
in the midland Counties of England; that of
"Gabriel's Hounds" appears to be very general
over Europe, being the same as the one upon
which the German Poet, Bürger, has founded his
ballad of the "Wild Huntsman." W. W. (note
to editions of 1807–15).

Page 359. SONG AT THE FEAST OF BROUGHAM
CASTLE.
Henry Lord Clifford, etc., who is the subject
of this Poem, was the son of John Lord Clifford,
who was slain at Towton Field, which John Lord
Clifford, as is known to the reader of English
history, was the person who after the battle of
Wakefield slew, in the pursuit, the young Earl of
Rutland, son of the Duke of York, who had
fallen in the battle, "in part of revenge" (say the
Authors of the *History of Cumberland and West-
moreland*); "for the Earl's Father had slain his."
A deed which worthily blemished the author
(saith Speed); but who, as he adds, "dare
promise any thing temperate of himself in the
heat of martial fury? chiefly, when it was re-
solved not to leave any branch of the York line
standing; for so one maketh this Lord to speak."
This, no doubt, I would observe by the bye, was
an action sufficiently in the vindictive spirit of
the times, and yet not altogether so bad as
represented; "for the Earl was no child, as some
writers would have him, but able to bear arms,
being sixteen or seventeen years of age, as is
evident from this (say the Memoirs of the
Countess of Pembroke, who was laudably anxious
to wipe away, as far as could be, this stigma
from the illustrious name to which she was born),
that he was the next Child to King Edward the
Fourth, which his mother had by Richard Duke
of York, and that King was then eighteen years
of age: and for the small distance betwixt her
children, see Austin Vincent, in his *Book of
Nobility*, p. 622, where he writes of them all."
It may further be observed, that Lord Clifford,
who was then himself only twenty-five years of
age, had been a leading man and commander two
or three years together in the army of Lancaster,
before this time; and, therefore, would be less
likely to think that the Earl of Rutland might
be entitled to mercy from his youth. — But, in-
dependent of this act, at best a cruel and savage
one, the Family of Clifford had done enough to
draw upon them the vehement hatred of the
House of York: so that after the Battle of
Towton there was no hope for them but in flight
and concealment. Henry, the subject of the

Poem, was deprived of his estate and honours during the space of twenty-four years; all which time he lived as a shepherd in Yorkshire, or in Cumberland, where the estate of his Father-in-law (Sir Lancelot Threlkeld) lay. He was restored to his estate and honours in the first year of Henry the Seventh. It is recorded that, "when called to Parliament, he behaved nobly and wisely; but otherwise came seldom to London or the Court; and rather delighted to live in the country, where he repaired several of his Castles, which had gone to decay during the late troubles." Thus far is chiefly collected from Nicholson and Burn; and I can add, from my own knowledge, that there is a tradition current in the village of Threlkeld and its neighbourhood, his principal retreat, that in the course of his shepherd-life he had acquired great astronomical knowledge. I cannot conclude this note without adding a word upon the subject of those numerous and noble feudal Edifices, spoken of in the Poem, the ruins of some of which are, at this day, so great an ornament to that interesting courtry. The Cliffords had always been distinguished for an honourable pride in these Castles; and we have seen that, after the wars of York and Lancaster, they were rebuilt; in the civil wars of Charles the First they were again laid waste, and again restored almost to their former magnificence by the celebrated Lady Anne Clifford, Countess of Pembroke, etc. Not more than twenty-five years after this was done, when the estates of Clifford had passed into the Family of Tufton, three of these Castles, namely, Brough, Brougham, and Pendragon, were demolished, and the timber and other materials sold by Thomas Earl of Thanet. We will hope that, when this order was issued, the Earl had not consulted the text of Isaiah, 58th chap., 12th verse, to which the inscription placed over the gate of Pendragon Castle by the Countess of Pembroke (I believe his Grandmother), at the time she repaired that structure, refers the reader: — "*And they that shall be of thee shall build the old waste places: thou shalt raise up the foundations of many generations; and thou shalt be called, The repairer of the breach, The restorer of paths to dwell in.*" The Earl of Thanet, the present possessor of the Estates, with a due respect for the memory of his ancestors, and a proper sense of the value and beauty of these remains of antiquity, has (I am told) given orders that they shall be preserved from all depredations. W. W.

Line 2. The River Emont flows past the ruins of Brougham Castle, the seat of the Cliffords. See *The Prelude*, VI.203–223.

Line 6. *The red rose.* Emblem of the House of Lancaster, and opposed to the white rose of York (line 11). The action of the poem takes place shortly after the accession of Henry Tudor, Henry VII, who ended the Wars of the Roses at Bosworth Field (line 25) in 1485, and restored the exiled Henry Clifford of Lancaster.

Line 27. *Earth helped him with the cry of blood.* This line is from "The Battle of Bosworth Field," by Sir John Beaumont (brother to the Dramatist), whose poems are written with

much spirit, elegance, and harmony, and have deservedly been reprinted lately in Chalmers's Collection of English Poets. W. W.

Lines 36–47. The castles of Skipton, Pendragon, Brough, and Appleby (on the River Eden) were estates of the Cliffords.

Line 89. *Mosedale.* A valley in the north of the Lake District, near the mountain Blencathara.

Line 95. Lancelot Threlkeld took young Clifford under his protection.

Line 122. *fish.* It is imagined by the people of the country that there are two immortal Fish, inhabitants of this Tarn, which lies in the mountains not far from Threlkeld. — Blencathara, mentioned before, is the old and proper name of the mountain vulgarly called Saddleback. W. W.

Lines 142, 143.

> *Armour rusting in his halls*
> *On the blood of Clifford calls.*

The martial character of the Cliffords is well known to the readers of English history; but it may not be improper here to say, by way of comment on these lines and what follows that besides several others who perished in the same manner, the four immediate Progenitors of the Person in whose hearing this is supposed to be spoken all died in the Field. W. W.

Page 361. THE WHITE DOE OF RYLSTONE. Composed in the winter of 1807–1808, and revised before publication in 1815. Wordsworth added the following notes to the poem:

"The Poem of 'The White Doe of Rylstone' is founded on a local tradition, and on the Ballad in Percy's Collection, entitled 'The Rising of the North.' The tradition is as follows: — 'About this time,' not long after the Dissolution, 'a White Doe,' say the aged people of the neighbourhood, 'long continued to make a weekly pilgrimage from Rylstone over the fells of Bolton, and was constantly found in the Abbey Churchyard during divine service; after the close of which she returned home as regularly as the rest of the congregation.'" — DR. WHITAKER'S *History of the Deanery of Craven.*

"Rylstone was the property and residence of the Nortons, distinguished in that ill-advised and unfortunate Insurrection; which led me to connect with this tradition the principal circumstances of their fate, as recorded in the Ballad.

"'Bolton Priory,' says Dr. Whitaker in his excellent book, *The History and Antiquities of the Deanery of Craven,* 'stands upon a beautiful curvature of the Wharf, on a level sufficiently elevated to protect it from inundations, and low enough for every purpose of picturesque effect.

"'Opposite to the East window of the Priory Church, the river washes the foot of a rock nearly perpendicular, and of the richest purple, where several of the mineral beds, which break out instead of maintaining their usual inclination to the horizon, are twisted by some inconceivable process into undulating and spiral lines. To the South all is soft and delicious; the eye reposes upon a few rich pastures, a moderate reach of the river, sufficiently tranquil to form a mirror to the sun, and the bounding hills beyond, neither too near nor too lofty to exclude, even in winter, any portion of his rays.

" 'But after all, the glories of Bolton are on the North. Whatever the most fastidious taste could require to constitute a perfect landscape, is not only found here, but in its proper place. In front, and immediately under the eye, is a smooth expanse of park-like enclosure, spotted with native elm, ash, etc., of the finest growth: on the right a skirting oak wood, with jutting points of grey rock; on the left a rising copse. Still forward are seen the aged groves of Bolton Park, the growth of centuries; and farther yet, the barren and rocky distances of Simon-seat and Barden Fell contrasted with the warmth, fertility, and luxuriant foliage of the valley below.

" 'About half a mile above Bolton the valley closes, and either side of the Wharf is overhung by solemn woods, from which huge perpendicular masses of grey rock jut out at intervals.

" 'This sequestered scene was almost inaccessible till of late, that ridings have been cut on both sides of the river, and the most interesting points laid open by judicious thinnings in the woods. Here a tributary stream rushes from a waterfall, and bursts through a woody glen to mingle its waters with the Wharf: there the Wharf itself is nearly lost in a deep cleft in the rock, and next becomes a horned flood enclosing a woody island — sometimes it reposes for a moment, and then resumes its native character, lively, irregular, and impetuous.

" 'The cleft mentioned above is the tremendous STRID. This chasm, being incapable of receiving the winter floods, has formed on either side a broad strand of naked gritstone full of rock-basins, or "pots of the Linn," which bear witness to the restless impetuosity of so many Northern torrents. But, if here Wharf is lost to the eye, it amply repays another sense by its deep and solemn roar, like "the Voice of the angry Spirit of the Waters," heard far above and beneath, amidst the silence of the surrounding woods.

" 'The terminating object of the landscape is the remains of Barden Tower, interesting from their form and situation, and still more so from the recollections which they excite.'' W. W. (1820).

In 1815 the following note was added:

THE RISING IN THE NORTH. The subject of this ballad is the great Northern Insurrection in the 12th year of Elizabeth, 1569, which proved so fatal to Thomas Percy, the seventh Earl of Northumberland.

There had not long before been a secret negociation entered into between some of the Scottish and English nobility, to bring about a marriage between Mary Q. of Scots, at that time a prisoner in England, and the Duke of Norfolk, a nobleman of excellent character. This match was proposed to all the most considerable of the English nobility, and among the rest to the Earls of Northumberland and Westmoreland, two noblemen very powerful in the North. As it seemed to promise a safe and speedy conclusion

of the troubles in Scotland, with many advantages to the crown of England, they all consented to it, provided it should prove agreeable to Queen Elizabeth. The Earl of Leicester (Elizabeth's favourite) undertook to break the matter to her, but before he could find an opportunity, the affair had come to her ears by other hands, and she was thrown into a violent flame. The Duke of Norfolk, with several of his friends, was committed to the Tower, and summons were sent to the Northern Earls instantly to make their appearance at court. It is said that the Earl of Northumberland, who was a man of a mild and gentle nature, was deliberating with himself whether he should not obey the message, and rely upon the Queen's candour and clemency, when he was forced into desperate measures by a sudden report at midnight, Nov. 14, that a party of his enemies was come to seize his person. The Earl was then at his house at Topcliffe in Yorkshire. When, rising hastily out of bed, he withdrew to the Earl of Westmoreland at Brancepeth, where the country came in to them, and pressed them to take up arms in their own defence. They accordingly set up their standards, declaring their intent to restore the ancient Religion, to get the succession of the crown firmly settled, and to prevent the destruction of the ancient nobility etc. Their common banner, (from which was displayed the cross, together with the five wounds of Christ) was borne by an ancient gentleman, Richard Norton, Esquire, who, with his sons, (among whom Christopher, Marmaduke, and Thomas are expressly named by Camden), distinguished himself on this occasion. Having entered Durham, they tore the Bible, etc., and caused mass to be said there; they then marched to Clifford-moor near Wetherby, where they mustered their men. . . . The two Earls, who spent their large estates in hospitality, and were extremely beloved on that account, were masters of little ready money; the E. of Northumberland bringing with him only 8000 crowns, and the E. of Westmoreland nothing at all, for the subsistence of their forces, they were not able to march to London, as they had at first intended. In these circumstances, Westmoreland began so visibly to despond that many of his men slunk away, though Northumberland still kept up his resolution, and was master of the field till December 13, when the Earl of Sussex, accompanied with Lord Hunsden and others, having marched out of York at the head of a large body of forces, and being followed by a still larger army under the command of Ambrose Dudley, Earl of Warwick, the insurgents retreated northward towards the borders, and there dismissing their followers made their escape into Scotland. Though this insurrection had been suppressed with so little bloodshed, the Earl of Sussex and Sir George Bowes, marshal of the army, put vast numbers to death by martial law, without any regular trial. The former of these caused at Durham sixty-three constables to be hanged at once. And the latter made his boast, for sixty miles in length, and forty in breadth, betwixt Newcastle and Wetherby, there was hardly a town or village wherein he had not executed some of the inhabitants. This exceeds the cruelties practised in the West after Monmouth's rebellion.

Such is the account collected from Stow, Speed, Camden, Guthrie, Carte, and Rapin; it agrees, in most particulars, with the following Ballad, apparently the production of some northern minstrel. —

> Listen, lively lordings all,
>   Lithe and listen unto mee,
> And I will sing of a noble earle,
>   The noblest earle in the north countrie.
>
> Earle Percy is into his garden gone,
>   And after him walkes his faire leddie:
> I heard a bird sing in mine ear,
>   That I must either fight, or flee.
>
> Now heaven forefend, my dearest lord,
>   That ever such harm should hap to thee:
> But goe to London to the court,
>   And fair fall truth and honestie.
>
> Now nay, now nay, my ladye gay,
>   Alas! thy counsell suits not mee;
> Mine enemies prevail so fast,
>   That at the court I may not bee.
>
> O goe to the court yet, good my lord,
>   And take thy gallant men with thee;
> If any dare to doe you wrong,
>   Then your warrant they may bee.
>
> Now nay, now nay, thou ladye faire,
>   The court is full of subtiltie;
> And if I goe to the court, ladye,
>   Never more I may thee see.
>
> Yet goe to the court, my lord, she sayes,
>   And I myselfe will ryde wi'thee:
> At court then for my dearest lord,
>   His faithfull borrowe I will bee.
>
> Now nay, now nay, my ladye deare;
>   Far lever had I lose my life,
> Than leave among my cruell foes
>   My love in jeopardy and strife.
>
> But come thou hither, my little foot-page,
>   Come thou hither unto mee,
> To Maister Norton thou must goe
>   In all the haste that ever may bee.
>
> Commend me to that gentleman,
>   And beare this letter here fro mee;
> And say that earnestly I praye,
>   He will ryde in my companie.
>
> One while the little foot-page went,
>   And another while he ran;
> Untill he came to his journeys end,
>   The little foot-page never blan.
>
> When to that gentleman he came,
>   Down he kneeled on his knee;
> And took the letter betwixt his hands,
>   And lett the gentleman it see.
>
> And when the letter it was redd
>   Affore that goodlye companie,
> I wis, if you the truthe wold know,
>   There was many a weeping eye.
>
> He sayd, Come thither, Christopher Norton,
>   A gallant youth thou seem'st to bee;
> What doest thou counsell me, my sonne,
>   Now that good earle's in jeopardy?
>
> Father, my counselle's fair and free;
>   That erle he is a noble lord,

> And whatsoever to him you hight,
>   I wold not have you breake your word,
>
> Gramercy, Christopher, my sonne,
>   Thy counsell well it liketh mee;
> And if we speed and 'scape with life,
>   Well advanced shalt thou bee.
>
> Come you hither, my nine good sonnes,
>   Gallant men I trowe you bee:
> How many of you, my children deare,
>   Will stand by that good erle and mee?
>
> Wi' them full many a gallant wight
>   They cruellye bereav'd of life:
> And many a childe made fatherlesse,
>   And widowed many a tender wife.

To Wordsworth's comment in the headnote should be added that in a letter of 1816: " 'The White Doe' starts from a high point of imagination, and comes round, through various wanderings of that faculty, to a still higher — nothing less than the Apotheosis of the Animal, who gives the first of the two titles to the Poem. And as the Poem thus begins and ends with pure and lofty Imagination, every motive and impulse that actuates the persons introduced is from the same source; a kindred spirit pervades, and is intended to harmonize, the whole. Throughout, objects (the Banner, for instance) derive their influence not from properties inherent in them, not from what they are actually in themselves, but from such as are bestowed upon them by the minds of those who are conversant with or affected by those objects. Thus the Poetry, if there be any in the work, proceeds whence it ought to do, from the soul of Man, communicating its creative energies to the images of the external world."

Dedication. *Action is transitory.* This and five lines that follow were either read or recited by me, more than thirty years since, to the late Mr. Hazlitt, who quoted some expressions in them (imperfectly remembered) in a work of his published several years ago. W. W. These six lines are from *The Borderers,* Act III. 405–410. The second motto is from Bacon's essay "Of Atheism."

CANTO FIRST. Line 1. *From Bolton's old monastic tower.* It is to be regretted that at the present day Bolton Abbey wants this ornament: but the Poem, according to the imagination of the Poet, is composed in Queen Elizabeth's time. "Formerly," says Dr. Whitaker, "over the Transept was a tower. This is proved not only from the mention of bells at the Dissolution, when they could have had no other place, but from the pointed roof of the choir, which must have terminated westward, in some building of superior height to the ridge." W. W.

Line 27. *A Chapel.* The Nave of the Church having been reserved at the Dissolution for the use of the Saxon Cure, is still a parochial Chapel: and, at this day, is as well kept as the neatest English Cathedral. W. W.

Line 34. *Prior's Oak.* At a small distance from the great gateway stood the Prior's Oak, which was felled about the year 1720, and sold for £70. According to the price of wood at that time, it could scarcely have contained less than 1400 feet of timber. W. W.

Line 226. *When Lady Aäliza mourned.* The

detail of this tradition may be found in Dr. Whitaker's book, and in a Poem of this Collection, "The Force of Prayer." W. W.

Line 242. *yon chantry door.* At the East end of the North aisle of Bolton Priory Church, is a chantry belonging to Bethmesly Hall, and a vault where, according to tradition, the Claphams (who inherited this estate, by the female line, from the Mauleverers) were interred upright. John de Clapham, of whom this ferocious act is recorded, was a man of great note in his time: he was a vehement partisan of the house of Lancaster, in whom the spirit of his chieftains, the Cliffords, seemed to survive. W. W.

Line 268. *Who loved the Shepherd-lord to meet.* Among these Poems will be found one entitled, "Song at the Feast of Brougham Castle, upon the Restoration of Lord Clifford, the Shepherd, to the Estates and Honours of his Ancestors." To that Poem is annexed an account of this personage, chiefly extracted from Burn and Nicholson's *History of Cumberland and Westmoreland.* It gives me pleasure to add these further particulars concerning him, from Dr. Whitaker, who says he "retired to the solitude of Barden, where he seems to have enlarged the tower out of a common keeper's lodge, and where he found a retreat equally favourable to taste, to instruction, and to devotion. The narrow limits of his residence show that he had learned to despise the pomp of greatness, and that a small train of servants could suffice him, who had lived to the age of thirty a servant himself. I think this nobleman resided here almost entirely when in Yorkshire, for all his charters which I have seen are dated at Barden.

"His early habits, and the want of those artificial measures of time which even shepherds now possess, had given him a turn for observing the motions of the heavenly bodies; and, having purchased such an apparatus as could then be procured, he amused and informed himself by those pursuits, with the aid of the Canons of Bolton, some of whom are said to have been well versed in what was then known of the science.

"I suspect this nobleman to have been sometimes occupied in a more visionary pursuit, and probably in the same company.

"For, from the family evidences, I have met with two MSS. on the subject of Alchemy, which, from the character, spelling, etc., may almost certainly be referred to the reign of Henry the Seventh. If these were originally deposited with the MSS. of the Cliffords, it might have been for the use of this nobleman. If they were brought from Bolton at the Dissolution, they must have been the work of those Canons whom he almost exclusively conversed with.

"In these peaceful employments Lord Clifford spent the whole reign of Henry the Seventh, and the first years of his son. But in the year 1513, when almost sixty years old, he was appointed to a principal command over the army which fought at Flodden, and showed that the military genius of the family had neither been chilled in him by age, nor extinguished by habits of peace.

"He survived the battle of Flodden ten years, and died April 23d, 1523, aged about 70. I shall endeavour to appropriate to him a tomb, vault, and chantry, in the choir of the church of Bolton, as I should be sorry to believe that he was deposited, when dead, at a distance from the place which in his lifetime he loved so well.

"By his last will he appointed his body to be interred at Shap, if he died in Westmoreland; or at Bolton, if he died in Yorkshire."

With respect to the Canons of Bolton, Dr. Whitaker shows from MSS. that not only alchemy but astronomy was a favourite pursuit with them. W. W.

CANTO THIRD. Line 2. *Of Brancepeth.* Brancepeth Castle stands near the river Were, a few miles from the city of Durham. It formerly belonged to the Nevilles, Earls of Westmoreland. See Dr. Percy's account. W. W.

Lines 123, 124. From the old ballad. W. W.

Line 203. From the old ballad. W. W.

Line 221. *mitred Thurston.* See the Historians for the account of this memorable battle, usually denominated the Battle of the Standard. W. W.

Line 235. *In that other day of Neville's Cross.* "In the night before the battle of Durham was strucken and begun, the 17th day of October, *anno* 1346, there did appear to John Fosser, then Prior of the abbey of Durham, a Vision, commanding him to take the holy Corporax-cloth, wherewith St. Cuthbert did cover the chalice when he used to say mass, and to put the same holy relique like to a banner-cloth upon the point of a spear, and the next morning to go and repair to a place on the west side of the city of Durham, called the Red Hills, where the Maid's Bower wont to be, and there to remain and abide till the end of the battle. To which vision the Prior obeying, and taking the same for a revelation of God's grace and mercy by the mediation of Holy St. Cuthbert, did accordingly the next morning, with the monks of the said abbey, repair to the said Red Hills, and there most devoutly humbling and prostrating themselves in prayer for the victory in the said battle: (a great multitude of the Scots running and pressing by them, with intention to have spoiled them, yet had no power to commit any violence under such holy persons, so occupied in prayer, being protected and defended by the mighty Providence of Almighty God, and by the mediation of Holy St. Cuthbert, and the presence of the holy relique). And, after many conflicts and warlike exploits there had and done between the English men and the King of Scots and his company, the said battle ended, and the victory was obtained, to the great overthrow and confusion of the Scots, their enemies: And then the said Prior and monks accompanied with Ralph Lord Nevil, and John Nevil his son, and the Lord Percy, and many other nobles of England, returned home and went to the abbey church, there joining in hearty prayer and thanksgiving to God and Holy St. Cuthbert for the victory achieved that day."

This battle was afterwards called the Battle of Neville's Cross from the following circumstance: —

"On the west side of the city of Durham, where two roads pass each other, a most notable, famous, and goodly cross of stone-work was erected and set up to the honour of God for the victory there obtained in the field of battle, and known by the name of Nevil's Cross, and built at the sole cost of the Lord Ralph Nevil, one of the most excellent and chief persons in the said battle." The Relique of St. Cuthbert afterwards became of great importance in military events. For soon after this battle, says the same author, "The Prior caused a goodly and sumptuous banner to be made" (which is then described at great length), "and in the midst of the same banner-cloth was the said holy relique and corporax-cloth enclosed, etc., and so sumptuously finished, and absolutely perfected, this banner was dedicated to Holy St. Cuthbert, of intent and purpose that for the future it should be carried to any battle, as occasion should serve; and was never carried and showed at any battle but by the especial grace of God Almighty, and the mediation of Holy St. Cuthbert, it brought home victory; which banner-cloth, after the dissolution of the abbey, fell into the possession of Dean WHITTINGHAM, whose wife, called KATHARINE, being a French woman (as is most credibly reported by eyewitnesses), did most injuriously burn the same in her fire, to the open contempt and disgrace of all ancient and goodly reliques." — Extracted from a book entitled *Durham Cathedral, as it stood before the Dissolution of the Monastery.* It appears from the old metrical History, that the above-mentioned banner was carried by the Earl of Surrey to Flodden Field. W. W.

CANTO FIFTH. Line 6. *Norton Tower.* It is so called to this day, and is thus described by Dr. Whitaker: — "Rylstone Fell yet exhibits a monument of the old warfare between the Nortons and the Cliffords. On a point of very high ground, commanding an immense prospect, and protected by two deep ravines, are the remains of a square tower, expressly said by Dodsworth to have been built by Richard Norton. The walls are of strong grout-work, about four feet thick. It seems to have been three stories high. Breaches have been industriously made in all the sides, almost to the ground, to render it untenable.

"But Norton Tower was probably a sort of pleasure-house in summer, as there are, adjoining to it, several large mounds (two of them are pretty entire), of which no other account can be given than that they were butts for large companies of archers.

"The place is savagely wild, and admirably adapted to the uses of a watch tower." W. W.

CANTO SEVENTH. Line 18. *despoil and desolation.* "After the attainder of Richard Norton, his estates were forfeited to the crown, where they remained till the 2d or 3d of James; they were then granted to Francis Earl of Cumberland." From an accurate survey made at that time, several particulars have been extracted by Dr. W. It appears that "the mansion-house was then in decay. Immediately adjoining is a close, called the Vivery, so called, undoubtedly, from the

French Vivier, or modern Latin Vivarium; for there are near the house large remains of a pleasure-ground, such as were introduced in the earlier part of Elizabeth's time, with topiary works, fish-ponds, an island, etc. The whole township was ranged by an hundred and thirty red deer, the property of the Lord, which, together with the wood, had, after the attainder of Mr. Norton, been committed to Sir Stephen Tempest. The wood, it seems, had been abandoned to depredations, before which time it appears that the neighbourhood must have exhibited a forest-like and sylvan scene. In this survey, among the old tenants is mentioned one Richard Kitchen, butler to Mr. Norton, who rose in rebellion with his master, and was executed at Ripon." W. W.

Line 157. *Amerdale.* "At the extremity of the parish of Burnsal, the valley of Wharf forks off into two great branches, one of which retains the name of Wharfdale, to the source of the river; the other is usually called Littondale, but more anciently and properly, Amerdale. Dernbrook, which runs along an obscure valley from the N.W., is derived from a Teutonic word, signifying concealment." — DR. WHITAKER. W. W.

Line 212. "God us ayde." On one of the bells of Rylstone church, which seems coeval with the building to the tower, is the Gothic cypher, "I.N." for John Norton, and the motto, "God us ayde." W. W.

Line 253. *rock-encircled Pound.* Which is thus described by Dr. Whitaker: "On the plain summit of the hill are the foundations of a strong wall stretching from the S.W. to the N.E. corner of the tower, and to the edge of a very deep glen. From this glen, a ditch, several hundred yards long, runs south to another deep and rugged ravine. On the N. and W., where the banks are very steep, no wall or mound is discoverable, paling being the only fence that could stand on such ground.

"From the Minstrelsy of the Scottish Border, it appears that such pounds for deer, sheep, etc., were far from being uncommon in the south of Scotland. The principle of them was something like that of a wire mouse-trap. On the declivity of a steep hill, the bottom and sides of which were fenced so as to be impassable, a wall was constructed nearly level with the surface on the outside, yet so high within, that without wings it was impossible to escape in the opposite direction. Care was probably taken that these enclosures should contain better feed than the neighbouring parks or forests; and whoever is acquainted with the habits of these sequacious animals, will easily conceive, that if the leader was once tempted to descend into the snare, herd would follow."

I cannot conclude without recommending to the notice of all lovers of beautiful scenery Bolton Abbey and its neighbourhood. This enchanting spot belongs to the Duke of Devonshire; and the superintendence of it has for some years been entrusted to the Rev. William Carr, who has most skilfully opened out its features; and, in whatever he has added, has done justice to the place, by working with an invisible hand of art in the very spirit of nature. W. W.

Page 382. Composed While the Author Was Engaged in Writing a Tract.
By the terms of the Convention of Cintra (1808) the English aided the French evacuation of Portugal, a favor to the enemy that Wordsworth attacked in the tract, published in 1809.

Page 382. George and Sarah Green.
Composed in 1808, and first published (by Thomas de Quincy) in Tait's *Edinburgh Magazine* for September 1839.

Page 383. Hofer.
Andreas Hofer was a Tyrolean innkeeper who led his countrymen against the French in 1796 and 1809.

Page 384. "And Is It among Rude Untutored Dales?"
Line 8. *Zaragoza*. The Spanish town of Saragossa, stubbornly defended against the French by Palafox (1780–1847).

Page 384. On the Final Submission of the Tyrolese.
The Tyrolean rebellion was suppressed and Hofer betrayed and shot in 1809.

Page 384. "Hail, Zaragoza."
In this Sonnet I am under some obligations to one of an Italian author, to which I cannot refer. W. W. Saragossa surrendered to the French in February 1809.

Page 385. "The Martial Courage of a Day Is Vain."
On Austria's submission to the French in late 1809.
Line 10. *A daughter of her Throne*. Napoleon married Archduchess Marie Louise, daughter of the Austrian Emperor, in April 1810.
Line 11. *Tyrolean Champion*. Andreas Hofer.

Page 385. "Brave Schill!"
Ferdinand von Schill (1773–1809) led a war of liberation against the French in April 1809. He died at the battle of Stralsund, in May.

Page 385. "Call Not the Royal Swede Unfortunate."
See "The King of Sweden," p. 286. Gustavus IV was arrested and forced to abdicate in March 1809.

Page 385. "Look Now on that Adventurer."
The "adventurer" is Napoleon.

Page 387. On a Celebrated Event in Ancient History.
After defeating Philip V of Macedon, the Roman general Titus Quintius Flamininus proclaimed the freedom of Greece at the Isthmian Games in 196 B.C.

Page 388. "O'erweening Statesmen."
See Laborde's *Character of the Spanish People*; from him the statement of these lines is taken. W. W.

Page 388. Epitaphs Translated from Chiabrera.
The nine Epitaphs that follow are from the Italian poet Chiabrera, who was born at Savona, in 1552.
II. Line 13.

Ivi vivea giocondo e i suoi pensieri
Erano tutti rose.

The Translator had not skill to come nearer to his original. W. W.
VIII. Line 15. In justice to the Author, I subjoin the original: —

—— e degli amici
Non lasciava languire i bei pensieri.
W. W.

IX. Line 1. *Balbi*. Wordsworth's incorrect spelling of Baldi, Italian poet and philosopher (1553–1617).

Page 391. Maternal Grief.
Line 28. *Leverets*. Young hares.

Page 393. Spanish Guerillas.
Line 10. *Virathus* (or Viriathus). A shepherd who led opposition (149–41 B.C.) to Roman occupation of Spain.
Line 11. *Mina*. Francisco Espoz y Mina (1781–1836), who led Spanish resistance to Napoleon, was educated for the priesthood.
Line 12. *That great Leader*. Sertorius, who opposed Roman dictatorship. See note to *Prelude*, I.191.

Page 393. Epistle to Sir George Howland Beaumont, Bart.
Line 166. Loughrigg Tarn, alluded to in the foregoing Epistle, resembles, though much smaller in compass, the Lake Nemi, or *Speculum Dianæ* as it is often called, not only in its clear waters and circular form, and the beauty immediately surrounding it, but also as being overlooked by the eminence of Langdale Pikes as Lake Nemi is by that of Monte Calvo. Since this Epistle was written Loughrigg Tarn has lost much of its beauty by the felling of many natural clumps of wood, relics of the old forest, particularly upon the farm called "The Oaks," so called from the abundance of that tree which grew there.
It is to be regretted, upon public grounds, that Sir George Beaumont did not carry into effect his intention of constructing here a Summer Retreat in the style I have described; as his taste would have set an example how buildings, with all the accommodations modern society requires, might be introduced even into the most secluded parts of this country without injuring their native character. W. W.

Page 399. Inscriptions in the Grounds of Coleorton.

Line 17. *The haunt of him.* Sir George's ancestor, the poet John Beaumont (1583-1627).
Line 19. *that famous Youth.* John's brother, Francis Beaumont the dramatist (1589-1616).

Page 401. COMPOSED ON THE EVE OF THE MARRIAGE OF A FRIEND.
Wordsworth's brother-in-law, Thomas Hutchinson, married Mary Monkhouse, the sister of a dear friend, on November 1, 1812.

Page 401. WATER-FOWL.
From *The Recluse*, lines 204-229.

Page 403. NOVEMBER 1813.
Line 14. *The triumphs of this hour.* The allied victory over Napoleon at Leipzig, October 1813.

Page 403. THE EXCURSION.
The bulk of Book I was composed in 1797-1799 as a separate poem, entitled "The Ruined Cottage." The remainder of *The Excursion* occupied Wordsworth for five years, from 1809 until its publication in 1814. As Wordsworth pointed out in the headnote, the main action of the poem takes place in a composite landscape made up of the Vale of Grasmere, its churchyard, and the more mountainous region about the valleys of Great and Little Langdale. On a barren ridge between the Langdales lies Blea Tarn, the site of the Solitary's cottage.
BOOK FIRST. Unlike the rest of the poem, this book is set in Dorset, where it was composed. See Wordsworth's note, pp. 403-404.
Lines 108-433. Much of the Wanderer's biography is drawn from Wordsworth's own early life. Composed in February-March 1798, it may be described as a first sketch for *The Prelude*.
Line 341. *much did he see of men.* At the risk of giving a shock to the prejudices of artificial society, I have ever been ready to pay homage to the aristocracy of nature; under a conviction that vigorous human-heartedness is the constituent principle of true taste. It may still, however, be satisfactory to have prose testimony how far a Character, employed for purposes of imagination, is founded upon general fact. I, therefore, subjoin an extract from an author who had opportunities of being well acquainted with a class of men, from whom my own personal knowledge emboldened me to draw this portrait.
"We learn from Caesar and other Roman Writers, that the travelling merchants who frequented Gaul and other barbarous countries, either newly conquered by the Roman arms, or bordering on the Roman conquests, were ever the first to make the inhabitants of these countries familiarly acquainted with the Roman modes of life, and to inspire them with an inclination to follow the Roman fashions, and to enjoy Roman conveniences. In North America, travelling merchants from the Settlements have done and continue to do much more towards civilising the Indian natives, than all the missionaries, papist or protestant, who have ever been sent among them.
"It is farther to be observed, for the credit of this most useful class of men, that they commonly contribute by their personal manners, no less than by the sale of their wares, to the refinement of the people among whom they travel. Their dealings form them to great quickness of wit and acuteness of judgment. Having constant occasion to recommend themselves and their goods, they acquire habits of the most obliging attention, and the most insinuating address. As in their peregrinations they have opportunity of contemplating the manners of various men and various cities, they become eminently skilled in the knowledge of the world. *As they wander, each alone, through thinly-inhabited districts, they form habits of reflection and of sublime contemplation.* With all these qualifications, no wonder that they should often be, in remote parts of the country, the best mirrors of fashion, and censors of manners; and should contribute much to polish the roughness and soften the rusticity of our peasantry. It is not more than twenty or thirty years since a young man going from any part of Scotland to England, of purpose to *carry the pack*, was considered as going to lead the life and acquire the fortune of a gentleman. When, after twenty years' absence in that honourable line of employment, he returned with his acquisitions to his native country, he was regarded as a gentleman to all intents and purposes." — Heron's *Journey in Scotland*, vol. i, p. 89. W. W.
Lines 344-47. Wordsworth's belief in an "essential and eternal" human nature that is revealed more plainly by rural manners and speech lies at the heart of his theory of poetic diction, as formulated in the Preface of 1800.
Lines 934-39. This late addition (1845) exemplifies the growing orthodoxy of Wordsworth's religious sentiments, and may have been a response to critics who noted, as did Christopher North in 1842, the "utter absence of Revealed Religion" in the poem.
BOOK SECOND. Line 443. *a Novel of Voltaire. Candide, ou L'Optimisme* (1759).
Line 484. *dull product of a scoffer's pen.* Many readers have defended *Candide* against the charge of dullness. De Selincourt cites the "immortal dinner" held by the painter Benjamin Robert Haydon, at which Charles Lamb put the question to Wordsworth: "Now, you old Lake poet, you rascally poet, why do you call Voltaire dull?" "We all defended Wordsworth," recalled Haydon, "and affirmed there was a state of mind when Voltaire would be dull."
Line 692. *two huge Peaks.* The Langdale Pikes, which dominate the valley of Greater Langdale.
Lines 738-826. For the source of this story, see Wordsworth's headnote, p. 405.
BOOK THIRD. Line 112. *Lost in unsearchable eternity!* Since this paragraph was composed, I have read with so much pleasure, in Burnet's Theory of the Earth, a passage expressing corresponding sentiments, excited by objects of a similar nature, that I cannot forbear to transcribe it.
"Siquod verò Natura nobis dedit spectaculum, in hâc tellure, verè gratum, et philosophe dignum, id semel mihi contigisse arbitror; cùm ex

celsissimâ rupe speculabundus ad oram maris Mediterranei, hinc æquor cæruleum, illine tractus Alpinos prospexi; nihil quidem magìs dispar aut dissimile, nec in suo genere, magìs egregium et singulare. Hoc theatrum ego facilè prætulerim Romanis cunctis, Græcisve; atque id quod natura hîc spectandum exhibet, scenicis ludis omnibus, aut amphitheatri certaminibus. Nihil hîc elegans aut venustum, sed ingens et magnificum, et quod placet magnitudine suâ et quâdam specie immensitatis. Hinc intuebar maris æquabilem superficiem, usque et usque diffusam, quantum maximùm oculorum acies ferri potuit; illinc disruptissimam terræ faciem, et vastas moles variè elevatas aut depressas, erectas, propendentes, reclinatas, coacervatas, omni situ inæquali et turbido. Placuit, ex hâc parte, Naturæ unitas et simplicitas, et inexhausta quædam planities; ex alterâ, multiformis confusio magnorum corporum et insanæ rerum strages: quas cùm intuebar, non urbis alicujus aut oppidi, sed confracti mundi rudera, ante oculos habere mihi visus sum.

"In singulis ferè montibus erat aliquid insolens et mirabile, sed præ cæteris mihi placebat illa, quâ sedebam, rupes; erat maxima et altissima, et quâ terram respiciebat, molliori ascensu altitudinem suam dissimulabat: quà verò mare, horrendúm præceps, et quasi ad perpendiculum facta, instar parietis. Prætereà facies illa marina adeò erat lævis ac uniformis (quod in rupibus aliquando observare licet) ac si scissa fuisset à summo ad imum, in illo plano; vel terræ motu aliquo, aut fulmine, divulsa.

"Ima pars rupis erat cava, recessusque habuit, et saxeos specus, euntes in vacuum montem; sive naturâ pridem factos, sive exesos mari, et undarum crebris ictibus: In hos enim cum impetu ruebant et fragore, æstuantis maris fluctus; quos iterum spumantes reddidit antrum, et quasi ab imo ventre evomuit.

"Dextrum latus montis erat præruptum, aspero saxo et nudâ caute: sinistrum non adeò neglexerat Natura, arboribus utpote ornatum: et prope pedem montis rivus limpidæ aquæ prorupit; qui cùm vicinam vallem irrigaverat, lento motu serpens, et per varios mæandros, quasi ad protrahendam vitam, in magno mari absorptus subito periit. Denique in summo vertice promontorii, commodè eminebat saxum, cui insidebam contemplabundus. Vale augusta sedes. Rege digna: Augusta rupes, semper mihi memoranda!"
P. 89. *Telluris Theoria sacra, etc., Editio secunda.* W. W.

Lines 636 ff. A reminiscence of the deaths, in quick succession, of two of Wordsworth's children, Thomas and Catherine, in 1812.

Lines 700-701. An echo of *The Borderers*, IV.125. Like that play, the following account reflects Wordsworth's own experience of the French Revolution.

Line 931. *Of Mississippi, or that northern stream.* "A man is supposed to improve by going out into the *World*, by visiting *London*. Artificial man does; he extends with his sphere; but, alas! that sphere is microscopic; it is formed of minutiæ, and he surrenders his genuine vision to the artist, in order to embrace it in his ken. His bodily senses grow acute, even to barren and inhuman pruriency; while his mental become proportionally obtuse. The reverse is the Man of Mind: he who is placed in the sphere of Nature and of God, might be a mock at Tattersall's and Brooks's, and a sneer at St. James's: he would certainly be swallowed alive by the first *Pizarro* that crossed him: — But when he walks along the river of Amazons; when he rests his eye on the unrivalled Andes; when he measures the long and watered savannah; or contemplates, from a sudden promontory, the distant, vast Pacific — and feels himself a freeman in this vast theatre, and commanding each ready produced fruit of this wilderness, and each progeny of this stream — his exultation is not less than imperial. He is as gentle, too, as he is great: his emotions of tenderness keep pace with his elevation of sentiment; for he says, 'These were made by a good Being, who, unsought by me, placed me here to enjoy them.' He becomes at once a child and a king. His mind is in himself; from hence he argues, and from hence he acts, and he argues unerringly, and acts magisterially: his mind in himself is also in his God; and therefore he loves, and therefore he soars." — From the notes upon "The Hurricane," a Poem, by William Gilbert.

The Reader, I am sure, will thank me for the above quotation, which, though from a strange book, is one of the finest passages of modern English prose. W. W.

Line 947. *Muccawiss.* The whip-poor-will.

Book Fourth. Line 130. *'Tis, by comparison,* etc. See, upon this subject, Baxter's most interesting review of his own opinions and sentiments in the decline of life. It may be found (lately reprinted) in Dr. Wordsworth's *Ecclesiastical Biography.* W. W.

Line 205. *Alas!* etc. This subject is treated at length in the Ode — "Intimations of Immortality." W. W.

Line 324. *Knowing the heart of man,* etc. The passage quoted from Daniel is taken from a poem addressed to the Lady Margaret, Countess of Cumberland, and the two last lines printed in Italics, are by him translated from Seneca. The whole Poem is very beautiful. I will transcribe four stanzas from it, as they contain an admirable picture of the state of a wise Man's mind in a time of public commotion.

"Nor is he moved with all the thunder-cracks
Of tyrant's threats, or with the surly brow
Of Power, that proudly sits on others' crimes;
Charged with more crying sins than those he
    checks.
The storms of sad confusion that may grow
Up in the present for the coming times,
Appal not him; that hath no side at all,
But of himself, and knows the worst can fall.

"Although his heart (so near allied to earth)
Cannot but pity the perplexed state
Of troublous and distressed mortality,
That thus make way unto the ugly birth
Of their own sorrows, and do still beget
Affliction upon Imbecility:
Yet seeing thus the course of things must run,
He looks thereon not strange, but as fore-done

"And whilst distraught ambition compasses,
And is encompassed, while as craft deceives
And is deceived: whilst man doth ransack man,
And builds on blood, and rises by distress;
And th' Inheritance of desolation leaves
To great-expecting hopes: He looks thereon,
As from the shore of peace, with unwet eye,
And bears no venture in Impiety.

"Thus, Lady, fares that man that hath prepared
A rest for his desires; and sees all things
Beneath him; and hath learned this book of man,
Full of the notes of frailty; and compared
The best of glory with her sufferings:
By whom, I see, you labour all you can
To plant your heart! and set your thoughts as
      near
His glorious mansion as your powers can bear."
                                                        W. W.

Line 859. *beardless Youth.* Apollo.
Line 865. *beaming Goddess.* Diana. The interpretation of classical myth here suggested exercised a strong influence on the young John Keats. "Poor Keats always used to prefer this passage [858 ff.] to all others," wrote B. R. Haydon. See, in particular, Keats's "I Stood Tip-toe."
Lines 910–11. Saints associated with or revered in Scotland.
Lines 958–68. This and other parts of the Wanderer's exhortations were composed in March 1798, when Wordsworth was beginning *The Recluse.*
Lines 978–92. Quoted by John Ruskin as the motto for *Modern Painters* (1843-60), these lines do not attack science *per se* but science that lacks reverence, humility, and (as Wordsworth argues) true objectivity. See lines 1251–63.
Lines 1207–74. Composed in 1798.
BOOK FIFTH. Lines 78 ff. As Wordsworth's headnote suggests, the scene is now the Vale of Grasmere.
Line 672. *a shining speck.* Hackett Cottage, described in the headnote (as are the church, the churchyard, and the pastor), pp. 405–406.
Line 975. *And gentle Nature,* etc.
"And suffering Nature grieved that one should die." Southey's *Retrospect.* W. W.
Line 978. *And whence that tribute.* The sentiments and opinions here uttered are in unison with those expressed in the following Essay upon Epitaphs, which was furnished by me for Mr. Coleridge's periodical work, *The Friend*; and as they are dictated by a spirit congenial to that which pervades this and the two succeeding books, the sympathising reader will not be displeased to see the Essay here annexed. W. W.
The following essay was first published in Coleridge's *The Friend* on February 22, 1810. A second and third essay on the same subject were composed, but never published in Wordsworth's lifetime.

ESSAY UPON EPITAPHS

It need scarcely be said, that an Epitaph presupposes a Monument, upon which it is to be engraven. Almost all Nations have wished that certain external signs should point out the places where their dead are interred. Among savage tribes unacquainted with letters this has mostly been done either by rude stones placed near the graves, or by mounds of earth raised over them. This custom proceeded obviously from a twofold desire; first, to guard the remains of the deceased from irreverent approach or from savage violation: and, secondly, to preserve their memory. "Never any," says Camden, "neglected burial but some savage nations; as the Bactrians, which cast their dead to the dogs; some varlet philosophers, as Diogenes, who desired to be devoured of fishes; some dissolute courtiers, as Mæcenas, who was wont to say, Non tumulum curo; sepelit natura relictos.

"I'm careless of a grave: — Nature her dead will save."

As soon as nations had learned the use of letters, epitaphs were inscribed upon these monuments; in order that their intention might be more surely and adequately fulfilled. I have derived monuments and epitaphs from two sources of feeling: but these do in fact resolve themselves into one. The invention of epitaphs, Weever, in his Discourse of Funeral Monuments, says rightly, "proceeded from the presage or fore-feeling of immortality, implanted in all men naturally, and is referred to the scholars of Linus the Theban poet, who flourished about the year of the world two thousand seven hundred; who first bewailed this Linus their Master, when he was slain, in doleful verses, then called of him Œlina, afterwards Epitaphia, for that they were first sung at burials, after engraved upon the sepulchres."
And, verily, without the consciousness of a principle of immortality in the human soul, Man could never have had awakened in him the desire to live in the remembrance of his fellows: mere love, or the yearning of kind towards kind, could not have produced it. The dog or horse perishes in the field, or in the stall, by the side of his companions, and is incapable of anticipating the sorrow with which his surrounding associates shall bemoan his death, or pine for his loss; he cannot pre-conceive this regret, he can form no thought of it; and therefore cannot possibly have a desire to leave such regret or remembrance behind him. Add to the principle of love which exists in the inferior animals, the faculty of reason which exists in Man alone; will the conjunction of these account for the desire? Doubtless it is a necessary consequence of this conjunction; yet not, I think, as a direct result, but only to be come at through an intermediate thought, viz. that of an intimation or assurance within us, that some part of our nature is imperishable. At least the precedence, in order of birth, of one feeling to the other, is unquestionable. If we look back upon the days of childhood, we shall find that the time is not in remembrance when, with respect to our own individual Being, the mind was without this assurance; whereas, the wish to be remembered by our friends or kindred after death, or even in absence, is, as we shall discover, a sensation that

does not form itself till the *social* feelings have been developed, and the Reason has connected itself with a wide range of objects. Forlorn, and cut off from communication with the best part of his nature, must that man be, who should derive the sense of immortality, as it exists in the mind of a child, from the same unthinking gaiety or liveliness of animal spirits with which the lamb in the meadow or any other irrational creature is endowed; who should ascribe it, in short, to blank ignorance in the child; to an inability arising from the imperfect state of his faculties to come, in any point of his being, into contact with a notion of death; or to an unreflecting acquiescence in what has been instilled into him! Has such an unfolder of the mysteries of nature, though he may have forgotten his former self, ever noticed the early, obstinate, and unappeasable inquisitiveness of children upon the subject of origination? This single fact proves outwardly the monstrousness of those suppositions: for, if we had no direct external testimony that the minds of very young children meditate feelingly upon death and immortality, these inquiries, which we all know they are perpetually making concerning the *whence*, do necessarily include correspondent habits of interrogation concerning the *whither*. Origin and tendency are notions inseparably co-relative. Never did a child stand by the side of a running stream, pondering within himself what power was the feeder of the perpetual current, from what never-wearied sources the body of water was supplied, but he must have been inevitably propelled to follow this question by another: "Towards what abyss is it in progress? what receptacle can contain the mighty influx?" And the spirit of the answer must have been, though the word might be sea or ocean, accompanied perhaps with an image gathered from a map, or from the real object in nature — these might have been the *letter*, but the *spirit* of the answer must have been *as* inevitably, — a receptacle without bounds or dimensions; — nothing less than infinity. We may, then, be justified in asserting, that the sense of immortality, if not a co-existent and twin birth with Reason, is among the earliest of her offspring: and we may further assert, that from these conjoined, and under their countenance, the human affections are gradually formed and opened out. This not the place to enter into the recesses of these investigations; but the subject requires here to make a plain avowal, that, for my own part, it is to me inconceivable, that the sympathies of love towards each other, which grow with our growth, could ever attain any new strength, or even preserve the old, after we had received from the outward senses the impression of death, and were in the habit of having that impression daily renewed and its accompanying feeling brought home to ourselves, and to those we love; if the same were not counteracted by those communications with our internal Being, which are anterior to all these experiences, and with which revelation coincides, and has through that coincidence alone (for otherwise it could not possess it) a power to

affect us. I confess, with me the conviction is absolute, that, if the impression and sense of death were not thus counterbalanced, such a hollowness would pervade the whole system of things, such a want of correspondence and consistency, a disproportion so astounding betwixt means and ends, that there could be no repose, no joy. Were we to grow up unfostered by this genial warmth, a frost would chill the spirit, so penetrating and powerful that there could be no motions of the life of love; and infinitely less could we have any wish to be remembered after we had passed away from a world in which each man had moved about like a shadow. — If, then, in a creature endowed with the faculties of foresight and reason, the social affections could not have unfolded themselves uncountenanced by the faith that Man is an immortal being; and if, consequently, neither could the individual dying have had a desire to survive in the remembrance of his fellows, nor on their side could they have felt a wish to preserve for future times vestiges of the departed; it follows, as a final inference, that without the belief in immortality, wherein these several desires originate, neither monuments nor epitaphs, in affectionate or laudatory commemoration of the deceased, could have existed in the world.

Simonides, it is related, upon landing in a strange country, found the corse of an unknown person lying by the seaside; he buried it, and was honoured throughout Greece for the piety of that act. Another ancient Philosopher, chancing to fix his eyes upon a dead body, regarded the same with slight, if not with contempt; saying, "See the shell of the flown bird!" But it is not to be supposed that the moral and tender-hearted Simonides was incapable of the lofty movements of thought, to which that other Sage gave way at the moment while his soul was intent only upon the indestructible being; nor, on the other hand, that he, in whose sight a lifeless human body was of no more value than the worthless shell from which the living fowl had departed, would not, in a different mood of mind, have been affected by those earthly considerations which had incited the philosophic Poet to the performance of that pious duty. And with regard to this latter we may be assured that, if he had been destitute of the capability of communing with the more exalted thoughts that appertain to human nature, he would have cared no more for the corse of the stranger than for the dead body of a seal or porpoise which might have been cast up by the waves. We respect the corporeal frame of Man, not merely because it is the habitation of a rational, but of an immortal Soul. Each of these Sages was in sympathy with the best feelings of our nature; feelings which, though they seem opposite to each other, have another and a finer connection than that of contrast. — It is a connection formed through the subtle progress by which, both in the natural and the moral world, qualities pass insensibly into their contraries, and things revolve upon each other. As, in sailing upon the orb of this planet, a voyage towards the regions where the sun sets conducts gradually to the quarter where we have been accustomed to behold it come forth at its rising; and, in like manner, a voyage towards the east, the birth-place in our imagination of the morning, leads finally to the quarter where the sun is last seen when he departs from our eyes; so the contemplative Soul, travelling in the direction of mortality, advances to the country of everlasting life; and, in like manner, may she continue to explore those cheerful tracts till she is brought back, for her advantage and benefit, to the land of transitory things — of sorrow and of tears.

On a midway point, therefore, which commands the thoughts and feelings of the two Sages whom we have represented in contrast, does the Author of that species of composition, the laws of which it is our present purpose to explain, take his stand. Accordingly, recurring to the twofold desire of guarding the remains of the deceased and preserving their memory, it may be said that a sepulchral monument is a tribute to a man as a human being; and that an epitaph (in the ordinary meaning attached to the word) includes this general feeling and something more; and is a record to preserve the memory of the dead, as a tribute due to his individual worth, for a satisfaction to the sorrowing hearts of the survivors, and for the common benefit of the living: which record is to be accomplished, not in a general manner, but, where it can, in *close connection with the bodily remains of the deceased:* and these, it may be added, among the modern nations of Europe, are deposited within, or contiguous to, their places of worship. In ancient times, as is well known, it was the custom to bury the dead beyond the walls of towns and cities; and among the Greeks and Romans they were frequently interred by the waysides.

I could here pause with pleasure, and invite the Reader to indulge with me in contemplation of the advantages which must have attended such a practice. We might ruminate upon the beauty which the monuments, thus placed, must have borrowed from the surrounding images of nature — from the trees, the wild flowers, from a stream running perhaps within sight or hearing, from the beaten road stretching its weary length hard by. Many tender similitudes must these objects have presented to the mind of the traveller leaning upon one of the tombs, or reposing in the coolness of its shade, whether he had halted from weariness or in compliance with the invitation, "Pause, Traveller!" so often found upon the monuments. And to its epitaph also must have been supplied strong appeals to visible appearances or immediate impressions, lively and affecting analogies of life as a journey — death as a sleep overcoming the tired wayfarer — of misfortune as a storm that falls suddenly upon him — of beauty as a flower that passeth away, or of the innocent pleasure as one that may be gathered — of virtue that standeth firm as a rock against the beating waves; — of hope "undermined insensibly like the poplar by the side of the river that has fed it," or blasted in a moment like a pine-tree by the stroke of lightning upon the mountain-top — of admonitions and heart-

stirring remembrances, like a refreshing breeze that comes without warning, or the taste of the waters of an unexpected fountain. These, and similar suggestions, must have given, formerly, to the language of the senseless stone a voice enforced and endeared by the benignity of that nature with which it was in unison. — We, in modern times, have lost much of these advantages; and they are but in a small degree counterbalanced to the inhabitants of large towns and cities, by the custom of depositing the dead within, or contiguous to, their places of worship; however splendid or imposing may be the appearance of those edifices, or however interesting or salutary the recollections associated with them. Even were it not true that tombs lose their monitory virtue when thus obtruded upon the notice of men occupied with the cares of the world, and too often sullied and defiled by those cares, yet still, when death is in our thoughts, nothing can make amends for the want of the soothing influences of nature, and for the absence of those types of renovation and decay, which the fields and woods offer to the notice of the serious and contemplative mind. To feel the force of this sentiment, let a man only compare in imagination the unsightly manner in which our monuments are crowded together in the busy, noisy, unclean, and almost grassless church-yard of a large town, with the still seclusion of a Turkish cemetery, in some remote place; and yet further sanctified by the grove of cypress in which it is embosomed. Thoughts in the same temper as these have already been expressed with true sensibility by an ingenuous Poet of the present day. The subject of his poem is "All Saints Church, Derby:" he has been deploring the forbidding and unseemly appearance of its burial-ground, and uttering a wish, that in past times the practice had been adopted of interring the inhabitants of large towns in the country: —

"Then in some rural, calm, sequestered spot,
Where healing Nature her benignant look
Ne'er changes, save at that lorn season, when,
With tresses drooping o'er her sable stole,
She yearly mourns the mortal doom of man,
Her noblest work, (so Israel's virgins erst,
With annual moan upon the mountains wept
Their fairest gone,) there in that rural scene,
So placid, so congenial to the wish
The Christian feels, of peaceful rest within
The silent grave, I would have stray'd.
                  *   *   *   *
— wandered forth, where the cold dew of heaven
Lay on the humbler graves around, what time
The pale moon gazed upon the turfy mounds,
Pensive, as though like me, in lonely muse,
'T were brooding on the dead inhumed beneath.
There while with him, the holy man of Uz,
O'er human destiny I sympathised,
Counting the long, long periods prophecy
Decrees to roll, ere the great day arrives
Of resurrection, oft the blue-eyed Spring
Had met me with her blossoms, as the Dove,
Of old, returned with olive leaf, to cheer
The Patriarch mourning o'er a world destroyed:
And I would bless her visit; for to me
'T is sweet to trace the consonance that links
As one, the works of Nature and the word
Of God. —"   JOHN EDWARDS.

A village church-yard, lying as it does in the lap of nature, may indeed be most favourably contrasted with that of a town of crowded population; and sepulture therein combines many of the best tendencies which belong to the mode practised by the Ancients, with others peculiar to itself. The sensations of pious cheerfulness, which attend the celebration of the sabbath-day in rural places, are profitably chastised by the sight of the graves of kindred and friends, gathered together in that general home towards which the thoughtful yet happy spectators themselves are journeying. Hence a parish-church, in the stillness of the country, is a visible centre of a community of the living and the dead; a point to which are habitually referred the nearest concerns of both.

As, then, both in cities and in villages, the dead are deposited in close connection with our places of worship, with us the composition of an epitaph naturally turns, still more than among the nations of antiquity, upon the most serious and solemn affections of the human mind; upon departed worth — upon personal or social sorrow and admiration — upon religion, individual and social — upon time, and upon eternity. Accordingly, it suffices, in ordinary cases, to secure a composition of this kind from censure, that it contain nothing that shall shock or be inconsistent with this spirit. But, to entitle an epitaph to praise, more than this is necessary. It ought to contain some thought or feeling belonging to the mortal or immortal part of our nature touchingly expressed; and if that be done, however general or even trite the sentiment may be, every man of pure mind will read the words with pleasure and gratitude. A husband bewails a wife; a parent breathes a sigh of disappointed hope over a lost child; a son utters a sentiment of filial reverence for a departed father or mother; a friend perhaps inscribes an encomium recording the companionable qualities, or the solid virtues, of the tenant of the grave, whose departure has left a sadness upon his memory. This and a pious admonition to the living, and a humble expression of Christian confidence in immortality, is the language of a thousand church-yards; and it does not often happen that anything, in a greater degree discriminate or appropriate to the dead or to the living, is to be found in them. This want of discrimination has been ascribed by Dr. Johnson, in his Essay upon the epitaphs of Pope, to two causes; first, the scantiness of the objects of human praise; and, secondly, the want of variety in the characters of men; or, to use his own words, "to the fact, that the greater part of mankind have no character at all." Such language may be holden without blame among the generalities of common conversation; but does not become a critic and a moralist speaking seriously upon a serious subject. The objects of admiration in human-nature are not scanty, but abundant: and every man has a character of his own, to the eye that has skill to perceive it. The real cause of the acknowledged want of discrimination in sepulchral memorials is this: That to analyse the characters of others, especially of those whom we love, is not a common or natural employment of men at any time. We are not anxious unerringly to understand the constitution of the minds of those who have soothed, who have cheered, who have supported us: with whom we have been long and daily pleased or delighted. The affections are their own justification. The light of love in our hearts is a satisfactory evidence that there is a body of worth in the minds of our friends or kindred, whence that light has proceeded. We shrink from the thought of placing their merits and defects to be weighed against each other in the nice balance of pure intellect; nor do we find much temptation to detect the shades by which a good quality or virtue is discriminated in them from an excellence known by the same general name as it exists in the mind of another; and, least of all, do we incline to these refinements when under the pressure of sorrow, admiration, or regret, or when actuated by any of those feelings which incite men to prolong the memory of their friends and kindred, by records placed in the bosom of the all-uniting and equalising receptacle of the dead.

The first requisite, then, in an Epitaph is, that it should speak, in a tone which shall sink into the heart, the general language of humanity as connected with the subject of death — the source from which an epitaph proceeds — of death, and of life. To be born and to die are the two points in which all men feel themselves to be in absolute coincidence. This general language may be uttered so strikingly as to entitle an epitaph to high praise; yet it cannot lay claim to the highest unless other excellencies be superadded. Passing through all intermediate steps, we will attempt to determine at once what these excellencies are, and wherein consists the perfection of this species of composition. — It will be found to lie in a due proportion of the common or universal feeling of humanity to sensations excited by a distinct and clear conception, conveyed to the reader's mind, of the individual, whose death is deplored and whose memory is to be preserved; at least of his character as, after death, it appeared to those who loved him and lament his loss. The general sympathy ought to be quickened, provoked, and diversified by particular thoughts, actions, images, — circumstances of age, occupation, manner of life, prosperity which the deceased had known, or adversity to which he had been subject; and these ought to be bound together and solemnised into one harmony by the general sympathy. The two powers should temper, restrain, and exalt each other. The reader ought to know who and what the man was whom he is called upon to think of with interest. A distinct conception should be given (implicitly where it can, rather than explicitly) of the individual lamented. — But the writer of an epitaph is not an anatomist, who dissects the internal frame of the mind; he is not even a painter, who executes a portrait at leisure and in entire tranquillity: his delineation, we must remember, is performed by the side of the grave; and, what is more, the grave of one whom he loves and admires. What purity and brightness is that virtue clothed in, the image of which must no longer bless our living eyes! The character of a deceased friend or beloved kinsman is not seen, no — nor ought to be seen, otherwise than as a tree through a tender haze or a luminous mist, that spiritualises and beautifies it; that takes away, indeed, but only to the end that parts which are not abstracted may appear more dignified and lovely; may impress and affect the more. Shall we say, then, that this is not truth, not a faithful image; and that, accordingly, the purposes of commemoration cannot be answered? — It *is* truth, and of the highest order; for, though doubtless things are not apparent which did exist; yet, the object being looked at through this medium, parts and proportions are brought into the distinct view which before had been only imperfectly or unconsciously seen: it is truth hallowed by love — the joint offspring of the worth of the dead and the affections of the living! This may easily be brought to the test. Let one, whose eyes have been sharpened by personal hostility to discover what was amiss in the character of a good man, hear the tidings of his death, and what a change is wrought in a moment! Enmity melts away; and, as it disappears, unsightliness, disproportion, and deformity, vanish; and, through the influence of commiseration, a harmony of love and beauty succeeds. Bring such a man to the tombstone on which shall be inscribed an epitaph on his adversary, composed in the spirit which we have recommended. Would he turn from it as from an idle tale? No; — the thoughtful look, the sigh, and perhaps the involuntary tear, would testify that it had a sane, a generous, and good meaning; and that on the writer's mind had remained an impression which was a true abstract of the character of the deceased; that his gifts and graces were remembered in the simplicity in which they ought to be remembered. The composition and quality of the mind of a virtuous man, contemplated by the side of the grave where his body is mouldering, ought to appear, and be felt as something midway between what he was on earth walking about with his living frailties, and what he may be presumed to be as a Spirit in heaven.

It suffices, therefore, that the trunk and the main branches of the worth of the deceased be boldly and unaffectedly represented. Any further detail, minutely and scrupulously pursued, especially if this be done with laborious and antithetic discriminations, must inevitably frustrate its own purpose; forcing the passing Spectator to this conclusion, — either that the dead did not possess the merits ascribed to him, or that they who have raised a monument to his memory, and must therefore be supposed to have been closely connected with him, were incapable of perceiving those merits; or at least during the act of composition had lost sight of them; for, the understanding having been so busy in its petty occupation, how could the heart of the mourner be other than cold? and in either of these cases, whether the fault be on the part of the buried person or the survivors, the memorial is unaffecting and profitless.

Much better is it to fall short in discrimination than to pursue it too far, or to labour it un-

feelingly. For in no place are we so much disposed to dwell upon those points, of nature and condition, wherein all men resemble each other, as in the temple where the universal Father is worshipped, or by the side of the grave which gathers all human Beings to itself, and 'equalises the lofty and the low.' We suffer and we weep with the same heart; we love and are anxious for one another in one spirit; our hopes look to the same quarter; and the virtues by which we are all to be furthered and supported, as patience, meekness, good-will, justice, temperance, and temperate desires, are in an equal degree the concern of us all. Let an Epitaph, then, contain at least these acknowledgments to our common nature; nor let the sense of their importance be sacrificed to a balance of opposite qualities or minute distinctions in individual character; which if they do not (as will for the most part be the case), when examined, resolve themselves into a trick of words, will, even when they are true and just, for the most part be grievously out of place; for, as it is probable that few only have explored these intricacies of human nature, so can the tracing of them be interesting only to a few. But an epitaph is not a proud writing shut up for the studious: it is exposed to all — to the wise and the most ignorant; it is condescending, perspicuous, and lovingly solicits regard; its story and admonitions are brief, that the thoughtless, the busy, and indolent, may not be deterred, nor the impatient tired: the stooping old man cons the engraven record like a second horn-book; — the child is proud that he can read it; — and the stranger is introduced through its mediation to the company of a friend: it is concerning all, and for all: — in the church-yard it is open to the day; the sun looks down upon the stone, and the rains of heaven beat against it.

Yet, though the writer who would excite sympathy is bound in this case, more than in any other, to give proof that he himself has been moved, it is to be remembered, that to raise a monument is a sober and a reflective act; that the inscription which it bears is intended to be permanent, and for universal perusal; and that, for this reason, the thoughts and feelings expressed should be permanent also — liberated from that weakness and anguish of sorrow which is in nature transitory, and which with instinctive decency retires from notice. The passions should be subdued, the emotions controlled; strong, indeed, but nothing ungovernable or wholly involuntary. Seemliness requires this, and truth requires it also: for how can the narrator otherwise be trusted? Moreover, a grave is a tranquillising object: resignation in course of time springs up from it as naturally as the wild flowers, besprinkling the turf with which it may be covered, or gathering round the monument by which it is defended. The very form and substance of the monument which has received the inscription, and the appearance of the letters, testifying with what a slow and laborious hand they must have been engraven, might seem to reproach the author who had given way upon this occasion to transports of mind, or to quick turns of conflicting passion; though the same might constitute the life and beauty of a funeral oration or elegiac poem.

These sensations and judgments, acted upon perhaps unconsciously, have been one of the main causes why epitaphs so often personate the deceased, and represent him as speaking from his own tomb-stone. The departed Mortal is introduced telling you himself that his pains are gone; that a state of rest is come; and he conjures you to weep for him no longer. He admonishes with the voice of one experienced in the vanity of those affections which are confined to earthly objects, and gives a verdict like a superior Being, performing the office of a judge, who has no temptations to mislead him, and whose decision cannot but be dispassionate. Thus is death disarmed of its sting, and affliction unsubstantialised. By this tender fiction, the survivors bind themselves to a sedater sorrow, and employ the intervention of the imagination in order that the reason may speak her own language earlier than she would otherwise have been enabled to do. This shadowy interposition also harmoniously unites the two worlds of the living and the dead by their appropriate affections. And it may be observed, that here we have an additional proof of the propriety with which sepulchral inscriptions were referred to the consciousness of immortality as their primal source.

I do not speak with a wish to recommend that an epitaph should be cast in this mould preferably to the still more common one, in which what is said comes from the survivors directly; but rather to point out how natural those feelings are which have induced men, in all states and ranks of society, so frequently to adopt this mode. And this I have done chiefly in order that the laws, which ought to govern the composition of the other, may be better understood. This latter mode, namely, that in which the survivors speak in their own persons, seems to me upon the whole greatly preferable: as it admits a wider range of notices; and, above all, because, excluding the fiction which is the groundwork of the other, it rests upon a more solid basis.

Enough has been said to convey our notion of a perfect epitaph; but it must be borne in mind that one is meant which will best answer the *general* ends of that species of composition. According to the course pointed out, the worth of private life, through all varieties of situation and character, will be most honourably and profitably preserved in memory. Nor would the model recommended less suit public men, in all instances save of those persons who by the greatness of their services in the employments of peace or war, or by the surpassing excellence of their works in art, literature, or science, have made themselves not only universally known, but have filled the heart of their country with everlasting gratitude. Yet I must here pause to correct myself. In describing the general tenour of thought which epitaphs ought to hold, I have

omitted to say, that if it be the *actions* of a man, or even some *one* conspicuous or beneficial art of local or general utility, which have distinguished him, and excited a desire that he should be remembered, then, of course, ought the attention to be directed chiefly to those actions or that act: and such sentiments dwelt upon as naturally arise out of them or it. Having made this necessary distinction, I proceed. — The mighty benefactors of mankind, as they are not only known by the immediate survivors, but will continue to be known familiarly to latest posterity, do not stand in need of biographic sketches, in such a place; nor of delineations of character to individualise them. This is already done by their Works, in the memories of men. Their naked means, and a grand comprehensive sentiment of civil gratitude, patriotic love, or human admiration — or the utterance of some elementary principle most essential in the constitution of true virtue; — or a declaration touching that pious humility and self-abasement, which are ever most profound as minds are most susceptible of genuine exaltation — or an intuition, communicated in adequate words, of the sublimity of intellectual power — these are their only tribute which can here be paid — the only offering that upon such an altar would not be unworthy.

"What needs my Shakspeare for his honoured bones
The labour of an age in piled stones,
Or that his hallowed reliques should be hid
Under a star-ypointing pyramid?
Dear Son of Memory, great Heir of Fame,
What need'st thou such weak witness of thy name?
Thou in our wonder and astonishment
Hast built thyself a livelong monument,
And so sepulchred, in such pomp dost lie,
That kings for such a tomb would wish to die."

BOOK SIXTH. Line 19. *and spires whose 'silent finger points to heaven.'* An instinctive taste teaches men to build their churches in flat countries with spire-steeples, which, as they cannot be referred to any other object, point as with silent finger to the sky and stars, and sometimes, when they reflect the brazen light of a rich though rainy sunset, appear like a pyramid of flame burning heavenward. See *The Friend*, by S. T. Coleridge, No. 14, p. 223. W. W.

Lines 95 ff. Wordsworth discusses the tales told of the church-yard in the headnote, p. 406.

BOOK SEVENTH. Line 111. *Priest.* See the headnote, p. 408.

Line 316. *Priest.* Robert Walker, described in Wordsworth's note to "The River Duddon," Sonnets XVII and XVIII.

Line 400. *a gentle Dalesman.* See the headnote, p. 408.

Line 616. *That sycamore, etc.*

"This Sycamore oft musical with Bees;
Such Tents the Patriarchs loved."
S. T. Coleridge W. W.

Line 758. *a boastful Tyrant.* Napoleon.

Line 980. *Perish the roses and the flowers of kings.* The "Transit gloria mundi" is finely expressed in the Introduction to the Foundation-charters of some of the ancient Abbeys. Some expressions here used are taken from that of the Abbey of St. Mary's, Furness, the translation of which is as follows: —

"Considering every day the uncertainty of life, that the roses and flowers of Kings, Emperors, and Dukes, and the crowns and palms of all the great wither and decay; and that all things, with an uninterrupted course, tend to dissolution and death: I therefore," etc. W. W.

BOOK EIGHTH. Line 87. *An inventive Age.* See headnote, pp. 408–409.

Line 111. *Earth has lent her waters,* etc. In treating this subject, it was impossible not to recollect with gratitude the pleasing picture which in his poem of the Fleece the excellent and amiable Dyer has given of the influences of manufacturing industry upon the face of this Island. He wrote at a time when machinery was first beginning to be introduced, and his benevolent heart prompted him to augur from it nothing but good. Truth has compelled me to dwell upon the baneful effects arising out of an ill-regulated and excessive application of powers so admirable in themselves. W. W.

Line 413. *Christ-cross-row.* The alphabet arranged in form of a cross in the old Hornbooks [G].

BOOK NINTH. Line 299. *Binding herself by statute,* etc. The discovery of Dr. Bell affords marvellous facilities for carrying this into effect; and it is impossible to overrate the benefit which might accrue to humanity from the universal application of this simple engine under an enlightened and conscientious government. W. W.
An educational reformer, Dr. Andrew Bell (1753–1832) proposed the use of student teachers.

Page 525. LAODAMIA.
A story told by Virgil, Ovid, and Euripides.
Lines 158–63. Much of the "trouble" this poem cost Wordsworth concerned the appropriate punishment for Laodamia. In the first version (1815) this stanza ran as follows:

Ah, judge her gently who as deeply love!
Her, who, in reason's spite, yet without crime,
Was in a trance of passion thus removed;
Delivered from the galling yoke of time
And these frail elements — to gather flowers
Of blissful quiet 'mid unfading bowers.

In 1827 he was less forgiving:

By no weak pity might the Gods be moved;
She who thus perished not without the crime
Of Lovers that in Reason's spite have loved,
Was doomed to wander in a grosser clime,
Apart from happy Ghosts, that gather flowers
Of blissful quiet 'mid unfading bowers.

In 1845 the stanza assumed its final form. "As first written," Wordsworth wrote to his son John in justification of the change, "the heroine was dismissed to happiness in Elysium. To what purpose then the mission of Protesilaus? he exhorts her to moderate her passion; the exhortation is fruitless, and no punishment follows. So it stood; at present she is placed among unhappy ghosts for disregard of the exhortation. Virgil

also places her there, but compare the two passages, and give me your opinion."
Line 169. *spiry trees,* etc. For the account of these long-lived trees, see Pliny's *Natural History,* lib. xvi. cap. 44; and for the features in the character of Protesilaus see the "Iphigenia in Aulis" of Euripides. Virgil places the Shade of Laodamia in a mournful region, among unhappy Lovers.

"——His Laodamia,
It comes.——"   W. W.

Page 527. DION.
This poem began with the following stanza, which has been displaced on account of its detaining the reader too long from the subject, and as rather precluding, than preparing for, the due effect of the allusion to the genius of Plato: —

"Fair is the Swan, whose majesty, prevailing
O'er breezeless water, on Locarno's lake,
Bears him on while proudly sailing
He leaves behind a moon-illumined wake:
Behold! the mantling spirit of reserve
Fashions his neck into a goodly curve;
An arch thrown back between luxuriant wings
Of whitest garniture, like fir-tree boughs
To which, on some unruffled morning, clings
A flaky weight of winter's purest snows!
— Behold! — as with a gushing impulse heaves
That downy prow, and softly cleaves
The mirror of the crystal flood,
Vanish inverted hill, and shadowy wood,
And pendent rocks, where'er, in gliding state,
Winds the mute Creature without visible Mate
Or Rival, save the Queen of night
Showering down a silver light,
From heaven, upon her chosen Favourite!"
                                        W. W.

Page 529. I. THE BROWNIE'S CELL.
Line 92. *Nysa's isle.* See *Paradise Lost,* IV. 275–79.

Page 530. II. COMPOSED AT CORA LINN.
The motto is taken from *The Prelude,* I.214–20.

Page 532. IV. YARROW VISITED.
A sequel to "Yarrow Unvisited" (p. 301). "Second parts," Wordsworth wrote in a letter, "if much inferior to the first are always disgusting, and as I had succeeded in 'Yarrow Unvisited,' I was anxious there should be no falling-off; but that was unavoidable, perhaps, from the subject, as imagination almost always transcends reality."

Page 534. To B. R. HAYDON.
A painter in the grand style, Benjamin Robert Haydon (1786–1846) is remembered for his diaries. He was a friend of Keats and Lamb as well as Wordsworth.

Page 534. ARTEGAL AND ELIDURE.
In Book I of his *History of England* (the reference, in the headnote, to the Preface is incorrect), Milton tells the story of the virtuous Elidure, who returned the crown to his deposed brother.

Line 2. *the Trojan.* Brutus, legendary founder of Britain.

Line 17. *Corineus.* Follower of Brutus, ruler of Cornwall.

Line 34. *Guendolen.* Declared war upon her husband, Locrine, who betrayed her for a German princess by whom he had a daughter, Sabrina.

Line 41. King Lear succeeded Locrine.

Line 97. *Troynovant.* London.

Lines 234–39. This passage closely follows Milton's language in the *History*: "Thus was a brother saved by a brother, to whom love of a crown, the thing that so often dazzles and vitiates mortal men, for which thousands of nearest blood have destroyed each other, was in respect of brotherly dearness, a contemptible thing."

Page 539. "WEAK IS THE WILL OF MAN."
Prefixed to "The White Doe" in 1815 and 1820.

Page 540. TO THE POET, JOHN DYER.
Line 1. "The Fleece," a didactic poem on sheep husbandry, was published in 1757.

Page 541. ODE — THE MORNING OF THE DAY APPOINTED FOR A GENERAL THANKSGIVING.
A celebration of the victorious end of the French war.

"Wholly unworthy of touching upon the momentous subject here treated would that Poet be, before whose eyes the present distresses under which this kingdom labours could interpose a veil sufficiently thick to hide, or even to obscure, the splendour of this great moral triumph. If I have given way to exultation, unchecked by these distresses, it might be sufficient to protect me from a charge of insensibility, should I state my own belief that the sufferings will be transitory. Upon the wisdom of a very large majority of the British nation rested that generosity which poured out the treasures of this country for the deliverance of Europe: and in the same national wisdom, presiding in time of peace over an energy not inferior to that which has been displayed in war, *they* confide, who encourage a firm hope that the cup of our wealth will be gradually replenished. There will, doubtless, be no few ready to indulge in regrets and repinings; and to feed a morbid satisfaction, by aggravating these burthens in imagination; in order that calamity so confidently prophesied, as it has not taken the shape which their sagacity alloted to it, may appear as grievous as possible under another. But the body of the nation will not quarrel with the gain, because it might have been purchased at a less price; and, acknowledging in these sufferings, which they feel to have been in a great degree unavoidable, a consecration of their noble efforts, they will vigorously apply themselves to remedy the evil.

"Nor is it at the expense of rational patriotism, or in disregard of sound philosophy, that I have given vent to feelings tending to encourage a martial spirit in the bosoms of my countrymen, at a time when there is a general outcry against the prevalence of these dispositions. The British army, both by its skill and valour in the field, and by the discipline which rendered it, to the inhabitants of the several countries where its operations were carried on, a protection from the violence of their own troops, has performed services that will not allow the language of gratitude and admiration to be suppressed or restrained (whatever be the temper of the public mind) through a scrupulous dread lest the tribute due to the past should prove an injurious incentive for the future. Every man deserving the name of Briton adds his voice to the chorus which extols the exploits of his countrymen, a consciousness, at times overpowering the effort, that they transcend all praise. — But this particular sentiment thus irresistibly excited, is not sufficient. The nation would err grievously if she suffered the abuse which other states have made of military power to prevent her from perceiving that no people ever was or can be independent, free, of secure, much less great, in any same application of the word, without a cultivation of military virtues. Nor let it be overlooked that the benefits derivable from these sources are placed within the reach of Great Britain, under conditions peculiarly favourable. The same insular position which, by rendering territorial incorporation impossible, utterly precludes the desire of conquest under the most seductive shape it can assume, enables her to rely, for her defence against foreign foes, chiefly upon a species of armed force from which her own liberties have nothing to fear. Such are the privileges of her situation; and, by permitting, they invite her to give way to the courageous instincts of human nature, and to strengthen and refine them by culture.

"But some have more than insinuated that a design exists to subvert the civil character of the English people by unconstitutional applications and unnecessary increase of military power. The advisers and abettors of such a design, were it possible that it should exist, would be guilty of the most heinous crime, which, upon this planet, can be committed. Trusting that this apprehension arises from the delusive influences of an honourable jealousy, let me hope that the martial qualities which I venerate will be fostered by adhering to those good old usages which experience has sanctioned, and by availing ourselves of new means of indisputable promise: particularly by applying, in its utmost possible extent, that system of tuition whose master-spring is a habit of gradually enlightened subordination; — by imparting knowledge, civil, moral, and religious, in such measure that the mind, among all classes of the community, may love, admire, and be prepared and accomplished to defend, that country under whose protection its faculties have been unfolded and its riches acquired; — by just dealing towards all orders of the state, so that, no members of it being trampled upon, courage may everywhere continue to rest immovably upon its ancient English foundation, personal self-respect; — by adequate rewards and permanent honours conferred upon the deserving; — by encouraging athletic exercises and manly sports among the peasantry of the country; — and by especial care to provide and support institutions in which, during a time of peace, a reasonable proportion of the youth of the country may be instructed in military science.

"I have only to add that I should feel little satisfaction in giving to the world these limited attempts to celebrate the virtues of my country, if I did not encourage a hope that a subject, which it has fallen within my province to treat only in the mass, will by other poets be illustrated in that detail which its importance calls for, and which will allow opportunities to give the merited applause in PERSONS as well as to THINGS.

"The ode was published along with other pieces, now interspersed through this volume." W. W.
Line 122.

"Discipline the rule whereof is passion."
LORD BROOKE. W. W.

Page 544. ODE.
Lines 106–109. A substitution for the following controversial lines, which stood from 1816 to 1832:

But Thy most dreaded instrument,
In working out a pure intent,
Is Man — arrayed for mutual slaughter,
— Yea, carnage is thy daughter!

Page 549. THE FRENCH ARMY IN RUSSIA.
On the disastrous retreat of the French from Russia in the winter of 1812–13.

Page 550. "BY MOSCOW SELF-DEVOTED TO A BLAZE."
Moscow was burned by the retreating Russians in September 1812.

Page 550. THE GERMANS ON THE HEIGHTS OF HOCHHEIM.
The event is thus recorded in the journals of the day: "When the Austrians took Hochheim, in one part of the engagement they got to the brow of the hill, whence they had their first view of the Rhine. They instantly halted — not a gun was fired — not a voice heard: they stood gazing on the river with those feelings which the events of the last fifteen years at once called up. Prince Schwartzenberg rode up to know the cause of this sudden stop; they then gave three cheers, rushed after the enemy, and drove them into the water." W. W.

Page 551. SIEGE OF VIENNA RAISED BY JOHN SOBIESKI.

Ond' è ch'Io grido e griderò: giugnesti,
Guerregiasti, e vincesti;
Si, si, vincesti, o Campion forte e pio,
Per Dio vincesti, e per te vinse Iddio.

See Filicaia's Canzone, addressed to John Sobieski, King of Poland, upon his raising the siege of Vienna. This, and his other poems on the same occasion, are superior perhaps to any lyrical pieces that contemporary events have ever given

birth to, those of the Hebrew Scriptures only excepted. W. W. (1820). Vienna was relieved in 1683.

Page 551. OCCASIONED BY THE BATTLE OF WATERLOO.
The Battle of Waterloo took place on June 18, 1815.
Line 9. Assoiled, etc.

"From all the world's encumbrance did himself assoil."
SPENSER. W. W. [Faerie Queene, VI.v.37]

Page 552. FEELINGS OF A FRENCH ROYALIST.
The Duc d'Enghien was shot for conspiring to assassinate Napoleon. In 1814 his remains were disinterred and transferred to the castle of Vincennes.

Page 552. TRANSLATION.
Wordsworth translated Books I–III of the Aeneid, together with other passages, but published only the following selections from Book I (lines 657–756).

Page 554. A FACT AND AN IMAGINATION.
Line 1. The Danish Conqueror. Canute, Danish King of England, 1017–35. The legend is famous.
Line 26. Alfred. King of Wessex, 871–901, Alfred led English resistance to the incursions of the Danes.

Page 555. To DORA.
Lines 1–2. From Milton's Samson Agonistes, lines 1–2.

Page 558. Ode to Lycoris.
The title is from Virgil's tenth and final Eclogue, in which the poet consoles his friend Gallus for the disappearance of the beautiful shepherdess Lycoris.

Page 563. SEQUEL TO THE "BEGGARS."
For the poem of 1802, see p. 275.

Page 566. COMPOSED UPON AN EVENING OF EXTRAORDINARY SPLENDOUR AND BEAUTY.
Headnote. The "class" of poems referred to is that of "Evening Voluntaries."
Line 49. Wings at my shoulders seem to play. In these lines I am under obligation to the exquisite picture of "Jacob's Dream," by Mr. Allston, now in America. It is pleasant to make this public acknowledgment to a man of genius, whom I have the honour to rank among my friends. W. W. Washington Allston, American painter (1779–1843).
Line 80. The multiplication of mountain-ridges, described at the commencement of the third Stanza of this Ode as a kind of Jacob's Ladder, leading to Heaven, is produced either by watery vapours, or sunny haze; — in the present instance by the latter cause. Allusions to the Ode entitled

"Intimations of Immortality" pervade the last Stanza of the foregoing poem. W. W.

Page 567. THIS, AND THE TWO FOLLOWING.
Line 14. Waters (as Mr. Westall informs us in the letterpress prefixed to his admirable views) are invariably found to flow through these caverns. W. W. The artist William Westall (1781–1850) was a friend of Wordsworth and Sir George Beaumont.

Page 569. WRITTEN UPON A BLANK LEAF.
Izaak Walton's *The Compleat Angler* (1653).

Page 570. To THE RIVER DERWENT.
Line 10. *Nemæan victor*. The Nemæan games were held in ancient Argos.

Page 571. "I HEARD (ALAS! 'T WAS ONLY IN A DREAM)."
See the Phædo of Plato, by which this Sonnet was suggested. W. W.

Page 572. SEPTEMBER 1819.
This and the following poem were named by Wordsworth in the headnote to "To the Same" (p. 559) as having been composed near Rydal Mount.

Page 572. UPON THE SAME OCCASION.
Lines 28–30. An allusion, perhaps, to Lord Byron, whom Wordsworth described in 1833 as "a Man of Genius whose heart is perverted." See "Not in the Lucid Intervals of Life," p. 725, and note.
Lines 38 ff. A list of famous classical lyric poets: Alcæus, Greek poet of the sixth century B.C.; Sappho (the "Lesbian Maid," line 46), lyric poet of the seventh century B.C., who lived on the island of Lesbos; Simonides (line 54), fifth century B.C.
Line 59. *Maro*. Virgil.

Page 573. "THERE IS A LITTLE UNPRETENDING RILL."
A reminiscence of the spring of 1794, when Wordsworth and his sister were reunited in the Lake District after a long separation.

Page 573. ON THE DEATH OF HIS MAJESTY.
George III died on January 28, 1820, after years of insanity.

Page 574. To THE LADY MARY LOWTHER.
Lady Mary was the daughter of Wordsworth's friend and patron, the Earl of Lonsdale, Lord Lowther.

Page 574. ON THE DETRACTION WHICH FOLLOWED THE PUBLICATION OF A CERTAIN POEM.
Composed in 1798, "Peter Bell" was published in 1819. It was severely criticized in the *Eclectic* and *Monthly Reviews*, among others.

Page 574. OXFORD, MAY 30, 1820.
Line 11. *Isis*. A name for the River Thames as it flows through the town of Oxford, which

Wordsworth, with his wife and sister, visited on their way to the continent in 1820.

Page 575. JUNE 1820.
Line 2. *Groves*. Wallachia. W. W.
Line 12. *Poet of the Seasons*. James Thomson (1700–48).

Page 575. MEMORIALS OF A TOUR ON THE CONTINENT.
The Wordsworths crossed the English Channel in July 1820 and returned to England in November. The poems were composed to supplement the journals kept by Mary and Dorothy.

Page 575. I. FISH-WOMEN.
If in this sonnet I should seem to have borne a little too hard upon the personal appearance of the worthy Poissards of Calais, let me take shelter under the authority of my lamented friend, the late Sir George Beaumont. He, a most accurate observer, used to say of them, that their features and countenances seemed to have conformed to those of the creatures they dealt in; at all events the resemblance was striking. W. W.

Page 576. II. BRUGÈS.
This is not the first poetical tribute which in our times has been paid to this beautiful city. Mr. Southey, in the "Poet's Pilgrimage," speaks of it in lines which I cannot deny myself the pleasure of connecting with my own.

"Time hath not wronged her, nor hath ruin sought
    Rudely her splendid structures to destroy,
Save in those recent days, with evil fraught,
    When mutability, in drunken joy
Triumphant, and from all restraint released,
Let loose her fierce and many-headed beast.

"But for the scars in that unhappy rage
    Inflicted, firm she stands and undecayed;
Like our first Sires, a beautiful old age
    Is hers in venerable years arrayed;
And yet, to her, benignant stars may bring,
What fate denies to man, — a second spring.

"When I have read of tilts in days of old,
    And tourneys graced by Chieftains of renown,
Fair dames, grave citizens, and warriors bold,
    If fancy would pourtray some stately town,
Which for such pomp fit theatre should be,
Fair Brugès, I shall then remember thee."

In this city are many vestiges of the splendour of the Burgundian Dukedom, and the long black mantle universally worn by the females is probably a remnant of the old Spanish connection, which, if I do not much deceive myself, is traceable in the grave deportment of its inhabitants. Brugès is comparatively little disturbed by that curious contest, or rather conflict, of Flemish with French propensities in matters of taste, so conspicuous through other parts of Flanders. The hotel to which we drove at Ghent furnished an odd instance. In the passages were paintings and statues, after the antique of Hebe and Apollo; and in the garden a little pond, about a yard and a half in diameter, with a weeping willow bending over it, and under the shade of that tree, in the centre of the pond, a wooden painted statue of a Dutch or Flemish boor, looking ineffably tender upon his mistress, and embracing her. A living duck, tethered at the feet of the sculptured lovers, alternately tormented a miserable eel and itself with endeavours to escape from its bonds and prison. Had we chanced to espy the hostess of the hotel in this quaint rural retreat, the exhibition would have been complete. She was a true Flemish figure, in the dress of the days of Holbein; her symbol of office, a weighty bunch of keys, pendent from her portly waist. In Brussels the modern taste in costume, architecture, etc., has got the mastery; in Ghent there is a struggle; but in Brugès old images are still paramount, and an air of monastic life among the quiet goings-on of a thinly-peopled city is inexpressibly soothing; a pensive grace seems to be cast over all, even the very children. — *Extract from Journal*. W. W.

Page 577. VI. AIX-LA-CHAPELLE.
Line 2. *Seat of Charlemaine*. A chair exhibited in the town cathedral, "on which the Emperors were formerly crowned" (Dorothy's journal).
Line 14. *Where unremitting frosts the rocky crescent bleach*. "Let a wall of rocks be imagined from three to six hundred feet in height, and rising between France and Spain, so as physically to separate the two kingdoms — let us fancy this wall curved like a crescent, with its convexity towards France. Lastly, let us suppose, that in the very middle of the wall, a breach of 300 feet wide has been beaten down by the famous *Roland*, and we may have a good idea of what the mountaineers call the 'BRECHE DE ROLAND.'" — *Raymond's Pyrenees*. W. W.

Page 578. HYMN FOR THE BOATMEN.
Line 24. *Miserere Domine*. See the beautiful Song in Mr. Coleridge's Tragedy, "The Remorse." Why is the harp of Quantock silent? W. W. Coleridge completed a first version of his tragedy (under the title of "Osorio") in 1797, when he lived in Somerset near the Quantock Hills.

Page 578. THE SOURCE OF THE DANUBE.
Lines 1, 2.

Not, like his great Compeers, indignantly Doth Danube spring to life!

Before this quarter of the Black Forest was inhabited, the source of the Danube might have suggested some of those sublime images which Armstrong has so finely described; at present, the contrast is most striking. The Spring appears in a capacious stone Basin in front of a Ducal palace, with a pleasure-ground opposite; then, passing under the pavement, takes the form of a little, clear, bright, black, vigorous rill, barely wide enough to tempt the agility of a child five years old to leap over it, — and entering the garden, it joins, after a course of a few hundred yards, a stream much more considerable than itself. The *copiousness* of the spring at *Doneschingen* must have procured for it the honour of

being named the Source of the Danube. W. W.
Line 3. *Crescent's gleam*. The Moslem territories at the mouth of the Danube.
Line 8. *gloomy sea*. The Black Sea, on which, according to Greek myth, the Argonauts sailed in search of the Golden Fleece, accompanied by Orpheus.

Page 578. ON APPROACHING THE STAUB-BACH, LAUTERBRUNNEN.
"The Staub-bach" is a narrow Stream, which, after a long course on the heights, comes to the sharp edge of a somewhat overhanging precipice, overleaps it with a bound, and after a fall of 930 feet, forms again a rivulet. The vocal powers of these musical Beggars may seem to be exaggerated; but this wild and savage air was utterly unlike any sounds I had ever heard; the notes reached me from a distance, and on what occasion they were sung I could not guess, only they seemed to belong, in some way or other, to the Waterfall — and reminded me of religious services chanted to Streams and Fountains in Pagan times. Mr. Southey has thus accurately characterised the peculiarity of this music: "While we were at the Waterfall, some half-score peasants, chiefly women and girls, assembled just out of reach of the Spring, and set up — surely, the wildest chorus that ever was heard by human ears, — a song not of articulate sounds, but in which the voice was used as a mere instrument of music, more flexible than any which art could produce, — sweet, powerful, and thrilling beyond description." See Notes to *A Tale of Paraguay*. W. W.

Page 580. ENGELBERG, THE HILL OF ANGELS.
The Convent whose site was pointed out, according to tradition, in this manner, is seated at its base. The architecture of the building is unimpressive, but the situation is worthy of the honour which the imagination of the mountaineers has conferred upon it. W. W.

Page 580. OUR LADY OF THE SNOW.
Line 3. *thy own mountain*. Mount Righi. W. W.

Page 580. EFFUSION.
The following stanzas were suggested by the "Tower of Tell," at Altdorf, on the outside walls of which the chief exploits of the Hero are painted. W. W. (note to edition of 1822).

Page 581. THE TOWN OF SCHWYTZ.
Nearly 500 years (says Ebel, speaking of the French Invasion) has elapsed, when, for the first time, foreign soldiers were seen upon the frontiers of this small Canton, to impose upon it the laws of their governors. W. W.

Page 581. ON HEARING THE "RANZ DES VACHES."
A Swiss folksong, the "Ranz des Vaches" was famous for its power to inspire patriotism. See *Descriptive Sketches*, line 527 and note.

Page 582. CHURCH OF SAN SALVADOR.
Line 20. The quotation is from Milton's *Comus*, lines 5–6.
Line 36. Arnold Winkelried, at the battle of Sempach, broke an Austrian phalanx in this manner. The event is one of the most famous in the annals of Swiss heroism; and pictures and prints of it are frequent throughout the country. W.W.

Page 584. THE LAST SUPPER.
Lines 1, 2.

*Tho' searching damps and many an envious flaw
Have marred this Work.*

This picture of the Last Supper has not only been grievously injured by time, but the greatest part of it, if not the whole, is said to have been retouched, or painted over again. These niceties may be left to connoisseurs, — I speak of it as I felt. The copy exhibited in London some years ago, and the engraving by Merghen, are both admirable; but in the original is a power which neither of those works has attained, or even approached. W. W.

Page 584. THE ECLIPSE OF THE SUN.
Line 40. *Of Figures human and divine.* The statues ranged round the spire and along the roof of the Cathedral of Milan have been found fault with by persons whose exclusive taste is unfortunate for themselves. It is true that the same expense and labour, judiciously directed to purposes more strictly architectural, might have much heightened the general effect of the building; for, seen from the ground, the Statues appear diminutive. But the *coup-d'œil*, from the best point of view, which is half way up the spire, must strike the unprejudiced person with admiration; and surely the selection and arrangement of the Figures is exquisitely fitted to support the religion of the country in the imaginations and feelings of the spectator. It was with great pleasure that I saw, during the two ascents which we made, several children, of different ages, tripping up and down the slender spire, and pausing to look around them, with feelings much more animated than could have been derived from these or the finest works of art, if placed within easy reach. — Remember also that you have the Alps on one side, and on the other the Appenines, with the plain of Lombardy between! W. W.
Line 52. Above the highest circle of figures is a zone of metallic stars. W. W.

Page 585. THE THREE COTTAGE GIRLS.
Lines 53–54. See "To a Highland Girl," p. 297.

Page 587. ECHO, UPON THE GEMMI.
The Gemmi is a steep pass across the mountains of the Bernese Oberland.

Page 587. PROCESSIONS.
Stanzas 1–4. A survey of pre-Christian religious rites, Persian, Hebrew, Egyptian, and Roman.

Line 45. *Argentière.* A glacier near the valley of Chamonix.
Lines 48–49.

*Still, with those white-robed Shapes — a living Stream,
The glacier Pillars join in solemn guise.*

This Procession is a part of the sacramental service performed once a month. In the valley of Engelberg we had the good fortune to be present at the *Grand Festival* of the Virgin — but the Procession on that day, though consisting of upwards of 1000 persons, assembled from all the branches of the sequestered valley, was much less striking (notwithstanding the sublimity of the surrounding scenery); it wanted both the simplicity of the other and the accompaniment of the Glacier-columns, whose sisterly resemblance to the *moving* Figures gave it a most beautiful and solemn peculiarity. W. W.

Page 588. ELEGIAC STANZAS.
Line 3. *Queen.* Mount Righi, — Regina Montium. W. W.
Line 64. Goldau is one of the villages desolated by the fall of part of the Mountain Rossberg. W. W. 1837.
Line 75. *This tribute*, etc. The persuasion here expressed was not groundless. The first human consolation that the afflicted mother felt, was derived from this tribute to her son's memory, a fact which the author learned, at his own residence, from her daughter, who visited Europe some years afterward. W. W.

Page 590. ON BEING STRANDED NEAR THE HARBOUR OF BOULOGNE.
Near the town of Boulogne, and overhanging the beach, are the remains of a tower which bears the name of Caligula, who here terminated his western expedition, of which these seashells were the boasted spoils. And at no great distance from these ruins, Buonaparte, standing upon a mound of earth, harangued his "Army of England," reminding them of the exploits of Caesar, and pointing towards the white cliffs, upon which their standards *were to float.* He recommended also a subscription to be raised among the Soldiery to erect on that ground, in memory of the foundation of the "Legion of Honour," a Column — which was not completed at the time we were there. W. W.

Page 590. AFTER LANDING — THE VALLEY OF DOVER, NOVEMBER 1820.
Lines 1–4. A reference to the scandal over the king's attempt to annul his marriage to Queen Caroline, during the months the Wordsworths were abroad.
Lines 6–7.

*We mark majestic herds of cattle, free
To ruminate.*

This is a most grateful sight for an Englishman returning to his native land. Everywhere one misses in the cultivated grounds abroad, the animated and soothing accompaniment of animals ranging and selecting their own food at will. W. W.

Page 591. DESULTORY STANZAS.
Lines 19–27. In the 3d of the Desultory Stanzas I am indebted to M. Ramond, who has written with genuine feeling on these subjects. W. W. 1822. Ramond de Carbonnières's comments on Switzerland provided an important source for *Descriptive Sketches*; see the notes to that poem.
Line 21. *diluvian power.* The Biblical flood, crested by the highest Alps.
Line 37. *Far as St. Maurice, from yon eastern Forks.* At the head of the Valais. LES FOURCHES, the point at which the two chains of mountains part, that inclose the Valais which terminates at ST. MAURICE. W. W.
Line 49–51. *ye that occupy*

> *Your council-seats beneath the open sky,*
> *On Sarnen's Mount.*

Sarnen, one of the two capitals of the Canton of Unterwalden; the spot here alluded to is close to the town, and is called the Landenberg, from the tyrant of that name, whose château formerly stood there. On the 1st of January 1308, the great day which the confederated Heroes had chosen for the deliverance of their country, all the castles of the Governors were taken by force or stratagem; and the Tyrants themselves conducted, with their creatures, to the frontiers, after having witnessed the destruction of their strongholds. From that time the Landenberg has been the place where the Legislators of this division of the Canton assemble. The site, which is well described by Ebel, is one of the most beautiful in Switzerland. W. W.
Line 56. *Calls me to pace her honoured Bridge.* The bridges of Lucerne are roofed, and open at the sides, so that the passenger has at the same time, the benefit of shade, and a view of the magnificent country. The pictures are attached to the rafters; those from Scripture History, on the Cathedral-bridge, amount, according to my notes, to 240. Subjects from the Old Testament face the passenger as he goes towards the Cathedral, and those from the New as he returns. The pictures on these bridges, as well as those in most other parts of Switzerland, are not to be spoken of as works of art; but they are instruments admirably answering the purpose for which they were designed. W. W.

Page 592. THE RIVER DUDDON.
The thirty-four sonnets in this series trace the River Duddon from its source high in the mountains of the Lake District to its meeting with the sea.
"A Poet, whose works are not yet known as they deserve to be, thus enters upon his description of the 'Ruins of Rome:' —

> 'The rising Sun
> Flames on the ruins in the purer air
> Towering aloft;'

and ends thus —

> 'The setting Sun displays
> His visible great round, between yon towers,
> As through two shady cliffs.'

"Mr. Crowe, in his excellent loco-descriptive Poem, 'Lewesdon Hill,' is still more expeditious, finishing the whole on a May-morning, before breakfast.

> 'To-morrow for severer thought, but now
> To breakfast, and keep festival to-day.'

"No one believes, or is desired to believe, that those Poems were actually composed within such limits of time; nor was there any reason why a prose statement should acquaint the reader with the plain fact, to the disturbance of poetic credibility. But, in the present case, I am compelled to mention, that this series of Sonnets was the growth of many years; — the one which stands the 14th was the first produced; and others were added upon occasional visits to the Stream, or as recollections of the scenes upon its banks awakened a wish to describe them. In this manner I had proceeded insensibly, without perceiving that I was trespassing upon ground pre-occupied, at least as far as intention went, by Mr. Coleridge; who, more than twenty years ago, used to speak of writing a rural Poem, to be entitled 'The Brook,' of which he has given a sketch in a recent publication. But a particular subject cannot, I think, much interfere with a general one; and I have been further kept from encroaching upon any right Mr. C. may still wish to exercise, by the restriction which the frame of the Sonnet imposed upon me, narrowing unavoidably the range of thought, and precluding, though not without its advantages, many graces to which a freer movement of verse would naturally have led.

"May I not venture, then, to hope, that, instead of being a hindrance by anticipation of any part of the subject, these Sonnets may remind Mr. Coleridge of his own more comprehensive design, and induce him to fulfil it? — There is a sympathy in streams, — 'one calleth to another;' and I would gladly believe, that 'The Brook' will, ere long, murmur in concert with 'The Duddon.' But, asking pardon for this fancy, I need not scruple to say that those verses must indeed be ill-fated which can enter upon such pleasant walks of nature without receiving and giving inspiration. The power of waters over the minds of Poets has been acknowledged from the earliest ages; — through the 'Flumina amem sylvasque inglorius' of Virgil, down to the sublime apostrophe to the great rivers of the earth by Armstrong, and the simple ejaculation of Burns (chosen, if I recollect right, by Mr. Coleridge, as a motto for his embryo 'Brook').

> 'The Muse nae Poet ever fand her,
> Till by himsel' he learned to wander,
> Adown some trotting burn's meander,
> AND NA' THINK LANG.' "   W. W.

Page 593. DEDICATION.
Dr. Wordsworth. Christopher, William's young-

est brother, had recently been appointed Master of Trinity College, Cambridge.

Page 593. SONNET I.
Line 4. *Sabine Bard.* Horace, who celebrated the Blandusian (or Bandusian) Spring in an ode (III.xiii).

Page 594. SONNET II.
Line 11. *huge deer.* The deer alluded to is the Leigh, a gigantic species long since extinct. W. W.

Page 595. SONNET VI.
Lines 9, 10. *There bloomed the strawberry of the wilderness,* etc. These two lines are in a great measure taken from "The Beauties of Spring, a Juvenile Poem," by the Rev. Joseph Sympson. He was a native of Cumberland, and was educated at Hawkshead school: his poems are little known, but they contain passages of splendid description; and the versification of his "Vision of Alfred" is harmonious and animated. In describing the motions of the Sylphs that constitute the strange machinery of his Poem, he uses the following illustrative simile:

"Glancing from their plumes
A changeful light the azure vault illumes.
Less varying hues beneath the Pole adorn
The streamy glories of the Boreal morn,
That wavering to and fro their radiance shed
On Bothnia's gulf with glassy ice o'erspread.
Where the lone native, as he homeward glides,
On polished sandals o'er the imprisoned tides,
And still the balance of his frame preserves,
Wheeled on alternate foot in lengthening curves,
Sees at a glance, above him and below,
Two rival heavens with equal splendour glow.
Sphered in the centre of the world he seems;
For all around with soft effulgence gleams;
Stars, moons, and meteors, ray opposed to ray,
And solemn midnight pours the blaze of day."

He was a man of ardent feeling, and his faculties of mind, particularly his memory, were extraordinary. Brief notices of his life ought to find a place in the History of Westmoreland. W. W.

Page 596. SONNET XIII.
Line 3. *Byre.* A barn or cowshed.

Page 597. SONNET XVI.
Line 2. *the sculptured shows.* Indian rock paintings along the upper Orinoco River and elsewhere in South America, which Wordsworth found described in Alexander von Humboldt's *Travels* (1814–26).

Pages 597, 598. SONNETS XVII, XVIII.
The EAGLE requires a large domain for its support: but several pairs, not many years ago, were constantly resident in this country, building their nests in the steeps of Borrowdale, Wastdale, Ennerdale, and on the eastern side of Helvellyn. Often have I heard anglers speak of the grandeur of their appearance, as they hovered over Red Tarn, in one of the coves of this mountain. The bird frequently returns, but is always destroyed.

Not long since, one visited Rydal lake, and remained some hours near its banks; the consternation which it occasioned among the different species of fowl, particularly the herons, was expressed by loud screams. The horse also is naturally afraid of the eagle. — There were several Roman stations among these mountains; the most considerable seems to have been in a meadow at the head of Windermere, established, undoubtedly, as a check over the passes of Kirkstone, Dunmail-raise, and of Hardknot and Wrynose. On the margin of Rydal lake, a coin of Trajan was discovered very lately. — The ROMAN FORT here alluded to, called by the country people "*Hardknot Castle*," is most impressively situated half-way down the hill on the right of the road that descends from Hardknot into Eskdale. It has escaped the notice of most antiquarians, and is but slightly mentioned by Lysons. — The DRUIDICAL CIRCLE is about half a mile to the left of the road ascending Stoneside from the vale of Duddon: the country people call it "*Sunken Church.*"

The reader who may have been interested in the foregoing Sonnets (which together may be considered as a Poem) will not be displeased to find in this place a prose account of the Duddon, extracted from Green's comprehensive *Guide to the Lakes*, lately published. "The road leading from Coniston to Broughton is over high ground, and commands a view of the River Duddon; which, at high water, is a grand sight, having the beautiful and fertile lands of Lancashire and Cumberland stretching each way from its margin. In this extensive view, the face of nature is displayed in a wonderful variety of hill and dale, wooded grounds and buildings; amongst the latter Broughton Tower, seated on the crown of a hill, rising elegantly from the valley, is an object of extraordinary interest. Fertility on each side is gradually diminished, and lost in the superior heights of Backcomb, in Cumberland, and the high lands between Kirkby and Ulverstone.

"The road from Broughton to Seathwaite is on the banks of the Duddon, and on its Lancashire side it is of various elevations. The river is an amusing companion, one while brawling and tumbling over rocky precipices, until the agitated water becomes again calm by arriving at a smoother and less precipitous bed, but its course is soon again ruffled, and the current thrown into every variety of foam which the rocky channel of a river can give to water." — *Vide* Green's *Guide to the Lakes*, vol. i. pp. 98–100.

After all, the traveller would be most gratified who should approach this beautiful Stream, neither at its source, as is done in the Sonnets, nor from its termination; but from Coniston over Walna Scar; first descending into a little circular valley, a collateral compartment of the long winding vale through which flows the Duddon. This recess, towards the close of September, when the after-grass of the meadows is still of a fresh green, with the leaves of many of the trees faded, but perhaps none fallen, is truly enchanting. At a point elevated enough to show the various objects in the valley, and not so high as to diminish their importance, the stranger will instinctively halt. On the foreground, a little below the most favourable station, a rude foot-bridge is thrown over the bed of the noisy brook foaming by the wayside. Russet and craggy hills, of bold and varied outline, surround the level valley, which is besprinkled with grey rocks plumed with birch trees. A few homesteads are interspersed, in some places peeping out from among the rocks like hermitages, whose site has been chosen for the benefit of sunshine as well as shelter; in other instances, the dwelling-house, barn, and byre, compose together a cruciform structure, which, with its embowering trees, and the ivy clothing part of the walls and root like a fleece, call to mind the remains of an ancient abbey. Time, in most cases, and nature everywhere, have given a sanctity to the humble works of man that are scattered over this peaceful retirement. Hence a harmony of tone and colour, a consummation and perfection of beauty, which would have been marred had aim or purpose interfered with the course of convenience, utility, or necessity. This unvitiated region stands in no need of the veil of twilight to soften or disguise its features. As it glistens in the morning sunshine, it would fill the spectator's heart with gladsomeness. Looking from our chosen station, he would feel an impatience to rove among its pathways, to be greeted by the milkmaid, to wander from house to house exchanging "goodmorrows" as he passed the open doors; but, at evening, when the sun is set, and a pearly light gleams from the western quarter of the sky, with an answering light from the smooth surface of the meadows; when the trees are dusky, but each kind still distinguishable; when the cool air has condensed the blue smoke rising from the cottage chimneys; when the dark mossy stones seem to sleep in the bed of the foaming brook; *then* he would be unwilling to move forward, not less from a reluctance to relinquish what he beholds, than from an apprehension of disturbing, by his approach, the quietness beneath him. Issuing from the plain of this valley, the brook descends a rapid torrent passing by the church-yard of Seathwaite. The traveller is thus conducted at once into the midst of the wild and beautiful scenery which gave occasion to the Sonnets from the 14th to the 20th inclusive. From the point where the Seathwaite brook joins the Duddon is a view upwards into the pass through which the river makes its way into the plain of Donnerdale. The perpendicular rock on the right bears the ancient British name of THE PEN; the one opposite is called WALLABARROW CRAG, a name that occurs in other places to designate rocks of the same character. The *chaotic* aspect of the scene is well marked by the expression of a stranger, who strolled out while dinner was preparing, and at his return, being asked by his host, "What way he had been wandering?" replied, "As far as it is *finished!*"

The bed of the Duddon is here strewn with large fragments of rocks fallen from aloft; which,

as Mr. Green truly says, "are happily adapted to the many-shaped waterfalls" (or rather waterbreaks, for none of them are high) "displayed in the short space of half a mile." That there is some hazard in frequenting these desolate places, I myself have had proof; for one night an immense mass of rock fell upon the very spot where, with a friend, I had lingered the day before. "The concussion," says Mr. Green, speaking of the event (for he also, in the practice of his art, on that day sat exposed for a still longer time to the same peril), "was heard, not without alarm, by the neighbouring shepherds." But to return to Seathwaite Churchyard: it contains the following inscription: —

"In memory of the Reverend Robert Walker, who died the 25th of June 1802, in the 93d year of his age, and 67th of his curacy at Seathwaite.

"Also, of Anne his wife, who died the 28th of January, in the 93d year of her age."

In the parish-register of Seathwaite Chapel is this notice: —

"Buried, June 28th, the Rev. Robert Walker. He was curate of Seathwaite sixty-six years. He was a man singular for his temperance, industry, and integrity."

This individual is the Pastor alluded to, in the 18th Sonnet, as a worthy compeer of the country parson of Chaucer, etc. In the seventh book of the "Excursion," an abstract of his character is given, beginning,

"A Priest abides before whose life such doubts
Fall to the ground; — "

and some account of his life, for it is worthy of being recorded, will not be out of place here.
W. W.

MEMOIR OF THE REV. ROBERT WALKER

In the year 1709, Robert Walker was born at Under-crag, in Seathwaite; he was the youngest of twelve children. His oldest brother, who inherited the small family estate, died at Under-crag, aged ninety-four, being twenty-four years older than the subject of this memoir, who was born of the same mother. Robert was a sickly infant; and, through his boyhood and youth, continuing to be of delicate frame and tender health, it was deemed best, according to the country-phrase, to *breed him a scholar*; for it was not likely that he would be able to earn a livelihood by bodily labour. At that period few of these dales were furnished with schoolhouses; the children being taught to read and write in the chapel; and in the same consecrated building, where he officiated for so many years both as preacher and schoolmaster, he himself received the rudiments of his education. In his youth he became schoolmaster at Loweswater; not being called upon, probably, in that situation to teach more than reading, writing, and arithmetic. But, by the assistance of a "Gentleman" in the neighbourhood, he acquired, at leisure hours, a knowledge of the classics, and became qualified for taking holy orders. Upon his ordination, he had the offer of two curacies: the one, Torver, in the vale of Coniston, — the other, Seathwaite, in his native vale. The value of each was the same, viz. five pounds *per annum*; but the cure of Seathwaite having a cottage attached to it, as he wished to marry, he chose it in preference. The young person on whom his affections were fixed, though in the condition of a domestic servant, had given promise, by her serious and modest deportment, and by her virtuous dispositions, that she was worthy to become the helpmate of a man entering upon a plan of life such as he had marked out for himself. By her frugality she had stored up a small sum of money, with which they began housekeeping. In 1735 or 1736, he entered upon his curacy; and, nineteen years afterwards, his situation is thus described, in some letters to be found in the Annual Register for 1760, from which the following is extracted: —

"To Mr. ——

"Coniston, July 26, 1754.

"SIR — I was the other day upon a party of pleasure, about five or six miles from this place, where I met with a very striking object, and of a nature not very common. Going into a clergyman's house (of whom I had frequently heard), I found him sitting at the head of a long square table, such as is commonly used in this country by the lower class of people, dressed in a coarse blue frock, trimmed with black horn buttons; a checked shirt, a leathern strap about his neck for a stock, a coarse apron, and a pair of great wooden-soled shoes plated with iron to preserve them (what we call clogs in these parts), with a child upon his knee, eating his breakfast; his wife, and the remainder of his children, were some of them employed in waiting upon each other, the rest in teasing and spinning wool, at which trade he is a great proficient; and moreover, when it is made ready for sale, will lay it by sixteen or thirty-two pounds' weight, upon his back, and on foot, seven or eight miles, will carry it to the market, even in the depth of winter. I was not much surprised at all this, as you may possibly be, having heard a great deal of it related before. But I must confess myself astonished with the alacrity and the good humour that appeared both in the clergyman and his wife, and more so at the sense and ingenuity of the clergyman himself." . . .

Then follows a letter from another person, dated 1755, from which an extract shall be given: —

"By his frugality and good management he keeps the wolf from the door, as we say; and if he advances a little in the world, it is owing more to his own care than to anything else he has to rely upon. I don't find his inclination is running after further preferment. He is settled among the people, that are happy among themselves; and lives in the greatest unanimity and friendship with them; and, I believe, the minister and people are exceedingly satisfied with each other; and indeed how should they be dissatisfied when they have a person of so much worth and probity for their pastor? A man who, for his candour and meekness, his sober, chaste, and virtuous conversation, his soundness in principle and practice, is an ornament to his profession, and an honour to the country he is in; and bear with me if I say, the plainness of his dress, the sanctity of his manners, the simplicity of his doctrine, and the vehemence of his expression, have a sort of resemblance to the pure practice of primitive Christianity."

We will now give his own account of himself, to be found in the same place.

FROM THE REV. ROBERT WALKER

"SIR — Yours of the 26th instant was communicated to me by Mr. C——, and I should have returned an immediate answer, but the hand of Providence, then laying heavy upon an amiable pledge of conjugal endearment, hath since taken from me a promising girl, which the disconsolate mother too pensively laments the loss of; though we have yet eight living, all healthful, hopeful children, whose names and ages are as follows: — Zaccheus, aged almost eighteen years; Elizabeth, sixteen years and ten months; Mary, fifteen; Moses, thirteen years and three months; Sarah, ten years and three months; Mabel, eight years and three months; William Tyson, three years and eight months; and Anne Esther, one year and three months; besides Anne, who died two years and six months ago, and was then aged between nine and ten; and Eleanor, who died the 23d inst., January, aged six years and ten months. Zaccheus, the eldest child, is now learning the trade of a tanner, and has two years and a half of his apprenticeship to serve. The annual income of my chapel at present, as near as I can compute it, may amount to about £17, of which is paid in cash, viz. £5 from the bounty of Queen Anne, and £5 from W. P., Esq., of P——, out of the annual rents, he being lord of the manor, and £3 from the several inhabitants of L——, settled upon the tenements as a rent-charge; the house and gardens I value at £4 yearly, and not worth more; and I believe the surplice fees and voluntary contributions, one year with another, may be worth £3; but as the inhabitants are few in number, and the fees very low, this last-mentioned sum consists merely in free-will offerings.

"I am situated greatly to my satisfaction with regard to the conduct and behaviour of my auditory, who not only live in the happy ignorance of the follies and vices of the age, but in mutual peace and goodwill with one another, and are seemingly (I hope really too) sincere Christians, and sound members of the established church, not one dissenter of any denomination being amongst them all. I got to the value of £40 for my wife's fortune, but had no real estate of my own, being the youngest son of twelve children, born of obscure parents; and, though my income has been but small, and my family large, yet, by a providential blessing upon my own diligent endeavours, the kindness of friends, and a cheap country to live in, we have always had the necessaries of life. By what I have written (which is a true and exact account, to the best of my knowledge) I hope you will not think your favour to me out of the late worthy Dr. Stratford's effects quite misbestowed, for which I must ever gratefully own myself, Sir, your much obliged and most obedient humble servant, "R. W., Curate of S——.

"To Mr. C., of Lancaster."

About the time when this letter was written, the Bishop of Chester recommended the scheme of joining the curacy of Ulpha to the contiguous one of Seathwaite, and the nomination was offered to Mr. Walker; but an unexpected difficulty arising, Mr. W., in a letter to the Bishop (a copy of which, in his own beautiful handwriting, now lies before me), thus expresses himself. "If he," meaning the person in whom the difficulty originated, "had suggested any such objection before, I should utterly have declined any attempt to the curacy of Ulpha: indeed, I was always apprehensive it might be disagreeable to my auditory at Seathwaite, as they have been always accustomed to double duty, and the inhabitants of Ulpha despair of being able to support a schoolmaster who is not curate there also; which suppressed all thoughts in me of serving them both." And in a second letter to the Bishop he writes: —

"MY LORD — I have the favour of yours of the 1st instant, and am exceedingly obliged on account of the Ulpha affair: if that curacy should lapse into your Lordship's hands, I would beg leave rather to decline than embrace it; for the chapels of Seathwaite and Ulpha, annexed together, would be apt to cause a general discontent among the inhabitants of both places; by either thinking themselves slighted, being only served alternately, or neglected in the duty, or attributing it to covetousness in me; all which occasions of murmuring I would willingly avoid." And in concluding his former letter, he expresses a similar sentiment upon the same occasion, "desiring, if it be possible, however, as much as in me lieth, to live peaceably with all men."

The year following, the curacy of Seathwaite was again augmented; and, to effect this augmentation, fifty pounds had been advanced by himself; and in 1760, lands were purchased with eight hundred pounds. Scanty as was his income, the frequent offer of much better benefices could not tempt Mr. W. to quit a situation where he had been so long happy, with a consciousness of being useful. Among his papers I find the following copy of a letter, dated 1775, twenty years after his refusal of the curacy of Ulpha, which will show what exertions had been made for one of his sons.

"MAY IT PLEASE YOUR GRACE. — Our remote situation here makes it difficult to get the necessary information for transacting business regularly; such is the reason of my giving your Grace the present trouble.

"The bearer (my son) is desirous of offering himself candidate for deacon's orders at your Grace's ensuing ordination; the first, on the 25th instant, so that his papers could not be transmitted in due time. As he is now fully at age, and I have afforded him education to the utmost of my ability, it would give me great satisfaction (if your Grace would take him, and find him qualified) to have him ordained. His constitution has been tender for some years; he entered the college of Dublin, but his health would not permit him to continue there, or I would have supported him much longer. He has been with me at home above a year, in which time he has gained great strength of body, sufficient, I hope, to enable him for performing the function. Divine Providence, assisted by liberal benefactors, has blest my endeavours, from a small income, to rear a numerous family; and as my time of life renders me now unfit for much future expectancy from this world, I should be glad to see my son settled in a promising way to acquire an honest livelihood for himself. His behaviour, so far in life, has been irreproachable; and I hope he will not degenerate, in principles or practice, from the precepts and pattern of an indulgent parent. Your Grace's favourable reception of this, from a distant corner of the diocese, and an obscure hand, will excite filial gratitude, and a due use shall be made of the obligation vouchsafed thereby to your Grace's very dutiful and most obedient Son and Servant,

"ROBERT WALKER."

The same man, who was thus liberal in education of his numerous family, was even munificent in hospitality as a parish priest. Every Sunday were served upon the long table, at which he has been described sitting with a child upon his knee, messes of broth for the refreshment of those of his congregation who came from a distance, and usually took their seats as parts of his own household. It seems scarcely possible that this custom could have commenced before the augmentation of his cure; and what would to many have been a high price of self-denial was paid, by the pastor and his family, for this gratification; as the treat could only be provided by dressing at one time the whole, perhaps, of their weekly allowance of fresh animal food; consequently, for a succession of days, the table was covered with cold victuals only. His generosity in old age may be still further illustrated by a little circumstance relating to an orphan grandson, then ten years of age, which I find in a copy of a letter to one of his sons; he requests that half a guinea may be left for "little Robert's pocket money," who was then at school: intrusting it to the care of a lady, who, as he says, "may sometimes frustrate his squandering it away foolishly," and promising to send him an equal allowance annually for the same purpose. The conclusion of the same letter is so characteristic, that I cannot forbear to transcribe it. "We," meaning his wife and himself, "are in our wonted state of health, allowing for the hasty strides of old age knocking daily at our door, and threateningly telling us we are not only mortal, but must expect ere long to take our leave of our ancient cottage, and lie down in our last dormitory. Pray pardon my neglect to answer yours: let us hear sooner from you, to augment the mirth of the Christmas holidays. Wishing you all the pleasures of the approaching season, I am, dear Son, with lasting sincerity, yours affectionately,   ROBERT WALKER."

He loved old customs and old usages, and in some instances stuck to them to his own loss; for, having had a sum of money lodged in the hands of a neighbouring tradesman, when long course of time had raised the rate of interest, and more was offered, he refused to accept it; an act not difficult to one, who, while he was drawing seventeen pounds a year from his curacy, declined, as we have seen, to add the profits of another small benefice to his own, lest he should be suspected of cupidity. From this vice he was utterly free; he made no charge for teaching school; such as could afford to pay gave him what they pleased. When very young, having kept a diary of his expenses, however trifling, the large amount, at the end of the year, surprised him; and from that time the rule of his life was to be economical, not avaricious. At his decease he left behind him no less a sum than £2000 and such a sense of his various excellences was prevalent in the country, that the epithet of WONDERFUL is to this day attached to his name.

There is in the above sketch something so extraordinary as to require further *explanatory* details. — And to begin with his industry; eight hours in each day, during five days in the week, and half of Saturday, except when the labours of husbandry were urgent, he was occupied in teaching. His seat was within the rails of the altar; the communion table was his desk; and, like Shenstone's schoolmistress, the master employed himself at the spinning-wheel, while the children were repeating their lessons by his side. Every evening, after school hours, if not more profitably engaged, he continued the same kind of labour, exchanging, for the benefit of exercise, the small wheel, at which he had sate, for the large one on which wool is spun, the spinner stepping to and fro. Thus was the wheel constantly in readiness to prevent the waste of a moment's time. Nor was his industry with the pen, when occasion called for it, less eager. Intrusted with extensive management of public and private affairs, he acted, in his rustic neighbourhood, as scrivener, writing out petitions, deeds of conveyance, wills, covenants, etc., with pecuniary gain to himself, and to the great benefit of his employers. These labours (at all times considerable) at one period of the year, viz. between Christmas and Candlemas, when money transactions are settled in this country, were often so intense, that he passed great part of the night, and sometimes whole nights, at his desk. His garden also was tilled by his own hand; he had a right of pasturage upon the mountains for a few sheep and a couple of cows, which required his attendance; with this pastoral occupation he joined the labours of husbandry upon a small scale, renting two or three acres in addition to his own less than one acre of glebe; and the humblest drudgery which the cultivation of these fields required was performed by himself.

He also assisted his neighbours in hay-making and shearing their flocks, and in the performance of this latter service he was eminently dexterous. They, in their turn, complimented him with the present of a haycock, or a fleece; less as a recompence for this particular service than as a general acknowledgment. The Sabbath was in a strict sense kept holy; the Sunday evenings being devoted to reading the Scripture and family prayer. The principal festivals appointed by the Church were also duly observed; but through every other day in the week, through every week in the year, he was incessantly occupied in work of hand or mind; not allowing a moment for recreation, except upon a Saturday afternoon, when he indulged himself with a Newspaper, or sometimes with a Magazine. The frugality and temperance established in his house were as admirable as the industry. Nothing to which the name of luxury could be given was there known; in the latter part of his life, indeed, when tea had been brought into almost general use, it was provided for visitors, and for such of his own family as returned occasionally to his roof, and had been accustomed to this refreshment elsewhere; but neither he nor his wife ever partook of it. The raiment worn by his family was comely and decent, but as simple as their diet; the home-spun materials were made up into apparel by their own hands. At the time of the decease of this thrifty pair, their cottage contained a large store of webs of woollen and linen cloth, woven from thread of their own spinning. And it is remarkable that the pew in the chapel in which the family used to sit, remains neatly lined with woollen cloth spun by the pastor's own hands. It is the only pew in the chapel so distinguished; and I know of no other instance of his conformity to the delicate accommodations of modern times. The fuel of the house, like that of their neighbours, consisted of peat, procured from the mosses by their own labour. The lights by which, in the winter evenings, their work was performed, were of their own manufacture, such as still continue to be used in these cottages; they are made of the pith of rushes dipped in any unctuous substance that the house affords. *White* candles, as tallow candles are here called, were reserved to honour the Christmas festivals, and were perhaps produced upon no other occasions. Once a month; during the proper season, a sheep was drawn from their small mountain flock, and killed for the use of the family; and a cow, towards the close of the year, was salted and dried for winter provision; the hide was tanned to furnish them with shoes. — By these various resources, this venerable clergyman reared a numerous family, not only preserving them, as he affectingly says, "from wanting the necessaries of life;" but affording them an unstinted education, and the means of raising themselves in society. In this they were eminently assisted by the effects of their father's example, his precepts, and injunctions; he was aware that truth-speaking, as a moral virtue, is best secured by inculcating attention to accuracy of report even on trivial occasions; and so rigid were the rules of honesty by which he endeavoured to bring up his family, that if one of them had chanced to find in the lanes or fields anything of the least use or value without being able to ascertain to whom it belonged, he always insisted upon the child's carrying it back to the place from which it had been brought.

No one, it might be thought, could, as has been described, convert his body into a machine, as it were, of industry for the humblest uses, and keep his thoughts so frequently bent upon secular concerns, without grievous injury to the more precious parts of his nature. How could the powers of intellect thrive, or its graces be displayed, in the midst of circumstances apparently so unfavourable, and where, to the direct cultivation of the mind, so small a portion of time was allotted? But, in this extraordinary man, things in their nature adverse were reconciled. His conversation was remarkable, not only for being chaste and pure, but for the degree in which it was fervent and eloquent; his written style was correct, simple, and animated. Nor did his *affections* suffer more than his intellect; he was tenderly alive to all the duties of his pastoral office: the poor and needy "he never sent empty away," — the stranger was fed and refreshed in passing that unfrequented vale — the sick were visited; and the feelings of humanity found further exercise among the distresses and embarrassments in the worldly estate of his neighbours, with which his talents for business made him acquainted; and the disinterestedness, impartiality, and uprightness which he maintained in the management of all affairs confided to him were virtures seldom separated in his own conscience from religious obligation. Nor could such conduct fail to remind those who witnessed it of a spirit nobler than law or custom: they felt convictions which, but for such intercourse, could not have been afforded, that as in the practice of their pastor there was no guile, so in his faith there was nothing hollow; and we are warranted in believing that upon these occasions selfishness, obstinacy, and discord would often give way before the breathings of his good-will and saintly integrity. It may be presumed also — while his humble congregation were listening to the moral precepts which he delivered from the pulpit, and to the Christian exhortations that they should love their neighbours as themselves, and do as they would be done unto — that peculiar efficacy was given to the preacher's labours by recollections in the minds of his congregation that they were called upon to do no more than his own actions were daily setting before their eyes.

The afternoon service in the chapel was less numerously attended than that of the morning, but by a more serious auditory; the lesson from the New Testament, on those occasions, was accompanied by Burkitt's Commentaries. These lessons he read with impassioned emphasis, frequently drawing tears from his hearers, and leaving a lasting impression upon their minds.

His devotional feelings and the powers of his own mind were further exercised, along with those of his family, in perusing the Scriptures: not only on the Sunday evenings, but on every other evening, while the rest of the household were at work, some one of the children, and in her turn the servant, for the sake of practice in reading, or for instruction, read the Bible aloud; and in this manner the whole was repeatedly gone through. That no common importance was attached to the observance of religious ordinances by his family, appears from the following memorandum by one of his descendants, which I am tempted to insert at length, as it is characteristic and somewhat curious. "There is a small chapel in the county palatine of Lancaster, where a certain clergyman has regularly officiated above sixty years, and a few months ago administered the sacrament of the Lord's Supper in the same, to a decent number of devout communicants. After the clergyman had received himself, the first company out of the assembly who approached the altar, and kneeled down to be partakers of the sacred elements, consisted of the parson's wife, to whom he had been married upwards of sixty years; one son and his wife; four daughters, each with her husband; whose ages, all added together, amount to above 714 years. The several and respective distances from the place of each of their abodes to the chapel where they all communicated, will measure more than 1000 English miles. Though the narration will appear surprising, it is without doubt a fact that the same persons, exactly four years before, met at the same place, and all joined in performance of the same venerable duty."

He was indeed most zealously attached to the doctrine and frame of the Established Church. We have seen him congratulating himself that he had no dissenters in his cure of any denomination. Some allowance must be made for the state of opinion when his first religious impressions were received, before the reader will acquit him of bigotry, when I mention that at the time of the augmentation of the cure, he refused to invest part of the money in the purchase of an estate offered to him upon advantageous terms, because the proprietor was a Quaker; — whether from scrupulous apprehension that a blessing would not attend a contract framed for the benefit of the church between persons not in religious sympathy with each other; or, as a seeker of peace, he was afraid of the uncomplying disposition which at one time was too frequently conspicuous in that sect. Of this an instance had fallen under his own notice; for, while he taught school at Loweswater, certain persons of that denomination had refused to pay annual interest due under the title of Church-stock;[1] a great hardship upon the incumbent, for the curacy of Loweswater was then scarcely less poor than that of Seathwaite. To what degree this preju-

---

[1] Mr. Walker's charity being that kind which "seeketh not her own," he would rather forego his rights than distrain for dues which the parties liable refused, as a point of conscience, to pay.

dice of his was blamable need not be determined; — certain it is, that he was not only desirous, as he himself says, to live in peace, but in love, with all men. He was placable, and charitable in his judgments; and, however correct in conduct and rigorous to himself, he was ever ready to forgive the trespasses of others, and to soften the censure that was cast upon their frailties. — It would be unpardonable to omit that, in the maintenance of his virtues, he received due support from the partner of his long life. She was equally strict, in attending to her share of their joint cares, nor less diligent in her appropriate occupations. A person who had been some time their servant in the latter part of their lives, concluded the panegyric of her mistress by saying to me, "She was no less excellent than her husband; she was good to the poor; she was good to everything!" He survived for a short time this virtuous companion. When she died, he ordered that her body should be borne to the grave by three of her daughters and one granddaughter; and, when the corpse was lifted from the threshold, he insisted upon lending his aid, and feeling about, for he was then almost blind, took hold of a napkin fixed to the coffin; and, as a bearer of the body, entered the chapel, a few steps from the lowly parsonage.

What a contrast does the life of this obscurely-seated, and, in point of worldly wealth, poorly-repaid Churchman, present to that of a Cardinal Wolsey!

"O 't is a burthen, Cromwell, 't is a burthen
Too heavy for a man who hopes for heaven!"

We have been dwelling upon images of peace in the moral world, that have brought us again to the quiet enclosure of consecrated ground in which this venerable pair lie interred. The sounding brook, that rolls close by the churchyard, without disturbing feeling or meditation, is now unfortunately laid bare; but not long ago it participated, with the chapel, the shade of some stately ash-trees, which will not spring again. While the spectator from this spot is looking round upon the girdle of stony mountains that encompasses the vale, — masses of rock, out of which monuments for all men that ever existed might have been hewn — it would surprise him to be told, as with truth he might be, the plain blue slab dedicated to the memory of this aged pair is a production of a quarry in North Wales. It was sent as a mark of respect by one of their descendants from the vale of Festiniog, a region almost as beautiful as that in which it now lies!

Upon the Seathwaite Brook, at a small distance from the parsonage, has been erected a mill for spinning yarn; it is a mean and disagreeable object, though not unimportant to the spectator, as calling to mind the momentous changes wrought by such inventions in the frame of society — changes which have proved especially unfavourable to these mountain solitudes. So much had been effected by those new powers, before the subject of the preceding biographical sketch closed his life, that their operation could

not escape his notice, and doubtless excited touching reflections upon the comparatively insignificant results of his own manual industry. But Robert Walker was not a man of times and circumstances; had he lived at a later period, the principle of duty would have produced application as unremitting; the same energy of character would have been displayed, though in many instances with widely different effects.

With pleasure I annex, as illustrative and confirmatory of the above account, extracts from a paper in the *Christian Remembrancer*, October 1819: it bears an assumed signature, but is known to be the work of the Rev. Robert Bamford, vicar of Bishopton, in the county of Durham; a great-grandson of Mr. Walker, whose worth it commemorates, by a record not the less valuable for being written in very early youth.

"His house was a nursery of virtue. All the inmates were industrious, and cleanly, and happy. Sobriety, neatness, quietness, characterised the whole family. No railings, no idleness, no indulgence of passion were permitted. Every child, however young, had its appointed engagements; every hand was busy. Knitting, spinning, reading, writing, mending clothes, making shoes, were by the different children constantly performing. The father himself sitting amongst them and guiding their thoughts, was engaged in the same occupations. . . .

"He sate up late, and rose early; when the family were at rest, he retired to a little room which he had built on the roof of his house. He had slated it, and fitted it up with shelves for his books, his stock of cloth, wearing apparel, and his utensils. There many a cold winter's night, without fire, while the roof was glazed with ice, did he remain reading or writing till the day dawned. He taught the children in the chapel, for there was no schoolhouse. Yet in that cold, damp place he never had a fire. He used to send the children in parties either to his own fire at home or make them run up the mountain side.

. . . .

"It may be further mentioned, that he was a passionate admirer of Nature; she was his mother and he was a dutiful child. While engaged in the mountains, it was his greatest pleasure to view the rising sun; and in tranquil evenings, as it slided behind the hills, he blessed its departure. He was skilled in fossils and plants; a constant observer of the stars and winds: the atmosphere was his delight. He made many experiments on its nature and properties. In summer he used to gather a multitude of flies and insects, and, by his entertaining description, amuse and instruct his children. They shared all his daily employments, and derived many sentiments of love and benevolence from his observations on the works and productions of nature. Whether they were following him in the field, or surrounding him in school, he took every opportunity of storing their minds with useful information. — Nor was the circle of his influence confined to Seathwaite. Many a distant mother has told her child of Mr. Walker, and begged him to be as good a man.

. . . .

"Once, when I was very young, I had the pleasure of seeing and hearing that venerable old man in his 90th year, and even then, the calmness, the force, the perspicuity of his sermon, sanctified and adorned by the wisdom of grey hairs, and the authority of virtue, had such an effect upon my mind, that I never see a hoary-headed clergyman, without thinking of Mr. Walker. . . . He allowed no dissenter or methodist to interfere in the instruction of the souls committed to his care: and so successful were his exertions, that he had not one dissenter of any denomination whatever in the whole parish. — Though he avoided all religious controversies, yet when age had silvered his head, and virtuous piety had secured to his appearance reverence and silent honour, no one, however determined in his hatred of apostolic descent, could have listened to his discourse on ecclesiastical history and ancient times, without thinking that one of the beloved apostles had returned to mortality, and in that vale of peace had come to exemplify the beauty of holiness in the life and character of Mr. Walker.

. . . .

"Until the sickness of his wife, a few months previous to her death, his health and spirits and faculties were unimpaired. But this misfortune gave him such a shock that his constitution gradually decayed. His senses, except sight, still preserved their powers. He never preached with steadiness after his wife's death. His voice faltered: he always looked at the seat she had used. He could not pass her tomb without tears. He became, when alone, sad and melancholy, though still among his friends kind and good-humoured. He went to bed about twelve o'clock the night before his death. As his custom was, he went, tottering and leaning upon his daughter's arm, to examine the heavens, and meditate a few moments in the open air. 'How clear the moon shines tonight!' He said these words, sighed, and laid down. At six next morning he was found a corpse. Many a tear, and many a heavy heart, and many a grateful blessing followed him to the grave."

Having mentioned in this narrative the vale of Loweswater as a place where Mr. Walker taught school, I will add a few memoranda from its parish register, respecting a person apparently of desires as moderate, with whom he must have been intimate during his residence there.

"Let him that would, ascend the tottering seat
Of courtly grandeur, and become as great
As are his mounting wishes; but for me,
Let sweet repose and rest my portion be.
                    HENRY FOREST, Curate."

"Honour, the idol which the most adore,
Receives no homage from my knee;
Content in privacy I value more
Than all uneasy dignity."

"Henry Forest came to Loweswater, 1708, being 25 years of age."

"This curacy was twice augmented by Queen Anne's Bounty. The first payment, with great difficulty, was paid to Mr. John Curwen of London, on the 9th of May, 1724, deposited by me, Henry Forest, Curate of Loweswater. Y^e said 9th of May, ye said Mr. Curwen went to the office, and saw my name registered there, &c. This, by the Providence of God, came by lot to this poor place.

                    "Hæc testor H. Forest."

In another place he records that the sycamore-trees were planted in the churchyard in 1710.

He died in 1741, having been curate thirty-four years. It is not improbable that H. Forest was the gentleman who assisted Robert Walker in his classical studies at Loweswater.

To this parish register is prefixed a motto, of which the following verses are a part:

"Invigilate viri, tacito nam tempora gressu
Diffugiunt, nulloque sono convertitur annus;
Utendum est ætate, cito pede præterit ætas."
                    W. W.

Page 600. SONNET XXVII.
For the tradition referred to, see the headnote.

Page 601. SONNET XXXIV.
Line 14. *We feel that we are greater than we know.*

"And feel that I am happier than I know."
                    MILTON.

The allusion to the Greek Poet will be obvious to the classical reader. W. W. The Greek poet is Moschus (ca. 150 B.C.) whose *Lament for Bion* Wordsworth had in part translated during his schooldays.

Page 602. A PARSONAGE IN OXFORDSHIRE.
Headnote. The note alluded to is that to "Ecclesiastical Sonnets," III. xvii.

Page 602. To ENTERPRISE.
Line 114. *living hill.*

                    — "awhile the living hill
Heaved with convulsive throes, and all was still."
                    DR. DARWIN. W. W.

Page 604. ECCLESIASTICAL SONNETS.
During the month of December 1820, I accompanied a much-beloved and honoured Friend in a walk through different parts of his estate, with a view to fix upon the site of a new Church which he intended to erect. It was one of the most beautiful mornings of a mild season, — our feelings were in harmony with the cherishing influences of the scene; and such being our purpose, we were naturally led to look back upon past events with wonder and gratitude, and on the future with hope. Not long afterwards, some of the Sonnets which will be found towards the close of this series were produced as a private memorial of that morning's occupation.

The Catholic Question, which was agitated in Parliament about that time, kept my thoughts in the same course; and it struck me that certain points in the Ecclesiastical History of our Country might advantageously be presented to view in verse. Accordingly, I took up the subject and what I now offer to the reader was the result.

When this work was far advanced, I was agreeably surprised to find that my friend, Mr. Southey, had been engaged with similar views in writing a concise History of the Church in England. If our Productions, thus unintentionally coinciding, shall be found to illustrate each other, it will prove a high gratification to me, which I am sure my friend will participate.

W. WORDSWORTH.

Rydal Mount, *January 24, 1822.*

For the convenience of passing from one point of the subject to another without shocks of abruptness, this work has taken the shape of a series of Sonnets: but the Reader, it is to be hoped, will find that the pictures are often so closely connected as to have jointly the effect of passages of a poem in a form of stanza to which there is no objection but one that bears upon the Poet only — its difficulty. W. W.

PART I.

Page 605. SONNET II.
Line 6. *Did holy Paul*, etc. Stillingfleet adduces many arguments in support of this opinion, but they are unconvincing. The latter part of this Sonnet refers to a favourite notion of Roman Catholic writers, that Joseph of Arimathea and his companions brought Christianity into Britain, and built a rude church at Glastonbury; alluded to hereafter, in a passage upon the dissolution of monasteries. W. W.

Page 605. SONNET III.
Line 1. *seamew — white.* This water-fowl was, among the Druids, an emblem of those traditions connected with the Deluge that made an important part of their mysteries. The Cormorant was a bird of bad omen. W. W.
Line 2. *Menai.* A strait in Wales.

Page 605. SONNET V.
Line 2. *Brigantian coves.* Celtic hill-dwellers in the north of England.
Line 4. *Sarum.* Salisbury Plain.
Line 8. *Iona.* An island off the west coast of Scotland, the site of an early Christian settlement.
Line 10. *Taliesin.* British bard of the sixth century, who celebrated his people's struggle against the invading Germans.

Page 605. SONNET VI.
Line 1. *Diocletian.* Roman Emperor (284–305 A.D.) and persecutor of Christians.
Line 9. Saint Alban was martyred by the Romans in 304 A.D.
Line 13. *That Hill, whose flowery platform,* etc.

This hill at St. Alban's must have been an object of great interest to the imagination of the venerable Bede, who thus describes it, with a delicate feeling, delightful to meet with in that rude age, traces of which are frequent in his works: — "Variis herbarum floribus depictus imò usquequaque vestitus, in quo nihil repentè arduum, nihil præceps, nihil abruptum, quem lateribus longè latèque deductum in modum æquoris natura complanat, dignum videlicet eum pro insitâ sibi specie venustatis jam olim reddens, qui beati martyris cruore dicaretur." W. W.

Page 606. SONNET IX.
Line 8. *Pictish cloud.* The Picts, Celtic inhabitants of the north of England, fell upon the withdrawing Romans in the fourth and fifth centuries A.D.

Page 606. SONNET X.
Line 1. *Aneurin.* Welsh bard of the sixth century.
Line 3. *Caractacus.* British hero who opposed the Roman invasion in the first century A.D.
Line 9. *Urien.* British chieftain, patron of Taliesin.
Line 12. *Plinlimmon.* A mountain in Wales.

Page 607. SONNET XI.
Line 2. Alluding to the victory gained under Germanus. See Bede. W. W. Germanus, Bishop of Auxerre, aided the Britons in their wars against the pagan Saxons and Picts. The story is told by Bede in his *History of the English Church and People*, I.20.
Line 4. *Second . . . shade.* The Anglo-Saxon invasion of England.
Lines 9–10.

By men yet scarcely conscious of a care
For other monuments than those of Earth.

The last six lines of this Sonnet are chiefly from the prose of Daniel; and here I will state (though to the Readers whom this Poem will chiefly interest it is unnecessary) that my obligations to other prose writers are frequent, — obligations which, even if I had not a pleasure in courting, it would have been presumptuous to shun, in treating an historical subject. I must, however, particularise Fuller, to whom I am indebted in the Sonnet upon Wicliffe and in other instances. And upon the acquittal of the Seven Bishops I have done little more than versify a lively description of that event in the MS. Memoirs of the first Lord Lonsdale. W. W.

Page 607. SONNET XII.
"Ethelforth reached the convent of Bangor, he perceived the Monks, twelve hundred in number, offering prayers for the success of their countrymen: 'If they are praying against us,' he exclaimed, 'they are fighting against us'; and he ordered them to be first attacked: they were destroyed; and, appalled by their fate, the courage of Brocmail wavered, and he fled from the field in dismay. Thus abandoned by their leader,

his army soon gave way, and Ethelforth obtained a decisive conquest. Ancient Bangor itself soon fell into his hands, and was demolished; the noble monastery was levelled to the ground; its library, which is mentioned as a large one, the collection of ages, the repository of the most precious monuments of the ancient Britons, was consumed; half-ruined walls, gates, and rubbish were all that remained of the magnificent edifice." — See Turner's valuable history of the Anglo-Saxons.

Taliesin was present at the battle which preceded this desolation.

The account Bede gives of this remarkable event suggests a most striking warning against National and Religious prejudices. W. W.

Page 607. SONNET XIII.
The story of Pope Gregory's pun is told by Bede, II.1.

Page 607. SONNET XIV.
Line 6. Saint Augustine of Canterbury led a Christian mission to England in 596.

Page 608. SONNET XV.
The person of Paulinus is thus described by Bede, from the memory of an eye-witness: — "Longæ staturæ, paululum incurvus, nigro capillo, facie macilentâ, naso adunco, pertenui, venerabilis simul et terribilis aspectu." W. W. Paulinus converted the pagan King Edwin of Northumbria.

Page 698. SONNET XVI.
Line 1. *"Man's life is like a Sparrow."* See the original of this speech in Bede. — The Conversion of Edwin, as related by him, is highly interesting — and the breaking up of this Council accompanied with an event so striking and characteristic, that I am tempted to give it at length in a translation.

"Who, exclaimed the King, when the Council was ended, shall first desecrate the altars and the temples? I, answered the Chief Priest; for who more fit than myself, through the wisdom which the true God hath given me, to destroy, for the good example of others, what in foolishness I worshipped? Immediately, casting away vain superstition, he besought the King to grant him what the laws did not allow to a priest, arms and a courser (equum emissarium); which mounting, and furnished with a sword and lance, he proceeded to destroy the Idols. The crowd, seeing this, thought him mad — he, however, halted not, but, approaching, he profaned the temple, casting against it the lance which he had held in his hand, and, exulting in acknowledgment of the worship of the true God, he ordered his companions to pull down the temple, with all its enclosures. The place is shown where those idols formerly stood, not far from York, at the source of the river Derwent, and is at this day called Gormund Gaham, ubi pontifex ille, inspirante Deo vero, polluit ac destruxit eas, *quas ipse sacraverat aras.*" The last expression is a pleasing proof that the venerable monk of

Wearmouth was familiar with the poetry of Virgil. W. W.

Page 608. SONNET XVII.
Line 11. *such the inviting voice,* etc. The early propagators of Christianity were accustomed to preach near rivers, for the convenience of baptism. W. W.

Page 609. SONNET XIX.
Having spoken of the zeal, disinterestedness, and temperance of the clergy of those times, Bede thus proceeds: — "Unde et in magna erat veneratione tempore illo religionis habitus, ita ut ubicunque clericus aliquis, aut monachus adveniret, gaudenter ab omnibus tanquam Dei famulus exciperetur. Etiam si in itinere pergens inveniretur, accurrebant, et flexâ cervice, vel manu signari, vel oro illius se benedicti, gaudebant. Verbis quoque horum exhortatoriis diligenter auditum præbebant." Lib. iii. cap. 26. W. W.

Page 610. SONNET XXIII.
A tribute to the venerable Bede (673?-735), a Benedictine monk at the monastery of Jarrow, on the coast of Northumberland.
Line 14. He expired dictating the last words of a translation of St. John's Gospel. W. W.

Page 610. SONNET XXIV.
Line 2. *The people work like congregated bees.* See, in Turner's History, vol. iii, p. 528, the account of the erection of Ramsey Monastery. Penances were removable by the performance of acts of charity and benevolence. W. W.

Page 610. SONNET XXVI.
Alfred the Great was King of Wessex from 871 to 899. For Wordsworth's admiration of him, see "A Fact and an Imagination," p. 554.
Line 10. *pain narrows not his cares.* Through the whole of his life, Alfred was subject to grievous maladies. W. W.

Page 611. SONNET XXVIII.
Line 6. St. Dunstan (924–988), powerful Archbishop of Canterbury.

Page 611. SONNET XXIX.
Line 1. *Woe to the Crown that doth the Cowl obey!* The violent measures carried on under the influence of Dunstan, for strengthening the Benedictine Order, were a leading cause of the second series of Danish invasions. — *See Turner.* W. W.
Line 3. *Rovers.* Danish marauders, who settled in the northeast of England in the ninth century A.D. and were converted to Christianity, largely through the efforts of Alfred.

Page 611. SONNET XXX.
From the ballad composed by Canute, "Merie sangen the Muneches binen Ely."

Page 611. SONNET XXXI.
Line 1. *Confessor.* Edward the Confessor,

King of England at the time of the Norman Conquest (1066).

Page 612. Sonnet XXXIII.
The initiation of the First Crusade, in 1095.
Line 14. The decision of the Council was believed to be instantly known in remote parts of Europe. W. W.

Page 612. Sonnet XXXV.
Richard the Lion-hearted, participant in the Third Crusade and King from 1189 to 1199.

Page 613. Sonnet XXXVI.
The interdiction was laid upon England by Pope Innocent III in 1208.

Page 613. Sonnet XXXVIII.
See the headnote to the series.

PART II.

Page 614. Sonnet III.
Line 1. *"Here Man more purely lives,"* etc. "Bonum est nos hic esse, quia homo vivit purius, cadit rarius, surgit velocius, incedit cautius, quiescit securius, moritur felicius, purgatur citius, præmiatur copiosius." BERNARD. "This sentence," says Dr. Whitaker, "is usually inscribed in some conspicuous part of the Cistertian houses." W. W.

Page 614. Sonnet IV.
Line 3. *villain-service.* Serfdom.

Page 616. Sonnet XI.
Line 9. *Valdo.* Peter Waldo, former merchant of Lyons who was excommunicated (1184) and persecuted by the Church for preaching voluntary poverty.

Page 616. Sonnet XIV.
Waldenses: followers of Peter Waldo.
Line 8. *Whom Obloquy pursues,* etc. The list of foul names bestowed upon those poor creatures is long and curious; — and, as is, alas! too natural, most of the opprobrious appellations are drawn from circumstances into which they were forced by their persecutors, who even consolidated their miseries into one reproachful term, calling them Patarenians, or Paturins, from *pati,* to suffer.

"Dwellers with wolves, she names them, for the pine
And green oak are their covert; as the gloom
Of night oft foils their enemy's design,
She calls them Riders on the flying broom;
Sorcerers, whose frame and aspect have become
One and the same through practices malign."
W. W.

Page 617. Sonnet XV.
Archbishop Chicheley persuaded Henry V to undertake a war against Normandy (the leopard) and France (the lily).

Page 617. Sonnet XVII.
An Oxford theologian and reformer of the church, John Wycliffe, was accused of heresy. His body was disinterred in 1428, burned, and his ashes thrown into a nearby river.

Page 618. Sonnet XIX.
Line 6. *Secular.* A member of the clergy, as opposed to one living in monastic seclusion.

Page 618. Sonnet XXI.
Henry VIII suppressed the monasteries in 1536.
Lines 7, 8. *And the green lizard,* etc. These two lines are adopted from a MS., written about the year 1770, which accidentally fell into my possession. The close of the preceding Sonnet on monastic voluptuousness is taken from the same source, as is the verse, "Where Venus sits," etc., and the line, "Once ye were holy, ye are holy still," in a subsequent Sonnet. W. W.

Page 619. Sonnet XXVI.
Line 8. Sir Thomas More and John Fisher, Bishop of Rochester, were beheaded in 1535 for refusing to swear allegiance to Henry VIII.

Page 620. Sonnet XXVIII.
Line 9. *Limbo Lake.* See *Paradise Lost,* III. 495.

Page 620. Sonnet XXXI.
Edward VI was crowned in 1547 at the age of ten.

Page 621. Sonnet XXXIII.
Mary, a Catholic, succeeded Edward VI in 1553.

Page 621. Sonnet XXXIV.
Hugh Latimer and Nicholas Ridley were burned for heresy in 1555.
Line 4. *One (like those prophets),* etc. "M. Latimer suffered his keeper very quietly to pull off his hose, and his other array, which to looke unto was very simple: and being stripped into his shrowd, he seemed as comely a person to them that were present, as one should lightly see: and whereas in his clothes hee appeared a withered and crooked sillie (weak) olde man, he now stood bolt upright, as comely a father as one might lightly behold. . . . Then they brought a faggotte, kindled with fire, and laid the same downe at doctor Ridley's feete. To whome M. Latimer spake in this manner, 'Bee of good comfort, master Ridley, and play the man: wee shall this day light such a candle by God's grace in England, as I trust shall never be put out.' " — *Fox's Acts, etc.*
Similar alterations in the outward figure and deportment of persons brought to like trial were not uncommon. See note to the above passage in Dr. Wordsworth's *Ecclesiastical Biography,* for an example in an humble Welsh fisherman. W. W.

Page 621. Sonnet XXXV.
Thomas Cranmer, Archbishop of Canterbury, was burned at the stake in 1556.
Line 14. For the belief in this fact, see the contemporary Historians. W. W.

Page 622. SONNET XXXIX.
Line 5. *The gift exalting*, etc. "On foot they
went, and took Salisbury in their way, purposely
to see the good Bishop, who made Mr. Hooker
sit at his own table; which Mr. Hooker boasted
of with much joy and gratitude when he saw his
mother and friends; and at the Bishop's parting
with him, the Bishop gave him good counsel and
his benediction, but forgot to give him money;
which when the Bishop had considered, he sent a
servant in all haste to call Richard back to him,
and at Richard's return, the Bishop said to him,
'Richard, I sent for you back to lend you a
horse which hath carried me many a mile, and I
thank God with much ease,' and presently de-
livered into his hand a walking-staff, with which
he professed he had travelled through many parts
of Germany; and he said, 'Richard, I do not
give, but lend you my horse; be sure you be
honest, and bring my horse back to me, at your
return this way to Oxford. And I do now give
you ten groats to bear your charges to Exeter;
and here is ten groats more, which I charge you
to deliver to your mother, and tell her I send her
a Bishop's benediction with it, and beg the
continuance of her prayers for me. And if you
bring my horse back to me, I will give you ten
groats more to carry you on foot to the college;
and so God bless you, good Richard.' " — See
Walton's Life of Richard Hooker. W. W.

Page 623. SONNET XLI.
Line 10. *craftily incites*, etc. A common device
in religious and political conflicts. — See Strype,
in support of this instance. W. W. Wordsworth's
reference is to Strype's *Annals of the Reforma-
tion* (1709), as de Selincourt points out.

Page 623. SONNET XLII.
Line 9. *an assembled Senate.* Conspirators in
the Gunpowder Plot (1605) sought to blow up the
Houses of Parliament.
Line 12. *that dismal night.* The Massacre of
St. Bartholomew in Paris and the French prov-
inces, August 24, 1572.

Page 624. SONNET XLV.
In this age a word cannot be said in praise of
Laud, or even in compassion for his fate, with-
out incurring a charge of bigotry; but fearless of
such imputation, I concur with Hume, "that it is
sufficient for his vindication to observe that his
errors were the most excusable of all those which
prevailed during that zealous period." A key to
the right understanding of those parts of his
conduct that brought the most odium upon him
in his own time, may be found in the following
passage of his speech before the bar of the House
of Peers: — "Ever since I came in place, I have
laboured nothing more than that the external
publick worship of God, so much slighted in
divers parts of this kingdom, might be preserved,
and that with as much decency and uniformity as
might be. For I evidently saw that the public
neglect of God's service in the outward face of
it, and the nasty lying of many places dedicated
to that service, *had almost cast a damp upon*

*the true and inward worship of God, which while
we live in the body, needs external helps, and all
little enough to keep it in any vigour."* W. W.
William Laud, Archbishop of Canterbury under
Charles I, was executed in 1645.

Page 625. SONNET III.
Line 2. *His kingdom to regain.* The Restoration
of Charles II, in 1660.

Page 625. SONNET IV.
Line 6. *One.* John Milton. See *Paradise Lost*,
VII.27-28.
Lines 13-14. *Paradise Lost*, III.54-55.

Page 625. SONNET V.
Izaak Walton published biographies of John
Donne (1640), Richard Hooker (1665), and George
Herbert (1670), among others.

Page 625. SONNET VI.
Line 2. *one rigorous day.* The proclamation, in
1662, of the Act of Uniformity, which forced
nonconforming clergy out of the English Church.

Page 626. SONNET VII.
A comparison of Cromwell's intervention on be-
half of the persecuted Vaudois (lines 1-4) and
the Anglican persecution, in 1666, of the dis-
senting Scotch Covenanters.

Page 626. SONNET VIII.
On the acquittal, in 1687, of seven bishops im-
prisoned for opposing the Catholic policies of
James II.

Page 626. SONNET IX.
Line 4. *Nassau.* Among William's ancestors
were the princes of Nassau, a German duchy.
Line 13. *Bondman of the Pope.* James II, a
Catholic.

Page 626. SONNET X.
Lines 3, 4. Algernon Sidney and William Russell
were executed in 1683 for conspiracy against the
crown.

Page 626. SONNET XI.
The preacher Henry Sacheverel (1674?-1734) was
tried in 1710 and found guilty of sedition in op-
posing the government's war against Holland.

Page 627. SONNET XIII.
American episcopacy, in union with the church
in England, strictly belongs to the general sub-
ject; and I here make my acknowledgments to
my American friends, Bishop Doane, and Mr.
Henry Reed of Philadelphia, for having suggested
to me the propriety of adverting to it, and
pointed out the virtues and intellectual qualities
of Bishop White, which so eminently fitted him
for the great work he undertook. Bishop White
was consecrated at Lambeth, Feb. 4, 1787, by
Archbishop Moore; and before his long life was
closed, twenty-six bishops had been consecrated
in America by himself. For his character and

opinions, see his own numerous works, and a "Sermon in commemoration of him, by George Washington Doane, Bishop of New Jersey." W. W.

Page 628. SONNET XVIII.
Line 1. *A genial hearth*, etc. Among the benefits arising, as Mr. Coleridge has well observed, from a Church establishment of endowments corresponding with the wealth of the country to which it belongs, may be reckoned as eminently important the examples of civility and refinement which the clergy stationed at intervals afford to the whole people. The established clergy in many parts of England have long been, as they continue to be, the principal bulwark against barbarism, and the link which unites the sequestered peasantry with the intellectual advancement of the age. Nor is it below the dignity of the subject to observe that their taste, as acting upon rural residences and scenery, often furnishes models which country gentlemen, who are more at liberty to follow the caprices of fashion, might profit by. The precincts of an old residence must be treated by ecclesiastics with respect, both from prudence and necessity. I remember being much pleased, some years ago, at Rose Castle, the rural seat of the See of Carlisle, with a style of garden and architecture which, if the place had belonged to a wealthy layman, would no doubt have been swept away. A parsonage house generally stands not far from the church; this proximity imposes favourable restraints, and sometimes suggests an affecting union of the accommodations and elegancies of life with the outward signs of piety and morality. With pleasure I recall to mind a happy instance of this in the residence of an old and much-valued Friend in Oxfordshire. The house and church stand parallel to each other, at a small distance; a circular lawn, or rather grass-plot, spreads between them; shrubs and trees curve from each side of the dwelling, veiling, but not hiding, the church. From the front of this dwelling no part of the burial-ground is seen; but as you wind by the side of the shrubs towards the steeple-end of the church, the eye catches a single, small, low, monumental headstone, moss-grown, sinking into and gently inclining towards the earth. Advance, and the churchyard, populous and gay with glittering tombstones, opens upon the view. This humble and beautiful parsonage called forth a tribute, for which see the sonnet entitled "A Parsonage in Oxfordshire," p. 602. W. W.

Page 630. SONNET XXVI.
Line 10. Spenser's *Epithalamion*, line 217.

Page 631. SONNET XXXII.
This is still continued in many churches in Westmoreland. It takes place in the month of July, when the floor of the stalls is strewn with fresh rushes; and hence it is called "Rush-bearing." W. W. The ceremony is still observed in Grasmere and other towns in the Lake District.

Page 632. SONNET XXXIV.
Line 14. *unimaginable*. Incapable of being imaged; invisible. This line appears in a fragmentary Gothic narrative written many years before, probably in 1796.

Page 632. SONNET XXXV.
Line 10. *Teaching us to forget them or forgive.* This is borrowed from an affecting passage in Mr. George Dyer's history of Cambridge. W. W.

Page 633. SONNET XXXVII.
Line 3. *the great Deliverer.* William III, whose ships landed at Torbay on November 5, 1688.
Lines 5–6. *— had we, like them, endured*, etc. See Burnet, who is unusually animated on this subject; the east wind, so anxiously expected and prayed for, was called the "Protestant wind." W. W.

Page 633. SONNET XL.
Line 9. *Yet will we not conceal*, etc. The Lutherans have retained the Cross within their churches: it is to be regretted that we have not done the same. W. W.

Page 634. SONNET XLIII.
Line 1. *Royal Saint.* Henry VI, who built the chapel.

Page 634. SONNET XLV.
Line 8. *that younger Pile.* St. Paul's Cathedral.

Page 635. SONNET XLVI.
Line 5. *Or like the Alpine Mount*, etc. Some say that Monte Rosa takes its name from a belt of rock at its summit — a very unpoetical and scarcely a probable supposition. W. W.

Page 635. MEMORY.
See the headnote to "Written in a Blank Leaf of Macpherson's Ossian," p. 715.

Page 636. To THE LADY FLEMING.
Wordsworth leased his home, Rydal Mount, from Sir Michael and Lady Fleming, who lived nearby at Rydal Hall.
Line 15. Bekangs Ghyll — or dell of Nightshade — in which stands St. Mary's Abbey in Low Furness. W. W.

Page 637. ON THE SAME OCCASION.
Lines 4, 5. St. Oswald's Church, in Grasmere.

Page 637. "A VOLANT TRIBE OF BARDS."
Line 3. *Macbeth*, I.vi.7.

Page 639. To ——
Addressed probably to Wordsworth's daughter Dora, as Ernest Dowden suggested.

Page 640. To THE LADY E. B. AND THE HON. MISS P.
"The ladies . . . were Lady Eleanor Butler, . . . and the Hon. Miss Ponsonby" [de Selincourt].

Page 640. To the Torrent.
Line 4. *Pindus*. A mountain range in Greece.
Line 8. *Viamala*. A chasm near the source of the Rhine, in Switzerland. See "Descriptive Sketches," line 162.

Page 643. To a Sky-lark.
A penciled addition to the note describes Rydal Mount as a place "where there are no skylarks, but the poet is everywhere."

Page 644. To May.
Lines 59–60. "Lycidas," line 142.

Page 646. "The Massy Ways, Carried across these Heights."
According to a lost manuscript, recorded by Knight, this inscription was "intended to be placed on the door of the further Gravel Terrace" if the Wordsworths left Rydal Mount.

Page 646. The Pillar of Trajan.
The Pillar, which stands in Rome, celebrates the victories of the Emperor Trajan (98–117 A.D.) in the Dacian Wars, north of the Danube.
Line 46. *more high, the Dacian force*, etc. Here and infra, see Forsyth. W. W. Wordsworth refers to Forsythe's *Remarks on Antiquities, Arts and Letters, during an Excursion in Italy in 1802–3.*

Page 647. Farewell Lines.
Lamb wrote Wordsworth in 1822: "I grow ominously tired of official confinement. Thirty years have I served the Philistines, and my neck is not subdued to the yoke." In March, 1825, he received his pension and the next year he settled at Enfield, where he wrote to Wordsworth: "How I look down on the slaves and drudges of the world! Its inhabitants are a vast cotton-web of spin-spin-spinners! O the carking cares! O the money-grabbers! Sempiternal muck-worms" [G].
Line 1. The quotation is from James Thomson's "To the Rev. Patrick Murdoch," line 10.

Page 648. On Seeing a Needlecase.
To Edith, daughter of Wordsworth's friend, the poet Robert Southey.

Page 648. To ——.
"Almost certainly, to Mary" [de Selincourt]. In 1827 and after, this sonnet served as dedication for Wordsworth's series of Miscellaneous Sonnets.
Line 14. "Something less than joy, but more than dull content." Countess of Winchilsea. W. W.

Page 649. To S. H.
To Sara Hutchinson, Mary's sister.

Page 650. "Scorn not the Sonnet."
In 1827 and after this sonnet introduced Part II of the Miscellaneous Sonnets.
Line 6. Luiz Vas de Camöens, Portuguese poet (1524–1580).

Page 650. "There Is a Pleasure."
Lines 1–2. The quotation is from Cowper's *Task*, II.285.

Page 651. "When Philoctetes in the Lemnian Isle."
In Greek mythology, Philoctetes was marooned on the island of Lemnos, his only possession the bow and arrows that had descended to him from Hercules.

Page 651. "While Anna's Peers and Early Playmates Tread."
Headnote. Wordsworth refers to Maria Jane Jewsbury (1800–1833), writer, friend of the Wordsworth family, and companion to Dora. See "Liberty" (p. 664) and note.

Page 652. To Rotha Q——.
Line 9. The River Rotha, that flows into Windermere from the Lakes of Grasmere and Rydal. W. W. See Matthew Arnold's "Memorial Verses":

"Keep fresh the grass upon his grave,
O Rotha, with thy living wave!
Sing him thy best! for few or none
Hears thy voice right, now he is gone."

Page 653. In the Woods of Rydal.
This Sonnet, as Poetry, explains itself, yet the scene of the incident having been a wild wood, it may be doubted, as a point of natural history, whether the bird was aware that his attentions were bestowed upon a human, or even a living creature. But a Redbreast will perch upon the foot of a gardener at work, and alight on the handle of the spade when his hand is half upon it — this I have seen. And under my own roof I have witnessed affecting instances of the creature's friendly visits to the chambers of sick persons, as described in the verses to the Redbreast, page 768. One of these welcome intruders used frequently to roost upon a nail in the wall, from which a picture had hung, and was ready, as morning came, to pipe his song in the hearing of the Invalid, who had been long confined to her room. These attachments to a particular person, when marked and continued, used to be reckoned ominous; but the superstition is passing away. W. W.
Line 1. *Jemima*. The eldest daughter of Edward Quillinan, who would become Dora's husband in 1841.

Page 653. Conclusion.
This sonnet concluded Part II of the Miscellaneous Sonnets.
Lines 2–3. *the strife . . . of public life*. The sonnets gathered under the title of "Poems Dedicated to National Independence and Liberty."

Page 653. A Morning Exercise.
Line 16. See Waterton's "Wanderings in South America." W. W.
Lines 43–48. Before 1845 these lines formed the

second stanza of "To a Sky-lark" ("Ethereal Minstrel").

Page 654. THE TRIAD.
"How strange that any one should be puzzled with the name *Triad*, *after* reading the poem! I have turned to Dr. Johnson [the *Dictionary*] and there find '*Triad*, *three united*,' and not a word more, as nothing more was needed. I should have been rather mortified if *you* had not liked the piece, as I think it contains some of the happiest verses I ever wrote. It had been promised several years to two of the party before a fancy fit for the performance struck me; it was then thrown off rapidly, and afterwards revised with care" W. W. (from a letter of 1828).
Line 90. *youngest*, etc. Dora Wordsworth. "There is truth in the sketch of Dora," says Sara Coleridge, "poetic truth, though such as none but a poet-father would have seen" [G].

Page 658. THE WISHING-GATE DESTROYED.
In the Vale of Grasmere, by the side of the old high-way leading to Ambleside, is a gate which, time out of mind, has been called the Wishing-gate.
Having been told, upon what I thought good authority, that this gate had been destroyed, and the opening, where it hung, walled up, I gave vent immediately to my feelings in these stanzas. But going to the place some time after, I found, with much delight, my old favourite unmolested. W. W.

Page 659. THE GLEANER.
The painter was James Holmes (1777–1860).

Page 664. LIBERTY.
The connection of this with the preceding Poem is sufficiently obvious. W. W.
Line 2. *Anna*. Miss Jewsbury, mentioned in the headnote to the preceding poem.
Line 113. The poet Abraham Cowley (1618–1667).
Line 140. *Shall with a thankful tear*, etc. There is now, alas! no possibility of the anticipation, with which the above Epistle concludes, being realised: nor were the verses ever seen by the Individual for whom they were intended. She accompanied her husband, the Rev. Wm. Fletcher, to India, and died of cholera, at the age of thirty-two or thirty-three years, on her way from Shalapore to Bombay, deeply lamented by all who knew her.
Her enthusiasm was ardent, her piety steadfast; and her great talents would have enabled her to be eminently useful in the difficult path of life to which she had been called. The opinion she entertained of her own performances, given to the world under her maiden name, Jewsbury, was modest and humble, and, indeed, far below their merits; as is often the case with those who are making trial of their powers, with a hope to discover what they are best fitted for. In one quality, viz. quickness in the motions of her mind, she had, within the range of the Author's acquaintance, no equal. W. W.

Page 666. HUMANITY.
Line 32. *Descending to the worm in charity*. I am indebted, here, to a passage in one of Mr. Digby's valuable works. W. W.

Page 669. THE ARMENIAN LADY'S LOVE.
See, in Percy's *Reliques*, that fine old ballad, "The Spanish Lady's Love;" from which Poem the form of stanza, as suitable to dialogue, is adopted. W. W.

Page 672. THE RUSSIAN FUGITIVE.
Peter Henry Bruce, having given in his entertaining Memoirs the substance of this Tale, affirms that, besides the concurring reports of others, he had the story from the lady's own mouth.
The Lady Catherine, mentioned towards the close, is the famous Catherine, then bearing that name as the acknowledged Wife of Peter the Great. W. W.
Part III, Lines 3–4. From Golding's Translation of Ovid's Metamorphoses. See also his Dedicatory Epistle prefixed to the same work. W. W. (1835).

Page 683. ELEGIAC MUSINGS.
Sir George Beaumont died in 1827. To her father's note Dora Wordsworth added: "My Father was on my pony which he rode all the way from Rydal to Cambridge that I might have the comfort and pleasure of a horse at Cambridge — the storm of wind and rain on this day was so violent that the coach in which my Mother and I travelled the same road was all but blown over . . . . My Father and his pony were several times actually blown out of the road. D. Q."

Page 685. YARROW REVISITED, AND OTHER POEMS.
See "Yarrow Unvisited," p. 301, and "Yarrow Visited," p. 532.

Page 687. II. ON THE DEPARTURE OF SIR WALTER SCOTT.
Line 14. *Parthenope*. Another name for Naples.

Page 689. VII.
Line 1. *pibroch*. The bagpipe.

Page 689. VIII. COMPOSED AFTER READING A NEWSPAPER OF THE DAY.
In 1845 included among the Sonnets Dedicated to Liberty and Order.

Page 690. XI. IN THE SOUND OF MULL.
Line 3. *strath*. A flat river valley.
Line 14. *Etive Glen*. In Gaelic, *Buachaill Eite*. W. W.

Page 692. XV. HIGHLAND HUT.
This sonnet describes the *exterior* of a Highland hut, as often seen under a morning or evening sunshine. To the authoress of the "Address to the Wind," and other poems, in this volume, who was my fellow-traveller in this tour, I am indebted for the following extract from her journal, which accurately describes, under particular cir-

cumstances, the beautiful appearance of the *interior* of one of these rude habitations.

"On our return from the Trosachs the evening began to darken, and it rained so heavily that we were completely wet before we had come two miles, and it was dark when we landed with our boatman, at his hut upon the banks of Loch Katrine. I was faint from cold: the good woman had provided, according to her promise, a better fire than we had found in the morning; and, indeed, when I had sat down in the chimney-corner of her smoky biggin, I thought I had never felt more comfortable in my life: a pan of coffee was boiling for us, and having put our clothes in the way of drying, we all sat down thankful for a shelter. We could not prevail upon our boatman, the master of the house, to draw near the fire, though he was cold and wet, or to suffer his wife to get him dry clothes till she had served us, which she did most willingly, though not very expeditiously.

"A Cumberland man of the same rank would not have had such a notion of what was fit and right in his own house, or, if he had, one would have accused him of servility; but in the Highlander it only seemed like politeness (however erroneous and painful to us), naturally growing out of the dependence of the inferiors of the clan upon their laird; he did not, however, refuse to let his wife bring out the whisky bottle for his refreshment, at our request. 'She keeps a dram,' as the phrase is: indeed, I believe there is scarcely a lonely house by the wayside, in Scotland, where travellers may not be accommodated with a dram. We asked for sugar, butter, barley-bread, and milk: and, with a smile and a stare more of kindness than wonder, she replied, 'Ye'll get that,' bringing each article separately. We caroused our cups of coffee, laughing like children at the strange atmosphere in which we were: the smoke came in gusts, and spread along the walls; and above our heads in the chimney (where the hens were roosting) it appeared like clouds in the sky. We laughed and laughed again, in spite of the smarting of our eyes, yet had a quieter pleasure in observing the beauty of the beams and rafters gleaming between the clouds of smoke: they had been crusted over and varnished by many winters, till, where the fire-light fell upon them, they had become as glossy as black roots, on a sunny day, cased in ice. When we had eaten our supper we sat about half an hour, and I think I never felt so deeply the blessing of a hospitable welcome and a warm fire. The man of the house repeated from time to time that we should often tell of this night when we got to our homes, and interposed praises of his own lake, which he had more than once, when we were returning in the boat, ventured to say was 'bonnier than Loch Lomond.' Our companion from the Trosachs, who, it appeared, was an Edinburgh drawing-master going, during the vacation, on a pedestrian tour to John O'Groat's House, was to sleep in the barn with my fellow-travellers, where the man said he had plenty of dry hay. I do not believe that the hay of the Highlands is ever very dry, but this year it had

a better chance than usual: wet or dry, however, the next morning they said they had slept comfortably. When I went to bed, the mistress, desiring me to '*go ben*,' attended me with a candle, and assured me that the bed was dry, though not 'sic as I had been used to.' It was of chaff; there were two others in the room, a cupboard and two chests, upon one of which stood milk in wooden vessels covered over. The walls of the house were of stone unplastered; it consisted of three apartments, the cow-house at one end, the kitchen or house in the middle, and the spence at the other end; the rooms were divided, not up to the rigging, but only to the beginning of the roof, so that there was a free passage for light and smoke from one end of the house to the other. I went to bed some time before the rest of the family; the door was shut between us, and they had a bright fire, which I could not see, but the light it sent up amongst the varnished rafters and beams, which crossed each other in almost as intricate and fantastic a manner as I have seen the under-boughs of a large beech-tree withered by the depth of shade above, produced the most beautiful effect that can be conceived. It was like what I should suppose an underground cave or temple to be with a dripping or moist roof, and the moonlight entering in upon it by some means or other; and yet the colours were more like those of melted gems. I lay looking up till the light of the fire faded away, and the man and his wife and child had crept into their bed at the other end of the room; I did not sleep much, but passed a comfortable night; for my bed, though hard, was warm and clean: the unusualness of my situation prevented me from sleeping. I could hear the waves beat against the shore of the lake; a little rill close to the door made a much louder noise, and, when I sat up in my bed, I could see the lake through an open window-place at the bed's head. Add to this, it rained all night. I was less occupied by remembrance of the Trosachs, beautiful as they were, than the vision of the Highland hut, which I could not get out of my head; I thought of the Faery-land of Spenser, and what I had read in romance at other times; and then what a feast it would be for a London Pantomime-maker could he but transplant it to Drury-lane, with all its beautiful colours!" — *MS.* W. W.

Page 692. XVIII. BOTHWELL CASTLE.
Line 4. *Once on those steeps I roamed.* The following is from the same MS., and gives an account of the visit to Bothwell Castle here alluded to: —

"It was exceedingly delightful to enter thus unexpectedly upon such a beautiful region. The castle stands nobly, overlooking the Clyde. When we came up to it, I was hurt to see that flower-borders had taken place of the natural over-growings of the ruin, the scattered stones, and wild plants. It is a large and grand pile of red freestone, harmonising perfectly with the rocks of the river, from which, no doubt, it has been hewn. When I was a little accustomed to the unnaturalness of a modern garden, I could not help admiring the excessive beauty and luxuriance of some of the plants, particularly the purple-flowered clematis, and a broad-leafed creeping plant without flowers, which scrambled up the castle wall, along with the ivy, and spread its vine-like branches so lavishly that it seemed to be in its natural situation, and one could not help thinking that, though not self-planted among the ruins of this country, it must somewhere have its native abode in such places. If Bothwell Castle had not been close to the Douglas mansion, we should have been disgusted with the possessor's miserable conception of *adorning* such a venerable ruin; but it is so very near to the house, that of necessity the pleasure-grounds must have extended beyond it, and perhaps the neatness of a shaven lawn, and the complete desolation natural to a ruin, might have made an unpleasing contrast; and, besides being within the precincts of the pleasure-grounds, and so very near to the dwelling of a noble family, it has forfeited, in some degree, its independent majesty, and becomes a tributary to the mansion: its solitude being interrupted, it has no longer the command over the mind in sending it back into past times, or excluding the ordinary feelings which we bear about us in daily life. We had then only to regret that the castle and the house were so near to each other; and it was impossible *not* to regret it; for the ruin presides in state over the river, far from city or town, as if it might have a peculiar privilege to preserve its memorials of past ages, and maintain its own character for centuries to come. We sat upon a bench under the high trees, and had beautiful views of the different reaches of the river, above and below. On the opposite bank, which is finely wooded with elms and other trees, are the remains of a priory built upon a rock; and rock and ruin are so blended, that it is impossible to separate the one from the other. Nothing can be more beautiful than the little remnant of this holy place; elm-trees (for we were near enough to distinguish them by their branches) grow out of the walls, and overshadow a small, but very elegant window. It can scarcely be conceived what a grace the castle and priory impart to each other; and the river Clyde flows on, smooth and unruffled, below, seeming to my thoughts more in harmony with the sober and stately images of former times, than if it had roared over a rocky channel, forcing its sound upon the ear. It blended gently with the warbling of the smaller birds, and the chattering of the larger ones that had made their nests in the ruins. In this fortress the chief of the English nobility were confined after the battle of Bannockburn. If a man *is* to be a prisoner, he scarcely could have a more pleasant place to solace his captivity; but I thought that, for close confinement, I should prefer the banks of a lake, or the seaside. The greatest charm of a brook or river is in the liberty to pursue it through its windings; you can then take it in whatever mood you like; silent or noisy, sportive or quiet. The beauties of a brook or river must be sought, and the pleasure is in going in search of them; those of a lake or of the sea come to you of themselves. These rude warriors cared little, perhaps, about either; and yet, if one may judge from the writings of Chaucer and from the old romances, more interesting passions were connected with natural objects in the days of chivalry than now; though going in search of scenery, as it is called, had not then been thought of. I had previously heard nothing of Bothwell Castle, at least nothing that I remembered; therefore, perhaps, my pleasure was greater, compared with what I received elsewhere, than others might feel." — *MS. Journal.* W. W.

Page 694. XXII. HART'S-HORN TREE.
"In the time of the first Robert de Clifford, in the year 1333 or 1334, Edward Baliol king of Scotland came into Westmoreland, and stayed some time with the said Robert at his castles of Appleby, Brougham, and Pendragon. And during that time they ran a stag by a single greyhound out of Whinfell Park to Redkirk, in Scotland, and back again to this place; where, being both spent, the stag leaped over the pales, but died on the other side; and the greyhound, attempting to leap, fell, and died on the contrary side. In memory of this fact the stag's horns were nailed upon a tree just by, and (the dog being named Hercules) this rhythm was made upon them: —

" 'Hercules killed Hart a greese,
And Hart a greese killed Hercules.'

The tree to this day bears the name of Hart's-horn Tree. The horns in process of time were almost grown over by the growth of the tree, and another pair was put up in their place." — Nicholson and Burns's *History of Westmoreland and Cumberland.*
The tree has now disappeared, but I well remember its imposing appearance as it stood, in a decayed state, by the side of the highroad leading from Penrith to Appleby. This whole neighbourhood abounds in interesting traditions and vestiges of antiquity, viz. Julian's Bower; Brougham and Penrith Castles; Penrith Beacon, and the curious remains in Penrith Churchyard; Arthur's Round Table, and, close by, Maybrough; the excavation, called the Giant's Cave, on the banks of the Emont; Long Meg and her Daughters, near Eden, etc. W. W.

Page 695. XXVI. APOLOGY.
Line 20. *a threshold.* Sir Walter Scott's, in the introductory poem of this series.
Line 30. *rash change.* Wordsworth strongly opposed the First Reform Bill, which after much agitation was passed by the House of Lords in June 1832.

Page 695. XXVII. THE HIGHLAND BROACH.
Lines 30-35. *Malvina, Fingal.* Characters mentioned in James Macpherson's forgery (1760-63) of the poems of Ossian, the ancient Welsh bard.

Page 696. DEVOTIONAL INCITEMENTS.
For the motto see *Paradise Lost,* V.78-80.

Page 699. Upon the Late General Fast.
The fast was called because of an outbreak of cholera.

Page 699. Filial Piety.
Headnote. The coachman mentioned here also provided the subject of "A Tradition of Oker Hill," p. 669.

Page 700. "If Thou Indeed Derive Thy Light from Heaven."
Placed by Wordsworth at the head of his collected poems in 1845 and after. Lines 2 and 14–16 were added in 1837.

Page 700. To the Author's Portrait.
The portrait still hangs in the hall of St. John's College.

Page 701. To——.
To Isabella Wordsworth, the poet's daughter-in-law. The motto is from Lucretius, *De Rerum Natura*, V.222-23.

Page 702. The Warning.
A note followed the poem in manuscript: "Aware that expressions of regret for the past are seldom of much use as a preventive of future evils, the Author has not admitted without reluctance the above into a Collection of Poems so different from it in character. But it was poured out in sincerity of heart — and the heart of a Poet may in some cases be trusted, where the opinion of a practical Statesman is erroneous: at all events, the Verses, however profitless or insignificant they may appear to many, could not have been suppressed, without shrinking from what the Writer felt (and he hopes without presumption) to be a duty to his Country in the present peril of her social Institutions."
The poem is referred to in a manuscript version of the Postscript of 1835: "It has from time to time been the practice of the Author of this volume, since he was first interested in public affairs, to express in verse the feelings with which he regarded them. Accordingly it is known to all who have read his poems, that he rejoiced in the opening of the French Revolution; and it will appear hereafter, from his unpublished works, how deeply he deplored the excesses into which the French people were betrayed in its progress. His *Excursion*, Sonnets and other Pieces afford abundant evidence how he abhorred the abuses of Power that Buonaparte fell into; how he sympathized with the Nations that suffered from the Despot's reckless ambitions; and how he exalted in their deliverance. After the battle of Waterloo, the course of public events, however interesting to an observing and thoughtful Mind, was of a less exciting and therefore of a less poetic character, and he confined himself to subjects not so discordant in their elements. The lines, however, in the present volume entitled 'The Warning', both by the occasion that suggested them, and the manner in which the subject is treated, show that recent events have intimately touched his affections, and thrown him back upon sensations akin to those he was troubled with in the early period of his life. That Poem is indeed so little in harmony with the general tenor of his writings and with the contents of this volume in particular, that it seems to require from him some notice in plain prose. It was written for one of the best reasons which in a poetical case can be given, viz. that the author could not help writing it; and it is published because, if there ever was a time when such a warning could be of the least service to any portion of his Countrymen, that time is surely not passed away.

"The agitation attendant upon the introduction, and carrying of the Reform Bill has there called forth a strain of reprehension, which as far as concerns the Leaders of that agitation requires neither explanation nor apology; they are spoken of with a warmth of indignant reproof which no man free in spirit will condemn, if it will appear that the feeling has been kindled by reflective patriotism: but as to the misled multitude, if there be a word that bears hard upon them, the Author would find a difficulty in forgiving himself; for even the *semblance* of such a thought would be a deviation from his habitual feelings towards the poor and humbly employed; the greater part of his life has been passed among them, he has not been an unthinking observer of their condition, and from the strongest conviction that so many of that Class are seeking their happiness in ways which cannot lead to it those admonitions proceeded."
Line 23. *Lay*,. In the edition of 1849–50 a period followed *lay*. The comma was suggested to de Selincourt by Nowell Smith.

Page 705. (By the Seaside).
Line 39. The quotation is from Young's *Night Thoughts*, II.95.

Page 707. IV. To the River Greta.
Line 5. *But if thou (like Cocytus)*, etc. Many years ago, when I was at Greta Bridge, in Yorkshire, the hostess of the inn, proud of her skill in etymology, said, that "the name of the river was taken from the *bridge*, the form of which, as every one must notice, exactly resembled a great A." Dr. Whitaker has derived it from the word of common occurrence in the north of England, "*to greet*;" signifying the lament aloud, mostly with weeping: a conjecture rendered more probable from the stony and rocky channel of both the Cumberland and Yorkshire rivers. The Cumberland Greta, though it does not, among the country people, take up *that* name till within three miles of its disappearance in the river Derwent, may be considered as having its source in the mountain cove of Wythburn, and thence flowing through Thirlmere. The beautiful features of that lake are known only to those who, travelling between Grasmere and Keswick, have quitted the main road in the vale of Wythburn, and, crossing over to the opposite side of the lake, have proceeded with it on the right hand. The channel of the Greta, immediately above Keswick, has, for the purposes of building, been in a great measure cleared of the immense stones

which, by their concussion in high floods, produced the loud and awful noises described in the sonnet.

"The scenery upon this river," says Mr. Southey in his Colloquies, "where it passes under the woody side of Latrigg, is of the finest and most rememberable kind : —

" '— ambiguo lapsu refluitque fluitque,
Occurrensque sibi venturas aspicit undas.' "
W. W.

Page 707. V. IN SIGHT OF THE TOWN OF COCKERMOUTH.
Line 2. *My buried Little-ones.* Thomas and Catherine, who died in 1812, were buried in Grasmere.

Page 708. VII. NUN'S WELL.
Line 11. *By hooded Votaresses,* etc. Attached to the church of Brigham was formerly a chantry, which held a moiety of the manor; and in the decayed parsonage some vestiges of monastic architecture are still to be seen. W. W.
Line 14. The quotation is from Pope's "Eloisa to Abelard," line 270.

Page 708. IX. MARY QUEEN OF SCOTS LANDING AT THE MOUTH OF THE DERWENT.
"The fears and impatience of Mary were so great," says Robertson, "that she got into a fisher-boat, and with about twenty attendants landed at Workington, in Cumberland; and thence she was conducted with many marks of respect to Carlisle." The apartment in which the Queen had slept at Workington Hall (where she was received by Sir Henry Curwen as became her rank and misfortunes) was long preserved, out of respect to her memory, as she had left it; and one cannot but regret that some necessary alterations in the mansion could not be effected without its destruction. W. W.
Line 14. *Fotheringay.* Mary was executed at Fotheringay Castle on February 8, 1587.

Page 709. X. STANZAS SUGGESTED IN A STEAM-BOAT OFF SAINT BEES' HEADS.
St. Bees' Heads, anciently called the Cliff of Baruth, are a conspicuous sea-mark for all vessels sailing in the N.E. parts of the Irish Sea. In a bay, one side of which is formed by the southern headland, stands the village of St. Bees; a place distinguished, from very early times, for its religious and scholastic foundations.

"St. Bees," say Nicholson and Burns, "had its name from Bega, an holy woman from Ireland, who is said to have founded here, about the year of our Lord 650, a small monastery, where afterwards a church was built in memory of her.

"The aforesaid religious house, being destroyed by the Danes, was restored by William de Meschiens, son of Ranulph, and brother of Ranulph de Meschiens, first Earl of Cumberland after the Conquest; and made a cell of a prior and six Benedictine monks to the Abbey of St. Mary at York."

Several traditions of miracles, connected with the foundation of the first of these religious houses, survive among the people of the neighbourhood; one of which is alluded to in these Stanzas; and another, of a somewhat bolder and more peculiar character, has furnished the subject of a spirited poem by the Rev. R. Parkinson, M.A., late Divinity Lecturer of St. Bees' College, and now Fellow of the Collegiate Church of Manchester.

After the dissolution of the monasteries, Archbishop Grindal founded a free school at St. Bees, from which the counties of Cumberland and Westmoreland have derived great benefit; and recently, under the patronage of the Earl of Lonsdale, a college has been established there for the education of ministers for the English Church. The old Conventual Church has been repaired under the superintendence of the Rev. Dr. Ainger, the Head of the College, and is well worthy of being visited by any strangers who might be led to the neighbourhood of this celebrated spot.

The form of stanza in this Poem, and something in the style of versification, are adopted from the "St. Monica," a poem of much beauty upon a monastic subject, by Charlotte Smith: a lady to whom English verse is under greater obligations than are likely to be either acknowledged or remembered. She wrote little, and that little unambitiously, but with true feeling for rural nature, at a time when nature was not much regarded by English Poets; for in point of time her earlier writings preceded, I believe, those of Cowper and Burns. W. W.

Line 73. *Are not, in sooth, their Requiem's sacred ties.* I am aware that I am here treading upon tender ground; but to the intelligent reader I feel that no apology is due. The prayers of survivors, during passionate grief for the recent loss of relatives and friends, as the object of those prayers could no longer be the suffering body of the dying, would naturally be ejaculated for the souls of the departed; the barriers between the two worlds dissolving before the power of love and faith. The ministers of religion, from their habitual attendance upon sick-beds, would be daily witnesses of these benign results; and hence would be strongly tempted to aim at giving to them permanence, by embodying them in rites and ceremonies, recurring at stated periods. All this, as it was in course of nature, so was it blameless, and even praiseworthy; some of its effects, in that rude state of society, could not but be salutary. No reflecting person, however, can view without sorrow the abuses which rose out of thus formalising sublime instincts, and disinterested movements of passion, and perverting them into means of gratifying the ambition and rapacity of the priesthood. But, while we deplore and are indignant at these abuses, it would be a great mistake if we imputed the origin of the offices to prospective selfishness on the part of the monks and clergy: *they* were at first sincere in their sympathy, and in their degree dupes rather of their own creed, than artful and designing men. Charity is, upon the whole, the safest guide that we can take in judging our fellow-men, whether of past ages or of the present time. W. W.

Line 162. *teaching of St. Bees.* See *The Excursion,* seventh part, and "Ecclesiastical Sonnets," second part, near the beginning. W. W.

Page 712. XIV. ON ENTERING DOUGLAS BAY.
The motto is from Horace, *Odes,* IV.viii.28.
Line 1. *Cohorn.* A Dutch military engineer (1641–1704).
Line 8. The Tower of Refuge, an ornament to Douglas Bay, was erected chiefly through the humanity and zeal of Sir William Hillary; and he also was the founder of the lifeboat establishment at that place; by which, under his superintendence, and often by his exertions at the imminent hazard of his own life, many seamen and passengers have been saved. W. W.
Line 14. *Hillary.* Under date of July 3, 1828, on the Isle of Man, Dorothy writes: "Sir Wm. Hillary saved a boy's life to-day in the harbour. He raised a regiment for the Government and chose his own reward — a Baronetcy" [G].

Page 712. XV. BY THE SEASHORE, ISLE OF MAN.
Line 14. The sea-water on the coast of the Isle of Man is singularly pure and beautiful. W. W.

Page 712. XVI. ISLE OF MAN.
Headnote. "William" is probably an error for John (see note, p. 706), but, as de Selincourt points out, this incident may have occurred when William visited the Isle of Man in 1828.

Page 713. XVII. ISLE OF MAN.
Line 8. *A veteran Marine.* Henry Hutchinson, Wordsworth's brother-in-law and author of the following sonnet.

Page 713. XVIII. BY A RETIRED MARINER, H.H.
This unpretending sonnet is by a gentleman nearly connected with me, and I hope, as it falls so easily into its place, that both the writer and the reader will excuse its appearance here. W. W.

Page 713. XIX. AT BALA-SALA, ISLE OF MAN.
Line 3. Rushen Abbey. W. W.

Page 713. XX. TYNWALD HILL.
Line 9. *Off with yon cloud, old Snafell.* The summit of this mountain is well chosen by Cowley as the scene of the "Vision," in which the spectral angel discourses with him concerning the government of Oliver Cromwell. "I found myself," says he, "on the top of that famous hill in the Island Mona, which has the prospect of three great, and not long since most happy, kingdoms. As soon as ever I looked upon them, they called forth the sad representation of all the sins and all the miseries that had overwhelmed them these twenty years." It is not to be denied that the changes now in progress, and the passions, and the way in which they work, strikingly resemble those which led to the disasters the philosophic writer so feelingly bewails. God grant that the re-

semblance may not become still more striking as months and years advance! W. W.

Page 715. XXIV. ON REVISITING DUNOLLY CASTLE.
This ingenious piece of workmanship, as I afterwards learned, had been executed for their own amusement by some labourers employed about the place. W. W.

Page 715. XXVI. WRITTEN IN A BLANK LEAF OF MACPHERSON'S OSSIAN.
James Macpherson (1736–96) published his forged translations of the Welsh bard Ossian in 1760–63. The "H.C." of the headnote is Hartley Coleridge (1796–1849), Coleridge's eldest son.
Line 39. *Musæus.* A legendary Greek poet said to have been the pupil of Orpheus.
Lines 47–48. *strayed from hope and promise.* Among Hartley Coleridge's recent disappointments had been his dismissal from Oriel College, Oxford, for intemperance.
Lines 77–79. *Morven, Fingal.* A mountain and a hero, respectively, in Macpherson's Ossianic poems.
Line 80. *Mæonides.* Homer.
Line 82. *Urania.* See *Paradise Lost,* VII.1, 31.

Page 716. XXVII. CAVE OF STAFFA.
The reader may be tempted to exclaim, "How came this and the two following sonnets to be written, after the dissatisfaction expressed in the preceding one?" In fact, at the risk of incurring the reasonable displeasure of the master of the steamboat, I returned to the cave, and explored it under circumstances more favourable to those imaginative impressions which it is so wonderfully fitted to make upon the mind. W. W. Staffa is a rocky islet off the west coast of Scotland.

Page 717. XXX. FLOWERS ON THE TOP OF THE PILLARS AT THE ENTRANCE OF THE CAVE.
Line 1. *Hope smiled when your nativity was cast,* etc. Upon the head of the columns which form the front of the cave rests a body of decomposed basaltic matter, which was richly decorated with that large bright flower, the ox-eyed daisy. I had noticed the same flower growing with profusion among the bold rocks on the western coast of the Isle of Man, making a brilliant contrast with their black and gloomy surfaces. W. W.

Page 717. XXXI. IONA.
An island off the west coast of Scotland, Iona was the site of an early Christian settlement.

Page 717. XXXII. IONA UPON LANDING.
The four last lines of this sonnet are adopted from a well-known sonnet of Russel, as conveying my feeling better than any words of my own could do. W. W. The Rev. Thomas Russell published his *Sonnets and Miscellaneous Poems* in 1789, as de Selincourt notes.

Page 718. XXXIV.
Line 1. *Columba's Cell.* An Irish saint and missionary, Columba (521–597) founded a church and monastery on Iona.
Line 6. *St. Kilda's.* An island off the Outer Hebrides.

Page 718. XXXV. GREENOCK.
The motto is from Dante's *Inferno*, III.1.

Page 718. XXXVI.
Line 9. "the random *bield.*" From Burns, "To a Mountain Daisy," iv.; "bield": a shelter.

Page 719. THE RIVER EDEN.
Line 3. "That verse of mine." "Song at the Feast of Brougham Castle," p. 359.
Line 5. *Yet fetched from Paradise.* It is to be feared that there is more of the poet than the sound etymologist in this derivation of the name Eden. On the western coast of Cumberland is a rivulet which enters the sea at Moresby, known also in the neighbourhood by the name of Eden. May not the latter syllable come from the word Dean, *a valley?* Langdale, near Ambleside, is by the inhabitants called Langden. The former syllable occurs in the name Emont, a principal feeder of the Eden; and the stream which flows, when the tide is out, over Cartmel Sands, is called the Ea — eau, French— aqua, Latin. W. W.

Page 719. XXXVIII. MONUMENT OF MRS. HOWARD.
The sculptor was Joseph Nollekens (1737–1823).

Page 720. XL. NUNNERY.
Line 2. *the Pennine Alps.* The chain of Crossfell. W. W.
Line 14. *Canal,* etc. At Corby, a few miles below Nunnery, the Eden is crossed by a magnificent viaduct; and another of these works is thrown over a deep glen or ravine at a very short distance from the main stream. W. W.

Page 721. THE MONUMENT COMMONLY CALLLED LONG MEG AND HER DAUGHTERS, NEAR THE RIVER EDEN.
Line 1. *A weight of awe, not easy to be borne.* The daughters of Long Meg, placed in a perfect circle eighty yards in diameter, are seventy-two in number above ground; a little way out of the circle stands Long Meg herself, a single stone, eighteen feet high. When I first saw this monument, as I came on it by surprise, I might overrate its importance as an object; but, though it will not bear a comparison with Stonehenge, I must say, I have not seen any other relique of those dark ages which can pretend to rival it in singularity and dignity of appearance. W. W.

Page 721. LOWTHER.
Lowther Castle was the seat of the Earl of Lonsdale, Wordsworth's patron and friend.

Page 721. XLIV. TO THE EARL OF LONSDALE.
This sonnet was written immediately after certain trials took place at the Cumberland Assizes when the Earl of Lonsdale, in consequence of repeated and long-continued attacks upon his character through the local press, had thought it right to prosecute the conductors and proprietors of three several journals. A verdict of libel was given in one case; and, in the others, the prosecutions were withdrawn, upon the individuals retracting and disavowing the charges, expressing regret that they had been made, and promising to abstain from the like in future. W. W. The motto is that of the Lowthers, as in lines 9–10.

Page 722. XLV. THE SOMNAMBULIST.
Line 1. *Lyulph's Tower.* A pleasure-house built by the late Duke of Norfolk upon the banks of Ullswater. W. W. These ruins are reached from Grasmere by the Grisdale path over Helvellyn. See "Airey-Force Valley" [G].
Line 3. *force.* A word used in the Lake District for Waterfall. W. W.
Line 83. *"That pale Queen."* Lady Macbeth.

Page 723. XLVI. TO CORDELIA M——
Cordelia Marshall was the daughter of Dorothy Wordsworth's old and good friend, Jane Marshall.

Page 725. "NOT IN THE LUCID INTERVALS OF LIFE."
It is interesting to note that when the *Edinburgh Review* was attacking Byron, Wordsworth wrote: "The young man will do something if he goes on as he has begun. But these reviews, just because he is a lord, set upon him." Although Byron in "English Bards and Scotch Reviewers" alluded to Wordsworth as —

"That mild apostate from poetic rule,"

yet later in life after meeting Wordsworth at a dinner on being asked how he was impressed, he replied: "Why, to tell the truth, I had but one feeling from the beginning of the visit to the end, and that was *reverence*" [G]. In 1826 a friend reported that Wordsworth "admitted the power of Byron in describing the workings of human passion, but denied that he knew anything of the beauties of Nature, or succeeded in describing them with fidelity." To Walter Scott he wrote in 1816: "Let me say only one word upon Lord Byron. The man is insane; and will probably end his career in a madhouse." See "Upon the Same Occasion," p. 572, and note.

Page 726. "THE LEAVES THAT RUSTLED."
Line 20. *tod.* A bushy clump.

Page 727. THE REDBREAST.
Line 45. *Matthew, Mark*, etc. These words are a part of a child's prayer, still in general use throughout the northern counties. W. W.
Line 70. *Lilt.* "Italicized by Wordsworth because he is using the word in the dialect (Lakeland) sense of 'walk with a light and springing step'" [de Selincourt].

Page 728. LINES.
Headnote. J. Q. is Jemima Quillinan, the

daughter of Wordsworth's future son-in-law.
Line 126. *Bethesda's pool.* See John 5:4.

Page 733. To the Moon, Rydal.
Line 50. The quotation is from Shakespeare, Sonnet 116, line 6.

Page 734. Written after the Death of Charles Lamb.
Lamb died on December 27, 1834. Lines 1–38 were written at the request of his sister, Mary, and were printed privately as an Epitaph, in 1835. The remainder of the poem was composed in December 1835, and printed privately in 1836.
Line 23. *From the most gentle creature nursed in fields.* This way of indicating the *name* of my lamented friend has been found fault with; perhaps rightly so; but I may say in justification of the double sense of the word, that similar allusions are not uncommon in epitaphs. One of the best in our language in verse I ever read, was upon a person who bore the name of Palmer; and the course of the thought, throughout, turned upon the Life of the Departed, considered as a pilgrimage. Nor can I think that the objection in the present case will have much force with any one who remembers Charles Lamb's beautiful sonnet addressed to his own name, and ending —

"No deed of mine shall shame thee, gentle name!" W. W.

Line 50. *a scorner of the fields.* In 1801 Wordsworth had invited Lamb to visit the Lake District. Lamb refused, writing: "Separate from the pleasure of your company, I don't much care if I never see a mountain in my life. — I have passed all my days in London, until I have formed as many and intense local attachments, as any of you Mountaineers have done with dead nature." Lamb did visit the Lakes in 1802, however, and was impressed despite himself.

Page 736. Extempore Effusion upon the Death of James Hogg.
Line 4. *Ettrick Shepherd.* James Hogg (1770–1835), Scottish poet.
Line 8. *Border-Minstrel.* Sir Walter Scott, who had died in 1832. See "Yarrow Revisited," p. 685.
Line 15. Coleridge died in 1834.
Line 31. George Crabbe, the poet (1754–1832).
Line 39. *Her.* Felicia Hemans (1793–1835), poet and translator, whom Wordsworth had met in 1829.

Page 737. Upon Seeing a Coloured Drawing of the Bird of Paradise.
Sara Hutchinson died on June 23, 1835.

Page 740. VII.
Published in 1838 as a protest against the ballot, and preceded by a note which ran in part: "Having in this notice alluded only in general terms to the mischief which, in my opinion, the Ballot would bring along with it,

without especially branding its immoral and anti-social tendency, (for which no political advantages, were they a thousand times greater than those presumed upon, could be a compensation) I have been impelled to subjoin a reprobation of it upon that score."
Line 14. In a manuscript Wordsworth refers to George Grote (1794–1871), historian and radical politician.

Page 741. November 1836.
Line 4. *Dear Sister.* Sara Hutchinson. See headnote to "Methought I Saw the Footsteps of a Throne," p. 351.

Page 741. "Six Months to Six Years Added He Remained."
Inscribed upon the gravestone of Thomas Wordsworth, the poet's son, in Grasmere churchyard. "It took him years to produce those six simple lines at the head of the earthly remains of our own dear Boy." — Mary Wordsworth.

Page 741. To Henry Crabb Robinson.
Lawyer, foreign correspondent, and diarist, Robinson (1775–1867) was acquainted with many of the notable literary figures of his day, including William Blake, Coleridge, Lamb, Hazlitt, and others.
Line 2. *In.* Originally "to," but changed after Robinson's objection. De Selincourt cites Wordsworth's letter on the change: "I trust *in* Providence, I trust in your or any man's *integrity*, but in matters of inferior importance, as companionship in a tour of pleasure must be reckoned, I prefer saying '*to.*' But, when the lines are reprinted, I shall be most happy to defer to your judgment and feeling. Let me say, however, that my ear is susceptible of the clashing of sounds almost to disease; and '*in*' and 'trusting,' unless the 'g' be well marked in pronunciation, which it often is not, make to me a disagreeable repetition."

Page 743. I. Musings near Aquapendente.
Composed in 1841, three years after the tour.
Lines 30–37. *Fairfield, Seat Sandal, Helvellyn.* Mountains near Wordsworth's home in the Lake District.
Line 57. *The Wizard of the North.* Walter Scott, who had journeyed to Italy in search of health in 1831. See "Yarrow Revisited," p. 685.
Line 76. *He said, "When I am there,"* etc. These words were quoted to me from "Yarrow Unvisited" by Sir Walter Scott when I visited him at Abbotsford, a day or two before his departure for Italy; and the affecting condition in which he was when he looked upon Rome from the Janicular Mount, was reported to me by a lady who had the honour of conducting him thither. W. W.
Line 158. *Sacred earth.* "Archbishop Ubaldo (1188–1200) founded the Campo Santo at Pisa, bringing fifty-three shiploads of earth from Mount Calvary in order that the dead might repose in holy ground" [William Knight].

Line 236. Gabriello Chiabrera (1552–1617), Italian poet born at Savona.

Line 241. *his sepulchral verse.* If any English reader should be desirous of knowing how far I am justified in thus describing the epitaphs of Chiabrera, he will find translated specimens of them on pages 388–391. W. W.

Line 264. *that delicious Bay.* The Bay of Naples.

Line 305. *Mamertine prison.* Where, according to legend, Sts. Peter and Paul were imprisoned.

Line 372. It would be ungenerous not to advert to the religious movement that, since the composition of these verses in 1837, has made itself felt, more or less strongly, throughout the English Church; — a movement that takes, for its first principle, a devout deference to the voice of Christian antiquity. It is not my office to pass judgment on questions of theological detail; but my own repugnance to the spirit and system of Romanism has been so repeatedly and, I trust, feelingly expressed, that I shall not be suspected of a leaning that way, if I do not join in the grave charge, thrown out, perhaps in the heat of controversy, against the learned and pious men to whose labours I allude. I speak apart from controversy; but, with strong faith in the moral temper which would elevate the present by doing reverence to the past, I would draw cheerful auguries for the English Church from this movement, as likely to restore among us a tone of piety more earnest and real than that produced by the mere formalities of the understanding, refusing, in a degree which I cannot but lament, that its own temper and judgment shall be controlled by those of antiquity. W. W.

Page 748. II. THE PINE OF MONTE MARIO.
Line 7. Within a couple of hours of my arrival at Rome, I saw from Monte Pincio the Pine tree as described in the Sonnet; and, while expressing admiration at the beauty of its appearance, I was told by an acquaintance of my fellow-traveller, who happened to join us at the moment, that a price had been paid for it by the late Sir G. Beaumont, upon condition that the proprietor should not act upon his known intention of cutting it down. W. W.

Page 748. IV. AT ROME — REGRETS.
Barthold Georg Niebuhr (1766–1831) had cast doubt on the legendary origins of Rome in his *History of Rome* (1827–28).

Page 749. V. CONTINUED.
Line 11. *Runic Scald.* A Norse bard.

Page 749. VI. PLEA FOR THE HISTORIAN.
Line 14.

Quem virum — lyra —
— sumes celebrare Clio?
W. W. (Horace, *Odes*, I. xii.)

Page 750. XI. FROM THE ALBAN HILLS.
Line 10. *twice exalted.* In the classical and Christian eras.

Page 751. XII. NEAR THE LAKE OF THRASYMENE.
Line 1. Hannibal of Carthage vanquished the Romans near this lake in 247 B.C.
Line 7. *Rill.* Sanguinetto. W. W.

Page 751. XIII. NEAR THE SAME LAKE.
Line 9. *vanquished Chief.* Flaminius, the defeated Roman consul.
Line 14. *death-cup.* Hannibal took poison to avoid capture (190 B.C.).

Page 751. XIV. THE CUCKOO AT LAVERNA.
The following note precedes a manuscript of the poem: "Laverna is one of the three famous Convents called the three Tuscan Sanctuaries — Camaldoli and Vallombrosa are the other two. Laverna was finished by St. Francis of Assisi, and the monks are Franciscans. In the following verses I am much indebted to a passage in a letter to one of Mrs. Corbelin's relations, the thought of which was suggested to that writer by my own Poem to the Cuckoo . . . transcribed in Munich, July 18, 1837."
Line 29. *far-famed Pile.* Monastery of St. Francis.
On entering we were courteously received by the poor and humble monks. W. W.

Page 753. XV. AT THE CONVENT OF CAMALDOLI.
This famous sanctuary was the original establishment of Saint Romualdo (or Rumwald, as our ancestors Saxonised the name), in the 11th century, the ground (campo) being given by Count Maldo. The Camaldolensi, however, have spread wide as a branch of Benedictines, and may therefore be classed among the *gentlemen* of the monastic orders. The society comprehends two orders, monks and hermits; symbolised by their arms, two doves drinking out of the same cup. The monastery in which the monks here reside is beautifully situated, but a large unattractive edifice, not unlike a factory. The hermitage is placed on a loftier and wider region of the forest. It comprehends between twenty and thirty distinct residences, each including for its single hermit an inclosed piece of ground and three very small apartments. There are days of indulgence when the hermit may quit his cell, and when old age arrives he descends from the mountain and takes his abode among the monks.
My companion had in the year 1831 fallen in with the monk, the subject of these two sonnets, who showed him his abode among the hermits. It is from him that I received the following particulars. He was then about forty years of age, but his appearance was that of an older man. He had been a painter by profession, but on taking orders changed his name from Santi to Raffaello, perhaps with an unconscious reference as well to the great Sanzio d'Urbino as to the archangel. He assured my friend that he had been thirteen years in the hermitage and had never known melancholy or ennui. In the little recess for study and prayer, there was a small collection of books. "I read only," said he, "books of asceticism and mystical theology." On

being asked the names of the most famous mystics, he enumerated *Scaramelli, San Giovanni della Croce, St. Dionysius the Areopagite* (supposing the work which bears his name to be really his), and with peculiar emphasis *Ricardo di San Vittori.* The works of *Saint Theresa* are also in high repute among ascetics. These names may interest some of my readers.

We heard that Raffaello was then living in the convent; my friend sought in vain to renew his acquaintance with him. It was probably a day of seclusion. The reader will perceive that these sonnets were supposed to be written when he was a young man. W. W.

Page 753. XVII. At the Eremite or Upper Convent of Camaldoli.
Line 1. *What aim had they, the Pair of Monks.* In justice to the Benedictines of Camaldoli, by whom strangers are so hospitably entertained, I feel obliged to notice that I saw among them no other figure at all resembling, in size and complexion, the two monks described in this Sonnet. What was their office, or the motive which brought them to this place of mortification, which they could not have approached without being carried in this or some other way, a feeling of delicacy prevented me from inquiring. An account has before been given of the hermitage they were about to enter. It was visited by us towards the end of the month of May; yet snow was lying thick under the pine-trees, within a few yards of the gate. W. W.

Page 753. XVIII. At Vallombrosa.
The name of Milton is pleasingly connected with Vallombrosa in many ways. The pride with which the monk, without any previous question from me, pointed out his residence, I shall not readily forget. It may be proper here to defend the poet from a charge which has been brought against him, in respect to the passage in "Paradise Lost," where this place is mentioned. It is said, that he has erred in speaking of the trees there being deciduous, whereas they are, in fact, pines. The faultfinders are themselves mistaken; the *natural* woods of the region of Vallombrosa *are* deciduous, and spread to a great extent; those near the convent are, indeed, mostly pines; but they are avenues of trees *planted* within a few steps of each other, and thus composing large tracts of wood; plots of which are periodically cut down. The appearance of those narrow avenues, upon steep slopes open to the sky, on account of the height which the trees attain by being *forced* to grow upwards, is often very impressive. My guide, a boy of about fourteen years old, pointed this out to me in several places. W. W. The motto is from *Paradise Lost*, I.302-304.
Lines 1-2. From "Stanzas Composed in the Simplon Pass," p. 586.

Page 756. XXII.
An early version of this sonnet appears in a manuscript of 1805.

Page 757. XXV. After Leaving Italy.
Headnote. *Carbonari.* The "Charcoal-burners," the most famous of the revolutionary secret societies that sprang up in Italy after the conservative settlement of 1815.

Page 757. At Bologna, in Remembrance of the Late Insurrections.
This and the following were suggested at Bologna, and other cities in the North of Italy. W. W., manuscript note. A fruitless uprising against the Papal government had taken place in Bologna in 1831. All three sonnets were included in 1845 and after among those Dedicated to Liberty and Order.

Page 759. Composed at Rydal.
In 1845 and 1849 placed at the conclusion of the series on the Tour of 1837.

Page 759. Composed on a May Morning, 1838.
Composed on the same morning [as the preceding]. W. W.

Page 760. "Oh What a Wreck!"
Robert Southey's wife died, insane, on November 16, 1837, two years after Wordsworth's sister had become mentally ill. A manuscript version of the last six lines runs as follows:

Such faith was thine, and now to me, dear Friend,
Whose trouble flows from some mysterious source,
While o'er my stricken Sister's couch I bend,
Like consolation comes with gentle force;
So may remembrance of thy patient course
Long proved, sustain me till my trials end.

"The thought in the sonnet as it now stands has ever been a consolation to me," he wrote to Dora in 1838, ". . . and [the] hope that, thus expressed, it may prove so to others makes one wish to print it; but your mother seems to think it would be applied at once to your dear aunt. I own I do not see the force of this objection; but if you and Miss Fenwick and others should be of the same mind, it shall be suppressed."

Page 760. A Plea for Authors.
Wordsworth used all his influence to secure an extension of the Copyright Act, which protected a work for only twenty-eight years from the date of its publication. Bills to this effect were introduced in Parliament in 1837 and 1838 by Thomas Noon Talfourd, an admirer of the poet, but were defeated. In 1842, due in part to Wordsworth's efforts, a more generous Bill was passed.

Page 760. A Poet to his Grandchild.
Line 4. The author of an animated article, printed in the Law Magazine, in favour of the principle of Serjant Talfourd's Copyright Bill, precedes me in the public expression of this feeling; which had been forced too often upon my own mind, by remembering how few descendants of men eminent in literature are even known to exist. W. W. (1838).

Page 761. "Blest Statesman He, Whose Mind's Unselfish Will."
Included, in 1845 and 1849, among the Sonnets Dedicated to Liberty and Order.
Line 14. "All change is perilous and all chance unsound." Spenser. — W. W. (*Faerie Queene,* V.ii.36).

Page 761. Sonnets upon the Punishment of Death.
Written to oppose Parliamentary proposals of total abolition of the death penalty.

Page 763. VIII.
Line 14. The quotation is from Bacon's essay, "On Revenge."

Page 764. On a Portrait of I. F.
Isabella Fenwick (1783-1856), friend of Wordsworth in his later years, and transcriber of the notes that precede his poems in this edition. She took a house near Rydal Mount in 1841. A. J. George cites her comment to Sir Henry Taylor: "I would be content to be a servant in his house to hear his wisdom." Mary Moorman reminds us that she did not "idolize or spoil him. 'I know *all* his faults,' she once said."

Page 765. Poor Robin.
The Poor Robin is the small wild geranium known by that name. W. W. Kept as it was in Wordsworth's day, Rydal Mount is now open to the public.

Page 766. "When Severn's Sweeping Flood Had Overthrown."
De Selincourt cites William Knight: "In 1842 a bazaar was held at Cardiff Castle to aid in the erection of a church, on the site of one which had been washed away by a flood in the river Severn (and a consequent influx of waters into the estuary of the Bristol Channel) two hundred years before. Wordsworth and James Montgomery were asked to write some verses which might be printed and sold to assist the cause."

Page 769. III. "Feel for the Wrongs to Universal Ken."
In Wordsworth's note the sonnet is recommended as well to "the Anti-Corn Law Leaguers, [and] the Political Economists."

Page 769. IV. In Allusion to Various Recent Histories . . . of the French Revolution.
Thomas Carlyle's *French Revolution* appeared in 1837.

Page 770. VII. "Men of the Western World!"
These lines were written several years ago, when reports prevailed of cruelties committed in many parts of America, by men making a law of their own passions. A far more formidable, as being a more deliberate mischief, has appeared among those States, which have lately broken faith with the public creditor in a manner so infamous. I cannot, however, but look at both evils under a similar relation to inherent good, and hope that the time is not distant when our brethren of the West will wipe off this stain from their name and nation.

ADDITIONAL NOTE

I am happy to add that this anticipation is already partly realised; and that the reproach addressed to the Pennsylvanians in the sonnet on page 784 is no longer applicable to them. I trust that those other States to which it may yet apply will soon follow the example now set them by Philadelphia, and redeem their credit with the world. — 1850. W. W.

Page 770. VIII. "Lo! Where She Stands Fixed in a Saint-like Trance."
On Dora Wordsworth, according to a note by Sara Coleridge.

Page 771. The Poet's Dream.
Line 28. *Chapel Oak of Allonville.* Among ancient Trees there are few, I believe, at least in France, so worthy of attention as an Oak which may be seen in the "Pays de Caux," about a league from Yvetot, close to the church, and in the burial-ground of Allonville.
The height of this Tree does not answer to its girth; the trunk, from the roots to the summit, forms a complete cone; and the inside of this cone is hollow throughout the whole of its height.
Such is the Oak of Allonville in its state of nature. The hand of Man, however, has endeavored to impress upon it a character still more interesting, by adding a religious feeling to the respect which its age naturally inspires.
The lower part of its hollow trunk has been transformed into a Chapel of six or seven feet in diameter, carefully wainscoted and paved, and an open iron gate guards the humble Sanctuary.
Leading to it there is a staircase, which twists round the body of the Tree. At certain seasons of the year, divine service is performed in this Chapel.
The summit has been broken off many years, but there is a surface at the top of the trunk, of the diameter of a very large tree, and from it rises a pointed roof, covered with slates, in the form of a steeple, which is surmounted with an iron Cross, that rises in a picturesque manner from the middle of the leaves, like an ancient hermitage above the surrounding Wood.
Over the entrance to the Chapel an Inscription appears, which informs us it was erected by the Abbé du Détroit, Curate of Allonville in the year 1696; and over a door is another, dedicating it "To our Lady of Peace."
Vide No. 14, Saturday Magazine. W. W.

Page 774. "Lyre! Though Such Power Do in Thy Magic Live."
See headnote to "The Forsaken," p. 313.

Page 776. "Wansfell! This Household Has a Favoured Lot."

Line 1. *Wansfell.* The hill that rises to the southeast, above Ambleside. W. W.

Page 776. THE EAGLE AND THE DOVE.
Published in *La Petite Chouannerie, ou Histoire d'un Collège Breton sous l'Empire*, 1842, and not republished by Wordsworth. De Selincourt cites a letter of Wordsworth's American publisher, Henry Reed, which describes the book's subject as "the romantic revolt of the royalist students of the college of Vannes in 1815, and their battles with the soldiers of the French Republic."

Page 776. GRACE DARLING.
The daughter of a lighthouse-keeper on the Northumbrian coast, Grace Darling aided him in the rescue of nine persons from the wreck of a steamship in September 1838. Privately printed in 1843 and published in 1845.

Page 778. "WHILE BEAMS OF ORIENT LIGHT SHOOT WIDE AND HIGH."
Line 2. *rural Town.* Ambleside. W. W.

Page 778. TO THE REVEREND CHRISTOPHER WORDSWORTH.
To Wordsworth's nephew, the son of his youngest brother, Christopher.

Page 778. INSCRIPTION.
For Robert Southey, who died in 1843.

Page 778. ON THE PROJECTED KENDAL AND WINDERMERE RAILWAY.
The degree and kind of attachment which many of the yeomanry feel to their small inheritances can scarcely be over-rated. Near the house of one of them stands a magnificent tree, which a neighbour once advised him to fell for profit's sake. "Fell it!" exclaimed the yeoman, "I had rather fall on my knees and worship it." It happens, I believe, that the intended railway would pass through this little property, and I hope that an apology for the answer will not be thought necessary by one who enters into the strength of the feeling. W. W.
Wordsworth vainly opposed the extension, in 1844, of the railway from Kendal to the lake of Windermere. Mary Moorman cites a friend's recollection of the composition of this sonnet: "In the autumn of 1844 my mother and I paid a morning call at Rydal Mount. . . . Presently the poet entered, having a sheet of paper in his hand; his face was flushed and his waistcoat in disarray as if he had been clutching at it under the stress of fervid thought. 'I have been writing a sonnet,' he said. After a few more words, standing up in front of the fire he recited it to us; it was the sonnet "Is there no nook of English ground secure." The force and intensity with which he uttered the lines breathed into his hearers a contagious fire, and to this hour I recollect the precise manner and tone of his delivery more exactly than in any case of any verses I ever heard. . . .'"

Page 779. AT FURNESS ABBEY.
Line 14. The Duke of Cavendish, owner of the Abbey.

Page 779. "FORTH FROM A JUTTING RIDGE."
Line 9. *two adventurous Sisters.* Mary and Sara Hutchinson.

Page 784. "SO FAIR, SO SWEET, WITHAL SO SENSITIVE."
De Selincourt cites R. P. Graves's recollection of the incident that gave rise to this poem during a walk to Loughrigg Tarn: "The splendour of a July noon surrounded us, and lit up the landscape with the Langdale Pikes soaring above, and the bright Tarn shining beneath; and when the poet's eyes were satisfied with their feast on the beauties familiar to them, they sought relief in the search . . . for new beauty in the flower-enamelled turf at his feet. There his attention was arrested by a fair smooth stone, of the size of an ostrich's egg, seeming to imbed at its centre, and at the same time to display a dark star-shaped fossil of most distinct outline. Upon closer inspection this proved to be the shadow of a daisy projected upon it with extraordinary precision by the intense light of an almost vertical sun."

Page 784. TO THE PENNSYLVANIANS.
"Wordsworth was much troubled by the stoppage of payment of Pennsylvanian Bonds, in which both his brother Christopher and Miss Fenwick had large holdings" [de Selincourt]. For Wordsworth's retraction, see "Men of the Western World" (p. 770) and note. The sonnet was included among those Dedicated to Liberty and Order.

Page 784. "YOUNG ENGLAND — WHAT IS THEN BECOME OF OLD."
Line 11. *servum pecus.* "Servile herd," a contemptuous phrase used by Horace and other Roman writers.

Page 786. SONNET.
This and the following sonnet were suggested by the death, in Rome, of a five-year-old grandson in late 1845.

Page 787. EVENING VOLUNTARIES.
A painting by Lucca Giordano (1632–1705) hung in Rydal Mount.

Page 788. ODE ON THE INSTALLATION OF HIS ROYAL HIGHNESS.
Grief-stricken over the death of his daughter Dora (July 9, 1847), Wordsworth was assisted in the composition of this ode by his son-in-law, Edward Quillinan. He never republished it.

Page 790. PREFACE.
This famous Preface was published in 1800, enlarged in 1802, and revised in subsequent editions of the *Lyrical Ballads* and the *Collected Works*. The present text is that of 1849–50. The

most substantial additions of 1802 are indicated in the notes. For detailed commentary on these essays, the reader should consult *The Prose Works*, edited by W. J. B. Owen and Jane Worthington Smyser.

Page 791. Column 1, paragraph 2, lines 3–9. *to relate or describe . . . an unusual aspect.* Added in 1802.

Page 791. Column 1, paragraph 2, lines 4–5 from the bottom. *a far more philosophical language.* A more accurate language. W. J. B. Owen cites Joseph Priestly's definition of a "philosophical language" as "the most natural and perfect expression of human ideas and sentiments."

Page 791. Column 2, paragraph 2, lines 22–23. *the spontaneous overflow of powerful feelings.* As this famous definition is often cited without the qualification that follows in the same sentence, it should be emphasized that Wordsworth is arguing on behalf of "thought" as well as "feeling." Both are essential to poetic excellence.

Page 793. Column 1. *"In vain to me the smiling mornings shine."* Thomas Gray's "Sonnet on the Death of Richard West."

Page 793. Column 1, paragraph 3. *"such as Angels weep."* From *Paradise Lost*, I.620.

Page 793. Column 1, paragraph 4, line 2 from the bottom, *The language of such Poetry . . .* to p. 796, column 1, paragraph 1, line 3, *to remind the Reader.* Added in 1802.

Page 796. Column 2, paragraph 2, last 17 lines. *and of feeling not strictly and necessarily connected with the passion* to *similar instances will be found in them.* Added in 1802.

Page 797. Column 1, paragraph 1. *the "Gamester."* A popular drama by Edward Moore (1753).

Page 798. Column 1. *"I put my hat upon my head."* As Wordsworth's probable source, Owen cites *The London Magazine*, April 1785.

Page 798. Column 1. *"Babes in the Wood."* A popular ballad known to Wordsworth since his youth.

Page 798. Column 1, paragraph 4, last 3 lines. *Why take pains to prove . . . that he is not a man?* An echo of Pope's *Essay on Man*, II.31–34.

Page 799. APPENDIX. Added in 1802 and reprinted in subsequent editions.

Page 801. PREFACE TO THE EDITION OF 1815. Prefixed to the collected poems in 1815, this essay reappeared in collected editions thereafter.

Page 801. Column 2, paragraph 2. *Epopœia.* The heroic epic.

Page 801. Column 2, paragraph 2. *Arma virumque cano.* "I sing of arms and a man," the first line of Virgil's *Aeneid*.

Page 803. Column 1. *"He murmurs near the running brooks."* "A Poet's Epitaph," page 114, lines 39–40.

Page 803. Column 2. *"Non ego vos post-hac . . ."* From Virgil's first *Eclogue*, lines 75–76.

Page 803. Column 2. *"half way down."* *King Lear*, IV.vi.14–15.

Page 803. Column 2. *"As when far off at sea a fleet descried."* From *Paradise Lost*, II.636–43.

Page 803. Column 2. *"Over his own sweet voice . . ."* "Resolution and Independence," page 280, line 5.

Page 803. Column 2. *"His voice was buried among trees."* "O Nightingale! Thou Surely Art," page 358, lines 13–14.

Page 803. Column 2. *"O Cuckoo! shall I call thee Bird."* "To the Cuckoo," page 310, lines 3–4.

Page 804. Column 1. *"As a huge stone is sometimes seen to lie."* "Resolution and Independence," page 281, lines 57–65, 75–77.

Page 804. Column 2. *"Modo me Thebis, . . ."* "Now [the Poet] puts me down in Thebes, now in Athens," from Horace, *Epistles*, II.i.213.

Page 804. Column 2. *"Attended by ten thousand thousand Saints."* *Paradise Lost*, VI.767–68.

Page 805. Column 1. *"I tax not you, ye Elements, with unkindness."* *King Lear*, III.ii.16–17.

Page 805. Column 1, paragraph 3. Coleridge replied to this criticism in Chapter IV of his *Biographia Literaria* (1817).

Page 805. Column 1. *"In shape no bigger than an agate-stone."* *Romeo and Juliet*, I.iv.55–56.

Page 805. Column 2. *"His stature reached the sky."* *Paradise Lost*, IV.988.

Page 805. Column 2. *"The dews of the evening most carefully shun."* From Chesterfield's *Advice to a Lady in Autumn*, II.248–49.

Page 806. Column 1. *"Sky lowered, and, muttering thunder, some sad drops."* *Paradise Lost*, IX.1002–1003.

Page 806. Column 2, paragraph 1. In all editions before that of 1836–37, this concluding paragraph was preceded by the following passage: "It remains that I should express my regret at the necessity of separating my compositions from some beautiful Poems of Mr. Coleridge, with which they have been long associated in publication. The feelings, with which that joint publication was made, have been gratified; its end is answered, and the time is come when considerations of general propriety dictate the separation. Three short pieces (now first published) are the work of a Female Friend; and the Reader, to whom they may be acceptable, is indebted to me for his pleasure; if any one regard them with dislike, or be disposed to condemn them, let the censure fall upon him, who, trusting in his own sense of their merit and their fitness for the place which they occupy, *extorted* them from the Authoress." The "Female Friend" was of course Dorothy Wordsworth.

Page 806. ESSAY, SUPPLEMENTARY TO THE PREFACE. This survey of the vagaries of literary reputation in England was first published in the edition of 1815. It reappeared in every edition of the collected works thereafter, although in those of 1836–37 and after it was presented, misleadingly, as supplementary to the Preface of 1800.

Page 809. Column 1. *"The laurel, meed of mighty conquerors."* From Spenser's *Faerie Queene*, I.i.9.

Page 810. Column 1, end of paragraph 1. *"there sitting where he durst not soar." Paradise Lost*, IV.829.

Page 810. Column 1, paragraph 3, line 8. *"Fit audience find though few." Paradise Lost*, VII.31.

Page 814. Column 1, paragraph 2, line 21. *the morning-star of English Poetry.* Chaucer.

Page 814. Column 2, paragraph 3, lines 9–10. *the philosophical Friend.* Coleridge, as Wordsworth explained in the deleted conclusion to the Preface of 1815 (see note).

Page 815. Column 2. *"Anger in hasty words or blows."* Adapted from Edmund Waller's "Of Love," lines 1–2.

Page 816. Column 2. *"Past and future, are the wings."* From *The Prelude* (1850), VI.448–50.

Page 816. Column 2, paragraph 2, line 12 from bottom. *the "Vision and the Faculty divine."* From *The Excursion*, I.79.

Page 817. POSTSCRIPT. First published in *Yarrow Revisited, and Other Poems*, in 1835, and reprinted in later editions.

Page 817. Column 1, paragraph 3, line 2. *the Poor-Law Amendment Act.* This act, which severely restricted state aid to the poor, had been passed in 1834.

Page 818. Column 1, paragraph 2. *"Did I request Thee, Maker, from my clay." Paradise Lost*, X.743–47.

Page 818. Column 2. *"Homeless, near a thousand homes they stood."* From "Guilt and Sorrow," page 19, lines 368–69.

Page 821. Column 1, paragraph 5, line 1. *a loud clamour for extensive change.* A Royal Commission, appointed in 1835, had been empowered to recommend reforms in the temporal structure of the church.

Page 821. Column 2, paragraph 3, line 1. *The order of curates.* J. W. Smyser points out that Wordsworth's son John had been a curate several years before.

Page 822. Column 2, paragraph 4. *"In the unreasoning progress of the world."* From *The Prelude*, V.359–61.

Page 825. Column 1. *"Here might I pause, and bend in reverence."* From *The Prelude*, XIII. 224–78.

THE BIBLIOGRAPHY OF WORDSWORTH

A Bibliographical List of the Principal Writings in Verse and Prose of William Wordsworth, published from 1793 to 1850; arranged in Chronological Order. (Notes signed T. were furnished in the first edition by J. R. Tutin.)

1

An Evening Walk. An Epistle; In verse. Addressed to a Young Lady, from the Lakes of the North of England. By W. Wordsworth, B. A., of St. John's, Cambridge. London: printed for J. Johnson, St. Paul's Church-yard, 1793. 4to.

2

Descriptive Sketches. In verse. Taken during a pedestrian tour in the Italian, Grison, Swiss, and Savoyard Alps. By W. Wordsworth, B. A., of St. John's, Cambridge. Loca pastorum deserta atque otia dia. — *Lucret*. Castella in tumulis — Et longe saltus lateque vacantes. — *Virgil*. London: printed for J. Johnson, St. Paul's Churchyard, 1793. 4to.

3

Lyrical Ballads, with a few other Poems. Printed by Biggs & Cottle, for T. N. Longman, Paternoster Row, London, 1798. 8vo.

Lyrical Ballads, with a few other Poems. London: printed for J. & A. Arch, Grace-church Street, 1798. 8vo.
Four of the poems in this Edition were by S. T. Coleridge, viz. "The Rime of the Ancyent Marinere;" "The Foster-Mother's Tale;" "The Nightingale, a Conversational Poem;" and "The Dungeon."

4

Lyrical Ballads, with other Poems. In two volumes. By W. Wordsworth. Quam nihil ad genium, Papiniane, tuum! Vol. I. Second Edition. [Vol. II.] London: printed for T. N. Longman and O. Rees, Paternoster Row, by Biggs and Co., Bristol. 1800. 8vo.

5

Lyrical Ballads, with Pastoral and other Poems. In two volumes. By W. Wordsworth. Quam nihil ad genium, Papiniane, tuum! Third Edition. London: printed for T. N. Longman & O. Rees, Paternoster-Row, by Biggs and Cottle, Crane-Court, Fleet-Street. 1802. 8vo.
These volumes were republished in Philadelphia, U. S. A., in one volume in 1802. (T.)

6

Lyrical Ballads, with Pastoral and other Poems. In two volumes. By W. Wordsworth. Quam nihil ad genium, Papiniane, tuum! Fourth Edition. London: printed for Longman, Hurst, Rees, & Orme, by R. Taylor and Co., 38 Shoe Lane. 1805. 8vo.

7

Poems, in two volumes, By William Wordsworth, Author of the Lyrical Ballads. *Posterius graviore sono tibi Musa loquetur Nostra: dabunt cum securos mihi tempora fructus*. Vol. I. [Vol. II.] London: printed for Longman, Hurst, Rees, and Orme, Paternoster Row. 1807. 12mo.

8

Concerning the Relations of Great Britain, Spain, and Portugal, to each Other, and to the Common Enemy, at this Crisis; and specifically as affected by the Convention of Cintra: *The whole brought to the test of those principles by which alone the Independence and Freedom of Nations can be Preserved or Recovered*. Qui didicit patriæ quid debeat; — Quod sit conscripti, quod judicis officium; quæ Partes in bellum missi ducis. By William Wordsworth. London: printed for Longman, Hurst, Rees, and Orme, Paternoster-Row. 1809. 8vo.

9

The Excursion, being a portion of The Recluse, a Poem. By William Wordsworth. London: printed for Longman, Hurst, Rees, Orme, and Brown, Paternoster Row. 1814. 4to.
The "Essay on Epitaphs" inserted in the Notes to this volume was originally published in *The Friend*, February 22, 1810. (T.)

10

Poems by William Wordsworth: including Lyrical Ballads, and the Miscellaneous Pieces of the Author. With additional Poems, a new Preface, and a Supplementary Essay. In two volumes. Vol. I. [Vol. II.] London: printed for Longman, Hurst, Rees, Orme, and Brown, Paternoster Row. 1815. 8vo.
This is the first *collected* Edition (to date) of Wordsworth's Poems, excluding "The Excursion." In it the poet for the first time arranges the pieces under various headings, viz. "Poems referring to the Period of Childhood," "Juvenile Pieces," "Poems founded on the Affections," etc. (T.)

11

THE WHITE DOE OF RYLSTONE ; or The Fate
of the Nortons. A Poem. By William
Wordsworth. London: printed for Longman,
Hurst, Rees, Orme, and Brown, Paternoster-
row, by James Ballantyne and Co., Edin-
burgh. 1815. 4to.

12

A LETTER TO A FRIEND OF ROBERT BURNS :
occasioned by an intended republication of
the account of the Life of Burns, by Dr.
Currie ; and of the Selection made by him
from his Letters. By William Wordsworth.
London: printed for Longman, Hurst, Rees,
Orme, and Brown, Paternoster Row. 1816.
8vo.

13.

THANKSGIVING ODE, January 18, 1816. With
other short Pieces, chiefly referring to Recent
Public Events. By William Wordsworth.
London: printed by Thomas Davison, White-
friars ; for Longman, Hurst, Rees, Orme,
and Brown, Paternoster-Row. 1816. 8vo.

14

TWO ADDRESSES TO THE FREEHOLDERS OF
WESTMORELAND. Kendal: Printed by Airey
and Bellingham, 1818. 8vo.

15

PETER BELL, a tale in verse, by William
Wordsworth. London: Printed by Strahan
and Spottiswoode, Printers Street ; for Long-
man, Hurst, Rees, Orme, and Brown, Pater-
noster Row. 1819. 8vo.

16

PETER BELL, A Tale in Verse, by William
Wordsworth. Second Edition. London:
printed by Strahan and Spottiswoode, Print-
ers-Street, for Longman, Hurst, Rees, Orme,
and Brown, Paternoster-Row. 1819. 8vo.

17

THE WAGGONER, a Poem, to which are added,
Sonnets. By William Wordsworth. " What's
in a NAME? Brutus will start a spirit as
soon as Cæsar." London : printed by Stra-
han & Spottiswoode, Printers-Street, for
Longman, Hurst, Rees, Orme, & Brown,
Paternoster-Row, 1819. 8vo.

18

THE RIVER DUDDON, a Series of Sonnets:
Vaudracour and Julia: and other Poems. To
which is annexed, a Topographical Descrip-
tion of the Country of the Lakes, in the North
of England. By William Wordsworth. Lon-
don : Printed for Longman, Hurst, Rees,
Orme, and Brown, Paternoster Row. 1820.
8vo.

19

THE MISCELLANEOUS POEMS OF WILLIAM
WORDSWORTH. In four volumes. Vol. I.

[Vol. II., Vol. III., Vol. IV.] London:
printed for Longman, Hurst, Rees, Orme, and
Brown, Paternoster Row. 1820. 12mo.

20

THE EXCURSION, being a portion of The Re-
cluse, A Poem. By William Wordsworth.
Second Edition. London : printed for Long-
man, Hurst, Rees, Orme, and Brown. 1820.
8vo.

21

MEMORIALS OF A TOUR ON THE CONTINENT,
1820. By William Wordsworth. London:
printed for Longman, Hurst, Rees, Orme, and
Brown, Paternoster Row, 1822. 8vo.

22

ECCLESIASTICAL SKETCHES By William Words-
worth. London: printed for Longman, Hurst,
Rees, Orme, and Brown, Paternoster-Row.
1822. 8vo.

23

A DESCRIPTION OF THE SCENERY OF THE
LAKES IN THE NORTH OF ENGLAND. Third
Edition (now first published separately), with
additions, and illustrative remarks upon
the Scenery of the Alps. By William Words-
worth. London : printed for Longman,
Hurst, Rees, Orme, and Brown, Paternoster-
Row. 1822. 12mo.

24

THE POETICAL WORKS OF WILLIAM WORDS-
WORTH. In five volumes. Vol. I. [Vol. II.-
V.] London: printed for Longman, Rees,
Orme, Brown, and Green, Paternoster-Row.
1827. 12mo.
" In these volumes will be found the whole
of the Author's published poems, for the first
time collected in a uniform edition, with several
new pieces interspersed." — Advertisement by
the Author.
This edition was republished, in one volume,
at Paris in 1828. (T.)

25

THE POETICAL WORKS OF WILLIAM WORDS-
WORTH. Complete in one volume. Paris,
published by A. and W. Galignani, No. 18,
Rue Vivienne. 1828. Demy 8vo.

26

SELECTIONS FROM THE POEMS OF WILLIAM
WORDSWORTH, ESQ., chiefly for the use of
schools and Young Persons. London : Ed-
ward Moxon, 64 New Bond Street, 1831.
12mo.

27

THE POETICAL WORKS OF WILLIAM WORDS-
WORTH. A new Edition. In four volumes.
Vol. I. [Vol. II., Vol. III., Vol. IV.] Lon-
don : Printed for Longman, Rees, Orme,
Brown, Green, & Longman. Paternoster-
Row. 1832. 8vo.
The Advertisement to this Edition is as fol-
lows : — " The contents of the last Edition in

five volumes are compressed into the present of four, with some additional pieces reprinted from miscellaneous publications."

28

SELECTIONS FROM THE POEMS OF WILLIAM WORDSWORTH, ESQ., chiefly for the use of Schools and young persons. London: Edward Moxon, Dover Street. MDCCCXXXIV. 8vo.

29

YARROW REVISITED, AND OTHER POEMS. By William Wordsworth. " Poets . . . dwell on earth To clothe whate 'er the soul admires and loves With language and with numbers." — *Akenside.* London : printed for Longman, Rees, Orme, Brown, Green, & Longman, Paternoster-Row ; and Edward Moxon, Dover-Street. 1835. 12mo.

30

A GUIDE THROUGH THE DISTRICT OF THE LAKES IN THE NORTH OF ENGLAND, with a Description of the Scenery &c. For the use of Tourists and Residents. Fifth Edition, with considerable additions. By William Wordsworth. Kendal : published by Hudson and Nicholson ; and in London by Longman & Co., Moxon, and Whittaker and Co., 1835. 12mo.

31

YARROW REVISITED, AND OTHER POEMS. By William Wordsworth. " Poets . . . dwell on earth To clothe whate'er the soul admires and loves With language and with numbers." — *Akenside.* Second Edition. London : printed for Longman, Rees, Orme, Brown, Green, & Longman, Paternoster Row ; and Edward Moxon, Dover Street. 1836. Fcap. 8vo. (T.)

32

THE EXCURSION. A Poem. By William Wordsworth. A New Edition. London : Edward Moxon, Dover Street. MDCCCXXXVI. 8vo.

33

THE POETICAL WORKS OF WILLIAM WORDSWORTH. A New Edition. In six volumes. Vol. I. (Vol. II.–VI.) London: Edward Moxon, Dover Street, MDCCCXXXVI.– MDCCCXXXVII. Fcap. 8vo. Cloth.
(In 1837 an American reprint of the poetical works of Wordsworth was published, edited by Professor Reed. It contained the poems issued in London in 5 vols. in 1827, and the contents of the Volume, " Yarrow Revisited," etc., published in 1835. It was a Royal 8vo double-column edition, and had a portrait from a painting by W. Boxall. After the Poet's death Professor Reed published a revised and complete Edition, which included not only the whole of the poems published by Wordsworth in 1849–50, but " The Prelude," and one or two pieces which have never been included in any other collective Edition of his works.) (T.)

34

THE SONNETS OF WILLIAM WORDSWORTH. Collected in one volume, with a few additional ones, now first published. London: Edward Moxon, Dover Street. 1838. 8vo.
This collective Edition of the Sonnets was reprinted, with an Essay on the History of the English Sonnet, by the late Archbishop Trench, in 1884. (T.)

35

YARROW REVISITED; and Other Poems. By William Wordsworth. [Woodcut, Cupid with a Harp.] London: Edward Moxon, Dover Street. MDCCCXXXIX. 18mo.

36

POEMS, CHIEFLY OF EARLY AND LATE YEARS; including The Borderers, a Tragedy. By William Wordsworth. London: Edward Moxon, Dover Street. 1842. 8vo.

37

SELECT PIECES FROM THE POEMS OF WILLIAM WORDSWORTH. London: James Burns 1843. Sq. 12mo.
[About this date (1843) there was a selection from Wordsworth's Poems made by Henry Reed, and published by Leavitt and Co., New York.] (T.)

38

KENDAL AND WINDERMERE RAILWAY. Two Letters, reprinted from the Morning Post. Revised, with additions. Kendal: printed by R. Branthwaite and Son (no date). (D.)

39

THE POEMS OF WILLIAM WORDSWORTH, D.C.L., Poet Laureate, etc. etc. A New Edition. London: Edward Moxon, Dover Street. MDCCCXLV. Royal 8vo.
Republished 1846, 1847, 1849, 1851. (D.)

40

ODE, performed in the Senate-House, Cambridge, on the sixth of July, M.DCCC.XLVII. At the first commencement after the Installation of his Royal Highness the Prince Albert, Chancellor of the University. Cambridge: printed at the University Press. 1847. 4to. Paper wrapper. (T.)

41

THE POETICAL WORKS OF WILLIAM WORDSWORTH, D.C.L., Poet Laureate, etc. etc. In six volumes. Vol. I. [Vol. II., Vol. III., Vol. IV., Vol. V., Vol. VI.] A new Edition. London: Edward Moxon, Dover Street. MDCCCXLIX. [—MDCCCL.] 12mo.
[This is the last Edition issued during the poet's lifetime.]

42

THE PRELUDE, OR GROWTH OF A POET'S MIND ; an Autobiographical Poem. By William Wordsworth. London: Edward Moxon, Dover Street. 1850. 8vo.

A CHRONOLOGICAL LIST OF POEMS

All of the poems in this volume are here listed according to the date of their composition, or, in conjectural cases, of their earliest probable composition. When the date of composition is unknown (indicated below by a question mark) that of publication is given. For the reader's convenience, poems composed in a given year are arranged in order of their appearance in this volume.

For further details the reader should consult the first two volumes of Professor Reed's *Chronology* (for dates before 1815) and de Selincourt's notes to the *Poetical Works* (for dates after 1815). Both works are listed in the Select Bibliography.

1821

A SELECT BIBLIOGRAPHY

A Bibliographical List of the Principal Writings in Verse and Prose of William Wordsworth, published from 1793 to 1850; arranged in Chronological Order. (Notes signed T. were furnished in the first edition by J. R. Tutin.)

1. Editions

The Poetical Works of William Wordsworth. Ed. Ernest de Selincourt and Helen Darbishire. 5 vols. Oxford: Clarendon Press, 1940–49.

The Prelude, or Growth of a Poet's Mind. Ed. Ernest de Selincourt. Oxford: Clarendon Press, 1926. 2nd ed. revised by Helen Darbishire, 1959.

The Prose Works of William Wordsworth. Ed. W. J. B. Owen and Jane Worthington Smyser. 3 vols. Oxford: Clarendon Press, 1974.

The Letters of William and Dorothy Wordsworth. Ed. Ernest de Selincourt. 6 vols. Oxford: Clarendon Press, 1935–39. Revised by Chester Shaver, Mary Moorman, and Alan G. Hill, 1967– .

Journals of Dorothy Wordsworth. Ed. Ernest de Selincourt. 2 vols. London: Macmillan & Co., 1941.

The serious student should also consult the editions published under the general title of The Cornell Wordsworth, which offer complete manuscript histories of particular texts. Six volumes have appeared to date:

Benjamin the Waggoner. Ed. Paul F. Betz. Ithaca: Cornell University Press, 1981.

The Borders. Ed. Robert Osborn. Ithaca: Cornell University Press, 1982.

Home at Grasmere. Ed. Beth Darlington. Ithaca: Cornell University Press, 1977.

The Prelude, 1798–1799. Ed. Stephen Parrish. Ithaca: Cornell University Press, 1977.

The Ruined Cottage and the Pedlar. Ed. James Butler. Ithaca: Cornell University Press, 1979.

The Salisbury Plain Poems of William Wordsworth. Ed. Stephen Gill. Ithaca: Cornell University Press, 1975.

2. Biographical Studies

Legouis, Émile. *The Early Life of William Wordsworth, 1770–1798: A Study of "The Prelude."* Trans. J. W. Matthews. 2nd ed. rev. New York: Russell and Russell, 1921.

Margoliouth, H. M. *Wordsworth and Coleridge, 1795–1834.* London, New York, Toronto: Oxford University Press, 1953.

Moorman, Mary. *William Wordsworth: A Biography.* 2 vols. Oxford: Clarendon Press, 1957, 1965.

Reed, Mark L. *Wordsworth: The Chronology of the Early Years, 1770–1799.* Cambridge, Mass.: Harvard University Press, 1967.

——. *Wordsworth: The Chronology of the Middle Years, 1800–1815.* Cambridge, Mass.: Harvard University Press, 1975.

Thompson, T. W. *Wordsworth's Hawkshead.* Ed. R. S. Woof. Oxford: Oxford University Press, 1970.

3. Criticism

Abrams, M. H. *Natural Supernaturalism: Tradition and Revolution in Romantic Literature.* New York: Norton, 1971.

Arnold, Matthew. "Wordsworth," in *Essays in Criticism, Second Series.* London: Macmillan & Co., 1888.

Bateson, F. W. *Wordsworth: A Re-interpretation.* London: Longmans, Green, 1954; 2nd ed., 1956.

Beatty, Arthur. *William Wordsworth: His Doctrine and Art in Their Historical Relations.* University of Wisconsin Studies in Language and Literature, No. 17. Madison: University of Wisconsin Press, 1922. 3rd ed. 1960.

Bloom, Harold. "Wordsworth," in *The Visionary Company: A Reading of English Romantic Poetry.* Garden City, N.Y.: Doubleday, 1961.

Bradley, A. C. "Wordsworth," in *Oxford Lectures on Poetry.* London: Macmillan & Co., 1909.

Coleridge, Samuel Taylor. *Biographia Literaria.* Ed. J. Shawcross. 2 vols. London: Oxford University Press, 1907.

Danby, John F. *The Simple Wordsworth: Studies in the Poems, 1797–1807.* London: Routledge and Kegan Paul, 1960.

Darbishire, Helen. *The Poet Wordsworth.* Oxford: Clarendon Press, 1950.

Ferguson, Frances. *Wordsworth: Language as Counter-Spirit.* New Haven: Yale University Press, 1977.

Ferry, David. *The Limits of Mortality: An Essay on Wordsworth's Major Poems.* Middletown, Conn.: Wesleyan University Press, 1959.

Hartman, Geoffrey H. *Wordsworth's Poetry 1787–1814.* New Haven and London: Yale University Press, 1964.

Havens, Raymond Dexter. *The Mind of a Poet: A Study of Wordsworth's Thought with Particular Reference to "The Prelude."* Baltimore: John Hopkins Press, 1941.

Jones, John. *The Egotistical Sublime: A History of Wordsworth's Imagination.* London: Chatto and Windus, 1954.

Lindenberger, Herbert. *On Wordsworth's Prelude.* Princeton: Princeton University Press, 1963.

Parrish, Stephen Maxfield. *The Art of the "Lyrical Ballads."* Cambridge, Mass.: Harvard University Press, 1973.

Perkins, David. *The Quest for Permanence: The Symbolism of Wordsworth, Shelley, and Keats.*

Cambridge, Mass.: Harvard University Press, 1959.

——. *Wordsworth and the Poetry of Sincerity.* Cambridge, Mass.: Harvard University Press, 1964.

Sheats, Paul D. *The Making of Wordsworth's Poetry, 1785–1798.* Cambridge, Mass.: Harvard University Press, 1973.

Trilling, Lionel. "The Immortality Ode," in *The Liberal Imagination.* New York: Viking, 1950.

Whitehead, Alfred North. "The Romantic Reaction," in *Science and the Modern World.* New York: Macmillan & Co., 1925.

Wordsworth: A Collection of Critical Essays. Ed. M. H. Abrams. Englewood Cliffs, N.J.: Prentice-Hall, 1972.

Wordsworth, Jonathan. *The Music of Humanity: A Critical Study of Wordsworth's "Ruined Cottage."* London and New York: Nelson, 1969.

MAP OF THE
LAKE DISTRICT

SCALE OF MILES

INDEX TO THE FIRST LINES

INDEX TO THE POEMS